Tennyson: A Selected Edition

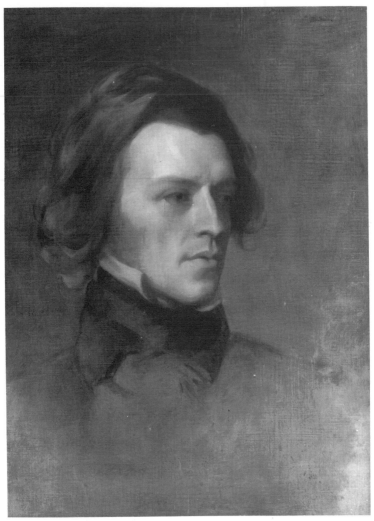

Tennyson aged about 31. By Samuel Laurence. (By kind permission of the National Portrait Gallery.)

TENNYSON

A Selected Edition

INCORPORATING THE TRINITY COLLEGE MANUSCRIPTS

Edited by

CHRISTOPHER
RICKS

UNIVERSITY OF CALIFORNIA PRESS
Berkeley and Los Angeles

University of California Press 1989
Berkeley and Los Angeles

Published by arrangement with Addison Wesley Longman Limited
Tennyson: A Selected Edition first appeared under the
auspices of the *Longman Annotated English Poets* series

© Longman Group UK Limited 1989

Library of Congress Cataloguing-In-Publication-Data
has been applied for

LC 88-40556

ISBN 0-520-06588-3 (cloth)
ISBN 0-520-06666-9 (paper)

Set in Linotron Bembo Medium 10 on 11pt

Produced by Longman Singapore Publishers (Pte) Ltd
Printed in Singapore

2 3 4 5 6 7 8 9

Contents

vi CONTENTS

Note by the General Editor

Longman Annotated English Poets was launched in 1965 with the publication of Kenneth Allott's edition of *The Poems of Arnold*. F. W. Bateson wrote that the 'new series is the first designed to provide university students and readers, and the general reader with complete and fully annotated editions of the major English poets'. That remains the aim of the series, and Bateson's original vision of its policy remains essentially the same. Its 'concern is primarily with the *meaning* of the extant texts in their various contexts'.

Bateson formulated the rationale of the series as follows:

'Our ideal of comprehension, for the reader, combined with comprehensiveness, for the poet, has three logical consequences:

1. Since an essential clue to an author's intentions at any point is provided on the one hand, by what he has already written, and, on the other hand, by what he will write later, an editor will print the poems as far as possible in the order in which they were composed.

2. A poet writing in a living language, such as English, requires elucidation of a different kind from that suitable to the poetry of a dead language such as Sanskrit, Latin or old English; with minor exceptions vocabulary and syntax can be taken for granted, but sources, allusions, implications and stylistic devices need to be spelled out.

3. Since the reader in any English-speaking country will tend to pronounce an English poety of the past (any rate to Chaucer) as if he was a contemporary, whatever impedes the sympathetic response that is implicit in that fact – whether of spelling, punctuation or the use of initial capitals – must be regarded as undesirable. A modern pronunciation demands a modern presentation, except occasionally for rhymes (e.g. *bind-wind*) or obsolete archaisms (*eremite*, hermit). Some exceptions have had to be admitted to the principle summarized above, but they have been few and unimportant.'

These broad principles still govern the series. Its primary purpose is to provide an annotated text giving the reader any necessary contextual information. However, flexibility in the detailed application has proved necessary in the light of experience and the needs of a particular case (and each poet is, by definition, a particular case). First, proper glossing of a poet's vocabulary has proved essential and not something which can be taken for granted. Second, modernization has presented difficulties, which have been resolved pragmatically, trying to reach a balance between sensitivity to the text in question and attention to the needs of a modern reader. Thus, to modernize Browning's text has a double redundancy: Victorian conventions are very close to modern conventions, and Browning had firm ideas on punctuation.

Equally, to impose modern pointing on the ambiguities of Herbert or Marvell, or onto the rhetorical punctuation of Dryden, would create a misleading clarity. Third, in the very early days of the series Bateson hoped that editors would be able in many cases to annotate a *textus receptus*. That has not always been possible, and where no accepted text exists or where the text is controversial, editors have been obliged to go back to the originals and create their own text. The series has taken, and will continue to take, the opportunity of not only providing thorough annotations not available elsewhere, but also of making important textual scholarly contributions where necessary. A case in point is the edition of *The Poems of Tennyson* by Christopher Ricks, the Second Edition of which (1987) takes into account a full collation of the 'Trinity College Manuscripts', not previously available for an edition of this kind. Yet the series' primary purpose remains annotation and editions do not attempt a comprehensive recording of textual variants.

The requirements of a particular author take precedence over 'principle'. It would make little sense to print Herbert's *Temple* in the order of composition even if it could be established. Where Ricks rightly decided that Tennyson's reader needs to be given the circumstances of composition, the attitude to Tennyson and his circle, allusions, and important variants, a necessary consequence was the exclusion of twentieth-century critical responses. Milton, however, is a very different case. John Carey and Alastair Fowler, looking to the needs of their readers, undertook synopses of the main lines of the critical debate over Milton's poetry. Finally, chronological ordering will almost always have a greater or lesser degree of speculation or arbitrariness. The evidence is usually partial, and confused further by the fact that poets do not always write one poem at a time, and frequently revise at a later period than that of composition.

John Barnard
University of Leeds
December 1987

Prefatory Note to this Selected Edition

This selected edition is excerpted from *The Poems of Tennyson*, second edition, three volumes (1987). Each poem here is reproduced in full, together with the entire annotation (headnotes, footnotes, and alternative drafts) of the complete edition. For every poem included, then, this edition is identical with that of 1987. Likewise for the Preface, below, and for the Acknowledgments; the Chronological Table of Tennyson's Life and Chief Publications; and the Abbreviations.

Tennyson's four long poems are here: *The Princess, In Memoriam, Maud*, and *Idylls of the King*. So are all the masterpieces: onwards from *Mariana, The Lady of Shalott, St Simeon Stylites, Ulysses, Tithonus* . . . The necessity of reducing, by more than half, the two thousand pages of the complete edition entailed the enforcing of one principle: the inclusion of no poem which Tennyson himself had not included in his final edition, whether left unpublished or published by him and later rescinded. But this did not retrench quite enough. Judgement has been exercised to represent all of Tennyson's genius, in his many kinds of poetry and throughout the phases of his publishing career of over sixty years.

The numbering of the poems in the complete edition has been retained, partly to facilitate the use of the two editions in conjunction, and partly because the footnotes were keyed to their poems through numbers; to change numbers would have been costly and might have introduced error as well as making for confusion in there being two distinct numberings.

Cross-references

In the complete edition, published in three separately-paginated volumes, cross-references are given as volume and page number, e.g. II 321. In this selected edition, cross-references to poems included are given as *page number in italics*, e.g. *p. 279*; cross-references to poems *not* selected continue to refer to the complete edition by volume and page number.

Appendices

There are two Appendices new to this edition, numbered I and II to avoid confusion with the Appendices in the complete edition. Appendix I is of Alternative Drafts; these are from the earlier Appendix A and for these, page references are given for this edition. Page references to the complete edition are retained for drafts cited but not included in this selected edition. Appendix I also includes two items which had figured originally not in Appendix A but in the body of the text as poems in their own right: 'Oh! that 'twere possible', which is given here as an alternative draft for *Maud*; and *Tithon*, an alternative draft for *Tithonus*.

Appendix II reproduces the Contents pages of the complete edition, enabling the reader to see at once the full sequence of Tennyson's poems.

In both Appendix II and the Index of Titles and First Lines the use of a dagger indicates a poem included in this selected edition.

Preface to the Complete Edition

This second edition

The first edition of *The Poems of Tennyson* in this series was published in 1969 (pp. xxxiv + 1835) when the important and various manuscripts at Trinity College, Cambridge, were still under interdiction (see below). This second edition corrects errors and omissions; it assimilates the Tennyson scholarship of the last fifteen years or so; and it incorporates the Trinity MSS. The numbering of the poems in the first edition is preserved, with newly-added poems (and fragments and drafts) inserted with a following A, as 151A. New to this edition are about a dozen poems, about a thousand lines of verse, and countless variants.

Text

The text is based on the Eversley edition of Tennyson's *Works* (nine volumes, Macmillan, 1907–8), which was carefully edited by Hallam Lord Tennyson. *Eversley* has been collated with the one-volume edition of *1894* (Macmillan), which includes Tennyson's late revisions, and the very few differences in wording between *1894* and *Eversley* are noted. When the text below departs in its wording from *Eversley*, this too is noted. But the punctuation has sometimes been silently corrected; *Eversley* omits punctuation, especially at the end of a line, and in such cases the punctuation has been supplied, usually from *1894*. Modern practice has been followed (in variants as well as text) in the spelling of such words as 'though' and 'through' (instead of 'tho'' and 'thro''); in supplying the *e* for such words as 'Heav'n' and 'th''; and in using ed/èd. But Tennyson's use of -*t* ('slipt') has been preserved. In a review of the 1969 edition, J. Pettigrew made some shrewd criticisms of the minor modernizings (*VP* viii, 1970, 161–8).

  The text for all the poems which were not included in Tennyson's final edition (such poems are marked★) is specified in each case. The present is the first collected edition to include all the poems which Tennyson published, together with those since published by his son Hallam and by his grandson Sir Charles Tennyson, and those surviving in MS. Quotations from Tennyson's notes expand his references (*Ael. Lamprid.* is given as *Aelius Lampridius*), and emend their system of reference to accord with the practice in the other notes. Not all of the notes in *Eversley* are reproduced, though most which still have much relevance, whether critical, historical or biographical. *Eversley* is the source of all statements by Tennyson, Hallam Tennyson or Edward FitzGerald for which no specific reference is given. Those poems such as *Locksley Hall* which use an exceptionally long line have been set in smaller print, to avoid what is usually an ugly and awkward breaking of the lines.

When a poem is described as 'not reprinted', this means in authorized English editions during Tennyson's lifetime. Without his blessing, uncollected poems were often reprinted in U.S. editions (e.g. *The Poetical Works*, Harper and Brothers, N. Y., 1873, kindly brought to my attention by Dr R. H. Lonsdale). In quotations (including the *Letters*) when the intention is unambiguous, I have given the titles of poems as in this edition (italicized), and similarly have abbreviated Tennyson to T.

Published variants

The footnotes record all differences in wording between Tennyson's first published text of a poem and that of *Eversley/1894*. Readings from his errata slips are silently incorporated except when the change of wording is a genuine revision (in which case both readings are given), not a correction of a printer's error. But no record is given of changes in wording which Tennyson introduced later than his first published text and then withdrew before *Eversley/1894*–except when such variants are of especial interest (e.g. the close of *The Vision of Sin*, where Tennyson, in *1865* alone, added two lines). Variants in punctuation, capitalization, spelling, etc. are not recorded. The notes follow Tennyson's own practice in speaking of *Poems* (published December 1832, with the title-page dated 1833) as *1832*. In certain cases, an earlier reading survived inadvertently in some editions though definitively amended in others. Thus 'blowing' in *Maud* i 582 was changed to the final reading, 'glowing', in *A Selection* (1865)–but 'blowing' is still to be found in the 1867 reprint of *Maud*. Since there can be no doubt of Tennyson's intentions, the textual point is one which may be left to the bibliographer. The formula adopted in such cases ignores the inadvertent lingerers:

> *glowing*] *1865 Selection*; blowing *1855–65*.

MS variants

The Tennyson Archive, a set of thirty volumes reproducing in facsimile all such poetical MSS of Tennyson as may be permitted (including those at Trinity, at Harvard, and at Lincoln), and comprehensively indexed, is published in 1987–9 by Garland Publishing, edited by Aidan Day and the present editor. One day there will be an edition of Tennyson which records all MS variants–in twenty volumes or so. But Longman Annotated English Poets do not aim to be textually all-inclusive. Until after the *1969* edition was published, the MSS at Trinity College, Cambridge, could not be copied or quoted (in perpetuity, it was then maintained), so that a complete record of variant readings was in any case not possible then. The lifting of the restriction makes such a record possible, and it would be enormously valuable as well as enormous. Yet there is not only room for, but a need for, many different kinds of edition, though editing on any large scale is always so onerous that those of us who undertake it can only keep going by pretending to ourselves and to others that ours is the only kind of edition really worth doing. There is still something to be said for giving a selection of MS variants, and the new incorporation of the Trinity MSS has not necessitated (though it would have permitted) a change in the *raison d'être*, the posited readership, and the scale of such an edition as this. The editor has tried to resist the temptation to find the Trinity MSS more interesting (than, say, the good old Harvard ones) simply because they used to be under interdiction.

Since the authenticity of the MSS is beyond question, no note is made of whose hand a particular MS is written in; most are in Tennyson's hand, and most of the rest are in those of his family. In selecting MS variants, the principles ordinarily were: that the poem for which such variants are given is important; or that the MS variant is important; or that many years elapsed between composition and publication. In the case of such poems as *Ulysses* or *In Memoriam*, it seemed right to quote all MS variants. For certain of the poems, it is specifically noted that all MS variants are given, but this has not been noted throughout. When printing poems from MS, Hallam Tennyson and Sir Charles Tennyson sometimes provided titles not deriving, apparently, from the MS. The family tradition is itself worth retaining in such cases (and there may have been MSS not now extant). In some few cases, however, where the authority of a title might be of some importance, the headnote records that the title is not in the MS cited. When it is noted that all MS variants have been given, the footnotes do not explicitly state (though they implicitly provide) the readings of MSS or trial editions when such readings agree with those of the first published editions. It is to be understood in such cases that the MS readings are those of the earliest published text (or cited trial edition) unless specifically noted otherwise.

MS 1st reading usually implies that a subsequent correction to the MS brought it into the wording of the first published text. In accordance with the practice of Hallam Tennyson and of Sir Charles Tennyson, MS material (whether poems, fragments or variants) is not reproduced *literatim*; spelling and capitalization have been modified, and punctuation has been amended and added. This applies to all poems which Tennyson left in MS, including those which have since been published; wherever possible such poems have been newly edited from the MSS. In a sympathetic review (*Notes and Queries*, September 1966) of Kenneth Allott's *Arnold* in this series, J. C. Maxwell expressed doubts about such modifying of MS material. But in an edition which does not seek to be a definitive record of all MS variants, it is best to give precedence to the reader's convenience. Tennyson used to write out whole stanzas without punctuation, but there is nothing sacred in the practice or in his occasional misspellings. Though he himself did not stumble through his draft, a modern reader probably would.

The Trinity MSS

These were almost all presented to Trinity College, Cambridge, in 1924, by Hallam Tennyson, on conditions which forbade copying or quotation in perpetuity. The continued efforts of the present Lord Tennyson and of Sir Charles Tennyson, the poet's grandson, against the interdiction, were seconded by the publication of this edition in 1969 (obliged to say on very many pages '*Trinity MS*, which may not be quoted'); and later in 1969 the College wisely chose one form of piety over another, and lifted the restriction. Particular gratitude is owed, by all who love Tennyson, to the College and to its Librarian Dr. Philip Gaskell. For not only do the Trinity MSS contain a wealth of unpublished material–poems, drafts, fragments (some of which were printed by the present editor in the *TLS*, 21 August 1969)–but it is only by recourse to them that Hallam Tennyson's many errors in the poems which he published can be authoritatively corrected. J. C. Yearwood's *Catalogue of the Trinity MSS* (D. Phil., Austin, 1977) is of great service. There are MSS at the University Library Cambridge, which were given with the same interdiction, likewise waived after 1969.

Tennyson permitted Hallam Tennyson to publish variants, and Hallam himself published poems from these MSS. Tennyson would probably have destroyed the MSS if he had dreaded quotation. True, Tennyson disliked variant readings, but he also said: 'I like those old

Variorum Classics–all the Notes make the Text look precious' (*Tennyson and His Friends*, 1911, p. 147).

Other collections

Fortunately there were no restrictions on the Commonplace Book kept by Tennyson's Cambridge friend, J. M. Heath, and now in the Fitzwilliam Museum. It was compiled from 1832 to 1834, and includes many of Tennyson's early poems. For a full description, see Sir Charles Tennyson, *Cornhill* cliii (1936) 426–49. The Allen Notebook at Trinity College (shelf-mark R.7.50) is similar, though less important.

The notebooks and loose papers in the Houghton Library at Harvard were formerly in the possession of Sir Charles, and they comprise a collection which rivals even that at Trinity College. The Harvard MSS are described and indexed by E. F. Shannon and W. H. Bond in the *Harvard Library Bulletin* x (1956) 254–74. Not susceptible of description or indexing, but of great interest, are the innumerable stubs of the notebooks, which offer evidence not only of known poems but also of many poems which have not survived. (Abb. *H.MS, H.Nbk, H.Lpr.*)

The Tennyson Research Centre in the City Library, Lincoln, though it has valuable MS material (especially letters), is remarkable chiefly as the repository of not only Tennyson's library but also that of his father and his brother Charles. This, and a MS of *In Memoriam*. There did not seem any need to differentiate two kinds of evidence showing that a particular book was in the library at Somersby: the presence now of the book itself in the Centre, and a copy of the Sale Inventory of George Clayton Tennyson's library, 8–9 June 1831, which is also now in the Centre. See S. Shatto, 'Tennyson's Library', *The Book Collector* xxvii (1978) 494–513.

See *Tennyson in Lincoln: A Catalogue of the Collections in the Research Centre*, ed. N. Campbell (vol. i, 1971; vol. ii, 1973); unfortunately much of the collection had to be sold in 1980; see R. A. Carroll, *TRB* iii (1980) 141–6; S. Shatto, *VP* xviii (1980) 309–12; and R. L. Collins, *TRB* iv (1984) 134.

Publication

T. J. Wise's *Bibliography of the Writings of Tennyson* (1908) is indispensable, but it is inaccurate and is corrupted by his forgeries. Until there exists a complete list of the myriad editions, no textual apparatus can hope to be impeccable.

The headnotes, in citing the first publication of a poem or volume, make no attempt to list all Tennyson's privately printed editions. 'Publication' is taken in its simplest sense: 'issued for sale to the public'.

But full details are given whenever a privately printed edition had real importance (e.g. *The Window*, II 697).

'In 1842 [before publishing *Poems*, 1842] he had eight of the blank verse poems printed for his private use, because he always liked to see his poems in print some months and sometimes some years before publication, "for", as he said, "poetry looks better, more convincing, in print". This little volume was entitled *Morte d'Arthur; Dora, and other Idyls*' (*Mem.* i 189–90*n*). These private volumes contain important textual evidence. Though Tennyson certainly used them as proofs, they had for him a function which goes beyond proof-correcting, and it therefore seemed best to refer to them as trial editions. A bibliographer of Tennyson may have to differentiate trial editions from proofs; for this edition no such differentiation seemed necessary. Hallam Tennyson speaks of 'the first unpublished edition' which included *Locksley Hall* (*Mem.* i 195), and the textual notes below likewise treat all such trial editions as essentially prepublication MS material, and so give only selected variants from them.

Hallam Tennyson had privately printed *Materials for a Life of A.T.*, a draft of his *Tennyson: A Memoir* (1897). The headnotes do not specify the first printing in *Materials* of poems and fragments which were first *published* in the *Memoir*.

The order of the poems

As is standard for this series, the poems are printed in their chronological order of composition. This removes many anomalies but it also creates some. Reviewing Kenneth Allott's *Arnold* in *Victorian Studies* ix (1966) 215–17, A. Dwight Culler conceded that there is no ideal order in which to print the poems, and he specified two problems. First, 'we simply do not know very precisely when many of Arnold's poems were written'. Second, 'Arnold seems to have kept a good many poems going simultaneously'. Yet Professor Culler on the whole approved: 'Having said all this, I am nonetheless glad that Professor Allott decided upon this arrangement; for, after all, we have the other in the Tinker and Lowry edition.'

All these considerations apply to Tennyson. The obstacles to a chronological ordering are that for many poems no precise date of composition exists (and this is particularly true of the extraordinarily fertile years till 1834), and that Tennyson kept many poems going simultaneously, often working on a poem for decades. Yet we do have the other arrangement, roughly by the original volumes, in other easily available editions–Macmillan's, or Oxford Standard Authors. Despite the anomalies, the advantages of a chronological ordering, even a tentative one, are considerable. With a poet whose active career was so long, no reader can avoid pondering the development of his art. For a discussion of advantages, disadvantages, and anomalies, see Ian Jack: 'A Choice of Orders: The Arrangement of "The Poetical Works"', in *Textual Studies and Their Meaning for Literary Criticism*, ed. J. J. McGann (1985).

An attempt is made to mitigate the anomalies by inserting cross-references at points where the ordering might mislead. The major problem has been the poems which comprise a linked series written over several years. *In Memoriam* was begun in 1833, and published in 1850; it is printed under 1850, with a note under 1833. *The Epic* could not be separated from *Morte d'Arthur* which it introduces, and this meant either placing *Morte d'Arthur* misleadingly under 1837, or *The Epic* misleadingly under 1833. The latter seemed preferable, with a note under 1837. Some other cases, where it seemed that linked poems did not *have* to be printed together (so violating chronology), could invoke the precedent set by Hallam Tennyson himself. In *Tennyson and His Friends* (pp. 75–7), he saw nothing objectionable in printing *To Edward FitzGerald* without *Tiresias*, and *To Professor Jebb*, etc., without the poems to which they act as introductions. In all such cases, chronological ordering is at odds with keeping the poems together. Which of the two has been allowed to win is a matter of each particular case. 'How grave is the violation of chronology?' has had to contend with 'How grave is it to divorce these two linked poems?'

There is little precise evidence for dating the early poems, and so the poems in the three volumes of *1827*, *1830* and *1832* have been kept in the sequence in which they appeared in their respective volumes. The chronological ordering therefore begins with the four poems which antedate *1827*; then come the poems of *1827* in the order in which they were originally printed; then a few intermediate poems; then the poems of *1830*; again a few intermediate poems; and then the poems of *1832*. After which (with No. 123) all poems are given in a suggested chronological order (with subsequent volumes therefore broken up). In the absence of evidence it would have been merely bluff to reorder the poems in *1827*, *1830* and *1832*; what needs to be borne in mind is that the chronological ordering from 1824 to 1833 is decidedly more approximate than thereafter. Throughout, though, there are unavoidably tentative datings. The contents of volumes later than *1832* are listed in Appendix D (III 648), so that such groupings by Tennyson may be reconstituted by the reader.

Since Tennyson would have wished it, *Crossing the Bar* has been placed at the end of the main chronology, with a cross-reference given in sequence.

Idylls of the King were written over a large span of years, and yet clearly needed to be printed as one sequence; they are therefore printed together at the end of the volume (Nos. 463–76), followed by *Songs from the Plays* (No. 477), also out of the main sequence, and by four Appendices containing respectively Alternative Drafts; Fragments, Trivia &c; Doubtful Poems; and Contents of Volumes.

The plays

Though it includes his early play, *The Devil and the Lady*, this edition omits the plays which Tennyson published from 1875. The decision was based only in part on a judgement of their quality; the fact that they are readily available not only in nineteenth-century but also in modern editions made it reasonable to omit them here. Tennyson himself authorized collected editions which omitted the plays, retaining only—as in the present case—the songs from the plays.

Parallel passages

The footnotes cite many parallel passages. As in any annotated edition these illustrate a range of possible likenesses. At one end is conscious allusion to another poet; then unconscious reminiscence; then phrasing which is only an analogue and not a source. Some of the instances cited here are probably analogues, not sources, but they are cited because Tennyson's phrasing can be illuminated by the comparison. Though eighteenth-century diction has been well studied, nineteenth-century late romantic diction has remained relatively unexplored. Parallel passages from, say, Keats and Shelley point not always to a source but to a common fund of poetic materials. What precisely Tennyson made of such materials may best be seen when we invoke—for comparison and contrast—his predecessors. Certainly Tennyson himself disliked such source-hunters as John Churton Collins:

> There is, I fear, a prosaic set growing up among us, editors of booklets, book-worms, index-hunters, or men of great memories and no imagination, who *impute themselves* to the poet, and so believe that *he*, too, has no imagination, but is for ever poking his nose between the pages of some old volume to see what he can appropriate. They will not allow one to say "Ring the bell" without finding that we have taken it from Sir P. Sidney, or even to use such a simple expression as the ocean "roars", without finding out the precise verse in Homer or

Horace from which we have plagiarised it (fact). (*Eversley* iv 239–40) But he was prepared nevertheless to quote such parallels himself. His note at *Eversley* i 334 says: 'Many of the parallelisms here given are accidental. The same idea must often occur independently to two men looking on the same aspects of Nature.' Accidental parallels may, then, have their own interest, even if the major interest still belongs to what is not accidental but a source.

Translations of the classics are from the Loeb editions whenever possible. As to acknowledging the work of previous scholars on this and similar matters, the principle has been to provide specific acknowledgements when a scholarly point was made for the first time during the last fifty years or so. It did not seem necessary to acknowledge by name the earlier discoverers, except when a particular interest or authority attaches to them. K. H. Beetz has edited *Tennyson: A Bibliography, 1827–1982* (1984).

Poems by Two Brothers (1827)

The only major problem of attribution concerns *Poems by Two Brothers*, by Tennyson and his brother Charles, with a few poems by their brother Frederick. It was published in April 1827 (the persistent statement that it was published late in 1826 is certainly an error, *pace* Hallam Tennyson, who wrote to J. E. Wetherell, 15 Oct. 1891: 'The publishers dated the book with the date of the year following the publication' (*Letters* iii), it being instead true that 'My father was 17 . . . when the book was published'). Tennyson later said to Sir James Knowles: 'There were twenty-six misprints, but the publisher would not make a longer list of errata' than the seven which appear (*Nineteenth Century* xxxiii (1893) 181). The epigraph was *Haec nos novimus esse nihil* (Martial, XIII ii 8: *nos haec* . . . 'We know these efforts of ours are nothing worth'). The poems were prefaced by an Advertisement dated March 1827:

The following Poems were written from the ages of fifteen to eighteen, not conjointly, but individually; which may account for their difference of style and matter. To light upon any novel combination of images, or to open any vein of sparkling thought untouched before, were no easy task: indeed the remark itself is as old as the truth is clear; and, no doubt, if submitted to the microscopic eye of periodical Criticism, a long list of inaccuracies and imitations would result from the investigation. But so it is: we have passed the Rubicon, and we leave the rest to fate; though its edict may create a fruitless regret that we ever emerged from "the shade," and courted notoriety.

Paul Turner, *Tennyson* (1976), p. 40, notes that this Advertisement 'is modelled on the Preface to Byron's first volume, *Hours of Idleness* (1807), even down to the statement "we have passed the Rubicon".' It is to be noted that many of Tennyson's best youthful poems 'were omitted from the *Poems by Two Brothers*, being thought too much out of the common for the public taste' (*Mem.* i 23).

There was a move to reissue the volume in 1865; Tennyson's brother Charles wrote to him about this, 6 Feb. (*Mat.* i 39n; *Letters* ii 391); Tennyson bought this off. William Allingham lent Tennyson a copy of T. Bayne's article on Charles and *1827* (*Fraser's Magazine*, Dec. 1881); Allingham records T. as saying, 13 Jan. 1882: 'I myself at that time had done far better things than any contained in that volume–but there were parts of would-be Epics 5000 lines long–all which thank God, and the Muses, are burnt' (*Letters* iii).

In 1893 Hallam Tennyson authorized a reprint of *1827*, and prefaced it by saying:

It is requested that none of the poems in this volume said to be by my father and consequently signed A.T., be included in any future edition of his Works, as my uncle, Frederick Tennyson, cannot be certain of the authorship of every poem, and as the hand-writing of the manuscript is known not to be a sure guide.

The Additional Poems at the end form part of the original manuscript of 1827, and were omitted for some forgotten reason.

My father writes, "The Preface states 'written from 15 to 18.' I was between 15 and 17, Charles between 15 and 18."

The following is from Frederick Tennyson, and explains itself: "I return you the Poems, with which I have been greatly interested, as I did not expect to find them so good as they really are. The initials are right as appended to my four poems, but *I cannot be sure of the others.*"

(The correspondence with Frederick is now at Yale.) Despite this Preface, Hallam Tennyson permitted W. J. Rolfe to include Tennyson's poems of *1827* in his edition of 1898; for this edition Hallam modified the attributions in some cases (the headnotes below indicate this where it is of importance).

Hallam Tennyson saw to the appending of initials (A.T., C.T. and F.T.) in 1893, some with queries. A letter from Robert Bowes to Hallam, 1 March 1893 (now at Lincoln), makes it clear that the main evidence was the handwriting of the MS of *1827* (watermarked 1823), despite the doubts expressed in the Preface. In addition to the memory of the aged Frederick, further evidence for the attributions exists in three surviving copies of *1827*.

Professor W. D. Paden studied two of these copies in an article in *The Library* xix (1964) 147–61, and the present edition is much indebted to him. First: the Haddelsey copy, with attributions by Tennyson, now in the Brotherton Collection at Leeds: 'This copy was presented by Lord Tennyson to Mr Haddelsey the family Solicitor with the poems marked by him showing that Three Brothers were concerned in the book.' Second: Charles's own copy in which he marked attributions (formerly in the possession of Mr Paden). The divergences between these three sources (*1893*, the Haddelsey copy, Charles's copy) are sufficient to suggest that the sources have independent authority, and this lends great weight to the fact that in most cases the attributions are identical. Mr Paden argued that the agreement of both the Haddelsey and Charles's copy should be considered to outweigh a dissenting attribution in *1893* (see Appendix C, Doubtful Poems, III 641). For full details, his article must be studied. Subsequent to it, a third copy of *1827* with attributions has turned up. This was given by Tennyson's Aunt Russell to a Mrs Robinson in 1827, and it includes Mrs Russell's attributions – only one of which (Frederick's *The Oak of the North*) is followed by a query. This, the Russell copy, now belongs to Mr Chilton Thomson, who has kindly allowed the use of it. As with the Haddelsey and Charles's copy, the divergences in the Russell copy are sufficient to suggest that it has independent authority, and this again lends important weight to the fact that most of its attributions concur with the three other sources.

When a headnote below quotes solely the *1893* attribution, it is to be understood that *1893* is supported by all three of the marked copies of *1827*. Whenever these four authorities do not agree, the headnote to a poem says so.

Addendum. For further parallel passages, see A. Burnett, 'Echoes and Parallels in Tennyson's Poetry', *Notes and Queries* (March 1987).

Acknowledgements

My greatest debt is to Sir Charles Tennyson, the poet's grandson, for his published work on Tennyson, which is here drawn on throughout; for his personal assistance which has been most generous; and for his permission to make use of Tennyson MSS. My thanks are also due to the present Lord Tennyson for the interest he has shown in the edition and for permission to quote a great deal of copyright material including Tennyson MSS.

Macmillan and Co. have kindly given permission to quote from the Eversley edition of Tennyson's *Works; Alfred Tennyson: A Memoir* by Hallam Tennyson (1897); and *Works* (1913); and to reprint *The Devil and the Lady* (1930) and *Unpublished Early Poems* (1931). The *Twentieth Century* has also kindly given permission to reprint *The Christ of Ammergau*, which was first published in its pages in January 1955.

For help of many kinds, my gratitude is due to: John Barnard; W. Rayner Batty; Sir Benjamin C. Brodie; A. N. Bryan-Brown; Rowland L. Collins; Martin Dodsworth; Miss M. J. Donahue (Mrs Ellmann); Philip L. Elliott; David Fleeman; William E. Fredeman; Miss Joyce Green (Mrs Garnier); Miss Elaine Hasløv; David Jeffcock; Mrs Catherine Barham Johnson; John Killham; Cecil Y. Lang; W. S. G. Macmillan; George O. Marshall, Jr; J. C. Maxwell; Stephen Orgel; W. D. Paden; R. L. Purdy; Ralph Wilson Rader; Edgar F. Shannon, Jr; B. C. Southam; John Sparrow; John Spedding; Mrs Marguerite Sussman; Alfred Tennyson d'Eyncourt; Mrs Ruth Tennyson d'Eyncourt; Chilton Thomson. The General Editor of this series, F. W. Bateson, has been most generous with his time, his knowledge and his vigilance.

Of the libraries which have made possible this edition, my greatest debts are due to the Tennyson Research Centre housed in the City Library, Lincoln, and its director, Mr F. T. Baker; to the Houghton Library at Harvard; to the Bodleian Library, Oxford; and to Trinity College, Cambridge. Among other libraries which have been of great assistance are: the Bapst Library, Boston College; the British Museum; the Brotherton Library, Leeds; the University Library, Cambridge; the Fitzwilliam Museum, Cambridge; the University of Hawaii; the Huntington Library; the Lincolnshire Archives Committee; the University of London Library; the Mitchell Library, Sydney; the Pierpont

Morgan Library; the National Library of Australia; the New York Public Library, especially the Berg Collection; the Royal College of Music; the University of Texas; the Victoria and Albert Museum; the University of Virginia; Yale University Library.

This second edition is indebted yet again to many of the above, and to: Michaël Alexander; Marilyn Butler; Philip Collins; Aidan Day; David De Laura; E. E. Duncan-Jones; Roger Evans; Philip Gaskell; J. M. Gray; Eric Griffiths; Philip Headley; Timothy Hobbs; Mary Barham Johnson; Jack Kolb; Jim McCue; Roderic Owen; Thomas R. Schuck; Joseph Sendry; Susan Shatto; Marion Shaw; Sir John Simeon; John Russell Taylor; and Hallam Tennyson. I owe a particular debt to Cecil Y. Lang and Edgar F. Shannon for their generosity with their work on the *Letters*.

The curator of the Robert H. Taylor Collection at Princeton University has kindly given permission to quote MSS, as have the Department of Rare Books and Special Collections at the University of Rochester Library, and the Syndics of Cambridge University for MSS in the University Library.

Quotations from the MSS at Trinity College, Cambridge, are by the permission of Lord Tennyson and Lord Tennyson's Trustees, and with the approval of the Master and Fellows.

Chronological Table of Alfred Tennyson's Life and Chief Publications

1809   (*6 August*) Born at Somersby, Lincolnshire, fourth son of Rev. George Clayton Tennyson the younger, Rector of Somersby, and of Elizabeth Tennyson (*née* Fytche). T.'s father had been virtually disinherited by T.'s grandfather in favour of a younger brother, and T.'s youth was overshadowed by this family feud between the Tennysons of Somersby and the grandparents with their favoured son (later Charles Tennyson d'Eyncourt) of Bayons Manor.

1816   Pupil at Louth Grammar School, where his elder brothers Frederick (b. 1807) and Charles (b. 1808) had started in 1814 and 1815.

1820   Leaves Louth, to be privately educated at home by his father.

1823-4   Writes *The Devil and the Lady*, in imitation of Elizabethan drama.

1824   Serious breakdown in the health, physical and mental, of his father.

1827   (*April*) Publishes *Poems by Two Brothers*, by T. and his brother Charles, with a few poems by Frederick. T.'s contributions were written 'between 15 and 17'.

      (*November*) Enters Trinity College, Cambridge, together with Charles (*October*), joining Frederick (1826) there.

1828   (*October*) Arthur Henry Hallam (b. 1811) enters Trinity, meeting T. probably in April 1829.

1829   Friendship with Hallam.

      (*June*) Wins the Chancellor's Gold Medal with his prize poem, *Timbuctoo*.

      (*October*) Elected a member of the 'Apostles', an undergraduate debating society to which most of his Cambridge friends belonged.

      (*December*) Hallam may first meet T.'s sister Emily (b. 1811), with whom he was to fall in love. (This traditional dating given by H. T. was vigorously contested by J. Kolb, *RES* n.s. xxviii (1977) 32–48, arguing for April 1830; it was re-affirmed by R. B. Martin.)

1830   (*June*) Publishes *Poems, Chiefly Lyrical*.

      (*July–September*) Visits the Pyrenees with Hallam.

1831   (*March*) Death of his father.
        Leaves Cambridge without taking a degree.
        (*August*) Hallam's essay 'On Some of the Characteristics of
        Modern Poetry and on the Lyrical Poems of Alfred Tennyson'
        in *Englishman's Magazine*.

1832   (*May*) Severe, though not indiscriminate, review of *1830* by
        'Christopher North' (John Wilson) in *Blackwood's Magazine*.
        (*July*) Visits the Rhine country with Hallam.
        (*Autumn*) Hallam's engagement to Emily grudgingly recognized
        by the Hallams.
        (*October*) Insanity, eventually incurable, of his brother Edward
        (b. 1813).
        (*December*) Publishes *Poems* (title-page dated 1833).

1833   Begins revising many poems of *1830* and *1832*.
        (*April*) Venomous review of *1832* by J. W. Croker in *Quarterly
        Review*.
        (*September*) Death of Hallam from a haemorrhage, while visiting
        Vienna.

1834   Falls in love with Rosa Baring, with whom he seems to have
        become disillusioned by 1835-6. (She married Robert Shafto in
        1838.)

1835   (*March*) His brother Charles inherits an estate and changes his
        name to Turner.

1836   (*May*) Marriage of Charles to Louisa Sellwood, and the beginning
        of T.'s love for her sister Emily Sellwood, whom T. had met in
        1830.

1837   (*May*) The Tennysons move from Somersby to High Beech,
        Epping.
        (*September*) Persuaded by Richard Monckton Milnes to contribute
        to *The Tribute*, in which he publishes *Oh! that 'twere possible*.
        Engagement to Emily Sellwood recognized by her family and
        his.

1840   Engagement broken off, partly or ostensibly because of T.'s
        financial insecurity. The Tennysons move to Tunbridge Wells
        (and in 1841 to Boxley).
        (*February*) Edward FitzGerald reports that T. is 'really ill, in a
        nervous way', a condition which persists into the late 1840s.

1840–41 Invests his fortune (about £3,000) in a wood-carving scheme,
        which has collapsed by 1843.

1842   (*May*) Publishes *Poems*. The first volume selects poems from *1830*
        and *1832* together with a few written *c*. 1833; the second volume
        consists of new poems.

1843–4 Receives treatment in a hydropathic hospital near Cheltenham.

1845 (*September*) Is granted a Civil List pension of £200 p.a.

1846 (*August*) Visits Switzerland with his publisher Edward Moxon.

1847 (*December*) Publishes *The Princess*.

1848 Visits Ireland and Cornwall, taking up again a projected Arthurian enterprise.

1849 Renews correspondence with Emily Sellwood.

1850 (*May*) Publishes *In Memoriam* anonymously in the last week of May (the first commercial announcement, 1 June).
(*June*) Marries Emily.
(*November*) Appointed Poet Laureate, Wordsworth having died in April.

1851 (*April*) A still-born baby boy.
(*July*) Visits Italy with Emily, returning in October.

1852 (*August*) Birth of his son Hallam Tennyson.
(*November*) Publishes *Ode on the Death of the Duke of Wellington*.

1853 (*November*) Moves to Farringford, Isle of Wight, which he buys in 1856.

1854 (*March*) Birth of his son Lionel.

1855 (*June*) Hon. D.C.L. at Oxford.
(*July*) Publishes *Maud, and Other Poems*.

1859 (*July*) Publishes *Idylls of the King*, namely *Enid*, *Vivien*, *Elaine* and *Guinevere*.
(*August*) Visits Portugal with F. T. Palgrave.

1860 Assists Palgrave in selecting poems for *The Golden Treasury*.

1861 (*June*) Visits the Pyrenees with his family.

1862 (*January*) Writes Dedication for a new edition of the *Idylls of the King*, in memory of Albert, Prince Consort (d. December 1861).
(*April*) First audience with Queen Victoria, at Osborne, Isle of Wight.

1864 (*April*) Visit by Garibaldi to Farringford.
(*August*) Publishes *Enoch Arden* [etc.].

1865 (*January*) Publishes *A Selection from the Works of Alfred Tennyson*. Refuses offer of a baronetcy.
(*February*) Death of his mother.

1868 (*April*) Foundation stone laid of his second home, Aldworth, at Blackdown, Haslemere.

1869 (*April*) Attends the meeting to organize a 'Metaphysical Society', which he joins and which flourishes until 1879.
(*December*) Publishes *The Holy Grail and Other Poems* (title-page dated 1870).

1870   (*December*) Reluctantly publishes *The Window* (title-page dated 1871), with music by Arthur Sullivan.

1872   (*October*) Publishes *Gareth and Lynette* [etc.]. The Imperial Library edition of the *Works* (1872–3) brings together the *Idylls of the King* (with a new Epilogue: *To the Queen*), virtually complete except for *Balin and Balan* (written 1874).

1873   (*April*) Again refuses offer of baronetcy, as also in 1874 and 1880.

1875   (*June*) Publishes *Queen Mary*, inaugurating his career as a playwright.

1876   (*April*) Production of *Queen Mary*.
        (*December*) Publishes *Harold* (title-page dated 1877).

1878   (*February*) Marriage of his son Lionel to Eleanor Locker.

1879   (*April*) Death of his brother Charles Tennyson Turner.
        (*May*) After repeated piracies, publishes *The Lover's Tale*, which had been omitted from *1832*.
        (*December*) Production of *The Falcon*.

1880   (*December*) Publishes *Ballads and Other Poems*.

1881   (*July*) Henry Irving's production of *The Cup*, with Ellen Terry and Irving.

1882   (*November*) Production of *The Promise of May*, his only published work in prose.

1883   (*September*) Visits Denmark with Gladstone.
        Accepts the offer of a barony, taking his seat in the House of Lords in March 1884.

1884   (*February*) Publishes *The Cup and The Falcon*.
        (*June*) Marriage of his son Hallam to Audrey Boyle.
        (*December*) Publishes *Becket*.

1885   (*November*) Publishes *Tiresias, and Other Poems*.

1886   (*April*) Death of his son Lionel, aged thirty-two, returning from India.
        (*December*) Publishes *Locksley Hall Sixty Years After*, which includes *The Promise of May*.

1888   Severe rheumatic illness, from which he does not recover till May 1889.

1889   (*December*) Publishes *Demeter and Other Poems*.

1890   (*May*) Makes a recording of some poems, by the kindness of Edison.

1892   (*March*) Production of *The Foresters* in New York.

(*April*) Publishes *The Foresters*. Irving at last agrees to produce *Becket* (acted February 1892).

(*July*) His last illness.

(*6 October*) Dies at Aldworth.

(*28 October*) Posthumous publication of *The Death of Œnone, Akbar's Dream, and Other Poems.*

Abbreviations

AHH = *The Letters of Arthur Henry Hallam*, edited by Jack Kolb (1981)

B.MS = *Berg Manuscript*

Buckley = Jerome Hamilton Buckley, *Tennyson: The Growth of a Poet* (1960)

CT = Sir Charles Tennyson, *Alfred Tennyson* (1949)

Culler = A. Dwight Culler, *The Poetry of Tennyson* (1977)

E. and S. = *Essays and Studies*

ELN = *English Language Notes*

E. T. = Emily Tennyson, the poet's wife

Eversley = Tennyson's *Works* (nine vols, Macmillan, 1907–8), edited by Hallam Lord Tennyson

FitzGerald, *Letters* = Edward FitzGerald, *The Letters*, edited by A. McK. and A. B. Terhune (1980)

Gray = J. M. Gray, *Thro' the Vision of the Night: A Study of Source, Evolution and Structure in Tennyson's Idylls of the King* (1980)

HLB = *Harvard Library Bulletin*

H. Lpr = *Harvard Loosepaper*

H. MS = *Harvard Manuscript*

H. Nbk = *Harvard Notebook*

HnMS = *Huntington Manuscript*

H. T. = Hallam Lord Tennyson

JEGP = *Journal of English and Germanic Philology*

Knowles = Gordon N. Ray, *Tennyson Reads 'Maud'* (1968), comments reported by James Knowles.

Letters = *The Letters of Alfred Lord Tennyson*, edited by Cecil Y. Lang and Edgar F. Shannon, i (1982), ii (1987), iii (forthcoming; no page-references therefore possible below).

L. MS = *Lincoln Manuscript*

Martin = Robert Bernard Martin, *Tennyson: The Unquiet Heart* (1980)

Mat. = Hallam Lord Tennyson, *Materials for a Life of A. T.* (privately printed, no date)

Mem. = Hallam Lord Tennyson, *Alfred Lord Tennyson: A Memoir* (1897). A few corrections were made in 1899.

MLN = *Modern Language Notes*

MLR = *Modern Language Review*

Motter = T. H. Vail Motter (ed.), *The Writings of Arthur Hallam* (1943)

MP = *Modern Philology*

OED = *Oxford English Dictionary*
Paden = W. D. Paden, *Tennyson in Egypt: A Study of the Imagery in His Earlier Work* (1942)
PL = *Paradise Lost*
PMLA = *Publications of the Modern Language Association of America*
PQ = *Philological Quarterly*
PR = *Paradise Regained*
QR = *Quarterly Review*
Rader = Ralph Wilson Rader, *Tennyson's 'Maud': The Biographical Genesis* (1963)
RES = *Review of English Studies*
Rosenberg = John Rosenberg, *The Fall of Camelot* (1973)
S & S = Susan Shatto and Marion Shaw (ed.), *In Memoriam* (1982)
SB = *Studies in Bibliography*
Shannon = Edgar Finlay Shannon, Jr., *Tennyson and the Reviewers* (1952)
T. = Tennyson
Charles Tennyson = *CT* above
TLS = *Times Literary Supplement*
T. MS = *Trinity Manuscript*
T. Nbk = *Trinity Notebook*
TRB = *Tennyson Research Bulletin*
Turner = Paul Turner, *Tennyson* (1976)
ULC MS = *University Library, Cambridge, Manuscript*
VN = *Victorian Newsletter*
VP = *Victorian Poetry*
VS = *Victorian Studies*
Y. MS = *Yale MS*

(*p. 135*) = page reference within this Selected Edition
(II 276) = page reference to Complete Edition

★ = a poem not included by Tennyson in his final edition
[relevant in this Selected Edition only to draft material in Appendix I]

1913 = The one-volume edition of Tennyson's *Works* (1913), edited by Hallam Lord Tennyson, based upon but slightly modifying the Eversley edition
1931 = *Unpublished Early Poems by Alfred Tennyson*, edited by Sir Charles Tennyson (1931)

THE POEMS

73 Mariana

Published *1830*; 'Juvenilia'. T. says: 'The *moated grange* was no particular grange, but one which rose to the music of Shakespeare's words.' The epigraph is from *Measure for Measure* III i 212ff: 'She should this Angelo have married: was affianced to her by oath, and the nuptial appointed. . . . Left her in her tears, and dried not one of them with his comfort. . . . What a merit were it in death to take this poor maid from the world! . . . There, at the moated grange, resides this dejected Mariana.' The poem was influenced by Keats's *Isabella* 233ff, where she waits in vain: 'She weeps alone for pleasures not to be; / Sorely she wept until the night came on . . . / And so she pined, and so she died forlorn.' Keats's 'aloof/roof' may have suggested the rhymes in ll. 73–5. Cp. Samuel Rogers, *Captivity* (1801): 'Caged in old woods, whose reverend echoes wake / When the hern screams along the distant lake, / Her little heart oft flutters to be free, / Oft sighs to turn the unrelenting key. / In vain! the nurse that rusted relic wears, / Nor moved by gold – nor to be moved by tears; / And terraced walls their black reflection throw / On the green-mantled moat that sleeps below.' These eight lines T. later praised to Palgrave 'for their delicate music' (*Mem.* ii 503). Rogers' *Poems* (1812) was at Somersby (*Lincoln*). Ian Kennedy compares *Wilhelm Meister's Apprenticeship*: 'Wilhelm's first love is an actress called Mariana . . . Goethe's Mariana finds no such happy consummation [as Shakespeare's] . . . she waits and watches for him in vain.' Kennedy notes: 'You came not', her 'weary life', 'I entreat thee, come, O come!' with the constant repetition of the word 'come'. He also suggests, as an influence on the refrain Lytton's *Falkland* (1827, p. 330): 'O God! O God! would that I were dead!' (*PQ* lvii, 1978, 93–4, 100; the source was suggested by C. Y. Lang, *Tennyson in Lincoln* i, 1971, xi).

T. seems to have invented the stanza form; J. F. A. Pyre remarks that the best of the early poems are those that stay most strictly with a stanza, as here (*The Formation of Tennyson's Style*, 1921, p. 26). Cp. *Mariana in the South* (p. 27). In a copy of *1830*, T. inserted the titles of additional poems, presumably considering, before *1832*, a revised edition of *1830*. Before *Mariana*, he wrote *Prologue to the Marianas*; this either has not survived or has not been recognized. After *Mariana*, he wrote *A Southern Mariana*. (See C. Sturman, *TRB* iv, 1984, 123–4.)

Mariana in the moated grange

(*Measure for Measure*)

' With blackest moss the flower-plots
    Were thickly crusted, one and all:

¶ **73.1–2.** Adapted from *The Outcast* 23 (1826): 'The wet moss crusts the parting wall', followed by 'knots'.

The rusted nails fell from the knots
That held the pear to the gable-wall.
5 The broken sheds looked sad and strange:
Unlifted was the clinking latch;
Weeded and worn the ancient thatch
Upon the lonely moated grange.
She only said, 'My life is dreary,
10 He cometh not,' she said;
She said, 'I am aweary, aweary,
I would that I were dead!'

Her tears fell with the dews at even;
Her tears fell ere the dews were dried;
15 She could not look on the sweet heaven,
Either at morn or eventide.
After the flitting of the bats,
When thickest dark did trance the sky,
She drew her casement-curtain by,
20 And glanced athwart the glooming flats.
She only said, 'The night is dreary,
He cometh not,' she said;
She said, 'I am aweary, aweary,
I would that I were dead!'

4. pear] *1862*; peach *1830–60*. T. says: '"peach" spoils the desolation of the picture. It is not a characteristic of the scenery I had in mind.'   *gable-wall*] *1869*; garden-wall *1830–68*.

13. Cp. Horace, *Odes* II ix 10–12: *nec tibi Vespero / surgente decedunt amores / nec rapidum fugiente solem.* ('Nor do thy words of love cease either when Vesper comes out at evening, or when he flies before the swiftly coursing sun'.) Cp. also 'Her tears are mixed with the beaded dews', from *Song* [*I' the glooming light*] (I 235), a poem comparable to *Mariana*: 'Death standeth by; / She will not die; / With glazèd eye / She looks at her grave: she cannot sleep; / Ever alone / She maketh her moan . . .'. John Churton Collins remarked that ll. 13–14 were evidently adapted from Cinna: *Te matutinus flentem conspexit Eous, / Te flentem paulo vidit post Hesperus idem.* Alongside this suggestion, T. wrote: 'I read this for the first time' (*Cornhill*, Jan. 1880, *Lincoln*).

15. Cp. the deserted Dido, *Aeneid* iv 451: *taedet caeli convexa tueri* ('she is weary of gazing on the arch of heaven').

18. *trance*: throw into a trance. T.'s is the earliest figurative use in *OED*.

20. Cp. *A Fragment* 17: 'Looking athwart the burning flats'; and *Fatima* 13: 'I looked athwart the burning drouth', where the suffering heroine awaits her lover. Keats has 'athwart the gloom', *Sleep and Poetry* 146.

25 Upon the middle of the night,
    Waking she heard the night-fowl crow:
    The cock sung out an hour ere light:
    From the dark fen the oxen's low
    Came to her: without hope of change,
30   In sleep she seemed to walk forlorn,
    Till cold winds woke the gray-eyed morn
    About the lonely moated grange.
    She only said, 'The day is dreary,
      He cometh not,' she said;
35   She said, 'I am aweary, aweary,
      I would that I were dead!'

    About a stone-cast from the wall
    A sluice with blackened waters slept,
    And o'er it many, round and small,
40   The clustered marish-mosses crept.
    Hard by a poplar shook alway,
    All silver-green with gnarlèd bark:
    For leagues no other tree did mark
    The level waste, the rounding gray.
45   She only said, 'My life is dreary,
      He cometh not,' she said;
    She said, 'I am aweary, aweary,
      I would that I were dead!'

    And ever when the moon was low,
50   And the shrill winds were up and away,
    In the white curtain, to and fro,
    She saw the gusty shadow sway.
    But when the moon was very low,
    And wild winds bound within their cell,

25. *Measure for Measure* IV i 35: 'Upon the heavy middle of the night'; and Keats, *Eve of St Agnes* 49: 'Upon the honey'd middle of the night'.
25–6. T. compares the ballad of Clerk Saunders: 'O cocks are crowing of merry midnight'; and H.T. adds *Oriana* 12: 'At midnight the cock was crowing'.
31. *gray-eyed morn*: *Romeo and Juliet* II iii 1.
40. *marish-mosses*: 'the little marsh-moss lumps that float on the surface of water' (T.). Cp. Crabbe, *The Lover's Journey*: 'Here the dwarf sallows creep, the septfoil harsh, / And the soft slimy mallow of the marsh.'
43. *mark*] *1845*; dark *1830–43*.
50. *and*] *1842*; an' *1830*.
54. The cave of Aeolus, mentioned in *Lycidas* 97 – cp. l. 80n.

55 The shadow of the poplar fell
Upon her bed, across her brow.
She only said, 'The night is dreary,
He cometh not,' she said;
She said, 'I am aweary, aweary,
60 I would that I were dead!'

All day within the dreamy house,
The doors upon their hinges creaked;
The blue fly sung in the pane; the mouse
Behind the mouldering wainscot shrieked,
65 Or from the crevice peered about.
Old faces glimmered through the doors,
Old footsteps trod the upper floors,
Old voices called her from without.
She only said, 'My life is dreary,
70 He cometh not,' she said;
She said, 'I am aweary, aweary,
I would that I were dead!'

The sparrow's chirrup on the roof,
The slow clock ticking, and the sound
75 Which to the wooing wind aloof
The poplar made, did all confound
Her sense; but most she loathed the hour
When the thick-moted sunbeam lay
Athwart the chambers, and the day
80 Was sloping toward his western bower.
Then, said she, 'I am very dreary,
He will not come,' she said;
She wept, 'I am aweary, aweary,
Oh God, that I were dead!'

55. Turner (p. 46) notes that the poplar 'comes from Ovid: Œnone, deserted by Paris, addresses a poplar, with "wrinkled bark", on which Paris has carved a promise never to desert her.'
63. in] 1850; i' 1830–48. Cp. the empty house in Maud i 257–60, with its 'shrieking rush of the wainscot mouse' (p. 534).
74. A. Burnett notes Pope, Epistle to Miss Blount, on her leaving the town 18: 'Count the slow clock' (Notes and Queries ccxxv, 1980, 208).
78. Burnett also notes Milton, Il Penseroso 7–8: 'As thick and numberless / As the gay motes that people the Sun Beams'.
80] 1842; Downsloped was westering in his bower. 1830. Echoing Lycidas 31: 'had slop'd his westering wheel'.

78 Supposed Confessions of a Second-Rate Sensitive Mind

Published *1830*, with the longer title . . . *Mind Not In Unity With Itself*; not reprinted till restored *1884*, 'Juvenilia'. Cp. *Remorse* (I 98); *Perdidi Diem* (I 293); and *Pierced through* (I 513). The doubts precede Arthur Hallam's death, and anticipate *The Two Voices* and *In Memoriam*. T. says: 'If some kind friend had taken him by the hand and said, "Come, work"–"Look not every man on his own things, but every man also on the things of others" (*Philippians* ii 4)–he might have been a happy man, though sensitive.' T. quarried it for *A Fragment* (I 313). Ian Kennedy compares the original title with *Wilhelm Meister's Travels* ch. viii (tr. Carlyle); 'the Confessions of some mind not yet in unity with itself' (*PQ* lvii, 1978, 87); Kennedy mounts a persuasive argument about the 'extraordinary correspondence between parts of Goethe's two novels and a number of T.'s poems of the Cambridge period'. In a copy of *1830*, T. inserted the titles of additional poems, presumably considering, before *1832*, a revised edition of *1830*. After *Supposed Confessions*, he wrote *St. Lawrence on the Gridiron* (I 324; C. Sturman, *TRB* iv, 1984, 123–4).

> O God! my God! have mercy now.
> I faint, I fall. Men say that Thou
> Didst die for me, for such as *me*,
> Patient of ill, and death, and scorn,
> 5 And that my sin was as a thorn
> Among the thorns that girt Thy brow,
> Wounding Thy soul.–That even now,
> In this extremest misery
> Of ignorance, I should require
> 10 A sign! and if a bolt of fire
> Would rive the slumbrous summer noon
> While I do pray to Thee alone,
> Think my belief would stronger grow!
> Is not my human pride brought low?
> 15 The boastings of my spirit still?
> The joy I had in my freewill
> All cold, and dead, and corpse-like grown?
> And what is left to me, but Thou,
> And faith in Thee? Men pass me by;

¶ 78.2. Cp. Shelley, *Indian Serenade* 18: 'I faint! I fail!'
9–10. *1 Corinthians* i 22, 'For the Jews require a sign'; *Matthew* xii 39, 'an evil and adulterous generation seeketh after a sign; and there shall no sign be given to it'.
11. the slumbrous summer noon : incorporated in *A Fragment* 11.

20   Christians with happy countenances –
     And children all seem full of Thee!
     And women smile with saint-like glances
     Like Thine own mother's when she bowed
     Above Thee, on that happy morn
25   When angels spake to men aloud,
     And Thou and peace to earth were born.
     Goodwill to me as well as all –
     I one of them: my brothers they:
     Brothers in Christ – a world of peace
30   And confidence, day after day;
     And trust and hope till things should cease,
     And then one Heaven receive us all.

     How sweet to have a common faith!
     To hold a common scorn of death!
35   And at a burial to hear
     The creaking cords which wound and eat
     Into my human heart, whene'er
     Earth goes to earth, with grief, not fear,
     With hopeful grief, were passing sweet!

40   Thrice happy state again to be
     The trustful infant on the knee!

36. Cp. *To-*[*Clear-headed friend*] 4: 'The wounding cords that bind and strain'.

39 ∧ 40]   A grief not uninformed, and dull,
                    Hearted with hope, of hope as full
                    As is the blood with life, or night
                    And a dark cloud with rich moonlight.
          [*5*]   To stand beside a grave, and see
                    The red small atoms wherewith we
                    Are built, and smile in calm, and say –
                    'These little motes and grains shall be
                    'Clothed on with immortality
          [*10*]   'More glorious than the noon of day.
                    'All that is passed into the flowers,
                    'And into beasts, and other men,
                    'And all the Norland whirlwind showers
                    'From open vaults, and all the sea
          [*15*]   'O'erwashes with sharp salts, again
                    'Shall fleet together all, and be
                    'Indued with immortality.' *1830*
Cp. l. [9] with *2 Corinthians* v 4, 'not for that we would be unclothed, but clothed upon, that mortality might be swallowed up of life'. 'The Norland whirlwind' of l. [13] is in *Oriana* 6.

Who lets his rosy fingers play
About his mother's neck, and knows
Nothing beyond his mother's eyes.
45 They comfort him by night and day;
They light his little life alway;
He hath no thought of coming woes;
He hath no care of life or death;
Scarce outward signs of joy arise,
50 Because the Spirit of happiness
And perfect rest so inward is;
And loveth so his innocent heart,
Her temple and her place of birth,
Where she would ever wish to dwell,
55 Life of the fountain there, beneath
Its salient springs, and far apart,
Hating to wander out on earth,
Or breathe into the hollow air,
Whose chillness would make visible
60 Her subtil, warm, and golden breath,
Which mixing with the infant's blood,
Fulfils him with beatitude.
Oh! sure it is a special care
Of God, to fortify from doubt,
65 To arm in proof, and guard about
With triple-mailèd trust, and clear
Delight, the infant's dawning year.

Would that my gloomèd fancy were
As thine, my mother, when with brows
70 Propt on thy knees, my hands upheld
In thine, I listened to thy vows,
For me outpoured in holiest prayer –
For me unworthy! – and beheld
Thy mild deep eyes upraised, that knew
75 The beauty and repose of faith,
And the clear spirit shining through.
Oh! wherefore do we grow awry
From roots which strike so deep? why dare
Paths in the desert? Could not I
80 Bow myself down, where thou hast knelt,
To the earth – until the ice would melt
Here, and I feel as thou hast felt?

42. *rosy*] *1884*; waxen *1830*.
56. *salient springs*: *Adeline* 26; as in Wordsworth, *The Borderers* 1788. Cp.
'the salient blood' (i.e. leaping), *Sonnet* [*Shall the hag*] 5.
65. *proof*: armour.

What Devil had the heart to scathe
Flowers thou hadst reared – to brush the dew
85 From thine own lily, when thy grave
Was deep, my mother, in the clay?
Myself? Is it thus? Myself? Had I
So little love for thee? But why
Prevailed not thy pure prayers? Why pray
90 To one who heeds not, who can save
But will not? Great in faith, and strong
Against the grief of circumstance
Wert thou, and yet unheard. What if
Thou pleadest still, and seest me drive
95 Through utter dark a full-sailed skiff,
Unpiloted i' the echoing dance
Of reboant whirlwinds, stooping low
Unto the death, not sunk! I know
At matins and at evensong,
100 That thou, if thou wert yet alive,
In deep and daily prayers wouldst strive
To reconcile me with thy God.
Albeit, my hope is gray, and cold
At heart, thou wouldest murmur still –
105 'Bring this lamb back into Thy fold,
My Lord, if so it be Thy will.'
Wouldst tell me I must brook the rod
And chastisement of human pride;
That pride, the sin of devils, stood
110 Betwixt me and the light of God!
That hitherto I had defied
And had rejected God – that grace
Would drop from his o'er-brimming love,
As manna on my wilderness,
115 If I would pray – that God would move
And strike the hard, hard rock, and thence,
Sweet in their utmost bitterness,
Would issue tears of penitence
Which would keep green hope's life. Alas!
120 I think that pride hath now no place
Nor sojourn in me. I am void,
Dark, formless, utterly destroyed.
Why not believe then? Why not yet
Anchor thy frailty there, where man

97. *reboant*: re-bellowing; T.'s is the earliest example in *OED*.
116. *Numbers* xx 11.
121–2. *void, dark*: Coleridge's *Dejection* 21. Cp. *On Sublimity* 70: 'formless

125   Hath moored and rested? Ask the sea
       At midnight, when the crisp slope waves
       After a tempest, rib and fret
       The broad-imbasèd beach, why he
       Slumbers not like a mountain tarn?
130   Wherefore his ridges are not curls
       And ripples of an inland mere?
       Wherefore he moaneth thus, nor can
       Draw down into his vexèd pools
       All that blue heaven which hues and paves
135   The other? I am too forlorn,
       Too shaken: my own weakness fools
       My judgment, and my spirit whirls,
       Moved from beneath with doubt and fear.

       'Yet,' said I, in my morn of youth,
140   The unsunned freshness of my strength,
       When I went forth in quest of truth,
       'It is man's privilege to doubt,
       If so be that from doubt at length,
       Truth may stand forth unmoved of change,
145   An image with profulgent brows,
       And perfect limbs, as from the storm
       Of running fires and fluid range
       Of lawless airs, at last stood out
       This excellence and solid form
150   Of constant beauty. For the Ox
       Feeds in the herb, and sleeps, or fills
       The hornèd valleys all about,
       And hollows of the fringèd hills

and still and dark'. Also several words are taken up from *Paradise Lost* iii
11–16: 'waters dark and deep, / Won from the void and formless infinite. /
Thee I re-visit now with bolder wing, / Escap't the *Stygian* Pool, though
long detain'd / In that obscure sojourn, while in my flight / Through utter
and through middle darkness borne . . .'.
126. slope: sloping.
126–9. A Fragment 10–11 has 'broadbased . . . sloped . . . slumbrous' (cp.
l. 11*n*).
129. Cp. *Ode: O Bosky Brook* 22: 'the mountain tarn's unbroken sleep'.
145. Adapted for *A Fragment* 3: 'A perfect Idol with profulgent brows'.
147–8. Cp. *The Princess* ii 101: 'This world was once a fluid haze of light'.
150–71. G. O. Marshall (*A Tennyson Handbook*, 1963, p. 32) notes the in-
fluence of Pope, *Essay on Man* i 77–86: 'Heav'n from all creatures hides the
book of Fate, / All but the page prescrib'd, their present state; / From
brutes what men, from men what spirits know: / Or who could suffer Being

In summer heats, with placid lows
155 Unfearing, till his own blood flows
About his hoof. And in the flocks
The lamb rejoiceth in the year,
And raceth freely with his fere,
And answers to his mother's calls
160 From the flowered furrow. In a time,
Of which he wots not, run short pains
Through his warm heart; and then, from whence
He knows not, on his light there falls
A shadow; and his native slope,
165 Where he was wont to leap and climb,
Floats from his sick and filmèd eyes,
And something in the darkness draws
His forehead earthward, and he dies.
Shall man live thus, in joy and hope
170 As a young lamb, who cannot dream,
Living, but that he shall live on?
Shall we not look into the laws
Of life and death, and things that seem,
And things that be, and analyse
175 Our double nature, and compare
All creeds till we have found the one,
If one there be?' Ay me! I fear
All may not doubt, but everywhere
Some must clasp Idols. Yet, my God,
180 Whom call I Idol? Let Thy dove
Shadow me over, and my sins
Be unremembered, and Thy love
Enlighten me. Oh teach me yet
Somewhat before the heavy clod
185 Weighs on me, and the busy fret
Of that sharp-headed worm begins
In the gross blackness underneath.

O weary life! O weary death!
O spirit and heart made desolate!
190 O damnèd vacillating state!

here below? / The lamb thy riot dooms to bleed to-day, / Had he thy
Reason, would he skip and play? / Pleas'd to the last, he crops the flow'ry
food, / And licks the hand just rais'd to shed his blood. / Oh blindness to
the future! kindly giv'n, / That each may fill the circle mark'd by Heav'n.'
158. fere: companion.
169. man] *1884*; men *1830*.
179. Idols: Turner (p. 53) notes 'used in the Baconian sense of false mental
images'.
181. Shadow: to protect with wings, a biblical sense.

86 Song [A spirit haunts the year's last hours]

Published *1830*; 'Juvenilia'. 'Written at Somersby' (H.T.). Stanza I appears in *T.Nbk 18* with poems of 1828; all variants are below.

I

A spirit haunts the year's last hours
Dwelling amid these yellowing bowers:
 To himself he talks;
For at eventide, listening earnestly,
5 At his work you may hear him sob and sigh
  In the walks;
  Earthward he boweth the heavy stalks
Of the mouldering flowers:
  Heavily hangs the broad sunflower
10   Over its grave i' the earth so chilly;
  Heavily hangs the hollyhock,
  Heavily hangs the tiger-lily.

II

The air is damp, and hushed, and close,
As a sick man's room when he taketh repose
15 An hour before death;
My very heart faints and my whole soul grieves
At the moist rich smell of the rotting leaves,
  And the breath
  Of the fading edges of box beneath,
20 And the year's last rose.
  Heavily hangs the broad sunflower
   Over its grave i' the earth so chilly;
  Heavily hangs the hollyhock,
  Heavily hangs the tiger-lily.

¶ 86. *5. you*] ye *T.MS.*
10] The sky is all white: the wind is chilly *T.MS.*
13. damp . . . hushed] hushed . . . damp *H.Nbk 4.*
16. very . . . whole] whole . . . very *H.MS.* Cp. *The Lover's Tale* i 261–2:
'My whole soul languishes / And faints'. Also *Maud* ii 237–8: 'weep / My
whole soul out to thee'.

88 A Character

Published *1830*; 'Juvenilia'. A 'character' after Theophrastus, epigram-matically combining a moral temperament and a personal sketch. It is on Thomas Sunderland (1808–67), who was at Trinity College with T. and was 'a very plausible, parliament-like, and self-satisfied speaker at the Union' (FitzGerald). He won the Trinity declamation prize in 1829. Hallam listed him among the 'crack speakers' at the Union, and called him 'wonderfully fluent: his principles appear to be Benthamite and but very ambiguously Christian' (to J. M. Gaskell, 5 Nov. 1828); Sunderland's mind failed shortly after he left Cambridge in 1830 (*AHH*, pp. 241–2). On Sunderland, see also P. Allen, *The Cambridge Apostles* (1978), ch. 3: 'Thomas Sunderland and the Cambridge Union'. Sterling wrote of 'his general cold superciliousness', and Kemble (to W. B. Donne, 13 Jan. 1829) wrote: 'he has already mounted up through presentations, sensations, conceptions and notions and cognitions within sight of the Deity, and thinks Christianity a very fair style of thing, and the Trinity a tolerably passable notion' (p. 41). Written 1829 or early 1830, when T.'s friends Richard Monckton Milnes and J. W. Blakesley complained of Sunderland's zest for 'perfect solitude' and his 'direct contemplation of the absolute' (Joyce Green, *The Development of the Poetic Image in Tennyson*, Cambridge thesis, 1954). In his review of *1842* in the *Church of England Quarterly Review* (Oct. 1842), Leigh Hunt wrote: 'We look upon the above, after its kind, as a faultless composition; and its kind is no mean one. Considered as a poetical satire, it brings an atmosphere of imagination round the coldest matter of fact; and the delicate *blank* effect of the disposition of the rhymes completes the seemingly passionless exposure of its passionless object.'

> With a half-glance upon the sky
> At night he said, 'The wanderings
> Of this most intricate Universe
> Teach me the nothingness of things.'
> 5   Yet could not all creation pierce
> Beyond the bottom of his eye.
>
> He spake of beauty: that the dull
> Saw no divinity in grass,
> Life in dead stones, or spirit in air;
> 10   Then looking as 'twere in a glass,
> He smoothed his chin and sleeked his hair,
> And said the earth was beautiful.

¶ 88.*11. sleeked*: smoothed, as in Milton, *Comus* 882: 'sleeking her soft alluring locks'.

He spake of virtue: not the gods
More purely, when they wish to charm
15   Pallas and Juno sitting by:
And with a sweeping of the arm,
And a lack-lustre dead-blue eye,
Devolved his rounded periods.

Most delicately hour by hour
20   He canvassed human mysteries,
And trod on silk, as if the winds
Blew his own praises in his eyes,
And stood aloof from other minds
In impotence of fancied power.

25   With lips depressed as he were meek,
Himself unto himself he sold:
Upon himself himself did feed:
Quiet, dispassionate, and cold,
And other than his form of creed,
30   With chiselled features clear and sleek.

97 The Dying Swan

Published *1830*; 'Juvenilia'. The widespread tradition of the swan's death-song was discussed in William Hone's *Every-Day Book* (1827 edn, ii 964–8), the acknowledged source of *St Simeon Stylites*. Turner (p. 47) notes that, in Ovid, 'Dido begins her complaint to Aeneas in the *Heroides*, by comparing herself to a white swan, singing by the river Maeander, just before its death . . . it is noticeable that [T.] makes his swan female (l. 28), and gives her a backcloth of snow-capped mountains, much more appropriate to the Maeander (overlooked by Mount Latmos) than to any English fen-country.' C. B. Stevenson studies the dying swan in mythology and throughout T., in relation to his hopes for art (*Studies in English Literature* xx, 1980, 621–35).

I

The plain was grassy, wild and bare,
Wide, wild, and open to the air,
Which had built up everywhere
An under-roof of doleful gray.

17. The moralizing fool in *As You Like It* II vii 21 had a 'lack-lustre eye'.
18. Thomson, *Autumn* 16–17: 'Devolving through the maze of eloquence /
A roll of periods'; from Horace's *verba devolvit* (*Odes* IV ii 11).
27. Cp. *Troilus and Cressida* II iii 153–4: 'He that is proud eats up himself:
pride is his own glass'; see l. 10.

5   With an inner voice the river ran,
     Adown it floated a dying swan,
          And loudly did lament.
     It was the middle of the day.
     Ever the weary wind went on,
10   And took the reed-tops as it went.

                    II
     Some blue peaks in the distance rose,
     And white against the cold-white sky,
          Shone out their crowning snows.
     One willow over the river wept,
15   And shook the wave as the wind did sigh;
     Above in the wind was the swallow,
          Chasing itself at its own wild will,
          And far through the marish green and still
          The tangled water-courses slept,
20   Shot over with purple, and green, and yellow.

                    III
     The wild swan's death-hymn took the soul
     Of that waste place with joy
     Hidden in sorrow: at first to the ear
     The warble was low, and full and clear;
25   And floating about the under-sky,
     Prevailing in weakness, the coronach stole
     Sometimes afar, and sometimes anear;
     But anon her awful jubilant voice,
     With a music strange and manifold,
30   Flowed forth on a carol free and bold;
     As when a mighty people rejoice
     With shawms, and with cymbals, and harps of gold,

¶ 97.7. *And*] *1850*; Which *1830–48*.

9. weary wind: *Ode to Memory* 113, and also three times in Shelley.

16. was] *1842*; sung *1830*.

17. Cp. Wordsworth, *Westminster Bridge* 12: 'The river glideth at his own sweet will'.

21. wild swan: since the tradition excluded the domestic swan (a point made by Hone).   *took*: enraptured.

26. coronach: 'Gaelic funeral-song' (T.). C. B. Stevenson notes that the word implies a group of people lamenting.

30. free and bold: cp. Hone, 'with the sentiment of entire liberty, it has also the tones'.

31–4. Based on *Iliad* iv 452–5. T. here anticipates *Ode on Wellington* 142–7 (*p. 494*).

And the tumult of their acclaim is rolled
Through the open gates of the city afar,
35 To the shepherd who watcheth the evening star.
And the creeping mosses and clambering weeds,
And the willow-branches hoar and dank,
And the wavy swell of the soughing reeds,
And the wave-worn horns of the echoing bank,
40 And the silvery marish-flowers that throng
The desolate creeks and pools among,
Were flooded over with eddying song.

113 The Kraken

Published *1830*, not reprinted until restored in *1872*, 'Juvenilia'. T. com-
ments: 'See the account which Erik Pontoppidan, the Norwegian bishop,
born 1698, gives of the fabulous sea-monster–the Kraken (*Biographie
Universelle*)' [1823]. Pontoppidan's account was summarized in the *English
Encyclopaedia* (1802), of which a copy was at Somersby (*Lincoln*). T. would
also have read of the kraken in Scott's *Ministrelsy* (Leyden's *The Mermaid*),
and in T. C. Croker's *Fairy Legends* ii (1828) 64, a book which he knew and
later owned (*Lincoln*). Paden (p. 155) observes that T.'s monster has only its
name in common with Pontoppidan's, and argues that T. associated it with
G. S. Faber's religious mythologizing, where the serpent (the evil prin-
ciple) leads to the deluge: hence the sea-snake, and hence the 'latter fire'.
On T.'s later owning books by Faber, see *p. 149*. D. Bush, *Major British
Writers* (1959) ii 380, cites *Revelation* xiii 1, 'And I stood upon the sand of
the sea, and saw a beast rise up out of the sea.' The adaptation of the sonnet
form is discussed by R. Pattison, *Tennyson and Tradition* (1979), pp. 41–2.
Ian Kennedy suggests adding to the sources a dream in Lytton's *Falkland*
(1827, p. 269), a book T. knew (*Letters* i 23): 'He was a thousand fathoms
beneath the sea . . . he saw the coral banks, which it requires a thousand
ages to form, rise slowly . . . and ever and ever, around and above him,
came vast and misshapen things, – the wonders of the secret deeps; and the
sea-serpent, the huge chimera of the north, made its resting place by his
side, glaring upon him with a livid and death-like eye, wan, yet burning as
an expiring sun' (*PQ* lvii, 1978, 97).

Below the thunders of the upper deep;
Far, far beneath in the abysmal sea,
His ancient, dreamless, uninvaded sleep
The Kraken sleepeth: faintest sunlights flee

33. Cp. 'tumult of acclaim', *In Memoriam* lxxv 20, and *To Poesy [Religion]* 8.
38. soughing: 'Anglo-Saxon *sweg*, a sound. Modified into an onomatopœic
word for the soft sound or the deep sighing of the wind' (T.).
42. Cp. *Timbuctoo* 9: 'were flooded over with clear glory'.

 5 About his shadowy sides: above him swell
    Huge sponges of millennial growth and height;
    And far away into the sickly light,
    From many a wondrous grot and secret cell
    Unnumbered and enormous polypi
10 Winnow with giant arms the slumbering green.
    There hath he lain for ages and will lie
    Battening upon huge seaworms in his sleep,
    Until the latter fire shall heat the deep;
    Then once by man and angels to be seen,
15 In roaring he shall rise and on the surface die.

[1830. *The Sleeping Beauty*–see *p. 172*]

159 The Lady of Shalott

Published *1832*, much revised *1842*. Written, at least in part, by 5–9 Oct. 1831 (Hallam to Frederick T.: 'I would fain know where the Lady of Shalott abides at present'; *AHH*, p. 487); then by 31 May 1832 (FitzGerald's *Letters*,

¶ 113.*7*. *sickly light*: *OED* 6, 'of light, colour', from Prior, *An English Ballad* 135 (1695).
9. Pontoppidan: 'This Krake must be of the Polypus kind, notwithstanding its enormous size' (*Natural History of Norway* (tr. 1755) ii 217).
10. *arms*] *1872*; fins *1830*. Pontoppidan ii 210: 'full of arms'.   *Winnow*: in this sense, influenced by Milton, *Paradise Lost* v 269–70: 'Then with quick Fann / Winnows the buxom Air'. T. probably observed Shelley's fondness for *winnow*. For the context, cp. *Timbuctoo* 146–51: 'My thoughts which long had grovelled in the slime / Of this dull world, like dusky worms which house / Beneath unshaken waters, but at once / Upon some Earth-awakening day of Spring / Do pass from gloom to glory, and aloft / Winnow the purple.'
12. Shelley, *Prometheus Unbound* IV 542: 'The dull weed some seaworm battens on'. The kraken's 'ability to feed while sleeping may have been suggested by [Pontoppidan's] account of a strong scent by which krakens attract fish into their clutches' (Paden, p. 155).
13–15. *Revelation* viii 8–9: 'And the second angel sounded, and as it were a great mountain burning with fire was cast into the sea; and the third part of the sea became blood; And the third part of the creatures which were in the sea, and had life, died.' In Faberian terms (see headnote), this was 'another in that series of dissolutions of which the mystae were taught' (Paden, p. 155).
14. *man*] *1830*, *1872*; men *correction in 1830 Errata*. Pontoppidan ii 211–12: 'Amongst the many great things which are in the ocean, and concealed from our eyes, or only presented to our view for a few minutes, is the Kraken', whose whole body 'in all likelihood no human eye ever beheld'.

i 112–3). T. says it was 'taken from an Italian novelette, *Donna di Scalotta*'.
T. noted in *T.Nbk 23*: 'Legends. / The Lady of Scalot. *Novelle Antiche*'. The
source is quoted in Italian, *Mat.* iv 461: 'The following is the Italian novella
on which *The Lady of Shalott* was founded: Novella LXXXI *Quì conta come la
Damigella di Scalot morì per amore di Lancialotto de Lac.* From the *Cento
Novelle Antiche*, dated conjecturally before 1321. Text from the Milan edn,
ed. G. Ferrario, 1804.' The source had been mentioned by F. T. Palgrave
and by John Churton Collins, and was investigated by L. S. Potwin, *MLN*
xvii (1902) 473–7, and by D. L. Chambers, *MLN* xviii (1903) 227–8. But
the story is very different; the poem has no Arthur, and no Queen; the
source has no mirror, weaving, curse, song, river, or island. Apart from the
Lady's death, the main links are that Camelot is the end of the funeral
voyage, and is – unusually – on the sea-shore, and that there is an astonished
crowd about the body. G. R. Jackson notes that, like the source, *1832* has
no Lancelot among the onlookers at the end. The *1832* text is slightly closer
in some details, e.g. her death-letter. F. J. Furnivall quotes T. in Jan. 1868:
'I met the story first in some Italian *novelle*: but the web, mirror, island,
etc., were my own. Indeed, I doubt whether I should ever have put it in
that shape if I had been then aware of the Maid of Astolat in *Mort Arthur*'
(*Rossetti Papers 1862–1870*, ed. W. M. Rossetti, 1903, p. 341). T. may have
seen Thomas Roscoe's translation (1825), where she is 'the Lady', not
'Damsel'. T. says: 'The Lady of Shalott is evidently the Elaine of the *Morte
d'Arthur* [cp. *Lancelot and Elaine, p. 834*], but I do not think that I had ever
heard of the latter when I wrote the former. Shalott was a softer sound than
"Scalott".' See Malory xviii. J. M. Gray (*TRB* ii, 1976, 210–11) suggests
that T. may have forgotten that Malory influenced the poem; he compares
l. 73 with Malory's distance, 'as nigh . . . as bow-draught', and ll. 78–80
with Malory's Lancelot and his 'shield all of sable, and a queen crowned in
the midst, all of silver, and a knight clene armed kneeling afore her'
(Malory i and xii). Paden (pp. 156–7) notes the general influence of T. C.
Croker's *Fairy Legends* (1825–8) and of Thomas Keightley's *Fairy Mythology*
(1828), both of which T. knew. He also argues for the influence of G. S.
Faber's religious mythologizing: 'It may be suggested that she is one of
those nymphs, occupied in weaving, whom Porphyry explained as human
souls about to be born into the world'; Faber claimed them as symbols for
the epoptae of the mysteries. 'Bishop Percy had affirmed, in a note at the
end of the ballad on the death of Arthur, that "*Ladies* was the word our old
English writers used for *Nymphs*". In a very Tennysonian revision of Faber,
the birth of a soul is identified with the coming of love, and love brings
with it the doom of God.' On T.'s later owning books by Faber, see
p. 149. R. Simpson takes up J. M. Gray's reference to Louisa Stuart
Costello's poem *The Funeral Boat* (1829), indebted to the same Italian
novella (*TRB* iv, 1984, 129–31). L. Stevenson (*Critical Essays on Tennyson*,
ed. Killham, pp. 129–30) suggests the influence of Shelley's *Witch of Atlas*,
for an onlooker who weaves, and who has a magic boat: ''Tis said in after
times her spirit free / Knew what love was, and felt itself alone.' T.

comments (*Mem*. i 117): 'The new-born love for something, for some one in the wide world from which she has been so long secluded, takes her out of the region of shadows into that of realities'. H.T. comments: 'The key to this tale of magic symbolism is of deep human significance and is to be found in the lines [69–72].' Culler (p. 44) notes that the authority for the comments by T. and H.T. is Canon Ainger's *Tennyson for the Young* (1891), where there is however no 'indication that they come from Tennyson'. Cp. the companion poem, *Life of the Life* (I 548). G. Cannon suggests that *The Arabian Nights* (269th Night) provided the mirror: that is, a magic jewel with five facets, one of which shows a river, another a knight on a steed; the story also has a funeral scroll. The tale was available in various English and French versions by 1832, but Cannon adds: 'Unfortunately, no version seems to contain details close enough to T.'s terminology to suggest an actual borrowing of phrases and images. The 269th Tale is not in Edward Forster's five-volume edition (London, 1802) which T. apparently knew' (*VP* viii, 1970, 344–6). S. C. Wilson (misprinted as 'Allen', *TRB* ii, 1975, 171–2) suggests the influence of Sappho, fragment 102, in particular for the weaving; he notes other similarities, along with the fact that T. later marked with a small pencilled cross this fragment in *Poetae Lyrici Graeci* (*Lincoln*). For an account of previous interpretations and a new reading, see E. F. Shannon, *VP* xix (1981) 207–23. M. A. Lourie argues for Shelley's influence on the poem, especially *Prometheus Unbound*, and describes T.'s new kind of Romanticism (*Studies in Romanticism* xviii, 1979, 19–21, 27): 'Between 1830 and 1833 T. had essentially invented Pre-Raphaelitism.'

PART I

On either side the river lie
Long fields of barley and of rye,
That clothe the wold and meet the sky;
And through the field the road runs by
· 5   To many-towered Camelot;
And up and down the people go,
Gazing where the lilies blow
Round an island there below,
The island of Shalott.

¶ 159.5. *many-towered*: followed by 'lilies', this suggests *Ilion, Ilion* (I 281).
6–9] *1842*; The yellowleavèd waterlily,
    The greensheathèd daffodilly,
    Tremble in the water chilly,
      Round about Shalott. *1832*

T. altered J. M. Heath's copy of *1832* (*Fitzwilliam Museum*) to 'The yellow globe o' the waterlily'. Cp. *Anacreontics* 2–3 (1830): 'And drooping daffodilly, / And silverleavèd lily.'

10 Willows whiten, aspens quiver,
    Little breezes dusk and shiver
    Through the wave that runs for ever
    By the island in the river
        Flowing down to Camelot.
15 Four gray walls, and four gray towers,
    Overlook a space of flowers,
    And the silent isle imbowers
        The Lady of Shalott.

    By the margin, willow-veiled,
20 Slide the heavy barges trailed
    By slow horses; and unhailed
    The shallop flitteth silken-sailed
        Skimming down to Camelot:
    But who hath seen her wave her hand?
25 Or at the casement seen her stand?
    Or is she known in all the land,
        The Lady of Shalott?

    Only reapers, reaping early
    In among the bearded barley,
30 Hear a song that echoes cheerly
    From the river winding clearly,
        Down to towered Camelot:

10. quiver] *1842*; shiver *1832*.
11–12] *1842*; The sunbeam-showers break and quiver
            In the stream that runneth ever *1832*
19–27, 28–36] *1842*; *transposed 1832*.
19–21] *1842*; The little isle is all inrailed
            With a rose-fence, and overtrailed
            With roses: by the marge unhailed *1832*
24–6] *1842*; A pearlgarland winds her head:
            She leaneth on a velvet bed,
            Full royally apparellèd, *1832*
27. Shalott?] *1842*; Shalott. *1832*.
28–34] *1842*; Underneath the bearded barley,
            The reaper, reaping late and early,
            Hears her ever chanting cheerly,
            Like an angel, singing clearly,
                O'er the stream of Camelot.
            Piling the sheaves in furrows airy,
            Beneath the moon, the reaper weary *1832*
30. cheerly: T. compares *Richard II* I iii 66: 'But lusty, young, and cheerly
drawing breath'.

And by the moon the reaper weary,
Piling sheaves in uplands airy,
35   Listening, whispers ''Tis the fairy
Lady of Shalott.'

PART II

There she weaves by night and day
A magic web with colours gay.
She has heard a whisper say,
40   A curse is on her if she stay
To look down to Camelot.
She knows not what the curse may be,·
And so she weaveth steadily,
And little other care hath she,
45   The Lady of Shalott.

And moving through a mirror clear
That hangs before her all the year,
Shadows of the world appear.
There she sees the highway near
50   Winding down to Camelot:

34. Thomas Warton has 'airy uplands' in his *Sonnet ii*, 'When late the
trees' (1777).
37–40] *1842*; No time hath she to sport and play:
            A charmèd web she weaves alway.
            A curse is on her, if she stay
            Her weaving, either night or day, *1832*
43. And so] *1842*; Therefore *1832.*
44. And little] *1842*; Therefore no *1832.*
46–51] *1842*; She lives with little joy or fear.
            Over the water, running near,
            The sheepbell tinkles in her ear.
            Before her hangs a mirror clear,
                Reflecting towered Camelot.
            And, as the mazy web she whirls,' *1832*
46. The mirror is not there simply for the fairy-tale; it was set behind the
tapestry so that the worker could see the effect from the right side. This was
slightly clearer in the sequence of lines in *1832.* T. was much influenced by
Spenser's *Faerie Queene* III ii, on Britomart and Artegall: 'The wondrous
myrrhour, by which she in love with him did fall'. Spenser mentions 'the
Towre, / Wherein th' Ægyptian *Phao* long did lurke / From all mens
vew, that none might her discoure, / Yet she might all men vew out of her
bowre.' Britomart looks in the mirror: 'Eftsoones there was presented to
her eye / A comely knight, all arm'd in complet wize.' She is then lan-
guishing: 'Till death make one end of my dayes and miserie'.

There the river eddy whirls,
And there the surly village-churls,
And the red cloaks of market girls,
    Pass onward from Shalott.

55 Sometimes a troop of damsels glad,
An abbot on an ambling pad,
Sometimes a curly shepherd-lad,
Or long-haired page in crimson clad,
    Goes by to towered Camelot;
60 And sometimes through the mirror blue
The knights come riding two and two:
She hath no loyal knight and true,
    The Lady of Shalott.

But in her web she still delights
65 To weave the mirror's magic sights,
For often through the silent nights
A funeral, with plumes and lights
    And music, went to Camelot:
Or when the moon was overhead,
70 Came two young lovers lately wed;
'I am half sick of shadows,' said
    The Lady of Shalott.

PART III

A bow-shot from her bower-eaves,
He rode between the barley-sheaves,
75 The sun came dazzling through the leaves,
And flamed upon the brazen greaves
    Of bold Sir Lancelot.
A red-cross knight for ever kneeled
To a lady in his shield,
80 That sparkled on the yellow field,
    Beside remote Shalott.

The gemmy bridle glittered free,
Like to some branch of stars we see
Hung in the golden Galaxy.

52. *And there*] *1842*; She sees *1832*.
68. *went to*] *1842;* came from *1832.*
69–70] At morning often journeyèd
        Two deepeyed lovers, lately wed *T.Nbk 16 1st reading*
78. *red-cross knight*: for the Spenserian influence, see l. 46n.
82ff. For the knight's appearance, T. takes up details from *Faerie Queene*
I vii st. 29 ff.

 85 The bridle bells rang merrily
        As he rode down to Camelot:
     And from his blazoned baldric slung
     A mighty silver bugle hung,
     And as he rode his armour rung,
 90   Beside remote Shalott.

     All in the blue unclouded weather
     Thick-jewelled shone the saddle-leather,
     The helmet and the helmet-feather
     Burned like one burning flame together,
 95   As he rode down to Camelot.
     As often through the purple night,
     Below the starry clusters bright,
     Some bearded meteor, trailing light,
        Moves over still Shalott.

100 His broad clear brow in sunlight glowed;
     On burnished hooves his war-horse trode;
     From underneath his helmet flowed
     His coal-black curls as on he rode,
        As he rode down to Camelot.
105 From the bank and from the river
     He flashed into the crystal mirror,
     'Tirra lirra,' by the river
        Sang Sir Lancelot.

     She left the web, she left the loom,
110 She made three paces through the room,
     She saw the water-lily bloom,
     She saw the helmet and the plume,
        She looked down to Camelot.
     Out flew the web and floated wide;
115 The mirror cracked from side to side;
     'The curse is come upon me,' cried
        The Lady of Shalott.

86. to] *1842*; from *1832*. Likewise in ll. 95, 104.

99. still] *1842*; green *1832*.

107] *1842*; 'Tirra lirra, tirra lirra,' *1832*. From *Winter's Tale* IV iii 9. Turner (p. 61) notes that T. 'faintly underlined the Damsel's sexual frustration by making Lancelot, at her first sight of him, sing "Tirra lirra, tirra lirra", taken from a song in *The Winter's Tale* where Autolycus thinks of "tumbling in the hay" with his "aunts" (whores)'. Cp. the fragment *I sent no ambassador forward* 16: 'Tirrala, Tirrala'.

111. water-lily] *1842*; waterflower *1832*.

PART IV

In the stormy east-wind straining,
The pale yellow woods were waning,
120 The broad stream in his banks complaining,
Heavily the low sky raining
Over towered Camelot;
Down she came and found a boat
Beneath a willow left afloat,
125 And round about the prow she wrote
The Lady of Shalott.

And down the river's dim expanse
Like some bold seër in a trance,
Seeing all his own mischance –
130 With a glassy countenance
Did she look to Camelot.
And at the closing of the day
She loosed the chain, and down she lay;
The broad stream bore her far away,
135 The Lady of Shalott.

Lying, robed in snowy white

123] *1842*; Outside the isle a shallow boat *1832*.
124. left] *1842*; lay *1832*.
126. And . . . prow] *1842*; Below the carven stern *1832*.
126 ∧ 7]   A cloudwhite crown of pearl she dight.
              All raimented in snowy white
              That loosely flew, (her zone in sight,
              Clasped with one blinding diamond bright,)
                Her wide eyes fixed on Camelot,
              Though the squally eastwind keenly
              Blew, with folded arms serenely
                By the water stood the queenly
                Lady of Shalott. *1832*
Cp. l. 136.
127] *1842*; With a steady, stony glance – *1832*.
129. Seeing] *1842*; Beholding *1832*.
130. With] *1842*; Mute, with *1832*.
131. Did she look] *1842*; She looked down *1832*.
132. And at] *1842*; It was *1832*. Gray (p. 149) notes *1 Henry IV* III ii 133: 'The closing of some glorious day'.
136–41] *1842*; As when to sailors while they roam,
              By creeks and outfalls far from home,
              Rising and dropping with the foam,
              From dying swans wild warblings come,
                Blown shoreward; so to Camelot
              Still as . . . *1832*

That loosely flew to left and right—
The leaves upon her falling light—
Through the noises of the night
140   She floated down to Camelot:
And as the boat-head wound along
The willowy hills and fields among,
They heard her singing her last song,
The Lady of Shalott.

145   Heard a carol, mournful, holy,
Chanted loudly, chanted lowly,
Till her blood was frozen slowly,
And her eyes were darkened wholly,
Turned to towered Camelot.
150   For ere she reached upon the tide
The first house by the water-side,
Singing in her song she died,
The Lady of Shalott.

Under tower and balcony,
155   By garden-wall and gallery,
A gleaming shape she floated by,
Dead-pale between the houses high,
Silent into Camelot.
Out upon the wharfs they came,
160   Knight and burgher, lord and dame,
And round the prow they read her name,
The Lady of Shalott.

---

143. singing her last song] *1842*; chanting her deathsong *1832*. With this stanza, especially *1832*, cp. *The Dying Swan (p. 15)*, and *Morte d'Arthur* 266–9 (*p. 163*).
145. Heard a] *1842*; A longdrawn *1832*.
146. Chanted] *1842*; She chanted *1832*.
147, 148] *1842*; *transposed 1832* (Till her eyes . . .).
148] *1842*; And her smooth face sharpened slowly *1832*. T. records that 'George Eliot liked my first [version] the best'.
156. gleaming shape] *1842*; pale, pale corpse *1832*.
157. Dead-pale] *1855*; Deadcold *1832*; A corse *1842–53*.
158] *1842*; Dead into towered Camelot. *1832*.
159, 160] *1842*; *transposed 1832*.
159] *1842*; To the plankèd wharfage came *1832*.
161. And . . . prow] *1842*; Below the stern *1832*. As E. F. Shannon points out, *Tennyson and the Reviewers* (1952), p. 41, J. W. Croker 'had noted with derision that the name, *The Lady of Shalott*, was "below the stern" of the boat'.

Who is this? and what is here?
And in the lighted palace near
165 Died the sound of royal cheer;
And they crossed themselves for fear,
All the knights at Camelot:
But Lancelot mused a little space;
He said, 'She has a lovely face;
170 God in his mercy lend her grace,
The Lady of Shalott.'

160 Mariana in the South

Published *1832*; 'Juvenilia'. It was considerably rewritten for *1842*; T. began such revision very soon after *1832* (*Mem.* i 141, 145). It was written 1830–31: 'the idea of this came into my head between Narbonne and Perpignan' (T.), during his tour of the Pyrenees with Arthur Hallam, summer 1830. Hallam sent it, as *The Southern Mariana*, the title in *H.Lpr 142*, to W. B. Donne, 13 Feb. 1831: 'It is intended, you will perceive, as a kind of pendant to his former poem of Mariana [*p. 3*], the idea of both being the expression of desolate loneliness, but with this distinctive variety in the second that it paints the forlorn feeling as it would exist under the influence of different impressions of sense. When we were journeying together this summer through the South of France we came upon a range of country just corresponding to his preconceived thought of a barrenness, so as in the South, and the portraiture of the scenery in this poem is most faithful. You will, I think, agree with me that the essential & distinguishing character of the conception requires in the Southern Mariana a greater lingering on the outward circumstances, and a less palpable transition of the poet into Mariana's feelings, than was the case in the former poem' (*AHH*, p. 401; *Mem.* i 500–1). Hallam wrote to T., 24 Sept. 1832: '*Mariana in the South* seems the right title; I perceive you mean to refer only to the former one, not to republish it' (*AHH*, p. 652). In a copy of

163–71] *1842*; They crossed themselves, their stars they blest,
Knight, minstrel, abbot, squire and guest.
There lay a parchment on her breast,
That puzzled more than all the rest,
The wellfed wits at Camelot.
'*The web was woven curiously*
The charm is broken utterly,
Draw near and fear not–this is I,
The Lady of Shalott.' *1832*
John Stuart Mill objected to the *1832* stanza, *London Review*, July 1835.
168. E. E. Duncan-Jones notes Scott, *Marmion* I xxi, 'The Captain mused a little space'.

1830, T. inserted the titles of additional poems, presumably considering, before *1832*, a revised edition of *1830*. Before *Mariana*, he wrote *Prologue to the Marianas*; this either has not survived or has not been recognized. After *Mariana*, he wrote *A Southern Mariana*. (See C. Sturman, *TRB* iv, 1984, 123–4.)

The reviewer of *1832* in *The True Sun* (19 Jan. 1833), probably John Forster, spoke of T.'s heroine as 'exceedingly lovely in her desertion, with the scenery around in keeping with her heart' (E. F. Shannon, *Tennyson and the Reviewers*, 1952, p. 18). The poem was influenced by Sappho's *Fragment 111*: Δέδυκε μὲν ἀ σελάννα / καὶ Πληιάδες, μέσαι δὲ / νύκτες, παρὰ δ'ἔρχετ' ὥρα, / ἔγω δὲ μόνα κατεύδω. ('The Moon is gone / And the Pleiads set, / Midnight is nigh; / Time passes on, / And passes; yet / Alone I lie.') (J. C. Maxwell noted that the attribution to Sappho now has little support.) Hallam referred to 'the fragments of Sappho, in which I see much congeniality to Alfred's peculiar power', when enclosing the poem. *Revision*: In *1832* the first stanza violated the scheme by having twelve lines plus refrain; the last stanza likewise, and with a false rhyme. *T.Nbk 23* shows that an earlier stage of the poem consisted of stanzas of sixteen lines plus refrain, i.e. joining two of the final stanzas. J. F. A. Pyre (*The Formation of Tennyson's Style*, 1921, pp. 59–60) shows that the *1842* revisions make for regularity of rhythm, which is apt to the persistent monotony.

> With one black shadow at its feet,
>   The house through all the level shines,
> Close-latticed to the brooding heat,
>   And silent in its dusty vines:

¶ 160. *Title*: *1832* note: 'See *Poems, chiefly Lyrical*'.

1–12] *1842*; Behind the barren hill upsprung
          With pointed rocks against the light,
        The crag sharpshadowed overhung
          Each glaring creek and inlet bright.
        Far, far, one lightblue ridge [hill *AHH*] was seen,
          Looming like baseless fairyland;
        Eastward a slip of burning sand,
        Dark-rimmed with sea, and bare of green.
        Down in the dry salt-marshes stood
          That house darklatticed. Not a breath
        Swayed the sick vineyard underneath,
        Or moved the dusty southernwood.
          'Madonna,' with melodious moan
          Sang Mariana, night and morn,
          'Madonna! lo! I am all alone,
          Love-forgotten and love-forlorn.' *1832*.

5   A faint-blue ridge upon the right,
    An empty river-bed before,
    And shallows on a distant shore,
    In glaring sand and inlets bright.
    But 'Ave Mary,' made she moan,
10   And 'Ave Mary,' night and morn,
    And 'Ah,' she sang, 'to be all alone,
    To live forgotten, and love forlorn.'

    She, as her carol sadder grew,
    From brow and bosom slowly down
15   Through rosy taper fingers drew
    Her streaming curls of deepest brown
    To left and right, and made appear
    Still-lighted in a secret shrine,
    Her melancholy eyes divine,
20   The home of woe without a tear.
    And 'Ave Mary,' was her moan,
    'Madonna, sad is night and morn,'
    And 'Ah,' she sang, 'to be all alone,
    To live forgotten, and love forlorn.'

25   Till all the crimson changed, and past
    Into deep orange o'er the sea,
    Low on her knees herself she cast,
    Before Our Lady murmured she;

H.Lpr 141 has an intermediate revision of ll. 1–28, close to *1842* but with
e.g. l. 1 'The beams on all the level beat'; l. 3 'Dark-latticed'; l. 4 'the
blighted vines'; l. 5 'The flats are far to left and right'. About l. 5 of *1832* in
MS, Hallam wrote to T., 24 Sept. 1832: 'Is "looming" rightly used? its
precise meaning I know not, but rather think it applies to ships at sea seen
through mist or fog' (*AHH*, p. 652).

9–11. Cp. *Song [I' the glooming light]* 12–17 (I 235): 'Death standeth by; /
She will not die; / With glazèd eye / She looks at her grave: she cannot
sleep; / Ever alone / She maketh her moan.'

14] 1842; From her warm brow and bosom down *1832*.

15. taper fingers: Keats, *I stood tip-toe* 59, as in T.'s *Madeline* 44.

17. To . . . right] 1842; On either side *1832*.

21–4] 1842; *1832* has the refrain as in its first stanza.

25. Till . . . crimson] 1842; When the dawncrimson *1832*. (mooncrimson
T.Nbk 23.)

28. Before . . . murmured] 1842; Unto . . . prayèd *1832*.

Complaining, 'Mother, give me grace
30   To help me of my weary load.'
And on the liquid mirror glowed
The clear perfection of her face.
'Is this the form,' she made her moan,
'That won his praises night and morn?'
35   And 'Ah,' she said, 'but I wake alone,
I sleep forgotten, I wake forlorn.'
Nor bird would sing, nor lamb would bleat,
Nor any cloud would cross the vault,

29–36] *1842*; She moved her lips, she prayed alone,
She praying disarrayed and warm
From slumber, deep her wavy form
In the darklustrous mirror shone.
'Madonna,' in a low clear tone
Said Mariana, night and morn,
Low she mourned, 'I am all alone,
Love-forgotten, and love-forlorn.' *1832*
T.MS has the last line without 'and'.
29] 'Madonna Mary lend me grace *Lincoln revision of 1832*.
31. liquid mirror: as in Shelley, *Alastor* 462, where it has the more common
application to water.
32] Her bounteous form and beauteous face. *Lincoln rev.*, *1st reading*.
33. form'; *she made her*] beauty,' she made *Lincoln rev.*, *1st reading*.
35] Yet mother look I wake alone, *Lincoln rev.*, *1st reading*.
37. lamb] herd *Lincoln rev.*, *2nd reading*.
37–48] *1842*; At noon she slumbered. All along
The silvery field, the large leaves talked
With one another, as among
The spikèd maize in dreams she walked.
The lizard leapt: the sunlight played:
She heard the callow nestling lisp,
And brimful meadow-runnels crisp,
In the full-leavèd platan-shade.
In sleep she breathed in a lower tone,
Murmuring as at night and morn,
'Madonna! lo! I am all alone,
Love-forgotten and love-forlorn.' *1832*
T.MS has the third and fourth lines as: '. . . as she walked / Browhigh the
spikèd maize among'. Cp. *Claribel* 17–19: 'The callow throstle lispeth . . . /
The babbling runnel crispeth.' *Lincoln rev. of 1832* has an intermediate version
of ll. 37–40:
And Day moved on with steps of Death
And Silence added heat to heat
In fields of drought without a breath
That never felt the shadow fleet.

But day increased from heat to heat,
40 On stony drought and steaming salt;
 Till now at noon she slept again,
 And seemed knee-deep in mountain grass,
 And heard her native breezes pass,
 And runlets babbling down the glen.
45 She breathed in sleep a lower moan,
  And murmuring, as at night and morn,
  She thought, 'My spirit is here alone,
  Walks forgotten, and is forlorn.'

 Dreaming, she knew it was a dream:
50 She felt he was and was not there.
 She woke: the babble of the stream
 Fell, and, without, the steady glare
 Shrank one sick willow sere and small.
 The river-bed was dusty-white;
55 And all the furnace of the light
 Struck up against the blinding wall.
 She whispered, with a stifled moan
  More inward than at night or morn,
  'Sweet Mother, let me not here alone
60 Live forgotten and die forlorn.'

 And, rising, from her bosom drew
 Old letters, breathing of her worth,
 For 'Love,' they said, 'must needs be true,
 To what is loveliest upon earth.'

On the *1832* dream, and Mariana's dream about Wilhelm and the sunshine, in *Wilhelm Meister's Apprenticeship*, see Ian Kennedy, *PQ* lvii (1978) 94.

42. knee-deep in] to walk on *Lincoln rev., 1st reading.*

44. runlets babbling] runnels crisping *Lincoln rev., 1st reading.*

49–50. dream: | She felt he] *1842*; dream | Most false: *he 1832.*

53. one] *1850*; the *1832-48. willow*] *1853*; olive *1832-51.*

55-6] *1842*; From the bald rock the blinding light
  Beat ever on the sunwhite wall. *1832*

59-60] *1842*; 'Madonna, leave me not all alone,
  To die forgotten and live forlorn.' *1832*

61-84] *1842; not 1832.* Possibly precipitated by the death of Hallam; cp. the 'letters' ('love', 'worth') with *In Memoriam* xcv; the 'image' which speaks makes use of the *In Memoriam* stanza in ll. 65–8. Ian Kennedy notes Mariana's dream in Goethe (see ll. 37–48*n.* above): 'till I observed your image sinking down, sinking, sinking'; Kennedy (pp. 98–9) also suggests the influence of Lytton's *Falkland* (1827) on the poem, for the letters here, the lattice-scenes (ll. 3, 87–92), and for 'weary load' (l. 30).

65 An image seemed to pass the door,
To look at her with slight, and say
'But now thy beauty flows away,
So be alone for evermore.'
'O cruel heart,' she changed her tone,
70   'And cruel love, whose end is scorn,
Is this the end to be left alone,
To live forgotten, and die forlorn?'

But sometimes in the falling day
An image seemed to pass the door,
75 To look into her eyes and say,
'But thou shalt be alone no more.'
And flaming downward over all
From heat to heat the day decreased,
And slowly rounded to the east
80 The one black shadow from the wall.
'The day to night,' she made her moan,
'The day to night, the night to morn,
And day and night I am left alone
To live forgotten, and love forlorn.'

85 At eve a dry cicala sung,
There came a sound as of the sea;
Backward the lattice-blind she flung,
And leaned upon the balcony.
There all in spaces rosy-bright

85–6] *1842*; One dry cicala's summer song
            At night filled all the gallery, *1832*
T.MS has: '. . . song / Filled all the corridor at night . . . / And leaned into
the purple [*lacuna*]'. T. says that the MS of l. 85 read: 'At fall of eve a cricket
sung'.
89–92. Cp. the opening of Beattie's *Retirement* (1758): 'When in the crim-
son cloud of even / The lingering light decays, / And Hesper on the front
of heaven / His glittering gem displays; / Deep in the silent vale . . .'
There was a copy of Beattie's *Minstrel* at Somersby (*Lincoln*).
89–96] *1842*; Ever the low wave seemed to roll
            Up to the coast: far on, alone
            In the East, large Hesper overshone
            The mourning gulf, and on her soul
            Poured divine solace, or the rise
            Of moonlight from the margin gleamed,
            Volcano-like, afar, and streamed
            On her white arm, and heavenward eyes.
            Not all alone she made her moan,
            Yet ever sang she, night and morn,
            'Madonna, lo! I am all alone,
            Love-forgotten and love-forlorn.' *1832*

90   Large Hesper glittered on her tears,
      And deepening through the silent spheres
      Heaven over Heaven rose the night.
      And weeping then she made her moan,
      'The night comes on that knows not morn,
95   When I shall cease to be all alone,
      To live forgotten, and love forlorn.'

163 Fatima

Published *1832*, with no title, but an epigraph from Sappho's *Fragment 2*: φαίνεταί μοι κῆνος ἶσος θέοισιν / ἔμμεν ὤνηρ. Especially in ll. 15–19, it closely imitates Sappho, the same poem adapted in *Eleänore* (I 401). Paden (p. 39) observes that Sappho merges with the story of Jemily from C.-E. Savary's *Letters on Egypt* (the acknowledged source of *Egypt*; T. used the 1799 translation, *Lincoln*). She waits for her lover who dare not come because of her husband: 'extending herself on the ground, [she] rolled among and crushed the tender flowers' (ll. 11–12). Though this stanza did not appear till *1842*, Paden (p. 132) points out that: 'It is not safe to assume that the added stanza was written after 1832, for Tennyson often returned from the published to the manuscript version of a poem.' The name 'Fatima' occurs in the poem of the *Moállakát* which inspired *Locksley Hall*; in Savary; and in the *Arabian Nights*. See the fragment *I sent no ambassador forward* (III 621), with its reference to 'Fatima, Selim's daughter'. For the scheme of rhyme and metre, cp. *The Lady of Shalott*, which simply adds rhyming refrains.

      O Love, Love, Love! O withering might!
      O sun, that from thy noonday height
      Shudderest when I strain my sight,
      Throbbing through all thy heat and light,
5   Lo, falling from my constant mind,
      Lo, parched and withered, deaf and blind,
      I whirl like leaves in roaring wind.

      Last night I wasted hateful hours
      Below the city's eastern towers:

90. Cp. *The Lover's Tale* i 248: 'I saw the moonlight glitter on their tears'. A reminiscence of Keats, *Hyperion* ii 5–6: 'light / Could glimmer on their tears'. Cp. Thomson, *Autumn* 200–1, where Lavinia's eyes 'like the dewy star / Of evening, shone in tears'.
90–2. tears . . . night: adapted from the third stanza of *The Voyage* (II 82), in *T.Nbk 21*.
¶ 163. *Title*] *1842; not 1832*.
2. from] *1842;* at *1832*.
8–14] *1842; not 1832*.

10 I thirsted for the brooks, the showers:
    I rolled among the tender flowers:
      I crushed them on my breast, my mouth;
      I looked athwart the burning drouth
      Of that long desert to the south.

15 Last night, when some one spoke his name,
    From my swift blood that went and came
    A thousand little shafts of flame
    Were shivered in my narrow frame.
    O Love, O fire! once he drew
20 With one long kiss my whole soul through
    My lips, as sunlight drinketh dew.

Before he mounts the hill, I know
    He cometh quickly: from below
    Sweet gales, as from deep gardens, blow
25 Before him, striking on my brow.
      In my dry brain my spirit soon,
      Down-deepening from swoon to swoon,
      Faints like a dazzled morning moon.

The wind sounds like a silver wire,
30 And from beyond the noon a fire
    Is poured upon the hills, and nigher
    The skies stoop down in their desire;
      And, isled in sudden seas of light,
      My heart, pierced through with fierce delight,
35 Bursts into blossom in his sight.

My whole soul waiting silently,
    All naked in a sultry sky,
    Droops blinded with his shining eye:

11–12. Cp., in addition to Savary (headnote), *Sense and Conscience* 57–8:
'crushed and massed / The pleasurable flowers'.

13. Adapted from *A Fragment* 17: 'Looking athwart the burning flats'; and
cp. *Mariana* 20: 'And glanced athwart the glooming flats'.

15–19. Cp., in addition to Sappho (headnote), *Eleänore* 122 ff.

19–21. A traditional notion, as in *Locksley Hall* 38. Cp. Marlowe's *Dr
Faustus* 1331: 'Her lips sucke forth my soule'; and Donne's *The Expiration*:
'So, so, breake off this last lamenting kisse, / Which sucks two soules, and
vapors both away.'

26–8. Cp. *Sonnet* [*Alas! how weary*] 3–4: 'Alas! how like the dazzled moon at
morn / My waning spirit after darkness sighs'.

I *will* possess him or will die.
40   I willl grow round him in his place,
    Grow, live, die looking on his face,
    Die, dying clasped in his embrace.

164 Œnone

Published *1832*, much revised for *1842*. The changes are well discussed by
P. F. Baum (*Tennyson Sixty Years After*, 1948, pp. 75–82). T. began such
changes soon after *1832*, as is clear from the copy presented to J. M. Heath
(*Fitzwilliam Museum*), which has various intermediate alterations to the
opening lines and elsewhere. T. wrote to Spedding in early March 1835 of
'my old poems most of which I have so corrected (particularly *Œnone*) as to
make them much less imperfect' (*Letters* i 130–1; *Mem.* i 145). It was
written 1830–32; the scenery was suggested by the Pyrenees, where
according to T. part of it was written, summer 1830. Hallam asked T.'s
sister Emily to send him 'the concluding lines of *Œnone*. Existing
manuscripts go no further than "I only saw great Here's angry eyes [186]
with the lines immediately following' (26 May 1832; *AHH*, p. 583). T.'s
note observes that Œnone was 'married to Paris, and afterwards deserted by
him for Helen. The sequel of the tale is poorly given in Quintus Calaber'
(which T. was to adapt in *The Death of Œnone*, III 220). The sources and
classical allusions – in particular Ovid's *Heroides* and Theocritus – have been
comprehensively discussed by P. Turner (*JEGP* lxi (1962) 57–72), who
subsumes previous commentators and on whom the following notes draw
extensively. Culler (pp. 78–9) discusses 'the traditional Renaissance
interpretation of the myth' and T.'s awareness of it; 'Paris's error is that in
choosing any one of the goddesses over another he has shown a lack of
harmony and balance.' 'The scene . . . has echoes of the temptation scenes in
Paradise Lost and *Paradise Regained*, and, indeed, it is less a judgment scene
than a temptation. It is a temptation *to* judge, as well as to judge wrong.' D.
Bush (*Mythology and the Romantic Tradition*, 1937, p. 204) describes the
poem as an epyllion, or minor epic, in the manner of Theocritus. Some
variants are selected from *Huntington MS* (HM 19501), ll. 54–124, which
was originally part of *T.Nbk 26*. The early version in *T.Nbk 23* (1830) is
much briefer, and omits e.g. ll. 52–84. P. Gaskell reproduces and discusses
eleven stages of the text of ll. 1–32, including five successive drafts in
T.Nbk 26 (*From Writer to Reader*, 1978, pp. 118–41). This is supplemented
by A. Day, *The Library* 6th Ser. ii (1980) 315–25, on two other stages of
revision (*Lincoln*) throughout the poem. Day also noted the revised *1832*, in
T.'s hand, in the Ashley Library (*British Library*). The MS variants are
innumerable and complex, beyond the scale of such an edition as this. See

39–42. Cp. the end of *Eleänore*: 'I *would* be dying evermore, / So dying
ever, Eleänore.'

Appendix B (III 611) for a passage–not in blank verse–which
contributed to *Œnone*. T. says: 'I had an idiotic hatred of hyphens in those
days, but though I printed such words as "glénríver," "téndríltwine" I
always gave them in reading their full two accents. Coleridge thought
because of these hyphened words that I could not scan.'

> There lies a vale in Ida, lovelier
> Than all the valleys of Ionian hills.
> The swimming vapour slopes athwart the glen,
> Puts forth an arm, and creeps from pine to pine,
> 5   And loiters, slowly drawn. On either hand
> The lawns and meadow-ledges midway down
> Hang rich in flowers, and far below them roars
> The long brook falling through the cloven ravine
> In cataract after cataract to the sea.
> 10 Behind the valley topmost Gargarus
> Stands up and takes the morning: but in front
> The gorges, opening wide apart, reveal
> Troas and Ilion's columned citadel,
> The crown of Troas.
>   Hither came at noon
> 15 Mournful Œnone, wandering forlorn
> Of Paris, once her playmate on the hills.

¶ 164.*1–14*] *1842;*   There is a dale in Ida, lovelier
                               Than any in old Ionia, beautiful
                               With emerald slopes of sunny sward, that lean
                               Above the loud glenriver, which hath worn
                               A path through steepdown granitewalls below
                               Mantled with flowering tendriltwine. In front
                               The cedarshadowy valleys open wide.
                               Far-seen, high over all the Godbuilt wall
                               And many a snowycolumned range divine,
                               Mounted with awful sculptures–men and Gods,
                               The work of Gods–bright on the darkblue sky
                               The windy citadel of Ilion
                               Shone, like the crown of Troas. Hither came *1832*
1. Ida: the mountain on the south of the Troas. Paris describes the scene of
the Judgment: *Est locus in mediis nemorosae vallibus Idae . . .* (Ovid, *Heroides*
xvi 53–8). T.'s opening paragraphs follow the pastoral love-lament: hope-
less lover, loved one, setting.
10. Gargarus: 'the highest part of Mount Ida'; T. compares Virgil's
Georgics i 103: *Ipsa suas mirantur Gargara messes.*
16–17] *1842;* . . . playmate. Round her neck, / Her neck all marblewhite
and marblecold, *1832.   forlorn of:* Spenserian and Miltonic.

Her cheek had lost the rose, and round her neck
Floated her hair or seemed to float in rest.
She, leaning on a fragment twined with vine,
20 Sang to the stillness, till the mountain-shade
Sloped downward to her seat from the upper cliff.

'O mother Ida, many-fountained Ida,
Dear mother Ida, harken ere I die.
For now the noonday quiet holds the hill:
25 The grasshopper is silent in the grass:
The lizard, with his shadow on the stone,
Rests like a shadow, and the winds are dead.

17–18. P. Turner suggests that this associates Œnone ominously with Cassandra: *diffusis comis* (*Heroides* v 114); and with Dido: *aut videt aut vidisse putat* (*Aeneid* vi 454).

19. fragment . . . vine] *1842*; vine-entwinèd stone *1832*.

20. -shade] *1842*; -shadow *1832*.

20–1. As in Virgil's *Eclogues* i 83: *maioresque cadunt altis de montibus umbrae*.

22. T. remarks that 'this sort of refrain is found in Theocritus'.   *mother* : because of Theocritus ix 15; in the source of 'many-fountained' (*Iliad* xiv 283), Ida is 'mother of wild beasts'; hence the pard and panther later. *ere I die* : a traditional feature of the pastoral love-poem.

24] *1842; not 1832.* In *Eversley*, T. quotes Callimachus, *Lavacrum Palladis* 72: μεσαμβρινὴ δ᾽ εἶχ᾽ ὄρος ἡσυχία ('and noontide quiet held all the hill'). And yet when John Churton Collins originally suggested this, T. wrote in the margin: 'not known to me' (*Cornhill*, Jan. 1880, *Lincoln*).

25–9. Based on Virgil's *Eclogues* ii 8–13, where *cicadis* suggested the cicala of *1832*. The antithesis, *rests/awake*, is from Theocritus ii 38–9; and the lizard, from vii 21–3. Alongside John Churton Collins's suggestion of Theocritus, T. wrote: 'from nature in the south of France' (*Cornhill*, Jan. 1880, *Lincoln*).

27] *1883*;   Sleeps like a shadow, and the scarletwinged
Cicala in the noonday leapeth not
Along the water-rounded granite-rock. *1832*;
Rests like a shadow, and the cicala sleeps *1842–82*. T. says: 'In these lines describing a perfect stillness, I did not like the jump, "Rests like a shadow –and the cicala sleeps". Moreover, in the heat of noon the cicala is generally at its loudest, though I have read that, in extreme heat, it is silent. Some one (I forget who) found them silent at noon on the slopes of Etna.' *1832* note: 'In the Pyrenees, where part of this poem was written, I saw a very beautiful species of Cicala, which had scarlet wings spotted with black. Probably nothing of the kind exists in Mount Ida.' T. emended J. M. Heath's copy of *1832* (*Fitzwilliam Museum*) to:
. . . and the garrulous
Cicala ceaseth now to burst the brake
With thick dry clamour chafed from griding wings.

The purple flower droops: the golden bee
Is lily-cradled: I alone awake.
30 My eyes are full of tears, my heart of love,
My heart is breaking, and my eyes are dim,
And I am all aweary of my life.

'O mother Ida, many-fountained Ida,
Dear mother Ida, harken ere I die.
35 Hear me, O Earth, hear me, O Hills, O Caves
That house the cold crowned snake! O mountain
    brooks,
I am the daughter of a River-God,
Hear me, for I will speak, and build up all
My sorrow with my song, as yonder walls
40 Rose slowly to a music slowly breathed,
A cloud that gathered shape: for it may be
That, while I speak of it, a little while
My heart may wander from its deeper woe.

'O mother Ida, many-fountained Ida,
45 Dear mother Ida, harken ere I die.
I waited underneath the dawning hills,
Aloft the mountain lawn was dewy-dark,
And dewy dark aloft the mountain pine:
Beautiful Paris, evil-hearted Paris,
50 Leading a jet-black goat white-horned, white-hooved,
Came up from reedy Simois all alone.

'O mother Ida, harken ere I die.
Far-off the torrent called me from the cleft:
Far up the solitary morning smote

---

28. *flower droops*] *1832, 1883*; flowers droop *1842–82* ('*misprint*', T.).
30. T. denied the influence of *2 Henry VI* II iii 17: 'Mine eyes are full of tears, my heart of grief'.
35–8. Echoing Aeschylus, *Prometheus Vinctus* 88–91; and Shelley, *Prometheus Unbound* I 25–9.
37. The claim made by Ovid's Œnone, *Heroides* v 9–10.
38–41. Suggested by Ovid's Œnone, who boasts that Apollo was her first lover (as in T.; ll. 61–2, *1832* text) – Apollo, *Troiae munitor* (*Heroides* v 139). For the building of Troy, cp. *Tithonus* 62–3: 'Like that strange song I heard Apollo sing, / While Ilion like a mist rose into towers.' Also *Ilion, Ilion* (I 281) throughout. H.T. compares *Heroides* xvi 182.
46] *1842; not 1832.*   *the dawning hills: Paradise Lost* vi 528.
50. With the apple of l. 65, the traditional rustic gifts of the pastoral; a goat, Theocritus iii 34–6.
51. *Simois*: one of the two rivers of the plain of Troy.

55   The streaks of virgin snow. With down-dropt eyes
      I sat alone: white-breasted like a star
      Fronting the dawn he moved; a leopard skin
      Drooped from his shoulder, but his sunny hair
      Clustered about his temples like a God's:
60   And his cheek brightened as the foam-bow brightens
      When the wind blows the foam, and all my heart
      Went forth to embrace him coming ere he came.

      'Dear mother Ida, harken ere I die.
      He smiled, and opening out his milk-white palm
65   Disclosed a fruit of pure Hesperian gold,

53–6] *1842*; I sate alone: the goldensandalled morn
                Rosehued the scornful hills: I sate alone
                With downdropt eyes: whitebreasted . . . *1832*.
T. emended ll. 53–4 in J. M. Heath's copy of *1832*:
                I sate alone: the torrent in the cleft
                Called me: far up, far on the rosy glows
                O'er trackless woods smote all the snowy streaks,
                Smote all the scarrèd spurs. I sat alone
Huntington MS of ll. 54–6 shows T.'s uncertainty:
                Far up the lonely morning lit the streaks
                Of virgin snow; with downdropt eyes I sat:
                I heard a voice: white-breasted . . .
56. Cp. the Homeric *Hymn to Aphrodite* 89–90; and Theocritus ii 79. T. uses
details from Theocritus and Virgil, but changes from the first meeting to
the last.
57. *moved*] *1842*; came *1832*. The leopard skin is from *Iliad* iii 17.
58] *1842*; From his white shoulder drooped: his sunny hair *1832*.
59–62. Based on Catullus lxiv 270–8, the arrival of the gods (cp. below) at a
wedding.
60. *foam-bow*: 'the rainbow in the cataract' (T.).
61–2] *1842*;   . . . and I called out,
                'Welcome Apollo, welcome home Apollo,
                Apollo, my Apollo, loved Apollo.' *1832*
Kemble wrote to T., ?Jan. 1833 (*Letters* i 85–6): 'let me ask whether Ovid or
you are in the right? You seem to know something about Œnone; was it the
strength of character that made her burn Troy which enabled her to call Paris
"her Apollo"? he knowing all things.' *Letters* notes that T. replaced the lines,
though Ovid was in fact his authority.
62. Cp. Venus, in *Who is it* 12–13 (see ll. 213–15n below): 'Whose coming
ere she comes doth strike / On expectation.' Also *PL* vi 768: 'He onward
came, farr off his coming shon'.
64. *smiled . . . out*] *1842*; mildly smiling, in *1832*.
65. A pastoral gift, as in Theocritus iii 10–11 (see l. 50n), but here the apple
of Discord. For the Hesperian apples, see *The Hesperides* (I 461).

That smelt ambrosially, and while I looked
And listened, the full-flowing river of speech
Came down upon my heart.

          "'My own Œnone,
Beautiful-browed Œnone, my own soul,
70   Behold this fruit, whose gleaming rind ingraven
'For the most fair,' would seem to award it thine,
As lovelier than whatever Oread haunt
The knolls of Ida, loveliest in all grace
Of movement, and the charm of married brows."

75   'Dear mother Ida, harken ere I die.
He prest the blossom of his lips to mine,

65–7] *1842*;   Close-held a golden apple, lightningbright
               With changeful flashes, dropt with dew of Heaven
               Ambrosially smelling. From his lip,
               Curved crimson, the fullflowing ... *1832*

69. *my*] *1842*; mine *1832*. For the meeting eyebrows (as in l. 74), T. compares Theocritus viii 72–3, of a beautiful girl watching from a cave (cp. l. 85).

71–87] *1842*;   'For the most fair,' in aftertime may breed
              Deep evilwilledness of heaven and sere
              Heartburning toward hallowèd Ilion;
              And all the colour of my afterlife
              Will be the shadow of today. Today
              Here [Herè] and Pallas and the floating grace
              Of laughterloving Aphrodite meet
              In manyfolded Ida to receive
              This meed of beauty, she to whom my hand
              Award the palm. Within the green hillside,
              Under yon whispering tuft of oldest pine,
              Is an ingoing grotto, strown with spar
              And ivymatted at the mouth, wherein
              Thou unbeholden mayst behold, unheard *1832*
Hn MS shows T.'s efforts; ll. 71–83:
              ... fair, hath bred dispute in Heaven
              For Hermes brought it, telling that today
              To me, chosen arbiter, would Herè come *1st reading*;
              ... fair, perplexes Heaven with feud
              For Hermes brought it, telling that today
              (So much they do me honour) unto me
              Selected arbiter, would Herè come *2nd reading*
72. *Oread*: mountain-nymph.
76. Ominously recalling Bion's *Lament for Adonis* 11–12: 'The rose departs from his lip, and the kiss that Cypris shall never have so again, that kiss dies upon it and is gone.' Cp. l. 17 above.

And added "This was cast upon the board,
When all the full-faced presence of the Gods
Ranged in the halls of Peleus; whereupon
80 Rose feud, with question unto whom 'twere due:
But light-foot Iris brought it yester-eve,
Delivering, that to me, by common voice
Elected umpire, Herè comes today,
Pallas and Aphroditè, claiming each
85 This meed of fairest. Thou, within the cave
Behind yon whispering tuft of oldest pine,
Mayst well behold them unbeheld, unheard
Hear all, and see thy Paris judge of Gods."

'Dear mother Ida, harken ere I die.
90 It was the deep midnoon: one silvery cloud
Had lost his way between the piney sides
Of this long glen. Then to the bower they came,
Naked they came to that smooth-swarded bower,
And at their feet the crocus brake like fire,

81. *Iris*: the messenger of the gods. T. translated *Iliad* xviii 202 as 'light-foot
Iris', *Achilles* 1.
86. *whispering . . . oldest*] sobbing growth of twisted *HnMS, to which T.
reverted in emending J. M. Heath's copy of 1832.* *whispering*: Theocritus i 1.
91. *sides*] *1842*; hills *1832*. Cp. Thomson, *Summer* 1303–4: 'Paris on the
piny top / Of Ida'.
92] *1842*; They came–all three–the Olympian goddesses: *1832*.
93. *that*] *1842*; the *1832*. The setting is from *Iliad* xiv 346–51, where the cloud
dropping dew (cp. ll. 103–4) envelops Herè (Hera) and not her peacock.
Cp. *PL* iv 700–702, the bower of Adam and Eve: 'underfoot the Violet, /
Crocus, and Hyacinth with rich inlay / Broiderd the ground.'
94–7] *1842*; Lustrous with lilyflower, violeteyed
              Both white and blue, with lotetree-fruit thickset,
              Shadowed with singing pine; and all the while,
              Above, the overwandering ivy and vine *1832*
T. emended J. M. Heath's copy of *1832*: 'Lustrous with lily and myrtle –
myriad-eyed / With violet-hues.' *HnMS* of ll. 94–5 included further
allusions to Milton:
              That darkened all with violets underneath
              Through which like fire the sudden crocus came,
              Amaracus, immortal asphodel,
A. Day notes *PL* ix 1036–41.
like fire: T. spoke of the 'flame-like petal . . . not only the colour'. This
note was written alongside John Churton Collins's remark that the com-
parison was not 'original' (*Cornhill*, Jan. 1880, *Lincoln*). Cp. 'The ground-
flame of the crocus', *The Progress of Spring* 1 and *n* (I 517). H.T. compares
Oedipus Coloneus 685.

95   Violet, amaracus, and asphodel,
      Lotos and lilies: and a wind arose,
      And overhead the wandering ivy and vine,
      This way and that, in many a wild festoon
      Ran riot, garlanding the gnarlèd boughs
      With bunch and berry and flower through and
100· through.
            'O mother Ida, harken ere I die.
      On the tree-tops a crested peacock lit,
      And o'er him flowed a golden cloud, and leaned
      Upon him, slowly dropping fragrant dew.
105   Then first I heard the voice of her, to whom
      Coming through Heaven, like a light that grows
      Larger and clearer, with one mind the Gods
      Rise up for reverence. She to Paris made
      Proffer of royal power, ample rule
110   Unquestioned, overflowing revenue
      Wherewith to embellish state, "from many a vale
      And river-sundered champaign clothed with corn,
      Or laboured mine undrainable of ore.
      Honour," she said, "and homage, tax and toll,

97–9. Cp. Leigh Hunt, *Rimini* ii 137–8: 'And still from tree to tree the early vines / Hung garlanding the way.' T. jotted down phrases from *Rimini* in *H.Nbk 4*.

101–8] *1842*;   On the treetops a golden glorious cloud
                  Leaned, slowly dropping down ambrosial dew.
                  How beautiful they were, too beautiful
                  To look upon! but Paris was to me
                  More lovelier than all the world beside.
                    'O mother Ida, hearken ere I die.
                  First spake the imperial Olympian
                  With archèd eyebrow smiling sovranly,
                  Fulleyèd Here. She to Paris made *1832*

102. *peacock*: 'sacred to Herè' (T.).

108. *Rise up*: as in *Iliad* xv 86.

113] *1882*; . . . mines . . . *1842–81*; Or upland glebe wealthy in oil and wine–*1832*.

114] *1842*; Honour and homage, tribute, tax and toll, *1832*.

In *1832*, ll. 113–4 bring out more clearly the debt to *Paradise Regained* iii 257–60, noted by D. Bush (*Major British Writers* (1959) ii 387): 'Fair Champain with less rivers interveind, / Then meeting joyn'd thir tribute to the Sea: / Fertil of corn the glebe, of oyl and wine, / With herds the pastures throng'd . . .'. The reminiscence is due to the similar situation, of tempting offers being made. Cp. *The Palace of Art* 79: 'upland, prodigal in oil'; *Hn MS* of *Œnone* 113 has 'Or upland prodigal of oil and wine'.

115 From many an inland town and haven large,
Mast-thronged beneath her shadowing citadel
In glassy bays among her tallest towers."

'O mother Ida, harken ere I die.
Still she spake on and still she spake of power,
120 "Which in all action is the end of all;
Power fitted to the season; wisdom-bred
And throned of wisdom—from all neighbour crowns
Alliance and allegiance, till thy hand
Fail from the sceptre-staff. Such boon from me,
125 From me, Heaven's Queen, Paris, to thee king-born,
A shepherd all thy life but yet king-born,
Should come most welcome, seeing men, in power
Only, are likest gods, who have attained
Rest in a happy place and quiet seats
130 Above the thunder, with undying bliss
In knowledge of their own supremacy."

'Dear mother Ida, harken ere I die.
She ceased, and Paris held the costly fruit
Out at arm's-length, so much the thought of power
135 Flattered his spirit; but Pallas where she stood
Somewhat apart, her clear and bared limbs
O'erthwarted with the brazen-headed spear
Upon her pearly shoulder leaning cold,
The while, above, her full and earnest eye
140 Over her snow-cold breast and angry cheek
Kept watch, waiting decision, made reply.

' "Self-reverence, self-knowledge, self-control,
These three alone lead life to sovereign power.

116. beneath] *1842*; below *1832*.
121] *1842*; . . . season, measured by / The height of the general feeling,
wisdomborn *1832*.
123–5] *1842*; . . . allegiance evermore. / Such boon from me Heaven's
Queen to thee kingborn, *1832*.
126. but] *1842*; and *1832*.
127. power] *1842*; this *1832*.
127–31. Based, as T. says, on Lucretius's account of the Epicurean gods,
iii 18–24; and on *Aeneid* iv 379–80. With a reminiscence of *PL* vi 301:
'Of Godlike Power: for likest Gods they seemd'.
131 ∧ 2]   The changeless calm of undisputed right,
                The highest height and topmost strength of power.' *1832*
135. spirit] *1842*; heart *1832*.
137. O'erthwarted: T. says it was founded on the Chaucerian word 'over-
thwart', across, *Troilus and Criseyde* iii 685.
142–3. Ian Kennedy compares *Wilhelm Meister's Travels* ch. x, on 'the "re-

Yet not for power (power of herself
145   Would come uncalled for) but to live by law,
Acting the law we live by without fear;
And, because right is right, to follow right
Were wisdom in the scorn of consequence."

'Dear mother Ida, harken ere I die.
150   Again she said: "I woo thee not with gifts.
Sequel of guerdon could not alter me
To fairer. Judge thou me by what I am,
So shalt thou find me fairest.
Yet, indeed,
If gazing on divinity disrobed
155   Thy mortal eyes are frail to judge of fair,

verence for oneself" which is at the heart of the educational philosophy of
"the Three" and by which they assert that "man attains the highest elevation
of which he is capable"' (*PQ* lvii, 1978, 91).
143] *1842*;   Are the three hinges of the gates of Life,
That open into power, everyway
Without horizon, bound or shadow or cloud. *1832*
145. Would] *1842*; Will *1832*.
148. Traditionally Pallas had offered Paris success in war, until (as D. Bush
noted, *Mythology and the Romantic Tradition*, 1937, p. 206) the fifth–sixth-
century writer Fulgentius made the offer that of wisdom.
150–64] *1842*;   Not as men value gold because it tricks
And blazons outward Life with ornament,
But rather as the miser, for itself.
Good for selfgood doth half destroy selfgood.
The means and end, like two coiled snakes, infect
Each other, bound in one with hateful love.
So both into the fountain and the stream
A drop of poison falls. Come hearken to me,
And look upon me and consider me,
So shalt thou find me fairest, so endurance,
Like to an athlete's arm, shall still become
Sinewed with motion, till thine active will
(As the dark body of the Sun robed round
With his own ever-emanating lights)
Be flooded o'er with her own effluences,
And thereby grow to freedom.' *1832*
There is an intermediate version of l. 163 in J. M. Heath's copy of *1832*,
which T. emended:
Circled through all experience, narrowing up
From orb to orb, still nigher rest, remain
A polestar fixt in truth and so made one
With effort, wholly one herself, pure law,
151. Sequel of guerdon: 'addition of reward' (T.).

Unbiased by self-profit, oh! rest thee sure
That I shall love thee well and cleave to thee,
So that my vigour, wedded to thy blood,
Shall strike within thy pulses, like a God's,
160　To push thee forward through a life of shocks,
Dangers, and deeds, until endurance grow
Sinewed with action, and the full-grown will,
Circled through all experiences, pure law,
Commeasure perfect freedom."
　　　　　　　　　　'Here she ceased,
165　And Paris pondered, and I cried, "O Paris,
Give it to Pallas!" but he heard me not,
Or hearing would not hear me, woe is me!

'O mother Ida, many-fountained Ida,
Dear mother Ida, harken ere I die.
170　Idalian Aphroditè beautiful,
Fresh as the foam, new-bathed in Paphian wells,
With rosy slender fingers backward drew
From her warm brows and bosom her deep hair
Ambrosial, golden round her lucid throat
175　And shoulder: from the violets her light foot
Shone rosy-white, and o'er her rounded form

160–64. Paraphrasing Horace's definition of a Stoic, *Satires* II vii 83–6.

162. *2 Henry IV* IV i 172: 'Insinewed to this action'.

165. and I cried] *1842*; I cried out *1832*.

166–7. The antithesis, *heard/hear*, is from Aeschylus, *Prometheus Vinctus* 448;
Turner observes that it 'carries the implication that Paris is in the same
state of primitive animalism as the human race before Prometheus began
to civilize it'.

170. beautiful] *1842*; oceanborn *1832*.

170–1. 'Idalium and Paphos in Cyprus are sacred to Aphrodite' (T.),
who was born from the sea-foam.

172. backward] *1842*; upward *1832*.

173. brows . . . deep] *1842*; brow . . . dark *1832*. Adapted from *Mariana
in the South* 14, *1832* text: 'From her warm brow and bosom down'.

174–6] *1842*;　Fragrant and thick, and on her head upbound
　　　　　　　In a purple band: below her lucid neck
　　　　　　　Shone ivorylike, and from the ground her foot
　　　　　　　Gleamed rosywhite . . . *1832*

T. emended ll. 174–5 in J. M. Heath's copy of *1832*:
　　　　　　　Deep, fragrant. Dimpled was her chin–her throat
　　　　　　　Shone pure, and from the all-flowering ground her foot

176–8. Cp. the Oread in *Lucretius* 188–90: 'how the sun delights / To
glance and shift about her slippery sides, / And rosy knees and supple
roundedness.'

Between the shadows of the vine-bunches
Floated the glowing sunlights, as she moved.

'Dear mother Ida, harken ere I die.
180   She with a subtle smile in her mild eyes,
The herald of her triumph, drawing nigh
Half-whispered in his ear, "I promise thee
The fairest and most loving wife in Greece,"
She spoke and laughed: I shut my sight for fear:
185   But when I looked, Paris had raised his arm,
And I beheld great Herè's angry eyes,
As she withdrew into the golden cloud,
And I was left alone within the bower;
And from that time to this I am alone,
190   And I shall be alone until I die.

'Yet, mother Ida, harken ere I die.
Fairest—why fairest wife? am I not fair?
My love hath told me so a thousand times.
Methinks I must be fair, for yesterday,
195   When I past by, a wild and wanton pard,
Eyed like the evening star, with playful tail
Crouched fawning in the weed. Most loving is she?
Ah me, my mountain shepherd, that my arms
Were wound about thee, and my hot lips prest
200   Close, close to thine in that quick-falling dew
Of fruitful kisses, thick as Autumn rains
Flash in the pools of whirling Simois.

'O mother, hear me yet before I die.
They came, they cut away my tallest pines,
205   My tall dark pines, that plumed the craggy ledge
High over the blue gorge, and all between

184] *1842; not 1832.*
185–6] *1842;* I only saw my Paris raise his arm: / I only saw great ... *1832.*
192–4. Using the pastoral convention of Theocritus vi 34–6 and Virgil's
Eclogues ii 25–6.
195–7. Based on Horace's *Odes* I xx 9–12. Cp. Keats, *Lamia* i 49–50:
'freckled like a pard, / Eyed like a peacock'. Turner remarks this as
'bringing with it associations of illusory and evanescent love'.
203] *1842;* 'Dear mother Ida, hearken ere I die. *1832.*
204–5. Suggested by *Heroides* v 41–2; but there, as Turner says, 'Œnone's
only objection to the felling of the pines is that it provides transport for
Paris and Helen'.
205. *tall dark] 1884; dark tall 1832–83.*
206] *1843;* ... gorge, or lower down / Filling greengulphèd Ida, all
between *1832–42.*

The snowy peak and snow-white cataract
Fostered the callow eaglet – from beneath
Whose thick mysterious boughs in the dark morn
210 The panther's roar came muffled, while I sat
Low in the valley. Never, never more
Shall lone Œnone see the morning mist
Sweep through them; never see them overlaid
With narrow moon-lit slips of silver cloud,
215 Between the loud stream and the trembling stars.

'O mother, hear me yet before I die.
I wish that somewhere in the ruined folds,
Among the fragments tumbled from the glens,
Or the dry thickets, I could meet with her
220 The Abominable, that uninvited came
Into the fair Peleïan banquet-hall,
And cast the golden fruit upon the board,
And bred this change; that I might speak my mind,
And tell her to her face how much I hate
225 Her presence, hated both of Gods and men.

'O mother, hear me yet before I die.
Hath he not sworn his love a thousand times,
In this green valley, under this green hill,
Even on this hand, and sitting on this stone?
230 Sealed it with kisses? watered it with tears?
O happy tears, and how unlike to these!
O happy Heaven, how canst thou see my face?
O happy earth, how canst thou bear my weight?
O death, death, death, thou ever-floating cloud,
235 There are enough unhappy on this earth,
Pass by the happy souls, that love to live:
I pray thee, pass before my light of life,
And shadow all my soul, that I may die.
Thou weighest heavy on the heart within,
240 Weigh heavy on my eyelids: let me die.

213–15. Adapted from *Amy* 54–6: 'Like streaks of cloud by night / That overlay the stars in January / But cannot hide their light.' Also from *Who is it* 14–16 (see l. 62n above): 'the unrisen moon below / Dark firs, when creeping winds by night / Lay the long mist in streaks and bars.'
216–25] *1842; not 1832.*
220. Eris, 'the goddess of strife' (T.).
225. Cp. Aeschylus, *Eumenides* 644: ὦ παντομισῆ κνώδαλα, στύγη θεῶν,
226] *1842*; 'Oh! mother Ida, hearken ere I die.' *1832*.
233. A classical commonplace; cp. *Odyssey* xx 379.

'O mother, hear me yet before I die.
I will not die alone, for fiery thoughts
Do shape themselves within me, more and more,
Whereof I catch the issue, as I hear
245 Dead sounds at night come from the inmost hills,
Like footsteps upon wool. I dimly see
My far-off doubtful purpose, as a mother
Conjectures of the features of her child
Ere it is born: her child!–a shudder comes
250 Across me: never child be born of me,
Unblest, to vex me with his father's eyes!

'O mother, hear me yet before I die.
Hear me, O earth. I will not die alone,
Lest their shrill happy laughter come to me
255 Walking the cold and starless road of Death
Uncomforted, leaving my ancient love
With the Greek woman. I will rise and go
Down into Troy, and ere the stars come forth
Talk with the wild Cassandra, for she says
260 A fire dances before her, and a sound
Rings ever in her ears of armèd men.
What this may be I know not, but I know

241] *1842*; 'Yet, mother Ida, hear me ere I die. *1832*.
246. The simile is from Theocritus v 50–1.
249–51] *1842*; Ere it is born. I will not die alone. *1832*.
252] *1842*; 'Dear mother Ida, hearken ere I die. *1832*.
253–6. The association of Œnone and Dido (cp. l. 18) was, as Turner says,
'inevitable, considering the similarity of their histories (both being de-
serted by Trojan lovers, and both committing suicide on funeral pyres)'.
The image here is from Dido's dream, *Aeneid* iv 465–8.
257. *the Greek woman*: *Heroides* v 117 etc.
259. Turner points out that 'Ovid's Œnone refers to Cassandra's prophecy
that Helen will be the ruin of Troy, but she is also perfectly aware . . . that
the rape of Helen is going to cause a major war'; T. gives Œnone 'some
of Cassandra's vague prophetic power . . . depriving her of any accurate
knowledge'.
260. T. compares Aeschylus, *Agamemnon* 1256: παπαῖ, οἷον τὸ πῦρ
ἐπέρχεται δέ μοι ('Oh, oh! What fire! It comes upon me').
260–64. Turner links *fire* as a traditional metaphor for love, with it as
magic for bringing back the faithless lover (Theocritus ii 23–4 etc.); with
Hecuba's dream before the birth of Paris (*Heroides* xvi 43–50); and with
the fires of Dido, including her funeral pyre (*Aeneid* iv 604–5, 661–2,
669–71).

That, wheresoe'er I am by night and day,
All earth and air seem only burning fire.'

166 To — . With the Following Poem [The Palace of Art]

Published *1832*. It is addressed to R. C. Trench (*Tennyson and His Friends*, p. 79), a remark by whom prompted *The Palace of Art* (see *p. 50*). It proclaims the view of poetry (morally opposed to aestheticism) which was strongly held by the Cambridge 'Apostles'. On Trench, see P. Allen, *The Cambridge Apostles* (1978), pp. 93–4, 126, in particular. On the affinities with Goethe, see Ian Kennedy, *PQ* lvii (1978) 91.

I send you here a sort of allegory,
(For you will understand it) of a soul,
A sinful soul possessed of many gifts,
A spacious garden full of flowering weeds,
5   A glorious Devil, large in heart and brain,
That did love Beauty only, (Beauty seen
In all varieties of mould and mind)
And Knowledge for its beauty; or if Good,
Good only for its beauty, seeing not
10   That Beauty, Good, and Knowledge, are three sisters
That doat upon each other, friends to man,
Living together under the same roof,
And never can be sundered without tears.
And he that shuts Love out, in turn shall be
15   Shut out from Love, and on her threshold lie

264. John Churton Collins compared Webster, *Duchess of Malfi* IV ii 25–6: 'Th' heaven o'er my head seems made of molten brass, / The earth of flaming sulphur.' Alongside this, T. wrote: 'Nonsense' (*Cornhill*, Jan. 1880, *Lincoln*).

¶ 166.1. here] *1842*; Friend, *1832*.

2] *1842*; (You are an artist and will understand
        Its many lesser meanings) of a soul, *1832*

7. Cp. 'variety', 'moulds of mind', in *The constant spirit* (I 317).

10. Cp. *Fragment: We have a rumour* 4 (III 616): 'If beauty, then true knowledge. Sisters fair'.

15–16. Cp. *Hamlet* V i 234–6: 'I tell thee, churlish priest, / A minist'ring angel shall my sister be, / When thou liest howling.' Hence 'he that shuts Love out' suggests the priest's 'She should in ground unsanctified have lodged'. *Matthew* viii 12, 'But the children of the kingdom shall be cast out into outer darkness: there shall be weeping and gnashing of teeth'.

Howling in outer darkness. Not for this
Was common clay ta'en from the common earth
Moulded by God, and tempered with the tears
Of angels to the perfect shape of man.

167 The Palace of Art

Published *1832*, much revised *1842*. Written by April 1832 (*Mem.* i 85).
Hallam wrote to T., 10 April 1832: 'All were anxious for the *Palace of Art*,
etc., and fierce with me for not bringing more' (*AHH*, p. 549). It was
probably not begun before Oct. 1831, the date of Arthur Hallam's
Theodicaea Novissima (see l. 223*n*, but also l. 180*n*). T. reports: R. C. Trench
'said, when we were at Trinity (Cambridge) together, "Tennyson, we
cannot live in Art". This poem is the embodiment of my own belief that
the Godlike life is with man and for man.' See the introductory poem,
To – (p. 49), which is to Trench. T. did not yet know Trench on 1 April
1830 (*AHH*, p. 539); J. Kolb suggests that the poem was begun 'perhaps
after T.'s visit to Cambridge (where Trench was also keeping a term) in
November 1831'; he adds that Culler's 'earlier supposition . . . that
Trench's remark might have been relayed to T. through common friends –
or the possibility that T. and Trench met in November 1831 – argues that
Trench inspired the poem' (*AHH*, p. 550); this (Culler in *Nineteenth-Century
Literary Perspectives*, ed. C. de L. Ryals, 1974, p. 87) as against Culler's later
suggestion: 'it seems possible that the introductory poem . . . was addressed
not to Trench but to Hallam or Spedding' (Culler, p. 260). Culler notes, of
Trench's remark, that 'Trench had himself in mind much more than' T.
(p. 64). In a copy of *1830*, T. inserted the titles of additional poems,
presumably considering, before *1832*, a revised edition of *1830*. After *The
Poet* (I 243), he wrote *The Palace of Art*. C. Sturman (*TRB* iv, 1984, 123–7)
notes: 'Whilst it is unwise to infer too much from the juxtaposition, on
reading the two poems in sequence, *The Palace of Art* does appear –
countrary to Culler's protestation that it cannot be read simply as a
recantation of earlier aestheticism – to some extent a palinode.' T. had many
sources or analogues. *Ecclesiastes* ii 1–17, 'I said in mine heart, Go to now, I
will prove thee with mirth, therefore enjoy pleasure. . . . I made me great
works; I builded me houses. . . . I gathered me also silver and gold, and the
peculiar treasure of kings. . . . And whatsoever mine eyes desired I kept not

18–19. Cp. *Genesis* ii 7. But T. uses Sir William Jones's translation of the
Khelassut ul Akhbar of Khondemeer. At the creation of Adam, Gabriel and
the other angels were 'compassionating the earth's distress' when the earth
feared it might be involved in any 'offence' caused by man; 'In the space
of forty days, the clay was kneaded into form by the hands of the angels'.
Jones's *Works* were at Somersby (*Lincoln*). It is T. who links the tears and
the actual making of man.

from them, I withheld not my heart from any joy. . . . Then I looked on all
the works that my hands had wrought, and on the labour that I had laboured
to do: and, behold, all was vanity and vexation of spirit, and there was no
profit under the sun. . . . Therefore I hated life.' *Luke* xii 19–20, 'And I will
say to my soul, Soul, thou hast much goods laid up for many years; take
thine ease, eat, drink, and be merry. But God said unto him, Thou fool,
this night thy soul shall be required of thee.' Herbert, *The World*: '*Love* built
a stately house . . . / Then *Pleasure* came, who, liking not the fashion, /
Began to make *Balcones, Terraces*, / Till she had weakened all by alteration
. . . / But *Love* and *Grace* took *Glorie* by the hand, / And built a braver
Palace than before.' Shelley, *Queen Mab* ii 56–64: the Fairy 'pointed to the
gorgeous dome, / "This is a wondrous sight / And mocks all human
grandeur; / But, were it virtue's only meed, to dwell / In a celestial palace,
all resigned / To pleasurable impulses, immured / Within the prison of itself,
the will / Of changeless Nature would be unfulfilled. / Learn to make others
happy".' (Noted by H. N. Fairchild, *TLS*, 11 Jan. 1947.) L. Stevenson
(*Critical Essays on Tennyson*, ed. Killham, pp. 131–2) cites more examples
from Shelley: the Elysian temple in *The Revolt of Islam* I li–liii, and the
setting in *The Witch of Atlas* xviii–xxi. T. was probably influenced by Sir
William Jones, a favourite of his when young. Jones's works were at
Somersby (*Lincoln*); his *The Palace of Fortune* has similar disillusionments. A
few touches suggest the futile splendours of Milton's Pandæmonium, *PL* i
710–30. There are also affinities with George Sandys's account of Egyptian
'Palaces' in his *Travels* (the 1658 edition was at Somersby, *Lincoln*). Sandys
moralizes the labyrinth: 'The first entrance was of white marble, within
thorowout adorned with marble columns, and diversity of figures. By this
defigured they the perplexed life of man, combred and intangled with
manifold mischiefs, one succeeding another' (p. 88). Turner (pp. 63–4)
suggests that 'The thought and the basic image come from Bacon, to
whom T. transfers Dante's title for Aristotle: "The first of those who
know" (l. 164). In *The Advancement of Learning* Bacon had said that one
should not seek in knowledge "a tarrasse, for a wandering and variable
mind to walk up and down with a fair prospect; or a tower of state, for a
proud mind to raise itself upon", but "a rich storehouse, for the glory of the
Creator and the relief of man's estate".' Culler (pp. 70–2) notes the likeness
of the architecture to Cambridge and particularly to T.'s college, Trinity,
and adds that 'the pantheon of wise men whose busts adorn the Palace of
Art is virtually that of the Apostles themselves. T. indicates that the
description of "large-browed Verulam" was suggested by the bust of Bacon
in the Trinity College Library'; 'Of the twenty names mentioned in the
1832 version . . . all but four appear in [Shelley's] *Defence of Poetry*.' 'With
all these local thoughts, feelings, and associations *The Palace of Art* was
peculiarly an "Apostolic" poem,' while also having 'reference to the great
country houses of England', which were then 'the great art palaces of
England'. The stanza was independently developed (T. approached it in *The
Poet*, and cp. *A Dream of Fair Women*), but it is that of Vaughan's *They are
all gone into the world of light*.

I built my soul a lordly pleasure-house,
    Wherein at ease for aye to dwell.
I said, 'O Soul, make merry and carouse,
    Dear soul, for all is well.'

5   A huge crag-platform, smooth as burnished brass
        I chose. The rangèd ramparts bright
    From level meadow-bases of deep grass
        Suddenly scaled the light.

    Thereon I built it firm. Of ledge or shelf
10   The rock rose clear, or winding stair.
    My soul would live alone unto herself
        In her high palace there.

    And 'while the world runs round and round,' I said,
        'Reign thou apart, a quiet king,
15 Still as, while Saturn whirls, his stedfast shade
        Sleeps on his luminous ring.'

    To which my soul made answer readily:
        'Trust me, in bliss I shall abide
    In this great mansion, that is built for me,
20   So royal-rich and wide.'

            *   *   *   *
            *   *   *   *

¶ 167. *1. a lordly pleasure-house*: W. Hellstrom notes Coleridge's opening: 'In Xanadu did Kubla Khan / A stately pleasure-dome decree', and argues that much of T.'s poem engages with Coleridge's conception of the poet (*On the Poems of Tennyson*, 1972, pp. 8–9).
6. The] *1842*; whose *1832*.
7. level] *1842*; great broad *1832*.
13. And 'while the] *1842*; 'While the great' *1832*.
15–16. H.T. comments: 'The shadow of Saturn thrown on the luminous ring, though the planet revolves in ten and a half hours, appears to be motionless.'
16 ∧ *17*]   'And richly feast within thy palacehall,
                Like to the dainty bird that sups,
            Lodged in the lustrous crown-imperial,
                Draining the honeycups.' *1832*
21–52] *1842*; *preceding l. 129 in 1832*.
21] *1842*; Four ample courts there were, East, West, South, North, *1832*.

Four courts I made, East, West and South and
    North,
  In each a squarèd lawn, wherefrom
  The golden gorge of dragons spouted forth
    A flood of fountain-foam.

25 And round the cool green courts there ran a row
      Of cloisters, branched like mighty woods,
    Echoing all night to that sonorous flow
      Of spouted fountain-floods.

    And round the roofs a gilded gallery
30   That lent broad verge to distant lands,
    Far as the wild swan wings, to where the sky
      Dipt down to sea and sands.

    From those four jets four currents in one swell
      Across the mountain streamed below
35 In misty folds, that floating as they fell
      Lit up a torrent-bow.

    And high on every peak a statue seemed
      To hang on tiptoe, tossing up

23. The . . . dragons] 1842; A golden-gorgèd dragon 1832.
24] 1842; The fountain's diamond foam. 1832. D. Bush (MLR, liv, 1959,
423) compares H. J. Weber's Tales of the East (1812), i 115: 'Four large gilded
dragons adorned the angles of the bason, which was of a square form; and
these dragons spouted out water clearer than rock crystal.'
25. And] 1842; All 1832.
29–32, 33–6] 1842; transposed 1832.
29. a gilded gallery] 1842; ran gilded galleries 1832.
30. lent broad verge] 1842; gave large view 1832. broad verge: 'a broad
horizon' (T.).
31–2] 1842; Tall towns and mounds, and close beneath the skies
                Long lines of amber sands. 1832
34. Across the mountain] 1842; Over the black rock 1832.
35. misty] 1842; steamy 1832.
37–47] 1842; Huge incense-urns along the balustrade,
                Hollowed of solid amethyst,
              Each with a different odour fuming, made
                The air a silver mist.

              Far-off 'twas wonderful to look upon
                Those sumptuous towers between the gleam

A cloud of incense of all odour steamed
40   From out a golden cup.

So that she thought, 'And who shall gaze upon
      My palace with unblinded eyes,
While this great bow will waver in the sun,
      And that sweet incense rise?'

45 For that sweet incense rose and never failed,
      And, while day sank or mounted higher,
The light aërial gallery, golden-railed,
      Burnt like a fringe of fire.

Likewise the deep-set windows, stained and traced,
50   Would seem slow-flaming crimson fires
From shadowed grots of arches interlaced,
      And tipt with frost-like spires.

                *   *   *   *

                *   *   *   *

Full of long-sounding corridors it was,
      That over-vaulted grateful gloom,
55 Through which the livelong day my soul did pass,
      Well-pleased, from room to room.

Full of great rooms and small the palace stood,
      All various, each a perfect whole
From living Nature, fit for every mood
60   And change of my still soul.

Of that great foambow trembling in the sun,
      And the argent incense-steam;

And round the terraces and round the walls,
      While day sank lower or rose higher,
To see those rails with all their knobs and balls, *1832*

48. *Burnt*] *1842*; Burn *1832*.
50. *Would seem*] *1842*; Burned, like *1832*.
52. *tipt*] *1842*; topped *1832*.
54. *gloom*] *1842*; glooms *1832*. Cp. *Inverlee* 15: 'vaulted glooms'.
55–6] *1842*;   Roofed with thick plates of green and orange·glass
                Ending in stately rooms. *1832*
58. *each . . . whole*] *1842*; all beautiful *1832*.
59. *From . . . for*] *1842*; Looking all ways, fitted to *1832*.

For some were hung with arras green and blue,
Showing a gaudy summer-morn,
Where with puffed cheek the belted hunter blew
His wreathèd bugle-horn.

65 One seemed all dark and red – a tract of sand,
And some one pacing there alone,
Who paced for ever in a glimmering land,
Lit with a low large moon.

One showed an iron coast and angry waves.
70 You seemed to hear them climb and fall
And roar rock-thwarted under bellowing caves,
Beneath the windy wall.

And one, a full-fed river winding slow
By herds upon an endless plain,

61ff. Cp. the scenes depicted in Thomson's *Castle of Indolence* I xxxvi ff,
where 'the rooms with costly tapestry were hung'.
64 ∧ 5] *1832* had its version of ll. *85–8.* In *Heath MS*, there are four 'Stanzas
omitted or altered in *The Palace of Art*'; the first is marked 'x', and if this
refers to *1832* numbering, then it belongs here:
          One seemed a place of mart. The seller held
               The buyer's hand, and winked and smiled,
          And pointed to his wares. The teeming field
               On stalls lay stored and piled.
65–8] *1842*;   Some were all dark and red, a glimmering land
               Lit with a low round moon,
          Among brown rocks a man upon the sand
               Went weeping all alone. *1832*
68 ∧ 9] *1832* had its version of ll. *81–4.* Heath *MS* has a stanza 'XII':
          One shewed deep floods with dusky shadows gloomed,
               A blissful island high and bright
          With three white peaks mythic Trinacria loomed
               Far off in gleaming light.
Trinacria: Sicily.
69–80] *1842*;   Some showed far-off thick woods mounted with towers,
               Nearer, a flood of mild sunshine
          Poured on long walks and lawns and beds and bowers
               Trellised with bunchy vine. *1832*
Cp. *Armageddon* ii 50 ∧ 51, MS: 'Shaded and cinctured with the bunchy vine'.
T.Nbk 23 has a separate unadopted stanza, perhaps for hereabouts:
          Or some broad cataract, a wide crescent white
               Of twisted torrents, rolling through
          Rainbows and clouds and thunders, round the height
               Built up the columned dew.
Cp. *The Vision of Sin* 32–42.

75 The ragged rims of thunder brooding low,
       With shadow-streaks of rain.

    And one, the reapers at their sultry toil.
       In front they bound the sheaves. Behind
    Were realms of upland, prodigal in oil,
80   And hoary to the wind.

    And one a foreground black with stones and slags,
       Beyond, a line of heights, and higher
    All barred with long white cloud the scornful crags,
       And highest, snow and fire.

85 And one, an English home–gray twilight poured
       On dewy pastures, dewy trees,
    Softer than sleep–all things in order stored,
       A haunt of ancient Peace.

    Nor these alone, but every landscape fair,
90   As fit for every mood of mind,
    Or gay, or grave, or sweet, or stern, was there
       Not less than truth designed.

            *   *   *   *

            *   *   *   *

75. Cp. *The Lover's Tale* ii 59–63 (I.364): 'palaces', 'brooded', 'Like to a
low-hung and a fiery sky . . . / Hung round with ragged rims'.
79–80. Cp. Wordsworth, *Descriptive Sketches* 8 (1793): 'Or moonlight
Upland lifts her hoary breast'. See *Œnone* 113, *1832* text (*p. 42*).
80. 'The underside of the olive leaf is white' (T.).
81–4] *See ll. 68* ∧ *9n.*
81. *And one*] *1842*; One seemed *1832*.
82] *1842*; Below sunsmitten icy spires *1832*.
83. *All barred*] *1842*; Rose striped *1832*. Cp. *1842* with Keats, *To Autumn*
25: 'barred clouds'. Cp. *1832* with *Œnone* 53–6, *1832*: 'Rosehued the scornful
hills'. Also *As to one who listeneth eagerly* 7–8: 'And the bare and scornful
cragginess / Overlaid with silvery cloud'.
84] *1842*; Deeptrenched with thunderfires. *1832*.
85–8] *See ll. 64* ∧ *5n.*
85. *And one,*] *1842*; One showed *1832*.
86–7. J. H. Buckley (p. 264) compares *Ode: O Bosky Brook* 56: 'Close
pastures soft as dewy sleep'. Virgil, *Eclogues* vii 45: *somno mollior herba*.
89–92] *1842*; not *1832*.
93] *1832 note*: 'When I first conceived the plan of the Palace of Art, I
intended to have introduced both sculptures and paintings into it; but it is

Or the maid-mother by a crucifix,
In tracts of pasture sunny-warm,
95 Beneath branch-work of costly sardonyx
Sat smiling, babe in arm.

Or in a clear-walled city on the sea,
Near gilded organ-pipes, her hair
Wound with white roses, slept St Cecily;
100   An angel looked at her.

the most difficult of all things to *devise* a statue in verse. Judge whether I
have succeeded in the statues of Elijah and Olympias.
One was the Tishbite whom the raven fed,
As when he stood on Carmel-steeps,
With one arm stretched out bare, and mocked and said,
'Come cry aloud–he sleeps.'

Tall, eager, lean and strong, his cloak windborne
Behind, his forehead heavenly-bright
From the clear marble pouring glorious scorn,
Lit as with inner light.

One was Olympias: the floating snake
Rolled round her ancles, round her waist
Knotted, and folded once about her neck,
Her perfect lips to taste

Round by the shoulder moved: she seeming blythe
Declined her head: on every side
The dragon's curves melted and mingled with
The woman's youthful pride

Of rounded limbs.'
1842 dropped this. Elijah, *1 Kings* xviii 27; 'Olympias was the mother of
Alexander the Great, and devoted to the Orphic rites' (T.). T. altered the
thirteenth line to 'Down by the shoulder' (F. T. Palgrave, *Lyrical Poems of
Tennyson*, 1885, p. 249), and later to 'Down from the shoulder . . .'
(*Eversley*).
94. *tracts of pasture*] *1842*; yellow pastures *1832*.
95. T. comments: 'The Parisian jewellers apply graduated degrees of heat
to the sardonyx, by which the original colour is changed to various colours.
They imitate thus, among other things, bunches of grapes with green
tendrils.'
96 ∧ 7]   Or Venus in a snowy shell alone,
Deepshadowed in the glassy brine,
Moonlike glowed double on the blue, and shone
A naked shape divine. *1832*

Or thronging all one porch of Paradise
A group of Houris bowed to see
The dying Islamite, with hands and eyes
That said, We wait for thee.

105   Or mythic Uther's deeply-wounded son
In some fair space of sloping greens
Lay, dozing in the vale of Avalon,
And watched by weeping queens.

Or hollowing one hand against his ear,
110   To list a foot-fall, ere he saw
The wood-nymph, stayed the Ausonian king to hear
Of wisdom and of law.

Heath MS has stanzas following the 'maid-mother' stanza:
Behind her rose blue hills, and at her feet
The star-led Kings of old Cologne
Laid myrrh, laid gold, laid precious oils, and sweet
Incense before her throne.
Or shamed Tarpeia mused with head-decline,
As one whom her own soul condemns,
In caverns of the dark Capitoline,
Hung round with baleful gems.
Arthur Hallam wrote to T., 10 Oct. 1832 (AHH, pp. 661–2): 'I hear Tennant
has written to dissuade you from publishing Kriemhilt, Tarpeia and
Pendragon. Don't be humbugged, they are very good.' See also ll. 105–8n,
109–116n. Cp. III 626 for T.'s lines on the Magi and Cologne.
101–4] 1842 (see l. 103n); not 1832.
103. hands] 1843; heads 1842.
105–8] 1842;   Or that deepwounded child of Pendragon
Mid misty woods on sloping greens
Dozed in the valley of Avilion,
Tended by crownèd queens. 1832
Cp. Morte d'Arthur (p. 148).
109–16] 1842 (see ll. 110, 111n) ;
Or blue-eyed Kriemhilt from a craggy hold,
Athwart the lightgreen rows of vine,
Poured blazing hoards of Nibelungen gold,
Down to the gulfy Rhine. 1832
See ll. 96 ∧ 7n. Hallam wrote to T., 24 Sept. 1832: 'I like extremely the new
stanzas in the Palace. You must put a note to Kriemhild' (AHH, p. 652).
110. list] 1843; listen for 1842.
111. Ausonian] 1850; Tuscan 1842–8. The nymph is 'Egeria, who gave the
laws to Numa Pompilius' (T.). The story is told in Rollin's Ancient History,
of which a copy was at Somersby (Lincoln).

Or over hills with peaky tops engrailed,
   And many a tract of palm and rice.
115   The throne of Indian Cama slowly sailed
   A summer fanned with spice.

Or sweet Europa's mantle blew unclasped,
   From off her shoulder backward borne:
   From one hand drooped a crocus: one hand grasped
120   The mild bull's golden horn.

Or else flushed Ganymede, his rosy thigh
   Half-buried in the Eagle's down,
Sole as a flying star shot through the sky
   Above the pillared town.

125   Nor these alone: but every legend fair
   Which the supreme Caucasian mind
Carved out of Nature for itself, was there,
   Not less than life, designed.

                    *   *   *   *
                    *   *   *   *

113. engrailed: 'heraldic term for serrated' (H.T.). Cp. *Pierced through* 40:
'With semblance of the peaky wave engrailed', from *Armageddon* ii 50 ∧ 51
(*T.MS*, I 82–3). T.'s is the earliest use of *peaky* in *OED*.
115. Cama: T. comments: 'The Hindu God of young love, son of Brahma'.
For Cama, or Camdeo, and his 'wingèd throne', see *Love* (I 266), and
Love (I 159) where T. quotes Sir William Jones's *Hymn to Camdeo*.
117] *1842*; Europa's scarf blew in an arch, unclasped, *1832*.
117–20. Turner (p. 64) suggests the influence of Moschus ii 125–8.
118. off her] *1842*; her bare *1832*.
120 ∧ 21] He through the streaming crystal swam, and rolled
                    Ambrosial breaths that seemed to float
                    In lightwreathed curls. She from the ripple cold
                        Updrew her sandalled foot. *1832*
124. Above] *1842*; Over *1832*.
125] *1842*; Not these alone: but many a legend fair, *1832*.
126. Caucasian: Indo-European (an early nineteenth-century sense).
128] *1842*; Broidered in screen and blind. *1832*. After this line, *1832* had:

          So that my soul beholding in her pride
             All these, from room to room did pass;
          And all things that she saw, she multiplied,
             A manyfacèd glass;

   [5]   And, being both the sower and the seed,
             Remaining in herself became

Then in the towers I placed great bells that swung,
130   Moved of themselves, with silver sound;
And with choice paintings of wise men I hung
The royal dais round.

All that she saw, Madonna, Ganymede,
Or the Asiatic dame –

Still changing, as a lighthouse in the night
[*10*]   Changeth athwart the gleaming main,
From red to yellow, yellow to pale white,
Then back to red again.

'From change to change four times within the womb
The brain is moulded,' she began,
[*15*]   'So through all phases of all thought I come
Into the perfect man.

'All nature widens upward: evermore
The simpler essence lower lies.
More complex is more perfect, owning more
[*20*]   Discourse, more widely wise.

'I take possession of men's minds and deeds.
I live in all things great and small.
I dwell apart, holding no forms of creeds,
But contemplating all.'

T. made the following revisions (*Eversley*): l. [13] 'From shape to shape at
first within the womb'. l. [15] *So*] And. l. [16] *Into*] Unto. Lines [21–4]
became ll. 209–12; and ll. [13–20] became ll. 193–204 (until revised in
1851). H.Lpr *182* includes another version of ll. [10–12]:
From hue to hue, from glow to glow;
O'er gleaming seas the pilot knows the light
And all the death below.
The scientific ideas in ll. [13–20] are well discussed by J. Killham (*Tennyson
and 'The Princess'*, 1958, pp. 234–41). 'The discovery of the fourfold re-
semblances of the foetal human brain to the brains of other vertebrates was
made by Friedrich Tiedemann.' Tennyson 'sought to exorcise those
[doubts] raised by Tiedemann's theory by making the erring Soul foolishly
base its own hubristic confidence upon it'.
129] See ll. *21–52n.*   *Then*] *1842*; Up *1832*.

For there was Milton like a seraph strong,
   Beside him Shakespeare bland and mild;
135 And there the world-worn Dante grasped his song,
   And somewhat grimly smiled.

And there the Ionian father of the rest;
   A million wrinkles carved his skin;

133–4. For . . . him] *1842*; There deephaired Milton like an angel tall
            Stood limnèd, *1832*
135–6] 1842; Grim Dante pressed his lips, and from the wall
            The bald blind Homer smiled. *1832*
137–64] 1842; And underneath freshcarved in cedarwood,
            Somewhat alike in form and face,
          The Genii of every climate stood,
            All brothers of one race:

          Angels who sway the seasons by their art,
            And mould all shapes in earth and sea;
          And with great effort build the human heart
            From earliest infancy.

          And in the sunpierced Oriel's coloured flame
            Immortal Michael Angelo
          Looked down, bold Luther, largebrowed Verulam,
            The king of those who know.

          Cervantes, the bright face of Calderon,
            Robed David touching holy strings,
          The Halicarnasseän, and alone,
            Alfred the flower of kings,

          Isaïah with fierce Ezekiel,
            Swarth Moses by the Coptic sea,
          Plato, Petrarca, Livy, and Raphaël,
            And eastern Confutzee: *1832*

A fragment in *H.Nbk 5* shows that T. thought also of including Pyrrho,
Averröes, Virgil, and Cicero. Hallam wrote to T., 24 Sept. 1832, about 'the
new stanzas in the *Palace*': 'I would hint a change of Livy into some other
body. What think you of "Goethe & Raffael"?' (*AHH*, p. 652). 'Our classical
tutor at Trinity College used to call [Livy] such a great poet that I suppose he
got into my palace through his recommendation' (T.).
137–40. T. adapted his description of Merlin, *Sir Launcelot and Queen
Guinevere* (MS, p. *99*):
            High brows above a little face
            Had Merlin – these in every place
            Ten million lines did cross and lace;
            Slow as the shadow was his pace,
            The shade that creeps from dawn to dusk.

A hundred winters snowed upon his breast,
140   From cheek and throat and chin.

Above, the fair hall-ceiling stately-set
    Many an arch high up did lift,
And angels rising and descending met
    With interchange of gift.

145 Below was all mosaic choicely planned
    With cycles of the human tale
Of this wide world, the times of every land
    So wrought, they will not fail.

The people here, a beast of burden slow,
150   Toiled onward, pricked with goads and stings;
Here played, a tiger, rolling to and fro
    The heads and crowns of kings;

Here rose, an athlete, strong to break or bind
    All force in bonds that might endure,
155 And here once more like some sick man declined,
    And trusted any cure.

But over these she trod: and those great bells
    Began to chime. She took her throne:
She sat betwixt the shining Oriels,
160   To sing her songs alone.

And through the topmost Oriels' coloured flame
    Two godlike faces gazed below;
Plato the wise, and large-browed Verulam,
    The first of those who know.

165 And all those names, that in their motion were
    Full-welling fountain-heads of change,
Betwixt the slender shafts were blazoned fair
    In diverse raiment strange:

    From cheek and mouth and throat a load
    Of beard–a hundred winters snowed
    Upon the pummel as he rode
    Thin as a spider's husk.

Cp. the statue of Homer in Pope's *Temple of Fame* 185: 'His Silver Beard wav'd gently o'er his Breast'.

161–4] *See ll. 137–64n for the placing in 1832.*

164. 1832 note: '*Il maëstro di color chi sanno*–Dante, *Inferno* iii'. T. remarks that this praise of Francis Bacon (Lord Verulam) was Dante's praise of Aristotle. (*Inferno* iv 131.)

165] *1842*; And many more, that in their lifetime were *1832*.

167. Betwixt . . . were] *1842*; Between the stone shafts glimmered, *1832*.

Through which the lights, rose, amber, emerald,
blue,
170 Flushed in her temples and her eyes,
And from her lips, as morn from Memnon, drew
Rivers of melodies.

No nightingale delighteth to prolong
Her low preamble all alone,
175 More than my soul to hear her echoed song
Throb through the ribbèd stone;

Singing and murmuring in her feastful mirth,
Joying to feel herself alive,
Lord over Nature, Lord of the visible earth,
180 Lord of the senses five;

Communing with herself: 'All these are mine,
And let the world have peace or wars,
'Tis one to me.' She–when young night divine
Crowned dying day with stars,

171. Memnon: the statue that made music when touched by the sun. Cp.
A Fragment 16 (I 315).
173–4. Adapted from *Sonnet* [*Check every outflash*] 9: 'The nightingale, with
long and low preamble'.
180. Hallam wrote to W. B. Donne, 13 Feb. 1831: '"an artist," as Alfred is
wont to say, "ought to be lord of the five senses," but if he lacks the inward
sense which reveals to him what is inward in the heart, he has left out the
part of Hamlet in the play' (*AHH*, p. 401).
181–3] 1842; As some rich tropic mountain, that infolds
              All change, from flats of scattered palms
          Sloping through five great zones of climate, holds
              His head in snows and calms –

          Full of her own delight and nothing else,
              My vainglorious, gorgeous soul
          Sat throned between the shining oriels,
              In pomp beyond control;

          With piles of flavorous fruits in basket-twine
              Of gold, upheapèd, crushing down
          Muskscented blooms–all taste–grape, gourd or pine–
              In bunch, or singlegrown–

          Our growths, and such as brooding Indian heats
              Make out of crimson blossoms deep,
          Ambrosial pulps and juices, sweets from sweets
              Sunchanged, when seawinds sleep.

185   Making sweet close of his delicious toils –
      Lit light in wreaths and anadems,
    And pure quintessences of precious oils
      In hollowed moons of gems,

    To mimic heaven; and clapt her hands and cried,
190   'I marvel if my still delight
    In this great house so royal-rich, and wide,
      Be flattered to the height.

    With graceful chalices of curious wine,
      Wonders of art – and costly jars,
    And bossèd salvers. Ere young night divine *1832*

186. anadems: 'crowns' (T.). H.T. compares Shelley, *Adonais* 94: 'the wreath upon him, like an anadem'.

186–92] 1842;   She lit white streams of dazzling gas,
    And soft and fragrant flames of precious oils
      In moons of purple glass

    Ranged on the fretted woodwork to the ground.
    Thus her intense untold delight,
    In deep or vivid colour, smell and sound,
      Was flattered day and night. *1832*

1832 continued with a note (omitted in *1842*): 'If the Poem were not already too long, I should have inserted in the text the following stanzas, expressive of the joy wherewith the soul contemplated the results of astronomical experiment. In the centre of the four quadrangles rose an immense tower.

    Hither, when all the deep unsounded skies
      Shuddered with silent stars, she clomb,
    And as with optic glasses her keen eyes
      Pierced through the mystic dome,

    Regions of lucid matter taking forms,
      Brushes of fire, hazy gleams,
    Clusters and beds of worlds, and bee-like swarms
      Of suns, and starry streams.

    She saw the snowy poles of moonless Mars,
      That marvellous round of milky light
    Below Orion, and those double stars
      Whereof the one more bright

    Is circled by the other, &c.'

(J. W. Croker, *QR*, April 1833, as in l. 93, ridiculed T.'s 'ingenious device . . . for reconciling the rigour of criticism with the indulgence of parental partiality'.) H.T. quotes T.'s revision of the last stanza, necessitated by astronomical discovery in 1877:

> She saw the snowy poles and moons of Mars,
>   That mystic field of drifted light
> In mid Orion and the married stars . . .

T. made this revision in F. T. Palgrave, *Lyrical Poems of Tennyson* (1885), p. 249 (as '. . . moons of Mars, / That marvellous field of drifted light . . .'), and in a copy óf W. J. Rolfe's edition of *Select Poems* (Boston, 1885, at Lincoln). The allusion is to the theory of the nebulous matter diffused throughout the universe; 'lucid', 'matter', and 'forms' are all scientific terms. Cp. *The Princess* ii 101–4 (*p. 243*). *H.Lpr 182* has deleted stanzas leading up to those on astronomy:

> Yet saw she shadowed in her vast abode
>   The secret entities of Faith,
> Those ethnic instincts of Eternal God
>   And epic dreams of Death.

> She saw them blind and vague in form and face,
>   Not yet mixt up with human deeds,
> But always waiting in a dusky place
>   To clothe themselves in creeds.

> And likewise many a fair philosophy
>   From Plato to the German, wrought
> In mystic groups as far as this might be
>   That served the central thought.

> Yet saw she Earth laid open. Furthermore
>   How the strong Ages had their will,
> A range of Giants breaking down the shore
>   And heaving up the hill.

> And likewise every life that Nature made,
>   What yet is left and what is gone
> To where the classes vanish, shade by shade,
>   Life and half-life, to none.

> And likewise every Science fair displayed
>   By which men work with Nature's power.
> And in the centre of the courts I made
>   With toil a wondrous tower,

> To which, when all the deep unsounded skies . . .

The ninth line was adapted as *In Memoriam* xxiii 21: 'And many an old philosophy'. The fourth stanza was adapted to form *Ode on Wellington* 259–61:

> For though the Giant Ages heave the hill
> And break the shore, and evermore
> Make and break, and work their will;

'O all things fair to sate my various eyes!
   O shapes and hues that please me well!
195 O silent faces of the Great and Wise,
    My Gods, with whom I dwell!

'O God-like isolation which art mine,
   I can but count thee perfect gain,
What time I watch the darkening droves of swine
200   That range on yonder plain.

'In filthy sloughs they roll a prurient skin,
   They graze and wallow, breed and sleep;
And oft some brainless devil enters in,
    And drives them to the deep.'

205 Then of the moral instinct would she prate
   And of the rising from the dead,
As hers by right of full-accomplished Fate;
    And at the last she said:

'I take possession of man's mind and deed.
210   I care not what the sects may brawl.
I sit as God holding no form of creed,
    But contemplating all.'

            *   *   *   *

            *   *   *   *

Full oft the riddle of the painful earth
   Flashed through her as she sat alone,

With the fifth stanza, cp. *In Memoriam* lv (*p. 396*). *H.Nbk 4* has a further
astronomical stanza between the second and third of *1832*:

    Bright points the centre of a hazy shroud,
      Cold Uranus, cold Jupiter,
    Girthed eight times round with slowly streaming cloud
      And through his red-brown air

    Sparkled the snowy poles . . .
188. 'Gems hollowed out for lamps' (H.T.).
193–204] *1851; not 1832; 1842–50* had the revised text of *ll.* [*13–20*] *of the
lines from 1832 quoted at l. 128n* (retaining Into, *and with* moulded] *modelled*).
205–8] *1842; not 1832*.
209–12] *1850; not 1832* (*see l. 128n*);
      'I take possession of men's minds and deeds.
        I live in all things great and small.
      I sit apart, holding no forms of creeds,
        But contemplating all.' *1842–8*
213. Full oft] *1842* ; Sometimes *1832*.

215 Yet not the less held she her solemn mirth,
　　And intellectual throne.

And so she throve and prospered: so three years
　　She prospered: on the fourth she fell,
Like Herod, when the shout was in his ears,
220　　Struck through with pangs of hell.

Lest she should fail and perish utterly,
　　God, before whom ever lie bare
The abysmal deeps of Personality,
　　Plagued her with sore despair.

225 When she would think, where'er she turned her
　　sight
The airy hand confusion wrought,
Wrote, 'Mene, mene,' and divided quite
　　The kingdom of her thought.

Deep dread and loathing of her solitude
230　　Fell on her, from which mood was born
Scorn of herself; again, from out that mood
　　Laughter at her self-scorn.

216–17] *1850*; . . . throne / Of fullsphered contemplation. So three years
1832–48.
218. *prospered:*] *1850*; throve, but *1832–48*.
219–20. *Acts* xii 21–3: 'And upon a set day Herod, arrayed in royal apparel,
sat upon his throne, and made an oration unto them. And the people
gave a shout, saying, It is the voice of a god, and not of a man. And im-
mediately the angel of the Lord smote him, because he gave not God the
glory: and he was eaten of worms, and gave up the ghost.'
223. T. points out that this was from Arthur Hallam's *Theodicaea Novis-
sima*: 'God's election, with whom alone rest the abysmal secrets of perso-
nality' (Motter, pp. 210–11). Cp. *Psalm* cxxxix 1–4: 'O Lord, thou hast
searched me and known me . . .'
227. As at the feast of Belshazzar, *Daniel* v 23–7: who 'hast praised the
gods of silver, and gold, of brass, iron, wood, and stone, which see not, nor
hear, nor know: and the God in whose hand thy breath is, and whose are
all thy ways, hast thou not glorified . . . This is the interpretation of the
thing: MENE; God hath numbered thy kingdom, and finished it. TEKEL;
Thou art weighed in the balances, and art found wanting. PERES; Thy
kingdom is divided . . .'
232 ∧ 3] 'Who hath drawn dry the fountains of delight,
　　　That from my deep heart everywhere
　　Moved in my blood and dwelt, as power and might
　　　Abode in Sampson's hair? *1832*

'What! is not this my place of strength,' she said,
   'My spacious mansion built for me,
235 Whereof the strong foundation-stones were laid
   Since my first memory?'

But in dark corners of her palace stood
   Uncertain shapes; and unawares
On white-eyed phantasms weeping tears of blood,
240   And horrible nightmares,

And hollow shades enclosing hearts of flame,
   And, with dim fretted foreheads all,
On corpses three-months-old at noon she came,
   That stood against the wall.

245 A spot of dull stagnation, without light
   Or power of movement, seemed my soul,
'Mid onward-sloping motions infinite
   Making for one sure goal.

A still salt pool, locked in with bars of sand,
250   Left on the shore; that hears all night
The plunging seas draw backward from the land
   Their moon-led waters white.

A star that with the choral starry dance
   Joined not, but stood, and standing saw
255 The hollow orb of moving Circumstance
   Rolled round by one fixed law.

239. Cp. another guilty soul, that of Faustus, in Marlowe's *Dr Faustus*
1386–8: 'I would weep, but the devil draws in my tears. Gush forth
blood, instead of tears.' Also Shelley, *Prologue to Hellas* 88: 'Whose pores
wept tears of blood'. Cp. *Armageddon* i 107 ∧ 8: 'phantasies / From whose
pale fronts and white unhallowed eyes'.
241. Beckford's *Vathek*, which has a palace, mentions spirits with hearts
like Soliman, 'discerned through his bosom, which was as transparent as
crystal, his heart enveloped in flames' (A. C. Howell, *SP* xxxiii (1936) 517).
But when Arthur Coleridge suggested this influence to Tennyson, he
replied: 'No, merely spectral visions' (*Tennyson and His Friends*, p. 264).
On possible echoes of *Vathek* see A. A. Mendilow, 'Tennyson's Palace of
the Sinful Muse', *Scripta Hierosolymitana* xvii (1966) 164–5.
242. *fretted*: 'worm-fretted' (T.).
247. *onward*-] *1842*; downward- *1832*.
255. T. comments: 'Some old writer calls the Heavens "the Circumstance"
.... Here it is more or less a play on the word.' Cp. Milton's astronomy:
'the hollow Universal Orb', *PL* vii 257.

Back on herself her serpent pride had curled.
'No voice,' she shrieked in that lone hall,
'No voice breaks through the stillness of this world:
260   One deep, deep silence all!'

She, mouldering with the dull earth's mouldering
    sod,
Inwrapt tenfold in slothful shame,
Lay there exilèd from eternal God,
    Lost to her place and name;

265 And death and life she hated equally,
    And nothing saw, for her despair,
But dreadful time, dreadful eternity,
    No comfort anywhere;

Remaining utterly confused with fears,
270   And ever worse with growing time,
And ever unrelieved by dismal tears,
    And all alone in crime:

Shut up as in a crumbling tomb, girt round
    With blackness as a solid wall,
275 Far off she seemed to hear the dully sound
    Of human footsteps fall.

As in strange lands a traveller walking slow,
    In doubt and great perplexity,
A little before moon-rise hears the low
280   Moan of an unknown sea;

And knows not if it be thunder, or a sound
    Of rocks thrown down, or one deep cry

257. Probably referring to the scorpion's stinging itself to death. T. calls a
scorpion a 'serpent' of the mind in *The Passions* 16. Cp. Byron, *The
Giaour* 422–3: 'The Mind, that broods o'er guilty woes, / Is like the
Scorpion girt by fire.'
277–84. Cp. a fragment of the poem in *H.Nbk 4*:
    And as a lated man that makes all night
        For some warm town, [but?] dazzled and cold,
    Finds but a wreath of straw that ploughmen light
        Upon a windy wold
    To scorch the glebe and he has far to go–
        Even so she seemèd to have strayed from love,
    The central [?] light of knowledge; [even so?]
        She had no strength to move.
281. *a*] *1842*; the *1832*.
282. *rocks*] *1850*; stones *1832–48*.

Of great wild beasts; then thinketh, 'I have found
   A new land, but I die.'
285 She howled aloud, 'I am on fire within.
   There comes no murmur of reply.
   What is it that will take away my sin,
   And save me lest I die?'

So when four years were wholly finishèd,
290 She threw her royal robes away.
   'Make me a cottage in the vale,' she said,
   'Where I may mourn and pray.

'Yet pull not down my palace towers, that are
   So lightly, beautifully built:
295 Perchance I may return with others there
   When I have purged my guilt.'

170 The Lotos-Eaters

Published *1832*. The important revisions in *1842* were the addition of
ll. 114–32 and the rewriting of ll. 150–73. Written 1830–32 (*Mem.* i 86);
T. dated ll. 8, 11, 42, as 1830. T.'s letter to W. H. Brookfield, mid-March 1832
(*Letters* i 70–1) has many filaments to the poem: 'Hollo! Brooks, Brooks! for
shame! what are you about–musing, and brooding and dreaming and
opiumeating yourself out of this life into the next? . . . I think you mentioned
a renewal of your acquaintance with the fishermen, which may possibly
occur if you will leave off the aforesaid drug, if you do not I can foresee
nothing for you but stupefaction, aneurism, confusion, horror and death'
(cp. ll. 105, 110, 128: 'Eating the Lotos day by day / . . . To muse and brood
and live again in memory / . . . There *is* confusion worse than death'). The
main source was *Odyssey* ix 82–104: 'We set foot on the land of the Lotus-
eaters, who eat a flowery food. . . . So they went straightway and mingled
with the Lotus-eaters, and the Lotus-eaters did not plan death for my
comrades, but gave them of the lotus to taste. And whosoever of them ate of
the honey-sweet fruit of the lotus, had no longer any wish to bring back
word or to return, but there they were fain to abide among the Lotus-eaters,
feeding on the lotus, and forgetful of their homeward way. These men,
therefore, I brought back perforce to the ships, weeping.' T. jotted in *H.Nbk*
4 (1831–2): 'Alzerbe's isle / Where dwelt the folk that lotos eat erewhile.'
From Fairfax's translation of Tasso, *Jerusalem Delivered* XV xviii. T. was
influenced by Washington Irving's *Columbus* (1828), the source of *Anacaona*
(I 308); Irving describes the idyllic life on Haiti. For T.'s interest in Islands

288. *And . . . lest*] *1842*; Dying the death *1832*.

of the Blest, see Paden (pp. 141–3). Cp. *The Hesperides* (I 461), which mentions the 'lotusflute'; and *The Sea-Fairies* (I 278). Spenser was the major influence on the style and tone; note in particular the cave of Morpheus, *Faerie Queene* I i st. 41; the blandishments of Despair, I ix st. 40; the 'Idle lake' and its enervating island, II vi st. 10; and the mermaids and the Bower of Bliss, II xii st. 32. There are a few touches from James Thomson's Spenserian imitation, *The Castle of Indolence* I v–vi: 'And up the hills, on either side, a wood / Of blackening pines, ay waving to and fro, / Sent forth a sleepy horror through the blood; / And where this valley winded out, below, / The murmuring main was heard, and scarcely heard, to flow. // A pleasing land of drowsyhed it was: / Of dreams that wave before the half-shut eye; / And of gay castles in the clouds that pass, / For ever flushing round a summer sky: / There eke the soft delights, that witchingly / Instil a wanton sweetness through the breast, / And the calm pleasures always hovered nigh; / But whate'er smacked of noyance, or unrest, / Was far far off expelled from this delicious nest.' The earliest MS is *H.Nbk 3*, which breaks off at l. 98 (all variants are below, *A*). *H.Lpr 131* (*B*) is likewise not in T.'s hand. There is a copy in Arthur Hallam's hand at the *University of Hawaii*. E. Griffiths suggests as one source Horace, *Odes* II xi, quoted by T. in his earliest surviving letter (Oct. 1821?; *Letters* i 2): 'Of which this is a free Translation "Why lie we not at random, under the shade of the plantain (sub platano) having our hoary head perfumed with rose-water"' (*Cambridge Review*, 28 Jan. 1983).

>   'Courage!' he said, and pointed toward the land,
>   'This mounting wave will roll us shoreward soon.'
>   In the afternoon they came unto a land
>   In which it seemèd always afternoon.
> 5   All round the coast the languid air did swoon,
>   Breathing like one that hath a weary dream.
>   Full-faced above the valley stood the moon;

¶ 170. *1.* Turner (p. 67): 'the note of heroism sounds in the first word, "'Courage!'", which refers to the fact that the "mariners" have been driven about in a storm for the last nine days.'
3. T. says: '"The strand" was, I think, my first reading, but the no rhyme of "land" and "land" was lazier.'
4. seemèd always] always seemèd *A*.
7] *1842 and A*; Above the valley burned the golden moon; *1832*. J. M. Kemble wrote to W. B. Donne, 22 June 1833: 'Some d—— friend or other told him that the full moon was never seen while the sunset lingered in the West; which is a lie, for I have seen it in Spain, and in the Lotos Land too!' *W. B. Donne*, ed. C. B. Johnson (1905) p. 16. Cp. *The Hesperides* 99: 'the fullfaced sunset'.

And like a downward smoke, the slender stream
Along the cliff to fall and pause and fall did seem.
10 A land of streams! some, like a downward smoke,
Slow-dropping veils of thinnest lawn, did go; .
And some through wavering lights and shadows
broke,
Rolling a slumbrous sheet of foam below.
They saw the gleaming river seaward flow
15 From the inner land: far off, three mountain-tops,
Three silent pinnacles of agèd snow,
Stood sunset-flushed: and, dewed with showery
drops,
Up-clomb the shadowy pine above the woven copse.

The charmèd sunset lingered low adown
20 In the red West: through mountain clefts the dale
Was seen far inland, and the yellow down
Bordered with palm, and many a winding vale
And meadow, set with slender galingale;
A land where all things always seemed the same!
25 And round about the keel with faces pale,
Dark faces pale against that rosy flame,
The mild-eyed melancholy Lotos-eaters came.

Branches they bore of that enchanted stem,
Laden with flower and fruit, whereof they gave
30 To each, but whoso did receive of them,
And taste, to him the gushing of the wave

8. T. says: 'Taken from the waterfall at Gavarnie, in the Pyrenees, when I
was 20 or 21', as was l. 11.
10–18] Not *A*.
11. 'When I printed this, a critic informed me that "lawn" was the
material used in theatres to imitate a waterfall, and graciously added, "Mr
T. should not go to the boards of a theatre but to Nature herself for his
suggestions." And I *had* gone to Nature herself' (*Mem.* i 259). Cp. Herrick,
Upon Julia's Washing Herself in the River 5–6: 'As in the River Julia did, /
Halfe with a Lawne of water hid.'
14. river] *1842*; river's *1832*.
16] *1842;* Three thundercloven thrones of oldest snow, *1832*.
20. red] flushed *A*.
23] Thickset with lavender and galingale–*A*.
24. Lucretius iii 945: *eadem sunt omnia semper.* See l. 155*n.* Turner (pp. 67–8)
notes that in Lucretius the phrase is 'used by Nature in a prolonged attempt
(iii 931–62) to make death seem acceptable, and life seem not worth living'.
26] Pale in the steady sunset's rosy flame, *A*.

Far far away did seem to mourn and rave
On alien shores; and if his fellow spake,
His voice was thin, as voices from the grave;
35 And deep-asleep he seemed, yet all awake,
And music in his ears his beating heart did make.

They sat them down upon the yellow sand,
Between the sun and moon upon the shore;
And sweet it was to dream of Fatherland,
40 Of child, and wife, and slave; but evermore
Most weary seemed the sea, weary the oar,
Weary the wandering fields of barren foam.
Then some one said, 'We will return no more;'
And all at once they sang, 'Our island home
45 Is far beyond the wave; we will no longer roam.'

CHORIC SONG

I

There is sweet music here that softer falls
Than petals from blown roses on the grass,
Or night-dews on still waters between walls
Of shadowy granite, in a gleaming pass;
50 Music that gentlier on the spirit lies,
Than tired eyelids upon tired eyes;
Music that brings sweet sleep down from the blissful
    skies.
Here are cool mosses deep,
And through the moss the ivies creep,

34. *His*] The *A*. Cp. the ghosts, *Aeneid* vi 492: *pars tollere vocem exiguam*.
40. *but*] that *A*.
41–2. Cp. *Home* 3–4: 'the weary sea, / Leagues of sounding foam'.
42. T. comments: 'Made by me on a voyage from Bordeaux to Dublin (1830)'.
44. *sang*] sung *A*.
48. *still*] smooth *A*.
51. *tired eyelids*] heavy eyelids *A*. T. comments: 'tiërd'; but also adds 'making the word neither monosyllabic nor disyllabic, but a dreamy child of the two'.
52. *down from the*] from the dark *A*.
53–4] Here are cool springs and mosses deep, *A*.
53–6. The effect of the rhymes, and the subject-matter, suggest the end of Marvell's *Thyrsis and Dorinda*, which – after 44 lines of couplets – concludes: 'Then let us give Carillo charge o' th Sheep, / And thou and I'le pick poppies and them steep / In wine, and drink on't even till we weep, / So shall we smoothly pass away in sleep.'

55   And in the stream the long-leaved flowers weep,
      And from the craggy ledge the poppy hangs in
        sleep.

                              II
      Why are we weighed upon with heaviness,
      And utterly consumed with sharp distress,
      While all things else have rest from weariness?
60   All things have rest: why should we toil alone,
      We only toil, who are the first of things,
      And make perpetual moan,
      Still from one sorrow to another thrown:
      Nor ever fold our wings,
65   And cease from wanderings,
      Nor steep our brows in slumber's holy balm;
      Nor harken what the inner spirit sings,
      'There is no joy but calm!'
      Why should we only toil, the roof and crown of
        things?

                             III
70   Lo! in the middle of the wood,
      The folded leaf is wooed from out the bud
      With winds upon the branch, and there
      Grows green and broad, and takes no care,
      Sun-steeped at noon, and in the moon
75   Nightly dew-fed; and turning yellow

57. Cp. *The Lover's Tale*, MS (Appendix A, III 588), draft iii 146–7: 'weighed upon / With this lovelethargy'.

60–9. Cp. *Faerie Queene* II vi st. 17, on the relaxing island: 'Why then dost thou, O man, that of them all / Art Lord, and eke of nature Soveraine, / Wilfully make thy selfe a wretched thrall, / And wast thy joyous houres in needlesse paine, / Seeking for daunger and adventures vaine?'

60–1. we . . . We [*rom.*] *1842*; [*ital.*] *1832*.

62. *moan*] moaning *A* (*slip?*).

65] Not *A*; [wings] Of thought from wanderings, *B*.

70. *Lo!*] For *A*.

70–83. For Nature's effortlessness, cp. *Faerie Queene* (again the island, II vi st. 15): 'Behold, O man, that toilesome paines doest take, / The flowres, the fields, and all that pleasant growes . . . / They spring, they bud, they blossome fresh and faire . . . / Yet no man for them taketh paines or care, / Yet no man to them can his carefull paines compare.'

72. *winds . . . branch*] dalliance of sweet winds *A*.

74–5] Nightly dew-steeped; and turning yellow *A*.

75–8. The rhyme *yellow/mellow* and the account of the apple recall *The Hesperides* 99–101 (I 466).

Falls, and floats adown the air.
Lo! sweetened with the summer light,
The full-juiced apple, waxing over-mellow,
Drops in a silent autumn night.
80 All its allotted length of days,
The flower ripens in its place,
Ripens and fades, and falls, and hath no toil,
Fast-rooted in the fruitful soil.

IV

Hateful is the dark-blue sky,
85 Vaulted o'er the dark-blue sea.
Death is the end of life; ah, why
Should life all labour be?
Let us alone. Time driveth onward fast,
And in a little while our lips are dumb.
90 Let us alone. What is it that will last?
All things are taken from us, and become
Portions and parcels of the dreadful Past.
Let us alone. What pleasure can we have
To war with evil? Is there any peace
95 In ever climbing up the climbing wave?
All things have rest, and ripen toward the grave
In silence; ripen, fall and cease:
Give us long rest or death, dark death, or dreamful
ease.
How sweet it were, hearing the downward stream,
100 With half-shut eyes ever to seem
Falling asleep in a half-dream!

76. *adown*] upon *A*.
80. Cp. *Psalm* xxi 4: 'He asked life of thee, and thou gavest it him, even length of days for ever and ever.'
82. E. Griffiths compares this passage with *Matthew* vi 28: 'consider the lilies of the field, how they grow; they toil not, neither do they spin'.
84–5. Cp. *Aeneid* iv 451: *taedet caeli convexa tueri*.
85. *Vaulted o'er*] Wearisome *A*.
86. A commonplace, but note the context of Spenser's 'Death is the end of woes': Despair's easeful seductions, I ix st. 47; ll. 96–8 below are tinged with Spenser's stanza 40: 'Sleepe after toyle, port after stormie seas, / Ease after warre, death after life does greatly please.'
88–92] Not *A*.
94] In warring with mischances, or what peace *A*.
97. *fall and cease*: J. McCue notes *King Lear* V iii 266.
98] *A breaks off here*.
100–101. Cp. Thomson (headnote).

To dream and dream, like yonder amber light,
Which will not leave the myrrh-bush on the height;
To hear each other's whispered speech;
105 Eating the Lotos day by day,
To watch the crisping ripples on the beach,
And tender curving lines of creamy spray;
To lend our hearts and spirits wholly
To the influence of mild-minded melancholy;
110 To muse and brood and live again in memory,
With those old faces of our infancy
Heaped over with a mound of grass,
Two handfuls of white dust, shut in an urn of brass!

VI

Dear is the memory of our wedded lives,
115 And dear the last embraces of our wives
And their warm tears: but all hath suffered change:
For surely now our household hearths are cold:
Our sons inherit us: our looks are strange:
And we should come like ghosts to trouble joy.
120 Or else the island princes over-bold
Have eat our substance, and the minstrel sings
Before them of the ten years' war in Troy,
And our great deeds, as half-forgotten things.
Is there confusion in the little isle?
125 Let what is broken so remain.
The Gods are hard to reconcile:
'Tis hard to settle order once again.
There *is* confusion worse than death,
Trouble on trouble, pain on pain,
130 Long labour unto agèd breath,
Sore task to hearts worn out by many wars
And eyes grown dim with gazing on the pilot-stars.

108–9. Adapted from 'give up wholly / Thy spirit to mild-minded
Melancholy', *Sonnet* [*Check every outflash*], as is perhaps 'dark and holy',
l. 136.
111. those] *1842*; the *1832*.
114–32] *1842; not 1832.*
116–9. A preoccupation of T.'s; cp. *The Coach of Death* 65–8 (I 88), *In
Memoriam* XC (*p. 433*), and the story of *Enoch Arden*.
120–21. Cp. *Odyssey* xi 115, the wooing of Penelope in Ithaca: 'proud men
that devour thy livelihood'.
131. by] *1865*; with *1842–64*.
132. Cp. *The Lover's Tale* i 480–82, *1832* text: 'whose eyes are dim /
With gazing on the light'.

VII

But, propt on beds of amaranth and moly,
How sweet (while warm airs lull us, blowing lowly)
135 With half-dropt eyelid still,
Beneath a heaven dark and holy,
To watch the long bright river drawing slowly
His waters from the purple hill—
To hear the dewy echoes calling
140 From cave to cave through the thick-twinèd vine—
To watch the emerald-coloured water falling
Through many a woven acanthus-wreath divine!
Only to hear and see the far-off sparkling brine,
Only to hear were sweet, stretched out beneath the
        pine.

VIII

145 The Lotos blooms below the barren peak:
The Lotos blows by every winding creek:
All day the wind breathes low with mellower tone:
Through every hollow cave and alley lone
Round and round the spicy downs the yellow
        Lotos-dust is blown.
150 We have had enough of action, and of motion we,
Rolled to starboard, rolled to larboard, when the
        surge was seething free,
Where the wallowing monster spouted his foam-
        fountains in the sea.
Let us swear an oath, and keep it with an equal
        mind,
In the hollow Lotos-land to live and lie reclined

133. But, propt on] *1842*; Or, propt on lavish *1832*. *amaranth*: 'the immortal
flower of legend' (T.), as in Milton's Heaven, *Paradise Lost* iii 352; *moly*:
'the sacred herb of mystical power, used as a charm by Odysseus against
Circe' mentioned in *Comus* 636.
134] Not B.
135. half-dropt eyelid] *1872*; half-dropt eyelids *1832-70*; half-shut eyelids B.
137. long bright] lacuna in B and Hawaii MS.
141. watch] *1851*; hear *1832-50*.
145. barren] *1851*; flowery *1832-50*.
149. yellow] Not B.
150-73]   We have had enough of motion,
                    Weariness and wild alarm,
                    Tossing on the tossing ocean,
                    Where the tuskèd seahorse walloweth

[5]   In a stripe of grassgreen calm,
      At noon tide beneath the lee;
      And the monstrous narwhale swalloweth
      His foamfountains in the sea.
      Long enough the winedark wave our weary bark did carry.
[10] This is lovelier and sweeter,
      Men of Ithaca, this is meeter,
      In the hollow rosy vale to tarry,
      Like a dreamy Lotos-eater, a delirious Lotos-eater!
      We will eat the Lotos, sweet
[15] As the yellow honeycomb,
      In the valley some, and some
      On the ancient heights divine;
      And no more roam,
      On the loud hoar foam,
[20] To the melancholy home
      At the limit of the brine,
      The little isle of Ithaca, beneath the day's decline.
      We'll lift no more the shattered oar,
      No more unfurl the straining sail;
[25] With the blissful Lotoseaters pale
      We will abide in the golden vale
      Of the Lotos-land, till the Lotos fail;
      We will not wander more.
      Hark! how sweet the horned ewes bleat
[30] On the solitary steeps,
      And the merry lizard leaps,
      And the foamwhite waters pour;
      And the dark pine weeps,
      And the lithe vine creeps,
[35] And the heavy melon sleeps
      On the level of the shore:
      Oh! islanders of Ithaca, we will not wander more.
      Surely, surely slumber is more sweet than toil, the shore
      Than labour in the ocean, and rowing with the oar.
[40] Oh! islanders of Ithaca, we will return no more. *1832*

B has the following variants: l. [4] *tuskèd*] broadmaned.   l. [9] *winedark*]
weary.   l. [12] *rosy*] golden.   l. [16] Where the briar never clomb.
l. [21] *limit*] limits.   l. [28] We will return no more.   l. [31] *merry*]
rapid.   l. [37] *not wander*] return no.   l. [39] *and*] or. J. M. Kemble
wrote (see l. 7n): 'Then again what think you of the "tusked sea-horse"
for the "broad-maned sea-horse"? Here also some *stumpf* told him that
the Walrus or sea-horse had no mane; as if he and you and I do not know
very well that he never meant the Walrus or any such Northern Brute,
but a good mythological, Neptunian charger! But Ælfred piques himself
upon Natural History, for which may a sound rope's end be his portion.'

155 On the hills like Gods together, careless of
     mankind.
For they lie beside their nectar, and the bolts are
     hurled
Far below them in the valleys, and the clouds are
     lightly curled
Round their golden houses, girdled with the gleaming
     world:
Where they smile in secret, looking over wasted
     lands,
160 Blight and famine, plague and earthquake, roaring
     deeps and fiery sands,
Clanging fights, and flaming towns, and
     sinking ships, and praying hands.
But they smile, they find a music centred in a
     doleful song
Steaming up, a lamentation and an ancient tale of
     wrong,
Like a tale of little meaning though the words are
     strong;
165 Chanted from an ill-used race of men that cleave the
     soil,
Sow the seed, and reap the harvest with enduring
     toil,
Storing yearly little dues of wheat, and wine and oil;
Till they perish and they suffer—some, 'tis
     whispered—down in hell
Suffer endless anguish, others in Elysian valleys
     dwell,
170 Resting weary limbs at last on beds of asphodel.
Surely, surely, slumber is more sweet than toil,
     the shore
Than labour in the deep mid-ocean, wind and wave
     and oar;
Oh rest ye, brother mariners, we will not wander
     more.

155–70. The Gods are based on Lucretius's account of Epicureanism. H.T.
compares *deos securum agere aevom* v 82; and iii 18–22: *apparet divum numen
sedesque quietae | quas neque concutiunt venti nec nubila nimbis | aspergunt neque
nix acri concreta pruina | cana cadens violat semperque innubilus aether | integit,
et large diffuso lumine ridet.* ('Before me appear the gods in their majesty,
and their peaceful abodes, which no winds ever shake nor clouds besprinkle
with rain, which no snow congealed by the bitter frost mars with its white
fall, but the air ever cloudless encompasses them and laughs with its light
spread wide abroad'.) Cp. T.'s *Lucretius* 109–10: 'Nor sound of human
sorrow mounts to mar | Their sacred everlasting calm!'

173 A Dream of Fair Women

Published *1832*, revised subsequently. Written 1831–2. Hallam wrote to
W. B. Donne, 13 Feb. 1831: 'It is observable in the mighty models of art, left
for the worship of ages by the Greeks, & those too rare specimens of Roman
production which breathe a Greek spirit, that their way of imaging a mood of
the human heart in a group of circumstances, each of which reciprocally
affects & is affected by the unity of that mood, resembles much Alfred's
manner of delineation, and should therefore give additional sanction to the
confidence of our praise. I believe you will find instances in all the Greek
poems of the highest order, at present I can only call into distinct recollection
the divine passage about the sacrifice of Iphigenia in Lucretius, the desolation
of Ariadne in Catullus, and the fragments of Sappho, in which I see much
congeniality to Alfred's peculiar power.' Hallam then transcribed *The
Southern Mariana* (*AHH*, pp. 401–2). She, and the other women, Iphigenia

¶ 173. *Opening] 1832 preceded l. 1 with four stanzas:*
> As when a man, that sails in a balloon,
> Downlooking sees the solid shining ground
> Stream from beneath him in the broad blue noon,–
> Tilth, hamlet, mead and mound:

> And takes his flags and waves them to the mob,
> That shout below, all faces turned to where
> Glows rubylike the far-up crimson globe,
> Filled with a finer air:

> So, lifted high, the Poet at his will
> Lets the great world flit from him, seeing all,
> Higher through secret splendours mounting still,
> Selfpoised, nor fears to fall,

> Hearing apart the echoes of his fame.
> While I spoke thus, the seedsman, memory,
> Sowed my deepfurrowed thought with many a name,
> Whose glory will not die.

E. F. Shannon (*PQ* xxxi (1952) 441–5) suggests that T.'s source was prob-
ably the participation of his friend Richard Monckton Milnes in a flight
from Cambridge, 19 May 1829. T. may also have remembered the plates
(under 'Aerostation') in the *English Encyclopaedia* (1802), of which there
was a copy at Somersby (*Lincoln*). It has two balloon ascents, plus 'A View
from a Balloon above the Clouds'. Cp. the seventh line with Keats,
Imitation of Spenser 13: 'Cast upward, through the waves, a ruby glow'.
Instead of these stanzas, *Allen MS* has:
> The poet's steadfast soul, poured out in songs,
> Unmoved moves all things with exceeding might,
> Fixed as between his wings the Eagle's lungs
> Unshook of his wide flight.

(for Lucretius's passage, see l. 107n.), Ariadne, and Sappho, perhaps constitute an early grouping of 'fair women'. In *Allen MS*, it is entitled *The Legend of Fair Women*; all variants are below. T. comments on l. 3: 'Chaucer, the first great English poet, wrote the *Legend of Good Women*. From among these Cleopatra alone appears in my poem.' J. F. A. Pyre points out that T.'s stanza form is used in Vaughan's *Psalm 104* (*The Formation of Tennyson's Style*, 1921, p. 44). Cp. the stanza of *The Poet* (I 243), and of *The Palace of Art* (*p. 50*).

> I read, before my eyelids dropt their shade,
> ' *The Legend of Good Women*', long ago
> Sung by the morning star of song, who made
> His music heard below;
>
> 5 Dan Chaucer, the first warbler, whose sweet breath
> Preluded those melodious bursts that fill
> The spacious times of great Elizabeth
> With sounds that echo still.
>
> And, for a while, the knowledge of his art
> 10 Held me above the subject, as strong gales
> Hold swollen clouds from raining, though my heart,
> Brimful of those wild tales,
>
> Charged both mine eyes with tears. In every land
> I saw, wherever light illumineth,
> 15 Beauty and anguish walking hand in hand
> The downward slope to death.
>
> Those far-renownèd brides of ancient song

1. my . . . their] I dropt my eyelids' *H.Nbk 4*.
3. Arthur Hallam had called Chaucer 'our beautiful morning star', in *The Influence of Italian upon English Literature* (1831; Motter, p. 227). He was echoing Denham, *On Cowley* 1: 'Old Chaucer, like the morning Star'.
5. H.T. compares *Faerie Queene* IV ii st. 32: 'Dan Chaucer, well of English undefyled'.
9–10. Cp. Marvell, *On Paradise Lost* 5–6: 'the Argument / Held me a while misdoubting his Intent.' There 'argument' means 'subject'.
16 ∧ 17]   In every land I thought that, more or less,
          The stronger sterner nature overbore
          The softer, uncontrolled by gentleness
          And selfish evermore:

          And whether there were any means whereby,
          In some far aftertime, the gentler [gentle *Allen MS*] mind
          Might reassume its just and full degree
          Of rule among mankind. *1832*
These lines anticipate the concerns of *The Princess* (1847).

Peopled the hollow dark, like burning stars,
And I heard sounds of insult, shame, and wrong,
20   And trumpets blown for wars;

And clattering flints battered with clanging hoofs;
And I saw crowds in columned sanctuaries;
And forms that passed at windows and on roofs
Of marble palaces;

25 Corpses across the threshold; heroes tall
Dislodging pinnacle and parapet
Upon the tortoise creeping to the wall;
Lances in ambush set;

And high shrine-doors burst through with heated
blasts
30   That run before the fluttering tongues of fire;
White surf wind-scattered over sails and masts,
And ever climbing higher;

Squadrons and squares of men in brazen plates,
Scaffolds, still sheets of water, divers woes,
35 Ranges of glimmering vaults with iron grates,
And hushed seraglios.

---

18. the hollow dark: *In deep and solemn dreams* 59. The phrase occurs in Keats,
The Fall of Hyperion i 455 (not published, though, till 1856), which suggests
the status of romantic poetic diction.
21–32] Not H.MS.
23. passed] 1842; screamed *1832.*
25–8] Not Allen MS.
27. tortoise: 'the "testudo" of ancient war. Warriors with shields upheld
on their heads' (T.).
29. Cp. *Semele* 3: 'The blast of Godhead bursts the doors'.
33. Squadrons and squares] And I saw files *Allen MS 1st reading.*
35. grates] rails *Allen MS (error).*   *iron grates*: T. said of 'Thorough the
iron gates of life', *To His Coy Mistress* 44: 'he could fancy *grates* would
have intensified Marvell's image' (*Mem.* ii 501).
36. seraglios: Paden (p. 136) remarks the influence, here and in other details,
of C.-E. Savary's *Letters on Egypt* (T. used the 1799 translation, *Lincoln*, for
Fatima and other poems).
36 ∧ 7]   And as a dog goes round and round again
                And eyes his place of rest before he sleep,
              So my s. s! [? sad soul] with a continual pain
                Flowed eddylike and deep,

              Returning on itself *H.MS.*

So shape chased shape as swift as, when to land
   Bluster the winds and tides the self-same way,
Crisp foam-flakes scud along the level sand,
40   Torn from the fringe of spray.

I started once, or seemed to start in pain,
   Resolved on noble things, and strove to speak,
As when a great thought strikes along the brain,
   And flushes all the cheek.

45 And once my arm was lifted to hew down
   A cavalier from off his saddle-bow,
That bore a lady from a leaguered town;
   And then, I know not how,

All those sharp fancies, by down-lapsing thought
50   Streamed onward, lost their edges, and did creep
Rolled on each other, rounded, smoothed, and
      brought
   Into the gulfs of sleep.

At last methought that I had wandered far
   In an old wood: fresh-washed in coolest dew
55 The maiden splendours of the morning star
   Shook in the stedfast blue.

Enormous elm-tree-boles did stoop and lean
   Upon the dusky brushwood underneath
Their broad curved branches, fledged with clearest
      green,
60   New from its silken sheath.

The dim red morn had died, her journey done,
   And with dead lips smiled at the twilight plain,
Half-fallen across the threshold of the sun,
   Never to rise again.

65 There was no motion in the dumb dead air,
   Not any song of bird or sound of rill;

37–40] *Added in H.MS, but beginning* So thought chased thought . . .
45–52] *Not H.MS; ll. 45–8 deleted in Allen MS.*
52. Cp. Shelley, *Queen Mab* ix 175: 'the transient gulf-dream of a startling
sleep'.
53–6, 69–72] *Added in H.MS, which does not have ll. 57–68.*
54. T. says: 'The wood is the Past', and ll. 83–4, 'i.e. time backward'.
56. *Shook . . . stedfast*] Throbbed . . . deepening *H.MS.*
61–4. T. comments: 'Refers to the early past. How magnificently old
Turner would have painted it'.
62. *twilight*] languid *Allen MS.*

Gross darkness of the inner sepulchre
Is not so deadly still

As that wide forest. Growths of jasmine turned
70   Their humid arms festooning tree to tree,
And at the root through lush green grasses burned
The red anemone.

I knew the flowers, I knew the leaves, I knew
The tearful glimmer of the languid dawn
75 On those long, rank, dark wood-walks drenched
in dew,
Leading from lawn to lawn.

The smell of violets, hidden in the green,
Poured back into my empty soul and frame
The times when I remember to have been
80   Joyful and free from blame.

And from within me a clear under-tone
Thrilled through mine ears in that unblissful
clime,
'Pass freely through: the wood is all thine own,
Until the end of time.'

67. Cp. *Ode: O Bosky Brook* 108–10: 'With stillness like the stillness of the tomb / And grossest gloom, / As it were of the inner sepulchre.' The sepulchre, as Paden says (p. 136), derives from Savary's *Letters on Egypt*, the interior of the great pyramid. Cp. *Isaiah* lx 2: 'The darkness shall cover the earth, and gross darkness the people.'
69. *As . . . of*] Black ivy, and star-flowered *H.MS.*   *Growths of*] *1842*; Clasping *1832*.
70. *Their humid*] *1842*; Its twinèd *1832*.
73–92] Not *H.MS* (*missing sheet?*).
77–80. Cp. *Song*, which immediately followed this poem in *1832*:
    Who can say
    Why Today
    Tomorrow will be yesterday?
    Who can tell
    Why to smell
    The violet, recalls the dewy prime
    Of youth and buried time?
    The cause is nowhere found in rhyme.
82. *mine . . . unblissful*] my . . . unjoyful *Allen MS.*
83. Paden (pp. 36, 52) contrasts the wood in Savary's *Letters on Egypt*: 'Thus abandoned to the delights of contemplation, and indulging those delicious sensations the time and place inspired, I incautiously proceeded towards the thickest part of the wood; when a terrifying voice suddenly exclaimed –

85 At length I saw a lady within call,
      Stiller than chiselled marble, standing there;
      A daughter of the gods, divinely tall,
      And most divinely fair.

      Her loveliness with shame and with surprise
90 Froze my swift speech: she turning on my face
      The star-like sorrows of immortal eyes,
      Spoke slowly in her place.

      'I had great beauty: ask thou not my name:
      No one can be more wise than destiny.
95 Many drew swords and died. Where'er I came
      I brought calamity.'

      'No marvel, sovereign lady: in fair field
      Myself for such a face had boldly died,'
      I answered free; and turning I appealed
100 To one that stood beside.

      But she, with sick and scornful looks averse,
      To her full height her stately stature draws;
      'My youth,' she said, 'was blasted with a curse:
      This woman was the cause.

105 'I was cut off from hope in that sad place,
      Which men called Aulis in those iron years:
      My father held his hand upon his face;
      I, blinded with my tears,

      'Still strove to speak: my voice was thick with sighs
110 As in a dream. Dimly I could descry
      The stern black-bearded kings with wolfish eyes,
      Waiting to see me die.

where are you going? Stand, or you are dead.–It was a slave who guarded
the entrance of the grove, that no rash curiosity might disturb the females
who reposed upon the verdant banks.'
87. Cp. *The Mystic* 26: 'Daughters of time, divinely tall'. Helen, 'daughter
of Zeus and Leda' (T.).
100. 'Iphigenia, who was sacrificed by Agamemnon to Artemis' (T.).
101. *sick . . . looks*] sad . . . eyes *Allen MS 1st reading*.
106] *1883*; Which yet to name my spirit loathes and fears: *1832–82*. T. says
that the revised 'line (as far as I recollect) is almost synchronous with the
old reading; but the inversion there . . . displeased me'.
107. H.T. comments: 'No doubt my father had in his mind the famous
picture by Timanthes, *The Sacrifice of Iphigeneia* (described by Valerius
Maximus, VIII ii 6), of which there is a Pompeiian wall-painting. Also the
passage in Lucretius, i 84 foll.' See headnote.

'The high masts flickered as they lay afloat;
   The crowds, the temples, wavered, and the shore;
115 The bright death quivered at the victim's throat;
   Touched; and I knew no more.'

Whereto the other with a downward brow:
   'I would the white cold heavy-plunging foam,
   Whirled by the wind, had rolled me deep below,
120 Then when I left my home.'

Her slow full words sank through the silence drear,
   As thunder-drops fall on a sleeping sea:
   Sudden I heard a voice that cried, 'Come here,
   That I may look on thee.'

125 I turning saw, throned on a flowery rise,
   One sitting on a crimson scarf unrolled;
   A queen, with swarthy cheeks and bold black eyes,
   Brow-bound with burning gold.

She, flashing forth a haughty smile, began:
130   'I governed men by change, and so I swayed
   All moods. 'Tis long since I have seen a man.
   Once, like the moon, I made

113–16] *1853*; 'The tall masts quivered as they lay afloat,
         The temples and the people and the shore.
         One drew a sharp knife through my tender throat
         Slowly,–and nothing more.' *1832–51*
'I thought [it] too ghastly realistic' (T.). It had been ridiculed by J. W.
Croker, *QR*, April 1833: 'what touching simplicity–what pathetic resig-
nation–he cut my throat–"*nothing more!*" One might indeed ask, "*What
more*" she would have?'
117–20. Cp. Helen, *Iliad* vi 345ff: 'I would that on the day when first
my mother gave me birth an evil storm-wind had borne me away to some
mountain or to the wave of the loud-resounding sea, where the wave
might have swept me away or ever these things came to pass.'
120] *H.MS breaks off here.*
127. T. comments: 'I was thinking of Shakespeare's Cleopatra: "Think
of me / That am with Phoebus' amorous pinches black" (*Antony and
Cleopatra* I v 28). Millais has made a mulatto of her in his illustration. I know
perfectly well that she was a Greek. "Swarthy" merely means sunburnt. I
should not have spoken of her breast as "polished silver" if I had not
known her as a white woman. Read "sunburnt" if you like it better.'
Cp. *Antony to Cleopatra* (I 102).
128. *Coriolanus* II ii 96: 'Brow-bound with the oak'.
129. haughty] subtle *Allen MS.*
132–4. John Churton Collins compared John Ford's *Witch of Edmonton* II ii:
'You are the powerful moon of my blood's sea, / To make it ebb or

'The ever-shifting currents of the blood
   According to my humour ebb and flow.
135   I have no men to govern in this wood:
   That makes my only woe.

'Nay – yet it chafes me that I could not bend
   One will; nor tame and tutor with mine eye
   That dull cold-blooded Cæsar. Prythee, friend,
140   Where is Mark Antony?

'The man, my lover, with whom I rode sublime
   On Fortune's neck: we sat as God by God:
   The Nilus would have risen before his time
   And flooded at our nod.

145   'We drank the Libyan Sun to sleep, and lit
   Lamps which out-burned Canopus. O my life
   In Egypt! O the dalliance and the wit,
   The flattery and the strife,

flow.' Alongside Collins's note (*Cornhill*, Jan. 1880), T. wrote: 'Not known
to me' (*Lincoln*).
139. dull] proud *Allen MS*.
141–4] *1843*;   'By him great [Beside him *Allen MS 1st reading*] Pompey
            dwarfs and suffers pain,
         A mortal man before immortal Mars;
         The glories of great Julius lapse and wane,
            And shrink from suns to stars. *1832–42*
145–8] *1845*;   'That man, of all the men I ever knew,
            Most touched my fancy. O! what days and nights
         We had in Egypt, ever reaping new
            Harvest [Harvests *Allen MS*] of ripe delights,

         'Realmdraining revels! Life was one long feast.
            What wit! what words! what sweet words, only made
         Less sweet by the kiss that broke 'em, liking best
            To be so richly stayed! *1832–42*;

         What nights we had in Egypt! I could hit
            His humours while I crossed them: O the life
            I led him, and the dalliance . . . *1843*
146. Canopus: 'in the constellation of Argo' (T.). Moore's *Lalla Rookh:
The Fire-Worshippers* had a footnote to 'the Star of Egypt': 'The brilliant
Canopus, unseen in European climates.' The index to Charles Rollin's
Ancient History has 'Canopus: a city of the Lower Egypt, remarkable for
lewdness'; there was a copy of Rollin (1789 translation) at Somersby
(*Lincoln*).

'And the wild kiss, when fresh from war's alarms,
150   My Hercules, my Roman Antony,
My mailèd Bacchus leapt into my arms,
Contented there to die!

'And there he died: and when I heard my name
Sighed forth with life I would not brook my fear
155   Of the other: with a worm I balked his fame.
What else was left? look here!'

(With that she tore her robe apart, and half
The polished argent of her breast to sight
Laid bare. Thereto she pointed with a laugh,
160   Showing the aspick's bite.)

'I died a Queen. The Roman soldier found
Me lying dead, my crown about my brows,
A name for ever!—lying robed and crowned,
Worthy a Roman spouse.'

165   Her warbling voice, a lyre of widest range
Struck by all passion, did fall down and glance
From tone to tone, and glided through all change
Of liveliest utterance.

When she made pause I knew not for delight;
170   Because with sudden motion from the ground
She raised her piercing orbs, and filled with light
The interval of sound.

Still with their fires Love tipt his keenest darts;
As once they drew into two burning rings

149. And . . . kiss] 1843; What dainty strifes 1832–42. Cp. these lines with
Antony and Cleopatra IV viii 14–16: 'Chain mine armed neck; leap thou,
attire and all, / Through proof of harness to my heart, and there / Ride
on the pants triumphing!'
150. Roman] 1843; gallant 1832–42.
151. Bacchus] 1843; captain 1832–42.
153. there . . . when] 1843; in those arms he died: 1832–42.
154. life . . . my] 1845; life: then I shook off all 1832–42; life: I had no
further 1843. Allen MS has fragmentary line: In his last sigh.
155] 1845; Oh what a little snake [worm 1843] stole Caesar's fame! 1832–
42.
160. aspick's] aspic– Allen MS, which breaks off with l. 160 (end of sheet), and
then has on following sheet ll. 249–56 only.
161–4. T. compares non humilis mulier, Horace's Odes I xxxvii 32, on the
death of Cleopatra.
166. Struck] 1843; Touched 1832–42.

175   All beams of Love, melting the mighty hearts
          Of captains and of kings.

          Slowly my sense undazzled. Then I heard
          A noise of some one coming through the lawn,
          And singing clearer than the crested bird
180   That claps his wings at dawn.

          'The torrent brooks of hallowed Israel
          From craggy hollows pouring, late and soon,
          Sound all night long, in falling through the dell,
          Far-heard beneath the moon.

185   'The balmy moon of blessèd Israel
          Floods all the deep-blue gloom with beams
                    divine:
          All night the splintered crags that wall the dell
          With spires of silver shine.'

          As one that museth where broad sunshine laves
190   The lawn by some cathedral, through the door
          Hearing the holy organ rolling waves
          Of sound on roof and floor

          Within, and anthem sung, is charmed and tied
          To where he stands, – so stood I, when that flow
195   Of music left the lips of her that died
          To save her father's vow;

178. A noise] The sound *H.MS extra sheet.*
179. singing] chanting *H.MS extra sheet.*
181–4, 216–20. Adapted from *Margaret* 35 ∧ 6, MS (I 495):
                    Or when the Gileadite returned,
                    Whether Jephtha's daughter mourned
                    Two moons beside the heavy flow
                    Of torrent brooks in purple glens
                    Of Judah, leaving far below,
                    Leaving the fruitful olive plains,
                    Leaving the hope of her bride bower
                    In royal Mizpeh's battled tower.
Jephtha's daughter was sacrificed by him because of his vow to God: 'If
thou shalt without fail deliver the children of Ammon into mine hands,
Then it shall be, that whatsoever cometh forth of the doors of my house to
meet me, when I return in peace from the children of Ammon, shall surely
be the Lord's, and I will offer it up for a burnt offering' (*Judges* xi 30–1).
She appears in Percy's *Reliques* (*Jephtha, Judge of Israel*), as do Rosamond
and Eleanor, ll. 250–6 (*Fair Rosamond*).

The daughter of the warrior Gileadite,
    A maiden pure; as when she went along
From Mizpeh's towered gate with welcome light,
200   With timbrel and with song.

My words leapt forth: 'Heaven heads the count
        of crimes
    With that wild oath.' She rendered answer high:
'Not so, nor once alone; a thousand times
    I would be born and die.

205 'Single I grew, like some green plant, whose root
    Creeps to the garden water-pipes beneath,
Feeding the flower; but ere my flower to fruit
    Changed, I was ripe for death.

'My God, my land, my father – these did move
210   Me from my bliss of life, that Nature gave,
Lowered softly with a threefold cord of love
    Down to a silent grave.

'And I went mourning, "No fair Hebrew boy
    Shall smile away my maiden blame among
215 The Hebrew mothers" – emptied of all joy,
    Leaving the dance and song,

'Leaving the olive-gardens far below,
    Leaving the promise of my bridal bower,
The valleys of grape-loaded vines that glow
220   Beneath the battled tower.

'The light white cloud swam over us. Anon
    We heard the lion roaring from his den;
We saw the large white stars rise one by one,
    Or, from the darkened glen,

225 'Saw God divide the night with flying flame,
    And thunder on the everlasting hills.
I heard Him, for He spake, and grief became
    A solemn scorn of ills.

'When the next moon was rolled into the sky,
230   Strength came to me that equalled my desire.
How beautiful a thing it was to die
    For God and for my sire!

211. *cord*] *1842*; chord *1832*.
222. *from*] *1853*; in *1832–51*.
225. H.T. compares Horace, *Odes* I xxxiv 5–6: *Diespiter | igni corusco
nubila dividens.*

'It comforts me in this one thought to dwell,
    That I subdued me to my father's will;
235 Because the kiss he gave me, ere I fell,
    Sweetens the spirit still.

'Moreover it is written that my race
    Hewed Ammon, hip and thigh, from Aroer
On Arnon unto Minneth.' Here her face
240 Glowed, as I looked at her.

She locked her lips: she left me where I stood:
    'Glory to God,' she sang, and past afar,
Thridding the sombre boskage of the wood,
    Toward the morning-star.

245 Losing her carol I stood pensively,
    As one that from a casement leans his head,
When midnight bells cease ringing suddenly,
    And the old year is dead.

'Alas! alas!' a low voice, full of care,
250 Murmured beside me: 'Turn and look on me:
I am that Rosamond, whom men call fair,
    If what I was I be.

'Would I had been some maiden coarse and poor!
    O me, that I should ever see the light!
255 Those dragon eyes of angered Eleanor
    Do hunt me, day and night.'

She ceased in tears, fallen from hope and trust:
    To whom the Egyptian: 'O, you tamely died!
You should have clung to Fulvia's waist, and thrust
260 The dagger through her side.'

With that sharp sound the white dawn's creeping
        beams,
    Stolen to my brain, dissolved the mystery

242–4. Cp. *Job* xxxviii 7: 'When the morning stars sang together, and all
the sons of God shouted for joy'.
243. T. compares *Comus* 313: 'every bosky bourn'.
251. Rosamond de Clifford, the mistress of Henry II, was said to have been
poisoned by Queen Eleanor. Cp. *Rosamund's Bower* (II 177). She appears in
T.'s play *Becket*. T. may have read of her in the *English Encyclopaedia* (1802),
of which there was a copy at Somersby (*Lincoln*).
253. *poor*] fair *Allen MS*.
259. *Fulvia*: 'wife of Antony, named by Cleopatra as a parallel to Eleanor'
(T.).

Of folded sleep. The captain of my dreams
Ruled in the eastern sky.

265   Morn broadened on the borders of the dark,
Ere I saw her, who clasped in her last trance
Her murdered father's head, or Joan of Arc,
A light of ancient France;

Or her who knew that Love can vanquish Death,
270   Who kneeling, with one arm about her king,
Drew forth the poison with her balmy breath,
Sweet as new buds in Spring.

No memory labours longer from the deep
Gold-mines of thought to lift the hidden ore
275   That glimpses, moving up, than I from sleep
To gather and tell o'er

Each little sound and sight. With what dull pain
Compassed, how eagerly I sought to strike
Into that wondrous track of dreams again!
280   But no two dreams are like.

As when a soul laments, which hath been blest,
Desiring what is mingled with past years,
In yearnings that can never be exprest
By signs or groans or tears;

285   Because all words, though culled with choicest art,
Failing to give the bitter of the sweet,
Wither beneath the palate, and the heart
Faints, faded by its heat.

---

263. The captain: 'Venus, the star of morning' (T.).
266. T. comments: 'Margaret Roper, daughter of Sir Thomas More, who is said to have transferred his headless corpse from the Tower to Chelsea Church. Sir Thomas More's head had remained for fourteen days on London Bridge after his execution, and was about to be thrown into the Thames to make room for others, when she claimed and bought it. . . . [Her] vault was opened, and it is stated that she was found in her coffin, clasping the small leaden box which inclosed her father's head.'
266–7. who . . . head] *1842*; that in her latest trance / Clasped her dead father's heart *1832*.
269–72. T. comments: 'Eleanor, wife of Edward I, went with him to the Holy Land (1269), where he was stabbed at Acre with a poisoned dagger. She sucked the poison from the wound.'

183 To J.S.

Published *1832*. T. noted: 'Addressed to James Spedding, the biographer of Bacon. His brother was Edward Spedding, a friend of mine, who died in his youth.' Edward died 24 Aug. 1832. Hallam wrote to T., 4 Sept. 1832: 'E[mily] has probably told you of the death of Edward Spedding, cut off in the prime of life & the freshness of ardent feelings. He was more sensitive than his brother, but tempered that susceptibility with something of James' calmness. He looked to a future life, I should think, as calmly as to a future day. His epitaph is "Peace"' (*AHH*, p. 638; cp. l. 69 below). Hallam wrote to T. in Oct.: 'The lines to J.S. are perfect. James, I am sure, will be most grateful' (31 Oct.–3 Nov.; *AHH*, p. 678; *Mem.* i 88). T. may have remembered Hallam's praise when he came to write *In Memoriam*, which is comparable in style and gravity. The belief that the dead 'sleep sweetly' is discussed in *In Memoriam* xliii (*p. 386*): 'If Sleep and Death be truly one'. For the opening of *To J.S.* T. adapted the opening (all he had written) of part ii of a poem which he had already sent to James Spedding; *Dear friend* (III 614) was quoted by Spedding in a letter to his brother Edward, 9 March 1831 (copy at *Lincoln*), and so will have been particularly appropriate. P. Allen shows 'how distasteful Spedding found the traditional modes of Christian consolation'; a month after his brother died, his uncle died, and Spedding wrote, 8 Sept. 1832: 'I suppose the first thing the good Garden [Francis Garden] would have done would have been to administer religious consolation after his own fashion – and I have already had some religious consolation from Blakesley, – which would have been amusing enough to any one not the object of it' (*The Cambridge Apostles*, 1978, p. 167).

> The wind, that beats the mountain, blows
> More softly round the open wold,
> And gently comes the world to those
> That are cast in gentle mould.
>
> 5 And me this knowledge bolder made,
> Or else I had not dared to flow
> In these words toward you, and invade
> Even with a verse your holy woe.
>
> 'Tis strange that those we lean on most,
> 10 Those in whose laps our limbs are nursed,
> Fall into shadow, soonest lost:
> Those we love first are taken first.

¶ 183.*1–4*. Adapted from *Dear friend* (see headnote): 'The wind that beats the mountain cold / All night in early April blows / Softly on the open wold, / And gently comes the world to those / That are of gentle mould.'
5. And me] *1842*; My heart *1832*.
6. I] *1842*; it *1832*.

God gives us love. Something to love
　　He lends us; but, when love is grown
15　To ripeness, that on which it throve
　　Falls off, and love is left alone.

This is the curse of time. Alas!
　　In grief I am not all unlearned;
Once through mine own doors Death did
　　　pass;
20　One went, who never hath returned.

He will not smile—not speak to me
　　Once more. Two years his chair is seen
Empty before us. That was he
　　Without whose life I had not been.

25　Your loss is rarer; for this star
　　Rose with you through a little arc
Of heaven, nor having wandered far
　　Shot on the sudden into dark.

I knew your brother: his mute dust
30　I honour and his living worth:
A man more pure and bold and just
　　Was never born into the earth.

I have not looked upon you nigh,
　　Since that dear soul hath fallen asleep.
35　Great Nature is more wise than I:
　　I will not tell you not to weep.

And though mine own eyes fill with dew,
　　Drawn from the spirit through the brain,
I will not even preach to you,
40　'Weep, weeping dulls the inward pain.'

Let Grief be her own mistress still.
　　She loveth her own anguish deep

19–24. T. comments: 'The death of my father', in March 1831.
31. bold] *1842*; mild *1832*.
37–44. Cp. *The Gardener's Daughter* 193: 'A thought would fill my eyes
with happy dew'. Cp. Gray's Alcaic fragment (which provided an epi-
graph for a poem by T.'s brother Charles in *1827*, p. 11): O lachrymarum
Fons, tenero sacros / Ducentium ortus ex animo; quater / Felix! in imo qui
scatentem / Pectore te, pia Nympha, sensit! ('O fountain of tears which have
their sacred sources in the sensitive soul! Four times blessed he who has felt
thee, holy Nymph, bubbling up from the depths of his heart!') Yet along-
side John Churton Collins's suggestion of this (*Cornhill*, Jan. 1880, *Lincoln*),
T. wrote 'no!'. Cp. *Fragment: Why are my moments* (III 617).

More than much pleasure. Let her will
Be done – to weep or not to weep.

45　I will not say, 'God's ordinance
Of Death is blown in every wind;'
For that is not a common chance
That takes away a noble mind.

His memory long will live alone
50　In all our hearts, as mournful light
That broods above the fallen sun,
And dwells in heaven half the night.

Vain solace! Memory standing near
Cast down her eyes, and in her throat
55　Her voice seemed distant, and a tear
Dropt on the letters as I wrote.

I wrote I know not what. In truth,
How *should* I soothe you anyway,
Who miss the brother of your youth?
60　Yet something I did wish to say:

For he too was a friend to me:
Both are my friends, and my true breast
Bleedeth for both; yet it may be
That only silence suiteth best.

65　Words weaker than your grief would make
Grief more. 'Twere better I should cease
Although myself could almost take
The place of him that sleeps in peace.

45–8. Cp. *In Memoriam* vi 1–4: 'One writes, that "Other friends remain," /
That "Loss is common to the race" – / And common is the common-
place, / And vacant chaff well meant for grain. Cp. *Coriolanus* IV i 5: 'That
common chances common men could bear' (with 'noble' in l. 9).
49–52. Cp. Vaughan's poem on the same theme, *They are all gone into the
world of light*: 'Their very memory is fair and bright . . . / Or those faint
beams in which this hill is drest, / After the Sun's remove.' John Churton
Collins said that this stanza by T. 'may have been distilled from two lines
in Dryden's noble tragedy of *Don Sebastian*, act I scene 1': 'If I fall, / I shall
be like myself; a setting sun / Should leave a track of glory in the skies.'
Alongside this suggestion, T. wrote: 'Nonsense' (*Cornhill*, Jan. 1880,
Lincoln).
51. *fallen*] *1842*; sunken *1832*.
56. *the letters*] *1845*; my tablets *1832–43*.
64. *only*] *1842*; holy *1832*.
67] *1842*; Although to calm you I would take *1832*. The original hyperbole
aroused FitzGerald's scepticism; he wrote in a copy of *1842* (*Trinity*

Sleep sweetly, tender heart, in peace:
70   Sleep, holy spirit, blessèd soul,
While the stars burn, the moons increase,
And the great ages onward roll.

Sleep till the end, true soul and sweet.
Nothing comes to thee new or strange.
75   Sleep full of rest from head to feet;
Lie still, dry dust, secure of change.

199 The Eagle

Fragment

Published *1851*. C. B. Thackeray printed it from M. Brookfield's papers, with the date 2 May 1846; this, 'the original version', began: '–to sit apart / And triumph in the Eagle's heart; // Who clasps the crag with crooked hands' (*London Mercury* xi, 1925, 620). The envelope of the *Widener MS* (Harvard) is dated 2 Oct. 1849; and the poem is in T.'s hand, inscribed and dated 30 Oct. 1849 (*Letters* i 307*n*). T. entered it in Dora Wordsworth's album when in the Lake District in summer 1850 (*CT*, p. 205, mistakenly suggests that this was in 1845, following F. V. Morley, *Dora Wordsworth: Her Book*, 1924, p. 164). T. entered too on this page of the album *The Two Voices* 436–8, also in triplets. The placing in *Eversley* suggests composition before 1842, and its triplets are those of *The Two Voices* and *Stanzas* (both 1833). R. C. Sutherland argues that there is a background of evangelical Johannine symbolism which relates the poem to T.'s religious and mystical experiences (*Studies in the Literary Imagination* i, 1968, 23–35).

He clasps the crag with crookèd hands;
Close to the sun in lonely lands,
Ringed with the azure world, he stands.

The wrinkled sea beneath him crawls;
5   He watches from his mountain walls,
And like a thunderbolt he falls.

College): 'I used to ask if this was not *un peu trop fort*. I think it's altered or omitted in future Editions. It is all rather affected.' On these notes by FitzGerald, and the damage done to them by H. T., see *Letters* i xix–xx.
76. Cp. *Paradise Lost* iv 791: 'asleep secure of harme'.
¶ 199.1. *crookèd*] 1865; hookèd *1851–63*. See headnote. Cp. *Aeneid* vi 360: *prensantemque uncis manibus capita aspera montis* ('I caught with bent fingers at the rugged cliff-peaks').
4. *The wrinkled sea*: occurs in *Two Visits to a Grave*, by T.'s friend Richard Monckton Milnes, *Athenaeum*, 4 March 1829. (Noted by Joyce Green, *The Development of the Poetic Image in Tennyson*, Cambridge thesis, 1954, p. 178.) Shelley had 'the wrinkled ocean', *Hellas* 139.
6. Cp. *Samson Agonistes* 1695-6: 'as an Eagle / His cloudless thunder bolted on thir heads'.

205 Sir Launcelot and Queen Guinevere

A Fragment

Published *1842*. 'Partly if not wholly written in 1830' (*Mem.* ii 122); but both *Heath MS* and *T.Nbk 15* (all variants are below) make it clear that T. was still working on it in 1833. *T.MS* explains T.'s subtitle *A Fragment*; it describes the meeting of Launcelot and Guinevere with Merlin, and their journey. T. later quarried these lines, e.g. for *The Princess* v 250–3. See *Life of the Life* (I 548), which was a song within *Sir Launcelot* and which was quoted in a letter from J. M. Kemble to W. B. Donne, 22 June 1833 (which came down to Mary Barham Johnson):

'A companion to *The Lady of Shalott* is in Progress, called the *Ballad of Sir Lancelot*; a most triumphant matter whereof I will give you a sketch; in the Spring, Queen Guinevere and Sir Lancelot ride through the forest green, fayre and amorous: And such a queen! such a knight! Merlin with spindle shanks, vast brows and beard and a forehead like a mundane egg, over a face wrinkled with ten thousand crow-feet meets them, and tells Sir L. that he's doing well for his fame to be riding about with a light o' love &c. Whereupon the knight, nowise backward in retort, tells him it is a shame such an old scandal to antiquity should be talking, since his own propensities are no secret, and since he very well knows what will become of him in the valley of Avilion some day. Merlin, who tropically is Worldly Prudence, is of course miserably floored. So are the representatives of Worldly Force, who in the shape of three knights, sheathed, Sir, in trap from toe to toe, run at Sir L. and are most unceremoniously shot from their saddles like stones from a sling. But the Garde Joyeuse is now in sight; the knight I confess is singing but a loose song, when his own son Sir Galahad (the type of Chastity) passes by; he knows his father but does not speak to him, *blushes and rides on his way!* Voila tout. Much of this is written and stupendous; I regret bitterly that I had not opportunity to take down what there is of it; as it is I can only offer you Sir L.'s song.'

Cp. *Sir Galahad* (p. 165). The affinities with *The Lady of Shalott* (p. 18) are emphasised by the use of the same stanza, except that here the fifth and ninth lines are not refrains. Cp. the ride of Lancelot and the Queen in *Guinevere* 377–97 (p. 952).

> Like souls that balance joy and pain,
> With tears and smiles from heaven again
> The maiden Spring upon the plain
> Came in a sun-lit fall of rain.
> 5   In crystal vapour everywhere

¶ 205.2. *tears . . . smiles*] *Transposed T.MS*.
4. *fall*] shower *Heath MS*.

Blue isles of heaven laughed between,
And far, in forest-deeps unseen,
The topmost elm-tree gathered green
    From draughts of balmy air.

10 Sometimes the linnet piped his song:
Sometimes the throstle whistled strong:
Sometimes the sparhawk, wheeled along,
Hushed all the groves from fear of wrong:
    By grassy capes with fuller sound
15 In curves the yellowing river ran,
And drooping chestnut-buds began
To spread into the perfect fan,
    Above the teeming ground.

Then, in the boyhood of the year,
20 Sir Launcelot and Queen Guinevere
Rode through the coverts of the deer,
With blissful treble ringing clear.
    She seemed a part of joyous Spring:
    A gown of grass-green silk she wore,
25 Buckled with golden clasps before;
A light-green tuft of plumes she bore
    Closed in a golden ring.

Now on some twisted ivy-net,

8. *elm-tree*] *1853*; linden *1842–51*.
10–11] Or jangling sparrows in a throng
    Chirped all in one – a storm of song –
               transposed with ll. 12–13, T.MS
14] As when you trill [?] a silver wire *T.MS 1st reading*; By tufted knolls on
wavy wolds *T.MS*. See *The Gardener's Daughter 29–31n* (I 555).
15. In curves] Fuller *T.MS*.
18. teeming] blooming *T.MS 1st reading.*   *ground*] brier *T.MS 1st reading*;
moulds *T.MS*.
27 ∧ 8] Each clasp, a point of sharpest light,
    Was made, a lady and a knight,
    And when the clasp was buckled tight
    The lady seemed to fold the knight.
      Robed like the meadows rode the Queen,
    As when a lawn new-mowed receives
    Bright lights, that wanton summer weaves,
    Through trelliswork of tremulous leaves,
      So seemed she garbed in green. *T.MS*
Heath MS has the first four lines ('brightest light') and then a lacuna. Cp. the
description of the Queen, *Merlin and Vivien 85–7*.
28–36] Not *T.MS*.

Now by some tinkling rivulet,
30 In mosses mixt with violet
Her cream-white mule his pastern set:
    And fleeter now she skimmed the plains
Than she whose elfin prancer springs
By night to eery warblings,
35 When all the glimmering moorland rings
    With jingling bridle-reins.

As fast she fled through sun and shade,
The happy winds upon her played,
Blowing the ringlet from the braid:
40 She looked so lovely, as she swayed
    The rein with dainty finger-tips,
A man had given all other bliss,
And all his worldly worth for this,
To waste his whole heart in one kiss
45   Upon her perfect lips.

30. In] *1851*; On *1842–50. mixt*] *1853*; thick *1842–51*; black *Heath MS.*
32. fleeter now] *1853*; now more fleet *1842–51*.
33. she] her *Heath MS.*
33–6. Paden (p. 157) cites a book which T. certainly knew, and later owned,
T. C. Croker's *Fairy Legends* (1825): 'the sound of bridles ringing through
the air accompanies the whirlwind which marks the progress of a fairy
journey'. D. L. Chambers (*MLN*, xviii, 1903, 231) suggests Carlyle's *Essay
on Goethe's Helena* (1828): 'these fine warblings and trippings on the light
fantastic toe . . . as perhaps of elfin-bells when the Queen of Faery rides by
moonlight'.
37. fast she fled] *1890*; she fled fast *1842–89*.
45] *T.MS has further stanzas:*

They came on one that rode alone,
Astride upon a lob-eared roan,
Wherefrom stood out the staring bone,
    The wizard Merlin wise and gray.
His shanks were thin as legs of pies,
The bloom that on an apple dries
Burnt underneath his catlike eyes
    That twinkled everyway.

High brows above a little face
Had Merlin—these in every place
Ten million lines did cross and lace;
Slow as the shadow was his pace,
    The shade that creeps from dawn to dusk.

From cheek and mouth and throat a load
Of beard—a hundred winters snowed
Upon the pummel as he rode
    Thin as a spider's husk.

He stopped full butt. 'God's death, Sir Knight,
Your fame will flourish pure and bright.
You spare no pains. 'Tis your delight
To seek the Sangraal day and night;
    It is no fable, by my troth;
We know you are the cream and pride
Of knighthood blazoned far and wide,
The talk of the whole countryside.
    Good morrow to you both.'

[lacuna]

At last, mid lindentufts that smiled
In newest foliage, fresh and wild,—
With haughty towers turret-piled
To Heaven—by one deep moat in-isled
    Shone the white walls of Joyeuse Garde.
Then saw they three   [lacuna]

They trampling through the woodland lone
In clanging armour flashed and shone
Like those three suns that flame alone
Chased in the airy giant's zone,
    And burnished by the frosty dark;
And as the dogstar changes hue,
And bickers into green and blue,
Each glittered laved in lucid dew
    That washed the grassy park.

The last stanza was adapted as *The Princess* v 248–54 (*p. 291*); and the
second as *The Palace of Art* 137–40 (*pp. 61–2*). *T.Nbk 20* has an unpublished
unidentified fragment (the page torn away), which is apparently in the same
stanza-form and which has appropriate subject-matter for this poem:

As with chaste glory from below
The dark wide East comes climbing slow
The Christmas moon with holy glow
When all the dells are dumb with snow
    So from the hill that closed their way
In cold white armour silverclad,
B[riding slow and sad
        night

209 The Two Voices

Published *1842*, dated '1833'. H.T. describes it as 'begun under the cloud of his overwhelming sorrow after the death of Arthur Hallam', news of which was sent to T. on 1 October 1833. This statement has not hitherto been disputed, but that T. had begun it before Hallam's death is clear from a letter by J. M. Kemble to W. B. Donne (which came down to Mary Barham Johnson). The letter is postmarked 22 June 1833: 'Next Sir are some superb meditations on Self destruction called *Thoughts of a Suicide* wherein he argues the point with his soul and is thoroughly floored. These are amazingly fine and deep, and show a mighty stride in intellect since the *Second-Rate Sensitive Mind.*' Clearly a version of *The Two Voices* was already in existence. Spedding wrote to T., 19 Sept. 1834: 'Last and greatest (though not most perfect in its kind), I have received [from Douglas and John Heath] *The thoughts of a suicide*. The design is so grand and the moral, if there is one, so important that I trust you will not spare any elaboration of execution. At all events let me have the rest of it and I will tell you at large what I think' (*Letters* i 118). In its origin, as Kemble points out, it is a poem like *Supposed Confessions* (*1830, p. 7*), and the earlier *Remorse* (*1827, I 98*). But T.'s writing of it may well have been affected by the death of Hallam. Both *Heath MS* (all variants are below) and *H.Lpr 254* (virtually identical with *Heath MS*) stop after l. 309 with three lines added. This would be a feasible ending, and conceivably a better one. The published ending was developed later; Edmund Lushington says that T. 'left it for some time unfinished. . . . The termination . . . I first heard him read' in 1837 or early 1838 (*Mat.* i 246). Miss M. J. Donahue quotes FitzGerald's note on l. 453: 'Composed as he walked about the Dulwich meadows'; she remarks that T. was there in 1835 (*Studies in the 10 Years' Silence*, Yale thesis, 1946, p. 142). *T.Nbk 15* includes two drafts (*T.MS A*); the first ends with l. 96, and the second runs from l. 229–321. (But sheets are missing from this notebook.) *T.Nbk 26* (*T.MS B*) has a fragment beginning at l. 298, and breaking off with l. 393. *T.Nbk 22* also has a draft (*T.MS C*). The *Hn MS* (HM 1320) ends with l. 174; all its variants that differ from *Heath MS* are given below.

H.T. says that the poem, 'describing the conflict in a soul between Faith and Scepticism, was begun under the cloud of his overwhelming sorrow after the death of Arthur Hallam, which, as my father told me, for a while blotted out all joy from his life, and made him long for death'. *Thoughts of a Suicide* is the title in *Heath MS*, as in Kemble's letter and in *T.Nbk 15*; Martin (p. 76) relates the poem to Arthur Hallam's impulse to suicide. T.'s later title may owe something, as Miss Donahue suggests, to Wordsworth's sonnet *Two voices are there*, which T. read in spring 1835 (*Mem.* i 151). In his handling of the theme, T. was indebted to Lucretius's discussion of death (iii 830–1094); to the solicitations of Despair in *Faerie Queene* I ix; and to Hamlet's 'To be or not to be . . .' T.'s tone was influenced by *Job*, as

Carlyle suggested in 1842 (*Mem* i 213), *Psalms*, and *Ecclesiastes*. There are many similarities, in idea and phrasing, to *In Memoriam*, especially xliii–xlvii: and to *On a Mourner*, on Hallam's death (*p. 135*). The triplet had been used by T.'s brother Charles in *1827* in *Ode on the Death of Lord Bryon*. T. used it in *Stanzas* (1833, I 536), and *The Eagle* (*p. 96*). R. Pattison argues that T. adapts the pastoral contest (amoeban idyll) of Virgil's seventh eclogue; this, which had been often changed by Christian writers into a debate between body and soul (as in Marvell), is here 'turned into an interior debate between the logic of despair and the assertion of hope' (*Tennyson and Tradition*, 1979, p. 58).

> A still small voice spake unto me,
> 'Thou art so full of misery,
> Were it not better not to be?'
>
> Then to the still small voice I said;
> 5   'Let me not cast in endless shade
> What is so wonderfully made.'
>
> To which the voice did urge reply;
> 'Today I saw the dragon-fly
> Come from the wells where he did lie.

¶ 209.*1*. Contrast *1 Kings* xix 12, where the 'still small voice' is the Lord's. Arthur Hallam's essay on Cicero (written 1831, published 1832), said: 'The voice of the critical conscience is still and small, like that of the moral' (Motter, p. 153). T. wrote, 11 Nov. 1832: 'it is a hope which is only whispered in a still small voice, though it may be returned to me realized in tones as musically clear as those of a trumpet' (*Letters* i 82–3).

2–3. Cp. *Remorse* 42–4: 'yet I cling / To life, whose every hour to me / Hath been increase of misery.'

5] I will not die and cast in shade *Heath MS 1st reading*.

5–6. *Psalm* cxxxix 11–14: 'If I say, Surely the darkness shall cover me; even the night shall be light about me . . . . I will praise thee; for I am fearfully and wonderfully made.'

8–15. T. adapts a traditional emblem, found in Jacob Bryant's *New System of Ancient Mythology* (1807 edn iii 247–8). Bryant's work was at Somersby (*Lincoln*). His Plate xx is of 'The Chrysalis . . . and other emblems relating to the renewal of life, and the immortality of the soul'. Bryant: 'The Aurelia, after its first stage as an Eruca, or worm, lies for a season in a manner dead; and is inclosed in a sort of a coffin. In this state of darkness it remains all the winter: but at the return of spring it bursts its bonds, and comes out with new life, and in the most beautiful attire. The Egyptians thought this a very proper picture of the soul of man, and of the immortality, to which it aspired.' Cp. Olinthus Gregory, *On the Evidences of the Christian Religion* (1811, often reprinted): 'On the Resurrection of the Body' uses the example of the dragonfly (described in detail) to support the likelihood of

10 'An inner impulse rent the veil
Of his old husk: from head to tail
Came out clear plates of sapphire mail.

'He dried his wings: like gauze they grew;
Through crofts and pastures wet with dew
15 A living flash of light he flew.'

I said, 'When first the world began,
Young Nature through five cycles ran,
And in the sixth she moulded man.

'She gave him mind, the lordliest
20 Proportion, and, above the rest,
Dominion in the head and breast.'

Thereto the silent voice replied;
'Self-blinded are you by your pride:
Look up through night: the world is wide.

25 'This truth within thy mind rehearse,
That in a boundless universe
Is boundless better, boundless worse.

'Think you this mould of hopes and fears
Could find no statelier than his peers
30 In yonder hundred million spheres?'

resurrection. Cp. *Timbuctoo* 146–54 (I 195), where the change from worm
to dragonfly is T.'s simile for the lifting of his thoughts from the earthly to
the infinite. Also *From the East of life* 20–24 (I 508): 'The dragonfly is born
from damps. // The quickwinged gnat doth make a boat / Of his old husk
wherewith to float / To a new life: all low things range / To higher but I
cannot change.'
9. Come] Rise *Heath MS 1st reading.*
10. An inner] An inward *Heath MS*; A sudden *T.MSS A, C.*
12] Burst blazing plates of crimson mail. *Heath MS*; Burst burnisht [burning
T.MS C] plates of sapphire mail. *HnMS, T.MS C.*
14. crofts] holts *Heath MS*; *T.MS A.*
16–18. Invoking science as well as religion, 'the "creative eras" which
Buffon and his English followers equated with the 6 creative days of
Genesis'. M. Millhauser, *PMLA* lxix (1954) 337.
19–21] *Added in margin T.MS A.*
21. head] heart *Heath MS. Psalm* viii 6: 'Thou madest him to have dominion
over the works of thy hands.'
23. by] with *Heath MS, T.MS A.*
24. up through] through the *Heath MS 1st reading.*
29. statelier] higher *T.MS A 1st reading.*

It spake, moreover, in my mind:
'Though thou wert scattered to the wind,
Yet is there plenty of the kind.'

Then did my response clearer fall:
35   'No compound of this earthly ball
Is like another, all in all.'

To which he answered scoffingly;
'Good soul! suppose I grant it thee,
Who'll weep for thy deficiency?

40   'Or will one beam be less intense,
When thy peculiar difference
Is cancelled in the world of sense?'

I would have said, 'Thou canst not know,'
But my full heart, that worked below,
45   Rained through my sight its overflow.

Again the voice spake unto me:
'Thou art so steeped in misery,
Surely 'twere better not to be.

'Thine anguish will not let thee sleep,
50   Nor any train of reason keep:
Thou canst not think, but thou wilt weep.'

I said, 'The years with change advance:
If I make dark my countenance,
I shut my life from happier chance.

32–3. Cp. *In Memoriam* lv–lvi (*pp. 396–400*).
34–6] And then my answer clearer came.
    'Be hushed, still voice: no soul or frame
    In all the world is just the same.' *T.MS A 1st reading*
39. *thy deficiency*: 'the want of thee' (T.).
40–42] *Added in margin T.MS A.*
45. Cp. *The Lover's Tale* i 23, *1832* text: 'for fear the mind / Rain through my sight'.
50. *Nor*] Or *Heath MS.*
52–7] *Not T.MSS A, C, Heath MS; added in margin HnMS. T.MS A has, deleted, ll. 229–31.*
52–3. Cp. *Job* xiv 20: 'Thou prevailest for ever against him, and he passeth: thou changest his countenance, and sendest him away.'

55 'Some turn this sickness yet might take,
   Even yet.' But he: 'What drug can make
   A withered palsy cease to shake?'

   I wept, 'Though I should die, I know
   That all about the thorn will blow
60 In tufts of rosy-tinted snow;

   'And men, through novel spheres of thought
   Still moving after truth long sought,
   Will learn new things when I am not.'

   'Yet,' said the secret voice, 'some time,
65 Sooner or later, will gray prime
   Make thy grass hoar with early rime.

   'Not less swift souls that yearn for light,
   Rapt after heaven's starry flight,
   Would sweep the tracts of day and night.

70 'Not less the bee would range her cells,
   The furzy prickle fire the dells,
   The foxglove cluster dappled bells.'

   I said that 'all the years invent;
   Each month is various to present
75 The world with some development.

59–60] That through green lanes the thorn will blow
       In spicy tufts of vernal snow; *Heath MS, T.MSS A, C*
66. thy] your *T.MS A 1st reading.*
67–9] *Transposed with ll. 70–72 in T.MSS A (1st reading), C, Heath MS;
emended HnMS.*
67] And spirits seeking truth and light, *T.MS A 1st reading.*   that] would
HnMS 1st reading.
70] Yet flies will weave their tinsel cells, *T.MS A 1st reading;* The umber sea
will strow her shells, *2nd reading.* Cp. *1st reading* with *In Memoriam* l 10–12:
'And men the flies of latter spring . . . And weave their petty cells and die'.
71] And [The *2nd reading*] thorny furze light up [inflame *2nd reading*] the dells
T.MS A 1st reading.
72. The] And *T.MS A 1st reading.*
73–5] *Not T.MSS A, C, Heath MS;*
           I said that every month invents
           And every various year presents
           The world with new developments. *HnMS*
76–8]   I murmured 'Through the space between
           New knowledge, shooting beams serene,
           Might curve new boughs of haler green.' *Heath MS 1st reading*

'Were this not well, to bide mine hour,
Though watching from a ruined tower
How grows the day of human power?'

'The highest-mounted mind,' he said,
80   'Still sees the sacred morning spread
The silent summit overhead.

'Will thirty seasons render plain
Those lonely lights that still remain,
Just breaking over land and main?

85   'Or make that morn, from his cold crown
And crystal silence creeping down,
Flood with full daylight glebe and town?

'Forerun thy peers, thy time, and let

T. revised l. [1] 'Yet' said I 'On the . . .   l. [2] *shooting beams*] dropping
dew l. [3] *curve new boughs*] feed fresh shoots. He then further revised
l. 76 '*Were this not*] I said 'twere   l. 78 *grows the day*] creep the tides. *T.MS
A* has the revised ll. [1, 2, 3] but with the last in *1st reading* as 'pamper
shoots'. *T.MS C* revised into *Heath MS 1st reading*.
80. *sees*] views *Heath MS, T.MS C.   sacred*] lonely *T.MS A 1st reading*.
82–4] The largest mind, his orb fulfilled,
        All round him sees a boundless field;
        What then would fifty winters yield?

    Moreover if the gold of joy
    In learning would not overbuy
    Thy grief, 'twere better thou shouldst die.

    Six thousand suns have failed to pour
    Clear lustre on the boundless shore.
    Will thirty seasons yield thee more?
                                        T.MS A, deleted
'Six thousand suns', because of Archbishop Ussher's Biblical archaeology,
estimating the date of the Creation – as in 'six thousand years of fear' (*The
Princess* iv 486). Cp. the first line with l. 138: 'That the whole mind might
orb about'; and the eighth line with *In Memoriam* lxx 12: 'And lazy lengths
on boundless shores'.
83] Ever those lonely lights remain *T.MS A 1st reading. The Outcast* 14:
'lonely light'.
85. *Or . . . his*] That morning from his high *T.MS A 1st reading*.
87. *Flood . . . daylight*] To flood with daybeams *T.MS A 1st reading*.
88–93] Not *T.MS C, Heath MS;* added in *Hn MS;*
        One step men mount into the air
        But from the landing of the stair
        Are equal-distant everywhere. *T.MS A*

Thy feet, millenniums hence, be set
90 In midst of knowledge, dreamed not yet.

'Thou hast not gained a real height,
Nor art thou nearer to the light,
Because the scale is infinite.

''Twere better not to breathe or speak,
95 Than cry for strength, remaining weak,
And seem to find, but still to seek.

'Moreover, but to seem to find
Asks what thou lackest, thought resigned,
A healthy frame, a quiet mind.'

100 I said, 'When I am gone away,
"He dared not tarry," men will say,
Doing dishonour to my clay.'

'This is more vile,' he made reply,
'To breathe and loathe, to live and sigh,
105 Than once from dread of pain to die.

'Sick art thou–a divided will
Still heaping on the fear of ill
The fear of men, a coward still.

'Do men love thee? Art thou so bound
110 To men, that how thy name may sound
Will vex thee lying underground?

'The memory of the withered leaf
In endless time is scarce more brief
Than of the garnered Autumn-sheaf.

96] *T.MS A ends its first fragment here.*
97–9] *Added in T.MS C.*
97] To enjoy the found, or seem to find *Heath MS, T.MS C.*
99] Strength, tempered will, a quiet mind. *Heath MS, T.MS C.*
106. *Sick art thou*] Thou sickenest *T.MS C 1st reading.*
107. *the*] thee *Heath MS.*
110. *may*] will *Heath MS 1st reading.*
111 ∧ 2]   Thou shrinkest from the probe of blame,
              Yet out of all that owns a name
              The vainest form is human fame. *T.MS C; Heath MS, deleted*
113. *more*] less *Heath MS 1st reading, T.MS C.*

115 'Go, vexèd Spirit, sleep in trust;
        The right ear, that is filled with dust,
        Hears little of the false or just.'

        'Hard task, to pluck resolve,' I cried,
        'From emptiness and the waste wide
120 Of that abyss, or scornful pride!

        'Nay–rather yet that I could raise
        One hope that warmed me in the days
        While still I yearned for human praise.

        'When, wide in soul and bold of tongue,
125 Among the tents I paused and sung,
        The distant battle flashed and rung.

        'I sung the joyful Pæan clear,
        And, sitting, burnished without fear
        The brand, the buckler, and the spear –

130 'Waiting to strive a happy strife,
        To war with falsehood to the knife,
        And not to lose the good of life –

        'Some hidden principle to move,
        To put together, part and prove,
135 And mete the bounds of hate and love –

        'As far as might be, to carve out

118–20] *Not T.MS C, added in Heath MS.*
119–20. Note the Miltonic 'abyss', and 'waste wide Anarchie', *PL* x 282–3.
121. *Nay–rather yet*] I groaned. 'Yet oh *Heath MS 1st reading, T.MS C;*
Oh–rather yet *Hn MS 1st reading.*
122. *One hope*] Those hopes *Heath MS 1st reading, T.MS C.*   *warmed me*]
flourished *Heath MS, T.MS C.*
124–45] *Missing from HnMS.*
124–56. On the moral certainties of battle, cp. *Locksley Hall* 103–4; *Thy
voice is heard* (*The Princess* iv ∧ v); and the conclusion of *Maud.*
126. *distant*] swaying *Heath MS, T.MS C.*
135. *hate*] hope *Heath MS.*
136–41] *Not Heath MS, which has, deleted:*
                My purposed thought, at full to weave,
                Then dying well all round to leave
                The sunset of a splendid eve.
T.MS C has these MS lines, square-bracketed for deletion, after l. 135.

Free space for every human doubt,
That the whole mind might orb about –

'To search through all I felt or saw,
140   The springs of life, the depths of awe,
And reach the law within the law:

'At least, not rotting like a weed,
But, having sown some generous seed,
Fruitful of further thought and deed,

145   'To pass, when Life her light withdraws,
Not void of righteous self-applause,
Nor in a merely selfish cause –

'In some good cause, not in mine own,
To perish, wept for, honoured, known,
150   And like a warrior overthrown;

'Whose eyes are dim with glorious tears,
When, soiled with noble dust, he hears
His country's war-song thrill his ears:

'Then dying of a mortal stroke,
155   What time the foeman's line is broke,
And all the war is rolled in smoke.'

'Yea!' said the voice, 'thy dream was good,
While thou abodest in the bud.
It was the stirring of the blood.

160   'If Nature put not forth her power
About the opening of the flower,
Who is it that could live an hour?

'Then comes the check, the change, the fall,
Pain rises up, old pleasures pall.
165   There is one remedy for all.

138. Cp. *In Memoriam* xxiv 15: 'And orb into the perfect star'.
142] Not rotting like an idle weed, *Heath MS, T.MS C 1st reading*. Cp. *Hamlet*
I v 32–3: 'Duller shouldst thou be than the fat weed / That rots itself in ease
on Lethe wharf.' See l. 280.
145–7] *Not Heath MS, T.MS C.*
148. good] great *Heath MS, T.MS C.*
151. with] through *Heath MS, T.MS C.*   *tears*] fears *Heath MS (error).*
152. Horace's *Odes* II i 22: *non indecoro pulvere sordidos*, which T. had quoted
as a note to 'Your brows with noble dust defiled', *The Vale of Bones* 88.
157. said] spake *Heath MS, T.MS C.*

'Yet hadst thou, through enduring pain,
Linked month to month with such a chain
Of knitted purport, all were vain.

'Thou hadst not between death and birth
170   Dissolved the riddle of the earth.
So were thy labour little-worth.

'That men with knowledge merely played,
I told thee – hardly nigher made,
Though scaling slow from grade to grade;

175   'Much less this dreamer, deaf and blind,
Named man, may hope some truth to find,
That bears relation to the mind.

'For every worm beneath the moon
Draws different threads, and late and soon
180   Spins, toiling out his own cocoon.

'Cry, faint not: either Truth is born
Beyond the polar gleam forlorn,
Or in the gateways of the morn.

'Cry, faint not, climb: the summits slope
185   Beyond the furthest flights of hope,
Wrapt in dense cloud from base to cope.

'Sometimes a little corner shines,
As over rainy mist inclines
A gleaming crag with belts of pines.

---

166. enduring] long toil and *T.MS C.*
170. The Palace of Art 213: 'The riddle of the painful earth'.
172–3] I told thee, men, like children, played / With science – hardly . . .
Heath MS, T.MS C.
177 ∧ *8*]   Where bides the false that thou would'st hate?
            The true, thou would'st elaborate?
            Meshed in the brazen toils of Fate.
                    T.MS C, del., which then substituted ll. 178–80
181–3] *Added in T.MS C.*
184] Thou seest not how the summits slope *T.MS C.*
187–9. Cp. *The Vale of Bones* 7–8: 'At times her partial splendour shines /
Upon the grove of deep-black pines.'

190 'I will go forward, sayest thou,
       I shall not fail to find her now.
       Look up, the fold is on her brow.

       'If straight thy track, or if oblique,
       Thou know'st not. Shadows thou dost strike,
195 Embracing cloud, Ixion-like;

       'And owning but a little more
       Than beasts, abidest lame and poor,
       Calling thyself a little lower

       'Than angels. Cease to wail and brawl!
200 Why inch by inch to darkness crawl?
       There is one remedy for all.'

       'O dull, one-sided voice,' said I,
       'Wilt thou make everything a lie,
       To flatter me that I may die?

205 'I know that age to age succeeds,
       Blowing a noise of tongues and deeds,
       A dust of systems and of creeds.

       'I cannot hide that some have striven,
       Achieving calm, to whom was given
210 The joy that mixes man with Heaven:

192. fold: 'cloud' (T.).
193. T. comments 'I pronounce "oblique" *oblīque*', on the analogy of
'*obleege*'/*oblige*. Wordsworth rhymed *strike*/*oblique* in the MS of *An Evening
Walk*.
194. Shadows] Phantoms *H.Lpr 254*.
195. 'Ixion embraced a cloud, hoping to embrace a goddess' (T.).
196–9. Combining *Ecclesiastes* iii 19, 'For that which befalleth the sons of
men befalleth beasts; even one thing befalleth them: as the one dieth, so
dieth the other'; with *Psalm* viii 4–5, 'What is man, that thou art mindful
of him? and the son of man, that thou visitest him? For thou hast made him
a little lower than the angels.'
199. Cease to wail] Why complain *Heath MS, T.MS C*.
200. Why] And *Heath MS, T.MS C*.
205–7] Not *Heath MS, T.MS C*. Cp. the two deleted stanzas of *The Vision
of Sin* 103–6, 114 ∧ 5, beginning 'Systems! . . .' and 'Creeds! . . .'
(*p. 214*).
210. Horace's *Odes* I i 30: *dis miscent superis*.

'Who, rowing hard against the stream,
Saw distant gates of Eden gleam,
And did not dream it was a dream;

'But heard, by secret transport led,
215 Even in the charnels of the dead,
The murmur of the fountain-head –

'Which did accomplish their desire,
Bore and forbore, and did not tire,
Like Stephen, an unquenchèd fire.

220 'He heeded not reviling tones,
Nor sold his heart to idle moans,
Though cursed and scorned, and bruised with
     stones:

'But looking upward, full of grace,
He prayed, and from a happy place
225 God's glory smote him on the face.'

The sullen answer slid betwixt:
'Not that the grounds of hope were fixed,
The elements were kindlier mixed.'

I said, 'I toil beneath the curse,
230 But, knowing not the universe,
I fear to slide from bad to worse.

211. Who, rowing] Which did row *Heath MS 1st reading, T.MS C*; Which
rowing *Heath MS.*
212–3] Making to one great light, nor seem / Ever to dream . . . *Heath MS
1st reading, T.MS C.*
215. Even] Deep *Heath MS, T.MS C.*
222–5. Acts vii 55, 'But he, being full of the Holy Ghost, looked up sted-
fastly into heaven, and saw the glory of God.'
228. Julius Caesar V v 73–5: 'The elements / So mixed in him that Nature
might stand up / And say to all the world "This was a man!"' T. comments
'Some have happier dispositions.'
228 ∧ 9]   For these two shadows stand afar –
                One, cloakt with night, and looking war,
                The other wears the morning star.

                One urn they hold; o'er land and sea
                They shake it, and disorderly
                The lots leap out to thee and me'. *Heath MS, T.MS C*
229–31] See ll. *52–7n.*
229. said] cried *T.MS A.*

'And that, in seeking to undo
One riddle, and to find the true,
I knit a hundred others new:

235   'Or that this anguish fleeting hence,
Unmanacled from bonds of sense,
Be fixed and frozen to permanence:

'For I go, weak from suffering here:
Naked I go, and void of cheer:
240   What is it that I may not fear?'

'Consider well,' the voice replied,
'His face, that two hours since hath died;
Wilt thou find passion, pain or pride?

'Will he obey when one commands?
245   Or answer should one press his hands?
He answers not, nor understands.

'His palms are folded on his breast:
There is no other thing expressed
But long disquiet merged in rest.

250   'His lips are very mild and meek:
Though one should smite him on the cheek,
And on the mouth, he will not speak.

'His little daughter, whose sweet face
He kissed, taking his last embrace,
255   Becomes dishonour to her race—

'His sons grow up that bear his name,
Some grow to honour, some to shame,—
But he is chill to praise or blame.

232–40] Not T.MSS A, C, Heath MS.
236–7. The rhyme *sense/permanence* and 'fixed' recall Arthur Hallam's sonnet *On the Picture of the Three Fates*, 1827 (Motter, p. 3).
239. *Ecclesiastes* v 15: 'naked shall he return to go as he came'.
243. *passion*] pleasure Heath MS, T.MS C; hatred T.MS A. Cp. Pope, *Epistle to Oxford* 24: 'Above all Pain, all Passion, and all Pride'.
244–6] Transposed with ll. 247–9 T.MS A.
245. *should*] if T.MS A.
247. *palms*] hands T.MS A.
248. *There . . . thing*] And there is nothing else T.MS A.   A Dirge 2: 'Fold thy palms across thy breast'.
251. As in *Come hither* (I 165).
253–8] Added in margin T.MS A.
254. *kissed, taking*] fondled in T.MS A.
256–7. *Job* xiv 21, on the dead man: 'His sons come to honour, and he

'He will not hear the north-wind rave,
260   Nor, moaning, household shelter crave
From winter rains that beat his grave.

'High up the vapours fold and swim:
About him broods the twilight dim:
The place he knew forgetteth him.'

265   'If all be dark, vague voice,' I said,
'These things are wrapt in doubt and dread,
Nor canst thou show the dead are dead.

knoweth it not; and they are brought low, but he perceiveth it not of
them.'
259–61] *Transposed with ll. 262–4 T.MS A.*
259. *north-wind*] winds that *T.MS A 1st reading.*
260. *Nor, moaning*] Above nor *T.MS A 1st reading.*
262. *High . . . and*] Above the summit vapours *T.MS A 1st reading.*
263. *broods*] sleeps *T.MS A 1st reading.*
264. *Psalm* ciii 16, 'the place thereof shall know it no more' – man as a dead
flower. *Job* vii 10: 'He shall return no more to his house, neither shall his place
know him any more.'
264 ʌ 5] *T.MS A has nine lines, following the deleted ll. 265–7 (which then
undeleted follow the nine lines):*

When thy best friend draws sobbing breath,
Plight thou a compact ere his death
And comprehend the words he saith.

Urge him to swear, distinct and plain,
That out of bliss or out of pain
He will draw nigh thee once again.

Is that his footstep on the floor?
Is this his whisper at the door?
Surely he comes. He comes no more.

The poem was in existence by June 1833, and this is an early draft. The strong
probability is therefore that this passage on the death of 'thy best friend'
preceded Hallam's death; it would subsequently have struck T. as a hideous
premonition. Cp. the first line with *In Memoriam* lix 8 ʌ 9, MS: 'Use other
means than sobbing breath'.
265–6] *Transposed T.MS A 1st reading.*
265] These are the outward signs' I said, *T.MS A.*
266. *These*] All *T.MS A.*
267. *Nor canst thou*] Thou canst not *Heath MS, T.MS A.*

'The sap dries up: the plant declines.
A deeper tale my heart divines.
270 Know I not Death? the outward signs?

'I found him when my years were few;
A shadow on the graves I knew,
And darkness in the village yew.

'From grave to grave the shadow crept:
275 In her still place the morning wept:
Touched by his feet the daisy slept.

'The simple senses crowned his head:
"Omega! thou art Lord," they said,
"We find no motion in the dead."

280 'Why, if man rot in dreamless ease,
Should that plain fact, as taught by these,
Not make him sure that he shall cease?

268–318] Not T.MS A, which has:

A little space the voice was husht,
Then spake: 'When first the firehill flusht
The midnight, and the torrent [fountain *1st reading*] gusht—

When Mammoth, in the primal woods,
Wore, trampling to the fountain-floods,
Broad roads through blooming solitudes—

Where wert thou with the other souls?
Rolled where the equal tradewind rolls?
Or wheeled about the glimmering poles?

Cp. the fourth and fifth lines with *Opening of the Indian and Colonial Exhibition*
5–6: 'Produce of your field and flood, / Mount and mine, and primal wood'.
271–3]   He stands among the graves, the floods
                 Speak of him – and the winds: the woods
                 Whisper his name among the buds. *Heath MS, T.MS C*
274] He rises from unsounded deeps: *Heath MS, T.MS C.*
275. *wept*] weeps *Heath MS, T.MS C.*
276. *slept*] sleeps *Heath MS, T.MS C.*
277–9] Not *Heath MS, T.MS C* (*bottom half of page cut away, lacking ll.* 277–97).
'The simple senses made death a king' (T.). Contrast *Revelation* i 8: 'I am
Alpha and Omega, the beginning and the ending, saith the Lord.'
280–2]   Yet if man find unconscious ease
                 Why should that glassy frame of peace
                 Fail to persuade him he shall cease? *Heath MS*
280. *Hamlet* I v 32–3: 'the fat weed / That rots itself in ease'; see l. 142.

'Who forged that other influence,
That heat of inward evidence,
285   By which he doubts against the sense?

'He owns the fatal gift of eyes,
That read his spirit blindly wise,
Not simple as a thing that dies.

'Here sits he shaping wings to fly:
290   His heart forebodes a mystery:
He names the name Eternity.

'That type of Perfect in his mind
In Nature can he nowhere find.
He sows himself on every wind.

295   'He seems to hear a Heavenly Friend,
And through thick veils to apprehend
A labour working to an end.

'The end and the beginning vex
His reason: many things perplex,
300   With motions, checks, and counterchecks.

'He knows a baseness in his blood
At such strange war with something good,
He may not do the thing he would.

283. other] mightier *Heath MS.*
284. That heat] What heats *Heath MS.* Cp. *In Memoriam* cxxiv 13–14: 'A warmth within the breast would melt / The freezing reason's colder part.' Wordsworth has two lines coincidentally, it seems, close to T. here: 'Involved a history of no doubtful sense, / History that proves by inward evidence' (*Memorials of a Tour in Italy, 1837* (1842) v 2–3).
285. By which he doubts] That makes him doubt *Heath MS.*
292–4] Not *Heath MS.*
297. To be found verbatim in *Youth* 60; cp. *In Memoriam* cxxviii 24: 'toil cöoperant to an end'.
300. Cp. the fragment, *This Nature* (III 620; *T.Nbk 20*, 1833); 'this complex life / Of checks and impulses and counterchecks'. Also *The Lover's Tale* i 736–43*n*, MS: 'sundered and withdrawn/ And broken – though a lovely scene, withdrawn –/ To open and let inward'.
301–3]   His faith, his fear in secret hours
                 Shock like the isles of ice – he cowers
                 Before uncomprehended powers. *Heath MS, T.MS B*
                                             1st reading, *T.MS C*
Cp. *Morte d'Arthur* 140 (also on Hallam's death): 'where the moving isles of winter shock'.
301–3. Combining *Romans* vii 18–19: 'For I know that in me (that is, in my

'Heaven opens inward, chasms yawn,
305 Vast images in glimmering dawn,
Half shown, are broken and withdrawn.

'Ah! sure within him and without,
Could his dark wisdom find it out,
There must be answer to his doubt,

310 'But thou canst answer not again.
With thine own weapon art thou slain,
Or thou wilt answer but in vain.

'The doubt would rest, I dare not solve.
In the same circle we revolve.
315 Assurance only breeds resolve.'

As when a billow, blown against,
Falls back, the voice with which I fenced
A little ceased, but recommenced.

'Where wert thou when thy father played
320 In his free field, and pastime made,
A merry boy in sun and shade?

flesh), dwelleth no good thing'; with *Galatians* v 17: 'For the flesh lusteth against the Spirit, and the Spirit against the flesh: and these are contrary the one to the other: so that ye cannot do the things that ye would.'
304] Stars shake – Heaven rolls in – chasms yawn, *Heath MS, T.MS C.   opens*] rolleth *T.MS B.*
304–6. Cp. *Paradise Lost* ii 1035–9: 'from the walls of Heav'n / Shoots farr into the bosom of dim Night / A glimmering dawn' – making Chaos a 'brok'n foe'. Cp. the end of *The Vision of Sin*: 'And on the glimmering limit far withdrawn / God made Himself an awful rose of dawn.'
307. him] *Heath MS, revised to* me.
308. his] *Heath MS, revised to* my.
309. must be] *is an Heath MS 1st reading, T.MS C.   his*] the *Heath MS.*
309 ∧ 10]   And every soul whatever wine
           Of thought fermenteth, coarse or fine,
           Infolds the elements of mine. *Added to Heath MS which then ends. T.MS C ends at* l. 310 (*bottom half of page cut away, then stubs*).
313. Cp. *Youth* 50: 'Unvext by doubts I cannot solve'.
320. free field] own fields *T.MS A.*
321. merry] happy *T.MS A.   sun*] light *T.MS A.*
321 ∧ 2]   When thy young mother placidly
           Kneeled, praying at her mother's knee,
           She took but little thought of thee. *T.MS A, which ends*

'A merry boy they called him then,
He sat upon the knees of men
In days that never come again.

325   'Before the little ducts began
To feed thy bones with lime, and ran
Their course, till thou wert also man:

'Who took a wife, who reared his race,
Whose wrinkles gathered on his face,
330   Whose troubles number with his days:

'A life of nothings, nothing-worth,
From that first nothing ere his birth
To that last nothing under earth!'

'These words,' I said, 'are like the rest:
335   No certain clearness, but at best
A vague suspicion of the breast:

'But if I grant, thou mightst defend
The thesis which thy words intend –
That to begin implies to end;

340   'Yet how should I for certain hold,
Because my memory is so cold,
That I first was in human mould?

'I cannot make this matter plain,
But I would shoot, howe'er in vain,
345   A random arrow from the brain.

'It may be that no life is found,
Which only to one engine bound
Falls off, but cycles always round.

328–30] Deleted in *T.MS B* but added later.
330 ∧ 1] From when his baby pulses beat
           To when his hands in their last heat
           Pick at the deathmote on the sheet. *T.MS B, del.*
H.T. says these were 'omitted . . . as too dismal' (*Mem.* i 109).
331–3] And rest for ever [Who passest also *2nd reading*] – nothing-worth
         His [Thine *2nd reading*] essence, nothing ere his [thy *2nd reading*]
           birth
         And nothing in the quiet earth. *T.MS B 1st reading*
334–9] Added to *T.MS B.*
340] I said 'but can I justly hold *T.MS B 1st reading.*
342. first was] began *T.MS B 1st reading.*
347–9] H.Nbk 11 has these lines as the centre of an important unadopted

passage of forty-five lines, of which ll. [28–9] became *In Memoriam* lxxxv 21–2:

The voice was something low and weak,
Replying 'dost thou answer seek,
Put one thing clear that I may speak.'

And as a man that choosing draws
[5] One thing from many, but because
He must choose one, I broke the pause.

'That individual unity
Which each calls I, may never flee
To many parts and cease to be.'

[10] 'Were this self-evident as seems,'
He answered, 'who had flown to schemes
Of revelations and of dreams?'

Again he said in crafty words
'And wilt thou grant it to the herds,
[15] The fishes and the tribe of birds?'

'Perchance' I said 'no life is found
That only to one engine bound
Falls off, but cycles always round.'

'And things' he said 'which thou mayst cleave
[20] To many parts that each receive
Another life, dost thou believe

They feel thus one? So Nature spins
A various web and knowledge wins
No surety where this sense begins.

[25] Nor whereabouts to fainter fades
Through tints and neutral tints and shades
Life and half-life, a million grades.

And those Intelligences fair,
That range above thy state, declare
[30] If thou canst fathom what they are.'

'This knowledge' said I thereupon,
'As self-inorbed and perfect, one
Derives not from comparison.'

He said 'it should be always clear
[35] And still the same, not but as mere
Result of parts made whole appear.

Yet step by step it grows, for can
The retrospection of the man
Remember when the child began?'

'As old mythologies relate,
350   Some draught of Lethe might await
The slipping through from state to state.

'As here we find in trances, men
Forget the dream that happens then,
Until they fall in trance again.

355   'So might we, if our state were such
As one before, remember much,
For those two likes might meet and touch.

'But, if I lapsed from nobler place,
Some legend of a fallen race
360   Alone might hint of my disgrace;

'Some vague emotion of delight
In gazing up an Alpine height,
Some yearning toward the lamps of night;

'Or if through lower lives I came—
365   Though all experience past became
Consolidate in mind and frame—

---

[40]   'And step by step I cease to keep
My consciousness' I said 'and creep
In the long gradual cloud of sleep.

It fadeth likewise when I swoon,
It dips and darkens as the moon
[45]   And comes again

349. Pythagoras's metempsychosis, and Plato's myth of Er (*Republic* x).
351. Cp. *In Memoriam* lxxxii 6: 'From state to state the spirit walks'.
355-7] Added to T.MS B.
355. we] he *T.MS B 1st reading.*
358. But] So *T.MS B 1st reading.*
364. G. R. Potter (*PQ* xvi (1937) 335-6) argues that T. 'is writing about the transmigration of souls, and the lines refer not so much to material as to spiritual progress – a sort of semi-evolutionary idea that appears more than once in the writings of eighteenth-century thinkers'. The word *frame* 'injects the idea of physical change into these speculations concerning the soul. But from the lines themselves we cannot be at all sure whether Tennyson was thinking of changes in species, or of the same idea that he reflects in his Cambridge discussion, that the human body in its embryonic stages has resemblances to lower organisms.'
365. Though] And *T.MS B 1st reading.*
366 ∧ 7]   In passing on from more to more
And up to higher out of lower
I might forget the things before. *T.MS B, deleted*

'I might forget my weaker lot;
For is not our first year forgot?
The haunts of memory echo not.

370   'And men, whose reason long was blind,
From cells of madness unconfined,
Oft lose whole years of darker mind.

'Much more, if first I floated free,
As naked essence, must I be
375   Incompetent of memory:

'For memory dealing but with time,
And he with matter, could she climb
Beyond her own material prime?

'Moreover, something is or seems,
380   That touches me with mystic gleams,
Like glimpses of forgotten dreams—

'Of something felt, like something here;
Of something done, I know not where;
Such as no language may declare.'

385   The still voice laughed. 'I talk,' said he,
'Not with thy dreams. Suffice it thee
Thy pain is a reality.'

'But thou,' said I, 'hast missed thy mark,
Who sought'st to wreck my mortal ark,
390   By making all the horizon dark.

'Why not set forth, if I should do
This rashness, that which might ensue
With this old soul in organs new?

367. I might] As men T.MS B 1st reading.   my] their T.MS B 1st reading.
370. And] As T.MS B 1st reading.
372. Oft lose] Forget T.MS B 1st reading.
373–8] Added in T.MS B.
377. he] Time T.MS B 1st reading.
378. Arthur Hallam spoke of 'the material prime', Written in View of Ben
Lomond 14, 1829 (Motter, p. 52).
378 ∧ 9]   And after all it might transcend [descend 1st reading, error]
          Thy little logic to defend
          That since I was not, I must end. T.MS B, deleted
379. Moreover] Though sometimes T.MS B 1st reading.

'Whatever crazy sorrow saith,
395   No life that breathes with human breath
Has ever truly longed for death.

' 'Tis life, whereof our nerves are scant,
Oh life, not death, for which we pant;
More life, and fuller, that I want.'

400   I ceased, and sat as one forlorn.
Then said the voice, in quiet scorn,
'Behold, it is the Sabbath morn.'

And I arose, and I released
The casement, and the light increased
405   With freshness in the dawning east.

Like softened airs that blowing steal,
When meres begin to uncongeal,
The sweet church bells began to peal.

On to God's house the people prest:
410   Passing the place where each must rest,
Each entered like a welcome guest.

One walked between his wife and child,
With measured footfall firm and mild,
And now and then he gravely smiled.

415   The prudent partner of his blood
Leaned on him, faithful, gentle, good,
Wearing the rose of womanhood.

And in their double love secure,
The little maiden walked demure,
420   Pacing with downward eyelids pure.

These three made unity so sweet,
My frozen heart began to beat,
Remembering its ancient heat.

395–6. *Job* iii 20–1, 'Wherefore is light given to him that is in misery, and
life unto the bitter in soul; Which long for death but it cometh not.'
397–9. Cp. *Life* [*Why suffers human life so soon eclipse?*] 5: 'Would I could
pile fresh life on life'; and *Ulysses* 24–5: 'Life piled on life / Were all too
little'.
399. *John* x 10, 'I am come that they might have life, and that they might
have it more abundantly.'

I blest them, and they wandered on:
425   I spoke, but answer came there none:
The dull and bitter voice was gone.

A second voice was at mine ear,
A little whisper silver-clear,
A murmur, 'Be of better cheer'.

430   As from some blissful neighbourhood,
A notice faintly understood,
'I see the end, and know the good'.

A little hint to solace woe,
A hint, a whisper breathing low,
435   'I may not speak of what I know'.

Like an Æolian harp that wakes
No certain air, but overtakes
Far thought with music that it makes:

Such seemed the whisper at my side:
440   'What is it thou knowest, sweet voice?' I cried.
'A hidden hope,' the voice replied:

So heavenly-toned, that in that hour
From out my sullen heart a power
Broke, like the rainbow from the shower,

445   To feel, although no tongue can prove,
That every cloud, that spreads above
And veileth love, itself is love.

And forth into the fields I went,
And Nature's living motion lent
450   The pulse of hope to discontent.

I wondered at the bounteous hours,
The slow result of winter showers:
You scarce could see the grass for flowers.

424. Cp. the Ancient Mariner's release from guilt when he 'blessed them
unaware. / The self-same moment I could pray' (ll. 287–8).
425. *answer came there none*: Scott, *The Bridal of Triermain* III x.
447. Cp. the unadopted lines for *The Miller's Daughter* 189–98n: 'Bless
Love, for blest are all his ways – / The fluttering doubt, the jealous cares, /
Transparent veils that drink his rays.'
453. John Churton Collins compared George Peele's *The Arraignment of
Paris*: 'Ye may ne see for peeping flowers the grass'. Alongside this sugges-

I wondered, while I paced along:
455 The woods were filled so full with song,
There seemed no room for sense of wrong;

And all so variously wrought,
I marvelled how the mind was brought
To anchor by one gloomy thought;

460 And wherefore rather I made choice
To commune with that barren voice,
Than him that said, 'Rejoice! Rejoice!'

210 St Simeon Stylites

Published *1842*. Written 1833 (dated, *Heath MS*), by 27 Nov. (*Letters* i 98; *Mem.* i 130). It is unlikely to have been written in Oct., the month when T. heard of Hallam's death. But W. H. Thompson wrote to J. W. Blakesley, 11 Nov. 1833, on Hallam's death. and said of T.: 'He seemed less overcome than one would have expected: though, when he first arrived, he was very low – He left among us some magnificent poems and fragments of poems. Among the rest a monologue or soliloquy of one Simeon Stylites: or as he calls himself Simeon of the Pillar: a poem which we hold to be a wonderful disclosure of that mixture of self-loathing self-complacence and self-sacrifice which caused our forefathers to do penance when alive and to be canonized when dead. It is to be feared however that the men of this generation will hold it to be somewhat too unwholesome; the description of his sufferings

---

tion, T. wrote: 'No – close as it seems. Made in the fields' (*Cornhill*, Jan. 1880, *Lincoln*). FitzGerald says: 'Composed as he walked about the Dulwich meadows.'
457] *1884*; So variously seemed all things wrought, *1842–83*.
462. Cp. *In Memoriam* cxxx 5–16, MS: 'I walk the meadows and rejoice / And prosper, compassed by thy voice.' *Philippians* iv 4: 'Rejoice in the Lord alway: and again I say, Rejoice'; *Ecclesiastes* xi 9: 'Rejoice, O young man, in thy youth.' Cp. Keats, *Sleep and Poetry* 37–9: 'Sometimes it gives a glory to the voice, / And from the heart up-springs "Rejoice! rejoice!" / Sounds which will reach the Framer of all things.' Also 'Barry Cornwall' (B. W. Procter), *The Little Voice* (*English Songs*, 1832): 'Once there was a little Voice, / Merry as the month of May, / That did cry "*Rejoice! Rejoice!*" / Now 'tis flown away! // Sweet it was, and very clear, / Chasing every thought of pain . . .' In *Friendship's Offering* for 1833, to which T. contributed, there is R. F. Housman's *Away to the Greenwood*: 'And at every pause, the lute-like voice / Of the cuckoo sings – "Rejoice! rejoice!"' Edmund Blunden points out in his selection (1960) from T. that Coleridge's *Dejection* ends with the word 'rejoice'.

being too minute for any but those whom the knowledge of the Art holds above the subject' (P. Allen, *The Cambridge Apostles*, 1978, pp. 162–3). The important MSS are: *H.Nbk 13:19*, an early much-corrected draft of ll. 1–68, with stubs that include ll. 108–10 (*A*); revised as *H.Nbk 13:13* (*B*); *T.Nbk 22*; and *Heath MS*. Simeon was the first and most famous of the pillar-hermits (*Stylites*, from Greek στῦλος, pillar). H.T. gives as the sources William Hone's *Every-Day Book* (1825), which supplied almost all the details (under 'January 5'), and Gibbon's *Decline and Fall of the Roman Empire*, Chapter 37. FitzGerald says that 'this is one of the Poems A.T would read with grotesque Grimness, especially at such passages as "Coughs, Aches, Stitches, etc." [ll. 13–16], laughing aloud at times'. H.T. describes *St Telemachus* (III 224) as its 'pendant'. Cp. *St Agnes' Eve* (I 605), and *St Lawrence* (I 324). J. H. Buckley (p. 26) suggests that it was influenced by contempt for Charles Simeon, a notoriously exclamatory and influential preacher at Cambridge. Culler (p. 24) quotes Cambridge contemporaries on 'a great saint called Simeon', and on 'many other humorous and harmless little sarcasms of a like kind'. Culler also (p. 257) notes that T. 'apparently did not know much about the figure who purports to be the original of his poem. W. E. H. Lecky wrote, "He once confessed to me that when he wrote his *Simeon Stylites* he did not know that the story was a Syrian one, and had accordingly given it a Northern colouring which he now perceived to be wrong"' (*Mat.* iii 324). R. Pattison suggests that 'the whole monologue is loosely based on Chaucer's Pardoner's Prologue' (*Tennyson and Tradition*, 1979, p. 79). In his review of *1842* in the *Church of England Quarterly Review* (Oct. 1842), Leigh Hunt called it 'a powerfully graphic, and in some respects appalling satire on the pseudo-aspirations of egotistical asceticism and superstition . . . . We do not recollect to have met with a more startling picture of the sordid and the aspiring – the selfish and the self-sacrificing – the wretched, weak body and mind and resolute soul – the abject, the dominant, the stupid, the imaginative – and, alas, the misgiving . . . all mixed up in the poor phantom-like person of the almost incredible Saint of the Pillar – the almost solitary Christian counterpart of the Yogees of the Hindoos, who let birds build in their hair, and the nails of their fingers grow through the palms of their hands. We say Christian, out of Christian charity; for though real Christianity is a quintessence of good sense, both in its human and angelical aspirations, as the flower of it in due time will make manifest, yet these and other dark absurdities have, no doubt, lurked about its roots, and for a time, with equal absurdity, been confounded with the flower.' On T. and the art of the penultimate, see W. E. Fredeman, *University of Toronto Quarterly* xxxviii (1968) 69–83.

> Although I be the basest of mankind,
> From scalp to sole one slough and crust of sin,
> Unfit for earth, unfit for heaven, scarce meet

¶ 210.1. *be . . . mankind*] *T.MS 1st reading*; was the lowest in the scale *T.MS*.

For troops of devils, mad with blasphemy,
5   I will not cease to grasp the hope I hold
Of saintdom, and to clamour, mourn and sob,
Battering the gates of heaven with storms of prayer,
Have mercy, Lord, and take away my sin.

Let this avail, just, dreadful, mighty God,
10   This not be all in vain, that thrice ten years,
Thrice multiplied by superhuman pangs,
In hungers and in thirsts, fevers and cold,
In coughs, aches, stitches, ulcerous throes and cramps,
A sign betwixt the meadow and the cloud,
15   Patient on this tall pillar I have borne
Rain, wind, frost, heat, hail, damp, and sleet, and
snow;

2] *Several drafts:*
  (i) Plunged to the throat in crime – polluted, blurred,
     Blained, rank, corrupt, one crust of noisome filth – *A*
  (ii) Plunged to the throat in slough of crime – pollute,
     Blained, blurred, corrupt – one crust of noisome filth – *Heath MS*
      1st reading
  (iii) Sloughed to the throat in crime – from scalp to sole
     Blood, bone, breath, sinew, pulse and motion, sin – *Heath MS*
T.MS had the first line of (i), revised to that of (ii).
Based on *Deuteronomy* xxviii 35: 'The Lord shall smite thee in the knees,
and in the legs, with a sore botch that cannot be healed, from the sole of
thy foot unto the top of thy head.' *Job* ii 7: 'and smote Job with sore boils
from the sole of his foot unto his crown.' *Isaiah* i 6: 'From the sole of the
foot even unto the head there is no soundness in it; but wounds, and bruises,
and putrifying sores.'
4. mad with] loud in *A*.
5–6] I will not cease to clamour, day and night *A–B*.
7] Not *A*. gates] ears *Heath MS correction by T*.
9–10] Let this avail, O God, that thrice ten years *A*.
11] Not *A–B*.
12–13] *Transposed at first in A:*
     . . . thirsts, hour after hour,
       In aches and stitches, cramps and ulcerous pangs,
A reminiscence of Prospero to Caliban: 'tonight thou shalt have cramps, /
Side-stitches . . . I'll rack thee with old cramps, / Fill all thy bones with
aches', *The Tempest* I ii 326–7, 370–1. See ll. 170–75*n*.
14] Not *A – B*. A sign] Here fixed *T.MS 1st reading*. betwixt] between *T.MS*,
Heath MS.
15. on . . . pillar] *A*; upon tall pillars *B*.

And I had hoped that ere this period closed
Thou wouldst have caught me up into thy rest,
Denying not these weather-beaten limbs
20   The meed of saints, the white robe and the palm.

O take the meaning, Lord: I do not breathe,
Not whisper, any murmur of complaint.
Pain heaped ten-hundred-fold to this, were still
Less burthen, by ten-hundred-fold, to bear,
25   Than were those lead-like tons of sin that crushed
My spirit flat before thee.
O Lord, Lord;
Thou knowest I bore this better at the first,
For I was strong and hale of body then;
And though my teeth, which now are dropt away,
30   Would chatter with the cold, and all my beard
Was tagged with icy fringes in the moon,
I drowned the whoopings of the owl with sound
Of pious hymns and psalms, and sometimes saw
An angel stand and watch me, as I sang.
35   Now am I feeble grown; my end draws nigh;
I hope my end draws nigh: half deaf I am,
So that I scarce can hear the people hum
About the column's base, and almost blind,
And scarce can recognise the fields I know;

---

17. closed] Not A–B.
18] Into thy rest thou wouldst have caught me up *A.*
20. Revelation vii 9, 'clothed with white robes, and palms in their hands'.
21. O . . . Lord] Mistake me not, my God. *A–B*; My God, mistake me not:
T.MS, Heath MS.
23–4] *Several drafts:*

    (i) *A is confused, but works towards* (ii)
    (ii) Pain summed tenfold to this – ten-hundredfold
        Heaped on to that – beyond all form and mode
        Of tolerance – were less ten-hundredfold
        Than I deserve; and heavier to endure,
        If not a little by thy finger stayed, *B*
    (iii) Pain summed tenfold to this – tenhundredfold
        Heaped on to that – beyond all agonies,
        All energies of tolerance – were less
        Tenhundredfold less burthensome to bear *T.MS, Heath MS*
25] These weights – these leadlike tons of sin that crush *B.*
29. dropt away] fallen out *A–B.*
37–9] *Added in A, which is very confused at this point.*

  40 And both my thighs are rotted with the dew;
        Yet cease I not to clamour and to cry,
        While my stiff spine can hold my weary head,
        Till all my limbs drop piecemeal from the stone,
        Have mercy, mercy: take away my sin.

  45   O Jesus, if thou wilt not save my soul,
        Who may be saved? who is it may be saved?
        Who may be made a saint, if I fail here?
        Show me the man hath suffered more than I.
        For did not all thy martyrs die one death?
  50 For either they were stoned, or crucified,
        Or burned in fire, or boiled in oil, or sawn
        In twain beneath the ribs; but I die here
        Today, and whole years long, a life of death.
        Bear witness, if I could have found a way
  55 (And heedfully I sifted all my thought)
        More slowly-painful to subdue this home
        Of sin, my flesh, which I despise and hate,
        I had not stinted practice, O my God.

           For not alone this pillar-punishment,
  60 Not this alone I bore: but while I lived
        In the white convent down the valley there,
        For many weeks about my loins I wore
        The rope that haled the buckets from the well,
        Twisted as tight as I could knot the noose;

40. 'One of his thighs rotted a whole year, during which time he stood on
one leg only' (Hone).
42] Added in A.
46. Matthew xix 25: 'When his disciples heard it, they were exceedingly
amazed, saying, Who then can be saved?'
47] Not A; preceding l. 45, B.
48] Added in A.
49–53] Not A; added to margin of B (l.52: In sunder by the ribs . . .).
52. In twain] Atwain *T.MS, Heath MS.*
55 ʌ *6]* Devising every means and mode of ill *A–B, T.MS, Heath MS.*
56. slowly-painful] painful-slow *A–B, T.MS, Heath MS 1st reading.   subdue]*
mortify *A–B, T.MS, Heath MS 1st reading.   this home]* my flesh *A first reading,
which then added l. 57.*
Based on *Romans* vii 17–18: 'sin that dwelleth in me. For I know that in
me (that is, in my flesh) dwelleth no good thing.'
60. lived] dwelt *A.*
61. Where according to Hone he was thought over-austere.
62. wore] bore *A.*
64] Added in A, where it appeared ll. 62 ʌ *3.*

65 And spake not of it to a single soul,
Until the ulcer, eating through my skin,
Betrayed my secret penance, so that all
My brethren marvelled greatly. More than this
I bore, whereof, O God, thou knowest all.

70 Three winters, that my soul might grow to thee,
I lived up there on yonder mountain side.
My right leg chained into the crag, I lay
Pent in a roofless close of ragged stones;
Inswathed sometimes in wandering mist, and twice
75 Blacked with thy branding thunder, and sometimes
Sucking the damps for drink, and eating not,
Except the spare chance-gift of those that came
To touch my body and be healed, and live:
And they say then that I worked miracles,
80 Whereof my fame is loud amongst mankind,
Cured lameness, palsies, cancers. Thou, O God,
Knowest alone whether this was or no.
Have mercy, mercy! cover all my sin.

Then, that I might be more alone with thee,
85 Three years I lived upon a pillar, high
Six cubits, and three years on one of twelve;
And twice three years I crouched on one that rose
Twenty by measure; last of all, I grew
Twice ten long weary weary years to this,
90 That numbers forty cubits from the soil.

I think that I have borne as much as this—

65] And told it not unto a single soul *A*.
67. *so that all*] by the scent *A–B, T.MS, Heath MS 1st reading*.
68] So that my brethren marvelled. More than this *A–B, T.MS, Heath MS 1st reading*; My brethren marvelled. More, much more than this *Heath MS*. *A breaks off here.*
70–71] . . . thee / More nigh, I lived on yonder mountain-top—*B, T.MS 1st reading*.
72. *crag, I lay*] solid crag *B first reading*.
74–5] Inswathed sometimes in wandering mist, sometimes *B*.
80. *amongst*] among *B, T.MS, Heath MS*.
81. *Acts* viii 7, 'Many taken with palsies, and that were lame, were healed'.
82. *this was*] I did *B, T.MS, Heath MS*.
83. *Psalm* lxxxv 2, 'Thou hast forgiven the iniquity of thy people, thou hast covered all their sin.'
86. *cubit*: about 18 inches.
91–102] Not *B, T.MS*; added on later page of *Heath MS*.

Or else I dream – and for so long a time,
If I may measure time by yon slow light,
And this high dial, which my sorrow crowns –
So much – even so.

95   And yet I know not well,
For that the evil ones come here, and say,
'Fall down, O Simeon: thou hast suffered long
For ages and for ages!' then they prate
Of penances I cannot have gone through,

100   Perplexing me with lies; and oft I fall,
Maybe for months, in such blind lethargies
That Heaven, and Earth, and Time are
      choked.
                  But yet
Bethink thee, Lord, while thou and all the saints
Enjoy themselves in heaven, and men on earth

105   House in the shade of comfortable roofs,
Sit with their wives by fires, eat wholesome food,
And wear warm clothes, and even beasts have stalls,
I, 'tween the spring and downfall of the light,
Bow down one thousand and two hundred times,

110   To Christ, the Virgin Mother, and the saints;
Or in the night, after a little sleep,
I wake: the chill stars sparkle; I am wet
With drenching dews, or stiff with crackling frost.

93. *light*] fire *Heath MS 1st reading*. Simeon thinks of the pillar as a sundial.

96. *For that*] Because *Heath MS*.

98. *then*] and *Heath MS*.

106] *Not B; added in T.MS.*

107. Simeon likens himself to Christ, *Matthew* viii 20: 'The foxes have holes, and the birds of the air have nests; but the Son of man hath not where to lay his head.'

108–9]   Between the rise and falling of the light
              I bow . . . *A*

109. According to Hone and Gibbon, one thousand two hundred and forty four.

111–13] *Not B.*

111–14]   I wear an undrest goatskin, crackling-stiff
              With frost, and often drenched in drifts of rain. *T.MS 1st reading*
T.MS revised l. 111, 'Or', to 'And', and then back to 'Or'.

112. *chill*] still *Heath MS*.

113. Cp. Gray, *The Descent of Odin* 31–3: 'Long on these mould'ring bones have beat / The winter's snow, the summer's heat, / The drenching dews, and driving rain!'

I wear an undressed goatskin on my back;
115 A grazing iron collar grinds my neck;
And in my weak, lean arms I lift the cross,
And strive and wrestle with thee till I die:
O mercy, mercy! wash away my sin.

O Lord, thou knowest what a man I am;
120 A sinful man, conceived and born in sin:
'Tis their own doing; this is none of mine;
Lay it not to me. Am I to blame for this,
That here come those that worship me? Ha! ha!
They think that I am somewhat. What am I?
125 The silly people take me for a saint,
    · And bring me offerings of fruit and flowers:
And I, in truth (thou wilt bear witness here)
Have all in all endured as much, and more
Than many just and holy men, whose names
130 Are registered and calendared for saints.

Good people, you do ill to kneel to me.
What is it I can have done to merit this?
I am a sinner viler than you all.
It may be I have wrought some miracles,
135 And cured some halt and maimed; but what of that?
It may be, no one, even among the saints,

114. on my back] hard and stiff B.
115] I wear an iron collar round my neck B.
116. weak, lean] withered B. As shown in the illustration to Hone.
117. And . . . wrestle] Wrestling and striving B. Genesis xxxii 24, 'And Jacob was left alone; and there wrestled a man with him until the breaking of the day.'
118 O] Have T.MS 1st reading. Acts xxii 16: 'Arise, and be baptized, and wash away thy sins.'
120. Psalm li 5: 'I was shapen in iniquity; and in sin did my mother conceive me.'
122. Contrast the martyrdom of Stephen, Acts vii 60: 'And he kneeled down, and cried with a loud voice, Lord, lay not this sin to their charge'.
124. somewhat . . . I?] somewhat on the earth. B, T.MS 1st reading.
126. of] and B 1st reading.
131. kneel to] worship B.
132. can] Not B, T.MS.
133] Not B, where it appears later; see ll. 166–82n.
134. wrought] worked B.
136–7] Added in T.MS.
136–9] Not B.

May match his pains with mine; but what of that?
Yet do not rise; for you may look on me,
And in your looking you may kneel to God.
140 Speak! is there any of you halt or maimed?
I think you know I have some power with Heaven
From my long penance: let him speak his wish.

Yes, I can heal him. Power goes forth from me.
They say that they are healed. Ah, hark! they shout
145 'St Simeon Stylites.' Why, if so,
God reaps a harvest in me. O my soul,
God reaps a harvest in thee. If this be,
Can I work miracles and not be saved?
This is not told of any. They were saints.
150 It cannot be but that I shall be saved;
Yea, crowned a saint. They shout, 'Behold a saint!'
And lower voices saint me from above.
Courage, St Simeon! This dull chrysalis
Cracks into shining wings, and hope ere death
155 Spreads more and more and more, that God hath now
Sponged and made blank of crimeful record all
My mortal archives.
                    O my sons, my sons,
I, Simeon of the pillar, by surname
Stylites, among men; I, Simeon,
160 The watcher on the column till the end;
I, Simeon, whose brain the sunshine bakes;

143–7] Hearken, my brethren, for the power of God
            Is strong in me to preach and save your souls. *B*
See ll. 157 ∧ 8*n.*
146–7. Suggesting *Leviticus* xxiii 10–11: 'reap the harvest thereof....
And he shall wave the sheaf before the Lord, to be accepted for you.'
149] *Added in T.MS.*
153 ∧ *4*] Hung o'er the abysses of immortal Death *T.MS deleted.*
154. wings, ∧*and*] Death mortal steals / A lengthening shade upon me *T.MS
deleted.*
156. of] the *Heath MS 1st reading.*
157. mortal archives] tablets up in Heaven *T.MS 1st reading.*
157 ∧ *8*] God's grace is strong through me to preach and save. *T.MS, Heath
MS. See ll. 143–7n.*
160 ∧ *61*] Whom the lark passeth in her road to Heaven –
            To whose chill ears bats hook their leathern wings, *B*
Heath MS has only the second line. *T.MS* has the lines transposed, with the
line 'Whom the lark . . .' deleted.
161. I . . . whose] Even I, whose withered *B.*

I, whose bald brows in silent hours become
Unnaturally hoar with rime, do now
From my high nest of penance here proclaim
165   That Pontius and Iscariot by my side
Showed like fair seraphs. On the coals I lay,
A vessel full of sin: all hell beneath
Made me boil over. Devils plucked my sleeve,
Abaddon and Asmodeus caught at me.
170   I smote them with the cross; they swarmed again.
In bed like monstrous apes they crushed my chest:
They flapped my light out as I read: I saw
Their faces grow between me and my book;
With colt-like whinny and with hoggish whine
175   They burst my prayer. Yet this way was left,
And by this way I 'scaped them. Mortify
Your flesh, like me, with scourges and with thorns;
Smite, shrink not, spare not. If it may be, fast
Whole Lents, and pray. I hardly, with slow steps,
180   With slow, faint steps, and much exceeding pain,
Have scrambled past those pits of fire, that still
Sing in mine ears. But yield not me the praise:

166. seraphs. ∧ *On*] Jesus caught one hand,
           The Devil grasped the other: I was torn
           In twain betwixt them. *T.MS deleted*
166–82] Show like fair Seraphs. O my sons, my sons
           I am a sinner viler than you all,
           The last and least of men. Give God the praise: *B*
See l. 133*n.*
168. over. ∧ *Devils*] Jesus grasped one hand,
           That Evil one the other. I was torn
           In twain betwixt them. *T.MS deleted*
plucked my sleeve] twitched my beard *T.MS 1st reading.* Cp. Bunyan's *Grace
Abounding*: 'I have in my bed been greatly afflicted, while asleep, with the
apprehensions of Devils, and wicked spirits.'
169. caught at me] plucked my sleeve *T.MS 1st reading. Revelation* ix 11: 'The
angel of the bottomless pit, whose name in the Hebrew tongue is
Abaddon.' *Tobit* iii 8: 'Asmodeus the evil spirit'.
170–1] Added in *T.MS.*
170–5. Cp. Caliban, on Prospero's 'spirits', *The Tempest* II ii 8–10: 'For
every trifle are they set upon me – / Sometime like apes, that mow and
chatter at me, / And after bite me.' See ll. 12–13*n.*
172. flapped] blew *T.MS 1st reading.*
178. Isaiah lviii 1: 'Cry aloud, spare not, lift up thy voice like a trumpet, and
shew my people their transgression, and the house of Jacob their sins.'
179. Whole Lents: as Simeon did in Hone.

God only through his bounty hath thought fit,
Among the powers and princes of this world,
185 To make me an example to mankind,
Which few can reach to. Yet I do not say
But that a time may come–yea, even now,
Now, now, his footsteps smite the threshold stairs
Of life–I say, that time is at the doors
190 When you may worship me without reproach;
For I will leave my relics in your land,
And you may carve a shrine about my dust,
And burn a fragrant lamp before my bones,
When I am gathered to the glorious saints.

195   While I spake then, a sting of shrewdest pain
Ran shrivelling through me, and a cloudlike change,
In passing, with a grosser film made thick
These heavy, horny eyes. The end! the end!
Surely the end! What's here? a shape, a shade,
200 A flash of light. Is that the angel there
That holds a crown? Come, blessèd brother, come.
I know thy glittering face. I waited long;
My brows are ready. What! deny it now?
Nay, draw, draw, draw nigh. So I clutch it. Christ!
205 'Tis gone: 'tis here again; the crown! the crown!
So now 'tis fitted on and grows to me,
And from it melt the dews of Paradise,

---

183. God . . . his] God in his grace and B; 'Tis God who in his *T.MS 1st reading* (*then retaining* in); *Heath MS.*
184] *Not B.*
187. yea] and *B.*
189. that] (*ital.*) *T.MS.*
191–3] I leave my bones, my relicks in your land *B.*
197–200. Cp. Keats, *Endymion* ii 323–4: 'Before mine eyes thick films and shadows float – / O let me 'noint them with the heaven's light!'
198. heavy, horny eyes] globes of arid horn *B.*
199. shape . . . shade] shade . . . shape *B.*
200. the] an *B, T.MS, Heath MS.* The angel is mentioned in Hone.
202] *Not B.*
204. So . . . Christ!] is it? is it not? *B*; So I have it–God! *T.MS 1st reading, Heath MS.*
205. the crown! the crown!] Give me the crown. *B.* Based on *Revelation* ii 7–10: 'To him that overcometh will I give to eat of the tree of life . . . and I will give thee a crown of life.' J. McCue compares *Hamlet* I i 141–2: ' 'Tis here.' ' 'Tis here'. / ' 'Tis gone'.

Sweet! sweet! spikenard, and balm, and frankincense.
  Ah! let me not be fooled, sweet saints: I trust
210 That I am whole, and clean, and meet for Heaven.

  Speak, if there be a priest, a man of God,
  Among you there, and let him presently
  Approach, and lean a ladder on the shaft,
  And climbing up into my airy home,
215. Deliver me the blessèd sacrament;
  For by the warning of the Holy Ghost,
  I prophesy that I shall die tonight,
  A quarter before twelve.
                              But thou, O Lord,
  Aid all this foolish people; let them take
220 Example, pattern: lead them to thy light.

[1833. *In Memoriam*–see *p. 331*]

216 On a Mourner

Published *1865*. Written Oct. 1833 (*Y.MS*), immediately after T. heard of
the death of Arthur Hallam. Spedding described it to T. as 'one of those
pieces which nobody except yourself can write, and I think the most
exquisite of an exquisite race' (19 Sept. 1834; *Letters* i 117–8). It is in the
T.MS of *In Memoriam*, *T.Nbk 13*. T. probably delayed publication because
it was too directly personal. In revising it for *1865*, he veiled and objectified
the poem by adding the title; by addressing it to another, changing 'my' to
'thy'; and by omitting two explicit stanzas, ll. 15 ∧ 16. All variants from
Heath MS and *T.MS* are below. T. had used the same unusual stanza for
My life is full (I 383), a comparable poem on death and Nature addressed to
Hallam in his lifetime.

208. 'When Simeon died, Anthony smelt a precious odour emanating
from his body' (Hone).
209] O Holy, Holy, Holy now I know *B*, *T.MS 1st reading*, *Heath MS*.
210. whole] white *B*.   *Heaven*] thee *T.MS 1st reading*, *Heath MS*.
214. my] *1846*; mine *1842–5*.
217. The prophecy is not in Gibbon or Hone. See *Bede*, ed. A. Hamilton
Thompson (1935), pp. 211–3: 'Sometimes the day was prophesied by the
appearance of angels in a vision . . . . This particular form of prophecy is
of course a commonplace in the lives of the saints from the Life of St.
Antony onwards . . . . The idea underlying this widespread tradition was
that the saint was thus granted time to prepare himself for the great change
and to be fortified by receiving the Communion.'
218–9. *Psalm* lxxiv 18: 'O Lord, and that the foolish people have blas-
phemed thy name.' *Jeremiah* v 21: 'Hear now this, O foolish people'.
220. Example, pattern:] Pattern from me–so *T.MS*, *Heath MS*.

I

Nature, so far as in her lies,
Imitates God, and turns her face
To every land beneath the skies,
Counts nothing that she meets with base,
5   But lives and loves in every place;

II

Fills out the homely quickset-screens,
And makes the purple lilac ripe,
Steps from her airy hill, and greens
The swamp, where hummed the dropping snipe,
10   With moss and braided marish-pipe;

III

And on thy heart a finger lays,
Saying, 'Beat quicker, for the time
Is pleasant, and the woods and ways
Are pleasant, and the beech and lime
15   Put forth and feel a gladder clime.'

¶ 216.6. *homely*] edging *Heath MS, T.MS*. The quickset (whitethorn) appears twice in *In Memoriam*, in lxxxviii 2 and in the consolation of spring in cxv: 'Now fades the last long streak of snow, / Now burgeons every maze of quick . . . / . . . and in my breast / Spring wakens too; and my regret / Becomes an April violet, / And buds and blossoms like the rest.'
9. hummed] *1889, Heath MS*; hums *T.MS, 1865–88*. The snipe's humming is caused by its vibrating tail-feathers.
10] And shoots the fringèd paddock-pipe – *Heath MS*; With braided moss and paddock-pipe *T.MS 1st reading*; With moss and braided paddock-pipe *T.MS. T.MS* has a note by T. below 'paddock-pipe': '(for marestail)'.
11. thy] my *Heath MS, T.MS*. The touch of Nature (who 'imitates God', l. 2) gives man life as did the finger of Michelangelo's God at the Creation. Cp. *From sorrow* 4: 'Touch me, great Nature, make me live' (on Hallam's death). Contrast *In Memoriam* lxxxv 20: 'God's finger touched him, and he slept'.
12. quicker, for], mournful heart! *Heath MS, T.MS*.
14. beech] elm *Heath MS, T.MS*.
15 ∧ 16]   'Come, beat a little quicker now,
        When all things own my quickening breath:
      Thy friend is mute: his brows are low:
      But I am with thee till thy death.'
      Some such kind words to me she saith.

      Yet is she [she is *T.MS*] mortal even as I,
      Or as that friend I loved in vain:

IV

And murmurs of a deeper voice,
   Going before to some far shrine,
Teach that sick heart the stronger choice,
   Till all thy life one way incline
20   With one wide Will that closes thine.

V

And when the zoning eve has died
   Where yon dark valleys wind forlorn,
Come Hope and Memory, spouse and bride,
   From out the borders of the morn,
25   With that fair child betwixt them born.

VI

And when no mortal motion jars
   The blackness round the tombing sod,

     She only whispering [Did she but whisper *1st reading*] low
     or high,
       Through this vast [all this *T.MS*] cloud of grief and pain
       I had not found my peace again. *Heath MS, T.MS*
Cp. *In Memoriam* xxxiv, where 'this round of green' would in itself, for all
its beauty, be as nothing: "Twere hardly worth my while to choose / Of
things all mortal'.
16. And . . . deeper] Deep . . . holier *Heath MS*; But . . . deeper [holier *1st
reading*] *T.MS.*
18] Are learning me the purer choice, *Heath MS, T.MS.*
19. thy] my *T.MS.*
19] Till all my soul concentric shine *Heath MS.* Cp. 'A will concentric with all
fate', in the unpublished section of *In Memoriam, Young is the grief* 15. T.
wrote to Spedding, early Oct. 1834: 'In your criticisms, I think your
objection to "concentric" is not valid – the why I have not "verge and room
enough" to explain' (*Letters* i 125).
20. one] that *Heath MS*; some *T.MS. thine*] mine *Heath MS, T.MS.*
21] For when the fringing eve hath died *Heath MS, T.MS.*   *zoning*: striping,
as in *The Progress of Spring* 69; it suggests the elegiac and speculative context
of Keats, *Fall of Hyperion* i 310–12: 'No stir of life / Was in this shrouded
vale, not so much air / As in the zoning of a summer's day . . .' Moneta had
just been addressed as 'Shade of Memory'. *The Fall of Hyperion* was
published posthumously in 1856, and so may have affected T.'s revision of
'fringing' into 'zoning'. Yet later T. objected specifically to Keats's lines
(*Mem.* ii 286).
24. out] forth *Heath MS.*
25. betwixt] between *Heath MS.*   *child*: presumably Love; cp. *The Lover's
Tale* i 802–10 (I 362).
26. mortal motion] human murmur *Heath MS.*
27. blackness] darkness *Heath MS, T.MS.*

Through silence and the trembling stars
Comes Faith from tracts no feet have trod,
30   And Virtue, like a household god

VII

Promising empire; such as those
Once heard at dead of night to greet
Troy's wandering prince, so that he rose
With sacrifice, while all the fleet
35   Had rest by stony hills of Crete.

217 Ulysses

Published *1842*. Written 20 Oct. 1833 (dated, *Heath MS*), soon after T. heard the news of Arthur Hallam's death. T. made two slightly different comments. First, 'The poem was written soon after Arthur Hallam's death, and it gives the feeling [gave my feeling *Mem.* i 196] about the need of going forward and braving the struggle of life perhaps more simply than anything in *In Memoriam*' (*Eversley*). Second, comparing *In Memoriam*, 'There is more about myself in *Ulysses*, which was written under the sense of loss and that all had gone by, but that still life must be fought out to the end. It was more written with the feeling of his loss upon me than many poems in *In Memoriam*' (to James Knowles, *Nineteenth Century* xxxiii (1893) 182). For T.'s other attempts at this date to find solace and under-standing in a classical figure, see *Tithonus* (*p. 583*), which he said was in-tended as a 'pendant' to *Ulysses*, and *Tiresias* (I 622).

28. silence and the] silences of *Heath MS*.
29. Comes] Slides *Heath MS*. As in l. 28, T. disliked the sibilants.
32] *1884*; That once at dead of night did greet *1865–83*; Which in the hush of night did greet *Heath MS, T.MS*. Cp. the elegiac 'dead calm', *In Memoriam* xi 19. Cp. ll. 28–32 with Keats, *To my Brothers*: 'o'er our silence creep / Like whispers of the household gods that keep / A gentle empire o'er fraternal souls. / . . . at fall of night'.
32–5. Aeneid iii 147–78: Aeneas's cares were dispelled by the voices which promised him empire and success, after which he offered gifts to the gods: *tum sic adfari et curas his demere dictis* . . . / *idem venturos tollemus in astra nepotes* / *imperiumque urbi dabimus* . . . / *surge age et haec laetus longaevo dicta parenti* / *haud dubitanda refer*. ('Then thus they spake to me and with these words dispelled my cares . . . . We too shall exalt to heaven thy sons that are to be, and give empire to their city . . . . Come, arise, and with good cheer bear to thine aged parent these certain tidings.') For T., this would be apt not only as divine assurance of certainty (*haud dubitanda*), but also be-cause *tollemus in astra nepotes* hinted at immortality.
35. Had rest by] Moored under *Heath MS*.

The text in *Heath MS* is virtually that of *1842*; *H.Nbk 16* is earlier. *T.Nbk 22* is later than both. It breaks off with l. 49 (then stubs). All variants are below. J. M. Kemble sent it to W. B. Donne (the poem dated 20 Oct. 1833) in March–April 1834, with the comment: 'I will fill up my paper with a grand thing of Alfred's, unfinished though it be.' Kemble's text is that of *Heath MS*, except for two slips.

Sources. T. specifies *Odyssey* xi 100–137, and Dante's *Inferno* xxvi 90 ff. Tiresias speaks, *Odyssey* xi 112–37: 'Late shalt thou come home and in evil case, after losing all thy comrades, in a ship that is another's, and thou shalt find woes in thy house – proud men that devour thy livelihood, wooing thy godlike wife, and offering wooers' gifts. Yet verily on their violent deeds shalt thou take vengeance when thou comest. But when thou hast slain the wooers in thy halls, whether by guile or openly with the sharp sword, then do thou go forth, taking a shapely oar, until thou comest to men that know naught of . . . ships . . . . And death shall come to thee thyself far from the sea [possibly 'from out of the sea'], a death so gentle, that shall lay thee low when thou art overcome with sleek old age, and thy people shall dwell in prosperity around thee.' On this 'mysterious voyage', H.T. comments: 'This is elaborated by the author of the *Telegoneia*. My father, like Eugammon, takes up the story of further wanderings at the end of the *Odyssey*. Ulysses has lived in Ithaca for a long while before the craving for fresh travel seizes him. The comrades he addresses are of the same heroic mould as his old comrades.' The last sentence is meant to meet the objection that Ulysses' companions were dead. In a note H.T. added: 'Perhaps the *Odyssey* has not been strictly adhered to, and some of the old comrades may be still left.'

Dante is the more important source. T. probably used H. F. Cary's translation (1805); there is a copy at *Lincoln*. (There is also a copy of Henry Boyd's translation.) E. H. Duncan argues that the translations by Boyd (1785), Cary, and perhaps Nathaniel Howard (1807) 'may be at least as important as the original' (*Essays in Memory of Christine Burleson*, ed. T. G. Burton, 1969). R. Pattison notes, though, that T. 'owned at least eleven copies of Dante', and that his 'favourite' was in Italian, 1818–9 (*Tennyson and Tradition*, 1979, p. 167). Ulysses speaks, xxvi 90–124 (Cary):

> When I escap'd
> From Circe, who beyond a circling year
> Had held me near Caieta, by her charms,
> Ere thus Eneas yet had nam'd the shore,
> Nor fondness for my son, nor reverence
> Of my old father, nor return of love,
> That should have crown'd Penelope with joy,
> Could overcome in me the zeal I had
> T' explore the world, and search the ways of life,
> Man's evil and his virtue. Forth I sail'd
> Into the deep illimitable main,

With but one bark, and the small faithful band
That yet cleav'd to me. As Iberia far,
Far as Marocco either shore I saw,
And the Sardinian and each isle beside
Which round that ocean bathes. Tardy with age
Were I and my companions, when we came
To the strait pass, where Hercules ordain'd
The bound'ries not to be o'erstepp'd by man.
The walls of Seville to my right I left,
On the' other hand already Ceuta past.
'O brothers!' I began, 'who to the west
'Through perils without number now have reach'd,
'To this the short remaining watch, that yet
'Our senses have to wake, refuse not proof
'Of the unpeopled world, following the track
'Of Phoebus. Call to mind from whence ye sprang:
'Ye were not form'd to live the life of brutes,
'But virtue to pursue and knowledge high.'
With these few words I sharpen'd for the voyage
The mind of my associates, that I then
Could scarcely have withheld them. To the dawn
Our poop we turn'd . . .

Ulysses then describes the last and fatal voyage. It has been much discussed whether or not we are to find T.'s Ulysses altogether noble; there is a scrupulous account of the arguments by J. Pettigrew, *Victorian Poetry* i (1963) 27–45. See also the subsequent articles by L. K. Hughes, *VP* xvii (1979) 192–203, and L. M. Findlay, *VP* xix (1981), 139–49; and, on the significance of the Homeric and Dantesque backgrounds, T. Robbins, *VP* xi (1973) 177–93. T. P. Adler (*TRB* ii, 1974, 128–30) suggests as a further source Samuel Daniel's *Ulysses and the Siren* (it is in Percy's *Reliques*; Somersby, Lincoln). B. J. Leggett (*Tennessee Studies in Literature* xv, 1970, 143–59) argues that Byron's influence is almost as pervasive as Dante's; particularly *Childe Harold's Pilgrimage* III xlii–xlv, a significant source for theme, imagery and language. Cp. T.'s ll. 22–4, and his larger context, with III xliv:

> Their breath is agitation, and their life
> A storm whereon they ride, to sink at last,
> And yet so nursed and bigoted to strife,
> That should their days, surviving perils past,
> Melt to calm twilight, they feel overcast
> With sorrow and supineness, and so die;
> Even as a flame unfed, which runs to waste
> With its own flickering, or a sword laid by,
> Which eats into itself, and rusts ingloriously.

(For a parallel in Byron earlier noted, see l. 18*n*.)

It little profits that an idle king,
By this still hearth, among these barren crags,
Matched with an agèd wife, I mete and dole
Unequal laws unto a savage race,
5   That hoard, and sleep, and feed, and know not me.

I cannot rest from travel: I will drink
Life to the lees: all times I have enjoyed
Greatly, have suffered greatly, both with those
That loved me, and alone; on shore, and when
10   Through scudding drifts the rainy Hyades
Vext the dim sea: I am become a name;
For always roaming with a hungry heart
Much have I seen and known; cities of men

¶ 217.2. *still*] dull *H.MS 1st reading*.

3. *an agèd wife*: Duncan (see headnote) compares Boyd's 'agèd sire' and
Howard's 'an aged sire'.

4. *Unequal*: not 'unjust', but 'not affecting all in the same manner or
degree', a primitive state of law consequent upon the Ithacans' being 'a
savage race'.

5. *not me*] me not *H.MS*. Cp. *Hamlet* IV iv *33–9*, which not only echoes
'sleep and feed', but is also apt to the theme of the poem: 'What is a man, /
If his chief good and market of his time / Be but to sleep and feed? a beast,
no more: / Sure he that made us with such large discourse, / Looking
before and after, gave us not / That capability and god-like reason / To
fust in us unused.'

6–9] Much have I suffered both on shore and when *H.MS*.

6–7. J. Pettigrew (see headnote) compares *Macbeth* II iii 94–5: 'The wine of
life is drawn, and the mere lees / Is left this vault to brag of'.

10. *scudding drifts*: *Pleiadum choro* / *scindente nubes* (Horace, *Odes* IV xiv 21–
2). T. quotes *pluviasque Hyadas* (*Aeneid* i 744); the rising of these stars was
thought to bring storm.

10–11. Cp. Shelley, *Revolt of Islam* III xxxii 3–4: 'the starry giant dips / His
zone in the dim sea'.

11. *Vext*: cp. *The Tempest* I ii 229: 'the still-vexed Bermoothes'; *Paradise
Lost* i 305–6: 'with fierce Winds *Orion* arm'd / Hath vext the Red-Sea
Coast'; and Pope's *Iliad* iii 5–6: 'When inclement Winters vex the plain /
With piercing frosts, or thick-descending rain.' This sense is common in
Shelley.

12] Not *H.MS*, *Heath MS*, *T.MS*. J. C. Maxwell (private communication)
suggests the influence of *avido . . . pectore* in Cicero's free version of the
song of the Sirens, *De Finibus* V xviii 49.

13. *and*], much *H.MS*.

13–14. *Odyssey* i 3–5: πολλῶν δ'ἀνθρώπων ἴδεν ἄστεα καὶ νόον ἔγνω, /
πολλὰ δ' ὅ γ'ἐν πόντῳ πάθεν ἄλγεα ὃν κατὰ θυμόν. ('Many were the

And manners, climates, councils, governments,
15 Myself not least, but honoured of them all;
And drunk delight of battle with my peers,
Far on the ringing plains of windy Troy.
I am a part of all that I have met;
Yet all experience is an arch wherethrough
20 Gleams that untravelled world, whose margin fades
For ever and for ever when I move.
How dull it is to pause, to make an end,
To rust unburnished, not to shine in use!

men whose cities he saw and whose mind he learned, aye, and many the woes he suffered in his heart upon the sea'.) Hence Horace on Ulysses, *Epistles* I ii 19–20: *qui . . . multorum providus urbes / et mores hominum inspexit.*

17. windy Troy: Homer's προτὶ Ἴλιον ἠνεμόεσσαν.

18] Not H.MS. T. cites Aeneas's account of his experiences, *Aeneid* ii 5–6: *quaeque ipse miserrima vidi / et quorum pars magna fui.* Cp. Byron, *Childe Harold* III lxxii 1–2: 'I live not in myself, but I become / Portion of that around me'. Byron's passage has lines relevant to *Ulysses* (lxx 6–9, lxxv 1–2): 'on the sea / The boldest steer but where their ports invite – / But there are wanderers o'er Eternity, / Whose bark drives on and on, and anchored ne'er shall be . . . / Are not the mountains, waves, and skies, a part / Of me and of my Soul.'

19. wherethrough] through which MSS. Duncan (see headnote) says that the 'arch' is not apparently indebted to Dante, and notes Boyd: 'I circled round the Celtiberian strand' (xvii 4).

19–21. Matthew Arnold, *On Translating Homer* (1861) iii, commented on these lines: 'It is no blame to their rhythm, which belongs to another order of movement than Homer's, but it is true that these three lines by themselves take up nearly as much time as a whole book of the *Iliad*'.

20–22] Gleams the untravelled world: how dull it is H.MS. J. Pettigrew compares 'the unpeopled world', Cary's Dante, *Inf.* xxvi 117. M. Alexander compares *Hamlet* III i 79–80: 'The undiscovered country, from whose bourn / No traveller returns'.

23. Cp. Ulysses's words, *Troilus and Cressida* III iii 150–53: 'Perseverance, dear my lord, / Keeps honour bright: to have done, is to hang / Quite out of fashion, like a rusty mail / In monumental mockery.' T. later cited this speech as one of 'the noblest things' in Shakespeare (*Tennyson and His Friends*, p. 265). D. Bush, *MLR* xxxviii (1943) 38, compares *Hamlet* IV iv 39 (see l. 5*n*). J. J. M. Tobin (*TRB* iii, 1979, 120–1) suggests that a great many of the words of the scene have a place in the poem, and that the play 'gives a richer understanding of the themes of withdrawal and second chance in the poem.'

As though to breathe were life. Life piled on life
25 Were all too little, and of one to me
Little remains: but every hour is saved
From that eternal silence, something more,
A bringer of new things; and vile it were
For some three suns to store and hoard myself,
30 And this gray spirit yearning in desire
To follow knowledge like a sinking star,
Beyond the utmost bound of human thought.

This is my son, mine own Telemachus,
To whom I leave the sceptre and the isle –
35 Well-loved of me, discerning to fulfil
This labour, by slow prudence to make mild
A rugged people, and through soft degrees
Subdue them to the useful and the good.
Most blameless is he, centred in the sphere

24] As though to live were all the end of life. *H.MS 1st reading*; As though to live were life. Little of life *H.MS*. J. H. Buckley (p. 267) quotes 'Would I could pile fresh life on life', in *Life*, a poem on mortality beginning 'Why suffers human life so soon eclipse' (I 321).

25] Not *H.MS*; Were all too little. Of one life to me *Heath MS 1st reading, T.MS*.

26] Little of life *H.MS 1st reading, deleted*; Remains, but every hour is something more *H.MS*.

27] Not *H.MS*.

28. *vile it were*] this were vile *H.MS*.

29. *store and hoard*] hoard and save *H.MS*.

30–2. Leggett (see headnote) compares *Childe Harold* III xlii: 'There is a fire / And motion of the Soul which will not dwell / In its own narrow being, but aspire / Beyond the fitting medium of desire'.

30. *gray spirit*] old heart yet *H.MS, Heath MS 1st reading, T.MS 1st reading*. F. J. Rowe and W. T. Webb, in their *Selections* (1888), described the syntax as 'absolute case'; T. wrote: 'No. The accusative after *store* etc.' (*Lincoln*). (H. T. confusingly notes: 'accusative absolute'.)

31–2. To be found verbatim in a draft (1833) of *Tiresias*, where they formed párt of the opening lines (*T.Nbk 15*). Cp. *The Lover's Tale* i 50 ∧ 1: 'O'er long loud waters, like a sinking star'. Cary's Dante has 'following the track / Of Phoebus', and 'virtue to pursue and knowledge high' (see headnote). Duncan compares Boyd's translation: 'I saw the sinking barriers of the west' (xviii 2), and 'Till ev'ry well-known star beneath the deep / Declin'd the radiant head' (xx 2–3, different from Dante).

33–42] *Added to H.MS*.

33. *mine own*] my child *H.MS*.

39. *Most*] *Added in T.MS*.

39–40] Decent and blameless is he, not to fail *H.MS deleted but without the*

40 Of common duties, decent not to fail
In offices of tenderness, and pay
Meet adoration to my household gods,
When I am gone. He works his work, I mine.

There lies the port; the vessel puffs her sail:
45 There gloom the dark broad seas. My mariners,
Souls that have toiled, and wrought, and thought with me—
That ever with a frolic welcome took
The thunder and the sunshine, and opposed
Free hearts, free foreheads—you and I are old;
50 Old age hath yet his honour and his toil;
Death closes all: but something ere the end,
Some work of noble note, may yet be done,
Not unbecoming men that strove with Gods.
The lights begin to twinkle from the rocks:
55 The long day wanes: the slow moon climbs: the deep
Moans round with many voices. Come, my friends,
'Tis not too late to seek a newer world.

revision.   *decent*: having a sense of what is fitting. Culler (pp. 95–6) notes the connotations 'of ancient political wisdom, of Greek and Roman discussions of justice and the state', in Ulysses' terms here in ll. 33–43.
42. Meet] Just *H.MS.*
43] Not *H.MS*, Heath *MS*; . . . gone. That work is his *T.MS 1st reading*; He works his work. I mine. All this is just. *T.MS.*
44. the vessel] yon vessel *H.MS 1st reading.*
45. :There gloom] Beyond *H.MS.*
47–9] My mariners, though I and you are old *H.MS.*
48–9] The thunder and the sunshine—we are old; Heath *MS*, *T.MS 1st reading.*
51 ∧ *2*] Not all unworthy of heroic souls *added as H.MS 1st reading*; [l. 53] *H.MS.*
53] *See previous note.*
54–7] Not *H.MS.*
55. D. Bush, *Major British Writers* (1959) ii 396, remarks that 'Homeric voyages commonly begin in the evening; here the accent is on the evening of life.' Compare Cary's Dante: 'To the dawn / Our poop we turn'd', where Ulysses' account of his fatal voyage goes on to mention the moon and the stars.
57. J. J. M. Tobin compares *tellure nova*, Horace's *Odes* I vii 25–31, Teucer's address to his comrades: 'Teucer is struggling to overcome the despair occasioned by a double loss: that of Ajax his (half-)brother by death in battle and of Telamon his father by rejection. This double loss brings Teucer closer even than Ulysses to Tennyson who had lost Hallam, his more than brother, in 1833 and his troubled and troubling father in 1831' (*Notes & Queries* ccxxi, 1976, 395).

Push off, and sitting well in order smite
The sounding furrows; for my purpose holds
60 To sail beyond the sunset, and the baths
Of all the western stars, until I die.
It may be that the gulfs will wash us down:
It may be we shall touch the Happy Isles,
And see the great Achilles, whom we knew.
65 Though much is taken, much abides; and though
We are not now that strength which in old days
Moved earth and heaven; that which we are, we are;
One equal temper of heroic hearts,
Made weak by time and fate, but strong in will
70 To strive, to seek, to find, and not to yield.

[1833. *Tithon*–see *p. 992*]

58–9. Translating, as T. noted, a Homeric commonplace: ἑξῆς δ᾽ ἑζόμενοι
πολιὴν ἅλα τύπτον ἐρετμοῖς (*Odyssey* iv 580 etc).
59. *my . . . holds*] I purpose now *H.MS 1st reading.*
60–61. Adapting *Odyssey* v 270–5:
αὐτὰρ ὁ πηδαλίῳ ἰθύνετο τεχνηέντως / ἥμενος, οὐδέ οἱ ὕπνος ἐπὶ
βλεφάροισιν ἔπιπτεν / Πληιάδας τ᾽ ἐσορῶντι καὶ ὀψὲ δύοντα
Βοώτην / ῎Αρκτον θ᾽, ἣν καὶ ῎Αμαξαν ἐπίκλησιν καλέουσιν. / ἥ τ᾽
αὐτοῦ στρέφεται καί τ᾽ ᾽Ωρίωνα δοκεύει, / οἴη δ᾽ ἄμμορός ἐστι
λοετρῶν ᾽Ωκεανοῖο·
(Odysseus 'watched the Pleiads, and late-setting Bootes, and the Bear,
which men also call the Wain, which ever circles where it is and watches
Orion, and alone has no part in the baths of Ocean.')
62–5] Not *H.MS.*
63. The Isles of the Blest were thought to lie beyond the Pillars of Hercules
(Gibraltar), and it is beyond the Pillars that Dante's Ulysses urges his com-
panions to sail with him.
65–6. Leggett compares *Childe Harold* III vii: ' 'Tis too late! / Yet am I
changed; though still enough the same / In strength to bear what Time
cannot abate'. (Cp. l. 57 above.)
66. *that . . . days*] the men that in one night *H.MS 1st reading*; that strength
that [which *Heath MS*] in one night *H.MS, Heath MS.*
66–9. Recalling Hallam's *To J.M.G.* [James Milnes Gaskell], written May
1829 and printed 1830 (Motter, p. 47): 'We are not as we were . . . / We
are not as we were: our silent tombs / Shall have us not, till we have drunk
our fill / Of a new glorious joy, restoring heart and will!' Cp. ll. 6–7
above.
67. *Moved . . . heaven*] Swathed Troy with flame *H.MS, Heath MS.*
68] Not *H.MS.*

225 The Epic [Morte d'Arthur]

Published *1842*; among 'English Idyls'. Written after 1835 (FitzGerald), probably 1837–8, judging by the references to skating and geology (*Mem.* i 150, 162 – noted by W. C. DeVane). The draft in *H.Lpr 53* is watermarked 1838. This frame for *Morte d'Arthur* (both introduction and conclusion – see *p. 163*) did not accompany the poem in T.'s trial-edition of *1842* (T.J. Wise, *Bibliography of Tennyson*, i 77). For Leigh Hunt's strictures on T.'s framing, see *Godiva* (II 171). FitzGerald says that it was added to *Morte d'Arthur* 'to anticipate or excuse the "faint Homeric echoes"', and 'to give a reason for telling an old-world [Fairy-] tale'; he compares the framework of *The Day-Dream* (*p. 168*). It hints at T.'s ambitions for an epic on Arthur, though the *Morte* was to be the last, not the penultimate, book (l. 41). The germ of such an introduction was probably *Morte d'Arthur 225*, *Fitzwilliam MS* (*p. 161*): 'Before the eyes of ladies thrice as fair / As those that win the love of modern men.' T. says: 'Mrs Browning wanted me to continue this: she has put my answer in *Aurora Leigh*.'

    At Francis Allen's on the Christmas-eve, –
    The game of forfeits done – the girls all kissed
    Beneath the sacred bush and past away –
    The parson Holmes, the poet Everard Hall,
5   The host, and I sat round the wassail-bowl,
    Then half-way ebbed: and there we held a talk,
    How all the old honour had from Christmas gone,
    Or gone, or dwindled down to some odd games
    In some odd nooks like this; till I, tired out
10 With cutting eights that day upon the pond,
    Where, three times slipping from the outer edge,
    I bumped the ice into three several stars,
    Fell in a doze; and half-awake I heard
    The parson taking wide and wider sweeps,
15 Now harping on the church-commissioners,
    Now hawking at Geology and schism;
    Until I woke, and found him settled down

¶ *225.1*] *H. Lpr 53 begins with its draft of ll. 35–8 (see below), and then returns to the opening.*
6–13. Cp. *Edwin Morris 68*, MS:
      He left his episode and on he went
    Like one that cuts an eight upon the ice
    Returning on himself.
15. An inquiry was set up in 1835; the Ecclesiastical Commissioners Act was passed in 1836, and revised in 1840–1.

Upon the general decay of faith
Right through the world, 'at home was little left,
20   And none abroad: there was no anchor, none,
To hold by.' Francis, laughing, clapt his hand
On Everard's shoulder, with 'I hold by him.'
'And I,' quoth Everard, 'by the wassail-bowl.'
'Why yes,' I said, 'we knew your gift that way
25   At college: but another which you had,
I mean of verse (for so we held it then),
What came of that?' 'You know,' said Frank, 'he
      burnt
His epic, his King Arthur, some twelve books'–
And then to me demanding why? 'Oh, sir,
30   He thought that nothing new was said, or else
Something so said 'twas nothing–that a truth
Looks freshest in the fashion of the day:
God knows: he has a mint of reasons: ask.
It pleased *me* well enough.' 'Nay, nay,' said Hall,
35   'Why take the style of those heroic times?
For nature brings not back the Mastodon,
Nor we those times; and why should any man
Remodel models? these twelve books of mine
Were faint Homeric echoes, nothing-worth,

27–8] *1850*; . . . he flung / His epic of King Arthur in the fire!' *1842–8*. Cp. the
note to Pope's *Dunciad*: 'The first sketch of this poem was snatch'd from the
fire by Dr. Swift, who persuaded his friend to proceed in it' (see ll. 40–42
below).
32 ∧ 3] Old things are gone: we are wiser than our Sires. *MS*. Incorporated
in *Love thou* 72: 'That we are wiser than our sires'.
35–8] *MS has two drafts. The first was intended to open the poem*:

Why, what you ask–if any writer now
May take the style of some heroic age
Gone like the mastodon–nay, why should he
Remodel models rather than the life?
Yet this belief was lately half-unhinged
At Edward Allen's–on the Christmas Eve . . .

The second draft follows l. 34:

You scarce have hit the nail upon the head.
Nor yet had I. No doubt some modern lights,
Indeed the rising suns of their own times,
Have touched the distance into fresh results.
I had not done it. Those twelve books of mine

38] *1845*;   Remodel models rather than the life?
And these twelve books of mine (to speak the truth) *1842–3*

40   Mere chaff and draff, much better burnt.' 'But I,'
    Said Francis, 'picked the eleventh from this hearth
    And have it: keep a thing, its use will come.
    I hoard it as a sugar-plum for Holmes.'
    He laughed, and I, though sleepy, like a horse
45   That hears the corn-bin open, pricked my ears;
    For I remembered Everard's college fame
    When we were Freshmen: then at my request
    He brought it; and the poet little urged,
    But with some prelude of disparagement,
50   Read, mouthing out his hollow oes and aes,
    Deep-chested music, and to this result.

226 Morte d'Arthur

Published *1842*. Written 1833–4 (*Mem.* i 129, 138, and *Heath MS*), under the shock of Arthur Hallam's death, the news of which was sent to T. on 1 Oct. 1833. Cp. *Merlin and the Gleam* 77–80: 'Arthur had vanished / I knew not whither, / The king who loved me, / And cannot die.' R. J. Tennant wrote to T., 30 Sept. 1834: 'You promised to send me your Mort d'Arthur if you could get it written out' (*Letters* i 119). T. wrote to Spedding, early Oct. 1834: 'I cannot write the Suicide for you – tis too long, nor Mort d'Arthur (which I myself think the best thing I have managed lately) for tis likewise too long' (*Letters* i 125). On 16 Oct. 1834, Hallam's sister Ellen noted the visit of T.'s sister Emily: 'My dear Emily read to me this morning a little poem of Alfred's – a kind of ballad upon the death of King Arthur', Martin (p. 195) comments: 'If this was the *Morte d'Arthur*, the description is a strange one'.

Text. There are two drafts in *T.Nbk 17* (*T.MS A* and *B*). In Fitzwilliam Museum, there is an early MS, not in T.'s hand, which is apparently earlier than *Heath MS*, itself earlier than *Hn MS* (HM 1320) which breaks off at l. 180. All variants from *T.MS* and *Heath MS* are given below, plus all the significant variants from *Fitzwilliam* and *Huntington*. The poem is T.'s first

45] *MS adds*:
        For having lately met with Everard Hall,
        I marvelled what an arch the brain had built
        Above his ear and what a settled mind
        Tempered the peaceful light of hazel eyes
        Observing all things.

T. incorporated these lines as *The Ante-Chamber* 10–14 (I 550), where they almost certainly describe Arthur Hallam.
50. 'This is something as A.T. read' (FitzGerald).

major Arthurian work, later incorporated in full into *Idylls of the King* as *The Passing of Arthur* (1869), when it was preceded by 169 lines and followed by 29 lines. Cp. *The Palace of Art* 105–8, *1832* text: 'Or that deepwounded child of Pendragon / Mid misty woods on sloping greens / Dozed in the valley of Avilion, / Tended by crownèd queens.' It is based closely on Malory's *Morte d'Arthur* xxi 4–5. T. seems to have used the 3 vol. edition of 1816 (*Lincoln*; and *Letters* i 99*n*), which is quoted throughout below, with Caxton's numbering added in square brackets. The critical implications of T.'s adaptations of Malory are discussed by W. Nash, *Cambridge Quarterly* vi (1975) 326–49. T.'s note refers also to Geoffrey of Monmouth and Walter Map. See R. S. Loomis, *The Development of Arthurian Romance* (1963). Paden (pp. 80–88) argues that 'the narrative of Malory was suffused with and heightened by connotations drawn' from G. S. Faber's *Origin of Pagan Idolatry* (1816). Faber's account of Helio-Arkite mythology implied 'that the legend of Arthur's death is a veiled but unmistakable account of a death of the transmigrating Great Father'. T. later owned Faber's *Horae Mosaicae* (1818 edn, but with advertisements dated March 1850), and *The Difficulties of Infidelity* (1833 edn, but probably acquired between 1845 and 1850); A. Day, *Notes and Queries* n.s. xxvii (1980) 520–22. Paden links details of setting and imagery; e.g. the change from Malory's death in summer to winter; 'the mighty bones of ancient men' (l. 47), suggesting the tribe of Cush who brought the Helio-Arkite mysteries to Britain; the symbolism of the Round Table (l. 234); and the dying swan (l. 266). All of these have Faberian associations. The poem is introduced in *The Epic* as including 'Homeric echoes'. Among these may be noted: set epithets, and set lines introducing and closing speeches; the words of one speaker being quoted by another; repetition of words and lines; and soliloquies.

Criticism. John Sterling's adverse comments on *Morte d'Arthur* in *QR* discouraged T. from continuing with his epic (E. F. Shannon, *Tennyson and the Reviewers*, 1952, p. 91). Sterling said that the poem's 'inferiority' was not compensated for 'by any stronger human interest'; 'the miraculous legend of "Excalibur" does not come very near to us, and as reproduced by any modern writer must be a mere ingenious exercise of fancy'. Shannon (p. 95) also quotes Leigh Hunt's criticisms in the *Church of England Quarterly Review*: 'It treats the modes and feelings of one generation in the style of another, always a fatal thing, unless it be reconciled with something of self-banter in the course of the poem itself, or the mixture of light with grave'. On the relations between *Morte d'Arthur, In Memoriam, Ode on the Death of the Duke of Wellington,* and *Idylls of the King* (each honouring an Arthur), see C. Y. Lang, *Tennyson's Arthurian Psycho-drama* (1983).

So all day long the noise of battle rolled
Among the mountains by the winter sea;
Until King Arthur's table, man by man,
Had fallen in Lyonnesse about their Lord,
5 King Arthur: then, because his wound was deep,
The bold Sir Bedivere uplifted him,
Sir Bedivere, the last of all his knights,
And bore him to a chapel nigh the field,
A broken chancel with a broken cross,
10 That stood on a dark strait of barren land.
On one side lay the Ocean, and on one
Lay a great water, and the moon was full.

Then spake King Arthur to Sir Bedivere:

¶ 226. *1–5*] After that [the *T.MS A*] battle, where King Arthur lost
The flower of all the Earth, his knights, which made
'The table round', because his wound was deep, *T.MS A, Heath MS*
flower of all the Earth] honour of the world *T.MS A 1st reading.*
1. One of the 'Homeric echoes' mentioned in *The Epic* 39: *Iliad* vi 1, xvii
384. Cp. T.'s translation: 'All day the men contend in grievous war',
Achilles 9.
4. Lyonnesse: 'the country of legend that lay between Cornwall and the
Scilly Islands' (T.), described in *The Passing of Arthur* (p. 963).
5–12. Malory III clxvi [xxi]: 'And the noble King Arthur fell in a swoon
to the earth. And there he swooned often times. And Sir Lucan and Sir
Bedivere oftentimes heaved him up, and so weakly they led him between
them both unto a little chapel not far from the sea side.'
8. nigh] from *T.MS A 1st reading.*
9. chancel] chapel *T.MS A 1st reading.*
13. spake] spoke *T.MS A.*
13 ∧ 14]   'Well said old Merlin ere his time was come,
"Experience never closes all-in-all
But there is always something to be learnt
Even in the gate of death". So clear a dream –
Which I neglected with my waking mind –
Came yesternight – Sir Gawain as he lived –
Most like Sir Gawain in his eyes and hair.
Bare-headed, circled with a gracious light,
Seven ladies, like the seven rainy stars,
For whom he fought and whom he saved from shame –
Beautiful, tearful: and he spoke and said
"Go thou not forth tomorrow to the fight" –
But I went forth, and fought it, and lie here.'
                              T.MS B, Heath MS, Fitzwilliam MS

'The sequel of today unsolders all
15   The goodliest fellowship of famous knights
     Whereof this world holds record. Such a sleep
     They sleep – the men I loved. I think that we
     Shall never more, at any future time,
     Delight our souls with talk of knightly deeds,
20   Walking about the gardens and the halls
     Of Camelot, as in the days that were.
     I perish by this people which I made, –
     Though Merlin sware that I should come again
     To rule once more – but let what will be, be,
25   I am so deeply smitten through the helm
     That without help I cannot last till morn.
     Thou therefore take my brand Excalibur,
     Which was my pride: for thou rememberest how
     In those old days, one summer noon, an arm

These MSS have these lines in brackets, T.'s tentative sign for deletion.
This draft of the dream of Gawain's ghost is based on Malory xxi; T. was
to adapt it for *The Passing of Arthur* (*p. 961*).

14] 'The issue of this day unsolders quite *T.MS A*.

14–17. Malory III cl [xx 9]: 'For I have now lost the fairest fellowship of
noble knights that ever held christian King together.'

16. this] the *T.MSS, Heath MS*.

17–46] Not *T.MS B (page cut away)*.

17–18] They sleep, I thi [*del.*] that we, I think, shall nevermore *T.MS A 1st
reading*.

17. loved . . . we] loved that we, I think, *T.MS A*.

20. about] among *T.MS A, Heath MS*.

22–4] Not *T.MS A, Heath MS; added in Huntington MS, which had as first
reading*:

            And I that taught this people all I know
            Have overlived myself, and overlived
            The grateful heart, and perish by their hands.

23. Malory III clxx [xxi 7]: 'Some men yet say in many parts of England
that King Arthur is not dead, but by the will of our Lord in another place.
And men say that he will come again.'

27. brand] sword *T.MS A 1st reading*.

28–33. Malory I xxiii [i 25]: 'So they rode till they came to a lake, which
was a fair water, and abroad [a broad], and in the midst of the lake King
Arthur was ware of an arm, clothed in white samite, that held a fair
sword in the hand.'

29] In the old days, one summer noon, there rose [came *T.MS A*] *T.MS A,
Heath MS*.

30   Rose up from out the bosom of the lake,
      Clothed in white samite, mystic, wonderful,
      Holding the sword – and how I rowed across
      And took it, and have worn it, like a king:
      And, wheresoever I am sung or told
35   In aftertime, this also shall be known:
      But now delay not: take Excalibur,
      And fling him far into the middle mere:
      Watch what thou seëst, and lightly bring me word.'

      To him replied the bold Sir Bedivere:
40   'It is not meet, Sir King, to leave thee thus,
      Aidless, alone, and smitten through the helm.
      A little thing may harm a wounded man.
      Yet I thy hest will all perform at full,
      Watch what I see, and lightly bring thee word.'

45   So saying, from the ruined shrine he stept
      And in the moon athwart the place of tombs,

---

30. Rose ... the] From forth the peaceful *T.MS A*; An arm from out the Heath *MS*.

31] An arm, clothed in white samite, wonderful *T.MS A*.

35. aftertime] after years *T.MS A*.

36–44. Malory III clxvii [xxi] (subsequent quotations from Malory, unless noted otherwise, run on consecutively without omissions): '"Therefore take you Excalibur, my good sword, and go with it unto yonder water side, and when thou comest there, I charge thee throw my sword into that water, and come again and tell me what thou shalt see there." "My lord," said Sir Bedivere, "your command shall be done, and lightly bring you word again."'

37. H. A. Mason notes Byron's use of the Latinism (*medium in aequor*), *Childe Harold* II xxix: 'the middle deep'.

43. Yet I] But yet *T.MS A.*   *all*] I *T.MS A.*

44. thee] the *Heath MS*; thee *T.MSS, Fitzwilliam MS, HnMS*.

45–65. Malory: 'And so Sir Bedivere departed, and by the way he beheld that noble sword, where the pomel and the haft were all of precious stones, and then he said to himself: "If I throw this rich sword into the water, thereof shall never come good, but harm and loss." And then Sir Bedivere hid Excalibur under a tree, and as soon as he might he came again unto King Arthur, and said he had been at the water, and had thrown the sword into the water.'

45. stept] *T.MS A 1st reading*; went *T.MS A, Heath MS*.

46. And ... athwart] Into the moonlight: through *T.MS A 1st reading*; And in the moonlight through *T.MS A*. Mason notes Southey, *Thalaba* IX xxxiii: 'And she hath reach'd the Place of Tombs'.

Where lay the mighty bones of ancient men,
Old knights, and over them the sea-wind sang
Shrill, chill, with flakes of foam. He, stepping down
50 By zig-zag paths, and juts of pointed rock,
Came on the shining levels of the lake.

There drew he forth the brand Excalibur,
And o'er him, drawing it, the winter moon,
Brightening the skirts of a long cloud, ran forth
55 And sparkled keen with frost against the hilt:
For all the haft twinkled with diamond sparks,
Myriads of topaz-lights, and jacinth-work
Of subtlest jewellery. He gazed so long
That both his eyes were dazzled, as he stood,
60 This way and that dividing the swift mind,
In act to throw: but at the last it seemed
Better to leave Excalibur concealed

48–50] Heroes–and stepping down from rock to rock T.MS A 1st reading;
Heroes and over [ll. 48–50] . . . rock T.MS A 2nd reading, with By] Through
(in l. 50).
51. Came on] He reached T.MS A 1st reading.   levels: cp. The Lover's Tale iii
4: 'the rippling levels of the lake'.
52. There] T.MS A 3rd reading, T.MS B; Then T.MS A 1st and 2nd reading,
Heath MS.
53–5]   And over him the frosty moon ran out
         So keenly, that he marvelled, though he bore
         A hard unbroken spirit in his breast: T.MS A 1st reading
54. Mason notes Paradise Lost xi 878:. 'The fluid skirts of that same watrie
Cloud'.
56. sparks] 1855; studs 1842–53.
57–8] Or glowed with topaz-stone. He gazed so long T.MS A 1st reading.
59. stood] mused T.MS A 1st reading.
60. T. compares Aeneid iv 285: atque animum nunc huc celerem, nunc dividit illuc
('And now hither, now thither, he swiftly throws his mind'). In Dryden's
translation (iv 411): 'This way, and that, he turns his anxious Mind' (noted
by Mason). From Iliad i 188: εν δε οι ητορ .... διανδιχα μερμηριξεν ('and
within his shaggy breast his heart was divided in counsel'). Cp. The Lover's
Tale iii 49–50 n, MS: 'dividing the swift mind/That way and this'. Turner
(p. 78) notes: 'Aeneas, when in doubt whether to obey the gods and throw
over Dido...both men are torn between obedience to a higher power and
attraction to physical beauty (Aeneas is actually wearing a sword, adorned
like Excalibur with jewels, which Dido has given him).'
61. but] and T.MS A 1st reading. G. G. Loane compares Pope's Iliad iv 570:
'In act to throw; but cautious, looked around' (Echoes in Tennyson, 1928,
p. 6).

There in the many-knotted waterflags,
That whistled stiff and dry about the marge.
65   So strode he back slow to the wounded King.

Then spake King Arthur to Sir Bedivere:
'Hast thou performed my mission which I gave?
What is it thou hast seen? or what hast heard?'

And answer made the bold Sir Bedivere:
70   'I heard the ripple washing in the reeds,
And the wild water lapping on the crag.'

To whom replied King Arthur, faint and pale:
'Thou hast betrayed thy nature and thy name,
Not rendering true answer, as beseemed
75   Thy fëalty, nor like a noble knight:
For surer sign had followed, either hand,
Or voice, or else a motion of the mere.
This is a shameful thing for men to lie.
Yet now, I charge thee, quickly go again
80   As thou art lief and dear, and do the thing
I bad thee, watch, and lightly bring me word'.

Then went Sir Bedivere the second time

63. *There in*] Amongst *T.MS A 1st reading.*
64] *Not T.MS A 1st reading.*
66–81. Malory: '"What sawest thou there?" said the King. "Sir," said he,
"I saw nothing but waves and wind." "That is untruly said of thee,"
said King Arthur, "therefore go thou lightly and do my command, as
thou art to me life [lief] and dear, spare not but throw it in."'
66. *spake*] spoke *T.MSS, Heath MS.*
71. *lapping*] wapping *T.MSS, Heath MS.* The archaic word is from Malory;
see ll. 113–32n.
73] *Not T.MS A.*
74. *Not...answer,*] Thou hast not spoken truly *T.MS A.*
76–7] *Not T.MS A 1st reading.*
78. *This*] It *T.MS A 1st reading.*
78 ∧ 9] For he betrays his nature and his Lord. *T.MS A 1st reading.*
79. *Yet*] But *T.MS A.*
80. *thing*] deed *T.MS A 1st reading.*
82–112. Malory: 'Then Sir Bedivere returned again, and took the sword
in his hand; and then he thought it sin and shame to throw away that
noble sword. And so after he hid the sword, and returned again, and told
to the King that he had been at the water, and done his command.'
82. *the*] a *Heath MS.*

Across the ridge, and paced beside the mere,
Counting the dewy pebbles, fixed in thought;
85 But when he saw the wonder of the hilt,
How curiously and strangely chased, he smote
His palms together, and he cried aloud,

'And if indeed I cast the brand away,
Surely a precious thing, one worthy note,
90 Should thus be lost for ever from the earth,
Which might have pleased the eyes of many men.
What good should follow this, if this were done?
What harm, undone? deep harm to disobey,
Seeing obedience is the bond of rule.
95 Were it well to obey then, if a king demand
An act unprofitable, against himself?
The King is sick, and knows not what he does.
What record, or what relic of my lord
Should be to aftertime, but empty breath
100 And rumours of a doubt? but were this kept,
Stored in some treasure-house of mighty kings,
Some one might show it at a joust of arms,
Saying, "King Arthur's sword, Excalibur,
Wrought by the lonely maiden of the Lake.
105 Nine years she wrought it, sitting in the deeps

83] *1853; not 1842–51.*
84] With eyes, counting the stones, fixt in resolve *T.MS A.*
88. *'And if indeed*] 'Ay me! and should *T.MSS, Heath MS.*
92–7] This done what good should follow? harm, undone. *T.MS A.*
93. *deep harm*] 'Twere well *T.MS B 1st reading.*
93 ∧ 4] And yet in disobedience lies great harm, *T.MS B del.*
94. *Seeing*] Because *T.MS B, Heath MS.*
95. *demand*] require *T.MS B 1st reading.*
96. *unprofitable*] which profits not *T.MS B 1st reading.*
97] A question to be answered without fear. *T.MSS (added), Heath MS.*
100. *but were this*] Say this were *T.MS B, Heath MS.*
104. *lonely maiden*] prudent Lady *T.MS, Heath MS.* The friendly sorceress of
Malory I xxiii [i 25, out of the sequence]: '"That is the *Lady of the Lake,*"
said Merlin, "and within that lake is a rock, and therein is as fair a place
[palace] as any is on earth, and richly beseen."'
105–6. Cp. Pope's *Iliad* xviii 468–72, where Vulcan is about to make the
shield of Achilles: 'Chains, bracelets, pendants, all their toys I wrought. /
Nine years kept secret in the dark abode, / Secure I lay concealed from man
and God. / Deep in a caverned rock my days were led; / The rushing
ocean murmured o'er my head.'
105. *sitting in the*] in the silent *T.MS A.*

Upon the hidden bases of the hills."
So might some old man speak in the aftertime
To all the people, winning reverence.
But now much honour and much fame were lost.'
110   So spake he, clouded with his own conceit,
And hid Excalibur the second time,
And so strode back slow to the wounded King.

Then spoke King Arthur, breathing heavily:
'What is it thou hast seen? or what hast heard?'
115   And answer made the bold Sir Bedivere:
'I heard the water lapping on the crag,
And the long ripple washing in the reeds.'

To whom replied King Arthur, much in wrath:
'Ah, miserable and unkind, untrue,
120   Unknightly, traitor-hearted! Woe is me!
Authority forgets a dying king,
Laid widowed of the power in his eye
That bowed the will. I see thee what thou art,
For thou, the latest-left of all my knights,
125   In whom should meet the offices of all,
Thou wouldst betray me for the precious hilt;

---

106. Upon] And by *T.MS A.*   *hidden . . . hills*] secret . . . rocks *T.MS A 1st reading. bases of the hills*: incorporated from *The Lover's Tale* ii 120. M. Y. Mason compares Charles Lyell, *Principles of Geology*, chap. xvi: 'the sea washed the base of the hills' (*VP* x, 1972, 175).
110. spake] spoke *T.MSS. conceit*: fancy.
113. breathing heavily] drawing thicker breath *T.MSS, Heath MS.*
113–32. Malory: '"What saw ye there," said the King. "Sir," said he, "I saw nothing but the water wap and the waves wan." "Ah traitor, untrue," said King Arthur, "now hast thou betrayed me two times, who would have wend [weened] that thou hast been unto me so self [lief] and dear, and thou art named a noble Knight, and wouldest betray me for the rich sword. But now, go again lightly, for thy long tarrying putteth me in great jeopardy of my life, for I have taken cold. And but if thou do as I command thee, and if ever I may see thee, I shall slay thee with mine own hands, for thou wouldest for my rich sword see me dead."'
116. lapping] wapping *T.MSS, Heath MS.*
118. much in wrath] red with scorn *T.MS A*; filled with scorn *T.MS B, Heath MS.*
120. traitor-] sordid- *T.MS A.*   *Woe . . . me!*] Now I see *T.MS A 1st reading.*
121. forgets] deserts *T.MS A.*
122–3] Not *T.MS A.*

Either from lust of gold, or like a girl
Valuing the giddy pleasure of the eyes.
Yet, for a man may fail in duty twice,
130 And the third time may prosper, get thee hence:
But, if thou spare to fling Excalibur,
I will arise and slay thee with my hands.'

Then quickly rose Sir Bedivere, and ran,
And, leaping down the ridges lightly, plunged
135 Among the bulrush-beds, and clutched the sword,
And strongly wheeled and threw it. The great brand
Made lightnings in the splendour of the moon,
And flashing round and round, and whirled in an
        arch,
Shot like a streamer of the northern morn,
140 Seen where the moving isles of winter shock
By night, with noises of the northern sea.

127. *from*] for *T.MS A.*
128. Cp. Horace, *Epistles* II i 188: *oculos et gaudia vana.*
129. *Yet*] But *T.MS A 1st reading.*
131. *spare*] fail *T.MS A.*
132. Gray (pp. 11, 139) notes the 'Biblical resonance', e.g. *2 Sam.* xvii 1: 'I will arise and pursue after David.'
133. *quickly*] lightly *T.MS A.*
133–66. Malory: 'Then Sir Bedivere departed, and went to the sword, and lightly took it up, and went to the water side, and there he bound the girdle about the hilt. And then he threw the sword into the water as far as he might, and there came an arm and an hand above the water, and met it and caught it, and so shook it thrice and brandished. And then the hand vanished away with the sword in the water. So Sir Bedivere came again to the King and told him what he had seen. "Alas," said the King, "help me from hence, for I dread me I have tarried over long."'
134] And, springing goatlike down the ledges, plunged *T.MS A.*
135. *Among*] Into *T.MS A 1st reading*; Amongst *T.MS A.* *bulrush-beds*] withered sedge *T.MS A.* *clutched*] took *T.MS A 1st reading.*
136. *wheeled and*] wheeling *T.MS A.*
136–61] *T.MS B has all but the opening words cut away.*
137] Not *T.MS A.*
138. *And*] Spun *T.MS A.*
139] Sunk, whizzing like a flight of fiery stones *T.MS A 1st reading;* Whizzed like a flying noise of fiery stones. *T.MS A.*
140. *isles*] thrones *Heath MS.* Cp. Thomas Gisborne, on the Arctic: 'With shock of floating isles', *Walks in a Forest* (1794). There was a copy of Gisborne at Somersby (*Lincoln*).
140–2] Shot [Flung *1st reading*] from the moon. So flasht Excalibur. *T.MS A.*

So flashed and fell the brand Excalibur:
But ere he dipt the surface, rose an arm
Clothed in white samite, mystic, wonderful,
145 And caught him by the hilt, and brandished him
Three times, and drew him under in the mere.
And lightly went the other to the King.

Then spoke King Arthur, drawing thicker breath:
'Now see I by thine eyes that this is done.
150 Speak out: what is it thou hast heard, or seen?'

And answer made the bold Sir Bedivere:
'Sir King, I closed mine eyelids, lest the gems
Should blind my purpose, for I never saw,
Nor shall see, here or elsewhere, till I die,
155 Not though I live three lives of mortal men,
So great a miracle as yonder hilt.
Then with both hands I flung him, wheeling him;
But when I looked again, behold an arm,
Clothed in white samite, mystic, wonderful,
160 That caught him by the hilt, and brandished him
Three times, and drew him under in the mere.'

And answer made King Arthur, breathing hard:
'My end draws nigh; 'tis time that I were gone.
Make broad thy shoulders to receive my weight,
165 And bear me to the margin; yet I fear
My wound hath taken cold, and I shall die.'

So saying, from the pavement he half rose,
Slowly, with pain, reclining on his arm,

Cp. this simile with Scott's *Lay of the Last Minstrel* II viii (of which there was a copy at Somersby, *Lincoln*): 'And red and bright the streamers light / Were dancing in the glowing north. / So had he seen, in fair Castile, / The youth in glittering squadrons start, / Sudden the flying jennet wheel, / And hurl the unexpected dart. / He knew, by the streamers that shot so bright, / That spirits were riding the northern light.'

147. And] So T.MS A.

148] Then spoke the wounded Arthur faint and pale: T.MS A, Heath MS.

150] What is it thou hast seen? or what hast heard? T.MS A, Heath MS.

151. And answer made] To whom replied T.MS A, Heath MS.

155. T. compares *Odyssey* iii 245, τρὶς γὰρ δή μίν φασιν ἀνάξασθαι γένε’ ἀνδρῶν. ('For thrice, men say, has he been King for a generation of men.')

163] Not T.MS A.

167–203. Malory: 'Then Sir Bedivere took King Arthur upon his back, and so went with him to the water's side. And when they were at the water's side, even fast by the bank, hoved a little barge, with many fair ladies in it,

And looking wistfully with wide blue eyes
170 As in a picture. Him Sir Bedivere
Remorsefully regarded through his tears,
And would have spoken, but he found not words,
Then took with care, and kneeling on one knee,
O'er both his shoulders drew the languid hands,
175 And rising bore him through the place of tombs.

But, as he walked, King Arthur panted hard,
Like one that feels a nightmare on his bed
When all the house is mute. So sighed the King,
Muttering and murmuring at his ear, 'Quick, quick!
180 I fear it is too late, and I shall die.'
But the other swiftly strode from ridge to ridge,
Clothed with his breath, and looking, as he walked,
Larger than human on the frozen hills.
He heard the deep behind him, and a cry
185 Before. His own thought drove him, like a goad.
Dry clashed his harness in the icy caves
And barren chasms, and all to left and right
The bare black cliff clanged round him, as he based
His feet on juts of slippery crag that rang

and among them all was a Queen, and all they had black hoods, and they
wept and shrieked when they saw King Arthur.'
171–2] Not *T.MS A*; *T.MS B* had the first line, and added the second as did
Heath MS (in *T.'s hand*).
173. Then . . . care] Gently received *T.MS A.*
174–91] *Torn away from T.MS B.*
176–89]   But ever as he went King Arthur breathed
     Against his shoulder heavily like one
     That hath not full an hour left to live.
     So stept he carefully from ledge to ledge
     Wrapt in his breath, and shunning where the rock
     Looked brighter glazed with ice, made firm his foot
     On juts of slippery crag that rang like tin *T.MS A*
177] Like one on whom a dusky nightmare leaps *Fitzwilliam MS.*
183. Larger than human: *humano maior*, like the ghost of Romulus in Ovid,
Fasti ii 503. Cp. *Hark! the dogs howl* 20–21, which is also on the death of
Hallam: 'Larger than human passes by / The shadow of the man I loved.'
Also T.'s projected essay on Ghosts for the Cambridge 'Apostles', quoted
by J. H. Buckley (p. 33): 'Forth issue from the inmost gloom the colossal
Presences of the Past *majores humano*, some as they lived, seemingly
pale with exhaustion and faintly smiling; some as they died in a still
agony . . .' (*H.Nbk* 7).
188. J. Kolb compares Shelley, *Alastor* 86: 'On black bare pointed islets ever
beat.'

190 Sharp-smitten with the dint of armèd heels—
    And on a sudden, lo! the level lake,
    And the long glories of the winter moon.
    Then saw they how there hove a dusky barge,
    Dark as a funeral scarf from stem to stern,
195 Beneath them; and descending they were ware
    That all the decks were dense with stately forms
    Black-stoled, black-hooded, like a dream—by these
    Three Queens with crowns of gold—and from them
        rose
    A cry that shivered to the tingling stars,
200 And, as it were one voice, an agony
    Of lamentation, like a wind, that shrills
    All night in a waste land, where no one comes,
    Or hath come, since the making of the world.

        Then murmured Arthur, 'Place me in the barge,'
205 And to the barge they came. There those three
        Queens

190. *armèd*] mailèd *T.MS A, which breaks off here at the foot of the page (then stubs).*

192. Betty Miller, *Twentieth Century* clxvii (1960) 526, compares Dryden, *Aeneis* i 10: 'And the long Glories of Majestick *Rome*'. Henry Boyd quoted Dryden's line prominently in his translation of Dante (1802), of which a copy was at Somersby (*Lincoln*); Boyd also mentions 'the long glories of his line' (i 97, 102).

194] *Added in T.MS B.*

202. Gray (p. 12) notes 'the potent name of the Queen that Malory has deliberately placed third, the "Queen of the Waste Lands"'.

204–25. Malory: '"Now put me into the barge," said the King. And so he did softly, and there received him three Queens with great mourning, and so these three Queens set him down, and in one of their laps King Arthur laid his head. And then that Queen said: "Ah, dear brother, why have ye tarried so long from me. Alas, this wound on your head hath taken over much cold."'

205–6] And those three Queens received him, weeping wild. *T.MS B, Heath MS.* G. G. Loane (*Echoes in Tennyson,* 1928, p. 5) compares Wordsworth, the death of *Lucy Gray*: 'And to the bridge they came'. Malory III clxix [xxi 6, out of the sequence]: 'Thus was he led away in a barge wherein were three Queens. That one was King Arthur's sister Morgan le Fay; the other was the Queen of Northgalis; and the third was the Queen of the Waste Lands.' T. commented: 'Some say that the three Queens are Faith, Hope, and Charity.... They are three of the noblest of wòmen. They are also those three Graces, but they are much more.'

Put forth their hands, and took the King, and wept.
But she, that rose the tallest of them all
And fairest, laid his head upon her lap,
And loosed the shattered casque, and chafed his hands,
210 And called him by his name, complaining loud,
And dropping bitter tears against his brow
Striped with dark blood: for all his face was white
And colourless, and like the withered moon
Smote by the fresh beam of the springing east;
215 And all his greaves and cuisses dashed with drops
Of onset; and the light and lustrous curls—
That made his forehead like a rising sun
High from the daïs-throne—were parched with dust;
Or, clotted into points and hanging loose,
220 Mixed with the knightly growth that fringed his lips.
So like a shattered column lay the King;
Not like that Arthur who, with lance in rest,
From spur to plume a star of tournament,
Shot through the lists at Camelot, and charged
225 Before the eyes of ladies and of kings.

Then loudly cried the bold Sir Bedivere,
'Ah! my Lord Arthur, whither shall I go?
Where shall I hide my forehead and my eyes?

---

207. *rose*] was *T.MS B 1st reading.*
215. *greaves and cuisses*: armour for shin and thigh.
217. *That*] Which *T.MS B, Heath MS.*
220. *knightly*] stubborn *T.MS B, Heath MS.*
221. B. Richards notes: 'It was traditional to refer to monarchs as columns, e.g. the pattern-poems on Queen Elizabeth as a pillar of state... For the notion of the broken column and the great man see Petrarch: "*Rotta e l'alta Colonna e'l verde lauro*"' (*English Verse 1830–1890,* 1980, p. 86).
222. *Not like*] Unlike *T.MS B 1st reading.*
224] Rapidly galloping at Camelot charged *T.MS B (which also has* charged [?] at Camelot), *Heath MS*; Rapidly galloping in the list, went by *T.MS B 1st reading, Fitzwilliam MS.*
225] Before the eyes of ladies thrice as fair
      As those that win the love of modern men. *T.MS B 1st reading,*
                                                  Fitzwilliam MS.
The germ of *The Epic.*
226–38. Malory: 'And so then they rowed from the land. And Sir Bedivere beheld all these ladies go from him, then Sir Bedivere cried: "Ah, my lord Arthur, what shall become of me now ye go from me, and leave me here alone among mine enemies."'

For now I see the true old times are dead,
230 When every morning brought a noble chance,
And every chance brought out a noble knight.
Such times have been not since the light that led
The holy Elders with the gift of myrrh.
But now the whole ROUND TABLE is dissolved
235 Which was an image of the mighty world;
And I, the last, go forth companionless,
And the days darken round me, and the years,
Among new men, strange faces, other minds.'

And slowly answered Arthur from the barge:
240 'The old order changeth, yielding place to new,
And God fulfils Himself in many ways,
Lest one good custom should corrupt the world.
Comfort thyself: what comfort is in me?
I have lived my life, and that which I have done
245 May He within Himself make pure! but thou,
If thou shouldst never see my face again,
Pray for my soul. More things are wrought by prayer
Than this world dreams of. Wherefore, let thy voice
Rise like a fountain for me night and day.
250 For what are men better than sheep or goats
That nourish a blind life within the brain,
If, knowing God, they lift not hands of prayer
Both for themselves and those who call them friend?
For so the whole round earth is every way

234–5. Malory III 1 [xiv 2, out of the sequence]: 'Also Merlin made the *Round Table* in token of the roundness of the world. For by the *Round Table* is the world signified by right.'
238. Arthur Hallam, to Gladstone, 13 Aug. 1827: 'I have been suffering much from headaches; and sometimes, when in low spirits, anticipate being laid up at some infernal [*AHH* informal] posthouse, among strange faces, and stupid doctors, so as to realise the "rapidi vicinia leti" [Ovid, *Met.* viii 225, "the swift proximity of death"]. If I die, before I see you again, I give you leave to print this in the Morning post, as a marvellous coincidence' (*AHH*, p. 164).
239. *slowly*] clearly *T.MS B 1st reading, Fitzwilliam MS (which accidentally omits* answered).
239–64. Malory: '"Comfort thyself," said King Arthur, "and do as well as thou mayest, for in me is no trust for to trust in, for I will into the vale of Avilion, for to heal me of my grievous wound. And if thou never hear more of me, pray for my soul."'
242. '*e.g.* chivalry, by formalism of habit or by any other means' (T.).
243] *T.MS B had this line 239 ∧ 40 deleted, then here.*
249. *like*] as *T.MS B, Heath MS.*

255 Bound by gold chains about the feet of God.
     But now farewell. I am going a long way
     With these thou seëst – if indeed I go –
     (For all my mind is clouded with a doubt)
     To the island-valley of Avilion;
260 Where falls not hail, or rain, or any snow,
     Nor ever wind blows loudly; but it lies
     Deep-meadowed, happy, fair with orchard-lawns
     And bowery hollows crowned with summer sea,
     Where I will heal me of my grievous wound.'

265 So said he, and the barge with oar and sail
     Moved from the brink, like some full-breasted swan
     That, fluting a wild carol ere her death,
     Ruffles her pure cold plume, and takes the flood
     With swarthy webs. Long stood Sir Bedivere
270 Revolving many memories, till the hull
     Looked one black dot against the verge of dawn,
     And on the mere the wailing died away.

                    [THE EPIC]
     Here ended Hall, and our last light, that long
     Had winked and threatened darkness, flared and fell:
275 At which the Parson, sent to sleep with sound,
     And waked with silence, grunted 'Good!' but we
     Sat rapt: it was the tone with which he read –

255.'My father said that this passage was not, as has been said, suggested by
Iliad viii 19 or by Plato, *Theaetetus* 153' (H.T.).
256–64] Farewell then: I (256); 259; 264: If I may ... *T.MS B 1st reading.*
259. 'From which he will some day return – the Isle of the Blest' (T.).
260–3. T. compares *Odyssey* iv 566ff, and Lucretius iii 18ff; adapted again
as *Lucretius* 104–10 (II 713).
262. *Deep-meadowed*: T. compared Pindar, *Pythian Odes* x 23, and *Iliad* ix
151.
263. T. compares *Odyssey* x 195, νῆσον, τὴν πέρι πόντος ἀπείριτος ἐστ-
εφάνωται ('the island, about which is set as a crown the boundless deep').
265–72. Malory: 'But evermore the Queens and the ladies wept and
shrieked, that it was pity for to hear them. And as soon as Sir Bedivere had
lost sight of the barge, he wept and wailed, and so took the forest, and so
he went all the night.'
267. *fluting*] piping *T.MS B, Heath MS.*
268. *plume*] plumes *T.MS B, Heath MS.*
270. *Revolving*: Miltonic, cp. 'much revolving', *Paradise Lost* iv 31;
deriving from *Aeneid* i 305: *per noctem plurima volvens.*

Perhaps some modern touches here and there
Redeemed it from the charge of nothingness –
280   Or else we loved the man, and prized his work;
I know not: but we sitting, as I said,
The cock crew loud; as at that time of year
The lusty bird takes every hour for dawn:
Then Francis, muttering, like a man ill-used,
285   'There now – that's nothing!' drew a little back,
And drove his heel into the smouldered log,
That sent a blast of sparkles up the flue:
And so to bed; where yet in sleep I seemed
To sail with Arthur under looming shores,
290   Point after point; till on to dawn, when dreams
Begin to feel the truth and stir of day,
To me, methought, who waited with a crowd,
There came a bark that, blowing forward, bore
King Arthur, like a modern gentleman
295   Of stateliest port; and all the people cried,
'Arthur is come again: he cannot die.'
Then those that stood upon the hills behind
Repeated – 'Come again, and thrice as fair;'
And, further inland, voices echoed – 'Come
300   With all good things, and war shall be no more.'
At this a hundred bells began to peal,
That with the sound I woke, and heard indeed
The clear church-bells ring in the Christmas-morn.

[*The Epic*]

282–3. *Hamlet* I i 157–60: 'It faded on the crowing of the cock. / Some say that ever 'gainst that season comes / Wherein our Saviour's birth is celebrated / This bird of dawning singeth all night long.' This passage was quoted in Thomas Keightley's *Fairy Mythology* (1828; 2nd edn, 1833, ii 137), which T. used when working on *Morte d'Arthur* in 1833 (*Mem.* i 129), and later owned (*Lincoln*).

286–7. John Churton Collins compared Dante's *Paradiso* xviii 100–1: '*Poi come nel percuoter de' ciocchi arsi / surgono innumerabili faville.*' ('Then, as when burning logs are struck rise innumerable sparks.') Alongside this, T. wrote '!!!' (*Cornhill*, Jan. 1880, *Lincoln*).

290–1. A traditional belief; cp. Shelley, *Hellas* 122: 'The truth of day lightens upon my dream'. H. A. Mason notes T.'s letter to Milnes, *c.* 21 Dec. 1836: 'the small hours, when dreams are true' (*Letters* i 146).

294. Anticipating the *Dedication* and *Epilogue* of the *Idylls*; cp. l. 225n.

300. H. A. Mason remarks the many Biblical echoes, including *Micah* iv 3: 'neither shall they learn war any more'.

228 'Break, break, break'

Published *1842*. Written in Lincolnshire one spring (*Mem.* i 190), so presumably before early 1837, when the Tennysons left Somersby, and after Sept. 1833, since it is on the death of Arthur Hallam. Probably spring 1834. Cecilia Tennyson recited it on 16 March 1839 (*Blackwood's* clv (1894) 609). Cp. *In Memoriam*, especially for ll. 11–12; and also the lines which H.T. gave as the germ of *In Memoriam*: 'Where is the voice I loved? ah where / Is that dear hand that I would press? / Lo! the broad heavens cold and bare, / The stars that know not my distress!' For these lines (*Mem.* i 107), see *Hark! the dogs howl!* (I 608). Hallam wrote to Gladstone: 'the loss of valuable time, and the constant breaking of the mental energies, like waves, on an immoveable obstacle, cannot but tend to oppress the moral spirit' (28 Feb. 1829; *AHH*, p. 276).

Break, break, break,
    On thy cold gray stones, O Sea!
And I would that my tongue could utter
    The thoughts that arise in me.

5 O well for the fisherman's boy,
    That he shouts with his sister at play!
O well for the sailor lad,
    That he sings in his boat on the bay!

And the stately ships go on
10   To their haven under the hill;
But O for the touch of a vanished hand,
    And the sound of a voice that is still!

Break, break, break,
    At the foot of thy crags, O Sea!
15 But the tender grace of a day that is dead
    Will never come back to me.

234 Sir Galahad

Published *1842*. Written by 19 Sept. 1834 when Spedding told T. he had 'received by Douglas and John Heath divers of your compositions, albeit too few for my appetite: to wit, *Sir Galahad* which enjoys my unlimited admiration ...' (*Letters* i 117; also *Heath MS, Mem.* i 139). T. says 'Sir Galahad who was intended for something of a male counterpart to St Agnes' (*Letters* i 125; I 605). See J. M. Kemble's letter, *Sir Launcelot* (p. 97). Cp. *The Holy Grail* (p. 875).

My good blade carves the casques of men,
  My tough lance thrusteth sure,
My strength is as the strength of ten,
  Because my heart is pure.
5 The shattering trumpet shrilleth high,
  The hard brands shiver on the steel,
The splintered spear-shafts crack and fly,
  The horse and rider reel:
They reel, they roll in clanging lists,
10   And when the tide of combat stands,
Perfume and flowers fall in showers,
  That lightly rain from ladies' hands.

How sweet are looks that ladies bend
  On whom their favours fall!
15 For them I battle till the end,
  To save from shame and thrall:
But all my heart is drawn above,
  My knees are bowed in crypt and shrine:
I never felt the kiss of love,
20   Nor maiden's hand in mine.
More bounteous aspects on me beam,
  Me mightier transports move and thrill;
So keep I fair through faith and prayer
  A virgin heart in work and will.

25 When down the stormy crescent goes,
  A light before me swims,
Between dark stems the forest glows,
  I hear a noise of hymns:
Then by some secret shrine I ride;
30   I hear a voice but none are there;
The stalls are void, the doors are wide,
  The tapers burning fair.
Fair gleams the snowy altar-cloth,
  The silver vessels sparkle clean,
35 The shrill bell rings, the censer swings,
  And solemn chaunts resound between.

Sometimes on lonely mountain-meres
  I find a magic bark;
I leap on board: no helmsman steers:
40   I float till all is dark.
A gentle sound, an awful light!
  Three angels bear the holy Grail:
With folded feet, in stoles of white,
  On sleeping wings they sail.

45 Ah, blessèd vision! blood of God!
My spirit beats her mortal bars,
As down dark tides the glory slides,
And star-like mingles with the stars.

When on my goodly charger borne
50 Through dreaming towns I go,
The cock crows ere the Christmas morn,
The streets are dumb with snow.
The tempest crackles on the leads,
And, ringing, springs from brand and mail;
55 But o'er the dark a glory spreads,
And gilds the driving hail.
I leave the plain, I climb the height;
No branchy thicket shelter yields;
But blessèd forms in whistling storms
60 Fly o'er waste fens and windy fields.

A maiden knight–to me is given
Such hope, I know not fear;
I yearn to breathe the airs of heaven
That often meet me here.

¶ 234.*50. dreaming*] sleeping *Heath MS 1st reading.* Here and below all
variants in *Heath MS* were altered in T.'s hand to *1842.* The variants are
discussed by M. J. Donahue, *PQ* xxviii (1949) 326–9.
53–4] The frostwind in my helmet hums,
The tempest crackles on my mail, *Heath MS*
Corrected by T. to *1842* except for 'spinning, rings' in l. 54.
54. springs] *1862*; spins *1842–60.*
55] Upon the dark a glory comes *Heath MS.*
56. And] That *Heath MS.*
60 ∧ *61*] Oh power outsoaring human ken!
Oh Knighthood chaste and true!
With God, with Angels, and with men
What is it I may not do?
Not only in the tourney-field
The unpure are beaten from the fray,
Not only evil customs yield,
The very stars give way.
Lo! those bright stars which thou hast made,
They tremble fanned on by thy breath:
Yea Lord! they shine, those lamps of thine
In Heaven and in the gulphs of Death. *Heath MS*
T. wrote to James Spedding in early Oct. 1834: 'I dare say you are right
about the stanza in *Sir Galahad*' (*Letters* i 125; *Mem.* i 142). There is an
earlier draft of this stanza in *T.Nbk 20.*
61 – 72] *Transposed at first with the final stanza in H.Nbk 15.*

65 I muse on joy that will not cease,
        Pure spaces clothed in living beams,
    Pure lilies of eternal peace,
        Whose odours haunt my dreams;
    And, stricken by an angel's hand,
70   This mortal armour that I wear,
    This weight and size, this heart and eyes,
        Are touched, are turned to finest air.

    The clouds are broken in the sky,
        And through the mountain-walls
75 A rolling organ-harmony
        Swells up, and shakes and falls.
    Then move the trees, the copses nod,
        Wings flutter, voices hover clear:
    'O just and faithful knight of God!
80   Ride on! the prize is near.'
    So pass I hostel, hall, and grange;
        By bridge and ford, by park and pale,
    All-armed I ride, whate'er betide,
        Until I find the holy Grail.

241 The Day-Dream

One section, *The Sleeping Beauty*, was published *1830*; the whole sequence
was published *1842*. R. J. Tennant wrote to T., 8 June 1834: 'Send me the
new Sleeping Beauty and whatever else you have written since the glorious
three days of my Christmas sojourn at Somersby' (*Letters* i 111–2); meaning
either *The Sleeping Palace* or the sequence from that to *The Departure*. The
Prologue and *Epilogue* (and therefore presumably also *Moral* and *L'Envoi*)
were 'added after 1835 (when the poem was written), for the same reason
that caused the Prologue of the *Morte d'Arthur*, giving an excuse for telling
an old-world [Fairy-] tale' (FitzGerald). This resemblance to *The Epic* might
suggest 1837–8 for the *Prologue* and *Epilogue*. Perhaps it became tinged with
T.'s feelings for Rosa Baring in 1833–4. The whole sequence is in *T.Nbk 26*
(except that *The Sleeping Beauty*, already published, is represented by its title
only), where *Moral* was at first called *Epilogue*, and where *L'Envoi* at one
stage concluded the sequence. All variants are below.

PROLOGUE

    O Lady Flora, let me speak:
        A pleasant hour has passed away
    While, dreaming on your damask cheek,

The dewy sister-eyelids lay.
5 As by the lattice you reclined,
    I went through many wayward moods
To see you dreaming–and, behind,
    A summer crisp with shining woods.
And I too dreamed, until at last
10   Across my fancy, brooding warm,
    The reflex of a legend past,
    And loosely settled into form.
And would you have the thought I had,
    And see the vision that I saw,
15 Then take the broidery-frame, and add
    A crimson to the quaint Macaw,
And I will tell it. Turn your face,
    Nor look with that too-earnest eye–
The rhymes are dazzled from their place,
20   And ordered words asunder fly.

THE SLEEPING PALACE

I

The varying year with blade and sheaf
    Clothes and reclothes the happy plains,

¶ 241. *Prologue*
1–8] I pored upon you as you dreamed
        Beside the casement till there grew
    I know not what of strange: you seemed
        No Lady Flora that I knew
    But some perfection of the Mind
        As minted in the golden moods
    Of some great Artist–and behind
        The summer crisp with shining woods.   *T.Nbk 26, del.*
Cp. the third line with *Tithonus* 61–2: 'Whispering I knew not what of wild
and sweet, / Like that strange song'.
2] For all my fancies were at play *T.MS.*
4. dewy sister-eyelids: To Rosa ii 10 (1836).
5–7] I watcht you on that couch reclined,
        Rich work of Nature's amorous moods.
    A happy foreground and behind *T.MS*
8. A] The *T.MS.* Adapted from *The Gardener's Daughter* 29–31, MS: 'crisp
with shining woods / And summer holts'. At one stage T. thought of using
this in *Edwin Morris* (*T.Nbk 26*).
9–10] I rose and shut the lattice fast.
        I turned and watcht you breathing warm: *T.MS*
12. loosely] slowly *T.MS.*
15. Then] *1853*; So *1842–51.*

Here rests the sap within the leaf,
　　Here stays the blood along the veins.
5　Faint shadows, vapours lightly curled,
　　Faint murmurs from the meadows come,
　　Like hints and echoes of the world
　　　To spirits folded in the womb.

II

Soft lustre bathes the range of urns
10　　On every slanting terrace-lawn.
　　The fountain to his place returns
　　Deep in the garden lake withdrawn.
　　Here droops the banner on the tower,
　　　On the hall-hearths the festal fires,
15　The peacock in his laurel bower,
　　　The parrot in his gilded wires.

III

Roof-haunting martins warm their eggs:
　　In these, in those the life is stayed.
　　The mantles from the golden pegs
20　　Droop sleepily: no sound is made,
　　Not even of a gnat that sings.
　　　More like a picture seemeth all
　　Than those old portraits of old kings,
　　　That watch the sleepers from the wall.

IV

25　Here sits the Butler with a flask
　　　Between his knees, half-drained; and there
　　The wrinkled steward at his task,
　　　The maid-of-honour blooming fair;

The Sleeping Palace
3. rests] stays *H.Nbk 15 1st reading.*
4. stays] sleeps *H.MS 1st reading.*
8. folded] dreaming *H.MS 1st reading.*
9. Cp. Shelley, *Rosalind* 832: 'lustre bright and soft', a passage which might
have come to T.'s mind because it describes how 'Sudden sleep would
seize him oft / Like death, so calm'.
13. droops] rests *H.MS 1st reading.*
17] He heard the ringdoves warm their eggs: *H.MS 1st reading.* Cp. *Macbeth*
l vi 4: 'temple-haunting martlet'.
21. gnat] midge *MSS.*
26. and there] by him *H.MS revision.*
28] The waiting woman tight and trim *H.MS*; The waiting woman spruce
and fair *H.MS 1st reading.* With *MS*, cp. *Edwin Morris* 46–7: 'a dame in-
doors that trims us up, / And keeps us tight'.

30   Her lips are severed as to speak:
His own are pouted to a kiss:
The blush is fixed upon her cheek.

V

Till all the hundred summers pass,
The beams, that through the Oriel shine,
35   Make prisms in every carven glass,
And beaker brimmed with noble wine.
Each baron at the banquet sleeps,
Grave faces gathered in a ring.
His state the king reposing keeps.
40   He must have been a jovial king.

VI

All round a hedge upshoots, and shows
At distance like a little wood;
Thorns, ivies, woodbine, mistletoes,
And grapes with bunches red as blood;
45   All creeping plants, a wall of green
Close-matted, bur and brake and briar,
And glimpsing over these, just seen,
High up, the topmost palace spire.

VII

When will the hundred summers die,
50   And thought and time be born again,
And newer knowledge, drawing nigh,
Bring truth that sways the soul of men?
Here all things in their place remain,
As all were ordered, ages since.
55   Come, Care and Pleasure, Hope and Pain,
And bring the fated fairy Prince.

33. *Till all*] When will *H.MS 1st reading.*
34. *through the Oriel*] o'er the dais *H.MS 1st reading.*
36. *noble*] glowing *H.MS revision.*
37. *baron*] noble *H.MS.*
37–40] The guests are strown on couch and floor,
His state the king reposing keeps.
They neither nod, or dream, or snore,
The mind, the heart, the breathing sleeps. *H.MS 1st reading*
Line 38 was inserted subsequently.
40. *jovial*] 1853; jolly *1842–51.*
46. *bur and brake*] tendril, brake *H.MS;* brake and bur *T.MS.*
54. *were*] was *H.MS 1st reading.*

THE SLEEPING BEAUTY

I

Year after year unto her feet,
   She lying on her couch alone,
Across the purple coverlet,
   The maiden's jet-black hair has grown,
5 On either side her trancèd form
   Forth streaming from a braid of pearl:
The slumbrous light is rich and warm,
   And moves not on the rounded curl.

II

The silk star-broidered coverlid
10 Unto her limbs itself doth mould
Languidly ever; and, amid
   Her full black ringlets downward rolled,
Glows forth each softly-shadowed arm
   With bracelets of the diamond bright:
15 Her constant beauty doth inform
   Stillness with love, and day with light.

III

She sleeps: her breathings are not heard
   In palace chambers far apart.
The fragrant tresses are not stirred
20 That lie upon her charmèd heart.
She sleeps: on either hand upswells
   The gold-fringed pillow lightly prest:
She sleeps, nor dreams, but ever dwells
   A perfect form in perfect rest.

THE ARRIVAL

I

All precious things, discovered late,
   To those that seek them issue forth;
For love in sequel works with fate,
   And draws the veil from hidden worth.

The Sleeping Beauty
2] *1842*; The while she slumbereth alone, *1830*.
3. *Across*] *1842*; Over *1830*.   *purple*] *1884*; purpled *1830–83*.
4. *has*] *1842*; hath *1830*.
9. *star-broidered*] *1842*; starbraided *1830*.
21. *hand*] *1842*; side *1830*.

The Arrival Headed *The Revival* in H.MS.
4. *veil*] cloud *MSS.*

5 He travels far from other skies –
　His mantle glitters on the rocks –
　A fairy Prince, with joyful eyes,
　And lighter-footed than the fox.

II

　The bodies and the bones of those
10 That strove in other days to pass,
　Are withered in the thorny close,
　Or scattered blanching on the grass.
　He gazes on the silent dead:
　'They perished in their daring deeds.'
15 This proverb flashes through his head,
　'The many fail: the one succeeds.'

III

　He comes, scarce knowing what he seeks:
　He breaks the hedge: he enters there:
　The colour flies into his cheeks:
20 He trusts to light on something fair;
　For all his life the charm did talk
　About his path, and hover near
　With words of promise in his walk,
　And whispered voices at his ear.

IV

25 More close and close his footsteps wind:
　The Magic Music in his heart

6] And lighter-footed than the pard, *H.MS.*
8] In azure samite silver starred. *H.MS.*
9–16] Not *H.MS.*
12. on] 1853; in 1842–51.
15. This] A *T.MS.*
18. he] and *H.MS.*
19. flies] comes *H.MS.*
21. talk] keep *MSS.*
22. his ... and] him and did *H.MS.*
23. walk] sleep *MSS.*
24. at] 1851; in 1842–50.
25. close and close] near and near *H.MS.*
26. Cp. 'magic music' as a Christmas game, *The Princess: Prologue* 192.
The music is loud and fast when the seeker is 'warm'; soft and slow when
he is 'cold'. FitzGerald turned the phrase in praise of T.: 'We have had Alfred
Tennyson here ... at which good hour we would get Alfred to give us some
of his magic music' (April 1838; his *Letters* i 211).

Beats quick and quicker, till he find
The quiet chamber far apart.
His spirit flutters like a lark,
30   He stoops–to kiss her–on his knee.
'Love, if thy tresses be so dark,
How dark those hidden eyes must be!'

THE REVIVAL

I

A touch, a kiss! the charm was snapt.
There rose a noise of striking clocks,
And feet that ran, and doors that clapt,
And barking dogs, and crowing cocks;
5   A fuller light illumined all,
A breeze through all the garden swept,
A sudden hubbub shook the hall,
And sixty feet the fountain leapt.

II

The hedge broke in, the banner blew,
10   The butler drank, the steward scrawled,
The fire shot up, the martin flew,
The parrot screamed, the peacock squalled,
The maid and page renewed their strife,
The palace banged, and buzzed and clackt,
15   And all the long-pent stream of life
Dashed downward in a cataract.

III

And last with these the king awoke,
And in his chair himself upreared,
And yawned, and rubbed his face, and spoke,
20   'By holy rood, a royal beard!
How say you? we have slept, my lords.
My beard has grown into my lap.'
The barons swore, with many words,
'Twas but an after-dinner's nap.

27. *Beats quick*] Plays quicker *H.MS.*
31. *be*] are *T.MS 1st reading.*

The Revival
1. *touch, a*] single *T.MS.*
13. *maid . . . their*] page renewed his amorous *T.MS.*
17. *with these*] 1853; of all *1842–51.   last . . . these*] in the hall *T.MS 1st reading*; all
at once *T.MS alternative.*
24. J. McCue compares *Measure for Measure* III i 33–4: 'But as it were an
after-dinner's sleep, / Dreaming on both'.

IV

25 'Pardy,' returned the king, 'but still
    My joints are somewhat stiff or so.
    My lord, and shall we pass the bill
      I mentioned half an hour ago?'
    The chancellor, sedate and vain,
30   In courteous words returned reply:
    But dallied with his golden chain,
      And, smiling, put the question by.

THE DEPARTURE

I

And on her lover's arm she leant,
    And round her waist she felt it fold,
And far across the hills they went
    In that new world which is the old:
5 Across the hills, and far away
    Beyond their utmost purple rim,
And deep into the dying day
    The happy princess followed him.

II

'I'd sleep another hundred years,
10   O love, for such another kiss;'
'O wake for ever, love,' she hears,
    'O love, 'twas such as this and this.'
And o'er them many a sliding star,
    And many a merry wind was borne,
15 And, streamed through many a golden bar,
    The twilight melted into morn.

III

'O eyes long laid in happy sleep!'
    'O happy sleep, that lightly fled!'
'O happy kiss, that woke thy sleep!'
20   'O love, thy kiss would wake the dead!'

---

26. *somewhat*] *1862*; something *1842–60*.

The Departure
4. 'The world of Love' (T.).
13. *sliding*: traditional diction in such a context. Cp. Dryden, *Palamon and Arcite* iii 129–33: 'Creator Venus, genial power of love, / The bliss of men below and gods above! / Beneath the sliding sun thou runn'st thy race, / Dost fairest shine, and best become thy place; / For thee the winds their eastern blasts forbear . . .'

And o'er them many a flowing range
    Of vapour buoyed the crescent-bark,
And, rapt through many a rosy change,
    The twilight died into the dark.

IV

25 'A hundred summers! can it be?
    And whither goest thou, tell me where?'
'O seek my father's court with me,
    For there are greater wonders there.'
And o'er the hills, and far away
30   Beyond their utmost purple rim,
Beyond the night, across the day,
    Through all the world she followed him.

MORAL

I

So, Lady Flora, take my lay,
    And if you find no moral there,
Go, look in any glass and say,
    What moral is in being fair.
5 Oh, to what uses shall we put
    The wildweed-flower that simply blows?
And is there any moral shut
    Within the bosom of the rose?

II

But any man that walks the mead,
10   In bud or blade, or bloom, may find,
According as his humours lead,
    A meaning suited to his mind.
And liberal applications lie
    In Art like Nature, dearest friend;
15 So 'twere to cramp its use, if I
    Should hook it to some useful end.

L'ENVOI

I

You shake your head. A random string
    Your finer female sense offends.
Well–were it not a pleasant thing
    To fall asleep with all one's friends;

Moral
6. blows] grows *T.MS 1st reading.*

5   To pass with all our social ties
        To silence from the paths of men;
      And every hundred years to rise
        And learn the world, and sleep again;
      To sleep through terms of mighty wars,
10   And wake on science grown to more,
      On secrets of the brain, the stars,
        As wild as aught of fairy lore;
      And all that else the years will show,
        The Poet-forms of stronger hours,
15   The vast Republics that may grow,
        The Federations and the Powers;
      Titanic forces taking birth
        In divers seasons, divers climes;
      For we are Ancients of the earth,
20   And in the morning of the times.

                     II
      So sleeping, so aroused from sleep
        Through sunny decads new and strange,
      Or gay quinquenniads would we reap
        The flower and quintessence of change.

                     III
25   Ah, yet would I—and would I might!
        So much your eyes my fancy take—
      Be still the first to leap to light
        That I might kiss those eyes awake!

L'Envoi

9–12] Not *T.MS 1st reading.*

10–12. Cp. *Locksley Hall* 12: 'With the fairy tales of science, and the long result of Time'.

13–14] To come on all the world will show,
              Opinions, Poets, novel hours, *T.MS 1st reading*

16. Cp. *Locksley Hall* 128: 'the Parliament of man, the Federation of the world'.

19–20. Turner (p. 92) notes Bacon, *The Advancement of Learning: Antiquitas saeculi juventus mundi.*

20. morning] twilight *T.MS.*

23. gay] light *T.MS.   would*] might *T.MS 1st reading.*

24. Cp. *In Memoriam* lxi 4, MS: 'The flower and quintessence of Time'.

25. -. . . might!] my claim advance *T.MS 1st reading.*

26. fancy] *T.MS 1st reading*; spirit *T.MS.*

27] Still to be first to break the trance, *T.MS 1st reading.*

For, am I right, or am I wrong,
30   To choose your own you did not care;
You'd have *my* moral from the song,
    And I will take my pleasure there:
And, am I right or am I wrong,
    My fancy, ranging through and through,
35 To search a meaning for the song,
    Perforce will still revert to you;
Nor finds a closer truth than this
    All-graceful head, so richly curled,
And evermore a costly kiss
40   The prelude to some brighter world.

IV

For since the time when Adam first
    Embraced his Eve in happy hour,
And every bird of Eden burst
    In carol, every bud to flower,
45 What eyes, like thine, have wakened hopes,
    What lips, like thine, so sweetly joined?
Where on the double rosebud droops
    The fulness of the pensive mind;
Which all too dearly self-involved,
50   Yet sleeps a dreamless sleep to me;
A sleep by kisses undissolved,
    That lets thee neither hear nor see:
But break it. In the name of wife,
    And in the rights that name may give,
55 Are clasped the moral of thy life,
    And that for which I care to live.

EPILOGUE

So, Lady Flora, take my lay,
    And, if you find a meaning there,

---

32. *take my pleasure*] ride my hobby *T.MS 1st reading.*
34. *through and*] nature *T.MS 1st reading.*
35. *search . . . for*] find . . . to *T.MS.*
37. *closer*] costlier *T.MS 1st reading*; dearer *T.MS 2nd reading.*
39. *And*] If *T.MS 1st reading.*
40. *The*] Were *T.MS 1st reading.*
41. *For*] And *T.MS.*
47. 'A recollection of the bust of Clyte' (T.). Clyte watches Apollo leaving her; T. had a bust of her at High Beech (*Mem.* i 151).
49. *Which . . . dearly*] *1843*; The pensive mind·that *1842.*
52. ·*That*] *1843*; Which *1842.*

O whisper to your glass, and say,
'What wonder, if he thinks me fair?'
5 What wonder I was all unwise,
To shape the song for your delight
Like long-tailed birds of Paradise
That float through Heaven, and cannot light?
Or old-world trains, upheld at court
10 By Cupid-boys of blooming hue—
But take it—earnest wed with sport,
And either sacred unto you.

261 'Move eastward, happy earth, and leave'

Published *1842*. It is an epithalamium; cp. *The Bridesmaid* (II 90), and perhaps it too dates from the marriage of T.'s brother Charles in May 1836. Alternatively, T.'s engagement to Emily Sellwood was recognized early in 1838 (*CT*, p. 177).

Move eastward, happy earth, and leave
Yon orange sunset waning slow:
From fringes of the faded eve,
O, happy planet, eastward go;

Epilogue
3. O] Go *T.MS*.
4–8]   The meaning is that I am fair.
And Beauty's self shall make amends
For Beauty's error making Art's [Art *1st reading*]
Like sheep with those preposterous ends
That follow trailed in little carts [*from* That travel in a little
                                                                cart] *T.MS 1st reading*
4–5]   It is but this that I am fair
And 'tis but this made me unwise *T.MS*
6. the ... your] a ... thy *T.MS*.
7–8. In legend they do not alight.
9] Or trains of Countesses upheld *T.MS 1st reading*; Or old-world trains at court upheld *T.MS*.
11–12]   Or like a lady's postscript swelled
With windy text beyond its due. *T.MS*
¶ 261.*1*. *happy earth*: Arthur Hallam's *Sonnet to a Lady on Her Marriage* (Motter, p. 77).
2. Turner (p. 99) notes that 'the sunset is appropriately given the colour of the bridal veil (*flammeum*) in Catullus' epithalamion (lxi)'.
3. Cp. *On a Mourner* 21, MS: 'the fringing eve'.

5   Till over thy dark shoulder glow
    Thy silver sister-world, and rise
    To glass herself in dewy eyes
    That watch me from the glen below.
    Ah, bear me with thee, smoothly borne,
10   Dip forward under starry light,
    And move me to my marriage-morn,
    And round again to happy night.

265 A Farewell

Published *1842*. It is to the brook at Somersby (H.T.), so it was presumably
written in early 1837 when the family left. R. J. Tennant wrote to T.'s
mother, 2 May 1837: 'I am grieved to think how deserted Somersby will
soon be' (*Brotherton Collection*). It is probably not later than 1837, since it is
in *H.Nbk 21* (watermarked *1836*). Cp. *In Memoriam* ci 9–10, on the same
parting (*p. 448*): 'Unloved, by many a sandy bar, / The brook shall babble
down the plain.'

> Flow down, cold rivulet, to the sea,
>   Thy tribute wave deliver:
> No more by thee my steps shall be,
>   For ever and for ever.
>
> 5 Flow, softly flow, by lawn and lea,
>   A rivulet then a river:
> No where by thee my steps shall be,
>   For ever and for ever.
>
> But here will sigh thine alder tree,
> 10   And here thine aspen shiver;
> And here by thee will hum the bee,
>   For ever and for ever.

6. sister-world: 'the moon' (T.). Perhaps hinting at Emily Sellwood, with
whom Tennyson fell in love at the wedding of Charles to her sister.
9. smoothly] *1853*; lightly *1842–53*. Cp. *Paradise Lost* viii 166, where the
earth, advancing from the west, 'beares thee soft with the smooth Air
along'.
¶ *265.10*. Leaving Somersby, T. may have remembered a book (*Lincoln*) in
the library there: Thomas Gisborne's *Walks in a Forest: Spring* (1794):
'And rustling aspens shiver by the brook'.

A thousand suns will stream on thee,
A thousand moons will quiver;
15   But not by thee my steps shall be,
For ever and for ever.

[1837. *Oh! that 'twere possible*–see *p. 988*]

271 Locksley Hall

Published *1842*. Written 1837–8; so Rader (pp. 41–2) argues convincingly. (i) Edmund Lushington thought he remembered that it was read to him in 1837 or early 1838 (*Mat.* i 246). (ii) It relates to T.'s disillusionment with Rosa Baring, and was probably influenced by the talk in 1837 of her engagement, and her marriage in Oct. 1838. (iii) T. read T. Pringle (the source of ll. 135–6) in 1837 (*Mem.* i 162), and l. 114 was written at High Beech where the Tennysons lived from 1837–40 (*Mem.* i 150). (iv) *Y.MS* is watermarked '1835' and is not likely to be very much later. (Rader (p. 41) mistakenly calls this 'the sole MS of the poem'; in fact the poem appears with the *1842* poems in *HnMS* (HM 1320), which at this point is watermarked 1838.) Rader adds, for those who wish to associate it with Lincolnshire, that T. was there in the spring of 1838. Furthermore Walter White says that it 'was written at High Beech' (*Journals*, 1898, pp. 151–2), and he corroborates Lushington in that much of it was seen and heard at Mitre Court Buildings, The Temple. W. D. Templeman's preference for 1840–1 is supported by J. H. Buckley (writing before Rader, however), who believes it refers to T.'s breaking off his engagement with Emily in 1840; Rader's discoveries make this unnecessary, as is Templeman's suggestion that T. was adapting the unhappy love affair in Carlyle's *Sartor Resartus* (*Booker Memorial Studies*, 1950). All variants from *Y.MS* are given below, as '*MS*'. In *T.Nbk 26* fragment, it is twice spelt 'Loxley Hall'; cp. 'Oxley Hall' (*Audley Court*) in this Nbk.
Biography. The main source from T.'s life is his unhappy love affair with Rosa; see *Thy rosy lips* (II 59) and *To Rosa* (II 75). T.'s experience of 'marriage-hindering Mammon' precipitated, among other poems, *Locksley Hall, Edwin Morris* and *Maud*. Rader points out that hers was an arranged marriage (cp. ll. 59–62), and that the Hall was suggested by her Harrington Hall (and see ll. 25–6n). Sir Charles Tennyson notes that the story of 'family estrangement owes much of its form and atmosphere to the feud between Somersby and Bayons' (p. 194), the latter being the home of Charles Tennyson-d'Eyncourt, in whose favour T.'s father had virtually been disinherited; also that the heroes of *Locksley Hall* and *Maud* 'have more than a little reference to Frederick', T.'s brother (again, Rader's discoveries suggest

13. *thousand*] *1843*; hundred *1842*.

that this might be modified). T., as so often, maintained that it was 'an imaginary place and imaginary hero': 'The whole poem represents young life, its good side, its deficiencies, and its yearnings.'

Sources. 'Sir William Jones's prose translation of the *Moâllakât*, the seven Arabic poems . . . hanging up in the temple of Mecca, gave the idea of the poem' (H.T.). Jones summarized the first Poem, of Amriolkais: 'The poet . . . supposes himself attended on a journey by a company of friends; and, as they pass near a place, where his mistress had lately dwelled . . . he desires them to stop awhile, that he might indulge the painful pleasure of weeping over the deserted remains of her tent. They comply with his request, but exhort him to show more strength of mind, and urge two topicks of consolation; namely, that he had before been equally unhappy, and that he had enjoyed his full share of pleasures: thus by the recollection of his passed delight his imagination is kindled, and his grief suspended.' Then follows an account of Amriolkais's amours (among them 'Fathima'; cp. *Fatima*); the poem ends, as does T.'s poem, with a violent storm. See below ll. 9–10n, 75–6n, 89–90n, 122n. E. F. Shannon (*Note and Queries*, June 1959) suggests that 'Locksley' is from Scott's *Ivanhoe*, where it is Robin Hood's pseudonym (from his birthplace): 'Locksley is the pseudonym of a man alienated from society . . . indict[ing] the corruption and self-seeking of his day.' He mentions the bugle-horn (ll. 2, 145) with its insistent association with Scott's Locksley; and see l. 50n. T. had earlier written of *Amy*: 'I love thee, Amy, / And woo thee for my wife'. Reminiscences of *Hamlet* were apt to an attack on a corrupt society, dealing with an unhappy love-affair; see ll. 43–4n, 69n, 133n, and cp. T.'s description of *Maud*, a poem similar in many ways to *Locksley Hall*, as 'a little *Hamlet*'.

F. E. L. Priestley discusses the poem as a dramatic monologue, and notes: 'The speaker has joined the Army, presumably as a private soldier, and has come to say a last farewell to Locksley Hall before sailing abroad with his regiment . . . His enlistment in the Army is not given to us explicitly, but by a collating of a number of details', including from *Locksley Hall Sixty Years After* (*Queen's Quarterly* lxxxi, 1974, 512–32).

Metre, 'Mr Hallam [Henry Hallam] said to me that the English people liked verse in trochaics, so I wrote the poem in this metre' (T.). J. F. A. Pyre, *The Formation of Tennyson's Style* (1921), pp. 110–12, points out that T. used this 8-stress trochaic line in sporadic couplets in the revised *1842* ending of *The Lotos-Eaters*, and that he came very near such a metre in a trochaic ballad like *The Lord of Burleigh*. Edmund Blunden in his selection (1960) points out that it was used in *Sabbation* (1838) by T.'s friend R. C. Trench. The spur to its use may well have been the fact that, in the poem of Amriolkais, Jones's prose fell naturally into it: 'Thus I spoke, when my companions stopped their course[r]s by my side.' Jones has approximations like 'Thy condition, they replied, is not more painful than when thou . . .'; and half-lines like 'On that day I killed my camel', 'On that happy day I entered'. T.'s acute receptiveness to rhythms is famous (see the headnote to *The Charge of the Light Brigade, p. 508*), and Jones's prose probably ran in

his head (C. Ricks, *Notes and Queries*, Aug. 1965). Cp. *Locksley Hall Sixty
Years After* (*p. 640*). Turner (p. 90) suggests that the poem 'was written
after May 1839, when W. E. Aytoun published in *Blackwood's* . . . a
translation of *Iliad* xxii in the *Locksley Hall* metre'.

> Comrades, leave me here a little, while as yet 'tis early morn:
> Leave me here, and when you want me, sound upon the bugle-horn.
>
> 'Tis the place, and all around it, as of old, the curlews call,
> Dreary gleams about the moorland flying over Locksley Hall;
>
> 5 Locksley Hall, that in the distance overlooks the sandy tracts,
> And the hollow ocean-ridges roaring into cataracts.
>
> Many a night from yonder ivied casement, ere I went to rest,
> Did I look on great Orion sloping slowly to the West.
>
> Many a night I saw the Pleiads, rising through the mellow shade,
> 10 Glitter like a swarm of fire-flies tangled in a silver braid.
>
> Here about the beach I wandered, nourishing a youth sublime
> With the fairy tales of science, and the long result of Time;

¶ 271.*1. while . . . morn*] 'tis the place where I was born *Y.MS.*
2. Leave . . . and] Comrades leave me: *MS.*
3. 'Tis . . . it] *1843*; 'Tis the place, and round the gables *1842*; Round the
gable, round the turret *MS.*
3–4. T. says that this means '*while* dreary gleams', not in apposition to
'curlews'. Marian Bradley, in her diary (11 Jan. 1870, British Museum),
reports: 'He wishes he had used "sweeping"–instead of "flying"–it
would have been more explicit' (quoted *Mem.* ii 93). G. G. Loane, *Echoes
in Tennyson* (1928), p. 6, compares John Leyden: 'But formless shadows
seemed to fly / Along the muir-land dun . . . / And round did float, with
clamorous note / And scream, the hoarse curlew.' Leyden's *The Cout of
Keeldar* is in Scott's *Minstrelsy of the Scottish Border*, which T. certainly knew.
5. that . . . overlooks] before me and behind *MS.*
6. Adapted from *The Lover's Tale* i 52–61, MS: 'The roaring ridges into
cataracts' (pointed out by Sir Charles Tennyson, *Cornhill* cliii (1936) 445).
8. Horace, *Odes* III xxvii 18: *pronus Orion*.
9–10. From the *Moâllakát* (see headnote): 'It was the hour, when the Pleiads
appeared in the firmament, like the folds of a silken sash variously decked
with gems.'
11–16] Not at first in MS. T. had simply the one visionary passage beginning
at l. 119. He then revised that passage, and moved the vision (ll. 11–16,
121–30, as one) to this early point. For publication, he split the vision into
two, and repeated ll. 15–16 as ll. 119–20.
12. long] great *MS.* The Miltonic 'great result' (*PL* ii 515) must have seemed
unapt.   *the long result: In Memoriam* i 14. Cp. *The Day-Dream: L'Envoi*
10–12: 'science . . . / As wild as aught of fairy lore.'

When the centuries behind me like a fruitful land reposed;
When I clung to all the present for the promise that it closed:

15 When I dipt into the future far as human eye could see;
Saw the Vision of the world, and all the wonder that would be.—

In the Spring a fuller crimson comes upon the robin's breast;
In the Spring the wanton lapwing gets himself another crest;

In the Spring a livelier iris changes on the burnished dove;
20 In the Spring a young man's fancy lightly turns to thoughts of love.

Then her cheek was pale and thinner than should be for one so young,
And her eyes on all my motions with a mute observance hung.

And I said, 'My cousin Amy, speak, and speak the truth to me,
Trust me, cousin, all the current of my being sets to thee.'

25 On her pallid cheek and forehead came a colour and a light,
As I have seen the rosy red flushing in the northern night.

And she turned–her bosom shaken with a sudden storm of sighs–
All the spirit deeply dawning in the dark of hazel eyes–

Saying, 'I have hid my feelings, fearing they should do me wrong;'
30 Saying, 'Dost thou love me, cousin?' weeping, 'I have loved thee
    long.'

Love took up the glass of Time, and turned it in his glowing hands;
Every moment, lightly shaken, ran itself in golden sands.

Love took up the harp of Life, and smote on all the chords with might;
Smote the chord of Self, that, trembling, passed in music out of sight.

35 Many a morning on the moorland did we hear the copses ring,
And her whisper thronged my pulses with the fulness of the Spring.

13–14. See ll. 117–18n.

18. another] a novel *MS intermediate reading.*

19–20. Recalling the effect of spring in Thomson's *Spring* 786–8: 'the cooing dove / Flies thick in amorous chase, and wanton rolls / The glancing eye, and turns the changeful neck.'

22. motions] movements *MS.*

25–6. Rader (p. 45) refers to Rosa's blush, remembered years after in *The Roses on the Terrace* (p. 664).

31. glowing hands: traditional; cp. Keats, *Eve of St Agnes* 271: 'These delicates he heaped with glowing hand / On golden dishes'. T. had used it, again with personification, in *Time* 59: 'Bright Fame, with glowing hand'; and *Mithridates* 10: 'The glowing hands of Honour'.

33–4. Cp. Goethe, *Wilhelm Meister's Apprenticeship*, I xvii: 'Love ran with a quivering hand, in a thousand moods, over all the chords of his Soul: it was as if the spheres stood mute above him, suspending their eternal song to watch the low melodies of his heart' (Carlyle's tr.; C. Y. Lang, introduction to *Tennyson in Lincoln*, i, 1971, xi).

Many an evening by the waters did we watch the stately ships,
And our spirits rushed together at the touching of the lips.

O my cousin, shallow-hearted! O my Amy, mine no more!
40 O the dreary, dreary moorland! O the barren, barren shore!

Falser than all fancy fathoms, falser than all songs have sung,
Puppet to a father's threat, and servile to a shrewish tongue!

Is it well to wish thee happy?—having known me—to decline
On a range of lower feelings and a narrower heart than mine!

45 Yet it shall be: thou shalt lower to his level day by day,
What is fine within thee growing coarse to sympathise with clay.

As the husband is, the wife is: thou art mated with a clown,
And the grossness of his nature will have weight to drag thee down.

He will hold thee, when his passion shall have spent its novel force,
50 Something better than his dog, a little dearer than his horse.

What is this? his eyes are heavy: think not they are glazed with wine.
Go to him: it is thy duty: kiss him: take his hand in thine.

It may be my lord is weary, that his brain is overwrought:
Soothe him with thy finer fancies, touch him with thy lighter thought.

55 He will answer to the purpose, easy things to understand—
Better thou wert dead before me, though I slew thee with my hand!

Better thou and I were lying, hidden from the heart's disgrace,
Rolled in one another's arms, and silent in a last embrace.

Cursèd be the social wants that sin against the strength of youth!
60 Cursèd be the social lies that warp us from the living truth!

37. *the stately ships*: *Break, break, break* 9.
38. A traditional notion; cp. *Fatima* 19–21 and *n*: 'he drew / With one long kiss my whole soul through / My lips' (*p. 34*).
38 ∧ 9] In the hall there hangs a painting, Amy's arms are round my neck,
Happy children in a sunbeam, sitting on the ribs of wreck.

In my life there is a picture: she that claspt my neck is flown.
I am left within the shadow, sitting on the wreck alone. *HnMS*
T. deleted these lines from the proofs of *1842* (*Lincoln*); they became the nucleus, ll. 13–16, of *Locksley Hall Sixty Years After*.
43. *having*⸱⸱⸱ *to*] now that thou hast dared *Y.MS 1st reading*.
44. *On*] To *MS 1st reading*.   *narrower*] lesser *MS*. Cp. these lines with *Hamlet* I v 50–52: 'To decline / Upon a wretch whose natural gifts were poor / To those of mine'.
48. *will*] shall *MS*.
50. A common indictment; E. F. Shannon compares *Ivanhoe*, Chapter 29: 'His war-horse—his hunting hound are dearer to him than the despised Jewess!'

Cursèd be the sickly forms that err from honest Nature's rule!
Cursèd be the gold that gilds the straitened forehead of the fool!

Well–'tis well that I should bluster!–Hadst thou less unworthy proved–
Would to God–for I had loved thee more than ever wife was loved.

65 Am I mad, that I should cherish that which bears but bitter fruit?
I will pluck it from my bosom, though my heart be at the root.

Never, though my mortal summers to such length of years should come
As the many-wintered crow that leads the clanging rookery home.

Where is comfort? in division of the records of the mind?
70 Can I part her from herself, and love her, as I knew her, kind?

I remember one that perished: sweetly did she speak and move:
Such a one do I remember, whom to look at was to love.

Can I think of her as dead, and love her for the love she bore?
No–she never loved me truly: love is love for evermore.

75 Comfort? comfort scorned of devils! this is truth the poet sings,
That a sorrow's crown of sorrow is remembering happier things.

Drug thy memories, lest thou learn it, lest thy heart be put to proof,
In the dead unhappy night, and when the rain is on the roof.

Like a dog, he hunts in dreams, and thou art staring at the wall,
80 Where the dying night-lamp flickers, and the shadows rise and fall.

63. Well . . . bluster!] Cursèd–No I curse not thee. O MS 1st reading; No–I
curse not thee, my cousin MS.
68. Cp. the 'treble dated Crow' in Shakespeare's The Phoenix and Turtle;
Horace, Odes III xvii 13, annosa cornix. T. comments: 'Rooks are called
crows in the Northern counties.' (Letters iii, to T. Watts, 12 March 1892:
'In my county and I believe all through the North Rooks are called "Crows".
I am not such a ninny as not to know a crow from a rook.')
69. Cp. Hamlet I v 98–9: 'From the table of my memory / I'll wipe away
all trivial fond records'.
70] Can I hate her falsehood now and love the days when she was kind?
MS 1st reading.
74. No] Nay MS.
75. Comfort . . . devils] Hollow, hollow, hollow comfort MS 1st reading.
75–6. the poet: Dante. T.'s note quotes Nessun maggior dolore, / Che ricordarsi
del tempo felice / Nella miseria (Inferno v 121–3). At the age of twelve, he had
quoted this, via Byron's Corsair (Mem. i 8; his earliest surviving letter, Letters
i 1). These lines are in effect a retort to the Moâllakát's 'consolation': 'that he
had enjoyed his full share of pleasures: thus by the recollection of his passed
delight his imagination is kindled, and his grief suspended.'
77. Drug . . . it] Thou shalt know it: drug thy memories MS.
79. The dreaming dog is from Lucretius; see Lucretius 44–6n (II 710).

Then a hand shall pass before thee, pointing to his drunken sleep,
To thy widowed marriage-pillows, to the tears that thou wilt weep.

Thou shalt hear the 'Never, never,' whispered by the phantom years,
And a song from out the distance in the ringing of thine ears;

85 And an eye shall vex thee, looking ancient kindness on thy pain.
Turn thee, turn thee on thy pillow: get thee to thy rest again.

Nay, but Nature brings thee solace; for a tender voice will cry.
'Tis a purer life than thine; a lip to drain thy trouble dry.

Baby lips will laugh me down: my latest rival brings thee rest.
90 Baby fingers, waxen touches, press me from the mother's breast.

O, the child too clothes the father with a dearness not his due.
Half is thine and half is his: it will be worthy of the two.

O, I see thee old and formal, fitted to thy petty part,
With a little hoard of maxims preaching down a daughter's heart.

95 'They were dangerous guides the feelings—she herself was not exempt—
Truly, she herself had suffered'—Perish in thy self-contempt!

Overlive it—lower yet—be happy! wherefore should I care?
I myself must mix with action, lest I wither by despair.

What is that which I should turn to, lighting upon days like these?
100 Every door is barred with gold, and opens but to golden keys.

Every gate is thronged with suitors, all the markets overflow.
I have but an angry fancy: what is that which I should do?

81–2] Every tear that slowly gathers but a ghastly jest shall seem.
    Then a hand shall pass before thee pointing to his drunken dream.
                                                                MS 1st reading
87. *Nay . . . thee*] Rise—there is a little *MS 1st reading*.
89–90] *Added to MS.* The baby as 'rival' should be contrasted with the
Moállakát's very different tone: 'Many a lovely mother have I diverted
from the care of her yearling infant . . . When the suckling behind her
cried, she turned round to him with half her body; but half of it, pressed
beneath my embrace, was not turned from me.'
92. *it will be*] God send it *MS 1st reading*.
93. *fitted . . . part*] verse't in many a vulgar art *MS 1st reading*.
96. *Truly . . . suffered*] She could speak from sad experience *MS 1st reading*.
T. had used 'sad experience' in l. 144.
97. *lower . . . happy!*] which is basest! wherefore, *MS*.
98. The theme developed in *Maud*, especially the closing section.
99–100. Turner (p. 90): 'modelled, both in theme and in tone, on Juvenal,
Satire iii'.
102. *an angry*] a wandering *MS*.

I had been content to perish, falling on the foeman's ground,
When the ranks are rolled in vapour, and the winds are laid with
sound.

105   But the jingling of the guinea helps the hurt that Honour feels,
And the nations do but murmur, snarling at each other's heels.

Can I but relive in sadness? I will turn that earlier page.
Hide me from my deep emotion, O thou wondrous Mother-Age!

Make me feel the wild pulsation that I felt before the strife,
110   When I heard my days before me, and the tumult of my life;

Yearning for the large excitement that the coming years would yield,
Eager-hearted as a boy when first he leaves his father's field,

And at night along the dusky highway near and nearer drawn,
Sees in heaven the light of London flaring like a dreary dawn;

115   And his spirit leaps within him to be gone before him then,
Underneath the light he looks at, in among the throngs of men:

Men, my brothers, men the workers, ever reaping something new:
That which they have done but earnest of the things that they shall do:

For I dipt into the future, far as human eye could see,
120   Saw the Vision of the world, and all the wonder that would be;

Saw the heavens fill with commerce, argosies of magic sails,
Pilots of the purple twilight, dropping down with costly bales;

103–4. Cp. the aspiration, contrasted with despair, in *The Two Voices*
149–56: 'To perish ... like a warrior overthrown' (also 'foeman',
'smoke'). *laid*: the notion that gunfire stills the waves.
105. jingling ... hurt] tightness of the purse-string salves the sore *MS*.
('tightness', because of the weight of the money.)
107. that earlier] the former *MS*.
107–8] ... sadness? Shall I not arise and fling / Fancy back a little further
through the freshness of the spring? *MS 1st reading*.
109] When I felt the wild pulsation that is prophet to the strife, *MS 1st
reading*.   *the wild pulsation*: In Memoriam xii 4.
111. years] age *MS*.
117–40] *Deleted in MS, then revised.* See ll. 11–16n for the change of plan as
to the visions.
117–18] *Appearing in MS ll.* 174 ∧ 5. *MS* at first had instead ll.13–14
('Then . . .').
119. For] Then *MS 1st reading*.
120. Saw ... wonder] I had visions in my head of all the wonders *MS 1st
reading*.
121] When a man shall range the spaces, using unimagined sails, *MS 1st
reading*.   *fill*] throng *MS*.
122. Pilots ... twilight] Merchants in a rosy sunset *MS 1st reading*; Argosies

Heard the heavens fill with shouting, and there rained a ghastly dew
From the nations' airy navies grappling in the central blue;

125 Far along the world-wide whisper of the south-wind rushing warm,
With the standards of the peoples plunging through the thunder-storm;

Till the war-drum throbbed no longer, and the battle-flags were furled
In the Parliament of man, the Federation of the world.

There the common sense of most shall hold a fretful realm in awe,
130 And the kindly earth shall slumber, lapt in universal law.

So I triumphed ere my passion sweeping through me left me dry,
Left me with the palsied heart, and left me with the jaundiced eye;

Eye, to which all order festers, all things here are out of joint:
Science moves, but slowly slowly, creeping on from point to point:

that roam the twilight *MS 2nd reading*. T.'s final version, since it omits
'merchants', is not quite so clearly related to the *Moâllakât*. T. translates
into prophetic fact the *Moâllakât's* beautiful simile for rain: 'The cloud
unloads its freight on the desert of Ghabeit, like a merchant of Yemen
alighting with his bales of rich apparel.' Cp. also *The Mermaid* 44: 'the
purple twilights under the sea'. After l. 122, *MS* had at first:

When the pilot of the whirlwind flying by the northern star
Showers through [along *1st reading*] the polar hollow, meteors of
aërial war.

123. Heard . . . and] Saw [When *1st reading*] the heavens fill with battle,
when *MS. rained*] rains *MS 1st reading*. Cp. the blood from the battle in
The Vale of Bones 77: 'the red dew o'er thee rained'. *The Oak of the North*
(*1827*), by T.'s brother Frederick, calls blood 'that deadly dew'. Also
Shelley, *Mask of Anarchy* 192: 'Blood is on the grass like dew'; and Byron,
Childe Harold IV cxxvi: 'The skies which rain their plagues on men like
dew'.
123-4, 125-6] *Transposed in MS 1st reading; ll. 125-6 then deleted.*
124. E. F. Shannon, *PQ* xxxi (1952) 441-5, compares the 'balloon' stanzas
that originally began *A Dream of Fair Women*, and argues that T. was
thinking mainly of balloons here.
126. standards of the] standard of his *MS 1st reading.*
127] Saw the peoples brother-minded laying battle-standards furled *MS.
throbbed . . . were*] throb . . . are *MS 1st reading.*
129. There] Where *MS.*
131. triumphed ere] dreamed before *MS 1st reading.*
133. Eye, to which all] Nothing pleases, *MS 1st reading*. Cp. *Hamlet* I v
188-9: 'The time is out of joint, O cursèd spite, / That ever I was born to set
it right.'
134. Science . . . creeping] Little moves but Science creeping slowly *MS 1st
reading.*

135 Slowly comes a hungry people, as a lion creeping nigher,
       Glares at one that nods and winks behind a slowly-dying fire.

       Yet I doubt not through the ages one increasing purpose runs,
       And the thoughts of men are widened with the process of the suns.

       What is that to him that reaps not harvest of his youthful joys,
140 Though the deep heart of existence beat for ever like a boy's?

       Knowledge comes, but wisdom lingers, and I linger on the shore,
       And the individual withers, and the world is more and more.

       Knowledge comes, but wisdom lingers, and he bears a laden breast,
       Full of sad experience, moving toward the stillness of his rest.

145 Hark, my merry comrades call me, sounding on the bugle-horn,
       They to whom my foolish passion were a target for their scorn:

       Shall it not be scorn to me to harp on such a mouldered string?
       I am shamed through all my nature to have loved so slight a thing.

       Weakness to be wroth with weakness! woman's pleasure, woman's
            pain—
150 Nature made them blinder motions bounded in a shallower brain:

       Woman is the lesser man, and all thy passions, matched with mine,
       Are as moonlight unto sunlight, and as water unto wine—

135] Or the crowd that stumbling forward in their hunger drawing near,
        With a lingering will divided by their famine and their fear,
        As a lion in his hunger and his anger creeping nigher, *MS 1st reading*
The lion is from Thomas Pringle's *Travels*, which T. read in 1837 (*Mem.* i
162). Miss M. J. Donahue notes that H.T. confused Pringle's *Travels* and
his *Poetical Works* when quoting T.'s letter of 1837 (*Mat.* i 200); but this
need not invalidate the statement in *Mem.* that T. read the *Travels* then.
T. wrote to Pringle in 1832, and subscribed in 1837 to Pringle's *Poetical Works*
(1838–9; *Letters* i 82, 85, 147).
136 ∧ *7*] Yet I doubt not that a glory waits upon some later morn—
        Every moment dies a man and every moment one is born.
                                                          MS 1st reading
The second line became *The Vision of Sin* 97–8: 'Every moment dies a
man, / Every moment one is born.'
137. Yet . . . ages] And through all the generations *MS 1st reading*; Yet I
know through all the ages *MS*.
139. youthful] natural *MS 1st reading*.
141. and . . . shore] like a beggar at the door *MS alternative*. 'Knowledge
comes', exclaims the lover of the age, Æonophilus; see *Mechanophilus*
4 ∧ 5n (I 534).
144. toward] towards *MS*.
149–50] Woman is the lesser being: all her pleasure and her pain
        Is a feebler blinder motion bounded by a shallower brain. *MS*

Here at least, where nature sickens, nothing. Ah, for some retreat
Deep in yonder shining Orient, where my life began to beat;

155 Where in wild Mahratta-battle fell my father evil-starred;–
I was left a trampled orphan, and a selfish uncle's ward.

Or to burst all links of habit–there to wander far away,
On from island unto island at the gateways of the day.

Larger constellations burning, mellow moons and happy skies,
160 Breadths of tropic shade and palms in cluster, knots of Paradise.

Never comes the trader, never floats an European flag,
Slides the bird o'er lustrous woodland, swings the trailer from the crag;

Droops the heavy-blossomed bower, hangs the heavy-fruited tree–
Summer isles of Eden lying in dark-purple spheres of sea.

165 There methinks would be enjoyment more than in this march of mind,
In the steamship, in the railway, in the thoughts that shake mankind.

There the passions cramped no longer shall have scope and breathing
    space;
I will take some savage woman, she shall rear my dusky race.

153–6] *Not MS.*
155. *Mahratta*: soldiers of Bombay who were conquered in 1818. *T.MS*
(0.15.42) has as *1st reading*: 'In the war with Tippoo Sahib'.
156. *orphan*: cp. the story of *Maud*.
157. *Or . . . to*] I will burst the links of habit–I will *MS.*
158. *On from island unto island*] Roaming Oriental islands *MS.*
160 ∧ 1] All about a summer ocean, leagues on leagues of golden calm,
            And within melodious waters rolling round the knolls of palm.
H.T. quotes these lines from the 'original MS'; *Y.MS* has *about*] around;
round] by. 'In the first unpublished edition . . . omitted lest the description
should be too long' (*Mem.* i 195).
162. *swings*] *1851*; droops *1842–50.*   *trailer*] garland *MS.* Adapted from
Anacaona 39–40, the 'birds . . . in the lustrous woodland', another poem
that shows T.'s lifelong interest in island paradises (see Paden, pp. 141–3).
163. *heavy-blossomed bower*] crimson-blossomed trailer *MS.*
167] There my heart should find expansion and my passions breathing space;
MS 1st reading.   *the*] my *MS.*
168–9. Cp. Beaumont's *Philaster* IV i: 'Oh, that I had been nourished in
these woods / . . . and not known / The right of Crowns, nor the dissembling
Trains / Of Women's looks . . . / And then had taken me some Mountain
Girl / . . . and have borne at her big breasts / My large coarse issue. This had
been a life / Free from vexation.' Alongside John Churton Collins's note
on this (*Cornhill*, Jan. 1880), T. wrote 'possibly' (*Lincoln*). The works of
Beaumont and Fletcher were at Somersby (*Lincoln*).

Iron jointed, supple-sinewed, they shall dive, and they shall run,
170 Catch the wild goat by the hair, and hurl their lances in the sun;

Whistle back the parrot's call, and leap the rainbows of the brooks,
Not with blinded eyesight poring over miserable books—

Fool, again the dream, the fancy! but I *know* my words are wild,
But I count the gray barbarian lower than the Christian child.

175 I, to herd with narrow foreheads, vacant of our glorious gains,
Like a beast with lower pleasures, like a beast with lower pains!

Mated with a squalid savage—what to me were sun or clime?
I the heir of all the ages, in the foremost files of time—

I that rather held it better men should perish one by one,
180 Than that earth should stand at gaze like Joshua's moon in Ajalon!

Not in vain the distance beacons. Forward, forward let us range,
Let the great world spin for ever down the ringing grooves of change.

Through the shadow of the globe we sweep into the younger day:
Better fifty years of Europe than a cycle of Cathay.

169. dive] ride *MS 1st reading.*
171. Whistle . . . leap] Shouting in the gorges, leaping through *MS 1st reading.*
173. Fool . . . but] What is this I utter? madness. Well *MS.*
174. But] Well *MS.*
174 ∧ 5] Were there any good in living if we reapt not something new?
That which we have done is earnest of the things that we shall do.
                                                                                MS
These became ll. 117–18.
175] Could I live with narrow foreheads! herd with these about the plains,
MS.
176. lower pains] lesser pains *MS.*
177–8] Could I wed a savage woman steept perhaps in monstrous crime?
Am I not a modern man, a leader of the files of Time? *MS.*
179. I . . . it] It were better, ten times *MS.*
180. Joshua x 12.
182. great world] *1843, MS*; peoples *1842.* T. comments: 'When I went by
the first train from Liverpool to Manchester (1830) I thought that the
wheels ran in a groove. It was a black night, and there was such a vast crowd
round the train at the station that we could not see the wheels. Then I made
this line.'
183. globe] *1843, MS*; world *1842.* This line stood originally as two lines of
The Voyage (*T.Nbk 21*).   *shadow . . . sweep*] shadows . . . rush *MS.*
184. Cathay: China.

185 Mother-Age (for mine I knew not) help me as when life begun:
Rift the hills, and roll the waters, flash the lightnings, weigh the Sun.

O, I see the crescent promise of my spirit hath not set.
Ancient founts of inspiration well through all my fancy yet.

Howsoever these things be, a long farewell to Locksley Hall!
190 Now for me the woods may wither, now for me the roof-tree fall.

Comes a vapour from the margin, blackening over heath and holt,
Cramming all the blast before it, in its breast a thunderbolt.

Let it fall on Locksley Hall, with rain or hail, or fire or snow;
For the mighty wind arises, roaring seaward, and I go.

[1838. *The Epic*–see *p. 146. The Day-Dream*–see *p. 168*]

274 Audley Court

Published *1842*; among 'English Idyls'. It was written autumn 1838 at
Torquay (*Mem.* i 165), 'partially suggested by Abbey Park at Torquay in
the old time' (T.). In *T.Nbk 26*, it opens with a description of Francis's
arrival by boat; see below. There are two early drafts in the *FitzGerald MS* at
Trinity (*MS* below). J. S. Hagen discusses T.'s revisions of ll. 73–88, using
and reproducing *1842* proofs with T.'s changes (*Costerus* n.s. iv, 1975, 39–
49). In form and mood, the poem is based on Theocritus's 7th Idyll, where
Simichidas's song (ll. 96–127) resembles Francis's. Cp. the setting of *The
Princess* with its picnic and songs, especially the swallow-song (iv). On T.s
modernizing and anglicizing of Theocritus, see Turner (p. 82). Culler
(p. 264) 'wonders whether the title of the poem was not suggested by the
well-known country house of Lord Braybrooke, Audley End, at Saffron
Walden near Cambridge. In 1836, just two years before the poem was
published [*read* written], Richard Lord Braybrooke published *The History of
Audley End* . . . in which William Whewell and J. S. Henslow of Cambridge
assisted.'

185–6] Not MS.
186 ∧ 7] Life is battle, let me fight it: win or lose it? lose it, nay!
    Block my paths with toil and danger, I will find or force a way!
Added to a copy belonging to James Knowles (*Nineteenth Century* xxxiii
(1893) 168).
190. roof-tree: the main beam; T.'s hero may include the meaning 'the
whole family, the house'.
¶ 274. *T.Nbk 26* has a version of the beginning of the poem:
    It was the Autumn-feast at Oxley quay,
    And I expected Francis by the boat:
    And while I paced the quay the boat came round
    The headland trailing half a league of smoke.
    She made her way with power up and stilled

'The Bull, the Fleece are crammed, and not a room
For love or money. Let us picnic there
At Audley Court.'
                    I spoke, while Audley feast
Hummed like a hive all round the narrow quay,
5   To Francis, with a basket on his arm,
To Francis just alighted from the boat,
And breathing of the sea. 'With all my heart,'
Said Francis. Then we shouldered through the swarm,
And rounded by the stillness of the beach
10   To where the bay runs up its latest horn.

We left the dying ebb that faintly lipped
The flat red granite; so by many a sweep

The plashing paddlewheels and overhead
The snoring funnel whizzed her silver steam.
    The plank was laid and breathing of the sea
Came Francis with a basket in his hand –
A dash of colour on his cheeks and nose
Won from the wind: and up the hill we went
Across the wake but all the causeway swarmed;
The showman ranted: thrice as large as truth
The black-barred tiger glared upon the poles,
The quack was roaring nostrums: all the street
Buzzed like a hive and over hollowed tubes
Purselipt the swarthy piper moved his beard.
    'O come' said Francis 'I am dinned to death.
The Bull, the Fleece are crammed and not a room
For love of money. Come 'tis not so far.
We two will picnic there at Oxley hall;
See here', and lifting up the basket lid
He showed me lapt in cloth two pullets trusst
With liver-wings and stowed with these a flask
Of cyder from his father's vats at home,
Prime, which I knew: and even while he spoke
We came on John the storyteller, John
The talker, steering downward with a thumb
In either armhole

3. *Audley Court*] Oxley-Hall *FitzGerald MS.*
4]   Hummed like a hive, and over hollowed tubes
                Purse-lipt the swarthy piper moved his beard. *MS*
The last line and a half were incorporated from *The Gardener's Daughter*
185–208, MS.
10. *runs . . . horn*] scoops out its latest curve *MS.*

Of meadow smooth from aftermath we reached
The griffin-guarded gates, and passed through all
15 The pillared dusk of sounding sycamores,
And crossed the garden to the gardener's lodge,
With all its casements bedded, and its walls
And chimneys muffled in the leafy vine.

There, on a slope of orchard, Francis laid
20 A damask napkin wrought with horse and hound,
Brought out a dusky loaf that smelt of home,
And, half-cut-down, a pasty costly-made,
Where quail and pigeon, lark and leveret lay,
Like fossils of the rock, with golden yolks
25 Imbedded and injellied; last, with these,
A flask of cider from his father's vats,
Prime, which I knew; and so we sat and eat
And talked old matters over; who was dead,
Who married, who was like to be, and how
30 The races went, and who would rent the hall:
Then touched upon the game, how scarce it was
This season; glancing thence, discussed the farm,
The four-field system, and the price of grain;
And struck upon the corn-laws, where we split,
35 And came again together on the king
With heated faces; till he laughed aloud;
And, while the blackbird on the pippin hung
To hear him, clapt his hand in mine and sang—

'Oh! who would fight and march and countermarch,
40 Be shot for sixpence in a battle-field,
And shovelled up into some bloody trench
Where no one knows? but let me live my life.
'Oh! who would cast and balance at a desk,
Perched like a crow upon a three-legged stool,

13. aftermath: after-mowing.
15. Cp. *Paradise Lost* ix 1106: 'Pillard shade'.
18. leafy vine: traditional, as in Shelley.
19] We found a slope of thyme where Francis laid *MS.*
28–9. over . . . Who], who was dead, and who / Was *MS.*
34–5. There was Corn-Law agitation in 1837, the year in which William
IV was gravely ill for a month and then died.
37–8]   He clapt his hand in mine: he cleared his pipes
              And while the blackbird on the rennet hung
              To hear him, sang me out a random song. *MS*
41. some] *1872*; a *1842–70*.

45 Till all his juice is dried, and all his joints
    Are full of chalk? but let me live my life.
      'Who'd serve the state? for if I carved my name
    Upon the cliffs that guard my native land,
    I might as well have traced it in the sands;
50 The sea wastes all: but let me live my life.
      'Oh! who would love? I wooed a woman once,
    But she was sharper than an eastern wind,
    And all my heart turned from her, as a thorn
    Turns from the sea; but let me live my life.'

55   He sang his song, and I replied with mine:
    I found it in a volume, all of songs,
    Knocked down to me, when old Sir Robert's pride,
    His books – the more the pity, so I said –
    Came to the hammer here in March – and this –
60 I set the words, and added names I knew.
      'Sleep, Ellen Aubrey, sleep, and dream of me:
    Sleep, Ellen, folded in thy sister's arm,
    And sleeping, haply dream her arm is mine.
      'Sleep, Ellen, folded in Emilia's arm;
65 Emilia, fairer than all else but thou,
    For thou art fairer than all else that is.
      'Sleep, breathing health and peace upon her breast:
    Sleep, breathing love and trust against her lip:
    I go tonight: I come tomorrow morn.
70   'I go, but I return: I would I were
    The pilot of the darkness and the dream.
    Sleep, Ellen Aubrey, love, and dream of me.'

      So sang we each to either, Francis Hale,
    The farmer's son, who lived across the bay,
75 My friend; and I, that having wherewithal,

47. carved] wrote *MS.*
51. love] wed *MS.*
56–60] Not *MS.*

73–7]   So sang we couch't in thyme while overhead
          The large peach fattened and the waxen plum
          Pampered his luscious cheek: tall hollyoaks
          Clustered their largest roses: orchard boughs
          Dragged earthward overburdened: every gust
          Tumbled the mellowing pear and at our feet
          Through two round stones, two cushions of dark moss,
          A pebbly runlet bubbled from the mound. *MS*

This adapts *The Gardener's Daughter* 216–20, MS.

And in the fallow leisure of my life
A rolling stone of here and everywhere,
Did what I would; but ere the night we rose
And sauntered home beneath a moon, that, just
80 In crescent, dimly rained about the leaf
Twilights of airy silver, till we reached
The limit of the hills; and as we sank
From rock to rock upon the glooming quay,
The town was hushed beneath us: lower down
85 The bay was oily calm; the harbour-buoy,
Sole star of phosphorescence in the calm,
With one green sparkle ever and anon
Dipt by itself, and we were glad at heart.

275 Edwin Morris

or, The Lake

Published 1851, *Poems*, 7th edn; among 'English Idyls'. Written 1839 (*Mem.* i 174), which is the date of the *FitzGerald MS* at Trinity. The *FitzGerald MS* begins (at the top of a page) with the closing lines of Edwin's speech (ll. 62–70), in this version adapting further lines from *The Gardener's Daughter*; see ll. 26–40*n*. The poem was inspired by T.'s disillusionment with Rosa Baring; on this love affair, see *Thy rosy lips* (II 59). She married Robert Duncombe Shafto. The complaint, here treated more lightly ('the rentroll Cupid'), is treated tragically as 'marriage-hindering Mammon' in *Aylmer's Field*, *Locksley Hall*, and *Maud*. T. criticizes his earlier manner in the poet Edwin Morris, most of whose lines are from the MS version (e.g. *T.Nbk 17*) of *The Gardener's Daughter*, another poem inspired by Rosa, of which the speaker is again a landscape painter. Edward Bull's views on women were to be more fully presented by the King in *The Princess*. There are three drafts in *T.Nbk 26*; in the first, there is no character Edward Bull; and Morris tells of

77] *1855; not 1842–53.*
78–80]   There sat we till night fell, and rose at last
            Returning home beneath a quarter-moon
            That dimly rained about the lisping leaf *MS*
81. *airy*] showery *MS*.
82–3]   The latest limit of the seaward hill.
            Then as we stept down toward the glooming quay *MS*
86] *1869; not 1842–68.* 'The little buoy appearing and disappearing in the dark sea' (T.).
88. Cp. the image of moon and stars ending *Iliad* viii, as in T.'s *Specimen of a Translation*: 'and the Shepherd gladdens in his heart'.

an episode, suggesting *Maud*, in which his lover's cousin jealously lies in wait for him with a cudgel, unsuccessfully. One important revision is that which eliminates too harsh a resentment against Rosa, cutting out 'O facile nose of wax!', and 'the doll' (ll. 122–5*n*). All variants are below.

O me, my pleasant rambles by the lake,
My sweet, wild, fresh three quarters of a year,
My one Oasis in the dust and drouth
Of city life! I was a sketcher then:
5   See here, my doing: curves of mountain, bridge,
Boat, island, ruins of a castle, built
When men knew how to build, upon a rock
With turrets lichen-gilded like a rock:
And here, new-comers in an ancient hold,
10   New-comers from the Mersey, millionaires,
Here lived the Hills – a Tudor-chimnied bulk
Of mellow brickwork on an isle of bowers.

O me, my pleasant rambles by the lake
With Edwin Morris and with Edward Bull
15   The curate; he was fatter than his cure.

But Edwin Morris, he that knew the names,
Long learnèd names of agaric, moss and fern,
Who forged a thousand theories of the rocks,
Who taught me how to skate, to row, to swim,
20   Who read me rhymes elaborately good,
His own – I called him Crichton, for he seemed
All-perfect, finished to the finger nail.

¶ 275. *1–12*] *Not T.MS.*
2–4] A dilettante sketcher I was then: *H.MS.*
5. *doing*] drawings *H.MS.*
14. Edwin] Edward *T.MS B. Edward Bull*] Edwin Ray *T.MS B 1st reading;* William Bull *T.MS B.*
14–18] With Walter Murray. What a man he was.
      He taught me how to dub the fly for trout: *T.MS A;*
        With Edward Morris: that all-perfect man. [What a man he was.
                              1st reading] *T.MS B*
17. agaric: a fungus.
18] *Added in H.MS.*
19. Who] He *T.MSS. skate . . . swim*] to sketch, to skate, to row, *T.MS A, B, H.MS;* to sketch, to row, to skate, *T.MS C.*
20–22] He taught me how to touch the flageolet: *T.MS A, B;* To touch the flute. He taught me all I know. *T.MS C.*
21. James (the Admirable) Crichton was a sixteenth-century Scottish prodigy; P. F. Tytler's life of him was published 1819.
22. Horace, *Satires* I v 32–3: *ad unguem factus homo.*

And once I asked him of his early life,
And his first passion; and he answered me;
25 And well his words became him: was he not
A full-celled honeycomb of eloquence
Stored from all flowers? Poet-like he spoke.

'My love for Nature is as old as I;
But thirty moons, one honeymoon to that,
30 And three rich sennights more, my love for her.
My love for Nature and my love for her,
Of different ages, like twin-sisters grew,
Twin-sisters differently beautiful.
To some full music rose and sank the sun,
35 And some full music seemed to move and change
With all the varied changes of the dark,
And either twilight and the day between;
For daily hope fulfilled, to rise again
Revolving toward fulfilment, made it sweet
40 To walk, to sit, to sleep, to wake, to breathe.'

Or this or something like to this he spoke.
Then said the fat-faced curate Edward Bull,

'I take it, God made the woman for the man,
And for the good and increase of the world.
45 A pretty face is well, and this is well,

23] I was a lover and I questioned him *T.MS A*; I askt him of his life and of
his love *T.MS B*; And once I askt him of his life, his love, *T.MS C*.
24. *And*] Of *T.MS A*.
25. *was he not*] for he was *T.MS A 1st reading*.
26–40. These lines were incorporated, with only minor modifications, from
MSS of *The Gardener's Daughter* (see headnote); some are in *Heath MS*
version, others in *T.MS* drafts. T. apparently added ll. 28–30, 33.
27. *Poet-like*] like to this *T.MS, H.MS*. *spoke*] spake *T.MSS*.
28–30] Not *T.MS A*.
28. *for*] of *T.MS A 1st reading, H.MS 1st reading*.
32. *grew*] *T.MS, 1853*; throve *1851*.
40. *to wake, to breathe*] *1853*; transposed *1851–3*.
41] Not *T.MSS, H.MS*.
42–57] 'A happy dream' I said 'which cannot last,
        Yet something to remember. You are one
        That look on all things through a coloured glass. *T.MS A*
42. *Edward Bull*] Edwin Ray *T.MS B 1st reading*; William Bull *T.MS B*.
45. *this*] it *T.MS B, C*.
45–7] I see my boys and prosper and I have
        A dame indoors that trims them up and keeps
        A sharp look out: but these unreal ways *T.MS B 1st reading*

To have a dame indoors, that trims us up,
And keeps us tight; but these unreal ways
Seem but the theme of writers, and indeed
Worn threadbare. Man is made of solid stuff.
50   I say, God made the woman for the man,
And for the good and increase of the world.'

'Parson,' said I, 'you pitch the pipe too low:
But I have sudden touches, and can run
My faith beyond my practice into his:
55   Though if, in dancing after Letty Hill,
I do not hear the bells upon my cap,
I scarce have other music: yet say on.
What should one give to light on such a dream?'
I asked him half-sardonically.
'Give?
60   Give all thou art,' he answered, and a light
Of laughter dimpled in his swarthy cheek;
'I would have hid her needle in my heart,
To save her little finger from a scratch
No deeper than the skin: my ears could hear
65   Her lightest breath; her least remark was worth
The experience of the wise. I went and came;
Her voice fled always through the summer land;
I spoke her name alone. Thrice-happy days!

47. *tight*: neat.
48. *writers*] poets *T.MS B, C.*
52. *Parson*] My God *T.MS B, C*; O sir *H.MS 1st reading.   said I*] I said *T.MS B
1st reading.*
55. *Letty*] Emma *T.MS B, C, H.MS.*
57. *have*} *1869*; hear *1851–68.   yet*] but *T.MS B, C.*
59] Not *T.MSS, H.MS.*
60. *he . . . light*] he said: 'for me I think *T.MS A.   light*] gleam *T.MS B, C.*
61] Not *T.MS A.*
62. *would*] could *T.MS A.*
62–70. Adapted from MSS of *The Gardener's Daughter*; see headnote and
ll. 26–40*n.*
65. *breath*] *1872*; breaths *1851–70.*
66. *wise* ∧ *I*] :her daily life / Like noble instance – and *T.MS A.*
68. *alone* ∧ *Thrice-*]   : to speak her name
                    Was like a violation of reserve
                    Where foreign sweetness in familiar sound
                    Made the voice precious: or I sketcht for her
                    A glimpse of [The summer *1st reading*] landskip crisp
                    with shining woods,

The flower of each, those moments when we met,
70 The crown of all, we met to part no more.'

And giving parted paid beyond all hope
By some stray-riband balmy with her curls,
A locket or a glove of primrose kid
Fit for the hands of spring – its worth to me
That it was airy-modelled with her own'.
So far he flowed and with a staff he struck
The wayside flowers: and I laught aloud.
My laugh a little froze him but he said
'It is a trick I have: one twines a thread,
One plucks a rose: I flourish with my staff.
But there is hidden virtue in the wood
And hereby hangs a tale: for Ellen had
A cousin with a cheek of spongy dough [blowzy grain
                                        1st reading],
A head so white he lookt old age in youth,
Nicknamed white Peter: and a grosser clown
Than slouching Peter never crost between
Lintel and threshold: this thing fell in love,
Grew jealous and laid watch for me one night
With this same cudgel: but I waited long.
The lout was overwatcht and when I past
As lies a sheep within a furrow lay
Rolled on his back and snoring to the moon.
And stooping, from his hand I pluckt the staff
To thwack his ribs: but spared him for her sake
And kept it as a relic of those times!'
He left his episode and on he went
Like one that cuts an eight upon the ice
Returning on himself. *T.MS A*

T.MS B has here the first few lines ('to speak . . . precious'); *T.MS C* ends
with l. 68 (foot of page; pages missing). Cp. 'But there is hidden virtue in the
wood' with *The Princess* vi 34: 'There dwelt an iron nature in the grain'; and
the relating of talking to skating with *The Epic* 6–13 ('cutting eights').
68. *Thrice*-] Three times *T.MS B 1st reading*.
69–70] The crown of all, those moments when I watcht
        The pure and maiden spirit fold by fold
        Open before me, till she read and knew
        The meaning of my glances: even until
        Silent, with eyelids drooping, she resigned
        Her bosom to the transport of mine arms –
        With drooping eyelids silent, when the storm
        Of my first welcome pouring kiss on kiss

Were not his words delicious, I a beast
To take them as I did? but something jarred;
Whether he spoke too largely; that there seemed
A touch of something false, some self-conceit,
75   Or over-smoothness: howsoe'er it was,
He scarcely hit my humour, and I said:

'Friend Edwin, do not think yourself alone
Of all men happy. Shall not Love to me,
As in the Latin song I learnt at school,
80   Sneeze out a full God-bless-you right and left?
But you can talk: yours is a kindly vein:
I have, I think, – Heaven knows – as much within;

Incessantly like flashes of soft light
Melted from lip to lip and from my heart
Sank fused in hers, then growing one with mine'. *T.MS A*;
  The crown of each, those moments, when the storm
  Of my full welcome pouring kiss on kiss
  Melted from lip to lip and from my heart
  Sank fused in hers then growing one with mine'. *T.MS B*
Cp. *The Gardener's Daughter* 185–208, MS, which has a version of this long
passage (I 564).
71–5] All this and more he said: but something jarred. *T.MS A*. Implicit
criticism by T. of his earlier poetic manner; see ll. 62–70n. The name
'Edwin' for such a poet may have been suggested by the hero of Beattie's
Minstrel (ii 524–6), which provided an epigraph for *1827* (p. 61), of which
there was a copy at Somersby (*Lincoln*) and of which T.'s mother was fond
(H. D. Rawnsley, *Memories of the Tennysons*, 1900, pp. 225–6): 'Of late,
with cumbersome, though pompous show, / Edwin would oft his flowery
rhyme deface, / Through ardour to adorn.' Cp. l. 27 above.
74. some] or *FitzGerald MS.*
75–6] I know not what: a screw was loose: I said: *T.MS B, H.MS, FitzGerald
MS.*
77. Friend] O *T.MS A*.   *Edwin*] Walter *T.MS A*; Edward *T.MS B*.
78. Shall . . . me,] I am happy too. *T.MS A*.
79] Not *T.MS A, B, H.MS, FitzGerald MS.*
80. H.T. compares Catullus xlv 8–9: *hoc ut dixit, Amor, sinistra, ut ante / dextra,
sternuit approbationem.* ('As he said this, Love on the left, as before on the
right, sneezed goodwill.')
80] Not *T.MS A*.
81] 'Tis true, I have not such a kindly vein: *T.MS A*.   *yours is*] you have
T.MS B, FitzGerald MS.   *kindly vein*: Horace, *Odes* II xviii 10: *benigna
vena.*
82–3] I have, I think, as much within – I have / Or I should . . . *T.MS A, B,
H.MS, FitzGerald MS.* Cp. *Hamlet* I ii 85: 'But·I have that within which
passes show.'

Have, or should have, but for a thought or two,
That like a purple beech among the greens
85 Looks out of place: 'tis from no want in her:
It is my shyness, or my self-distrust,
Or something of a wayward modern mind
Dissecting passion. Time will set me right.'

So spoke I knowing not the things that were.
90 Then said the fat-faced curate, Edward Bull:
'God made the woman for the use of man,
And for the good and increase of the world.'
And I and Edwin laughed; and now we paused
About the windings of the marge to hear
95 The soft wind blowing over meadowy holms
And alders, garden-isles; and now we left
The clerk behind us, I and he, and ran
By ripply shallows of the lisping lake,
Delighted with the freshness and the sound.

100   But, when the bracken rusted on their crags,
My suit had withered, nipt to death by him
That was a God, and is a lawyer's clerk,
The rentroll Cupid of our rainy isles.
'Tis true, we met; one hour I had, no more:

84. *purple*] *1853*; copper *1851*.   *greens*] green *T.MS A*.
85. *from*] for *T.MS B, FitzGerald MS*.   *want*] fault *T.MS A*.
87. *Or*] 'Tis *T.MS A*.
87–8. *Or . . . passion:* originally in the MS of *The Gardener's Daughter* (*T.Nbk 17*); see ll. *62–70n*.
90. *Edward Bull*] Edwin Ray *T.MS B 1st reading*; William Bull *T.MS B*.
90–3] And in such talk we wore the random day. *T.MS A*.
93. *Edwin*] *T.MS B 1st reading*; Edward *T.MS B*.
94. *About . . . of*] And now we paused about *T.MS A*.
95. *over . . . holms*] in the osiered aits *T.MS A, B, H.MS, FitzGerald MS*. (As in *To the Vicar of Shiplake* 30.)
96. *left*] *1853*; ran *1851*.
97] *1853*; not *1851*.
100] But ere November [December *T.MS A, B, FitzGerald MS*] came, my own suit failed [my suit had failed *T.MS A*], *T.MS B, H.MS*.
101–2] Nipt by the true magician of the ring, *T.MS B, FitzGerald MS*.
101–3] Not *T.MS A*; Nipt by the rentroll Cupid of the realms. *H.MS*.
103. *our*] *1853*; the *1851*.
104–14] 'Tis true, we met: we kisst: swore faith: I breathed *T.MS B, FitzGerald MS*.
104–15] 'Tis true: we met: we kist: we broke a ring.
            Not those two Heavens in air and water touch

105 She sent a note, the seal an *Elle vous suit,*
       The close, 'Your Letty, only yours;' and this
       Thrice underscored. The friendly mist of morn
       Clung to the lake. I boated over, ran
       My craft aground, and heard with beating heart
110 The Sweet-Gale rustle round the shelving keel;
       And out I stept, and up I crept: she moved,
       Like Proserpine in Enna, gathering flowers:
       Then low and sweet I whistled thrice; and she,
       She turned, we closed, we kissed, swore faith, I breathed
115 In some new planet: a silent cousin stole
       Upon us and departed: 'Leave,' she cried,
       'O leave me!' 'Never, dearest, never: here
       I brave the worst:' and while we stood like fools
       Embracing, all at once a score of pugs
120 And poodles yelled within, and out they came
       Trustees and Aunts and Uncles. 'What, with him!
       Go' (shrilled the cotton-spinning chorus); 'him!'

And kiss each other to a perfect sphere
So sweetly. Was I happy? for an hour.
A brother came upon us unawares. *T.MS A*
105–8] She sent a note: I boated over, ran *H.MS.*
105. Byron, *Don Juan* I cxcviii: 'The seal a sunflower: "*Elle vous suit partout*"', a moment in Don Juan's 'earliest scrape'.
111] And out I leapt and hid myself. She walked *H.MS.*
112. Eve in Paradise, *Paradise Lost* iv 269, with suggestions of precariousness. T. had praised Rosa with the allusion in *The Gardener's Daughter* 187.
114. *we closed*] she came *H.MS.*
115. *cousin*] brother *T.MS B*, *FitzGerald MS*, *H.MS 1st reading*. An interesting parallel with the situation in *Maud*, where the brother steals upon the lovers.
115–20]   . . . silent brother came
            Upon us: ere a man could clap his hands,
            The cat was in the creampot. Out they came, *T.MS B,*
                                            FitzGerald MS
116–25]   The cat was in the creampot. All was blown.
          I might as well have tried to filch the comb
          From some full hive. A palsy shake [The Devil take *1st reading*]
              them all.
          A bib-and-tucker love, a doll of wax! *T.MS A*
116–18. 'Leave . . . worst:'] 'O', she said,
            'O leave me, leave me.' 'Never, let us brave
            The worst at once' *H.MS*
122] *1853; not 1851. cotton-spinning*: possibly this refers to one of Rosa's uncles (Rader, p. 135); 'cotton' is used with contempt in *Maud* i 370, and 'cotton-spinners' in *The Third of February, 1852,* but there in dislike of the

I choked. Again they shrieked the burthen – 'Him!'
Again with hands of wild rejection 'Go! –
125 Girl, get you in!' She went – and in one month
They wedded her to sixty thousand pounds,
To lands in Kent and messuages in York,
And slight Sir Robert with his watery smile
And educated whisker. But for me,
130 They set an ancient creditor to work:
It seems I broke a close with force and arms:
There came a mystic token from the king
To greet the sheriff, needless courtesy!
I read, and fled by night, and flying turned:
135 Her taper glimmered in the lake below:
I turned once more, close-buttoned to the storm;
So left the place, left Edwin, nor have seen
Him since, nor heard of her, nor cared to hear.

peace-loving politics of Manchester. Rader also remarks that 'trustees'
(l. 121) is unexplained in Letty's case, but that Rosa's rich father had died.
122–5]   'Go, Sir!' and 'collar him' and 'let him go'
          And 'get you in' ['hit him down' *1st reading*] O facile [O doll! o
                    1st reading] nose of wax! *T.MS B;*
          'Go, Sir' and 'collar him' and 'get you in'
          And 'let him go.' O facile nose of wax! *FitzGerald MS;*
          They clamoured, and again in chorus, 'him!',
          'Go, Sir' and 'collar him' and 'let him go'
          And 'get *you* in' – the doll – and in one month *H.MS*
'nose of wax': *OED* under *nose* 4, 'a thing easily turned or moulded in any
way desired; a person easily influenced, one of a weak character'.
123. *I choked.*] *1853;* 'Go Sir!' *1851.*
125. *She went*] *1853;* to her *1851.*
127] Not *T.MS A, B, FitzGerald MS.* Cp. Byron, *Don Juan* I xxxvii 1–2:
'sole heir / To a chancery suit and messuages and lands'.
128. *And ... watery*] To ... sickly *T.MS A;* To ... vapid *T.MS B,
FitzGerald MS. H.MS* ends with l. 128 at the bottom of a page, so a page is
probably missing).
130] Not *T.MS A.*
131–6] Not *T.MS A, B, FitzGerald MS.*
132. 'Writ from the old Court of Common Pleas' (T.).
134] *1853;*   I read and wished to crush the race of man,
                And fled by night; turned once upon the hills; *1851*
135. *below*] *1853;* and then *1851.*
136] *1853; not 1851.*
137. *So*] *1853;* I *1851.* ,*left*] and *T.MS A. Edwin*] Walter *T.MS A;* Edward
T.MS B.
138. *cared to hear.*] care to hear *T.MS A.*

Nor cared to hear? perhaps: yet long ago
140 I have pardoned little Letty; not indeed,
It may be, for her own dear sake but this,
She seems a part of those fresh days to me;
For in the dust and drouth of London life
She moves among my visions of the lake,
145 While the prime swallow dips his wing, or then
While the gold-lily blows, and overhead
The light cloud smoulders on the summer crag.

276 The Golden Year

Published *1846*. Sir Charles Tennyson (p. 211) says that, like *Edwin Morris*, it was written at Llanberis in summer 1845. But it was almost certainly written on the visit there in 1839. It is in *T.Nbk 26*; *Edwin Morris* is to be dated 1839; the song in *The Golden Year* (ll. 22–51), which is the core of the poem, is to be found on a sheet of the *Y.MS* of *Locksley Hall* (1837–8); and the discussion of free trade resembles, as does the poem in general, *Audley Court* (1838) and *Walking to the Mail* (1837–8). See also the reference to Charles Babbage (1837), ll. 59–64n. The incorporated song suggests Theocritus, especially vi. Cp. *Audley Court* (p. 193). The idea of the golden year is based on the classical conception of the great new era, as in Virgil, *Eclogue* iv. In the earlier draft (*H.Lpr 72*), Leonard too had doubts about progress; see ll. 59–64n. All variants from *T.MS* are below; it ends with l. 21 (foot of page).

Well, you shall have that song which Leonard wrote:
It was last summer on a tour in Wales:
Old James was with me: we that day had been
Up Snowdon; and I wished for Leonard there,
5 And found him in Llanberis: then we crost
Between the lakes, and clambered half way up

139–43] Not *T.MS A, B, FitzGerald MS.*
144] Nor evermore shall pace beside the lake *T.MS A*; Yet comes at times a vision of the lake, *T.MS B, FitzGerald MS.*
145. While] When *T.MS A, B, FitzGerald MS. or*] nor *T.MS A.*
146. While] When *T.MS A, B.*
¶ 276. *1. song which*] Poem *T.MS.*
2–7] Not *T.MS;   I came with James upon him while he sat*
                    Beside the mere; and that same song of his *H.MS*
5–7] 1851; And found him in Llanberis; and that same song *1846–50.*
12. Proverbs xxx 15: 'The horse-leech hath two daughters, crying, Give, give.'

The counter side; and that same song of his
He told me; for I bantered him, and swore
They said he lived shut up within himself,
10 A tongue-tied Poet in the feverous days,
That, setting the *how much* before the *how*,
Cry, like the daughters of the horseleech, 'Give,
Cram us with all,' but count not me the herd!

To which 'They call me what they will,' he said:
15 'But I was born too late: the fair new forms,
That float about the threshold of an age,
Like truths of Science waiting to be caught –
Catch me who can, and make the catcher crowned –
Are taken by the forelock. Let it be.
20 But if you care indeed to listen, hear
These measured words, my work of yestermorn.

'We sleep and wake and sleep, but all things move;
The Sun flies forward to his brother Sun;
The dark Earth follows wheeled in her ellipse;
25 And human things returning on themselves
Move onward, leading up the golden year.
    'Ah, though the times, when some new thought can
        bud,
Are but as poets' seasons when they flower,
Yet oceans daily gaining on the land,
30 Have ebb and flow conditioning their march,
And slow and sure comes up the golden year.
    'When wealth no more shall rest in mounded heaps,

14–15] And Leonard said, half earnest half in jest,
'They call me what they will – but I, Sir, born
Here at the fag end of a brassy term
With half its freshness gone – the common brain
And so my part within it overworn
From too-long exercise to fatuousness –
I shall not reap my name. Fresh forms and fair *T.MS*
1st reading of the second and third lines: '... will – a Poet, no. / Born at ...'
19 ∧ 20] The thought itself implies a barren soul. *T.MS.*
29] *1890*; Yet seas that daily gain upon the shore *1846–89*. Shakespeare,
Sonnet 64: 'the hungry ocean gain / Advantage on the kingdom of the
shore'.
32–33. Cp. a fragment in *H.Lpr 210*, from 'an old idyll never published'
(William Allingham, *Diary*, 1907, p. 303): 'The rich shall wed the rich, the
poor the poor, / So shall this mount of wealth be higher still, / So shall
this gulf of want be deeper still, / Until this mountain melt into this gulf /
With all confusion.'

But smit with freër light shall slowly melt
In many streams to fatten lower lands,
35 And light shall spread, and man be liker man
Through all the season of the golden year.
'Shall eagles not be eagles? wrens be wrens?
If all the world were falcons, what of that?
The wonder of the eagle were the less,
40 But he not less the eagle. Happy days
Roll onward, leading up the golden year.
'Fly, happy happy sails, and bear the Press;
Fly happy with the mission of the Cross;
Knit land to land, and blowing havenward
45 With silks, and fruits, and spices, clear of toll,
Enrich the markets of the golden year.
'But we grow old. Ah! when shall all men's good
Be each man's rule, and universal Peace
Lie like a shaft of light across the land,
50 And like a lane of beams athwart the sea,
Through all the circle of the golden year?'

Thus far he flowed, and ended; whereupon
'Ah, folly!' in mimic cadence answered James –
'Ah, folly! for it lies so far away,
55 Not in our time, nor in our children's time,
'Tis like the second world to us that live;
'Twere all as one to fix our hopes on Heaven
As on this vision of the golden year.'

With that he struck his staff against the rocks
60 And broke it, – James, – you know him, – old, but full

37. The antithesis *wrens* / *eagles* suggests *Richard III* I iii 71.
42. Cp. Washington Irving's *Columbus* (1828) I vi, on the new uniting forces in the world: 'light . . . would still shine on, dispensed to happier parts of the world, by the diffusive powers of the press.' T. used the book for *Anacaona* and *Columbus*.
48–52. Cp. Shelley, *Queen Mab* viii 53–7: 'O human Spirit! spur thee to the goal / Where virtue fixes universal peace, / And midst the ebb and flow of human things, / Shew somewhat stable, somewhat certain still, / A lighthouse o'er the wild of dreary waves.' Cp. also l. 30.
53] Right in his rhythm and cadence answered James. *H.MS.* James speaks as a Carlylean, as W. C. DeVane observes.
59–64]   He said; and having business in the town
             Departed, leaving Leonard, who began
             To ponder: 'will it come or, being come,

Of force and choler, and firm upon his feet,
And like an oaken stock in winter woods,
O'erflourished with the hoary clematis:
Then added, all in heat:
                              'What stuff is this!
65 Old writers pushed the happy season back,—
The more fools they,—we forward: dreamers both:
You most, that in an age, when every hour
Must sweat her sixty minutes to the death,
Live on, God love us, as if the seedsman, rapt
70 Upon the teeming harvest, should not plunge
His hand into the bag: but well I know
That unto him who works, and feels he works,
This same grand year is ever at the doors.'

Be felt as gain? this age of ours is gold
To much before it; yet no happier we,
Nor may our sons be happier than ourselves.
O grand old sires, who wagged their beards in hall
And laughed and let the earth go round, nor knew
The noiseless ether curdling into worlds
And complicated clockwork of the suns.
Motion: why motion? were it not as well
To fix a point, to rest? again, it seems
Most adverse to the nature of a man
To rest if there be any more to gain.
And there is all but what he is: no rest:
Why then, to be resolved into the all.
That will not do, being to lose myself.
What else?'—And here, methought he seemed to grasp
A pair of shadowy compasses, with these
To plant a centre and about it round
A wide and wider circle: and while he mused
Came James, his business ended, and resumed: H.MS

An important passage in *MS*, because of its close correspondence with T.'s
thinking. For the astronomy, cp. Babbage, *The Ninth Bridgewater Treatise*
(1837, p. 91), of which T. had a copy (*Lincoln*); of the heavens, Babbage says
'nebulous light is just curdling, as it were, into separate systems'. T.'s
'complicated clockwork' may owe something to the fact that Babbage
passes on to his clockwork 'calculating engine'.

63. Cp. *Twelfth Night* III iv 368: 'empty trunks o'erflourished'.

70. *plunge*] *1865 Selection*; dip *1846–65*.

72 ∧ 3] Howe'er it be, by some true art of Life, *H.MS*.

He spoke; and, high above, I heard them blast
75 The steep slate-quarry, and the great echo flap
And buffet round the hills, from bluff to bluff.

277 The Vision of Sin

Published *1842*. *HnMS* (HM 1320) is watermarked 1835. Not completed till after 1839. The fountain (ll. 8–32) was 'partly suggested by Turner's "Fountain of Fallacy"' (F. T. Palgrave's note from T.; see C. Ricks, *MP* lxii (1964) 139–40). This was exhibited in 1839, and J. M. W. Turner's verse-fragment in the catalogue spoke of 'its rainbow-dew' (cp. ll. 32, 42). Turner (p. 97) quotes contemporary descriptions of the Turner picture, which has not survived, and speculates on what it is likely to have given to T. T. comments: 'This describes the soul of a youth who has given himself up to pleasure and Epicureanism. He at length is worn out and wrapt in the mists of satiety. Afterwards he grows into a cynical old man afflicted with the "curse of nature", and joining in the Feast of Death. Then we see the landscape which symbolizes God, Law and the future life.' In a letter (*Brotherton Collection*), T. described it as 'one of my poems, which I confess has always been a favourite with myself'. Allingham quotes Patmore, 18 Aug. 1849: '"Tennyson perhaps likes the *Vision of Sin* best of his own poems. He said it was suggested to him by a line rejected from another poem." (This line is, I afterwards learned, "A little grain of conscience made him sour".)' (*Diary*, 1907, p. 54). FitzGerald remarks that 'Johnson's "Long-expected one-and-twenty" has the swing, and something of the spirit of the old sinner's lyric.' Cp. section iv with the drinking-song at the end of Burns's *The Jolly Beggars*: 'What is title? what is treasure? / What is reputation's care? / If we lead a life of pleasure, / 'Tis no matter, how or where!' J. H. Buckley (p. 72) tentatively compares Keats's *Lamia* ii, 'purple-lined palace of sweet sin'. A few details suggest Shelley's *The Triumph of Life*. All variants from *HnMS* (HM 1320) are given below. The use of the heroic couplet is very unusual for T.

I

I had a vision when the night was late:
A youth came riding toward a palace-gate.

74. above] *1851*; above us *1846–50*; o'erhead *Eversley* 'original reading'.
76. T. comments: 'Onomatopoeic. "Bluff to bluff" gives the echo of the blasting as I heard it from the mountain on the counter side, opposite to Snowdon.' Cp. *The Princess* vii 229–30, MS: 'Till the last fire shall catch and flap from peak / To peak across the world.'
¶ *277.1. vision . . . was*] dream when night was wearing *HnMS 1st reading*.

He rode a horse with wings, that would have flown,
But that his heavy rider kept him down.
5 And from the palace came a child of sin,
And took him by the curls, and led him in,
Where sat a company with heated eyes,
Expecting when a fountain should arise:
A sleepy light upon their brows and lips –
10 As when the sun, a crescent of eclipse,
Dreams over lake and lawn, and isles and capes –
Suffused them, sitting, lying, languid shapes,
By heaps of gourds, and skins of wine, and piles of
   grapes.

II
Then methought I heard a mellow sound,
15 Gathering up from all the lower ground;
Narrowing in to where they sat assembled
Low voluptuous music winding trembled,
Woven in circles: they that heard it sighed,
Panted hand-in-hand with faces pale,
20 Swung themselves, and in low tones replied;
Till the fountain spouted, showering wide
Sleet of diamond-drift and pearly hail;
Then the music touched the gates and died;
Rose again from where it seemed to fail,
25 Stormed in orbs of song, a growing gale;

3–4. Turner (p. 95) notes that 'in Plato's *Phaedrus* the soul is a chariot (with Reason as charioteer) drawn around heaven by two winged horses, one good and one bad. The weight of the bad horse brings the soul down to earth'.
6. A. A. Mendilow suggests that this ironically adapts the angel of *Ezekiel* viii 3, 'And he put forth the form of a hand, and took me by a lock of mine head; and the spirit lifted me up between the earth and the heaven, and brought me in the visions of God to Jerusalem', *Scripta Hierosolymitana* xvii (1966) 177.
8. Turner suggests the influence of 'the *Bacchae* of Euripides (which T. probably read in connection with his *Semele*), which one Bacchant produces a spring of water by sticking a thyrsus into a rock, and another creates a fountain of wine by planting her thyrsus in the earth'.
9] A glooming trance of light on brows and lips – *MS 1st reading*.
12. *Suffused*] Rained round *MS 1st reading*.
14. *mellow sound*: rhyming with 'ground', in Keats, *Endymion* i 146.
17–45. Cp. the Bacchantes in *Semele* (*c*.1833, I 630): 'voluptuous', 'throbbed', 'melody', 'giddiest'. 'Music-rolling orbs' suggests l. 25, 'orbs of song'.

Till thronging in and in, to where they waited,
As 'twere a hundred-throated nightingale,
The strong tempestuous treble throbbed and palpitated;
Ran into its giddiest whirl of sound,
30   Caught the sparkles, and in circles,
Purple gauzes, golden hazes, liquid mazes,
Flung the torrent rainbow round:
Then they started from their places,
Moved with violence, changed in hue,
35   Caught each other with wild grimaces,
Half-invisible to the view,
Wheeling with precipitate paces
To the melody, till they flew,
Hair, and eyes, and limbs, and faces,
40   Twisted hard in fierce embraces,
Like to Furies, like to Graces,
Dashed together in blinding dew:
Till, killed with some luxurious agony,
The nerve-dissolving melody
45   Fluttered headlong from the sky.

III

And then I looked up toward a mountain-tract,
That girt the region with high cliff and lawn:
I saw that every morning, far withdrawn
Beyond the darkness and the cataract,
50   God made Himself an awful rose of dawn,
Unheeded: and detaching, fold by fold,
From those still heights, and, slowly drawing near,
A vapour heavy, hueless, formless, cold,
Came floating on for many a month and year,
55   Unheeded: and I thought I would have spoken,
And warned that madman ere it grew too late:
But, as in dreams, I could not. Mine was broken,
When that cold vapour touched the palace gate,

30–2. Cp. *Those worldly goods* (*1827*), by T.'s brother Charles: 'As torrent-
rainbows, which appear / Still dwindling as we still draw near; / And yet
contracting on the eye, / Till the bright circling colours die.'
31. *liquid*] lucid MS *1st reading.*
32–42. Cp. the unadopted stanza of *The Palace of Art* (p. 55).
35–6] *Added in MS.*
40 ∧ 1] Fierce embraces, wild grimaces, MS, *deleted.*
52] The brooding burthen of a nameless fear, MS *1st reading.*
58. *touched*] swam MS.

And linked again. I saw within my head
60 A gray and gap-toothed man as lean as death,
Who slowly rode across a withered heath,
And lighted at a ruined inn, and said:

IV

'Wrinkled ostler, grim and thin!
Here is custom come your way;
65 Take my brute, and lead him in,
Stuff his ribs with mouldy hay.

'Bitter barmaid, waning fast!
See that sheets are on my bed;
What! the flower of life is past:
70 It is long before you wed.

'Slip-shod waiter, lank and sour,
At the Dragon on the heath!
Let us have a quiet hour,
Let us hob-and-nob with Death.

75 'I am old, but let me drink;
Bring me spices, bring me wine;
I remember, when I think,
That my youth was half divine.

'Wine is good for shrivelled lips,
80 When a blanket wraps the day,
When the rotten woodland drips,
And the leaf is stamped in clay.

'Sit thee down, and have no shame,
Cheek by jowl, and knee by knee:
85 What care I for any name?
What for order or degree?

'Let me screw thee up a peg:
Let me loose thy tongue with wine:
Callest thou that thing a leg?
90 Which is thinnest? thine or mine?

'Thou shalt not be saved by works:
Thou hast been a sinner too:

75-8] MS has, faintly, a half-worked version as well.
87-8] Screw thy fancies up a peg,
     Neither take my moods amiss. MS alternative fragment
91. Galatians ii 16.

Ruined trunks on withered forks,
Empty scarecrows, I and you!

95 'Fill the cup, and fill the can:
Have a rouse before the morn:
Every moment dies a man,
Every moment one is born.

'We are men of ruined blood;
100   Therefore comes it we are wise.
Fish are we that love the mud,
Rising to no fancy-flies.

'Name and fame! to fly sublime
Through the courts, the camps, the schools,
105 Is to be the ball of Time,
Bandied by the hands of fools.

'Friendship!–to be two in one–
Let the canting liar pack!
Well I know, when I am gone,
110   How she mouths behind my back.

'Virtue!–to be good and just–
Every heart, when sifted well,
Is a clot of warmer dust,
Mixed with cunning sparks of hell.

115 'O! we two as well can look
Whited thought and cleanly life

97 and 98. moment] *1851*; minute *1842–50*. *Locksley Hall* 136 ∧ 7, MS
(*p. 190*), included the line: 'Every moment dies a man and every
moment one is born.'
103–6]   Systems! we whose bones are chalk
                Hear to these when made complete
            As to odds and ends of talk
                Heard in passing through the street. *MS 1st reading*
Together with the MS stanza, ll. 114 ∧ 5, cp. *The Two Voices* 207: 'A dust
of systems and of creeds'. Lines 103–6 were adapted from *Wherefore, in these*
dark ages of the Press 11–13: 'my name / Shot like a racketball from mouth
to mouth / And bandied in the barren lips of fools'.
106. by] *1855*; in *1842–53*.
114 ∧ *15*]   Creeds! go up: make straight the hair,
                Give the chapter and the verse,
            Whine the text and drawl the prayer–
                Flee, belovèd, from the curse. *MS, deleted*

As the priest, above his book
Leering at his neighbour's wife.

'Fill the cup, and fill the can:
120   Have a rouse before the morn:
Every moment dies a man,
    Every moment one is born.

'Drink, and let the parties rave:
    They are filled with idle spleen;
125   Rising, falling, like a wave,
    For they know not what they mean.

'He that roars for liberty
    Faster binds a tyrant's power;
And the tyrant's cruel glee
130   Forces on the freer hour.

'Fill the can, and fill the cup:
    All the windy ways of men
Are but dust that rises up,
    And is lightly laid again.

135   'Greet her with applausive breath,
    Freedom, gaily doth she tread;
In her right a civic wreath,
    In her left a human head.

'No, I love not what is new;
140   She is of an ancient house:
And I think we know the hue
    Of that cap upon her brows.

'Let her go! her thirst she slakes
    Where the bloody conduit runs,
145   Then her sweetest meal she makes
    On the first-born of her sons.

'Drink to lofty hopes that cool–
    Visions of a perfect State:
Drink we, last, the public fool,
150   Frantic love and frantic hate.

117. his] the MS 1st reading.
121 and 122. moment] 1851; minute 1842–50.
128. a] 1845; the 1842–3.
141–2. S. Shatto and M. Shaw compare In Memoriam cxxvii, MS: 'The red-capt harlot of the Seine'.

'Chant me now some wicked stave,
　　Till thy drooping courage rise,
And the glow-worm of the grave
　　Glimmer in thy rheumy eyes.

155 'Fear not thou to loose thy tongue;
　　Set thy hoary fancies free;
What is loathsome to the young
　　Savours well to thee and me.

'Change, reverting to the years,
160　　When thy nerves could understand
What there is in loving tears,
　　And the warmth of hand in hand.

'Tell me tales of thy first love –
　　April hopes, the fools of chance;
165 Till the graves begin to move,
　　And the dead begin to dance.

'Fill the can, and fill the cup:
　　All the windy ways of men
Are but dust that rises up,
170　　And is lightly laid again.

'Trooping from their mouldy dens
　　The chap-fallen circle spreads:
Welcome, fellow-citizens,
　　Hollow hearts and empty heads!

175 'You are bones, and what of that?
　　Every face, however full,
Padded round with flesh and fat,
　　Is but modelled on a skull.

'Death is king, and Vivat Rex!
180　　Tread a measure on the stones,
Madam – if I know your sex,
　　From the fashion of your bones.

'No, I cannot praise the fire
　　In your eye – nor yet your lip:
185 All the more do I admire
　　Joints of cunning workmanship.

'Lo! God's likeness – the ground-plan –
　　Neither modelled, glazed, nor framed:

175–8, 179–82] *Transposed at first in MS.*
188. *nor*] *1874*; or *1842–72.*

Buss me, thou rough sketch of man,
190 Far too naked to be shamed!
'Drink to Fortune, drink to Chance,
While we keep a little breath!
Drink to heavy Ignorance!
Hob-and-nob with brother Death!
195 'Thou art mazed, the night is long,
And the longer night is near:
What! I am not all as wrong
As a bitter jest is dear.

'Youthful hopes, by scores, to all,
200 When the locks are crisp and curled;
Unto me my maudlin gall
And my mockeries of the world.

'Fill the cup, and fill the can:
Mingle madness, mingle scorn!
205 Dregs of life, and lees of man:
Yet we will not die forlorn.'

v

The voice grew faint: there came a further change:
Once more uprose the mystic mountain-range:
Below were men and horses pierced with worms,
210 And slowly quickening into lower forms;
By shards and scurf of salt, and scum of dross,

190 ∧ *1*]   Death is king, and Vivat Rex!
          Dance with me, ideal men—
        Vivat Rex and Curat Lex,
          Hands across and back again. MS, *deleted*
Alluding to the saying, De minimis non curat lex.
193. heavy Ignorance: Shakespeare, *Sonnet 78.*
197-8] Drink! I know that I am wrong / But . . . MS *1st reading*; What! I
reck not I am wrong . . . MS *2nd reading*, then *1842.*
199. , by scores,] are free MS *1st reading.*
208. Once more uprose] *1851*; Again arose *1842-50.*
209-10] Methought the men and horse with other forms
        Lay under, slowly quickening [*from* festering] into worms;
                                        MS *1st reading*
209. Cp. *Perdidi Diem* 8: 'Pierced through with loathly worms of utter
Death'. This line is also in *Pierced through* (I 513).
211. Cp. the landscape of Milton's Hell, *Paradise Lost* i 672, 704: 'shon with
a glossie scurff', 'scum'd the Bullion dross'.

Old plash of rains, and refuse patched with moss.
Then some one spake: 'Behold! it was a crime
Of sense avenged by sense that wore with time.'
215   Another said: 'The crime of sense became
The crime of malice, and is equal blame.'
And one: 'He had not wholly quenched his power;
A little grain of conscience made him sour.'
At last I heard a voice upon the slope
220   Cry to the summit, 'Is there any hope?'
To which an answer pealed from that high land,
But in a tongue no man could understand;
And on the glimmering limit far withdrawn
God made Himself an awful rose of dawn.

213. spake] *1843*; said *1842*.
214] Of sense and it was well avenged by time.' *MS 1st reading*.
213–14. 'The sensualist becomes worn out by his senses' (T.).
214 ∧ 15]   Another answered 'But a crime of sense?
        Give him new nerves with old experience.' *1865 Selection*
These lines are in *HnMS*; F. T. Palgrave reports T. as saying they were
'omitted from fear of overlength' (C. Ricks, *MP* lxii (1964) 140). Since this
was at Christmas 1863, it was presumably Palgrave who persuaded T. to
include them in *1865*.
215. Another said] A third rejoined *MS 1st reading*.
219] At last a voice called upward from the slope *MS 1st reading*.   *voice*]
trumpet voice *MS jotting*.   *upon*] from off *MS 2nd reading*.
220. Cry to] Unto *MS 1st reading*.
220–4. H. T. relates this to *In Memoriam* lv 20 (*p. 398* and *n.*): 'When he speaks
of "faintly trusting the larger hope", he means by "the larger hope" that the
whole human race would through, perhaps, ages of suffering be at length
purified and saved, even those who "better not with time"; so at the end of
this Vision we read: "God made Himself an awful rose of dawn".' G. G. Loane
(*Echoes in Tennyson*, 1928, p. 7) compares Keats, *Hyperion* i 203–12: 'Hyperion,
leaving twilight in the rear, / Came slope upon the threshold of the west; /
Then, as was wont, his palace-door flew ope . . . / And like a rose in vermeil
tint and shape, / In fragrance soft, and coolness to the eye, / That inlet to
severe magnificence/ Stood full blown, for the God to enter in.' Cp. also *The
Two Voices* 304–6: 'Heaven opens inward, chasms yawn, / Vast images in
glimmering dawn, / Half shown, are broken and withdrawn.' The 'voice' is a
traditional folk-motif, cp. *The Voyage of Maildun* (trans. in P. W. Joyce's *Old
Celtic Romances*, 1879, p. 151): 'After this they heard some one speaking on
the top of the pillar, in a loud, clear, glad voice; but they knew neither what
he said, nor in what language he spoke.'

286 The Princess

A Medley

Published 25 Dec. 1847.

Composition. 'He talked over the plan of the poem with my mother in 1839' (*Mem.* i 248): 'The plan of *The Princess* may have suggested itself when the project of a Women's College was in my father's mind (1839) [was in the air *Mem.*], or it may have arisen in its mock-heroic form from a Cambridge joke, such as he commemorated in the lines, *The Doctor's Daughter*' (I 307). Sir Charles Tennyson, *Cornhill* cliii (1936) 673, deduces from *H.Nbk 22* that T. 'began work on *The Princess* certainly not later than 1839 . . . and it may be several years earlier'. This MS has the title *The New University*. Aubrey de Vere 'listened to the *University of Women*' on 18 April 1845 (W. Ward, *Aubrey de Vere*, 1904, p. 71). FitzGerald (his *Letters* i 494) wrote to T.'s brother Frederick, 12 June 1845: 'Alfred was in London the first week of my stay there. He was looking well, and in good spirits; and had got two hundred lines of a new poem in a butcher's book.' In the summer of 1845, Edmund Lushington reports that T. 'was engaged on *The Princess*, of which I had heard nothing before. He read or showed me the first part, beyond which it had then hardly advanced' (*Mem.* i 203). On 30 Jan. 1846, Elizabeth Barrett wrote to Browning (*Letters*, ed. E. Kintner, 1969, i 427) that T. was ill: 'Which does not prevent his writing a new poem – he has finished the second book of it – and it is in blank verse & a fairy tale, & called the *University*, the university-members being all females. . . . I dont know what to think – it makes me open my eyes. Now isn't the world too old & fond of steam, for blank verse poems, in ever so many books, to be written on the fairies?' On 7 May 1847, T. had 'finished his University of Women: and read me three Books of it the other night' (FitzGerald, i 599), but in Nov. 1847 he wrote to Moxon: 'I am putting the last touches to *The Princess*. I trust there will still be time when I come up to get the book out by Xmas' (*Letters* i 279). There are MSS in the University Library, Cambridge (*ULC MS*), Add. MSS 6345, 6346 and 2588 (E) 585. *H.Nbks 22–5* have lengthy sections; *H.Lprs 191–7* have a few scraps and some of the songs. See Sir Charles Tennyson, *Nineteenth Century* cix (1931) 632–6, and *Cornhill* cliii (1936) 672–80.

Revisions after publication. These were more extensive than with any other of T.'s long poems; see E. F. Shannon, *Tennyson and the Reviewers* (1952), pp. 97–140. Since only a month or two elapsed between the 1st edition (Dec. 1847) and the 2nd (Jan.–Feb. 1848, dedicated to Henry Lushington), T. was able to make little more than stylistic changes–but he had already started on removing those extra syllables which now seemed to have become something of a mannerism in the blank verse. For the 3rd edition (1850), T. revised considerably; on 2 April 1849 he had read to Palgrave 'certain songs which he thought he might do well to place between the sections' (*Mem.* ii 486). These six songs have been since *1850* placed between the sections of the poem (not to be confused with the blank-verse lyrics, like *Tears, idle tears,* which have been since *1847* part of the body of the narrative). T. comments: 'The child is the link through the parts, as shown in the Songs (inserted 1850), which are the best interpreters of the poem. . . . Before the first edition came out, I deliberated with myself whether I should put songs between the separate divisions of the poem; again I thought that the poem would explain itself, but the public did not see the drift.' For alternative songs drafted by T. see Appendix I (*pp. 976–80*). In the 4th edition (1851), T. made the major additions due to the 'weird seizures' of the Prince, with their stress on a world of 'shadows'; this revision has been often deplored. T. says that 'the words "dream, shadow", "were and were not" doubtless refer to the anachronisms and improbabilities of the story'. The proofs for P. M. Wallace's edition of *The Princess* (1891, *Lincoln*) were seen by T. Wallace had said: 'It must be clearly shown that it was not the glamour of [the Prince's] physical or moral brilliance that won his lady from her isolation. His too emotional temperament and susceptibility to cataleptic seizures, added for the first time in the fourth Edition of the Poem, was no doubt intended partly to emphasise this point.' T. changed 'no doubt' to 'probably,' and deleted 'partly'. Cp. the fainting in *The Lover's Tale* i 586 and ii 205 (I 352; I 369). J. E. Sait suggests a link between the Prince's seizures and mesmerism (*Yearbook of English Studies* iv, 1974, 203–11). For the 5th edition (1853), T. enlarged the *Prologue,* and the poem reached virtually its final form. Shannon mentions the 'remarkable extent' to which T. was affected by his reviewers in these changes.

Sources. T. had long anticipated many of the concerns of *The Princess.* In his definitive study of *Tennyson and 'The Princess': Reflections of an Age* (1958), John Killham draws attention to lines in the *1832* text of *A Dream of Fair Women* (*p. 81,* dropped in *1842*): 'In every land I thought that, more or less, / The stronger sterner nature overbore / The softer, uncontrolled by gentleness / And selfish evermore: // And whether there were any means whereby, / In some far aftertime, the gentler mind / Might reassume its just and full degree / Of rule among mankind.' Killham (pp. 179–84) also shows the relevance of *Recollections of the Arabian Nights.* The blunt views of the King in *The Princess* had been those of Edward Bull the curate in *Edwin Morris* (*p. 197*). As a spur to T.'s writing, Herbert Grierson suggested (in his selection, 1907) that T. may have been influenced by the reviewer of *1830* in *Westminster Review,* Jan. 1831, who spoke warmly on female education. It should be added that Hannah More's *Female Education* (1799) is at *Lincoln,* and that *English Encyclopaedia* (1802), which was at Somersby (*Lincoln*), includes a lengthy discussion 'Of the Education of Females', under both 'Education' and 'Sex'.

Killham studies in detail the relation between the poem and the feminism of the age. 'Whether the marriage-relationship could survive the fulfilment of women's aspirations is the real point at issue' (p. 65). Hence T.'s stress on the child, both in the narrative (Aglaïa) and in the intercalated songs. On Arthur Hallam and 'Feminism at Cambridge', see Killham's Chapter iv. Culler (p. 132) suggests the influence of Caroline Norton's campaign in 1839 (when T. first thought of writing the poem) to award the custody of infant children to their mother.

Killham is sceptical about the sources suggested for the story (as distinct from the topical theme), and he singles out Wallace's edition, which 'mentioned that some had traced it to a passage in *Rasselas* wherein Nekayah, herself a Princess, contemplates founding a College for women. He also mentioned Defoe's *Project for an Academy for Women*, and the Duchess of Newcastle's play *The Female Academy* (1662). For good measure he threw in *Love's Labour's Lost*' (p. 16). But Killham is a little severe; the proofs of Wallace's edition now show that T. did not try to delete Wallace's paragraphs (as he did elsewhere). T.'s final suggestion for the wording was: 'Most likely Tennyson did not derive the idea of his College from any one of these [Johnson, Defoe, Newcastle]. But perhaps it was suggested to him by [the obverse side of the matter that forms the plot of Shakespeare's *Love's Labour's Lost*, in which, though there it is a strictly male Academy that is invaded by a band of ladies . . .].' Killham points to the importance of eastern tales (pp. 198–230). Turner (p. 101) suggests: 'The central idea of the poem . . . seems to have come from a novel that he "dipped into" in 1834, F. D. Maurice's *Eustace Conway*, which shares many features with the poem's Prologue: a country house owned by a squire called "Vivyan", a touchy maiden-aunt, undergraduate son, and a daughter of independent character, who replies to her brother's grumbles about university life: "Well, Eustace, I think as universities are so mischievous to men, you must make them over to us." Eustace gives his "full consent to the transfer".'

A medley. T. comments: 'In the Prologue the "Tale from mouth to mouth" was a game which I have more than once played when I was at Trinity College, Cambridge, with my brother-undergraduates. Of course, if he "that inherited the tale" had not attended very carefully to his predecessors, there were contradictions; and if the story were historical, occasional anachronisms.

'In defence of what some have called the too poetical passages, it should be recollected that the poet of the party was requested to "dress the tale up poetically," and he was full of the "gallant and heroic chronicle." A parable is perhaps the teacher that can most surely enter in at all doors. . . .

'It may be remarked that there is scarcely anything in the story which is not prophetically glanced at in the Prologue.' T.'s letter to S. E. Dawson, his Canadian editor, is given in *Eversley*: 'You have seen amongst other things that if women ever were to play such freaks, the burlesque and the tragic might go hand in hand.' See *Letters* iii, 21 Nov. 1882. Frederick Locker-Lampson records in 1869 (*Mem.* ii 70–1): 'He talked of *The Princess* with something of regret, of its fine blank verse, and the many good things in it: "but," said he, "though truly original, it is, after all, only a medley." He added that it was very difficult in blank verse to give descriptions, such as

[*Prologue* 79–138], and at the same time to retain poetical elevation. Tennyson insisted that the employment of rhyme would have made it much easier.' *Science.* G. G. Wickens discusses 'The Two Sides of Early Victorian Science and the Unity of *The Princess*' (*VS* xxiii, 1980, 369–88), and 'the controversy ... between different scientific perspectives, between a bright side of science – which maintains a teleology (and usually a theology as well) while considering the evidence of destruction and change in the material world – and a dark side of science – which is not interested in such formulations, but simply describes the mechanisms'; Wickens seeks 'to show that T. uses the distinction between the two sides of science to organize the plot of *The Princess*'. See also D. R. Dean, *Tennyson and Geology* (1985), pp. 14–17.

PROLOGUE

Sir Walter Vivian all a summer's day
Gave his broad lawns until the set of sun
Up to the people: thither flocked at noon
His tenants, wife and child, and thither half
5   The neighbouring borough with their Institute
Of which he was the patron. I was there
From college, visiting the son, – the son
A Walter too, – with others of our set,
Five others: we were seven at Vivian-place.

10   And me that morning Walter showed the house,
Greek, set with busts: from vases in the hall
Flowers of all heavens, and lovelier than their names,
Grew side by side; and on the pavement lay
Carved stones of the Abbey-ruin in the park,

¶ 286. *Prologue*
'The Prologue was written about a feast of the Mechanics' Institute held in the Lushingtons' grounds at Park House, near Maidstone, 6th July 1842' (T.). Killham (pp. 61–2) quotes from the *Maidstone and Kentish Advertiser*, 12 July 1842, which is very close to T.'s description of the occasion. Cp. T.'s 'English Idyls', especially *Audley Court* (*p. 193*). On the 'wonderfully apt location' (architecturally and in other ways), see Turner (pp. 103–4).
1. Cp. *Paradise Lost* i 449: 'In amorous dittyes all a Summers day' – from a passage which T. 'would repeatedly chant out with the deepest admiration, as the finest of all', *Nineteenth Century* xxxiii (1893) 172.
9] *1850; not 1847–8.*
11–12]   Greek, set with statues. Out of urn and vase
          Flamed the Cape-lily, the light Azalea shone,
          The balsam glowed. On fair mosaics lay *ULC MS 1st reading*

15 Huge Ammonites, and the first bones of Time;
    And on the tables every clime and age
    Jumbled together; celts and calumets,
    Claymore and snowshoe, toys in lava, fans
    Of sandal, amber, ancient rosaries,
20 Laborious orient ivory sphere in sphere,
    The cursed Malayan crease, and battle-clubs
    From the isles of palm: and higher on the walls,
    Betwixt the monstrous horns of elk and deer,
    His own forefathers' arms and armour hung.

25   And 'this' he said 'was Hugh's at Agincourt;
    And that was old Sir Ralph's at Ascalon:
    A good knight he! we keep a chronicle
    With all about him'–which he brought, and I
    Dived in a hoard of tales that dealt with knights,
30 Half-legend, half-historic, counts and kings
    Who laid about them at their wills and died;
    And mixt with these, a lady, one that armed
    Her own fair head, and sallying through the gate,
    Had beat her foes with slaughter from her walls.

35   'O miracle of women,' said the book,
    'O noble heart who, being strait-besieged
    By this wild king to force her to his wish,
    Nor bent, nor broke, nor shunned a soldier's death,

15. *Ammonites*: whorled fossil-stones.

17. *celts*: stone or bronze hatchets.   *calumets*: 'Longfellow sent me one of these pipes of peace, which belonged to a Red Indian chief' (T.).

19. *sandal*: a scented wood.

21. *crease*: kris, Malayan dagger.

26. *Ascalon*: Richard I's victory over the Saracens in 1192.

32–4]. Turner (p. 102) notes Froissart's *Chronicle* (Lord Berners's translation, chap. 80): 'how "the countesse of Mountfort", besieged in "Hanybont", led a sortie from the town, riding in armour on horseback, and set fire to the enemy's "lodgings"'. Turner adds that 'the lady's name, Mountfort, suggested a relevant image and an apt use of Theocritus', since the heroine is 'named Ida (after the mountain in *Œnone*)'; see also *p. 319*.

35–49] *1853; not 1847–51*. Cp. *Faerie Queene* III iv st. 1: 'Where is the Antique glory now become, / That whilome wont in women to appeare? / Where be the brave atchievements doen by some? / Where be the battels, where the shield and speare, / And all the conquests, which them high did reare, / That matter made for famous Poets verse, / And boastfull men so oft abasht to heare? / Bene they all dead, and laid in dolefull herse? / Or doen they onely sleepe, and shall againe reverse?'

But now when all was lost or seemed as lost—
40   Her stature more than mortal in the burst
Of sunrise, her arm lifted, eyes on fire—
Brake with a blast of trumpets from the gate,
And, falling on them like a thunderbolt,
She trampled some beneath her horses' heels,
45   And some were whelmed with missiles of the wall,
And some were pushed with lances from the rock,
And part were drowned within the whirling brook:
O miracle of noble womanhood!'

So sang the gallant glorious chronicle;
50   And, I all rapt in this, 'Come out,' he said,
'To the Abbey: there is Aunt Elizabeth
And sister Lilia with the rest.' We went
(I kept the book and had my finger in it)
Down through the park: strange was the sight to me;
55   For all the sloping pasture murmured, sown
With happy faces and with holiday.
There moved the multitude, a thousand heads:
The patient leaders of their Institute
Taught them with facts. One reared a font of stone
60   And drew, from butts of water on the slope,
The fountain of the moment, playing, now
A twisted snake, and now a rain of pearls,
Or steep-up spout whereon the gilded ball
Danced like a wisp: and somewhat lower down
65   A man with knobs and wires and vials fired
A cannon: Echo answered in her sleep
From hollow fields: and here were telescopes
For azure views; and there a group of girls
In circle waited, whom the electric shock
70   Dislinked with shrieks and laughter: round the lake
A little clock-work steamer paddling plied
And shook the lilies: perched about the knolls
A dozen angry models jetted steam:
A petty railway ran: a fire-balloon
75   Rose gem-like up before the dusky groves
And dropt a fairy parachute and past:
And there through twenty posts of telegraph

---

63. steep-up: cp. Shakespeare, *Sonnet 7*: 'And having climbed the steep-up
heavenly hill . . . / Attending on his golden pilgrimage.'
64. :and]   or metal Harlequin
       Pirouetted glittering: *ULC MS 1st reading*
74. fire-balloon: raised by heated air, not gas.

They flashed a saucy message to and fro
Between the mimic stations; so that sport
80 Went hand in hand with Science; otherwhere
Pure sport: a herd of boys with clamour bowled
And stumped the wicket; babies rolled about
Like tumbled fruit in grass; and men and maids
Arranged a country dance, and flew through light
85 And shadow, while the twangling violin
Struck up with Soldier-laddie, and overhead
The broad ambrosial aisles of lofty lime
Made noise with bees and breeze from end to end.

Strange was the sight and smacking of the time;
90 And long we gazed, but satiated at length
Came to the ruins. High-arched and ivy-claspt,
Of finest Gothic lighter than a fire,
Through one wide chasm of time and frost they gave
The park, the crowd, the house; but all within
95 The sward was trim as any garden lawn:
And here we lit on Aunt Elizabeth,
And Lilia with the rest, and lady friends
From neighbour seats: and there was Ralph himself,
A broken statue propt against the wall,
100 As gay as any. Lilia, wild with sport,
Half child half woman as she was, had wound
A scarf of orange round the stony helm,
And robed the shoulders in a rosy silk,
That made the old warrior from his ivied nook
105 Glow like a sunbeam: near his tomb a feast
Shone, silver-set; about it lay the guests,
And there we joined them: then the maiden Aunt
Took this fair day for text, and from it preached
An universal culture for the crowd,
110 And all things great; but we, unworthier, told
Of college: he had climbed across the spikes,
And he had squeezed himself betwixt the bars,
And he had breathed the Proctor's dogs; and one
Discussed his tutor, rough to common men,
115 But honeying at the whisper of a lord;

80. Went . . . Science] *1853*; With Science hand in hand went *1847–51*.
83. Like] For *ULC MS 1st reading.*
92. finest Gothic] purest Norman *ULC MS. fire*] flame *ULC MS.*
97–8] *1850*; And Lilia with the rest, and Ralph himself, *1847–8*.
113. 'Made the proctor's attendants out of breath' (T.).
114. Discussed] He slurred *ULC MS 1st reading.*

And one the Master, as a rogue in grain
Veneered with sanctimonious theory.
     But while they talked, above their heads I saw
The feudal warrior lady-clad; which brought
120   My book to mind: and opening this I read
Of old Sir Ralph a page or two that rang
With tilt and tourney; then the tale of her
That drove her foes with slaughter from her walls,
And much I praised her nobleness, and 'Where,'
125   Asked Walter, patting Lilia's head (she lay
Beside him) 'lives there such a woman now?'

     Quick answered Lilia 'There are thousands now
Such women, but convention beats them down:
It is but bringing up; no more than that:
130   You men have done it: how I hate you all!
Ah, were I something great! I wish I were
Some mighty poetess, I would shame you then,
That love to keep us children! O I wish
That I were some great princess, I would build
135   Far off from men a college like a man's,
And I would teach them all that men are taught;
We are twice as quick!' And here she shook aside
The hand that played the patron with her curls.

     And one said smiling 'Pretty were the sight
140   If our old halls could change their sex, and flaunt
With prudes for proctors, dowagers for deans,
And sweet girl-graduates in their golden hair.
I think they should not wear our rusty gowns,
But move as rich as Emperor-moths, or Ralph
145   Who shines so in the corner; yet I fear,
If there were many Lilias in the brood,
However deep you might embower the nest,
Some boy would spy it.'
                                   At this upon the sward

125–6. patting . . . him)] 1850; not 1847–8.
130. how . . . all!] who would marry men! ULC MS 1st reading.
131–3] 1850; not 1847–8.
134. That I were] 1850; O were I 1847–8.
135. like a man's] 1850; of my own 1847–8.
136. that . . . taught] 1850; things: you should see.' 1847–8.
137–8] 1850; not 1847–8.
142. Cp. Keats, Lamia i 197–8: 'As though in Cupid's college she had spent / Sweet days a lovely graduate'.

She tapt her tiny silken-sandaled foot:
150 'That's your light way; but I would make it death
For any male thing but to peep at us.'

Petulant she spoke, and at herself she laughed;
A rosebud set with little wilful thorns,
And sweet as English air could make her, she:
155 But Walter hailed a score of names upon her,
And 'petty Ogress', and 'ungrateful Puss',
And swore he longed at college, only longed,
All else was well, for she-society.
They boated and they cricketed; they talked
160 At wine, in clubs, of art, of politics;
They lost their weeks; they vext the souls of deans;
They rode; they betted; made a hundred friends,
And caught the blossom of the flying terms,
But missed the mignonette of Vivian-place,
165 The little hearth-flower Lilia. Thus he spoke,
Part banter, part affection.
                    'True,' she said,
'We doubt not that. O yes, you missed us much.
I'll stake my ruby ring upon it you did.'

She held it out; and as a parrot turns
170 Up through gilt wires a crafty loving eye,
And takes a lady's finger with all care,
And bites it for true heart and not for harm,
So he with Lilia's. Daintily she shrieked
And wrung it. 'Doubt my word again!' he said.
175 'Come, listen! here is proof that you were missed:
We seven stayed at Christmas up to read;
And there we took one tutor as to read:
The hard-grained Muses of the cube and square
Were out of season: never man, I think,
180 So mouldered in a sinecure as he:
For while our cloisters echoed frosty feet,
And our long walks were stript as bare as brooms,

161. *weeks*: of required attendance.
172] And nibbles it for love and not to hurt *ULC MS*.
177–9] *1850*; We seven took one tutor. Never man *1847–8*.
179] No churchman deep in some neglected fen *H.Nbk 24*.
181. *frosty*] studious *H.Nbk 24*. T. disliked the echo of *Il Penseroso* 155–6: 'But let my due feet never fail, / To walk the studious Cloysters pale.'
182. *were stript*] stuck up *H.Nbk 24*.

We did but talk you over, pledge you all
In wassail; often, like as many girls—
185   Sick for the hollies and the yews of home—
As many little trifling Lilias—played
Charades and riddles as at Christmas here,
And *what's my thought* and *when* and *where* and *how*,
And often told a tale from mouth to mouth
As here at Christmas.'
190   She remembered that:
A pleasant game, she thought: she liked it more
Than magic music, forfeits, all the rest.
But these—what kind of tales did men tell men,
She wondered, by themselves?
                    A half-disdain
195   Perched on the pouted blossom of her lips:
And Walter nodded at me; '*He* began,
The rest would follow, each in turn; and so
We forged a sevenfold story. Kind? what kind?
Chimeras, crotchets, Christmas solecisms,
200   Seven-headed monsters only made to kill
Time by the fire in winter.'
                  'Kill him now,
The tyrant! kill him in the summer too,'
Said Lilia; 'Why not now?' the maiden Aunt.
'Why not a summer's as a winter's tale?

183–4] We roused the fire and pledged you all in floods / Of wassail ... *ULC MS 1st reading*; We got great logs of Yule and pledged you all / In wassail ... *ULC MS*.

190. She remembered] *1850*; 'I remember *1847–8*.

191. , she thought: she] *1850*; ,'she said; 'I *1847–8*.

192. magic music: a game like hunt the thimble, with music played fast and loud when the seeker is 'warm', and slow and soft when he is 'cold'. Cp. *The Day-Dream: Arrival* 26 (p. *173*).

193. did] *1850*; do *1847–8*.

194. She wondered] *1850*; I wonder *1847–8*.   *She ... themselves?*] Not fit for us to hear *ULC MS 1st reading*.

194 ∧ 5] That only wanted scaring with a kiss *ULC MS 1st reading*.

197. , each ... so] *1850*; ; so we tost the ball: *1847–8*.

198–200] *1850*; What kind of tales? why, such as served to kill *1847–8*. Shannon (p. 125) observes that the change is to escape accusations of oddity or inconsistency.

202–3] *1850*;   Tell one' she said 'kill him in summer too,'
            And 'tell one' cried the solemn maiden aunt. *1847–8*

204–5. Cp. *Winter's Tale* II i 25: 'A sad tale's best for winter'. See l. 231.

205 A tale for summer as befits the time,
    And something it should be to suit the place,
    Heroic, for a hero lies beneath,
    Grave, solemn!'
                        Walter warped his mouth at this
    To something so mock-solemn, that I laughed
210 And Lilia woke with sudden-thrilling mirth
    An echo like a ghostly woodpecker,
    Hid in the ruins; till the maiden Aunt
    (A little sense of wrong had touched her face
    With colour) turned to me with 'As you will;

On *The Princess*'s relation to contemporary Shakespearean acting, production, and criticism (including of Shakespeare's women), see D. B. Mantell, *Texas Studies in Literature and Language* xx (1978) 48–67.

204–8] When better? all is quiet: only there
        At the high altar baaes the mother ewe:
        The shouters are scarce heard; the ruin sweet
        And solemn: tell us one, a solemn tale,
        As fits the scene. *ULC MS, which has in another draft*:
            The shouters in the park are faintly heard;
            And sweet the ruin is and solemn.

207–8] *1850*; Grave, moral, solemn, like the mouldering walls / About us.' *1847–8*. Shannon (p. 127) observes that this is to meet the objection by reviewers that the poem was pitched too unheroically at the beginning.

210–11. Cp. *Kate 3–4*: 'Her rapid laughters wild and shrill, / As laughters of the woodpecker.'

211. a ghostly] *1853*; an April *1848–51*.

214–39] *1850 (except ll. 222, 229–30)*;
        With colour) turned to me: 'Well–as you will–
        Just as you will,' she said; 'be, if you will,
        Yourself your hero.'
                            'Look then' added he
        'Since Lilia would be princess, that you stoop
        No lower than a prince.'
                            To which I said,
        'Take care then that my tale be followed out
        By all the lieges in my royal vein:
        But one that really suited time and place
        Were such a medley, we should . . . [*ll. 230–1, 225–9
            (reading* yonder] *there with l. 228*)]
        The nineteenth century gambols on the grass.
        [*l. 232*]
        Here are we seven: if each man take his turn
        We make a sevenfold story:' then began. *1847–8*

215   Heroic if you will, or what you will,
        Or be yourself your hero if you will.'

            'Take Lilia, then, for heroine' clamoured he,
        'And make her some great Princess, six feet high,
        Grand, epic, homicidal; and be you
        The Prince to win her!'
220   'Then follow me, the Prince,'
        I answered, 'each be hero in his turn!
        Seven and yet one, like shadows in a dream. –
        Heroic seems our Princess as required –
        But something made to suit with Time and place,
225   A Gothic ruin and a Grecian house,
        A talk of college and of ladies' rights,
        A feudal knight in silken masquerade,
        And, yonder, shrieks and strange experiments
        For which the good Sir Ralph had burnt them all –
230   This *were* a medley! we should have him back
        Who told the "Winter's tale" to do it for us.
        No matter: we will say whatever comes.
        And let the ladies sing us, if they will,
        From time to time, some ballad or a song
        To give us breathing-space.'
235   So I began,
        And the rest followed: and the women sang
        Between the rougher voices of the men,
        Like linnets in the pauses of the wind:
        And here I give the story and the songs.

                            I
        A prince I was, blue-eyed, and fair in face,

220. her!' ∧ *'Then*]   'I'll not be won', she said,
                              Not though they kissed my feet a thousand years,
                              By prince or peasant. Never! I will be
                              A heroine all in earnest' *ULC MS 1st reading, differing*
                                                          much in this section
Cp. *Three Sonnets to a Coquette* ii 13: 'And if you kissed her feet a thousand
years'.
222] *1851; not 1850.*
229] *1851, 1847–8; not 1850.*
230. This were] *1851*; Were such *1847–50.*
232 ∧ *3*] Like Shakespeare's recklings playing at papa *ULC MS.*
238. Cp. *The Miller's Daughter* 122: 'And, in the pauses of the wind'.
239. See Appendix I (*p. 976*), for the earlier introductory fragments.

Of temper amorous, as the first of May,
With lengths of yellow ringlet, like a girl,
For on my cradle shone the Northern star.

5   There lived an ancient legend in our house.
Some sorcerer, whom a far-off grandsire burnt
Because he cast no shadow, had foretold,
Dying, that none of all our blood should know
The shadow from the substance, and that one
10   Should come to fight with shadows and to fall.
For so, my mother said, the story ran.
And, truly, waking dreams were, more or less,
An old and strange affection of the house.
Myself too had weird seizures, Heaven knows what:
15   On a sudden in the midst of men and day,
And while I walked and talked as heretofore,
I seemed to move among a world of ghosts,
And feel myself the shadow of a dream.
Our great court-Galen poised his gilt-head cane,
20   And pawed his beard, and muttered 'catalepsy'.
My mother pitying made a thousand prayers;
My mother was as mild as any saint,
Half-canonized by all that looked on her,
So gracious was her tact and tenderness:
25   But my good father thought a king a king;
He cared not for the affection of the house;
He held his sceptre like a pedant's wand

i 2] *1850; not 1847–8.*
i 5–21] *1851 (except l. 20); not 1847–50.*
i 12–22]   And truly I had glamourish waking-dreams
             That sometimes held me for an hour or twain
             (They were an old affection of our house)
             And sudden weird seizures when I seemed
             To walk among a world of hollow shows,
             And framed a thousand monstrous fantasies,
             And felt myself the shadow of a dream.
                No shadow was my mother, clear throughout
             As genial daylight, mild as any saint,
                                                  ULC MS
The Princess vii 120 adopted 'hollow shows'.
i 19. *Galen*: 'the great doctor of Pergamus, 131 to 200 A.D.' (T.).
i 20. *muttered*] *1853;* called it *1851.*
i 23] *1850;* And nearly canonized by all she knew, *1847–8.*
i 26] *1851; not 1847–50.*
i 27. *pedant*: schoolmaster.

To lash offence, and with long arms and hands
Reached out, and picked offenders from the mass .
For judgment.
30   Now it chanced that I had been,
While life was yet in bud and blade, betrothed
To one, a neighbouring Princess: she to me
Was proxy-wedded with a bootless calf
At eight years old; and still from time to time
35 Came murmurs of her beauty from the South,
And of her brethren, youths of puissance;
And still I wore her picture by my heart,
And one dark tress; and all around them both
Sweet thoughts would swarm as bees about their queen.

40   But when the days drew nigh that I should wed,
My father sent ambassadors with furs
And jewels, gifts, to fetch her: these brought back
A present, a great labour of the loom;
And therewithal an answer vague as wind:
45 Besides, they saw the king; he took the gifts;
He said there was a compact; that was true:
But then she had a will; was he to blame?
And maiden fancies; loved to live alone
Among her women; certain, would not wed.

50   That morning in the presence room I stood
With Cyril and with Florian, my two friends:
The first, a gentleman of broken means
(His father's fault) but given to starts and bursts
Of revel; and the last, my other heart,
55 And almost my half-self, for still we moved
Together, twinned as horse's ear and eye.

i 33. 'The proxy of the king used to place his bare leg under the coverlet of the king's betrothed' (T.); H.T. adds: 'Bacon in his *Henry VII* writes of the proxy marriage of Maximilian, the king of the Romans, with Anne of Brittany, 1489: "For she was not only publicly contracted, but stated as a bride, and solemnly bedded; and after she was laid, there came in Maximilian's ambassador, with letters of procuration, and in the presence of sundry noble personages, men and women, put his leg, stript naked to the knee, between the espousal sheets; to the end that the ceremony might be thought to amount to a consummation and actual knowledge."'
i 36. youths] *1850*; knights *1847–8*.   youths of puissance] mighty men of war ULC MS *1st reading*; knights of puissance ULC MS.
i 54. ;and] ,such as made Arcturus wink,
      A double sun: ULC MS
i 55. And almost] *1851*; My shadow, *1847–50*.
i 56. twinned] *1851*; kin *1847–50*.

Now, while they spake, I saw my father's face
Grow long and troubled like a rising moon,
Inflamed with wrath: he started on his feet,
60 Tore the king's letter, snowed it down, and rent
The wonder of the loom through warp and woof
From skirt to skirt; and at the last he sware
That he would send a hundred thousand men,
And bring her in a whirlwind: then he chewed
65 The thrice-turned cud of wrath, and cooked his spleen,
Communing with his captains of the war.

At last I spoke. 'My father, let me go.
It cannot be but some gross error lies
In this report, this answer of a king,
70 Whom all men rate as kind and hospitable:
Or, maybe, I myself, my bride once seen,
Whate'er my grief to find her less than fame,
May rue the bargain made.' And Florian said:
'I have a sister at the foreign court,
75 Who moves about the Princess; she, you know,
Who wedded with a nobleman from thence:
He, dying lately, left her, as I hear,
The lady of three castles in that land:
Through her this matter might be sifted clean.'
80 And Cyril whispered: 'Take me with you too.'
Then laughing 'what, if these weird seizures come
Upon you in those lands, and no one near
To point you out the shadow from the truth!
Take me: I'll serve you better in a strait;
85 I grate on rusty hinges here:' but 'No!'
Roared the rough king, 'you shall not; we ourself
Will crush her pretty maiden fancies dead
In iron gauntlets: break the council up.'

But when the council broke, I rose and past
90 Through the wild woods that hung about the town;

---

i 65. *cooked his spleen*: Iliad iv 513: ἐπὶ νηυσὶ χόλον θυμαλγέα πέσσει.
i 72. Horace, *Epistles* I xi 3: *maiora minorave fama* ('whether above or below their fame').
i 80. *And . . . whispered*] *1851*; Then whispered Cyril *1847–50*.
i 81–3] *1851*; not *1847–50*.
i 84. *Take*] *1851*; Trust *1847–50*.
i 86] *1850*; Replied the king, 'you shall not; I myself *1847–8*.
i 87. *her*] *1851*; these *1847–50*.

Found a still place, and plucked her likeness out;
Laid it on flowers, and watched it lying bathed
In the green gleam of dewy-tasselled trees:
What were those fancies? wherefore break her troth?
95   Proud looked the lips: but while I meditated
A wind arose and rushed upon the South,
And shook the songs, the whispers, and the shrieks
Of the wild woods together; and a Voice
Went with it, 'Follow, follow, thou shalt win.'

100   Then, ere the silver sickle of that month
Became her golden shield, I stole from court
With Cyril and with Florian, unperceived,
Cat-footed through the town and half in dread
To hear my father's clamour at our backs
105   With Ho! from some bay-window shake the night;
But all was quiet: from the bastioned walls
Like threaded spiders, one by one, we dropt,
And flying reached the frontier: then we crost
To a livelier land; and so by tilth and grange,
110   And vines, and blowing bosks of wilderness,
We gained the mother-city thick with towers,
And in the imperial palace found the king.

i *93. dewy-tasselled*: with catkins; cp. *In Memoriam* lxxxvi 6.
i *96–9*. Cp. *Prometheus Unbound* II i 156–9: 'A wind arose among the pines;
it shook / The clinging music from their boughs, and then / Low, sweet,
faint sounds, like the farewell of ghosts, / Were heard: "O, follow,
follow, follow me!"' T. wrote to S. E. Dawson (*Eversley*, p. 240): 'I believe
the resemblance which you note is just a chance one. Shelley's lines are not
familiar to me, though of course, if they occur in the *Prometheus*, I must
have read them.' T. wished P. M. Wallace to delete a reference to this
parallel passage from his edition of *The Princess* (proofs, 1891, *Lincoln*).
i *103–5*] *1851; not 1847–50*.
i *106–7*] *1851*; Down from the bastioned walls we dropt by night, *1847–
8*;

          Down from the bastioned wall, suspense by night,
          Like threaded spiders from a balk, we dropt, *1850*
i *109. tilth and grange*] *1850*; town and thorpe *1847–8*.
i *110. vines*] *1850*; tilth *1847–8*.   *blowing bosks*: 'blossoming thickets'
(T.).
i *111–12*]   We crost into a land where mile-high towers
          Pufft out a night of smoke that drowsed the sun;
          Huge pistons rose and fell, and everywhere
          We heard the clank of chains, the creak of cranes,

His name was Gama; cracked and small his voice,
But bland the smile that like a wrinkling wind
115 On glassy water drove his cheek in lines;
A little dry old man, without a star,
Not like a king: three days he feasted us,
And on the fourth I spake of why we came,
And my betrothed. 'You do us, Prince,' he said,
120 Airing a snowy hand and signet gem,
'All honour. We remember love ourselves
In our sweet youth: there did a compact pass
Long summers back, a kind of ceremony—
I think the year in which our olives failed.
125 I would you had her, Prince, with all my heart,
With my full heart: but there were widows here,
Two widows, Lady Psyche, Lady Blanche;
They fed her theories, in and out of place
Maintaining that with equal husbandry
130 The woman were an equal to the man.
They harped on this; with this our banquets rang;
Our dances broke and buzzed in knots of talk;
Nothing but this; my very ears were hot
To hear them: knowledge, so my daughter held,
'135 Was all in all: they had but been, she thought,
As children; they must lose the child, assume
The woman: then, Sir, awful odes she wrote,
Too awful, sure, for what they treated of,
But all she is and does is awful; odes
140 About this losing of the child; and rhymes
And dismal lyrics, prophesying change

Ringing of blocks and throb of hammers mixt
With water split and spilt on groaning wheels,
Until we reacht the court. *H.Nbk 22*
i *114–15*] *1851; not 1847–8;* But bland the smile that puckered up his
cheeks; *1850.* Cp. *Paradise Lost* xi 842–4: 'Drivn by a keen North-winde,
that blowing drie / Wrinkl'd the face of Deluge, as decai'd; / And the
cleer Sun on his wide watrie Glass . . .'
i *120.* Cp. Juvenal, *Satires* i 28–9: *ventilet aestivum digitis sudantibus aurum, /
nec sufferre queat maioris pondera gemmae* ('whilst on his sweating finger he
airs a summer ring of gold, unable to endure the weight of a heavier
gem').
i *122.* Horace, *Odes* I xvi 23: *in dulci iuventa.*
i *134–45*] *1850 (except ll. 138–9);* To hear them. Last, my daughter begged
a boon, *1847–8.*
i *138–9*] *1851; not 1850.*

Beyond all reason: these the women sang;
And they that know such things–I sought but peace;
No critic I–would call them masterpieces:
145   They mastered *me*. At last she begged a boon,
A certain summer-palace which I have
Hard by your father's frontier: I said no,
Yet being an easy man, gave it: and there,
All wild to found an University
150   For maidens, on the spur she fled; and more
We know not,–only this: they see no men,
Not even her brother Arac, nor the twins
Her brethren, though they love her, look upon her
As on a kind of paragon; and I
155   (Pardon me saying it) were much loth to breed
Dispute betwixt myself and mine: but since
(And I confess with right) you think me bound
In some sort, I can give you letters to her;
And yet, to speak the truth, I rate your chance
Almost at naked nothing.'
160   Thus the king;
And I, though nettled that he seemed to slur
With garrulous ease and oily courtesies
Our formal compact, yet, not less (all frets
But chafing me on fire to find my bride)
165   Went forth again with both my friends. We rode
Many a long league back to the North. At last
From hills, that looked across a land of hope,
We dropt with evening on a rustic town
Set in a gleaming river's crescent-curve,
170   Close at the boundary of the liberties;
There, entered an old hostel, called mine host

---

i *151. only this*] *1850*; have not been *1847–8*.
i *152. Arac*] Eric *H.MS*.
i *153. her brethren*: 'accusative after "see"' (T.).
i *165*] *1851*; Set out once more with those two gallant boys; *1847–50*.
i *165* ∧ *6*] Then pushing onward under sun and stars *1847–8*.
i *166. At last*] *1851*; we came *1847–8*; we past *1850*.
i *167*] *1851*; When the first fern-owl whirred about the copse, *1847–8*; And came (the fern-owl whirring in the copse) *1850*.
i *168–9*] *1851*; Upon a little town within a wood *1847–50*.
i *170*. H.T. comments: 'Blackstone in his *Commentaries*, ii 37, defines a "liberty" as a "Royal privilege or branch of the King's prerogative, subsisting in the hands of a subject." The term "liberties" is here applied to the estate over which the privilege can be exercised.'

To council, plied him with his richest wines,
And showed the late-writ letters of the king.

He with a long low sibilation, stared
175   As blank as death in marble; then exclaimed
Averring it was clear against all rules
For any man to go: but as his brain
Began to mellow, 'If the king,' he said,
'Had given us letters, was he bound to speak?
180   The king would bear him out;' and at the last –
The summer of the vine in all his veins –
'No doubt that we might make it worth his while.
She once had past that way; he heard her speak;
She scared him; life! he never saw the like;
185   She looked as grand as doomsday and as grave:
And he, he reverenced his liege-lady there;
He always made a point to post with mares;
His daughter and his housemaid were the boys:
The land, he understood, for miles about
190   Was tilled by women; all the swine were sows,
And all the dogs' –
But while he jested thus,
A thought flashed through me which I clothed in act,
Remembering how we three presented Maid
Or Nymph, or Goddess, at high tide of feast,
195   In masque or pageant at my father's court.
We sent mine host to purchase female gear;
He brought it, and himself, a sight to shake
The midriff of despair with laughter, holp
To lace us up, till, each, in maiden plumes
200   We rustled: him we gave a costly bribe
To guerdon silence, mounted our good steeds,
And boldly ventured on the liberties.

i *171. entered an old] 1850;* entering in an *1847–8.*

i *183] 1850; not 1847–8.*

i *184] 1851; not 1847–50.*

i *185] 1850; not 1847–8.*

i *186. And he] 1850;* For him *1847–8.*

i *188. boys:* postilions.

i *197–200] 1850;* Which brought and clapt upon us, we tweezered out
What slender blossom lived on lip or cheek
Of manhood, gave mine host a costly bribe *1847–8.*
Shannon (p. 118) points out that QR had ridiculed this.

i *201. guerdon:* to reward.

        We followed up the river as we rode,
        And rode till midnight when the college lights
205   Began to glitter firefly-like in copse
        And linden alley: then we past an arch,
        Whereon a woman-statue rose with wings
        From four winged horses dark against the stars;
        And some inscription ran along the front,
210   But deep in shadow: further on we gained
        A little street half garden and half house;
        But scarce could hear each other speak for noise
        Of clocks and chimes, like silver hammers falling
        On silver anvils, and the splash and stir
215   Of fountains spouted up and showering down
        In meshes of the jasmine and the rose:
        And all about us pealed the nightingale,
        Rapt in her song, and careless of the snare.

        There stood a bust of Pallas for a sign,
220   By two sphere lamps blazoned like Heaven and Earth
        With constellation and with continent,
        Above an entry: riding in, we called;
        A plump-armed Ostleress and a stable wench
        Came running at the call, and helped us down.
225   Then stept a buxom hostess forth, and sailed,
        Full-blown, before us into rooms which gave
        Upon a pillared porch, the bases lost
        In laurel: her we asked of that and this,
        And who were tutors. 'Lady Blanche' she said,
230   'And Lady Psyche.' 'Which was prettiest,
        Best-natured?' 'Lady Psyche.' 'Hers are we,'
        One voice, we cried; and I sat down and wrote,
        In such a hand as when a field of corn
        Bows all its ears before the roaring East;

235   'Three ladies of the Northern empire pray
        Your Highness would enroll them with your own,

---

i 203] 1851; not 1847–50.
i 204. And] 1851; We 1847–50.
i 206. then] 1850; and then 1847–8.
i 207–10] 1850; Inscribed too dark for legible, and gained 1847–8. Shannon
(p. 119) points out that the reviewers had objected.
i 212. scarce could] 1850; could not 1847–8.
i 222. entry] 1850; archway 1847–8.
i 227. a pillared porch: Keats, Lamia i 379.
i 231. Hers are] 1850; Her pupils 1847–8.

As Lady Psyche's pupils.'
                        This I sealed:
The seal was Cupid bent above a scroll,
And o'er his head Uranian Venus hung,
240 And raised the blinding bandage from his eyes:
I gave the letter to be sent with dawn;
And then to bed, where half in doze I seemed
To float about a glimmering night, and watch
A full sea glazed with muffled moonlight, swell
245 On some dark shore just seen that it was rich.

                    [I ∧ II]
        As through the land at eve we went,
            And plucked the ripened ears,
        We fell out, my wife and I,
        O we fell out I know not why,
5   And kissed again with tears.
        And blessings on the falling out
            That all the more endears,
        When we fall out with those we love
            And kiss again with tears!
10   For when we came where lies the child
            We lost in other years,
        There above the little grave,
        O there above the little grave,
            We kissed again with tears.

                    II
At break of day the College Portress came:
She brought us Academic silks, in hue
The lilac, with a silken hood to each,
And zoned with gold; and now when these were on,
5 And we as rich as moths from dusk cocoons,
She, curtseying her obeisance, let us know
The Princess Ida waited: out we paced,
I first, and following through the porch that sang
All round with laurel, issued in a court

i *238–41*] *1850* (*except l. 239*); (A Cupid reading) to be sent with dawn;
1847–8.
i *239. o'er his head*] *1851*; over him *1850.*   *Uranian*: the higher love of
Plato's *Symposium.*

i ∧ ii Like the other songs between Parts of the poem, it was written 1849,
added *1850.* Cp. *The Miller's Daughter* 228–30 (I 417).
i ∧ ii *4, 13*] *1851; not 1850.*
i ∧ ii *6–9*] *1850, 1862; not 1851–61.* These lines, which he had temporarily
discarded, T. thought of using in *Maud*; see p. 531.

10 Compact of lucid marbles, bossed with lengths
   Of classic frieze, with ample awnings gay
   Betwixt the pillars, and with great urns of flowers.
   The Muses and the Graces, grouped in threes,
   Enringed a billowing fountain in the midst;
15 And here and there on lattice edges lay
   Or book or lute; but hastily we past,
   And up a flight of stairs into the hall.

   There at a board by tome and paper sat,
   With two tame leopards couched beside her throne,
20 All beauty compassed in a female form,
   The Princess; liker to the inhabitant
   Of some clear planet close upon the Sun,
   Than our man's earth; such eyes were in her head,
   And so much grace and power, breathing down
25 From over her arched brows, with every turn
   Lived through her to the tips of her long hands,
   And to her feet. She rose her height, and said:

   'We give you welcome: not without redound
   Of use and glory to yourselves ye come,
30 The first-fruits of the stranger: aftertime,
   And that full voice which circles round the grave,
   Will rank you nobly, mingled up with me.
   What! are the ladies of your land so tall?'
   'We of the court' said Cyril. 'From the court'
35 She answered, 'then ye know the Prince?' and he:
   'The climax of his age! as though there were
   One rose in all the world, your Highness that,
   He worships your ideal:' she replied:
   'We scarcely thought in our own hall to hear
40 This barren verbiage, current among men,
   Light coin, the tinsel clink of compliment.
   Your flight from out your bookless wilds would seem
   As arguing love of knowledge and of power;
   Your language proves you still the child. Indeed,
45 We dream not of him: when we set our hand

ii 29. *use and glory to*] *1850*; fame and profit unto *1847–8*.
ii 36. *climax of his age*] summit of his time *ULC MS.*
ii 38. *she*] *1850*; and she *1847–8*.
ii 39. *scarcely thought*] *1850*; did not think *1847–8*.
ii 42–4] *1850 (except l. 44); not 1847–8.*
ii 44. *Indeed*] *1851*; For us *1850*.
ii 45. *dream*] *1850*; think *1847–8*.

To this great work, we purposed with ourself
Never to wed. You likewise will do well,
Ladies, in entering here, to cast and fling
The tricks, which make us toys of men, that so,
50   Some future time, if so indeed you will,
You may with those self-styled our lords ally
Your fortunes, justlier balanced, scale with scale.'

At those high words, we conscious of ourselves,
Perused the matting; then an officer
55   Rose up, and read the statutes, such as these:
Not for three years to correspond with home;
Not for three years to cross the liberties;
Not for three years to speak with any men;
And many more, which hastily subscribed,
60   We entered on the boards: and 'Now,' she cried,
'Ye are green wood, see ye warp not. Look, our hall!
Our statues!—not of those that men desire,
Sleek Odalisques, or oracles of mode,
Nor stunted squaws of West or East; but she
65   That taught the Sabine how to rule, and she
The foundress of the Babylonian wall,
The Carian Artemisia strong in war,
The Rhodope, that built the pyramid,

ii *53–4.* Turner (p. 102) suggests that this 'bowdlerized' a moment in
Juvenal, Satire vi, referring 'to the intrusion of Clodius, disguised as a girl-
musician, into the all-female rites of the Bona Dea, "from which even the
buck-mouse runs away, conscious of its testicles"'.

ii *55–8.* Cp. the decrees in *Love's Labour's Lost* I i, among them not to see
a woman.

ii *60. boards*: the college register.

ii *62. not ... desire*] are they cooks or nursery maids *ULC MS.*

ii *63. Sleek*] Fat *ULC MS.* *Odalisques*: 'female slaves of the harem' (T.).

ii *64–5.* 'The wood-nymph Egeria, who was said to have given the laws to
Numa Pompilius' (T.). Cp. *The Palace of Art* 109–12.

ii *64*] The things that men would have us; no, but she *ULC MS.*

ii *66.* 'Semiramis' (T.).

ii *67.* 'She who fought so bravely for Xerxes at Salamis that he said that
his women had become men and his men women' (T.).

ii *68.* 'A celebrated Greek courtesan of Thracian origin, who was said to
have built a pyramid near Memphis' (T.). T. cites *1 Henry VI* I vi 21–2:
'A statelier pyramis to her I'll rear / Than Rhodope's of Memphis ever
was.'

Clelia, Cornelia, with the Palmyrene
70 That fought Aurelian, and the Roman brows
Of Agrippina. Dwell with these, and lose
Convention, since to look on noble forms
Makes noble through the sensuous organism
That which is higher. O lift your natures up:
75 Embrace our aims: work out your freedom. Girls,
Knowledge is now no more a fountain sealed:
Drink deep, until the habits of the slave,
The sins of emptiness, gossip and spite
And slander, die. Better not be at all
80 Than not be noble. Leave us: you may go:
Today the Lady Psyche will harangue
The fresh arrivals of the week before;
For they press in from all the provinces,
And fill the hive.'
                          She spoke, and bowing waved
85 Dismissal: back again we crost the court
To Lady Psyche's: as we entered in,
There sat along the forms, like morning doves
That sun their milky bosoms on the thatch,
A patient range of pupils; she herself
90 Erect behind a desk of satin-wood,
A quick brunette, well-moulded, falcon-eyed,
And on the hither side, or so she looked,
Of twenty summers. At her left, a child,
In shining draperies, headed like a star,
95 Her maiden babe, a double April old,
Aglaïa slept. We sat: the Lady glanced:

ii 69. *Clelia*: 'who swam the Tiber in escaping from Porsenna's camp
(Livy ii 13)' (T.).   *Cornelia*: 'mother of the Gracchi' (T.).   *Palmy-
rene*: 'Zenobia, Queen of Palmyra' (T.); H.T. refers to Gibbon, Chapter xi,
A.D. 272.
ii 71. *Agrippina*: 'grand-daughter of Augustus, married to Germanicus'
(T.).
ii 71–4. *Dwell . . . higher*] *1850; not 1847–8.*
ii 74–80. *O . . . noble*] *1851; not 1847–50.*
ii 76. Cp. *Song of Solomon* iv 12: 'A garden inclosed is my sister, my
spouse; a spring shut up, a fountain sealed.'
ii 84. *She . . . bowing*] *1850;* So saying, she bowed and *1847–8.*
ii 94. *headed like a star*: 'with bright golden hair' (T.); H.T. compares
Iliad vi 401, the description of Astyanax.
ii 96. *Aglaïa*: Brightness, the name of one of the Graces.

Then Florian, but no livelier than the dame
That whispered 'Asses' ears', among the sedge,
'My sister.' 'Comely, too, by all that's fair,'
100 Said Cyril. 'O hush, hush!' and she began.

'This world was once a fluid haze of light,
Till toward the centre set the starry tides,
And eddied into suns, that wheeling cast
The planets: then the monster, then the man;
105 Tattooed or woaded, winter-clad in skins,
Raw from the prime, and crushing down his mate;
As yet we find in barbarous isles, and here
Among the lowest.'
Thereupon she took
A bird's-eye-view of all the ungracious past;
110 Glanced at the legendary Amazon
As emblematic of a nobler age;
Appraised the Lycian custom, spoke of those
That lay at wine with Lar and Lucumo;
Ran down the Persian, Grecian, Roman lines
115 Of empire, and the woman's state in each,
How far from just; till warming with her theme
She fulmined out her scorn of laws Salique
And little-footed China, touched on Mahomet
With much contempt, and came to chivalry:
120 When some respect, however slight, was paid
To woman, superstition all awry:

ii 97–8. 'Midas in The Wyf of Bathe's Tale confides the secret of his hairy
asses' ears only to his wife' (T.).
ii 101. 'The nebular theory as formulated by Laplace' (T.). H.T. compares
In Memoriam cxviii 9–12, and lxxxix 45–8. Cp. The Palace of Art 186–92n
(p. 64).
ii 110. On feminism, 19th and 20th century, and the Amazons, see M. R.
Lefkowitz, TLS 27 Nov. 1981.
ii 112. 'Herodotus (i 73) says that the Lycians took their names from their
mothers instead of their fathers' (T.).
ii 113. Lar: 'noble' (H.T.).   Lucumo: 'an Etruscan prince or priest' (T.).
ii 117. fulmined: cp. Paradise Regained iv 268–70, on the orators 'whose
resistless eloquence / Wielded at will that fierce Democratie, / Shook the
Arsenal and fulmin'd over Greece.'   Salique: 'the laws of the Salian
Franks forbad inheritance by women' (T.).
ii 118. little-footed: the custom of deforming the feet.
ii 118–19. 'Had she heard that, according to the Mohammedan doctrine,
hell was chiefly occupied by women?' (T.).

However then commenced the dawn: a beam
Had slanted forward, falling in a land
Of promise; fruit would follow. Deep, indeed,
125   Their debt of thanks to her who first had dared
To leap the rotten pales of prejudice,
Disyoke their necks from custom, and assert
None lordlier than themselves but that which made
Woman and man. She had founded; they must build.
130   Here might they learn whatever men were taught:
Let them not fear: some said their heads were less:
Some men's were small; not they the least of men;
For often fineness compensated size:
Besides the brain was like the hand, and grew
135   With using; thence the man's, if more was more;
He took advantage of his strength to be
First in the field: some ages had been lost;
But woman ripened earlier, and her life
Was longer; and albeit their glorious names
140   Were fewer, scattered stars, yet since in truth
The highest is the measure of the man,
And not the Kaffir, Hottentot, Malay,
Nor those horn-handed breakers of the glebe,
But Homer, Plato, Verulam; even so
145   With woman: and in arts of government
Elizabeth and others; arts of war
The peasant Joan and others; arts of grace
Sappho and others vied with any man:
And, last not least, she who had left her place,
150   And bowed her state to them, that they might grow
To use and power on this Oasis, lapt
In the arms of leisure, sacred from the blight
Of ancient influence and scorn.
                                    At last
She rose upon a wind of prophecy
155   Dilating on the future; 'everywhere
Two heads in council, two beside the hearth,
Two in the tangled business of the world,
Two in the liberal offices of life,
Two plummets dropt for one to sound the abyss
160   Of science, and the secrets of the mind:

---

ii *123–4. land of promise: Hebrews* xi 9.
ii *135. more was more*: 'greater in size meant greater in power' (T.).
ii *144.* Cp. *The Palace of Art* 163 (*p. 62*).
ii *149., last ... she*] *1850*; she, though last not least, *1847–8.*

Musician, painter, sculptor, critic, more:
And everywhere the broad and bounteous Earth
Should bear a double growth of those rare souls,
Poets, whose thoughts enrich the blood of the world.'

165 She ended here, and beckoned us: the rest
Parted; and, glowing full-faced welcome, she
Began to address us, and was moving on
In gratulation, till as when a boat
Tacks, and the slackened sail flaps, all her voice
170 Faltering and fluttering in her throat, she cried
'My brother!' 'Well, my sister.' 'O,' she said,
'What do you here? and in this dress? and these?
Why who are these? a wolf within the fold!
A pack of wolves! the Lord be gracious to me!
175 A plot, a plot, a plot, to ruin all!'
'No plot, no plot,' he answered. 'Wretched boy,
How saw you not the inscription on the gate,
LET NO MAN ENTER IN ON PAIN OF DEATH?'
'And if I had,' he answered, 'who could think
180 The softer Adams of your Academe,
O sister, Sirens though they be, were such
As chanted on the blanching bones of men?'
'But you will find it otherwise' she said.
'You jest: ill jesting with edge-tools! my vow
185 Binds me to speak, and O that iron will,
That axelike edge unturnable, our Head,
The Princess.' 'Well then, Psyche, take my life,
And nail me like a weasel on a grange
For warning: bury me beside the gate,
190 And cut this epitaph above my bones;
Here lies a brother by a sister slain,
All for the common good of womankind.'
'Let me die too,' said Cyril, 'having seen
And heard the Lady Psyche.'
                            I struck in:
195 'Albeit so masked, Madam, I love the truth;
Receive it; and in me behold the Prince
Your countryman, affianced years ago
To the Lady Ida: here, for here she was,
And thus (what other way was left) I came.'

ii *184–5. my ... that*] *1850*; I am bound / To tell her. O, she has an
1847–8. Cp. *The Devil and the Lady* II iv 160: 'The Devil is an ill thing to be
jested with', where the context is also of disguise.
ii *186. That*] *1850*; An *1847–8*.

200 'O Sir, O Prince, I have no country; none;
      If any, this; but none. Whate'er I was
      Disrooted, what I am is grafted here.
      Affianced, Sir? love-whispers may not breathe
      Within this vestal limit, and how should I,
205 Who am not mine, say, live: the thunderbolt
      Hangs silent; but prepare: I speak; it falls.'
      'Yet pause,' I said: 'for that inscription there,
      I think no more of deadly lurks therein,
      Than in a clapper clapping in a garth,
210 To scare the fowl from fruit: if more there be,
      If more and acted on, what follows? war;
      Your own work marred: for this your Academe,
      Whichever side be Victor, in the halloo
      Will topple to the trumpet down, and pass
215 With all fair theories only made to gild
      A stormless summer.' 'Let the Princess judge
      Of that' she said: 'farewell, Sir–and to you.
      I shudder at the sequel, but I go.'

        'Are you that Lady Psyche,' I rejoined,
220 'The fifth in line from that old Florian,
      Yet hangs his portrait in my father's hall
      (The gaunt old Baron with his beetle brow
      Sun-shaded in the heat of dusty fights)
      As he bestrode my Grandsire, when he fell,
225 And all else fled? we point to it, and we say,
      The loyal warmth of Florian is not cold,
      But branches current yet in kindred veins.'
      'Are you that Psyche,' Florian added; 'she
      With whom I sang about the morning hills,
230 Flung ball, flew kite, and raced the purple fly,
      And snared the squirrel of the glen? are you
      That Psyche, wont to bind my throbbing brow,
      To smoothe my pillow, mix the foaming draught
      Of fever, tell me pleasant tales, and read
235 My sickness down to happy dreams? are you
      That brother-sister Psyche, both in one?
      You were that Psyche, but what are you now?'
      'You are that Psyche,' Cyril said, 'for whom
      I would be that for ever which I seem,

ii *209. garth*: enclosed ground.
ii *224. bestrode*: 'in defence' (T.). H.T. compares *1 Henry IV* V i 122, and
Comedy of Errors V i 192: 'When I bestrid thee in the wars'.

240 Woman, if I might sit beside your feet,
And glean your scattered sapience.'
Then once more,
'Are you that Lady Psyche,' I began,
'That on her bridal morn before she past
From all her old companions, when the king
245 Kissed her pale cheek, declared that ancient ties
Would still be dear beyond the southern hills;
That were there any of our people there
In want or peril, there was one to hear
And help them? look! for such are these and I.'
250 'Are you that Psyche,' Florian asked, 'to whom,
In gentler days, your arrow-wounded fawn
Came flying while you sat beside the well?
The creature laid his muzzle on your lap,
And sobbed, and you sobbed with it, and the blood
255 Was sprinkled on your kirtle, and you wept.
That was fawn's blood, not brother's, yet you wept.
O by the bright head of my little niece,
You were that Psyche, and what are you now?'
'You are that Psyche,' Cyril said again,
260 'The mother of the sweetest little maid,
That ever crowed for kisses.'
'Out upon it!'
She answered, 'peace! and why should I not play
The Spartan Mother with emotion, be
The Lucius Junius Brutus of my kind?
265 Him you call great: he for the common weal,
The fading politics of mortal Rome,
As I might slay this child, if good need were,
Slew both his sons: and I, shall I, on whom
The secular emancipation turns
270 Of half this world, be swerved from right to save
A prince, a brother? a little will I yield.
Best so, perchance, for us, and well for you.
O hard, when love and duty clash! I fear
My conscience will not count me fleckless; yet—

ii 240. *Woman*] *1850*; A woman *1847–8*.
ii 251–6. J. Killham, *Critical Essays on Tennyson*, pp. 229–30, compares
Marvell's *Nymph Complaining for the Death of her Faun*. Cp. also Silvia's
wounded stag, *Aeneid* vii 500–4.
ii 264. 'Who condemned his sons to death for conspiracy against the
city (Livy, ii 5)' (T.).
ii 269. *secular*: lasting through ages.

275   Hear my conditions: promise (otherwise
       You perish) as you came, to slip away
       Today, tomorrow, soon: it shall be said,
       These women were too barbarous, would not learn;
       They fled, who might have shamed us: promise, all.'

280   What could we else, we promised each; and she,
       Like some wild creature newly-caged, commenced
       A to-and-fro, so pacing till she paused
       By Florian; holding out her lily arms
       Took both his hands, and smiling faintly said:
285   'I knew you at the first: though you have grown
       You scarce have altered: I am sad and glad
       To see you, Florian. *I* give thee to death
       My brother! it was duty spoke, not I.
       My needful seeming harshness, pardon it.
       Our mother, is she well?'
290   With that she kissed
       His forehead, then, a moment after, clung
       About him, and betwixt them blossomed up
       From out a common vein of memory
       Sweet household talk, and phrases of the hearth,
295   And far allusion, till the gracious dews
       Began to glisten and to fall: and while
       They stood, so rapt, we gazing, came a voice,
       'I brought a message here from Lady Blanche.'
       Back started she, and turning round we saw
300   The Lady Blanche's daughter where she stood,
       Melissa, with her hand upon the lock,
       A rosy blonde, and in a college gown,
       That clad her like an April daffodilly
       (Her mother's colour) with her lips apart,
305   And all her thoughts as fair within her eyes,
       As bottom agates seen to wave and float
       In crystal currents of clear morning seas.

ii *285–6*] *1850*;   You are grown, and yet I knew you at the first.
                 I am very glad, and I am very vext *1847–8*
ii *291. then,*] *1850*; and *1847–8*.
ii *304. colour*: that worn by her pupils, her 'side'.
ii *306. seen*] *1850*; seem *1847–8*.
ii *306–7*. 'It has been said that I took this simile partly from Beaumont and
Fletcher, partly from Shakespeare, whereas I made it while I was bathing
in Wales' (T.).

So stood that same fair creature at the door.
Then Lady Psyche, 'Ah – Melissa – you!
310   You heard us?' and Melissa, 'O pardon me
I heard, I could not help it, did not wish:
But, dearest Lady, pray you fear me not,
Nor think I bear that heart within my breast,
To give three gallant gentlemen to death.'
315   'I trust you,' said the other, 'for we two
Were always friends, none closer, elm and vine:
But yet your mother's jealous temperament –
Let not your prudence, dearest, drowse, or prove
The Danaïd of a leaky vase, for fear
320   This whole foundation ruin, and I lose
My honour, these their lives.' 'Ah, fear me not'
Replied Melissa; 'no – I would not tell,
No, not for all Aspasia's cleverness,
No, not to answer, Madam, all those hard things
325   That Sheba came to ask of Solomon.'
'Be it so' the other, 'that we still may lead
The new light up, and culminate in peace,
For Solomon may come to Sheba yet.'
Said Cyril, 'Madam, he the wisest man
330   Feasted the woman wisest then, in halls
Of Lebanonian cedar: nor should you
(Though, Madam, *you* should answer, *we* would ask)
Less welcome find among us, if you came
Among us, debtors for our lives to you,
335   Myself for something more.' He said not what,

ii *311. wish*] *1850*; mean *1847–8*.

ii *312. pray*] *1850*; I pray *1847–8*.

ii *319*. The Danaids, who murdered their husbands, were punished in Hades by having to carry water in sieves.

ii *323. Aspasia*: hostess to the finest literary and philosophical minds in Athens, and (as Turner notes) a hetaera and the mistress of Pericles.

ii *325. 1 Kings* x 1: 'And when the queen of Sheba heard of the fame of Solomon concerning the name of the Lord, she came to prove him with hard questions.'

ii *326. still may*] *1850*; may live to *1847–8*.

ii *331*. Cp. T.'s letter to James Spedding, 15 Feb. 1835 (*Letters* i 127; *Mem.* i 143–4): 'I will come to thee as Sheba came to Solomon. "She travelled far from Indian streams, / And he a royal welcome made / In ample chambers overlaid / With Lebanonian cedar-beams." I forget where I read this.' Apparently T. had made up the lines.

ii *333. if*] *1850*; if e'er *1847–8*.

But 'Thanks,' she answered 'Go: we have been too long
Together: keep your hoods about the face;
They do so that affect abstraction here.
Speak little; mix not with the rest; and hold
340   Your promise: all, I trust, may yet be well.'

      We turned to go, but Cyril took the child,
And held her round the knees against his waist,
And blew the swollen cheek of a trumpeter,
While Psyche watched them, smiling, and the child
345   Pushed her flat hand against his face and laughed;
And thus our conference closed.
                                        And then we strolled
For half the day through stately theatres
Benched crescent-wise. In each we sat, we heard
· The grave Professor. On the lecture slate
350   The circle rounded under female hands
With flawless demonstration: followed then
A classic lecture, rich in sentiment,
With scraps of thundrous Epic lilted out
By violet-hooded Doctors, elegies
355   And quoted odes, and jewels five-words-long
That on the stretched forefinger of all Time
Sparkle for ever: then we dipt in all
That treats of whatsoever is, the state,
The total chronicles of man, the mind,
360   The morals, something of the frame, the rock,
The star, the bird, the fish, the shell, the flower,
Electric, chemic laws, and all the rest,
And whatsoever can be taught and known;
Till like three horses that have broken fence,
365   And glutted all night long breast-deep in corn,
We issued gorged with knowledge, and I spoke:
'Why, Sirs, they do all this as well as we.'
'They hunt old trails' said Cyril 'very well;
But when did woman ever yet invent?'
370   'Ungracious!' answered Florian; 'have you learnt
No more from Psyche's lecture, you that talked
The trash that made me sick, and almost sad?'
'O trash' he said, 'but with a kernel in it.

ii 347] *1850; not 1847–8.*
ii 348. *Benched crescent-wise*] *1850*; From room to room *1847–8.*
ii 356. Cp *Love and Duty* 45–6, MS: 'The stretcht forefinger of the hand of
some / Old Goddess'.
ii 360. *something of the frame*: physiology.

Should I not call her wise, who made me wise?
375   And learnt? I learnt more from her in a flash,
Than if my brainpan were an empty hull,
And every Muse tumbled a science in.
A thousand hearts lie fallow in these halls,
And round these halls a thousand baby loves
380   Fly twanging headless arrows at the hearts,
Whence follows many a vacant pang; but O
With me, Sir, entered in the bigger boy,
The Head of all the golden-shafted firm,
The long-limbed lad that had a Psyche too;
385   He cleft me through the stomacher; and now
What think you of it, Florian? do I chase
The substance or the shadow? will it hold?
I have no sorcerer's malison on me,
No ghostly hauntings like his Highness. I
390   Flatter myself that always everywhere
I know the substance when I see it. Well,
Are castles shadows? Three of them? Is she
The sweet proprietress a shadow? If not,
Shall those three castles patch my tattered coat?
395   For dear are those three castles to my wants,
And dear is sister Psyche to my heart,
And two dear things are one of double worth,
And much I might have said, but that my zone
Unmanned me: then the Doctors! O to hear
400   The Doctors! O to watch the thirsty plants
Imbibing! once or twice I thought to roar,
To break my chain, to shake my mane: but thou,
Modulate me, Soul of mincing mimicry!

ii 384. The legend of Cupid and Psyche.
ii 386–7] 1851; What think you of it, Florian? will it hold? 1847–50.
ii 388–93] 1851; not 1847–50.
ii 394 ʌ 5] 'Oh but,' he answered, 'women's fancies hook
          On rusty props. Remember her we called
          The "Star of midnight", how she used to hang
          On that flat-headed and bush-cheeked baboon,
          Lost to all else and peering up to find
          Her God within that blur he called his eye,
          The greasy casement of a vacant house.' MS
Quoted by Sir Charles Tennyson, Nineteenth Century cix (1931) 632.
ii 398. zone: girdle.
ii 402. thou] 1850; come 1847–8.
ii 403. Modulate me, Soul] Infect me, spirit ULC MS.

Make liquid treble of that bassoon, my throat;
405   Abase those eyes that ever loved to meet
Star-sisters answering under crescent brows;
Abate the stride, which speaks of man, and loose
A flying charm of blushes o'er this cheek,
Where they like swallows coming out of time
410   Will wonder why they came: but hark the bell
For dinner, let us go!'
                    And in we streamed
Among the columns, pacing staid and still
By twos and threes, till all from end to end
With beauties every shade of brown and fair
415   In colours gayer than the morning mist,
The long hall glittered like a bed of flowers.
How might a man not wander from his wits
Pierced through with eyes, but that I kept mine own
Intent on her, who rapt in glorious dreams,
420   The second-sight of some Astræan age,
Sat compassed with professors: they, the while,
Discussed a doubt and tost it to and fro:
A clamour thickened, mixt with inmost terms
Of art and science: Lady Blanche alone
425   Of faded form and haughtiest lineaments,
With all her autumn tresses falsely brown,
Shot sidelong daggers at us, a tiger-cat
In act to spring.
                    At last a solemn grace
Concluded, and we sought the gardens: there
430   One walked reciting by herself, and one
In this hand held a volume as to read,

ii *404* ∧ *5*] And plump me out with female to the tips: *ULC MS.*

ii *416.* 'Lady Psyche's "side" (pupils) wore lilac robes, and Lady Blanche's robes of daffodil colour' (T.).

ii *419*] *1851*; Intent upon the Princess, where she sat *1847–8*; Intent on her, who rapt in awful dreams, *1850*.

ii *420–23*] *1850*; Among her grave Professors, scattering gems *1847–8*. Aubrey de Vere had objected to the impression of lordliness given by the original (Shannon, p. 136).

ii *420. Astræan*: 'Astræa, daughter of Zeus and Themis, is to come back first of the celestials on the return of the Golden Age' (T.).

ii *424. Lady Blanche alone*] *1850*; only Lady Blanche, *1847–8*.

ii *425*] *1850*; A double-rouged and treble-wrinkled Dame, *1847–8*.

ii *426. autumn tresses*] *1850*; faded Autumns *1847–8*.

And smoothed a petted peacock down with that:
Some to a low song oared a shallop by,
Or under arches of the marble bridge
435 Hung, shadowed from the heat: some hid and sought
In the orange thickets: others tost a ball
Above the fountain-jets, and back again
With laughter: others lay about the lawns,
Of the older sort, and murmured that their May
440 Was passing: what was learning unto them?
They wished to marry; they could rule a house;
Men hated learned women: but we three
Sat muffled like the Fates; and often came
Melissa hitting all we saw with shafts
445 Of gentle satire, kin to charity,
That harmed not: then day droopt; the chapel bells
Called us: we left the walks; we mixt with those
Six hundred maidens clad in purest white,
Before two streams of light from wall to wall,
450 While the great organ almost burst his pipes,
Groaning for power, and rolling through the court
A long melodious thunder to the sound
Of solemn psalms, and silver litanies,
The work of Ida, to call down from Heaven
455 A blessing on her labours for the world.

[II ∧ III]
Sweet and low, sweet and low,
Wind of the western sea,
Low, low, breathe and blow,
Wind of the western sea!
5 Over the rolling waters go,
Come from the dying moon, and blow,

ii 442–3] *1850*; Men hated learned women: and to us came *1847–8*.

ii 446. then . . . bells] *1850*; so we sat; and now when day *1847–8*.

ii 447. Called . . . mixt] *1850*; Drooped, and the chapel tinkled, mixt *1847–8*.

ii 451–2. Adapted from *What did it profit me* 7–8 (Appendix B, III 620): 'through inexplorable ravines / Rolling melodious thunders'; see also *Lines on Cambridge of 1830* 9 and 11 *n.* (I 311).

ii 452. Cp. *The Poet's Mind* 27: 'a low melodious thunder'. Also *Semele* 10.

ii ∧ iii Written 1849, added *1850*. Cp. the lullaby in Theocritus xxiv 7–9. For alternative versions, see Appendix I (*p. 977*).

ii ∧ iii 1. Cp. *Hero to Leander* 33: 'Thy voice is sweet and low' (contrasted with the sea). Also *The Lover's Tale* i 530: 'Held converse sweet and low— low converse sweet'; i 552: 'her voice was very sweet and low'.

ii ∧ iii 6. dying] *1851*; dropping *1850*.

Blow him again to me;
While my little one, while my pretty one, sleeps.

Sleep and rest, sleep and rest,
10   Father will come to thee soon;
Rest, rest, on mother's breast,
      Father will come to thee soon;
Father will come to his babe in the nest,
Silver sails all out of the west
15   Under the silver moon:
Sleep, my little one, sleep, my pretty one, sleep.

III

Morn in the white wake of the morning star
Came furrowing all the orient into gold.
We rose, and each by other drest with care
Descended to the court that lay three parts
5 In shadow, but the Muses' heads were touched
Above the darkness from their native East.

   There while we stood beside the fount, and watched
Or seemed to watch the dancing bubble, approached
Melissa, tinged with wan from lack of sleep,
10 Or grief, and glowing round her dewy eyes
The circled Iris of a night of tears;
'And fly,' she cried, 'O fly, while yet you may!
My mother knows:' and when I asked her 'how,'
'My fault' she wept 'my fault! and yet not mine;
15 Yet mine in part. O hear me, pardon me.
My mother, 'tis her wont from night to night
To rail at Lady Psyche and her side.
She says the Princess should have been the Head,
Herself and Lady Psyche the two arms;
20 And so it was agreed when first they came;
But Lady Psyche was the right hand now,
And she the left, or not, or seldom used;

iii *1–2.* Cp. the end of *Love and Duty*: '. . . and morning driven her plow
of pearl / Far furrowing into light the mounded rack, / Beyond the fair
green field and eastern sea.'
iii *7. There*] *1850*; And *1847–8*.
iii *10. grief*] *1850*; sorrow *1847–8*.
iii *11. Iris*: rainbow. Cp. *All's Well* I iii 147–50: 'What's the matter, /
That this distempered messenger of wet, / The many-coloured Iris, rounds
thine eye? / Why? that you are my daughter?'
iii *13. when I asked her*] *1850*; we demanding *1847–8*.

Hers more than half the students, all the love.
And so last night she fell to canvass you:
25 *Her* countrywomen! she did not envy her.
"Who ever saw such wild barbarians?
Girls?—more like men!" and at these words the snake,
My secret, seemed to stir within my breast;
And oh, Sirs, could I help it, but my cheek
30 Began to burn and burn, and her lynx eye
To fix and make me hotter, till she laughed:
"O marvellously modest maiden, you!
Men! girls, like men! why, if they had been men
You need not set your thoughts in rubric thus
35 For wholesale comment." Pardon, I am shamed
That I must needs repeat for my excuse
What looks so little graceful: "men" (for still
My mother went revolving on the word)
"And so they are,—very like men indeed—
40 And with that woman closeted for hours!"
Then came these dreadful words out one by one,
"Why—these—*are*—men:" I shuddered: "and you know
            it."
"O ask me nothing," I said: "And she knows too,
And she conceals it." So my mother clutched
45 The truth at once, but with no word from me;
And now thus early risen she goes to inform
The Princess: Lady Psyche will be crushed;
But you may yet be saved, and therefore fly;
But heal me with your pardon ere you go.'

50   'What pardon, sweet Melissa, for a blush?'
Said Cyril: 'Pale one, blush again: than wear
Those lilies, better blush our lives away.
Yet let us breathe for one hour more in Heaven'
He added, 'lest some classic Angel speak
55 In scorn of us, "They mounted, Ganymedes,
To tumble, Vulcans, on the second morn."
But I will melt this marble into wax
To yield us farther furlough:' and he went.

iii 34. *rubric*: red letters.
iii 34-8] *1850*; And in their fulsome fashion wooed you, child,
            You need not take so deep a rouge: like men—*1847-8*
iii 40] *1850*; And closeted with her for hours. Aha!' *1847-8*.
iii 55-6. Ganymede, snatched up to heaven; Vulcan, hurled from it.
iii 58. *furlough*: leave of absence, here permission in general.

Melissa shook her doubtful curls, and thought
60 He scarce would prosper. 'Tell us,' Florian asked,
'How grew this feud betwixt the right and left.'
'O long ago,' she said, 'betwixt these two
Division smoulders hidden; 'tis my mother,
Too jealous, often fretful as the wind
65 Pent in a crevice: much I bear with her:
I never knew my father, but she says
(God help her) she was wedded to a fool;
And still she railed against the state of things.
She had the care of Lady Ida's youth,
70 And from the Queen's decease she brought her up.
But when your sister came she won the heart
Of Ida: they were still together, grew
(For so they said themselves) inosculated;
Consonant chords that shiver to one note;
75 One mind in all things: yet my mother still
Affirms your Psyche thieved her theories,
And angled with them for her pupil's love:
She calls her plagiarist; I know not what:
But I must go: I dare not tarry,' and light,
80 As flies the shadow of a bird, she fled.

Then murmured Florian gazing after her,
'An open-hearted maiden, true and pure.
If I could love, why this were she: how pretty
Her blushing was, and how she blushed again,
85 As if to close with Cyril's random wish:
Not like your Princess crammed with erring pride,
Nor like poor Psyche whom she drags in tow.'

'The crane,' I said, 'may chatter of the crane,
The dove may murmur of the dove, but I

---

iii 67. help] 1850; pardon 1847-8.

iii 71. heart] 1850; love 1847-8.

iii 72. Ida] 1850; the Princess 1847-8.

iii 73. inosculated: intertwined, kissing.

iii 74. Adapted from the blank-verse setting for Who can say (I 493). 'If two stringed instruments are together, and a note is struck on one, the other will vibrate with the same harmony' (T.).

iii 75. yet . . . still] 1850; only Lady Blanche 1847-8.

iii 77. her pupil's love] 1850; the Royal heart 1847-8.

iii 88-90. Cp. Theocritus ix 31-2: 'O cricket is to cricket dear, and ant for ant doth long, / The hawk's the darling of his fere, and o' me the Muse and her song.' Also Isaiah xxxviii 14: 'Like a crane or a swallow, so did

90 An eagle clang an eagle to the sphere.
    My princess, O my princess! true she errs,
    But in her own grand way: being herself
    Three times more noble than three score of men,
    She sees herself in every woman else,
95 And so she wears her error like a crown
    To blind the truth and me: for her, and her,
    Hebes are they to hand ambrosia, mix
    The nectar; but–ah she–whene'er she moves
    The Samian Herè rises and she speaks
100 A Memnon smitten with the morning Sun.'

    So saying from the court we paced, and gained
    The terrace ranged along the Northern front,
    And leaning there on those balusters, high
    Above the empurpled champaign, drank the gale
105 That blown about the foliage underneath,
    And sated with the innumerable rose,
    Beat balm upon our eyelids. Hither came
    Cyril, and yawning 'O hard task,' he cried;
    'No fighting shadows here! I forced a way
110 Through solid opposition crabbed and gnarled.
    Better to clear prime forests, heave and thump
    A league of street in summer solstice down,
    Than hammer at this reverend gentlewoman.
    I knocked and, bidden, entered; found her there
115 At point to move, and settled in her eyes
    The green malignant light of coming storm.
    Sir, I was courteous, every phrase well-oiled,
    As man's could be; yet maiden-meek I prayed

I chatter: I did mourn as a dove: mine eyes fail with looking upward.'
iii *90. clang*: cp. Leigh Hunt, *Hero and Leander* 201–2: 'The crane / Began
to clang against the coming rain.'
iii *92*] *1850*; For being, and wise in knowing that she is, *1847–8*.
iii *97. Hebes are they*] *1850*; They are Hebes meet *1847–8*.
iii *99.* 'The Greek Herè, whose favourite abode was Samos' (T.).
iii *100.* 'The statue in Egypt which gave forth a musical note when
"smitten with the morning sun"' (T.).
iii *101. from*] *1850*; from out *1847–8*.
iii *109–10*] *1851; not 1847–50.*
iii *111. prime*: primeval.
iii *114. entered;*] *1850*; went in: I *1847–8*.
iii *115. move*] *1850*; sally *1847–8*.
iii *116. malignant light*: *Perdidi Diem* 22.
iii *118. man's*] *1851*; man *1847–50*.

Concealment: she demanded who we were,
120 And why we came? I fabled nothing fair,
But, your example pilot, told her all.
Up went the hushed amaze of hand and eye.
But when I dwelt upon your old affiance,
She answered sharply that I talked astray.
125 I urged the fierce inscription on the gate,
And our three lives. True–we had limed ourselves
With open eyes, and we must take the chance.
But such extremes, I told her, well might harm
The woman's cause. "Not more than now," she said,
130 "So puddled as it is with favouritism."
I tried the mother's heart. Shame might befall
Melissa, knowing, saying not she knew:
Her answer was "Leave me to deal with that."
I spoke of war to come and many deaths,
135 And she replied, her duty was to speak,
And duty duty, clear of consequences.
I grew discouraged, Sir; but since I knew
No rock so hard but that a little wave
May beat admission in a thousand years,
140 I recommenced; "Decide not ere you pause.
I find you here but in the second place,
Some say the third–the authentic foundress you.
I offer boldly: we will seat you highest:
Wink at our advent: help my prince to gain
145 His rightful bride, and here I promise you
Some palace in our land, where you shall reign
The head and heart of all our fair she-world,
And your great name flow on with broadening time
For ever." Well, she balanced this a little,
150 And told me she would answer us today,
Meantime be mute: thus much, nor more I gained.'

He ceasing, came a message from the Head.
'That afternoon the Princess rode to take
The dip of certain strata to the North.
155 Would we go with her? we should find the land
Worth seeing; and the river made a fall
Out yonder:' then she pointed on to where

iii *120. fabled . . . fair*] *1850*; minted . . . false *1847–8*. A review had objected
(Shannon, p. 119).
iii *126. True–*] *1850*; She said *1847–8*.   *limed*: ensnared.
iii *146. Some palace in our*] *1850*; A palace in our own *1847–8*.
iii *153. That*] *1850*; In the *1847–8*.

A double hill ran up his furrowy forks
Beyond the thick-leaved platans of the vale.
160 Agreed to, this, the day fled on through all
Its range of duties to the appointed hour.
Then summoned to the porch we went. She stood
Among her maidens, higher by the head,
Her back against a pillar, her foot on one
165 Of those tame leopards. Kittenlike he rolled
And pawed about her sandal. I drew near;
I gazed. On a sudden my strange seizure came
Upon me, the weird vision of our house:
The Princess Ida seemed a hollow show,
170 Her gay-furred cats a painted fantasy,
Her college and her maidens, empty masks,
And I myself the shadow of a dream,
For all things were and were not. Yet I felt
My heart beat thick with passion and with awe;
175 Then from my breast the involuntary sigh
Brake, as she smote me with the light of eyes
That lent my knee desire to kneel, and shook
My pulses, till to horse we got, and so
Went forth in long retinue following up
180 The river as it narrowed to the hills.

I rode beside her and to me she said:
'O friend, we trust that you esteemed us not
Too harsh to your companion yestermorn;
Unwillingly we spake.' 'No—not to her,'
185 I answered, 'but to one of whom we spake
Your Highness might have seemed the thing you say.'
'Again?' she cried, 'are you ambassadresses
From him to me? we give you, being strange,
A license: speak, and let the topic die.'

190 I stammered that I knew him—could have wished—
'Our king expects—was there no precontract?
There is no truer-hearted—ah, you seem
All he prefigured, and he could not see
The bird of passage flying south but longed

---

iii *158. furrowy*] *1851*; dark-blue *1847–50.*
iii *159. thick-*] *1851*; full- *1847–50.* Adapted from *Mariana in the South*
44, *1832* text: 'the full-leavèd platan-shade'.
iii *167–73*] *1851; not 1847–50.*
iii *175. Then*] *1850*; And *1847–8.*
iii *178. got*] *1851*; clomb *1847–50.*

195   To follow: surely, if your Highness keep
Your purport, you will shock him even to death,
Or baser courses, children of despair.'
'Poor boy,' she said, 'can he not read—no books?
Quoit, tennis, ball—no games? nor deals in that
200   Which men delight in, martial exercise?
To nurse a blind ideal like a girl,
Methinks he seems no better than a girl;
As girls were once, as we ourself have been:
We had our dreams; perhaps he mixt with them:
205   We touch on our dead self, nor shun to do it,
Being other—since we learnt our meaning here,
To lift the woman's fallen divinity
Upon an even pedestal with man.'

She paused, and added with a haughtier smile
210   'And as to precontracts, we move, my friend,
At no man's beck, but know ourself and thee,
O Vashti, noble Vashti! Summoned out
She kept her state, and left the drunken king
To brawl at Shushan underneath the palms.'

215   'Alas your Highness breathes full East,' I said,
'On that which leans to you. I know the Prince,
I prize his truth: and then how vast a work
To assail this gray preëminence of man!
You grant me license; might I use it? think;
220   Ere half be done perchance your life may fail;
Then comes the feebler heiress of your plan,
And takes and ruins all; and thus your pains
May only make that footprint upon sand
Which old-recurring waves of prejudice
225   Resmooth to nothing: might I dread that you,
With only Fame for spouse and your great deeds
For issue, yet may live in vain, and miss,
Meanwhile, what every woman counts her due,

iii *199. tennis*: the earlier game, played in a walled court.
iii *200. exercise*] *1851*; exercises *1847–50*.
iii *203. ourself*] *1864*; ourselves *1847–62*.
iii *205*] We do not shame to speak of what we were, *ULC MS 1st reading.*
iii *207. lift*] *1850*; uplift *1847–8*.
iii *211. ourself*] *1864*; ourselves *1847–62*.
iii *212–4. Esther* i 11–12.
iii *215*. 'A playful reference to the cold manner of an Eastern queen and the east wind' (T.).

Love, children, happiness?'
                     And she exclaimed,
230 'Peace, you young savage of the Northern wild!
What! though your Prince's love were like a God's,
Have we not made ourself the sacrifice?
You are bold indeed: we are not talked to thus:
Yet will we say for children, would they grew
235 Like field-flowers everywhere! we like them well:
But children die; and let me tell you, girl,
Howe'er you babble, great deeds cannot die;
They with the sun and moon renew their light
For ever, blessing those that look on them.
240 Children–that men may pluck them from our hearts,
Kill us with pity, break us with ourselves–
O–children–there is nothing upon earth
More miserable than she that has a son
And sees him err: nor would we work for fame;
245 Though she perhaps might reap the applause of Great,
Who learns the one POU STO whence after-hands
May move the world, though she herself effect
But little: wherefore up and act, nor shrink
For fear our solid aim be dissipated
250 By frail successors. Would, indeed, we had been,
In lieu of many mortal flies, a race
Of giants living, each, a thousand years,
That we might see our own work out, and watch
The sandy footprint harden into stone.'

255   I answered nothing, doubtful in myself
If that strange Poet-princess with her grand
Imaginations might at all be won.
And she broke out interpreting my thoughts:

---

iii *232. ourself*] *1850*; ourselves *1847–8*.

iii *237–9*. Adopted from *Tiresias* 136, *T.Nbk 20*: 'for great acts perish not/ But with [like *1st reading*] the sun and moon renew their light / For ever blessing those that look on them'. Cp. *O mother Britain* 21–4: 'But thy good deed shall never die, / It spreads from shore to shore, / And with the sun and moon renews / Its light for evermore.'

iii *242–4*. *Proverbs* x 1, 'A wise son maketh a glad father: but a foolish son is the heaviness of his mother.'

iii *246*. 'δὸς ποῦ στῶ καὶ κόσμον κινήσω ('Give me where I may stand and I will move the world'), an often-quoted saying of Archimedes' (T.).

iii *250. By*] *1851*; Of *1847–50*.

iii *256–7*] *1851*; If that strange maiden could at all be won. *1847–50*.

'No doubt we seem a kind of monster to you;
260 We are used to that: for women, up till this
Cramped under worse than South-sea-isle taboo,
Dwarfs of the gynæceum, fail so far
In high desire, they know not, cannot guess
How much their welfare is a passion to us.
265 If we could give them surer, quicker proof—
Oh if our end were less achievable
By slow approaches, than by single act
Of immolation, any phase of death,
We were as prompt to spring against the pikes,
270 Or down the fiery gulf as talk of it,
To compass our dear sisters' liberties.'

She bowed as if to veil a noble tear;
And up we came to where the river sloped
To plunge in cataract, shattering on black blocks
275 A breadth of thunder. O'er it shook the woods,
And danced the colour, and, below, stuck out
The bones of some vast bulk that lived and roared
Before man was. She gazed awhile and said,
'As these rude bones to us, are we to her
280 That will be.' 'Dare we dream of that,' I asked,
'Which wrought us, as the workman and his work,
That practice betters?' 'How,' she cried, 'you love
The metaphysics! read and earn our prize,
A golden brooch: beneath an emerald plane
285 Sits Diotima, teaching him that died
Of hemlock; our device; wrought to the life;
She rapt upon her subject, he on her:
For there are schools for all.' 'And yet' I said
'Methinks I have not found among them all
290 One anatomic.' 'Nay, we thought of that,'
She answered, 'but it pleased us not: in truth
We shudder but to dream our maids should ape
Those monstrous males that carve the living hound,

iii 262. *gynæceum*: 'women's quarters in a Greek house' (T.).
iii 269–70. The acts of self-sacrifice by Publius Decius Mus and by Marcus Curtius.
iii 272 ∧ 3] And then she smote her horse upon the flanks *ULC MS 1st reading*.
iii 274–5. Adapted from *The Lover's Tale* iii 21 ∧ 2, MS: 'Shaking the woods, shattering the air with sound'.
iii 285. *Diotima*: 'Said to have been an instructress of Socrates. She was a priestess of Mantinea. (Cf. Plato's *Symposium*.)' (T.).
iii 293–4. 'See Hogarth's picture in the "Stages of Cruelty". It was

And cram him with the fragments of the grave,
295   Or in the dark dissolving human heart,
And holy secrets of this microcosm,
Dabbling a shameless hand with shameful jest,
Encarnalize their spirits: yet we know
Knowledge is knowledge, and this matter hangs:
300   Howbeit ourself, foreseeing casualty,
Nor willing men should come among us, learnt,
For many weary moons before we came,
This craft of healing. Were you sick, ourself
Would tend upon you. To your question now,
305   Which touches on the workman and his work.
Let there be light and there was light: 'tis so:
For was, and is, and will be, are but is;
And all creation is one act at once,
The birth of light: but we that are not all,
310   As parts, can see but parts, now this, now that,
And live, perforce, from thought to thought, and make
One act a phantom of succession: thus
Our weakness somehow shapes the shadow, Time;
But in the shadow will we work, and mould
The woman to the fuller day.'
315   She spake
With kindled eyes; we rode a league beyond,
And, o'er a bridge of pinewood crossing, came
On flowery levels underneath the crag,
Full of all beauty. 'O how sweet' I said
320   (For I was half-oblivious of my mask)
'To linger here with one that loved us.' 'Yea,'
She answered, 'or with fair philosophies

asserted that they used to give dogs the remnants of the dissecting-room'
(T.).
iii *300. ourself*] *1850*; ourselves *1847–8*. Likewise in l. 303.
iii *303. This ... healing*] Imbibed large leech-craft *ULC MS 1st reading*; To
deal with leech-craft *2nd reading*; To handle leech-craft *MS*.
iii *305. Ephesians* ii 10: 'For we are his workmanship, created in Christ
Jesus unto good works.'
iii *316. league beyond*] *1850*; little higher *1847–8*.
iii *317*] *1850*; To cross the flood by a narrow bridge, and came *1847–8*. A
review had objected to the rhythm (Shannon, p. 120).
iii *318*. Cp. Akenside's *Pleasures of Imagination (Lincoln)* ii: 'flowery level',
which occurs in *Ilion, Ilion 6*.
iii *319*. 'O] *1848*; ; and 'O *1847*.

That lift the fancy; for indeed these fields
Are lovely, lovelier not the Elysian lawns,
325 Where paced the Demigods of old, and saw
The soft white vapour streak the crownèd towers
Built to the Sun:' then, turning to her maids,
'Pitch our pavilion here upon the sward;
Lay out the viands.' At the word, they raised
330 A tent of satin, elaborately wrought
With fair Corinna's triumph; here she stood,
Engirt with many a florid maiden-cheek,
The woman-conqueror; woman-conquered there
The bearded Victor of ten-thousand hymns,
335 And all the men mourned at his side: but we
Set forth to climb; then, climbing, Cyril kept
With Psyche, with Melissa Florian, I
With mine affianced. Many a little hand
Glanced like a touch of sunshine on the rocks,
340 Many a light foot shone like a jewel set
In the dark crag: and then we turned, we wound
About the cliffs, the copses, out and in,
Hammering and clinking, chattering stony names
Of shale and hornblende, rag and trap and tuff,
345 Amygdaloid and trachyte, till the Sun
Grew broader toward his death and fell, and all
The rosy heights came out above the lawns.

iii *331. Corinna*: 'She is the Boeotian poetess who is said to have triumphed over Pindar in poetical competition (Pausanias, ix 22). The Princess probably exaggerates' (T.).

iii *337. with Melissa Florian,*] *1850*; Florian with the other, and *1847–8*.

iii *338* ∧ *9*] They mounting, from the rough rocks up the path
                  Hung like a drooping wreath of mountain flowers *ULC MS 1st*
                                                                      reading

iii *344–5*. The glossary to vol. i of Lyell's *Principles of Geology* (4th edn, 1835), which T. read in 1837, gives: *shale*: 'indurated slaty clay'.   *hornblende*: 'a simple mineral of a dark green or black colour'.   *trap*: 'volcanic rocks'.   *tuff*: 'a variety of volcanic rock of an earthy texture'. *amygdaloid*: 'one of the forms of the trap-rocks'.   *trachyte*: 'a variety of lava'. To these, add *rag*: a hard coarse kind of stone.

iii ∧ iv Added *1850*. 'Written after hearing the echoes at Killarney in 1848. When I was there I heard a bugle blown beneath the "Eagle's Nest," and eight distinct echoes' (T.). Cp. *The Vale of Bones* 3–7 (I 109). H.T. excised (*MS Mat., Lincoln*) Locke's comment: 'I think if, while reading the *Bugle Song* you listen attentively, you will detect a very faint echo which will convince you that Tennyson also admired Moore's very pretty poem called *Echo*' (P. L. Elliott, *The Making of the Memoir*, 1978, p. 28).

[III ∧ IV]

The splendour falls on castle walls
    And snowy summits old in story:
The long light shakes across the lakes,
    And the wild cataract leaps in glory.
5 Blow, bugle, blow, set the wild echoes flying,
Blow, bugle; answer, echoes, dying, dying, dying.

    O hark, O hear! how thin and clear,
        And thinner, clearer, farther going!
    O sweet and far from cliff and scar
10   The horns of Elfland faintly blowing!
    Blow, let us hear the purple glens replying:
    Blow, bugle; answer, echoes, dying, dying, dying.

    O love, they die in yon rich sky,
        They faint on hill or field or river:
15   Our echoes roll from soul to soul,
            And grow for ever and for ever.
    Blow, bugle, blow, set the wild echoes flying,
    And answer, echoes, answer, dying, dying, dying.

IV

'There sinks the nebulous star we call the Sun,
If that hypothesis of theirs be sound'
Said Ida; 'let us down and rest;' and we
Down from the lean and wrinkled precipices,
5 By every coppice-feathered chasm and cleft,
Dropt through the ambrosial gloom to where below
No bigger than a glow-worm shone the tent
Lamp-lit from the inner. Once she leaned on me,
Descending; once or twice she lent her hand,

iii ∧ iv *1–3*. Cp. Byron, *The Prisoner of Chillon* 83–5: 'A sunset till its summer's gone, / Its sleepless summer of long light, / The snow-clad offspring of the sun' (Byron's poem has its castle walls and its lake). H.T. wrote: 'My father remembered her [T.'s grandmother] reading to him, when a boy, *The Prisoner of Chillon* very tenderly' (*Mem.* i 12).

iii ∧ iv *3. long*] red *MS (formerly Gully)*. This reading is from family tradition; the whereabouts of this MS not now known; see E. Jenkins, *Tennyson and Dr Gully* (1974), p. 8.

iv *1–2*. 'Norman Lockyer says that this is a true description of the sun' (T.). The second line was added at the suggestion of G. S. Venables (F. M. Brookfield, *The Cambridge 'Apostles'*, 1906, p. 349). On Laplace's cosmogony and the nebular hypothesis, see E. A. Mooney, *MLN* lxiv (1949) 98–102, and M. Millhauser, *PMLA* lxix (1954) 337–43.

iv *6. ambrosial gloom*: cp. the fragment of an early play (*Mem.* i 24), 'In your high pomp of shade, and make beneath ye / Ambrosial gloom' (III 607).

10   And blissful palpitations in the blood,
       Stirring a sudden transport rose and fell.

       But when we planted level feet, and dipt
       Beneath the satin dome and entered in,
       There leaning deep in broidered down we sank
15   Our elbows: on a tripod in the midst
       A fragrant flame rose, and before us glowed
       Fruit, blossom, viand, amber wine, and gold.

       Then she, 'Let some one sing to us: lightlier move
       The minutes fledged with music:' and a maid,
20   Of those beside her, smote her harp, and sang.

               'Tears, idle tears, I know not what they mean,
               Tears from the depth of some divine despair
               Rise in the heart, and gather to the eyes,
               In looking on the happy Autumn-fields,
25   And thinking of the days that are no more.

iv *10–11.* Incorporated verbatim from *The Gardener's Daughter* 66 ∧ 7,
MS (I 557).

iv *16. fragrant flame*: *The Palace of Art* 187, *1832* text.

iv *17. blossom, viand,*] *1850*; viand, blossom, and *1847–8*.

iv *21. Tears, idle*] Ah foolish *MS in Eversley 1st reading.* Cp. the song in
The Miller's Daughter 210–11: 'Love is made a vague regret. / Eyes with
idle tears are wet'; and Virgil, *Aeneid* iv 449, x 465: *lacrimae inanes*.

iv *21–40.* On *Tears, idle tears*, T. remarks: 'This song came to me on the
yellowing autumn-tide at Tintern Abbey, full for me of its bygone
memories. It is the sense of the abiding in the transient.' Among the
memories (Douglas Bush suggests, *Major British Writers*, 1959) may have
been that Arthur Hallam is buried near Tintern; cp. *In Memoriam* xix
(*p. 364*). T. told G. F. Watts 'that it had seemed to flow from his mind
without difficulty' (L. Ormond, *TRB* iv, 1983, 53). Frederick Locker-
Lampson reports (*Mem.* ii 73): 'He told me that he was moved to write *Tears,
idle tears* at Tintern Abbey; and that it was not real woe, as some people might
suppose; "it was rather the yearning that young people occasionally
experience for that which seems to have passed away from them for ever."
That in him it was strongest when he was quite a youth.' To James Knowles,
T. said: 'It is in a way like St Paul's "groanings which cannot be uttered." ' . . .
It is what I have always felt even from a boy, and what as a boy I called the
"passion of the past." And it is so always with me now; it is the distance that
charms me in the landscape, the picture and the past, and not the immediate
to-day in which I move', *Nineteenth Century* xxxiii (1893) 170. Cp. *No More*
(1826, I 175): 'Oh sad *No More!* Oh sweet *No More!* / Oh strange *No More!*'.
On the diction, see *Tithonus* 59n (*p. 589*). Southey's *Remembrance* has 'The
days that are no more' as the concluding line of the first and last stanzas; its

'Fresh as the first beam glittering on a sail,
That brings our friends up from the underworld,
Sad as the last which reddens over one
That sinks with all we love below the verge;
30   So sad, so fresh, the days that are no more.

'Ah, sad and strange as in dark summer dawns
The earliest pipe of half-awakened birds
To dying ears, when unto dying eyes
The casement slowly grows a glimmering square;
35   So sad, so strange, the days that are no more.

'Dear as remembered kisses after death,
And sweet as those by hopeless fancy feigned
On lips that are for others; deep as love,
Deep as first love, and wild with all regret;
40   O Death in Life, the days that are no more.'

She ended with such passion that the tear,
She sang of, shook and fell, an erring pearl
Lost in her bosom: but with some disdain
Answered the Princess, 'If indeed there haunt
45   About the mouldered lodges of the Past
So sweet a voice and vague, fatal to men,
Well needs it we should cram our ears with wool

epigraph is 'The remembrance of Youth is a sigh', and it ends: 'Its idle hopes
are o'er, / Yet age remembers with a sigh / The days that are no more.'
J. Rutter notes another poem by Southey, *To a Friend, inquiring if I would live
over my youth again*: 'Why is it pleasant then to sit and talk / Of days that are no
more?' (and 'With no unmanly tears'). Cp. Hallam's poem (Motter, p. 108),
Scene at Rome 41, 45, 53, which was probably written on the Rhine journey
taken with T. It describes remembered thoughts as friends, 'Borne to the
silent things that are no more . . . / There they lie dead, and here I'd weep for
them . . . / These friends once harboured with me, now departed.' John
Sparrow, *RES* n.s. xiv (1963) 59, compares Gray's Alcaic fragment, *O
lachrymarum Fons*; this had provided an epigraph in *1827*. On the nexus of the
words 'idle', 'idol' and 'idyl' in T., see N. Hilton, *Essays in Criticism* xxxv
(1985) 223–37.
iv *26*. Cp. *Egypt* 13: 'But the first glitter of his rising beam'.
iv *34*. Cp. Leigh Hunt, *Hero and Leander* 284–5: 'And when the casement,
at the dawn of light, / Began to show a square of ghastly white.' Hero is
about to kill herself.
iv *35. so*] and MS Eversley 1st reading. Cp. *The Lover's Tale* iv 301: 'Sad,
sweet, and strange together'.
iv *36*. Cp. Moschus, *Lament for Bion* 68–9 ('and Cypris, she's fainer far of
you than the kiss she gave Adonis when he died the other day').
iv *47–8*. Odysseus stopped the ears of his crew with wax so that they
could not hear the song of the Sirens.

And so pace by: but thine are fancies hatched
In silken-folded idleness; nor is it
50   Wiser to weep a true occasion lost,
But trim our sails, and let old bygones be,
While down the streams that float us each and all
To the issue, goes, like glittering bergs of ice,
Throne after throne, and molten on the waste
55   Becomes a cloud: for all things serve their time
Toward that great year of equal mights and rights,
Nor would I fight with iron laws, in the end
Found golden: let the past be past; let be
Their cancelled Babels: though the rough kex
        break
60   The starred mosaic, and the beard-blown goat
Hang on the shaft, and the wild figtree split
Their monstrous idols, care not while we hear
A trumpet in the distance pealing news
Of better, and Hope, a poising eagle, burns
65   Above the unrisen morrow:' then to me;
    ' 'Know you no song of your own land,' she said,
'Not such as moans about the retrospect,
But deals with the other distance and the hues
Of promise; not a death's-head at the wine.'

70   Then I remembered one myself had made,
What time I watched the swallow winging south

iv 50. lost] 1850; gone 1847–8.
iv 51. old bygones be] 1850; the old proverb serve 1847–8.
iv 52. float . . . all] 1850; buoy each separate craft 1847–8.
iv 53–4. Cp. In Memoriam cxxvii 9–13: 'But ill for him that wears a
crown, / And him, the lazar, in his rags: / They tremble, the sustaining
crags; / The spires of ice are toppled down, // And molten up, and roar in
flood.'
iv 59. kex: 'hemlock' (T.).
iv 60. beard-blown goat] 1860; wild goat hang 1847–58.
iv 61. Hang on the shaft] 1860; Upon the pillar 1847–8; Upon the shaft
1850–58. 'The wind blew his beard on the height of the ruined pillar'
(T.). Cp. Samuel Rogers, Pleasures of Memory ii: 'High hung in air the
hoary goat reclined, / His streaming beard the sport of every wind.'
figtree split: H.T. compares Juvenal, Satires x 145: discutienda valent sterilis
mala robora fici ('. . . stones which may be rent asunder by the rude strength
of the barren fig-tree').
iv 65. then] 1848; and then 1847.

From mine own land, part made long since, and
part
Now while I sang, and maidenlike as far
As I could ape their treble, did I sing.

75 'O Swallow, Swallow, flying, flying South,
Fly to her, and fall upon her gilded eaves,
And tell her, tell her, what I tell to thee.

'O tell her, Swallow, thou that knowest each,
That bright and fierce and fickle is the South,
80 And dark and true and tender is the North.

'O Swallow, Swallow, if I could follow, and light
Upon her lattice, I would pipe and trill,
And cheep and twitter twenty million loves.

'O were I thou that she might take me in,
85 And lay me on her bosom, and her heart
Would rock the snowy cradle till I died.

'Why lingereth she to clothe her heart with love,
Delaying as the tender ash delays
To clothe herself, when all the woods are green?

90 'O tell her, Swallow, that thy brood is flown:
Say to her, I do but wanton in the South,
But in the North long since my nest is made.

'O tell her, brief is life but love is long,
And brief the sun of summer in the North,
95 And brief the moon of beauty in the South.

'O Swallow, flying from the golden woods,
Fly to her, and pipe and woo her, and make her mine,
And tell her, tell her, that I follow thee.'

I ceased, and all the ladies, each at each,
100 Like the Ithacensian suitors in old time,
Stared with great eyes, and laughed with alien lips,
And knew not what they meant; for still my voice
Rang false: but smiling 'Not for thee,' she said,

iv 75–98. This song was 'first composed in rhyme' (*Mem.* ii 74). Cp. the
isometric songs in Theocritus iii and xi.
iv 85–6. Cp. *Venus and Adonis* 1185–6: 'Lo, in this hollow cradle take thy
rest; / My throbbing heart shall rock thee day and night.'
iv 100–101. Alluding, as H.T. says, to *Odyssey* xx 347 (οἱ δ' ἤδη γναθμοῖσι
γελώων ἀλλοτρίοισιν), 'And now they laughed with alien lips'–there too
introducing a critical moment for the suitors.

'O Bulbul, any rose of Gulistan
105   Shall burst her veil: marsh-divers, rather, maid,
Shall croak thee sister, or the meadow-crake
Grate her harsh kindred in the grass: and this
A mere love-poem! O for such, my friend,
We hold them slight: they mind us of the time
110   When we made bricks in Egypt. Knaves are men,
That lute and flute fantastic tenderness,
And dress the victim to the offering up,
And paint the gates of Hell with Paradise,
And play the slave to gain the tyranny.
115   Poor soul! I had a maid of honour once;
She wept her true eyes blind for such a one,
A rogue of canzonets and serenades.
I loved her. Peace be with her. She is dead.
So they blaspheme the muse! But great is song
120   Used to great ends: ourself have often tried
Valkyrian hymns, or into rhythm have dashed
The passion of the prophetess; for song
Is duer unto freedom, force and growth
Of spirit than to junketing and love.
125   Love is it? Would this same mock-love, and this
Mock-Hymen were laid up like winter bats,
Till all men grew to rate us at our worth,
Not vassals to be beat, nor pretty babes
To be dandled, no, but living wills, and sphered
130   Whole in ourselves and owed to none. Enough!
But now to leaven play with profit, you,
Know you no song, the true growth of your soil,
That gives the manners of your country-women?'

      She spoke and turned her sumptuous head with
        eyes

---

iv *104. Bulbul*: nightingale.   *Gulistan*: rose-garden. Both Persian.

iv *106. meadow-crake*: 'corn-crake or landrail' (T.).

iv *109. hold*] *1850*; prize *1847–8*.

iv *115–24*] *1850*; not *1847–8*.

iv *115* ∧ *6*] Who let herself be twangled out of life *ULC MS, deleted*.

iv *121*. 'Like those sung by the Valkyrian maidens, "the choosers of the slain," in the Northern mythology' (H.T.).

iv *122. Exodus* xv 20, 'And Miriam the prophetess, the sister of Aaron, took a timbrel in her hand; and all the women went out after her with timbrels and with dances.' See v 500.

iv *125. Would*] *1850*; I would *1847–8*.

iv *129*. Cp. *In Memoriam* cxxxi: 'O living will'.

135 Of shining expectation fixt on mine.
Then while I dragged my brains for such a song,
Cyril, with whom the bell-mouthed glass had wrought,
Or mastered by the sense of sport, began
To troll a careless, careless tavern-catch
140 Of Moll and Meg, and strange experiences
Unmeet for ladies. Florian nodded at him,
I frowning; Psyche flushed and wanned and shook;
The lilylike Melissa drooped her brows;
'Forbear,' the Princess cried; 'Forbear, Sir' I;
145 And heated through and through with wrath and
    love,
I smote him on the breast; he started up;
There rose a shriek as of a city sacked;
Melissa clamoured 'Flee the death;' 'To horse'
Said Ida; 'home! to horse!' and fled, as flies
150 A troop of snowy doves athwart the dusk,
When some one batters at the dovecote-doors,
Disorderly the women. Alone I stood
With Florian, cursing Cyril, vext at heart,
In the pavilion: there like parting hopes
155 I heard them passing from me: hoof by hoof,
And every hoof a knell to my desires,
Clanged on the bridge; and then another shriek,
'The Head, the Head, the Princess, O the Head!'
For blind with rage she missed the plank, and rolled
160 In the river. Out I sprang from glow to gloom:
There whirled her white robe like a blossomed
    branch
Rapt to the horrible fall: a glance I gave,
No more; but woman-vested as I was
Plunged; and the flood drew; yet I caught her;
    then
165 Oaring one arm, and bearing in my left
The weight of all the hopes of half the world,
Strove to buffet to land in vain. A tree
Was half-disrooted from his place and stooped

iv *137. Cyril*] *1850*; Did Cyril *1847–8*.   *glass*] *1862*; flask *1847–61*.
iv *138. began*] *1850*; begin *1847–8*.
iv *149*] *1850*; Said Lady Ida; and fled at once, as flies *1847–8*.
iv *163*. Turner (p. 113) notes T.'s adaptation of Shakespeare's 'accoutred as I
was'; T. is 'parodying Cassius' speech in *Julius Caesar*, describing a similar
rescue of the great dictator'.
iv *164*. Cp. the drowning in *The Lover's Tale* ii 194–205 (I 368).

To drench his dark locks in the gurgling wave
170 Mid-channel. Right on this we drove and caught,
And grasping down the boughs I gained the shore.

There stood her maidens glimmeringly grouped
In the hollow bank. One reaching forward drew
My burthen from mine arms; they cried 'she lives:'
175 They bore her back into the tent: but I,
So much a kind of shame within me wrought,
Not yet endured to meet her opening eyes,
Nor found my friends; but pushed alone on foot
(For since her horse was lost I left her mine)
180 Across the woods, and less from Indian craft
Than beelike instinct hiveward, found at length
The garden portals. Two great statues, Art
And Science, Caryatids, lifted up
A weight of emblem, and betwixt were valves
185 Of open-work in which the hunter rued
His rash intrusion, manlike, but his brows
Had sprouted, and the branches thereupon
Spread out at top, and grimly spiked the gates.

A little space was left between the horns,
190 Through which I clambered o'er at top with pain,
Dropt on the sward, and up the linden walks,
And, tost on thoughts that changed from hue
    to hue,
Now poring on the glowworm, now the star,
I paced the terrace, till the Bear had wheeled
Through a great arc his seven slow suns.
195   A step
Of lightest echo, then a loftier form
Than female, moving through the uncertain gloom,
Disturbed me with the doubt 'if this were she,'
But it was Florian. 'Hist O Hist,' he said,

iv *174. ; they cried*] *1850*; , and crying *1847–8*.
iv *180. woods*] *1848*; thicket *1847*.
iv *182. garden portals*] *1850*; gates of the garden *1847–8*.
iv *183. Caryatids*: '"female figures used as bearing shafts" (Vitruvius i), e.g.
the maidens supporting the light entablature of the portico of the Erech-
theum at Athens' (T.).
iv *184. valves*: gates.
iv *185. open-work*] *1848*; open metal *1847*.   *hunter*] *1848*; old hunter *1847*.
iv *185–6*. 'Actaeon turned into a stag for looking on Diana bathing' (T.).
iv *196. then*] *1848*; and then *1847*.

200 'They seek us: out so late is out of rules.
 Moreover "seize the strangers" is the cry.
 How came you here?' I told him: 'I' said he,
 'Last of the train, a moral leper, I,
 To whom none spake, half-sick at heart, returned.
205 Arriving all confused among the rest
 With hooded brows I crept into the hall,
 And, couched behind a Judith, underneath
 The head of Holofernes peeped and saw.
 Girl after girl was called to trial: each
210 Disclaimed all knowledge of us: last of all,
 Melissa: trust me, Sir, I pitied her.
 She, questioned if she knew us men, at first
 Was silent; closer prest, denied it not:
 And then, demanded if her mother knew,
215 Or Psyche, she affirmed not, or denied:
 From whence the Royal mind, familiar with her,
 Easily gathered either guilt. She sent
 For Psyche, but she was not there; she called
 For Psyche's child to cast it from the doors;
220 She sent for Blanche to accuse her face to face;
 And I slipt out: but whither will you now?
 And where are Psyche, Cyril? both are fled:
 What, if together? that were not so well.
 Would rather we had never come! I dread
225 His wildness, and the chances of the dark.'

 'And yet,' I said, 'you wrong him more than I
 That struck him: this is proper to the clown,
 Though smocked, or furred and purpled, still the
    clown,
 To harm the thing that trusts him, and to shame
230 That which he says he loves: for Cyril, howe'er
 He deal in frolic, as tonight–the song
 Might have been worse and sinned in grosser lips
 Beyond all pardon–as it is, I hold
 These flashes on the surface are not he.
235 He has a solid base of temperament:
 But as the waterlily starts and slides

iv 202] 1850; I found the key in the doors: how came you here? 1847–8.
iv 207–8. Judith xiii.
iv 215. Psyche, she] 1850; Lady Psyche, 1847–8.
iv 236–8. 'Water-lilies in my own pond, seen on a gusty day with my own
eyes', said T., denying the influence of Wordsworth's Excursion v 567–9:

Upon the level in little puffs of wind,
Though anchored to the bottom, such is he.'

Scarce had I ceased when from a tamarisk near
240 Two Proctors leapt upon us, crying, 'Names:'
He, standing still, was clutched; but I began
To thrid the musky-circled mazes, wind
And double in and out the boles, and race
By all the fountains: fleet I was of foot:
245 Before me showered the rose in flakes; behind
I heard the puffed pursuer; at mine ear
Bubbled the nightingale and heeded not,
And secret laughter tickled all my soul.
At last I hooked my ankle in a vine,
250 That claspt the feet of a Mnemosyne,
And falling on my face was caught and known.

They haled us to the Princess where she sat
High in the hall: above her drooped a lamp,
And made the single jewel on her brow
255 Burn like the mystic fire on a mast-head,
Prophet of storm: a handmaid on each side
Bowed toward her, combing out her long black hair
Damp from the river; and close behind her stood
Eight daughters of the plough, stronger than men,
260 Huge women blowzed with health, and wind, and
         rain,
And labour. Each was like a Druid rock;
Or like a spire of land that stands apart
Cleft from the main, and wailed about with mews.

Then, as we came, the crowd dividing clove
265 An advent to the throne: and therebeside,

'And, like the water-lily, lives and thrives, / Whose root is fixed in stable
earth, whose head / Floats on the tossing waves.'
iv 242. *the musky-circled*] *1850*; through all the musky *1847–8*. Cp. *Rape of
the Lock* ii 139: 'Some thrid the mazy Ringlets of her Hair'. Also Shelley,
The Triumph of Life 347: 'and threaded all the forest's maze'.
iv 249. *hooked*] *1850*; took *1847–8*.
iv 250. *Mnemosyne*: 'goddess of memory, mother of the Muses' (T.).
iv 255. *fire*: 'St Elmo's fire' (T.). H.T. adds: 'St Elmo's phosphorescent
light flickers on the tops of masts when a storm is brewing', and compares
The Tempest I ii 199.
iv 260. *blowzed*: 'blown-red' (T.).
iv 263. *wailed*] *1851*; clanged *1847–50*. Cp. *Paradise Lost* xi 835: 'Sea-mews
clang'.

Half-naked as if caught at once from bed
And tumbled on the purple footcloth, lay
The lily-shining child; and on the left,
Bowed on her palms and folded up from wrong,
270   Her round white shoulder shaken with her sobs,
Melissa knelt; but Lady Blanche erect
Stood up and spake, an affluent orator.

'It was not thus, O Princess, in old days:
You prized my counsel, lived upon my lips:
275   I led you then to all the Castalies;
I fed you with the milk of every Muse;
I loved you like this kneeler, and you me
Your second mother: those were gracious times.
Then came your new friend: you began to change—
280   I saw it and grieved—to slacken and to cool;
Till taken with her seeming openness
You turned your warmer currents all to her,
To me you froze: this was my meed for all.
Yet I bore up in part from ancient love,
285   And partly that I hoped to win you back,
And partly conscious of my own deserts,
And partly that you were my civil head,
And chiefly you were born for something great,
In which I might your fellow-worker be,
290   When time should serve; and thus a noble scheme
Grew up from seed we two long since had sown;
In us true growth, in her a Jonah's gourd,
Up in one night and due to sudden sun:
We took this palace; but even from the first
295   You stood in your own light and darkened mine.
What student came but that you planed her path
To Lady Psyche, younger, not so wise,
A foreigner, and I your countrywoman,
I your old friend and tried, she new in all?
300   But still her lists were swelled and mine were lean;
Yet I bore up in hope she would be known:
Then came these wolves: *they* knew her: *they*
                   endured,
Long-closeted with her the yestermorn,
To tell her what they were, and she to hear:

iv 273. *old*] *1850*; the old *1847–8*.
iv 275. Castaly, a fountain on Parnassus sacred to the Muses.
iv 283. *To...froze*] *1850*; You froze to me *1847–8*.
iv 292. *Jonah* iv 6–10, the gourd 'which came up in a night, and perished
in a night'.

305   And me none told: not less to an eye like mine
     A lidless watcher of the public weal,
     Last night, their mask was patent, and my foot
     Was to you: but I thought again: I feared
     To meet a cold "We thank you, we shall hear of it
310   From Lady Psyche:" you had gone to her,
     She told, perforce; and winning easy grace,
     No doubt, for slight delay, remained among us
     In our young nursery still unknown, the stem
     Less grain than touchwood, while my honest heat
315   Were all miscounted as malignant haste
     To push my rival out of place and power.
     But public use required she should be known;
     And since my oath was ta'en for public use,
     I broke the letter of it to keep the sense.
320   I spoke not then at first, but watched them well,
     Saw that they kept apart, no mischief done;
     And yet this day (though you should hate me for it)
     I came to tell you; found that you had gone,
     Ridden to the hills, she likewise: now, I thought,
325   That surely she will speak; if not, then I:
     Did she? These monsters blazoned what they were,
     According to the coarseness of their kind,
     For thus I hear; and known at last (my work)
     And full of cowardice and guilty shame,
330   I grant in her some sense of shame, she flies;
     And I remain on whom to wreak your rage,
     I, that have lent my life to build up yours,
     I that have wasted here health, wealth, and time,
     And talent, I–you know it–I will not boast:
335   Dismiss me, and I prophesy your plan,
     Divorced from my experience, will be chaff
     For every gust of chance, and men will say
     We did not know the real light, but chased
     The wisp that flickers where no foot can tread.'

340   She ceased: the Princess answered coldly, 'Good:
     Your oath is broken: we dismiss you: go.

iv *306. lidless*: 'wakeful, wide-eyed' (T.). In this sense, *OED* quotes only
Coleridge and Shelley before T.
iv *319. 2 Corinthians* iii 6, 'Not of the letter, but of the spirit: for the letter
killeth, but the spirit giveth life'.
iv *323. came . . . that*] *1850*; judged it best to speak; but *1847–8*.
iv *325. speak*] *1850*; tell you *1847–8*.
iv *330. some sense*] *1850*; the merit *1847–8*.

For this lost lamb (she pointed to the child)
Our mind is changed: we take it to ourself.'

Thereat the Lady stretched a vulture throat,
345   And shot from crooked lips a haggard smile.
'The plan was mine. I built the nest' she said
'To hatch the cuckoo. Rise!' and stooped to updrag
Melissa: she, half on her mother propt,
Half-drooping from her, turned her face, and cast
350   A liquid look on Ida, full of prayer,
Which melted Florian's fancy as she hung,
A Niobëan daughter, one arm out,
Appealing to the bolts of Heaven; and while
We gazed upon her came a little stir
355   About the doors, and on a sudden rushed
Among us, out of breath, as one pursued,
A woman-post in flying raiment. Fear
Stared in her eyes, and chalked her face, and winged
Her transit to the throne, whereby she fell
360   Delivering sealed dispatches which the Head
Took half-amazed, and in her lion's mood
Tore open, silent we with blind surmise
Regarding, while she read, till over brow
And cheek and bosom brake the wrathful bloom
365   As of some fire against a stormy cloud,
When the wild peasant rights himself, the rick
Flames, and his anger reddens in the heavens;
For anger most it seemed, while now her breast,
Beaten with some great passion at her heart,
370   Palpitated, her hand shook, and we heard
In the dead hush the papers that she held
Rustle: at once the lost lamb at her feet
Sent out a bitter bleating for its dam;
The plaintive cry jarred on her ire; she crushed
375   The scrolls together, made a sudden turn
As if to speak, but, utterance failing her,

iv 343. take] 1850; assume 1847–8.   ourself] 1864; ourselves 1847–62.
iv 352. 'Niobe was proud of her twelve children, and in consequence
boasted herself as superior to Leto, mother of Apollo and Artemis, who in
revenge shot them all dead' (T.).
iv 355. rushed] 1848; ran in 1847.
iv 356] 1850; Among us, all out of breath, as pursued, 1847–8. A review
had objected to the rhythm (Shannon, p. 120).
iv 366. the rick] 1850; and the rick 1847–8. 'I remember seeing thirty ricks.
burning near Cambridge, and I helped to pass the bucket from the well to
help to quench the fire' (T.).

She whirled them on to me, as who should say
'Read,' and I read – two letters – one her sire's.

'Fair daughter, when we sent the Prince your
            way
380 We knew not your ungracious laws, which learnt,
We, conscious of what temper you are built,
Came all in haste to hinder wrong, but fell
Into his father's hands, who has this night,
You lying close upon his territory,
385 Slipt round and in the dark invested you,
And here he keeps me hostage for his son.'

The second was my father's running thus:
'You have our son: touch not a hair of his head:
Render him up unscathed: give him your hand:
390 Cleave to your contract: though indeed we hear
You hold the woman is the better man;
A rampant heresy, such as if it spread
Would make all women kick against their Lords
Through all the world, and which might well
            deserve
395 That we this night should pluck your palace down;
And we will do it, unless you send us back
Our son, on the instant, whole.'
                      So far I read;
And then stood up and spoke impetuously.

'O not to pry and peer on your reserve,
400 But led by golden wishes, and a hope
The child of regal compact, did I break
Your precinct; not a scorner of your sex
But venerator, zealous it should be
All that it might be: hear me, for I bear,
405 Though man, yet human, whatsoe'er your wrongs,
From the flaxen curl to the gray lock a life
Less mine than yours: my nurse would tell me of
            you;
I babbled for you, as babies for the moon,
Vague brightness; when a boy, you stooped to me
410 From all high places, lived in all fair lights,
Came in long breezes rapt from inmost south
And blown to inmost north; at eve and dawn
With Ida, Ida, Ida, rang the woods;

iv *389. Render*] *1850*; Deliver *1847–8*.
iv *411. inmost*] *1850*; the inmost *1847–8*. Likewise in l. *412*.

The leader wildswan in among the stars
Would clang it, and lapt in wreaths of glowworm
415   light
The mellow breaker murmured Ida. Now,
Because I would have reached you, had you been
Sphered up with Cassiopëia, or the enthroned
Persephonè in Hades, now at length,
420   Those winters of abeyance all worn out,
A man I came to see you: but, indeed,
Not in this frequence can I lend full tongue,
O noble Ida, to those thoughts that wait
On you, their centre: let me say but this,
425   That many a famous man and woman, town
And landskip, have I heard of, after seen
The dwarfs of presage: though when known, there
    grew
Another kind of beauty in detail
Made them worth knowing; but in you I found
430   My boyish dream involved and dazzled down
And mastered, while that after-beauty makes
Such head from act to act, from hour to hour,
Within me, that except you slay me here,
According to your bitter statute-book,
435   I cannot cease to follow you, as they say
The seal does music; who desire you more
Than growing boys their manhood; dying lips,
With many thousand matters left to do,
The breath of life; O more than poor men wealth,
Than sick men health–yours, yours, not mine–but
440   half
Without you; with you, whole; and of those halves
You worthiest; and howe'er you block and bar
Your heart with system out from mine, I hold
That it becomes no man to nurse despair,
445   But in the teeth of clenched antagonisms
To follow up the worthiest till he die:
Yet that I came not all unauthorized
Behold your father's letter.'
                    On one knee

iv 417. *had you*] *1850*; though you had *1847–8*.
iv 418. *Cassiopëia*: a mythical Queen of Ethiopia, subsequently a constellation.
iv 422. *Paradise Regained* i 128–9: 'in full frequence bright / Of Angels'.
iv 427. *dwarfs of presage*: 'afterwards seen to be far short of expectation' (H.T.).
iv 430. *My boyish dream*] *1850*; Mine old ideal *1847–8*.

Kneeling, I gave it, which she caught, and dashed
450   Unopened at her feet: a tide of fierce
Invective seemed to wait behind her lips,
As waits a river level with the dam
Ready to burst and flood the world with foam:
And so she would have spoken, but there rose
455   A hubbub in the court of half the maids
Gathered together: from the illumined hall
Long lanes of splendour slanted o'er a press
Of snowy shoulders, thick as herded ewes,
And rainbow robes, and gems and gemlike eyes,
460   And gold and golden heads; they to and fro
Fluctuated, as flowers in storm, some red, some pale,
All open-mouthed, all gazing to the light,
Some crying there was an army in the land,
And some that men were in the very walls,
465   And some they cared not; till a clamour grew
As of a new-world Babel, woman-built,
And worse-confounded: high above them stood
The placid marble Muses, looking peace.

Not peace she looked, the Head: but rising up
470   Robed in the long night of her deep hair, so
To the open window moved, remaining there
Fixt like a beacon-tower above the waves
Of tempest, when the crimson-rolling eye
Glares ruin, and the wild birds on the light
Dash themselves dead. She stretched her arms and
475   called
Across the tumult and the tumult fell.

'What fear ye, brawlers? am not I your Head?
On me, me, me, the storm first breaks: *I* dare
All these male thunderbolts: what is it ye fear?
480   Peace! there are those to avenge us and they come:
If not,–myself were like enough, O girls,
To unfurl the maiden banner of our rights,
And clad in iron burst the ranks of war,

iv *450. at her feet*] *1850*; on the marble *1847–8*.
iv *468. looking peace*: P. M. Wallace's edition, of which T. saw the proofs
(1891, *Lincoln*), remarks: 'half "looking peacefully", half "shedding
peace"'.
iv *472–5*. H.T. compares *Enoch Arden* 724–6: 'Allured him, as the beacon-
blaze allures / The bird of passage, till he madly strikes / Against it, and
beats out his weary life.'
iv *474. birds*] *1848*; sea-birds *1847*.

Or, falling, protomartyr of our cause,
485 Die: yet I blame you not so much for fear:
Six thousand years of fear have made you that
From which I would redeem you: but for those
That stir this hubbub–you and you–I know
Your faces there in the crowd–tomorrow morn
490 We hold a great convention: then shall they
That love their voices more than duty, learn
With whom they deal, dismissed in shame to live
No wiser than their mothers, household stuff,
Live chattels, mincers of each other's fame,
495 Full of weak poison, turnspits for the clown,
The drunkard's football, laughing-stocks of Time,
Whose brains are in their hands and in their heels,
But fit to flaunt, to dress, to dance, to thrum,
To tramp, to scream, to burnish, and to scour,
500 For ever slaves at home and fools abroad.'

She, ending, waved her hands: thereat the
      crowd
Muttering, dissolved: then with a smile, that looked
A stroke of cruel sunshine on the cliff,
When all the glens are drowned in azure gloom
505 Of thunder-shower, she floated to us and said:

'You have done well and like a gentleman,
And like a prince: you have our thanks for all:
And you look well too in your woman's dress:
Well have you done and like a gentleman.
510 You saved our life: we owe you bitter thanks:
Better have died and spilt our bones in the flood–
Then men had said–but now–What hinders me
To take such bloody vengeance on you both?–
Yet since our father–Wasps in our good hive,
515 You would-be quenchers of the light to be,
Barbarians, grosser than your native bears–
O would I had his sceptre for one hour!

iv 485. you] 1862; ye 1847–61. Likewise in ll. 486, 487.
iv 486. Lionel Stevenson (Darwin among the Poets, 1932, p. 73) points out
that Ida's grasp of evolution is not consistently maintained, since 6,000
years is the chronology of Archbishop Ussher.
iv 490. hold ... convention] 1850; meet to elect new tutors 1847–8.
iv 506. You] 1848; Ye 1847.
iv 510. saved] 1850; have saved 1847–8.
iv 514. our good] 1850; the wholesome 1847–8.

You that have dared to break our bound, and gulled
Our servants, wronged and lied and thwarted us—
520 I wed with thee! I bound by precontract
Your bride, your bondslave! not though all the gold
That veins the world were packed to make your
     crown,
And every spoken tongue should lord you. Sir,
Your falsehood and yourself are hateful to us:
525 I trample on your offers and on you:
Begone: we will not look upon you more.
Here, push them out at gates.'
                              In wrath she spake.
Then those eight mighty daughters of the plough
Bent their broad faces toward us and addressed
530 Their motion: twice I sought to plead my cause,
But on my shoulder hung their heavy hands,
The weight of destiny: so from her face
They pushed us, down the steps, and through the
     court,
And with grim laughter thrust us out at gates.

535 We crossed the street and gained a petty mound
Beyond it, whence we saw the lights and heard
The voices murmuring. While I listened, came
On a sudden the weird seizure and the doubt:
I seemed to move among a world of ghosts;
540 The Princess with her monstrous woman-guard,
The jest and earnest working side by side,
The cataract and the tumult and the kings
Were shadows; and the long fantastic night
With all its doings had and had not been,
And all things were and were not.

iv 518. *and gulled*] seduced *ULC MS 1st reading.*
iv 519. *servants*] *1850*; tutors *1847–8.*
iv 524. *yourself are hateful*] *1851*; your face are loathsome *1847–50.*
iv 537–46. *While . . . came,*] *1851*; not *1847–50.*
iv 538–9] *ULC MS has a draft of these 'seizure' lines:*
          And at this touch my sudden seizure came
          Upon me, that weird daydream of our house.
          I moved among a world of hollow masks,
          Until I scarcely knew my hands for mine,
          Like one that hardly knows the things he knows
          And moves in hollow haze that makes his mound
          A mountain and lifts up his ships at sea.
Cp. *In Memoriam* lxx 3: 'And mix with hollow masks of night'.

545   This went by
As strangely as it came, and on my spirits
Settled a gentle cloud of melancholy;
Not long; I shook it off; for spite of doubts
And sudden ghostly shadowings I was one
550 To whom the touch of all mischance but came
As night to him that sitting on a hill
Sees the midsummer, midnight, Norway sun
Set into sunrise; then we moved away.

[IV ∧ V]
Thy voice is heard through rolling drums,
    That beat to battle where he stands;
Thy face across his fancy comes,
    And gives the battle to his hands:
5   A moment, while the trumpets blow,
    He sees his brood about thy knee;
The next, like fire he meets the foe,
    And strikes him dead for thine and thee.

So Lilia sang: we thought her half-possessed,
10 She struck such warbling fury through the words;
And, after, feigning pique at what she called
The raillery, or grotesque, or false sublime –
Like one that wishes at a dance to change
The music – clapt her hands and cried for war,
15 Or some grand fight to kill and make an end:
And he that next inherited the tale
Half turning to the broken statue, said,
'Sir Ralph has got your colours: if I prove

iv 546. *and on*] *1851*; till upon *1847–50*.
iv 548] *1851*; Which I shook off, for I was young, and one *1847–8*;
Which I shook off, for I was ever one *1850*.
iv 549] *1851*; not *1847–50*.
iv 550. *touch*] *1851*; shadow *1847–50*.
iv 551–3. There is a draft of these lines in the descriptive jottings of *H.Lpr 191*
(see Appendix B, III 631).

iv ∧ v The 26 lines of song and interlude were added *1850*. For alternative
versions of the song, see Appendix I (p. *978*), and *The Tourney* (II 301).
On the nobility of a just war, cp. *The Two Voices* 124–56 (pp. *108–9*), and
the conclusion of *Maud*.
iv ∧ v 1–2] *1851*;   When all among the thundering drums
                Thy soldier in the battle stands, *1850*
iv ∧ v 8. *And strikes*] *1851*; Strikes *1850*.   *thine*] *1851*; them *1850*.
1850 follows this line with 'Tara ta tantara!'

Your knight, and fight your battle, what for me?'
20   It chanced, her empty glove upon the tomb
Lay by her like a model of her hand.
She took it and she flung it. 'Fight' she said,
'And make us all we would be, great and good.'
He knightlike in his cap instead of casque,
25   A cap of Tyrol borrowed from the hall,
Arranged the favour, and assumed the Prince.

V

Now, scarce three paces measured from the mound,
We stumbled on a stationary voice,
And 'Stand, who goes?' 'Two from the palace' I.
'The second two: they wait,' he said, 'pass on;
5   His Highness wakes:' and one, that clashed in arms,
By glimmering lanes and walls of canvas led
Threading the soldier-city, till we heard
The drowsy folds of our great ensign shake
From blazoned lions o'er the imperial tent
Whispers of war.
10   Entering, the sudden light
Dazed me half-blind: I stood and seemed to hear,
As in a poplar grove when a light wind wakes
A lisping of the innumerous leaf and dies,
Each hissing in his neighbour's ear; and then
15   A strangled titter, out of which there brake
On all sides, clamouring etiquette to death,
Unmeasured mirth; while now the two old kings
Began to wag their baldness up and down,
The fresh young captains flashed their glittering teeth,
20   The huge bush-bearded Barons heaved and blew,
And slain with laughter rolled the gilded Squire.

At length my Sire, his rough cheek wet with tears,
Panted from weary sides 'King, you are free!
We did but keep you surety for our son,
25   If this be he,—or a draggled mawkin, thou,

v 2. *stationary*: pertaining to a military post (*OED* 4b).
v 6. *glimmering lanes*: 'the lines of tents just visible in the darkness' (T.).
v 7. *till*] *1850*; until *1847–8*.
v 12–13. Cp. Keats, *To Autumn* 29: 'as the light wind lives or dies'. Milton describes boughs as 'innumerous', *Comus* 349.
v 15. *there brake*] *1850*; outbrake *1847–8*.
v 23. *King . . . free*] *1850*; You are free, O King! *1847–8*.
v 25. *mawkin*: kitchen-wench. H.T. compares *Coriolanus* II i 205.

That tends her bristled grunters in the sludge:'
For I was drenched with ooze, and torn with briers,
More crumpled than a poppy from the sheath,
And all one rag, disprinced from head to heel.
30   Then some one sent beneath his vaulted palm
A whispered jest to some one near him, 'Look,
He has been among his shadows.' 'Satan take
The old women and their shadows! (thus the King
Roared) make yourself a man to fight with men.
Go: Cyril told us all.'
35   As boys that slink
From ferule and the trespass-chiding eye,
Away we stole, and transient in a trice
From what was left of faded woman-slough
To sheathing splendours and the golden scale
40   Of harness, issued in the sun, that now
Leapt from the dewy shoulders of the Earth,
And hit the Northern hills. Here Cyril met us.
A little shy at first, but by and by
We twain, with mutual pardon asked and given
45   For stroke and song, resoldered peace, whereon
Followed his tale. Amazed he fled away
Through the dark land, and later in the night
Had come on Psyche weeping: 'then we fell
Into your father's hand, and there she lies,
But will not speak, nor stir.'
50   He showed a tent
A stone-shot off: we entered in, and there
Among piled arms and rough accoutrements,
Pitiful sight, wrapped in a soldier's cloak,
Like some sweet sculpture draped from head to foot,
55   And pushed by rude hands from its pedestal,
All her fair length upon the ground she lay:
And at her head a follower of the camp,
A charred and wrinkled piece of womanhood,
Sat watching like a watcher by the dead.

Then Florian knelt, and 'Come' he whispered
60   to her,

v 30–34] 1851; 'But hence' he said 'indue yourselves like men. 1847–50.
v 35. Go:] 1851; Your 1847–50.
v 36. ferule: cane.
v 37. transient: 'passing from one thing or person to another. Now rare'
(OED 3).

'Lift up your head, sweet sister: lie not thus.
What have you done but right? you could not slay
Me, nor your prince: look up: be comforted:
Sweet is it to have done the thing one ought,
65   When fallen in darker ways.' And likewise I:
'Be comforted: have I not lost her too,
In whose least act abides the nameless charm
That none has else for me?' She heard, she moved,
She moaned, a folded voice; and up she sat,
70   And raised the cloak from brows as pale and smooth
As those that mourn half-shrouded over death
In deathless marble. 'Her,' she said, 'my friend—
Parted from her—betrayed her cause and mine—
Where shall I breathe? why kept ye not your faith?
75   O base and bad! what comfort? none for me!'
To whom remorseful Cyril, 'Yet I pray
Take comfort: live, dear lady, for your child!'
At which she lifted up her voice and cried.

'Ah me, my babe, my blossom, ah, my child,
80   My one sweet child, whom I shall see no more!
For now will cruel Ida keep her back;
And either she will die from want of care,
Or sicken with ill-usage, when they say
The child is hers—for every little fault,
85   The child is hers; and they will beat my girl
Remembering her mother: O my flower!
Or they will take her, they will make her hard,
And she will pass me by in after-life
With some cold reverence worse than were she dead.
90   Ill mother that I was to leave her there,
To lag behind, scared by the cry they made,
The horror of the shame among them all:
But I will go and sit beside the doors,
And make a wild petition night and day,
95   Until they hate to hear me like a wind
Wailing for ever, till they open to me,
And lay my little blossom at my feet,
My babe, my sweet Aglaïa, my one child:
And I will take her up and go my way,
100   And satisfy my soul with kissing her:
Ah! what might that man not deserve of me
Who gave me back my child?' 'Be comforted,'
Said Cyril, 'you shall have it:' but again
She veiled her brows, and prone she sank, and so
105   Like tender things that being caught feign death,
Spoke not, nor stirred.

By this a murmur ran
Through all the camp and inward raced the scouts
With rumour of Prince Arac hard at hand.
We left her by the woman, and without
110 Found the gray kings at parle: and 'Look you' cried
My father 'that our compact be fulfilled:
You have spoilt this child; she laughs at you and man:
She wrongs herself, her sex, and me, and him:
But red-faced war has rods of steel and fire;
She yields, or war.'
115   Then Gama turned to me:
'We fear, indeed, you spent a stormy time
With our strange girl: and yet they say that still
You love her. Give us, then, your mind at large:
How say you, war or not?'
                              'Not war, if possible,
120 O king,' I said, 'lest from the abuse of war,
The desecrated shrine, the trampled year,
The smouldering homestead, and the household
      flower
Torn from the lintel – all the common wrong –
A smoke go up through which I loom to her
125 Three times a monster: now she lightens scorn
At him that mars her plan, but then would hate
(And every voice she talked with ratify it,
And every face she looked on justify it)
The general foe. More soluble is this knot,
130 By gentleness than war. I want her love.
What were I nigher this although we dashed
Your cities into shards with catapults,

v 110. you] 1850; to it 1847–8.
v 111. be fulfilled] 1850; is performed 1847–8.
v 112. child] 1850; girl 1847–8.
v 113] 1850; She shall not legislate for Nature, king, 1847–8.
v 114] 1850; not 1847–8.
v 115. She] 1850; But 1847–8.
v 117. girl] 1850; child 1847–8.
v 121. year: crop.
v 126. him that mars] 1850; the enemy of 1847–8.
v 129 ∧ 30] Like almost all the rest if men were wise, 1847–8.
v 132. shards: fragments. Cp. Cowley (whose works were at Somersby, Lincoln), Davideis ii 714–15: 'And scarce ought now of that vast Cities' found / But shards and rûbbish'.
v 132 ∧ 3] And dusted down your domes with mangonels; 1847–8.

She would not love;–or brought her chained, a
    slave,
The lifting of whose eyelash is my lord,
135 Not ever would she love; but brooding turn
The book of scorn, till all my flitting chance
Were caught within the record of her wrongs,
And crushed to death: and rather, Sire, than this
I would the old God of war himself were dead,
140 Forgotten, rusting on his iron hills,
Rotting on some wild shore with ribs of wreck,
Or like an old-world mammoth bulked in ice,
Not to be molten out.'
               And roughly spake
My father, 'Tut, you know them not, the girls.
145 Boy, when I hear you prate I almost think
That idiot legend credible. Look you, Sir!
Man is the hunter; woman is his game:
The sleek and shining creatures of the chase,
We hunt them for the beauty of their skins;
150 They love us for it, and we ride them down.
Wheedling and siding with them! Out! for shame!
Boy, there's no rose that's half so dear to them
As he that does the thing they dare not do,
Breathing and sounding beauteous battle, comes
155 With the air of the trumpet round him, and leaps in
Among the women, snares them by the score
Flattered and flustered, wins, though dashed with
    death
He reddens what he kisses: thus I won
Your mother, a good mother, a good wife,

v *134* ∧ *5*] For whose round arm all crystal and the clasps
        Of emerald and of chrysoprase were coarse–*ULC MS*
v *136. flitting*] *1870*; little *1847–68*.
v *140.* Cp. *In Memoriam* lvi 20: 'Or sealed within the iron hills'.
v *142.* 'Bulky mammoth buried in ice' (T.). Lyell's *Principles of Geology*
(4th edn, 1835), i 147, mentions that 'The entire carcass of a mammoth
was obtained in 1803. . . . It fell from a mass of ice, in which it had been
encased, on the banks of the Lena.'
v *145–51*] *1850* (*except ll. 145–6*); They prize hard knocks and to be won
by force. *1847–8*.
v *145–6*] *1851; not 1850*.
v *152–3*] There's nothing in the passive charm of flowers
        So dear a rose to them, as the bold youth,
        That having done the thing they dare not do, *ULC MS*

160   Worth winning; but this firebrand – gentleness
     To such as her! if Cyril spake her true,
     To catch a dragon in a cherry net,
     To trip a tigress with a gossamer,
     Were wisdom to it.'
                'Yea but Sire,' I cried,
165   'Wild natures need wise curbs. The soldier? No:
     What dares not Ida do that she should prize
     The soldier? I beheld her, when she rose
     The yesternight, and storming in extremes,
     Stood for her cause, and flung defiance down
170   Gagelike to man, and had not shunned the death,
     No, not the soldier's: yet I hold her, king,
     True woman: but you clash them all in one,
     That have as many differences as we.
     The violet varies from the lily as far
175   As oak from elm: one loves the soldier, one
     The silken priest of peace, one this, one that,
     And some unworthily; their sinless faith,
     A maiden moon that sparkles on a sty,
     Glorifying clown and satyr; whence they need
180   More breadth of culture: is not Ida right?
     They worth it? truer to the law within?
     Severer in the logic of a life?
     Twice as magnetic to sweet influences
     Of earth and heaven? and she of whom you speak,
185   My mother, looks as whole as some serene
     Creation minted in the golden moods
     Of sovereign artists; not a thought, a touch,
     But pure as lines of green that streak the white
     Of the first snowdrop's inner leaves; I say,
190   Not like the piebald miscellany, man,
     Bursts of great heart and slips in sensual mire,
     But whole and one: and take them all-in-all,
     Were we ourselves but half as good, as kind,
     As truthful, much that Ida claims as right

v *168–70*]   When, daring all and rushing on extremes,
     She laid her black mane on her shining neck,
     And neighed defiance at mankind: and yet
                         ULC MS, deleted

v *190–91*] *1850*; Not like strong bursts of sample among men, *1847–8*.
v *192–3*. J. McCue compares *Hamlet* I ii 186–7: "A was a goodly king'. "A was a man, take him for all in all'.
v *192. whole and one*] *1850*; all one piece *1847–8*.

195   Had ne'er been mooted, but as frankly theirs
        As dues of Nature. To our point: not war:
        Lest I lose all.'
                            'Nay, nay, you spake but sense'
        Said Gama. 'We remember love ourself
        In our sweet youth; we did not rate him then
200   This red-hot iron to be shaped with blows.
        You talk almost like Ida: *she* can talk;
        And there is something in it as you say:
        But you talk kindlier: we esteem you for it.–
        He seems a gracious and a gallant Prince,
205   I would he had our daughter: for the rest,
        Our own detention, why, the causes weighed,
        Fatherly fears–you used us courteously–
        We would do much to gratify your Prince–
        We pardon it; and for your ingress here
210   Upon the skirt and fringe of our fair land,
        You did but come as goblins in the night,
        Nor in the furrow broke the ploughman's head,
        Nor burnt the grange, nor bussed the milking-maid,
        Nor robbed the farmer of his bowl of cream:
215   But let your Prince (our royal word upon it,
        He comes back safe) ride with us to our lines,
        And speak with Arac: Arac's word is thrice
        As ours with Ida: something may be done–
        I know not what–and ours shall see us friends.
220   You, likewise, our late guests, if so you will,
        Follow us: who knows? we four may build some plan
        Foursquare to opposition.'
                                    Here he reached
        White hands of farewell to my sire, who growled
        An answer which, half-muffled in his beard,
225   Let so much out as gave us leave to go.

        Then rode we with the old king across the lawns
        Beneath huge trees, a thousand rings of Spring
        In every bole, a song on every spray
        Of birds that piped their Valentines, and woke
230   Desire in me to infuse my tale of love
        In the old king's ears, who promised help, and oozed

v *195. frankly*] *1850*; easily *1847–8*.
v *198. ourself*] *1864*; ourselves *1847–62*.
v *211–4*. Cp. *L'Allegro*, including ll. 105–6: 'Tells how the drudging
Goblin swet, / To ern his Cream-bowle duly set.'
v *231–2*. Cp. *Sea Dreams* 150–1: 'And then began to bloat himself, and
ooze / All over with the fat affectionate smile ...'

All o'er with honeyed answer as we rode
And blossom-fragrant slipt the heavy dews
Gathered by night and peace, with each light air
On our mailed heads: but other thoughts than
235   Peace
Burnt in us, when we saw the embattled squares,
And squadrons of the Prince, trampling the flowers
With clamour: for among them rose a cry
As if to greet the king; they made a halt;
240   The horses yelled; they clashed their arms; the drum
Beat; merrily-blowing shrilled the martial fife;
And in the blast and bray of the long horn
And serpent-throated bugle, undulated
The banner: anon to meet us lightly pranced
245   Three captains out; nor ever had I seen
Such thews of men: the midmost and the highest
Was Arac: all about his motion clung
The shadow of his sister, as the beam
Of the East, that played upon them, made them
      glance
250   Like those three stars of the airy Giant's zone,
That glitter burnished by the frosty dark;
And as the fiery Sirius alters hue,
And bickers into red and emerald, shone
Their morions, washed with morning, as they came.

255   And I that prated peace, when first I heard
War-music, felt the blind wildbeast of force,
Whose home is in the sinews of a man,

v 241. Cp. *Semele* 20: 'And melody o' the merrily-blowing flute'.
v 248–54. Adapted from *Sir Launcelot and Queen Guinevere*, MS (*p. 100*):
      They trampling through the woodland lone
      In clanging armour flashed and shone
      Like those three suns that flame alone
      Chased in the airy giant's zone,
          And burnished by the frosty dark;
      And as the dogstar changes hue,
      And bickers into green and blue,
      Each glittered laved in lucid dew
          That washed the grassy park.
v 250. 'The stars in the belt of Orion' (T.).
v 252–3. Cp. *The Lover's Tale* i 52–61n, MS: 'The bickering Dog-star
danced in sparkles'. The comparison of armour to starlight suggests
Iliad v 5.
v 254. *morions*: 'steel helmets' (H.T.). Cp. Dryden, *Palamon and Arcite* iii

Stir in me as to strike: then took the king
His three broad sons; with now a wandering hand
260   And now a pointed finger, told them all:
A common light of smiles at our disguise
Broke from their lips, and, ere the windy jest
Had laboured down within his ample lungs,
The genial giant, Arac, rolled himself
265   Thrice in the saddle, then burst out in words.

'Our land invaded, 'sdeath! and he himself
Your captive, yet my father wills not war:
And, 'sdeath! myself, what care I, war or no?
But then this question of your troth remains:
270   And there's a downright honest meaning in her;
She flies too high, she flies too high! and yet
She asked but space and fairplay for her scheme;
She prest and prest it on me—I myself,
What know I of these things? but, life and soul!
275   I thought her half-right talking of her wrongs;
I say she flies too high, 'sdeath! what of that?
I take her for the flower of womankind,
And so I often told her, right or wrong,
And, Prince, she can be sweet to those she loves,
280   And, right or wrong, I care not: this is all,
I stand upon her side: she made me swear it—
'Sdeath—and with solemn rites by candle-light—
Swear by St something—I forget her name—

450–52: 'glittring Arms, too dazling to behold; / And polish'd Steel that cast the View aside, / And Crested Morions, with their Plumy Pride.'
v 262–5. , ere . . . words.] 1850; Arac turning said; 1847–8.
v 266. 'sdeath! and he] 1851; life and soul! 1847–50.
v 268] 1851; not 1847–8; And, life! myself I care not, war or no: 1850.
v 269. then this] 1850; , Prince, the 1847–8.
v 271] 1850; not 1847–8.
v 273. I myself,] 1850; life! I felt 1847–8.
v 274] 1850; not 1847–8.
v 275. I thought her] 1850; That she was 1847–8.
v 276–88] 1850 (except ll. 276–9, 280, 282, 288);
        And I'll stand by her. Waive your claim, or else
        Decide it here: why not? we are three to three.' 1847–8
See l. 300n.
v 276–9] 1851; not 1850.
v 280. And] 1851; Yet 1850.
v 282. 'Sdeath] 1851; Life 1850. Likewise in l. 288.

Her that talked down the fifty wisest men;
285   *She* was a princess too; and so I swore.
Come, this is all; she will not: waive your claim:
If not, the foughten field, what else, at once
Decides it, 'sdeath! against my father's will.'

I lagged in answer loth to render up
290   My precontract, and loth by brainless war
To cleave the rift of difference deeper yet;
Till one of those two brothers, half aside
And fingering at the hair about his lip,
To prick us on to combat 'Like to like!
295   The woman's garment hid the woman's heart.'
A taunt that clenched his purpose like a blow!
For fiery-short was Cyril's counter-scoff,
And sharp I answered, touched upon the point
Where idle boys are cowards to their shame,
300   'Decide it here: why not? we are three to three.'

Then spake the third 'But three to three? no more?
No more, and in our noble sister's cause?
More, more, for honour: every captain waits
Hungry for honour, angry for his king.
305   More, more, some fifty on a side, that each
May breathe himself, and quick! by overthrow
Of these or those, the question settled die.'

'Yea,' answered I, 'for this wild wreath of air,
This flake of rainbow flying on the highest
310   Foam of men's deeds–this honour, if ye will.
It needs must be for honour if at all:

v *284.* 'St Catherine of Alexandria, niece of Constantine the Great' (T.).
H.T. adds: 'The Emperor Maxentius during his persecution is related to
have sent fifty of his wisest men to convert her from Christianity, but she
combated and confuted them all.'

v *289. render up*] *1850*; strike her kin, *1847–8.*

v *290*] *1850; not 1847–8.*

v *291. To*] *1850*; And *1847–8.*

v *294. Like to like!*] *1850*; Three to three? *1847–8.*

v *295*] *1850*; But such a three to three were three to one.' *1847–8.*

v *296. taunt*] *1850*; boast *1847–8.*

v *298. point*] *1850*; sense *1847–8.*

v *300*] *1850*;   And tipt with sportive malice to and fro
                    Like pointed arrows leapt the taunts and hit. *1847–8*

See ll. 276–88*n.*

Since, what decision? if we fail, we fail,
And if we win, we fail: she would not keep
Her compact.' ''Sdeath! but we will send to her,'
315 Said Arac, 'worthy reasons why she should
Bide by this issue: let our missive through,
And you shall have her answer by the word.'

'Boys!' shrieked the old king, but vainlier than
a hen
To her false daughters in the pool; for none
320 Regarded; neither seemed there more to say:
Back rode we to my father's camp, and found
He thrice had sent a herald to the gates,
To learn if Ida yet would cede our claim,
Or by denial flush her babbling wells
325 With her own people's life: three times he went:
The first, he blew and blew, but none appeared:
He battered at the doors; none came: the next,
An awful voice within had warned him thence:
The third, and those eight daughters of the plough
Came sallying through the gates, and caught his
330   hair,
And so belaboured him on rib and cheek
They made him wild: not less one glance he caught
Through open doors of Ida stationed there
Unshaken, clinging to her purpose, firm
335 Though compassed by two armies and the noise
Of arms; and standing like a stately Pine
Set in a cataract on an island-crag,
When storm is on the heights, and right and left
Sucked from the dark heart of the long hills roll
340 The torrents, dashed to the vale: and yet her will
Bred will in me to overcome it or fall.

But when I told the king that I was pledged
To fight in tourney for my bride, he clashed
His iron palms together with a cry;
345 Himself would tilt it out among the lads:
But overborne by all his bearded lords
With reasons drawn from age and state, perforce

v 312. J. McCue compares *Macbeth* I vii 59: 'If we should fail?' 'We fail?'
v 314. *'Sdeath . . . her,'*] *1851*; 'We will send to her' Arac said, *1847–8*;
Life! but we will send to her,' *1850*.
v 315. *Said Arac,'*] *1850*; 'A score of *1847–8*.
v 333. *open*] *1850*; the open *1847–8*.
v 336–7. 'Taken from a torrent above Cauteretz' (T.).

He yielded, wroth and red, with fierce demur:
And many a bold knight started up in heat,
350 And sware to combat for my claim till death.

All on this side the palace ran the field
Flat to the garden-wall: and likewise here,
Above the garden's glowing blossom-belts,
A columned entry shone and marble stairs,
355 And great bronze valves, embossed with Tomyris
And what she did to Cyrus after fight,
But now fast barred: so here upon the flat
All that long morn the lists were hammered up,
And all that morn the heralds to and fro,
360 With message and defiance, went and came;
Last, Ida's answer, in a royal hand,
But shaken here and there, and rolling words
Oration-like. I kissed it and I read.

'O brother, you have known the pangs we felt,
365 What heats of indignation when we heard
Of those that iron-cramped their women's feet;
Of lands in which at the altar the poor bride
Gives her harsh groom for bridal-gift a scourge;
Of living hearts that crack within the fire
370 Where smoulder their dead despots; and of those,–
Mothers,–that, all prophetic pity, fling
Their pretty maids in the running flood, and
    swoops
The vulture, beak and talon, at the heart
Made for all noble motion: and I saw
375 That equal baseness lived in sleeker times
With smoother men: the old leaven leavened all:

v 355. Tomyris: 'queen of the Massagetæ, who cut off the head of Cyrus the Great after defeating him, and dipped it in a skin which she had filled with blood and bade him, as he was insatiate of blood, to drink his fill, gorge himself with blood' (T.). H.T. adds the reference to Herodotus i 212.
v 364. 'O . . . known] 1850; 'You have known, O brother, all 1847–8.
v 365. indignation] 1850; moral anger 1847–8.
v 366 ∧ 7] Of those that shattered their girl-children's hands; ULC MS.
v 368. 'An old Russian custom' (T.). H.T. adds: 'See Hakluyt's Naviga-
tions, 1599–1600'.
v 369. 'Suttee in India' (T.).
v 372. flood: 'Ganges' (T.).
v 375] 1850; That it was little better in better times 1847–8.
v 376. 1 Corinthians v 6–7, 'Know ye not that a little leaven leaveneth the whole lump. Purge out therefore the old leaven.'

Millions of throats would bawl for civil rights,
No woman named: therefore I set my face
Against all men, and lived but for mine own.
380 Far off from men I built a fold for them:
I stored it full of rich memorial:
I fenced it round with gallant institutes,
And biting laws to scare the beasts of prey
And prospered; till a rout of saucy boys
385 Brake on us at our books, and marred our peace,
Masked like our maids, blustering I know not what
Of insolence and love, some pretext held
Of baby troth, invalid, since my will
Sealed not the bond–the striplings!–for their
              sport!–
390 I tamed my leopards: shall I not tame these?
Or you? or I? for since you think me touched
In honour–what, I would not aught of false–
Is not our cause pure? and whereas I know
Your prowess, Arac, and what mother's blood
395 You draw from, fight; you failing, I abide
What end soever: fail you will not. Still
Take not his life: he risked it for my own;
His mother lives: yet whatsoe'er you do,
Fight and fight well; strike and strike home. O dear
400 Brothers, the woman's Angel guards you, you

v *380. I*] *1850*; we *1847–8*. Likewise in ll. 381, 382, 386.

v *382. institutes*: laws.

v *383*. Cp. *Measure for Measure* I iii 19–23: 'We have strict statutes and most biting laws, / The needful bits and curbs for headstrong wills, / Which for these fourteen years we have let sleep, / Even like an o'ergrown lion in a cave, / That goes not out to prey.'

v *384–9. boys . . . for their sport*: J. McCue compares *King Lear* IV i 36–7: 'As flies to wanton boys are we to th' gods; / They kill us for their sport'.

v *384. rout*] *1850*; set *1847–8*.

v *388. baby troth*] *1850*; old affiance *1847–8*. *my*] *1850*; our *1847–8*.

v *390. I . . . I*] *1850*; We have tamed our leopards: shall we *1847–8*.

v *391. I*] *1850*; we *1847–8*.   *me*] *1850*; we are *1847–8*.

v *392. what, I*] *1850*; nay, we *1847–8*.

v *393. I*] *1850*; we *1847–8*.

v *395. you . . . abide*] *1850*; we abide what end soe'er *1847–8*.

v *396. What . . . fail*] *1851*; You failing: but we know *1847–8*; What end soever: but *1850*.

v *397*] *1850*; You must not slay him: he risked his life for ours, *1847–8*.

The sole men to be mingled with our cause,
The sole men we shall prize in the after-time,
Your very armour hallowed, and your statues
Reared, sung to, when, this gad-fly brushed aside,
405 We plant a solid foot into the Time,
And mould a generation strong to move
With claim on claim from right to right, till she
Whose name is yoked with children's, know
        herself;
And Knowledge in our own land make her free,
410 And, ever following those two crownèd twins,
Commerce and conquest, shower the fiery grain
Of freedom broadcast over all that orbs
Between the Northern and the Southern morn.'

Then came a postscript dashed across the rest.
415 'See that there be no traitors in your camp:
We seem a nest of traitors—none to trust
Since our arms failed—this Egypt-plague of men!
Almost our maids were better at their homes,
Than thus man-girdled here: indeed I think
420 Our chiefest comfort is the little child
Of one unworthy mother; which she left:
She shall not have it back: the child shall grow
To prize the authentic mother of her mind.
I took it for an hour in mine own bed
425 This morning: there the tender orphan hands
Felt at my heart, and seemed to charm from thence
The wrath I nursed against the world: farewell.'

I ceased; he said, 'Stubborn, but she may sit
Upon a king's right hand in thunder-storms,

v 407 ∧ 8] The woman-phantom, she that seemed no more
        Than the man's shadow in a glass, her name 1847–50
v 408. Whose ... yoked] 1851; Yoked in his mouth 1847–50.
v 409. in ... free] 1850; liberate her, nor only here 1847–8.
v 410–13. There is a draft of these lines in the descriptive jottings of H.Lpr 191
(see Appendix B, III 631), where the reference is to 'Our English empire'.
v 410. And] 1850; But 1847–8.
v 419. I] 1850; we 1847–8.
v 424. I] 1850; We 1847–8.   in ... bed] 1850; this morning to us,
1847–8.
v 425. This ... there] 1850; In our own bed: 1847–8.
v 426. my] 1850; our 1847–8.
v 427. I] 1850; we 1847–8.

430 And breed up warriors! See now, though yourself
Be dazzled by the wildfire Love to sloughs
That swallow common sense, the spindling king,
This Gama swamped in lazy tolerance.
When the man wants weight, the woman takes
      it up,
435 And topples down the scales; but this is fixt
As are the roots of earth and base of all;
Man for the field and woman for the hearth:
Man for the sword and for the needle she:
Man with the head and woman with the heart:
440 Man to command and woman to obey;
All else confusion. Look you! the gray mare
Is ill to live with, when her whinny shrills
From tile to scullery, and her small goodman
Shrinks in his arm-chair while the fires of Hell
445 Mix with his hearth: but you—she's yet a colt—
Take, break her: strongly groomed and straitly
      curbed
She might not rank with those detestable
That let the bantling scald at home, and brawl
Their rights or wrongs like potherbs in the street.
450 They say she's comely; there's the fairer chance:
I like her none the less for rating at her!
Besides, the woman wed is not as we,
But suffers change of frame. A lusty brace
Of twins may weed her of her folly. Boy,
455 The bearing and the training of a child
Is woman's wisdom.'
                    Thus the hard old king:
I took my leave, for it was nearly noon:
I pored upon her letter which I held,
And on the little clause 'take not his life:'
460 I mused on that wild morning in the woods,
And on the 'Follow, follow, thou shalt win:'
I thought on all the wrathful king had said,
And how the strange betrothment was to end:
Then I remembered that burnt sorcerer's curse

v *441. you!*] *1850*; to it: *1847–8*. The proverb, 'the grey mare is the better
horse', said of the domineering wife.
v *445. you . . . colt*–] *1850*; take and break her, you! *1847–8*.
v *446*] *1850*; She's yet a colt. Well groomed and strongly curbed *1847–8*.
v *448. let . . . home*] *1850*; to the hireling leave their babe *1847–8*.
v *457–71. for . . . woke*] *1851; not 1847–50*.

That one should fight with shadows and should
465　　fall;
And like a flash the weird affection came:
King, camp and college turned to hollow shows;
I seemed to move in old memorial tilts,
And doing battle with forgotten ghosts,
470　To dream myself the shadow of a dream:
And ere I woke it was the point of noon,
The lists were ready. Empanoplied and plumed
We entered in, and waited, fifty there
Opposed to fifty, till the trumpet blared
475　At the barrier like a wild horn in a land
Of echoes, and a moment, and once more
The trumpet, and again: at which the storm
Of galloping hoofs bare on the ridge of spears
And riders front to front, until they closed
480　In conflict with the crash of shivering points,
And thunder. Yet it seemed a dream, I dreamed
Of fighting. On his haunches rose the steed,
And into fiery splinters leapt the lance,
And out of stricken helmets sprang the fire.
Part sat like rocks: part reeled but kept their
485　　seats:
Part rolled on the earth and rose again and drew:
Part stumbled mixt with floundering horses. Down
From those two bulks at Arac's side, and down
From Arac's arm, as from a giant's flail,
490　The large blows rained, as here and everywhere
He rode the mellay, lord of the ringing lists,
And all the plain, – brand, mace, and shaft, and
　　shield –
Shocked, like an iron-clanging anvil banged

v 472ff. Killham (pp. 272–4) discusses the Eglinton tournament, Sept.
1839, which took place in armour and was widely reported: 'to one con-
sidering the position of women in a changing world the interest provoked
in 1839 by the Eglinton tournament, especially among women, would have
seemed bizarre in the extreme'. There is much in Mark Girouard's *The Return
to Camelot: Chivalry and the English Gentleman* (1981) that is apt to the poem.
v 474] *1850*; To fifty, till the terrible trumpet blared *1847–8*. A review had
objected to the rhythm (Shannon, p. 121).
v 475–6. like . . . echoes] *1851*; not *1847–50*.
v 476. and a] *1851*; yet a *1847–50*.
v 480. conflict] *1850*; the middle *1847–8*.
v 481–2. Yet . . . fighting] *1851*; not *1847–50*.

With hammers; till I thought, can this be he
495   From Gama's dwarfish loins? if this be so,
The mother makes us most—and in my dream
I glanced aside, and saw the palace-front
Alive with fluttering scarfs and ladies' eyes,
And highest, among the statues, statuelike,
500   Between a cymballed Miriam and a Jael,
With Psyche's babe, was Ida watching us,
A single band of gold about her hair,
Like a Saint's glory up in heaven: but she
No saint—inexorable—no tenderness—
505   Too hard, too cruel: yet she sees me fight,
Yea, let her see me fall! with that I drave
Among the thickest and bore down a Prince,
And Cyril, one. Yea, let me make my dream
All that I would. But that large-moulded man,
510   His visage all agrin as at a wake,
Made at me through the press, and, staggering back
With stroke on stroke the horse and horseman, came
As comes a pillar of electric cloud,
Flaying the roofs and sucking up the drains,
515   And shadowing down the champaign till it strikes
On a wood, and takes, and breaks, and cracks, and
         splits,
And twists the grain with such a roar that Earth
Reels, and the herdsmen cry; for everything
Gave way before him: only Florian, he
520   That loved me closer than his own right eye,
Thrust in between; but Arac rode him down:
And Cyril seeing it, pushed against the Prince,
With Psyche's colour round his helmet, tough,
Strong, supple, sinew-corded, apt at arms;

v 496. *in my dream*] *1851*; thinking thus *1847–50*.

v 497. *aside*] *1850*; to the left *1847–8*.

v 500. *Exodus* xv 20 (see iv *122n*); *Judges* iv 21 (Jael slays Sisera with the nail).

v 506. *fall!*] *1851*; die. *1847–50*.

v 508–9. *Yea . . . would.*] *1851; not 1847–50*.

v 510] *1850; not 1847–8*.

v 514. *Flaying*] *1850*; Flaying off *1847–8*. A review had objected to the rhythm, and in l. 517 (Shannon, p. 121).

v 517. *Earth*] *1850*; the Earth *1847–8*.

v 518]   Reels and the beldam shrieks beside her fire
            The last day of the Lord for everything *ULC MS*

525 But tougher, heavier, stronger, he that smote
     And threw him: last I spurred; I felt my veins
     Stretch with fierce heat; a moment hand to hand,
     And sword to sword, and horse to horse we hung,
     Till I struck out and shouted; the blade glanced,
530 I did but shear a feather, and dream and truth
     Flowed from me; darkness closed me; and I fell.

[V ∧ VI]
Home they brought her warrior dead:
    She nor swooned, nor uttered cry:
All her maidens, watching, said,
    'She must weep or she will die.'

5   Then they praised him, soft and low,
            Called him worthy to be loved,
        Truest friend and noblest foe;
            Yet she neither spoke nor moved.

        Stole a maiden from her place,
10   Lightly to the warrior stept,
        Took the face-cloth from the face;
            Yet she neither moved nor wept.

        Rose a nurse of ninety years,
            Set his child upon her knee–
15   Like summer tempest came her tears–
            'Sweet my child, I live for thee.'

VI
My dream had never died or lived again.
As in some mystic middle state I lay;

v 525. *heavier*] *1850*; suppler *1847–8*.
v 530. *dream and truth*] *1851*; life and love *1847–50*.

v ∧ vi Written 1849, added *1850*. For an alternative version, see Appendix I
(*p. 980*). Both versions resemble Scott's *Lay of the Last Minstrel* I ix: 'In
sorrow o'er Lord Walter's bier / The warlike foresters had bent; / And
many a flower and many a tear / Old Teviot's maids and matrons lent: /
But o'er her warrior's bloody bier / The Ladye dropp'd nor flower nor
tear! / Vengeance, deep-brooding o'er the slain, / Had lock'd the source of
softer woe; / And burning pride and high disdain / Forbade the rising tear
to flow; / Until, amid his sorrowing clan, / Her son lisp'd from the nurse's
knee– / "And if I live to be a man, / My father's death reveng'd shall
be!" / Then fast the mother's tears did seek / To dew the infant's kindling
cheek.' T.'s song is also close to the Icelandic *Guþrunarkviþa I*, which J. S.
Conybeare translated in *Illustrations of Anglo-Saxon Poetry* (1826); see
R. M. Lumiansky, *Notes and Queries* clxxix (1940) 23–4.

vi 1–4] *1851*; What followed, though I saw not, yet I heard *1847–50*.

Seeing I saw not, hearing not I heard:
Though, if I saw not, yet they told me all
5   So often that I speak as having seen.

    For so it seemed, or so they said to me,
That all things grew more tragic and more strange;
That when our side was vanquished and my cause
For ever lost, there went up a great cry,
10   The Prince is slain. My father heard and ran
In on the lists, and there unlaced my casque
And grovelled on my body, and after him
Came Psyche, sorrowing for Aglaïa.
    But high upon the palace Ida stood
15   With Psyche's babe in arm: there on the roofs
Like that great dame of Lapidoth she sang.

        'Our enemies have fallen, have fallen: the seed,
    The little seed they laughed at in the dark,
    Has risen and cleft the soil, and grown a bulk
20   Of spanless girth, that lays on every side
    A thousand arms and rushes to the Sun.

        'Our enemies have fallen, have fallen: they came;
    The leaves were wet with women's tears: they heard
    A noise of songs they would not understand:
25   They marked it with the red cross to the fall,
    And would have strown it, and are fallen themselves.

        'Our enemies have fallen, have fallen: they came,
    The woodmen with their axes: lo the tree!
    But we will make it faggots for the hearth,
30   And shape it plank and beam for roof and floor,
    And boats and bridges for the use of men.

---

vi 6–7] *1851*; *not 1847–50.*

vi 8. *That*] *1850*; *For 1847–8.*

vi 16. *Judges* iv 4, 'And Deborah, a prophetess, the wife of Lapidoth, she judged Israel at that time.' v 1–2, 'Then sang Deborah and Barak the son of Abinoam on that day, saying, Praise ye the Lord for the avenging of Israel.' Ida's song may also recall v 14, 'Out of Ephraim was there a root of them against Amalek'; and v 31, 'So let all thine enemies perish, O Lord.'

vi 17. *Isaiah* xxi 9, 'Babylon is fallen, is fallen'; also *Revelation* xviii 2, xiv 8. The song's theme of the seed is linked by Killham (p. 118) with Anna Jameson's *Woman's Mission and Woman's Position* (in *Memoirs and Essays*, 1846), which is prefaced with the story of Donna Maria d'Escobar, who planted a few grains of wheat in her garden at Lima, and thence produced all the wheat in Peru.

'Our enemies have fallen, have fallen: they struck;
With their own blows they hurt themselves, nor knew
There dwelt an iron nature in the grain:
35   The glittering axe was broken in their arms,
Their arms were shattered to the shoulder blade.

'Our enemies have fallen, but this shall grow
A night of Summer from the heat, a breadth
Of Autumn, dropping fruits of power: and rolled
40   With music in the growing breeze of Time,
The tops shall strike from star to star, the fangs
Shall move the stony bases of the world.

'And now, O maids, behold our sanctuary
Is violate, our laws broken: fear we not
45   To break them more in their behoof, whose arms
Championed our cause and won it with a day
Blanched in our annals, and perpetual feast,
When dames and heroines of the golden year
Shall strip a hundred hollows bare of Spring,
50   To rain an April of ovation round
Their statues, borne aloft, the three: but come,
We will be liberal, since our rights are won.
Let them not lie in the tents with coarse mankind,
Ill nurses; but descend, and proffer these
55   The brethren of our blood and cause, that there
Lie bruised and maimed, the tender ministries
Of female hands and hospitality.'

She spoke, and with the babe yet in her arms,
Descending, burst the great bronze valves, and led
60   A hundred maids in train across the Park.
Some cowled, and some bare-headed, on they came,
Their feet in flowers, her loveliest: by them went
The enamoured air sighing, and on their curls
From the high tree the blossom wavering fell,
65   And over them the tremulous isles of light
Slided, they moving under shade: but Blanche

vi *34*. Cp. *Edwin Morris* 68, MS: 'But there is hidden virtue in the wood'.
vi *40*. *growing*] *1850*; Æonian *1847–8*.
vi *41*. Cp. *The Hesperides* 37 ʌ 8, MS: 'the fangèd root'.
vi *47*. *Blanched*: marked in white chalk as propitious days.
vi *48*. Cp. *The Golden Year* (p. *206*).
vi *59*. *valves*: leaves of a door.
vi *65–6*. 'Spots of sunshine coming through the leaves, and seeming to slide from one to the other, as the procession of girls "moves under

At distance followed: so they came: anon
Through open field into the lists they wound
Timorously; and as the leader of the herd
70   That holds a stately fretwork to the Sun,
And followed up by a hundred airy does,
Steps with a tender foot, light as on air,
The lovely, lordly creature floated on
To where her wounded brethren lay; there
         stayed;
75   Knelt on one knee, – the child on one, – and prest
Their hands, and called them dear deliverers,
And happy warriors, and immortal names,
And said 'You shall not lie in the tents but here,
And nursed by those for whom you fought, and
         served
80   With female hands and hospitality.'

Then, whether moved by this, or was it chance,
She past my way. Up started from my side
The old lion, glaring with his whelpless eye,
Silent; but when she saw me lying stark,
85   Dishelmed and mute, and motionlessly pale,
Cold even to her, she sighed; and when she saw
The haggard father's face and reverend beard
Of grisly twine, all dabbled with the blood
Of his own son, shuddered, a twitch of pain
90   Tortured her mouth, and o'er her forehead past
A shadow, and her hue changed, and she said:
'He saved my life: my brother slew him for it.'
No more: at which the king in bitter scorn
Drew from my neck the painting and the tress,
95   And held them up: she saw them, and a day
Rose from the distance on her memory,
When the good Queen, her mother, shore the tress
With kisses, ere the days of Lady Blanche:
And then once more she looked at my pale face:
100 Till understanding all the foolish work
Of Fancy, and the bitter close of all,

shade"' (T.).   *isles of light*: as in Thomas Gisborne's *Walks in a Forest*
('Summer.–Moonlight'), which was at Somersby (*Lincoln*). Shelley has
'slide / Tremulous . . . isle' in *A Vision of the Sea* 131–3.
vi *68. open*] *1850*; the open *1847–8*.
vi *77.* Cp. Wordsworth's *Who is the happy Warrior?*
vi *91. her*] *1848*; all her *1847*.

Her iron will was broken in her mind;
Her noble heart was molten in her breast;
She bowed, she set the child on the earth; she laid
105 A feeling finger on my brows, and presently
'O Sire,' she said, 'he lives: he is not dead:
O let me have him with my brethren here
In our own palace: we will tend on him
Like one of these; if so, by any means,
110 To lighten this great clog of thanks, that make
Our progress falter to the woman's goal.'

She said: but at the happy word 'he lives'
My father stooped, re-fathered o'er my wounds.
So those two foes above my fallen life,
115 With brow to brow like night and evening mixt
Their dark and gray, while Psyche ever stole
A little nearer, till the babe that by us,
Half-lapt in glowing gauze and golden brede,
Lay like a new-fallen meteor on the grass,
120 Uncared for, spied its mother and began
A blind and babbling laughter, and to dance
Its body, and reach its fatling innocent arms
And lazy lingering fingers. She the appeal
Brooked not, but clamouring out 'Mine—mine—
          not yours,
125 It is not yours, but mine: give me the child'
Ceased all on tremble: piteous was the cry:
So stood the unhappy mother open-mouthed,
And turned each face her way: wan was her cheek
With hollow watch, her blooming mantle torn,
130 Red grief and mother's hunger in her eye,
And down dead-heavy sank her curls, and half
The sacred mother's bosom, panting, burst
The laces toward her babe; but she nor cared
Nor knew it, clamouring on, till Ida heard,
135 Looked up, and rising slowly from me, stood
Erect and silent, striking with her glance
The mother, me, the child; but he that lay
Beside us, Cyril, battered as he was,

vi *110. make*] *1850*; makes *1847–8.*
vi *118–19. brede*: 'embroidery' (T.). Cp. Keats, *Lamia* i 157–60: 'And, as the
lava ravishes the mead, / Spoilt all her silver mail, and golden brede . . . /
Eclips'd her crescents, and lick'd up her stars.'
vi *137. he that*] *1850*; Cyril, who *1847–8.*
vi *138*] *1850*; Bruised, where he fell, not far off, much in pain, *1847–8.*

Trailed himself up on one knee: then he drew
140 Her robe to meet his lips, and down she looked
At the armed man sideways, pitying as it seemed,
Or self-involved; but when she learnt his face,
Remembering his ill-omened song, arose
Once more through all her height, and o'er him
    grew
145 Tall as a figure lengthened on the sand
When the tide ebbs in sunshine, and he said:

'O fair and strong and terrible! Lioness
That with your long locks play the Lion's mane!
But Love and Nature, these are two more terrible
150 And stronger. See, your foot is on our necks,
We vanquished, you the Victor of your will.
What would you more? give her the child! remain
Orbed in your isolation: he is dead,
Or all as dead: henceforth we let you be:
155 Win you the hearts of women; and beware
Lest, where you seek the common love of these,
The common hate with the revolving wheel
Should drag you down, and some great Nemesis
Break from a darkened future, crowned with fire,
160 And tread you out for ever: but howsoe'er
Fixed in yourself, never in your own arms
To hold your own, deny not hers to her,
Give her the child! O if, I say, you keep
One pulse that beats true woman, if you loved
165 The breast that fed or arm that dandled you,
Or own one port of sense not flint to prayer,
Give her the child! or if you scorn to lay it,
Yourself, in hands so lately claspt with yours,
Or speak to her, your dearest, her one fault
170 The tenderness, not yours, that could not kill,
Give *me* it: *I* will give it her.'
                   He said:
At first her eye with slow dilation rolled
Dry flame, she listening; after sank and sank

---

vi *159*. Cp. *Ode on Wellington* 170 ∧ 71, *1852* text: 'a darkening future'.
vi *165. arm*] *1850*; the arm *1847–8*.
vi *166. port*] *1880*; part *1847–78*. T. says this was a misprint, and glosses
port as 'haven'. Cp. *2 Henry IV* IV v 24: 'That keep'st the ports of slumber
open wide', where the meaning is 'portals'.
vi *168*. Cp. *In Memoriam* x 19: 'And hands so often clasped in mine'.
vi *171. I*] *1850*; and I *1847–8*.

And, into mournful twilight mellowing, dwelt
175 Full on the child; she took it: 'Pretty bud!
Lily of the vale! half opened bell of the woods!
Sole comfort of my dark hour, when a world
Of traitorous friend and broken system made
No purple in the distance, mystery,
180 Pledge of a love not to be mine, farewell;
These men are hard upon us as of old,
We two must part: and yet how fain was I
To dream thy cause embraced in mine, to think
I might be something to thee, when I felt
185 Thy helpless warmth about my barren breast
In the dead prime: but may thy mother prove
As true to thee as false, false, false to me!
And, if thou needs must bear the yoke, I wish it
Gentle as freedom'—here she kissed it: then—
190 'All good go with thee! take it Sir,' and so
Laid the soft babe in his hard-mailèd hands,
Who turned half-round to Psyche as she sprang
To meet it, with an eye that swum in thanks;
Then felt it sound and whole from head to foot,
195 And hugged and never hugged it close enough,
And in her hunger mouthed and mumbled it,
And hid her bosom with it; after that
Put on more calm and added suppliantly:

'We two were friends: I go to mine own land
200 For ever: find some other: as for me
I scarce am fit for your great plans: yet speak to me,
Say one soft word and let me part forgiven.'

But Ida spoke not, rapt upon the child.
Then Arac. 'Ida—'sdeath! you blame the man;
205 You wrong yourselves—the woman is so hard
Upon the woman. Come, a grace to me!
I am your warrior: I and mine have fought

vi 178. broken system] broken purpose H.Nbk 25. As in the song, vii 199.
vi 179. Cp. In Memoriam xxxviii 3: 'The purple from the distance dies'.
vi 185. helpless . . . barren] 1851; waxen . . . milkless 1847–50. barren
breast: L'Allegro 73.
vi 186. dead prime: 'earliest dawn' (T.).
vi 193. meet] 1850; embrace 1847–8.
vi 204. Ida—'sdeath] 1851; Soul and life! 1847–50.
vi 205–6] I hate the sight of female difference ULC MS.
vi 206 ∧ 7] I am your brother; I advise you well: 1847–8.

Your battle: kiss her; take her hand, she weeps:
'Sdeath! I would sooner fight thrice o'er than see it.'

210   But Ida spoke not, gazing on the ground,
And reddening in the furrows of his chin,
And moved beyond his custom, Gama said:

'I've heard that there is iron in the blood,
And I believe it. Not one word? not one?
215   Whence drew you this steel temper? not from me,
Not from your mother, now a saint with saints.
She said you had a heart—I heard her say it—
"Our Ida has a heart"—just ere she died—
"But see that some one with authority
220   Be near her still" and I—I sought for one—
All people said she had authority—
The Lady Blanche: much profit! Not one word;
No! though your father sues: see how you stand
Stiff as Lot's wife, and all the good knights
            maimed,
225   I trust that there is no one hurt to death,
For your wild whim: and was it then for this,
Was it for this we gave our palace up,
Where we withdrew from summer heats and state,
And had our wine and chess beneath the planes,
230   And many a pleasant hour with her that's gone,
Ere you were born to vex us? Is it kind?
Speak to her I say: is this not she of whom,
When first she came, all flushed you said to me
Now had you got a friend of your own age,
Now could you share your thought; now should
235   men see
Two women faster welded in one love

vi 209. 'Sdeath] 1851; Life 1847–50.

vi 225] 1850; not 1847–8. T. wrote to Aubrey de Vere, late Jan. 1850 (Letters i
320), who had reviewed the poem in the Edinburgh Review, Oct. 1849: 'There
were only one or two little things in it which I did not like; for instance that
about "the dying and the dead" which is quite wide of the mark and you will
see that I have inserted a line to guard against such an interpretation in
future.' Again, mid-Feb. 1850 (Letters i 320–21; Mem. i 282): 'Now I certainly
did not mean to kill anyone and therefore I put this new line into the old
king's mouth. "I trust that there is no one hurt to death" and in the old
tourneys it really did happen now and then that there was only a certain
amount of bruises, and bangs and no death.'

Than pairs of wedlock; she you walked with, she
You talked with, whole nights long, up in the tower,
Of sine and arc, spheroid and azimuth,
240 And right ascension, Heaven knows what; and now
A word, but one, one little kindly word,
Not one to spare her: out upon you, flint!
You love nor her, nor me, nor any; nay,
You shame your mother's judgment too. Not one?
245 You will not? well–no heart have you, or such
As fancies like the vermin in a nut
Have fretted all to dust and bitterness.'
So said the small king moved beyond his wont.

But Ida stood nor spoke, drained of her force
250 By many a varying influence and so long.
Down through her limbs a drooping languor wept:
Her head a little bent; and on her mouth
A doubtful smile dwelt like a clouded moon
In a still water: then brake out my sire,
255 Lifting his grim head from my wounds. 'O you,
Woman, whom we thought woman even now,
And were half fooled to let you tend our son,
Because he might have wished it–but we see
The accomplice of your madness unforgiven,
260 And think that you might mix his draught with death,
When your skies change again: the rougher hand
Is safer: on to the tents: take up the Prince.'

He rose, and while each ear was pricked to attend
A tempest, through the cloud that dimmed her broke
265 A genial warmth and light once more, and shone
Through glittering drops on her sad friend.
                                        'Come hither.
O Psyche,' she cried out, 'embrace me, come,
Quick while I melt; make reconcilement sure
With one that cannot keep her mind an hour:
270 Come to the hollow heart they slander so!
Kiss and be friends, like children being chid!
I seem no more: I want forgiveness too:
I should have had to do with none but maids,
That have no links with men. Ah false but dear,

vi 239. 'The azimuth of any point on a horizontal plane is the angle between
a line drawn to that point, and a fixed line in the horizontal plane, usually
chosen to be a line drawn due North' (H.T.).
vi 269] With one no firmer than a whimpering girl: ULC MS.

Dear traitor, too much loved, why?–why?–
275   Yet see,
Before these kings we embrace you yet once more
With all forgiveness, all oblivion,
And trust, not love, you less.
                                 And now, O sire,
Grant me your son, to nurse, to wait upon him,
280   Like mine own brother. For my debt to him,
This nightmare weight of gratitude, I know it;
Taunt me no more: yourself and yours shall have
Free adit; we will scatter all our maids
Till happier times each to her proper hearth:
What use to keep them here–now? grant my
285   prayer.
Help, father, brother, help; speak to the king:
Thaw this male nature to some touch of that
Which kills me with myself, and drags me down
From my fixt height to mob me up with all
290   The soft and milky rabble of womankind,
Poor weakling even as they are.'
                                 Passionate tears
Followed: the king replied not: Cyril said:
'Your brother, Lady,–Florian,–ask for him
Of your great head–for he is wounded too–
295   That you may tend upon him with the prince.'
'Ay so,' said Ida with a bitter smile,
'Our laws are broken: let him enter too.'
Then Violet, she that sang the mournful song,
And had a cousin tumbled on the plain,
300   Petitioned too for him. 'Ay so,' she said,
'I stagger in the stream: I cannot keep
My heart an eddy from the brawling hour:
We break our laws with ease, but let it be.'
'Ay so?' said Blanche: 'Amazed am I to hear
Your Highness: but your Highness breaks with
305   ease
The law your Highness did not make: 'twas I.
I had been wedded wife, I knew mankind,
And blocked them out; but these men came to woo
Your Highness–verily I think to win.'

vi *283*. *adit*: access (T.'s is the earliest example in *OED* in precisely this sense).
vi *304*. *Amazed am I*] *1850*; I am all amaze *1847–8*.

310   So she, and turned askance a wintry eye:
       But Ida with a voice, that like a bell
       Tolled by an earthquake in a trembling tower,
       Rang ruin, answered full of grief and scorn.

       'Fling our doors wide! all, all, not one, but all,
315   Not only he, but by my mother's soul,
       Whatever man lies wounded, friend or foe,
       Shall enter, if he will. Let our girls flit,
       Till the storm die! but had you stood by us,
       The roar that breaks the Pharos from his base
320   Had left us rock. She fain would sting us too,
       But shall not. Pass, and mingle with your likes.
       We brook no further insult but are gone.'
         She turned; the very nape of her white neck

vi *313* ∧ *4*]   'What! in our time of glory when the cause
         Now stands up, first, a trophied pillar–now
         So clipt, so stinted in our triumph–barred
         Even from our free heart-thanks, and every way
         Thwarted and vext, and lastly catechised
         By our own creature! one that made our laws!
         Our great she-Solon! her that built the nest
         To hatch the cuckoo! whom we called our friend!
         But we will crush the lie that glances at us
         As cloaking in the larger charities
         Some baby predilection: all amazed!
         We must amaze this legislator more. *1847–8*

vi *321* ∧ *2*]   Go, help the half-brained dwarf, Society,
         To find low motives unto noble deeds,
         To fix all doubt upon the darker side;
         Go, fitter thou for narrowest neighbourhoods,
         Old talker, haunt where gossip breeds and seethes
         And festers in provincial sloth: and, you,
         That think we sought to practise on a life
         Risked for our own and trusted to our hands,
         What say you, Sir? you hear us: deem ye not
         'Tis all too like that even now we scheme,
         In one broad death confounding friend and foe,
         To drug them all? revolve it: you are man,
         And therefore no doubt wise; but after this *1847–8*

ULC MS included:
         . . . sloth and slips
     From hearth to hearth the petty venomous hint
     To blister household health and peace: and you . . .

Cp. *In Memoriam* xxi 8 ∧ 9, MS: 'to find / Low motives for a noble deed.'

Was rosed with indignation: but the Prince
325 Her brother came; the king her father charmed
Her wounded soul with words: nor did mine own
Refuse her proffer, lastly gave his hand.

       Then us they lifted up, dead weights, and bare
Straight to the doors: to them the doors gave way
330 Groaning, and in the Vestal entry shrieked
The virgin marble under iron heels:
And on they moved and gained the hall, and there
Rested: but great the crush was, and each base,
To left and right, of those tall columns drowned
335 In silken fluctuation and the swarm
Of female whisperers: at the further end
Was Ida by the throne, the two great cats
Close by her, like supporters on a shield,
Bow-backed with fear: but in the centre stood
340 The common men with rolling eyes; amazed
They glared upon the women, and aghast
The women stared at these, all silent, save
When armour clashed or jingled, while the day,
Descending, struck athwart the hall, and shot
345 A flying splendour out of brass and steel,
That o'er the statues leapt from head to head,
Now fired an angry Pallas on the helm,
Now set a wrathful Dian's moon on flame,
And now and then an echo started up,
350 And shuddering fled from room to room, and died
Of fright in far apartments.
                                  Then the voice
Of Ida sounded, issuing ordinance:
And me they bore up the broad stairs, and through
The long-laid galleries past a hundred doors
355 To one deep chamber shut from sound, and due
To languid limbs and sickness; left me in it;
And others otherwhere they laid; and all
That afternoon a sound arose of hoof
And chariot, many a maiden passing home
360 Till happier times; but some were left of those
Held sagest, and the great lords out and in,
From those two hosts that lay beside the walls,
Walked at their will, and everything was changed.

---

vi *332. on they moved*] *1850*; they moved on *1847–8*.

[VI ∧ VII]

Ask me no more: the moon may draw the sea;
The cloud may stoop from heaven and take the shape
With fold to fold, of mountain or of cape;
But O too fond, when have I answered thee?
5   Ask me no more.

Ask me no more: what answer should I give?
I love not hollow cheek or faded eye:
Yet, O my friend, I will not have thee die!
Ask me no more, lest I should bid thee live;
10   Ask me no more.

Ask me no more: thy fate and mine are sealed:
I strove against the stream and all in vain:
Let the great river take me to the main:
No more, dear love, for at a touch I yield;
15   Ask me no more.

VII

So was their sanctuary violated,
So their fair college turned to hospital;
At first with all confusion: by and by

vi ∧ vii Written 1849, added *1850*. Cp. Thomas Carew's *Song*, of which each stanza begins 'Aske me no more': 'Aske me no more where Jove bestowes, / When June is past, the fading rose: / For in your beauties orient deepe, / These flowers as in their causes, sleepe. . . .'.
ULC MS has, as a separate draft:

Bid me be gone and I obey you
    Even to the wild west's latest shore
But if a touch of passion sway you
Fly me no more, dearest, I pray you
    Fly me no more, fly me no more.

vi ∧ vii *2. cloud . . . and*] chill gray cloud may stoop to *HnMS (HM 19486).*
vi ∧ vii *5 ∧ 6*]   Ask me no more: it is not that I hate,
        But I, shall I that cared not for thy bloom
        Be captive to thy paleness and thy gloom?
        Ask me no more or thou wilt seal thy fate;
            Ask me no more. *HnMS*
vi ∧ vii *7–8*]   It cannot be that I would have thee die.
        My life were all too short for my reply. *HnMS*
vi ∧ vii *11. Ask . . . more*] What use to ask? *HnMS*; No more – for now *ULC MS.*
vi ∧ vii *12. all*] strove *HnMS*. Cp. *Venus and Adonis* 772: 'And all in vain you strive against the stream'.
vi ∧ vii *13*] The mighty current sweeps me to the main. *ULC MS.*
vi ∧ vii *14. No . . . love,*] But ask no more *HnMS.*

Sweet order lived again with other laws:
5   A kindlier influence reigned; and everywhere
Low voices with the ministering hand
Hung round the sick: the maidens came, they
        talked,
They sang, they read: till she not fair began
To gather light, and she that was, became
10   Her former beauty treble; and to and fro
With books, with flowers, with Angel offices,
Like creatures native unto gracious act,
And in their own clear element, they moved.

But sadness on the soul of Ida fell,
15   And hatred of her weakness, blent with shame.
Old studies failed; seldom she spoke: but oft
Clomb to the roofs, and gazed alone for hours
On that disastrous leaguer, swarms of men
Darkening her female field: void was her use,
20   And she as one that climbs a peak to gaze
O'er land and main, and sees a great black cloud
Drag inward from the deeps, a wall of night,
Blot out the slope of sea from verge to shore,
And suck the blinding splendour from the sand,
25   And quenching lake by lake and tarn by tarn
Expunge the world: so fared she gazing there;
So blackened all her world in secret, blank
And waste it seemed and vain; till down she came,
And found fair peace once more among the sick.

And twilight dawned; and morn by morn the
30   lark
Shot up and shrilled in flickering gyres, but I
Lay silent in the muffled cage of life:
And twilight gloomed; and broader-grown the
        bowers
Drew the great night into themselves, and Heaven,
35   Star after star, arose and fell; but I,
Deeper than those weird doubts could reach me,
        lay
Quite sundered from the moving Universe,
Nor knew what eye was on me, nor the hand
That nursed me, more than infants in their sleep.

vii *19. void was her use*: her usual occupations neglected.
vii *36] 1851; not 1847–50.*
vii *37. Quite] 1851; Lay 1847–50.*

40   But Psyche tended Florian: with her oft,
        Melissa came; for Blanche had gone, but left
        Her child among us, willing she should keep
        Court-favour: here and there the small bright head,
        A light of healing, glanced about the couch,
45   Or through the parted silks the tender face
        Peeped, shining in upon the wounded man
        With blush and smile, a medicine in themselves
        To wile the length from languorous hours, and draw
        The sting from pain; nor seemed it strange that soon
50   He rose up whole, and those fair charities
        Joined at her side; nor stranger seemed that hearts
        So gentle, so employed, should close in love,
        Than when two dewdrops on the petal shake
        To the same sweet air, and tremble deeper down,
55   And slip at once all-fragrant into one.

        Less prosperously the second suit obtained
        At first with Psyche. Not though Blanche had
                sworn
        That after that dark night among the fields
        She needs must wed him for her own good name;
60   Not though he built upon the babe restored;
        Nor though she liked him, yielded she, but feared
        To incense the Head once more; till on a day
        When Cyril pleaded, Ida came behind
        Seen but of Psyche: on her foot she hung
65   A moment, and she heard, at which her face
        A little flushed, and she past on; but each
        Assumed from thence a half-consent involved
        In stillness, plighted troth, and were at peace.

        Nor only these: Love in the sacred halls
70   Held carnival at will, and flying struck
        With showers of random sweet on maid and man.
        Nor did her father cease to press my claim,
        Nor did mine own, now reconciled; nor yet
        Did those twin-brothers, risen again and whole;
75   Nor Arac, satiate with his victory.

        But I lay still, and with me oft she sat:
        Then came a change; for sometimes I would catch

vii 56. *obtained*: 'prevailed' (T.).
vii 60. *upon the babe restored*] *1850*; on what she said of the child *1847–8*.
Cp. T.'s Latinism with *Comus* 48: 'After the Tuscan Mariners transform'd'.
vii 61. *yielded she*] *1850*; would she yield *1847–8*.

Her hand in wild delirium, gripe it hard,
And fling it like a viper off, and shriek
80 'You are not Ida;' clasp it once again,
And call her Ida, though I knew her not,
And call her sweet, as if in irony,
And call her hard and cold which seemed a truth:
And still she feared that I should lose my mind,
85 And often she believed that I should die:
Till out of long frustration of her care,
And pensive tendance in the all-weary noons,
And watches in the dead, the dark, when clocks
Throbbed thunder through the palace floors, or
  called
90 On flying Time from all their silver tongues –
And out of memories of her kindlier days,
And sidelong glances at my father's grief,
And at the happy lovers heart in heart –
And out of hauntings of my spoken love,
95 And lonely listenings to my muttered dream,
And often feeling of the helpless hands,
And wordless broodings on the wasted cheek –
From all a closer interest flourished up,
Tenderness touch by touch, and last, to these,
100 Love, like an Alpine harebell hung with tears
By some cold morning glacier; frail at first
And feeble, all unconscious of itself,
But such as gathered colour day by day.

Last I woke sane, but well-nigh close to death
105 For weakness: it was evening: silent light
Slept on the painted walls, wherein were wrought
Two grand designs; for on one side arose
The women up in wild revolt, and stormed
At the Oppian law. Titanic shapes, they crammed
110 The forum, and half-crushed among the rest
A dwarf-like Cato cowered. On the other side

vii 89. Cp. *Semele* 19: 'To throbbings of the thunderous gong'.
vii 90. Cp. *Amy* 5: 'The silver tongues of featherfooted rumour'.
vii 109. 'When Hannibal was nearing Rome a law was carried by C.
Oppius, Trib. Pleb., B.C. 215, forbidding women to wear more than half
an ounce of gold, or brilliant dresses, and no woman was to come within a
mile of Rome or of any town save on account of public sacrifices in a
conveyance drawn by horses' (T.). H.T. adds: 'In B.C. 195 the Oppian Law
was, in spite of Cato's protests, repealed. Livy xxxiv 8.'
vii 111. *dwarf-like*] *1850*; little *1847–8*.

Hortensia spoke against the tax; behind,
A train of dames: by axe and eagle sat,
With all their foreheads drawn in Roman scowls,
115   And half the wolf's-milk curdled in their veins,
The fierce triumvirs; and before them paused
Hortensia pleading: angry was her face.

I saw the forms: I knew not where I was:
They did but look like hollow shows; nor more
120   Sweet Ida: palm to palm she sat: the dew
Dwelt in her eyes, and softer all her shape
And rounder seemed: I moved: I sighed: a touch
Came round my wrist, and tears upon my hand:
Then all for languor and self-pity ran
125   Mine down my face, and with what life I had,
And like a flower that cannot all unfold,
So drenched it is with tempest, to the sun,
Yet, as it may, turns toward him, I on her
Fixt my faint eyes, and uttered whisperingly:

'If you be, what I think you, some sweet
130   dream,
I would but ask you to fulfil yourself:
But if you be that Ida whom I knew,
I ask you nothing: only, if a dream,
Sweet dream, be perfect. I shall die tonight.
135   Stoop down and seem to kiss me ere I die.'

I could no more, but lay like one in trance,
That hears his burial talked of by his friends,
And cannot speak, nor move, nor make one sign,
But lies and dreads his doom. She turned; she
            paused;
140   She stooped; and out of languor leapt a cry;
Leapt fiery Passion from the brinks of death;

vii 112. *Hortensia*: 'she pleaded against the proposed tax on Roman
matrons after the assassination of Julius Caesar which was to be raised in
order to pay for the expenses of the war against Brutus and Cassius' (H.T.).
vii 119] 1854;   Sad [Strange 1850] phantoms conjured out of
                    circumstance,
            Ghosts of the fading brain, they seemed; nor more
                                            1847–50;
They did but seem as hollow shows; nor more 1851–3.
vii 122. *seemed*] 1854; showed 1847–53.
vii 140] 1850;   She stooped; and with a great shock of the heart
            Our mouths met: out of languor leapt a cry, 1847–8
vii 141] 1850; Crowned [Leapt 1848] Passion from the brinks of death
and up 1847–8. A review had objected to the rhythm (Shannon, p. 120).

And I believed that in the living world
My spirit closed with Ida's at the lips;
Till back I fell, and from mine arms she rose
145   Glowing all over noble shame; and all
Her falser self slipt from her like a robe,
And left her woman, lovelier in her mood
Than in her mould that other, when she came
From barren deeps to conquer all with love;
150   And down the streaming crystal dropt; and she
Far-fleeted by the purple island-sides,
Naked, a double light in air and wave,
To meet her Graces, where they decked her out
For worship without end; nor end of mine,
155   Stateliest, for thee! but mute she glided forth,
Nor glanced behind her, and I sank and slept,
Filled through and through with Love, a happy
        sleep.

Deep in the night I woke: she, near me, held
A volume of the Poets of her land:
160   There to herself, all in low tones, she read.

'Now sleeps the crimson petal, now the white;
Nor waves the cypress in the palace walk;
Nor winks the gold fin in the porphyry font:
The fire-fly wakens: waken thou with me.

165   Now droops the milkwhite peacock like a ghost,
And like a ghost she glimmers on to me.

---

vii *142*] *1851; not 1847–50.*
vii *143*] *1850;* Along the shuddering senses struck the soul,
                And closed on fire with Ida's at the lips; *1847–8*
vii *147–8.* 'Aphrodite passed before his brain, drowsy with weakness' (T.).
The lines that follow refer to Aphrodite's rising from the sea.
vii *150. the streaming crystal: The Palace of Art* 120 ∧ 21, *1832* text.
vii *161–74.* This song draws on eastern sources; the best summary is by
Killham (pp. 219–20). The form is that of a ghazal–'the requisite number of
couplets, the repetition of a single final word at short intervals to produce
what is tantamount to rhyme, and . . . the standard images and ornaments
of the Persian love poem, roses, lilies, peacocks, the stars, the cypress'. T.
probably learnt of the ghazal from the works of Sir William Jones (*Lincoln*).
On the controversy as to how much Persian T. knew (listed in Killham),
there should be added T.'s own jotting: 'I don't read Persian' (C. Ricks,
ELN iv (1966) 46–7).
vii *165.* Cp. *The Day-Dream: The Sleeping Palace* 15,.where droops 'The

Now lies the Earth all Danaë to the stars,
And all thy heart lies open unto me.

Now slides the silent meteor on, and leaves
170   A shining furrow, as thy thoughts in me.

Now folds the lily all her sweetness up,
And slips into the bosom of the lake:
So fold thyself, my dearest, thou, and slip
Into my bosom and be lost in me.'

175   I heard her turn the page; she found a small
Sweet Idyl, and once more, as low, she read:

peacock in his laurel bower', the setting that of the urns and the lake.
There too a prince enters to rescue a princess.
vii *167*. 'Zeus came down to Danaë when shut up in the tower in a
shower of golden stars' (T.). J. H. Buckley (p. 269) suggests that T. may
have been inspired by a memory of Arthur Hallam's last letter to him,
6 Sept. 1833 (*Mem.* i 104): 'and oh Alfred such Titians! by Heaven, that
man could paint! I wish you could see his Danaë. Do you just write as
perfect a Danaë!' (*AHH*, p. 785).
vii *169–70*. D. H. Jones (*TRB* ii, 1976, 214) compares Victor Hugo, *Les
Feuilles d'Automne* (1831) xxiii: 'Et, comme un météore au sein des nuits
funèbres, / Vous laissez dans le coeur un sillon radieux'. (Note too the 'bosom'
of ll. 172, 174.)
vii *170*. Cp. *A Dream of Fair Women, 1832* opening: 'my deepfurrowed
thought'.
vii *171*. R. Warren compares Edward Fairfax: 'The rose within her selfe her
sweetnes closed' (translating Tasso; *Godfrey of Bulloigne* II xviii 4); T. owned an
edition, and Warren notes the lily / rose connection elsewhere in T. (*TRB* iv,
1982, 28).
vii *177–207*. '*Come down, O maid* is said to be taken from Theocritus, but
there is no real likeness except perhaps in the Greek Idyllic feeling' (T.).
H.T. adds: 'For simple rhythm and vowel music my father considered this
Idyllic song, written in Switzerland–chiefly at Lauterbrunnen and Grindel-
wald–and descriptive of the waste Alpine heights and gorges and of the
sweet rich valleys below, as among his most successful work.' Turner
(p. 102) describes the poem as 'pervasively Theocritean, but most closely
related to *Idyll* xi'; he relates the maid and the mountain not only to the
Jungfrau, but also to the names Ida and Mountfort – see *p. 223*. ULC MS
has several drafts of the poem (*A, B, C, D* below) and a fragmentary
reworking of a few lines. Drafts *A* and *B* are not simply successive; for
instance *A* has the last two lines while *B* does not, but *B* has l. 189 in its final
form whereas *A* does not.

'Come down, O maid, from yonder mountain height:
What pleasure lives in height (the shepherd sang)
In height and cold, the splendour of the hills?
180   But cease to move so near the Heavens, and cease
To glide a sunbeam by the blasted Pine,
To sit a star upon the sparkling spire;
And come, for Love is of the valley, come,
For Love is of the valley, come thou down
185   And find him; by the happy threshold, he,
Or hand in hand with Plenty in the maize,
Or red with spirted purple of the vats,
Or foxlike in the vine; nor cares to walk
With Death and Morning on the silver horns,

vii *177*]   O Daughter of the height and of the cold
          Come to us, mountain shepherdess and say *B*;
             Descend, descend from yonder mountain height. *C 1st reading*
vii *177–80*]   Descend, O maiden, from thy mountain home.
          Why art thou fond to move so near the Heaven?
          What pleasure lives in height? in height and cold? *A*
vii *178–80*]   What pleasure lives in height, in height and cold
          And splendour: come for Love is of the vale
          And waits thee. Cease to move so near the Heavens *B*
vii *180*]   Descend, descend and move no more in Heaven, *C.*
vii *180–82*]   *A fragmentary draft at first lineated these lines differently:* '...
Heavens, to glide / A sunbeam ... Pine, to sit / A star ... spire, but come'.
vii *181. To*] Nor *C.*   J. McCue compares *Paradise Lost* iv 555–6: 'Thither came
Uriel, gliding through the Eeven / On a Sun beam, swift as a shooting starr'.
vii *182. To*] Nor *C.   spire*] spires *A.*
vii *183–4*]   But come, for Love is of the vale, descend *C.*
vii *183–8*]   And come O come for Love is of the Vale.
          And come, for Love is of the Vale, nor walks *B*
vii *183–95*]   To hang a flower on furrowed stairs of ice
          That roll the torrent from their dusky doors
          Where there is death among the silver horns
          And madness in the stream and in the snow.
             But leave the cold, the death, and let the wild *A*
vii *186–7*] Not *C.*
vii *188. Or*] And *C 1st reading. Song of Solomon* ii 15, 'Take us the foxes, the
little foxes, that spoil the vines; for our vines have tender grapes.' Turner
suggests the influence of Theocritus i 48–9.   *walk*: H.T. compares *Hamlet* I i
166–7: 'But look, the morn in russet mantle clad / Walks o'er the dew of yon
high eastward hill.'
vii *189. silver horns*] *1854*; Silver Horns *1847–53*. T. wrote (mid-Nov. 1852?):
'The silver horns of the mountain range before which the shepherd stands are
simply the snowy peaks. You know there is a Silberhorn in Switzerland so

190   Nor wilt thou snare him in the white ravine,
       Nor find him dropt upon the firths of ice,
       That huddling slant in furrow-cloven falls
       To roll the torrent out of dusky doors:
       But follow; let the torrent dance thee down
195   To find him in the valley; let the wild
       Lean-headed Eagles yelp alone, and leave
       The monstrous ledges there to slope, and spill
       Their thousand wreaths of dangling water-smoke,
       That like a broken purpose waste in air:
200   So waste not thou; but come; for all the vales

called from its beautifully shaped snow peak. Silver (by the bye) ought not to be spelt as it is with a capital letter in that passage. The Shepherd personifying Love personifies likewise the lifelessness of those high places where not a lichen grows as Death and as to Morning which is personified too. No doubt he has for years seen its earliest light moving on the mountains when all the valleys were in shade. He says figuratively Love cannot live in those snowy heights, where all is lifeless in the cold lights of Morning. I have expressed myself clumsily, but I hope you see what I mean' (*Letters* ii 49). John Churton Collins had noticed Silberhorn, and pointed to a suggestion of Diana's crescent.

vii *190* ∧ *1*] Or couched behind the shower of spouted brooks *C, deleted*.
vii *190*] Nor wilt thou find him clinging to the cleft *B*.   snare] catch *C 1st reading*.
vii *191*]   Nor couched behind the shower of spouted brooks
        Nor lies he flushed upon the firths of ice *B*
vii *192*. Cp. *Comus* 495: 'the huddling brook'.
vii *193*. 'The opening of the gorge is called dusky as a contrast with the snows all about' (T.).
vii *194–5*]   But follow from the dusky doors and let
        The torrent lead thee till thou light on Love
        [The torrent dance thee down and find him here: *C*]
        And leave the height the death and let the wild *B, C*
vii *196–7*. Cp. Theocritus xi, the apostrophe of Polyphemus to Galatea – e.g. l. 42: 'O leave it be, the blue blue sea, to gasp an't will o' the shore'.
vii *196*. leave] come *B*.
vii *197*] And let the monstrous ledges lean to spill *B*.   slope] slant *D*.
vii *199*. Cp. John Armstrong's *Art of Preserving Health* (1744, *Lincoln*) ii 427–8: 'The virgin stream / In boiling wastes its finer soul in air'. Also Sir William Jones (whose works, too, are at *Lincoln*), *The Palace of Fortune*: 'To catch each rising wish, each ardent prayer, / And some to grant, and some to waste in air.'   a broken] a failing *A, B*; an idle *C, D*.   broken purpose: see vi *178n*.
vii *200*. So] But *B 1st reading, C 1st reading*.   but come] descend *A, C 1st reading*. for ... vales] the happy vale *B*.   vales] vale *C*.

Await thee; azure pillars of the hearth
Arise to thee; the children call, and I
Thy shepherd pipe, and sweet is every sound,
Sweeter thy voice, but every sound is sweet;
205 Myriads of rivulets hurrying through the lawn,
The moan of doves in immemorial elms,
And murmuring of innumerable bees.'

So she low-toned; while with shut eyes I lay
Listening; then looked. Pale was the perfect face;
210 The bosom with long sighs laboured; and meek
Seemed the full lips, and mild the luminous eyes,
And the voice trembled and the hand. She said
Brokenly, that she knew it, she had failed
In sweet humility; had failed in all;
215 That all her labour was but as a block
Left in the quarry; but she still were loth,
She still were loth to yield herself to one
That wholly scorned to help their equal rights
Against the sons of men, and barbarous laws.
220 She prayed me not to judge their cause from her
That wronged it, sought far less for truth than power
In knowledge: something wild within her breast,
A greater than all knowledge, beat her down.
And she had nursed me there from week to week:
225 Much had she learnt in little time. In part
It was ill counsel had misled the girl

---

vii *201. Await*] Awaits B, C.   *azure . . . hearth*] many a hearth and many
a home A.

vii *201.* Adapted from *The Invasion of Russia by Napoleon Buonaparte* 15–16: 'no
exulting smoke / From her high halls in azure column broke' Cp. Ovid,
Pontic Epistles I iii 33–4, on Ulysses: *non dubia est Ithaci prudentia, sed tamen
optat / fumum de patriis posse videre focis.* ('None doubt the Ithacan's wisdom,
but yet he prays that he may see the smoke from his native hearth.')

vii *202. Arise to thee*] Await thee: come: A.

vii *205. lawn*] lawns A.

vii *205–7*]   The household hum of many a matron's wheel,
              The bleat of ewe, the breeze, the low of kine B, *bracketed for
              deletion*

Cp. *Sense and Conscience* 46–9: 'hum of murmurous bees . . . moan of
waterfalls . . . voice of doves'.

vii *206.* T. compares Virgil, *Eclogues* i 58: *nec gemere aëria cessabit turtur ab ulmo.*

vii *207.* A creative oddity may have transformed T.'s journal-note in
Switzerland, 10 Aug. 1846 (where he then wrote this poem): 'infernal chatter
of innumerous apes' (*Letters* i 260), *apes* being Latin bees.

To vex true hearts: yet was she but a girl –
'Ah fool, and made myself a Queen of farce!
When comes another such? never, I think,
Till the Sun drop, dead, from the signs.'
230   Her voice
Choked, and her forehead sank upon her hands,
And her great heart through all the faultful Past
Went sorrowing in a pause I dared not break;
Till notice of a change in the dark world
235 Was lispt about the acacias, and a bird,
That early woke to feed her little ones,
Sent from a dewy breast a cry for light:
She moved, and at her feet the volume fell.

'Blame not thyself too much,' I said, 'nor
    blame
240 Too much the sons of men and barbarous laws;
These were the rough ways of the world till now.
Henceforth thou hast a helper, me, that know
The woman's cause is man's: they rise or sink
Together, dwarfed or godlike, bond or free:
245 For she that out of Lethe scales with man
The shining steps of Nature, shares with man
His nights, his days, moves with him to one goal,
Stays all the fair young planet in her hands –
If she be small, slight-natured, miserable,

vii *229–30*]   To lapse so far from sweet humility
              The mother of all virtues, to desire
              Knowledge for power, power more than truth!
              When comes another such? Never I think
              Till the last fire shall catch and flap from peak
              To peak across the world, and the sun hang
              Dead in the signs. *H.Nbk 25*
vii *243–6*]   The cause of man and woman one: they rise,
              They sink, are free or thralls at once: if she
              That steps with man from the vast silence, shares *ULC MS*
vii *244*. Cp. *1 Corinthians* xii 13, 'whether we be Jews or Gentiles, whether
we be bond or free'.
vii *249–50*. Killham (pp. 262–5) quotes from Robert Chambers's *Vestiges
of Creation* 'two passages . . . which have a direct bearing upon feminism.
The first discusses in general terms the evils present in keeping classes of
societies in an unjust subordination; the other takes this much further by
stating as an indisputable fact that if women suffer weak health or misery,
they may fail to transmit acquired characteristics to their children, and the
whole society will in time revert to a lower condition.'

250 How shall men grow? but work no more alone!
     Our place is much: as far as in us lies
     We two will serve them both in aiding her –
     Will clear away the parasitic forms
     That seem to keep her up but drag her down –
255 Will leave her space to burgeon out of all
     Within her – let her make herself her own
     To give or keep, to live and learn and be
     All that not harms distinctive womanhood.
     For woman is not undevelopt man,
260 But diverse: could we make her as the man,
     Sweet Love were slain: his dearest bond is this,
     Not like to like, but like in difference.
     Yet in the long years liker must they grow;
     The man be more of woman, she of man;
265 He gain in sweetness and in moral height,
     Nor lose the wrestling thews that throw the world;
     She mental breadth, nor fail in childward care,
     Nor lose the childlike in the larger mind;
     Till at the last she set herself to man,
270 Like perfect music unto noble words;
     And so these twain, upon the skirts of Time,

vii 250–3] 1850;   How shall men grow? We two will serve them both
                    In aiding her, strip off, as in us lies,
                    (Our place is much) the parasitic forms 1847–8
vii 255. space . . . all] 1850; field to burgeon and to bloom 1847–8.
vii 256] 1850; From all within her, make herself her own 1847–8.
vii 261. : his] 1850; , whose 1847–8.
vii 264. Cp. a draft by T.
            And if aught be comprising in itself
            The man, the woman, let it sit [apart]
            Godlike, alone, or only rapt on heaven –
            What need for such to wed? or if there be
            Men-women, let them wed with women-men
            And make a proper marriage. H.Nbk 25
Quoted by Sir Charles Tennyson, Nineteenth Century cix (1931) 633. Cp.
On One who Affected an Effeminate Manner (III 217), and Locksley Hall Sixty
Years After 48n (p. 643)
vii 268] 1850; More as the double-natured Poet each: 1847–8. Cp. Wherefore, in
these dark ages of the Press 16–17: 'And if I be, as truecast Poets are, / Half
woman-natured, typing all mankind'.
vii 271] ULC MS has, as deleted drafts hereabouts:
            For yet the world is hardly grown but I
            Foresee them on the Titan knees of Time

            For all is yet the giant babe that strives
            To strangle dragons in his crib but I

Sit side by side, full-summed in all their powers,
Dispensing harvest, sowing the To-be,
Self-reverent each and reverencing each,
275 Distinct in individualities,
But like each other even as those who love.
Then comes the statelier Eden back to men:
Then reign the world's great bridals, chaste and
    calm:
Then springs the crowning race of humankind.
May these things be!'
280   Sighing she spoke 'I fear
They will not.'
         'Dear, but let us type them now
In our own lives, and this proud watchword rest
Of equal; seeing either sex alone
Is half itself, and in true marriage lies
285 Nor equal, nor unequal: each fulfils
Defect in each, and always thought in thought,
Purpose in purpose, will in will, they grow,
The single pure and perfect animal,
The two-celled heart beating, with one full stroke,
Life.'
290   And again sighing she spoke: 'A dream
That once was mine! what woman taught you this?'

'Alone,' I said, 'from earlier than I know,
Immersed in rich foreshadowings of the world,
I loved the woman: he, that doth not, lives
295 A drowning life, besotted in sweet self,
Or pines in sad experience worse than death,
Or keeps his winged affections clipt with crime:
Yet was there one through whom I loved her, one
Not learnèd, save in gracious household ways,
300 Not perfect, nay, but full of tender wants,
No Angel, but a dearer being, all dipt

---

vii 272. Cp. PR i 14–15: 'With prosperous wing full summ'd to tell of deeds /
Above Heroic'.
vii 275. Killham (p. 260) points out that this line was originally written as
The Ante-Chamber 27 in Heath MS, but that H.T. dropped it in Mem. i 199.
(Mat. i 243 had included it.)
vii 282. rest: be no more mentioned (H.T. in Wallace's edition, 1891,
Lincoln).
vii 295. A ... life,] All rotted and ULC MS.

In Angel instincts, breathing Paradise,
Interpreter between the Gods and men,
Who looked all native to her place, and yet
305 On tiptoe seemed to touch upon a sphere
Too gross to tread, and all male minds perforce
Swayed to her from their orbits as they moved,
And girdled her with music. Happy he
With such a mother! faith in womankind
310 Beats with his blood, and trust in all things high
Comes easy to him, and though he trip and fall
He shall not blind his soul with clay.'
                              'But I,'
Said Ida, tremulously, 'so all unlike–
It seems you love to cheat yourself with words:
315 This mother is your model. I have heard
Of your strange doubts: they well might be: I seem
A mockery to my own self. Never, Prince;
You cannot love me.'
                    'Nay but thee' I said
'From yearlong poring on thy pictured eyes,
320 Ere seen I loved, and loved thee seen, and saw
Thee woman through the crust of iron moods
That masked thee from men's reverence up,
             and forced
Sweet love on pranks of saucy boyhood: now,
Given back to life, to life indeed, through thee,
325 Indeed I love: the new day comes, the light
Dearer for night, as dearer thou for faults
Lived over: lift thine eyes; my doubts are dead,
My haunting sense of hollow shows: the change,
This truthful change in thee has killed it. Dear,
330 Look up, and let thy nature strike on mine,
Like yonder morning on the blind half-world;
Approach and fear not; breathe upon my brows;
In that fine air I tremble, all the past

vii *313. tremulously,*'] *1850*; 'so unlike, *1847–8.*
vii *315-7. I . . . self*] *1851; not 1847–50.*
vii *319* ∧ *20*] Or some mysterious or magnetic touch, *1847–8.*
vii *320* ∧ *1*] (So much my faith was euphrasy to sight) *ULC MS.*
vii *325–32*]   I love indeed: thine image falls upon me
              As sunrise through the blazon of a saint
              On clouds of incense: breathe... *ULC MS*
vii *327–9. my . . . Dear*] *1851*; doubt me no more *1847–50.* 'You have
become a real woman to me' (T.).

Melts mist-like into this bright hour, and this
335 Is morn to more, and all the rich to-come
Reels, as the golden Autumn woodland reels
Athwart the smoke of burning weeds. Forgive me,
I waste my heart in signs: let be. My bride,
My wife, my life. O we will walk this world,
340 Yoked in all exercise of noble end,
And so through those dark gates across the wild
That no man knows. Indeed I love thee: come,
Yield thyself up: my hopes and thine are one:
Accomplish thou my manhood and thyself;
345 Lay thy sweet hands in mine and trust to me.'

CONCLUSION

So closed our tale, of which I give you all
The random scheme as wildly as it rose:
The words are mostly mine; for when we ceased
There came a minute's pause, and Walter said,
5   'I wish she had not yielded!' then to me,
'What, if you drest it up poetically?'
So prayed the men, the women: I gave assent:
Yet how to bind the scattered scheme of seven
Together in one sheaf? What style could suit?
10   The men required that I should give throughout
The sort of mock-heroic gigantesque,
With which we bantered little Lilia first:

vii *335. Is . . . more*] *1851*; I scarce believe *1847–50*.
vii *335–7*. Adapted from *In Memoriam: Epilogue* 96 ∧ 7, MS (*p. 481*).
vii *337. weeds*] *1851*; flowers *1847–8*; leaves *1850*.

Conclusion
c 1–35] *1850*; Here closed our compound story which at first
Had only [Perhaps, but *1848*] meant to banter little
     maids
With mock-heroics and with parody:
But slipt in some strange way, crost with burlesque,
From mock to earnest, even into tones
Of tragic, and with less and less of jest
To such a serious end that Lilia fixt
A showery glance upon her Aunt and said
'You–tell us what we are;' who there began
A treatise, growing with it, and might have flowed
In axiom worthier to be graven on rock,
Than all that lasts of old-world hieroglyph,
Or lichen-fretted Rune and arrowhead; *1847–8*

The women–and perhaps they felt their power,
For something in the ballads which they sang,
15   Or in their silent influence as they sat,
Had ever seemed to wrestle with burlesque,
And drove us, last, to quite a solemn close–
They hated banter, wished for something real,
A gallant fight, a noble princess–why
20   Not make her true-heroic–true-sublime?
Or all, they said, as earnest as the close?
Which yet with such a framework scarce could be.
Then rose a little feud betwixt the two,
Betwixt the mockers and the realists:
25   And I, betwixt them both, to please them both,
And yet to give the story as it rose,
I moved as in a strange diagonal,
And maybe neither pleased myself nor them.

But Lilia pleased me, for she took no part
30   In our dispute: the sequel of the tale
Had touched her; and she sat, she plucked the
        grass,
She flung it from her, thinking: last, she fixt
A showery glance upon her aunt, and said,
'You–tell us what we are' who might have told,
35   For she was crammed with theories out of books,
But that there rose a shout: the gates were closed
At sunset, and the crowd were swarming now,
To take their leave, about the garden rails.

So I and some went out to these: we climbed
40   The slope to Vivian-place, and turning saw
The happy valleys, half in light, and half
Far-shadowing from the west, a land of peace;
Gray halls alone among their massive groves;
Trim hamlets; here and there a rustic tower
45   Half-lost in belts of hop and breadths of wheat;
The shimmering glimpses of a stream; the seas;
A red sail, or a white; and far beyond,
Imagined more than seen, the skirts of France.

c 27. In the proofs of Wallace's edition (1891, *Lincoln*), T. deleted 'perhaps'
in the note: 'The expression was perhaps suggested by the principle of the
Parallelogram of Forces.'
c 37. sunset] *1850*; sundown *1847–8*.
c 39] *1850*; And I and some went out, and mingled with them. *1847–8*.
c 40–80] *1850 (except l. 65); not 1847–8*. 'Written just after the disturbances
in France, February 1848, when Louis Philippe was compelled to abdicate'
(T.).

'Look there, a garden!' said my college friend,
50 The Tory member's elder son, 'and there!
God bless the narrow sea which keeps her off,
And keeps our Britain, whole within herself,
A nation yet, the rulers and the ruled—
Some sense of duty, something of a faith,
55 Some reverence for the laws ourselves have made,
Some patient force to change them when we will,
Some civic manhood firm against the crowd—
But yonder, whiff! there comes a sudden heat,
The gravest citizen seems to lose his head,
60 The king is scared, the soldier will not fight,
The little boys begin to shoot and stab,
A kingdom topples over with a shriek
Like an old woman, and down rolls the world
In mock heroics stranger than our own;
65 Revolts, republics, revolutions, most
No graver than a schoolboys' barring out;
Too comic for the solemn things they are,
Too solemn for the comic touches in them,
Like our wild Princess with as wise a dream
70 As some of theirs—God bless the narrow seas!
I wish they were a whole Atlantic broad.'

'Have patience,' I replied, 'ourselves are full
Of social wrong; and maybe wildest dreams
Are but the needful preludes of the truth:
75 For me, the genial day, the happy crowd,
The sport half-science, fill me with a faith.
This fine old world of ours is but a child
Yet in the go-cart. Patience! Give it time
To learn its limbs: there is a hand that guides.'

80   In such discourse we gained the garden rails,
And there we saw Sir Walter where he stood,
Before a tower of crimson holly-hoaks,
Among six boys, head under head, and looked
No little lily-handed Baronet he,
85 A great broad-shouldered genial Englishman,
A lord of fat prize-oxen and of sheep,
A raiser of huge melons and of pine,
A patron of some thirty charities,

c 65. *most*] *1853*; all *1850–51*.
c 84. 'An imaginary character' (T.).
c 87. *pine*: 'pine-apple' (T.).

A pamphleteer on guano and on grain,
90 A quarter-sessions chairman, abler none;
Fair-haired and redder than a windy morn;
Now shaking hands with him, now him, of those
That stood the nearest – now addressed to speech –
Who spoke few words and pithy, such as closed
95 Welcome, farewell, and welcome for the year
To follow: a shout rose again, and made
The long line of the approaching rookery swerve
From the elms, and shook the branches of the deer
From slope to slope through distant ferns, and rang
100 Beyond the bourn of sunset; O, a shout
More joyful than the city-roar that hails
Premier or king! Why should not these great Sirs
Give up their parks some dozen times a year
To let the people breathe? So thrice they cried,
105 I likewise, and in groups they streamed away.

But we went back to the Abbey, and sat on,
So much the gathering darkness charmed: we sat
But spoke not, rapt in nameless reverie,
Perchance upon the future man: the walls
110 Blackened about us, bats wheeled, and owls whooped,
And gradually the powers of the night,
That range above the region of the wind,
Deepening the courts of twilight broke them up
Through all the silent spaces of the worlds,
115 Beyond all thought into the Heaven of Heavens.

Last little Lilia, rising quietly,
Disrobed the glimmering statue of Sir Ralph
From those rich silks, and home well-pleased we
went.

c 96. rose] 1850; arose 1847–8.
c 102. should not] 1850; don't 1847–8.   great] 1850; acred 1847–8.
c 103. Give] 1850; Throw 1847–8.
c 104. To] 1850; And 1847–8.
c 108. But spoke not] 1850; Saying little 1847–8.
c 111–15. Incorporated verbatim from The Lover's Tale i 52–61n, MS (I 330).
c 115. the Heaven of Heavens: Nehemiah ix 6.
c 116. quietly] 1850; without sound 1847–8.

296 In Memoriam A. H. H.

OBIIT MDCCCXXXIII

Published, anonymously, *1850*.

The edition of *In Memoriam* by S. Shatto and M. Shaw (1982, abbreviated S & S) is notable, first, for its full collation of all MSS (including the *Trinity MS*, released from interdiction), with variants of punctuation; and second, for its consideration of sequences of sections within the poem; there is also a full commentary, with particular attention to classical precedent. (But strictures on many of the editorial decisions are voiced by W. E. Fredeman, *The Library* 6th ser. vi, 1984, 306–15.)

Arthur Hallam. On 15 Sept. 1833, T.'s friend Arthur Henry Hallam died at Vienna. On 1 Oct. T. was sent the news: 'Your friend Sir, and my much loved Nephew, Arthur Hallam, is no more – it has pleased God, to remove him from this his first scene of Existence, to that better World, for which he was Created. He died at Vienna on his return from Buda, by Apoplexy, and I believe his Remains come by Sea from Trieste' (*AHH*, p. 792; *Mem.* i 105). Kolb notes: 'Since mail was delivered only three times a week to the Spilsby postoffice, the Tennysons may not have learned of AHH's death until toward the end of the week, close to the date (6 October) of the composition of *In Memoriam* ix. The news reached the Hallam family on 28 September 1833' (*AHH*, p. 793). He was buried at Clevedon, Somerset, 3 Jan. 1834. No event in T.'s life was of greater importance. Arthur Hallam was born 1 Feb. 1811, and so was eighteen months younger than T. They met soon after Hallam came up to Trinity College, Cambridge, in Oct. 1828. 'Alfred was already a prominent figure in the College by that time and Hallam's passion for poetry must almost certainly have brought the two together before long' (*CT*, p. 66). Hallam's background was sufficiently different from T.'s for T. to find in him not only a lovable person but a largeness of aspiration and moneyed culture. The son of Henry Hallam the historian, he had been at Eton, where he made the friendship of Gladstone and J. Milnes Gaskell; since leaving Eton in 1827, he had spent some months in Italy and had become a proficient scholar and even poet in the language. But, as Sir Charles Tennyson notes in his excellent account of the friendship, Hallam had need of friends at Cambridge (Gladstone and Gaskell had gone to Oxford), and 'Alfred's need of a friend was even greater. The early months of 1829 were a time of peculiar distress for him, owing to the disastrous effect on Dr Tennyson of Frederick's rustication and the misery which the Doctor's condition was causing at Somersby.' Later in 1829, Hallam wrote a poem to T., and also praised him warmly in a poem to R. J. Tennant of Trinity College (*CT*, p. 77). At Christmas 1829 (April 1830, on Kolb's arguments; *AHH*, p. 673 *n*), Hallam met T.'s sister Emily, to whom he wrote a sonnet before the end of the year and with whom he was soon in love. In 1830 he went on a trip to the Pyrenees with T., which T. was to remember in detail for the rest of his life. Hallam's love for Emily, however, ran into difficulties; Henry Hallam tried to discourage the match (Arthur had already been rapturously in love elsewhere) by insisting that Hallam should not see Emily or correspond with her till after his 21st birthday. In Aug. 1831 Hallam wrote a eulogistic but perceptive review of T.'s *1830* volume in the *Englishman's Magazine*, 'On Some of the Characteristics of Modern Poetry and on the Lyrical Poetry of Alfred Tennyson'. The influence upon T. of Hallam's writings was not limited to this. His *Theodicæa Novissima* (1831) was a considerable influence on the religious thinking of *In Memoriam*, though in general terms. It was to be at T.'s request that the *Theodicæa* was included in Hallam's *Remains* (1834). P. Flynn studies Hallam's arguments in relation to T., *Studies in English Literature* xix (1979) 705–20. Hallam and T. spent July 1832 in a tour of the Rhine country. In 1833 Hallam's engagement to Emily was recognised. During all this period, the background to T.'s friendship for Hallam was one of dark family troubles and hostile reviews (both for *1830* and *1832*) which wounded T. deeply. On 15 Sept. 1833 Hallam died – 'a blood-vessel near the brain had suddenly burst' (*Mem.* i 105).

In the words of Sir Charles Tennyson (p. 145):

'The shock to all Arthur's friends was terrible. The Cambridge circle had for so long regarded him as their centre. With his vivacity, unselfishness and breadth of interests he touched all their lives at so many points, that they seemed almost to have lost a part of themselves. The letters which passed between them as the news reached one after another, and the references in memoirs and poems written years afterwards by Gladstone, Alford, Trench, Milnes and others, all show their deep affection for him as a friend and their profound admiration for his intellectual powers.

'To both Alfred and Emily the blow was overwhelming. On Arthur's betrothed it fell at a moment when, after years of trial and disappointment, there seemed good prospect that their hopes would at last be crowned with marriage. For Alfred, a sudden and brutal stroke had annihilated in a moment a love "passing the love of women". The prop, round which his own growth had twined itself for four fruitful years, was suddenly removed. A lifelong prospect, founded on his own friendship and Emily's hoped-for union with his friend, was blotted out instantly and for ever.'

And, as Sir Charles adds (p. 146), 'The wretched state of poor Edward, the fears about Charles and Septimus [T.'s brothers] and the disastrous reception of his own work added to his misery.' Yet the misery spurred him almost immediately into writing some of his greatest work, much of it not explicitly about Hallam. (But see *On a Mourner*, p. 135.)

The very high estimate which T. had of Hallam's gifts was fully shared by the other friends. John Kemble wrote to his sister (*Mem.* i 106):

'This is a loss which will most assuredly be felt by this age, for if ever man was born for great things he was. Never was a more powerful intellect joined to a purer and holier heart; and the whole illuminated with the richest imagination, with the most sparkling yet the kindest wit.'

Gladstone wrote at the time (*Mem.* i 108): 'When much time has elapsed, when most bereavements will be forgotten, he will still be remembered, and his place, I fear, will be felt to be still vacant, singularly as his mind was calculated by its native tendencies to work powerfully and for good, in an age full of import to the nature and destinies of man.' Gladstone later reiterated this praise when writing of *In Memoriam* (*Mem.* i 299). See J. Kolb, 'The Hero and His Worshippers: The History of Arthur Henry Hallam's Letters', *Bulletin of the John Rylands Library* lvi (1973) 150–73.

The growth of the poem. It is clear from the MSS that T. set about some sections of *In Memoriam* in Oct. 1833. He will have been affected by the plans to publish Hallam's works. R. J. Tennant wrote to him, 26 Nov. 1833 (*Letters* i 97; *Mem.* i 498):

'It appears to be a universal wish among them, that whatever writings Arthur has left should be collected and published, that there may be some memorial of him amongst us, which though it will fall very far short of what was hoped and expected of him, will yet be highly gratifying to his friends, and as we think will not be without interest and value to many others'.

Henry Hallam wrote to T. about the *Remains* (*Letters* i 106–7; *Mem.* i 108): 'It will be necessary to prefix a short Memoir. I must rely on his contemporaries and most intimate friends to furnish me with part of my materials; and I should wish to have any thing that may be thought most worthy of being mentioned, communicated to me by letter. Perhaps you would do something. I should desire to have the character of his mind, his favourite studies and pursuits, his habits and views, delineated'.

T.'s reply to this (14 Feb. 1834, *Letters* i 108; *Eversley* iii 258) makes clear his long-term project:

'I attempted to draw up a memoir of his life and character, but I failed to do him justice. I failed even to please myself. I could scarcely have pleased you. I hope to be able at a future period to concentrate whatever powers I may possess on the construction of some tribute to those high speculative endowments and comprehensive sympathies which I ever loved to contemplate; but at present, though somewhat ashamed at my own weakness, I find the object yet is too near me to permit of any very accurate delineation. You, with your clear insight into human nature, may perhaps not wonder that in the dearest service I could have been employed in, I should be found most deficient.'

T. sent to his grandfather a copy of Hallam's *Remains*, mid-July 1834: 'I thought it would not be unpleasing to you, as the Head of that family to which had he lived he would have been allied yet more closely than he was by the bonds of friendship, to receive a copy from me. I wish indeed that he had had more frequent opportunities of conversing with and seeing you. I am sure you could not have failed of loving and admiring the many excellent qualities for which his contemporaries esteemed him: but Life and Death are in the hands of God.

Mr. Hallam wrote to me some time ago to draw up a memoir of his son's Life and character: but at that time my heart seemed too crushed and all my energies too paralysed to permit me any compliance with his request, otherwise I had not been found wanting in the dearest office I could discharge to the memory of one whom I can never forget' (*Letters* i 112).

That T. had the idea of a sequence as early as 1834 is supported by M. Mason's observation: 'T.'s decision, whenever it occurred, to reserve the special ABBA stanza for all poems on Hallam's death, and only those poems, must have followed on some kind of plan to assemble these as a group . . . The latest of the non-*In Memoriam* poems cast in the stanza . . . cannot be dated after 1834. And the last stanzaic poem relating to Hallam's death that does *not* use the *In Memoriam* rhyme scheme is probably *Break, break, break*, ascribed . . . to the spring of 1834' (*Studies in Tennyson*, ed. H. Tennyson, 1981, p. 160).

On the relations between *Morte d'Arthur, In Memoriam, Ode on the Death of the Duke of Wellington*, and *Idylls of the King* (each honouring an Arthur), see C. Y. Lang, *Tennyson's Arthurian Psycho-drama* (1983). On T.'s state of mind immediately after Hallam's death, see R. W. Rader (pp. 11–21). Also *Hark! the dogs howl!* (I 607), which H.T. described as 'the germ of *In Memoriam*'. (Details of the MSS are in the next section.) The marriage, in Jan. 1842, of T.'s sister Emily (who had been betrothed to Hallam) to Richard Jesse aroused anger in some members of the Hallam family (see *Letters* i 194–5), and may have played some part in T.'s continued reluctance to publish the poem.

Of a visit to T. at Christmas 1841 (*Mem.* i 202), Edmund Lushington wrote: 'In the meantime [since 1840?] the number of the memorial poems had rapidly increased since I had seen the poet, his book containing many that were new to me. Some I heard him repeat before I had seen them in writing, others I learnt to know first from the book itself which he kindly allowed me to look through without stint.' On 17 April 1842, Aubrey de Vere records that T. 'read me some beautiful Elegies' (Wilfrid Ward, *Aubrey de Vere*, 1904, p. 71). T. wrote to Venables, 16 July 1844: 'You had better keep the MSS which you mention till I see you. I suppose I must myself have slipt it behind your books to keep it out of people's way, for I scarcely liked everyone who came in to overhaul those poems and moreover the volume itself was not fit to be seen, foul with the rust dust and mildew of innumerable moons' (*Letters* i 226). On 30 Nov. 1844, T. wrote to Aunt Russell (*Letters* i 231, correcting *Mem.* i 243): 'With respect to the non-publication of those poems which you mention, it is partly occasioned by the considerations you speak of, and partly by my sense of their present imperfectness: perhaps they will not see the light till I have ceased to be. I cannot tell, but I have no wish to send them out yet.' On 29 Jan. 1845, FitzGerald reported that Spedding was putting pressure on T. to publish the elegies (his *Letters* i 478): 'A.T. has near a volume of poems – elegiac – in memory of Arthur Hallam. Don't you think the world wants other notes than elegiac now? Lycidas is the utmost length an elegiac should reach. But

Spedding praises: and I suppose the elegiacs will see daylight – public daylight – one day.' Of the summer of 1845, Lushington reported: 'He had then completed many of the cantos in *In Memoriam* .... He said to me, "I have brought in your marriage at the end of *In Memoriam*," and then showed me those poems of *In Memoriam* which were finished and which were a perfectly novel surprise to me' (*Mem.* i 203). Before 24 Jan. 1849, T. had promised de Vere 'to *print* at least his exquisite Elegies, and let his friends have a few copies'. T. wrote to Patmore about the MS, 28 Feb. 1849 (*Letters* i 297 and *n.*). Under 18 Aug. 1849, William Allingham's *Diary* records that Patmore showed him the MS of *In Memoriam*: 'Mrs Patmore had copied it out for the press, and Tennyson gave her the original.' On 7 Dec. 1849, FitzGerald reported to Frederick T. that T. 'was about to print but (I think) not to publish, those Elegiacs on Hallam' (i 657). W. D. Paden, in his important study of the final stages of *In Memoriam* (*The Library*, 5th ser. viii (1953) 259–73), suggested that T.'s letter to de Vere (*Mem.* i 282) was written soon after 13 Nov. 1849; *Letters* i 321 dates it mid-Feb. 1850.

'With respect to the Elegies, I cannot say that I have turned my attention to them lately – I do not know whether I have done anything new in that quarter since you saw them, but I believe I am going to print them and then I needn't tell you that you will be perfectly welcome to a copy – on the condition that when the book is published, this vaunt courier of it shall be either sent back to me, or die the death by fire in Curragh Chase. I shall print about 25 copies and let them out among friends under the same condition of either return or cremation.'

In early March 1850, T. wrote to Moxon: 'You may print these and distribute the types. I have not been able from the state of my head to do anything more to them and there is a great deal that wants doing – however print ½ dozen copies and send me them. Give none away and retain none yourself' (*Letters* i 321–2). By 21 March, Patmore had 'one out of some half-dozen copies of Tennyson's Elegies that have been printed strictly for private perusal' (*The P.R.B. Journal*, ed. W. E. Fredeman, 1975, p. 64). For this private issue or trial edition, *Mem.* i 297 says 'May' in error; and half a dozen, not twenty five, were printed. Patmore wrote to Allingham, 17 April 1850: 'His elegies are printed. I have one of the *only* half dozen copies at present in existence. He talks of publishing them next Christmas' (B. Champneys, *Memoir of Patmore*, 1900, ii 173). Very few copies are in existence: Professor Paden used one belonging to C. B. Tinker; there is one in the Bodleian Library, and one in the Tennyson Research Centre at Lincoln. All variants are given below. Mrs E. B. Mattes was the first to comment critically on the significance of the differences between the trial edition and *1850*; she remarks that the additions seem mainly meant to qualify an over-assurance, e.g. T. added lvi (the most openly sceptical) and xcvi on doubt (*In Memoriam: The Way of a Soul*, 1951). It has been said (*CT*, p. 241) that the trial edition was entitled *Fragments of an Elegy*; though T. certainly considered this title (*Mem.* i 293), it does not appear on the surviving copies. T. sometimes called it *The Way of the Soul* (*Mem.* i 393). It has also been said that the title *In Memoriam* was suggested by Emily Sellwood, whom T. married in June 1850 (*CT*, pp. 247, 350; S & S, p. 22); but the letter by E.T. (26 June 1864) does not make clear whether she suggested or preferred the title: 'Idylls Chiefly of Seventy Years Ago. I am anxious about the title, dearest, will this do? In Memoriam has proved a good title so perhaps I may be right in this too. Idylls of the King too' (E.T., *Letters*, p. 181). Emily Sellwood wrote to Catherine Rawnsley, 1 April 1850, incorporating a letter from herself to T., expressing her gratitude; her letter also incorporated Charles Kingsley's praise of the poem (*Letters* i 322–4). The copy Emily read may have been a trial edition, not MS (S & S, p. 160). The poem was published at the end of May 1850. W. D. Paden notes that though the poem was anonymous, the first commercial announcement, by an error (a helpful error), gave T. as the author (*Publishers' Circular*, 1 June). The 2nd edition appeared in the latter half of July; the 3rd, end of August; the 4th, Jan. 1851. Martin (p. 341) notes that 'during his lifetime he never allowed an edition to appear with his name on the title-page'. But the poem appeared in 1870, and thereafter, in collected editions of T.

Manuscripts. Many sections can be dated, but we lack evidence for much more than that. The earliest group is in *T.Nbk 17* (*T.Nbk 17* in footnotes below), which dates from 1833–4 and has: xxx, ix, xvii (headed 'II'), xviii (headed 'III'), xxxi–xxxii (a version), lxxxv, and xxviii. H.T. attempted lists of the 'first written sections', but there are discrepancies between the lists which he gave (*Lincoln leaf*, *Mat.* i 127–8, *Mem.* i 109, and *Eversley*). Nevertheless, ix, xxxi, and xxviii appear in all three lists; and lxxxv in both *Mem.* and *Eversley*. (*Mem.* has also xxx, correctly; *Eversley* has also xvii–xviii, correctly. *Mat.* errs in listing i and ii, a mistake probably due to the numbering in *T.Nbk 17*; *Mat.*'s listing xxvi is inexplicable. On these lists, see S. Shatto, *Notes and Queries* June 1978.)

Heath MS (compiled 1833–4) has: ix, xvii–xix, xxx–xxxi, and lxxxv. Of these, only xix is not in *T.Nbk 17*, and is therefore probably of 1834.

Both the later, full-scale *Trinity MS* (*T.MS* in footnotes below) and the similar *Lincoln MS* (*L.MS* in footnotes below) deserve to be described in some detail, but neither is of much help in dating, because of the time-span which they cover. Both these MSS are dated Nov. 1842; the significance is uncertain, but it may indicate that it was then that *Lincoln MS* took over from *Trinity MS*. On the Huntington MSS see S & S, p. 11.

T.MS is watermarked 1834, and dated Nov. 1842. It began, but did not remain, a fair copy, and often has more than one section on a page. It includes some of the earliest sections (e.g. xxx), but there are sheets missing at the beginning of the notebook. (We know from *T.Nbk 17* that ix, xvii–xviii were in existence.) From such evidence as we have, the latest written section included in *T.MS* appears to be li, apparently written Christmas 1841 (*Mem.* i 202–3). It includes cii, which refers to the move from Somersby in 1837, but not ci and ciii on the same subject; nor does it have civ–cv about residence from 1837 at High Beech, or lxxxvi (probably 1839). The likelihood is that *T.MS* mainly represents sections written between 1833 and 1837, but that T. kept it by him at least till 1841. Its sections are not in the published order. The sections it does *not* have are: *Prologue*, ii–xii, xiv–xxii, xxvi–xxvii, xxxix, xlvii, l, lv–lvi, lviii–lix, lxiv, lxix–lxx, lxxii, lxxxiv, lxxxvi–lxxxvii, lxxxix–xc, xcv–ci, ciii, cvi–cvii, cix–cx, cxiii–cxvi, cxviii–cxxii, cxxiv, cxxvii, cxxix–cxxxi, *Epilogue*.

Lincoln MS sets out as virtually a fair copy, with minor corrections and with one section only on the recto of each leaf. But this gradually breaks down, and soon the MS has become altogether less neat and finished. Its first 42 pages are watermarked 1814. The sections are not precisely in the published order. The notebook is dated 3–4–5 Nov. 1842. It adds to *T.MS* many sections which cannot be pre-1837 (on leaving Somersby, on High Beech); it also adds such sections on Evolution as cxxiii. T. read Lyell's *Principles of Geology* at the end of 1836 (*Letters* i 145) and in 1837 (*Mem.* i 162), and these sections were written 'some years before the publication of [Chambers's] *Vestiges of Creation* in 1844' (*Mem.* i 223). The *Lincoln MS* therefore adds to *T.MS* sections from *c.* 1837, but the MS itself may well have been compiled in 1842 (as dated). Its latest written section is even harder to pinpoint. It includes a draft of the *Epilogue*, on the marriage of T.'s sister Cecilia to Edmund Lushington, 10 Oct. 1842. Lushington says, of the summer of 1845: 'He had then completed many of the cantos in *In Memoriam*. . . . He said to me, " I have brought in your marriage at the end of *In Memoriam*, and then showed me those poems of *In Memoriam* which were finished and which were a perfectly novel surprise to me' (*Mem.* i 203). The similarities to Chambers's *Vestiges*, though by no means decisive, suggest that T. may not have written the *Epilogue* till 1844–5, shortly before showing it to Lushington. But since the draft of the *Epilogue* is an early one, the MS may belong to the month after the wedding. (Mrs Mattes – who used only a description of the MS – mistakenly says the *Lincoln MS* does not include the *Epilogue*, by which she dates all that it does include as pre-1845.) As for the date of the earliest of those sections *not* in *Lincoln MS*, which might provide a *terminus ad quem*, the following are *not* in *Lincoln MS*: *Prologue* (dated '1849'); vii–viii; xxxix (published 1869); lix (published 1851); lxxxviii (but in *T.MS*); xci (but in *T.MS*); xcvi–xcvii; cvi; cxiv; cxvi; cxix–cxxi; cxxv (but in *T.MS*); cxxviii (but in *T.MS*); cxxix. Of these, vii–viii, xcvi–xcvii, and cxix–cxxi are not in the trial edition of 1850 either, and so may well not have been written till 1850. Of the remaining sections not in *Lincoln MS*, only cvi can be even tentatively dated; it may belong to *c.* 1845–6. In view of the date of the *Epilogue*, the likelihood is therefore that *Lincoln MS* adds to *T.MS* many of the sections which were written between 1837 and 1845–6. Possibly it was originally compiled in 1842, and it may carry through till 1850.

The other MSS are more fragmentary. There are sections in *Harvard Notebooks* and *Loosepapers*, in the Huntington Library, and in the possession of John Sparrow and of Richard Purdy. All variants from the trial edition and MSS are given below. On the MSS see also S. F. C. Niermeier, *HLB* xix

(1971) 149–59; and J. Sendry, *HLB* xxi (1973) 202–20, and xxvii (1979) 36–64.

T. left unpublished eight drafted sections of the poem; since they might distract a reader from the sequence of the poem, they are printed in Appendix I (*pp. 980–86*).

The stanza. T. says: 'As for the metre of *In Memoriam* I had no notion till 1880 that Lord Herbert of Cherbury had written his occasional verses in the same metre. I believed myself the originator of the metre, until after *In M·m·oriam* came out, when some one told me that Ben Jonson and Sir Philip Sidney had used it.' (But see *Letters* ii 553, 8 Aug. 1870, where T. mentions Jonson and Lord Herbert. Also S & S, pp. 158–9.) The year 1880 refers to John Churton Collins's article in *The Cornhill* (Jan.); T. wrote alongside Collins's reference to Lord Herbert 'I had no notion till I saw it here that such a poem existed' (*Lincoln*). Before *In Memoriam*, T. had used the stanza for many political poems of *c.* 1832, including *Hail Briton.* Early fragments of *In Memoriam* use the *abab* stanza. On T.'s predecessors in using the stanza, and on T.'s approaches to it in his earlier poems, see A. C. Bradley, *A Commentary on In Memoriam* (3rd edn, 1910, pp. 67–70). Culler (p. 159) suggests a relation between the poem's gradual movements and 'the verse form which he had already devised to express his political gradualism'.

The structure. The best discussion is still that in Bradley's *Commentary*, to which should be added T. S. Eliot's essay (*Essays Ancient and Modern*, 1936, and reprinted in J. Killham's collection). See also the chapter on the poem in *Mem.*, which reports T. as saying (i 304–5):

'It must be remembered that this is a poem, *not* an actual biography. It is founded on our friendship, on the engagement of Arthur Hallam to my sister, on his sudden death at Vienna, just before the time fixed for their marriage, and on his burial at Clevedon Church. The poem concludes with the marriage of my youngest sister Cecilia. It was meant to be a kind of *Divina Commedia*, ending with happiness. The sections were written at many different places, and as the phases of our intercourse came to my memory and suggested them. I did not write them with any view of weaving them into a whole, or for publication, until I found that I had written so many. The different moods of sorrow as in a drama are dramatically given, and my conviction that fear, doubts, and suffering will find answer and relief only through Faith in a God of Love. "I" is not always the author speaking of himself, but the voice of the human race speaking through him. After the Death of A.H.H., the divisions of the poem are made by First Xmas Eve (Section xxviii), Second Xmas (lxxviii), Third Xmas Eve (civ and cv etc.).'

To James Knowles, when reading the poem, T. said (*Nineteenth Century* xxxiii (1893) 182):

'It is rather the cry of the whole human race than mine. In the poem altogether private grief swells out into thought of, and hope for, the whole world. It begins with a funeral and ends with a marriage–begins with death and ends in promise of a new life–a sort of Divine Comedy, cheerful at the close. It is a very impersonal poem as well as personal. There is more about myself in *Ulysses*, which was written under the sense of loss and that all had gone by, but that still life must be fought out to the end. It was more written with the feeling of his loss upon me than many poems in *In Memoriam* ... [*sic*] It's too hopeful, this poem, more than I am myself ... [*sic*] The general way of its being written was so queer that if there were a blank space I would put in a poem ... [*sic*] I think of adding another to it, a speculative one, bringing out the thoughts of *The Higher Pantheism*, and showing that all the arguments are about as good on one side as the other, and thus throw man back more on the primitive impulses and feelings.'

These remarks to Knowles were made in Aug. 1870 and March 1871; see G. N. Ray, *Tennyson Reads 'Maud'* (1968), for the notes by Knowles which were the basis of his 1893 article; the important variants in T.'s general comments on the poem are (i) Knowles's recording 'It is rather the cry of the whole human race than mine'; (ii) 'and thus throw man back more and more on the primitive impulses and feelings'. (Quotations below as *Knowles*.) P. L. Elliott has noted that H.T. wrote to Henry Sidgwick (23 May 1893) denying that T. had ever said 'It's too hopeful this poem, more than I am myself' (*The Making of the Memoir*, 1978, pp. 16–17).

T. explained to Knowles that there were nine natural groups or divisions in the poem, as follows: i–viii, ix–xx ('all connected–about the Ship'), xxi–xxvii, xxviii–xlix, l–lviii, lix–lxxi, lxxii–xcviii, xcix–ciii, civ–cxxxi. On the time-sequence in the poem, see *CT* (p. 177). T. refused permission for excerpts in 1867: '*In Memoriam* is an anonymous work and not to be meddled with' (20 April; *Letters* ii 459). But T. permitted F. T. Palgrave to print a selection from the poem in his *Lyrical Poems* from T. (1885), with the sections in a different order. Palgrave reports that the selections 'from *In Memoriam* (peculiarly difficult to frame, from the reasons which I have noted above in regard to Shakespeare's Sonnets) follow a list which he gave me' (*Mem.* ii 503). On this selection, see S & S (p. 25). On likeness and unlikeness to Keble's *The Christian Year* (1827), see Culler (p. 156); and on what it is to read the poem consecutively and cumulatively, Timothy Peltason, *Reading "In Memoriam"* (1985).

Shakespeare's Sonnets. Important both as a source and as an analogue. Benjamin Jowett records (*Mat.* iv 460):

'Once again, perhaps in his weaker moments, he had thought of Shakespeare as happier in having the power to draw himself for his fellow men, and used to think Shakespeare greater in his sonnets than in his plays. But he soon returned to the thought which is indeed the thought of all the world. He would have seemed to me to be reverting for a moment to the great sorrow of his own mind. It would not have been manly or natural to have lived in it always. But in that peculiar phase of mind he found the sonnets a deeper expression of the never to be forgotten love which he felt more than any of the many moods of many minds which appear among his dramas. The love of the sonnets which he so strikingly expressed was a sort of sympathy with Hellenism.'

Fearing a homosexual misconstruction, H.T. cut this for *Mem.*, removing the last sentence and that which begins 'It would not have been manly ...' Arthur Hallam's own love for the *Sonnets* will also have played its part; he had written in his *Influence of Italian Upon English Literature* (1831; Motter, p. 229):

'It would have been strange, however, if, in the most universal mind that ever existed, there had been no express recognition of that mode of sentiment, which had first asserted the character, and designated the direction, of modern literature. I cannot help considering the Sonnets of Shakspeare as a sort of homage to that Genius of Christian Europe, necessarily exacted, although voluntarily paid, before he was allowed to take in hand the sceptre of his endless dominion.'

It seems likely that Arthur's father, Henry Hallam, was remembering the opinions of Arthur and of T. when he gave his very influential opinion of the *Sonnets* in 1839, between the death of Arthur and the publication of *In Memoriam*. Henry Hallam wrote in his *Introduction to the Literature of Europe*, iii 501–4:

'Perhaps there is now a tendency, especially among young men of poetical tempers, to exaggerate the beauties of these remarkable productions .... An attachment to some female, which seems to have touched neither his heart nor his fancy very sensibly, was overpowered, without entirely ceasing, by one to a friend; and this last is of such an enthusiastic character, and so extravagant in the phrases that the author uses, as to have thrown an unaccountable mystery over the whole work. It is true that in the poetry as well as in the fictions of early ages, we find a more ardent tone of affection in the language of friendship than has since been usual; and yet no instance has been adduced of such rapturous devotedness, such an idolatry of admiring love, as the greatest being whom nature ever produced in the human form pours forth to some unknown youth in the majority of these sonnets .... Notwithstanding the frequent beauties of these sonnets, the pleasure of their perusal is greatly diminished by these circumstances; and it is impossible not to wish that Shakspeare had never written them. There is a weakness and folly in all excessive and mis-placed affection, which is not redeemed by the touches of nobler sentiments that abound in this long series of sonnets.'

H.T. records T. as saying of the *Sonnets*: 'Henry Hallam made a great mistake about them: they are noble' (*Mem.* ii 289).

Sources and analogues. On the classical influences, including Horace, see Turner (pp. 116–18); and on Dante (pp. 127–9). Ian Kennedy shows the poem to be 'a work which absorbs and transforms the English pastoral elegy in a way that acknowledges the virtues of the tradition and at the same time renders the intellectual and religious spirit of the age with unparalleled fullness and accuracy' (*VP* xv, 1977, 351–66). W. Nash studies the general and particular affinities of Horace and the poem (*Neophilologus* lix, 1975, 466–75).

On twentieth-century criticism of the poem, see J. Sendry, *VP* xviii (1980) 105–18.

Theology and Evolution. 'They are always speaking of me', T. remarked, 'as if I were a writer of philosophical treatises' (*Mat.* ii 17). For his relationship to the thought of his day, see: G. R. Potter, 'Tennyson and the biological theory of mutability in species', *PQ* xvi (1937) 321–43; W. R. Rutland, 'Tennyson and the theory of evolution', *E and S* xxvi (1940) 7–29; G. Hough, 'The Natural Theology of *In Memoriam*', *RES* xxxiii (1947) 244–56; E. B. Mattes, *In Memoriam: The Way of a Soul* (1951); and J. Killham, *Tennyson and 'The Princess'* (1958). On T. as 'elusively vague as to just what kind of evolution he did envisage', see J. Harrison, *Durham University Journal* lxiv (1971) 26–31. S. Gliserman discusses T.'s language and its relation to early Victorian science writers (*VS* xviii, 1975, 277–308, 437–59). For an insistence that T.'s thinking is non-evolutionary, and derives from the progressivism of 'the English school of geology', see N. Rupke, *The Great Chain of History* (1983), pp. 225–30. On contemporary theology and the poem, see Culler (pp. 169–75). See also D. R. Dean, *Tennyson and Geology* (1985), pp. 8–19. Of his poetic predecessors, the most important is James Thomson, whose *Autumn* includes a long passage on geology (ll. 743–833). The footnotes below give the more important of the sources and analogues from Lyell's *Principles of Geology* and Chambers's *Vestiges of Creation.*

[PROLOGUE]

Strong Son of God, immortal Love,
　　Whom we, that have not seen thy face,
　　By faith, and faith alone, embrace,
Believing where we cannot prove;

¶ 296. [*Prologue*] Dated '1849' from trial edition and *1850.* Not *T.MS* and *L.MS.* The present edition follows A. C. Bradley in referring to this as the *Prologue,* though T. gave it no title. (S & S follow Alfred Gatty in preferring *Introductory stanzas.* On this decision, and on the relation of this to the poem as a whole, see W. E. Fredeman, *The Library* 6th ser. vi, 1984, 309.) Mrs E. B. Mattes suggests a general indebtedness to the religious teaching of F. D. Maurice, and describes the *Prologue* as 'a conclusion more truly than an

5   Thine are these orbs of light and shade;
    Thou madest Life in man and brute;
    Thou madest Death; and lo, thy foot
    Is on the skull which thou hast made.

    Thou wilt not leave us in the dust:
10   Thou madest man, he knows not why,
    He thinks he was not made to die;
    And thou hast made him: thou art just.

opening to *In Memoriam*. Insofar as it is a prologue, it is one not so much to
the poems it precedes as to the new way of life Tennyson was about to enter.'
She notes that the trial edition had the *Prologue* before, and not after, the title
In Memoriam A.H.H. Obiit [*Sept.* here in trial edition] *MDCCCXXXIII*,
which made a considerable break and gave a more accurate impression of the
relationship of the *Prologue* to the succeeding poems (*In Memoriam: The Way
of a Soul*, 1951, p. 98). S & S note the resemblance to Hallam's *Theodicœa
Novissima*, which T. had pressed Henry Hallam to include in the *Remains*;
also that these stanzas would have been welcome to Emily Sellwood.
P 1. immortal Love: 'This might be taken in a St John sense' (T.); H.T.
refers to *1 John* iv and v.
P 1–12. John Churton Collins called T.'s *Prologue* 'obviously a trans-
fusion' from verses by George Herbert. Alongside this suggestion (*Corn-
hill*, Jan. 1880, *Lincoln*), T. wrote 'No'. Collins compared l. 12 with
Herbert, *The Discharge* 55: 'My God hath promis'd; he is just'; T. wrote:
'No, close as it seems.' Cp. also T.'s opening with Herbert's *Love* [*I*] 1–4:
'Immortall Love, authour of this great frame, / Sprung from that beautie
which can never fade; / How hath man parcel'd out thy glorious name, /
And thrown it on that dust which thou hast made.' Also T.'s ll. 9, 12, with
Herbert's *The Temper* [*I*] 25–6: 'Whether I flie with angels, fall with dust, /
Thy hands made both.' (Collins suggested these too.) Coventry Patmore,
reviewing *In Memoriam*, said that it contained 'the best religious poetry that
has ever been written in our language – if we except a very few of the lovely
and too seldom appreciated effusions of George Herbert' (E. F. Shannon,
Tennyson and the Reviewers, 1952, p. 145).
P 2–3. 1 Peter i 8: 'Whom having not seen, ye love; in whom, though
now ye see him not, yet believing.'
P 5. orbs: 'sun and moon' (T.).
P 7–8. E. B. Mattes (p. 97) refers to Christ's victory over death as symbol-
ized in medieval paintings of the Crucifixion in which his feet rest on a
skull. J. Kolb compares *1 Corinthians* xv 25–6: 'For he must reign, till he
hath put all enemies under his feet. The last enemy that shall be destroyed is
death. For he hath put all things under his feet'.
P 9. Cp. *Psalm* xvi 10: 'Thou wilt not leave my soul in hell'.
P 9–12. The rhymes suggest *Why should we weep for those who die?* 1–4
(*1827*, I 97): die, dust, eternally, just.

Thou seemest human and divine,
The highest, holiest manhood, thou:
15   Our wills are ours, we know not how;
Our wills are ours, to make them thine.

Our little systems have their day;
They have their day and cease to be:
They are but broken lights of thee,
20 And thou, O Lord, art more than they.

We have but faith: we cannot know;
For knowledge is of things we see;
And yet we trust it comes from thee,
A beam in darkness: let it grow.

25 Let knowledge grow from more to more,
But more of reverence in us dwell;
That mind and soul, according well,
May make one music as before,

P 14–16]   Thou madest man, without, within:
Yet who shall say thou madest sin?
For who shall say 'it is not mine' *MS quoted in Eversley, corrected*
H.T.'s source was 'Daily Prayers by Emily Tennyson' (*Lincoln*), where
ll. 13–16 are in T.'s hand.

P 15. Cp. Sir Thomas Browne, *Religio Medici* i 36: 'Thus we are men, and
we know not how'.

P 17. Cp. *The Two Voices* 207: 'dust of systems'.

P 19. broken lights: S & S compare a fragment: 'This Nature full of hints and
mysteries, / Untrackt conclusions, broken lights and shapes' (III 620). Cp.
also *Will Waterproof* 59. Arthur Hallam has 'broken light', *On Free Submission
to God's Will* 4 (Motter, p. 67). B. Richards notes: 'figurative use of a painting
term (*OED* 12)' (*English Verse 1830–1890*, 1980, p. 103).

P 22–4. Cp. Charles Lyell on 'doubt and perplexity' in relation to geo-
logical knowledge: 'It has been justly said, that the greater the circle of
light, the greater the boundary of darkness by which it is surrounded'
(*Principles of Geology*, 4th edn, 1835, ii 291). T. read Lyell at the end of 1836
(*Letters* i 145) and in 1837 (*Mem.* i 162).

P 25–6. Cp. *Love thou thy land* 17–18: 'Make knowledge circle with the
winds; / But let her herald, Reverence, fly . . .' The antithesis is a common-
place, but T. may have been affected by Robert Chambers's use of it in
speaking specifically of geological knowledge: 'The acquisition of this
knowledge is consequently an available means of our growing in a genuine
reverence for him [God]' (*Vestiges of Creation*, 1844, p. 233). S & S note T.'s
recommending a long ō, 'knōwledge'.

P 28. as before: 'As in the ages of faith' (T.).

But vaster. We are fools and slight;
30   We mock thee when we do not fear:
But help thy foolish ones to bear;
Help thy vain worlds to bear thy light.

Forgive what seemed my sin in me;
What seemed my worth since I began;
35   For merit lives from man to man,
And not from man, O Lord, to thee.

Forgive my grief for one removed,
Thy creature, whom I found so fair.
I trust he lives in thee, and there
40 I find him worthier to be loved.

Forgive these wild and wandering cries,
Confusions of a wasted youth;
Forgive them where they fail in truth,
And in thy wisdom make me wise.

1849

I

I held it truth, with him who sings
To one clear harp in divers tones,
That men may rise on stepping-stones
Of their dead selves to higher things.

P 36. Psalm cxliii 2: 'in thy sight shall no man living be justified'.

P 41–4. Turner (p. 119) suggests the influence of the Sonnets of Petrarch.
P 41. wild and wandering: Troilus and Cressida I i 104. Cp. A Dirge 43:
'Wild words wander here and there'.

i Probably not completed till after 1846. Mat. i 127–8 listed it as one of the
earliest sections, apparently in error (II 310).

i 1–4] T. and L.MSS and H.Lpr 101 have only this stanza. T. says: 'I alluded to
Goethe's creed. Among his last words were... "from changes to higher
changes"'. (S & S note: 'These words have not been found among all the
reported "last words" of Goethe in the final months of his life, nor in the
letters of this time'.)   divers tones: 'Goethe is consummate in so many different
styles' (T.). Cp. Wilhelm Meister's Apprenticeship, I xvii: 'Love ran with a
quivering hand, in a thousand moods, over all the chords of his Soul'
(Carlyle's tr.; C. Y. Lang, introduction to Tennyson in Lincoln, i, 1971, xi).
On T. and Goethe see Culler (pp. 160, 265). G. G. Loane (Echoes in
Tennyson, 1928, p. 9) compares Byron, Siege of Corinth 239–41: 'Or pave the
path with many a corse, / O'er which the following brave may rise, / Their

5   But who shall so forecast the years
      And find in loss a gain to match?
      Or reach a hand through time to catch
      The far-off interest of tears?

      Let Love clasp Grief lest both be drowned,
10   Let darkness keep her raven gloss:
      Ah, sweeter to be drunk with loss,
      To dance with death, to beat the ground,

      Than that the victor Hours should scorn
      The long result of love, and boast,
15   'Behold the man that loved and lost,
      But all he was is overworn.'

stepping-stone – the last who dies!' Cp. *Timbuctoo* 194: 'And step by step to scale that mighty stair'. Also *To – [Thou mayst remember]* 3–6, 10–11: 'From the tomb / And charnel-place of purpose dead, / Through spiritual death we come / Into the light of spiritual life. . . . / Thy thought did scale a purer range / Of prospect up to self-control.' C. Y. Lang compares T.'s letter to Emily Sellwood, 24 Oct. 1839: 'Thou hast proved Time and space very prettily. So mayst thou and I and all of us ascend stepwise to Perfection' (*Letters* i 174; *Tennyson in Lincoln* i, p. xi).
i *4. their dead selves*: to be found in R. C. Trench's poem *To W. B. Donne* (both were Cambridge friends of T.), written 18 Oct. 1829 and in *Heath MS* alongside poems by T. S & S note *The Princess* iii 205: 'We touch on our dead self'.
i *5–8.* Cp. *Tiresias* 122–3 (begun on the death of Hallam): 'their examples reach a hand / Far through all years'. Based on *Hail Briton* 81–4: 'They wrought a work which time reveres, / A precedent to all the lands, / And an example reaching hands / For ever into coming years.'
i *7–8.* Three apparent reminiscences of Shakespeare. *Sonnet 31* 5–7: 'How many a holy and obsequious tear / Hath dear religious love stolen from mine eye, / As interest of the dead.'   *Rape of Lucrece* 1796–8: 'do not take away / My sorrow's interest; let no mourner say / He weeps for her.'   *Richard III* IV iv 322–4: 'The liquid drops of tears that you have shed / Shall come again, transformed to orient pearl, / Advantaging their loan with interest.' T.: 'The good that grows for us out of grief'.
i *10. Comus* 251–2: 'Raven doune / Of darkness'.
i *12.* Cp. *Comus* 143: 'Come, knit hands, and beat the ground', and Horace, *Odes* I xxxvii 1–2, *pulsanda tellus*. Cp. 'beat the floor', cv 17.
i *13. the victor Hours*: as in the unpublished section, *Are these the far-famed Victor Hours?* (p. 985).
i *14.* Cp. *Locksley Hall* 12: 'the long result of Time'.
i *16. was*] loves *trial edition*.

II

Old Yew, which graspest at the stones
That name the under-lying dead,
Thy fibres net the dreamless head,
Thy roots are wrapt about the bones.

5   The seasons bring the flower again,
And bring the firstling to the flock;
And in the dusk of thee, the clock
Beats out the little lives of men.

O not for thee the glow, the bloom,
10   Who changest not in any gale,
Nor branding summer suns avail
To touch thy thousand years of gloom:

And gazing on thee, sullen tree,
Sick for thy stubborn hardihood,
15   I seem to fail from out my blood
And grow incorporate into thee.

III

O Sorrow, cruel fellowship,
O Priestess in the vaults of Death,
O sweet and bitter in a breath,
What whispers from thy lying lip?

ii Not *T.MS. Mat.* i 127–8 listed it as one of the earliest sections, apparently in error (*p. 336*).

ii 3. T. compares: Νεκύων ἀμενηνὰ κάρηνα (*Odyssey* x 521 etc., 'the powerless heads of the dead').

ii 4. *Job* viii 17: 'His roots are wrapped about the heap, and seeth the place of stones.'

ii 6. S & S note *Genesis* iv 4: 'And Abel, he also brought of the firstlings of his flock'.

ii 9–16. 'Yet it is better to bear the wild misery of extreme grief than that Time should obliterate the sense of loss and deaden the power of love' (T.)

ii 9. 'Sorrow only saw the winter gloom of the foliage' (T.).

ii 11. On T. and the Victorian study of language, especially of etymology, P. G. Scott argues for the main sense of 'branding' here as from Old English *brinnan* or *byrn* to scorch or burn (*VP* xviii, 1980, 379–80).

ii 12. Cp. *The Lover's Tale* iv 194: 'a hundred years of gloom'.

ii 13. *thee,*] *1851*; the trial edition, *1850*; thy *corrected to* the *L.MS.*

ii 14. *stubborn hardihood*: Scott, *The Lord of the Isles* VI xxiii.

ii 15. *fail from out*: die away from (A. C. Bradley); cp. 'fail from thy desire', iv 6; 'Thy spirit should fail from off the globe', lxxxiv 36.

iii Not *T.MS*; but see 9*n.* The germ of it is in *H.Nbk 17* (1833).

5   'The stars,' she whispers, 'blindly run;
       A web is woven across the sky;
       From out waste places comes a cry,
     And murmurs from the dying sun:

     'And all the phantom, Nature, stands –
10   With all the music in her tone,
       A hollow echo of my own, –
     A hollow form with empty hands.'

     And shall I take a thing so blind,
       Embrace her as my natural good;
15   Or crush her, like a vice of blood,
     Upon the threshold of the mind?

iii 5–6. Cp. Shelley, *Adonais* 482: 'Which through the web of being blindly wove', on Love versus mortality.

iii 5–8] *H.Nbk 17* has an early fragment, rhyming *abab*:

> A cloud was drawn across the sky,
>   The stars their courses blindly run.
> Out of waste places came a cry
>   And murmurs from the dying sun.
>
> In every form the sense receives
>   A something hitherto unmet,
> In every motion of the leaves
>   The shadow of a vain regret.
>
> The whole house shaken to its fall,
>   This travelled mind a foreign land,
> Love mixt with all – love lord of all,
>   Thought drifting like the hills of sand.

The ninth line was echoed in 'And travelled men from foreign lands', x 6. Cp. the *1850* text with *Armageddon* i 36–7: 'Spirits of discord seemed to weave across / His fiery disk a web of bloody haze.'

iii 7. S & S note *Isaiah* li 3: 'For the Lord shall comfort Zion: he will comfort all her waste places'.

iii 9. *And all*] Because *H.Lpr 100*. S & S note that this is a detached leaf from *T.MS*.

iii 10. *the*] *1851* (*5th*), *H.Lpr 100*, *L.MS*; her *1850–51* (*4th*).

iii 11. Cp. Spenser: *Shepherd's Calendar*: *August* 160: 'The hollow Echo of my carefull cryes'.

iii 14–15. Cp. Shelley, *Queen Mab* iv 115–20, which mentions blood , 'vice', and 'Stifling with rudest grasp all natural good'; 'natural good' recurs in Shelley five lines later.

iii 15. Cp. *Othello* I iii 123: 'I do confess the vices of my blood'.

iii 16] *H.Lpr 100* has a further stanza, deleted:

> But Sorrow cares not for my frown,
>   And Sorrow says, 'We must not part,
>   For if I die upon thy heart,
> Then my dead weight will draw thee down.'

IV

To Sleep I give my powers away;
  My will is bondsman to the dark;
  I sit within a helmless bark,
And with my heart I muse and say:

5 O heart, how fares it with thee now,
  That thou should'st fail from thy desire,
  Who scarcely darest to inquire,
'What is it makes me beat so low?'

Something it is which thou hast lost,
10 Some pleasure from thine early years.
  Break, thou deep vase of chilling tears,
That grief hath shaken into frost!

Such clouds of nameless trouble cross
  All night below the darkened eyes;
15 With morning wakes the will, and cries,
'Thou shalt not be the fool of loss.'

V

I sometimes hold it half a sin
  To put in words the grief I feel;
  For words, like Nature, half reveal
And half conceal the Soul within.

iv Not *T.MS.*

iv *11–12*. T. comments: 'Water can be brought below freezing-point and not turn into ice – if it be kept still; but if it be moved suddenly it turns into ice and may break the vase.' An important source has been noted by Elaine Jordan (*Notes and Queries*, Nov. 1968): Goethe's *Dichtung und Wahrheit*. 'While my thoughts were thus employed, the death of young Jerusalem took place. The most minute and circumstantial details of the event were immediately circulated. The plan of *Werther* was instantly conceived. The elements of that composition seemed now to amalgamate, to form a whole, just as water, on the point of freezing in a vase, receives from the slightest concussion the form of a compact piece of ice' (*Memoirs*, 1824 tr., 44–5). On the importance of Goethe to the poem, see Turner (pp. 122–3), including that Goethe 'was an authority for linking spiritual with physical, or scientific evolution'.

v Not *T.MS.* J.C. Hixson and P. Scott compare Keble's argument about the value of poetry; T. owned his lectures *De Poeticae vi medica*, 1844 (*TRB* ii, 1976, 191).

5 But, for the unquiet heart and brain,
   A use in measured language lies;
   The sad mechanic exercise,
   Like dull narcotics, numbing pain.

   In words, like weeds, I'll wrap me o'er,
10 Like coarsest clothes against the cold:
   But that large grief which these enfold
   Is given in outline and no more.

VI

   One writes, that 'Other friends remain,'
   That 'Loss is common to the race' –
   And common is the commonplace,
   And vacant chaff well meant for grain.

5 That loss is common would not make
   My own less bitter, rather more:
   Too common! Never morning wore
   To evening, but some heart did break.

v 7. *sad*] set *L.MS.*
v 8. S & S note Keats, *Ode to a Nightingale* 1–3: 'a drowsy numbness pains /
My sense, as though of hemlock I had drunk, / Or emptied some dull opiate
to the drains'.
v 9. *weeds*: garments, with a suggestion of mourning (widow's weeds).

vi Not *T.MS.* The poem is mentioned by E. Lushington, as if it were one
of the many new sections written between summer 1840 and Christmas
1841 (*Mem.* i 201–2).
vi *1–8.* T. compares Lucretius ii 578–80: *nec nox ulla diem neque noctem
aurora secutast / quae non audierit mixtos vagitibus aegris / ploratus mortis
comites et funeris atri.* ('No night ever followed day, or dawn followed
night, but has heard mingled with their sickly wailings the lamentations
that attend upon death and the black funeral.') Cp. *Hamlet* I ii 72: 'Thou
know'st 'tis common, all that lives must die'. Also T.'s earlier elegiac poem,
To J. S. 45–8: 'I will not say, "God's ordinance / Of Death is blown in every
wind;" / For that is not a common chance / That takes away a noble mind.'
At an early stage of the *Memoir*, H.T. wrote: 'One of the poems in the 1832
volume which had been the least noticed, and which Hallam now ranked
among the best, was that to James Spedding, who afterwards took the place
of Arthur Hallam as my father's literary advisor'; this was excised for *Mem.*
(P. L. Elliott, *The Making of the Memoir*, 1978, p. 27). For Hallam's words to
T., see p. 93. Cp. *Why should we weep for those who die?* 12 (*1827*): 'They die
the common death of man'.

O father, wheresoe'er thou be,
10   Who pledgest now thy gallant son;
    A shot, ere half thy draught be done,
    Hath stilled the life that beat from thee.

O mother, praying God will save
    Thy sailor,—while thy head is bowed,
15   His heavy-shotted hammock-shroud
    Drops in his vast and wandering grave.

Ye know no more than I who wrought
    At that last hour to please him well;
    Who mused on all I had to tell,
20   And something written, something thought;

Expecting still his advent home;
    And ever met him on his way
    With wishes, thinking, 'here today,'
    Or 'here tomorrow will he come.'

vi *9–12*. Cp. *Aeneid* xi 49–52: *et nunc ille quidem spe multum captus inani | fors et vota facit cumulatque altaria donis; | nos iuvenem exanimum et nil iam caelestibus ullis | debentem vano maesti comitamur honore.* ('And now he, much beguiled by idle hope, perchance is offering vows and heaping the altars high with gifts; we, in sorrow, attend with bootless rites the lifeless son, who no more owes aught to any gods of heaven.')

vi *10*. *Who*] *1855*; That *1850–51*.

vi *16*. Cp. Clarence's dream of drowning, 'To find the empty, vast, and wand'ring air', *Richard III* I iv 39. M. Y. Mason says of these references to loss at sea and their relation to geology in the poem: 'Of course water is associated with geology primarily through its erosive action, but the references to human remains at sea are not simply metaphorical. Lyell [*Principles of Geology*] devotes a good deal of space in chapter sixteen to the question of how human remains can come to be found in "subaqueous strata", mentioning such things as "burial of human bodies at sea" and "loss of life by shipwreck"' (*VP* x, 1972, 175).

vi *17–18*. Turner (p. 128) notes that 'Dante was composing a poem in Beatrice's honour at the moment of her death'; and compares (p. 115) Hallam on Petrarch: 'It is the luxury of grief to connect the memory of the dead with our thoughts, and employments . . . at the moment of their death' (Motter, p. 290).

vi *19*. H.T. records that T. 'was writing to Arthur Hallam in the hour that he died'.

vi *21–40*. Cp. Juvenal, *Satires* iii 261–5: *domus interea secura patellas | iam lavat et bucca-foculum excitat et sonat unctis | striglibus et pleno componit lintea guto. | haec inter pueros varie properantur, at ille | iam sedet in ripa taetrumque novicius horret.* ('At home meanwhile the folk, unwitting, are washing the

25　O somewhere, meek, unconscious dove,
　　　That sittest ranging golden hair;
　　　And glad to find thyself so fair,
　　　Poor child, that waitest for thy love!

　　For now her father's chimney glows
30　　In expectation of a guest;
　　　And thinking 'this will please him best,'
　　　She takes a riband or a rose;

　　For he will see them on tonight;
　　　And with the thought her colour burns;
35　　And, having left the glass, she turns
　　　Once more to set a ringlet right;

　　And, even when she turned, the curse
　　　Had fallen, and her future Lord
　　　Was drowned in passing through the ford,
40　Or killed in falling from his horse.

　　O what to her shall be the end?
　　　And what to me remains of good?
　　　To her, perpetual maidenhood,
　　And unto me no second friend.

VII

Dark house, by which once more I stand
　　Here in the long unlovely street,

dishes, blowing up the fire with distended cheek, clattering over the greasy
flesh-scrapers, filling the oil-flasks and laying out the towels. And while
each of them is thus busy over his own task, their master is already sitting,
a new arrival, upon the bank, and shuddering at the grim ferryman.')
vi 32. A friend described T.'s sister Emily, 'the first day since her loss that
she had been able to meet anyone, and she came at last, dressed in deep
mourning, a shadow of her former self, but with one white rose in her
black hair as her Arthur loved to see her' (Mem. i 109).
vi 37–40. T.'s friend W. F. Rawnsley said that 'all his early life Tennyson
had heard "horse" in Lincolnshire pronounced "hurse"', Nineteenth
Century xcvii (1925) 190. But Hail Briton 113–6 rhymes 'perforce' /
'horse'.

vii Not T.MS, L.MS, trial edition. For the arguments supporting a date of
composition between 1848 and 1850, see S & S.　T. said that vii and cxix were
'pendant poems' (Knowles). Cp. The Deserted House 9–12 (1830, I 261), in
which the house is a corpse and which falls into something resembling the In
Memoriam stanza: 'Close the door, the shutters close, / Or through the

Doors, where my heart was used to beat
So quickly, waiting for a hand,

5   A hand that can be clasped no more –
Behold me, for I cannot sleep,
And like a guilty thing I creep
At earliest morning to the door.

He is not here; but far away
10   The noise of life begins again,
And ghastly through the drizzling rain
On the bald street breaks the blank day.

VIII

A happy lover who has come
To look on her that loves him well,

windows we shall see / The nakedness and vacancy / Of the dark deserted house.' J. H. Buckley (p. 111) quotes R. M. Milnes's poem on the death of Hallam (1838), which has interesting similarities. Turner (p. 122) notes that in Goethe's *Wilhelm Meister*, 'Wilhelm visits the front door of his beloved Mariana in the early morning, leaving only when the business of the town begins to come "alive" again (*lebendig*)'. On the precedents in Latin poetry (the lover excluded from the house), see S & S.

vii *1*. T. comments: '67 Wimpole Street', Henry Hallam's house at this time.

vii *3*. Doors] Door *H.Lpr 104*.

vii *4*] In expectation of his hand, *H.MS 1st reading*; So quickly, waiting for the hand, *H.MS*. The first reading was probably rejected as too like 'In expectation of a guest', l. 30 of the preceding section. Cp. *Break, break, break* 11: 'But O for the touch of a vanished hand'.

vii *5*. A] The *H.MS*. Cp. *If I were loved* 9 (*1832*, probably to Hallam): 'Claspt hand-in-hand with thee'. Also *The Princess* vi 168: 'In hands so lately claspt with yours'.

vii *7*. And] But *H.MS*. Cp. the ghost in *Hamlet* I i 148: 'And then it started like a guilty thing'. Also Wordsworth's *Immortality Ode* 148–51 (note the subject, and 'blank'): 'Blank misgivings of a Creature / Moving about in worlds not realised, / High instincts before which our mortal Nature / Did tremble like a guilty Thing surprised.'

vii *9*. J. D. Rosenberg, *JEGP* lviii (1959) 230, suggests an allusion to *Luke* xxiv 6, with the angel before the empty sepulchre: 'He is not here, but is risen'. Cp. Crabbe, *The School-Fellow* (published 1834), which begins 'Yes! I must leave thee, brother of my heart', and of which section II begins: 'He is not here: the Youth I loved so well / Dwells in some place where kindred spirits dwell: / But I shall learn. Oh! tell me of my Friend, / With whom I hoped life's evening-calm to spend'.

vii *11*. drizzling] dripping *H.MS*.

Who 'lights and rings the gateway bell,
And learns her gone and far from home;

5   He saddens, all the magic light
Dies off at once from bower and hall,
And all the place is dark, and all
The chambers emptied of delight:

So find I every pleasant spot
10   In which we two were wont to meet,
The field, the chamber and the street,
For all is dark where thou art not.

Yet as that other, wandering there
In those deserted walks, may find
15   A flower beat with rain and wind,
Which once she fostered up with care;

So seems it in my deep regret,
O my forsaken heart, with thee
And this poor flower of poesy
20   Which little cared for fades not yet.

But since it pleased a vanished eye,
I go to plant it on his tomb,
That if it can it there may bloom,
Or dying, there at least may die.

IX

Fair ship, that from the Italian shore
Sailest the placid ocean-plains

viii Not *T.MS, L.MS, trial edition.* Written 1850 (?).
viii 5. *magic light*: S & S note Coleridge, *France: an Ode* 35.
viii 5–6. *light / Dies*: E. Griffiths compares Popé, *Dunciad* iv 654: 'Light dies
before thy uncreating word'.
viii 8. Bradley noted Keats, *Lamia* ii 307: 'And Lycius' arms were empty of
delight'.
viii *12*. Cp. Arthur Hallam, *To Two Sisters* (to T.'s sisters Mary and Emily;
Motter, p. 90) i 42–4: 'Sick and lone, / Roaming the weary desert of my
doom, / Where thou art not.'

ix Not *T.MS* (missing sheets). S & S note that *H.Lpr 100* is a detached leaf
from *T.MS*. Dated '6 Oct. 1833' in *Heath MS* and *Y.MS. H.Nbk 16* (1833)
has an earlier draft than *Heath MS. H.Nbk 17* has ll. 1–6 only. The poem is in
T.Nbk 17 (1833).
    Cp. Horace, *Odes* I iii, with its prayer for a safe crossing for the ship
carrying his poet friend Virgil: *Sic te diva potens Cypri, / sic fratres Helenae,*

With my lost Arthur's loved remains,
Spread thy full wings, and waft him o'er.

5   So draw him home to those that mourn
In vain; a favourable speed
Ruffle thy mirrored mast, and lead
Through prosperous floods his holy urn.

All night no ruder air perplex
10   Thy sliding keel, till Phosphor, bright
As our pure love, through early light
Shall glimmer on the dewy decks.

Sphere all your lights around, above;
Sleep, gentle heavens, before the prow;
15   Sleep, gentle winds, as he sleeps now,
My friend, the brother of my love;

My Arthur, whom I shall not see
Till all my widowed race be run;

lucida sidera, / ventorumque regat pater / obstrictis aliis praeter Iapyga, / navis . . .
('May the goddess who rules over Cyprus, may Helen's brothers, gleaming
fires, and the father of the winds, confining all but Iapyx, guide thee so,
O ship . . .'). Theocritus vii 52–62 also implores fair weather for a crossing
to Mitylene. S & S note Henry Elton's letter: 'I believe his remains come by Sea
from Trieste'; T. told Knowles that ix was 'the first written'.
ix 2. *placid*] glassy H.Nbk 16 1st reading. Cp. Aeneid x 103: *placida aequora.*
ix 4. J. Sendry notes 'waft' in *Lycidas* 164, and argues for the importance of
Milton's poem to T.'s (*PMLA* lxxxii, 1967, 437–43).
ix 5. *So . . . home*] Convoy thy charge H.MS 1st reading; Draw thy dear
freight Heath MS 1st reading, H.MS 2nd reading. Cp. 'thy dark freight',
l. 8 of the following section.
ix 6. *; a favourable*] for him. A happy H.MS 1st reading.
ix 7] All day strain all thy cords, and lead H.MS 1st reading. T. also jotted
down '[cords] are tight'.   *thy mirrored*] H.MS, 1850; the mirrored trial
edition.   *Ruffle*: cp. Shelley, *Queen Mab* viii 65 (see too l. 2 above): 'Ruffle
the placid ocean-deep'. Also Crabbe, *The Library*:
    On the smooth mirror of the deep resides
    Reflected woe, and o'er unruffled tides
    The ghost of every former danger glides.
ix 8. *prosperous*: used similarly by Shelley, of the wind, *Rosalind* 817.
ix 10. *Phosphor*: T. comments 'star of dawn'.
ix 13. *lights*] light H.MS. (Also H.Lpr 98.) Cp. Enoch Arden 593: 'Then the
great stars that globed themselves in Heaven'; and Virgil, Georgics iv 79:
magnum mixtae glomerantur in orbem.
ix 15. *winds*] waves H.MS, Heath MS, H.Lpr 98.
ix 18. D. S. Hair compares *Hebrews* xii 1: 'Let us lay aside every weight, and

> Dear as the mother to the son,
> 20 More than my brothers are to me.

X

> I hear the noise about thy keel;
> I hear the bell struck in the night:
> I see the cabin-window bright;
> I see the sailor at the wheel.
>
> 5 Thou bring'st the sailor to his wife,
> And travelled men from foreign lands;
> And letters unto trembling hands;
> And, thy dark freight, a vanished life.
>
> So bring him: we have idle dreams:
> 10 This look of quiet flatters thus
> Our home-bred fancies: O to us,
> The fools of habit, sweeter seems

the sin which doth so easily beset us, and let us run with patience the race that is set before us' (*Domestic and Heroic in Tennyson's Poetry*, 1981, p. 23).

ix 20. T.'s brother Frederick wrote to J. Frere, 10 Feb. 1834: 'The number of a man's friends can never be great, but since he who was more than Brother to us has been taken away out of humanity, methinks indeed we have marvellous few remaining' (*Letters* i 107). S & S note Hallam, *Meditative Fragments* vi 102–3: 'I felt as of two brothers I were one, / And he of all men nearest to my soul'; also *Proverbs* xviii 24: 'there is a friend that sticketh closer than a brother'.

x Not *T.MS.*

x 6. Cp. 'This travelled mind a foreign land', iii 5–8n, MS.

x 8. *thy dark freight*] dearer yet *L.MS 1st reading*. See ix 5n.

x 11–14. S & S cp. Collins, *Ode, Written in the beginning of the year 1746* 1–6:
> How sleep the Brave, who sink to Rest,
> By all their Country's Wishes blest!
> When Spring, with dewy Fingers cold,
> Returns to deck their hallow'd Mold,
> She there shall dress a sweeter Sod,
> Than Fancy's Feet have ever trod.

(To which might be added that 'trod' may have suggested T.'s 'grapes' in l. 16.)

x 11. :O] that MS 1st reading.   *home-bred fancies*: 'the wish to rest in the churchyard or in the chancel' (H.T.).

x 12–20. Cp. Ovid, *Tristia* I ii 53–4: *est aliquid, fatove suo ferrove cadentem / in solida moriens ponere corpus humo.* ('Tis something worth if falling by fate or by the steel one rests in death upon the solid ground'–this then contrasted with being lost at sea.) The passage is also echoed in xviii 1–4.

To rest beneath the clover sod,
  That takes the sunshine and the rains,
15   Or where the kneeling hamlet drains
  The chalice of the grapes of God;

Than if with thee the roaring wells
  Should gulf him fathom-deep in brine;
  And hands so often clasped in mine,
20 Should toss with tangle and with shells.

XI

Calm is the morn without a sound,
  Calm as to suit a calmer grief,
  And only through the faded leaf
The chestnut pattering to the ground:

5 Calm and deep peace on this high wold,
  And on these dews that drench the furze,
  And all the silvery gossamers
That twinkle into green and gold:

Calm and still light on yon great plain
10   That sweeps with all its autumn bowers,
  And crowded farms and lessening towers,
To mingle with the bounding main:

Calm and deep peace in this wide air,
  These leaves that redden to the fall;
15   And in my heart, if calm at all,
  If any calm, a calm despair:

x *17. wells*: S & S suggest that wells as whirlpools may derive from Scott, *The Pirate* xxxviii.

x *19*. Cp. *The Princess* vi 168: 'hands so lately claspt with yours'.

x *20. tangle*: 'oar-weed' (T.). G. Tillotson, noting that this is *laminaria digitata*, says T. 'cannot bear the thought that seaweed might clasp with its fingers (*digitata*) the hands so often clasped in his' (*A View of Victorian Literature*, 1978, p. 304).

xi Not *T.MS*.
xi *6. these*] the *L.MS 1st reading*.
xi *7–8*. Adapted from *The Ruined Kiln* 1–2: 'A million gossamers in field and fold / Were twinkling into green and gold.'
xi *11*. Cp. Samuel Rogers, *The Sailor* (1786): 'The Sailor sighs as sinks his native shore, / As all its lessening turrets bluely fade'.
xi *14. These*] And *L.MS 1st reading*.

Calm on the seas, and silver sleep,
And waves that sway themselves in rest,
And dead calm in that noble breast
20 Which heaves but with the heaving deep.

XII

Lo, as a dove when up she springs
To bear through Heaven a tale of woe,
Some dolorous message knit below
The wild pulsation of her wings;

5   Like her I go; I cannot stay;
I leave this mortal ark behind,
A weight of nerves without a mind,
And leave the cliffs, and haste away

O'er ocean-mirrors rounded large,
10   And reach the glow of southern skies,
And see the sails at distance rise,
And linger weeping on the marge,

And saying; 'Comes he thus, my friend?
Is this the end of all my care?'
15   And circle moaning in the air:
'Is this the end? Is this the end?'

And forward dart again, and play
About the prow, and back return
To where the body sits, and learn
20   That I have been an hour away.

xi 20. Cp. Byron, *Bride of Abydos* 1088: 'His head heaves with the heaving billow'.

xii Not *T.MS*. Suggested by *Genesis* viii 8–9, 'Also he sent forth a dove from him, to see if the waters were abated from off the face of the ground; but the dove found no rest for the sole of her foot, and she returned unto him into the ark, for the waters were on the face of the whole earth.'
xii 6. ark] arc *L.MS 1st reading.   mortal ark*: *The Two Voices* 389. T. comments: 'My spirit flies from out my material self.' Cp. the visionary journey ('I leave the dreaming world below') in *Hark! the dogs howl!* (1833, I 607), the germ of *In Memoriam*.
xii 9. Incorporated from an early draft of *The Voyage* 40 ∧ 1 (*T.Nbk 20*):
　　Or plowed the broadening glare that basks
　　　On that smooth Ocean rounded large
　　Where sometimes like a chain of casks
　　　The long sea-serpent moved the marge.

XIII

Tears of the widower, when he sees
 A late-lost form that sleep reveals,
 And moves his doubtful arms, and feels
Her place is empty, fall like these;

5   Which weep a loss for ever new,
 A void where heart on heart reposed;
 And, where warm hands have prest and closed,
Silence, till I be silent too.

Which weep the comrade of my choice,
10   An awful thought, a life removed,
 The human-hearted man I loved,
A Spirit, not a breathing voice.

Come Time, and teach me, many years,
 I do not suffer in a dream;
15   For now so strange do these things seem,
Mine eyes have leisure for their tears;

My fancies time to rise on wing,
 And glance about the approaching sails,
 As though they brought but merchants' bales,
20 And not the burthen that they bring.

XIV

If one should bring me this report,
 That thou hadst touched the land today,
 And I went down unto the quay,
And found thee lying in the port;

xiii *3–4.* Cp. Milton's *Sonnet 19*, 'Methought I saw my late espoused Saint', which ends: 'But O as to embrace me she enclin'd / I wak'd, she fled, and day brought back my night.' Also Ovid, *Heroides* x 9–12, Ariadne reaching out for the phantom of Theseus.
xiii *15*] But now so strange does this thing seem, *T.MS.* James Spedding had put '(?)' against l. 15 (or ll. 15–16); T. heeded many of these queries and criticisms by Spedding in *T.MS*; see C. Ricks, *TRB* iv (1984) 110–13.
xiii *17–20*] *Not T.MS.*
xiii *18–19.* Cp. *Locksley Hall* 121–2, MS: 'unimagined sails, / Merchants in a rosy sunset, dropping down with costly bales.'

xiv Not *T.MS*. S & S discuss the section's relation to the classical genre of the speech of welcome to a traveller.
xiv *2–3.* OED shows that Swift rhymed 'quay' and 'day', *Stella at Wood-Park* 46.

5   And standing, muffled round with woe,
        Should see thy passengers in rank
        Come stepping lightly down the plank,
    And beckoning unto those they know;

    And if along with these should come
10   The man I held as half-divine;
        Should strike a sudden hand in mine,
    And ask a thousand things of home;

    And I should tell him all my pain,
        And how my life had drooped of late,
15   And he should sorrow o'er my state
    And marvel what possessed my brain;

    And I perceived no touch of change,
        No hint of death in all his frame,
        But found him all in all the same,
20 I should not feel it to be strange.

XV

    Tonight the winds begin to rise
        And roar from yonder dropping day:
        The last red leaf is whirled away,
    The rooks are blown about the skies;

5   The forest cracked, the waters curled,
        The cattle huddled on the lea;
        And wildly dashed on tower and tree
    The sunbeam strikes along the world:

    And but for fancies, which aver
10   That all thy motions gently pass
        Athwart a plane of molten glass,
    I scarce could brook the strain and stir

xv Not *T.MS.* Henry Hallam wrote to T., 30 Dec. 1833: 'You may have
been apprehensive for the safety of the vessel' (*Letters* i 105). There are many
small similarities to *On Sublimity* (*1827*, I 128): 'to pore'; 'the labouring
vessel'; 'doats on solitude'; 'wild'; 'While the black clouds in strange and
uncouth forms, / Come hurrying onward'; the winds at midnight; 'roar';
'whirling'.
xv 1. *begin*] *1855*, *L.MS*; began *1850–51*.
xv 3. Cp. Coleridge, *Christabel* 48–9: 'There is not wind enough to twirl /
The one red leaf, the last of its clan.'
xv 11. *plane*: 'a calm sea' (T.). Cp. *Job* xxxvii 18: the sky 'as a molten
looking glass'; *Revelation* iv 6: 'a sea of glass like unto crystal'; xv 2: 'a sea of
glass mingled with fire'. Cp. ix 2, MS: 'the glassy ocean-plains.'

That makes the barren branches loud;
And but for fear it is not so,
15   The wild unrest that lives in woe
Would dote and pore on yonder cloud

That rises upward always higher,
And onward drags a labouring breast,
And topples round the dreary west,
20   A looming bastion fringed with fire.

XVI

What words are these have fallen from me?
Can calm despair and wild unrest
Be tenants of a single breast,
Or sorrow such a changeling be?

5   Or doth she only seem to take
The touch of change in calm or storm;
But knows no more of transient form
In her deep self, than some dead lake

That holds the shadow of a lark
10   Hung in the shadow of a heaven?
Or has the shock, so harshly given,
Confused me like the unhappy bark

xv *14–16*. 'The stormy night, except it were for my fear for the "sacred bark", would be in sympathy with me' (H.T.). *it is not so*: T. glossed this 'all is not peace with thee' (University of London Library, *Works*, 1884).
xv *15*. *wild unrest*: *Timbuctoo* 127.
xv *15–20*. Cp. Arthur Hallam, *The Garden Trees* 10–11 (Motter, p. 98): 'The wild gray light that fronts yon massive cloud, / Or the half bow, rising like pillared fire.' This sonnet's opening ('The garden trees are busy with the shower / That fell ere sunset') was by T.: 'The commencement of a sonnet by me, which I requested my dear friend Arthur to continue [to] its conclusion" (R. Adicks, *TRB* i, 1971, 147).
xv *18*. Cp. *L'Allegro* 73–4: 'Mountains on whose barren brest / The labouring clouds do often rest.' Keats, *Hyperion* i 39–41: clouds and 'stored thunder labouring up'. Cp. 'The vapour labours up the sky', *Hark! the dogs howl!* 18, a poem which is the germ of *In Memoriam* (I 607). Sir William Jones's translation of the *Moállakát* (the acknowledged source of *Locksley Hall*), Amriolkais's poem, tells how night seemed 'to drag on her unwieldy length, and to advance slowly with her breast'.
xv *19–20*. Cp. *The Palace of Art* 48: 'Burnt like a fringe of fire'. Also *Armageddon* i 133–5: 'the livid West . . . melancholy red that fringed the sky'.

xvi Not *T.MS.*

That strikes by night a craggy shelf,
  And staggers blindly ere she sink?
15 And stunned me from my power to think
  And all my knowledge of myself;

And made me that delirious man
  Whose fancy fuses old and new,
  And flashes into false and true,
20 And mingles all without a plan?

XVII

Thou comest, much wept for: such a breeze
  Compelled thy canvas, and my prayer
  Was as the whisper of an air
To breathe thee over lonely seas.

5 For I in spirit saw thee move
  Through circles of the bounding sky,
  Week after week: the days go by:
Come quick, thou bringest all I love.

Henceforth, wherever thou mayst roam,
10 My blessing, like a line of light,

xvi *13–16.* Cp. Herbert, *Miserie* 76–7: 'A sick toss'd vessel, dashing on each thing; / Nay, his own shelf.' John Churton Collins wrote: 'For this graphic touch see Napier, *History of the Peninsular War* (Battle of Albuera): "The Fusileer battalions, struck by the iron tempest, *reeled and staggered like a sinking ship.*"' Alongside this suggestion, T. wrote: '! ! !' (*Cornhill*, Jan. 1880, *Lincoln*).
xvi *18. fuses:* S & S note Hallam's praise of T.: 'his vivid, picturesque delineation of objects, and the peculiar skill with which he holds all of them *fused*, to borrow a metaphor from science, in a medium of strong emotion'.
xvi *20. And mingles all*] In all his words *L.MS 1st reading*.

xvii Not *T.MS.* Written 1833–4. The chronology of the MSS is *H.Nbk 17* (1833–4), *T.Nbk 17, Heath MS, Purdy MS.* Henry Hallam wrote to T., 30 Dec. 1833: 'You may have been apprehensive for the safety of the vessel'.
xvii *2–3*] Was on thee, hollowing all the sail.
      My prayer was, likewise, as a gale *H.MS, T.Nbk 17, Heath MS 1st*
                                      reading
H.MS then changed 'likewise, as' to 'also like'.   *thy canvas*] the canvas *Heath MS, Purdy MS.*
xvii *8. quick*] quiet *Heath MS (error).*
xvii *9–12.* Cp. Thomas Moore, *How dear to me the hour* 5–8: 'And, as I watch the line of light, that plays / Along the smooth wave t'ward the burning west, / I long to tread that golden path of rays, / And think 'twould lead to some bright isle of rest.'
xvii *10. like*] *H.MS 1st reading;* as *H.MS 2nd reading.*

Is on the waters day and night,
And like a beacon guards thee home.

So may whatever tempest mars
　　Mid-ocean, spare thee, sacred bark;
15　　And balmy drops in summer dark
　　Slide from the bosom of the stars.

So kind an office hath been done,
　　Such precious relics brought by thee;
　　The dust of him I shall not see
20　Till all my widowed race be run.

XVIII

'Tis well; 'tis something; we may stand
　　Where he in English earth is laid,
　　And from his ashes may be made
The violet of his native land.

xvii *12. guards*] leads MSS.
xvii *13-16*]　　May never adverse wind incline,
　　　　　Thee moving swift thy burnisht sides
　　　　　From port to port in glassy tides
　　　Whose loudest motion comes from thine. *H.MS*

Cp. ciii 37–40 on the 'great ship' and her 'shining sides'; also the thought
in xv 9–13. With the *1850* text, cp. Horace, *Odes* I iii (which influenced ix
above); Shelley, *Queen Mab* i 114–17: 'Stars! your balmiest influence shed!/
Elements! your wrath suspend! / Sleep, Ocean, in the rocky bounds /
That circle thy domain!' Also *The Talking Oak* 267–8: 'All starry cul-
mination drop / Balm-dews'.
xvii *19*] More than my brothers are to me, *H.MS, Purdy MS*; Dear as a
brother is to me, *T.Nbk 17, Heath MS*.
xvii *20*] Dear as the mother to the son. *MSS except L.MS*. Echoing the end of
ix.

xviii Not *T.MS*. (S & S note that *Sparrow MS* is a detached leaf from *T.MS*.)
H.Nbk 10 (1832–4) lacks ll. 1–12 (though see l. *20n*) but numbers ll. 13–16 as
stanza 'V', which means that there was an extra stanza. Written 1834, since it
refers to Hallam's burial (3 Jan.).
xviii *1–4*. Cp. Ovid, *Tristia* I ii 53–4: *est aliquid, fatove suo ferrove cadentem /
in solida moriens ponere corpus humo*. ('Tis something worth if falling by
fate or by the steel one rests in death upon the solid ground'.)
xviii *2–4*. T. compares *Hamlet* V i 232–4: 'Lay her i' the earth, / And from
her fair and unpolluted flesh / May violets spring!' Arthur Hallam had

5   'Tis little; but it looks in truth
        As if the quiet bones were blest
        Among familiar names to rest
        And in the places of his youth.

        Come then, pure hands, and bear the head
10   That sleeps or wears the mask of sleep,
        And come, whatever loves to weep,
        And hear the ritual of the dead.

        Ah yet, even yet, if this might be,
        I, falling on his faithful heart,
15   Would breathing through his lips impart
        The life that almost dies in me;

        That dies not, but endures with pain,
        And slowly forms the firmer mind,
        Treasuring the look it cannot find,
20   The words that are not heard again.

quoted, in praise of T. (*Englishman's Magazine*, Aug. 1831), Persius's
Satires i 39–40: *Nunc non e tumulo fortunataque favilla / nascentur violae.* 'When
this Poet dies, will not the Graces and the Loves mourn over him?' Cp.
Aylmer's Field 845n (II 682). T. wrote to Charlotte Burton, 24 Nov. 1846:
'Nothing could be sweeter than Cathy's Somersby violets and doubt not but
that I shall keep them as a sacred treasure. The violets of one's native place
gathered by the hands of a pure innocent child must needs be precious to me'
(*Letters* i 267).
xviii 7. *familiar names*: those of the Eltons, his mother's family. Arthur
Hallam's *Remains* (1834, p. xxxv) spoke of the place of burial, Clevedon, as
having been selected 'not only from the connexion of kindred' (Hallam's
maternal grandmother). The wording of Henry Hallam (*Mem.* i 107) is
close to T.: 'brought him home to rest among his kindred and in his own
country'.
xviii *10. mask*] *MSS, 1850*; mark *trial edition* (error).
xviii *13*] Oh yet that–though it cannot be–*H.MS.*   *might*] may *T.Nbk 17,
Purdy MS, Sparrow MS, Heath MS*.
xviii *13–16.* Cp. 2 *Kings* iv 34, Elisha's miracle: 'And he went up, and lay
upon the child, and put his mouth upon his mouth . . . and the flesh of the
child waxed warm.'
xviii *15. Would*] Will *T.Nbk 17, Heath MS 1st reading*; Could *H.MS.*
xviii *20. that*] which *MSS except L.MS. H.MS* concludes with ll. 1–4 (as
stanza 'VII'), beginning 'And yet 'tis something here to stand'.

XIX

The Danube to the Severn gave
    The darkened heart that beat no more;
    They laid him by the pleasant shore,
And in the hearing of the wave.

5   There twice a day the Severn fills;
    The salt sea-water passes by,
    And hushes half the babbling Wye,
And makes a silence in the hills.

The Wye is hushed nor moved along,
10   And hushed my deepest grief of all,
    When filled with tears that cannot fall,
I brim with sorrow drowning song.

The tide flows down, the wave again
    Is vocal in its wooded walls;
15   My deeper anguish also falls,
And I can speak a little then.

XX

The lesser griefs that may be said,
    That breathe a thousand tender vows,
    Are but as servants in a house
Where lies the master newly dead;

5   Who speak their feeling as it is,
    And weep the fulness from the mind:

xix Not T.MS. (S & S note that *Sparrow MS* is a detached leaf from *T.MS.*)
'Written at Tintern Abbey' (H.T.); but what T. said of ll. 9–12 was 'Written
at Tintern (supposed to be)' (*Knowles*). See the unpublished section, *I keep no
more a lone distress* (p. 984). xix is the only section in *Heath MS* but not in
T.Nbk 17; it refers to Hallam's burial (3 Jan. 1834), so was written 1834. S & S
date it, erroneously, May 1839, because of T.'s travels; but T. had visited
Tintern Abbey in autumn 1834 (Martin, pp. 193–4). T. said: 'After the burial
these thoughts come' (*Knowles*).
xix 1. 'He died at Vienna and was brought to Clevedon to be buried' (T.).
xix 3. S & S note Keats, *Hyperion* ii 262: 'a pleasant shore'.
xix 5–8. 'Taken from my own observation–the rapids of the Wye are
stilled by the incoming sea' (T.).
xix 12. *sorrow*] sorrows *Heath MS*.

xx Not *T.MS*.

'It will be hard,' they say, 'to find
Another service such as this.'

My lighter moods are like to these,
10   That out of words a comfort win;
But there are other griefs within,
And tears that at their fountain freeze;

For by the hearth the children sit
Cold in that atmosphere of Death,
15   And scarce endure to draw the breath,
Or like to noiseless phantoms flit:

But open converse is there none,
So much the vital spirits sink
To see the vacant chair, and think,
20   'How good! how kind! and he is gone.'

XXI

I sing to him that rests below,
    And, since the grasses round me wave,
    I take the grasses of the grave,
And make them pipes whereon to blow.

5   The traveller hears me now and then,
    And sometimes harshly will he speak:
    'This fellow would make weakness weak,
And melt the waxen hearts of men.'

xx *12.* Cp. Byron, *There's not a joy* 11: 'That heavy chill has frozen o'er the
fountain of our tears'.

xxi Not *T.MS.* S & S note that *H.Lpr 103* is a detached leaf from *T.MS*; and
that above this section in *HnMS* are the words 'This yearning', deleted (see
p. *986*).

xxi *6. sometimes*] pausing *Purdy MS.*

xxi *8 ∧ 9*] Yet I as soon would preach a creed
            Whose baseness levels humankind
            Or help an old man's vice to find
            Low motives for a noble deed. *H.Lpr 103, deleted*

Purdy MS ends at this point with these lines for ll. 9–12, with variants:
preach] use; *baseness*] hatred; *an old man's vice*] a cankered heart. Cp. *The
Princess* vi 321 ∧ 2, *1847–8* text: 'To find low motives unto noble deeds'.

Another answers, 'Let him be,
10   He loves to make parade of pain,
That with his piping he may gain
The praise that comes to constancy.'

A third is wroth: 'Is this an hour
For private sorrow's barren song,
15   When more and more the people throng
The chairs and thrones of civil power?

'A time to sicken and to swoon,
When Science reaches forth her arms
To feel from world to world, and charms
20   Her secret from the latest moon?'

Behold, ye speak an idle thing:
Ye never knew the sacred dust:
I do but sing because I must,
And pipe but as the linnets sing:

25   And one is glad; her note is gay,
For now her little ones have ranged;
And one is sad: her note is changed,
Because her brood is stolen away.

xxi *15–16*. Probably alluding to Chartism and, as so often in T., to the French Revolution. Carlyle in *The French Revolution* (1837, ii V xii), for example, told of the Procession of the Black Breeches, describing how 'Blind lake of Sansculottism welters stagnant through the King's Château, for the space of three hours'.

xxi *18–20*. Quoted à propos the spectroscope, *Mem.* ii 336. But it is not clear whether T. or H.T. made the application, and still less clear as to whether or not the lines are *referring* to the spectroscope. No specific astronomical allusion seems needed; for example J. Jacobs's suggestion of the discovery of Neptune (Sept. 1846) seems unfoundedly late for this section.

xxi *23–4*. Turner (p. 122) notes Carlyle's translation (1824–7) of Goethe's *Wilhelm Meister*: 'I sing but as the linnet sings'.

xxi *25. one is glad;*] *1855*; unto one *1850–51*.

xxi *27. one is sad;*] *1855*; unto one *1850–51*. The revisions were prompted by Palgrave's criticism of 'unto' as 'slightly feeble. Here it comes *twice*' (J. O. Waller, *VN* No. 52, 1977, 13–17).

XXII

The path by which we twain did go,
Which led by tracts that pleased us well,
Through four sweet years arose and fell,
From flower to flower, from snow to snow:

5   And we with singing cheered the way,
And, crowned with all the season lent,
From April on to April went,
And glad at heart from May to May:

But where the path we walked began
10   To slant the fifth autumnal slope,
As we descended following Hope,
There sat the Shadow feared of man;

Who broke our fair companionship,
And spread his mantle dark and cold,
15   And wrapt thee formless in the fold,
And dulled the murmur on thy lip,

---

xxii Not *T.MS.* S & S note that *H.Lpr 103* is a detached leaf from *T.MS.* Cp. *Prometheus Unbound* II ii 1: 'The path through which that lovely twain'. See the unpublished section on the same page of *H.MS: The path by which I walkt alone* (p. *980*). Possibly influenced by Petrarch's 47th Sonnet.

xxii *3. four*] three *H.Lpr 103, L.MS.* H.T. comments '1828–32'; rather, 1829–33.

xxii *4 ∧ 5*] *H.MS* has xxiii 21–4, deleted.

xxii *6. lent*] sent *H.MS.*

xxii *8. glad at heart*] gaily stept *H.MS.*

xxii *9. where*] when *H.MS 1st reading.*

xxii *10. To . . . fifth*] Its fourth aut [*del.*] long *H.MS*; Its fourth long *L.MS.* S & S say: 'The MS reading is a syllable short'; but T. apparently gave two syllables to 'four' (and so to 'fourth'); *The Gardener's Daughter* 205–7, MS: 'I heard the bell toll four when I reacht'. *autumnal*: Hallam died 15 Sept. 1833.

xxii *11*] And we came down it high in hope, *H.MS.*

xxii *12.* Adapted from a line of *Tithon* 40 ∧ 41 (p. *993*), *T.MS*: 'the uncertain shadow feared / Of Gods and men'. Suggesting 'the valley of the shadow of death', *Psalm* xxiii 4.

xxii *13. our*] the *H.MS.*

xxii *14–15.* Cp. *Supposed Confessions* 121–2: 'I am void, / Dark, formless, utterly destroyed'. Also *On Sublimity* 70: 'formless and still and dark'.

xxii *14. his*] a *H.MS 1st reading.*

xxii *15. the*] its *H.MS.*

And bore thee where I could not see
Nor follow, though I walk in haste,
And think, that somewhere in the waste
20   The Shadow sits and waits for me.

XXIII

Now, sometimes in my sorrow shut,
Or breaking into song by fits,
Alone, alone, to where he sits,
The Shadow cloaked from head to foot,

5   Who keeps the keys of all the creeds,
I wander, often falling lame,
And looking back to whence I came,
Or on to where the pathway leads;

And crying, How changed from where it ran
10   Through lands where not a leaf was dumb;
But all the lavish hills would hum
The murmur of a happy Pan:

When each by turns was guide to each,
And Fancy light from Fancy caught,
15   And Thought leapt out to wed with Thought
Ere Thought could wed itself with Speech;

And all we met was fair and good,
And all was good that Time could bring,
And all the secret of the Spring
20   Moved in the chambers of the blood;

And many an old philosophy
On Argive heights divinely sang,
And round us all the thicket rang
To many a flute of Arcady.

xxiii See the unpublished section, *H.MS: The path by which I walkt alone* (p. *980*).

xxiii *1. Now,*] And *T.MS.*

xxiii *3. Alone,*] I move *T.MS 1st reading.*

xxiii *5*. John Churton Collins noted: 'Milton has described Death as the "keeper of the keys of all creeds."' Alongside this suggestion, T. wrote: 'Not known to me' (*Cornhill*, Jan. 1880, *Lincoln*). Known to no-one.

xxiii *6*] The secret. Oft I falter lame, *T.MS 1st reading.*

xxiii *7. And looking*] In lookings *T.MS 1st reading.*

xxiii *21–4*. See xxii 4 ∧ *5n.* Adapted from *The Palace of Art*, MS (p. *65*): 'And likewise many a fair philosophy'. S & S compare *Comus* 476: 'How charming is divine Philosophy!'.

XXIV

And was the day of my delight
As pure and perfect as I say?
The very source and fount of Day
Is dashed with wandering isles of night.

5   If all was good and fair we met,
This earth had been the Paradise
It never looked to human eyes
Since our first Sun arose and set.

And is it that the haze of grief
10   Makes former gladness loom so great?
The lowness of the present state,
That sets the past in this relief?

Or that the past will always win
A glory from its being far;
15   And orb into the perfect star
We saw not, when we moved therein?

XXV

I know that this was Life,—the track
Whereon with equal feet we fared;
And then, as now, the day prepared
The daily burden for the back.

5   But this it was that made me move
As light as carrier-birds in air;

xxiv 3. *The . . . fount*] We know the very Lord *trial edition*. S & S note *Macbeth*
II iii 96–7: 'The spring, the head, the fountain of your blood, / Is stopped; the
very source of it is stopped'.
xxiv 4. *wandering isles*: Shelley, *Prologue to Hellas* 18, *Witch of Atlas* 474. Here,
'sun-spots' (T.).
xxiv 6. *been*] seemed *T.MS 1st reading*.
xxiv 8] *1875*; Since Adam left his garden yet. *1850–74*.
xxiv 10] *1851*; Hath stretched [made *T.MS*] my former joy so great? *1850*.
xxiv 11. *the*] my *T.MS*.
xxiv 12. *in*] *L.MS*; on *trial edition* (*error*). *this*] such *T.MS*.
xxiv 15–16. H.T. compares *Locksley Hall Sixty Years After* 187–8:
Hesper–Venus–were we native to that splendour or in Mars,
We should see the Globe we groan in, fairest of their evening stars.

xxv 1. *Life*: 'chequered, but the burden was shared' (T.).
xxv 2. *with equal feet*: *Aeneid* ii 724, *non passibus aequis*.

I loved the weight I had to bear,
Because it needed help of Love:

Nor could I weary, heart or limb,
10   When mighty Love would cleave in twain
The lading of a single pain,
And part it, giving half to him.

XXVI

Still onward winds the dreary way;
I with it; for I long to prove
No lapse of moons can canker Love,
Whatever fickle tongues may say.

5   And if that eye which watches guilt
And goodness, and hath power to see
Within the green the mouldered tree,
And towers fallen as soon as built—

Oh, if indeed that eye foresee
10   Or see (in Him is no before)
In more of life true life no more
And Love the indifference to be,

Then might I find, ere yet the morn
Breaks hither over Indian seas,
15   That Shadow waiting with the keys,
To shroud me from my proper scorn.

xxv 9. *could*] was *T.MS.*

xxv 10–12. S & S note *If I were loved* 5–6: 'All the inner, all the outer world of pain / Clear Love would pierce and cleave, if thou wert mine'.

xxvi Not *T.MS. Mat.* i 127–8 listed it as one of the earliest sections, apparently in error (*p. 336*).

xxvi 5. *which*] that *L.MS.*

xxvi 9–10. Cp. Marston, *Sophonisba* II i 134–5: 'Gods naught foresee, but see, for to their eyes / Naught is to come or past'.

xxvi 11] In Being that it is no more, *L.MS 1st reading.*

xxvi 12. *And*] In *L.MS 1st reading.*

xxvi 13. *Then*] *1851(5th)*; So *1850–51(4th)*.

xxvi 14. *Indian*] Eastern *trial edition.* H.T. compares *Comus* 139: 'The nice Morn on th' *Indian* steep'.

xxvi 16. *shroud*] *1855*; cloak *1850–51.* Probably altered because of an objection by *The Times*, 28 Nov. 1851 (E. F. Shannon, *Tennyson and the Reviewers*, 1952, p. 162).   *proper*: 'scorn of myself' (T.).

XXVII

I envy not in any moods
    The captive void of noble rage,
    The linnet born within the cage,
That never knew the summer woods:

5 I envy not the beast that takes
    His license in the field of time,
    Unfettered by the sense of crime,
To whom a conscience never wakes;

Nor, what may count itself as blest,
10   The heart that never plighted troth
    But stagnates in the weeds of sloth;
Nor any want-begotten rest.

I hold it true, whate'er befall;
    I feel it, when I sorrow most;
15   'Tis better to have loved and lost
Than never to have loved at all.

XXVIII

The time draws near the birth of Christ:
    The moon is hid; the night is still;
    The Christmas bells from hill to hill
Answer each other in the mist.

xxvii Not *T.MS.*
xxvii *2–3.* Cp. Gray, *Elegy* 51: 'Chill Penury repress'd their noble rage'
(note the context); and Scott, *Lady of the Lake* VI xxii (a funeral lament):
'The captive thrush may brook the cage, / The prison'd eagle dies for
rage.'
xxvii *11.* Cp. *Sonnet [Conrad!]* 14: 'This sloth-sprung weed'.
xxvii *15–16.* Many analogues have been found, among them Congreve:
''Tis better to be left, than never to have been lov'd', *Way of the World* II i;
and Thomas Campbell's *The Jilted Nymph* 19–20: 'Better be courted and
jilted / Than never be courted at all.'

xxviii One of the earliest sections, begun 1833 (*Mem.* i 109, substantiated by
the fact that xxviii is one of the eight sections in *T.Nbk 17*, 1833–4).
xxviii *1. The time draws*] It draweth *T.Nbk 17.*
xxviii *2–4.* S & S note Coleridge, *Christabel* ii 360–61: 'The air is still! through
mist and cloud / That merry peal comes ringing loud'. T. said of the bells:
'They always used to ring on Xmas Eve'.
xxviii *4. in*] through *T.MS.*

5   Four voices of four hamlets round,
        From far and near, on mead and moor,
        Swell out and fail, as if a door
     Were shut between me and the sound:

     Each voice four changes on the wind,
10   That now dilate, and now decrease,
         Peace and goodwill, goodwill and peace,
     Peace and goodwill, to all mankind.

     This year I slept and woke with pain,
         I almost wished no more to wake,
15   And that my hold on life would break
     Before I heard those bells again:

     But they my troubled spirit rule,
         For they controlled me when a boy;
         They bring me sorrow touched with joy,
20   The merry merry bells of Yule.

                    XXIX

     With such compelling cause to grieve
         As daily vexes household peace,
         And chains regret to his decease,
     How dare we keep our Christmas-eve;

5   Which brings no more a welcome guest
         To enrich the threshold of the night

xxviii 6. *From far and*] Some far, some *T.MSS.*
xxviii 7. *Swell out and*] Voices that *T.Nbk 17*; They rise and *T.MS.*
xxviii 15] I almost thought my heart would break *T.Nbk 17, T.MS 1st reading. on*] of *T.MS.*
xxviii 16. *Before . . . those*] To hear those merry *T.Nbk 17, T.MS 1st reading.*

xxix 1] My sister with such cause to grieve *T.MS alternative stanza, deleted.*
xxix 2] As that which drains our days of peace, *T.MS alternative stanza, del. daily*] that which *T.MS 1st reading. household peace: PL* x 908.
xxix 4] We scarce can keep this Christmas-eve; *T.MS.*
xxix 5. *Which . . . more*] The last brought here *T.MS.*
xxix 6–7] *Transposed T.MS.*
xxix 6. *To enrich*] Enriched *T.MS. the threshold of the night: The Voyage* 18.

With showered largess of delight
In dance and song and game and jest?

Yet go, and while the holly boughs
10   Entwine the cold baptismal font,
Make one wreath more for Use and Wont,
That guard the portals of the house;

Old sisters of a day gone by,
Gray nurses, loving nothing new;
15   Why should they miss their yearly due
Before their time? They too will die.

XXX

With trembling fingers did we weave
The holly round the Christmas hearth;
A rainy cloud possessed the earth,
And sadly fell our Christmas-eve.

5   At our old pastimes in the hall
We gambolled, making vain pretence
Of gladness, with an awful sense
Of one mute Shadow watching all.

xxix 7. *With showered*] And showering *T.MS.*
xxix 8. *In*] With *T.MS.*
xxix 8 ∧ 9] But this—to keep it like the last,
          To keep it even for his sake
          Lest one more link should seem to break,
          And Death sweep all into the Past. *T.MS*
xxix 9. *Yet go*] So be it *T.MS.*
xxix 11. *Use and Wont*: Alfred Gatty quotes the motto to Scott's *Pirate*,
Chapter 14: 'What religion . . . / Save the good use and wont that carries
them / To worship how and where their fathers worshipp'd?'
xxix 15. *Why should they*] They shall not *T.MS.*

xxx In *T.Nbk* 17 (1833–4), and therefore one of the earliest sections; also in
T.MS. Entitled in *Heath MS* 'Christmas Eve. 1833'. Hallam had written to
T.'s sister Emily about the prospect of having to leave Somersby: 'I fear the
shadow of the coming event will be on your spirit; but really you must try
to pluck up a bit; & make me properly merry for the Eve. If you set up a
"reg'lar good cry" because it is your *last* Eve at Somersby, how shall I
remember it is my *first*?' (20 Dec. 1832; *AHH*, p. 706).
xxx 7] Despite of that restraining sense *T.Nbk* 17 *1st reading.*

We paused: the winds were in the beech:
10   We heard them sweep the winter land;
And in a circle hand-in-hand
Sat silent, looking each at each.

Then echo-like our voices rang;
We sung, though every eye was dim,
15   A merry song we sang with him
Last year: impetuously we sang:

We ceased: a gentler feeling crept
Upon us: surely rest is meet:
'They rest,' we said, 'their sleep is sweet,'
20   And silence followed, and we wept.

Our voices took a higher range;
Once more we sang: 'They do not die
Nor lose their mortal sympathy,
Nor change to us, although they change;

25   'Rapt from the fickle and the frail
With gathered power, yet the same,
Pierces the keen seraphic flame
From orb to orb, from veil to veil.'

Rise, happy morn, rise, holy morn,
30   Draw forth the cheerful day from night:
O Father, touch the east, and light
The light that shone when Hope was born.

xxx *9. paused*] ceased *Heath MS.*
xxx *17. ceased*] paused *Heath MS.*
xxx *19. rest . . . sleep*] sleep . . . rest *Heath MS 1st reading.*
xxx *20. And . . . followed*] We kissed each other *T.MSS, Heath MS, HnMS 1st reading, H.Lpr 101, L.MS 1st reading.*
xxx *22. Once more*] Again *Heath MS 1st reading.*
xxx *23.* S & S note Hallam's essay *On Sympathy.*
xxx *24*] Though burning up from change to change. *T.Nbk 17 1st reading.*
xxx *26. yet*] still *Heath MS 1st reading.*
xxx *27. Pierces*] Pierceth *Heath MS.* Cp. Shelley, *Revolt of Islam* xii 45: 'Pierce like reposing flames the tremulous atmosphere'.
xxx *28. From orb to orb*: *Œnone* 163–4, MS.
xxx *28–32.* Cp. the last lines of Shelley's *Adonais* (noting the elegiac context): 'Whilst, burning through the inmost veil of Heaven, / The soul of Adonais, like a star, / Beacons from the abode where the Eternal are.'
xxx *29.* S & S note Milton, *On the Morning of Christ's Nativity* 1: 'This is the Month, and this the happy morn'.
xxx *30.* S & S note Gray, *Elegy* 87: 'the warm precincts of the cheerful day'.
xxx *32. Hope*] truth *HnMS 1st reading. T.MS* has ll. 1–13 of an unpublished section, '*The light that shone when Hope was born*' (p. *982*).

XXXI

When Lazarus left his charnel-cave,
And home to Mary's house returned,
Was this demanded–if he yearned
To hear her weeping by his grave?

5 'Where wert thou, brother, those four days?'
There lives no record of reply,
Which telling what it is to die
Had surely added praise to praise.

From every house the neighbours met,
10 The streets were filled with joyful sound,
A solemn gladness even crowned
The purple brows of Olivet.

Behold a man raised up by Christ!
The rest remaineth unrevealed;
15 He told it not; or something sealed
The lips of that Evangelist.

xxxi One of the earliest sections (*Mem.* i 109, substantiated by *T.Nbk 17*), written in 1833–4. It is in *Heath MS. T.Nbk 17* shows that xxxi and xxxii were originally envisaged as one section; this draft at first consisted of xxxi 1–8 plus xxxii 5–16, and was then revised to xxxi 1–8 plus xxxii 1–12. Cp. *Thou mayst remember* (I 306), which in *T.Nbk 23* has a concluding stanza on the joy of Mary at the resurrection of Lazarus, the stanza deleted apparently by H.T. T. quotes: 'She goeth unto the grave to weep there', *John* xi 31. S & S note T.'s admiration for Sebastiano del Piombo's painting *The Raising of Lazarus*.

xxxi *1. his*] *T.Nbk 17 B*; the *H.Lpr 106, H.Nbk 21, Heath MS.*

xxxi *1–3*] When rose the corpse from out his cave,
           Did Mary ask of him she loved,
           If any time the spirit moved *T.Nbk 17 A*

xxxi *4. by*] at *MSS except L.MS.*

xxxi *5–6, 7–8*] *Transposed T.Nbk 17 A.*

xxxi *7–8*] Or told he what it is to die,
           An answer adding praise to praise? *T.Nbk 17*

xxxi *7. is*] was *H.Lpr 106.*

xxxi *8*] Had filled the measure of her praise. *T.Nbk 17 B.*

xxxi *9–16*] *Not T.Nbk 17.*

xxxi *9. every house*] all the lands *H.Nbk 21.*

xxxi *10. filled*] lined *H.Lpr 101.* S & S note *Psalm* lxxxix 15: 'Blessed is the people that know the joyful sound'.

xxxi *13. raised up*] upraised *H.Lpr 106, H.Nbk 21, Heath MS, Moxon MS.*

xxxi *13–16.* Cp. Pope, *Eloisa to Abelard* 9–10: 'rest ever unreveal'd, / Nor pass these lips in holy silence seal'd.'

XXXII

Her eyes are homes of silent prayer,
    Nor other thought her mind admits
    But, he was dead, and there he sits,
And he that brought him back is there.

5   Then one deep love doth supersede
    All other, when her ardent gaze
    Roves from the living brother's face,
And rests upon the Life indeed.

All subtle thought, all curious fears,
10   Borne down by gladness so complete,
    She bows, she bathes the Saviour's feet
With costly spikenard and with tears.

Thrice blest whose lives are faithful prayers,
    Whose loves in higher love endure;
15   What souls possess themselves so pure,
Or is there blessedness like theirs?

XXXIII

O thou that after toil and storm
    Mayst seem to have reached a purer air,
    Whose faith has centre everywhere,
Nor cares to fix itself to form,

xxxii Begun 1833–4; see xxxi *n.*

xxxii *1–4*] Not *T.Nbk 17 A.*

xxxii *1. are*] were *T.Nbk 17 B.*

xxxii *2*] She musing moved not lips or hands. *T.Nbk 17 B.*

xxxii *3. But, he*] For 'he *T.Nbk 17 B.*   *sits*] stands *T.Nbk 17 B.*

xxxii *4. there*] there' *T.Nbk 17 B.*

xxxii *5. Then . . . love*] One deeper love *T.Nbk 17 A.*   *doth*] did *T.Nbk 17.*

xxxii *7. Roves*] Roved *T.Nbk 17.*

xxxii *8. rests upon*] rested on *T.Nbk 17.*

xxxii *11. bows, she bathes*] bowed, she bathed *T.Nbk 17.*   , *she*] and *H.Lpr 101,* *T.MS.*

xxxii *11–12.* John xii 3.

xxxii *13–16*] Not *T.Nbk 17 B.*

xxxii *13. Thrice blest*] Happy, *T.Nbk 17 A.*

xxxii *15. What*] No *T.Nbk 17 A.*

xxxii *16. Or*] Nor *T.Nbk 17 A.*   *theirs?*] theirs. *T.Nbk 17 A.*

5   Leave thou thy sister when she prays,
      Her early Heaven, her happy views;
      Nor thou with shadowed hint confuse
   A life that leads melodious days.

   Her faith through form is pure as thine,
10   Her hands are quicker unto good:
      Oh, sacred be the flesh and blood
   To which she links a truth divine!

   See thou, that countest reason ripe
      In holding by the law within,
15   Thou fail not in a world of sin,
   And even for want of such a type.

XXXIV

   My own dim life should teach me this,
      That life shall live for evermore,
      Else earth is darkness at the core,
   And dust and ashes all that is;

5   This round of green, this orb of flame,
      Fantastic beauty; such as lurks
      In some wild Poet, when he works
   Without a conscience or an aim.

   What then were God to such as I?
10   'Twere hardly worth my while to choose
      Of things all mortal, or to use
   A little patience ere I die;

xxxiii 6. *early*] local *trial edition*. H.T. corrected 'local' to 'early' in *T.MS*.
xxxiii 8. T. compares Statius, *Silvae* I iii 22–3: *ceu [placidi] veritus turbare Vopisci / Pieriosque dies et habentes carmina somnos*. ('As if afraid to disturb the Pierian days and music-haunted slumbers of tranquil Vopiscus.')
xxxiii 10] Nor could thy vision bring her good: *H.Lpr 101, T.MS, L.MS*.
xxxiii 11. *Oh*,] So *MSS*.

xxxiv 1. *dim life*] dark heart *H.Lpr 101, T.MS 1st reading*.   *should*] can *trial edition*.
xxxiv 5–8. On the same subject but in a different mood, cp. *On a Mourner* 15 ∧ 16 (*p. 136*), on Hallam's death, which says how slight the comforts of Nature are: 'Yet is she mortal even as I, / Or as that friend I loved in vain: / She only whispering low or high, / Through this vast cloud of grief and pain / I had not found my peace again.'

'Twere best at once to sink to peace,
    Like birds the charming serpent draws,
15   To drop head-foremost in the jaws
Of vacant darkness and to cease.

XXXV

Yet if some voice that man could trust
    Should murmur from the narrow house,
    'The cheeks drop in; the body bows;
Man dies: nor is there hope in dust:'

5   Might I not say? 'Yet even here,
    But for one hour, O Love, I strive
    To keep so sweet a thing alive:'
But I should turn mine ears and hear

The moanings of the homeless sea,
10   The sound of streams that swift or slow
    Draw down Æonian hills, and sow
The dust of continents to be;

And Love would answer with a sigh,
    'The sound of that forgetful shore
15   Will change my sweetness more and more,
Half-dead to know that I shall die.'

xxxiv *14.* Cp. Shelley, *Revolt of Islam* ii 414: 'as the charmed bird that haunts the serpent's den'.

xxxv *1. man*] men *T.MS.*

xxxv *9. the homeless sea*: Shelley, *The Cyclops* 709. Cp. *Alastor* 566 (noting l. 10): 'The thunder and the hiss of homeless streams'. John Churton Collins suggested that T.'s line was 'partly from Horace, *Odes* II xx: *Visam gementis litora Bospori*'. Alongside this suggestion, T. wrote: 'Nonsense' (*Cornhill*, Jan. 1880, *Lincoln*). M. Millhauser comments: 'The sea is homeless in a double sense: it affords no man a home (except those who are buried in it); and in geologic time . . . it shifts its bed, or "home". It is also, of course, in constant, restless motion' (*Fire and Ice: The Influence of Science on T.'s Poems*, 1971, p. 18).

xxxv *9–12.* T. commented to J. Knowles, *Nineteenth Century* xxxiii (1893) 182: 'The vastness of the future–the enormity of the ages to come after your little life would act against that love.'

xxxv *10–11.* Cp. *The Ring* 41: 'Æonian Evolution, swift or slow'.

xxxv *11*] For millions of millenniums, sow *T.MS 1st reading.* Spedding underlined 'millenniums' and put '(?)'.

xxxv *13–16*] *Added to T.MS in margin.*

xxxv *14. that forgetful shore*: T. comments: 'the land where all things are forgotten'. Cp. *Paradise Lost* ii 74: 'that forgetful Lake'.

O me, what profits it to put
     An idle case? If Death were seen
     At first as Death, Love had not been,
20   Or been in narrowest working shut,

Mere fellowship of sluggish moods,
     Or in his coarsest Satyr-shape
     Had bruised the herb and crushed the grape,
And basked and battened in the woods.

XXXVI

Though truths in manhood darkly join,
     Deep-seated in our mystic frame,
     We yield all blessing to the name
Of Him that made them current coin;

5   For Wisdom dealt with mortal powers,
     Where truth in closest words shall fail,
     When truth embodied in a tale
Shall enter in at lowly doors.

And so the Word had breath, and wrought
10   With human hands the creed of creeds
     In loveliness of perfect deeds,
More strong than all poetic thought;

Which he may read that binds the sheaf,
     Or builds the house, or digs the grave,
15   And those wild eyes that watch the wave
In roarings round the coral reef.

xxxv *23–4.* Cp. *Sonnet* [*Alas! how weary*] 9–10: 'laughing cheerily / Bruise his gold grain upon his threshing-floor'. Also *PL* v 344–5: 'For drink the Grape / She crushes'; and *Comus* 46–7.

xxxvi *1. manhood*] Nature *trial edition.*
xxxvi *2. our*] her *trial edition.*
xxxvi 5] Oh wisdom of eternal Powers! *H.Lpr 101, T.MS 1st reading. powers*] hours *T.MS.*
xxxvi *5–8.* T. comments: 'For divine Wisdom had to deal with the limited powers of humanity, to which truth logically argued out would be ineffectual, whereas truth coming in the story of the Gospel can influence the poorest.'
xxxvi *6. Where truth*] Truth chased *H.MS, T.MS 1st reading.*
xxxvi *9. Word had breath*] Logos breathed *H.MS, T.MS 1st reading.* S & S note *John* i 14: 'And so the Word became flesh, and dwelt among us'.
xxxvi *11. In*] Pure *H.MS, T.MS 1st reading.*
xxxvi *15. wild eyes*: 'the Pacific Islanders' (T.).

XXXVII

Urania speaks with darkened brow:
    'Thou pratest here where thou art least;
    This faith has many a purer priest,
And many an abler voice than thou.

5 'Go down beside thy native rill,
    On thy Parnassus set thy feet,
    And hear thy laurel whisper sweet
About the ledges of the hill.'

And my Melpomene replies,
10   A touch of shame upon her cheek:
    'I am not worthy even to speak
Of thy prevailing mysteries;

'For I am but an earthly Muse,
    And owning but a little art
15   To lull with song an aching heart,
And render human love his dues;

'But brooding on the dear one dead,
    And all he said of things divine,

xxxvii Arthur Hallam had remarked in his *Essay on the Philosophical Writings of Cicero* (1831; Motter, pp. 150–51): 'Poetry, indeed, is seductive by exciting in us that mood of feeling which conjoins all mental states that pass in review before it, according to congruity of sentiment, not agreement of conceptions; and it is with justice, therefore, that the Muses are condemned by the genius of a profound philosophy. But though poetry encourages a wrong condition of feeling with respect to the discovery of truth, its enchantments tend to keep the mind within that circle of contemplative enjoyment, which is not less indispensably necessary to the exertions of a philosophic spirit. We may be led wrong by the sorcery; but that wrong is contiguous to the right.' S & S cp. Propertius, *Elegies* III iii.

xxxvii 9. *Melpomene*: the Muse of Tragedy, here of Elegy, as in *Shepherd's Calendar: November* 53–4: 'Up then *Melpomene* thou mournefulst Muse of nyne, / Such cause of mourning never hadst afore.' As in Horace, *Odes* I xxiv 2–3, on the death of a friend: *praecipe lugubres / cantus, Melpomene* ('Teach me a song of mourning, O Melpomene').

xxxvii 11. *even*] ev'n *1855*; but *1850–51*.

xxxvii 12. *prevailing*: probably in the sense of the Latin *praevalens*, 'very strong', since there is no reason why Urania should prevail over Melpomene.

xxxvii 16. *human love his*] love his human *T.MS*.

(And dear to me as sacred wine
20 To dying lips is all he said),

'I murmured, as I came along,
Of comfort clasped in truth revealed;
And loitered in the master's field,
And darkened sanctities with song.'

XXXVIII

With weary steps I loiter on,
Though always under altered skies
The purple from the distance dies,
My prospect and horizon gone.

5 No joy the blowing season gives,
The herald melodies of spring,
But in the songs I love to sing
A doubtful gleam of solace lives.

If any care for what is here
10 Survive in spirits rendered free,
Then are these songs I sing of thee
Not all ungrateful to thine ear.

xxxvii *19. to me as sacred*] *1855*; as sacramental *1850–51*. Probably altered because of an objection in *The Times*, 28 Nov. 1851 (E. F. Shannon, *Tennyson and the Reviewers*, 1952, p. 161). S & S note that T. wrote (of the original reading), beside Gatty's discussion, 'sounds too commonplace'.

xxxvii *23. master's field*: T. comments: 'God's acre' (*Works, 1884*, University of London Lib.).

xxxvii *24.* Cp. Horace, *Odes* III iii 69: *non hoc iocosae conveniet lyrae* ('But this will not befit the sportive lyre').

xxxviii *3.* Cp. *The Princess* vi 179: 'No purple in the distance'.

xxxviii *5. blowing*: 'blossoming' (T.).

xxxviii *6.* Cp. Shakespeare, *Sonnet 1*: 'Herald to the gaudy spring'.

xxxviii *9–12.* H.T. (*1913*) compares *Aeneid* iv 34: *id cinerem aut manis credis curare sepultos?* ('Thinkest thou that dust or buried shades give heed to that?') Cp. Catullus xcvi 1–2: *Si quicquam mutis gratum acceptumve sepulcris / accidere a nostro, Calve, dolore potest.* ('If the silent grave can receive any pleasure, or sweetness at all from our grief, Calvus'.) The theme is that of *My life is full* (I 383).

xxxviii *11. of*] to *T.MS 1st reading*.

XXXIX

Old warder of these buried bones,
　And answering now my random stroke
　With fruitful cloud and living smoke,
Dark yew, that graspest at the stones

5　And dippest toward the dreamless head,
　　To thee too comes the golden hour
　　When flower is feeling after flower;
　But Sorrow – fixt upon the dead,

　And darkening the dark graves of men, –
10　　What whispered from her lying lips?
　　Thy gloom is kindled at the tips,
　And passes into gloom again.

xxxix Written 1 April 1868 (*Mem.* ii 53), and so not in *T.MS* and *L.MS*.
Published 1869, as a pendant to ii.

xxxix *3*. T. comments: 'The yew, when flowering, in a wind or if struck
sends up its pollen like smoke'; H.T. compares *The Holy Grail* 13–15:
'Beneath a world-old yew-tree, darkening half / The cloisters, on a gustful
April morn / That puffed the swaying branches into smoke.' The yew
figures in Lyell's *Principles of Geology* (4th edn, 1835, iii 8): 'How often,
during the heat of a summer's day, do we see the males of diœcious plants,
such as the yew-tree, standing separate from the females, and sending off
into the air, upon the slightest breath of wind, clouds of buoyant pollen.'
Turner (p. 125) speaks of T.'s 'giving a serious significance to Lyell's jocular
comparison of yew trees in spring to the mares mentioned by Virgil
(*Georgics*, iii 271–5) that are impregnated by the wind, when "the warmth
returns to their bones". The warmed bones of the mares, with their promise
of new life, become the "buried bones" watched over by the yew tree; thus
Lyell's flippant allusion is made to hint delicately at the question put to
Ezekiel, the central question of the poem: "Can these bones live?"'

xxxix *7*. H.T. remarks: 'The yew is diœcious' (having the unisexual male
and female flowers on separate plants).

xxxix *11*. This is more likely to refer to the shoots than to the flowers of the
yew. ii 11–12 is about foliage. Cp. *Sonnet* [*Alas! how weary*] 5: 'kindling
buds', a phrase used by Shelley, *Adonais* 137. Cp. Shelley's *Triumph of Life*
309–10: 'When all the forest-tips began to burn / With kindling green'.
In 1838 T. spoke of 'the tops of the elms . . . beginning to kindle into green'
(*Mem.* i 167). But 'kindling buds' might point to flowers; the section speaks
of flowers; and tips would imply that the green tips of the yew are con-
spicuous while the yew blooms, which is not so.

XL

Could we forget the widowed hour
And look on Spirits breathed away,
As on a maiden in the day
When first she wears her orange-flower!

5   When crowned with blessing she doth rise
To take her latest leave of home,
And hopes and light regrets that come
Make April of her tender eyes;

And doubtful joys the father move,
10   And tears are on the mother's face,
As parting with a long embrace
She enters other realms of love;

Her office there to rear, to teach,
Becoming as is meet and fit
15   A link among the days, to knit
The generations each with each;

And, doubtless, unto thee is given
A life that bears immortal fruit
In those great offices that suit
20   The full-grown energies of heaven.

Ay me, the difference I discern!
How often shall her old fireside

xl T. said: 'See Poem xcvii where the writer is compared to the female – *here* the spirit becomes the female in the parable' (*Knowles*).

xl 5. *doth*] does *T.MS.*

xl 7–8. *Antony and Cleopatra* III ii 43: 'The April's in her eyes'. Cp. Arthur Hallam's poem to Emily Tennyson, *Oh best and fairest of the things that seem:* 'light of tender eyes' (*Victorian Poetry*, Supplement to vol. iii, 1965).

xl 9. *doubtful*] thoughtful *T.MS.*

xl 12. *other*] novel *trial edition.*

xl 19. *those . . . that*] *1877*; such . . . as *1850–75*. T. said of the earlier reading: 'I hate that. I should not write so *now.* I'd almost rather sacrifice a meaning than let two S'S come together' (*Knowles*).

xl 20. L. Poston compares Robert Montgomery's *Satan* (1830) ii: 'no energies which pant for heaven' (*TRB* iii, 1980, 162–3).

xl 21. *Ay*] Oh *T.MS.*

xl 21–32] *T.MS* ends with one stanza which it then revised to form these three:

Be cheered with tidings of the bride,
How often she herself return,

25 And tell them all they would have told,
    And bring her babe, and make her boast,
    Till even those that missed her most
    Shall count new things as dear as old:

But thou and I have shaken hands,
30 Till growing winters lay me low;
    My paths are in the fields I know,
And thine in undiscovered lands.

XLI

Thy spirit ere our fatal loss
Did ever rise from high to higher;
As mounts the heavenward altar-fire,
As flies the lighter through the gross.

5 But thou art turned to something strange,
   And I have lost the links that bound

But ah the bitter difference
    That knowledge here is left to hope
    And that imaginative scope
That seeks for truths beyond the sense.

xl 25. *would have told*: would desire to be told (H.T.).

xl 30. *Till*] The *T.MS 1st reading*.

xl 32. Cp. Shelley, *Alastor* 77: 'To seek strange truths in undiscovered lands'.
Also *Hamlet* III i 79–80: 'The undiscovered country, from whose bourn /
No traveller returns'.

xli 3. *Judges* xiii 20: 'For it came to pass, when the flame went up toward
heaven from off the altar, that the angel of the Lord ascended in the flame
of the altar.'

xli 4–8. T. said: 'Love fears to be lost in the advance of the dead beyond the
Survivor' (*Knowles*).

xli 4. *flies*] goes *HnMS, T.MS*.

xli 5. Cp. *The Tempest* I ii 405: 'something rich and strange'.

xli 6. *links*: Turner (p. 115) relates these lines to Hallam, *On Cicero*: 'Of that
immense chain of mental successions, which extends from the cradle to the
death-bed, how few links . . . are visible to any other person?' He also noted in
Crabbe's *The Parting Hour* 'strange', 'change', 'links', 'bind'.

Thy changes; here upon the ground,
No more partaker of thy change.

Deep folly! yet that this could be –
10   That I could wing my will with might
To leap the grades of life and light,
And flash at once, my friend, to thee.

For though my nature rarely yields
To that vague fear implied in death;
15   Nor shudders at the gulfs beneath,
The howlings from forgotten fields;

Yet oft when sundown skirts the moor
An inner trouble I behold,
A spectral doubt which makes me cold,
20   That I shall be thy mate no more,

Though following with an upward mind
The wonders that have come to thee,
Through all the secular to-be,
But evermore a life behind.

XLII

I vex my heart with fancies dim:
He still outstript me in the race;
It was but unity of place
That made me dream I ranked with him.

xli 8 ∧ 9]   How far, how far gone upward now?
Too far for me to catch the while
The sweetness of thy proper smile
Through those new splendours of thy brow! *HnMS*
deleted

Cp. the third line with 'Thy sweetness from its proper place', lxxxiii 6.
xli *10*. *I could*] God would *HnMS 1st reading.*
xli *11*. Cp. *The Two Voices* 347–9, MS (*pp. 118–20*): 'Life and half-life,
a million grades'.
xli *16*. 'The eternal miseries of the Inferno' (T.). H.T. comments: 'forgotten,
and consigned to everlasting nothingness', referring to *Inferno* iii 25–51.
Cp. *Measure for Measure* III i 126–7: 'those that lawless and incertain
thoughts / Imagine howling'; and *Hamlet* V i 235–6: 'A minist'ring angel
shall my sister be, / When thou liest howling.' Also *To—with* [*The Palace
of Art*] 15–16: 'Lie / Howling in outer darkness.'
xli *19*. *which*] that *HnMS*, *T.MS 1st reading.*
xli *23*. *secular to-be*: 'æons of the future' (T.).

5 And so may Place retain us still,
   And he the much-beloved again,
   A lord of large experience, train
To riper growth the mind and will:

And what delights can equal those
10   That stir the spirit's inner deeps,
   When one that loves but knows not, reaps
   A truth from one that loves and knows?

XLIII

If Sleep and Death be truly one,
   And every spirit's folded bloom
   Through all its intervital gloom
In some long trance should slumber on;

5 Unconscious of the sliding hour,
   Bare of the body, might it last,
   And silent traces of the past
Be all the colour of the flower:

---

xlii *4–8*. T. said: 'Sympathy of the teacher & taught' (*Knowles*).
xlii *10*. *spirit's inner*] spirit through its Hn MS.

xliii *T.MS* and *L.MS* show that this originally consisted of ll. 1–8 plus a version of the last stanza (below). On the arguments during the Renaissance as to whether or not the dead 'sleep', see Helen Gardner, *Donne's Divine Poems* (1952), pp. xliii–xlvi. There was ample scriptural authority for the belief, e.g. *1 Thessalonians* iv 13–15. But it still excited controversy, e.g. O. Gregory's *On the Evidences of the Christian Religion* (1811; 3rd edn, 1815): 'There are some who contend that the soul *sleeps*, utterly void of sense, consciousness, and activity, from the time of death till the day of judgment' (p. 269). Gregory attacked this view, and the 'still more dangerous error' of not believing in eternal punishment. Cp. *To J.S.* (*p. 93*).
xliii *3*. *intervital*: the first usage in OED.
xliii *4–8*. T. said: 'Sympathy of equal learning in the new life' (*Knowles*).
xliii *5–8*. Spedding put '(?)' against l. 6, possibly referring to the whole stanza, and of ll. 7–8 he wrote: 'The two last lines of the 2d Stanza I do not understand. Do you mean this?'
xliii *5*. *sliding*: a traditional epithet, as in Dryden's 'the sliding Sun', *Palamon and Arcite* iii 131; and 'the sliding year', Virgil's *Pastorals* iii 62.
xliii *7*. *silent traces*] only memories *trial edition*.
xliii *8*. *all . . . of*] scent and colour to *trial edition*.

So then were nothing lost to man;
10   So that still garden of the souls
        In many a figured leaf enrolls
        The total world since life began;

        And love will last as pure and whole
        As when he loved me here in Time,
15   And at the spiritual prime
        Rewaken with the dawning soul.

XLIV

How fares it with the happy dead?
For here the man is more and more;
But he forgets the days before
God shut the doorways of his head.

xliii 9–12] Not T.MS, not originally L.MS.
xliii 10. So] 1855; But 1850–51. that still garden: The Gardener's Daughter
196; cp. The Lover's Tale i 263: 'A man in some still garden'.
xliii 10–12. Behind T.'s choice of this metaphor for xliii may be Lyell's
remark on the bones of men: 'Even if the more solid parts of our species
had disappeared, the impression of their form would have remained en-
graven on the rocks, as have the traces [l. 7] of the tenderest leaves of plants'
(Principles of Geology, 4th edn, 1835, i 241). T. said of l. 11: 'painted
with the past life' (Knowles).
xliii 13–16]   And thus our love, for ever new,
                Would last through all; and pure and whole,
                Within the centre of the soul
                Lie lapt till dawn like golden dew. trial edition
L.MS likewise, but beginning 'And therefore that our love was true'.
T.MS opens as L.MS, and has: last] live; centre] bosom. Cp. Richard III IV i
84: 'the golden dew of sleep'.
xliii 13. will] 1855; would 1850–51.
xliii 15. prime: daybreak. Cp. The Two Voices 378: 'material prime'.

xliv 1. John Sparrow, London Mercury xxi (1930) 429, compares James
Thomson's Song: 'Tell me, thou soul of her I love, / Ah! tell me, whither
art thou fled; / To what delightful world above, / Appointed for the
happy dead?'
xliv 2. Cp. Locksley Hall 142: 'The world is more and more'.
xliv 3. days] day HnMS, H.Lpr 101, T.MS.
xliv 4. doorways of] doors within HnMS, H.Lpr 101, T.MS. Spedding
underlined 'within', put '(?)', and wrote: 'First Stanza obscure. You told me
what you meant by the shutting of the doors'. Incorporated from Hail Briton
175–6, as Sir Charles Tennyson notes: 'ere yet / God shuts the doors within
his head.' T. remarks: 'Closing of the skull after babyhood. The dead after

5 The days have vanished, tone and tint,
    And yet perhaps the hoarding sense
    Gives out at times (he knows not whence)
    A little flash, a mystic hint;

    And in the long harmonious years
10   (If Death so taste Lethean springs),
    May some dim touch of earthly things
    Surprise thee ranging with thy peers.

    If such a dreamy touch should fall,
    O turn thee round, resolve the doubt;
15   My guardian angel will speak out
    In that high place, and tell thee all.

XLV

The baby new to earth and sky,
    What time his tender palm is prest
    Against the circle of the breast,
    Has never thought that 'this is I:'

5 But as he grows he gathers much,
    And learns the use of 'I', and 'me',

this life may have no remembrance of life, like the living babe who forgets
the time before the sutures of the skull are closed, yet the living babe grows in
knowledge, and though the remembrance of his earliest days has vanished,
yet with his increasing knowledge there comes a dreamy vision of what has
been.' Cp. *The Two Voices* 368: 'For is not our first year forgot?' Also
Wordsworth, *Immortality Ode* 58: 'Our birth is but a sleep and a forgetting'.
xliv *5. have vanished*] of many a *HnMS*.
xliv *6*] Have ceased to haunt the hoarding sense. *HnMS*; Yet send from
out the hoarding sense *H.MS, T.MS*.
xliv *7*] Yet comes [At times *H.MS, T.MS*], he hardly knows from whence
HnMS, T.MS.
xliv *8. little flash*] flash from these *HnMS*.
xliv *10*. Shelley, *Rosalind* 409: 'Lethean spring'. Cp. *The Two Voices* 350:
'Some draught of Lethe'.
xliv *13–16*. T. said: 'if you *have* forgot all earthly things – yet as a man has
faint memories, even so in the new life a sort of vague memory of the past
would come. This is fortified by considering that the use of flesh & blood
were lost if they do not establish an identity' (*Knowles*; see xlv).
xliv *13. such*] ever *HnMS 1st reading*.
xliv *15*. The 'guardian angel' is to be distinguished from Hallam.

xlv Turner (p. 115) notes that this paraphrases a passage in Hallam's essay *On
Sympathy*.

And finds 'I am not what I see,
And other than the things I touch.'

So rounds he to a separate mind
10   From whence clear memory may begin,
As through the frame that binds him in
His isolation grows defined.

This use may lie in blood and breath,
Which else were fruitless of their due,
15   Had man to learn himself anew
Beyond the second birth of Death.

XLVI

We ranging down this lower track,
The path we came by, thorn and flower,
Is shadowed by the growing hour,
Lest life should fail in looking back.

xlv 8. And] But *HnMS, T.MS.*
xlv 10. From ... clear] And thence his *HnMS.*
xlv 12. grows] is *HnMS.*
xlv 14] And Life were pilfered of her due, *HnMS.* Spedding underlined the
last words (*T.MS*), and put '(?)', but T. made no change.
xlv 15. man ... himself] men ... themselves *HnMS.*
xlv 16. Incorporated from lix 8 ∧ 9, MS:

    Use other means than sobbing breath,
      And other charms than misted eyes,
      And broodings on the change that lies
    Shut in the second birth of death.

xlvi 1-4] In travelling through this lower clime,
      With reason our memorial power
    Is shadowed by the growing hour,
    Lest this should be too much for time.
                H.Lpr 101, T.MS, L.MS 1st reading
xlvi 1. Cp. Spenser, *Muiopotmos* 42: 'this lower tract'.
xlvi 2. Cp. Arthur Hallam, *On My Sister's Birthday* 41–4 (Motter, p. 60):
'My own dear sister, thy career / Is all before thee, thorn and flower: /
Scarce hast thou known by joy or fear / The still heart-pride of Friendship's
hour.'
xlvi 3. shadowed: cp. Shelley, *Hellas* 805: 'The coming age is shadowed on
the Past'. *the growing hour: Love thou thy land* 61.
xlvi 4–5. Spedding underlined 'this' (*T.MS*), and wrote 'what?'; he
underlined 'Yet' (*T.MS*) and put '(?)'.
xlvi 4. T. said: 'If there were a perfect memory of all sorrows & sins we
should not be able to bear it' (*Knowles*).

5   So be it: there no shade can last
     In that deep dawn behind the tomb,
     But clear from marge to marge shall bloom
     The eternal landscape of the past;

     A lifelong tract of time revealed;
10   The fruitful hours of still increase;
     Days ordered in a wealthy peace,
     And those five years its richest field.

     O Love, thy province were not large,
     A bounded field, nor stretching far;
15   Look also, Love, a brooding star,
     A rosy warmth from marge to marge.

XLVII

     That each, who seems a separate whole,
     Should move his rounds, and fusing all
     The skirts of self again, should fall
     Remerging in the general Soul,

5   Is faith as vague as all unsweet:
     Eternal form shall still divide
     The eternal soul from all beside;
     And I shall know him when we meet:

xlvi 5. *So be it:*] Yet surely *H.MS, T.MS, L.MS 1st reading.*
xlvi 9. *tract*] *L.MS, 1850*; track *trial edition* (error). tract of time: *Paradise Lost* v 498.
xlvi 12. *five*] four *H.MS, T.MS, L.MS 1st reading.*
xlvi 13. *O Love, thy*] O me, Love's *H.MS, T.MS, L.MS 1st reading* (the 'original reading', T.). T. glossed this by adding 'then' after 'were' (*Knowles*).
xlvi 15. T. comments: 'As if Lord of the whole life', H.T. adding: 'not merely of those five years of friendship'. H.T. (*1913*) compares 'looks a flower', *A Dedication* 13.

xlvii Not *T.MS.* T. comments: 'The individuality lasts after death, and we are not utterly absorbed into the Godhead. If we are to be finally merged in the Universal Soul, Love asks to have at least one more parting before we lose ourselves.' 'Love protests against the loss of identity in the theory of absorption' (*Knowles*).
xlvii 1. *who*] which *L.MS 1st reading.*
xlvii 2. *his*] its *MS 1st reading.*
xlvii 5. *Is faith . . . as*] Such faith as vague and *MS 1st reading.*

And we shall sit at endless feast,
10   Enjoying each the other's good:
    What vaster dream can hit the mood
    Of Love on earth? He seeks at least

Upon the last and sharpest height,
    Before the spirits fade away,
15   Some landing-place, to clasp and say,
    'Farewell! We lose ourselves in light.'

XLVIII

If these brief lays, of Sorrow born,
    Were taken to be such as closed
    Grave doubts and answers here proposed,
    Then these were such as men might scorn:

5 Her care is not to part and prove;
    She takes, when harsher moods remit,
    What slender shade of doubt may flit,
    And makes it vassal unto love:

And hence, indeed, she sports with words,
10   But better serves a wholesome law,
    And holds it sin and shame to draw
    The deepest measure from the chords:

Nor dare she trust a larger lay,
    But rather loosens from the lip

---

xlvii *11. vaster*] dimmer *MS 1st reading.*

xlvii *14.* T. noted for James Knowles: 'into the Universal Spirit–but at least one last parting! and always would want it again–of course' (*Nineteenth Century* xxxiii (1893) 183).

xlvii *15–16.* Cp. *Timbuctoo* 194–6: 'And step by step to scale that mighty stair / Whose landing-place is wrapt about with clouds / Of glory' of heaven. With earliest light of Spring . . .' T.'s use of 'landing-place' in a religious context may owe something to Coleridge's use of it prominently in *The Friend* (of which the 1844 edition is at *Lincoln*).

xlviii *1. brief*] light *H.Lpr 101, T.MS.*

xlviii *5. part and prove: The Two Voices* 134.

xlviii *7. slender shade*] random ghost *H.MS, T.MS 1st reading.*

xlviii *8.* Cp. 'Lord of my love, to whom in vassalage', Shakespeare's *Sonnet 26*, a poem similar in its self-depreciation.

15   Short swallow-flights of song, that dip
        Their wings in tears, and skim away.

XLIX

From art, from nature, from the schools,
    Let random influences glance,
    Like light in many a shivered lance
That breaks about the dappled pools:

5   The lightest wave of thought shall lisp,
        The fancy's tenderest eddy wreathe,
        The slightest air of song shall breathe
    To make the sullen surface crisp.

And look thy look, and go thy way,
10   But blame not thou the winds that make
        The seeming-wanton ripple break,
    The tender-pencilled shadow play.

Beneath all fancied hopes and fears
        Ay me, the sorrow deepens down,
15   Whose muffled motions blindly drown
    The bases of my life in tears.

L

Be near me when my light is low,
    When the blood creeps, and the nerves prick

xlviii *15–16.* Adapted from *Dear friend* 19–22, which falls into something
resembling the *In Memoriam* stanza: 'By thy placid scorns that play / Round
the surfaces of things / And like swallows dip their wings / Evermore, and
skim away.' Lines from *Dear friend* were also adapted for another elegiac
poem, *To J.S.*

xlix *6. tenderest*] lightest *T.MS, L.MS 1st reading.*
xlix *7. slightest*] lightest *T.MS.*
xlix *9.* T. said: 'the reader' (*Knowles*).
xlix *11. seeming-wanton ripple*: 'wanton ripples', *The Miller's Daughter*
48 ∧ 9, MS.
xlix *12. The*] And *T.MS. tender-pencilled*: cp. *The Daisy* 67: 'shadowy-
pencilled'.
xlix *13. Beneath all fancied*] Aye me! beneath all *T.MS 1st reading.*

l Not *T.MS.* Cp. Arthur Hallam, *Meditative Fragments* vi 128–32 (Motter,
pp. 73–4): 'But when our feelings coil upon themselves / At time's rude
pressure; when the heart grows dry, / And burning with immedicable
thirst / As though a plague-spot seared it, while the brain / Fevers with
cogitations void of love.'

And tingle; and the heart is sick,
And all the wheels of Being slow.

5   Be near me when the sensuous frame
        Is racked with pangs that conquer trust;
        And Time, a maniac scattering dust,
    And Life, a Fury slinging flame.

    Be near me when my faith is dry,
10   And men the flies of latter spring,
        That lay their eggs, and sting and sing
    And weave their petty cells and die.

    Be near me when I fade away,
        To point the term of human strife,
15   And on the low dark verge of life
    The twilight of eternal day.

LI

    Do we indeed desire the dead
        Should still be near us at our side?
        Is there no baseness we would hide?
    No inner vileness that we dread?

5   Shall he for whose applause I strove,
        I had such reverence for his blame,

l 1. *my light*] the pulse *L.MS 1st reading.*
l 2–3. Cp. Shelley, *The Cenci* IV i 163–5: 'My blood is running up and down
my veins; / A fearful pleasure makes it prick and tingle: / I feel a giddy
sickness of strange awe.'
l 4. *the wheels of Being*: Shelley, *Queen Mab* ix 151–2: 'urge / The restless
wheels of being on their way', noted by J. D. Jump, *Notes and Queries*
cxcvi (1951) 540–41.
l 5–6. Cp. *Suggested by Reading* 56: 'the social frame is racked'.
l 8. The Furies carried torches.
l 10–12. Cp. *The Two Voices* 70, MS: 'Yet flies will weave their tinsel cells'.

li It had just been composed at Christmas 1841, according to one
interpretation of the words of E. Lushington (*Mem.* i 202–3): 'On one other
occasion he came and showed me a poem he had just composed, saying he
liked it better than most he had done lately'. But S & S note that this is
ambiguous, and suggest an earlier date because of *H.Lpr 101*.

See with clear eye some hidden shame
And I be lessened in his love?

I wrong the grave with fears untrue:
10   Shall love be blamed for want of faith?
There must be wisdom with great Death:
The dead shall look me through and through.

Be near us when we climb or fall:
Ye watch, like God, the rolling hours
15   With larger other eyes than ours,
To make allowance for us all.

LII

I cannot love thee as I ought,
For love reflects the thing beloved;
My words are only words, and moved
Upon the topmost froth of thought.

5 'Yet blame not thou thy plaintive song,'
The Spirit of true love replied;
'Thou canst not move me from thy side,
Nor human frailty do me wrong.

'What keeps a spirit wholly true
10 To that ideal which he bears?
What record? not the sinless years
That breathed beneath the Syrian blue:

li 7. *eye . . . hidden*] sight my secret *H.Lpr 101. T.MS* has a *1st reading* heavily deleted (probably as *H.Lpr*).
li *10.* Cp. *Gareth and Lynette* 293: 'Let love be blamed for it, not she, nor I'.

lii 3. *only words, and*] words and lightly *T.MS.* T. said: 'There is so much evil in me that I don't really reflect you & all my talk is only words' (*Knowles*).
lii 4. John Churton Collins compared Persius, *Satires* i 104-5: *Summa delumbe saliva / hoc natat in labris.* ('Floating and spluttering on the lips, on the top of the spittle.') (This satire is apparently alluded to in xviii 3-4.) But T. wrote 'Nonsense' at this point on his copy of Collins's article, *Cornhill*, Jan. 1880 (*Lincoln*).
lii 5-6. T. said: 'Then the Spirit of true love replies – all life fails in some measure' (*Knowles*).
lii 5. *Yet*] Oh *T.MS.*
lii 8. *human*] casual *T.MS 1st reading.*
lii 9] What record keeps a spirit true *T.MS.*
lii 11. *What . . . the*] No – not the thirty *T.MS.*

'So fret not, like an idle girl,
    That life is dashed with flecks of sin.
15   Abide: thy wealth is gathered in,
    When Time hath sundered shell from pearl.'

LIII

How many a father have I seen,
    A sober man, among his boys,
    Whose youth was full of foolish noise,
Who wears his manhood hale and green:

5 And dare we to this fancy give,
    That had the wild oat not been sown,
    The soil, left barren, scarce had grown
The grain by which a man may live?

Or, if we held the doctrine sound
10   For life outliving heats of youth,
    Yet who would preach it as a truth
To those that eddy round and round?

Hold thou the good: define it well:
    For fear divine Philosophy
15   Should push beyond her mark, and be
Procuress to the Lords of Hell.

lii *15. Abide*: 'wait without wearying' (T.).
lii *16. Time hath sundered*] years have rotted *trial edition*.

liii T. said: 'There is a passionate heat of nature in a rake sometimes – The
nature that yields emotionally may come straighter than a prig's'; 'Yet don't
you be making excuses for this kind of thing – it's unsafe. You must set a rule
before youth'; 'There's need of rule to men also – though no particular one
that I know of – it may be arbitrary' (*Knowles*).
liii *5. fancy*] *1850* (*3rd*); doctrine *1850* (*1st – 2nd*).
liii *7. scarce had*] *1850* (*3rd*); had not *1850* (*1st – 2nd*).
liii *8*. B. Richards notes: 'the grain reminiscent both of "Man shall not live by
bread alone" (*Matthew* iv 4) and the parable of the wheat and the tares'
(*English Verse 1830–1890*, 1980, p. 115).
liii *9. Or,*] *1883*; Oh! *1850–82* (T. made this change in a copy of *Works*, 1881,
Lincoln).
liii *12. those*] lives *trial edition*.
liii *14. divine Philosophy: Comus* **476**. Cp. *Colossians* ii 8: 'Beware lest any
man spoil you through philosophy and vain deceit, after the tradition of
men, after the rudiments of the world, and not after Christ.'
liii *16. Procuress*] A pandar *T.MS, L.MS*.

LIV

Oh yet we trust that somehow good
  Will be the final goal of ill,
  To pangs of nature, sins of will,
Defects of doubt, and taints of blood;

5 That nothing walks with aimless feet;
  That not one life shall be destroyed,
  Or cast as rubbish to the void,
When God hath made the pile complete;

That not a worm is cloven in vain;
10   That not a moth with vain desire
  Is shrivelled in a fruitless fire,
Or but subserves another's gain.

Behold, we know not anything;
  I can but trust that good shall fall
15   At last—far off—at last, to all,
And every winter change to spring.

So runs my dream: but what am I?
  An infant crying in the night:
  An infant crying for the light:
20 And with no language but a cry.

LV

The wish, that of the living whole
  No life may fail beyond the grave,
  Derives it not from what we have
The likest God within the soul?

liv *1. we*] I *T.MS.*
liv *12* ∧ *13*] For hope at awful distance set
        Oft whispers of a kindlier plan
        Though never prophet came to man
        Of such a revelation yet. *T.MS, deleted*
liv *13–14*] Behold, I know not anything
        But that I would that good should fall *T.MS*
liv *18. infant: infans,* unable to speak. Cp. *Jeremiah* i 6: 'Then said I, Ah,
Lord God! behold, I cannot speak: for I am a child.'

lv Not *T.MS.* The sections about evolution were written 'some years'
before the publication of Robert Chambers's *Vestiges of Creation* in 1844

5 Are God and Nature then at strife,
   That Nature lends such evil dreams?
   So careful of the type she seems,
   So careless of the single life;

(*Mem.* i 223). The use of 'type' and 'life' suggests the influence of Charles
Lyell's *Principles of Geology*, which T. read at the end of 1836 (*Letters* i 145)
and in 1837 (*Mem.* i 162, noted by J. Killham, *Tennyson and 'The Princess'*,
1958, p. 248). Cp. the MS of *The Palace of Art* 186–92*n* (*p.* 65): 'And likewise
every life that Nature made, / What yet is left and what is gone / To where the
classes vanish, shade by shade, / Life and half-life, to none.' Also *The Two
Voices* 32–3: 'Though thou wert scattered to the wind, / Yet is there plenty of
the kind.'
lv 7–8. Cp. Chambers (p. 377): 'It is clear, moreover, from the
whole scope of the natural laws, that the individual, as far as the present
sphere of being is concerned, is to the Author of Nature a consideration of
inferior moment. Everywhere we see the arrangements for the species
perfect; the individual is left, as it were, to take his chance amidst the *mêlée* of
the various laws affecting him. If he be found inferiorly endowed, or ill
befalls him, there was at least no partiality against him. The system has the
fairness of a lottery, in which every one has the like chance of drawing the
prize.' Sections liii–lv should be compared with T.'s letter to Emily
Sellwood, 24 Oct. 1839 (*Letters* i 174–5): 'So mayst thou and I and all of us
ascend stepwise to Perfection ... the hope that conquers all things ... but
there is no answer to the question except in a great hope of universal good.
And even then one might ask why God has made one to suffer more than
another, why is it not meted equally to all. Let us be silent for we know
nothing of these things and we trust there is one who knows all ... Who
knows whether revelation be not itself a veil to hide the glory of that love
which we could not look upon without marring our own sight and our own
onward progress. If it were proclaimed as a truth "no man shall perish: all
shall live after a certain time have gone by in bliss with God" such a truth
might tell well with one or two lofty spirits but would be the hindrance of the
world. I dare say my own progress is impeded by holding this hope however
dimly.'
    N. Rupke, writing on 'William Buckland and the English School of
Geology', has argued that the traditional interpretation of T.'s science is the
opposite of the truth: 'Neither organic evolution nor Lyellian geology occurs
in *The Princess* or in *In Memoriam*. The reading of organic evolution into these
poems is based on the elementary mistake of confusing the theory of
progressive succession with that of evolution.' The 'distinctive features' of
the English school of geology 'are all present, namely an interest in vertebrate
fossils (especially giant reptiles), an emphasis on the finite duration of species
shown by episodic extinctions, a reluctant acceptance of the nebular
hypothesis with its corollary of a central heat, and a committed belief in
progressive change. These sharply contrasted with the views of Lyell' (*The
Great Chain of History*, 1983, pp. 226–7).

That I, considering everywhere
10   Her secret meaning in her deeds,
    And finding that of fifty seeds
    She often brings but one to bear,

I falter where I firmly trod,
    And falling with my weight of cares
15   Upon the great world's altar-stairs
    That slope through darkness up to God,

I stretch lame hands of faith, and grope,
    And gather dust and chaff, and call
    To what I feel is Lord of all,
20 And faintly trust the larger hope.

LVI

'So careful of the type?' but no.
    From scarpèd cliff and quarried stone
    She cries, 'A thousand types are gone:
I care for nothing, all shall go.

lv *11.* '"Fifty" should be "myriad"' (T.).
lv *20.* See *The Vision of Sin* 220–4n (*p. 218*).

lvi Not *T.MS* and *trial edition. Mem.* i 223 says that the sections about
evolution existed some years before the publication of Chambers's *Vestiges
of Creation* in 1844. E. B. Mattes (*In Memoriam: The Way of a Soul,* 1951,
p. 58) remarks: 'It was almost certainly his reading in the *Principles of
Geology* that led Tennyson to write lvi. Lyell's second volume has this dis-
concerting quotation on its title-page: "The inhabitants of the globe, like
all the other parts of it, are subject to change. It is not only the individual
that perishes, but whole species".' Lyell also says: 'Species cannot be
immortal, but must perish, one after the other, like the individuals which
compose them' (4th edn, 1835, iii 155). 'And even when they have been
included in rocky strata, . . . they must nevertheless eventually perish; for
every year some portion of the earth's crust is shattered by earthquakes or
melted by volcanic fire, or ground to dust by the moving waters on the
surface' (iii 280). T.read Lyell at the end of 1836 (*Letters* i 145) and in 1837
(*Mem.* i 162), which was also the date of publication of C. Babbage's *Ninth
Bridgewater Treatise* (*Lincoln*). Babbage praised God's foreseeing 'that the
extinction of every race should be as certain as the death of each individual;
and the advent of new genera be as inevitable as the destruction of their
predecessors' (p. 46). T. said: 'There's a deeper tone about these than
the last lot (of speculative stanzas)' (*Knowles*).
lvi *1. but no*] not so *L.MS 1st reading.*

5   'Thou makest thine appeal to me:
      I bring to life, I bring to death:
      The spirit does but mean the breath:
      I know no more.' And he, shall he,

      Man, her last work, who seemed so fair,
10   Such splendid purpose in his eyes,
      Who rolled the psalm to wintry skies,
      Who built him fanes of fruitless prayer,

      Who trusted God was love indeed
      And love Creation's final law –
15   Though Nature, red in tooth and claw
      With ravine, shrieked against his creed –

      Who loved, who suffered countless ills,
      Who battled for the True, the Just,
      Be blown about the desert dust,
20   Or sealed within the iron hills?

lvi 5–8] *Added to L.MS in margin.*

lvi 8–16. Cp. Thomson's *Spring* 349–58: 'But man, whom Nature formed of milder clay, / With every kind emotion in his heart, / And taught alone to weep . . . shall he, fair form! / Who wears sweet smiles, and looks erect on Heaven, / E'er stoop to mingle with the prowling herd, / And dip his tongue in gore? The beast of prey, / Blood-stained, deserves to bleed.'

lvi 9] Shall he that seemed so grand and fair, *L.MS 1st reading.*

lvi 11. *wintry*] Sabbath *L.MS.* Cp. T.'s childhood translation of Horace (*Lincoln*): 'roll away / Along yon wintry skies' (I 4).

lvi 12. *fruitless*] praise and *L.MS.* S & S note *The Death of Œnone* 40–41: 'The Gods / Avenge on stony hearts a fruitless prayer'.

lvi 15. *in*] with *L.MS.*

lvi 16. *With . . . shrieked*] And . . . cried *L.MS.*

lvi 18] Who yearned for True and Good and Just, *L.MS.*

lvi 19. Turner (pp. 124–5) notes that Lyell 'has a whole section entitled "Imbedding of Organic Bodies and Human Remains in Blown Sand"'.

lvi 20. *iron hills. The Princess* v 140. J. S. Kebabian notes: 'the sandstone hills of Scotland, as described in Hugh Miller's *The Old Red Sandstone*, 1841. They are coloured red by the iron oxide which they contain'; *sealed*, because of 'the fossil fishes discovered by Miller in these sandstones' (*TLS*, 11 June 1982). To which may be added that a jotting by T. in *H.Nbk 18* acknowledges this book.

No more? A monster then, a dream,
    A discord. Dragons of the prime,
    That tare each other in their slime,
Were mellow music matched with him.

25 O life as futile, then, as frail!
    O for thy voice to soothe and bless!
    What hope of answer, or redress?
Behind the veil, behind the veil.

LVII

Peace; come away: the song of woe
    Is after all an earthly song:
    Peace; come away: we do him wrong
To sing so wildly: let us go.

5   Come; let us go: your cheeks are pale;
    But half my life I leave behind:

lvi *22. prime*: B. Richards notes 'the first age of the world (*OED* 6b)' (*English Verse 1830–1890*, 1980, p. 117).

lvi *23. tare*] tore *L.MS*.

lvi *28.* The 'veil' has attracted much commentary. E. B. Mattes (pp. 62–3) suggests that T. probably 'had in mind the myth of the veiled statue of Truth at Sais, which one might unveil only at the cost of one's life'; Arthur Hallam had alluded to this in a sonnet either to Emily Tennyson (Motter, p. 83) or to Fanny Kemble (as J. Kolb argues): 'Who in my Sais-temple wast a light / Behind all veils of thought.' T. may have learned of it from William Heckford's *Succinct Account of All the Religions* (1791), of which a copy was at Somersby (*Lincoln*): 'on whose temple at Sais was the following remarkable inscription: "I am all that hath been, is, and shall be, and my veil hath no mortal yet uncovered"' (p. 5). Cp. also *Hebrews* vi 19: 'Which hope we have as an anchor of the soul, both sure and stedfast, and which entereth into that within the veil.' The word was a favourite of Shelley's. S. Gliserman points out that 'The word occurs with great frequency in science writing in exactly the same way that T. uses it', in 'the kind of book which was intended to mediate between the results of scientific observation and the wish of a general audience to understand scientific information and theories' (*VS* xviii, 1975, 439). J. Beer notes that Coleridge has 'behind the veil' in *Aids to Reflection*.

lvii *L.MS* introduces this with an unpublished section, *O Sorrower for the faded leaf* (p. 981). S & S note that this section comes at the end of *T.MS* and may have been intended to close the whole poem.

lvii *5. Come*] Peace *T.MS*. T. said of 'your': 'the auditor's' (*Knowles*).

> Methinks my friend is richly shrined;
> But I shall pass; my work will fail.
>
> Yet in these ears, till hearing dies,
> 10 One set slow bell will seem to toll
> The passing of the sweetest soul
> That ever looked with human eyes.
>
> I hear it now, and o'er and o'er,
> Eternal greetings to the dead;
> 15 And 'Ave, Ave, Ave,' said,
> 'Adieu, adieu' for evermore.

LVIII

> In those sad words I took farewell:
> Like echoes in sepulchral halls,
> As drop by drop the water falls
> In vaults and catacombs, they fell;

lvii 7. T. said of 'richly shrined': 'in half a life!' (*Knowles*).

lvii 8. T. comments: 'The poet speaks of these poems. Methinks I have built a rich shrine to my friend, but it will not last.'

lvii 8 ∧ 9] So might it last and guard thy dust
For ever! would indeed [O I would *1st reading*] for this,
My skill were greater than it is!
But let it be. The years are just. *T.MS*

Spedding wrote: 'It seems to me that the 3^d Stanza is not wanted and w^d be better cut. The second does not quite please me. I s^d like it better if it contained a simple expression of fear that these songs are too perishable to preserve the memory of their subject. Something in this way – "The songs in which I build a shrine for his memory will soon die away in men's ears. They cannot perpetuate his name – yet in these ears &c" With this exception I think it beautiful –'

lvii 13–16. T. said: 'I thought this was too sad for an ending' (*Knowles*).

lvii 15–16. T. compares Catullus ci, 'these terribly pathetic lines': *Accipe fraterno multum manantia fletu, / atque in perpetuum, frater, ave atque vale.* ('Take them, wet with many tears of a brother, and for ever, O my brother, hail and farewell!') T. added: 'Nor can any modern elegy, so long as men retain the least hope in the after-life of those whom they loved, equal in pathos the desolation of that everlasting farewell.' Cp. *Frater Ave Atque Vale* (*p. 627*). On the importance of Catullus' poem to T., see J. Ferguson, *English Studies in Africa* xii (1969) 54–5.

lviii Not *T.MS.*

lviii 1–3. Bradley compared *The Lover's Tale* i 564–6: 'While her words, syllable by syllable, / Like water, drop by drop upon my ear / Fell'.

5   And, falling, idly broke the peace
      Of hearts that beat from day to day,
      Half-conscious of their dying clay,
    And those cold crypts where they shall cease.

    The high Muse answered: 'Wherefore grieve
10   Thy brethren with a fruitless tear?
      Abide a little longer here,
    And thou shalt take a nobler leave.'

LIX

    O Sorrow, wilt thou live with me
    No casual mistress, but a wife,
    My bosom-friend and half of life;
    As I confess it needs must be;

5   O Sorrow, wilt thou rule my blood,
      Be sometimes lovely like a bride,
      And put thy harsher moods aside,
    If thou wilt have me wise and good.

lviii *9–12*]   The grave Muse answered: 'Go not yet.
                 A speechless child can move the heart,
                 But thine, my friend, is nobler Art.
               I lent thee force, and pay the debt.

               Why wouldst thou make thy brethren grieve?
                 Depart not with an idle tear
                 But wait: there comes a stronger year
               When thou shalt take a nobler leave.' *L.MS 1st reading*

lix Not published till *1851* (*4th*), 'as a pendant to iii' (H.T.). Not *T.MS*,
L.MS. *H.Lpr 99* antedates *Sparrow MS* (which has no variants). T. said:
'Added afterwards but one of the old poems nevertheless' (*Knowles*).
lix *1. wilt*] would'st *H.MS*.
lix *1–2*. Cp. *Richard II* V i 93–4: 'Come, come, in wooing sorrow let's be
brief, / Since, wedding it, there is such length in grief.'
lix *4 ∧ 5*]   I cannot put thee forth again,
                 Nor lose thee in the cloud of change,
                 The times that grow to something strange,
                 The faces and the minds of men. *H.MS*
These became lxxi 10–11: 'Of men and minds, the dust of change, / The
days that grow to something strange.' Cp. *Morte d'Arthur* 238: 'Among new
men, strange faces, other minds'.
lix *6. like*] as *H.MS*.
lix *7. harsher*] deeper *H.MS*. T. said: 'A time has now elapsed & he treats
sorrow in a more familiar and less dreading way' (*Knowles*).
lix *8. wilt*] would'st *H.MS*.

My centred passion cannot move,
10   Nor will it lessen from today;
But I'll have leave at times to play
As with the creature of my love;

And set thee forth, for thou art mine,
    With so much hope for years to come,
15   That, howsoe'er I know thee, some
Could hardly tell what name were thine.

LX

He past; a soul of nobler tone:
    My spirit loved and loves him yet,
    Like some poor girl whose heart is set
On one whose rank exceeds her own.

5 He mixing with his proper sphere,
    She finds the baseness of her lot,
    Half jealous of she knows not what,
And envying all that meet him there.

The little village looks forlorn;
10   She sighs amid her narrow days,
    Moving about the household ways,
In that dark house where she was born.

lix 8 ∧ 9]   Use other means than sobbing breath,
        And other charms than misted eyes,
        And broodings on the change that lies
    Shut in the second birth of death.

    Nor shalt thou only wear the rue,
        But there are daisies on the grave,
        And sweeter blooms which thou shalt have,
    Not dipt with tears but dasht with dew. *H.MS*

Cp. the first line with 'When thy best friend draws sobbing breath', *The Two Voices* 244–6, MS.

l. [8] *dipt*] dasht with *H.MS 1st reading*, suggesting that 'with tears' was inadvertently left for 'in tears'. l. [3] was adapted as 'But brooding on the dear one dead', xxxvii 17. l. [4] was adapted as 'Beyond the second birth of Death', xlv 16. l. [8] was adapted as 'Deep tulips dashed with fiery dew', lxxxiii 11. For the daisy, dew, and grave, cp. the unpublished section, *I keep no more a lone distress* (p. 984).

lix *9. centred*] deepset *H.MS*.

lix *10*] Be less tomorrow than today; *H.MS*.

lix *11*] But sometimes I'll take leave *H.MS 1st reading, broken off.*

lix *13*] And set thee forth so trim and fine, *H.MS*.

lix *15*] That though I know thee well yet some *H.MS*.

The foolish neighbours come and go,
And tease her till the day draws by:
15   At night she weeps, 'How vain am I!
How should he love a thing so low?'

LXI

If, in thy second state sublime,
Thy ransomed reason change replies
With all the circle of the wise,
The perfect flower of human time;

5   And if thou cast thine eyes below,
How dimly charactered and slight,
How dwarfed a growth of cold and night,
How blanched with darkness must I grow!

Yet turn thee to the doubtful shore,
10   Where thy first form was made a man;
I loved thee, Spirit, and love, nor can
The soul of Shakspeare love thee more.

LXII

Though if an eye that's downward cast
Could make thee somewhat blench or fail,
Then be my love an idle tale,
And fading legend of the past;

lxi *1. state sublime*: Gray, *Ode for Music* 25. Also Crabbe, *The Borough: The Church*: 'All are departed from their state sublime, / Mangled and wounded in their war with Time'.

lxi *4*] The flower and quintessence of Time; *HnMS, T.MS 1st reading*. The MS line is *The Day Dream: L'Envoi* 24, which suggests that lxi was written *c.* 1833–4.

lxi *12*. Arthur Hallam speaks of Shakespeare in a context of Heaven and friendship, in a poem with many affinities to *In Memoriam: To One Early Loved*, stanza xiii (Motter, p. 82): 'Brave spirits are, whom I will have to friend ... / ... to whom th'approach is free / Of unbarred Heaven, and the full mystery / Unfolded to the penetrative mind. / Such is the mighty Florentine, and He / Who saw the solar angel, nor was blind; / Such the deep, simple Shakespeare, greatest of mankind.' Hallam also spoke of Shakespeare as 'the most universal mind that ever existed' in praising the *Sonnets* (*The Influence of Italian upon English Literature*, 1831; Motter, p. 229). For *In Memoriam* and the *Sonnets*, see headnote (*p. 339*). T. said of ll. 11–12: 'perhaps he might, if he were a greater soul' (*Knowles*).

lxii *3. Then*] *1851*; So *1850*.

5 And thou, as one that once declined,
    When he was little more than boy,
    On some unworthy heart with joy,
But lives to wed an equal mind;

    And breathes a novel world, the while
10   His other passion wholly dies,
    Or in the light of deeper eyes
Is matter for a flying smile.

LXIII

Yet pity for a horse o'er-driven,
    And love in which my hound has part,
    Can hang no weight upon my heart
In its assumptions up to heaven;

5 And I am so much more than these,
    As thou, perchance, art more than I,
    And yet I spare them sympathy,
And I would set their pains at ease.

    So mayst thou watch me where I weep,
10   As, unto vaster motions bound,
    The circuits of thine orbit round
A higher height, a deeper deep.

LXIV

Dost thou look back on what hath been,
    As some divinely gifted man,

lxii 5–7. Cp. *Locksley Hall* 43–4: 'Having known me—to decline / On a range of lower feelings and a narrower heart than mine'. Based on *Hamlet* I v 50–52: 'to decline / Upon a wretch whose natural gifts were poor / To those of mine.'

lxiii 1–4. T. said: 'Man can love below as well as above himself; So surely it cannot be a weight on the Spirit to remember the writer' (*Knowles*).

lxiii 4. *assumptions*: including the theological suggestion as in the Virgin Mary's reception into heaven.

lxiii 8. *I would*] will to *T.MS 1st reading.*

lxiv Not *T.MS*. 'Composed by my father when he was walking up and down the Strand and Fleet Street' (H.T.). R. Pattison suggests that the diction is reminiscent of Gray's *Elegy*, and that this section is a critique of 'Gray's form of elegy' (*Tennyson and Tradition*, 1979, p. 120).

Whose life in low estate began
And on a simple village green;

5 Who breaks his birth's invidious bar,
And grasps the skirts of happy chance,
And breasts the blows of circumstance,
And grapples with his evil star;

Who makes by force his merit known
10 And lives to clutch the golden keys,
To mould a mighty state's decrees,
And shape the whisper of the throne;

And moving up from high to higher,
Becomes on Fortune's crowning slope
15 The pillar of a people's hope,
The centre of a world's desire;

Yet feels, as in a pensive dream,
When all his active powers are still,
A distant dearness in the hill,
20 A secret sweetness in the stream,

The limit of his narrower fate,
While yet beside its vocal springs
He played at counsellors and kings,
With one that was his earliest mate;

25 Who ploughs with pain his native lea
And reaps the labour of his hands,
Or in the furrow musing stands;
'Does my old friend remember me?'

LXV

Sweet soul, do with me as thou wilt;
I lull a fancy trouble-tost
With 'Love's too precious to be lost,
A little grain shall not be spilt.'

5 And in that solace can I sing,
Till out of painful phases wrought

lxiv 3. S & S cp. *Psalm* cxxxvi 23: 'Who remembered us in our low estate'.
lxiv 6. *skirts*] skirt *L.MS.*
lxiv 21. *limit*] limits *MS 1st reading.*
lxiv 22. *its vocal*] his native *MS 1st reading. Chorus* 15 has 'vocal spring'.
lxv T. said: 'Another higher thought now comes – a great lift-up – part of mine will live in thee' (*Knowles*).
lxv 2. *fancy*] spirit *T.MS.*

There flutters up a happy thought,
Self-balanced on a lightsome wing:

Since we deserved the name of friends,
10   And thine effect so lives in me,
A part of mine may live in thee
And move thee on to noble ends.

LXVI

You thought my heart too far diseased;
You wonder when my fancies play
To find me gay among the gay,
Like one with any trifle pleased.

5   The shade by which my life was crost,
Which makes a desert in the mind,
Has made me kindly with my kind,
And like to him whose sight is lost;

Whose feet are guided through the land,
10   Whose jest among his friends is free,
Who takes the children on his knee,
And winds their curls about his hand:

He plays with threads, he beats his chair
For pastime, dreaming of the sky;
15   His inner day can never die,
His night of loss is always there.

LXVII

When on my bed the moonlight falls,
I know that in thy place of rest
By that broad water of the west,
There comes a glory on the walls;

lxv 6. *phases*] changes *T.MS.*

lxvi *1*. T. said of 'You': 'the auditor' (*Knowles*).
lxvi *9*] Like one gone blind within the land, *HnMS, T.MS, L.MS 1st reading*.

lxvii has a general likeness to *On the Moon-Light Shining upon a Friend's Grave*
(*1827*, III 643). Cp. also *Inverlee* (I 174), with its chancel, church,
moonlight, coffin and dusk. T. said: 'One I like very much. The visions of
the night' (*Knowles*).
lxvii *3*. *broad*] great *T.MS.* *water*] river *T.MS, L.MS.* 'The Severn' (T.).
lxvii *4*. *walls;*] *Eversley*; walls: *1850–84*. S & S (p. 33) say of the semi-colon:
'Either this is a change made by the poet's son or it is an error made by the
printing-house. In either case it is not authoritative'. The semi-colon may

5   Thy marble bright in dark appears,
     As slowly steals a silver flame
     Along the letters of thy name,
     And o'er the number of thy years.

     The mystic glory swims away;
10   From off my bed the moonlight dies;
     And closing eaves of wearied eyes
     I sleep till dusk is dipt in gray:

     And then I know the mist is drawn
     A lucid veil from coast to coast,
15   And in the dark church like a ghost
     Thy tablet glimmers to the dawn.

LXVIII

     When in the down I sink my head,
       Sleep, Death's twin-brother, times my breath;
       Sleep, Death's twin-brother, knows not Death,
     Nor can I dream of thee as dead:

well be a mistake, as J. Sendry also believes. But it could have been
introduced by H.T. with T.'s authority; S & S themselves record that *T.MS*
has a full stop, *L.MS* no punctuation, and trial edition a semi-colon; and
W. E. Fredeman points out that the Golden Treasury text of *In Memoriam*
(1885) has the semi-colon, and T. 'almost certainly vetted the volume'.

lxvii *5. marble*] tab *T.MS 1st reading (presumably* tablet). Cp. Shakespeare,
Sonnet 43: 'And darkly bright are bright in dark directed'.

lxvii *9. The*] *L.MS*; Thy *trial edition (error)*.

lxvii *14. lucid veil*: as in Thomson's *Autumn* 962, and Thomas Moore, *Odes
of Anacreon* (1800), xvi. Also Thomas Gisborne, *Walks in a Forest: Autumn:*
'The rime / Floats thin diffused in air ... / Twinkling in the sun its lucid
veil'. The 4th edn is at *Lincoln*, having belonged to T.'s mother. A.C.
Bradley (pp. 247–8) noted that Wordsworth speaks of 'a lucid veil' in
Poems During a Tour of 1833 xxxv (1835). But the earlier instances preclude
using this to date lxvii.

lxvii *15. dark church*] *1855*; chancel *1850–51*. T. remarks: 'I myself did not
see Clevedon till years after the burial of A.H.H. (January 3, 1834), and then
in later editions ... I altered the word "chancel" (which was the word used
by Mr Hallam in his *Memoir* [1834]) to "dark church"'. See T.'s letter to E.
Malan, 14 Nov. 1883 (*Letters* iii). Cp. *The Walk at Midnight* 38: 'The
chancel's lettered stone above'.

lxvii *15–16*. Cp. *The Princess* vii 165–6: 'Now droops the milkwhite
peacock like a ghost, / And like a ghost she glimmers on to me.' Also *To
the Queen*, MS (*p. 986*): 'And glimmers to the Northern morn'.

lxviii *2*. T. compares *Aeneid* vi 278: *Consanguineus Leti Sopor.*

5 I walk as ere I walked forlorn,
   When all our path was fresh with dew,
   And all the bugle breezes blew
   Reveillée to the breaking morn.

   But what is this? I turn about,
10   I find a trouble in thine eye,
   Which makes me sad I know not why,
   Nor can my dream resolve the doubt:

   But ere the lark hath left the lea
   I wake, and I discern the truth;
15   It is the trouble of my youth
   That foolish sleep transfers to thee.

LXIX

   I dreamed there would be Spring no more,
   That Nature's ancient power was lost:
   The streets were black with smoke and frost,
   They chattered trifles at the door:

5 I wandered from the noisy town,
   I found a wood with thorny boughs:
   I took the thorns to bind my brows,
   I wore them like a civic crown:

   I met with scoffs, I met with scorns
10   From youth and babe and hoary hairs:
   They called me in the public squares
   The fool that wears a crown of thorns:

lxviii 5–8] *Not HnMS, T.MS 1st reading.*
lxviii 5. Cp. *Mariana* 30: 'In sleep she seemed to walk forlorn'.
lxviii 9] Again with thee I wander out *HnMS, T.MS 1st reading.*
lxviii 10. *I find a*] But there is *HnMS, T.MS 1st reading.*
lxviii 13] But when the bird is in the tree *HnMS, T.MS.*
lxviii 15. *trouble*] sorrow *HnMS.*

lxix *Not T.MS* and *trial edition,* but this section is in *L.MS* where it comes
between lxvi and lxvii.
lxix 2. *That . . . ancient*] I dreamed that Nature's *L.MS.* For the darkness
this causes, cp. *The Two Voices* 160–62: 'If Nature put not forth her power /
About the opening of the flower, / Who is it that could live an hour?'
lxix 5. Cp. *The Gardener's Daughter* 185–208n (I 563): 'Tired of the
noisy town I wandered there'.
lxix 10. *youth and babe*] babe and youth *MS.*
lxix 12. T. comments: 'To write poems about death and grief is "to wear
a crown of thorns," which the people say ought to be laid aside.' 'I tried to
make my grief into a crown of these poems – but it is not to be taken too

They called me fool, they called me child:
I found an angel of the night;
15   The voice was low, the look was bright;
He looked upon my crown and smiled:

He reached the glory of a hand,
That seemed to touch it into leaf:
The voice was not the voice of grief,
20 The words were hard to understand.

LXX

I cannot see the features right,
When on the gloom I strive to paint
The face I know; the hues are faint
And mix with hollow masks of night;

5 Cloud-towers by ghostly masons wrought,
A gulf that ever shuts and gapes,
A hand that points, and pallèd shapes
In shadowy thoroughfares of thought;

closely – To write verses about sorrow grief & death is to wear a crown of thorns which ought to be put by – as people say' (*Knowles*). Cp. *Pierced through with knotted thorns of barren pain* (I 513).

lxix *14. I . . . angel*] There came a Vision *MS.* T. comments: 'But the Divine Thing in the gloom brought comfort.'

lxix *15. look was*] eyes were *MS.*

lxx Not *T.MS. L.MS* has two drafts (*A,B* below).

lxx *1. see*] get *A.*   *the*] *A – B*; thy *trial edition* (*error*).

lxx *1–4.* Cp. *Ah! yes, the lip may faintly smile* 7–9, on 'the rainbow of the night': 'But seldom seen, it dares to bloom / Upon the bosom of the gloom. / Its tints are sad and coldly pale.' Also Arthur Hallam, *Sonnets to Emily Tennyson* i 6: 'And paint upon the gloom thy mimic form' (Motter, p. 87). A. Day notes *Oh! that 'twere possible* 78–80: 'And I paint the beauteous face / Of the maiden, that I lost, / In my inner eyes again'. Cp. 1.3 with *The Princess* iv 538–9, MS: 'I moved among a world of hollow masks'.

lxx *5. Cloud-towers*] A fort *B.* Cp. this nightmare scene with Carlyle on the taking of Fort L'Eguillette, *The French Revolution* (1837), iii V iii: 'Toulon sees fusillading, grapeshotting in mass, as Lyons saw; and "death is poured out in great floods, *vomie à grands flots*''; and Twelve-thousand Masons are requisitioned from the neighbouring country, to raze Toulon from the face of the Earth. . . . There in black death-cloud we must leave it.' See l. 10n.

lxx *7. hand . . . and*] long long train of *A.*

lxx *8. In shadowy*] That sweep the *A.* John Churton Collins said that this line 'was obviously inspired by that weird line in Sophocles [*Oedipus Rex* 67], so infinite in its suggestiveness – πολλὰς δ'ὁδοὺς ἐλθόντα φροντίδος πλάνοις ['And threaded many a maze of weary thought'] – on which Shelley has written an admirable commentary' [Note on *Prometheus Unbound*]. Alongside this suggestion, T. wrote: 'Nonsense' (*Cornhill*, Jan. 1880, Lincoln).

And crowds that stream from yawning doors,
10   And shoals of puckered faces drive;
Dark bulks that tumble half alive,
And lazy lengths on boundless shores;

Till all at once beyond the will
I hear a wizard music roll,
15   And through a lattice on the soul
Looks thy fair face and makes it still.

LXXI

Sleep, kinsman thou to death and trance
And madness, thou hast forged at last
A night-long Present of the Past
In which we went through summer France.

5   Hadst thou such credit with the soul?
Then bring an opiate trebly strong,

lxx 8 ∧ 9]   Revolving spheres and weltering waves,
          And gusts of sand and foam and snow
          That down a dreary margin go,
          And lamps that wink at yawning graves; B
lxx 9] High shadows crossing dreary moors, A; lacuna B.
lxx 10. Cp. Carlyle: 'the victims tumble confusedly ... ravens darken the
river', The French Revolution iii V iii, alluded to in Aylmer's Field 765–8.
lxx 11. bulk: a word with evolutionary suggestions for T.; 'The bones of
some vast bulk that lived and roared / Before man was', The Princess iii 277–8;
and 'an old-world mammoth bulked in ice', ibid v 142.
lxx 12. Cp. The Two Voices 82–4, MS: 'Clear lustre on that boundless shore'.
lxx 13–16. Cp. the end of cxxvii and n (p. 474), which seems to allude to the
French Revolution: 'And compassed by the fires of Hell; / While thou, dear
spirit, happy star, / O'erlook'st the tumult from afar, / And smilest, knowing
all is well.'
lxx 16] Look thy fair eyes and make it still. B.

lxxi 1–2]   Kinsman of madness, waking trance,
          And death, O Sleep! thou hast forged at last trial edition;
          Old things are clear in waking trance,
          And thou, O Sleep, hast made at last T.MS
lxxi 4. went] T.MS; paced trial edition. summer] sunny T.MS. Alluding to
T.'s tour in the south of France with Arthur Hallam in 1830; see In the Valley
of Cauteretz (p. 590).
lxxi 5. Hadst] Hast T.MS.
lxxi 6–7]   So canst thou not put back and blight
          The sense that something is not right T.MS
lxxi 6. Then] 1851 (5th); So 1850–51 (4th). trebly strong] 1855; treble strong
1850–51.

Drug down the blindfold sense of wrong
That so my pleasure may be whole;

While now we talk as once we talked
10   Of men and minds, the dust of change,
The days that grow to something strange,
In walking as of old we walked

Beside the river's wooded reach,
The fortress, and the mountain ridge,
15   The cataract flashing from the bridge,
The breaker breaking on the beach.

LXXII

Risest thou thus, dim dawn, again,
And howlest, issuing out of night,
With blasts that blow the poplar white,
And lash with storm the streaming pane?

5   Day, when my crowned estate begun
To pine in that reverse of doom,
Which sickened every living bloom,
And blurred the splendour of the sun;

Who usherest in the dolorous hour
10   With thy quick tears that make the rose
Pull sideways, and the daisy close
Her crimson fringes to the shower;

Who might'st have heaved a windless flame
Up the deep East, or, whispering, played

lxxi 7. T. refers this back to lxviii 10 (*Knowles*).
lxxi 8. *so . . . may*] *1851*; thus . . . might *1850*.
lxxi *10–11*. Adapted from lix 4 ∧ 5, MS:
    Nor lose thee in the cloud of change,
    The times that grow to something strange,
lxxi *13. Beside*] Besides *L.MS.*
lxxi *14*] The meadow set with summer flags, *T.MS.*
lxxi *15. flashing . . . bridge*] clashing . . . crags *T.MS.*

lxxii Not *T.MS.* T. said: 'Another death day Sept 15th', and referred to xcix (*Knowles*).
lxxii *8. blurred*] sucked *L.MS 1st reading*.   *of*] from *L.MS.*
lxxii *10. quick tears*: Shelley, *Rosalind* 366.

15   A chequer-work of beam and shade
        Along the hills, yet looked the same,

        As wan, as chill, as wild as now;
          Day, marked as with some hideous crime,
          When the dark hand struck down through time,
20   And cancelled nature's best: but thou,

        Lift as thou mayst thy burthened brows
          Through clouds that drench the morning star,
          And whirl the ungarnered sheaf afar,
        And sow the sky with flying boughs,

25   And up thy vault with roaring sound
          Climb thy thick noon, disastrous day;
          Touch thy dull goal of joyless gray,
        And hide thy shame beneath the ground.

LXXIII

        So many worlds, so much to do,
          So little done, such things to be,
          How know I what had need of thee,
        For thou wert strong as thou wert true?

5   The fame is quenched that I foresaw,
          The head hath missed an earthly wreath:
          I curse not nature, no, nor death;
        For nothing is that errs from law.

lxxii *15. L'Allegro* 96: 'Chequer'd shade'.

lxxii *16. Along the hills*] *1855*; From hill to hill *1850–51.   yet*] and *L.MS.   same,*] same. *1884, Eversley.* Like S & S, this edition (1969) followed the authoritative edns. (or elsewhere authoritative), and printed a full stop, not a comma. But J. D. Rosenberg (*TRB* iv, 1982, 3–7) has persuasively argued that 'any full stop short of the very end clearly defeats T.'s rhetorical intention'; that the full stop in *1884* is a misprint or a tail-less comma; and that editions should revert to the comma that 'appears in every printed edition . . . from the Trial issue of March 1850 through the Kegan Paul edition of 1883'.

lxxii *26.* Cp. *Armageddon* iii 13–14: 'A day / Of darkness riseth on ye, a thick day'. Also T.'s *Sonnet:* 'Though Night hath climbed her peak of highest noon, / And bitter blasts the screaming autumn whirl.'

lxxii *28.* Cp. Shakespeare's *Sonnet 33*, on the sun: 'And from the forlorn world his visage hide / Stealing unseen to west with this disgrace.'

lxxiii *6. hath*] has *H.Lpr 101, T.MS.*

lxxiii *8.* 'Zoroaster's saying, "Nought errs from law"' (T.).

We pass; the path that each man trod
10   Is dim, or will be dim, with weeds:
What fame is left for human deeds
In endless age? It rests with God.

O hollow wraith of dying fame,
Fade wholly, while the soul exults,
15   And self-infolds the large results
Of force that would have forged a name.

LXXIV

As sometimes in a dead man's face,
To those that watch it more and more,
A likeness, hardly seen before,
Comes out—to some one of his race:

5   So, dearest, now thy brows are cold,
I see thee what thou art, and know
Thy likeness to the wise below,
Thy kindred with the great of old.

But there is more than I can see,
10   And what I see I leave unsaid,
Nor speak it, knowing Death has made
His darkness beautiful with thee.

LXXV

I leave thy praises unexpressed
In verse that brings myself relief,
And by the measure of my grief
I leave thy greatness to be guessed;

lxxiii *13. wraith*] wreath *H.MS.*

lxxiv *3.   , hardly*] comes, scarce *HnMS.*
lxxiv *4. Comes . . . one*] Unto some other *HnMS.*
lxxiv *5. dearest . . . thy*] now thy massy *T.MS 1st reading.   brows are*] brain is
T.MS.
lxxiv *6. art*] wert *HnMS.*
lxxiv *9. But*] And *HnMS.*
lxxiv *11–12.* Turner (p. 119) notes that 'Hallam's four surviving essays on
Italian literature include a life of Petrarch, containing a translation of
Petrarch's line on the dead Laura: "Death appeared lovely in that lovely
face", the probable source' of these lines.
lxxiv *11. knowing*] seeing *HnMS, T.MS 1st reading.*

5   What practice howsoe'er expert
       In fitting aptest words to things,
       Or voice the richest-toned that sings,
    Hath power to give thee as thou wert?

    I care not in these fading days
10   To raise a cry that lasts not long,
       And round thee with the breeze of song
    To stir a little dust of praise.

    Thy leaf has perished in the green,
       And, while we breathe beneath the sun,
15   The world which credits what is done
    Is cold to all that might have been.

    So here shall silence guard thy fame;
       But somewhere, out of human view,
       Whate'er thy hands are set to do
20 Is wrought with tumult of acclaim.

LXXVI

    Take wings of fancy, and ascend,
       And in a moment set thy face
       Where all the starry heavens of space
    Are sharpened to a needle's end;

5   Take wings of foresight; lighten through
       The secular abyss to come,

lxxv 8. *Hath*] Has *HnMS, T.MS.*

lxxv 9. *these*] our *HnMS, T.MS.*

lxxv 11] And with the breeze of lyric song *HnMS 1st reading.*

lxxv 13. Cp. *I loving Freedom* 11–12: 'But that which prospers in the green / May perish in the dry.'

lxxv 17. *So here*] *HnMS 1st reading*; Here then *HnMS.*

lxxv 20. *tumult of acclaim*: a phrase from *To Poesy* 8, written by Hallam and T. Cp. 'The tumult of their acclaim', *The Dying Swan* 33; and *Ode on Wellington* 142–6 (*p. 494*).

lxxvi 1. John Churton Collins compared Petrarch, *Sonnet 82*; T. wrote alongside this suggestion, '!!! nonsense' (*Cornhill*, Jan. 1880, *Lincoln*).

lxxvi 3. *starry heavens*] milky girths *T.MS, L.MS.* Spedding underlined 'milky girths' and put '(?)'.

lxxvi 3–4. Cp. *Cymbeline* I iii 18–19: 'Till the diminution / Of space had pointed him sharp as my needle'.

And lo, thy deepest lays are dumb
Before the mouldering of a yew;

And if the matin songs, that woke
10   The darkness of our planet, last,
Thine own shall wither in the vast,
Ere half the lifetime of an oak.

Ere these have clothed their branchy bowers
With fifty Mays, thy songs are vain;
15   And what are they when these remain
The ruined shells of hollow towers?

LXXVII

What hope is here for modern rhyme
To him, who turns a musing eye
On songs, and deeds, and lives, that lie
Foreshortened in the tract of time?

5   These mortal lullabies of pain
May bind a book, may line a box,
May serve to curl a maiden's locks;
Or when a thousand moons shall wane

A man upon a stall may find,
10   And, passing, turn the page that tells
A grief, then changed to something else,
Sung by a long-forgotten mind.

lxxvi 7. *And*] But *T.MS*.

lxxvi 8. *Before*] Ere half *L.MS 1st reading*.

lxxvi 9. *matin songs*: 'the great early poets' (T.). Spedding underlined 'if' and wrote 'qy though?'.

lxxvi 10. *our*] the *T.MS 1st reading*.

lxxvi 11. Cp. *Epilogue to The Charge of the Heavy Brigade* 39: 'But Song will vanish in the Vast'.

lxxvi 13. *clothed*] changed *T.MS 1st reading*.   *bowers*] towers *T.MS 1st reading*. Spedding marked this slip.

lxxvi 14. *With fifty*] A hundred *T.MS, L.MS*.

lxxvii 1–2. S & S note Campbell, *The Pleasures of Hope* i 3: 'Why to yon mountain turns the musing eye'.

lxxvii 2. *musing eye*: Arthur Hallam's *To Two Sisters* i 13 (to T.'s sisters Emily and Mary; Motter, p. 89).

lxxvi 4. Cp. Marvell, *First Anniversary* 139: 'Fore-shortned Time its useless Course would stay'; also *Paradise Lost* v 498: 'tract of time'.

lxxvii 6. *bind . . . line*] be the lining of *T.MS 1st reading*.   *may*] or *trial edition*.

lxxvii 7. *May*] Or *trial edition*.

lxxvii 8. *a thousand moons*: *A Farewell* 14, a poem resembling *In Memoriam*.

> But what of that? My darkened ways
>   Shall ring with music all the same;
> 15   To breathe my loss is more than fame,
>   To utter love more sweet than praise.

LXXVIII

Again at Christmas did we weave
  The holly round the Christmas hearth;
  The silent snow possessed the earth,
And calmly fell our Christmas-eve:

5 The yule-clog sparkled keen with frost,
  No wing of wind the region swept,
  But over all things brooding slept
The quiet sense of something lost.

As in the winters left behind,
10   Again our ancient games had place,
  The mimic picture's breathing grace,
And dance and song and hoodman-blind.

Who showed a token of distress?
  No single tear, no mark of pain:
15   O sorrow, then can sorrow wane?
  O grief, can grief be changed to less?

lxxvii *13. darkened*] mortal *T.MS 1st reading.* *ways*] days *T.MS.*

lxxviii *5.* The Yule-Clog (log) was placed on the fire on Christmas Eve. T. may have recalled J. Brand's *Popular Antiquities* (1810, *Lincoln*), which spoke of 'its being burnt as an Emblem of the returning Sun' (p. 174).
lxxviii *11.* 'Tableaux vivants' (T.).
lxxviii *12. hoodman-blind*: blind man's buff (T.). H.T. compares *Hamlet* III iv 76–7: 'What devil was't / That thus hath cozened you at hoodman-blind?'.
lxxviii *14. mark*] *1855*; type *1850–51*.   *tear*] *MSS*; tears *trial edition* (*error*). S & S note Hallam, *On Sympathy*: 'Pleasure, therefore, will be the surest sign of life to the soul ... Marks of pain, in a less degree, will also be proofs' (Motter, p. 135).
lxxviii *16. be changed to*] become the *HnMS, T.MS, L.MS 1st reading*; decline to *L.MS 2nd reading.* Spedding wrote: 'Stanza 4. l 4. "*the* less" I doubt whether this is good English. As far as I can remember "the" is never prefixed except when a [*deleted*] "because of" or some equivalent expression follows, – exprest or understood – "Never the less" means I think "not the less on that account". When will you do it? on Monday. Will you not do it sooner? *The* sooner sweet for you! I hope you are better (not *the* better). How are you? Never *the* better for seeing you?'

O last regret, regret can die!
No–mixt with all this mystic frame,
Her deep relations are the same,
20   But with long use her tears are dry.

LXXIX

'More than my brothers are to me,'–
Let this not vex thee, noble heart!
I know thee of what force thou art
To hold the costliest love in fee.

5   But thou and I are one in kind,
As moulded like in Nature's mint;
And hill and wood and field did print
The same sweet forms in either mind.

For us the same cold streamlet curled
10   Through all his eddying coves; the same
All winds that roam the twilight came
In whispers of the beauteous world.

At one dear knee we proffered vows,
One lesson from one book we learned,
15   Ere childhood's flaxen ringlet turned
To black and brown on kindred brows.

And so my wealth resembles thine,
But he was rich where I was poor,
And he supplied my want the more
20   As his unlikeness fitted mine.

LXXX

If any vague desire should rise,
That holy Death ere Arthur died

lxxviii *17–20*] Not HnMS.
lxxviii *20. But*] Though *T.MS.*

lxxix 'Addressed to my brother Charles (Tennyson Turner)' (T.). Cp.
Prefatory Poem to My Brother's Sonnets (p. *625*).
lxxix *1.* ix 20.
lxxix *9.* Cp. Crabbe, *Delay Has Danger* 707: 'And the cold stream curl'd
onward'.
lxxix *11. that roam the twilight*: incorporated from *Locksley Hall* 122, MS.
lxxix *16. kindred*] either *T.MS 1st reading*; brother *trial edition.*
lxxix *17. And*] Even *T.MS. wealth*] mould *T.MS 1st reading.*

lxxx *10–11*]   I see him in familiar ways;
           He bears about a weight of days *T.MS*

Had moved me kindly from his side,
And dropt the dust on tearless eyes;
5 Then fancy shapes, as fancy can,
The grief my loss in him had wrought,
A grief as deep as life or thought,
But stayed in peace with God and man.

I make a picture in the brain;
10 I hear the sentence that he speaks;
He bears the burthen of the weeks
But turns his burthen into gain.

His credit thus shall set me free;
And, influence-rich to soothe and save,
15 Unused example from the grave
Reach out dead hands to comfort me.

LXXXI

Could I have said while he was here,
'My love shall now no further range;
There cannot come a mellower change,
For now is love mature in ear.'

5 Love, then, had hope of richer store:
What end is here to my complaint?
This haunting whisper makes me faint,
'More years had made me love thee more.'

lxxx 14. *influence-rich*] rich in force *T.MS.*
lxxx 15–16. Adapted from *Hail Briton* 81–4: 'They wrought a work which time reveres, / A precedent to all the lands, / And an example reaching hands / For ever into coming years.' Cp. *Tiresias* 122–23: 'their examples reach a hand / Far through all years'.

lxxxi 1. *Could I have said*: 'Would that I could have said' (T.); Spedding wrote: '"Could I have said" meaning "I wish I could" – see above [*deleted*] a former note. I suspect it would be better without the first stanza'.
lxxxi 3–4. Adapted from *The Gardener's Daughter* 234–9*n*, MS: 'Beyond a mellower growth mature in ear'.
lxxxi 3. *There . . . a*] Oh! now there comes no *T.MS.*
lxxxi 4.*ear.*] H.T. reports: 'he told me, as far as I remember, that a note of exclamation had been omitted by accident after "ear" (thus, "ear!")'. But H.T. did not change the text; S & S note that the full stop is also in *T.MS*, *L.MS*, and *trial edition.*
lxxxi 5. *Love, then,*] If Love *T.MS.*
lxxxi 8 ∧ 9]   Scarce in my love can I rejoice
                By that conjectured loss dismayed,

But Death returns an answer sweet:
10   'My sudden frost was sudden gain,
And gave all ripeness to the grain,
It might have drawn from after-heat.'

LXXXII

I wage not any feud with Death
For changes wrought on form and face;
No lower life that earth's embrace
May breed with him, can fright my faith.

5 Eternal process moving on,
From state to state the spirit walks;
And these are but the shattered stalks,
Or ruined chrysalis of one.

Nor blame I Death, because he bare
10   The use of virtue out of earth:
I know transplanted human worth
Will bloom to profit, otherwhere.

For this alone on Death I wreak
The wrath that garners in my heart;
15   He put our lives so far apart
We cannot hear each other speak.

LXXXIII

Dip down upon the northern shore,
O sweet new-year delaying long;

Like some blind boy whose life is made
Dejected by his mother's voice. *T.MS, which then has,
interpolated* A sorrow through
lxxxi 9] Yet mighty Death speaks out at once. *T.MS.*
lxxxi *12. after-heat*] future Suns *T.MS.*

lxxxii *6. From . . . state*] Through other states *T.MS. From state to state: The
Two Voices* 351 (a similar context), and *Demeter and Persephone* 7. S & S add
Thomson's *Seasons, Winter* 605–8, where 'the mind . . . / Rises from state to
state, and world to world'.
lxxxii *7–8. shattered . . . ruined*] Transposed *T.MS.*
lxxxii *10. out of*] from the *T.MS, L.MS.*
lxxxii *12. Will*] Must *T.MS.*
lxxxii *14. Othello* IV ii 58: 'where I have garner'd up my heart'.

lxxxiii *2.* Cp. Shelley, *Prometheus Unbound* II i 15: 'Too long desired, too
long delaying, come'.

Thou doest expectant nature wrong;
Delaying long, delay no more.

5   What stays thee from the clouded noons,
Thy sweetness from its proper place?
Can trouble live with April days,
Or sadness in the summer moons?

Bring orchis, bring the foxglove spire,
10   The little speedwell's darling blue,
Deep tulips dashed with fiery dew,
Laburnums, dropping-wells of fire.

O thou, new-year, delaying long,
Delayest the sorrow in my blood,
15   That longs to burst a frozen bud
And flood a fresher throat with song.

LXXXIV

When I contemplate all alone
The life that had been thine below,
And fix my thoughts on all the glow
To which thy crescent would have grown;

5   I see thee sitting crowned with good,
A central warmth diffusing bliss
In glance and smile, and clasp and kiss,
On all the branches of thy blood;

lxxxiii 5–8, 9–12] *Transposed T.MS.*
lxxxiii 5–6] Dark nights, dim morrows, clouded noons –
                    Art thou too stayed within thy place? *T.MS 1st reading*
lxxxiii 6. Adapted from 'The sweetness of thy proper smile', xli 8 ∧ 9,
MS (p. 385).
lxxxiii 9–12. Cp. (noting the context) the flower-passage, *Lycidas* 142–51:
'Bring the rathe Primrose that forsaken dies . . .'
lxxxiii 11. See lix 8 ∧ 9n.
lxxxiii 11, 15. From Shelley, *Epipsychidion* 110–111: 'Beyond the sense,
like fiery dews that melt / Into the bosom of a frozen bud.'
lxxxiii 12. *dropping-wells*: wells formed by the dropping of water from above.
lxxxiii 16. *The Dying Swan* 42: 'Were flooded over with eddying song'.

lxxxiv Not *T.MS* (but there are leaves missing). T. said: 'I like that one'
(*Knowles*).
lxxxiv 1. *contémplate*: as cxviii 1.

Thy blood, my friend, and partly mine;
10   For now the day was drawing on,
       When thou shouldst link thy life with one
Of mine own house, and boys of thine

Had babbled 'Uncle' on my knee;
       But that remorseless iron hour
15   Made cypress of her orange flower,
Despair of Hope, and earth of thee.

I seem to meet their least desire,
       To clap their cheeks, to call them mine.
       I see their unborn faces shine
20   Beside the never-lighted fire.

I see myself an honoured guest,
       Thy partner in the flowery walk
       Of letters, genial table-talk,
Or deep dispute, and graceful jest;

25   While now thy prosperous labour fills
       The lips of men with honest praise,
       And sun by sun the happy days
Descend below the golden hills

With promise of a morn as fair;
30   And all the train of bounteous hours
       Conduct by paths of growing powers,
To reverence and the silver hair;

Till slowly worn her earthly robe,
       Her lavish mission richly wrought,
35   Leaving great legacies of thought,
Thy spirit should fail from off the globe;

What time mine own might also flee,
       As linked with thine in love and fate,
       And, hovering o'er the dolorous strait
40   To the other shore, involved in thee,

lxxxiv 25–6. Cp. *Hail Briton* 139–40, MS: 'An evil scorn / Has filled the lips of men with lies'.
lxxxiv 37–44. Cp. Horace, *Odes* II xvii 5–8: *a, te meae si partem animae rapit / maturior vis, quid moror altera, / nec carus aeque nec superstes / integer?* ('Alas, if some untimely blow snatches thee, the half of my own life, away, why do I, the other half, still linger on, neither so dear as before nor surviving whole?'). Cp. lxxxv 63–4.

Arrive at last the blessèd goal,
And He that died in Holy Land
Would reach us out the shining hand,
And take us as a single soul.

45 What reed was that on which I leant?
Ah, backward fancy, wherefore wake
The old bitterness again, and break
The low beginnings of content.

LXXXV

This truth came borne with bier and pall,
I felt it, when I sorrowed most,
'Tis better to have loved and lost,
Than never to have loved at all—

5 O true in word, and tried in deed,
Demanding, so to bring relief
To this which is our common grief,
What kind of life is that I lead;

And whether trust in things above
10   Be dimmed of sorrow, or sustained;

lxxxiv 41. Cp. *Paradise Lost* ii 409–10: 'Ere he arrive / The happy Ile'.
lxxxiv 43. Cp. *Maud* i 382–8, MS: 'Reached me a shining hand of help'.
lxxxiv 45. *Isaiah* xxxvi 6: 'Lo, thou trustest in the staff of this broken reed,
on Egypt; whereon if a man lean, it will go into his hand, and pierce it.'
lxxxiv 47. break] shake *L.MS 1st reading*.

lxxxv The version in *T.Nbk 17* (1833–4) is in eleven numbered stanzas; that
in *Heath MS* and *H.Lpr 106* has 48 lines. For a study of the *Heath* version, see
M. J. Ellmann, *MLN* lxv (1950) 22–30. *T.MS* has leaves missing and begins
at l. 93. Except in l. 74, *L.MS* has the final version, and so is not included in
references to MSS below. In *Eversley*, H.T. notes: 'addressed to Edmund
Lushington'; but he dropped this note in *1913* possibly because he came
across the 1833 version. Mrs Ellmann (without pointing out that H.T.
dropped his note) suggests 1841 as a probable date for the revision, since T.'s
friendship with Lushington was then strong. H.T. added a note in *1913* on
ll. 115–6: 'refers to his "bride to be", Emily Sellwood'; this suggests that the
revision of the poem will have been later than 1838, when they became
engaged. But S & S note that T. wrote alongside Gatty's comment on
ll. 113–16 ('the lady who became Mrs Tennyson') the words: 'no – a friend.
Apparently the one to whom the epithalamion is addressed'. S & S cp.
Hallam's poem *To A.T.*
lxxxv 5–40] *Not H.MS, Heath MS, T.Nbk 17.*

And whether love for him have drained
My capabilities of love;

Your words have virtue such as draws
A faithful answer from the breast,
15   Through light reproaches, half exprest,
And loyal unto kindly laws.

My blood an even tenor kept,
Till on mine ear this message falls,
That in Vienna's fatal wall
20   God's finger touched him, and he slept.

The great Intelligences fair
That range above our mortal state,
In circle round the blessèd gate,
Received and gave him welcome there;

25   And led him through the blissful climes,
And showed him in the fountain fresh
All knowledge that the sons of flesh
Shall gather in the cycled times.

But I remained, whose hopes were dim,
30   Whose life, whose thoughts were little worth,
To wander on a darkened earth,
Where all things round me breathed of him.

O friendship, equal-poised control,
O heart, with kindliest motion warm,
35   O sacred essence, other form,
O solemn ghost, O crownèd soul!

lxxxv *20.* J. H. Buckley (p. 114) observes: 'an image reversing Michel-angelo's view of the Creation'. Cp. *On a Mourner* II (on Hallam's death): 'And on thy heart a finger lays'.

lxxxv *21–4.* Adapted from a passage unadopted in *The Two Voices* (p. *119*): 'And those Intelligences fair, / That range above thy state, declare / If thou canst fathom what they are'. Cp. Arthur Hallam, *On the Madonna* 1–3 (Motter, p. 3): 'Not with a glorry of stars, a throne inwrought / With elemental splendors, and a host / Of rare intelligences'. The words 'intelligences fair' occur in Spenser, *Tears of the Muses* 509–10: 'The Spirites and Intelligences fayre, / And Angels waighting on th'Almighties chayre.' With the account here of Hallam's reception in Heaven, T. compares *Lycidas* 178–82.

lxxxv *33.* S & S note *The Gardener's Daughter* 4–5, MS: on 'a friendship so complete . . . justlier poised'.

Yet none could better know than I,
　　How much of act at human hands
　　The sense of human will demands
40　By which we dare to live or die.

Whatever way my days decline,
　　I felt and feel, though left alone,
　　His being working in mine own,
The footsteps of his life in mine;

45　A life that all the Muses decked
　　With gifts of grace, that might express
　　All-comprehensive tenderness,
All-subtilising intellect:

And so my passion hath not swerved
50　To works of weakness, but I find
　　An image comforting the mind,
And in my grief a strength reserved.

Likewise the imaginative woe,
　　That loved to handle spiritual strife,
55　Diffused the shock through all my life,
But in the present broke the blow.

My pulses therefore beat again
　　For other friends that once I met;
　　Nor can it suit me to forget
60　The mighty hopes that make us men.

I woo your love: I count it crime
　　To mourn for any overmuch;

lxxxv 40. Cp. Pope, *Essay on Man* iv 4: 'For which we bear to live, or
dare to die'.
lxxxv *41–4*] Not *T.Nbk 17*.
lxxxv *41. days decline*] life incline *H.MS, Heath MS*.
lxxxv *45–8*] Not *MSS*.
lxxxv *51. the*] my *MSS*.
lxxxv *53–6*] Not *MSS*.
lxxxv *57. My ... therefore*] These mortal pulses *MSS*.
lxxxv *58. that*] whom *H.MS*.
lxxxv *59. can*] doth *MSS*.
lxxxv *60. mighty hopes*: Shelley, *Revolt of Islam* iv 127.

I, the divided half of such
A friendship as had mastered Time;

65   Which masters Time indeed, and is
Eternal, separate from fears:
The all-assuming months and years
Can take no part away from this:

But Summer on the steaming floods,
70   And Spring that swells the narrow brooks,
And Autumn, with a noise of rooks,
That gather in the waning woods,

And every pulse of wind and wave
Recalls, in change of light or gloom,
75   My old affection of the tomb,
And my prime passion in the grave:

My old affection of the tomb,
A part of stillness, yearns to speak:
'Arise, and get thee forth and seek
80   A friendship for the years to come.

'I watch thee from the quiet shore;
Thy spirit up to mine can reach;
But in dear words of human speech
We two communicate no more.'

85   And I, 'Can clouds of nature stain
The starry clearness of the free?
How is it? Canst thou feel for me
Some painless sympathy with pain?'

And lightly does the whisper fall;
90   ''Tis hard for thee to fathom this;
I triumph in conclusive bliss,
And that serene result of all.'

lxxxv 63-4. See Horace's *Odes* II xvii 5-8 (quoted under lxxxiv 37-44*n*).
lxxxv 72. Cp. *The Lady of Shalott* 119: 'The pale yellow woods were waning'.
lxxxv 74. Recalls] Recall *L.MS.*
lxxxv 77-96] Not *MSS.*

So hold I commerce with the dead;
　　Or so methinks the dead would say;
95　　Or so shall grief with symbols play
　　And pining life be fancy-fed.

Now looking to some settled end,
　　That these things pass, and I shall prove
　　A meeting somewhere, love with love,
100　I crave your pardon, O my friend;

If not so fresh, with love as true,
　　I, clasping brother-hands, aver
　　I could not, if I would, transfer
The whole I felt for him to you.

105　For which be they that hold apart
　　The promise of the golden hours?
　　First love, first friendship, equal powers,
That marry with the virgin heart.

Still mine, that cannot but deplore,
110　That beats within a lonely place,
　　That yet remembers his embrace,
But at his footstep leaps no more,

My heart, though widowed, may not rest
　　Quite in the love of what is gone,

lxxxv 93. *commerce*] commune *T.MS*.
lxxxv 95. Cp. *Song* [*Every day*] 25–6: 'Grief and Sadness steal / Symbols of each other'.
lxxxv 97. *Now* ... *some*] Yet ... a *MSS except T.MS*.
lxxxv 98. *I*] we *H.MS*.
lxxxv 104. *whole*] all *MSS except T.MS*.
lxxxv 105. *which be they*] who are those *MSS except T.MS*.
lxxxv 109–20]   But yet I love you–count it crime
　　　　　　　　　　To mourn for any overmuch;
　　　　　　　　　　I, the divided half of such
　　　　　　　　　　A friendship as had mastered time. *MSS*
Repeating ll. 61–4. *T.Nbk 17* had originally placed this repetition as ll. 104 ∧ 5 there beginning 'And'.
lxxxv 113. R. W. Rader (p. 16) quotes Rashdall's diary, 14 Jan. 1834, speaking of T.: 'Hallam seems to have left his heart a widowed one.' Rader notes that if we did not know that this particular stanza was probably not composed till much later, the similarity might lead us to think that during his visit Tennyson had read Rashdall this very early elegy.

115   But seeks to beat in time with one
         That warms another living breast.

         Ah, take the imperfect gift I bring,
           Knowing the primrose yet is dear,
           The primrose of the later year,
120   As not unlike to that of Spring.

LXXXVI

         Sweet after showers, ambrosial air,
           That rollest from the gorgeous gloom
           Of evening over brake and bloom
         And meadow, slowly breathing bare

5   The round of space, and rapt below
           Through all the dewy-tasselled wood,
           And shadowing down the hornèd flood
         In ripples, fan my brows and blow

         The fever from my cheek, and sigh
10   The full new life that feeds thy breath
           Throughout my frame, till Doubt and Death,
         Ill brethren, let the fancy fly

         From belt to belt of crimson seas
           On leagues of odour streaming far,

lxxxv *115–16*. See general note above.

lxxxvi Not *T.MS*. 'Written at Barmouth' (T.). He was there in 1839, and apparently not previously (*Mem.* i 173). S & S note that he was there in July 1844 too. Knowles reported T. as saying 'Bournemouth', but this was presumably misheard (*Nineteenth Century* xxxiii (1893) 185). Cp. *The Lover's Tale* iii 3 (I 369): 'A morning air, sweet after rain [showers *1st reading*]'. T. said: 'This is one I like too – The West wind'; of l. 12, 'Imagination – *The Fancy* – no particular fancy' (*Knowles*).

lxxxvi *1–4, 9*. S & S note Coleridge, *The Destiny of Nations* 384–6: 'sweet, / As after showers the perfumed gale of eve, / That flings the cool drops on a feverous cheek'.

lxxxvi *1. ambrosial*] delicious *L.MS 1st reading*. Cp. 'Ambrosial gloom', fragment of a play (*Mem.* i 24); and *The Princess* iv 6.

lxxxvi *6*. Cp. *The Princess* i 93: 'dewy-tasselled trees'.

lxxxvi *7. the hornèd flood*: 'between two promontories' (T.). As in *Paradise Lost* xi 827.

lxxxvi *11. Throughout*] Through all *L.MS 1st reading*.

lxxxvi *13–16*. T. remarked to Knowles: 'The west wind rolling to the

15   To where in yonder orient star
      A hundred spirits whisper 'Peace.'

LXXXVII

I past beside the reverend walls
    In which of old I wore the gown;
    I roved at random through the town,
And saw the tumult of the halls;

5   And heard once more in college fanes
    The storm their high-built organs make,
    And thunder-music, rolling, shake
The prophet blazoned on the panes;

And caught once more the distant shout,
10   The measured pulse of racing oars
    Among the willows; paced the shores
And many a bridge, and all about

The same gray flats again, and felt
    The same, but not the same; and last
15   Up that long walk of limes I past
To see the rooms in which he dwelt.

Another name was on the door:
    I lingered; all within was noise
    Of songs, and clapping hands, and boys
20   That crashed the glass and beat the floor;

Where once we held debate, a band
    Of youthful friends, on mind and art,

Eastern seas till it meets the evening star'. Cp. *Milton* 13–16: 'Where some refulgent sunset of India / Streams o'er a rich ambrosial ocean isle, / And crimson-hued the stately palm-woods / Whisper in odorous heights of even.'

lxxxvii Not *T.MS.* P. Allen's *The Cambridge Apostles: The Early Years* (1978) is relevant to this section as to much else in this poem and others.

lxxxvii 6–7]   The silver anthem trilling wake
           And that melodious thunder shake *L.MS 1st reading*

lxxxvii 8. *prophet*] *1884*; prophets *1850–83.*

lxxxvii 15. The limes at Trinity College; 'that walk of limes', *To the Rev. W. H. Brookfield* 6.

lxxxvii 20. *beat*] smote *trial edition.*

lxxxvii 21–4. T. said to James Knowles: 'The "Water Club," because there was no wine. They used to make speeches–I never did'. *Nineteenth Century* xxxiii (1893) 185.

<blockquote>
And labour, and the changing mart,
And all the framework of the land;
</blockquote>

25   When one would aim an arrow fair,
      But send it slackly from the string;
      And one would pierce an outer ring,
      And one an inner, here and there;

      And last the master-bowman, he,
30   Would cleave the mark. A willing ear
      We lent him. Who, but hung to hear
      The rapt oration flowing free

      From point to point, with power and grace
      And music in the bounds of law,
35   To those conclusions when we saw
      The God within him light his face,

      And seem to lift the form, and glow
      In azure orbits heavenly-wise;
      And over those ethereal eyes
40   The bar of Michael Angelo.

lxxxvii 25. *When*] And *MS 1st reading.*

lxxxvii 25–30. The same metaphor is used in another poem to Arthur Hallam, *If I were loved* 5–6:

      All the inner, all the outer world of pain
      Clear Love would pierce and cleave, if thou wert mine.

lxxxvii 36. Motter (p. 43) compares Arthur Hallam's *Timbuctoo* 190: 'God triumphed in her face'.

lxxxvii 39. *ethereal*] seraphic *L.MS.*

lxxxvii 40. T. comments: 'the broad bar of frontal bone over the eyes of Michael Angelo.' 'These lines I wrote from what Arthur Hallam said after reading of the prominent ridge of bone over the eyes of Michael Angelo: "Alfred, look over my eyes; surely I have the bar of Michael Angelo!"' (*Mem.* i 38). On the significance of such a bar, cp. Coleridge: 'A few whose eyes were bright, and either piercing or steady, and whose ample foreheads, with the weighty bar, ridge-like, above the eyebrows, bespoke observation followed by meditative thought' (*A Lay Sermon*, 1817, 'Allegoric Vision'). R. G. Laird notes George Combe, *A System of Phrenology* (published April 1843), on the Organ of Individuality and its sign of a 'talent for observation, curiosity to know, and aptitude for acquiring knowledge of details': 'When large it produces breadth, projection, and descent between the eye-brows . . . It is very large in the portrait of Michael Angelo' (accompanied by an engraving); 'Such persons are learned, and, owing to the store of facts with which their memories are replenished, the great definiteness and precision of

LXXXVIII

Wild bird, whose warble, liquid sweet,
    Rings Eden through the budded quicks,
    O tell me where the senses mix,
O tell me where the passions meet,

5   Whence radiate: fierce extremes employ
    Thy spirits in the darkening leaf,
    And in the midmost heart of grief
Thy passion clasps a secret joy:

And I – my harp would prelude woe –
10   I cannot all command the strings;
    The glory of the sum of things
Will flash along the chords and go.

LXXXIX

Witch-elms that counterchange the floor
    Of this flat lawn with dusk and bright;
    And thou, with all thy breadth and height
Of foliage, towering sycamore;

their ideas, and the readiness with which they command them, they often take
a lead in public business' (*VP* xiv, 1976, 253–5).

lxxxviii Not *L.MS* but in *T.MS*. S & S note that in *T.MS* it is marked 'X' for
omission.
lxxxviii *1. Wild bird*: 'To the Nightingale' (T.).
lxxxviii *2. Eden*: 'a paradisal song' (T., copy of *Works, 1884*, Univ. of
London Library). *quicks*: quickset thorn (H.T.). Cp. 'Fills out the homely
quickset-screens', *On a Mourner* 6 (on the death of Hallam).
lxxxviii *5. fierce extremes*: *King John* V vii 13; *Paradise Lost* ii 599, vii 272
(note 'Eden', l. 2); Wordsworth, *Ecclesiastical Sonnets* III xi 12.
lxxxviii *6. darkening*] *1855*; *dusking 1850–51*.
lxxxviii *7. heart*] *pith T.MS*.
lxxxviii *11. the sum of things*: *Paradise Lost* vi 673.

lxxxix Not *T.MS*. It has many affinities, both in phrasing and in mood,
with *An Idle Rhyme* (II 91).
lxxxix *1. counterchange*: chequer (heraldic). J. H. Buckley (p. 264) com-
pares *Ode: O Bosky Brook* 58–9: 'woods, whose counterchanged em-
broidery / Of light and darkness chequered the old moss'. Also *Recol-
lections of the Arabian Nights* 84–6: 'counterchanged / The level lake with
diamond-plots / Of dark and bright'. Hallam wrote to T.'s mother, 20–30
June 1830, of 'the vicissitudes that have been changing and counter-changing
"the summervault of leaden weather' (*AHH*, p. 366, quoting T.'s *Dualisms*
17–18).
lxxxix *2.* Cp. *Marion* 48, MS: 'stealing shadows dusk and bright'.

5   How often, hither wandering down,
　　　My Arthur found your shadows fair,
　　　And shook to all the liberal air
　　The dust and din and steam of town:

　　He brought an eye for all he saw;
10   He mixt in all our simple sports;
　　　They pleased him, fresh from brawling courts
　　And dusty purlieus of the law.

　　O joy to him in this retreat,
　　　Immantled in ambrosial dark,
15   To drink the cooler air, and mark
　　The landscape winking through the heat:

　　O sound to rout the brood of cares,
　　　The sweep of scythe in morning dew,
　　　The gust that round the garden flew,
20 And tumbled half the mellowing pears!

　　O bliss, when all in circle drawn
　　　About him, heart and ear were fed
　　　To hear him, as he lay and read
　　The Tuscan poets on the lawn:

25 Or in the all-golden afternoon
　　　A guest, or happy sister, sung,
　　　Or here she brought the harp and flung
　　A ballad to the brightening moon:

　　Nor less it pleased in livelier moods,
30 　Beyond the bounding hill to stray,

lxxxix 7. *shook*] flung *L.MS 1st reading*.　　*the liberal air*: Byron, *Manfred*
I ii 50.
lxxxix 8. Cp. *Playfellow Winds* 7: 'With steam of this dull town'; and
To the Rev. F. D. Maurice 13: 'Where, far from noise and smoke of town'.
From Horace, *Odes* III xxix 12: *fumum et opes strepitumque Romae* ('The
smoke, the riches, and the din of Rome').
lxxxix 12. *dusty*] *1855, trial edition, L.MS*; dusky *1850–51*. Cp. *Will Water-
proof* 183, where 'dusty crypt' had originally been 'dusky crypt'.
lxxxix 15. *To ... air*] With me to suck the cool *L.MS*.
lxxxix 19–20. Adapted from the MS of *The Gardener's Daughter* 216–20n
(Sir Charles Tennyson, *Cornhill* cliii (1936) 441): 'The wind was fitful:
every musky gust / Tumbled the mellow pear'.
lxxxix 25. *all-golden*] golden *L.MS 1st reading*.

And break the livelong summer day
With banquet in the distant woods;

Whereat we glanced from theme to theme,
Discussed the books to love or hate,
35   Or touched the changes of the state,
Or threaded some Socratic dream;

But if I praised the busy town,
He loved to rail against it still,
For 'ground in yonder social mill
40   We rub each other's angles down,

'And merge' he said 'in form and gloss
The picturesque of man and man.'
We talked: the stream beneath us ran,
The wine-flask lying couched in moss,

45   Or cooled within the glooming wave;
And last, returning from afar,
Before the crimson-circled star
Had fallen into her father's grave,

And brushing ankle-deep in flowers,
50   We heard behind the woodbine veil
The milk that bubbled in the pail,
And buzzings of the honied hours.

XC

He tasted love with half his mind,
Nor ever drank the inviolate spring
Where nighest heaven, who first could fling
This bitter seed among mankind;

lxxxix *31–2*. Horace, *Odes* II vii 6–7: *cum quo morantem saepe diem mero /
fregi* ('with whom I many a time have beguiled the lagging day with
wine').
lxxxix *35. touched*] grazed *L.MS 1st reading.*
lxxxix *36. threaded ... Socratic*] handled ... Platonic *L.MS 1st reading.* S & S:
'T. probably substituted "Socratic" because "Platonic" was sometimes
understood to mean "homosexual" (*OED* a. A. 2.)'.
lxxxix *47–8*. T. comments: 'Before Venus, the evening star, had dipt into
the sunset. The planets, according to Laplace, were evolved from the sun.'
lxxxix *48. Had*] *L.MS*; Has *trial edition (error).*
lxxxix *49*. S & S note Keats, *Hyperion* iii 35: 'Full ankle-deep in lilies of the
vale'.

xc Not *T.MS.*

5   That could the dead, whose dying eyes
          Were closed with wail, resume their life,
          They would but find in child and wife
     An iron welcome when they rise:

     'Twas well, indeed, when warm with wine,
10   To pledge them with a kindly tear,
          To talk them o'er, to wish them here,
     To count their memories half divine;

     But if they came who past away,
          Behold their brides in other hands;
15   The hard heir strides about their lands,
     And will not yield them for a day.

     Yea, though their sons were none of these,
          Not less the yet-loved sire would make
          Confusion worse than death, and shake
20   The pillars of domestic peace.

     Ah dear, but come thou back to me:
          Whatever change the years have wrought,
          I find not yet one lonely thought
     That cries against my wish for thee.

XCI

     When rosy plumelets tuft the larch,
          And rarely pipes the mounted thrush;
          Or underneath the barren bush
     Flits by the sea-blue bird of March;

xc 13–20. A recurrent theme in T. Cp. *The Lotos-Eaters* 114–19: 'Dear is the memory of our wedded lives, / And dear the last embraces of our wives / And their warm tears: but all hath suffered change: / For surely now our household hearths are cold: / Our sons inherit us: our looks are strange: / And we should come like ghosts to trouble joy.' 'Confusion worse than death' (l. 19) is incorporated from *The Lotos-Eaters* 128. The theme is also that of *Enoch Arden*.

xc 21–4]   Alas–but could I gaze on him
                   Reclothed with human life from dust,
                   My friend should share my latest crust,
              Though famine tore me limb from limb. *L.MS 1st reading*

xci Not *L.MS* but in *T.MS*. S & S give reasons for thinking it was cut away from *L.MS*.

xci 4. T. comments: '"Darts the sea-shining bird of March" would

5 Come, wear the form by which I know
   Thy spirit in time among thy peers;
   The hope of unaccomplished years
   Be large and lucid round thy brow.

   When summer's hourly-mellowing change
10   May breathe, with many roses sweet,
   Upon the thousand waves of wheat,
   That ripple round the lonely grange;

   Come: not in watches of the night,
   But where the sunbeam broodeth warm,
15   Come, beauteous in thine after form,
   And like a finer light in light.

XCII

   If any vision should reveal
   Thy likeness, I might count it vain
   As but the canker of the brain;
   Yea, though it spake and made appeal

5 To chances where our lots were cast
   Together in the days behind,
   I might but say, I hear a wind
   Of memory murmuring the past.

   Yea, though it spake and bared to view
10   A fact within the coming year;
   And though the months, revolving near,
   Should prove the phantom-warning true,

   They might not seem thy prophecies,
   But spiritual presentiments,
15   And such refraction of events
   As often rises ere they rise.

best suit the Kingfisher. I used to see him in our brook first in March . . .
ἀλιπόρφυρος εἴαρος ὄρνις ["sea-flashing bird of spring"] (Alcman)'.
xci 5. *know*] knew *H.Lpr 101* (*error*).
xci 7-8. The nimbus of Iulus, *Aeneid* ii 681-4.
xci 12. Cp. 'the lonely moated grange' of *Mariana*.

xcii 1. *If any*] Yet if a *T.MS, L.MS 1st reading*.
xcii 3. *the brain*] my brain *T.MS*. Cp. *Maud* ii 200: 'the blot upon the brain'.
xcii 5. *where*] when *T.MS, L.MS*.
xcii 12. *-warning*] -warnings *T.MS*.
xcii 13-16. Cp. Coleridge, *Death of Wallenstein* (1800) V i 98-102: 'As the

XCIII

I shall not see thee. Dare I say
  No spirit ever brake the band
  That stays him from the native land
Where first he walked when claspt in clay?

5 No visual shade of some one lost,
  But he, the Spirit himself, may come
  Where all the nerve of sense is numb;
Spirit to Spirit, Ghost to Ghost.

O, therefore from thy sightless range
10 With gods in unconjectured bliss,
  O, from the distance of the abyss
Of tenfold-complicated change,

Descend, and touch, and enter; hear
  The wish too strong for words to name;
15 That in this blindness of the frame
My Ghost may feel that thine is near.

XCIV

How pure at heart and sound in head,
  With what divine affections bold
  Should be the man whose thought would hold
An hour's communion with the dead.

sun, / Ere it is risen, sometimes paints its image / In the atmosphere, so often do the spirits / Of great events stride on before the events, / And in to-day already walks to-morrow.' Hallam had written to T.'s sister Emily about the prospect of having to leave Somersby: 'I fear the shadow of the coming event will be on your spirit' (20 Dec. 1832; *AHH*, p. 706).

xciii 7. *all . . . is*] sense is deaf and blind and *T.MS 1st reading.*
xciii 9–12. H.T. comments: 'the ten heavens of Dante. Cf. *Paradiso* **xxviii** 15 ff.'   *sightless*: invisible, as cxv 8.
xciii 13] Stoop soul and touch me: wed me: hear *T.MS, L.MS 1st reading.*
xciii 15. *blindness*] darkness *T.MS 1st reading.*
xciii 16. *Ghost . . . thine is*] soul . . . thou art *T.MS 1st reading.*

xciv John Churton Collins said that 'The whole of this piece is little else than a translation of the noble passage about the mood in which man is fitted for communion with his God in Jeremy Taylor's Fifth Golden Grove Sermon.' Alongside this suggestion, T. wrote: 'Not known to me' (*Cornhill*, Jan. 1880, *Lincoln*).
xciv 3. *be the man*] that man be *T.MS.*   *thought*] thoughts *T.MS, L.MS.*
xciv 3–4. Cp. Arthur Hallam, *Who has not dreamt* 3–4 (Motter, p. 5):

5   In vain shalt thou, or any, call
      The spirits from their golden day,
      Except, like them, thou too canst say,
      My spirit is at peace with all.

      They haunt the silence of the breast,
10   Imaginations calm and fair,
      The memory like a cloudless air,
      The conscience as a sea at rest:

      But when the heart is full of din,
      And doubt beside the portal waits,
15   They can but listen at the gates,
      And hear the household jar within.

XCV

      By night we lingered on the lawn,
      For underfoot the herb was dry;
      And genial warmth; and o'er the sky
      The silvery haze of summer drawn;

5   And calm that let the tapers burn
      Unwavering: not a cricket chirred:
      The brook alone far-off was heard,
      And on the board the fluttering urn:

'Spirits that but seem / To hold communion with the dead'. Cp. *On Sublimity* 67: 'For thou dost hold communion with the dead'. G. G. Loane, *Notes and Queries* clxxix (1940) 275, compares *Duchess of Malfi* IV ii 20–21: 'O that it were possible we might / But hold some two days' conference with the dead.'

xciv *6.* Cp. Young, *Night Thoughts* iv 144: 'The spirit of the golden day'.
xciv *9–12.* T. said to Knowles: 'I figure myself in this rather' (*Nineteenth Century* xxxiii (1893) 185).
xciv *14–16.* The metaphor suggests Herbert's *The Family.* S & S add Cowper, *The House of Prayer.*

xcv Not *T.MS.* Possibly written 1841–2, since Dean Bradley 'was greatly struck by his describing to us on one singularly still starlit evening, how he and his friends had once sat out far into the night having tea at a table on the lawn beneath the stars, and that the candles had burned with steady upright flame, disturbed from time to time by the inrush of a moth or cockchafer, as tho' in a closed room. I do not know whether he had already written, or was perhaps even then shaping, the lines in *In Memoriam*, which so many years afterwards brought back to me the incident' (*Mem.*

And bats went round in fragrant skies,
10   And wheeled or lit the filmy shapes
That haunt the dusk, with ermine capes
And woolly breasts and beaded eyes;

While now we sang old songs that pealed
From knoll to knoll, where, couched at ease,
15   The white kine glimmered, and the trees
Laid their dark arms about the field.

But when those others, one by one,
Withdrew themselves from me and night,
And in the house light after light
20   Went out, and I was all alone,

A hunger seized my heart; I read
Of that glad year which once had been,
In those fallen leaves which kept their green,
The noble letters of the dead:

25   And strangely on the silence broke
The silent-speaking words, and strange
Was love's dumb cry defying change
To test his worth; and strangely spoke

The faith, the vigour, bold to dwell
30   On doubts that drive the coward back,
And keen through wordy snares to track
Suggestion to her inmost cell.

i 205). See *Mariana in the South* 61–84n (*p. 31*). T. said: 'This happened in my native place' (*Knowles*).

xcv *10*. 'Moths' (T.).   *lit*: alighted (H.T.). From Shelley, *Unfinished Drama* 236–8: 'And on it little quaint and filmy shapes, / With dizzy motion, wheel and rise and fall, / Like clouds of gnats with perfect lineaments.'

xcv *18*. The setting and mood suggest Gray's *Elegy* 1–4: '. . . And leaves the world to darkness and to me.'

xcv *24*. Perhaps, though the scene has its differences, T. recalled one of Hallam's letters to T.'s sister Emily, 28 Aug. 1831: 'Beautiful this harvest moon must have been with you, and I have fancied it many a night shedding abundant tenderness of light on the garden at Somersby, whose old trees and dark, tufted corners rejoice in that lonely radiance, and seem, as the wind murmurs through them, to utter inarticulate sounds of greeting and love' (*AHH*, p. 477). Turner (p. 122) notes that in Goethe's *Wilhelm Meister*, 'the dead Mariana "speaks to" her lover through her letters'.

xcv *28*. Of 'his', T. said: 'its' (*Knowles*).

xcv *32*. *inmost cell*: as in Gray's translation from Tasso; Shelley, *The Cenci* V ii 163, and *Epipsychidion* 569.

So word by word, and line by line,
    The dead man touched me from the past,
35 And all at once it seemed at last
    The living soul was flashed on mine,

And mine in this was wound, and whirled
    About empyreal heights of thought,
    And came on that which is, and caught
40 The deep pulsations of the world,

Æonian music measuring out
    The steps of Time – the shocks of Chance –
    The blows of Death. At length my trance
Was cancelled, stricken through with doubt.

45 Vague words! but ah, how hard to frame
    In matter-moulded forms of speech,
    Or even for intellect to reach
Through memory that which I became:

Till now the doubtful dusk revealed
50 The knolls once more where, couched at ease,
    The white kine glimmered, and the trees
Laid their dark arms about the field:

xcv 33. *Isaiah* xxviii 13: 'But the word of the Lord was unto them precept upon precept, precept upon precept; line upon line, line upon line.'
xcv 36. *The*] *1872*; *His 1850–70*. T. comments: 'The Deity, maybe. The first reading . . . troubled me, as perhaps giving a wrong impression.' H.T. quotes T., 'The greater Soul may include the less', and 'I have often had that feeling of being whirled up and rapt into the Great Soul.' Similarly, 'my conscience was troubled by "his". I've often had a strange feeling of being wound & wrapped in the Great Soul' (*Knowles*). Cp. *The Ancient Sage* (III 138).
xcv 37. *this*] *1872*; *his 1850–70*.
xcv 38. *heights*] heigths [?heighths] *L.MS.*
xcv 39. *that which is*: 'Tὸ'όν, the Absolute Reality' (H.T.). On the Platonic sources and implications, see A. Sinfield, *VP* xiv (1976) 247–52. S & S note it elsewhere in T. and in Hallam.
xcv 40. Incorporated from *An Idle Rhyme* 40 (II 92). Cp. *Armageddon* iv 29–31: 'An indefinable pulsation / Inaudible to outward sense, but felt / Through the deep heart of every living thing.'
xcv 42–3. Cp. Milton, *On Time* 22: 'Triumphing over Death, and Chance, and thee O Time'.

And sucked from out the distant gloom
A breeze began to tremble o'er
55   The large leaves of the sycamore,
And fluctuate all the still perfume,

And gathering freshlier overhead,
Rocked the full-foliaged elms, and swung
The heavy-folded rose, and flung
60   The lilies to and fro, and said

'The dawn, the dawn,' and died away;
And East and West, without a breath,
Mixt their dim lights, like life and death,
To broaden into boundless day.

XCVI

You say, but with no touch of scorn,
Sweet-hearted, you, whose light-blue eyes
Are tender over drowning flies,
You tell me, doubt is Devil-born.

5   I know not: one indeed I knew
In many a subtle question versed,
Who touched a jarring lyre at first,
But ever strove to make it true:

xcv 54–5. Adapted, as Sir Charles Tennyson observes, from *In deep and solemn dreams* 47–8 (I 303): 'And the sweet winds tremble o'er / The large leaves of the sycamore.'
xcv 63. Cp. Pope, *Elegy to the Memory of an Unfortunate Lady* 19: 'Dim lights of life'.

xcvi Not *T.MS, L.MS, trial edition*.
xcvi 1. *You say, but*] Dear Lady H.*Nbk 19 1st reading*. This variant and that in l. 2 show that, in so far as a particular person is addressed, it is more likely to be Emily Sellwood (whose religious scruples about T. had been one factor in delaying their marriage; H. D. Rawnsley, *Memories of the Tennysons*, 1900, p. 71), and not T.'s mother.
xcvi 2. *, you,*] maid *MS 1st reading*.
xcvi 4. *tell me,*] say that *MS*.
xcvi 5. *one*: Arthur Hallam, as T. says. Cp. *He was too good* 2–4: 'in his hour / Of darkest doubt, and in his power, / To fling his doubts into the street.' T. refers, as Motter says (p. 92), to Hallam's sonnet, *Then what is Life*, which wrestles with his doubts and ends: 'Those who know and feel that it is Night'. Hallam, to Milnes: 'I had many grapples with Atheism, but beat the monster back, taking my stand on strongholds of Reason' (1 Sept. 1829; *AHH*, p. 312); cp. l. 10.

Perplext in faith, but pure in deeds,
10   At last he beat his music out.
There lives more faith in honest doubt,
Believe me, than in half the creeds.

He fought his doubts and gathered strength,
He would not make his judgment blind,
15   He faced the spectres of the mind
And laid them: thus he came at length

To find a stronger faith his own;
And Power was with him in the night,
Which makes the darkness and the light,
20 And dwells not in the light alone,

But in the darkness and the cloud,
As over Sinaï's peaks of old,
While Israel made their gods of gold,
Although the trumpet blew so loud.

XCVII

My love has talked with rocks and trees;
He finds on misty mountain-ground
His own vast shadow glory-crowned;
He sees himself in all he sees.

xcvi *10. At last he*] Till he had MS *1st reading.*
xcvi *11–12.* In his copy of P. J. Bailey's *Festus* (2nd edn, 1845; *Lincoln*), T.
marked in the margin the line 'Who never doubted never half believed'
(p. 63).
xcvi *15. faced*] met MS *1st reading.*
xcvi *17. find*] make MS *1st reading.*
xcvi *19. makes*] made MS *1st reading.*
xcvi *21–4.* T. compares *Exodus* xix 16, 'And it came to pass on the third
day in the morning, that there were thunders and lightnings, and a thick
cloud upon the mount, and the voice of the trumpet exceeding loud.'

xcvii Not *T.MS, L.MS, trial edition.* There are two drafts in *H.Nbk 19*
(*A, B* below). *A* opens with the isolated line: 'Long married souls, dear
friend, are we,' and has the lines–with variants–in the order: 9–12; 33,
18–20; 13–16; 21–24; 29, 31, 30, 32; 25–28; 33–36. *B* lacks ll. 1–4 but
follows the line-order of *1850.* T. says: 'The relation of one on earth to
one in the other and higher world. Not my relation to him here. He
looked up to me as I looked up to him.
    'The spirit yet in the flesh but united in love with the spirit out of the

5 Two partners of a married life –
    I looked on these and thought of thee
    In vastness and in mystery,
  And of my spirit as of a wife.

  These two – they dwelt with eye on eye,
10   Their hearts of old have beat in tune,
    Their meetings made December June,
  Their every parting was to die.

  Their love has never past away;
    The days she never can forget
15   Are earnest that he loves her yet,
  Whate'er the faithless people say.

  Her life is lone, he sits apart,
    He loves her yet, she will not weep,
    Though rapt in matters dark and deep
20 He seems to slight her simple heart.

flesh resembles the wife of a great man of science. She looks up to him – but what he knows is a mystery to her' (*1913*). 'A running comment on life. The Soul left behind is only acquainted with the narrow circle of the old house – thus resembling a wife married to a mighty man of Science' (*Knowles*). J. Kolb, calling in evidence xcvi too, compares xcvii with Hallam's letter to T.'s sister Emily, 22 Jan. 1832: 'I was half inclined to be sorry that you looked into that Theodicaea of mine. It must have perplexed rather than cleared your sight of those high matters. I do not think women ought to trouble themselves much with theology: we, who are more liable to the subtle objections of the Understanding, have more need to handle the weapons that lay them prostrate. But where there is greater innocence, there are larger materials for a singlehearted faith' (*AHH*, pp. 509–10). Cp. xxxiii (*p. 376*).
xcvii *1–4*] Not *A–B*.
xcvii *3*. 'Like the spectre of the Brocken' (T.).
xcvii *5–8*] Not *A*.
xcvii *5*. *married*] common *B*.
xcvii *6*. *looked . . . and*] saw them and I *B*.
xcvii *8*. *spirit as of a*] soul as of thy *B*.
xcvii *9–12*]   They madly drank each other's breath
            With breast to breast in early years.
        They met with passion and with tears,
            Their every parting was a death. *A*
B likewise, with *They madly drank*] These two have drunk.
xcvii *13*. *Their*] His *A*.   *past*] died *A–B*.
xcvii *17*] Her faith is fixt and cannot move [rove *B*], *A–B* (l. 33).
xcvii *18*. T. notes: '*She* says' (*Knowles*).
xcvii *20*. *heart*] love *A–B*.

He thrids the labyrinth of the mind,
  He reads the secret of the star,
  He seems so near and yet so far,
He looks so cold: she thinks him kind.

25 She keeps the gift of years before,
  A withered violet is her bliss:
  She knows not what his greatness is,
For that, for all, she loves him more.

For him she plays, to him she sings
30   Of early faith and plighted vows;
  She knows but matters of the house,
And he, he knows a thousand things.

Her faith is fixt and cannot move,
  She darkly feels him great and wise,
35   She dwells on him with faithful eyes,
'I cannot understand: I love.'

XCVIII

You leave us: you will see the Rhine,
  And those fair hills I sailed below,
  When I was there with him; and go
By summer belts of wheat and vine

xcvii 24. *she ... him*] she knows so A; and is so A *1st reading.*
xcvii 25. *keeps ... of*] dwells upon the A.
xcvii 26] To think he loves her is her bliss, A.
xcvii 27. *knows*] knowing A.
xcvii 28. *For ... all,*] And yet for that A.
xcvii 29–32. T. notes: 'Just as this poor gift of Poesy is exercised because he loved it' (*Knowles*). T. glossed l. 31, 'of earth', and l. 32, 'of Heaven'.
xcvii 30–31] *Transposed A.*
xcvii 30] She looks upon his ample brows, A.
xcvii 32. *And he,*] And thinks A.
xcvii 33] His thoughts in vaster orbits move, B *1st reading.* Cp. 'orbits', lxxxvii 38.
xcvii 34. *darkly feels him*] feels him, darkly A. The MS is even closer to Pope's 'A being darkly wise, and rudely great', *Essay on Man* ii 4.

xcviii Not *T.MS.*
xcviii 1. '"You" is imaginary' (T.). But *Mem.* i 148 says that it alludes to the honeymoon of T.'s brother Charles, on the Rhine in 1836.
xcviii 2] And watch the impetuous current flow L.*MS 1st reading.*
xcviii 3. *When ... there*] That once I watched *MS 1st reading.*

5   To where he breathed his latest breath,
       That City. All her splendour seems
       No livelier than the wisp that gleams
       On Lethe in the eyes of Death.

    Let her great Danube rolling fair
10   Enwind her isles, unmarked of me:
       I have not seen, I will not see
       Vienna; rather dream that there,

    A treble darkness, Evil haunts
       The birth, the bridal; friend from friend
15   Is oftener parted, fathers bend
       Above more graves, a thousand wants

    Gnarr at the heels of men, and prey
       By each cold hearth, and sadness flings
       Her shadow on the blaze of kings:
20 And yet myself have heard him say,

    That not in any mother town
       With statelier progress to and fro
       The double tides of chariots flow
       By park and suburb under brown

25 Of lustier leaves; nor more content,
       He told me, lives in any crowd,
       When all is gay with lamps, and loud
    With sport and song, in booth and tent,

    Imperial halls, or open plain;
30   And wheels the circled dance, and breaks

xcviii 7. T. noted: 'the ghosts' (*Knowles*).
xcviii 12. *rather dream*] but methinks MS *1st reading*.
xcviii 13. *A . . . darkness*] In tenfold frequence MS *1st reading*.
xcviii 14. *birth, the bridal*] threshold, oftener MS *1st reading*.
xcviii 15. *oftener . . . fathers*] plucked asunder, parents MS *1st reading*.
xcviii 16. *more graves*] their dead MS *1st reading*.
xcviii 17. *Gnarr*: 'snarl' (T.).
xcviii 20] And Pain [Death *1st reading*] is lord; albeit they say MS.
xcviii 21. *mother town*: 'metropolis' (T.).
xcviii 26. *He . . . any*] Sits on the foreheads of the MS *1st reading*; They tell me, lives in any MS.
xcviii 28. *and tent*] or tent MS.

The rocket molten into flakes
Of crimson or in emerald rain.

XCIX

Risest thou thus, dim dawn, again,
  So loud with voices of the birds,
  So thick with lowings of the herds,
Day, when I lost the flower of men;

5 Who tremblest through thy darkling red
  On yon swollen brook that bubbles fast
  By meadows breathing of the past,
And woodlands holy to the dead;

Who murmurest in the foliaged eaves
10 A song that slights the coming care,
  And Autumn laying here and there
A fiery finger on the leaves;

Who wakenest with thy balmy breath
  To myriads on the genial earth,
15 Memories of bridal, or of birth,
And unto myriads more, of death.

O wheresoever those may be,
  Betwixt the slumber of the poles,

xcviii *30. And*] As *MS 1st reading*; While *MS.* The MS originally ended as *1850*, but another stanza was added:

> As once I watched them at his side
> And heard him breathe a broken line
> From that stronghearted Florentine:
> '*O vana gloria!*', thus he cried.

Hallam had spoken of the influence of 'the mighty Florentine' upon himself, in the last paragraph of *The Influence of Italian upon English Literature* (Motter, p. 234). *Purgatorio* xi 91: *oh vana gloria dell'umane posse!* ('O empty glory of human powers!').

xcix Not *T.MS. L.MS* has a first draft (*A*, below), deleted, between lxxxv and lxxxvi; a later draft (*B*) in its final position. T. noted: 'The *death* day September' (*Knowles*).

xcix *5–8*] Not *A*.

xcix *6. swollen*] wild *B*.

xcix *9. foliaged eaves*: cp. Shelley, *Alastor* 464: 'foliaged lattice'.

xcix *9–10*] Who risest not as one that grieves
      In silence for a world of care, *A*

xcix *13. balmy breath: Othello* V ii 16 (a context both of bridal and of death).

Today they count as kindred souls;
20   They know me not, but mourn with me.

C

I climb the hill: from end to end
Of all the landscape underneath,
I find no place that does not breathe
Some gracious memory of my friend;

xcix *19. they count as*] I count them *A*.

c Not *T.MS.* c–ciii allude to the Tennysons' move from Somersby in 1837, as T. observes. All four poems ask comparison with Hallam's reiterated letters to T.'s sister Emily about the prospect: 'Nay sometimes I cannot help thinking that if the name of Tennyson should pass from that little region, which all your life long has been to you home – that blessed little region "bosomed in a kindlier air, than the outer realm of care & dole" – the very fields & lanes will feel sorrow, as if part of their appointed being had been reft from them. Yet after all a consecration has come upon them from the dwellers at Somersby, which I think is not of the things that fail. Many years perhaps, or shall I say many ages, after we have all been laid in dust, young lovers of the beautiful & the true may seek in faithful pilgrimage the spot where Alfred's mind was moulded in silent sympathy with the everlasting forms of nature. Legends will perhaps be attached to the places, that are near it. Some Mariana, it will be said, lived wretched & alone in a dreary house on the top of the opposite hill. Some Isabel may with more truth be sought nearer yet. The belfry in which the white owl sat "warming his five wits" will be shown for sixpence to such travellers as have lost their own. Critic after critic will track the wanderings of the brook, or mark the groupings of elm & poplar in order to verify the Ode to Memory in its minutest particulars' (1–14 April 1831; *AHH*, p. 418). 'If you must take a farewell of that "happy spot," which seems to you "the only desirable place on earth," let it not be till I can take that farewell too. Its charms are not, and cannot be the same for me, but though different, they are not less holy. You look at those fields and wolds, and in your sight they are invested with a thousand hues of life's early morning: the "glory is on the grass," and "the splendor on the flower": feelings of what has been haunt every object around you, and you could as well prevent your senses from distinguishing their forms, as bereave them of the natural magic with which they affect your soul' (17 April 1831; *AHH*, p. 420). 'I am much grieved to think what your grief must be in leaving Somersby. I hardly dare endeavor to console you, but I trust you feel the necessity of summoning up all the powers of your mind to meet the event with composure & patience, if not with fortitude. Surely it must be some relief to you that you go not to a distant place, but to Dalby, the *second home*

5   No gray old grange, or lonely fold,
     Or low morass and whispering reed,
     Or simple stile from mead to mead,
     Or sheepwalk up the windy wold;

     Nor hoary knoll of ash and haw
10   That hears the latest linnet trill,
     Nor quarry trenched along the hill
     And haunted by the wrangling daw;

     Nor runlet tinkling from the rock;
     Nor pastoral rivulet that swerves
15   To left and right through meadowy curves,
     That feed the mothers of the flock;

     But each has pleased a kindred eye,
     And each reflects a kindlier day;
     And, leaving these, to pass away
20   I think once more he seems to die.

CI

Unwatched, the garden bough shall sway,
     The tender blossom flutter down,

of your childhood, a spot endeared by numberless early associations, &
having the same neighbourhood as Somersby itself. This must comfort you,
I think; and since you must indeed go to Dalby, it is well that you should
keep it much before your mind, as I doubt not you do. Yet–shall I own it,
Emily? I could bring myself to wish it were not so, and that when you left
your home you had left altogether the country. There is a hunger of
imagination preying upon your mind which I want to see blunted by a
complete, or at least considerable change of circumstances. Do you think me
cruel for saying this? I speak only in what I think your real & permanent
interest. To secure your welfare I would assent to anything &
everything–even to the temporary wounding of your feelings. I too love
Somersby. How dearly! But I love it *principally* for your sake. I trust I am not
too late to see it once more, to take a farewell of it with you–a last farewell of
objects & places eternally engraven on my heart, because connected with a
passion that has made the destiny of my life. I will not sadden myself more
by writing more about it' (12 Dec. 1832; *AHH*, p. 700).
c *1. climb the hill*] *1855*; wake, I rise *1850–51*.
c *8. the windy wold: Who claps the gate* 3 (*The Princess* ii ∧ iii, *p. 977*).
c *12. wrangling*] jangling *L.MS.*
c *13. runlet tinkling*] fountain sparkling *MS.*

ci Not *T.MS.* c–ciii allude to the Tennysons' move from Somersby in
1837, as T. observes. Cp. *A Farewell* (*p. 180*), on the same theme. J. Kolb

Unloved, that beech will gather brown,
This maple burn itself away;

5   Unloved, the sun-flower, shining fair,
Ray round with flames her disk of seed,
And many a rose-carnation feed
With summer spice the humming air;

Unloved, by many a sandy bar,
10   The brook shall babble down the plain,
At noon or when the lesser wain
Is twisting round the polar star;

Uncared for, gird the windy grove,
And flood the haunts of hern and crake;
15   Or into silver arrows break
The sailing moon in creek and cove;

Till from the garden and the wild
A fresh association blow,
And year by year the landscape grow
20 Familiar to the stranger's child;

As year by year the labourer tills
His wonted glebe, or lops the glades;
And year by year our memory fades
From all the circle of the hills.

CII

We leave the well-belovèd place
Where first we gazed upon the sky;
The roofs, that heard our earliest cry,
Will shelter one of stranger race.

compares Thomas Campbell, *Lines on Leaving a Scene in Bavaria* 64–72:
'Unheeded spreads thy blossomed bud / Its milky bosom to the bee; /
Unheeded falls along the flood / Thy desolate and aged tree ...'.
ci *3. that beech*] those elms *L.MS 1st reading*. The MS is even closer to *Sir
Launcelot and Queen Guinevere* 8, 'The topmost elm-tree gathered green'.
ci *8.* Cp. Arthur Hallam, *A Scene in Summer* 20–21 (Motter, p. 99):
'humming things that summer loves, / Through the warm air'.
ci *14.* Cp. *The Brook* 23: 'I come from haunts of coot and hern'.
ci *19*] And all the landskip slowly grow *MS 1st reading*.

cii *2. gazed*] lookt *T.MS*.

5   We go, but ere we go from home,
      As down the garden-walks I move,
      Two spirits of a diverse love
   Contend for loving masterdom.

   One whispers, 'Here thy boyhood sung
10   Long since its matin song, and heard
      The low love-language of the bird
   In native hazels tassel-hung.'

   The other answers, 'Yea, but here
      Thy feet have strayed in after hours
15   With thy lost friend among the bowers,
   And this hath made them trebly dear.'

   These two have striven half the day,
      And each prefers his separate claim,
      Poor rivals in a losing game,
20   That will not yield each other way.

   I turn to go: my feet are set
      To leave the pleasant fields and farms;
      They mix in one another's arms
   To one pure image of regret.

CIII

   On that last night before we went
      From out the doors where I was bred,
      I dreamed a vision of the dead,
   Which left my after-morn content.

5   Methought I dwelt within a hall,
      And maidens with me: distant hills

cii *7–8.* T. comments: 'First, the love of the native place; second, this enhanced by the memory of A. H. H.' The phrasing suggests Shakespeare's *Sonnet 144*: 'Two loves I have of comfort and despair, / Which like two spirits do suggest me still.'

cii *7. Two*] The *T.MS 1st reading.*

cii *19.* Cp. Shelley, *Queen Mab* iii 172–3: 'mutual foes, forever play / A losing game into each other's hands'.

cii *20. yield*] give *T.MS 1st reading.*

cii *22.* Cp. *Paradise Lost* ix 448: 'the pleasant Villages and Farmes'.

ciii Not *T.MS.* c–ciii allude to the Tennysons' move from Somersby in 1837, as T. observes.

ciii *6. maidens*: 'They are the Muses, poetry, arts–all that made life beautiful here, which we hope will pass with us beyond the grave' (T.).

From hidden summits fed with rills
A river sliding by the wall.

The hall with harp and carol rang.
10   They sang of what is wise and good
And graceful. In the centre stood
A statue veiled, to which they sang;

And which, though veiled, was known to me,
The shape of him I loved, and love
15   For ever: then flew in a dove
And brought a summons from the sea:

And when they learnt that I must go
They wept and wailed, but led the way
To where a little shallop lay
20   At anchor in the flood below;

And on by many a level mead,
And shadowing bluff that made the banks,
We glided winding under ranks
Of iris, and the golden reed;

25   And still as vaster grew the shore
And rolled the floods in grander space,
The maidens gathered strength and grace
And presence, lordlier than before;

And I myself, who sat apart
30   And watched them, waxed in every limb;

ciii 7. *summits*: 'the divine' (T.).
ciii 8. *river*: 'life' (T.).
ciii 12. *Letters* i 166 suggests affinities with T.'s words to Emily Sellwood, ? Oct. or Nov. 1838: 'Sculpture is particularly good for the mind: there is a height and divine stillness about it which preaches peace to our stormy passions. Methinks that in looking upon a great statue like the Theseus (maim'd and defaced as it is) one becomes as it were Godlike to feel things in the Idea'. L. D. Wiggins suggests the influence of Hallam's adaptation of Schiller on the 'Sais-temple', in which case the 'statue veiled' would represent Truth (*English Studies* xlix, 1968, 444–5).
ciii 16. *sea*: 'eternity' (T.).
ciii 25–8. 'The progress of the Age' (T.). 'The great progress of the age as well as the opening of another world' (*Knowles*). J. C. Maxwell compares l. 25 with Thomas Campbell, *Lord Ullin's Daughter* 29: 'But still, as wilder blew the wind'.
ciii 31. *Anakim*: the giants of *Deuteronomy* ii 10. Cp. *A Fragment* 20: 'the strong and sunborn Anakim'.

I felt the thews of Anakim,
The pulses of a Titan's heart;

As one would sing the death of war,
And one would chant the history
35   Of that great race, which is to be,
And one the shaping of a star;

Until the forward-creeping tides
Began to foam, and we to draw
From deep to deep, to where we saw
40   A great ship lift her shining sides.

The man we loved was there on deck,
But thrice as large as man he bent
To greet us. Up the side I went,
And fell in silence on his neck:

45   Whereat those maidens with one mind
Bewailed their lot; I did them wrong:
'We served thee here,' they said, 'so long,
And wilt thou leave us now behind?'

So rapt I was, they could not win
50   An answer from my lips, but he
Replying, 'Enter likewise ye
And go with us:' they entered in.

And while the wind began to sweep
A music out of sheet and shroud,
55   We steered her toward a crimson cloud
That landlike slept along the deep.

CIV

The time draws near the birth of Christ;
The moon is hid, the night is still;

ciii *33–6*. 'The great hopes of humanity and science' (T.).
ciii *37*. Cp. *Recollections of the Arabian Nights* 4: 'The forward-flowing tide
of time'.
ciii *40*. Cp. Arthur Hallam, of a ship: 'Did not the sides **wear** brilliance',
Lines Written at Brighton 21 (Motter, p. 49).
ciii *41. there on*] on the *L.MS 1st reading.*
ciii *45–8*. T. commented to James Knowles: 'He was wrong to drop his
earthly hopes and powers–they will be still of use to him', *Nineteenth
Century* xxxiii (1893) 187.

civ *2. hid*] out *T.MS.*

A single church below the hill
Is pealing, folded in the mist.

5   A single peal of bells below,
That wakens at this hour of rest
A single murmur in the breast,
That these are not the bells I know.

Like strangers' voices here they sound,
10   In lands where not a memory strays,
Nor landmark breathes of other days,
But all is new unhallowed ground.

CV

Tonight ungathered let us leave
This laurel, let this holly stand:
We live within the stranger's land,
And strangely falls our Christmas-eve.

5   Our father's dust is left alone
And silent under other snows:
There in due time the woodbine blows,
The violet comes, but we are gone.

No more shall wayward grief abuse
10   The genial hour with mask and mime;
For change of place, like growth of time,
Has broke the bond of dying use.

Let cares that petty shadows cast,
By which our lives are chiefly proved,
15   A little spare the night I loved,
And hold it solemn to the past.

civ 3. *church*: 'Waltham Abbey church' (T.).
civ 10. *lands*] fields *T.MS, L.MS 1st reading.*
civ 11. *other*] older *T.MS.*
civ 12. 'High Beech, Epping Forest (where we were living)' (T.).

cv Referring to Christmas 1837, at High Beech, Epping Forest.
cv *1–2] 1863*; This holly by the cottage-eave,
         To night, ungathered, shall it stand: *1850–62*
(*This*] The *H.Lpr 101.* -*eave*]-case *H.Lpr 101* (error).) S & S discuss the
grounds for the revision.
cv 7. *woodbine*: pronounced 'wood bin' by T. (and a very common word in
his poetry); *Tennyson at Aldworth*, ed. E. A. Knies, 1984, p. 69).

But let no footstep beat the floor,
  Nor bowl of wassail mantle warm;
  For who would keep an ancient form
20 Through which the spirit breathes no more?

Be neither song, nor game, nor feast;
  Nor harp be touched, nor·flute be blown;
  No dance, no motion, save alone
  What lightens in the lucid east

25 Of rising worlds by yonder wood.
  Long sleeps the summer in the seed;
  Run out your measured arcs, and lead
  The·closing cycle rich in good.

CVI

Ring out, wild bells, to the wild sky,
  The flying cloud, the frosty light:
  The year is dying in the night;
  Ring out, wild bells, and let him die.

5 Ring out the old, ring in the new,
  Ring, happy bells, across the snow:
  The year is going, let him go;
  Ring out the false, ring in the true.

Ring out the grief that saps the mind,
10 For those that here we see no more;

cv 22. *Nor*] No *H.MS.*
cv 23. *no*] nor *T.MS.*
cv 28. Bradley notes that T. 'uses the language of the Roman poets, e.g.
Horace in the *Carmen Saeculare*, or Virgil, *Ecl.* iv . . . Time is said to have
been divided in the books of the Cumaean Sybil into cycles or saecula, and
Virgil makes the golden age return with the closing cycle'.

cvi Not *T.MS, L.MS.* This was the only section of *In Memoriam* included
in *Songs* (1872). H. N. Fairchild, *MLN* lxiv (1949) 256–8, observes the
general similarity to a passage in P. J. Bailey's *Festus.* This would suggest
composition in 1846, since there is a copy of the 2nd edition of *Festus* (1845) at
Lincoln, with T.'s marginal markings; T. wrote for a copy on 5 Nov., and
urged FitzGerald to read *Festus* on 12 Nov. 1846 (*Letters* i 265; *Mem.* i 234). On
T. and *Festus*, see J. O. Waller, who discusses too the details of T.'s marking
of his copy (*Lincoln*); *Bulletin of Research in the Humanities* (formerly *Bulletin of
the N.Y. Public Library*) lxxxii (1979) 105–23. C. Baker, remarking Milton's
title, compares *On the Morning of Christ's Nativity* 125: 'Ring out ye Crystall
sphears' (*VP* xviii, 1980, 202–3).

Ring out the feud of rich and poor,
Ring in redress to all mankind.

Ring out a slowly dying cause,
  And ancient forms of party strife;
15 Ring in the nobler modes of life,
With sweeter manners, purer laws.

Ring out the want, the care, the sin,,
  The faithless coldness of the times;
Ring out, ring out my mournful rhymes,
20 But ring the fuller minstrel in.

Ring out false pride in place and blood,
  The civic slander and the spite;
Ring in the love of truth and right,
Ring in the common love of good.

25 Ring out old shapes of foul disease;
  Ring out the narrowing lust of gold;
  Ring out the thousand wars of old,
Ring in the thousand years of peace.

Ring in the valiant man and free,
30 The larger heart, the kindlier hand;
  Ring out the darkness of the land,
Ring in the Christ that is to be.

CVII

It is the day when he was born,
  A bitter day that early sank
  Behind a purple-frosty bank
Of vapour, leaving night forlorn.

cvi *15. modes of life: Lisette* 30.
cvi *28. Revelation* xx 2–4 tells of the binding of Satan for 'a thousand years'.
cvi *32.* 'The broader Christianity of the future' (T.).

cvii Not *T.MS. L.MS* has it between lxxxiii and lxxxiv. A. C. Bradley compares Horace, *Odes* I ix, for the setting, and Alcaeus's *Fragment 34* on which the Ode was based.
cvii *1.* 'February 1, 1811' (T.).

5   The time admits not flowers or leaves
         To deck the banquet. Fiercely flies
     The blast of North and East, and ice
     Makes daggers at the sharpened eaves,

     And bristles all the brakes and thorns
10   To yon hard crescent, as she hangs
     Above the wood which grides and clangs
     Its leafless ribs and iron horns

     Together, in the drifts that pass
         To darken on the rolling brine
15   That breaks the coast. But fetch the wine,
     Arrange the board and brim the glass;

     Bring in great logs and let them lie,
         To make a solid core of heat;
     Be cheerful-minded, talk and treat.
20   Of all things even as he were by;

     We keep the day. With festal cheer,
         With books and music, surely we
     Will drink to him, whate'er he be,
     And sing the songs he loved to hear.

CVIII

     I will not shut me from my kind,
         And, lest I stiffen into stone,
     I will not eat my heart alone,
     Nor feed with sighs a passing wind:

cvii *11*. Cp. *Chorus* 13 (*1830*): 'The heavy thunder's griding might'. In
H.Nbk 4 (1830), T.'s glossary includes 'griding–rubbing', noting 'Sax.
Chr.' (Saxon Chronicle). The sense of grating, rather than piercing, sug-
gests *Prometheus Unbound* III i 47–8: 'the thunder of the fiery wheels /
Griding the winds'. The word 'iron' suggests Wordsworth, *Guilt and
Sorrow* 492–3, where however the sense follows that in Milton, 'piercing':
'Through his brain / At once the griding iron passage found'. T. had used
it of sound in *Œnone* 27, MS, where the 'cicala ceaseth now to burst the
brake / With thick dry clamour chafed from griding wings' (note 'brake').
cvii *13*. 'Fine snow which passes in squalls to fall into the breaker, and
darkens before melting in the sea' (H.T.).

cviii *1*. Ian Kennedy compares Lytton's *Falkland* (1827, pp. 308–9), a work T.
knew: 'I have separated myself from my kind' (*PQ* lvii, 1978, 98).
cviii *3*. *OED* 6c: '*To eat one's own heart*: to suffer from silent grief or
vexation'. Most commonly, of envy or jealousy, as in *Faerie Queene* I ii

5 What profit lies in barren faith,
    And vacant yearning, though with might
    To scale the heaven's highest height,
    Or dive below the wells of Death?

What find I in the highest place,
10   But mine own phantom chanting hymns?
    And on the depths of death there swims
    The reflex of a human face.

I'll rather take what fruit may be
    Of sorrow under human skies:
15   'Tis held that sorrow makes us wise,
    Whatever wisdom sleep with thee.

CIX

Heart-affluence in discursive talk
    From household fountains never dry;
    The critic clearness of an eye,
    That saw through all the Muses' walk;

5 Seraphic intellect and force
    To seize and throw the doubts of man;
    Impassioned logic, which outran
    The hearer in its fiery course;

st. 6, where the Red Cross Knight 'could not rest, but did his stout heart
eat'.
cviii 4. Nor] And L.MS.
cviii 5–8. Cp. Romans x 6–7: 'But the righteousness which is of faith
speaketh on this wise, Say not in thine heart, Who shall ascend into
heaven? (that is, to bring Christ down from above;) or, Who shall
descend into the deep? (that is, to bring up Christ again from the dead)'.
cviii 6. yearning] yearnings T.MS.
cviii 7. highest height: Œnone 131 ∧ 2, 1832 text, on the gods' calm.
cviii 16] Yet how much wisdom sleeps with thee. T.MS 1st reading. Spedding
wrote (verso): 'You might give the thought a turn of this kind–"The
wisdom that died with you is lost for ever, but out of the loss itself some
other wisdom may be gained"–or (to speak as a poet)
        Even from the grave where Wisdom lies
    May some new wisdom sprout for me.
                                            J. S. Nov 11'.

cix Not T.MS.
cix 1. Heart-affluence] Heart-effluence L.MS.
cix 6. Cp. xcvi 5 and n.

High nature amorous of the good,
10   But touched with no ascetic gloom;
And passion pure in snowy bloom
Through all the years of April blood;

A love of freedom rarely felt,
Of freedom in her regal seat
15   Of England; not the schoolboy heat,
The blind hysterics of the Celt;

And manhood fused with female grace
In such a sort, the child would twine
A trustful hand, unasked, in thine,
20   And find his comfort in thy face;

All these have been, and thee mine eyes
Have looked on: if they looked in vain,
My shame is greater who remain,
Nor let thy wisdom make me wise.

CX

Thy converse drew us with delight,
The men of rathe and riper years:
The feeble soul, a haunt of fears,
Forgot his weakness in thy sight.

5   On thee the loyal-hearted hung,
The proud was half disarmed of pride,
Nor cared the serpent at thy side
To flicker with his double tongue.

cix 15–16. Cp. *The Princess: Conclusion* 66, on revolutions in France: 'No graver than a schoolboys' barring out'. Also *Hail Briton* 19: 'that unstable Celtic blood'.
cix 17. Cp. *Locksley Hall Sixty Years After* 48 and *n*. T. spoke of 'what he called the "man-woman" in Christ, the union of tenderness and strength' (*Mem.* i 326).
cix 21. *been, and thee*] vanished from *L.MS 1st reading*.
cix 22] All these have been, and if in vain *L.MS 1st reading*.
cix 24. *Nor*: 'If I do not . . .' (T.). Echoing the last line of the *Prologue*.

cx Not *T.MS*.
cx 2. *rathe*: early.
cx 7. *cared*] loved *L.MS*.
cx 8. *double*] *1855*; treble *1850–51*. *Aeneid* ii 475: *linguis trisulcis*.

The stern were mild when thou wert by,
10   The flippant put himself to school
        And heard thee, and the brazen fool
        Was softened, and he knew not why;

        While I, thy nearest, sat apart,
        And felt thy triumph was as mine;
15   And loved them more, that they were thine,
        The graceful tact, the Christian art;

        Nor mine the sweetness or the skill,
        But mine the love that will not tire,
        And, born of love, the vague desire
20   That spurs an imitative will.

                        CXI

        The churl in spirit, up or down
        Along the scale of ranks, through all,
        To him who grasps a golden ball,
        By blood a king, at heart a clown;

5   The churl in spirit, howe'er he veil
        His want in forms for fashion's sake,
        Will let his coltish nature break
        At seasons through the gilded pale:

        For who can always act? but he,
10   To whom a thousand memories call,
        Not being less but more than all
        The gentleness he seemed to be,

        Best seemed the thing he was, and joined
        Each office of the social hour
15   To noble manners, as the flower
        And native growth of noble mind;

cx 13. nearest] 1875; dearest 1850–74.
cx 16. art] heart MS 1st reading.
cx 17. Nor] 1864; Not 1850–63.
cx 20. Adapted from 'She spurs an imitative will', Young is the grief 6, an unpublished section of In Memoriam.
cxi 2. scale] scales L.MS 1st reading.
cxi 3. him who grasps] 1855; who may grasp 1850–51.
cxi 13. Best . . . was] 1855; So wore his outward best 1850–51.
cxi 15–16. Cp. Guinevere 333–4: 'For manners are not idle, but the fruit / Of loyal nature, and of noble mind'. On the importance of this link

Nor ever narrowness or spite,
Or villain fancy fleeting by,
Drew in the expression of an eye,
20 Where God and Nature met in light;

And thus he bore without abuse
The grand old name of gentleman,
Defamed by every charlatan,
And soiled with all ignoble use.

CXII

High wisdom holds my wisdom less,
That I, who gaze with temperate eyes
On glorious insufficiencies,
Set light by narrower perfectness.

5 But thou, that fillest all the room
Of all my love, art reason why

(and with *In Memoriam* xcix 4, 'the flower of men', and the Latin epigraph to *Idylls of the King*, 'Flos Regum Arthurus'), see C. Y. Lang, *Tennyson's Arthurian Psycho-drama* (1983), pp. 2–3.

cxi 21–4] *T.MS has these lines only.*

cxi 21. *And . . . bore*] He best might bear *T.MS.*

cxi 22. C. Y. Lang (see ll. 15–16 *n*; p. 15) notes that a cancelled reading in *Dedication* to *Idylls of the King* referred to Prince Albert: 'the great old name of gentleman'.

cxi 23. *Defamed*] Profaned *T.MS. charlatan*: T. observes: 'From Ital. *ciarlatano*, a mountebank; hence the accent on the last syllable.' T. may have learnt this from the *English Encyclopaedia* (1802), of which a copy was at Somersby (*Lincoln*).

cxii 1–4. H.T. comments: '*High wisdom* is ironical. "High wisdom" has been twitting the poet that although he gazes with calm and indulgent eyes on unaccomplished greatness, yet he makes light of narrower natures more perfect in their own small way.'

cxii 3. *glorious insufficiencies*: 'unaccomplished greatness such as Arthur Hallam's' (T.).

cxii 4. *set light by*: 'make light of' (T.). Hallam had written of 'Reason's perfectness, / To our deject and most imbased eye', his *Timbuctoo* 117–18 (Mottèr, p. 41).

cxii 5–8]   For souls, the lesser lords of doom,
            Are worth all praise from young and old,
            Though those are quick to judge that hold
      Completion in a little room. *H.Lpr 101, T.MS 1st reading*

(Echoing Marlowe: 'Infinite riches in a little room', *The Jew of Malta* I i 37.) Spedding wrote: 'I cannot quite satisfy myself which wisdom it is that speaks

I seem to cast a careless eye
On souls, the lesser lords of doom.

For what wert thou? some novel power
10   Sprang up for ever at a touch,
        And hope could never hope too much,
In watching thee from hour to hour,

Large elements in order brought,
        And tracts of calm from tempest made,
15   And world-wide fluctuation swayed
In vassal tides that followed thought.

CXIII

'Tis held that sorrow makes us wise;
        Yet how much wisdom sleeps with thee
        Which not alone had guided me,
But served the seasons that may rise;

5   For can I doubt, who knew thee keen
        In intellect, with force and skill
        To strive, to fashion, to fulfil —
I doubt not what thou wouldst have been:

A life in civic action warm,
10   A soul on highest mission sent,
        A potent voice of Parliament,
A pillar steadfast in the storm,

in the 2ᵈ Stanza, – high wisdom or your wisdom. If, as I suppose, the former,
I do not think it speaks quite in character. "The *lesser* lords of doom" are (I
presume) the perfectly narrow'. H.T. added with a caret the words 'in an
ironic sense' after Spedding's quoted 'high wisdom'.
cxii *8*. 'Those that have free-will, but less intellect' (T.).
cxii *9*. *For . . . thou?*] Such wert not thou: *H.MS, T.MS 1st reading.*
novel power: cp. Hallam: 'What novel power is mine that makes me bold?', *How
is it that I look toward the swell*, which uses nautical imagery to describe fear
(*Victorian Poetry*, Supplement to Vol. iii, 1965).
cxii *14*. Hallam had described himself as one who 'faced / Himself the
tempest, and can prize the calm', *Lines for Ellen Hallam* 11–12 (Motter,
p. 103).
cxii *16*. Cp. Shelley, *Daemon* ii 46: 'The mighty tide of thought'.

cxiii Not *T.MS.*
cxiii *11*. *potent voice: Paradise Lost* vii 100.

Should licensed boldness gather force,
Becoming, when the time has birth,
15   A lever to uplift the earth
And roll it in another course,

With thousand shocks that come and go,
With agonies, with energies,
With overthrowings, and with cries,
20 And undulations to and fro.

CXIV

Who loves not Knowledge? Who shall rail
Against her beauty? May she mix
With men and prosper! Who shall fix
Her pillars? Let her work prevail.

5   But on her forehead sits a fire:
She sets her forward countenance
And leaps into the future chance,
Submitting all things to desire.

Half-grown as yet, a child, and vain—
10   She cannot fight the fear of death.

cxiii *13–20*. Incorporated from *Hail Briton* 96 ∧ 7 (I 526), a very important borrowing.

cxiii *17. thousand*] *1855*; many *1850–51*. The final version suggests 'The thousand natural shocks / That flesh is heir to', *Hamlet* III i 62–3.

cxiii *18.* Cp. *Youth* 59: 'An energy, an agony'; *St Simeon Stylites* 23–4, MS: 'All agonies, / All energies'. Hallam had joined the two, his *Timbuctoo* 74–6 (Motter, p. 40): 'the energies / Of Guilt, and desolate the poor man's sleep. / Yet not alone for torturing agonies . . .'

cxiv Not *T.MS, L.MS.* Turner (p. 126) notes that Julius Hare's University Sermon, Advent Sunday 1828, 'anticipates many features' of cxiv; the sermon was published in *The Victory of Faith* (1840).

cxiv *1–4.* Incorporated verbatim from *Hail Briton* 133–6, as Sir Charles Tennyson notes. T. compares *Proverbs* ix 1: 'Wisdom hath builded her house, she hath hewn out her seven pillars.' On 'knowledge' and 'Reverence', cp. *Love thou thy land* 17–20. A. C. Bradley quotes H. C. Beeching's elucidation: 'The pillars of Hercules represented the farthest boundary of the ancient mariners'.

cxiv *5.* S & S compare xcviii 26, MS: 'Sits on the foreheads of the crowd'; and *King John* V ii 176–7: 'in his forehead sits / A bare-ribbed death'.

What is she, cut from love and faith,
  But some wild Pallas from the brain

Of Demons? fiery-hot to burst
  All barriers in her onward race
15   For power. Let her know her place;
  She is the second, not the first.

A higher hand must make her mild,
  If all be not in vain; and guide
  Her footsteps, moving side by side
20 With wisdom, like the younger child:

For she is earthly of the mind,
  But Wisdom heavenly of the soul.
  O, friend, who camest to thy goal
  So early, leaving me behind,

25 I would the great world grew like thee,
  Who grewest not alone in power
  And knowledge, but by year and hour
  In reverence and in charity.

CXV

Now fades the last long streak of snow,
  Now burgeons every maze of quick
  About the flowering squares, and thick
  By ashen roots the violets blow.

5 Now rings the woodland loud and long,
  The distance takes a lovelier hue,
  And drowned in yonder living blue
  The lark becomes a sightless song.

Now dance the lights on lawn and lea,
10 The flocks are whiter down the vale,
  And milkier every milky sail
  On winding stream or distant sea;

cxiv 27. *by year and*] *1855*; from hour to *1850–51*.

cxv Not *T.MS.* Cp. *On a Mourner* (p. *135*).
cxv 2. *quick*: quickset thorn (T.).
cxv 3. *flowering*] greening *L.MS 1st reading.* Cp. *The Gardener's Daughter*
75: 'flowery squares'.

Where now the seamew pipes, or dives
In yonder greening gleam, and fly
15   The happy birds, that change their sky
To build and brood; that live their lives

From land to land; and in my breast
Spring wakens too; and my regret
Becomes an April violet,
20 And buds and blossoms like the rest.

CXVI

Is it, then, regret for buried time
That keenlier in sweet April wakes,
And meets the year, and gives and takes
The colours of the crescent prime?

5 Not all: the songs, the stirring air,
The life re-orient out of dust,
Cry through the sense to hearten trust
In that which made the world so fair.

Not all regret: the face will shine
10   Upon me, while I muse alone;
And that dear voice, I once have known,
Still speak to me of me and mine:

Yet less of sorrow lives in me
For days of happy commune dead;
15   Less yearning for the friendship fled,
Than some strong bond which is to be.

CXVII

O days and hours, your work is this
To hold me from my proper place,
A little while from his embrace,
For fuller gain of after bliss:

cxv *15*. Horace's *caelum . . . mutant* (*Epistles* I xi 27).
cxv *16. that*] and L.*MS* 1st reading.

cxvi Not T.*MS*, L.*MS*. But see the unpublished section from L.*MS*, *Let Death and Memory* (p. 984).
cxvi *4. crescent prime*: 'growing spring' (T.).
cxvi *11*] *1855*; The dear, dear voice that I have known, *1850–51*.
cxvi *12. Still*] *1855*; Will *1850–51*. This line is adapted from *Let Death and Memory* 8.

5   That out of distance might ensue
    Desire of nearness doubly sweet;
    And unto meeting when we meet,
    Delight a hundredfold accrue,

    For every grain of sand that runs,
10   And every span of shade that steals,
    And every kiss of tootht̀ed wheels,
    And all the courses of the suns.

CXVIII

Contemplate all this work of Time,
    The giant labouring in his youth;
    Nor dream of human love and truth,
    As dying Nature's earth and lime;

5   But trust that those we call the dead
    Are breathers of an ampler day
    For ever nobler ends. They say,
    The solid earth whereon we tread

    In tracts of fluent heat began,
10   And grew to seeming-random forms,
    The seeming prey of cyclic storms,
    Till at the last arose the man;

cxvii *10*. 'The sun-dial' (T.). Cp. Shakespeare, *Sonnet 77*: 'thy dial's shady stealth'.
cxvii *12*. Cp. Shakespeare, *Sonnet 59*: 'five hundred courses of the sun'.

cxviii Not *T.MS*. 'The sections of *In Memoriam* about Evolution had been read by his friends some years before the publication of [Robert Chambers's] *Vestiges of Creation* in 1844' (*Mem.* i 223). T. read Charles Lyell's *Principles of Geology* at the end of 1836 (*Letters* i 145) and in 1837 (*Mem.* i 162).
cxviii *1*. *all*] thou *L.MS 1st reading*.
cxviii *9*. *tracts of fluent*] fields of fluid *L.MS 1st reading.*   *heat*] fire *L.MS*.
cxviii *9–11*. As W. R. Rutland, *Essays and Studies* xxvi (1940) 13, shows, this refers to Cuvier's cataclysmic theory. J. Killham (*Tennyson and "The Princess"*, 1958, p. 246) remarks that 'the resemblances between the anatomical structures of present-day animals and fossils of extinct species were to be explained by the occurrence of fresh creations after each of a series of cataclysms, of which the Flood was perhaps one'. This theory, as Killham says, is incompatible with others that T. mentions, e.g. marine erosion.
cxviii *12–17*. G. R. Potter, *PQ* xvi (1937) 337, shows that though this is close to a theory of mutability of species, the concept is still of 'an evolving

Who throve and branched from clime to clime,
The herald of a higher race,
15   And of himself in higher place,
If so he type this work of time

Within himself, from more to more;
Or, crowned with attributes of woe
Like glories, move his course, and show
20   That life is not as idle ore,

But iron dug from central gloom,
And heated hot with burning fears,
And dipt in baths of hissing tears,
And battered with the shocks of doom

25   To shape and use. Arise and fly
The reeling Faun, the sensual feast;
Move upward, working out the beast,
And let the ape and tiger die.

CXIX

Doors, where my heart was used to beat
So quickly, not as one that weeps
I come once more; the city sleeps;
I smell the meadow in the street;

Nature'. 'Branched' means divided into different races, but still as man.
There is no clear-cut belief in mutability of species here. T.'s wording
resembles Chambers, *Vestiges of Creation* (despite T.'s denial—see above):
'It may only have been when a varied climate arose, that the originally
few species branched off into the present extensive variety' (p. 262).
cxviii *18*. Or] *1850* (*2nd*); And *1850* (*1st*).
cxviii *21–3*. Cp. *Chorus from The Devil and the Lady*, printed *Cornhill*
cliii (1936) 443–4: 'And our frequent tears / Hiss into drought on the
burning cheek'. Also *Sense and Conscience* 119–22: 'Which would not fall
because his burning eyes / Did hiss them into drought. Aloud he wept, /
Loud did he weep, for now the iron had come / Into his soul.'
cxviii *26. sensual feast*: Shakespeare, *Sonnet 141*.
cxix Not *T.MS, L.MS, trial edition*. But based on an unpublished section
from *L.MS, Let Death and Memory* (*p. 984*). A pendant to vii.
cxix *9–12*. Adapted from *Let Death and Memory* 9–12 (p. *984*).
cxx Not *T.MS, L.MS, trial edition*.
cxx *3*. J. Killham compares Robert Chambers's account of the seemingly
electrical nature of nervous and cerebral action, mentioning magnetism
(*Vestiges of Creation*, 1844, p. 333). See also M. Millhauser, *ELN* v (1967)

5   I hear a chirp of birds; I see
       Betwixt the black fronts long-withdrawn
       A light-blue lane of early dawn,
     And think of early days and thee,

     And bless thee, for thy lips are bland,
10   And bright the friendship of thine eye;
       And in my thoughts with scarce a sigh
     I take the pressure of thine hand.

                    CXX

     I trust I have not wasted breath:
       I think we are not wholly brain,
       Magnetic mockeries; not in vain,
     Like Paul with beasts, I fought with Death;

5   Not only cunning casts in clay:
       Let Science prove we are, and then
       What matters Science unto men,
     At least to me? I would not stay.

     Let him, the wiser man who springs
10   Hereafter, up from childhood shape
       His action like the greater ape,
     But I was *born* to other things.

                   CXXI

     Sad Hesper o'er the buried sun
       And ready, thou, to die with him,
       Thou watchest all things ever dim
     And dimmer, and a glory done:

108–13, and his *Fire and Ice: The Influence of Science on T.'s Poetry* (1971), pp. 16–17.

cxx *4*. T. compares *1 Corinthians* xv 32: 'If after the manner of men I have fought with beasts at Ephesus, what advantageth it me?'

cxx *9–11*. 'Spoken ironically against mere materialism, not against evolution' (T.).

cxx *12. born*] [ital.] *1872*; born [rom.] *1850–70*.

cxxi Not *T.MS, L.MS, trial edition*. In H. D. Rawnsley's *Memories of the Tennysons* (1900), p. 121, W. F. Rawnsley reports: 'My earliest remembrance of him is of his visiting my parents at Shiplake, before 1850, when I was turned out of my little room in order that he might have a place of his own to smoke in. He was then still working on *In Memoriam*, and it

5   The team is loosened from the wain,
        The boat is drawn upon the shore;
        Thou listenest to the closing door,
    And life is darkened in the brain.

    Bright Phosphor, fresher for the night,
10   By thee the world's great work is heard
        Beginning, and the wakeful bird;
    Behind thee comes the greater light:

    The market boat is on the stream,
        And voices hail it from the brink;
15   Thou hear'st the village hammer clink,
    And see'st the moving of the team.

    Sweet Hesper-Phosphor, double name
        For what is one, the first, the last,
        Thou, like my present and my past,
20 Thy place is changed; thou art the same.

                    CXXII

    Oh, wast thou with me, dearest, then,
        While I rose up against my doom,

was in this little room of mine that he wrote the "Hesper Phosphor"
canto.' Cp. Shelley's translation of an epigram attributed to Plato:
'Thou wert the morning star among the living, / Ere thy fair light had
fled; – / Now, having died, thou art as Hesperus, giving / New splendour
to the dead.' And Horace, *Odes* II ix 10–12: *nec tibi Vespero | surgente
decedunt amores | nec rapidum fugiente solem.* ('Nor do thy words of love
cease either when Vesper comes out at evening, or when he flies before the
swiftly coursing sun.')
cxxi *1–4.* T. said: 'The grief over the the end of things' (*Knowles*).
cxxi *8.* T. said: 'sleep, image of death' (*Knowles*).
cxxi *9–12.* T. said: 'The progress of mankind is the undermeaning which he
has before referred to, alluding – all the previous poem – to the greater thing
which is to come' (*Knowles*).
cxxi *11. the wakeful bird: Paradise Lost* iii 38.
cxxi *12.* Cp. *Genesis* i 16, 'The greater light to rule the day'.
cxxi *17–20.* S & S note that, beside Gatty's comment ('Hallam has only been
removed: he is not altered into something else'), T. wrote: 'the writer is
rather referring to himself'.
cxxi *18. Revelation* i 11, 'Alpha and Omega, the first and the last'.

cxxii Not *T.MS.*
cxxii *1.* T. said to James Knowles: 'If anybody thinks I ever called him

And yearned to burst the folded gloom,
To bare the eternal Heavens again,

5   To feel once more, in placid awe,
The strong imagination roll
A sphere of stars about my soul,
In all her motion one with law;

If thou wert with me, and the grave
10   Divide us not, be with me now,
And enter in at breast and brow,
Till all my blood, a fuller wave,

Be quickened with a livelier breath,
And like an inconsiderate boy,
15   As in the former flash of joy,
I slip the thoughts of life and death;

And all the breeze of Fancy blows,
And every dew-drop paints a bow,
The wizard lightnings deeply glow,
20 And every thought breaks out a rose.

CXXIII

There rolls the deep where grew the tree.
O earth, what changes hast thou seen!
There where the long street roars, hath been
The stillness of the central sea.

"dearest" in his life they are much mistaken, for I never even called him "dear"', *Nineteenth Century* xxxiii (1893) 187.

cxxii 2. *doom*: 'that of grief' (T.).

cxxii 3. *yearned*] *1850* (*2nd*); strove *1850* (*1st*).

cxxii 9. T. said: 'at all helping me–then' (*Knowles*)

cxxii 10–12. Cp. Arthur Hallam: 'Th' innumerable waves divide us now', *To One Early Loved* 2, a poem similar in theme to *In Memoriam* (Motter, p. 78).

cxxii 17. *breeze*] storm *L.MS 1st reading*.

cxxii 18. 'Every dew-drop turns into a miniature rainbow' (T.).

cxxiii The sections on Evolution (or some of them) were written 'some years' before the publication of Chambers's *Vestiges of Creation* in 1844 (*Letters* i 230; *Mem.* i 223). T. read Charles Lyell's *Principles of Geology* at the end of 1836

5   The hills are shadows, and they flow
     From form to form, and nothing stands;
     They melt like mist, the solid lands,
     Like clouds they shape themselves and go.

     But in my spirit will I dwell,
10   And dream my dream, and hold it true;
     For though my lips may breathe adieu,
     I cannot think the thing farewell.

CXXIV

That which we dare invoke to bless;
   Our dearest faith; our ghastliest doubt;
   He, They, One, All; within, without;
   The Power in darkness whom we guess;

(*Letters* i 145) and in 1837 (*Mem.* i 162); E. B. Mattes (p. 61) compares Lyell: 'many flourishing inland towns, and a still greater number of ports, now stand where the sea rolled its waves' (4th edn, 1835, i 375 – the concluding paragraph of vol. i).

cxxiii 4 ∧ 5] Like days and hours the cycles fleet,
          The deep seas pass away like steam,
          But Love hath such a real dream
     It cannot pass, it is so sweet. *T.MS, deleted*
These lines are in H.T.'s hand in a copy of *Works* (1884, *Lincoln*), as 'Unpublished verse (your epitaph)'. In the second line, T. changed 'roll' to 'pass'.
cxxiii 5. *and they flow*] *T.MS 1st reading;* flowing by *T.MS.*   S & S note *Babylon* 31: 'And the mountains shall flow at my presence', where T.'s note acknowledges *Isaiah* lxiv 1 and *Judges* v 5.
cxxiii 8. *go*] *T.MS 1st reading;* fly *T.MS.* Cp. Wordsworth, *White Doe* 969–70: 'A thousand, thousand rings of light / That shape themselves and disappear'.
cxxiii 8 ∧ 9] But in my love will I rejoice,
          Nor should my song of love be mute,
          Though Earth should shake beneath my foot,
          And Heaven's axle break with noise. *T.MS*
cxxiii 9. *But*] And *T.MS.   will I*] I will *T.MS.*

cxxiv Not *T.MS.* The poem originally began at l. 9, as is clear from *H.Lpr 102, L.MS,* and *trial edition.*
cxxiv *1–8*] *Not trial edition.* T. rejected Paley's arguments for the existence of God, based on design in the natural world. Paley (whose *Natural Theology* was at Somersby, *Lincoln*) wrote: 'we have made choice of the eye as an instance upon which to rest the argument of this chapter' (1803 edn, p. 44). At a meeting of the 'Apostles' at Cambridge, T. had voted 'No' to the question 'Is an intelligible First Cause deducible from the phenomena of the Universe?' (*Mem.* i 44).

5 I found Him not in world or sun,
  Or eagle's wing, or insect's eye;
  Nor through the questions men may try,
  The petty cobwebs we have spun:

  If e'er when faith had fallen asleep,
10 I heard a voice 'believe no more'
  And heard an ever-breaking shore
  That tumbled in the Godless deep;

  A warmth within the breast would melt
  The freezing reason's colder part,
15 And like a man in wrath the heart
  Stood up and answered 'I have felt.'

  No, like a child in doubt and fear:
  But that blind clamour made me wise;
  Then was I as a child that cries,
20 But, crying, knows his father near;

  And what I am beheld again
  What is, and no man understands;
  And out of darkness came the hands
  That reach through nature, moulding men.

cxxiv *9. had*] L.MS; hath *trial edition (error).*
cxxiv *10. I . . . voice*] And doubt began L.MS *1st reading.*
cxxiv *11*] I heard upon the crumbling shore L.MS *1st reading.*
cxxiv *12. That . . . in*] The long roll of L.MS *1st reading.*
cxxiv *13–14.* Cp. 'That heat of inward evidence', *The Two Voices* 284. S & S
compare the stanza with Carlyle, *Sartor Resartus* ch. vii, 'The Everlasting
No': 'then was it that my whole ME stood up, in God-created majesty, and
with emphasis rendered its Protest'.
cxxiv *17–20*] Not trial edition. E. B. Mattes notes the bearing of this on
Henry Sidgwick's praise of this section: 'At this point, if the stanzas had
stopped here ["I have felt"], we should have shaken our heads and said,
"Feeling must not usurp the function of Reason. Feeling is not knowing.
It is the duty of a rational being to follow truth wherever it leads." But
the poet's instinct knows this; he knows that this usurpation by Feeling of
the function of Reason is too bold and confident; accordingly in the next
stanza he gives the turn to humility in the protest of Feeling which is
required (I think) to win the assent of the "man in men" at this stage of
human thought' (*Mem.* i 303).
cxxiv *21. am*] *1859*; seem *1850–56.* *what I am*] the inner eye *trial edition.*
cxxiv *22–3*] The form which no one understands,
    And glimpses of the shadowy hands, *trial edition*

CXXV

Whatever I have said or sung,
  Some bitter notes my harp would give,
  Yea, though there often seemed to live
A contradiction on the tongue,

5 Yet Hope had never lost her youth;
  She did but look through dimmer eyes;
  Or Love but played with gracious lies,
Because he felt so fixed in truth:

And if the song were full of care,
10   He breathed the spirit of the song;
  And if the words were sweet and strong
He set his royal signet there;

Abiding with me till I sail
  To seek thee on the mystic deeps,
15   And this electric force, that keeps
A thousand pulses dancing, fail.

CXXVI

Love is and was my Lord and King,
  And in his presence I attend
  To hear the tidings of my friend,
Which every hour his couriers bring.

5 Love is and was my King and Lord,
  And will be. though as yet I keep

cxxv Not *L.MS* but in *T.MS*. S & S note that in *T.MS* this section and the
next are marked 'X' for omission.
cxxv *3. Yea,*] And *T.MS 1st reading.*
cxxv *5. had ... her*] was ever hale in *T.MS 1st reading.*
cxxv *6. She*] And *T.MS.   look through*] borrow *T.MS 1st reading.*
cxxv *7. Or ... gracious*] And ... graceful *T.MS 1st reading.*
cxxv *9. song ... of care*] lay ... and strong *T.MS 1st reading.*
cxxv *11. words*] lay *T.MS 1st reading.   sweet*] full *T.MS.*
cxxv *15. electric:* see M. Millhauser, *Fire and Ice* (1971), pp. 16–17.

cxxvi *L.MS* has only the words 'Love is my', but this section is in *T.MS.*
cxxvi *1. and ... and*] my Lord and Love my *T.MS 1st reading.*
cxxvi *2–3.* Cp. Herbert, *The Holy Communion* 23–4: 'While those to
spirits refin'd, at doore attend / Dispatches from their friend.'
cxxvi *5–8*]   Love is my king, nor here alone,
                But where I see the distance loom,
                For on the field behind the tomb
                There rest the shadows of his throne. *T.MS, deleted*

Within his court on earth, and sleep
Encompassed by his faithful guard,

And hear at times a sentinel
10   Who moves about from place to place,
And whispers to the worlds of space,
In the deep night, that all is well.

CXXVII

And all is well, though faith and form
Be sundered in the night of fear;
Well roars the storm to those that hear
A deeper voice across the storm,

cxxvi 9. a] the *T.MS 1st reading.*
cxxvi 10. Who] *1855;* That *1850–51.*
cxxvi 11. worlds] *1855;* vast *1850–51.*
cxxvi 12] A distant notice 'All is well'. *T.MS 1st reading. In . . . night] 1855;*
Among the worlds *1850–51.*

cxxvii Not *T.MS.* S & S note that this is a substitute for *Are these the far-famed Victor Hours (p. 985).* There is no specific reference to any particular revolution, but Arthur Hallam's words in his *Influence of Italian upon English Literature* (1831; Motter, p. 233) have obvious affinities:

'Looking, then, to the lurid presages of the times that are coming; believing that amidst the awful commotions of society, which few of us do not expect,–the disruption, it may be, of those common bands which hold together our social existence, necessarily followed by an occurrence on a larger scale of the same things that were witnessed in France forty years ago . . . that, in such a desolation, nothing possibly can be found to support men but a true spiritual Christianity, I am not entirely without hope, that round such an element of vital light, constrained once more to put forth its illuminating energies for protection and deliverance to its children, may gather once again the scattered rays of human knowledge.'

The close of the poem also suggests Hallam's *A·Farewell to the South* 679–83 (Motter, p. 26): 'as when mountains fling / Their central fire aloft, strugglings and rout, /Which uproar all our being's harmony, / And yoke our very consciousness to doubt. /Who smiles on such a scene? Yes, poesy!'

Such sentiments as Hallam's and T.'s may now sound complacent but they were in line with serious geological study. In *Principles of Geology* (4th edn, 1835, ii 290–1), Lyell insists that 'the general tendency of sub-terranean movements, when their effects are considered for a sufficient lapse of ages, is eminently beneficial, and that they constitute an essential part of that mechanism by which the integrity of the habitable surface is

5   Proclaiming social truth shall spread,
       And justice, even though thrice again
       The red fool-fury of the Seine
     Should pile her barricades with dead.

     But ill for him that wears a crown,
10   And him, the lazar, in his rags:
       They tremble, the sustaining crags;
     The spires of ice are toppled down,

preserved, and the very existence and perpetuation of dry land secured.
Why the working of this same machinery should be attended with so much
evil, is a mystery far beyond the reach of our philosophy, and must prob-
ably remain so until we are permitted to investigate, not our planet alone
and its inhabitants, but other parts of the moral and material universe with
which they may be connected.' Another paragraph by Lyell (ii 403)
suggests the geological-political analogy: 'Causes acting in the interior
of the earth; which, although so often the source of death and terror to the
inhabitants of the globe – visiting, in succession, every zone, and filling
the earth with monuments of ruin and disorder – are, nevertheless, the
agents of a conservative principle above all others essential to the stability
of the system.'
cxxvii 4. Cp. Revelation xvi 17–18: 'And the seventh angel poured out his
vial into the air; and there came a great voice out of the temple of heaven,
from the throne, saying, It is done. And there were voices, and thunders,
and lightnings; and there was a great earthquake, such as was not since
men were upon the earth.'
cxxvii 6. even] yea L.MS 1st reading.   thrice] once trial edition. S & S note:
'Perhaps revised so as to allude to the latest revolution in France, that of
1848'.
cxxvii 7. red fool-fury] red-capt harlot L.MS. Cp. Switzerland 28–9
(Appendix C, III 645): 'And bid the Seine / Be choked with slain.' Cp.
Beautiful City (III 216).
cxxvii 9. But . . . him] 1850 (2nd); Woe to the head L.MS 1st reading; But
woe to him 1850 (1st). Cp. 2 Henry IV III i 31: 'Uneasy lies the head that
wears a crown.'
cxxvii 12. Cp. 'icy spires', The Palace of Art 82, 1832 text. Cp. (noting
ll. 10–17) This Earth is wondrous 22–4: 'Set round with many a toppling
spire / And monstrous rocks from craggy snouts / Disploding globes of
roaring fire.' Also Shelley, Prometheus Unbound II iii 28–30: 'mountains /
From icy spires of sun-like radiance fling / The dawn'; Shelley then applies
this to revolution: 'and the nations echo round, / Shaken to their roots,
as do the mountains now.' The revolutionary situation recurs in The
Princess iv 53–4: 'Like glittering bergs of ice, / Throne after throne, and
molten on the waste.'

And molten up, and roar in flood;
The fortress crashes from on high,
15   The brute earth lightens to the sky,
And the great Æon sinks in blood,

And compassed by the fires of Hell;
While thou, dear spirit, happy star,
O'erlook'st the tumult from afar,
20   And smilest, knowing all is well.

CXXVIII

The love that rose on stronger wings,
Unpalsied when he met with Death,
Is comrade of the lesser faith
That sees the course of human things.

5   No doubt vast eddies in the flood
Of onward time shall yet be made,
And thronèd races may degrade;
Yet O ye mysteries of good,

Wild Hours that fly with Hope and Fear,
10   If all your office had to do
With old results that look like new;
If this were all your mission here,

To draw, to sheathe a useless sword,
To fool the crowd with glorious lies,

cxxvii *14. fortress*] mountain *L.MS.*
cxxvii *15. Comus* 797–9: 'And the brute Earth would lend her nerves, and shake, / Till all thy magick structures rear'd so high, /Were shatter'd into heaps.' T. said: 'The back stroke of lightning–The people rise' (*Knowles*).
cxxvii *16. great*] *1851*; vast *1850*.
cxxvii *18. happy star*] from afar *trial edition*.
cxxvii *19. O'erlook'st*] Look'st o'er *L.MS.*   *from afar*] like a star *trial edition*.

cxxviii Not *L.MS, trial edition. T.MS* begins at l. *9; H.Lpr 102* at l. *5*.
cxxviii *1–4*] Not *T.MS, H.MS.*
cxxviii *5–8*] Not *T.MS.*
cxxviii *8. mysteries*] *1850 (2nd)*; ministers *1850 (1st)*.
cxxviii *11.* Cp. *The constant spirit* 4: 'Old principles still working new results'.
cxxviii *14–15*]   To split a creed in barren sects,
                        Heap simple goodness with neglects, *T.MS*
cxxviii *14*] To choke a creed with mythic lies, *H.MS.*   *glorious lies*: Horace's *splendide mendax* (*Odes* III xi 35). John Churton Collins said that

15   To cleave a creed in sects and cries,
      To change the bearing of a word,

      To shift an arbitrary power,
      To cramp the student at his desk,
      To make old bareness picturesque
20   And tuft with grass a feudal tower;

      Why then my scorn might well descend
      On you and yours. I see in part
      That all, as in some piece of art,
      Is toil cöoperant to an end.

                    CXXIX
      Dear friend, far off, my lost desire,
      So far, so near in woe and weal;
      O loved the most, when most I feel
      There is a lower and a higher;

 5   Known and unknown; human, divine;
      Sweet human hand and lips and eye;
      Dear heavenly friend that canst not die,
      Mine, mine, for ever, ever mine;

      Strange friend, past, present, and to be;
10   Loved deeplier, darklier understood;

'glorious lies' 'is probably a mistranslation of Plato's θεῖα ψευδῆ'. Along-
side this suggestion, T. wrote: '!!' (Cornhill, Jan. 1880, Lincoln).
cxxviii 15. To . . . in] Or cleave it into H.MS.
cxxviii 16. To] Or T.MS, H.MS.
cxxviii 18. cramp] bow T.MS 1st reading.
cxxviii 19. bareness] 1850 (2nd); baseness 1850 (1st), T.MS, H.MS. Cp. 'She
finds the baseness of her lot', i.e. lowliness, lx 6.
cxxviii 21. Why] Oh T.MS.   well descend] largely blend T.MS 1st reading.
cxxviii 22. On] With T.MS.   S & S note 1 Corinthians xiii 12: 'For now
we see . . . now I know in part'.
cxxviii 23. piece] work T.MS.
cxxviii 24. cöoperant] cöoperate T.MS. Cp. Youth 60: 'A labour working to an
end', which was incorporated as The Two Voices 297.

cxxix Not T.MS, L.MS. Transposed with cxxx in trial edition.
cxxix 2. So far] Sweet friend trial edition.
cxxix 3. O loved the] Dear friend, loved trial edition.
cxxix 6. hand and lips] voice, and hand trial edition. Cp. 'Dear lips, loved
eyes, ye fade, ye fly', from In deep and solemn dreams 57, a poem with many
affinities with In Memoriam.
cxxix 8. Mine, mine] My friend trial edition.

Behold, I dream a dream of good,
And mingle all the world with thee.

CXXX

Thy voice is on the rolling air;
 I hear thee where the waters run;
 Thou standest in the rising sun,
And in the setting thou art fair.

5 What art thou then? I cannot guess;
 But though I seem in star and flower
 To feel thee some diffusive power,
I do not therefore love thee less:

My love involves the love before;
10 My love is vaster passion now;
 Though mixed with God and Nature thou,
I seem to love thee more and more.

cxxix 11–12]   Let me not lose my faith in good
             Lest I make less my love for thee. *trial edition*

cxxx Not *T.MS*. Transposed with cxxix in *trial edition*.
cxxx 1. on] in *L.MS 1st reading*. Cp. Arthur Hallam's poem to T.'s sister
Emily, *Lady, I bid thee* 6 (Motter, p. 97): 'Old Dante's voice encircles
all the air'. Also Shelley, *Adonais* 370–87, beginning: 'He is made one with
Nature: there is heard / His voice in all her music'.
cxxx 3. Cp. *Revelation* xix 17, 'And I saw an angel standing in the sun;
and he cried with a loud voice'. Hallam himself had alluded to this verse,
in speaking of friendship and Heaven, *To One Early Loved* stanza xiii
(Motter, p. 82): 'Brave spirits are, whom I will have to friend . . . / . . . to
whom th' approach is free / Of unbarred Heaven, and the full mystery /
Unfolded to the penetrative mind. / Such is the mighty Florentine, and
He / Who saw the solar angel, nor was blind; / Such the deep, simple
Shakespeare, greatest of mankind.' Hallam's note to the penultimate
line: 'St John, *Revelations*, Chap. x'.
cxxx 4. setting] flowers *L.MS 1st reading*.
cxxx 5–16]   No more I yearn, no longer grieve:
             I walk the meadows and rejoice
             And prosper, compassed by thy voice
             For ever. Strange that I should live

             To say such wondrous things of thee!
             I know the beauty which thou wast,
             Thy single sweetness in the Past,
             Yet art thou oft as God to me. *L.MS 1st reading, deleted*
Cp. the end of *The Two Voices* (p. 124).

Far off thou art, but ever nigh;
I have thee still, and I rejoice;
15   I prosper, circled with thy voice;
I shall not lose thee though I die.

CXXXI

O living will that shalt endure
When all that seems shall suffer shock,
Rise in the spiritual rock,
Flow through our deeds and make them pure,

5   That we may lift from out of dust
A voice as unto him that hears,
A cry above the conquered years
To one that with us works, and trust,

With faith that comes of self-control,
10   The truths that never can be proved
Until we close with all we loved,
And all we flow from, soul in soul.

cxxx *13. Far . . . art*] O thou far off *L.MS.*
cxxx *15. circled*] compassed *L.MS.*

cxxxi Not *T.MS.*
cxxxi *1.* 'That which we know as Free-will in man' (T.).
cxxxi *1–4. I loving Freedom* 14–16: 'May well surmount the coming shock /
By climbing steps their fathers carved / Within the living rock.'
cxxxi *2*] When mountains *[lacuna]* shock *H.Nbk 18.*
cxxxi *3. 1 Corinthians* x 4: 'for they drank of that spiritual Rock that
followed them: and that Rock was Christ.'
cxxxi *5. lift*] speak *H.MS.*   *of*] *1850* (*2nd*); the *1850* (*1st*).
cxxxi *5–6. Isaiah* xxix 4: 'And thou shalt be brought down, and shalt
speak out of the ground, and thy speech shall be low out of the dust, and
thy voice shall be, as of one that hath a familiar spirit, out of the ground,
and thy speech shall whisper out of the dust.'
cxxxi *6*] As unto one that hears and see *H.MS.*   *him*] one *L.MS 1st*
reading.
cxxxi *7*] Some little of the vast to be *H.MS.*
cxxxi *8*] *[lacuna]* & *[lacuna]* trust *H.MS.*
cxxxi *8. Mark* xvi 20: 'And they went forth, and preached every where,
the Lord working with them, and confirming the word with signs
following' (the concluding verse of the Gospel).
cxxxi *9*] With ever more of [ever-growing *1st reading*] strength and grace,
H.MS. Cp. 'The maidens gathered strength and grace', ciii 27.

[EPILOGUE]

O true and tried, so well and long,
    Demand not thou a marriage lay;
    In that it is thy marriage day
Is music more than any song.

5   Nor have I felt so much of bliss
    Since first he told me that he loved
    A daughter of our house; nor proved
Since that dark day a day like this;

Though I since then have numbered o'er
10   Some thrice three years: they went and came,
    Remade the blood and changed the frame,
And yet is love not less, but more;

No longer caring to embalm
    In dying songs a dead regret,
15   But like a statue solid-set,
And moulded in colossal calm.

Regret is dead, but love is more
    Than in the summers that are flown,
    For I myself with these have grown
20 To something greater than before;

cxxxi *11–12*]   And come to look on those we loved
                And That which made us, face to face. *H.MS*
Cp. *Crossing the Bar* 15: 'I hope to see my Pilot face to face'. From *1
Corinthians* xiii 12: 'For now we see through a glass, darkly; but then face
to face: now I know in part; but then shall I know even as also I am
known.' Hallam's poem *To Two Sisters* (Mary and at this point Emily T.)
had said: 'Till our souls see each other face to face' (Motter, p. 90).

[*Epilogue*] Not *T.MS*. The present edition follows A. C. Bradley in refer-
ring to this as the Epilogue, though T. gave it no title. It describes the
marriage of T.'s sister Cecilia to his friend Edmund Lushington, 10 Oct.
1842. The version in *L.MS* could belong to 1842 (see ll. 9–10), but the
similarities to Chambers's *Vestiges of Creation* (1844) in the conclusion,
though not decisive, suggests that T. did not write it till 1844–5. Lushington
says, of the summer of 1845: 'He had then completed many of the cantos in
In Memoriam. ... He said to me, "I have brought in your marriage at the
end of *In Memoriam*," and then showed me those poems of *In Memoriam*
which were finished and which were a perfectly novel surprise to me'
(*Mem*. i 203).
E 2. Demand not thou] Why ask of me *L.MS 1st reading.*
E 7] Her elder sister: no, nor proved *MS 1st reading.*
E 10. they ... came] have seen them go *MS 1st reading.*
E 11] With change of blossom, fruit and snow; *MS 1st reading.*

Which makes appear the songs I made
　　As echoes out of weaker times,
　　As half but idle brawling rhymes,
The sport of random sun and shade.

25　But where is she, the bridal flower,
　　That must be made a wife ere noon?
　　She enters, glowing like the moon
Of Eden on its bridal bower:

On me she bends her blissful eyes
30　And then on thee; they meet thy look
　　And brighten like the star that shook
Betwixt the palms of paradise.

O when her life was yet in bud,
　　He too foretold the perfect rose.
35　For thee she grew, for thee she grows
For ever, and as fair as good.

And thou art worthy; full of power;
　　As gentle; liberal-minded, great,
　　Consistent; wearing all that weight
40　Of learning lightly like a flower.

But now set out: the noon is near,
　　And I must give away the bride;
　　She fears not, or with thee beside
And me behind her, will not fear.

45　For I that danced her on my knee,
　　That watched her on her nurse's arm,
　　That shielded all her life from harm
At last must part with her to thee;

Now waiting to be made a wife,
50　Her feet, my darling, on the dead;
　　Their pensive tablets round her head,
And the most living words of life

E 21. *appear*] me deem *MS 1st reading.*
E 24 ∧ 5]　　　　For if the wisest rule, to rest
　　　　　　　In Him, is wisest; all are His;
　　　　　　　And so we leave whatever is
　　　　　　To Him the Wisest and the Best; *MS deleted*
E 39. *Consistent:* in the sense of having qualities that 'stand well' together.
E 41. *now set out*] we must go *MS 1st reading.*

Breathed in her ear. The ring is on,
 The 'wilt thou' answered, and again
55 The 'wilt thou' asked, till out of twain
Her sweet 'I will' has made you one.

Now sign your names, which shall be read,
 Mute symbols of a joyful morn,
 By village eyes as yet unborn;
60 The names are signed, and overhead

Begins the clash and clang that tells
 The joy to every wandering breeze;
 The blind wall rocks, and on the trees
The dead leaf trembles to the bells.

65 O happy hour, and happier hours
 Await them. Many a merry face
 Salutes them – maidens of the place,
That pelt us in the porch with flowers.

O happy hour, behold the bride
70 With him to whom her hand I gave.
 They leave the porch, they pass the grave
That has today its sunny side.

Today the grave is bright for me,
 For them the light of life increased,
75 Who stay to share the morning feast,
Who rest tonight beside the sea.

Let all my genial spirits advance
 To meet and greet a whiter sun;
 My drooping memory will not shun
80 The foaming grape of eastern France.

E 56. you] 1872; ye 1850–70.
E 58. joyful] blissful MS.
E 65] Come out: a day of happy hours MS 1st reading.
E 66. Await them] Awaits you MS 1st reading.
E 67. Salutes them] Will greet you MS 1st reading; Salute them MS.
E 68. That] They MS 1st reading.
E 69] Return with him: return a bride MS 1st reading.
E 70. her] thy MS 1st reading.
E 71] Step lightly by the sunny grave, MS 1st reading.
E 72. That] It MS 1st reading.
E 73-6]   For all is light and life increased
    For you and so for us today,
     Albeit you leave us here: but stay
      A little: share the morning feast. MS 1st reading
See ll. 88 ∧ 9n.

It circles round, and fancy plays,
And hearts are warmed and faces bloom,
As drinking health to bride and groom
We wish them store of happy days.

85 Nor count me all to blame if I
Conjecture of a stiller guest,
Perchance, perchance, among the rest,
And, though in silence, wishing joy.

But they must go, the time draws on,
90 And those white-favoured horses wait;
They rise, but linger; it is late;
Farewell, we kiss, and they are gone.

A shade falls on us like the dark
From little cloudlets on the grass,
95 But sweeps away as out we pass
To range the woods, to roam the park,

Discussing how their courtship grew,
And talk of others that are wed,
And how she looked, and what he said,
100 And back we come at fall of dew.

E 77–9. *Samson Agonistes* 594: 'my genial spirits droop'.
E 78. *whiter sun: candidi soles,* Catullus viii 3.
E 81. *and*] the *MS 1st reading.*
E 82. *And . . . and*] The . . . the *MS 1st reading.*
E 86. *a stiller*] another *MS 1st reading.*
E 87. *Perchance, perchance*] As here unseen *MS 1st reading.*
E 88 ∧ 9]   A passing fancy, let it be:
        However wished, their joy will grow
        Beyond the wish: but they must go:
        They rest tonight beside the sea. *MS deleted*
The last line became l. 76.
E 89] Farewell–and yet they linger on: *MS 1st reading.*
E 91. *linger*] go not *MS 1st reading.*
E 94. *grass*] sun *MS 1st reading.*
E 95–6]   But out we go, we walk, we run,
        We loiter in and out the park: *MS 1st reading*
E 96 ∧ 7]   We pace the stubble bare of sheaves,
        We watch the brimming river steal
        And half the golden woodland reel
        Athwart the smoke of burning leaves. *MS deleted*
Adapted as *The Princess* vii 335–7: 'all the rich to-come / Reels, as the
golden Autumn woodland reels / Athwart the smoke of burning weeds'
[*1851*; leaves *1850*].
E 97. *Discussing*] We talk of *MS 1st reading.*
E 98. *And talk*] We speak *MS 1st reading.*

Again the feast, the speech, the glee,
   The shade of passing thought, the wealth
   Of words and wit, the double health,
   The crowning cup, the three-times-three,

105 And last the dance;–till I retire:
   Dumb is that tower which spake so loud,
   And high in heaven the streaming cloud,
   And on the downs a rising fire:

And rise, O moon, from yonder down,
110 Till over down and over dale
   All night the shining vapour sail
   And pass the silent-lighted town,

The white-faced halls, the glancing rills,
   And catch at every mountain head,
115 And o'er the friths that branch and spread
   Their sleeping silver through the hills;

And touch with shade the bridal doors,
   With tender gloom the roof, the wall;
   And breaking let the splendour fall
120 To spangle all the happy shores

By which they rest, and ocean sounds,
   And, star and system rolling past,
   A soul shall draw from out the vast
   And strike his being into bounds,

E 102–3. the wealth of words: Œnone 105, MS.
E 104. The . . . cup] And close on that MS *1st reading.*
E 109. down] downs MS *1st reading.*
E 109–20. There are many affinities with *The Vale of Bones* 1–10 (*1827,* (I 108).
E 110] And over tower and grove and vale MS *1st reading.*
E 112. pass] cross MS *alternative.*   *town*] towns MS *1st reading.*
E 113. The . . . the] And cross with gloom with MS *1st reading.*
E 114. catch] touch MS *1st reading.*
E 114–5. Cp. the visionary flight in the 'germ' of *In Memoriam, Hark! the dogs howl!* (I 607).
E 117. touch with shade the] o'er the blessèd MS *1st reading.*
E 118] And pausing fall in sparks of dew, MS *1st reading.*   *sparks of dew*: *The Progress of Spring* 58.   *tender gloom*: Thomson's *Castle of Indolence* i 507.
E 119. fall] through MS *1st reading.* Cp. *The Princess* iii ∧ iv: 'The splendour falls'.
E 121. they rest] Love rests MS *1st reading.*
E 122] And night delays, until at last MS *1st reading.* Cp. *1850* with *God and the Universe* 3: 'Rush of Suns, and roll of systems'; also *The Devil*

125   And, moved through life of lower phase,
        Result in man, be born and think,
        And act and love, a closer link
        Betwixt us and the crowning race

        Of those that, eye to eye, shall look
130   On knowledge; under whose command
        Is Earth and Earth's, and in their hand
        Is Nature like an open book;

and the Lady II i 40: 'Suns and spheres and stars and belts and systems'.
rolling] wh[eeling] *MS 2nd reading del.*
E 123–4. Cp. *Crossing the Bar* 7: 'When that which drew from out the
boundless deep'.
E 124. strike] smite *MS 1st reading.*
E 125. And,] Who *MS 1st reading.*   *life*] lives *MS.* G. R. Potter, *PQ*
xvi (1937) 339, notes that in these concluding lines there is no certain
implication of change of species, and that 'life of lower phase' refers to
Von Baer's (and Tiedemann's) theory that the embryo reproduces the
stages of the different forms of life. See also J. Killham, *Tennyson and
'The Princess'* (1958), pp. 234–40. The phrase 'the crowning race' in
l. 128 also occurs in *The Princess* vii 279. W. R. Rutland, *Essays and
Studies* xxvi (1940) 22, suggested the influence of Robert Chambers's
Vestiges of Creation, for which T. asked Moxon in 1844 (*Mem.* i 222);
he noted Chambers's question, 'Is our race but the initial of the grand crown-
ing type ?'. Killham observes that this, with other relevant passages, was
quoted in a review in *The Examiner*, 9 Nov. 1844. Killham (p. 257) remarks
the association of Tiedemann's foetal theory with evolutionary hypotheses,
and quotes Chambers: 'There may then be occasion for a nobler type of
humanity.' *The Examiner* 'specially emphasized that the operation of the
law of development depended entirely upon the "generative system". It
is in consequence of this, I suggest, that a marriage concludes *In Memoriam*;
in marriage we come closest to participating in the cosmic purpose,
though we must continually seek to "type" the qualities we desire to make
permanent in man.' T.'s *Epilogue* has a clear link with Chambers's insistence
(p. 71) on the 'parity of law affecting the progress of general creation, and
the progress of an individual foetus of one of the more perfect animals',
and also on the 'parity, or rather identity, of laws presiding over the
development of the animated tribes on the face of the earth, and that of
the individual in embryo' (p. 202). The *Epilogue* may well have been
suggested by such remarks of Chambers as: 'The production of new
forms . . . has never been anything more than a new stage of progress in
gestation, an event as simply natural, and attended as little by any circum-
stances of a wonderful or startling kind, as the silent advance of an ordinary
mother from one week to another of her pregnancy' (pp. 222–3). See also
E. B. Mattes (pp. 84–5) and J. Harrison, *Bulletin de l'Association Canadienne
des Humanités* xxiii (1972) 28–32.
E 126. Result] Shall end *MS 1st reading.*

> No longer half-akin to brute,
>   For all we thought and loved and did,
> *135*   And hoped, and suffered, is but seed
>   Of what in them is flower and fruit;
>
> Whereof the man, that with me trod
>   This planet, was a noble type
>   Appearing ere the times were ripe,
> *140* That friend of mine who lives in God,
>
> That God, which ever lives and loves,
>   One God, one law, one element,
>   And one far-off divine event,
>   To which the whole creation moves.

E 128–30. Cp. Chambers's *Vestiges of Creation*, p. 6: 'A time may come when we shall be much more in the thick of the stars of our astral system than we are now, and have of course much more brilliant nocturnal skies; but it may be countless ages before the eyes which are to see this added resplendence shall exist.'

E 129. Of those] The men *MS 1st reading.* Cp. Shakespeare, *Sonnet 81*: 'Your monument shall be my gentle verse, / Which eyes not yet created shall o'er-read.' (Cp. l. 59.)

E 130. whose] their *MS 1st reading.*

E 131. hand] hands *MS 1st reading.*

E 132. This traditional metaphor was invigorated by its geological aptness. Chambers (p. 57) speaks of fossils and 'the leaves of the *Stone Book*', just as he speaks often of 'the Divine Author'. Lyell (*Principles of Geology*, 4th edn, 1835, i 27) writes: 'The ancient history of the globe was to them a sealed book ... although written in characters of the most striking and imposing kind'; and he mentions 'the alphabet and grammar of geology' (iii 332).

E 137–8]   In them whereof the friend, that trod
                This Earth with me, was once a type *MS 1st reading*

E 140. who] *MS*; that *trial edition.   lives in*] walks with *MS 1st reading.*

E 141–4. Cp. Arthur Hallam's *On the Picture of the Three Fates* 12–13 (Motter, p. 3): 'The Love / Toward which all being solemnly doth move'. Also *Revelation* x 6–7: 'And sware by him that liveth for ever and ever, who created heaven, and the things that therein are, and the earth, and the things that therein are, and the sea, and the things which are therein, that there should be time no longer: But in the days of the voice of the seventh angel, when he shall begin to sound, the mystery of God should be finished.' As Mrs Mattes observes, T. much admired these verses (*Mem.* i 279). J. Kolb compares *Acts* xvii 27–8: 'That they should seek the Lord, if haply they might feel after him, and find him, though he be not far from every one of us: for in him we live, and move, and have our being; as certain also of your own poets have said, For we are also his offspring.'

299 To the Queen

Published as dedication of *Poems*, 7th edn (1851). Dated 'March 1851', it was T.'s first publication as Poet Laureate. The revisions and the many drafts (see Appendix I, p. *986*) show that the poem cost T. much difficulty. T.'s friendship and respect for Queen Victoria are traced in *Mem.* and in *CT.* It is apt that the poem uses the *In Memoriam* stanza since T. 'was appointed Poet Laureate, owing chiefly to Prince Albert's admiration for *In Memoriam*' (*Mem.* i 334). Moreover T. had long used it for major patriotic poems, e.g. *Hail Briton.*

> Revered, beloved – O you that hold
>   A nobler office upon earth
>   Than arms, or power of brain, or birth
> Could give the warrior kings of old,
>
> 5   Victoria, – since your Royal grace
>   To one of less desert allows
>   This laurel greener from the brows
> Of him that uttered nothing base;
>
> And should your greatness, and the care
> 10   That yokes with empire, yield you time
>   To make demand of modern rhyme
> If aught of ancient worth be there;
>
> Then – while a sweeter music wakes,
>   And through wild March the throstle calls,
> 15   Where all about your palace-walls
> The sun-lit almond-blossom shakes –
>
> Take, Madam, this poor book of song;
>   For though the faults were thick as dust
>   In vacant chambers, I could trust
> 20   Your kindness. May you rule us long,

¶299. *1. , beloved–O*] *1853*; Victoria, *1851*.
5. Victoria,–since] *1853*; I thank you that *1851*.
8. him: Wordsworth, T.'s predecessor as Poet Laureate.
9–12] Nor should I dare to flatter state,
    Nor such a lay would you receive,
    Were I to shape it, who believe
  Your nature true as you are great. *proof quoted in Eversley*
H.Lpr *105* has this unadopted stanza only, with variants: *lay*] strain; *shape*] give; *nature*] taste as.
11. modern rhyme: *In Memoriam* lxxvii 1.
13–16] *1853*; not *1851*.
20. kindness] *1853*; sweetness *1851*.

And leave us rulers of your blood
As noble till the latest day!
May children of our children say,
'She wrought her people lasting good;

25   'Her court was pure; her life serene;
God gave her peace; her land reposed;
A thousand claims to reverence closed
In her as Mother, Wife, and Queen;

'And statesmen at her council met
30   Who knew the seasons when to take
Occasion by the hand, and make
The bounds of freedom wider yet

'By shaping some august decree,
Which kept her throne unshaken still,
35   Broad-based upon her people's will,
And compassed by the inviolate sea.'

March 1851

301 To E.L., on His Travels in Greece

Published *Poems*, 8th edn (1853). In praise of Edward Lear's *Journals of a Landscape Painter in Albania and Illyria* (1851). It was written 1851-2 (*H.Nbk 26* has two drafts, the first of which is quoted below; the first has no title, the second: *To – on his book about Greece*). T.'s friend Lear is now best known for his nonsense verse, but he had a considerable reputation as a

28 ∧ 9]   'She brought a vast design to pass,
When Europe and the scattered ends
Of our fierce world were mixt as friends
And brethren in her halls of glass; *1851*
The topical allusion to the Great Exhibition in the Crystal Palace (1851) had lost its point by 1853.
32. *wider*] *1853*; broader *1851*.
32-3. Cp. *I loving Freedom* 25-8:
What nobler than an ancient land
That passing an august decree
Makes wider in a settled peace
The lists of liberty?
35. Cp. *Sonnet* [*Woe to the double-tongued*] 4-5: 'England's ancient ease / Built on broad bases'.

traveller and as a painter, especially of landscapes. (*Poems by Tennyson Illustrated by Lear*, 1889, is still of some interest.) T. was to use the *In Memoriam* stanza to congratulate another author on his travel-book, in *To Ulysses* (*p. 651*).

> Illyrian woodlands, echoing falls
>   Of water, sheets of summer glass,
>   The long divine Peneïan pass,
>   The vast Akrokeraunian walls,
>
> 5   Tomohrit, Athos, all things fair,
>   With such a pencil, such a pen,
>   You shadow forth to distant men,
>   I read and felt that I was there:
>
>   And trust me while I turned the page,
> 10   And tracked you still on classic ground,
>   I grew in gladness till I found
>   My spirits in the golden age.
>
>   For me the torrent ever poured
>   And glistened – here and there alone
> 15   The broad-limbed Gods at random thrown
>   By fountain-urns; – and Naiads oared

¶301. *1. woodlands*] olives *H.MS.*   *echoing*] foaming *MS 1st reading.*
2. sheets] lakes *MS.*
3. Illustrated by Lear (facing p. 410).
4. From Horace, *Odes* I iii 20: *scopulos Acrocerauniae*. Lear spoke of 'the Acroceraunian range' (p. 210).
6] So well with pencil and with pen, *MS.* T. courteously repudiates Lear's self-depreciation: 'No pen or pencil can do justice to the scenery of Metéora' (p. 397).
8] I could but feel that I was there. *MS.*
9] And while [as *1st reading*] I turned the [your *1st reading*] storied page, *MS.*
10. tracked you still] mapped your course *MS.*   *classic ground*: a classic phrase; cp. Addison's *Letter from Italy* 11–12 (written 1701): 'Poetic fields encompass me around, / And still I seem to tread on Classic ground.'
11. grew . . . till] grew so joyful that *MS 1st reading*; waxt in gladness till *MS.*
13] Through sacred clefts the torrent poured *MS.*
14. glistened] glittered *MS.*
15. broad-limbed] broad-browed *MS.* Cp. *Samson Agonistes* 118: 'See how he lies at random, carelessly diffus'd'. In his earliest surviving letter (Oct. 1821?; *Letters* i 1), T. quoted this, and Newton on 'this beautiful application of the word "diffused"' from Horace.
16. urns] heads *MS.*

A glimmering shoulder under gloom
Of cavern pillars; on the swell
The silver lily heaved and fell;
20   And many a slope was rich in bloom

From him that on the mountain lea
By dancing rivulets fed his flocks
To him who sat upon the rocks,
And fluted to the morning sea.

309 Ode on the Death of the Duke of Wellington

Published in 1852

Published 16 Nov. 1852; 2nd edn, Feb.–March 1853 (it is twenty-nine lines longer and has many changes); then *1855*. It was T.'s first separate publication since becoming Poet Laureate. (While T. was still a child at Somersby, 'the doings of Wellington and Napoleon were the themes of story and verse', *Mem.* i 5.) On the background, reception, and T.'s response in revision, see E. F. Shannon, *Studies in Bibliography* xiii (1960) 149–77. The textual history of the poem, including a full account of the MSS and a record of all substantive variants, along with a critical discussion, is told in E. F. Shannon and C. Ricks, *SB* xxxii (1979) 125–57. (Supplemented by A. Day and P. G. Scott, *SB* xxxv, 1982, 320–23). The Duke of Wellington died 14 Sept. 1852; the funeral was on 18 Nov. Shannon in his earlier study connects ll. 8–9 with the protracted discussion of 'when, where, and with what state … the great Duke of Wellington shall be buried' (*Illustrated London News*). He quotes the Prime Minister's letter of 20 Sept. that the Duke would be buried in St Paul's, 'there to rest by the side of Nelson – the greatest military by the side of the greatest naval chief who ever reflected lustre upon the annals of England'; cp. ll. 80–4. Shannon also relates the poem to T.'s many patriotic verses of 1852; see l. 171*n*. He notes that T. had been pressed for time for the 1st edition, and that it was to be an advantage to him to commemorate rather than anticipate the funeral. Many of the reviews were hostile; T. seems to have paid little attention to specific complaints (except perhaps for the opening lines), but he paid some attention to general suggestions. He also intensified the religious note. The early draft in *T.Nbk 25* includes, deleted,

18. *cavern pillars;*] columned caves, as *MS*.
19. *lily*] lilies *MS*.
20] And all the region burst in bloom *MS*.
22. *dancing*] leaping *MS*.
23. *who*] that *MS*.

the final stanza of *England and America in 1782* (written 1832–4; published 1872). See Shannon and Ricks, *SB* 143–4, 154, on these lines in MS in VII. Immediately following the poem in *T.MS* is *Will* 10–20 (pp. *500–1*), which has clear affinities with the *Ode* and which T. may well have considered incorporating. Martin (p. 368) notes that, strictly speaking, the poem 'was not written as Poet Laureate, since it was not requested by the Queen and had no official publication, but T. none the less felt that it was his public duty. "I wrote it because it was expected of me to write", he told his aunt Russell' (*Letters* ii 50).

On the relations between *Morte d'Arthur, In Memoriam, Ode on the Death of the Duke of Wellington*, and *Idylls of the King* (each honouring an Arthur), see C. Y. Lang, *Tennyson's Arthurian Psycho-drama* (1983). B. Richards argues that the first six lines of *To the Duke of Argyll* (III 85), of which a draft is in *T.Nbk 21* (*c.* 1833), were originally written about the Duke of Wellington.

I

Bury the Great Duke
   With an empire's lamentation,
Let us bury the Great Duke
   To the noise of the mourning of a mighty nation,
5 Mourning when their leaders fall,
Warriors carry the warrior's pall,
And sorrow darkens hamlet and hall.

II

Where shall we lay the man whom we deplore?
Here, in streaming London's central roar.
10 Let the sound of those he wrought for,
And the feet of those he fought for,
Echo round his bones for evermore.

III

Lead out the pageant: sad and slow,
As fits an universal woe,
15 Let the long long procession go,

¶309. *1. Bury*] 1855; Let us bury 1852–3.
5] 1853; When laurel-garlanded leaders fall, 1852.
6. *Warriors*] 1853; And warriors 1852.
7. Cp. the conclusion of *The Sea-Fairies*, 1830 text: 'sorrow shall darken ye ... no more'.
8–12] *Not T.MS.*
8 ∧ 9] He died on Walmer's lonely shore, 1853. On this revision, see Shannon and Ricks, *SB* 146.
9] 1855; *not* 1852; But here ... 1853. *London:* on naming and the poem's revisions, see ll. 80–83*n*.

And let the sorrowing crowd about it grow,
And let the mournful martial music blow;
The last great Englishman is low.

IV

Mourn, for to us he seems the last,
20 Remembering all his greatness in the Past.
No more in soldier fashion will he greet
With lifted hand the gazer in the street.
O friends, our chief state-oracle is mute:
Mourn for the man of long-enduring blood,
25 The statesman-warrior, moderate, resolute,
Whole in himself, a common good.
Mourn for the man of amplest influence,
Yet clearest of ambitious crime,
Our greatest yet with least pretence,
30 Great in council and great in war,
Foremost captain of his time,
Rich in saving common-sense,
And, as the greatest only are,
In his simplicity sublime.
35 O good gray head which all men knew,
O voice from which their omens all men drew,
O iron nerve to true occasion true,
O fallen at length that tower of strength
Which stood four-square to all the winds that blew!
40 Such was he whom we deplore.
The long self-sacrifice of life is o'er.
The great World-victor's victor will be seen no more.

20] 1853; Our sorrow draws but on the golden Past. 1852.
21–22] 1853; not 1852.
26. Horace, Satires II vii 86: in se ipso totus.
27. amplest] 1853; largest 1852.
28. clearest of] 1853; freëst from 1852.
35. Claudian, Venerandus apex et cognita cunctis canities, was quoted in a speech by Disraeli on Wellington's death. But in a copy of F. J. Rowe and W. T. Webb's Selections from his poems (1888, Lincoln), T. commented: 'never heard of Claudian's line!'
38–9. Adapted from Young is the grief 16: 'A life four-square to all the winds'. On the importance of this link, see C. Y. Lang, Tennyson's Arthurian Psycho-drama (1983), pp. 4–5. For the epithet, T. compares Simonides (τετράγωνος), 'though I did not think of this parallel when I wrote it'. Cp. Dante's Purgatorio v 14–15: sta come torre ferma, che non crolla / già mai la cima per soffiar de' venti. ('Stand like a firm tower that never shakes its top for blast of wind.')
42. World-victor: Napoleon.

V

All is over and done:
Render thanks to the Giver,
45   England, for thy son.
Let the bell be tolled.
Render thanks to the Giver,
And render him to the mould.
Under the cross of gold
50   That shines over city and river,
There he shall rest for ever
Among the wise and the bold.
Let the bell be tolled:
And a reverent people behold
55   The towering car, the sable steeds:
Bright let it be with its blazoned deeds,
Dark in its funeral fold.
Let the bell be tolled:
And a deeper knell in the heart be knolled;
60   And the sound of the sorrowing anthem rolled
Through the dome of the golden cross;
And the volleying cannon thunder his loss;
He knew their voices of old.
For many a time in many a clime
65   His captain's-ear has heard them boom
Bellowing victory, bellowing doom:
When he with those deep voices wrought,
Guarding realms and kings from shame;
With those deep voices our dead captain taught
70   The tyrant, and asserts his claim
In that dread sound to the great name,
Which he has worn so pure of blame,
In praise and in dispraise the same,
A man of well-attempered frame.

---

46. A special honour, since the Great Bell was tolled only for the Royal
Family, the Bishop, the Dean, and the Lord Mayor.
49. the cross of gold: C. Y. Lang (see note to ll. 38–9) relates this to Tennyson's
early prose-sketch 'King Arthur' (*Mem.* ii 122), 'the Holy Minster with the
Cross of gold', and to *Merlin and the Gleam* 67–8: 'the golden / Cross of the
churches'.
56. its] *1859*; his *1852–6*.
59] *1855*; not *1852*; A deeper ... *1853*. Cp. the praise of the brave dead,
'God's soldier', *Macbeth* V viii 50–51: '"And so his knell is knolled."
"He's worth more sorrow, / And that I'll spend for him."' T. probably
recalled Shelley's lines *On the Death of Napoleon* 11, 22 (1821): 'Is not *his*
death-knell knolled? ... / All my sons when their knell is knolled.'

75 O civic muse, to such a name,
    To such a name for ages long,
    To such a name,
    Preserve a broad approach of fame,
    And ever-echoing avenues of song.

                    VI
80 Who is he that cometh, like an honoured guest,
    With banner and with music, with soldier and with
        priest,
    With a nation weeping, and breaking on my rest?
    Mighty Seaman, this is he
    Was great by land as thou by sea.
85 Thine island loves thee well, thou famous man,
    The greatest sailor since our world began.
    Now, to the roll of muffled drums,
    To thee the greatest soldier comes;
    For this is he
90 Was great by land as thou by sea;
    His foes were thine; he kept us free;
    O give him welcome, this is he
    Worthy of our gorgeous rites,
    And worthy to be laid by thee;
95 For this is England's greatest son,
    He that gained a hundred fights,
    Nor ever lost an English gun;
    This is he that far away
    Against the myriads of Assaye
100 Clashed with his fiery few and won;

75–9. Adapted, as Sir Charles Tennyson observes (*1931*, p. 74), from *Hail
Briton* 169–72: 'O civic Muse, for such a name, / Deep-minded Muse, for
ages long / Preserve a broad approach of song / And ringing avenues of
fame.' *T.MS* has 'ringing'.

79. *ever-echoing*] *1865*; ever-ringing *1852–64*.

80–83. Nelson speaks. On the revisions of this section in MS, see Shannon
and Ricks, *SB* 139–40; and on T.'s finally not naming Nelson (or Wellington
within the poem) and other aspects of naming (London; England), *SB* 141–6.

91] *1853*; His martial wisdom kept us free; *1852*.

92. *give . . . welcome*] *1853*; warrior-seaman *1852*.

95] *1852 has this line ll.* 92 ∧ 3, *beginning* This . . . .

97. *Nor ever*] *1853*; And never *1852*. Disraeli's speech on Wellington also
mentions that he 'captured 3,000 cannon from the enemy, and never lost a
single gun'.

98] *1853*; He that in his earlier day *1852*.

99. Hindustan, 1803.

And underneath another sun,
Warring on a later day,
Round affrighted Lisbon drew
The treble works, the vast designs
105 Of his laboured rampart-lines,
Where he greatly stood at bay,
Whence he issued forth anew,
And ever great and greater grew,
Beating from the wasted vines
110 Back to France her banded swarms,
Back to France with countless blows,
Till o'er the hills her eagles flew
Beyond the Pyrenean pines,
Followed up in valley and glen
115 With blare of bugle, clamour of men,
Roll of cannon and clash of arms,
And England pouring on her foes.
Such a war had such a close.
Again their ravening eagle rose
120 In anger, wheeled on Europe-shadowing wings,
And barking for the thrones of kings;
Till one that sought but Duty's iron crown
On that loud sabbath shook the spoiler down;
A day of onsets of despair!
125 Dashed on every rocky square
Their surging charges foamed themselves away;
Last, the Prussian trumpet blew;
Through the long-tormented air

101–8. C. Y. Lang (see note to ll. 38–9; p. 6) shows that T.'s lines summarizing the Peninsular Campaign echo Corneille, *Le Cid* (IV iii), 'the famous recital of his victory against the Moors by Don Rodrigue'.

101. The Latin *alio sole*.

102] *1853*; Made the soldier, led him on, *1852*.

103–7] *1853*; *not 1852*.

105. Torres Vedras, 1810.

110] *1853*; All their marshals' bandit swarms, *1852*.

112] *1853*; Till their host of eagles flew *1852*.   *eagles*: Napoleon's ensigns.

113. Beyond] *1864*; Past *1852–62*.

118 ∧ *9*] He withdrew to brief repose. *1852–3*.

121. barking: as in *Boädicea* 13.

123. Waterloo, Sunday 18 June 1815.

124–5. C. Y. Lang (see note to ll. 38–9; p. 8) compares the face of the dying Arthur: 'dashed with drops / Of onset' (*Morte d'Arthur* 215–16).

Heaven flashed a sudden jubilant ray,
130 And down we swept and charged and overthrew.
So great a soldier taught us there,
What long-enduring hearts could do
In that world-earthquake, Waterloo!
Mighty Seaman, tender and true,
135 And pure as he from taint of craven guile,
O saviour of the silver-coasted isle,
O shaker of the Baltic and the Nile,
If aught of things that here befall
Touch a spirit among things divine,
140 If love of country move thee there at all,
Be glad, because his bones are laid by thine!
And through the centuries let a people's voice
In full acclaim,
A people's voice,
145 The proof and echo of all human fame,
A people's voice, when they rejoice
At civic revel and pomp and game,
Attest their great commander's claim
With honour, honour, honour, honour to him,
150 Eternal honour to his name.

VII
A people's voice! we are a people yet.
Though all men else their nobler dreams forget,
Confused by brainless mobs and lawless Powers;
Thank Him who isled us here, and roughly set
155 His Briton in blown seas and storming showers,

129. 'The setting sun glanced on this last charge of the English and Prussians' (T.). *T.MS* had not acknowledged the Prussians. The line is adapted from *The Christian Penitent* 14n (I 511).

130. C. Y. Lang: T. 'must have meant *down* from the little fortress of Hougoumont (particularized, years later, in *To the Queen*)'.

133. *world-earthquake*] *1872*; world's-earthquake *1852-70*.

137. The defeat of the Danish fleet (1801), and of Napoleon at Aboukir (1798).

139. T. says: 'Dwell upon the word "touch" and make it as long as "can touch."'

142-6. Cp. the 'death-hymn' in *The Dying Swan* 31-3: 'As when a mighty people rejoice ... / And the tumult of their acclaim is rolled.' Cp. l. 4 above.

154-5] *1853*; *not 1852*.

155. *Briton*] *1864*; Saxon *1853-62*. On this belated revision, see Shannon and Ricks, *SB* 145.

We have a voice, with which to pay the debt
Of boundless love and reverence and regret
To those great men who fought, and kept it ours.
And keep it ours, O God, from brute control;
160 O Statesmen, guard us, guard the eye, the soul
Of Europe, keep our noble England whole,
And save the one true seed of freedom sown
Betwixt a people and their ancient throne,
That sober freedom out of which there springs
165 Our loyal passion for our temperate kings;
For, saving that, ye help to save mankind
Till public wrong be crumbled into dust,
And drill the raw world for the march of mind,
Till crowds at length be sane and crowns be just.
170 But wink no more in slothful overtrust.
Remember him who led your hosts;

157. *Of boundless love and*] *1855*; Of most unbounded *1852*; Of boundless *1853*.

159] *1853*; not *1852*.

166. *help to*] *1853*; not *1852*.

168] *1853*; And help the march of human mind *1852*.

169. *at length*] *1855*; not *1852–3*.

170 ∧ 1]   Perchance our greatness will increase;
         Perchance a darkening future yields
         Some reverse from worse to worse,
         The blood of men in quiet fields,
         And sprinkled on the sheaves of peace. *1852*

These lines are adapted, as Shannon remarks, from *Hail Briton* 121–4: 'For who may frame his thought at ease / Mid sights that civil contest yields– / The blood of men in quiet fields / And sprinkled on the sheaves of peace.'

171. *Remember*] *1853*; And O remember *1852*. Shannon prints from *Pierpont Morgan MS* an attack on Napoleon III which links with ll. 171, 185–6. Emily T.'s note added: 'This might perhaps have been altered had it been intended for publication–made stronger I mean.' (The lines are in *T.MS*, virtually identical.) On the deletion of this passage, see Shannon and Ricks, *SB* 131–4, 155.

         But O remember him who led your hosts
         And take his counsel ere too late.
         There sits a silent man beyond the strait–
         Guard guard guard your coasts.
         His are all the powers of the state,
         His are all the passions of the rabble–
         A man of silence in a world of babble.
         Sudden blows are strokes of fate,

He bad you guard the sacred coasts.
Your cannons moulder on the seaward wall;
His voice is silent in your council-hall
175 For ever; and whatever tempests lour
For ever silent; even if they broke
In thunder, silent; yet remember all
He spoke among you, and the Man who spoke;
Who never sold the truth to serve the hour,
180 Nor paltered with Eternal God for power;
Who let the turbid streams of rumour flow
Through either babbling world of high and low;
Whose life was work, whose language rife
With rugged maxims hewn from life;
185 Who never spoke against a foe;
Whose eighty winters freeze with one rebuke
All great self-seekers trampling on the right:
Truth-teller was our England's Alfred named;
Truth-lover was our English Duke;
190 Whatever record leap to light
He never shall be shamed.

Yet to be true is more than half of great.
By the hollow blatant cry,
Half-godded underneath a scornful sky
Their great Napoleons live and die
With rolling echoes by the nations heard.
But shall we count them Gods who break their word?
The word is God: thou shalt not lie.
Was our great Chief (his life is bare from youth
To all men's comment till his latest hour)
A man to dodge and shuffle with the Truth
And palter with Eternal God for power?
His eighty winters &c.

Walter White observed, 5 Nov. 1852, that it 'contains a grand invective against Louis Napoleon of France which will be omitted' (*Journals*, 1898, p. 147). Cp. T.'s patriotic poems of 1852, especially *Britons, Guard Your Own* (II 470).

172] *1855*; Respect his sacred warning; guard your coasts. *1852*; Revere his warning; guard your coasts. *1853*.

173] *1853*; *not 1852*.

181–2] *1855*; *not 1852–3*.

183–4] *1853*; *not 1852*.

185] *1855*; *not 1852–3*.

186. Whose] *1853*; His *1852*.

188. On names, see ll. 80–83*n*.

VIII

Lo, the leader in these glorious wars
Now to glorious burial slowly borne,
Followed by the brave of other lands,
195 He, on whom from both her open hands
Lavish Honour showered all her stars,
And affluent Fortune emptied all her horn.
Yea, let all good things await
Him who cares not to be great,
200 But as he saves or serves the state.
Not once or twice in our rough island-story,
The path of duty was the way to glory:
He that walks it, only thirsting
For the right, and learns to deaden
205 Love of self, before his journey closes,
He shall find the stubborn thistle bursting
Into glossy purples, which outredden
All voluptuous garden-roses.
Not once or twice in our fair island-story,
210 The path of duty was the way to glory:
He, that ever following her commands,
On with toil of heart and knees and hands,
Through the long gorge to the far light has won
His path upward, and prevailed,
215 Shall find the toppling crags of Duty scaled
Are close upon the shining table-lands
To which our God Himself is moon and sun.
Such was he: his work is done.
But while the races of mankind endure,
220 Let his great example stand
Colossal, seen of every land,
And keep the soldier firm, the statesman pure:
Till in all lands and through all human story
The path of duty be the way to glory:
225 And let the land whose hearths he saved from shame

195–7. 'These are full-vowelled lines to describe Fortune emptying her Cornucopia' (T.).
202. Cp. Gray's *Elegy* 36: 'The paths of glory lead but to the grave.'
209–15. Based on the 15th fragment of Simonides, an influence suggested by H. G. Dakyns (tutor to T.'s sons), in *Tennyson and His Friends*, p. 200.
217. *Revelation* xxi 23: 'And the city had no need of the sun, neither of the moon, to shine in it: for the glory of God did lighten it.'
218] *1853*; He has not failed: he hath prevailed: *1852*.
219–24] *1853*; not *1852*.
225. *And*] *1853*; So *1852*.   *land*] *1853*; men *1852*.

For many and many an age proclaim
At civic revel and pomp and game,
And when the long-illumined cities flame,
Their ever-loyal iron leader's fame,
230   With honour, honour, honour, honour to him,
Eternal honour to his name.

IX

Peace, his triumph will be sung
By some yet unmoulded tongue
Far on in summers that we shall not see:
235   Peace, it is a day of pain
For one about whose patriarchal knee
Late the little children clung:
O peace, it is a day of pain
For one, upon whose hand and heart and brain
240   Once the weight and fate of Europe hung.
Ours the pain, be his the gain!
More than is of man's degree
Must be with us, watching here
At this, our great solemnity.
245   Whom we see not we revere;
We revere, and we refrain
From talk of battles loud and vain,
And brawling memories all too free
For such a wise humility
250   As befits a solemn fane:
We revere, and while we hear
The tides of Music's golden sea
Setting toward eternity,
Uplifted high in heart and hope are we,
255   Until we doubt not that for one so true
There must be other nobler work to do
Than when he fought at Waterloo,
And Victor he must ever be.
For though the Giant Ages heave the hill

226. For] *1853*; Through *1852*.
241] *1853*; not *1852*.
251–3] *1853*; not *1852*.
254] *1855*; For solemn, too, this day are we, *1852*; Lifted up in heart are we, *1853*.
255. Until] *1853*; O friends, *1852*.
259–61] *1853*; not *1852*. The lines are adapted from a cancelled stanza of *The Palace of Art* (H. Lpr *182*):

260 And break the shore, and evermore
Make and break, and work their will;
Though world on world in myriad myriads roll
Round us, each with different powers,
And other forms of life than ours,
265 What know we greater than the soul?
On God and Godlike men we build our trust.
Hush, the Dead March wails in the people's ears:
The dark crowd moves, and there are sobs and tears:
The black earth yawns: the mortal disappears;
270 Ashes to ashes, dust to dust;
He is gone who seemed so great. –
Gone; but nothing can bereave him
Of the force he made his own
Being here, and we believe him
275 Something far advanced in State,
And that he wears a truer crown
Than any wreath that man can weave him.
Speak no more of his renown,
Lay your earthly fancies down,
280 And in the vast cathedral leave him.
God accept him, Christ receive him.

1852

Yet saw she Earth laid open. Furthermore
How the strong Ages had their will,
A range of Giants breaking down the shore
And heaving up the hill.

The military context suggests Wordsworth, *To Enterprise* 114–16: 'An Army now, and now a living hill / That a brief while heaves with convulsive throes–/Then all is still'. Wordsworth's note (1822) runs: ' "Awhile the living hill / Heaved with convulsive throes, and all was still." Dr Darwin describing the destruction of the army of Cambyses'. (*The Botanic Garden* I ii 497–8.)
262. *world on world*] *1856*; worlds on worlds *1852–5*.
266–70] *1853*; not *1852*. 'God and Godlike men', from *Suggested by Reading* 84, as Sir Charles Tennyson says (p. 266). Cp. *Love and Duty* 31: 'But then most Godlike being most a man'. Also *Paradise Regained* iv 348: 'Where God is prais'd aright, and Godlike men'; and Byron, *Childe Harold* II lxxxv 2: 'Gods and godlike men'.
267. *wails*] *1855*; sounds *1853*.
271. *He*] *1853*; The man *1852*.
278. *Speak*] *1864*; But speak *1852–62*.
281. Romans xiv 3: 'God hath received him.'

310 Will

Published *1855*. There are two drafts of the second stanza in *T.Nbk 25*, immediately following the MS of the *Ode on Wellington* (1852); T. probably considered using these lines as part of the *Ode*, with which the first stanza too has affinities. A MS of the second stanza only is at the *University of Sydney* (all variants from the MSS are below). H.T. relates the second stanza to T.'s religious thinking, especially that of *The Vision of Sin* (*Mem.* i 322).

I

O well for him whose will is strong!
He suffers, but he will not suffer long;
He suffers, but he cannot suffer wrong:
For him nor moves the loud world's random mock,
5 Nor all Calamity's hugest waves confound,
Who seems a promontory of rock,
That, compassed round with turbulent sound,
In middle ocean meets the surging shock,
Tempest-buffeted, citadel-crowned.

II

10 But ill for him who, bettering not with time,
Corrupts the strength of heaven-descended Will,

¶310. *1–9*. Cp. Horace, *Odes* III iii 1–8: *Iustum et tenacem propositi virum / non civium ardor prava iubentium, / non vultus instantis tyranni / mente quatit solida neque Auster, // dux inquieti turbidus Hadriae, / nec fulminantis magna manus Iovis; / si fractus inlabatur orbis, / impavidum ferient ruinae.* ('The man tenacious of his purpose in a righteous cause is not shaken from his firm resolve by the frenzy of his fellow-citizens bidding what is wrong, not by the face of threatening tyrant, not by Auster, stormy master of the restless Adriatic, not by the mighty hand of thundering Jove. Were the vault of heaven to break and fall upon him, its ruins would smite him undismayed.') See T.'s schoolboy translation of this ode (I 4).
4. mock: mockery, with an archaic ring by this date. Cp. Shelley, *The Cenci* IV i 156–7: 'the clamorous scoffs / Of the loud world'.
5–9. Cp. *Aeneid* x 693–6: *ille velut rupes, vastum quae prodit in aequor, / obvia ventorum furiis expostaque ponto, / vim cunctam atque minas perfert caelique marisque, / ipsa immota manens.* ('Even as a cliff that juts into the vast deep, exposed to the raving winds and braving the main, that endures all the stress, all the menace of sky and sea, itself fixed unshaken.')
8–9. Sir Charles Tennyson remarks the adaptation of *Ode: O Bosky Brook* 76, 79: 'Citadel-crowned and tempest-buffeted . . . / And in the middle ocean meets the surging shock.'
10] Alas for him whose will [*lacuna*] vile crime *T.MS A*. *But ill*] Alas *MSS*.
11] *Not T.MS A. strength of heaven-descended*] God-given force [strength *T.MS B*] of his own *Sydney MS, T.MS B*.

And ever weaker grows through acted crime,
Or seeming-genial venial fault,
Recurring and suggesting still!
15 He seems as one whose footsteps halt,
Toiling in immeasurable sand,
And o'er a weary sultry land,
Far beneath a blazing vault,
Sown in a wrinkle of the monstrous hill,
20 The city sparkles like a grain of salt.

311 The Daisy
Written at Edinburgh

Published *1855*. Written Aug. 1853 (*Mem.* i 364; *Mat.* ii 85). T. says it was written to his wife Emily, remembering their Italian tour of 1851: 'In a metre which I invented, representing in some measure the grandest of metres, the Horatian Alcaic.' T. was to modify the stanza for other epistolary poems, *To the Rev. F. D. Maurice* (p. 505) and *To Professor Jebb* (III 162), and still further for *To the Master of Balliol* (III 219).

O love, what hours were thine and mine,
In lands of palm and southern pine;
  In lands of palm, of orange-blossom,
Of olive, aloe, and maize and vine.

5 What Roman strength Turbia showed
In ruin, by the mountain road;
  How like a gem, beneath, the city
Of little Monaco, basking, glowed.

How richly down the rocky dell
10 The torrent vineyard streaming fell
  To meet the sun and sunny waters,
That only heaved with a summer swell.

12] Is ever weaker made by some one fault *T.MS A.* *And*] Which *Sydney MS*; That *T.MS B.* *acted*] some vile *Sydney MS, T.MS B.*
13] Added in *T.MS A.* *seeming-genial venial*] only seeming-venial *MSS.*
14. *suggesting*: tempting. Cp. Shakespeare, *Sonnet 144*: 'Which like two spirits do suggest me still.'
15. halt] ever halt *MS.*
16. Cp. Shelley, *Queen Mab* viii 70: 'Those deserts of immeasurable sand'.
17. And] While *Sydney MS, T.MS A.* *a*] Not *T.MS B* (*slip?*). *sultry*] weary *MSS.*
18. Far] Far on *MSS.*
20. Perhaps suggested by 'the city of salt', *Joshua* xv 62.
¶**311. 8.** *Mónaco.*

What slender campanili grew
By bays, the peacock's neck in hue;
15   Where, here and there, on sandy beaches
A milky-belled amaryllis blew.

How young Columbus seemed to rove,
Yet present in his natal grove,
    Now watching high on mountain cornice,
20   And steering, now, from a purple cove,

Now pacing mute by ocean's rim;
Till, in a narrow street and dim,
    I stayed the wheels at Cogoletto,
And drank, and loyally drank to him.

25   Nor knew we well what pleased us most,
Not the clipt palm of which they boast;
    But distant colour, happy hamlet,
A mouldered citadel on the coast,

Or tower, or high hill-convent, seen
30   A light amid its olives green;
    Or olive-hoary cape in ocean;
Or rosy blossom in hot ravine,

Where oleanders flushed the bed
Of silent torrents, gravel-spread;
35   And, crossing, oft we saw the glisten
Of ice, far up on a mountain head.

We loved that hall, though white and cold,
Those nichèd shapes of noble mould,
    A princely people's awful princes,
40   The grave, severe Genovese of old.

At Florence too what golden hours,
In those long galleries, were ours;
    What drives about the fresh Cascinè,
Or walks in Boboli's ducal bowers.

---

13. *campanili*: bell-towers.
14. T. in Cornwall, 8 June 1848: 'sea purple and green like a peacock's neck' (*Mem.* i 275).
36. *up*] *1856*; off *1855*.
37. 'The Palazzo Ducale' (T.).
43. 'The Park of Florence' (T.).

45 In bright vignettes, and each complete,
Of tower or duomo, sunny-sweet,
    Or palace, how the city glittered,
Through cypress avenues, at our feet.

But when we crost the Lombard plain
50 Remember what a plague of rain;
    Of rain at Reggio, rain at Parma;
At Lodi, rain, Piacenza, rain.

And stern and sad (so rare the smiles
Of sunlight) looked the Lombard piles;
55   Porch-pillars on the lion resting,
And sombre, old, colonnaded aisles.

O Milan, O the chanting quires,
The giant windows' blazoned fires,
    The height, the space, the gloom, the glory!
60 A mount of marble, a hundred spires!

I climbed the roofs at break of day;
Sun-smitten Alps before me lay.
    I stood among the silent statues,
And statued pinnacles, mute as they.

65 How faintly-flushed, how phantom-fair,
Was Monte Rosa, hanging there
    A thousand shadowy-pencilled valleys
And snowy dells in a golden air.

Remember how we came at last
70 To Como; shower and storm and blast
    Had blown the lake beyond his limit,
And all was flooded; and how we past

From Como, when the light was gray,
And in my head, for half the day,
75   The rich Virgilian rustic measure
Of Lari Maxume, all the way,

51. *Reggio, rain*] *1856*; Reggio *1855*.
57. *Milan.*
60–62. Cp. *The Palace of Art* 82, *1832* text: 'Below sunsmitten icy spires'.
75–6. Virgil, *Georgics* ii 159–60: *Anne lacus tantos? te, Lari maxime, teque /
fluctibus et fremitu adsurgens, Benace, marino?* ('Or of our mighty lakes?
Of thee, Larius, our greatest; and thee, Benacus, with the roaring, surging
swell of the sea?') Lake Como was the Lacus Larius of the Romans.

Like ballad-burthen music, kept,
As on The Lariano crept
   To that fair port below the castle
80 Of Queen Theodolind, where we slept;

Or hardly slept, but watched awake
A cypress in the moonlight shake,
   The moonlight touching o'er a terrace
One tall Agavè above the lake.

85 What more? we took our last adieu,
And up the snowy Splugen drew,
   But ere we reached the highest summit
I plucked a daisy, I gave it you.

It told of England then to me,
90 And now it tells of Italy.
   O love, we two shall go no longer
To lands of summer across the sea;

So dear a life your arms enfold
Whose crying is a cry for gold:
95   Yet here tonight in this dark city,
When ill and weary, alone and cold,

I found, though crushed to hard and dry,
This nurseling of another sky
   Still in the little book you lent me,
100 And where you tenderly laid it by:

And I forgot the clouded Forth,
The gloom that saddens Heaven and Earth,
   The bitter east, the misty summer
And gray metropolis of the North.

105 Perchance, to lull the throbs of pain,
Perchance, to charm a vacant brain,
   Perchance, to dream you still beside me,
My fancy fled to the South again.

79. 'Varenna' (T.).
80. *Theodolind*: wife of a sixth-century king of the Lombards.
84. *Agavè*: a handsome tropical plant.
93. H.T. was born Aug. 1852.
98. Shelley, *The Cloud* 74: 'the nursling of the Sky'.

312 To the Rev. F. D. Maurice

Published *1855*, dated 'January, 1854'. *H. Lpr 245* shows T. changing the order of the stanzas. H.T. says of this 'invitation to Farringford' that 'Mr Maurice had been ejected from his professorship at King's College for non-orthodoxy. He had especially alarmed some of the "weaker brethren" by pointing out that the word "eternal" in "eternal punishment" (αἰώνιος), strictly translated, referred to the quality not the duration of the punishment.' Maurice (1805–72) had argued in *Theological Essays* (1853) that the popular belief in the endlessness of future punishment was superstitious; in Oct. 1853 a council of King's College, London, forced his resignation. T. abhorred the belief in eternal punishment (*Despair* 26, *Faith* 7–8). Maurice had agreed to be godfather of H.T. in Aug. 1852, the month of birth. Apparently he did not see the poem till it was published in *1855*, to judge from his letter of 27 July 1855 (*Mat.* ii 147–8). Cp. Horace, *Epistle* I v, and, e.g., Ben Jonson's *Inviting a Friend to Supper*. Cp. the stanza form of *The Daisy* (p. *501*), and *To Professor Jebb* (III 162).

> Come, when no graver cares employ,
> Godfather, come and see your boy:
>   Your presence will be sun in winter,
> Making the little one leap for joy.
>
> 5 For, being of that honest few,
> Who give the Fiend himself his due,
>   Should eighty-thousand college-councils
> Thunder 'Anathema,' friend, at you;

¶ 312. *1–4*] *T.Nbk 36 has these following l. 12, and begins:*
    With loathsome, loveless prate of Hell
    Each bigot makes his infidel,
       Claps Calvin in God's chair and bids us
    Honour the Devil and all is well.
1. when] if *H.MS.*
3. will] would *T.MS. sun in winter*] light among us *H.MS.*
5–6] But you are of that honest few
    Who give both God and men their due. *T.MS*
7. eighty-] thirty *T.MS.*
8] Dare to decide on a man like you *T.MS. Anathema*: the curse of the church, denouncing a doctrine as damnable. (Ironic, in view of Maurice's doctrine.)

         Should all our churchmen foam in spite
   10   At you, so careful of the right,
              Yet one lay-hearth would give you welcome
         (Take it and come) to the Isle of Wight;

         Where, far from noise and smoke of town,
         I watch the twilight falling brown
   15   All round a careless-ordered garden
         Close to the ridge of a noble down.

         You'll have no scandal while you dine,
         But honest talk and wholesome wine,
              And only hear the magpie gossip
   20   Garrulous under a roof of pine:

         For groves of pine on either hand,
         To break the blast of winter, stand;
              And further on, the hoary Channel
         Tumbles a billow on chalk and sand;

9–10]   Should half our churchmen bear a spite
            To one so loving of the light *T.MS*;
            The bigot needs must bear a spite
            To priests so faithful to the light, *H.MS*
11. Yet one lay-hearth] There's yet one hearth *T.MS*; But there is one *H.MS*.
12. (Take . . . the] Here in the sweet little *H.MS*.
12 ∧ *13*]   *T.MS has ll. 1–4 and then:*
            Listen. I see the golden ray
            Of sunrise on three headlands play,
              Here falling over elm and ilex
            There on the curve of a lovely bay.
13] And here far off from noise of town *T.MS*; Far off from hum and noise of
town, *H.MS*. Horace's *fumum et opes strepitumque Romae* (*Odes* III xxix 12), as
in *In Memoriam* lxxxix 8: 'The dust and din and steam of town'.
14. falling] mellowing *MSS*.
15. All round] About *MSS*.
17–20. N. Rudd compares Horace, *Satires* II vi 65–78, of which, too, l. 35
below is an adaptation.
17. You'll . . . you] We'll . . . we *MSS*.   *scandal*] slander *T.MS*.
18. wholesome] an honest *H.MS*.
19. only] sitting *H.MS*.
20 ∧ *21*]   For these are frequent here with me—
            O not ill-omened may they be.
              Here comes the fieldfare, here the starling,
            Mixt with a clangorous bird of sea. *H.MS*
This stanza appears on its own; it was presumably intended to follow the
magpie, but would have disrupted the sequence in ll. 20–1.
24. billow] *1872*; breaker *1855–70*.

25 Where, if below the milky steep
    Some ship of battle slowly creep,
       And on through zones of light and shadow
    Glimmer away to the lonely deep,

    We might discuss the Northern sin
30 Which made a selfish war begin;
       Dispute the claims, arrange the chances;
    Emperor, Ottoman, which shall win:

    Or whether war's avenging rod
    Shall lash all Europe into blood;
35   Till you should turn to dearer matters,
    Dear to the man that is dear to God;

    How best to help the slender store,
    How mend the dwellings, of the poor;
       How gain in life, as life advances,
40 Valour and charity more and more.

    Come, Maurice, come: the lawn as yet
    Is hoar with rime, or spongy-wet;

25. *Where,*] Here *T.MS*; Or *H.MS*.
27] And moving, charged with silent thunders, *T.MS*; And bearing on her towers of silver *H.MS*.
28. *lonely*] silent *H.MS*.
29–32]   We would not scruple to discuss
              The claims that shake the Bosporus,
                 Nor Oltenitza, nor Sinope,
              Ottoman, Emperor, Turk and Russ. *H.MS*
T.MS has the second line as 'Our fleet that keeps the Bosporus'; and breaks off after the third line. The Russo–Turkish war began in Oct. 1853; l. [3] mentions two battles. It was Russia's destruction of the Turkish ships in Nov. that shocked British opinion; by the end of March 1854 England was to find herself at war with Russia in the Crimea.
33–6] Nor how the chance of war may fall *H.MS with lacuna*.
37. *best to help*] to eke out *H.MS*.
41–5. Recalling Horace's invitation to enjoy the springtime (*Odes* I iv), and also Milton's *Sonnet 17* (which makes use of Horace): 'Now that the Fields are dank, and ways are mire, / Where shall we sometimes meet, and by the fire / Help wast a sullen day; what may be won / From the hard Season gaining: time will run / On smoother, till *Favonius* re-inspire / The frozen earth; and cloth in fresh attire / The Lillie and Rose, that neither sow'd nor spun. / What neat repast shall feast us . . .'
41. *lawn*] park *H.MS*.
42. *spongy-wet*] dank with wet *H.MS*.

But when the wreath of March has blossomed,
Crocus, anemone, violet,
45 Or later, pay one visit here,
For those are few we hold as dear;
Nor pay but one, but come for many,
Many and many a happy year.

January, 1854

315 The Charge of the Light Brigade

Published *The Examiner*, 9 Dec. 1854, signed 'A.T.'; then *1855*. The Crimean charge took place 25 Oct. 1854; cp. *The Charge of the Heavy Brigade* (III 92). Written 2 Dec. 1854, 'in a few minutes, after reading . . . . *The Times* in which occurred the phrase "some one had blundered", and this was the origin of the metre of his poem' (*Mem.* i 381). The editorial (13 Nov.) in fact spoke of 'some hideous blunder'. T. also drew on the report (14 Nov.), where – as he says –'only 607 sabres are mentioned'. T. wrote to Forster, 6 Dec.: 'Six is much better than seven hundred (as I think) metrically so keep it' (*Letters* ii 101).
The textual history of the poem, including a full account of the MSS and a record of all variants, along with a critical discussion (including of the relation to *The Times*), is told in E. F. Shannon and C. Ricks, *SB* xxxviii (1985) 1–44. On the relation of the poem to history and ideology, see J. J. McGann, *The Beauty of Inflections* (1985), pp. 190–203. T. soon deplored the *1855* revision, which omitted ll. 5–12 ('Some one had blundered') and closed feebly. He reverted in *1856* to earlier readings. 'Not a poem on which I pique myself' (*Mem.* i 409–10); at one stage he intended to omit it from the 2nd edition of *Maud, and Other Poems* (*Virginia*).
Sources: Drayton's *Ballad of Agincourt* was suggested at least as early as 1872; T. said it 'was not in my mind; my poem is dactyllic'. Chatterton's *Song to Ælla* is similar in rhythm, form, and theme, e.g., 'Down to the depth of hell/Thousands of Dacyanns went . . . .'. T. may have remembered it unconsciously.
On T.'s recording made in 1890, see B. Maxwell, *TRB* iii (1980) 150–57.

I
Half a league, half a league,
Half a league onward,

43. *wreath*] pride *H.MS.*
46. *as*] so *H.MS.*
47. *pay but*] only *H.MS.*

All in the valley of Death
Rode the six hundred.
5 'Forward, the Light Brigade!
Charge for the guns!' he said:
Into the valley of Death
Rode the six hundred.

II
'Forward, the Light Brigade!'
10 Was there a man dismayed?
Not though the soldier knew
Some one had blundered:
Their's not to make reply,
Their's not to reason why,
15 Their's but to do and die:
Into the valley of Death
Rode the six hundred.

III
Cannon to right of them,
Cannon to left of them,
20 Cannon in front of them
Volleyed and thundered;
Stormed at with shot and shell,
Boldly they rode and well,
Into the jaws of Death,
25 Into the mouth of Hell
Rode the six hundred.

¶ 315. 3. *the valley of Death: The Times* called it 'that valley of death'
(13 Nov.).
5–8] *1856*;   Into the valley of Death
                               Rode the six hundred,
                               For up came an order which
                               Some one had blundered.
                               'Forward, the Light Brigade!
                               Take the guns,' Nolan said:
                               Into the valley of Death
                               Rode the six hundred. *1854 as separate stanza;*
'Charge,' was the captain's cry; *1855.*
9–12] *1856*; . . . / No man was there dismayed, / . . . *1854; not 1855.*
13–14] *Transposed 1855.*
17. *hundred:* pronounced 'hunderd' in Lincolnshire, according to T.'s
friend W. F. Rawnsley.

IV

Flashed all their sabres bare,
Flashed as they turned in air
Sabring the gunners there,
30   Charging an army, while
All the world wondered:
Plunged in the battery-smoke
Right through the line they broke;
Cossack and Russian
35   Reeled from the sabre-stroke
Shattered and sundered.
Then they rode back, but not
Not the six hundred.

V

Cannon to right of them,
40   Cannon to left of them,
Cannon behind them
Volleyed and thundered;
Stormed at with shot and shell,
While horse and hero fell,
45   They that had fought so well
Came through the jaws of Death,
Back from the mouth of Hell,
All that was left of them,
Left of six hundred.

27–32. 'Through the clouds of smoke we could see their sabres flashing'
(*The Times*).
28. *as they turned*] *1856*; all at once *1854–5*.
33] *1856*; With many a desperate stroke *1854*; Fiercely the line . . . *1855*.
34] *1856*; The Russian line they broke; *1854*; Strong was the sabre-stroke;
1855.
35–6] *1856*; *not 1854*;   Making an army reel
                              Shaken and sundered. *1855*
44] *1854, 1856*; *not 1855*.
45. *fought*] *1854, 1856*; struck *1855*.
46. *Came*] *1854, 1856*; Rode *1855*.   *through*] *1855*; from *1854*.
46 ∧ 7] Half a league back again, *1855*.
47. *Back*] *1854, 1856*; Up *1855*.
49. 'Only 195 returned' (T.).

VI

50   When can their glory fade?
      O the wild charge they made!
      All the world wondered.
      Honour the charge they made!
      Honour the Light Brigade,
55   Noble six hundred!

316 Maud

A MONODRAMA

Published *1855*.
Composition. T. worked on *Maud*, 'morning and evening', in 1854 (*Mem.*
i 377). On 10 Jan. 1855, he had 'finished, and read out, several lyrics of
Maud' (*Mem.* i 382); in Feb. 1855, 'he made the mad scene in *Maud* in
twenty minutes' (*Mat.* ii 108). On 25 April 1855, he 'copied out *Maud* for
the press', and put 'the last touch' to it on 7 July (*Mem.* i 384–5). On the
trial edition or proofs see T. J. Wise, *Bibliography* i 126–31. S. Shatto (see
below) argues that Wise's variants are from proofs, not strictly a trial edition;
Wise used R. H. Shepherd's collations, and the volume itself, a copy of *1855*, is
in the *Huntington*. A copy of a (subsequent) trial edition is now in *Lincoln*. The
germ of *Maud* was the early lyric *Oh! that 'twere possible* (p. *988*) (now *Maud* ii
141–238), which T. had written in 1833–4 soon after the death of Arthur
Hallam. There are two drafts of this in *Heath MS* and T. published an
expansion in *The Tribute*, Sept. 1837 (for details, see *p. 569*), apparently
with reluctance. R. W. Rader (p. 6) comments: 'Tennyson finished and
published his poem in 1837 against his will, cobbling up an ending for it
under pressure because he wished to pacify Milnes and had no other poem to
do it with. But that he continued to think of his poem as incomplete (the 1834
version ended unsatisfactorily with "And weep / My whole soul out to
thee") is suggested by the existence of a fair copy, dated April, 1838, in which
it has been returned to its pre-1837 form; and by the fact that he did not
reprint this lovely lyric in the *1842* volumes or in any other collection before
Maud.' In *Eversley*, T. records: 'Sir John Simeon years after begged me to'
weave a story round this poem, and so *Maud* came into being.' Aubrey de
Vere's account in *Mem.* i 379 differs slightly: 'Its origin and composition
were, as he described them, singular. He had accidentally lighted upon a

50–55] *1854, 1856;*   Honour the brave and bold!
                        Long shall the tale be told,
                        Yea, when our babes are old–
                        How they rode onward. *1855*

poem of his own which begins, "O that 'twere possible", and which had long before been published in a selected volume got up by Lord Northampton for the aid of a sick clergyman. It had struck him, in consequence, I think, of a suggestion made by Sir John Simeon, that, to render the poem fully intelligible, a preceding one was necessary. He wrote it; the second poem too required a predecessor: and thus the whole poem was written, as it were, *backwards.*' But in H.T.'s notes (*Lincoln*) for the early version in *Mat.* the phrase 'in consequence ... Simeon' does not appear. Rader argues, persuasively, that though Simeon's remark may well have spurred T. on, it would be wrong to give it too much weight, since T. must have long thought of doing something more with *Oh! that 'twere possible.* 'Tennyson plainly intended to do something with the piece eight months before his friendship with Simeon began', since in Oct. 1853 his father-in-law, Henry Sellwood, sent by request to Emily T. a copy of the poem from *The Tribute.* See Rader, pp. 1–11. In *1913*, H.T. records: 'My father told [Simeon] that the poem had appeared years before in *The Tribute*, but that it was really intended to be part of a dramatic poem' (p. xxxix). The lyric beginning 'See what a lovely shell' (II ii) had also been written in the 1830s and laid aside (*CT*, p. 281; the authority is the memory of D. D. Heath in 1894, quoting Spedding); and 'Go not happy day' (l xvii) had originally been intended as a song for *The Princess* (MS, *University Library, Cambridge*). The fierce social criticism of his society was begun in T.'s political poems of 1852. The original title was *Maud or the Madness* (*Mem.* i 402); T. 'intended to revert to the original title, as the words "or the Madness" are added in his hand in the present copy' (1855, *Virginia*). E. F. Shannon notes that the addition of 'A Monodrama' to the title in 1875 was probably suggested by R. J. Mann's calling it a monodrama in 1856 (*Maud Vindicated*), a term echoed by Alexander Macmillan in 1859 ('The Critical Reception of *Maud*', *PMLA* lxviii (1953) 397–417). On the traditions of the monodrama (invented by Rousseau in 1762, *Pygmalion*), see Culler (pp. 194–6): 'The form was introduced into England by William Taylor of Norwich and his friend Dr Frank Sayers in 1792 and was quickly imitated by Southey and "Monk" Lewis. Because it did not often achieve stage representation, however, it soon lost the connection with music, and by the 1840s the term *monodrama* was commonly used of any dramatic performance intended for a single actor or, indeed, any dramatic poem placed in the mouth of a single speaker. It was used where we would use the term *dramatic monologue*. R. H. Horne, for instance, speaks of T.'s "powerful monodrama of *St. Simeon Stylites*"' T. wrote to R. C. Hall, 17 Jan. 1873: '*Maud* is a drama, i.e. a monodrama and one sui generis. I once thought of calling it *Maud or the Madness* but again I thought, "the countrymen of Shakespeare are not fools," in your case at least I had not miscalculated' (*Letters* iii). Culler suggests that Mann in 1856 probably received the word *monodrama* from T. as well as 'the entire substance' of his pamphlet, from which Culler quotes compellingly (pp. 200–202). Shannon shows that the reception of *Maud* was on the whole unfavourable, though there were more favourable reviews than is usually said. By Oct. 1855, more than 8,000 copies had been sold. Only one of the passages castigated was altered in the 2nd edition (1856), namely, iii 50. On the other hand, as Shannon says, the additions in *1856* improved the logic of the poem; T. added three stanzas to the opening section; mitigated the attack on the peace-party in I x; and added a stanza at the very close of the poem. He also added I xix (on the mother's death-bed), and II iii (on Maud's death). The division into Parts I and II was made in *1859*; the further division into a Part III was made in *1865*. The fullest MS is *T.Nbk 36*. There are MSS in Harvard (Notebooks 13, 20–21, 27, 29–31; Loosepapers 145–9, 274); the Huntington Library (HM 19495–6, the latter apparently six leaves detached from Trinity MS); and the Berg Collection. There is an edition of *Maud*, with a full commentary and collation, by Susan Shatto (1986).

Sources. J. H. Buckley observes that *Maud* 'in form, theme, and substance recalled the more ambitious efforts of Alexander Smith and Sydney Dobell', the so-called 'Spasmodics' (*The Victorian Temper*, 1952, p. 63). See also Turner (pp. 140–41). Smith published *A Life Drama* in 1852, and Dobell published *Balder* in 1853. T. owned the edition of 1854 (*Lincoln*), and he spoke of Smith as 'a poet of considerable promise' (*Mem.* ii 73, i 468) and pointed out 'the real merits of *Balder*' (*Mem.* ii 506). The plot of *Maud* Edward FitzGerald spoke of as 'leaving something of a Bride of Lammermoor Gloom on one' (15 July 1856, *Letters* ii 234). Andrew Lang later stressed the similarity to Scott's novel (which T. alludes to in *The Flight* 57): the hero 'is merely The Master of Ravenswood in modern costume, and without Lady Ashton. Her part is taken by Maud's brother. The situations are nearly identical – ruin; dawdling by a lost ancestral home; love; and duelling (*Alfred Tennyson*, 1901, p. 89). T. P. Harrison, '*Maud* and Shakspere', *Shakespeare Association Bulletin* xvii (1942) 80–5, points out that only Part I has much affinity with *Hamlet* (which T. invoked), and that the erotic theme is from *Romeo and Juliet* – feud, dance, duel, and flight, with the brother similar to Tybalt. G. O. Marshall, *Georgia Review* xvi (1962) 463–4, remarks on a ballad which appeared in *The Tribute* (along with *Oh! that 'twere possible*) in 1837: 'For the name "Maud" if not for part of his story he was possibly indebted to one of the contributions, an anonymous ballad entitled *The Wicked Nephew*, in which the Lady Maud waits for her lover .... There are several elements common to both poems: murder for material gain, overseas flight after a murder, madness caused by having committed a murder, presence of ghost, and death after a fall.' (As to the name 'Maud', it is an odd coincidence at least that the year before publishing *The Princess* T. travelled on the 'Princess Maude'; *Mem.* i 230; cp. 'Queen Maud', I xx 836.) Turner (p. 133) adds further 'striking parallels between *Maud* and other poems in *The Tribute*'; he compares Aubrey de Vere's *The Passion Flower* with I xiv 496, and he particularly stresses Lady Northampton's *The Idiot Boy*, which 'shares with Maude'; *Mem.* i 230; cp. 'Queen Maud', I xx 836.) Turner Cp. 133) adds "thirst of gold"), the main features of its plot (a mentally deranged boy falls in love with "a damsel brighter than the rose", with "rosy cheeks", and a "rightful heir" has been robbed of his "manor" by "treacherous wiles"), its seaside setting, and two notable images: the waves beat against the rocks in "madd'ning fury' [cp. I iii 98], and the dead hero, like Maud's dying brother [I ii 117], is called a "poor worm"'. The importance of another literary source, Charles Kingsley's *Alton Locke* (1850), was suggested by Sir Charles Tennyson: 'Alfred and Emily both read *Alton Locke*, and the story of the tailor poet particularly moved Alfred' (p. 260). On the parallels, see Turner (p. 140). Sir Charles suggests that the social denunciations in *Maud* 'sprang from his long talks with Charles Kingsley and F. D. Maurice about the terrible conditions in the rapidly growing industrial cities' (p. 281). The detailed resemblances to *Alton Locke* are described by J. B. Steane, *Tennyson* (1966), pp. 93–4, 111–12. T.'s attitudes are close to those of the political poems of 1852, and he was also influenced by 'Peace and War: A Dialogue', in *Blackwood's* lxxvi (Nov. 1854) 589–98. R. C. Schweik, *Notes and Queries* ccv (1960) 457–8, points out the parallels, including the mention of 'civil war'; the adulteration of food; and the Quaker. See also C. Ricks, *Notes and Queries* ccvii (1962) 230. W. Collins (*TRB* ii, 1974, 126–8) notes the influence of a pamphlet, *Points of War*, by T.'s friend Franklin Lushington; there are 'similarities in thought, imagery, phrasing, and even rhythm', and E.T.'s copy is inscribed 'May 15, 1854'.

T. wrote to Archer Gurney, 6 Dec. 1855: 'I wish to say one word about *Maud* which you and others so strangely misinterpret. I have had Peace party papers sent to me claiming me as being on their side because I had put the cry for war into the mouth of a madman. Surely that is not half so wrong a criticism as some I have seen. Strictly speaking I do not see how from the poem I could be pronounced with çertainty either peace man or war man. I wonder that you and others did not find out that all along the man was intended to have an hereditary vein of insanity, and that he falls foul on the swindling, on the times, because he feels that his father has been killed by the work of the lie, and that all through he fears the coming madness. How could you or anyone suppose that if I had had to speak in my own person my own opinion of this war or war generally I should have spoken with so little moderation. The whole was intended to be a new form of dramatic composition. I took a man constitutionally diseased and dipt him into the circumstances of the time and took him out on fire. I shall show this better in a second edition ... I do not mean that my madman does not speak truths too' (*Letters* ii 137). Henry van Dyke reports T. as speaking in similar terms in 1892 (*Studies in Tennyson*, 1920, p. 97): 'You must remember always, in reading it, what it is meant to be – a drama in lyrics. It shows the unfolding of a lonely, morbid soul, touched with inherited madness ... The things which seem like faults belong not so much to the poem as to the character of the hero.

He is wrong, of course, in much that he says. If he had been always wise and just he would not have been himself. He begins with a false comparison – "blood-red heath". There is no such thing in nature; but he sees the heather tinged like blood because his mind has been disordered ... He is

wrong in thinking that war will transform the cheating tradesman into a
great-souled hero, or that it will sweep away the dishonesties and lessen the
miseries of humanity. The history of the Crimean War proves his error. But
this very delusion is natural to him: it is in keeping with his morbid,
melancholy, impulsive character to see a cure for the evils of peace in the
horrors of war.' The attack on Mammonism clearly owes something to
Carlyle as well as to Kingsley (G. O. Marshall, *Notes and Queries* cciv (1959)
77–8).

Biographical relevance. See R. W. Rader, *Tennyson's 'Maud'* (1963),
passim; he shows that T. here draws together all the strands of his early
life–the hero's father and his rage, the lonely mother, the old man ('of
the wolds'), the politician son, and above all the love for Rosa Baring–
though Maud herself blends Rosa, Sophy Rawnsley, and T.'s wife Emily
(everything about Maud in the last part of the poem recalls Emily rather
than Rosa). The story of a love thwarted by Mammonism resembles that
of *Edwin Morris*, *Aylmer's Field*, *Locksley Hall*, and *The Flight*; and there
are many likenesses to the poems about Rosa, such as *The Rosebud*,
Three Sonnets to a Coquette, and *To Rosa*, 1836. Sir Charles Tennyson
observes that the mad scenes are based on T.'s recollections of Dr Matthew
Allen's asylum at High Beech (p. 286); furthermore T. owned a copy of
Allen's *Essay on the Classification of the Insane* (1837, Lincoln). H.T. records:

'My father liked reading aloud this poem, a "Drama of the Soul", set in a
landscape glorified by Love, and, according to Lowell, "The antiphonal
voice to *In Memoriam*", which is the "Way of the Soul" . . . . My father
said, "This poem of *Maud or the Madness* is a little *Hamlet*, the history of a
morbid, poetic soul, under the blighting influence of a recklessly specu-
lative age. He is the heir of madness, an egoist with the makings of a
cynic, raised to a pure and holy love which elevates his whole nature,
passing from the height of triumph to the lowest depth of misery, driven
into madness by the loss of her whom he has loved, and, when he has
at length passed through the fiery furnace, and has recovered his reason,
giving himself up to work for the good of mankind through the unselfish-
ness born of a great passion. The peculiarity of this poem is that different
phases of passion in one person take the place of different characters.'
(Quoted here from *Eversley*, where it is all within quotation-marks as T.'s,
and where the next sentence has a reference to 'me', i.e. T.; in *Mem.* i 396,
there are quotation-marks after *Hamlet*, and again at 'The peculiarity . . .
characters'.)

T. said to Knowles in 1870–71: 'No other poem (a monotone with
plenty of change and no weariness) has been made into a drama where
successive phases of passion in one person take the place of successive persons.
It is slightly akin to *Hamlet*'; 'I've always said that *Maud* and *Guinevere* were
the finest things I've written'. (See G. N. Ray, *Tennyson Reads 'Maud'*, 1968,
pp. 43, 45; abbreviated below to *Knowles*.) Turner (p. 139) says of the

poem's hero: 'Like Hamlet he is obsessed by a wish to avenge his father's death . . . Like Hamlet he is profoundly disgusted by himself and the whole human race, is haunted by a ghost, and kills the brother of the girl he loves in a duel.'

W. E. Gladstone modified in *Gleanings of Past Years* (1879, ii 146–7; quoted in *Mem.* i 398–9) his earlier criticisms of *Maud* (*QR*, Oct. 1859):

'I can now see, and I at once confess, that a feeling, which had reference to the growth of the war-spirit in the outer world at the date of this article, dislocated my frame of mind, and disabled me from dealing even tolerably with the work as a work of imagination. Whether it is to be desired that a poem should require from common men a good deal of effort in order to comprehend it; whether all that is put into the mouth of the Soliloquist in *Maud* is within the lines of poetical verisimilitude, whether this poem has the full moral equilibrium which is so marked a characteristic of the sister-works; are questions open, perhaps, to discussion. But I have neither done justice in the text to its rich and copious beauties of detail, nor to its great lyrical and metrical power. And what is worse, I have failed to comprehend rightly the relation between particular passages in the poem and its general scope. This is, I conceive, not to set forth any coherent strain, but to use for poetical ends all the moods and phases allowable under the laws of the art, in a special form of character, which is impassioned, fluctuating, and ill-grounded. The design, which seems to resemble that of the Ecclesiastes in another sphere, is arduous; but Mr Tennyson's power of execution is probably nowhere greater. Even as regards the passages devoted to war-frenzy, equity should have reminded me of the fine lines in the *latter* portion of X iii (Part I), and of the emphatic words [ii 332–3]: "I swear to you, lawful and lawless war / Are scarcely even akin."'

J. R. Bennett elucidates the arguments for dissociating T. from the speaker and from Crimean war-fever (*English Studies* lxii, 1981, 34–45).

See also J. Killham, in his *Critical Essays on the Poetry of Tennyson.*

PART I

I

1

I hate the dreadful hollow behind the little wood,
Its lips in the field above are dabbled with blood-red
    heath,
The red-ribbed ledges drip with a silent horror of
    blood,

¶ 316. i *1–3*. 'My father would say that in calling heath "blood"-red the hero showed his extravagant fancy, which is already on the road to mad-

And Echo there, whatever is asked her, answers
'Death.'

II
For there in the ghastly pit long since a body was
5   found,
His who had given me life – O father! O God! was it
     well? –
Mangled, and flattened, and crushed, and dinted into
     the ground:
There yet lies the rock that fell with him when he fell.

III
Did he fling himself down? who knows? for a vast
     speculation had failed,
And ever he muttered and maddened, and ever
10   wanned with despair,
And out he walked when the wind like a broken
     worldling wailed,
And the flying gold of the ruined woodlands drove
     through the air.

IV
I remember the time, for the roots of my hair were
     stirred
By a shuffled step, by a dead weight trailed, by a
     whispered fright,
And my pulses closed their gates with a shock on my
15   heart as I heard
The shrill-edged shriek of a mother divide the
     shuddering night.

ness' (H.T.). Cp. *The Vale of Bones* 81–2, where the flowers 'Blush with the
big and purple drops, / That dribbled from the leafy copse.' Also *The
Lover's Tale* i 388–9: 'heath and hill, / And hollow lined and wooded to the
lips'. T. in Switzerland saw 'little coves and wooded shores and villages
under vast red ribs of rock' (10 Aug. 1846; *Letters* i 260).
i *4*. W. E. Buckler notes: 'The myth of Narcissus and Echo, with variations,
is one of the subtexts of *Maud*, as the fiction suggests and as the fourth line
. . . and the adoration of the "beautiful voice" [I v] signal'; Buckler remarks
the change from the trial edition, 'sweet Narcissus', to the published 'shining
daffodil' [i 101, iii 6]: 'it may have been to keep his subtext from surfacing too
obviously' (*The Victorian Imagination*, 1980, p. 226).
i *9*. *vast*] *1856*; great *1855*.   *fling himself down*] slay [kill *alternative*]
himself *HnMS*.

V

Villainy somewhere! whose? One says, we are villains
    all.
Not he: his honest fame should at least by me be
    maintained:
But that old man, now lord of the broad estate and
    the Hall,
Dropt off gorged from a scheme that had left us flaccid
20   and drained.

VI

Why do they prate of the blessings of Peace? we have
    made them a curse,
Pickpockets, each hand lusting for all that is not its
    own;
And lust of gain, in the spirit of Cain, is it better or
    worse
Than the heart of the citizen hissing in war on his own
    hearthstone?

VII

But these are the days of advance, the works of the
25   men of mind,

i *17*. Turner (p. 139) compares Hamlet's 'We are arrant knaves all' (III i 128).
i *21-8*. Valerie Pitt (*Tennyson Laureate*, 1962, p. 175) compares Carlyle,
Past and Present (1843), IV i: '"Violence", "war", "disorder": well,
what is war, and death itself, to such a perpetual life-in-death, and "peace,
peace, where there is no peace!"' In his edition (1896) of *Sartor Resartus*,
A. MacMechan had compared III v: 'Where each, isolated, regardless of
his neighbour; turned against his neighbour, clutches what he can get, and
cries "Mine!" and calls it Peace, because, in the cut-purse and cut-throat
Scramble, no steel knives, but only a far cunninger sort, can be employed?'
P. Scott notes *Jeremiah* vi 14: 'Peace, peace, where there is no peace'; and 2
Kings ix 17, 18, 19, 22: 'Is it peace?'; 'the repetition of the question in *Maud*
[ll. 27 and 47 here] draws attention to the passage from 2 *Kings*, with its
similar repetition'. Scott also notes Martin Tupper's poem *A Commentary*
(1851): 'Tupper's stridency (indeed, the obsession in his tone) seems
surprisingly similar to the *Maud* passage': 'Is it peace, thou child of reason?/Is
it peace, ye men of earth?' (etc.) 'One wonders if the connection between the
Biblical question "Is it peace?", and a denunciation of the hypocrisy of "civil
war", had become a commonplace in the early 1850s. If so, perhaps T.'s hero
is ranting out a kind of rhetoric which T. hoped would be recognisable, and
"placeable", by his readers' (*TRB* iii, 1978, 83–4).

When who but a fool would have faith in a tradesman's
    ware or his word?
Is it peace or war? Civil war, as I think, and that of a
    kind
The viler, as underhand, not openly bearing the sword.

VIII

Sooner or later I too may passively take the print
Of the golden age – why not? I have neither hope nor
    trust;
30

May make my heart as a millstone, set my face as a
    flint,
Cheat and be cheated, and die: who knows? we are
    ashes and dust.

IX

Peace sitting under her olive, and slurring the days
    gone by,
When the poor are hovelled and hustled together,
    each sex, like swine,
When only the ledger lives, and when only not all men
    lie;
35

Peace in her vineyard – yes! – but a company forges the
    wine.

X

And the vitriol madness flushes up in the ruffian's
    head,
Till the filthy by-lane rings to the yell of the trampled
    wife,

---

i *31. Job* xli 24: 'His heart is as firm as a stone: yea, as hard as a piece of the
nether millstone.' *Isaiah* l 7: 'Therefore have I set my face like a flint, and
I know that I shall not be ashamed.'
i *33, 36. Micah* iv 3–4: 'Neither shall they learn war any more. But they
shall sit every man under his vine and under his fig tree; and none shall
make them afraid.'
i *35.* Cp. *Hands All Round!* 20: 'Too much we make our Ledgers, Gods'.
Psalm cxvi 11: 'I said in my haste, All men are liars.'
i *37.* Turner (p. 142) notes: 'partly from *Alton Locke*, where gin is called
"vitriol", and partly, perhaps, from a *Times* report (8 Dec. 1854) of a "Vitriol
Man" with "a monomania" for squirting vitriol on ladies' dresses'.

And chalk and alum and plaster are sold to the poor
for bread,
And the spirit of murder works in the very means of
40 life,

XI

And Sleep must lie down armed, for the villainous
centre-bits
Grind on the wakeful ear in the hush of the moonless
nights,
While another is cheating the sick of a few last gasps,
as he sits
To pestle a poisoned poison behind his crimson lights.

XII

When a Mammonite mother kills her babe for a burial
45 fee,

i 39. And] 1865; While 1855-64. A notorious scandal. E. F. Shannon
refers to A. H. Hassall's articles (*The Lancet*, 1851-4) on the adulteration of
food, published as a book in 1855. J. B. Steane compares *Alton Locke*:
'Bread full o' alum and bones, and sic filth.' Turner (p. 134) says that this is
'unlikely to have been written before April 1854, when the adulteration of
food and drugs to which it refers was first highlighted by John Postgate's
revelations at a special conference held at Birmingham to discuss the subject
(20 April); and the date of composition was probably after the second
Birmingham meeting (28 Nov. 1854), which was brought to the attention of
readers, not only of the *Lancet*, but also of *The Times*, the *Morning Post* and
Punch.' On l. 40, Turner (p. 142) notes: 'may derive from "The Poisoners of
the Present Century", *Punch* (9 Dec. 1854)'.
i 41. *centre-bits*: 'An instrument used for making cylindrical holes. (Noted
as a burglar's tool.)', *OED*, which quotes *Oliver Twist*: '"None", said
Sikes, "'Cept a centre-bit and a boy."'
i 43] While the chemist cheats the sick of his last poor sleep and sits
HnMS 1st reading.
i 44. *poison*: the drug wantonly dispensed.
i 45. W. C. DeVane's selection (1947) points out that T.'s use of Mam-
monite derives from Carlyle; G. O. Marshall adds from *Past and Present*,
I i, how in 1841, 'a Mother and a Father are arraigned and found guilty of
poisoning three of their children, to defraud a "burial-society" of some
£3.8s. due on the death of each child: they are arraigned, found guilty;
and the official authorities, it is whispered, hint that perhaps the case is not
solitary, that perhaps you had better not probe farther into that department
of things'. Marshall's suggestion is supported by the variant: *kills*] poisons
HnMS 1st reading.

And Timour-Mammon grins on a pile of children's
    bones,
Is it peace or war? better, war! loud war by land and
    by sea,
War with a thousand battles, and shaking a hundred
    thrones.

XIII

For I trust if an enemy's fleet came yonder round by
    the hill,
And the rushing battle-bolt sang from the three-decker
50   out of the foam,
That the smooth-faced snubnosed rogue would leap
    from his counter and till,
And strike, if he could, were it but with his cheating
    yardwand, home.—

XIV

What! am I raging alone as my father raged in his
    mood?
Must *I* too creep to the hollow and dash myself down
    and die
Rather than hold by the law that I made, nevermore
55   to brood
On a horror of shattered limbs and a wretched
    swindler's lie?

XV

Would there be sorrow for *me?* there was *love* in the
    passionate shriek,
Love for the silent thing that had made false haste to
    the grave—
Wrapt in a cloak, as I saw him, and thought he would
    rise and speak
60   And rave at the lie and the liar, ah God, as he used to
    rave.

i *46. grins*] sits *HnMS 1st reading.*   *Timour*: or Tamerlane the conqueror
credited with atrocities in such works as M. G. Lewis's *Timour* (1811).
i *53–64*] *1856; not 1855.*
i *53. What!*] O God *H.Lpr 149. raging . . . raged*] raving . . . raved *H.Lpr.*
i *54. hollow*] pit *H.Lpr.*
i *60* ∧ *61*]
    So that I hardly believed there was nothing further to dread
    From the furious moods of the man and his ever restless eye,
    But over and over again these words flasht into my head:
    The work of the lie—the work of the lie—the work of the lie. *H.Lpr*

XVI

I am sick of the Hall and the hill, I am sick of the
    moor and the main.
Why should I stay? can a sweeter chance ever come to
    me here?
O, having the nerves of motion as well as the nerves
    of pain,
Were it not wise if I fled from the place and the pit
    and the fear?

XVII

Workmen up at the Hall!—they are coming back from
65   abroad;
The dark old place will be gilt by the touch of a
    millionaire:
I have heard, I know not whence, of the singular
    beauty of Maud;
I played with the girl when a child; she promised then
    to be fair.

XVIII

Maud with her venturous climbings and tumbles and
    childish escapes,
Maud the delight of the village, the ringing joy of the
70   Hall,
Maud with her sweet purse-mouth when my father
    dangled the grapes,
Maud the beloved of my mother, the moon-faced
    darling of all,—

i *61–2*]
    Why should I stay? is it habit, but habit, that makes me remain?
    That, or a dream of a better chance that may come to me here? *H.Lpr*
i *65. Workmen*] *1862*; There are workmen *1855–61*.
i *69. venturous climbings*] crowings and creepings *T.Nbk 36 (which has a draft of
ll. 68–76 only of this section). childish*] pretty *HnMS.*
i *70. the ... village,*] in her aftersummers *HnMS, T.MS.*
i *71. sweet*] red *T.MS.*
i *72. beloved*] delight *HnMS, T.MS. the*] and *T.MS.*

XIX

What is she now? My dreams are bad. She may bring
   me a curse.
No, there is fatter game on the moor; she will let me
   alone.

1 *73–6*] *Not HnMS*. But T. selected these four lines from two expanded versions which are in this MS. Shatto notes that (*a*) precedes II, and (*b*) follows it, that is, after and not before the hero has seen Maud.

(*a*) Comes she not out of a race that my wrongs have made me despise?
   I to be taken with Maud! it would only have turned to a curse.
   Now am I proof, heartproof to her unseen beautiful eyes,
   Proof for a hundred summers to whatsoever is hers.
   Not to be dragged in her shining wake as a rustic prize,
   Not to be trapt in her tresses however redundantly curled,
   Proof to it all, thank God; so in time I may hope to be wise.
   I will bury myself in my books and the Devil may dance through his
         world.

The second version is vituperative; T.'s indignation after losing Rosa Baring could not find a true place in *Maud*, but the lines have a fierce impulse:

(*b*) What is she now that to see her a moment provokes me to spite?
   One of the monkeys who mimic wisdom, whom nothing can shake?
   One whom earthquake and deluge would touch with a feeble delight?
   One who can hate so sweetly with mannerly polish, and make
   Pointed with 'love' and 'my dearest' a sweet innuendo bite?
   One who has travelled, is knowing? a beauty and ruined with praise?
   Well, I was half-afraid but I shall not die for her sake,
   Not be her 'savage' and 'O the monster'! their delicate ways!
   Their finical interlarding of French and the giggle and shrug!
   Taken with Maud – not so – for what could she prove but a curse.
   Being so hard, she has hardly a decent regard for her pug.
   Thanks! there is fatter game on the moor; she will let me alone;
   Thanks, for the Devil best knows whether woman or man be the worse.
   I will bury myself in my books and the Devil may pipe to his own.

   Eyes, what care I for her eyes, those eyes that I did not behold.
   Can they be more whether black or blue, fullrolling or small,
   More than the beldam-tutored Demos commonplace eyes,
   Lying a splendid whoredom to full-fed heirs at the Ball,
   'Buy me, O buy me and have me, for I am here to be sold'.

T.MS has a later version of the first section of (*b*), with minor variants and without the second and third lines.

75 Thanks, for the fiend best knows whether woman or
    man be the worse.
I will bury myself in myself, and the Devil may pipe
    to his own.

II

Long have I sighed for a calm: God grant I may find it
    at last!
It will never be broken by Maud, she has neither
    savour nor salt,
But a cold and clear-cut face, as I found when her
    carriage past,
Perfectly beautiful: let it be granted her: where is the
80   fault?
All that I saw (for her eyes were downcast, not to be
    seen)
Faultily faultless, icily regular, splendidly null,
Dead perfection, no more; nothing more, if it had not
    been
For a chance of travel, a paleness, an hour's defect of
    the rose,
Or an underlip, you may call it a little too ripe, too
85   full,
Or the least little delicate aquiline curve in a sensitive
    nose,
From which I escaped heart-free, with the least little
    touch of spleen.

i 76. *in myself*] *1865*; in my books *1855–64*.
i 78. *Matthew* v 13: 'But if the salt have lost his savour, wherewith shall it
be salted?'
i 79. The ensuing description of Maud recalls the Rosa Baring of the early
poems. Sonnet [*I lingered yet awhile*]: 'And yet a jewel only made to shine, /
And icy-cold although 'tis rosy-clear– / Why did I linger? I myself
condemn, / For ah! 'tis far too costly to be mine, / And Nature never dropt
a human tear / In those chill dews whereof she froze the gem.' Sonnet
[*How thought you*] 13: 'A perfect-featured face, expressionless.'
i 80] Perfectly beautiful–that, no doubt; but there is the fault. *HnMS 1st
reading.*
i 81. *downcast*,] down and could *HnMS 1st reading.*
i 84. *an hour's*] a slight *HnMS 1st reading.*
i 84 ∧ 5] That will blossom again to the surface as bright, with an hour's
repose, *HnMS deleted.*

/

III

Cold and clear-cut face, why come you so cruelly meek,
Breaking a slumber in which all spleenful folly was
    drowned,
Pale with the golden beam of an eyelash dead on the
90   cheek,
Passionless, pale, cold face, star-sweet on a gloom
    profound;
Womanlike, taking revenge too deep for a transient
    wrong

i *88–101*] *T.MS* has three drafts of section III:

  (*a*) Cold and clear-cut face
      Why have you taken a deep revenge for a trifling wrong
      Pale with a close-shut eye   without a sound
      Vexing me and the night and haunting [return *del.*] me o'er
        and o'er
      [l. 95, with 'all the night']
      [l. 96]
      But waking paced by the beds of my own dark garden
        ground
      And heard the swell of the tide as it shrieked in a long sea
        cave
      And walked in a feeble [light *omitted, presumably*] and a wind
        like a wail and found
      [l. 101, as trial edition]

  (*b*) Cold and clear-cut face, star-sweet in a gloom profound
      Take you so deep a revenge, pale face, for a trifling wrong
      Pale with a close-shut eye, coming on me without a sound,
      Scaring me [the darkn *del.*] and the darkness and vexing me
        o'er and o'er
      [ll. 95–6]
      But sprang from the mistress of Terror, and went (my fear
        was so strong) [*line bracketed for del.*]
      But arising paced by the beds of my own dark garden
        ground
      And smelt the storm of a tide that plunged and clashed in the
        cave
      And walked in a feeble light and a wind like a wail and found
      [l. 101, as trial edition]

  (*c*) *ll. 88–97 as published but with the following variants:*
      88] Passionless, clear-cut face, why came you ...
      90. golden ... an] beam of a golden
      91] Pale, how pale yet how sweet, star-sweet ...

Done but in thought to your beauty, and ever as pale
    as before
Growing and fading and growing upon me without a
    sound,
Luminous, gemlike, ghostlike, deathlike, half the night
95   long
Growing and fading and growing, till I could bear it
    no more,
But arose, and all by myself in my own dark garden
    ground,
Listening now to the tide in its broad-flung
    shipwrecking roar,
Now to the scream of a maddened beach dragged
    down by the wave,
Walked in a wintry wind by a ghastly glimmer, and
100   found
The shining daffodil dead, and Orion low in his grave.

IV

I

A million emeralds break from the ruby-budded lime
In the little grove where I sit—ah, wherefore cannot I
    be
Like things of the season gay, like the bountiful season
    bland,
When the far-off sail is blown by the breeze of a
105   softer clime,
Half-lost in the liquid azure bloom of a crescent of sea,
The silent sapphire-spangled marriage ring of the land?

II

Below me, there, is the village, and looks how quiet
    and small!

92. *too*] so   *transient*] trifling
95. *half*] all
97] But arising paced by the plots of my . . .
i *99–101.* Cp. *Oh! ye wild winds* 22–4: 'The shrilly wailings of the grave!
And mingle with the maddened skies, / The rush of wind, and roar of
wave.'
i *101. shining daffodil*] sweet Narcissus *trial edition or proofs (proofs below).* (T. J.
Wise, *Bibliography* i 126–31, derived this and other variants from R. H.
Shepherd.)
i *104. bountiful*] blossoming *T.MS 1st reading.*
i *107. -spangled*] -sparkling *T.MS 1st reading.*

And yet bubbles o'er like a city, with gossip, scandal,
   and spite;
And Jack on his ale-house bench has as many lies as a
110   Czar;
And here on the landward side, by a red rock,
   glimmers the Hall;
And up in the high Hall-garden I see her pass like a
   light;
But sorrow seize me if ever that light be my leading
   star!

III
When have I bowed to her father, the wrinkled head
   of the race?
I met her today with her brother, but not to her
115   brother I bowed:
I bowed to his lady-sister as she rode by on the moor;
But the fire of a foolish pride flashed over her beautiful
   face.
O child, you wrong your beauty, believe it, in being so
   proud;
Your father has wealth well-gotten, and I am nameless
   and poor.

IV
I keep but a man and a maid, ever ready to slander
120   and steal;
I know it, and smile a hard-set smile, like a stoic, or
   like
A wiser epicurean, and let the world have its way:
For nature is one with rapine, a harm no preacher can
   heal;
The Mayfly is torn by the swallow, the sparrow
   speared by the shrike,

i *110. Czar*: Nicholas I and the Crimean war.
i *114*] Her father has plundered the people and so he has wealth and place
T.MS 1st reading (bracketed for del.); Once I met with her father – to him I never
will bow *T.MS 2nd reading*.
i *115. I . . . today*] I met her abroad *T.MS 1st reading*; Today I met *T.MS 2nd
reading.   today*] *1856*; abroad *1855*.
i *117. face*] brow *T.MS 2nd reading (from and reverting to* face).
i *118. so*] Not *T.MS*.
i *119. Your*] The *T.MS 1st reading.   well-gotten*] and title *T.MS 1st reading*.
i *120*] I keep but one little maid readyripe to plunder and steal *H.MS*.
i *124. torn . . . swallow*] rent by the robin *H.MS*. The MS reading suggests

And the whole little wood where I sit is a world of
125   plunder and prey.

V
We are puppets, Man in his pride, and Beauty fair in
        her flower;
Do we move ourselves, or are moved by an unseen
        hand at a game
That pushes us off from the board, and others ever
        succeed?
Ah yet, we cannot be kind to each other here for an
        hour;
We whisper, and hint, and chuckle, and grin at a
130   brother's shame;
However we brave it out, we men are a little breed.

VI
A monstrous eft was of old the Lord and Master of
        Earth,

Keats, *To Reynolds* 93–105 (published 1848): 'I saw / Too far into the sea;
where every maw / The greater on the less feeds evermore:– / But I saw
too distinct into the core / Of an eternal fierce destruction, / And so from
Happiness I far was gone. / Still am I sick of it: and though today / I've
gathered young spring-leaves, and flowers gay / Of Periwinkle and wild
strawberry, / Still do I that most fierce destruction see, / The Shark at
savage prey–the hawk at pounce, / The gentle Robin, like a pard or
ounce, / Ravening a worm.'   *sparrow*] swallow *T.MS 1st reading.*
i *125. a world*] full *T.MS.*
i *127. Do . . . moved*] We do not play but are played *H.Nbk 29.*
i *127–8.* John Churton Collins thought T. owed these lines to FitzGerald's
Rubáiyát, stanza xlix; but T. wrote in the margin: 'I don't read Persian and
F.'s translation was not published when this was written' (*Cornhill,* Jan.
1880, *Lincoln*). FitzGerald published in 1859.
i *128. from*] Added in *T.MS.*
i *129. Ah*] And *T.MS.*
i *132.* 'The great old lizards of geology' (T.)
i *132–7.* W. R. Rutland, *Essays and Studies* xxvi (1940) 23, suggests the
influence of Chambers's *Vestiges of Creation:* 'Are there yet to be species
superior to us in organization, purer in feeling, more powerful in
device and act, and who shall take a rule over us?' J. Killham adds from
Chambers: 'The gestation of a single organism is the work of but a few
days, weeks or months; but the gestation, so to speak, of a whole creation
is a matter probably involving enormous spaces of time' (*Tennyson and
'The Princess',* p. 258).

For him did his high sun flame, and his river billowing
    ran,
And he felt himself in his force to be Nature's crowning
    race.
As nine months go to the shaping an infant ripe for
135   his birth,
So many a million of ages have gone to the making of
    man:
He now is first, but is he the last? is he not too base?

VII

The man of science himself is fonder of glory, and
    vain,
An eye well-practised in nature, a spirit bounded and
    poor;
The passionate heart of the poet is whirled into folly
140   and vice.
I would not marvel at either, but keep a temperate
    brain;
For not to desire or admire, if a man could learn it,
    were more
Than to walk all day like the sultan of old in a garden
    of spice.

VIII

For the drift of the Maker is dark, an Isis hid by the
    veil.
Who knows the ways of the world, how God will bring
145   them about?
Our planet is one, the suns are many, the world is
    wide.

i *133. river billowing*] *Transposed T.MS 1st reading.*

i *137. He*] Who *T.MS.*

i *138. himself . . . glory*] is greedy of glory and selfish *H.MS.*

i *139. spirit bounded*] soul that is narrow *H.MS.*

i *142.* Horace's *Nil admirari* (*Epistles* I vi 1).

i *143.* Cp. *Song of Solomon* iv 16: 'Blow upon my garden, that the spices thereof may flow out. Let my beloved come into his garden, and eat his pleasant fruits.'

i *144.* 'The great Goddess of the Egyptians' (T.).

i *146*] We are not first, our planet is one, and the worlds are wide. *H.MS.*

Shall I weep if a Poland fall? shall I shriek if a
    Hungary fail?
Or an infant civilisation be ruled with rod or with
    knout?
I have not made the world, and He that made it will
    guide.

IX

Be mine a philosopher's life in the quiet woodland
150   ways,
Where if I cannot be gay let a passionless peace be my
    lot,
Far-off from the clamour of liars belied in the hubbub
    of lies;
From the long-necked geese of the world that are ever
    hissing dispraise
Because their natures are little, and, whether he heed it
    or not,
Where each man walks with his head in a cloud of
155   poisonous flies.

X

And most of all would I flee from the cruel madness of
    love,
The honey of poison-flowers and all the measureless ill.
Ah Maud, you milkwhite fawn, you are all unmeet for
    a wife.
Your mother is mute in her grave as her image in
    marble above;
Your father is ever in London, you wander about at
160   your will;
You have but fed on the roses and lain in the lilies of
    life.

V

I

A voice by the cedar tree
.In the meadow under the Hall!

i *147–8*. Referring to the Russian and Austrian occupation of Cracow in
1846, and the defeat of the Hungarians in 1849. Cp. *Hands All Round!* 18*n*
(II 476): 'The Russian whips and Austrian rods.'
i *150–52*]
    O green little wood, O quiet of winding woodland ways,
    If I cannot be merry yet here shall peace be my lot,
    I shall hear no more the liar belied in the hubbub of lies; *H.MS*

She is singing an air that is known to me,
165 A passionate ballad gallant and gay,
A martial song like a trumpet's call!
Singing alone in the morning of life,
In the happy morning of life and of May,
Singing of men that in battle array,
170 Ready in heart and ready in hand,
March with banner and bugle and fife
To the death, for their native land.

II

Maud with her exquisite face,
And wild voice pealing up to the sunny sky,
175 And feet like sunny gems on an English green,
Maud in the light of her youth and her grace,
Singing of Death, and of Honour that cannot die,
Till I well could weep for a time so sordid and mean,
And myself so languid and base.

III

180 Silence, beautiful voice!
Be still, for you only trouble the mind
With a joy in which I cannot rejoice,
A glory I shall not find.
Still! I will hear you no more,
185 For your sweetness hardly leaves me a choice
But to move to the meadow and fall before
Her feet on the meadow grass, and adore,
Not her, who is neither courtly nor kind,
Not her, not her, but a voice.

i *166. martial*] passionate *T.MS earlier draft of V (A), 1st reading*; fiery *T.MS A, T.MS later draft (B), 1st reading.*
i *174. And*] And her *T.MS A, B.*
i *175*] And into the woodland green, *T.MS A, B.*
i *178*] Till I feel the foolish tears running [coming *B*] over my face
To think that I live in a time ... *T.MS A, B 1st reading*
i *180. beautiful*] exquisite *T.MS A 1st reading.*
i *186. move*] run *T.MS A.*
i *188. nor*] or *T.MS A, B.*
i *189. H.Nbk 30* has a passage of a very different tone about singing. This edition (*1969*) erred badly in its placing of the lines (now corrected thanks to S. Shatto), but the attribution – which Shatto does not accept – of the lines to *Maud* (because of movement, plot and tone) still holds, especially as *H.Nbk 30*

VI

I

190   Morning arises stormy and pale,
No sun, but a wannish glare
In fold upon fold of hueless cloud,
And the budded peaks of the wood are bowed
Caught and cuffed by the gale:
195   I had fancied it would be fair.

II

Whom but Maud should I meet
Last night, when the sunset burned
On the blossomed gable-ends
At the head of the village street,
200   Whom but Maud should I meet?
And she touched my hand with a smile so sweet,
She made me divine amends
For a courtesy not returned.

mostly consists of *Maud*. It is not clear where the lines would have been used by T.

> 'My blessing on the falling out
> That all the more endears,
> When we fall out with those we love
> And kiss again with tears'

> That is the song: I have heard it before:
> Boy, I love not songs at the door:
> *She* told you to sing at the house below?
> *She* told you to sing me this!
> Well, there is money: take it: go:
> O God what a riddle she is. *H.MS*

An example of T.'s self-borrowing, since the song is from *The Princess* i ∧ ii (*p. 239*). These four lines were part of the song in *The Princess* in *1850*; T. then dropped them from *1851* to *1861*, but restored them in *1862*. The passage could not have been entertained for *The Princess* or for *Idylls of the King* (the other poems, with *The Charge of the Light Brigade*, in *H.Nbk 30* with *Maud*), since the six lines after the excerpted song are not in blank verse, but in rhymed stanzaic lines; the lines are spoken by a man in love and in doubt as to whether he is loved back, who is given to such a reflection as 'O God what a riddle she is'. 'The house below': cp. 'up at the Hall', and the descent of the brook from the Hall (i 837–9). No other poem than *Maud* suggests itself as able to have been in mind for such a passage, and T.'s hand in the MS is perfectly consonant with that of *Maud* in the same Nbk.

i *191*. Cp. Keats, *Lamia* i 57: 'wannish fire'.

III

And thus a delicate spark
205   Of glowing and growing light
Through the livelong hours of the dark
Kept itself warm in the heart of my dreams,
Ready to burst in a coloured flame;
Till at last when the morning came
210   In a cloud, it faded, and seems
But an ashen-gray delight.

IV

What if with her sunny hair
And smile as sunny as cold,
She meant to weave me a snare
215   of some coquettish deceit,
Cleopatra-like as of old
To entangle me when we met,
To have her lion roll in a silken net
And fawn at a victor's feet.

V

220   Ah, what shall I be at fifty
Should Nature keep me alive,
If I find the world so bitter
When I am but twenty-five?
Yet, if she were not a cheat,
225   If Maud were all that she seemed,
And her smile were all that I dreamed,
Then the world were not so bitter
But a smile could make it sweet.

VI

What if though her eye seemed full
230   Of a kind intent to me,
What if that dandy-despot, he,
That jewelled mass of millinery,
That oiled and curled Assyrian Bull
Smelling of musk and of insolence,

i *206*. Cp. *The Lover's Tale* i 798: 'All through the livelong hours of utter dark'.
i *209*. the] *Added in T.MS.*
i *233*. 'With hair curled like that of the bulls on Assyrian sculpture' (T.). T. had read Layard's *Nineveh* in 1852 (*Mem.* i 356).
i *234*. The zeugma suggests *Paradise Lost* i 501–2: 'the Sons / Of Belial, flown with insolence and wine'.

235   Her brother, from whom I keep aloof,
         Who wants the finer politic sense
         To mask, though but in his own behoof,
         With a glassy smile his brutal scorn –
         What if he had told her yestermorn
240   How prettily for his own sweet sake
         A face of tenderness might be feigned,
         And a moist mirage in desert eyes,
         That so, when the rotten hustings shake
         In another month to his brazen lies,
245   A wretched vote may be gained.

                              VII

         For a raven ever croaks, at my side,
         Keep watch and ward, keep watch and ward,
         Or thou wilt prove their tool.
         Yea, too, myself from myself I guard,
250   For often a man's own angry pride
         Is cap and bells for a fool.

                             VIII

         Perhaps the smile and tender tone
         Came out of her pitying womanhood,
         For am I not, am I not, here alone
255   So many a summer since she died,
         My mother, who was so gentle and good?
         Living alone in an empty house,
         Here half-hid in the gleaming wood,
         Where I hear the dead at midday moan,
260   And the shrieking rush of the wainscot mouse,
         And my own sad name in corners cried,
         When the shiver of dancing leaves is thrown
         About its echoing chambers wide,
         Till a morbid hate and horror have grown
265   Of a world in which I have hardly mixt,
         And a morbid eating lichen fixt
         On a heart half-turned to stone.

                              IX

         O heart of stone, are you flesh, and caught
         By that you swore to withstand?

i 243. Cp. *Hail Briton!* 88: 'To which the slight-built hustings shake'
i 260. Cp. *Mariana* 63–4: 'the mouse / Behind the mouldering wainscot
shrieked'.

270   For what was it else within me wrought
        But, I fear, the new strong wine of love,
        That made my tongue so stammer and trip
        When I saw the treasured splendour, her hand,
        Come sliding out of her sacred glove,
275   And the sunlight broke from her lip?

                        X
        I have played with her when a child;
        She remembers it now we meet.
        Ah well, well, well, I *may* be beguiled
        By some coquettish deceit.
280   Yet, if she were not a cheat,
        If Maud were all that she seemed,
        And her smile had all that I dreamed,
        Then the world were not so bitter
        But a smile could make it sweet.

                    VII
                     I
285   Did I hear it half in a doze
            Long since, I know not where?
        Did I dream it an hour ago,
            When asleep in this arm-chair?

i *277. it*] *Added in T.MS.*
i *280. Yet*] But *T.MS 1st reading.*
i *285–300.* 'He remembers his father and her father talking just before the
birth of Maud' (T.), W. D. Paden (pp. 93, 161) points out that the reference
in ll. 293–6 is to *The Story of Nourredin Ali and Bedreddin Hassan*, in
Galland's translation of the *Arabian Nights*; the brothers agree to pair their
children if of opposite sexes; they quarrel, but the children finally marry.
'The hero vaguely remembers, or believes that he remembers, from his
childhood that his father and Maud's father betrothed them, over the wine,
when Maud was born . . . . The betrothal, as a matter of fact, had taken
place. Maud had been told of the compact by her dying mother, for whose
sake she now desires to be reconciled to the man that her father had
wronged.'
i *285. half . . . doze*] ,long years back *T.MS earlier draft of VII (A), which
transposes ll. 285–8, 289–92.*
i *286*] Half-dozing who knows where *T.MS A.*
i *287. Did I*] Or *T.MS later draft (B).*
i *288. When asleep*] Sleeping *T.MS A.*

II

Men were drinking together,
Drinking and talking of me;
'Well, if it prove a girl, the boy
Will have plenty: so let it be.'

290

III

Is it an echo of something
Read with a boy's delight,
Viziers nodding together
In some Arabian night?

295

IV

Strange, that I hear two men,
Somewhere, talking of me;
'Well, if it prove a girl, my boy
Will have plenty: so let it be.'

300

VIII

She came to the village church,
And sat by a pillar alone;
An angel watching an urn
Wept over her, carved in stone;
And once, but once, she lifted her eyes,
And suddenly, sweetly, strangely blushed
To find they were met by my own;

305

i 289. Men] Who T.MS B.   together] and talking T.MS A.
i 291. the] my T.MS A.
i 293–6] Not T.MS A.
i 293] Is it a part of a tale T.MS B 1st reading.
i 297–8]   Strange that the words come back
           With such a force upon me T.MS A
i 298. Somewhere,] Talking and T.MS B 1st reading.
i 299. my] the T.MS A.
i 301. She came] I went T.MS 1st reading.
i 302] She was there: she was not alone, T.MS 1st reading.
i 303. An] A silent T.MS 1st reading.
i 305] Added in T.MS.
i 306. And] Added in T.MS.   sweetly, strangely] Transposed T.MS.   blushed]
she blushed T.MS 1st reading.
i 307] When her eyes met once with my own T.MS 1st reading.

And suddenly, sweetly, my heart beat stronger
And thicker, until I heard no longer
310   The snowy-banded, dilettante,
Delicate-handed priest intone;
And thought, is it pride, and mused and sighed
'No surely, now it cannot be pride.'

IX

I was walking a mile,
315   More than a mile from the shore,
The sun looked out with a smile
Betwixt the cloud and the moor,
And riding at set of day
Over the dark moor land,
320   Rapidly riding far away,
She waved to me with her hand.
There were two at her side,
Something flashed in the sun,
Down by the hill I saw them ride,
325   In a moment they were gone:
Like a sudden spark
Struck vainly in the night,
Then returns the dark
With no more hope of light.

X

I

330   Sick, am I sick of a jealous dread?
Was not one of the two at her side
This new-made lord, whose splendour plucks
The slavish hat from the villager's head?
Whose old grandfather has lately died,
335   Gone to a blacker pit, for whom

i *308. And] Added in T.MS.*
i *312]* She looked no more but I thought and sighed *T.MS 1st reading.*
i *313. No . . . now]* What is it? no *T.MS 1st reading.* 'It cannot be pride that she did not return his bow', *T.*–alluding to i 116–17.
i *316. The]* And the *T.MS 1st reading.*
i *322. There were two]* Two others were *T.MS 1st reading.*
i *328. Then] 1865;* And back *1855–64.*
i *330. Sick, am I]* I think I am *T.MS.*
i *331. Was]* For was *T.MS.*
i *335. Gone to]* Now in *T.MS.*

Grimy nakedness dragging his trucks
And laying his trams in a poisoned gloom
Wrought, till he crept from a gutted mine
Master of half a servile shire,
340   And left his coal all turned into gold
To a grandson, first of his noble line,
Rich in the grace all women desire,
Strong in the power that all men adore,
And simper and set their voices lower,
345   And soften as if to a girl, and hold
Awe-stricken breaths at a work divine,
Seeing his gewgaw castle shine,
New as his title, built last year,
There amid perky larches and pine,
350   And over the sullen-purple moor
(Look at it) pricking a cockney ear.

II

What, has he found my jewel out?
For one of the two that rode at her side
Bound for the Hall, I am sure was he:
355   Bound for the Hall, and I think for a bride.
Blithe would her brother's acceptance be.
Maud could be gracious too, no doubt
To a lord, a captain, a padded shape,

i *341. a . . . his*] *Transposed T.MS.*
i *342*] Rich in the beauty all maidens admire *T.MS.*
i *344–5.* T. told J. H. Mangles in 1871 that this passage was 'from a conversation of Rogers' (*Tennyson at Aldworth,* ed. E. A. Knies, 1984, p. 70).
i *344*] *Not T.MS.*
i *345–7*] Who address him sweet like a woman and hold
     Their breath but to see his castle shine *T.MS*
i *347–8.* Probably a memory of the rebuilding of Bayons Manor in 1835 by T.'s favoured uncle, Charles Tennyson d'Eyncourt (J. H. Buckley, p. 69).
i *349. amid . . . larches*] on a knoll of perky larch *T.MS, preceded by* There *del.*
i *353–4*] This bantam lord–I am . . . *T.MS earlier draft (A) of X ii, and later draft (B);* This babe-faced lord, I am sure it was he, *proofs, Wise's trial edition* (supported by *Berg MS*–abbreviated hereafter to *B.MS*).
i *355*] *Not T.MS A. I think*] perhaps *T.MS B.*
i *356*] *Not T.MS B.*
i *357. could*] will *T.MS B.*
i *357 ∧ 8*] Maud could be very gracious too *T.MS A.*
i *358–60*]   To the dawdling drawl of the tender ape,
           His bought commission and padded shape,

A bought commission, a waxen face,
360   A rabbit mouth that is ever agape –
         Bought? what is it he cannot buy?
         And therefore splenetic, personal, base,
         A wounded thing with a rancorous cry,
         At war with myself and a wretched race,
365   Sick, sick to the heart of life, am I.

His one half-grain of sense, and his three
    Straw-coloured hairs upon either side
    Of a rabbit mouth ... *proofs*
T.MS B as proofs but with variants 'his padded' and 'a baby mouth';
followed, after a space, by l. 359.
i *358–9*] Not *T.MS A*.
i *359. A*] His *T.MS B*.
i *360*] To the rabbit mouth and the baby face. *T.MS A*.
i *360* ∧ *1*] What ails me that I cannot be cool *T.MS A*.
i *361*] *T.MS A* has its version of this line following l. *365*.
i *362–5*. Cp. Crabbe, *The Old Bachelor*: 'But is not man, the solitary, sick / Of
his existence, sad and splenetic?'
i *362. And therefore*] Harsh *T.MS A*.
i *363–4*] *1856*; not *1855*;
         I am not worthy of her – a fool
         And most unworthy – yet it is true
         That I checked my maid who wantonly smiled
         As at some fair jest when she called him wild –
         Poor worm she meant it half in his praise
         For there is nothing he may not do; *T.MS A*
i *365*]   And sick to the heart of life am I
         To think there is nothing he may not buy. *T.MS A*
i *365* ∧ *6*]   Now are they serf-like, horribly bland,
         To this lord-captain up at the Hall:
         Will she smile if he presses her hand?
         Captain! he to hold a command!
    [*5*]   He can hold a cue, he can pocket a ball;
         And sure not a bantam cockerel lives
         With a weaker crow upon English land,
         Whether he boast of a horse that gains,
         Or cackle his own applause, when he gives
    [*10*]   A filthy story at second-hand,
         Where the point is missed, and the filth remains.
         Bought commission! can such as he
         Be wholesome guards for an English throne,
         When if France but make a lunge, why she,
    [*15*]   God knows, might prick us to the backbone?

III

Last week came one to the county town,
To preach our poor little army down,
And play the game of the despot kings,
Though the state has done it and thrice as well:
370   This broad-brimmed hawker of holy things,
Whose ear is crammed with his cotton, and rings

What use for a single mouth to rage
At the rotten creak of the old machine;
Though it makes friends weep and enemies smile,
That here in the face of a watchful age,
[20] The sons of a gray-beard-ridden isle
Should dance in a round of an old routine,
And a few great families lead the reels,
While pauper manhood lies in the dirt,
And Favour and Wealth with gilded heels
[25] Trample service and tried desert.   *proofs*

T. quotes ll. [2–9], [16–21], in the *Eversley* notes. *Mat.* ii 131 prints ll.
[12–15]. *T.MS B* has a draft of this:

Now is she smiling up at the hall
Now this new soldier presses her hand
Commission! he to hold . . .

Then lines [5–11], [12–15], with variants: [6] For I know not; [11] And the;
[13] An ancient. Then [16–25], with variants: [17] state machine
(State-machine *Eversley*); [18] Which makes friend weep and enemy; [19]
That men; [20] Here in the gray-; [21] of old; [22] While; [23] And.

i 366–73. 'The *Westminster Review* said this was an attack on John Bright. I did
not even know at the time that he was a Quaker' (T.). See *The Third of
February* 43, MS (II 475), and *The Penny-Wise* 33, MS (II 472). T.
probably took over the Quaker, as the type of peace-at-any-price, from
Blackwood's (see headnote).

i 366] *T.MS earlier draft (A) of X iii precedes this line with its version of l. 368*: We
tickle the lust of tyrant kings. *T.MS A then has the sequence, ll. 366, 370, 367,
369, 371–4 (only).*

Last . . . one] Last week there came *T.MS A 1st reading*; One came last week
T.MS A, T.MS later draft (B) of ll. 366–74.

i 367–8] *Transposed in T.MS B.*

i 367. *To preach*] Preaching *T.MS B.*

i 368. *And play*] Playing *T.MS B.*

i 369. *Though*] Not *T.MS A, B.*

i 370. *This broad-brimmed*] A broad brimmed *T.MS A*; This broadbrim
T.MS B.

i 371–2] 374 ∧ 5 *T.MS B.*

i 371. *Whose*] His *T.MS B.*   *crammed*] *1859*; stuffed *1855–6*.

Even in dreams to the chink of his pence,
This huckster put down war! can he tell
Whether war be a cause or a consequence?
375   Put down the passions that make earth Hell!
Down with ambition, avarice, pride,
Jealousy, down! cut off from the mind
The bitter springs of anger and fear;
Down too, down at your own fireside,
380   With the evil tongue and the evil ear,
For each is at war with mankind.

IV
I wish I could hear again
The chivalrous battle-song
That she warbled alone in her joy!
385   I might persuade myself then
She would not do herself this great wrong,
To take a wanton dissolute boy
For a man and leader of men.

V
Ah God, for a man with heart, head, hand,
390   Like some of the simple great ones gone
For ever and ever by,
One still strong man in a blatant land,
Whatever they call him, what care I,

i 372. dreams] a dream T.MS A, B.
i 373] He put down war! can the huckster tell T.MS A.   huckster] hawker
T.MS B 1st reading.
i 376. avarice] envy T.MS.
i 377. Jealousy] Avarice T.MS.
i 378. anger and] hate and of T.MS.
i 382–8] 1856; not 1855;

    And Maud, who when I had languished long,
    Reached me a shining hand of help
    To arouse me, that May morning, when
    She chanted a chivalrous battle-song,
    Maud, can she do herself so much wrong
    As to take this waxen effeminate whelp
    For a man and leader of men. *proofs*
(supported by B.MS and by T.MS with variants: 'Can she' and 'As take').
The second MS line will have seemed too close to *In Memoriam* lxxxiv 43:
'Would reach us out the shining hand'.

395   Aristocrat, democrat, autocrat–one
                 Who can rule and dare not lie.

                              VI
                 And ah for a man to arise in me,
                 That the man I am may cease to be!

                              XI

                              I
                 O let the solid ground
                    Not fail beneath my feet
400   Before my life has found
                    What some have found so sweet;
                 Then let come what come may,
                 What matter if I go mad,
                 I shall have had my day.

                              II
405   Let the sweet heavens endure,
                    Not close and darken above me
                 Before I am quite quite sure
                    That there is one to love me;
                 Then let come what come may
410   To a life that has been so sad,
                 I shall have had my day.

i *394. Aristocrat*, the usual nineteenth-century pronunciation.
i *396–7] 1856; not 1855.*
i *398–411.* T. said of XI: 'The poor madman–He begins to soften', and of the
fifth to seventh lines, 'It's terrible–isn't it?' (*Knowles*).
i *398*] Let not the sound earth fail *British Museum [British Library] first draft (as
below throughout)*; Let not the solid ground *T.MS 1st reading.*
i *399*] And open under my feet *BM MS.*   *Not fail] Fail T.MS 1st reading.*
i *400. has found*] finds out *BM MS.*
i *401. some*] others *BM MS.*
i *402–4.* Cp. *Macbeth* I iii 146–7: 'Come what come may, / Time and the
hour runs through the roughest day.'
i *403*] To a life that has been so sad, *BM MS.*
i *405*] Let not the sweet Heaven fail, *BM MS.* Cp. *Lear* I v 45–6: 'O, let
me not be mad, not mad, sweet heaven! / Keep me in temper; I would
not be mad!'
i *406. Not close*] Close *BM MS.*
i *408*] That Maud *does* love me; *BM MS.*
i *410*] What matter if I go mad, *BM MS.*
i *411. had*] lived *BM MS, T.MS.*

XII

I

Birds in the high Hall-garden
When twilight was falling,
Maud, Maud, Maud, Maud,
415   They were crying and calling.

II

Where was Maud? in our wood;
And I, who else, was with her,
Gathering woodland lilies,
Myriads blow together.

III

420   Birds in our wood sang
Ringing through the valleys,
Maud is here, here, here
In among the lilies.

IV

I kissed her slender hand,
425   She took the kiss sedately;
Maud is not seventeen,
But she is tall and stately.

V

I to cry out on pride
Who have won her favour!
430   O Maud were sure of Heaven
If lowliness could save her.

VI

I know the way she went
Home with her maiden posy,
For her feet have touched the meadows
435   And left the daisies rosy.

VII

Birds in the high Hall-garden
Were crying and calling to her,

i *414*. 'Like the rooks' caw' (T.).
i *422*. 'Like the call of the little birds' (T.).
i *426. not seventeen*] but sixteen *T.MS.*
i *428*. Turner (p. 139) compares Jaques, 'whose phrase the speaker borrows':
'Why, who cries out on pride / That can therein tax any private party?' (*As You Like It* II vii 70–71).
i *435*. 'Because if you tread on the daisy, it turns up a rosy underside' (T.).

> Where is Maud, Maud, Maud?
> One is come to woo her.

VIII

440   Look, a horse at the door,
    And little King Charley snarling,
  Go back, my lord, across the moor,
    You are not her darling.

XIII

I

  Scorned, to be scorned by one that I scorn,
445 Is that a matter to make me fret?
  That a calamity hard to be borne?
  Well, he may live to hate me yet.
  Fool that I am to be vext with his pride!
  I past him, I was crossing his lands;
450 He stood on the path a little aside;
  His face, as I grant, in spite of spite,
  Has a broad-blown comeliness, red and white,
  And six feet two, as I think, he stands;
  But his essences turned the live air sick,
455 And barbarous opulence jewel-thick
  Sunned itself on his breast and his hands.

II

  Who shall call me ungentle, unfair,
  I longed so heartily then and there

i *441. Charley*] *1864*; Charles is *1855–62*. A spaniel. Cp. i 441–3 with 'Charley is my darling'.

i *444*. T. said of XIII: 'a counter passion – passionate & furious' (*Knowles*). i *444–8*] *Added in T.MS.*

i *448. Fool*] Ass *T.MS. vext with*] hurt by *T.MS.*

i *449*] I met him walking over his lands; *T.MS 1st reading.*

i *450–53*]   His face is a servant maid's delight,
    A vulgar comeliness, red and white, *T.MS*

i *454*] But a gust of his essences made me sick *B.MS, T.MS*; For his essences made the morning sick *proofs.*

i *455*] And those fat fingers foolishly thick *B.MS, T.MS.*

i *456*] With jewels, stunted obstinate hands. *B.MS, T.MS*; Flashed on his obstinate-fingered hands. *proofs.*

i *457–9*] *Not T.MS.*

i *458. heartily*] *1856*; earnestly *1855.*

To give him the grasp of fellowship;
460 But while I past he was humming an air,
Stopt, and then with a riding-whip
Leisurely tapping a glossy boot,
And curving a contumelious lip,
Gorgonised me from head to foot
465 With a stony British stare.

III

Why sits he here in his father's chair?
That old man never comes to his place:
Shall I believe him ashamed to be seen?
For only once, in the village street,
470 Last year, I caught a glimpse of his face,
A gray old wolf and a lean.
Scarcely, now, would I call him a cheat;
For then, perhaps, as a child of deceit,
She might by a true descent be untrue;
475 And Maud is as true as Maud is sweet:
Though I fancy her sweetness only due

i 460. But] Not T.MS.
i 461. Stopt] But stopt T.MS 1st reading.
i 462. tapping a glossy] tapt on a polished T.MS.
i 463. curving a contumelious] making a supercilious T.MS 1st reading.
i 464–5. T. (in 1849?) 'made a line on the Oxford "masher's" general reception of a stranger: "With one Oxonian stare from heel to head"' (Mem. ii 485).
i 465. British] execrable T.MS.
i 466] Not T.MS earlier draft (A) of XIII iii.
i 467–8] Is he ashamed to be seen
        That he never comes to his Place. T.MS A
i 468. Shall ... him] What is he T.MS later draft (B).
i 469] Only once in the street T.MS A.
i 470. Last year] Long since proofs. Last ... caught] I caught T.MS A; I caught, long since T.MS B 1st reading.
i 472. Scarcely ... I] I will not T.MS A; I dare not T.MS B 1st reading; For now I dare not T.MS B.
i 473] Not T.MS A, B.
i 474] For then might Maud be untrue T.MS A; Then perhaps might Maud be untrue. T.MS B.
i 475. And] Not T.MS B. as Maud is] as T.MS A, B 1st reading.
i 476–7] But this, I doubt not is due
        To her blood ... T.MS A which has these lines ll. 477 ∧ 8
i 476. Though] But T.MS B. only due] due T.MS B 1st reading.

To the sweeter blood by the other side;
Her mother has been a thing complete,
However she came to be so allied.
480　And fair without, faithful within,
Maud to him is nothing akin:
Some peculiar mystic grace
Made her only the child of her mother,
And heaped the whole inherited sin
485　On the huge scapegoat of the race,
All, all upon the brother.

IV

Peace, angry spirit, and let him be!
Has not his sister smiled on me?

XIV

I

Maud has a garden of roses
490　And lilies fair on a lawn;
There she walks in her state
And tends upon bed and bower,
And thither I climbed at dawn
And stood by her garden-gate;

<hr>

i *477. the sweeter*] the *T.MS B 1st reading.*
i *478–9*] And think her mother too [?] was some
　　　　　Ideal, as mother and bride. *T.MS B 1st reading*
i *478. Her . . . has*] She must have *T.MS A.*
i *479*] *T.MS A breaks off at* came.
i *480*] *T.MS A has this line ll. 482 ∧ 3, as:* Made my Maud without and within
And fair] Fair *T.MS B 1st reading;* She is fair *T.MS B (which had ll. 480–81 in
that order but then marked for transposition).*
i *481*] Not *T.MS A.* Maud] *T.MS B 1st reading;* And Maud *T.MS B.*
i *482*] I think that some peculiar grace *T.MS A (which then has its version of
l. 480).* Cp. *PL* iii 183: 'peculiar grace'; v 15: 'peculiar Graces'.
i *483*] Only the child of a gracious mother *T.MS A.*
i *484. And*] But *T.MS A.*
i *487–8*. T. said: 'He makes allowances for the man – Yet he is called a mere
brute!' (*Knowles*).
i *490. fair*] bright *T.MS earlier draft (A) of XIV.*
i *491–2*] *Transposed in T.MS A.*
i *492*] Bright is the bed and the bower. *T.MS A.*

495 A lion ramps at the top,
     He is claspt by a passion-flower.

                              II
     Maud's own little oak-room
     (Which Maud, like a precious stone
     Set in the heart of the carven gloom,
500 Lights with herself, when alone
     She sits by her music and books
     And her brother lingers late
     With a roystering company) looks
     Upon Maud's own garden-gate:
505 And I thought as I stood, if a hand, as white
     As ocean-foam in the moon, were laid
     On the hasp of the window, and my Delight
     Had a sudden desire, like a glorious ghost, to glide,
     Like a beam of the seventh Heaven, down to my side,
510 There were but a step to be made.

                             III
     The fancy flattered my mind,
     And again seemed overbold;
     Now I thought that she cared for me,
     Now I thought she was kind
515 Only because she was cold.

i 495. PL iv 343: 'Sporting the Lion rampd'. T. said of ll. 495–6: 'A token – I
hardly write anything without some meaning of that kind' (Knowles).
i 496 ∧ 7]   Maud has an old oak-room,
                A room that is all her own   T.MS later draft (B), del.
i 497] Maud's little carven room T.MS A.
i 498. Maud,]   ,set T.MS A.
i 499] In panels of oaken gloom T.MS A.
i 500. Lights] She lights T.MS A.
i 501. by] with T.MS A.
i 503. With a roystering] By his bacchanal T.MS A.
i 505. as I stood,] Not T.MS A.
i 507–8. T. said: 'alludes to the time when she did come out' (Knowles).
i 507. hasp . . . window] window handle T.MS A.
i 508. like . . . ghost] Not BM MS; not T.MS A here, but see l. 509; added in
T.MS B.
i 509. beam . . . down] glorious ghost T.MS A.
i 511–15] Not T.MS A.

IV

I heard no sound where I stood
But the rivulet on from the lawn
Running down to my own dark wood;
Or the voice of the long sea-wave as it swelled
520   Now and then in the dim-gray dawn;
But I looked, and round, all round the house I beheld
The death-white curtain drawn;
Felt a horror over me creep,
Prickle my skin and catch my breath,
525   Knew that the death-white curtain meant but sleep,
Yet I shuddered and thought like a fool of the sleep
of death.

XV

So dark a mind within me dwells,
    And I make myself such evil cheer,
That if *I* be dear to some one else,
530   Then some one else may have much to fear;
But if *I* be dear to some one else,
    Then I should be to myself more dear.
Shall I not take care of all that I think,
Yea even of wretched meat and drink,
535   If I be dear,
If I be dear to some one else.

i 517. *on from*] over *T.MS A.*

i 518. *own dark*] little *T.MS A.*

i 518 ∧ 9] And so by the village out to the sea; *T.MS A.*

i 519. *long sea-wave*] sea itself *T.MS A.*

i 520 ∧ 1] But a morbid fancy belongs to me: *T.MS A.*

i 521. *But I*] I *T.MS A.*

i 523. *Felt*] And I felt *T.MS A.*

i 525. *Knew*] For I knew *T.MS A.*

i 526. *like a fool*] Not *T.MS A;* added in *T.MS B.*

i 530. *may have*] has *T.MS 1st reading.*

i 533–6. T. said: 'He begins with universal hatred of all things & gets more human by the influence of Maud' (*Knowles*).

i 533. *Shall I not*] I will *T.MS 1st reading.*

i 534. *wretched meat*] what I eat *T.MS 1st reading.*

i 537–8. Turner (p. 138) notes: 'adapting a Homeric phrase, "a useless weight on the earth", applied to himself by Achilles . . . The brother . . . turns out at the end to be the more magnanimous (" 'The fault was mine', he whispered, 'fly!'"), and the Homeric allusion already hints at this truth. It is the speaker himself who is the "useless weight", the caricature of Achilles.'

XVI

I

This lump of earth has left his estate
The lighter by the loss of his weight;
And so that he find what he went to seek,
540   And fulsome Pleasure clog him, and drown
His heart in the gross mud-honey of town,
He may stay for a year who has gone for a week:
But this is the day when I must speak,
And I see my Oread coming down,
545   O this is the day!
O beautiful creature, what am I
That I dare to look her way;
Think I may hold dominion sweet,
Lord of the pulse that is lord of her breast,
550   And dream of her beauty with tender dread,
From the delicate Arab arch of her feet
To the grace that, bright and light as the crest
Of a peacock, sits on her shining head,
And she knows it not: O, if she knew it,
555   To know her beauty might half undo it.
I know it the one bright thing to save
My yet young life in the wilds of Time,
Perhaps from madness, perhaps from crime,
Perhaps from a selfish grave.

II

560   What, if she be fastened to this fool lord,
Dare I bid her abide by her word?

i 537] This clod has left his broad estate *T.MS 1st reading.*
i 539] *Added in T.MS.*
i 540. *And*] Let *T.MS 1st reading.*
i 542. *He may*] Till he *T.MS 1st reading.*
i 543. *when*] that *T.MS 1st reading.*
i 544-5] *Transposed in T.MS.*
i 544. T.: 'She lives on the hill near him' (*Knowles*).
i 548. *Think ... hold*] To think of holding *T.MS.*
i 549. *pulse ... of*] pulses that move *T.MS.*
i 550. *And*] To *T.MS.*
i 551. Like the arched neck of an Arab horse.
i 552. *grace ... and*] *T.MS 1st reading;* splendid grace, that *T.MS.*
i 556-9] *Added in T.MS.*
i 559. *a selfish*] the *T.MS.*
i 560-66. T. said: 'You see he is the most conscientious fellow – a perfect

                    Should I love her so well if she
                    Had given her word to a thing so low?
                    Shall I love her as well if she
565   Can break her word were it even for me?
                    I trust that it is not so.

                                        III
                    Catch not my breath, O clamorous heart,
                    Let not my tongue be a thrall to my eye,
                    For I must tell her before we part,
570   I must tell her, or die.

                                    XVII
                            Go not, happy day,
                                From the shining fields,
                            Go not, happy day,
                                Till the maiden yields.
575   Rosy is the West,
                                Rosy is the South,
                            Roses are her cheeks,
                                And a rose her mouth.
                            When the happy Yes
580   Falters from her lips,
                            Pass and blush the news
                                Over glowing ships;
                            Over blowing seas,
                                Over seas at rest,
585   Pass the happy news,
                                Blush it through the West;
                            Till the red man dance
                                By his red cedar-tree,

gentleman though semi-insane! he would not have been so, had he met with
happiness' (*Knowles*).

i *571–98*. This appears with the songs written in 1849 for the 3rd edition
of *The Princess* (1850) in the MS at *University Library, Cambridge*. T.
recited this poem, 'which found a place in *Maud*', to Palgrave in 1853
(*Mem.* ii 504). In the 1865 *Selection*, T. placed this song, not with *Come into
the garden, Maud*, but immediately after *Three Sonnets to a Coquette* (which
are about Rosa Baring). It is relevant that this lyric in *Maud* was much
ridiculed by the critics. Cp. *Early Verses* (II 60) to Rosa.

i *576–8*. Cp. Byron, *Don Juan* VI xxvii 7–8: 'That womankind had but one
rosy mouth, / To kiss them all at once from north to south'.

i *578. mouth.*] *T.MS, 1855*; mouth *1884, Eversley* (presumably an error).

i *582. Over glowing*] *1865 Selection*; O'er the blowing *1855–65*. E. F
Shannon points out that a reviewer had objected to 'blowing'.

And the red man's babe
590   Leap, beyond the sea.
          Blush from West to East,
            Blush from East to West,
          Till the West is East,
595   Blush it through the West.
          Rosy is the West,
            Rosy is the South,
          Roses are her cheeks,
            And a rose her mouth.

XVIII

I

I have led her home, my love, my only friend.
600   There is none like her, none.
       And never yet so warmly ran my blood
       And sweetly, on and on
       Calming itself to the long-wished-for end,
       Full to the banks, close on the promised good.

II

605   None like her, none.
       Just now the dry-tongued laurels' pattering talk
       Seemed her light foot along the garden walk,
       And shook my heart to think she comes once more;
       But even then I heard her close the door,
610   The gates of Heaven are closed, and she is gone.

III

There is none like her, none.
Nor will be when our summers have deceased.
O, art thou sighing for Lebanon
In the long breeze that streams to thy delicious East,

---

i *599–683*. T. said of XVIII i–iii: 'These might not be divided' (*Knowles*).
i *599*. *led*] brought *H.Nbk 30*.
i *601*. *warmly*] sweetly *H.MS, T.MS*.
i *602*] So like a sunwarm river on and on *H.MS*.
i *605–6*. A reminiscence of Hallam's sonnet *The Garden Trees* (1831; Motter, p. 98), which says of the trees: 'Now methinks they talk, / Lowly and sweetly as befits the hour, / One to another down the grassy walk'. The sonnet has 'whisper light', and (of the trees) 'Or are they sighing faintly for desire' – cp. i 613. The first line and a half of the sonnet were written by T., who requested Hallam to finish it (R. Adicks, *TRB* i, 1971, 147).
i *607*. *Seemed*] Like *H.MS*.   *foot*] feet *H.MS*.
i *608*. *And . . . heart*] Made my heart shake *H.MS*.

615   Sighing for Lebanon,
    Dark cedar, though thy limbs have here increased,
    Upon a pastoral slope as fair,
    And looking to the South, and fed
    With honeyed rain and delicate air,
620   And haunted by the starry head
    Of her whose gentle will has changed my fate,
    And made my life a perfumed altar-flame;
    And over whom thy darkness must have spread
    With such delight as theirs of old, thy great
625   Forefathers of the thornless garden, there
    Shadowing the snow-limbed Eve from whom she
     came.

IV

    Here will I lie, while these long branches sway,
    And you fair stars that crown a happy day
    Go in and out as if at merry play,
630   Who am no more so all forlorn,
    As when it seemed far better to be born
    To labour and the mattock-hardened hand,
    Than nursed at ease and brought to understand
    A sad astrology, the boundless plan

i *615. Psalm* civ 16: 'The trees of the Lord are full of sap; the cedars of Lebanon, which he hath planted.'

i *617. Upon*] Here on *T.MS.*

i *619. rain and delicate*] showers and tender *H.MS. The Brook* 202 speaks of 'tender air'. *rain*] shower *T.MS 1st reading*.

i *626.* T. said: 'Snow in contrast with the dark black cedars' (*Knowles*).

i *627. these*] thy *T.MS.*

i *628. you fair*] watch the *H.MS, T.MS.*

i *629.* D. Mermin compares Spenser, *Epithalamion* 368: 'All night therefore attend your merry play'; this section is coloured by the *Epithalamion*, she argues (*Texas Studies in Literature and Language* xv, 1973, 272).

i *632. mattock*: farm tool.

i *634*] The huge uncomfortable plan *T.MS 1st reading*;   A [Some *H.MS*] cheerless fragment of the boundless plan *H.MS, T.MS.* T. comments: 'The *sad astrology* is modern astronomy, for of old astrology was thought to sympathise with and rule man's fate. The stars are "cold fires", for though they emit light of the highest intensity, no perceptible warmth reaches us. His newer astrology describes them [l. 677] as "soft splendours."' Cp. *Time* 52–6: 'All human grandeur fades away / Before their flashing, fiery, hollow eyes; / Beneath the terrible control / Of those vast armèd orbs, which roll / Oblivion on the creatures of a day.'

635   That makes you tyrants in your iron skies,
        Innumerable, pitiless, passionless eyes,
        Cold fires, yet with power to burn and brand
        His nothingness into man.

                            V
        But now shine on, and what care I,
640   Who in this stormy gulf have found a pearl
        The countercharm of space and hollow sky,
        And do accept my madness, and would die
        To save from some slight shame one simple girl.

                            VI
        Would die; for sullen-seeming Death may give
645   More life to Love than is or ever was
        In our low world, where yet 'tis sweet to live.
        Let no one ask me how it came to pass;
        It seems that I am happy, that to me
        A livelier emerald twinkles in the grass,
650   A purer sapphire melts into the sea.

                            VII
        Not die; but live a life of truest breath,
        And teach true life to fight with mortal wrongs.
        O, why should Love, like men in drinking-songs,
        Spice his fair banquet with the dust of death?
655   Make answer, Maud my bliss,
        Maud made my Maud by that long loving kiss,

i 635. That . . . your] Of your tyrannic T.MS 1st reading.   That . . . in] Which is
the despot [tyrant T.MS] of H.MS, T.MS.
i 636-7. PL vii 87-8: Heaven 'with moving Fires adornd / Innumerable'.
i 640. stormy] Not H.MS.
i 641. hollow] Not H.MS.
i 644-6] Not H.MS.
i 644. Would die] Die, yes T.MS 1st reading.
i 645. More] Some sweeter T.MS 1st reading.   than is or] than T.MS 1st
reading.
i 646. low] sweet T.MS 1st reading.
i 647. Let no one] For let none T.MS 1st reading.
i 651-61] Not H.MS.
i 651. 'This is the central idea – the holy power of Love' (T.).
i 652. fight with] conquer T.MS 1st reading.
i 653. O,] For T.MS 1st reading.
i 656. loving] 1882; lover's 1855-81.

Life of my life, wilt thou not answer this?
'The dusky strand of Death inwoven here
With dear Love's tie, makes Love himself more dear.'

VIII

660   Is that enchanted moan only the swell
Of the long waves that roll in yonder bay?
And hark the clock within, the silver knell
Of twelve sweet hours that past in bridal white,
And died to live, long as my pulses play;
665   But now by this my love has closed her sight
And given false death her hand, and stolen away
To dreamful wastes where footless fancies dwell
Among the fragments of the golden day.
May nothing there her maiden grace affright!
670   Dear heart, I feel with thee the drowsy spell.
My bride to be, my evermore delight,
My own heart's heart, my ownest own, farewell;
It is but for a little space I go:
And ye meanwhile far over moor and fell
675   Beat to the noiseless music of the night!
Has our whole earth gone nearer to the glow
Of your soft splendours that you look so bright?
I have climbed nearer out of lonely Hell.

i 657. *Life of my*] Maud my true *T.MS 1st reading.* Cp. *Life of the Life* (I 548).
i 658. 'He suddenly dropped his voice and asked after the line ... "What is
that strand?" "Shore", was replied. "You missed the word 'inwoven'; it is
the woven strand of a rope"' (Blanche Warre-Cornish; *London Mercury* v,
1921, 153).
i 659. *With dear*] With *T.MS 1st reading. Love's*] life-*T.MS 1st reading. makes*]
made *T.MS 1st reading.*
i 660] I scarce can think this music but the swell *T.MS 1st reading*; What
threefold meaning echoes from the swell *T.MS 2nd reading.*
i 662. *And ... within*] The clock within strikes twelve *H.MS.*
i 663. *that ... bridal*] for ever marked with [in *T.MS*] *H.MS, T.MS.*
i 664] And yet I scarce have heart to break the spell *H.MS. And ... live*] So
marked at least *T.MS 1st reading.*
i 669] 666 ∧ 7 *T.MS. grace*] heart *H.MS.*
i 670] Not *H.MS*; I likewise droop and feel the drowsy spell. *T.MS 1st reading.*
i 672. *My ... heart*] Dear heart's mid-heart *T.MS. own ... heart*] life's own
life *H.MS, T.MS 1st reading. my*] 1872, *T.MS*; and 1855–70, *T.MS 1st
reading.*
i 674. *ye*] you *T.MS. moor*] fold *H.MS.*
i 677. *you look*] they stream *H.MS.*
i 678] Added in *T.MS.*

Beat, happy stars, timing with things below,
680   Beat with my heart more blest than heart can tell,
Blest, but for some dark undercurrent woe
That seems to draw – but it shall not be so:
Let all be well, be well.

XIX

I

Her brother is coming back tonight,
685   Breaking up my dream of delight.

II

My dream? do I dream of bliss?
I have walked awake with Truth.
O when did a morning shine
So rich in atonement as this
690   For my dark-dawning youth,
Darkened watching a mother decline
And that dead man at her heart and mine:
For who was left to watch her but I?
Yet so did I let my freshness die.

III

695   I trust that I did not talk
To gentle Maud in our walk
(For often in lonely wanderings
I have cursed him even to lifeless things)
But I trust that I did not talk,
700   Not touch on her father's sin:
I am sure I did but speak
Of my mother's faded cheek
When it slowly grew so thin,
That I felt she was slowly dying
705   Vext with lawyers and harassed with debt:
For how often I caught her with eyes all wet,
Shaking her head at her son and sighing
A world of trouble within!

i 679. *Beat, happy*] Beat on, true *H.MS.*
i 681–2] But for some strange and misconjectured woe,
          Some undercurrent – may it not be so: *H.MS*
i 682. *shall*] may *T.MS 1st reading.*
i 683. Turner (p. 139) notes: 'ominously echoes Claudius's "All may be well"
before praying to be forgiven for "a brother's murder"' (*Hamlet* III iii 72).
i 684–786] *1856; not 1855.*

IV
And Maud too, Maud was moved
710   To speak of the mother she loved
As one scarce less forlorn,
Dying abroad and it seems apart
From him who had ceased to share her heart,
And ever mourning over the feud,
715   The household Fury sprinkled with blood
By which our houses are torn:
How strange was what she said,
When only Maud and the brother
Hung over her dying bed–
720   That Maud's dark father and mine
Had bound us one to the other,
Betrothed us over their wine,
On the day when Maud was born;
Sealed her mine from her first sweet breath.
725   Mine, mine by a right, from birth till death.
Mine, mine–our fathers have sworn.

V
But the true blood spilt had in it a heat
To dissolve the precious seal on a bond,
That, if left uncancelled, had been so sweet;
730   And none of us thought of a something beyond,
A desire that awoke in the heart of the child,
As it were a duty done to the tomb,
To be friends for her sake, to be reconciled;
And I was cursing them and my doom,
735   And letting a dangerous thought run wild
While often abroad in the fragrant gloom
Of foreign churches–I see her there,

i 715–16. Turner (pp. 144–5) notes, with II i 22, the relating of *Maud* to the
Oresteia; this from *Blackwood's* on 'Peace and War' (see headnote, p. 514),
'which quoted in Greek three lines from the *Eumenides* of Aeschylus . . .
spoken by Athena, when trying to persuade the Furies to stop tormenting
Orestes for the murder of his mother'.
i 727. H.Nbk 31 (then deleted) precedes l. 727 with:
            Was he not bound the more,
            After the horrible end
            Of the man that he called his friend,
            By the promise sworn to before?
            Were his feelings then so fine and so sweet
            That the true blood . . .

Bright English lily, breathing a prayer
To be friends, to be reconciled!

VI

740   But then what a flint is he!
Abroad, at Florence, at Rome,
I find whenever she touched on me
This brother had laughed her down,
And at last, when each came home,
745   He had darkened into a frown,
Chid her, and forbid her to speak
To me, her friend of the years before;
And this was what had reddened her cheek
When I bowed to her on the moor.

VII

750   Yet Maud, although not blind
To the faults of his heart and mind,
I see she cannot but love him,
And says he is rough but kind,
And wishes me to approve him,
755   And tells me, when she lay
Sick once, with a fear of worse,
That he left his wine and horses and play,
Sat with her, read to her, night and day,
And tended her like a nurse.

VIII

760   Kind? but the deathbed desire
Spurned by this heir of the liar—
Rough but kind? yet I know
He has plotted against me in this,
That he plots against me still.
765   Kind to Maud? that were not amiss.
Well, rough but kind; why let it be so:
For shall not Maud have her will?

IX

For, Maud, so tender and true,
As long as my life endures
770   I feel I shall owe you a debt,
That I never can hope to pay;
And if ever I should forget
That I owe this debt to you
And for your sweet sake to yours;

775   O then, what then shall I say?—
         If ever I *should* forget,
         May God make me more wretched
         Than ever I have been yet!

X

         So now I have sworn to bury
780   All this dead body of hate,
         I feel so free and so clear
         By the loss of that dead weight,
         That I should grow light-headed, I fear,
         Fantastically merry;
785   But that her brother comes, like a blight
         On my fresh hope, to the Hall tonight.

X X
I

         Strange, that I felt so gay,
         Strange, that *I* tried today
         To beguile her melancholy;
790   The Sultan, as we name him,—
         She did not wish to blame him—
         But he vext her and perplext her
         With his worldly talk and folly:
         Was it gentle to reprove her
795   For stealing out of view
         From a little lazy lover
         Who but claims her as his due?
         Or for chilling his caresses
         By the coldness of her manners,
800   Nay, the plainness of her dresses?
         Now I know her but in two,
         Nor can pronounce upon it

i *787–8*] I am not often gay
         Yet so I seemed today *T.MS*
i *790–91*] Because the lubber dandy *H.MS, T.MS.*
i *792. But he*] Had *H.MS, T.MS 1st reading.*
i *794. Was it gentle*] Ah booby *H.MS, T.MS.*
i *795*] *T.MS has its l. 798*: For chilling the caresses
i *796*] Of a little lord her lover *T.MS 1st reading.*
i *800. Nay,*] And *T.MS 1st reading.*
i *801. Now*] For *T.MS.*
i *802–3*] O Maud I know not whether
         Had I to pronounce upon it
         T.Nbk 18 (which has only i 802–8 of Maud)

If one should ask me whether
The habit, hat, and feather,
805   Or the frock and gipsy bonnet
Be the neater and completer;
For nothing can be sweeter
Than maiden Maud in either.

II

But tomorrow, if we live,
810   Our ponderous squire will give
A grand political dinner
To half the squirelings near;
And Maud will wear her jewels,
And the bird of prey will hover,
815   And the titmouse hope to win her
With his chirrup at her ear.

III

A grand political dinner
To the men of many acres,
A gathering of the Tory,
820   A dinner and then a dance
For the maids and marriage-makers,
And every eye but mine will glance
At Maud in all her glory.

IV

For I am not invited,
825   But, with the Sultan's pardon,
I am all as well delighted,
For I know her own rose-garden,
And mean to linger in it
Till the dancing will be over;
830   And then, oh then, come out to me
For a minute, but for a minute,
Come out to your own true lover,
That your true lover may see

i *806–8*] Is the dearer to my mind
       For I love you well in either *T.Nbk 18*
i *814*] Not *T.Nbk 36.*
i *825. the Sultan's*] her brother's *T.MS.*
i *832–6.* T. said: 'The verse should be read here as if it were prose – Nobody
can read it naturally enough!' (*Knowles*).
i *832*] O come [Come *1st reading*] if you can to your lover *T.MS.*

835
Your glory also, and render
All homage to his own darling,
Queen Maud in all her splendour.

XXI

840

845
Rivulet crossing my ground,
And bringing me down from the Hall
This garden-rose that I found,
Forgetful of Maud and me,
And lost in trouble and moving round
Here at the head of a tinkling fall,
And trying to pass to the sea;
O Rivulet, born at the Hall,
My Maud has sent it by thee
(If I read her sweet will right)
On a blushing mission to me,
Saying in odour and colour, 'Ah, be
Among the roses tonight.'

XXII

I

850
Come into the garden, Maud,
For the black bat, night, has flown,

i *840*] *Not T.MS.*
i *841–2*] *Transposed in T.MS.*
i *841. And lost in*] In doubt and *T.MS.*
i *842. tinkling*] poppling *T.MS.*
i *848. Ah*] O *T.MS.*
i *849. the roses*] my sisters *T.MS alternative in another draft.*
i *850–923.* The stanzaic and rhythmical likeness to Dryden was pointed out as
long ago as 1873 (*Notes and Queries*, 4th series, xi 105); see his Song for *The
Pilgrim*: 'Song of a Scholar and his Mistress, who being Cross'd by their
Friends, fell Mad for one another; and now first meet in Bedlam'. Phyllis
sings: 'Shall I Marry the Man I love? / And shall I conclude my Pains? / Now
blest be the Powers above, / I feel the Blood bound in my Veins . . .' Phyllis
has said 'For, like him, there is none'; cp. i 600, etc. Cp. *The Rosebud* (II 61).
J. H. Mangles recorded, in 1871, T.'s saying that 'Come into the garden,
Maud' 'had, & was intended to have, a taint of madness'; 'Hated the valse to
which "Come into the garden, Maud", was made to dance. Nothing fit for it
but the human voice' (*Tennyson at Aldworth*, ed. E. A. Knies, pp. 69–71). Ian
Kennedy compares *Wilhelm Meister's Apprenticeship*: T.'s lover 'waits at night
as Wilhelm waits . . . outside the house of his beloved and listening to music,
which is finally stilled in the late hours, while his lady-love within deals with
the undesirable attentions of another suitor' (*PQ* lvii, 1978, 92). *T.MS* has
i 850–61, but *HnMS* is then its missing leaves.

Come into the garden, Maud,
   I am here at the gate alone;
And the woodbine spices are wafted abroad,
855   And the musk of the rose is blown.

II

For a breeze of morning moves,
   And the planet of Love is on high,
Beginning to faint in the light that she loves
   On a bed of daffodil sky,
860   To faint in the light of the sun she loves,
   To faint in his light, and to die.

III

All night have the roses heard
   The flute, violin, bassoon;
All night has the casement jessamine stirred
865   To the dancers dancing in tune;
Till a silence fell with the waking bird,
   And a hush with the setting moon.

IV

I said to the lily, 'There is but one
   With whom she has heart to be gay.
870   When will the dancers leave her alone?
   She is weary of dance and play.'
Now half to the setting moon are gone,
   And half to the rising day;
Low on the sand and loud on the stone
875   The last wheel echoes away.

V

I said to the rose, 'The brief night goes
   In babble and revel and wine.

i *855. rose is*] *1872*; roses *1855–70*.
i *859.* Cp. 'One dark heron flew over the sea, backed by a daffodil sky' (Nov.
1853; *Mem.* i 365).
i *861. to*] Not *HnMS*.
i *866. fell* ... *waking*] came ... morning *HnMS 1st reading (as below throughout).*
i *870*] O dancers leave my darling alone, *HnMS.*
i *873. rising*] breaking *HnMS.*
i *874. sand*] grass *HnMS.*
i *876–7*]   'O leave her a little to sweet repose.
             You are merry with feast and wine. *HnMS*

O young lord-lover, what sighs are those,
    For one that will never be thine?
880   But mine, but mine,' so I sware to the rose,
    'For ever and ever, mine.'

VI

And the soul of the rose went into my blood,
    As the music clashed in the hall;
And long by the garden lake I stood,
885   For I heard your rivulet fall
From the lake to the meadow and on to the wood,
    Our wood, that is dearer than all;

VII

From the meadow your walks have left so sweet
    That whenever a March-wind sighs
890   He sets the jewel-print of your feet
    In violets blue as your eyes,
To the woody hollows in which we meet
    And the valleys of Paradise.

VIII

The slender acacia would not shake
895   One long milk-bloom on the tree;
The white lake-blossom fell into the lake
    As the pimpernel dozed on the lea;
But the rose was awake all night for your sake,
    Knowing your promise to me;
900   The lilies and roses were all awake,
    They sighed for the dawn and thee.

i *878–9*. T. said: 'No reproach for the young lover – now that he feels successful' (*Knowles*).
i *878. sighs*] looks *HnMS*.
i *879. one*] a heart *HnMS*.
i *880–81*. J. Kolb compares *In Memoriam* cxxix 8: 'Mine, mine, for ever, ever mine'.
i *880. so I sware*] I said *HnMS*.
i *888. your . . . left*] you pace and have made *HnMS*.
i *889. whenever*] it sets when *HnMS*.
i *890. He sets the*] The dewy *HnMS*.
i *896. white lake-*] water *HnMS*.
i *897. As the pimpernel*] The daisy *HnMS*.
i *898. all . . . your*] for thy sweet *HnMS*.
i *899. Knowing your*] And felt thy *HnMS*.
i *901. sighed for the*] waited for *HnMS*.

IX

Queen rose of the rosebud garden of girls,
  Come hither, the dances are done,
In gloss of satin and glimmer of pearls,
905   Queen lily and rose in one;
Shine out, little head, sunning over with curls,
  To the flowers, and be their sun.

X

There has fallen a splendid tear
  From the passion-flower at the gate.
910 She is coming, my dove, my dear;
  She is coming, my life, my fate;
The red rose cries, 'She is near, she is near;'
  And the white rose weeps, 'She is late;'
The larkspur listens, 'I hear, I hear;'
915   And the lily whispers, 'I wait.'

XI

She is coming, my own, my sweet;
  Were it ever so airy a tread,
My heart would hear her and beat,
  Were it earth in an earthy bed;
920 My dust would hear her and beat,
  Had I lain for a century dead;
Would start and tremble under her feet,
  And blossom in purple and red.

i *902. rosebud*] muskrose *HnMS.*
i *906. out,*] sweet *HnMS.*
i *916–23.* Cp. *To Rosa* i 6–8: 'But all my blood in time to thine shall
beat, / Henceforth I lay my pride within the dust / And my whole heart is
vassal at thy feet.' Cp. *My life is full* 8–10 (I 384); and *The May Queen:
New-Year's Eve* 31–2 (I 457). The romantic prophecy in *Maud* is ironically
answered in ii 239–58.
i *918. her*] it *HnMS.*
i *919. earth*] hushed *HnMS.* Cp. St Paul on the resurrection of the dead,
1 *Corinthians* xv 47, 'The first man is of the earth, earthy: the second man is the
Lord from heaven.'
i *920–21.* J. C. Maxwell compares Propertius, I xix 5–6: *non adeo leviter noster
puer haesit ocellis, / ut meus oblito pulvis amore vacet.*
i *920. her*] it *HnMS. and beat*] and beat, and beat *HnMS.*

PART II

I

I

'The fault was mine, the fault was mine' –
Why am I sitting here so stunned and still,
Plucking the harmless wild-flower on the hill? –
It is this guilty hand! –
5   And there rises ever a passionate cry
From underneath in the darkening land –
What is it, that has been done?
O dawn of Eden bright over earth and sky,
The fires of Hell brake out of thy rising sun,
10   The fires of Hell and of Hate;
For she, sweet soul, had hardly spoken a word,
When her brother ran in his rage to the gate,
He came with the babe-faced lord;
Heaped on her terms of disgrace,
15   And while she wept, and I strove to be cool,
He fiercely gave me the lie,
Till I with as fierce an anger spoke,
And he struck me, madman, over the face,
Struck me before the languid fool,
20   Who was gaping and grinning by:
Struck for himself an evil stroke;
Wrought for his house an irredeemable woe;
For front to front in an hour we stood,
And a million horrible bellowing echoes broke
25   From the red-ribbed hollow behind the wood,
And thundered up into Heaven the Christless code,
That must have life for a blow.

ii *1. was ... was*] is ... is *T.MS earlier draft* (A) *of II i.*
ii *1* ∧ *2*] Why do I stare at the far sea-line? *T.MS A.*
ii *2. am I sitting*] sit I *T.MS A.*
ii *5. there ... ever*] I seem to hear *T.MS A.*
ii *6. From ... in*] That rings about *T.MS A.*
ii *12.* Cp. *Edwin Morris* (p. *197*).
ii *17*] Not *T.MS A.   anger*] answer *T.MS later draft* (B) *1st reading.*
ii *18. he*] Not *T.MS A.*
ii *19. Struck me*] Not *T.MS A.*
ii *21*] Laid on me an unbearable load, *T.MS A.*
ii *22. Wrought*] And wrought *T.MS A.*
ii *23–6*] For he fell at noon, by the Christless code *T.MS A.*
ii *27–9. blow ... eye?*] blow, / Poor angry wretch – in the little wood;
                                                                    T.MS A

Ever and ever afresh they seemed to grow.
Was it he lay there with a fading eye?
30 'The fault was mine,' he whispered, 'fly!'
Then glided out of the joyous wood
The ghastly Wraith of one that I know;
And there rang on a sudden a passionate cry,
A cry for a brother's blood:
35 It will ring in my heart and my ears, till I die, till I die.

II

Is it gone? my pulses beat—
What was it? a lying trick of the brain?
Yet I thought I saw her stand,
A shadow there at my feet,
40 High over the shadowy land.
It is gone; and the heavens fall in a gentle rain,
When they should burst and drown with deluging
storms
The feeble vassals of wine and anger and lust,
The little hearts that know not how to forgive:
45 Arise, my God, and strike, for we hold Thee just,
Strike dead the whole weak race of venomous worms,
That sting each other here in the dust;
We are not worthy to live.

ii *30. was*] is *T.MS A.*
ii *31–2*] Not *T.MS A.*
ii *33. And*] But *T.MS A.*
ii *36–48.* T. said: 'It all has to be read like passionate prose' (*Knowles*).
ii *36–41*] Not *T.MS A* (*presumably once there, since it has ll. 43–8*).
ii *38. her*] it *T.MS B 1st reading.*
ii *41.* J. Skedd, noting ii *44*, compares *The Merchant of Venice* IV i 182–4: 'The quality of mercy is not strained; / It droppeth as the gentle rain from heaven / Upon the place beneath'.
ii *42*] Break forth in earthquake and in storms *T.MS A.*
ii *43*] Kill kill the feeble vassals of anger and lust *T.MS A.*
ii *44. The little hearts*] Not *T.MS A.*
ii *45. Arise . . . strike*] Strike dead, O God *T.MS A*; Rise, strike, my God, strike dead *T.MS B.*
ii *46. Strike dead*] Not *T.MS A, B.*
ii *47. here*] Not *T.MS A.*
ii *48. worthy*] fit *T.MS A.*
ii *49.* 'In Brittany. The shell undestroyed amid the storm perhaps symbolises to him his own first and highest nature preserved amid the storms of passion' (T.). This lyric had been written in the 1830s (see headnote). Turner (p. 134) says that these lines were written 'doubtless in response to Lyell's remark (ii

II

I

50
See what a lovely shell,
Small and pure as a pearl,
Lying close to my foot,
Frail, but a work divine,
Made so fairily well
With delicate spire and whorl,

55
How exquisitely minute,
A miracle of design!

II

What is it? a learned man
Could give it a clumsy name.
Let him name it who can,

60
The beauty would be the same.

III

The tiny cell is forlorn,
Void of the little living will
That made it stir on the shore.
Did he stand at the diamond door

65
Of his house in a rainbow frill?
Did he push, when he was uncurled,
A golden foot or a fairy horn
Through his dim water-world?

IV

Slight, to be crushed with a tap

70
Of my finger-nail on the sand,
Small, but a work divine,
Frail, but of force to withstand,
Year upon year, the shock
Of cataract seas that snap

281): "It sometimes appears extraordinary when we observe the violence of
the breakers on our coast ... that many tender and fragile shells should
inhabit the sea in the immediate vicinity of this turmoil"'.
ii 57. *What is it?*] If I were *T.MS 1st reading.*
ii 58. *Could*] I could *T.MS 1st reading.*
ii 67–8. Cp. Keats, *Endymion* iii 101–3: 'A moon-beam to the deep, deep
water-world, / To find Endymion. On gold sand impearl'd / With lily shells,
and pebbles milky white ...'.
ii 67. *golden*] rosy *T.MS.*

75　　　　The three decker's oaken spine
　　　　　Athwart the ledges of rock,
　　　　　Here on the Breton strand!

　　　　　　　　　　v

　　　　　Breton, not Briton; here
　　　　　Like a shipwrecked man on a coast
80　　　　Of ancient fable and fear–
　　　　　Plagued with a flitting to and fro,
　　　　　A disease, a hard mechanic ghost
　　　　　That never came from on high
　　　　　Nor ever arose from below,
85　　　　But only moves with the moving eye,
　　　　　Flying along the land and the main–
　　　　　Why should it look like Maud?
　　　　　Am I to be overawed
　　　　　By what I cannot but know
90　　　　Is a juggle born of the brain?

　　　　　　　　　　VI

　　　　　Back from the Breton coast,
　　　　　Sick of a nameless fear,
　　　　　Back to the dark sea-line
　　　　　Looking, thinking of all I have lost;
95　　　　An old song vexes my ear;
　　　　　But that of Lamech is mine.

ii *78–80*] Here on the Breton coast
　　　　　　Pacing beside the main *T.MS earlier drafts (A) of II v–vi, ix only*
ii *81–2*] Vext with a hard mechanic ghost *T.MS A.*
ii *82, 90.* Adapted from *Oh! that 'twere possible* 83–4 (1837): 'By a dull mechanic ghost / And a juggle of the brain.' See l. 141*n.*
ii *83–6*] *Not T.MS A.*
ii *87–8*] That looks a little like Maud
　　　　　　But I will not be overawed *T.MS A*
ii *89–90*] By a juggle born of the brain. *T.MS A and later draft (B), B ending with ?*
ii *92*] *Not T.MS A. nameless fear: The Vision of Sin 52, MS.*
ii *93. to*] over *T.MS A 1st reading.*
ii *94. ,thinking of*] and sighing for *T.MS A.*
ii *95*] *Not T.MS A.*
ii *96. But that*] The song *T.MS A.* T. cites *Genesis* iv 23, 'I have slain a man to my wounding, and a young man to my hurt.'

VII

For years, a measureless ill,
For years, for ever, to part –
But she, she would love me still;
100   And as long, O God, as she
Have a grain of love for me,
So long, no doubt, no doubt,
Shall I nurse in my dark heart,
However weary, a spark of will
105   Not to be trampled out.

VIII

Strange, that the mind, when fraught
With a passion so intense
One would think that it well
Might drown all life in the eye, –
110   That it should, by being so overwrought,
Suddenly strike on a sharper sense
For a shell, or a flower, little things
Which else would have been past by!
And now I remember, I,
115   When he lay dying there,
I noticed one of his many rings
(For he had many, poor worm) and thought
It is his mother's hair.

IX

Who knows if he be dead?
120   Whether I need have fled?
Am I guilty of blood?
However this may be,
Comfort her, comfort her, all things good,
While I am over the sea!
125   Let me and my passionate love go by,

ii *104*] One spark of a fiery will *T.MS B.*
ii *106–18*] *Cut away from T.MS B.*
ii *108*. T. said: 'I remember that *shell* did rhyme to *well* – but I forget how it
dropped out of the rhyme' (*Knowles*).
ii *119*] I have not heard he is dead. *T.MS A 1st reading.*
ii *120–22*]   Perhaps I need not have fled.
              I may not be guilty of blood
              But howsoever it be *T.MS A*
ii *124, 127*] *Transposed in T.MS A.*
ii *125*] *T.MS A has this as l. 128.*

But speak to her all things holy and high,
Whatever happen to me!
Me and my harmful love go by;
But come to her waking, find her asleep,
130 Powers of the height, Powers of the deep,
And comfort her though I die.

III

Courage, poor heart of stone!
I will not ask thee why
Thou canst not understand
135 That thou art left for ever alone:
Courage, poor stupid heart of stone. –
Or if I ask thee why,
Care not thou to reply:
She is but dead, and the time is at hand
140 When thou shalt more than die.

IV

i

O that 'twere possible
After long grief and pain

ii *126. But] Not T.MS A.*
ii *128 ∧ 9] T.MS A has ll. 123, 126 deleted (and see l. 125 n).*
ii *129. But] Added in T.MS A.*
ii *130. height,] height and T.MS A.*
ii *131 And] Not T.MS A.*
ii *132–40] 1856; not 1855.* T.'s wife Emily (30 Aug. 1855) told Edward Lear that
this ('the saddest possible little poem') was written prior to 11 Aug. *(Lincoln).*
But the sadness is tempered by *Ezekiel* xi 19: 'And I will give them one heart,
and I will put a new spirit within you; and I will take the stony heart out of
their flesh, and will give them an heart of flesh.' Cp. i 268. T. said of III:
'Here he comes back to England and London. There was another poem about
London & the streets at night – "When all the scum of night & hell boils from
the cellar & the sewer" was part of it' *(Knowles).* T. told J. H. Mangles in
1871 that 'The passage beginning "Courage, poor heart of stone" was put in
after first publication because people would not understand that Maud was
dead' *(Tennyson at Aldworth,* ed. E. A. Knies, p. 70).
i *141–238.* This section, 'O that 'twere possible', was written 1833–4, and
published 1837 (p. 988). All variants from *Heath MS* (two drafts, A, B)
and from *1837* are given below. (Unless differentiated, *1837* subsumes
H.MS, Heath MS A–B in the following notes.) *H.Nbk 13* (which has a draft
of the original *Oh! that 'twere possible* 1–16, 23–35, 42–8, 58–64; see p. 988)
has therein the text of *Heath A* and *Heath A 1st reading. T. Nbk 21* has the text

To find the arms of my true love
Round me once again!

II

145   When I was wont to meet her
In the silent woody places
By the home that gave me birth,
We stood tranced in long embraces
Mixt with kisses sweeter sweeter
150   Than anything on earth.

III

A shadow flits before me,
Not thou, but like to thee:
Ah Christ, that it were possible
For one short hour to see
155   The souls we loved, that they might tell us
What and where they be.

IV

It leads me forth at evening,
It lightly winds and steals
In a cold white robe before me,
160   When all my spirit reels
At the shouts, the leagues of lights,
And the roaring of the wheels.

V

Half the night I waste in sighs,
Half in dreams I sorrow after

of *Heath MS* except at i 153, 205. The links with *In Memoriam* have often been
noticed; see G. O. Marshall, *PMLA* lxxviii (1963) 225–9. The opening
resembles the famous early sixteenth-century lyric: 'Westron winde, when
wilt thou blow, / The smalle raine downe can raine? / Christ if my love were
in my armes, / And I in my bed againe.'

ii *147. By the home*] *1856*; Of the land *1837, 1855.*

ii *151.* Shelley, *Hellas* 716–7: 'What shadow flits / Before?'

ii *153. Ah*] Oh *T.Nbk 21. Christ*] *Heath A–B*; God *1837.* In 'Tennyson and
Musset' (1881), Swinburne compared these lines with Webster's *Duchess of
Malfi* IV ii 20–24: 'O that it were possible we might / But hold some two
days' conference with the dead, / From them I should learn somewhat, I am
sure / I never shall know here: – I'll tell thee a miracle – / I am not mad yet, to
my cause of sorrow.'

ii *157–62*] Not *Heath A.*

ii *158. It*] And *Heath B.*

ii *164*] *Heath A–B*; not *1837.*   *Half*] Or *Heath A 1st reading.*

165   The delight of early skies;
In a wakeful doze I sorrow
For the hand, the lips, the eyes,
For the meeting of the morrow,
The delight of happy laughter,
170   The delight of low replies.

VI

'Tis a morning pure and sweet,
And a dewy splendour falls
On the little flower that clings
To the turrets and the walls;
175   'Tis a morning pure and sweet,
And the light and shadow fleet;
She is walking in the meadow,
And the woodland echo rings;
In a moment we shall meet;
180   She is singing in the meadow
And the rivulet at her feet
Ripples on in light and shadow
To the ballad that she sings.

VII

Do I hear her sing as of old,
185   My bird with the shining head,
My own dove with the tender eye?
But there rings on a sudden a passionate cry,

ii *165*] Her hands, her lips, her eyes, *Heath A*; The hand, the lips, the eyes, *Heath B*; not *1837*.
ii *166–7*] Not *Heath A-B* (*see l. 165n*).
ii *168*] Not *Heath A-B*.   *the morrow*] tomorrow *1837*.
ii *169*] The [Her *Heath A*] winsome laughter. *Heath B*.
ii *170*] Not *Heath A-B*.   *low replies*: *Life of the Life 8*.
ii *171–83*] Not *1837*.
ii *172. a dewy splendour*: Shelley, *Witch of Atlas* 78, which goes on to describe 'A lovely lady garmented in light'. Cp. the song in *The Princess*, 'The splendour falls on castle walls'.
ii *176.* Cp. *Mariana in the South* 40, MS: 'That never felt the shadow fleet'.
ii *184–90*]   Do [And *Heath A-B*] I hear the pleasant ditty,
          That I heard her [She was wont to *Heath A*] chant of old?
                                        1837
I hear] the sound of *Heath A 1st reading*.
ii *187–9*. T. said: 'Perhaps the sound of a cab in the street suggests this cry of recollection' (*Knowles*).

There is some one dying or dead,
And a sullen thunder is rolled;
190   For a tumult shakes the city,
And I wake, my dream is fled;
In the shuddering dawn, behold,
Without knowledge, without pity,
By the curtains of my bed
195   That abiding phantom cold.

VIII

Get thee hence, nor come again,
Mix not memory with doubt,
Pass, thou deathlike type of pain,
Pass and cease to move about!
200   'Tis the blot upon the brain
That *will* show itself without.

IX

Then I rise, the eavedrops fall,
And the yellow vapours choke
The great city sounding wide;
205   The day comes, a dull red ball
Wrapt in drifts of lurid smoke
On the misty river-tide.

X

Through the hubbub of the market
I steal, a wasted frame,

ii *189. sullen thunder*: Shelley, *Revolt of Islam* VI xlv 5.
ii *191. And*] But *1837*.
ii *192. shuddering*] glimmering *Heath A.*   *dawn*] grey *Heath A-B*.
1837 transposes ll. 192, 193; the original order in *Heath MS* was: 191,
192, 194, 193, 195.
ii *195. abiding*] dreadful *Heath A-B*.
ii *196–207*] Not *Heath A*. *1837* (unlike *Heath B*) places ll. 196–201 after
l.238.
ii *197, 199*] Transposed in *1837* (unlike *Heath B*).
ii *197. Mix not*] Mixing *Heath B*.
ii *198.* Cp. *In Memoriam* lxxviii 14 (*1850* reading): 'type of pain'.
ii *200.* Cp. *In Memoriam* xcii 1–3: 'If any vision should reveal / Thy
likeness, I might count it vain / As but the canker of the brain.'
ii *205. The*] And *Heath B; not T.Nbk* 21.
ii *206. Wrapt in drifts*] In a drift *Heath B*.   *lurid smoke*: Shelley, *Prometheus Unbound* II iv 151.
ii *208. the hubbub of the market*: *The Ante-Chamber* 21.

210 It crosses here, it crosses there,
Through all that crowd confused and loud,
The shadow still the same;
And on my heavy eyelids
My anguish hangs like shame.

XI

215 Alas for her that met me,
That heard me softly call,
Came glimmering through the laurels
At the quiet evenfall,
In the garden by the turrets
220 Of the old manorial hall.

XII

Would the happy spirit descend,
From the realms of light and song,
In the chamber or the street,
As she looks among the blest,
225 Should I fear to greet my friend
Or to say 'Forgive the wrong,'
Or to ask her, 'Take me, sweet,
To the regions of thy rest'?

XIII

But the broad light glares and beats,
230 And the shadow flits and fleets
And will not let me be;
And I loathe the squares and streets,
And the faces that one meets,
Hearts with no love for me:

ii *210. crosses . . . crosses*] crosseth . . . crosseth *1837*.
ii *215–20*] Not *Heath A*.
ii *221–8*] Not *Heath A-B*; *1837* after l. 220 runs: 229–38, 196–201, 221–8
(but omitting 222 and 226); it then adds a further thirty-four lines (see
p. *991*).
ii *228. regions*] region *1837*.
ii *229–31*] Not *Heath A*.
ii *229. But the*] The *Heath B*; Then the *1837*.
ii *230. shadow*] sunk eye *1837*.
ii *232–4*. Cp. Hallam to J. Frere: 'There is a rapture truly in walking about the
streets without knowing a face one meets!' (23 Dec. 1828; *AHH*, p. 260).
ii *232. And*] Not *1837*.

235   Always I long to creep
     Into some still cavern deep,
     There to weep, and weep, and weep
     My whole soul out to thee.

· V

I

    Dead, long dead,
240   Long dead!
    And my heart is a handful of dust,
    And the wheels go over my head,
    And my bones are shaken with pain,
    For into a shallow grave they are thrust,
245   Only a yard beneath the street,
    And the hoofs of the horses beat, beat,

ii *235–8*. T. said: 'I've often felt this in London' (*Knowles*).

ii *236*. *Into*] To *1837*.

ii *237*. *There to*] And *Heath A–B*; And to *1837*.

ii *238*. Cp. *Song* [*A spirit haunts*] 16: 'My very heart faints and my whole soul grieves'.

ii *239 ff.* T. said of II v: 'This was written in 20 minutes' (*Knowles*; likewise to J. H. Mangles in 1871: 'He called out to his wife, "Now I am going to begin the mad scene", & in 20 minutes it was done', *Tennyson at Aldworth*, ed. E. A. Knies, p. 69). 'About the mad-scene one of the best-known doctors for the insane wrote that it was "the most faithful representation of madness since Shakespeare' (*Mem.* i 398). Campbell's *The Death-Boat of Heligoland* (written 1828) begins: 'Can restlessness reach the cold sepulchred head?– / Ay, the quick have their sleep-walkers, so have the dead. / There are brains, though they moulder, that dream in the tomb, / And that maddening forehear the last trumpet of doom.' The eleventh line of Campbell's poem says: 'The foam of the Baltic had sparkled like fire'; cp. iii 51. J. C. Maxwell compares *The Old Curiosity Shop*, chapter I: 'That constant pacing to and fro, that never-ending restlessness, that incessant tread of feet wearing the rough stones smooth and glossy – is it not a wonder how the dwellers in narrow ways can bear to hear it! Think of a sick man . . . think of the hum and noise being always present to his senses, and of the stream of life that will not stop, pouring on, on, on, through all his restless dreams, as if he were condemned to lie, dead but conscious, in a noisy churchyard, and had no hope of rest for centuries to come!'

ii *241*. *heart*] brain *T.MS 1st reading*. Cp. *The Lotos-Eaters* 113: 'Two handfuls of white dust, shut in an urn of brass'.

ii *243*. *are . . . with*] though dead are full of *T.MS 1st reading*.

The hoofs of the horses beat,
Beat into my scalp and my brain,
With never an end to the stream of passing feet,
250   Driving, hurrying, marrying, burying,
Clamour and rumble, and ringing and clatter,
And here beneath it is all as bad,
For I thought the dead had peace, but it is not so;
To have no peace in the grave, is that not sad?
255   But up and down and to and fro,
Ever about me the dead men go;
And then to hear a dead man chatter
Is enough to drive one mad.

II

Wretchedest age, since Time began,
260   They cannot even bury a man;
And though we paid our tithes in the days that are gone,
Not a bell was rung, not a prayer was read;
It is that which makes us loud in the world of the dead;
There is none that does his work, not one;
265   A touch of their office might have sufficed,
But the churchmen fain would kill their church,
As the churches have killed their Christ.

III

See, there is one of us sobbing,
No limit to his distress;
270   And another, a lord of all things, praying
To his own great self, as I guess;

ii 248 ∧ 9] All the roar of the street *T.MS del.*
ii 249–50] *Transposed in T.MS but then marked for reversal.*
ii 249. *With never an*] There is no *T.MS 1st reading.*
ii 251. *rumble . . . ringing*] gabble . . . cackle *T.MS 1st reading.*
ii 252. *beneath*] in the grave *T.MS 1st reading.*
ii 256] The dead men trample as they go *T.MS 1st reading.*
ii 257. Cp. *The Coach of Death* 95: 'The chattering of the fleshless jaws'.
ii 261. *And though*] Not *T.MS.*
ii 262. *Not . . . rung,*] But over us *T.MS.*
ii 263. *It . . . us*] That makes us so *T.MS.*
ii 265. *their*] his *T.MS.*
ii 268. *See,*] *T.MS 1st reading*; Lo! *T.MS.*
ii 270. *a . . . praying*] musical puppet [fool *1st reading*] is playing *T.MS.* T.: 'I put "a God Almighty" first, which is a usual form of madness' (*Knowles*).
ii 271] Not *T.MS.*

And another, a statesman there, betraying
His party-secret, fool, to the press;
And yonder a vile physician, blabbing
275   The case of his patient–all for what?
To tickle the maggot born in an empty head,
And wheedle a world that loves him not,
For it is but a world of the dead.

IV

Nothing but idiot gabble!
280   For the prophecy given of old
And then not understood,
Has come to pass as foretold;
Not let any man think for the public good,
But babble, merely for babble.
285   For I never whispered a private affair
Within the hearing of cat or mouse,
No, not to myself in the closet alone,
But I heard it shouted at once from the top of the house;
Everything came to be known.
290   Who told *him* we were there?

ii 272. *another, a*] a silly *T.MS 1st reading*.
ii 273. *, fool,*] *Added in T.MS*.
ii 274–5. T. said: 'the doctor of the madhouse' (*Knowles*). Possibly recalling
Dr Allen; in Allen's *Essay on the Classification of the Insane* (*Lincoln*, 1837),
Case No. 22 is one 'whose mind was instantly wrecked by the female of his
heart unexpectedly marrying another the very day previous to that on which
she had promised to be made his own for ever'.
ii 275. *The . . . –*] His patient's ailment [case *1st reading*]–and *T.MS*.
ii 276–8] To tickle [please *1st reading*] a world of the dead that loves [heeds *1st
reading*] him not. *T.MS*.
ii 281] Discredited by the rabble *T.MS 1st reading*; Is now fulfilled by the
rabble *T.MS 2nd reading*.
ii 282. *Has*] It has *T.MS 2nd reading*.
ii 283–4] But not virtue's sake, merely for babble *T.MS 1st reading*.
ii 285. *For . . . whispered*] Wilt [Darest *1st reading*] thou whisper *T.MS*.
ii 286] But tell not thou thy secret to the mouse *T.MS*.
ii 287–8. Luke xii 3: 'Therefore whatsoever ye have spoken in darkness shall
be heard in the light; and that which ye have spoken in the ear in closets shall
be proclaimed upon the house-tops.'
ii 287. *myself*] thyself *T.MS*.
ii 288. *But . . . it*] It is *T.MS*.
ii 289] And everything is known. *T.MS del., with nothing then supplied*.
ii 290. *Who*] For who *T.MS*.

V

Not that gray old wolf, for he came not back
From the wilderness, full of wolves, where he used to lie;
He has gathered the bones for his o'ergrown whelp to
    crack;
Crack them now for yourself, and howl, and die.

VI

295 Prophet, curse me the blabbing lip,
And curse me the British vermin, the rat;
I know not whether he came in the Hanover ship,
But I know that he lies and listens mute
In an ancient mansion's crannies and holes:
300 Arsenic, arsenic, sure, would do it,
Except that now we poison our babes, poor souls!
It is all used up for that.

VII

Tell him now: she is standing here at my head;
Not beautiful now, not even kind;
305 He may take her now; for she never speaks her mind,
But is ever the one thing silent here.
She is not *of* us, as I divine;

ii *291–302*] *Not T.MS.*
ii *291*. See i 471.
ii *294*. 'For his son is, he thinks, dead' (T.).
ii *296–7*. 'The Norwegian rat has driven out the old English rat' (T.). H.T.
adds: 'The Jacobites asserted that the brown Norwegian rat came to England
with the House of Hanover, 1714, and hence called it "the Hanover rat".'
ii *300. sure*] *1856*; *sir 1855*. Cp. Lear IV vi 89–90: 'Peace, peace; this piece of
toasted cheese will do it'.
ii *301. babes*] wives *proofs.*
ii *303*] She is here at my bed. *Simeon MS (draft of ll. 303–320, 334)*; Why is she
always standing at my head *T.MS, which then adds*: They may tell him now.
The *Simeon MS* was printed, with a facsimile, by W. E. Fredeman,
Christmas 1982.   *him*: 'her old Father'; tell 'how we met in the garden' (T.,
Knowles).
ii *304*] She is ghostly [ghastly?] now she is not kind *Simeon MS*; She is not
beautiful now she is not kind *T.MS 1st reading.*
ii *305*] What ails her she never tells her mind *Simeon MS, and T.MS which has
that she. T.MS then adds*: Let him take her now
ii *306*] She alone is silent here. *Simeon MS.   ever*] *Not T.MS.*
ii *307*] *Not Simeon MS.   as*] *Added in T.MS.*

She comes from another stiller world of the dead,
Stiller, not fairer than mine.

VIII

310 But I know where a garden grows,
Fairer than aught in the world beside,
All made up of the lily and rose
That blow by night, when the season is good,
To the sound of dancing music and flutes:
315 It is only flowers, they had no fruits,
And I almost fear they are not roses, but blood;
For the keeper was one, so full of pride,
He linkt a dead man there to a spectral bride;
For he, if he had not been a Sultan of brutes,
320 Would he have that hole in his side?

IX

But what will the old man say?
He laid a cruel snare in a pit

ii *308. stiller*] *Not Simeon MS; added in T.MS.*

ii *309*] That is stiller than mine *Simeon MS which has above* not sweeter. *Stiller, not fairer*] That is stiller, not sweeter *T.MS*; But it seems no fairer *T.MS alternative.*

ii *310*] I know [   ] Garden where the rose tree shoots *Simeon MS.*

ii *311–12*] More sweeter than in all the world wide *Simeon MS*; Sweeter than all in the whole world wide *T.MS.*

ii *313–14*] *Transposed in T.MS.*

ii *313. blow by night,*] is *Simeon MS, T.MS.*

ii *314*] *Not Simeon MS.* To] Blows to *T.MS.* music] *Not T.MS.*

ii *315*] A garden of flowers, for it had [flowers: it has *Simeon MS*] no fruits *Simeon MS, T.MS.*

ii *316. I almost fear*] *Not Simeon MS 1st reading.* almost] *Not T.MS.*

ii *317*] *Not Simeon MS, T.MS.*

ii *318*] For there a dead man wooed a dying bride *Simeon MS.* He linkt] For there did *T.MS.* dead man: 'himself in his fancy' (T.). there to] woo for *T.MS.*

ii *319*] If he had not been the prince of brutes *Simeon MS.* For] And *T.MS.* a Sultan] the prince *T.MS, proofs.* (A later *T.MS* draft of ll. 310–20 is as published except for this last variant.)

ii *320.* Turner (pp. 146–7) discusses Dr Allen's influence on the madhouse lines, and says here: 'suggested by the patient who "thought he was Jesus Christ", but was cured of the delusion when told that the "hole in the side" that he was always pointing at was on the wrong side'.

ii *322. laid*] that *T.MS, presumably for* that laid. cruel] *Not T.MS.*

To catch a friend of mine one stormy day;
Yet now I could even weep to think of it;
325   For what will the old man say
When he comes to the second corpse in the pit?

X

Friend, to be struck by the public foe,
Then to strike him and lay him low,
That were a public merit, far,
330   Whatever the Quaker holds, from sin;
But the red life spilt for a private blow –
I swear to you, lawful and lawless war
Are scarcely even akin.

XI

O me, why have they not buried me deep enough?
335   Is it kind to have made me a grave so rough,
Me, that was never a quiet sleeper?
Maybe still I am but half-dead;
Then I cannot be wholly dumb;
I will cry to the steps above my head
340   And somebody, surely, some kind heart will come
To bury me, bury me
Deeper, ever so little deeper.

ii *323. a friend of mine*: 'his own father' (T., *Knowles*).
ii *324. weep*] cry *T.MS.*
ii *326. comes to*] finds *T.MS.*   *second corpse*: 'of his own son' (T., *Knowles*).
ii *327*] To kill the public foe, *T.MS 1st reading. Friend*] Sir *T.MS.*
ii *328. Then*] *Added in T.MS.*
ii *329*] Is a public merit I hold and far *T.MS 1st reading.*
ii *330. holds*] says *T.MS 1st reading.*
ii *331. the ... spilt*] murder done *T.MS 1st reading.*
ii *332–3*. T. said: 'He feels that he is getting a little too sensible in this remark' (*Knowles*).
ii *332. swear to*] tell *T.MS 1st reading.*
ii *334–42*. See i 916–23n.
ii *334. why have they*] they have *T.MS 1st reading, with no final* ?
ii *335. Is*] Was *T.MS. Is ... to*] Or they *T.MS 1st reading. me*] *Added in T.MS.*
ii *336*] For one that never was a quiet sleeper *T.MS 1st reading, with no final* ?
ii *337. Maybe still*] Or maybe yet *T.MS 1st reading.*
ii *338. Then*] And then *T.MS.*
ii *339. steps*] feet *T.MS 1st reading.*
ii *340. surely*] *Added in T.MS. will*] may *T.MS 1st reading.*
ii *341*] *Added in T.MS.*
ii *342. Deeper,*] And bury me *T.MS 1st reading;* Bury me *T.MS.*

PART III

VI

I

My life has crept so long on a broken wing
Through cells of madness, haunts of horror and fear,
That I come to be grateful at last for a little thing:
My mood is changed, for it fell at a time of year
5   When the face of night is fair on the dewy downs,
And the shining daffodil dies, and the Charioteer
And starry Gemini hang like glorious crowns
Over Orion's grave low down in the west,
That like a silent lightning under the stars
10   She seemed to divide in a dream from a band of the
        blest,
And spoke of a hope for the world in the coming wars –
'And in that hope, dear soul, let trouble have rest,
Knowing I tarry for thee,' and pointed to Mars
As he glowed like a ruddy shield on the Lion's breast.

II

15   And it was but a dream, yet it yielded a dear delight
To have looked, though but in a dream, upon eyes so
      fair,
That had been in a weary world my one thing bright;
And it was but a dream, yet it lightened my despair
When I thought that a war would arise in defence of
      the right,
20   That an iron tyranny now should bend or cease,
The glory of manhood stand on his ancient height,
Nor Britain's one sole God be the millionaire:
No more shall commerce be all in all, and Peace

iii 'Sane, but shattered. Written when the cannon was heard booming
from the battleships in the Solent before the Crimean War' (T.). When T.
made the division for Part III in *1865*, he did not start again with the
numbering of sections, as he had with Part II; this may have been an
omission, but it has the effect of linking Parts II and III more closely than
I and II.

iii *2. cells of madness*: The Two Voices 371.

iii **6.** *shining daffodil*] sweet Narcissus *trial edition.*

iii *13–14.* T. wrote, 17 March 1854 (*Trinity College*): 'A boy was born last
night – a stout little fellow. Mars was culminating in the Lion – does that
mean soldiership?' The Lion represents Britain.

iii *19 ff.* For war in a just cause as contrasted with despairing self-absorp-
tion, cp. *The Two Voices* 124–56 (*pp. 108–9*).

iii *23–8.* B. Richards notes: 'For a representation in Victorian painting of the

Pipe on her pastoral hillock a languid note,
25 And watch her harvest ripen, her herd increase,
Nor the cannon-bullet rust on a slothful shore,
And the cobweb woven across the cannon's throat
Shall shake its threaded tears in the wind no more.

III

And as months ran on and rumour of battle grew,
30 'It is time, it is time, O passionate heart,' said I
(For I cleaved to a cause that I felt to be pure and
          true),
'It is time, O passionate heart and morbid eye,
That old hysterical mock-disease should die.'
And I stood on a giant deck and mixed my breath
35 With a loyal people shouting a battle cry,
Till I saw the dreary phantom arise and fly
Far into the North, and battle, and seas of death.

IV

Let it go or stay, so I wake to the higher aims
Of a land that has lost for a little her lust of gold,
40 And love of a peace that was full of wrongs and shames,
Horrible, hateful, monstrous, not to be told;
And hail once more to the banner of battle unrolled!
Though many a light shall darken, and many shall weep
For those that are crushed in the clash of jarring claims,
45 Yet God's just wrath shall be wreaked on a giant liar;
And many a darkness into the light shall leap,
And shine in the sudden making of splendid names,
And noble thought be freer under the sun,

image of peace, similarly portrayed, see Edwin Landseer's *Time of Peace*
(1846), reproduced in Allen Staley, *The Pre-Raphaelite Landscape* (1973) plate
29b' (*English Verse 1830–1890*, 1980, p. 172). Turner (p. 138) notes:
'Theocritus, *Idyll* xvi, which complains of the age's commercial greed,
celebrates the approach of war against the Phoenicians (traditionally as
dishonest as the Russian Czar), and contains a prototype for T.'s image of
cobwebs "woven across the cannon's throat" (as well as for his earlier phrase
"the mattock-hardened hand", I xviii 632).'
iii *36. phantom*: 'of Maud' (T., *Knowles*). As G. O. Marshall points out,
Maud's ghost takes a dual form; the 'ghastly Wraith' of ii 32, 82, 90, and the
blessed spirit of iii 10.
iii *43–5*] For many shall triumph and some shall fall asleep
              In wreaking Heaven's just doom on a crafty liar
                                        ULC MS (draft of iii 43–53)
iii *45. wrath*] *1856*; doom *1855*. *liar*: 'The Czar' (T., *Knowles*).
iii *46–7. And ... the*] *Not ULC MS.*
iii *48*] *Not ULC MS.*

And the heart of a people beat with one desire;
For the peace, that I deemed no peace, is over and
50   done,
And now by the side of the Black and the Baltic deep,
And deathful-grinning mouths of the fortress, flames
The blood-red blossom of war with a heart of fire.

v

Let it flame or fade, and the war roll down like a wind,
We have proved we have hearts in a cause, we are
55   noble still,
And myself have awaked, as it seems, to the better
    mind;
It is better to fight for the good than to rail at the ill;
I have felt with my native land, I am one with my
    kind,
I embrace the purpose of God, and the doom assigned.

[1857. *The Marriage of Geraint, Geraint and Enid,* and *Merlin and Vivien*—see *pp. 735, 761, 805.*
1859. *Lancelot and Elaine* and *Guinevere*—see *pp. 834, 941*]

iii *50. peace ... no*] *1856;* long, long canker of *1855.* The original reading had been deplored by *Tait's Edinburgh Magazine,* Sept. 1855: 'If any man comes forward to say or sing that the slaughter of 30,000 Englishmen in the Crimea tends to prevent women poisoning their babies, for the sake of the burial fees, in Birmingham, he is bound to show cause, and not bewilder our notions of morals and of lexicography by calling thirty years of intermitted war (absolute peace we have *not* had during the interval) a "long, long *canker* of peace".' Turner (p. 141) notes: 'A leader in *The Times* asked (14 Feb. 1855): "What if ... 'the cankers of a long peace' should be found almost as destructive as the more confessed plagues of war?'"'; the phrase being quoted from Falstaff: 'the cankers of a calm world and a long peace' (*2 Henry IV* IV ii 29).

iii *51. side*] shore *ULC MS. and the*] and *ULC MS.*

iii *52. And*] And the *ULC MS.*

iii *54–9*] *1856; not 1855.* A British Library copy of *1855* (first American edition) has cancelled drafts of this last stanza, which show T. attempting to relate the war to the love for Maud:

    Let it go or stay, so I walk henceforth resigned
    By the light of a love not lost, with a purer mind
    And rejoice in my native land, and am one with my kind.

Also: 'And I rise from a life half-lost with a better mind ...'. Of l. 57, T. said: 'Take this with the first where he railed at everything—He is not quite sane—a little shattered' (*Knowles*).

324 Tithonus

Published *Cornhill Magazine*, Feb. 1860; then *1864*.
In 1859 Thackeray importuned T. for a poem to be published in his *Cornhill* (first number, Jan. 1860; *Letters*, ed. G. N. Ray, iv (1946) 168). T. says: 'My friend Thackeray and his publishers had been so urgent with me to send them something, that I ferreted among my old books and found this *Tithonus*, written upwards of a quarter of a century ago. . . . It was originally a pendent to the *Ulysses* in my former volumes, and I wanted Smith to insert a letter, not of mine, to the editor stating this, and how long ago it had been written, but he thought it would lower the value of the contribution in the public eye' (*Mem.* i 459; see *Letters* ii 605, 26 Dec. 1859). At the end of a proof of *1860*, T. added the date '1833' and then deleted it (*Lincoln*). The poem was originally written in a shorter form, *Tithon*, in 1833 (p. 992); all the revisions from the *Heath MS* are below, given as *Tithon*. There is a discussion of them by M. J. Donahue, *PMLA* lxiv (1949) 400–16, where *Tithon* was first printed, and by L. K. Hughes, *PQ* lviii (1979) 82–9. There are two earlier drafts in *T. Nbk 20* (1833; *T.MS A* and *B*). *T. Nbk 21* is as *Heath MS* except for the variants given at l. 4. T. revised it in Nov. – Dec. 1859 (*Mem.* i 443, *Mat.* ii 240), which suggests that T.'s mind may have been turned to the poem by a letter, 10 April 1859, from Jowett who had just visited the grave of Arthur Hallam: 'It is a strange feeling about those who are taken young that while we are getting old and dusty they are as they were' (*Lincoln*). T. wrote to Sarah Prinsep, late March or early April 1859, in terms which are like a comic counterpart to the poem's sorrow: 'And O princess, with respect to the Heavens and the Earth, have regard to me, a silverheaded many wrinkled man, if you that are everblooming, always believed to be your own daughter, and know no touch of time, can sympathize with decadence and infirmity' (*Letters* ii 220). For the delay in publication, cp. *On a Mourner* (p. *135*), which is also on the death of Hallam, written 1833 but not published till *1865*.

Written after the shock of Hallam's death, the poem is a companion to *Ulysses* (p. *138*) and *Tiresias* (I 622), begun at the same time. T. turned to a classical story for an insight into mortality, and here explores the possibility that immortality would not simply in itself be a blessing. Cp. *Ulysses* (the need for the courage of life), and *Tiresias* (the courage of self-sacrifice). The theme may have been influenced by the grief of T.'s sister Emily (Hallam's betrothed); she wrote to T., 12 July 1834: 'What is life to me! if I die (which the Tennysons never do)' (*Mem.* i 135, cited by Miss Donahue). As Miss Donahue says, 'It is not that anything so obvious and simple as the identification of Eos [Aurora] with Hallam is possible or that the emotional relationship between Tennyson and Hallam is wholly clarified by *Tithonus*. But it is clear that, in choosing the mask of Tithonus, Tennyson reached out to two of the most basic symbols, those of love between man and woman and the frustration of love by age, to express the

peculiar and individual nature of his own emotional injury.' Moreover
Tithonus is as much a fear as to the *nature* of Hallam's immortality (a fear
which recurs in *In Memoriam*) as a mask for T. Robert Monteith wrote to T.,
?14 Dec. 1833: 'Since Hallam's death I almost feel like an old man looking
back on many friendships as something bygone' (*Letters* i 103).
   Tithonus, as T. remarks, was 'beloved by Aurora [goddess of the dawn],
who gave him eternal life but not eternal youth. He grew old and infirm,
and as he could not die, according to the legend, was turned into a grass-
hopper.' Cp. *The Grasshopper* 5, 28 (*1830*): 'No Tithon thou as poets
feign . . . / No withered immortality.' The story is told in the Homeric
Hymn to Aphrodite where it ends (l. 239 ff.) with words that are apt to T.'s
feelings: 'I would not have you be deathless among the deathless gods and
live continually after such sort. Yet if you could live on such as now you are
in look and in form, and be called my husband, sorrow would not then
enfold my careful heart.' Also apt to T.'s feelings were two appearances of
Tithonus in Horace's *Odes*. I xxviii is on the universality of death, appar-
ently the dramatic monologue of a ghost: *nec quicquam tibi prodest // aërias
temptasse domos animoque rotundum / percurrisse polum morituro. / occidit et
Pelopis genitor, conviva deorum, / Tithonusque remotus in auras . . . // sed omnes
una manet nox, / et calcanda semel via leti.* ('Nor doth it aught avail thee that
thou didst once explore the gods' ethereal homes and didst traverse in
thought the circling vault of heaven. For thou wast born to die! Death
befell also Pelops' sire, though once he sat at the table of the gods; Tit-
honus, too, translated to the skies . . . . But a common night awaiteth
every man, and Death's path must be trodden once for all.') II xvi is on
patience in adversity: *nihil est ab omni / parte beatum. // abstulit clarum cita
mors Achillem, / longa Tithonum minuit senectus; / et mihi forsan, tibi quod
negarit, / porriget hora.* ('Nothing is happy altogether. Achilles for all his
glory was snatched away by an early death; Tithonus, though granted a
long old age, wasted to a shadow; and to me mayhap the passing hour will
grant what it denies to thee.') T.'s translations of some of the *Odes*, written
at school, are at *Lincoln*. For the theme of the danger of loving a deity,
cp. *Semele*, written *c*. 1833 (I 630).

   The woods decay, the woods decay and fall,
   The vapours weep their burthen to the ground,
   Man comes and tills the field and lies beneath,

¶324. *1. The woods decay,*] *1864*; Ay me! ay me! *1860*. The revision
suggests the influence of one of T.'s favourite passages of Wordsworth
(*Mem.* i 151), the account of the Simplon Pass, *The Prelude* vi 624–5
(published 1845): 'The immeasurable height / Of woods decaying, never
to be decayed'. This is apt to Tithonus's immortal decay.
1 ∧ *2*] The stars blaze out and never rise again, *T.MS A, del.*
2. burthen] substance *Tithon, T.MSS.*
3. field] *1864*; earth *1860*.

And after many a summer dies the swan.
5   Me only cruel immortality
Consumes: I wither slowly in thine arms,
Here at the quiet limit of the world,
A white-haired shadow roaming like a dream
The ever-silent spaces of the East,
10 Far-folded mists, and gleaming halls of morn.

Alas! for this gray shadow, once a man –
So glorious in his beauty and thy choice,
Who madest him thy chosen, that he seemed
To his great heart none other than a God!
15 I asked thee, 'Give me immortality.'
Then didst thou grant mine asking with a smile,
Like wealthy men who care not how they give.
But thy strong Hours indignant worked their wills,
And beat me down and marred and wasted me,
20 And though they could not end me, left me maimed
To dwell in presence of immortal youth,
Immortal age beside immortal youth,

4] And after many summers dies the rose. *Tithon. T.MS A* revised 'rose' to 'swan', as did *T.Nbk 21* which also revised to 'many a summer'. The swan was noted for its longevity, and was taken as a type of white-haired age (F. L. Lucas, *Tennyson*, 1957, p. 27). Its singing too is suggested; cp. *The Dying Swan* (p. 15).

5. *cruel*] fatal *Tithon, T.MSS.*

7. Adapted from a fragment of *The Lover's Tale, Heath MS* (I 325): 'Down to the quiet limit of the world'. Cp. the *Hymn to Aphrodite* 225–7: 'He lived rapturously with golden-throned Eos, the early-born, by the streams of Ocean, at the ends of the earth.'

8. *shadow*] *T.MS A 1st reading*; shade yet *T.MS A*. Euripides, *Phoenissae* 1543–5: 'A white-haired shape, like a phantom that fades / On the sight, or a ghost from the underworld shades, / Or a dream that hath wings.' A. Day (*TRB* iii, 1981, 206) notes that T. glossed Euripides' lines, in a copy of the *Pentalogia* inscribed 'Somersby / July 6th 1825': 'grey-headed, an obscure phantom of air – a dead body beneath the earth – a flitting dream'.

11–23]   Ay me! ay me! what everlasting pain,
                Being immortal with a mortal heart,
                To live confronted with eternal youth:
                To look [gaze *T.MS A*] on what is beautiful nor know
                Enjoyment save through memory. Can thy love, *Tithon,*
                                                                 T.MSS

21. Cp. Shelley, *Prometheus Unbound* III iii 88–9: 'And through my withered, old, and icy frame / The warmth of an immortal youth shoots down.'

And all I was, in ashes. Can thy love,
Thy beauty, make amends, though even now,
25   Close over us, the silver star, thy guide,
Shines in those tremulous eyes that fill with tears
To hear me? Let me go: take back thy gift:
Why should a man desire in any way
To vary from the kindly race of men,
30   Or pass beyond the goal of ordinance
Where all should pause, as is most meet for all?

A soft air fans the cloud apart; there comes
A glimpse of that dark world where I was born.
Once more the old mysterious glimmer steals
35   From thy pure brows, and from thy shoulders pure,
And bosom beating with a heart renewed.
Thy cheek begins to redden through the gloom,
Thy sweet eyes brighten slowly close to mine,

23. The image was suggested by the comparable tragedy in *Semele*: 'When I am ashes'.

25. star: 'Venus' (T.).

26. Shines] Gleams *T.MS B.   tears*] tears? *Tithon, T.MS B.   tremulous*] dewy *T.MS A.   tremulous eyes*: as in *The Invasion of Russia by Napoleon Buonaparte* 58, and the song in *The Miller's Daughter* (*1832* text, I 416), which perhaps suggested 'dewy', l. 58 (*T.MS A* supports this). Cp. Keats, *I stood tip-toe* 146–7, on Cupid and Psyche: 'And how they kist each other's tremulous eyes: / The silver lamp, – '. Also Shelley, *Revolt of Islam* XII xiv 1–2: 'The warm tears burst in spite of faith and fear / From many a tremulous eye'. The phrase occurs in Keble's best-seller, *The Christian Year* (1827), xviii; T.'s copy is at *Lincoln.*

26–7. that . . . go] Not *T.MS A.*

27] Take back thy dreadful gift, immortal age. *T.MS B.   To hear me?*] Release me: *Tithon.*

28. way] shape *Tithon, T.MSS.*

29] To vary from his kind, or beat the roads *Tithon, T.MSS.*

30. Or pass] Of life, *Tithon, T.MSS.   goal of ordinance*: 'appointed limit' (T.). Cp. *Cymbeline* IV ii 145–6: 'Let ordinance / Come as the gods fore-say it'.

31 ∧ 2]   Or [O *T.MS A*] let me call thy ministers, the hours,
                  To take me up, to wind me [*not T.MS B, error*] in their arms,
                  To shoot the sunny interval of day,
                  And lap me deep within the lonely west. *Tithon, T.MSS*

32. cloud . . . comes] curtained cloud apart *T.MS A*; curtained cloud: there comes *T.MS B 1st reading.*

33–6] Not *T.MS A.*

36] And bosom throbbing with a fresher heart. *Tithon, T.MS B.*

37. redden . . . gloom] to bloom a fuller [purer *T.MS A*] red *Tithon, T.MSS.*

Ere yet they blind the stars, and the wild team
40　Which love thee, yearning for thy yoke, arise,
And shake the darkness from their loosened manes,
And beat the twilight into flakes of fire.

Lo! ever thus thou growest beautiful
In silence, then before thine answer given
45　Departest, and thy tears are on my cheek.

Why wilt thou ever scare me with thy tears,
And make me tremble lest a saying learnt,
In days far-off, on that dark earth, be true?
'The Gods themselves cannot recall their gifts.'
50　Ay me! ay me! with what another heart

39. Ere yet] As when *T.MS A.　the wild*] *1864*; that wild *1860*; thy wild *Tithon*;
thy swift *T.MS B.*
39–42. and . . . fire] 'Tis ever thus *T.MS A.*
40] Not *Tithon*, *T.MSS.*
41] Spreading a rapid glow [light *T.MS B*] with loosened manes, *Tithon,*
T.MS B.
42. And beat the] Fly, trampling *Tithon*, *T.MS B.　*Traditional for the dawn; cp.
a poem which T. used for *Boädicea*, Catullus lxiii 41: *pepulitque noctis umbras
vegetis sonipedibus.* Also *The Coach of Death* 128: 'They broke the ground with
hoofs of fire.' Apparently also a reminiscence of Marston's *Antonio's Revenge*
I ii 120, i 107–8; 'flakes of fire', 'coursers of the morn / Beat up the light with
their bright silver hooves' (noted by C. R. Forker, *Notes and Queries*, Dec.
1959).
43] And when thou growest the most beautiful, *T.MS A*; 'Tis ever thus: thou
growest more [*not T.MS B*] beautiful, *Tithon*, *T.MS B.*
44] Thou partest: when a little warmth returns *Tithon*, *T.MSS.*
45. Departest] Thou partest *Tithon*, *T.MSS.*
46–9] Not *Tithon*, *T.MSS.*
49. Paradise Lost ix 926–7: 'But past who can recall, or don undoe? / Not
God Omnipotent, nor Fate.' John Churton Collins said that T.'s line 'is,
of course, from Agathon, as quoted by Aristotle (*Eth.N.* vi 2)'. Alongside
this suggestion, T. wrote: 'not known to me' (*Cornhill*, Jan. 1880, *Lincoln*).
50–76] *T.MS A has fragmentary drafts:*
　　　Release me lest I rise, go forth and call
　　　From under yon dark fields that dream below
　　　The Shape I seek – he thus implored invade
　　　The Incorruptible and thou some time
　　　Returning on thy silver wheels behold
　　　Even on these cool and gleaming thresholds Him
　　　Thou knowest not, the uncertain shadow feared
　　　Of Gods and men.

In days far-off, and with what other eyes
I used to watch – if I be he that watched –
The lucid outline forming round thee; saw
The dim curls kindle into sunny rings;
55   Changed with thy mystic change, and felt my blood
Glow with the glow that slowly crimsoned all

Take back thy gift lest I go forth and call
From under yon still fields that dream below
[*lacuna*]   he implored invade
The incorruptible and thou some time
Returning on thy silver wheels behold
Even on these glimmering thresholds, mute and dark
Him whom thou knowest not, the uncertain shape
Not loved of Gods.

Cp. ll. 58, 64. *T.MS B* has a torn draft of this. The top of the opposite page
of *T.MS A* is torn away; it ends:

Not loved of Gods.
                              In vain: he would not [come?]
Why wilt thou keep me ever in the East?
How can my nature longer mix with thine?
Take back thy fatal gift – so let me die.
Meanwhile thy dappled coursers without noise
Scaling the twilight to the morning star
Will draw thee and with dewy breast divide
The rosy shadows flowing either way.
Thou wilt renew thy beauty with the morn,
I earth in earth abide with easeful night.

Cp. ll. 39–42, 54–6, 62–3.
50 ∧ 51] Drowned deep in rapturous trances, beating fast, *T.MS B.*
51–3] By thy divine embraces circumfused, *Tithon, T.MS B.*
53. *forming*] growing *1860* proof (*Lincoln, but altered by T.*).
54] Thy golden tresses shining more and more, *T.MS B.*   *The ... kindle*] Thy
black curls burning *Tithon.* Cp. the final version with 'My long tresses, run
in sunny rings', *The Gardener's Daughter* 75–80, *Heath MS.*
55–7]   I felt thy blood run quicker: felt and saw
                These glows that gradually blooming flusht
                All thy pale limbs: what time my mortal frame
                Molten in thine immortal, I lay wooed *T.MS B*;
                With thy change changed, I felt this wondrous glow
                That, gradually blooming, flushes all
                Thy pale fair limbs: what time my mortal frame
                Molten in thine immortal, I lay wooed, *Tithon*
J. C. Maxwell compares Keats, *Hyperion* iii 124–5: 'and made flush / All the
immortal fairness of his limbs'.

Thy presence and thy portals, while I lay,
Mouth, forehead, eyelids, growing dewy-warm
With kisses balmier than half-opening buds
60 Of April, and could hear the lips that kissed
Whispering I knew not what of wild and sweet,
Like that strange song I heard Apollo sing,
While Ilion like a mist rose into towers.

Yet hold me not for ever in thine East:
65 How can my nature longer mix with thine?
Coldly thy rosy shadows bathe me, cold
Are all thy lights, and cold my wrinkled feet
Upon thy glimmering thresholds, when the steam
Floats up from those dim fields about the homes
70 Of happy men that have the power to die,
And grassy barrows of the happier dead.
Release me, and restore me to the ground;
Thou seëst all things, thou wilt see my grave:
Thou wilt renew thy beauty morn by morn;

58. *Mouth*] Lips *Tithon, T.MS.B.*
59. *half-opening buds*] opening buds; *Tithon, T.MS B.* The change in this erotic image suggests the similarity in sound of the 'half-awakened birds' in *Tears, idle tears* – a poem which, as F. L. Gwynn says (*PMLA* lxvii (1952) 572–5), employs to a remarkable extent the same vocabulary as *Tithon* and *Tithonus*.
60–1]   Anon the lips that dealt them moved themselves
              In wild and airy whisperings more sweet *Tithon*;
         ... airy whispers sweeter far *T.MS B*
62. *Like*] Than *Tithon, T.MS B*. Cp. ll. 61–2 with Shelley, *To Constantia, Singing* 12: 'Wild, sweet, but uncommunicably strange'. Also *The Day-Dream: Prologue* 3, MS: 'I know not what of strange'.
63. Troy was built by the music of Apollo; see *Ilion, Ilion* (I 281), where it is 'melody born'. Cp. T.'s translation from Horace (I 7): 'that god-built wall'. Cp. Milton's Pandaemonium, *PL* i 711–12: 'Rose like an Exhalation, with the sound / Of Dulcet Symphonies and voices sweet.' The mythologist Jacob Bryant wrote of 'towers' in his *New System of Ancient Mythology* (1807 edn, ii 127–8): 'Tithonus, whose longevity is so much celebrated, was nothing more than one of these structures, a Pharos, sacred to the sun, as the name plainly shews.' There was a copy of Bryant at Somersby (*Lincoln*), and he influenced *A Fragment* (I 313) and *Pierced through* (I 513).
64] Ah! keep me not for ever in the East: *Tithon*.
68. *thy*] these *Tithon*.
69. *dim ... homes*] still fields that dream below. *Tithon*.
70–1] Not *Tithon*.
72. *, and*] ! so *Tithon*.
74. *morn by*] with the *Tithon*.

75   I earth in earth forget these empty courts,
      And thee returning on thy silver wheels.

326 In the Valley of Cauteretz

Published *1864*. Written 6–8 Sept. 1861, visiting 'a valley in the Pyrenees, where I had been with Arthur Hallam' (T.) in 1830. Hallam wrote to T.'s brother Charles, 12 Sept. 1830: 'we remained at Cauterets, and recruited our strength with precipitous defiles, jagged mountain tops, forests of solemn pine, travelled by dewy clouds, and encircling lawns of the greenest freshness, waters, in all shapes, and all powers, from the clear runnel bubbling down over our mountain paths at intervals, to the blue little lake whose deep, cold waters are fed eternally from neighbouring glaciers, and the impetuous cataract, fraying its way over black, beetling rocks' (*AHH*, p. 375). Also Hallam's letter to T.'s sister Emily, from Salzburg, 24 Aug. 1833: 'waters flashing into white foam along the rocky channel . . . & seeming, as I stopped to listen, like the voices of the eternal hills' (*AHH*, p. 773).

J.C. Hixson notes the word 'life' in E.T.'s Journal entry, Sept. 1861: 'It is pleasant to see Ally absorbed as he is by the beauty of the scene where the green Pau river dashes by, breaking into little joyous-looking fountains, seemingly fuller of life than any river I have ever seen' (*TRB* ii, 1975, 146). T. sent the poem to the Duchess of Argyll, 11 March 1863: 'This is a little lyrical flash, an impromptu which I sent to the Queen and for which she returned me the warmest thanks' (*Letters* ii 323). 'After hearing the voice of the torrent seemingly sound deeper as the night grew' (T., *Mem.* i 474–5). T. said in 1863: 'Altogether I like the little piece as well as anything I have written' (*Letters* ii 327, 12 May; *Mem.* i 492). Cp. the elegy *In the Garden at Swainston* (p. 619). All variants from *H.Lpr 113* are below.

> All along the valley, stream that flashest white,
> Deepening thy voice with the deepening of the night,
> All along the valley, where thy waters flow,

75] *T.MS A ended with this line;* see ll. 50–76*n.* T. quotes '*terra in terra* (Dante)'. He wrote this alongside John Churton Collins's observation that: 'This happy Hellenism is in Stephen Hawes' *Pastime of Pleasure*, capit. xlv.: "When *earth in earth* hath ta'en his corrupt taste"' (*Cornhill*, Jan. 1880, *Lincoln*). T.'s reference is to *Paradiso* xxv 124–6: *In terra terra è'l mio corpo, e saràgli / tanto con li altri, che'l numero nostro / con l'etterno proposito s'agguagli.* ('My body is earth in the earth, and it will be there with the rest till our number tallies with the eternal purpose.')

¶326. 1] Brook that runnest madly, brook that flashest white, *H.MS*. 3. *waters flow*] mad waters go *MS*.

I walked with one I loved two and thirty years ago.
5   All along the valley, while I walked today,
    The two and thirty years were a mist that rolls away;
    For all along the valley, down thy rocky bed,
    Thy living voice to me was as the voice of the dead,
    And all along the valley, by rock and cave and tree,
10   The voice of the dead was a living voice to me.

330 Enoch Arden

Published *1864*. Written Nov. 1861–April 1862 (A. Woolner, *Thomas Woolner*, 1917, p. 208; *Mat.* ii 351). After discussing *Idylls of the King*, T. wrote to the Duke of Argyll, Feb. 1862: 'I am now about my Fisherman which is heroic too in its way' (*Letters* ii 297). T. wrote to his wife Emily, 26 April 1862: 'Spedding is coming to hear me read the Fisherman' (*Letters* ii 305). Walter White, 13 Feb. 1864, reports T. as saying that 'he had had a proof more than a year, could not yet make up his mind to publish' (*Journals*, 1898, p. 155). At one stage the poem was to be called simply *Enoch* (early mock-up, *Lincoln*). The many biblical echoes in the poem suggest also *Genesis* v 24: 'And Enoch walked with God: and he was not; for God took him'. Like *Aylmer's Field* (II 657), it was based on a prose sketch sent by T.'s friend Thomas Woolner (pp. 208–12), who had read the story in 1854 and had since told it to T. (For a faint doubt as to Amy Woolner's text, see P. G. Scott, *TRB* i, 1968, item C6; and for a reassurance, L. Ormond, *Tennyson and Thomas Woolner* (1981), pp. 25–6.) T. took the outline and many details from Woolner's *The Fisherman's Story*, but in Woolner there were no names; no episode with Philip seeing Enoch and Annie in love (ll. 61–78); and none of the pressures on Enoch to make the voyage (ll. 101–10). The 'sickly' babe (l. 229) was deduced from

4. *one I loved*] Arthur Hallam *MS*. 'My father was vexed that he had written "two and thirty years ago"..... instead of "one and thirty years ago," and as late as 1892 wished to alter it since he hated inaccuracy. I persuaded him to let his first reading stand, for the public had learnt to love the poem in its present form: and besides "two and thirty" was more melodious' (*Mem.* i 475). Martin (pp. 439–41) quotes T.'s complaint, 'A brute of a – has discovered that it was thirty-one years and not thirty-two'. Martin adds: 'But it was not true. Clough's letters [in 1861] prove that T. had known all along how many years it had been since his first visit.' (Clough: 'T. was here with Arthur Hallam 31 years ago'; and again: '... of which he retained a recollection from his visit of 31 years ago'.)
5–7] All along the valley thou ravest down thy bed, *MS*.
8. *was*] is *MS*, as in l. 10.
9. *And all*] All *MS*.

Woolner's reference to its death; Woolner gave no details of the parting, or of Philip's courtship; no praying for a sign (ll. 485–504); no details of life on the tropical island; and no details of the journey home. Woolner's ending was much expanded by T., who omitted Woolner's detail of 'no news ... beyond the fact that the ship ... was wrecked, ... and all hands lost'.

T. applied to FitzGerald in order to authenticate the seafaring details (*Mem.* i 515–16). The poem was also influenced by Crabbe's verse tale *The Parting Hour* (*Tales*, 1812); T. read it in 1859 and again in 1862 (*Mat.* ii 212, 341); in Crabbe, the rival is also called Philip. Mrs Gaskell's tale *Sylvia's Lovers* (1863) has a somewhat similar story, and seems to have suggested, presumably as an inserted detail, the ship's name *Good Fortune* (l. 524); her tale had an epigraph from T. on the title-page. Mrs Marian Bradley commented in her diary, 4 Jan. 1864, after hearing T. read *Enoch the Fisherman*: 'A great resemblance in the story to *Sylvia's Lovers* – singular' (*British Library*). Adelaide Anne Procter's poem *Homeward Bound* (*Legends and Lyrics*, 1858) is an interesting analogue. There is a copy at *Lincoln*, but H.T. has a note (*Mem.* ii 1): 'Adelaide Procter wrote a poem on a similar subject, but this my father did not know until after *Enoch Arden* had been published.' T. also had a presentation copy of *The Morning Watch* (N.Y., 1850): 'the scene is in a tropic land'; see l. 131*n* below. On the process of composition (including the probable influence of Clough) and on the poem's reception, see P. G. Scott, *Tennyson's Enoch Arden: A Victorian Best-Seller* (1970).

The poem brings to a climax a lifelong preoccupation of T.'s; cp. the ghosts in *The Coach of Death* 65–8: 'They see the light of their blest firesides, / They hear each household voice: / The whispered love of the fair young wives; / And the laugh of their rose-lipped boys.' The Lotos-Eaters (ll. 117–9) knew it would be better not to return to Ithaca: 'For surely now our household hearths are cold: / Our sons inherit us: our looks are strange: / And we should come like ghosts to trouble joy.' Again, *In Memoriam* xc 13–20: 'But if they came who past away, / Behold their brides in other hands; / The hard heir strides about their lands, / And will not yield them for a day. // Yea, though their sons were none of these, / Not less the yet-loved sire would make / Confusion worse than death, and shake / The pillars of domestic peace.' Turner (p. 179) notes parallels with the *Odyssey* and 'equivalents of several features in the Homeric narrative'.

Long lines of cliff breaking have left a chasm;
And in the chasm are foam and yellow sands;
Beyond, red roofs about a narrow wharf
In cluster; then a mouldered church; and higher

¶ 330. *4–8.* E. Griffiths, noting 'clusters', 'hazelwood' and 'nutters', compares Wordsworth, *Nutting* 19–20.

5   A long street climbs to one tall-towered mill;
     And high in heaven behind it a gray down
     With Dan'sh barrows; and a hazelwood,
     By autumn nutters haunted, flourishes
     Green in a cuplike hollow of the down.

10   Here on this beach a hundred years ago,
     Three children of three houses, Annie Lee,
     The prettiest little damsel in the port,
     And Philip Ray the miller's only son,
     And Enoch Arden, a rough sailor's lad
15   Made orphan by a winter shipwreck, played
     Among the waste and lumber of the shore,
     Hard coils of cordage, swarthy fishing-nets,
     Anchors of rusty fluke, and boats updrawn;
     And built their castles of dissolving sand
20   To watch them overflowed, or following up
     And flying the white breaker, daily left
     The little footprint daily washed away.

     A narrow cave ran in beneath the cliff:
     In this the children played at keeping house.
25   Enoch was host one day, Philip the next,
     While Annie still was mistress; but at times
     Enoch would hold possession for a week:
     'This is my house and this my little wife.'
     'Mine too' said Philip 'turn and turn about:'
30   When, if they quarrelled, Enoch stronger-made
     Was master: then would Philip, his blue eyes
     All flooded with the helpless wrath of tears,
     Shriek out 'I hate you, Enoch,' and at this
     The little wife would weep for company,
35   And pray them not to quarrel for her sake,
     And say she would be little wife to both.

     But when the dawn of rosy childhood past,
     And the new warmth of life's ascending sun
     Was felt by either, either fixt his heart
40   On that one girl; and Enoch spoke his love,
     But Philip loved in silence; and the girl
     Seemed kinder unto Philip than to him;
     But she loved Enoch; though she knew it not,
     And would if asked deny it. Enoch set
45   A purpose evermore before his eyes,
     To hoard all savings to the uttermost,
     To purchase his own boat, and make a home
     For Annie: and so prospered that at last
     A luckier or a bolder fisherman,

50 A carefuller in peril, did not breathe
    For leagues along that breaker-beaten coast
    Than Enoch. Likewise had he served a year
    On board a merchantman, and made himself
    Full sailor; and he thrice had plucked a life
55 From the dread sweep of the down-streaming seas:
    And all men looked upon him favourably:
    And ere he touched his one-and-twentieth May
    He purchased his own boat, and made a home
    For Annie, neat and nestlike, halfway up
60 The narrow street that clambered toward the mill.

        Then, on a golden autumn eventide,
    The younger people making holiday,
    With bag and sack and basket, great and small,
    Went nutting to the hazels. Philip stayed
65 (His father lying sick and needing him)
    An hour behind; but as he climbed the hill,
    Just where the prone edge of the wood began
    To feather toward the hollow, saw the pair,
    Enoch and Annie, sitting hand-in-hand,
70 His large gray eyes and weather-beaten face
    All-kindled by a still and sacred fire,
    That burned as on an altar. Philip looked,
    And in their eyes and faces read his doom;
    Then, as their faces drew together, groaned,
75 And slipt aside, and like a wounded life
    Crept down into the hollows of the wood;
    There, while the rest were loud in merrymaking,
    Had his dark hour unseen, and rose and past
    Bearing a lifelong hunger in his heart.

80   So these were wed, and merrily rang the bells,
    And merrily ran the years, seven happy years,
    Seven happy years of health and competence,
    And mutual love and honourable toil;
    With children; first a daughter. In him woke,
85 With his first babe's first cry, the noble wish
    To save all earnings to the uttermost,
    And give his child a better bringing-up
    Than his had been, or hers; a wish renewed,
    When two years after came a boy to be
90 The rosy idol of her solitudes,
    While Enoch was abroad on wrathful seas,
    Or often journeying landward; for in truth
    Enoch's white horse, and Enoch's ocean-spoil

In ocean-smelling osier, and his face,
95 Rough-reddened with a thousand winter gales,
Not only to the market-cross were known,
But in the leafy lanes behind the down,
Far as the portal-warding lion-whelp,
And peacock-yewtree of the lonely Hall,
100 Whose Friday fare was Enoch's ministering.

Then came a change, as all things human change.
Ten miles to northward of the narrow port
Opened a larger haven: thither used
Enoch at times to go by land or sea;
105 And once when there, and clambering on a mast
In harbour, by mischance he slipt and fell:
A limb was broken when they lifted him:
And while he lay recovering there, his wife
Bore him another son, a sickly one:
110 Another hand crept too across his trade
Taking her bread and theirs: and on him fell,
Although a grave and staid God-fearing man,
Yet lying thus inactive, doubt and gloom.
He seemed, as in a nightmare of the night,
115 To see his children leading evermore
Low miserable lives of hand-to-mouth,
And her, he loved, a beggar: then he prayed
'Save them from this, whatever comes to me.'
And while he prayed, the master of that ship
120 Enoch had served in, hearing his mischance,
Came, for he knew the man and valued him,
Reporting of his vessel China-bound,
And wanting yet a boatswain. Would he go?
There yet were many weeks before she sailed,
125 Sailed from this port. Would Enoch have the place?
And Enoch all at once assented to it,
Rejoicing at that answer to his prayer.

So now that shadow of mischance appeared
No graver than as when some little cloud
130 Cuts off the fiery highway of the sun,
And isles a light in the offing: yet the wife –

131. Makes 'islands of light on the sea' (T.).   offing: 'in the sea-language, that part of the sea, a good distance from shore, where there is deep water, and no need of a pilot to conduct the ship' (*English Encyclopaedia,* 1802, of which there was a copy at Somersby, Lincoln). Cp. *The Morning Watch* (see headnote): 'A small white cloud is seen in the offing.' From 'as when' to 'offing' had at first been a separate nature jotting by T. (*H.Nbk 18*).

When he was gone – the children – what to do?
Then Enoch lay long-pondering on his plans;
To sell the boat – and yet he loved her well –
135 How many a rough sea had he weathered in her!
He knew her, as a horseman knows his horse –
And yet to sell her – then with what she brought
Buy goods and stores – set Annie forth in trade
With all that seamen needed or their wives –
140 So might she keep the house while he was gone.
Should he not trade himself out yonder? go
This voyage more than once? yea twice or thrice –
As oft as needed – last, returning rich,
Become the master of a larger craft,
145 With fuller profits lead an easier life,
Have all his pretty young ones educated,
And pass his days in peace among his own.

Thus Enoch in his heart determined all:
Then moving homeward came on Annie pale,
150 Nursing the sickly babe, her latest-born.
Forward she started with a happy cry,
And laid the feeble infant in his arms;
Whom Enoch took, and handled all his limbs,
Appraised his weight and fondled fatherlike,
155 But had no heart to break his purposes
To Annie, till the morrow, when he spoke.

Then first since Enoch's golden ring had girt
Her finger, Annie fought against his will:
Yet not with brawling opposition she,
160 But manifold entreaties, many a tear,
Many a sad kiss by day by night renewed
(Sure that all evil would come out of it)
Besought him, supplicating, if he cared
For her or his dear children, not to go.
165 He not for his own self caring but her,
Her and her children, let her plead in vain;
So grieving held his will, and bore it through.

For Enoch parted with his old sea-friend,
Bought Annie goods and stores, and set his hand
170 To fit their little streetward sitting-room
With shelf and corner for the goods and stores.
So all day long till Enoch's last at home,
Shaking their pretty cabin, hammer and axe,
Auger and saw, while Annie seemed to hear
175 Her own death-scaffold raising, shrilled and rang,

Till this was ended, and his careful hand, –
The space was narrow, – having ordered all
Almost as neat and close as Nature packs
Her blossom or her seedling, paused; and he,
180 Who needs would work for Annie to the last,
Ascending tired, heavily slept till morn.

And Enoch faced this morning of farewell
Brightly and boldly. All his Annie's fears,
Save, as his Annie's, were a laughter to him.
185 Yet Enoch as a brave God-fearing man
Bowed himself down, and in that mystery
Where God-in-man is one with man-in-God,
Prayed for a blessing on his wife and babes
Whatever came to him: and then he said
190 'Annie, this voyage by the grace of God
Will bring fair weather yet to all of us.
Keep a clean hearth and a clear fire for me,
For I'll be back, my girl, before you know it.'
Then lightly rocking baby's cradle 'and he,
195 This pretty, puny, weakly little one, –
Nay – for I love him all the better for it –
God bless him, he shall sit upon my knees
And I will tell him tales of foreign parts,
And make him merry, when I come home again.
200 Come, Annie, come, cheer up before I go.'

Him running on thus hopefully she heard,
And almost hoped herself; but when he turned
The current of his talk to graver things
In sailor fashion roughly sermonizing
205 On providence and trust in Heaven, she heard,
Heard and not heard him; as the village girl,
Who sets her pitcher underneath the spring,
Musing on him that used to fill it for her,
Hears and not hears, and lets it overflow.

210   At length she spoke 'O Enoch, you are wise;
And yet for all your wisdom well know I
That I shall look upon your face no more.'

185–9] *Added in T.Nbk 35, with (deleted, ll. 186 ∧ 7)* 'Daily defamed
by formalist and fool,'.
212. Cp. *Acts* xx 38: 'Sorrowing most of all for the words which he spake,
that they should see his face no more. And they accompanied him unto the
ship.'

'Well then,' said Enoch, 'I shall look on yours.
Annie, the ship I sail in passes here
215 (He named the day) get you a seaman's glass,
Spy out my face, and laugh at all your fears.'

But when the last of those last moments came,
'Annie, my girl, cheer up, be comforted,
Look to the babes, and till I come again
220 Keep everything shipshape, for I must go.
And fear no more for me; or if you fear
Cast all your cares on God; that anchor holds.
Is He not yonder in those uttermost
Parts of the morning? if I flee to these
225 Can I go from Him? and the sea is His,
The sea is His: He made it.'
                              Enoch rose,
Cast his strong arms about his drooping wife,
And kissed his wonder-stricken little ones;
But for the third, the sickly one, who slept
230 After a night of feverous wakefulness,
When Annie would have raised him Enoch said
'Wake him not; let him sleep; how should the child
Remember this?' and kissed him in his cot.
But Annie from her baby's forehead clipt
235 A tiny curl, and gave it: this he kept
Through all his future; but now hastily caught
His bundle, waved his hand, and went his way.

She when the day, that Enoch mentioned, came,
Borrowed a glass, but all in vain: perhaps
240 She could not fix the glass to suit her eye;
Perhaps her eye was dim, hand tremulous;
She saw him not: and while he stood on deck
Waving, the moment and the vessel past.

Even to the last dip of the vanishing sail
245 She watched it, and departed weeping for him;

222–6. *1 Peter* v 7: 'Casting all your care upon him, for he careth for you';
Hebrews vi 19: 'Which hope we have as an anchor of the soul both sure
and stedfast'; *Psalm* cxxxix 9: 'If I take the wings of the morning, and
dwell in the uttermost parts of the sea'; *Psalm* xcv 5: 'The sea is his, and he
made it'.
228. Cp. Shelley, *Revolt of Islam* V xliii 5: 'Which now the wonder-
stricken breezes kissed'.

Then, though she mourned his absence as his grave,
Set her sad will no less to chime with his,
But throve not in her trade, not being bred
To barter, nor compensating the want
250 By shrewdness, neither capable of lies,
Nor asking overmuch and taking less,
And still foreboding 'what would Enoch say?'
For more than once, in days of difficulty
And pressure, had she sold her wares for less
255 Than what she gave in buying what she sold:
She failed and saddened knowing it; and thus,
Expectant of that news which never came,
Gained for her own a scanty sustenance,
And lived a life of silent melancholy.

260 Now the third child was sickly-born and grew
Yet sicklier, though the mother cared for it
With all a mother's care: nevertheless,
Whether her business often called her from it,
Or through the want of what it needed most,
265 Or means to pay the voice who best could tell
What most it needed – howsoe'er it was,
After a lingering, – ere she was aware, –
Like the caged bird escaping suddenly,
The little innocent soul flitted away.

270 In that same week when Annie buried it,
Philip's true heart, which hungered for her peace
(Since Enoch left he had not looked upon her),
Smote him, as having kept aloof so long.
'Surely,' said Philip, 'I may see her now,
275 May be some little comfort;' therefore went,
Past through the solitary room in front,
Paused for a moment at an inner door,
Then struck it thrice, and, no one opening,
Entered; but Annie, seated with her grief,
280 Fresh from the burial of her little one,
Cared not to look on any human face,
But turned her own toward the wall and wept.
Then Philip standing up said falteringly
'Annie, I came to ask a favour of you.'

---

246. 'She mourned as if his absence were his grave' (Woolner).
248–9. 'Not having been bred to barter' (Woolner).
249. compénsating: apparently the usual pronunciation till the mid-nineteenth century.

285 He spoke; the passion in her moaned reply
'Favour from one so sad and so forlorn
As I am!' half abashed him; yet unasked,
His bashfulness and tenderness at war,
He set himself beside her, saying to her:

290 'I came to speak to you of what he wished,
Enoch, your husband: I have ever said
You chose the best among us – a strong man:
For where he fixt his heart he set his hand
To do the thing he willed, and bore it through.
295 And wherefore did he go this weary way,
And leave you lonely? not to see the world –
For pleasure? – nay, but for the wherewithal
To give his babes a better bringing-up
Than his had been, or yours: that was his wish.
300 And if he come again, vext will he be
To find the precious morning hours were lost.
And it would vex him even in his grave,
If he could know his babes were running wild
Like colts about the waste. So, Annie, now –
305 Have we not known each other all our lives?
I do beseech you by the love you bear
Him and his children not to say me nay –
For, if you will, when Enoch comes again
Why then he shall repay me – if you will,
310 Annie – for I am rich and well-to-do.
Now let me put the boy and girl to school:
This is the favour that I came to ask.'

 Then Annie with her brows against the wall
Answered 'I cannot look you in the face;
315 I seem so foolish and so broken down.
When you came in my sorrow broke me down;
And now I think your kindness breaks me down;
But Enoch lives; that is borne in on me:
He will repay you: money can be repaid;
Not kindness such as yours.'
320   And Philip asked
'Then you will let me, Annie?'
         There she turned,
She rose, and fixt her swimming eyes upon him,
And dwelt a moment on his kindly face,
Then calling down a blessing on his head
325 Caught at his hand, and wrung it passionately,
And past into the little garth beyond.
So lifted up in spirit he moved away.

Then Philip put the boy and girl to school,
And bought them needful books, and everyway,
330 Like one who does his duty by his own,
Made himself theirs; and though for Annie's sake,
Fearing the lazy gossip of the port,
He oft denied his heart his dearest wish,
And seldom crost her threshold, yet he sent
335 Gifts by the children, garden-herbs and fruit,
The late and early roses from his wall,
Or conies from the down, and now and then,
With some pretext of fineness in the meal
To save the offence of charitable, flour
340 From his tall mill that whistled on the waste.

But Philip did not fathom Annie's mind:
Scarce could the woman when he came upon her,
Out of full heart and boundless gratitude
Light on a broken word to thank him with.
345 But Philip was her children's all-in-all;
From distant corners of the street they ran
To greet his hearty welcome heartily;
Lords of his house and of his mill were they;
Worried his passive ear with petty wrongs
350 Or pleasures, hung upon him, played with him
And called him Father Philip. Philip gained
As Enoch lost; for Enoch seemed to them
Uncertain as a vision or a dream,
Faint as a figure seen in early dawn
355 Down at the far end of an avenue,
Going we know not where: and so ten years,
Since Enoch left his hearth and native land,
Fled forward, and no news of Enoch came.

It chanced one evening Annie's children longed
360 To go with others, nutting to the wood,
And Annie would go with them; then they begged
For Father Philip (as they called him) too:
Him, like the working bee in blossom-dust,
Blanched with his mill, they found · and saying to him
365 'Come with us Father Philip' he denied;
But when the children plucked at him to go,
He laughed, and yielded readily to their wish,
For was not Annie with them? and they went.

But after scaling half the weary down,
370 Just where the prone edge of the wood began
To feather toward the hollow, all her force

Failed her; and sighing, 'Let me rest' she said:
So Philip rested with her well-content;
While all the younger ones with jubilant cries
375   Broke from their elders, and tumultuously
Down through the whitening hazels made a plunge
To the bottom, and dispersed, and bent or broke
The lithe reluctant boughs to tear away
Their tawny clusters, crying to each other
380   And calling, here and there, about the wood.

But Philip sitting at her side forgot
Her presence, and remembered one dark hour
Here in this wood, when like a wounded life
He crept into the shadow: at last he said,
385   Lifting his honest forehead, 'Listen, Annie,
How merry they are down yonder in the wood.
Tired, Annie?' for she did not speak a word.
'Tired?' but her face had fallen upon her hands;
At which, as with a kind of anger in him,
390   'The ship was lost,' he said, 'the ship was lost!
No more of that! why should you kill yourself
And make them orphans quite?' And Annie said
'I thought not of it: but – I know not why –
Their voices make me feel so solitary.'

395   Then Philip coming somewhat closer spoke.
'Annie, there is a thing upon my mind,
And it has been upon my mind so long,
That though I know not when it first came there,
I know that it will out at last. O Annie,
400   It is beyond all hope, against all chance,
That he who left you ten long years ago
Should still be living; well then – let me speak:
I grieve to see you poor and wanting help:
I cannot help you as I wish to do
405   Unless – they say that women are so quick –
Perhaps you know what I would have you know –
I wish you for my wife. I fain would prove
A father to your children: I do think
They love me as a father: I am sure
410   That I love them as if they were mine own;
And I believe, if you were fast my wife,
That after all these sad uncertain years,
We might be still as happy as God grants
To any of his creatures. Think upon it:
415   For I am well-to-do – no kin, no care,

No burthen, save my care for you and yours:
And we have known each other all our lives,
And I have loved you longer than you know.'

Then answered Annie; tenderly she spoke:
420 'You have been as God's good angel in our house.
God bless you for it, God reward you for it,
Philip, with something happier than myself.
Can one love twice? can you be ever loved
As Enoch was? what is it that you ask?'
425 'I am content' he answered 'to be loved
A little after Enoch.' 'O' she cried,
Scared as it were, 'dear Philip, wait a while:
If Enoch comes – but Enoch will not come –
Yet wait a year, a year is not so long:
430 Surely I shall be wiser in a year:
O wait a little!' Philip sadly said
'Annie, as I have waited all my life
I well may wait a little.' 'Nay' she cried
'I am bound: you have my promise – in a year:
435 Will you not bide your year as I bide mine?'
And Philip answered 'I will bide my year.'

Here both were mute, till Philip glancing up
Beheld the dead flame of the fallen day
Pass from the Danish barrow overhead;
440 Then fearing night and chill for Annie, rose
And sent his voice beneath him through the wood.
Up came the children laden with their spoil;
Then all descended to the port, and there
At Annie's door he paused and gave his hand,
445 Saying gently 'Annie, when I spoke to you,
That was your hour of weakness. I was wrong,
I am always bound to you, but you are free.'
Then Annie weeping answered 'I am bound.'

She spoke; and in one moment as it were,
450 While yet she went about her household ways,
Even as she dwelt upon his latest words,
That he had loved her longer than she knew,
That autumn into autumn flashed again,
And there he stood once more before her face,
455 Claiming her promise. 'Is it a year?' she asked.
'Yes, if the nuts' he said 'be ripe again:
Come out and see.' But she – she put him off –
So much to look to – such a change – a month –
Give her a month – she knew that she was bound –

460   A month – no more. Then Philip with his eyes
         Full of that lifelong hunger, and his voice
         Shaking a little like a drunkard's hand,
         'Take your own time, Annie, take your own time.'
         And Annie could have wept for pity of him;
465   And yet she held him on delayingly
         With many a scarce-believable excuse,
         Trying his truth and his long-sufferance,
         Till half-another year had slipt away.

         By this the lazy gossips of the port,
470   Abhorrent of a calculation crost,
         Began to chafe as at a personal wrong.
         Some thought that Philip did but trifle with her;
         Some that she but held off to draw him on;
         And others laughed at her and Philip too,
475   As simple folk that knew not their own minds,
         And one, in whom all evil fancies clung
         Like serpent eggs together, laughingly
         Would hint at worse in either. Her own son
         Was silent, though he often looked his wish;
480   But evermore the daughter prest upon her
         To wed the man so dear to all of them
         And lift the household out of poverty;
         And Philip's rosy face contracting grew
         Careworn and wan; and all these things fell on her
         Sharp as reproach.

485   At last one night it chanced
         That Annie could not sleep, but earnestly
         Prayed for a sign 'my Enoch is he gone?'
         Then compassed round by the blind wall of night
         Brooked not the expectant terror of her heart,
490   Started from bed, and struck herself a light,
         Then desperately seized the holy Book,
         Suddenly set it wide to find a sign,
         Suddenly put her finger on the text,
         'Under the palm-tree.' That was nothing to her:
495   No meaning there: she closed the Book and slept:
         When lo! her Enoch sitting on a height,
         Under a palm-tree, over him the Sun:
         'He is gone,' she thought, 'he is happy, he is singing

---

487–96. Cp. *Judges* vi 17: 'If now I have found grace in thy sight, then
show me a sign'.
494. the] *1870*; a *1864–9*. Misquoting *Judges* iv 5: 'And she dwelt under the
palm tree of Deborah'.

Hosanna in the highest: yonder shines
500 The Sun of Righteousness, and these be palms
Whereof the happy people strowing cried
"Hosanna in the highest!"'' Here she woke,
Resolved, sent for him and said wildly to him
'There is no reason why we should not wed.'
505 'Then for God's sake,' he answered, 'both our sakes,
So you will wed me, let it be at once.'

 So these were wed and merrily rang the bells,
Merrily rang the bells and they were wed.
But never merrily beat Annie's heart.
510 A footstep seemed to fall beside her path,
She knew not whence; a whisper on her ear,
She knew not what; nor loved she to be left
Alone at home, nor ventured out alone.
What ailed her then, that ere she entered, often
515 Her hand dwelt lingeringly on the latch,
Fearing to enter: Philip thought he knew:
Such doubts and fears were common to her state,
Being with child: but when her child was born,
Then her new child was as herself renewed,
520 Then the new mother came about her heart,
Then her good Philip was her all-in-all,
And that mysterious instinct wholly died.

 And where was Enoch? prosperously sailed
The ship 'Good Fortune', though at setting forth
525 The Biscay, roughly ridging eastward, shook
And almost overwhelmed her, yet unvext
She slipt across the summer of the world,
Then after a long tumble about the Cape
And frequent interchange of foul and fair,
530 She passing through the summer world again,
The breath of heaven came continually
And sent her sweetly by the golden isles,
Till silent in her oriental haven.

 There Enoch traded for himself, and bought
535 Quaint monsters for the market of those times,
A gilded dragon, also, for the babes.

 Less lucky her home-voyage: at first indeed
Through many a fair sea-circle, day by day,
Scarce-rocking, her full-busted figure-head

500. *The Sun of Righteousness*: *Malachi* iv 2. *palms*: *John* xii 13.
527. 'The Equator' (T.).

540 Stared o'er the ripple feathering from her bows:
      Then followed calms, and then winds variable,
      Then baffling, a long course of them; and last
      Storm, such as drove her under moonless heavens
      Till hard upon the cry of 'breakers' came
545 The crash of ruin, and the loss of all
      But Enoch and two others. Half the night,
      Buoyed upon floating tackle and broken spars,
      These drifted, stranding on an isle at morn
      Rich, but the loneliest in a lonely sea.

550 No want was there of human sustenance,
      Soft fruitage, mighty nuts, and nourishing roots;
      Nor save for pity was it hard to take
      The helpless life so wild that it was tame.
      There in a seaward-gazing mountain-gorge
555 They built, and thatched with leaves of palm, a hut,
      Half hut, half native cavern. So the three,
      Set in this Eden of all plenteousness,
      Dwelt with eternal summer, ill-content.

      For one, the youngest, hardly more than boy,
560 Hurt in that night of sudden ruin and wreck,
      Lay lingering out a five-years' death-in-life.
      They could not leave him. After he was gone,
      The two remaining found a fallen stem;
      And Enoch's comrade, careless of himself,
565 Fire-hollowing this in Indian fashion, fell
      Sun-stricken, and that other lived alone.
      In those two deaths he read God's warning 'wait'.

      The mountain wooded to the peak, the lawns
      And winding glades high up like ways to Heaven,
570 The slender coco's drooping crown of plumes,
      The lightning flash of insect and of bird,
      The lustre of the long convolvuluses
      That coiled around the stately stems, and ran
      Even to the limit of the land, the glows

542. 'Having met a long course of baffling winds' (Woolner).
561. five-] *1869*; three- *1864–7*.
568–95. Cp. *The Lover's Tale*, MS (Appendix A, III 581), draft iii
61–82.
570. The coco-palm appears in *The Progress of Spring* 68.
571] The flash and flicker of insect and bird, *T.MS 1st reading*.
574–5. Cp. *The Deity* 12 (by T.'s brother Charles, *1827*): 'the broad glow
of glory'; and *The Lover's Tale* i 392, ii 109: 'glory of broad waters',
'glows and glories of the moon'.

575 And glories of the broad belt of the world,
     All these he saw; but what he fain had seen
     He could not see, the kindly human face,
     Nor ever hear a kindly voice, but heard
     The myriad shriek of wheeling ocean-fowl,
580 The league-long roller thundering on the reef,
     The moving whisper of huge trees that branched
     And blossomed in the zenith, or the sweep
     Of some precipitous rivulet to the wave,
     As down the shore he ranged, or all day long
585 Sat often in the seaward-gazing gorge,
     A shipwrecked sailor, waiting for a sail:
     No sail from day to day, but every day
     The sunrise broken into scarlet shafts
     Among the palms and ferns and precipices;
590 The blaze upon the waters to the east;
     The blaze upon his island overhead;
     The blaze upon the waters to the west;
     Then the great stars that globed themselves in Heaven,
     The hollower-bellowing ocean, and again
595 The scarlet shafts of sunrise – but no sail.

     There often as he watched or seemed to watch,
     So still, the golden lizard on him paused,
     A phantom made of many phantoms moved
     Before him haunting him, or he himself
600 Moved haunting people, things and places, known
     Far in a darker isle beyond the line;
     The babes, their babble, Annie, the small house,
     The climbing street, the mill, the leafy lanes,
     The peacock-yewtree and the lonely Hall,
605 The horse he drove, the boat he sold, the chill
     November dawns and dewy-glooming downs,
     The gentle shower, the smell of dying leaves,
     And the low moan of leaden-coloured seas.

     Once likewise, in the ringing of his ears,
610 Though faintly, merrily – far and far away –
     He heard the pealing of his parish bells;

575. *belt*] waist *T.MS 1st reading.*
579] The cries of cormorants and albatrosses, *T.MS 1st reading. ocean-*]
water- *T.MS 2nd reading.*
606–8. Shelley's *Alastor* 555–7 has 'seas', 'gloom', 'leaden-coloured'.
611. T. says 'Kinglake told me that he had heard his own parish bells in
the midst of an Eastern desert'; and refers to *Eothen*, chapter xvii. See also
Letters ii 485, 24 March 1868, to E. C. Tainsh.

Then, though he knew not wherefore, started up
Shuddering, and when the beauteous hateful isle
Returned upon him, had not his poor heart
615   Spoken with That, which being everywhere
Lets none, who speaks with Him, seem all alone,
Surely the man had died of solitude.

Thus over Enoch's early-silvering head
The sunny and rainy seasons came and went
620   Year after year. His hopes to see his own,
And pace the sacred old familiar fields,
Not yet had perished, when his lonely doom
Came suddenly to an end. Another ship
(She wanted water) blown by baffling winds,
625   Like the Good Fortune, from her destined course,
Stayed by this isle, not knowing where she lay:
For since the mate had seen at early dawn
Across a break on the mist-wreathen isle
The silent water slipping from the hills,
630   They sent a crew that landing burst away
In search of stream or fount, and filled the shores
With clamour. Downward from his mountain gorge
Stept the long-haired long-bearded solitary,
Brown, looking hardly human, strangely clad,
635   Muttering and mumbling, idiotlike it seemed,
With inarticulate rage, and making signs
They knew not what: and yet he led the way
To where the rivulets of sweet water ran;
And ever as he mingled with the crew,
640   And heard them talking, his long-bounden tongue
Was loosened, till he made them understand;
Whom, when their casks were filled they took aboard:
And there the tale he uttered brokenly,
Scarce-credited at first but more and more,
645   Amazed and melted all who listened to it:
And clothes they gave him and free passage home;
But oft he worked among the rest and shook
His isolation from him. None of these
Came from his country, or could answer him,

613. The theme of *The Islet* (II 685).

638. T. compares *Aeneid* i 167: *intus aquae dulces vivoque sedilia saxo* ('within are fresh waters and seats in the living stone').

640–1. Cp. *Luke* i 64: 'And his mouth was opened immediately, and his tongue loosed, and he spake, and praised God.'

649. *country*] *1875*; county *1864–72*.

650   If questioned, aught of what he cared to know.
        And dull the voyage was with long delays,
        The vessel scarce sea-worthy; but evermore
        His fancy fled before the lazy wind
        Returning, till beneath a clouded moon
655   He like a lover down through all his blood
        Drew in the dewy meadowy morning-breath
        Of England, blown across her ghostly wall:
        And that same morning officers and men
        Levied a kindly tax upon themselves,
660   Pitying the lonely man, and gave him it:
        Then moving up the coast they landed him,
        Even in that harbour whence he sailed before.

        There Enoch spoke no word to any one,
        But homeward—home—what home? had he a home?
665   His home, he walked. Bright was that afternoon,
        Sunny but chill; till drawn through either chasm,
        Where either haven opened on the deeps,
        Rolled a sea-haze and whelmed the world in gray;
        Cut off the length of highway on before,
670   And left but narrow breadth to left and right
        Of withered holt or tilth or pasturage.
        On the nigh-naked tree the robin piped
        Disconsolate, and through the dripping haze
        The dead weight of the dead leaf bore it down:
675   Thicker the drizzle grew, deeper the gloom;
        Last, as it seemed, a great mist-blotted light
        Flared on him, and he came upon the place.

        Then down the long street having slowly stolen,
        His heart foreshadowing all calamity,
680   His eyes upon the stones, he reached the home
        Where Annie lived and loved him, and his babes
        In those far-off seven happy years were born;
        But finding neither light nor murmur there
        (A bill of sale gleamed through the drizzle) crept
685   Still downward thinking 'dead or dead to me!'

        Down to the pool and narrow wharf he went,
        Seeking a tavern which of old he knew,
        A front of timber-crost antiquity,
        So propt, worm-eaten, ruinously old,
690   He thought it must have gone; but he was gone
        Who kept it; and his widow Miriam Lane,

663–5] Bright was that afternoon as Enoch walked *T.MS 1st reading.*

With daily-dwindling profits held the house;
A haunt of brawling seamen once, but now
Stiller, with yet a bed for wandering men.
695   There Enoch rested silent many days.

But Miriam Lane was good and garrulous,
Nor let him be, but often breaking in,
Told him, with other annals of the port,
Not knowing—Enoch was so brown, so bowed,
700   So broken—all the story of his house.
His baby's death, her growing poverty,
How Philip put her little ones to school,
And kept them in it, his long wooing her,
Her slow consent, and marriage, and the birth
705   Of Philip's child: and o'er his countenance
No shadow past, nor motion: any one,
Regarding, well had deemed he felt the tale
Less than the teller: only when she closed
'Enoch, poor man, was cast away and lost'
710   He, shaking his gray head pathetically,
Repeated muttering 'cast away and lost;'
Again in deeper inward whispers 'lost!'

But Enoch yearned to see her face again;
'If I might look on her sweet face again
715   And know that she is happy.' So the thought
Haunted and harassed him, and drove him forth,
At evening when the dull November day
Was growing duller twilight, to the hill.
There he sat down gazing on all below;
720   There did a thousand memories roll upon him,
Unspeakable for sadness. By and by
The ruddy square of comfortable light,
Far-blazing from the rear of Philip's house,
Allured him, as the beacon-blaze allures
725   The bird of passage, till he madly strikes
Against it, and beats out his weary life.

For Philip's dwelling fronted on the street,
The latest house to landward; but behind,
With one small gate that opened on the waste,
730   Flourished a little garden square and walled:
And in it throve an ancient evergreen,
A yewtree, and all round it ran a walk
Of shingle, and a walk divided it:
But Enoch shunned the middle walk and stole
735   Up by the wall, behind the yew; and thence

That which he better might have shunned, if griefs
Like his have worse or better, Enoch saw.

For cups and silver on the burnished board
Sparkled and shone; so genial was the hearth:
740 And on the right hand of the hearth he saw
Philip, the slighted suitor of old times,
Stout, rosy, with his babe across his knees;
And o'er her second father stoopt a girl,
A later but a loftier Annie Lee,
745 Fair-haired and tall, and from her lifted hand
Dangled a length of ribbon and a ring
To tempt the babe, who reared his creasy arms,
Caught at and ever missed it, and they laughed;
And on the left hand of the hearth he saw
750 The mother glancing often toward her babe,
But turning now and then to speak with him,
Her son, who stood beside her tall and strong,
And saying that which pleased him, for he smiled.

Now when the dead man come to life beheld
755 His wife his wife no more, and saw the babe
Hers, yet not his, upon the father's knee,
And all the warmth, the peace, the happiness,
And his own children tall and beautiful,
And him, that other, reigning in his place,
760 Lord of his rights and of his children's love,—
Then he, though Miriam Lane had told him all,
Because things seen are mightier than things heard,
Staggered and shook, holding the branch, and feared
To send abroad a shrill and terrible cry,
765 Which in one moment, like the blast of doom,
Would shatter all the happiness of the hearth.

He therefore turning softly like a thief,
Lest the harsh shingle should grate underfoot,
And feeling all along the garden-wall,
770 Lest he should swoon and tumble and be found,
Crept to the gate, and opened it, and closed,
As lightly as a sick man's chamber-door,
Behind him, and came out upon the waste.

738–9] 753 ∧ 4, *T.MS 1st reading* ('And . . .').
742. 'He saw the miller, stout rosy and happy, with a two years old child
on his knee' (Woolner).

And there he would have knelt, but that his knees
775 Were feeble, so that falling prone he dug
His fingers into the wet earth, and prayed.

'Too hard to bear! why did they take me thence?
O God Almighty, blessèd Saviour, Thou
That didst uphold me on my lonely isle,
780 Uphold me, Father, in my loneliness
A little longer! aid me, give me strength
Not to tell her, never to let her know.
Help me not to break in upon her peace.
My children too! must I not speak to these?
785 They know me not. I should betray myself.
Never: No father's kiss for me – the girl
So like her mother, and the boy, my son.'

There speech and thought and nature failed a little,
And he lay tranced; but when he rose and paced
790 Back toward his solitary home again,
All down the long and narrow street he went
Beating it in upon his weary brain,
As though it were the burthen of a song,
'Not to tell her, never to let her know.'

795 He was not all unhappy. His resolve
Upbore him, and firm faith, and evermore
Prayer from a living source within the will,
And beating up through all the bitter world,
Like fountains of sweet water in the sea,
800 Kept him a living soul. 'This miller's wife'
He said to Miriam 'that you spoke about,
Has she no fear that her first husband lives?'
'Ay, ay, poor soul' said Miriam, 'fear enow!
If you could tell her you had seen him dead,
805 Why, that would be her comfort;' and he thought
'After the Lord has called me she shall know,
I wait His time,' and Enoch set himself,
Scorning an alms, to work whereby to live.
Almost to all things could he turn his hand.
810 Cooper he was and carpenter, and wrought
To make the boatmen fishing-nets, or helped

---

780. *Psalm* cxlv 14: 'The Lord upholdeth all that fall'.
795. *He . . . unhappy*] The man that strongly wills and truly loves / Cannot be called unhappy *T.MS 1st reading.*
800–807. '*This . . . Enoch*] *Added in T.MS* ('. . . and set himself').
801. *spoke about*] *1872*; told me of *1864–70.*

At lading and unlading the tall barks,
That brought the stinted commerce of those days;
Thus earned a scanty living for himself:
815 Yet since he did but labour for himself,
Work without hope, there was not life in it
Whereby the man could live; and as the year
Rolled itself round again to meet the day
When Enoch had returned, a languor came
820 Upon him, gentle sickness, gradually
Weakening the man, till he could do no more,
But kept the house, his chair, and last his bed.
And Enoch bore his weakness cheerfully.
For sure no gladlier does the stranded wreck
825 See through the gray skirts of a lifting squall
The boat that bears the hope of life approach
To save the life despaired of, than he saw
Death dawning on him, and the close of all.

For through that dawning gleamed a kindlier hope
830 On Enoch thinking 'after I am gone,
Then may she learn I loved her to the last.'
He called aloud for Miriam Lane and said
'Woman, I have a secret – only swear,
Before I tell you – swear upon the book
835 Not to reveal it, till you see me dead.'
'Dead,' clamoured the good woman, 'hear him talk!
I warrant, man, that we shall bring you round.'
'Swear,' added Enoch sternly 'on the book.'
And on the book, half-frighted, Miriam swore.
840 Then Enoch rolling his gray eyes upon her,
'Did you know Enoch Arden of this town?'
'Know him?' she said 'I knew him far away.
Ay, ay, I mind him coming down the street;
Held his head high, and cared for no man, he.'
845 Slowly and sadly Enoch answered her;
'His head is low, and no man cares for him.
I think I have not three days more to live;
I am the man.' At which the woman gave
A half-incredulous, half-hysterical cry.
850 'You Arden, you! nay, – sure he was a foot
Higher than you be.' Enoch said again
'My God has bowed me down to what I am;

816. Cp. Coleridge, *Work without Hope* 13-14: 'Work without Hope
draws nectar in a sieve, / And Hope without an object cannot live.'

My grief and solitude have broken me;
Nevertheless, know you that I am he
855 Who married – but that name has twice been changed –
I married her who married Philip Ray.
Sit, listen.' Then he told her of his voyage,
His wreck, his lonely life, his coming back,
His gazing in on Annie, his resolve,
860 And how he kept it. As the woman heard,
Fast flowed the current of her easy tears,
While in her heart she yearned incessantly
To rush abroad all round the little haven,
Proclaiming Enoch Arden and his woes;
865 But awed and promise-bounden she forbore,
Saying only 'See your bairns before you go!
Eh, let me fetch 'em, Arden,' and arose
Eager to bring them down, for Enoch hung
A moment on her words, but then replied:
870 'Woman, disturb me not now at the last,
But let me hold my purpose till I die.
Sit down again; mark me and understand,
While I have power to speak. I charge you now,
When you shall see her, tell her that I died
875 Blessing her, praying for her, loving her;
Save for the bar between us, loving her
As when she laid her head beside my own.
And tell my daughter Annie, whom I saw
So like her mother, that my latest breath
880 Was spent in blessing her and praying for her.
And tell my son that I died blessing him.
And say to Philip that I blest him too;
He never meant us any thing but good.
But if my children care to see me dead,
885 Who hardly knew me living, let them come,
I am their father; but she must not come,
For my dead face would vex her after-life.
And now there is but one of all my blood
Who will embrace me in the world-to-be:
890 This hair is his: she cut it off and gave it,
And I have borne it with me all these years,
And thought to bear it with me to my grave;
But now my mind is changed, for I shall see him,
My babe in bliss: wherefore when I am gone,
895 Take, give her this, for it may comfort her:

891. *years,*] *1864*; years. *Eversley.*

It will moreover be a token to her,
That I am he.'
          He ceased; and Miriam Lane
Made such a voluble answer promising all,
That once again he rolled his eyes upon her
900 Repeating all he wished, and once again
She promised.
          Then the third night after this,
While Enoch slumbered motionless and pale,
And Miriam watched and dozed at intervals,
There came so loud a calling of the sea,
905 That all the houses in the haven rang.
He woke, he rose, he spread his arms abroad
Crying with a loud voice 'A sail! a sail!
I am saved;' and so fell back and spoke no more.

So past the strong heroic soul away.
910 And when they buried him the little port
Had seldom seen a costlier funeral.

[1862. *Dedication* to *Idylls of the King*–see *p. 667*]

334 Hendecasyllabics

Published *Cornhill*, Dec. 1863, as the third of 'Attempts at Classic Metres in
Quantity'; then *1864*, among 'Experiments in Quantity'. Written autumn
1863 (*CT*, p. 346). All variants from *HnMS* (HM 19498) are below.
'These must be read with the English accent' (T.). He used the metre
again for an attack on a critic, *The Gentle Life* (III 12). Cp. Campion's
epigrams in his *Observations in the Art of English Poesy* (1602).

904. *calling*: 'a ground swell' (T.). Cp. the death in 'Barry Cornwall',
A Sicilian Story (1820): 'The seas / Did rise and fall, and then that fearful
swell / Came silently which seamen know so well; / And all was like an
Omen.' T. gave 'calling of the sea' as an example of the difficulty of
translation: 'a clear night with a sea-sound on the shore in calm. A German
translator rendered it "Geschrei," which suggested storm, etc., wrongly.
He meant a big voice of the sea, but coming through the calm' (1865;
J. A. Symonds, *Letters and Papers*, 1923, p. 10).
911. T. replied to criticism of this line: 'The costly funeral is all that poor
Annie could do for him after he was gone. This is entirely introduced for
her sake, and, in my opinion, quite necessary to the perfection of the Poem
and the simplicity of the narrative.'

O you chorus of indolent reviewers,
Irresponsible, indolent reviewers,
Look, I come to the test, a tiny poem
All composed in a metre of Catullus,
5   All in quantity, careful of my motion,
Like the skater on ice that hardly bears him,
Lest I fall unawares before the people,
Waking laughter in indolent reviewers.
Should I flounder awhile without a tumble
10   Through this metrification of Catullus,
They should speak to me not without a welcome,
All that chorus of indolent reviewers.
Hard, hard, hard is it, only not to tumble,
So fantastical is the dainty metre.
15   Wherefore slight me not wholly, nor believe me
Too presumptuous, indolent reviewers.
O blatant Magazines, regard me rather —
Since I blush to belaud myself a moment —
As some rare little rose, a piece of inmost
20   Horticultural art, or half coquette-like
Maiden, not to be greeted unbenignly.

¶334. 2] Not HnMS.
3. Look, I] Here I MS.
4. 'The Phalaecian hendecasyllable, the metre in which all but seventeen of the short poems 1–60 are written' (C. J. Fordyce, Catullus, 1961, p. 83). On the metre and an echo of Catullus, see J. Ferguson, English Studies in Africa xii (1969) 43–4.
10. metrification] versification MS.
14. fantastical] tyrannical MS.
15. slight] scorn MS.
17. blatant] loud-lung'd MS.
19. rare little] 1864; exquisite 1863. Presumably changed because of the doubt as to éxquisite or exquísite.
19–20] As some exquisite rose, or half-coquettish MS.
19–21. Cp. Catullus lxii 39–45: ut flos in saeptis secretus nascitur hortis . . . / sic virgo dum intacta manet, dum cara suis est. ('As a flower springs up secretly in a fenced garden . . . so a maiden, whilst she remains untouched, so long is she dear to her own.')
21. greeted] treated MS.

344 Northern Farmer

NEW STYLE

Published *1869* ('*1870*'). The Duke of Argyll wrote to T., 18 Feb. 1865: 'I hear you have got something new to match the *Lincolnshire Farmer*' (*Lincoln*). Walter White refers to it, 9 July 1865 (*Journals*, 1898, p. 160). T. says it was 'founded on a single sentence: "When I canters my 'erse along the ramper (highway) I 'ears 'proputty, proputty, proputty'".' Cp. *Northern Farmer, Old Style* (II 619). Contrast this comic treatment of 'marriage-hindering Mammon' with that in *Maud* and in the other poems connected with Rosa Baring. All glossarial notes below are by T.

I

Dosn't thou 'ear my 'erse's legs, as they canters awaäy?
Proputty, proputty, proputty—that's what I 'ears 'em saäy.
Proputty, proputty, proputty—Sam, thou's an ass for thy paaïns:
Theer's moor sense i' one o' 'is legs nor in all thy braaïns.

II

5 Woä—theer's a craw to pluck wi' tha, Sam: yon's parson's 'ouse—
Dosn't thou knaw that a man mun be eäther a man or a mouse?
Time to think on it then; for thou'll be twenty to weeäk.
Proputty, proputty—woä then woä—let ma 'ear mysén speäk.

III

Me an' thy muther, Sammy, 'as beän a-talkin' o' thee;
10 Thou's beän talkin' to muther, an' she beän a tellin' it me.
Thou'll not marry for munny—thou's sweet upo' parson's lass—
Noä—thou'll marry for luvv—an' we boäth on us thinks tha an ass.

IV

Seeä'd her todaäy goä by—Saäint's-daäy—they was ringing the bells.
She's a beauty thou thinks—an' soä is scoors o' gells,
15 Them as 'as munny an' all—wot's a beauty?—the flower as blaws.
But proputty, proputty sticks, an' proputty, proputty graws.

V

Do'ant be stunt: taäke time: I knaws what maäkes tha sa mad.
Warn't I craäzed fur the lasses mysén when I wur a lad?
But I knawed a Quaäker feller as often 'as towd ma this:
20 'Doänt thou marry for munny, but goä wheer munny is!'

¶344. *7. to weeäk*: this week.
17. stunt: obstinate.

VI

An' I went wheer munny war: an' thy muther coom to 'and,
Wi' lots o' munny laaïd by, an' a nicetish bit o' land.
Maäybe she warn't a beauty:–I niver giv it a thowt–
But warn't she as good to cuddle an' kiss as a lass as 'ant nowt?

VII

25   Parson's lass 'ant nowt, an' she weänt 'a nowt when 'e's deäd,
Mun be a guvness, lad, or summut, and addle her breäd:
Why? fur 'e's nobbut a curate, an' weänt niver git hissen clear,
An' 'e maäde the bed as 'e ligs on afoor 'e coomed to the shere.

VIII

An' thin 'e coomed to the parish wi' lots o' Varsity debt,
30   Stook to his taaïl they did, an' 'e 'ant got shut on 'em yet.
An' 'e ligs on 'is back i' the grip, wi' noän to lend 'im a shuvv,
Woorse nor a far-weltered yowe: fur, Sammy, 'e married fur luvv.

IX

Luvv? what's luvv? thou can luvv thy lass an' 'er munny too,
Maakin' 'em goä togither as they've good right to do.
35   Could'n I luvv thy muther by cause o' 'er munny laaïd by?
Naäy–fur I luvved 'er a vast sight moor fur it: reäson why.

X

Ay an' thy muther says thou wants to marry the lass,
Cooms of a gentleman burn: an' we boäth on us think tha an ass.
Woä then, proputty, wiltha?–an ass as near as mays nowt–
40   Woä then, wiltha? dangtha!–the bees is as fell as owt.

XI

Breäk me a bit o' the esh for his 'eäd lad, out o' the fence!
Gentleman burn! what's gentleman burn? is it shillins an' pence?
Proputty, proputty's ivrything 'ere, an', Sammy, I'm blest
If it isn't the saäme oop yonder, fur them as 'as it's the best.

XII

45   Tis'n them as 'as munny as breäks into 'ouses an' steäls,
Them as 'as coäts to their backs an' taäkes their regular meäls.
Noä, but it's them as niver knaws wheer a meäl's to be 'ad.
Taäke my word for it, Sammy, the poor in a loomp is bad.

XIII

Them or thir feythers, tha sees, mun 'a beän a laäzy lot,
50   Fur work mun 'a gone to the gittin' whiniver munny was got.

26. *addle*: earn.
27. *hissen clear*] *1888*; naw 'igher *1869–86*.
32. *far-weltered*: or fow-weltered,–said of a sheep lying on its back.
39. *mays nowt*: makes nothing.
40. *the bees is as fell as owt*: the flies are as fierce as anything.

Feyther 'ad ammost nowt; leästways 'is munny was 'id.
But 'e tued an' moiled 'issén deäd, an 'e died a good un, 'e did.

xiv

Look thou theer wheer Wrigglesby beck cooms out by the 'ill!
Feyther run oop to the farm, an' I runs oop to the mill;
55 An' I'll run oop to the brig, an' that thou'll live to see;
And if thou marries a good un I'll leäve the land to thee.

xv

Thim's my noätions, Sammy, wheerby I means to stick;
But if thou marries a bad un, I'll leäve the land to Dick.–
Coom oop, proputty, proputty–that's what I 'ears 'im saäy–
60 Proputty, proputty, proputty–canter an' canter awaäy.

349 'Flower in the crannied wall'

Published *1869* ('*1870*'). 'The flower was plucked out of a wall at "Waggoners Wells", near Haslemere' (T.).

Flower in the crannied wall,
I pluck you out of the crannies,
I hold you here, root and all, in my hand,
Little flower–but *if* I could understand
5 What you are, root and all, and all in all,
I should know what God and man is.

[1869. *The Coming of Arthur, The Holy Grail, Pelleas and Ettarre, The Passing of Arthur*–see *pp. 677, 875, 903, 959*]

357 In the Garden at Swainston

Published 1874, Cabinet Edition. Written or pondered 31 May 1870 (*Mem.* ii 97–8; see *CT*, p. 389), on the occasion of the funeral of T.'s friend and neighbour Sir John Simeon, who died 21 May at Fribourg. E.T. wrote to

¶349. *3. I hold*] *1882*; Hold *1869–81*. Corrected by T. in his copy of *Works, 1881* (*Lincoln*).
5. T. wrote to Spedding, 19 Jan. 1870: 'Where is the difficulty of that line in the Flower? it is rather rough certainly, but had you followed the clue of "little flower" in the preceding line you would not have stumbled over this, which is accentual anapaest–"What you afe–root and áll"–rough, doubtless' (*Letters* ii 540).

H.T.: 'Nightingales were singing, beautiful roses were all about the house and gardens and lilacs were in full bloom and the contrast only added to the sadness' (1 June 1870); and 28 Nov. 1871: 'Thou wilt be glad to hear that Papa has done a little song about the day of our dear Sir John's burial. It is not quite finished yet, perhaps' (*Letters of E.T.*, pp. 258, 279). The 'three dead men' (l. 15) were Arthur Hallam, Henry Lushington and Simeon (T.). Cp. the elegy *In the Valley of Cauteretz* (*p. 590*).

> Nightingales warbled without,
>   Within was weeping for thee:
> Shadows of three dead men
>   Walked in the walks with me,
>   Shadows of three dead men and thou wast one
> 5   of the three.
>
> Nightingales sang in his woods:
>   The Master was far away:
> Nightingales warbled and sang
>   Of a passion that lasts but a day;
>   Still in the house in his coffin the Prince of
> 10   courtesy lay.
>
> Two dead men have I known
>   In courtesy like to thee:
> Two dead men have I loved
>   With a love that ever will be:
>   Three dead men have I loved and thou art last
> 15   of the three.

[1871. *The Last Tournament*—see *p. 920*.
1872. *Gareth and Lynette*, and *To the Queen: Idylls of the King*—See *pp. 693, 973*.
1874. *Balin and Balan*—See *p. 787*]

¶ 357. 6–7. L. G. Whitbread notes the fame (long before the Simeon family came) of the nightingales at Swainston, and says of 'The Master': 'the title by which Sir John had been regularly addressed ... Before his conversion to Rome in 1851 he had been a prominent Island Freemason, several times Master of the Newport lodge; and for three successive seasons, in 1854–6, he served as Master of the Isle of Wight Foxhounds' (*VP* xiii, 1975, 61–9). 10. Martin (p. 495*n*) compares *Balin and Balan* 252, where 'Arthur is described as "the king of courtesy", as if to establish Hallam's primacy in the trinity of T.'s affections'. T. wrote of Simeon as 'the very Prince of Courtesy' in a letter to Lady Simeon, 27 June 1870 (*Letters* ii 551).

366 Battle of Brunanburh

Published *1880*; among 'Translations'. Knowles requested it, 6 Jan. 1877, for the first number of the *Nineteenth Century* (see III 23; *Lincoln*; P. Metcalf, *TLS*, 23 June 1972; also her *James Knowles*, 1980, p. 277). T. said: 'I have more or less availed myself of my son's [H.T.'s] prose translation of this poem in the *Contemporary Review* (Nov. 1876).' T. takes over much from H.T., e.g. ll. 23, 30, 'the bark's bosom' (49), 'on the fallow flood' (61), 99, 110; but it is clear that T. also studied the original. Like H.T., he used the text and translation in E. Guest's *History of English Rhythms* (1838); the copy at *Lincoln* has annotations by H.T. In *Harold*, written and published 1876, T. twice refers to 'that old song of Brunanburg / Where England conquered' (V i), and the verse (IV iii) breaks into such a style: 'Marked how the war-axe swang, / Heard how the war-horn sang, / Marked how the spear-head sprang, / Heard how the shield-wall rang, / Iron on iron clang, / Anvil on hammer bang –.' The tenth-century Old English poem is one of a group of panegyrics on royalty, using an earlier style both in metre and diction. T.'s is in general a close translation. His metre is unrhymed dactylics and trochaics: 'In rendering this Old English war-song into modern language and alliterative rhythm I have made free use of the dactylic beat. I suppose that the original was chanted to a slow, swinging recitative' (*Harold*, Eversley). T. wrote a few lines of a translation of *Beowulf* 258–63, including 'The army's leader / His wordhoard unlocked ...' *H.Nbk 4* (*c.* 1830–1). T.'s headnote: 'Constantinus, King of the Scots, after having sworn allegiance to Athelstan, allied himself with the Danes of Ireland under Anlaf, and invading England, was defeated by Athelstan and his brother Edmund with great slaughter at Brunanburh in the year 937.' T. had a copy of Joseph Bosworth's *Anglo-Saxon Dictionary* (J. Hixson and P. Scott, *TRB* ii, 1976, 197). On T.'s poem as a translation, see M. Alexander, *TRB* iv (1985).

I
Athelstan King,
Lord among Earls,
Bracelet-bestower and
Baron of Barons,
5   He with his brother,
Edmund Atheling,
Gaining a lifelong
Glory in battle,
Slew with the sword-edge
10   There by Brunanburh,
Brake the shield-wall,
Hewed the lindenwood,
Hacked the battleshield,
Sons of Edward with hammered brands.

II

15
          Theirs was a greatness
          Got from their Grandsires –
          Theirs that so often in
          Strife with their enemies
     Struck for their hoards and their hearths and their
          homes.

III

20
          Bowed the spoiler,
          Bent the Scotsman,
          Fell the shipcrews
          Doomed to the death.
     All the field with blood of the fighters
25
          Flowed, from when first the great
          Sun-star of morningtide,
          Lamp of the Lord God
          Lord everlasting,
     Glode over earth till the glorious creature
30
          Sank to his setting.

IV

          There lay many a man
          Marred by the javelin,
          Men of the Northland
          Shot over shield.
35
          There was the Scotsman
          Weary of war.

V

          We the West-Saxons,
          Long as the daylight
          Lasted, in companies
40
     Troubled the track of the host that we hated,
     Grimly with swords that were sharp from the
          grindstone,
     Fiercely we hacked at the flyers before us.

¶366. *3–4*. T.'s expansion of *beorna beahgifa*, ring-giver of warriors.
6. Atheling: a member of an English royal family.
12. 1880 note: 'Shields of lindenwood.'
29. Glode: glided, suggested by the original's *glad* and probably by
Shelley's usage, three times in *The Revolt of Islam* (M. L. Woods, *Poetry
Review* xxxiii (1942) 277).
30. Sank] *1882*; Sunk *1880–81*. Corrected by T. in his copy of *Works*,
1881 (*Lincoln*).
37. We: added by T., as in l. 42.

VI

Mighty the Mercian,
Hard was his hand-play,
45   Sparing not any of
Those that with Anlaf,
Warriors over the
Weltering waters
Borne in the bark's-bosom,
50   Drew to this island:
Doomed to the death.

VII

Five young kings put asleep by the sword-stroke,
Seven strong Earls of the army of Anlaf
Fell on the war-field, numberless numbers,
55 Shipmen and Scotsmen.

VIII

Then the Norse leader,
Dire was his need of it,
Few were his following,
Fled to his warship:
60 Fleeted his vessel to sea with the king in it,
Saving his life on the fallow flood.

IX

Also the crafty one,
Constantinus,
Crept to his North again,
65   Hoar-headed hero!

X

Slender warrant had
He to be proud of
The welcome of war-knives —
He that was reft of his
70   Folk and his friends that had
Fallen in conflict,
Leaving his son too
Lost in the carnage,

43. *Mighty*: added by T.
50. *this island*: in the original simply 'land'.
61. *fallow*: yellowish, *fealo*.
66. *warrant*] 1882; reason 1880–81. Corrected by T. in his copy of *Works*,
1881 (*Lincoln*).
68. *welcome of war-knives*: literally 'fellowship or meeting of . . .', a kenning
for battle.

Mangled to morsels,
75   A youngster in war!

XI

Slender reason had
He to be glad of
The clash of the war-glaive—
Traitor and trickster
80   And spurner of treaties—
He nor had Anlaf
With armies so broken
A reason for bragging
That they had the better
85   In perils of battle
On places of slaughter—
The struggle of standards,
The rush of the javelins,
The crash of the charges,
90   The wielding of weapons—
The play that they played with
The children of Edward.

XII

Then with their nailed prows
Parted the Norsemen, a
95   Blood-reddened relic of
Javelins over
The jarring breaker, the deep-sea billow,
Shaping their way toward Dyflen again,
Shamed in their souls.

XIII

100   Also the brethren,
King and Atheling,
Each in his glory,
Went to his own in his own West-Saxonland,
Glad of the war.

79–80. T. freely adapts the original, literally 'the grey-haired man, the old deceiver'.
88. rush: literally 'meeting'.
89. 1880 note: 'Literally "the gathering of men"'.
96–7. over | The jarring breaker: the original has *on Dingesmere*, probably the name of a part of the sea, but possibly from *dinnes*, noise.
98. 1880 note: 'Dublin'.
102. The original has simply 'both together'.

XIV

105 Many a carcase they left to be carrion,
Many a livid one, many a sallow-skin –
Left for the white tailed eagle to tear it, and
Left for the horny-nibbed raven to rend it, and
Gave to the garbaging war-hawk to gorge it, and
110 That gray beast, the wolf of the weald.

XV

Never had huger
Slaughter of heroes
Slain by the sword-edge –
Such as old writers
115 Have writ of in histories –
Hapt in this isle, since
Up from the East hither
Saxon and Angle from
Over the broad billow
120 Broke into Britain with
Haughty war-workers who
Harried the Welshman, when
Earls that were lured by the
Hunger of glory gat
125 Hold of the land.

377 Prefatory Poem to My Brother's Sonnets

Midnight, June 30, 1879

Published 1880, with Charles Tennyson Turner's *Collected Sonnets*, where the title was simply the subsequent subtitle; then *1885*. In 1880 it has the subtitle only, which provides the date of composition; Charles died 25 April 1879. There are drafts in *H.Nbk 33* (*A* below) and *Lpr 186* (*B*). Cp. 'Frater Ave atque Vale' (*p. 627*). R. Evans (*TRB* iv, 1983, 81–91) relates T.'s poem to his brother's poems, citing parallels (including in the movement of T.'s poem): 'poised at that moment when day succeeds day, when June passes into July ... for at midnight on 30 June we are exactly at the year's centre'.

106. The original is agreed to apply not to the corpses, but to the eagle (dun-coated) and the raven (dark-coated). Cp. *Boädicea* 11–15; eagle, raven, carrion, carcase, 'kite and kestrel, wolf and wolfkin, from the wilderness, wallow in it'.
123–4. The original is agreed to mean simply 'glorious Earls'.

I

Midnight–in no midsummer tune
The breakers lash the shores:
The cuckoo of a joyless June
Is calling out of doors:

5 And thou hast vanished from thine own
To that which looks like rest,
True brother, only to be known
By those who love thee best.

II

Midnight–and joyless June gone by,
10 And from the deluged park
The cuckoo of a worse July
Is calling through the dark:

But thou art silent underground,
And o'er thee streams the rain,
15 True poet, surely to be found
When Truth is found again.

III

And, now to these unsummered skies
The summer bird is still,
Far off a phantom cuckoo cries
20 From out a phantom hill;

And through this midnight breaks the sun
Of sixty years away,
The light of days when life begun,
The days that seem today,

25 When all my griefs were shared with thee,
As all my hopes were thine–
As all thou wert was one with me,
May all thou art be mine!

¶377. *17–20*] Not *A*.
17] Midnight. The ceaseless shower falls, *B*.
18. summer] sunless *B*.
19] Flown! But [At last *1st reading*] a phantom cuckoo calls [falls *1st reading*] *B*.
23] The days when life had just begun, *A*.
24 ∧ *25*]   Our brother-days that will not die–
                  And, now thou art withdrawn
                  So far I cannot follow, I cry
                  To that first light of dawn *B*
26. As] *1885*; And *1880*.
27 ∧ *28*] So, brother, whatsoe'er thou be, *A*.

384 To Alfred Tennyson
My Grandson

Published as the dedication of *1880*. It was added by pen to a *Lincoln* trial edition of *1880*. T.'s grandson was born 20 Nov. 1878, so this poem was written *c*. May 1880 (l. 3). Cp. *Little Aubrey* (III 637). The title in *H.Lpr 236* is *To Alfred Tennyson, babe, from Alfred Tennyson, Septuagenarian*.

Golden-haired Ally whose name is one with mine,
Crazy with laughter and babble and earth's new wine,
Now that the flower of a year and a half is thine,
O little blossom, O mine, and mine of mine,
5   Glorious poet who never hast written a line,
Laugh, for the name at the head of my verse is thine.
Mayst thou never be wronged by the name that is mine!

385 'Frater Ave atque Vale'

Published *Nineteenth Century*, March 1883; then *1885*. Written on a visit to Sirmio, June 1880 (*Mem.* ii 247). It alludes to T.'s brother Charles, who had died in 1879 (cp. *Prefatory Poem to My Brother's Sonnets*, p. 625). The beauty of Sirmio is the subject of Catullus's *Poem* xxxi, which begins *Paene insularum, Sirmio, insularumque / ocelle* (T.'s 'all-but-island'); exclaims *o venusta Sirmio* (T.'s l. 2); and ends *o Lydiae lacus undae: / ridete, quicquid est domi cachinnorum* (T.'s l. 8). T. characteristically combines this poem of joy (*o quid solutis est beatius curis*) with the sadness of Catullus's *Poem* ci, an elegy for his dead brother, beginning *Multas per gentes et multa per aequora vectus* (apt to T.'s travels), and ending *atque in perpetuum, frater, ave atque vale*. The mingling of the two moods resembles *Tears, idle tears*: '. . . gather to the eyes, / In looking on the happy Autumn-fields'.

T. wrote to Gladstone, 3 Nov. 1880 (*Letters* iii; *Mem.* ii 239): 'I am glad too that you are touched by my little prefatory poem [*Prefatory Poem to My Brother's Sonnets*], so far as to honour it by a comparison with those lovely lines "Multas per terras [*for* gentes] et multa per aequora vectus", of which as you truly say neither I "nor any other can surpass the beauty" – no, nor can any modern elegy, so long as men retain the least hope in the afterlife of those whom they loved, equal in pathos the desolation of that everlasting farewell, "Atque in perpetuum frater Ave atque Vale" ' On the importance of Catullus' poem to T., see J. Ferguson, *English Studies in Africa* xii (1969) 54–7.

Row us out from Desenzano, to your Sirmione row!
So they rowed, and there we landed–'O venusta
   Sirmio!'
There to me through all the groves of olive in the summer
   glow,
There beneath the Roman ruin where the purple flowers
   grow,
5 Came that 'Ave atque Vale' of the Poet's hopeless woe,
Tenderest of Roman poets nineteen-hundred years ago,
'Frater Ave atque Vale'–as we wandered to and fro
Gazing at the Lydian laughter of the Garda Lake below
Sweet Catullus's all-but-island, olive-silvery Sirmio!

394 To Virgil
Written at the Request of the Mantuans for the Nineteenth Centenary of Virgil's Death

Published *Nineteenth Century*, Sept. 1882; then *1885*. T. wrote to Knowles, Aug. 1882: 'you can put To Virgil if you like–I don't think it matters much. I am not quite satisfied with the VIth–but the thing must go' (*Letters* iii). The letter of request from the Vergilian Academy of Mantua was dated 23 June 1882: 'One verse of yours, one writing however small, that could be published in the Vergilian Album will be agreeable, not only to us ...' (*Mat.* iv 26–7). The poem was acknowledged 10 Sept. Cp. *To Dante* (II 691). D. Bush points out that the 'rolling trochaic lines suggest something of the sound of the Virgilian hexameter' (*Major British Writers*, 1959, ii 463). J. B. Trapp reproduces the MS from the Academy's files (*TLS*, 18 Sept. 1981); he notes the variants, of which the most important is that 'the lay-out of the manuscript poem differs from all the published versions, which print it in ten numbered stanzas of two lines each, broken at the caesura, so that they look like twice two ... When he sent it to Mantua, T. clearly intended it as a single unit of twenty long trochaic lines, rhyming in couplets'.

I
Roman Virgil, thou that singest
   Ilion's lofty temples robed in fire,

¶385. *3. through all*] among *H.Nbk 47 1st reading.*
6. T. had apparently called Catullus 'tenderest of Roman poets' in 1846–7 (*Mem.* i 266).
8. *laughter*] laughters MS. D. Bush, *Major British Writers* (1959) ii 463, observes that the ancient Etruscans of this region were said to be descended from the Lydians of Asia Minor.
¶394. *1–2. Aeneid:* 'temples', Book ii; Dido, iv; 'faith', vi.

Ilion falling, Rome arising,
  wars, and filial faith, and Dido's pyre;

II
Landscape-lover, lord of language
  more than he that sang the Works and Days,
All the chosen coin of fancy
  flashing out from many a golden phrase;

III
Thou that singest wheat and woodland,
5   tilth and vineyard, hive and horse and herd;
All the charm of all the Muses
  often flowering in a lonely word;

IV
Poet of the happy Tityrus
  piping underneath his beechen bowers;
Poet of the poet-satyr
  whom the laughing shepherd bound with
    flowers;

V
Chanter of the Pollio, glorying
  in the blissful years again to be,
Summers of the snakeless meadow,
10   unlaborious earth and oarless sea;

---

3. *he*: Hesiod, Virgil's predecessor in writing of rural life.
5. *Georgics*, as summarized at i 1–5: *Quid faciat laetas segetes, quo sidere terram* . . . . *tilth*] tithe MS. H.T. curiously said that 'There was at first a curious misprint in the poem', tithe (*Mem.* ii 320).
7. *Eclogue* i 1: *Tityre, tu patulae recubans sub tegmine fagi.* ('You, Tityrus, lie under your spreading beech's covert.')
8. Silenus, seized in *Eclogue* vi 19: *iniciunt ipsis ex vincula sertis.* ('They cast him into fetters made from his own garlands.')
9. *Eclogue* iv, prophetic of a golden age, often taken as anticipating the birth of Christ.
10. *Eclogue* iv: *occidet et serpens* (24); *At tibi prima, puer, mullo munuscula cultu / errantis hederas passim cum baccare tellus* . . . (18–19: 'But for thee, child, shall the earth untilled pour forth, as her first pretty gifts, straggling ivy with foxglove everywhere'); *cedet et ipse mari vector* (38: 'even the trader shall quit the sea').

VI

Thou that seëst Universal
Nature moved by Universal Mind;
Thou majestic in thy sadness
at the doubtful doom of human kind;

VII

Light among the vanished ages;
star that gildest yet this phantom shore;
Golden branch amid the shadows,
kings and realms that pass to rise no more;

VIII

Now thy Forum roars no longer,
15   fallen every purple Cæsar's dome –
Though thine ocean-roll of rhythm
sound for ever of Imperial Rome –

IX

Now the Rome of slaves hath perished,
and the Rome of freemen holds her place,
I, from out the Northern Island
sundered once from all the human race,

X

I salute thee, Mantovano,
I that loved thee since my day began,
Wielder of the stateliest measure
20   ever moulded by the lips of man.

11. Aeneid vi 727: *mens agitat molem* ('mind sways the mass').
12. Aeneid i 462: *sunt lacrimae rerum et mentem mortalia tangunt* ('there are tears for misfortune and mortal sorrows touch the heart').
14. Praising Virgil as himself the golden bough that gives mysterious access to the underworld, *Aeneid* vi 208.
15–16] Quoted in the halls of Council,
          speaking yet in every schoolboy's home,
Only living Imperator
          left of all thine own imperial Rome.
                              H.Nbk 66, early draft
15. purple Cæsar: Horace's *Odes* I xxxv 12: *purpurei tyranni.*
18. H.T. cited *Eclogue* i 66: *et penitus toto divisos orbe Britannos* ('and the Britons, wholly sundered from all the world').
19. Mantovano: Mantuan. H.T. cited Dante, *Purgatorio* vi 74: *Mantovano*, which allows T. to join Dante in venerating Virgil.

398 To E. FitzGerald

Published *1885*, introducing *Tiresias* (I 622). Written June 1883; Edward FitzGerald died 14 June, and T. wrote to Frederick Pollock: 'I had written a poem to him within the last week – a dedication – which he will never see' (17 June 1883; *Letters* iii). T. therefore concluded *Tiresias* by returning to FitzGerald and mourning his death (below). The poem recalls the last visit by T. and H.T. to FitzGerald in Sept. 1876, as H.T. points out. For T.'s change of conception, see ll. 50–6n (*H.Nbk 46*).

> Old Fitz, who from your suburb grange,
>   Where once I tarried for a while,
> Glance at the wheeling Orb of change,
>   And greet it with a kindly smile;
> 5   Whom yet I see as there you sit
>   Beneath your sheltering garden-tree,
> And while your doves about you flit,
>   And plant on shoulder, hand and knee,
> Or on your head their rosy feet,
> 10   As if they knew your diet spares
> Whatever moved in that full sheet
>   Let down to Peter at his prayers;
> Who live on milk and meal and grass;
>   And once for ten long weeks I tried
> 15   Your table of Pythagoras,
>   And seemed at first 'a thing enskied'
> (As Shakespeare has it) airy-light
>   To float above the ways of men,
> Then fell from that half-spiritual height
> 20   Chilled, till I tasted flesh again
> One night when earth was winter-black,
>   And all the heavens flashed in frost;

¶398. *1. grange*: FitzGerald's home, Little Grange, Woodbridge, Suffolk.
3. the wheeling Orb: as in *On golden evenings* (1827), by T.'s brother Charles.
11–12. Acts x 11–13: 'And a certain vessel descending unto him, as it had been a great sheet knit at the four corners, and let down to the earth: Wherein were all manner of four-footed beasts of the earth, and wild beasts, and creeping things, and fowls of the air. And there came a voice to him, Rise, Peter: kill, and eat.'
15. Pythagoras's vegetarianism is connected with the belief that the transmigration of souls included animals.
16. Measure for Measure I iv 34–5: 'I hold you as a thing enskied and sainted / By your renouncement – an immortal spirit.' 'Renouncement' (Isabella's nunhood) calls out the allusion, which leads into ll. 18–19.

And on me, half-asleep, came back
That wholesome heat the blood had lost,
25 And set me climbing icy capes
And glaciers, over which there rolled
To meet me long-armed vines with grapes
Of Eshcol hugeness; for the cold
Without, and warmth within me, wrought
30 To mould the dream; but none can say
That Lenten fare makes Lenten thought,
Who reads your golden Eastern lay,
Than which I know no version done
In English more divinely well;
35 A planet equal to the sun
Which cast it, that large infidel
Your Omar; and your Omar drew
Full-handed plaudits from our best
In modern letters, and from two,
40 Old friends outvaluing all the rest,
Two voices heard on earth no more;
But we old friends are still alive,
And I am nearing seventy-four,
While you have touched at seventy-five,

23–8. 'One of the most wonderful experiences I ever had was this. I had
gone without meat for six weeks, living only on vegetables; and at the end
of the time, when I came to eat a mutton-chop, I shall never forget the
sensation. I never felt such joy in my blood. When I went to sleep, I
dreamt that I saw the vines of the South, with huge Eschol branches,
trailing over the glaciers of the North' (*Mem.* ii 317).

28. *Numbers* xiii 23: 'And they came unto the brook of Eshcol, and cut
down from thence a branch with one cluster of grapes, and they bare it
between two upon a staff' (Eshcol, meaning 'a cluster of grapes').

32. *The Rubáiyát of Omar Khayyám*, published 1859 and subsequently
revised.

41. James Spedding, died 1881; and W. H. Brookfield, died 1874.

43–5. A Horatian touch; cp. *Epistles* I xx 27: *me quater undenos sciat
implevisse Decembris* ('let him know that I completed my forty-fourth
December in …'). T. would be 74 on 6 Aug. 1883; since FitzGerald was
born 31 March 1809 and died 14 June 1883, he never 'touched at seventy-
five', nor are these two ages compatible. T. thought that FitzGerald was 75 in
March 1883, and his 'birthday greeting' was going to be a month or two late.
T. made the mistake because of misreading the end of FitzGerald's letter of 19
April 1883, as 'Yours and all yours as ever at 75' (*Mem.* ii 275–6); the letter,
pinned into *Mat. (Lincoln)*, ends 'as ever – æt: 75'; *anno ætatis suae*: in his 75th
year. (C. Ricks, *The Library* 5th ser. xxv, 1970, 156.) A. M. and A. B.

45   And so I send a birthday line
       Of greeting; and my son, who dipt
    In some forgotten book of mine
       With sallow scraps of manuscript,
       And dating many a year ago,
50   Has hit on this, which you will take

Terhune retain the error in their edition of FitzGerald's *Letters*, and then say
that FitzGerald calculated eccentrically. T.'s lines resemble Peacock's *Letter to
Lord Broughton*, a copy of which is among T.'s papers (*Lincoln*): 'Old friend,
whose rhymes so kindly mix / Thoughts grave and gay with seventy-six, / I
hope it may to you be given / To do the same at seventy-seven; / Whence
your still living friends may date / A new good wish for seventy-eight; / And
thence again extend the line, / Until it passes seventy-nine.'

45–6]   At seventy-five! I asked a friend
             What I should send you on the day
             When you were born. He answered, 'Send
             Bound in the sumptuousest way
             Your books'–'He knows them line by line'–
             'Well then, send this', for he had dipt
                                    H.Nbk 46 1st draft

49. *many a*] forty *MS 1st reading.*
50. *this*: Tiresias.
50–6] *There are many fragmentary drafts in MS:*

(i)   And found these lines, which you will take,
             Old Fitz, and value, as I know,
               Less for their own than for my sake,
             Who love you,
                      Yours

(ii) *includes as ll.* 53–4:
             Of me remembering gracious times,
               Who keep the love of older days.

(iii)   Has hit on this, which you will take,
              My Fitz, and welcome, as I know,
               Less for its own, than for my sake,
             Who love you always.
                     Ah if I
             Should play Tiresias to the times,
             I fear I might but prophesy
             Of faded faiths, and civic crimes,
              And fierce Transition's blood-red morn,
             And years with lawless voices loud,
             Old vessels from their moorings torn,
             And cataclysm and thundercloud,

My Fitz, and welcome, as I know
    Less for its own than for the sake
Of one recalling gracious times,
    When, in our younger London days,
55 You found some merit in my rhymes,
    And I more pleasure in your praise.

'One height and one far-shining fire'
    And while I fancied that my friend
For this brief idyll would require
60   A less diffuse and opulent end,
And would defend his judgment well,
    If I should deem it over nice—
The tolling of his funeral bell
    Broke on my Pagan Paradise,

And one lean hope, that at the last
    Perchance—if this small world endures—
Our heirs may find the stormy Past
    Has left their Present purer.
                            Yours

An earlier draft of the last four lines reads:
And yet if our poor earth should last,
    And evolution still endures,
Our heirs may find that stormy Past
    True mother of their Present.
                            Yours

T. and FitzGerald had been friends since about 1835. Cp. FitzGerald's
letter of 1862: 'You can't remember this: in old Charlotte Street, ages ago'
(*Tennyson and His Friends*, p. 130). The passage of political prophecy in
(iii) links the dedication and *Tiresias* itself (cp. *Tiresias* 71–5), but T. must
have decided that its fierceness and lack of connection with FitzGerald
would obtrude. Cp. ll. 54–6 with Byron, *Don Juan* XVI lxxxii 1: 'I knew
him in his livelier London days', rhyming with 'earned its praise' (in a stanza
which rhymes on 'Lincoln' and so is the more likely to have lodged with T.).
57. From the closing line of *Tiresias* (l 630), which followed l. 56 in *1885*.
64 ∧ 5]   And drove the shadows far apart
                    With echoes of our College hall—
                Old voices. Hushed the loyal heart,
                    The wit, truth, delicate humour, all. *MS, deleted*
This *MS* also has a deleted passage that continues from l. 80:
                Who, sorrowing, send you, to be laid
                    Upon your coffin, flowers, a sign
                You flower in me and will not fade
                    While my few years on earth are mine.

65 And mixt the dreams of classic times,
    And all the phantoms of the dream,
  With present grief, and made the rhymes,
    That missed his living welcome, seem
  Like would-be guests an hour too late,
70   Who down the highway moving on
  With easy laughter find the gate
    Is bolted, and the master gone.
  Gone into darkness, that full light
    Of friendship! past, in sleep, away
75 By night, into the deeper night!
    The deeper night? A clearer day
  Than our poor twilight dawn on earth—
    If night, what barren toil to be!
  What life, so maimed by night, were worth
80   Our living out? Not mine to me
  Remembering all the golden hours
    Now silent, and so many dead,
  And him the last; and laying flowers,
    This wreath, above his honoured head,
85 And praying that, when I from hence
    Shall fade with him into the unknown,
  My close of earth's experience
    May prove as peaceful as his own.

400 The Dead Prophet

182–

Published *1885*. Written 1882–4, judging from MSS in *H.Nbks 52* and *68* and from its probably being occasioned by J. A. Froude's frank revelations about Carlyle's private life (1882–4). In a letter to Watts, 10 Dec. 1885, H.T. said that it was one of 'the old ones' that he had made T. touch up, and that it was 'written ten or twelve years ago' (*Letters* iii); but this is unlikely and may be protective. T. said it was 'about no particular prophet', but H.T.'s note goes on: 'At this time he said of Mr and Mrs Carlyle: "I am sure that Froude is wrong. I saw a great deal of them. They were always 'chaffing' one another, and they could not have done that if they had got on so 'badly together' as Froude thinks."' Froude's Preface (1882) had spoken of Carlyle as a 'teacher and a prophet in the Jewish sense of the word', and in 1884 his introductory note described Carlyle as 'a man who could thus take on himself the character of a prophet'. Cp. the beldam's argument in ll. 44–56 with Froude:

'When a man has exercised a large influence on the minds of his contemporaries, the world requires to know whether his own actions have corresponded with his teaching, and whether his moral and personal character entitles him to confidence. This is not idle curiosity; it is a legitimate demand. In proportion to a man's greatness is the scrutiny to which his conduct is submitted.'

Froude's introductory note spoke too of vague biographies as leaving great men 'a prey to be torn in pieces'. Moreover M. D. Conway (who himself had preceded Froude with a study of Carlyle) wrote of this controversy: 'Tennyson's main trouble seemed to be that the bones of Carlyle should be flung about' (*Autobiography*, 1904, ii 192)–note the metaphor. Froude protested, 20 March 1882, at T.'s having said Froude 'had sold [his] Master for thirty pieces of silver'; H.T. placated him, denying the rumour since T. had said no more than that 'it would have been better if you had omitted 3 or 4 pages' (*Lincoln*).
The poem does not appear in No. 1 of the *British Museum* trial editions of *1885*. No. 2 followed the poem with *By a Darwinian* (III 10), entitled *Reversion*, which is on the same subject. The fact that *Reversion* was, in this trial edition, on the same page is probably due to the printer; in the earlier trial edition (*Lincoln*), *Reversion* is in MS on the verso of the last page of the MS of *The Dead Prophet*. No. 3 added the note: 'It may be as well to state that this allegory is not in any way personal. The speaker in it is as imaginary as the prophet'. The false date '182–' does not appear in the *BM* trial editions; when T. first added a date to a *Lincoln* trial edition, he put '17—'. (Like *Aylmer's Field*, '1793', this suggests the French Revolution.) Cp. the veiling of *To——, After Reading a Life and Letters* (II 297), which is on the same theme of the intrusive biography, and which includes the germ of *The Dead Prophet*: 'For whom the carrion vulture waits / To tear his heart before the crowd!' Since this was about Keats, '182–' may have been suggested by Keats's death (1821). Cp. also T.'s poem of *1827*, *Come hither* (I 165), on the mocked corpse of Henri IV: 'There came a woman from the crowd and smote / The corpse upon the cheek.' (See l. 25n.) Since *Come hither* is about the French Revolution, by 1882 it might have come to suggest Carlyle. T.'s source for *Come hither* (*Quarterly Review* xxi (1819) 376) included: 'When the King is dead, his body was placed upon a carriage in such a position that the head hung down to the ground and the hair dragged upon the ground; a woman followed and with a besom threw dust upon the head of the corpse. At the same time, a cryer proclaimed, with a loud voice, O men! behold your King! he was your master yesterday, but the empire which he possessed is passed away.' Cp. also the MS versions of *Locksley Hall Sixty* 134: 'Pillory the dead face . . .', 'Pillory the dumb corpse . . .' A *Lincoln* trial edition added as epigraph (slightly misquoted) *Henry V* IV i 229–31: 'O hard condition, / Twin-born with greatness, subject to the breath / Of every fool.'

I

Dead!
And the Muses cried with a stormy cry
'Send them no more, for evermore.
Let the people die.'

II

5 Dead!
'Is it *he* then brought so low?'
And a careless people flocked from the fields
With a purse to pay for the show.

III

Dead, who had served his time,
10   Was one of the people's kings,
Had laboured in lifting them out of slime,
And showing them, souls have wings!

IV

Dumb on the winter heath he lay.
His friends had stript him bare,
15 And rolled his nakedness everyway
That all the crowd might stare.

V

A storm-worn signpost not to be read,
And a tree with a mouldered nest
On its barkless bones, stood stark by the dead;
20   And behind him, low in the West,

VI

With shifting ladders of shadow and light,
And blurred in colour and form,
The sun hung over the gates of Night,
And glared at a coming storm.

¶400. 1] There lay a prophet [dead man *1st reading*] on the heath, *H.Nbk 68*.
5–12] A prophet dead upon the heath *MS*.
14. *friends had*] best friend *MS*. The MS points to Froude.
15] Tore all the decent coverings off *MS*.
17–24] Not *MS*.

VII

25   Then glided a vulturous Beldam forth,
     That on dumb death had thriven;
    They called her 'Reverence' here upon earth,
     And 'The Curse of the Prophet' in Heaven.

VIII

    She knelt–'We worship him'–all but wept–
30   'So great so noble was he!'
    She cleared her sight, she arose, she swept
     The dust of earth from her knee.

IX

  'Great! for he spoke and the people heard,
     And his eloquence caught like a flame
35   From zone to zone of the world, till his Word
     Had won him a noble name.

X

  Noble! he sung, and the sweet sound ran
     Through palace and cottage door,
  For he touched on the whole sad planet of man,
40   The kings and the rich and the poor;

XI

  And he sung not alone of an old sun set,
     But a sun coming up in his youth!
  Great and noble–O yes–but yet–
     For man is a lover of Truth,

XII

45   And bound to follow, wherever she go
     Stark-naked, and up or down,
  Through her high hill-passes of stainless snow,
     Or the foulest sewer of the town–

XIII

  Noble and great–O ay–but then,
50   Though a prophet should have his due,
  Was he noblier-fashioned than other men?
    Shall we see to it, I and you?

25] There came a beldam from the crowd *MS*. Cp. 'There came a woman from the crowd', *Come hither* 21. See headnote.
26. dumb death] dead flesh *MS*.
27. here] *Not MS*.
29–68] *Not MS*.

XIV

For since he would sit on a Prophet's seat,
 As a lord of the Human soul,
55 We needs must scan him from head to feet
 Were it but for a wart or a mole?'

XV

His wife and his child stood by him in tears,
 But she–she pushed them aside.
'Though a name may last for a thousand years,
60 Yet a truth is a truth,' she cried.

XVI

And she that had haunted his pathway still,
 Had often truckled and cowered
When he rose in his wrath, and had yielded her
 will
 To the master, as overpowered,

XVII

65 She tumbled his helpless corpse about.
 'Small blemish upon the skin!
But I think we know what is fair without
 Is often as foul within.'

XVIII

She crouched, she tore him part from part,
70 And out of his body she drew
The red 'Blood-eagle' of liver and heart;
 She held them up to the view;

54] And preached of a deathless soul H.Nbk 52 *1st reading*. This MS has
pages missing, and consists only of ll. 49–56, plus two stanzas on different
pages:

  He found his truth in an old shadow-land,
   In a ghost-tale told us afresh.
  We prize a truth that is closer at hand,
   The Truth, my friends, in the flesh.'

  And one of the People arose with a frown,
   'Will you help the People to be
  By pulling the People's leaders down
   To the People's level?' but she,

69] She tore the Prophet's hidden part *Nbk 68*.
71. *Blood-eagle*: *1885* note: 'Old Viking term for lungs, liver, etc., when
torn by the conqueror out of the body of the conquered.'

XIX

She gabbled, as she groped in the dead,
   And all the people were pleased;
75 'See, what a little heart,' she said,
   'And the liver is half-diseased!'

XX

She tore the Prophet after death,
   And the people paid her well.
Lightnings flickered along the heath;
80   One shrieked 'The fires of Hell!'

417 Locksley Hall
Sixty Years After

Published *1886*. Written 1886, recited 27 Oct. (*Mem.* ii 324, 506). The title in the trial edition of *1886* (*British Library*) is *Locksley Hall 1886*. See *Locksley Hall* and headnote (p. *181*). H.*Nbks* 51, 53 (1885–6) and *Lpr 128* contain many drafts; some of the more important variants are given below, but without distinguishing in general between first and final readings. J. H. Buckley (p. 234) points out that T. 'strove through heavy revision of several early drafts to control the invective . . . late in the composition of the poem he added several lines' [151–4] of retreat, as he did in *Maud*. 'The nucleus of the poem' (T.) was ll. 13–15, which had been dropped from *Locksley Hall*. The idea of a sequel probably owed something to a comment by A. H. Japp in 1865 (*Three Great Teachers*, p. 132):

'The poet has here carried the poem to the strict limit of his experience at the time it was written. It closes, but does not cease. It abounds with suggestions as to a higher result in prospect. It points to a region of lofty possibility. In one respect, however, it was unsafe for the poet to leave his hero here; that is, when viewed simply from the formally moral stand-point, which requires that a direct lesson be drawn from everything. If, however, the poet ever again wrote on a kindred theme, it would test at once his insight and fuller experience, – whether he would conduct his hero to a more worthy goal.'

73] Her talons raked into the dead *MS.*
76 ∧ 7]   'The People! the People!' a thin ghost-cry
     Fled over the blasted tree,
    Far away to be lost in a stormy sky,
     'I had lifted them up:' but she, *BM trial edition 2*
80] They were the fires of Hell. *MS.* Perhaps suggested by Froude's introductory note: 'The fire in his soul burnt red to the end, and sparks flew from it which fell hot on those about him.'

Possibly T. was again influenced by the *Moállakát*, the acknowledged source of *Locksley Hall*; Amriolkais says, 'O how oft have I rejected the admonitions of a morose adviser, vehement in censuring my passion for thee; nor have I been moved by his reproaches!' For an important reply to T.'s onslaught on the age, see W. E. Gladstone, *Nineteenth Century*, Jan. 1887. On the biographical level, Rader (p. 58) suggests that T. was reappraising Rosa Baring and her husband (ll. 239-40). 'Edith' is T.'s wife Emily ('very woman of very woman,' l. 51, is applied to her, *Mem.* i 331), to whom the volume was dedicated. Sir Charles Tennyson (p. 493) stresses the reconciliation with the other branch of T.'s family at Bayons (e.g. ll. 43-4). For the death of T.'s son Lionel, see l. 55*n*. T. said that it was 'a dramatic poem, and the Dramatis Personae are imaginary'. 'My father said that the old man in the second *Locksley Hall* had a stronger faith in God and in human goodness than he had had in his youth; but he had also endeavoured to give the moods of despondency which are caused by the decreased energy of life.' T. said: 'There is not one touch of biography in it from beginning to end' (*Mem.* ii 329-31). T. wrote to C. Esmarch, 18 April 1888: 'I must object and strongly to the statement in your preface that *I* am the hero in either poem. I never had a cousin Amy. Locksley Hall is an entirely imaginative edifice. My grandsons are little boys. I am not even white-haired, I never had a gray hair in my head. The whole thing is a dramatic impersonation, but I find in almost all modern criticism this absurd tendency to personalities. Some of my thought *may* come out in the poem but am I therefore the hero? *There is not one* touch of *autobiography in it from end to end*' (*Letters* iii).

Late, my grandson! half the morning have I paced these sandy tracts,
Watched again the hollow ridges roaring into cataracts,

Wandered back to living boyhood while I heard the curlews call,
I myself so close on death, and death itself in Locksley Hall.

5 So–your happy suit was blasted–she the faultless, the divine;
And you liken–boyish babble–this boy-love of yours with mine.

I myself have often babbled doubtless of a foolish past;
Babble, babble; our old England may go down in babble at last.

'Curse him!' curse your fellow-victim? call him dotard in your rage?
10 Eyes that lured a doting boyhood well might fool a dotard's age.

Jilted for a wealthier! wealthier? yet perhaps she was not wise;
I remember how you kissed the miniature with those sweet eyes.

In the hall there hangs a painting–Amy's arms about my neck–
Happy children in a sunbeam sitting on the ribs of wreck.

¶417. *9-10*] Curse the old goat, you say? poor goat, that through the desert bears the curse.
Should be yours! the would-be widow thinks he bears the longer purse. *H.MS*

15 In my life there was a picture, she that clasped my neck had flown;
I was left within the shadow sitting on the wreck alone.

Yours has been a slighter ailment, will you sicken for her sake?
You, not you! your modern amourist is of easier, earthlier make.

Amy loved me, Amy failed me, Amy was a timid child;
20 But your Judith—but your worldling—*she* had never driven me wild.

She that holds the diamond necklace dearer than the golden ring,
She that finds a winter sunset fairer than a morn of Spring.

She that in her heart is brooding on his briefer lease of life,
While she vows 'till death shall part us,' she the would-be-widow wife.

25 She the worldling born of worldlings—father, mother—be content,
Even the homely farm can teach us there is something in descent.

Yonder in that chapel, slowly sinking now into the ground,
Lies the warrior, my forefather, with his feet upon the hound.

Crossed! for once he sailed the sea to crush the Moslem in his pride;
30 Dead the warrior, dead his glory, dead the cause in which he died.

Yet how often I and Amy in the mouldering aisle have stood,
Gazing for one pensive moment on that founder of our blood.

There again I stood today, and where of old we knelt in prayer,
Close beneath the casement crimson with the shield of Locksley—there,

35 All in white Italian marble, looking still as if she smiled,
Lies my Amy dead in child-birth, dead the mother, dead the child.

Dead—and sixty years ago, and dead her agèd husband now—
I this old white-headed dreamer stoopt and kissed her marble brow.

Gone the fires of youth, the follies, furies, curses, passionate tears,
Gone like fires and floods and earthquakes of the planet's dawning
40 years.

Fires that shook me once, but now to silent ashes fallen away.
Cold upon the dead volcano sleeps the gleam of dying day.

Gone the tyrant of my youth, and mute below the chancel stones,
All his virtues—I forgive them—black in white above his bones.

45 Gone the comrades of my bivouac, some in fight against the foe,
Some through age and slow diseases, gone as all on earth will go.

13–16. The nucleus of the poem, deleted in proof from *Locksley Hall.*
Cp. the painting in *The Lover's Tale* ii 165ff.
42. Cp. *Mariana in the South* 89–96n, *1832* text: 'gleamed, volcano-like'.
Here influenced by T.'s memories of 'the still more magnificent view of
the dead volcanoes' in 1861 (*Mem.* i 476). 'My father always quoted this
line as the most imaginative in the poem' (H.T.).
43–4. Martin (pp. 212–13) adduces the tablet to the memory of T.'s
grandfather, 'the Old Man of the Wolds', erected by T.'s uncle Charles
Tennyson d'Eyncourt and slighting the Somersby Tennysons.

Gone with whom for forty years my life in golden sequence ran,
She with all the charm of woman, she with all the breadth of man,

Strong in will and rich in wisdom, Edith, yet so lowly-sweet,
50 Woman to her inmost heart, and woman to her tender feet,

Very woman of very woman, nurse of ailing body and mind,
She that linked again the broken chain that bound me to my kind.

Here today was Amy with me, while I wandered down the coast,
Near us Edith's holy shadow, smiling at the slighter ghost.

55 Gone our sailor son thy father, Leonard early lost at sea;
Thou alone, my boy, of Amy's kin and mine art left to me.

Gone thy tender-natured mother, wearying to be left alone,
Pining for the stronger heart that once had beat beside her own.

Truth, for Truth is Truth, he worshipt, being true as he was brave;
60 Good, for Good is Good, he followed, yet he looked beyond the grave,

Wiser there than you, that crowning barren Death as lord of all,
Deem this over-tragic drama's closing curtain is the pall!

Beautiful was death in him, who saw the death, but kept the deck,
Saving women and their babes, and sinking with the sinking wreck,

65 Gone for ever! Ever? no – for since our dying race began,
Ever, ever, and for ever was the leading light of man.

Those that in barbarian burials killed the slave, and slew the wife,
Felt within themselves the sacred passion of the second life.

48] As our greatest is man-woman, so was she the woman-man. *MS.*
'What he called "the man-woman" in Christ, the union of tenderness and strength' (*Mem.* i 326). A recurring aspiration of T.'s; cp. *The Princess*, and contrast *On One Who Affected an Effeminate Manner* (III 217).
49. *yet so lowly-sweet*] *1888*; loyal, lowly, sweet *1886*.
50. *Woman . . . woman*] *1888*; Feminine . . . feminine *1886*.
55. Suggested by the death of T.'s son Lionel (a name cognate with Leonard) at sea, on his return from India in April 1886; ll. 59–60, 71–2, 'were written immediately after the death of my brother, and described his chief characteristics' (*Mem.* ii 329).
59–60] She in him was wise and truthful, she in him was good and brave.
    Love your father. She had taught him not to shudder at the grave.
                                                                            MS
61–2. Cp. *The Play* (III 217).
66 ∧ 7] Prove that all the race will perish wholly, worst and best,
    Give me chloroform, set me free of it – without pain – and let me
        rest. *MS*
Mem. ii 35 tells of a man chloroforming himself: '"That's what I should do," my father said, "if I thought there was no future life".'

Indian warriors dream of ampler hunting grounds beyond the night;
70 Even the black Australian dying hopes he shall return, a white.

Truth for truth, and good for good! The Good, the True, the Pure, the Just—
Take the charm 'For ever' from them, and they crumble into dust.

Gone the cry of 'Forward, Forward,' lost within a growing gloom;
Lost, or only heard in silence from the silence of a tomb.

75 Half the marvels of my morning, triumphs over time and space,
Staled by frequence, shrunk by usage into commonest commonplace!

'Forward' rang the voices then, and of the many mine was one.
Let us hush this cry of 'Forward' till ten thousand years have gone.

Far among the vanished races, old Assyrian kings would flay
80 Captives whom they caught in battle—iron-hearted victors they.

Ages after, while in Asia, he that led the wild Moguls,
Timur built his ghastly tower of eighty thousand human skulls,

Then, and here in Edward's time, an age of noblest English names,
Christian conquerors took and flung the conquered Christian into flames.

85 Love your enemy, bless your haters, said the Greatest of the great;
Christian love among the Churches looked the twin of heathen hate.

From the golden alms of Blessing man had coined himself a curse:
Rome of Cæsar, Rome of Peter, which was crueller? which was worse?

France had shown a light to all men, preached a Gospel, all men's good;
90 Celtic Demos rose a Demon, shrieked and slaked the light with blood.

Hope was ever on her mountain, watching till the day begun—
Crowned with sunlight—over darkness—from the still unrisen sun.

Have we grown at last beyond the passions of the primal clan?
'Kill your enemy, for you hate him,' still, 'your enemy' was a man.

95 Have we sunk below them? peasants maim the helpless horse, and drive
Innocent cattle under thatch, and burn the kindlier brutes alive.

Brutes, the brutes are not your wrongers—burnt at midnight, found at morn,
Twisted hard in mortal agony with their offspring, born-unborn,

70. 'Some Negros, who believe the Resurrection, think that they shall rise white', Thomas ꓶrowne's *Christian Morals* ii 6 (where it derives from the traveller Mandelslo).
72 ʌ 3] So at least it seems to me, that man can never wholly die *MS.*
74–5] *Transposed in the earlier MS.*
95–8. 'The modern Irish cruelties' (T.); he had deplored them in 1883 (*Mem.* ii 457).
97. *wrongers*] landlord *MS.*

Clinging to the silent mother! Are we devils? are we men?
100 Sweet St Francis of Assisi, would that he were here again,

He that in his Catholic wholeness used to call the very flowers
Sisters, brothers – and the beasts – whose pains are hardly less than ours!

Chaos, Cosmos! Cosmos, Chaos! who can tell how all will end?
Read the wide world's annals, you, and take their wisdom for your
friend.

105 Hope the best, but hold the Present fatal daughter of the Past,
Shape your heart to front the hour, but dream not that the hour will
last.

Ay, if dynamite and revolver leave you courage to be wise:
When was age so crammed with menace? madness? written, spoken
lies?

Envy wears the mask of Love, and, laughing sober fact to scorn,
110 Cries to Weakest as to Strongest, Ye a   equals, equal-born.'

Equal-born? O yes, if yonder hill be level with the flat.
Charm us, Orator, till the Lion look no larger than the Cat,

Till the Cat through that mirage of overheated language loom
Larger than the Lion, – Demos end in working its own doom.

115 Russia bursts our Indian barrier, shall we fight her? shall we yield?
Pause! before you sound the trumpet, hear the voices from the field.

Those three hundred millions under one Imperial sceptre now,
Shall we hold them? shall we loose them? take the suffrage of the plow.

Nay, but these would feel and follow Truth if only you and you,
120 Rivals of realm-ruining party, when you speak were wholly true.

Plowmen, Shepherds, have I found, and more than once, and still could
find,
Sons of God, and kings of men in utter nobleness of mind,

Truthful, trustful, looking upward to the practised hustings-liar;
So the Higher wields the Lower, while the Lower is the Higher.

125 Here and there a cotter's babe is royal-born by right divine;
Here and there my lord is lower than his oxen or his swine.

99] Falling from their roasted bowels . . .; Jutting from the silent
mother . . . *MSS.*
110 ∧ *1*] Nature, Caesar, and Napoleon give your equal men the lie. *MS.*
115. Indian] Afghan *MS.* Russia attacked Penjdeh, 30 March 1885, and
for some weeks war seemed imminent.
116. Pause . . . trumpet] What is Afghan? wars are taxes *MS.*
118] Subject to the voice of one who sees one yard beyond his plow. *MS.*
122. Cp. *John* i 12–13: 'But as many as received him, to them gave he power
to become the sons of God, even to them that believe on his Name:
Which were born, not of blood, nor of the will of the flesh, nor of the
will of man, but of God.'

Chaos, Cosmos! Cosmos, Chaos! once again the sickening game;
Freedom, free to slay herself, and dying while they shout her name.

Step by step we gained a freedom known to Europe, known to all;
130   Step by step we rose to greatness, – through the tonguesters we may fall.

You that woo the Voices – tell them 'old experience is a fool,'
Teach your flattered kings that only those who cannot read can rule.

Pluck the mighty from their seat, but set no meek ones in their place;
Pillory Wisdom in your markets, pelt your offal at her face.

135   Tumble Nature heel o'er head, and, yelling with the yelling street,
Set the feet above the brain and swear the brain is in the feet.

Bring the old dark ages back without the faith, without the hope,
Break the State, the Church, the Throne, and roll their ruins down the
        slope.

Authors – essayist, atheist, novelist, realist, rhymester, play your part,
140   Paint the mortal shame of nature with the living hues of Art.

Rip your brothers' vices open, strip your own foul passions bare;
Down with Reticence, down with Reverence – forward – naked –
        let them stare.

Feed the budding rose of boyhood with the drainage of your sewer;
Send the drain into the fountain, lest the stream should issue pure.

145   Set the maiden fancies wallowing in the troughs of Zolaism, –
Forward, forward, ay and backward, downward too into the abysm.

130. See *Freedom* 21–4*n* (III 130).

131. Suggesting (with l. 134) *Coriolanus* II iii, where Coriolanus solicits
votes.

133. Luke i 52.

134] Pillory the dead face . . .; Pillory the dumb corpse . . . *MSS.* These
suggest that T. is remembering the indignities inflicted by the mob in the
French Revolution; he had written about such in *Come hither* (I 165).
Cp. *The Dead Prophet* (p. 635). Cp. T.'s letter: 'Burlesque, the true enemy
of humour, the thin bastard sister of poetical caricature who I verily believe
from her utter want of human feeling would in a revolution be the first to
dabble her hands in blood' (*Letters* iii, mid-Nov. 1882; *Mem.* ii 423).

137. Cp. *Despair* 88: 'For these are the new dark ages'.

139. essayist, atheist] 1888; *transposed 1886.*

139–40]   Wild young Poet, glancing forward, drag us backward,
                play your part,
            Crown the dying filths of Nature with the living flowers of Art.

            Dying are they? No, nor will, and would that I myself were dead
            Ere the living body of Britain die beneath her dying head. *MS*

140. Cp. *Art for Art's sake* (III 12).   *living hues:* as in Shelley, *West
Wind* 12.

145] Till the delicate lady wallow in the sewer of Zolaism, *MS.*

Do your best to charm the worst, to lower the rising race of men;
Have we risen from out the beast, then back into the beast again?

Only 'dust to dust' for me that sicken at your lawless din,
150   Dust in wholesome old-world dust before the newer world begin.

Heated am I? you–you wonder–well, it scarce becomes mine age–
Patience! let the dying actor mouth his last upon the stage.

Cries of unprogressive dotage ere the dotard fall asleep?
Noises of a current narrowing, not the music of a deep?

155   Ay, for doubtless I am old, and think gray thoughts, for I am gray:
After all the stormy changes shall we find a changeless May?

After madness, after massacre, Jacobinism and Jacquerie,
Some diviner force to guide us through the days I shall not see?

When the schemes and all the systems, Kingdoms and Republics fall,
160   Something kindlier, higher, holier–all for each and each for all?

All the full-brain, half-brain races, led by Justice, Love, and Truth;
All the millions one at length with all the visions of my youth?

All diseases quenched by Science, no man halt, or deaf or blind;
Stronger ever born of weaker, lustier body, larger mind?

165   Earth at last a warless world, a single race, a single tongue–
I have seen her far away–for is not Earth as yet so young?–

148. Cp. *Passing of Arthur* 25–6: 'All my realm / Reels back into the beast'.

149–50]   Only this worldweary being, sick of senseless rage and sin
Fain would lie below the surface ere this newer world begin. *MS*

152 ∧ 3]   Who'd have thought of so much blood–to quote our Lady of
       Macbeth–
'So much blood in the old man' yet, who stumbles down the
       steps of death. *MS*

153–4] *Added later to MS.*

156] Earth may come to iceless winters, Earth may find a deathless May.
MS.

157. Jacquerie: 'Originally a revolt in 1358 against the Picardy nobles; and
afterwards applied to insurrections of the mob' (T.).

159] Light on some new form of Power, after Europe's rulers fall, *MS.*

165. Cp. *Isaiah* ii 4: 'Neither shall they learn war any more'.

165–6. T. adapts an unadopted stanza of *Freedom*:
On Earth so old, but yet so young,
Of equal day from pole to pole,
A warless world, a single tongue . . .

166 ∧ 7]   When the great elastick name will flash through all from end to
       end,
Make, as in the simple body, every member friend with friend.
                                                        MS

Every tiger madness muzzled, every serpent passion killed,
Every grim ravine a garden, every blazing desert tilled,

Robed in universal harvest up to either pole she smiles,
170   Universal ocean softly washing all her warless Isles.

Warless? when her tens are thousands, and her thousands millions,
    then–
All her harvest all too narrow–who can fancy warless men?

Warless? war will die out late then. Will it ever? late or soon?
Can it, till this outworn earth be dead as yon dead world the moon?

175   Dead the new astronomy calls her. . . . On this day and at this hour,
In this gap between the sandhills, whence you see the Locksley tower,

Here we met, our latest meeting–Amy–sixty years ago–
She and I–the moon was falling greenish through a rosy glow,

Just above the gateway tower, and even where you see her now–
Here we stood and claspt each other, swore the seeming-deathless
180   vow. . . .

Dead, but how her living glory lights the hall, the dune, the grass!
Yet the moonlight is the sunlight, and the sun himself will pass.

Venus near her! smiling downward at this earthlier earth of ours,
Closer on the Sun, perhaps a world of never fading flowers.

185   Hesper, whom the poet called the Bringer home of all good things.
All good things may move in Hesper, perfect peoples, perfect kings.

Hesper–Venus–were we native to that splendour or in Mars,
We should see the Globe we groan in, fairest of their evening stars.

Could we dream of wars and carnage, craft and madness, lust and spite,
190   Roaring London, raving Paris, in that point of peaceful light?

178. The tints at twilight were due to the eruption of Krakatoa in Aug.
1883; cp. the opening of *St Telemachus* (III 224).
185–6. T. compares Sappho (as in *Leonine Elegiacs* 13): ϝέσπερε, πάντα
φέρεις, ὅσα φαίνολις ἐσκέδασ' αὔως, φέρεις ὄϊν, φέρεις αἶγα, φέρεις
ματέρι παῖδα. ('Evening Star that bringest back all that lightsome Dawn
hath scattered afar, thou bringest the sheep, thou bringest the goat, thou
bringest her child home to the mother'.)
187–92. Cp. T.'s words to Emily Sellwood (?c. 1 Oct. 1839): 'To me often the
far-off world seems nearer than the present, for in the present is always
something unreal and indistinct, but the other seems a good solid planet,
rolling round its green hills and paradises to the harmony of more steadfast
laws. There steam up from about me mists of weakness, or sin, or
despondency, and roll between me and the far planet, but it is there still'
(*Letters* i 174).

Might we not in glancing heavenward on a star so silver-fair,
Yearn, and clasp the hands and murmur, 'Would to God that
    we were there'?

Forward, backward, backward, forward, in the immeasurable sea,
Swayed by vaster ebbs and flows than can be known to you or me.

195 All the suns—are these but symbols of innumerable man,
Man or Mind that sees a shadow of the planner or the plan?

Is there evil but on earth? or pain in every peopled sphere?
Well be grateful for the sounding watchword, 'Evolution' here,

Evolution ever climbing after some ideal good,
200 And Reversion ever dragging Evolution in the mud.

What are men that He should heed us? cried the king of sacred song;
Insects of an hour, that hourly work their brother insect wrong,

While the silent Heavens roll, and Suns along their fiery way,
All their planets whirling round them, flash a million miles a day.

205 Many an Æon moulded earth before her highest, man, was born,
Many an Æon too may pass when earth is manless and forlorn,

Earth so huge, and yet so bounded—pools of salt, and plots of land—
Shallow skin of green and azure—chains of mountain, grains of sand!

Only That which made us, meant us to be mightier by and by,
210 Set the sphere of all the boundless Heavens within the human eye,

Sent the shadow of Himself, the boundless, through the human soul;
Boundless inward, in the atom, boundless outward, in the Whole.

                *   *   *   *

Here is Locksley Hall, my grandson, here the lion-guarded gate.
Not tonight in Locksley Hall—tomorrow—you, you come so late.

Wrecked—your train—or all but wrecked? a shattered wheel? a vicious
215   boy!
Good, this forward, you that preach it, is it well to wish you joy?

Is it well that while we range with Science, glorying in the Time,
City children soak and blacken soul and sense in city slime?

There among the glooming alleys Progress halts on palsied feet,
220 Crime and hunger cast our maidens by the thousand on the street.

There the Master scrimps his haggard sempstress of her daily bread,
There a single sordid attic holds the living and the dead.

193. *the immeasurable sea*: Shelley, *Daemon of the World* i 190.
201. *Psalm* viii 4.
204. Cp. *The Window: Marriage Morning*: 'Flash for a million miles'.
217–24] *Added later on separate sheet of MS.*
217] Well that while we range with Science glorying through the field of
Time, *MS.*
219. *glooming*] squalid *MS.*

There the smouldering fire of fever creeps across the rotted floor,
And the crowded couch of incest in the warrens of the poor.

Nay, your pardon, cry your 'forward,' yours are hope and youth, but
225   I –
Eighty winters leave the dog too lame to follow with the cry,

Lame and old, and past his time, and passing now into the night;
Yet I would the rising race were half as eager for the light.

Light the fading gleam of Even? light the glimmer of the dawn?
230 Agèd eyes may take the growing glimmer for the gleam withdrawn.

Far away beyond her myriad coming changes earth will be
Something other than the wildest modern guess of you and me.

Earth may reach her earthly-worst, or if she gain her earthly-best,
Would she find her human offspring this ideal man at rest?

235 Forward then, but still remember how the course of Time will swerve,
Crook and turn upon itself in many a backward streaming curve.

Not the Hall tonight, my grandson! Death and Silence hold their own
Leave the Master in the first dark hour of his last sleep alone.

Worthier soul was he than I am, sound and honest, rustic Squire,
240 Kindly landlord, boon companion – youthful jealousy is a liar.

Cast the poison from your bosom, oust the madness from your brain.
Let the trampled serpent show you that you have not lived in vain.

Youthful! youth and age are scholars yet but in the lower school,
Nor is he the wisest man who never proved himself a fool.

245 Yonder lies our young sea-village – Art and Grace are less and less:
Science grows and Beauty dwindles – roofs of slated hideousness!

There is one old Hostel left us where they swing the Locksley shield,
Till the peasant cow shall butt the 'Lion passant' from his field.

Poor old Heraldry, poor old History, poor old Poetry, passing hence,
250 In the common deluge drowning old political common-sense!

Poor old voice of eighty crying after voices that have fled!
All I loved are vanished voices, all my steps are on the dead.

All the world is ghost to me, and as the phantom disappears,
Forward far and far from here is all the hope of eighty years.

*   *   *   *

255 In this Hostel – I remember – I repent it o'er his grave –
Like a clown – by chance he met me – I refused the hand he gave.

From that casement where the trailer mantles all the mouldering
    bricks –

222] There among his living orphans lies the still-unburied dead. *MS.*
236 ∧ 7] Like our earthly streams that lapse into the level from the steep,
    Time is not a still canal that moves still forward to the deep. *MS*
250. Cp. *Far shines that land* 21 (III 633): 'to drown in deluge all the Old.'

I was then in early boyhood, Edith but a child of six –

While I sheltered in this archway from a day of driving showers –
260 Peept the winsome face of Edith like a flower among the flowers.

Here tonight! the Hall tomorrow, when they toll the Chapel bell!
Shall I hear in one dark room a wailing, 'I have loved thee well.'

Then a peal that shakes the portal – one has come to claim his bride,
Her that shrank, and put me from her, shrieked, and started from my
side –

265 Silent echoes! You, my Leonard, use and not abuse your day,
Move among your people, know them, follow him who led the way,

Strove for sixty widowed years to help his homelier brother men,
Served the poor, and built the cottage, raised the school, and drained
the fen.

. Hears he now the Voice that wronged him? who shall swear it cannot
be?
270 Earth would never touch her worst, were one in fifty such as he.

Ere she gain her Heavenly-best, a God must mingle with the game:
Nay, there may be those about us whom we neither see nor name,

Felt within us as ourselves, the Powers of Good, the Powers of Ill,
Strowing balm, or shedding poison in the fountains of the Will.

275 Follow you the Star that lights a desert pathway, yours or mine.
Forward, till you see the highest Human Nature is divine.

Follow Light, and do the Right – for man can half-control his doom –
Till you find the deathless Angel seated in the vacant tomb.

Forward, let the stormy moment fly and mingle with the Past.
280 I that loathed, have come to love him. Love will conquer at the last.

Gone at eighty, mine own age, and I and you will bear the pall;
Then I leave thee Lord and Master, latest Lord of Locksley Hall.

423 To Ulysses

Published *1889*. Written early 1888 (ll. 6–8), and read to F. T. Palgrave in
Nov. (*Mem.* ii 507). T. comments that *Ulysses* was 'the title of a number of
essays by W. G. Palgrave. He died at Monte Video before seeing my poem'.
Palgrave was the brother of F. T. Palgrave (friend of T., and editor of
The Golden Treasury); T. had met him many times since 1860. His *Ulysses*

267–8] I that never turned away the truthful pauper from my door,
I that being poor myself have ever striven to raise the poor! *MS*
269–76, 279–80] *Added later on separate sheet of MS.*

was published in Nov. 1887, and T. was presented with a copy; he died 30 Sept. 1888 (*Mem.* ii 507). T. uses the *In Memoriam* stanza to praise the book, as in *To E.L.* (*p. 486*). On Palgrave and his book, *Ulysses: or, Scenes and Studies in Many Lands*, see W. N. Rogers, *VP* xix (1981) 351–66.

I
Ulysses, much-experienced man,
    Whose eyes have known this globe of ours,
    Her tribes of men, and trees, and flowers,
From Corrientes to Japan,

II
5 To you that bask below the Line,
    I soaking here in winter wet—
    The century's three strong eights have met
To drag me down to seventy-nine

III
    In summer if I reach my day—
10   To you, yet young, who breathe the balm
    Of summer-winters by the palm
And orange grove of Paraguay,

IV
I tolerant of the colder time,
    Who love the winter woods, to trace
15   On paler heavens the branching grace
Of leafless elm, or naked lime,

V
And see my cedar green, and there
    My giant ilex keeping leaf
    When frost is keen and days are brief—
20 Or marvel how in English air

¶423. *1–3.* Palgrave's epigraph (in explanation of his title) had been *Qui multorum hominum mores et vidit et urbes,* i.e. Horace's *Epistles* I ii 19–20: *qui . . . multorum providus urbes | et mores hominum inspexit,* from *Odyssey* i 3. Cp. *Ulysses* 13: 'Much have I seen and known; cities of men . . .'.
4. Corrientes: in Argentina.
10–11. Cp. *The Brook* 196: 'breathes in April–autumns'.
11. summer-winters] sunnier summers *H.Nbk 55.*
14. the winter woods,] with careful [patient *1st reading*] eye *MS.*
17. And] Who *MS.*
20. Or . . . how] While yonder out *MS 1st reading.*

VI

My yucca, which no winter quells,
    Although the months have scarce begun,
    Has pushed toward our faintest sun
A spike of half-accomplished bells –

VII

25 Or watch the waving pine which here
    The warrior of Caprera set,
    A name that earth will not forget
Till earth has rolled her latest year –

VIII

I, once half-crazed for larger light
30   On broader zones beyond the foam,
    But chaining fancy now at home
Among the quarried downs of Wight,

IX

Not less would yield full thanks to you
    For your rich gift, your tale of lands
35   I know not, your Arabian sands;
Your cane, your palm, tree-fern, bamboo,

X

The wealth of tropic bower and brake;
    Your Oriental Eden-isles,

---

21. My] One *MS 1st reading.*
23. our faintest] the hazy *MS 1st reading*; our feeblest *MS 2nd reading.*
25. Or] Who *MS 1st reading.*   *waving pine*] slim pine wave *MS 1st reading.*
26. 1889 note: 'Garibaldi said to me, alluding to his barren island, "I wish I had your trees."' T. noted that Garibaldi planted a Wellingtonia at Farringford, April 1864.   *Caprera*: Garibaldi's home, an island off Sardinia.
29. once half-crazed] yearning once *MS 1st reading*; once half-mad *MS 2nd reading.* Cp. *You ask me, why* 26–8: 'I seek a warmer sky, / And I will see before I die / The palms and temples of the South.' Recalled perhaps because it uses the *In Memoriam* stanza.
31. chaining fancy now] now with fancy chained *MS 1st reading.*
33. Not less] I yet *MS 1st reading.*
34. 1889 note: 'The tale of Nejd' (in Arabia).
38. 1889 note: 'The Philippines'. Cp. *Locksley Hall* 164: 'summer isles of Eden'. Palgrave may have been thinking of this (he was certainly thinking of *The Lotos-Eaters*) when he called the Philippines 'isles of Eden, lotus-lands' (p. 113). T., as it were, returns the compliment.

Where man, nor only Nature smiles;
40 Your wonder of the boiling lake;

XI

Phra-Chai, the Shadow of the Best,
Phra-bat the step; your Pontic coast;
Crag-cloister; Anatolian Ghost;
Hong-Kong, Karnac, and all the rest;

XII

45 Through which I followed line by line
Your leading hand, and came, my friend,
To prize your various book, and send
A gift of slenderer value, mine.

425 To Mary Boyle

With the Following Poem
[The Progress of Spring]

Published *1889*, introducing *The Progress of Spring* (I 516). Written spring
1888 (l. 13*n*, and l. 45), it is not in the *Virginia* trial edition of *1889*. H.T.
says: 'Mary Boyle was an aunt of my wife's (Audrey Tennyson, *née*
Boyle)'; T. first met her in 1882 (*Mem.* ii 294).

I

'Spring-flowers'! While you still delay to take
Your leave of Town,
Our elmtree's ruddy-hearted blossom-flake
Is fluttering down.

40. wonder] marvel *MS 1st reading*. *1889* note: 'In Dominica' (West
Indies).
40–44. The listing of the natural wonders suggests *On Sublimity* 81–100
(I 131).
41. 1889 note: 'The Shadow of the Lord. Certain obscure markings on a
rock in Siam, which express the image of Buddha to the Buddhist more or
less distinctly according to his faith and his moral worth.'
42. Phra-bat: 1889 note: 'The footstep of the Lord on another rock.'
43. 1889 notes: 'The monastery of Sumelas', and 'Anatolian Spectre
stories'.
44. Hong-Kong: 1889 note: 'The Three Cities' (the title of Palgrave's
chapter on Hong-Kong).   *Karnac: 1889* note: 'Travels in Egypt'.
rest;] rest. *1889*, *1894*, *Eversley*. Rogers (see headnote) puts the case against the
full stop; to his argument should be added that *H.MS* has no punctuation here.

II

5 Be truer to your promise. There! I heard
       Our cuckoo call.
   Be needle to the magnet of your word,
       Nor wait, till all

III

   Our vernal bloom from every vale and plain
10   And garden pass,
   And all the gold from each laburnum chain
       Drop to the grass.

IV

   Is memory with your Marian gone to rest,
       Dead with the dead?
15 For ere she left us, when we met, you prest
       My hand, and said

V

   'I come with your spring-flowers.' You came not,
       friend;
           My birds would sing,
   You heard not. Take then this spring-flower I send,
20   This song of spring,

VI

   Found yesterday–forgotten mine own rhyme
       By mine old self,
   As I shall be forgotten by old Time,
       Laid on the shelf–

¶ 425. 5–20] You sit conversing with your private grief
               While Nature smiles,
           And you should watch the bursting of the leaf
               Not bricks and tiles.

       You hear the milkman's cry, but not, my friend,
           Our throstle sing.
       To quicken your half-dead resolve I send
           This ode to Spring. *H.Nbk 55 (which has then other drafts*
                                    which include ll. 5–12)

13. 'Lady Marian Alford' (T.). She died 9 Feb. 1888.
27–37. The Progress of Spring was begun in the early 1830s, in the days of
political upheaval and Reform agitation; see *Mem.* i 41, and T.'s recurring
memory of rick-burning in *The Princess* iv 366, and *The Grandmother* 39.
T. says that the 'homestead' was near Cambridge, 1830.

VII

25 A rhyme that flowered betwixt the whitening sloe
         And kingcup blaze,
    And more than half a hundred years ago,
         In rick-fire days,

VIII

    When Dives loathed the times, and paced his land
30   In fear of worse,
    And sanguine Lazarus felt a vacant hand
         Fill with *his* purse.

IX

    For lowly minds were maddened to the height
         By tonguester tricks,
35 And once – I well remember that red night
         When thirty ricks,

X

    All flaming, made an English homestead Hell –
         These hands of mine
    Have helpt to pass a bucket from the well
40   Along the line,

XI

    When this bare dome had not begun to gleam
         Through youthful curls,
    And you were then a lover's fairy dream,
         His girl of girls;

XII

45 And you, that now are lonely, and with Grief
         Sit face to face,
    Might find a flickering glimmer of relief
         In change of place.

XIII

    What use to brood? this life of mingled pains
50   And joys to me,
    Despite of every Faith and Creed, remains
         The Mystery.

XIV

    Let golden youth bewail the friend, the wife,
         For ever gone.
55 He dreams of that long walk through desert life
         Without the one.

XV

The silver year should cease to mourn and sigh—
　　　Not long to wait—
So close are we, dear Mary, you and I
60　　　To that dim gate.

XVI

Take, read! and be the faults your Poet makes
　　　Or many or few,
He rests content, if his young music wakes
　　　A wish in you

XVII

65　To change our dark Queen-city, all her realm
　　　Of sound and smoke,
For his clear heaven, and these few lanes of elm
　　　And whispering oak.

426 Far—Far—Away

(For Music)

Published *1889*. Recited Aug. 1888 (*Mem.* ii 346), though H.T. also says
that it was written after T.'s severe illness, which began Sept. 1888. T.
presumably revised it. 'The words "far, far away" had always a strange
charm for me' (T. on his early childhood). He made many changes to the
drafts in *H.Nbks 54* and *87* (*A* and *B* below), including the change from
'I' to 'he' throughout. He altered the sequence of lines and stanzas, and
the poem cost him great difficulty. Stanzas that found no place in *1889* are
given below, l. 18n. A trial edition of *1889* (*Virginia*) has only four stanzas.
T. rewrote the poem in the *Trinity* trial edition or proofs (*T.Nbk 27*).

63–8] And send my youthful ode which hopes to wake
　　　Desire in you

　　To leave at once your million-chimneyed realm
　　　Of noise and smoke
　　For streets of whispering beech and lanes of elm,
　　　And lime and oak.　　*H.MS, early draft*

What sight so lured him through the fields he knew
As where earth's green stole into heaven's own hue,
Far–far–away?

What sound was dearest in his native dells?
5   The mellow lin-lan-lone of evening bells
Far–far–away.

What vague world-whisper, mystic pain or joy,
Through those three words would haunt him
when a boy,
Far–far–away?

10 A whisper from his dawn of life? a breath
From some fair dawn beyond the doors of death
Far–far–away?

Far, far, how far? from o'er the gates of Birth,
The faint horizons, all the bounds of earth,
15   Far–far–away?

What charm in words, a charm no words could
give?
O dying words, can Music make you live
Far–far–away?

¶426. 1] What field so witched him in the land he knew *Harvard B 1st reading.*
2. *hue*] blue *Harvard B 1st reading.*
5. Sir Charles Tennyson (*1931*, p. 78) compares 'lin, lan, lone', *New Year's Eve*, from *c.* 1837.
7–8]   That strange world-whisper came to me, a boy,
            A haunting notice, neither grief, nor joy, *Harvard A*
14] And all the faint horizons of the earth, *Harvard A*; Beyond the faint horizons of his earth, *Harvard B 1st reading.*
17. *dying*] poor dead *Harvard B 1st reading.*
18] *The following stanzas appear in the MSS (the sequences of which are quite different from 1889):*
        (i) That weird soul-phrase of something half-divine,
            In earliest youth, in latest age is mine,
                Far – far – away. *Harvard A*
        (ii) Ghost, do the men that walk this planet seem
            [Ghost, can you see us, hear us? do we seem *1st reading*]
            Far, far away, a truth and yet a dream,
                Far – far – away? *Harvard B*
        (iii) What whisper? whence? from summers long gone by
            And twilight times when I was growing I,
                Far–far–away?   *T.MS*
Cp. ll. 10–12.

427 To the Marquis of Dufferin and Ava

Published *1889*. It is not in the *Virginia* trial edition of *1889*. Its subject is the death in April 1886 of T.'s son Lionel (born 1854) in the Red Sea when returning from India where he had caught fever. His host had been Lord Dufferin (1826–1902), the Governor-General of India (1884–8) and an old friend of T.'s. Dufferin took care of Lionel for the months of his illness before the fatal journey. Since the poem acts as the introduction to *1889* (see ll. 15–16), it was probably written in that year or in 1888 (supported by its placing in *H.Nbk 55*). T. would have had it in mind since 1886. He uses the *In Memoriam* stanza. Martin (pp. 558–9) compares *In Memoriam* vi 13–16 (*p. 350*).

I

At times our Britain cannot rest,
    At times her steps are swift and rash;
    She moving, at her girdle clash
The golden keys of East and West.

II

5   Not swift or rash, when late she lent
    The sceptres of her West, her East,
    To one, that ruling has increased
Her greatness and her self-content.

III

Your rule has made the people love
10   Their ruler. Your viceregal days
    Have added fulness to the phrase
Of 'Gauntlet in the velvet glove.'

IV

But since your name will grow with Time,
    Not all, as honouring your fair fame
15   Of Statesman, have I made the name
A golden portal to my rhyme:

¶427. *1–4.* Sir Charles Tennyson (*1931*, p. 74) points out that these lines had been *Hail Briton!* 21–4: 'For Britain had an hour of rest; / But now her steps' etc., *verbatim* (I 521).
2. At . . . steps] Her steps at times *T.Nbk 27, trial edition or proofs, corrected then.*
6. Dufferin had been Governor-General of Canada, 1872–8.
7–8. Cp. *Ode on Wellington* 170 ∧ 71: 'Perchance our greatness will increase'.
10–12. Dufferin's rule in India was characterized by a strengthening of the army and by many military operations.

V

But more, that you and yours may know
From me and mine, how dear a debt
We owed you, and are owing yet
20   To you and yours, and still would owe.

VI

For he – your India was his Fate,
And drew him over sea to you –
He fain had ranged her through and
          through,
To serve her myriads and the State, –

VII

25   A soul that, watched from earliest youth,
And on through many a brightening year,
Had never swerved for craft or fear,
By one side-path, from simple truth;

VIII

Who might have chased and claspt Renown
30   And caught her chaplet here – and there
In haunts of jungle-poisoned air
The flame of life went wavering down;

IX

But ere he left your fatal shore,
And lay on that funereal boat,
35   Dying, 'Unspeakable' he wrote
'Their kindness,' and he wrote no more;

19. *owed you, and*] feel that we *trial edn, corrected then.*
21–4. Lionel's work in the India Office, including a Blue Book, had been very
successful (*Mem.* ii 322–3). Jowett wrote to the Tennysons, 12 Dec. 1858
(*Mem.* i 434) suggesting a subject for T.: 'The subject I mean is "In
Memoriam" for the dead in India. It might be done so as to include some
scenes of Cawnpore and Lucknow; or quite simply and slightly, "Relatives in
India", the Schemings and hopings and imaginings about them, and the fatal
missive suddenly announcing their death. They leave us in the fairness and
innocence of youth, with nothing but the vision of their childhood and
boyhood to look back upon, and return no more. Perhaps you know what
sets my thoughts upon this, the death of my dear brother, the second who
had died in India.'
25–8. Cp. the similar praise of the dead Lionel in *Locksley Hall Sixty Years
After* 59–60 (p. 643).

X

And sacred is the latest word;
And now the Was, the Might-have-been,
And those lone rites I have not seen,
40   And one drear sound I have not heard,

XI

Are dreams that scarce will let me be,
Not there to bid my boy farewell,
When That within the coffin fell,
Fell–and flashed into the Red Sea,

XII

45   Beneath a hard Arabian moon
And alien stars. To question, why
The sons before the fathers die,
Not mine! and I may meet him soon;

XIII

But while my life's late eve endures,
50   Nor settles into hueless gray,
My memories of his briefer day
Will mix with love for you and yours.

39. lone] last *trial edn, corrected then.*
41–2] But sounds, shapes, shadows, trouble me,
    Black decks, sea-whirl, muffled bell, *H.Nbk 55 1st reading*
42–6. F. T. Palgrave, in an article set up in type but not published (*Lincoln*),
juxtaposed these lines with an extract from 'the *Melbourne Argus* of the 24th of
July [1886], written by a fellow-passenger on board the vessel; as the short
personal description gave a sad pleasure to the bereaved father: "No
mistaking the likeness [to Lord Tennyson] in the massive head, the flowing
beard and hair, as he lay, pale and wan, on a couch on deck. Six hours
afterwards, at nine o'clock, the crew is mustered by the tolling of a muffled
bell ... A reverend clergyman and missionary reads the beautiful Burial
Service of the Church of England, which seems more impressive here than
on shore. There are many wet eyes at the words 'We therefore commit' ...
Then the coffin slides with a solemn splash into the dark water, a bubble of
phosphorescent light is seen for a moment, the waves close over it, and
broken voices repeat *Our Father*" ...' (*TRB* ii, 1972, 20). T.'s 'flashed' is
illuminated by the phosphorescence; and cp. also ll. 34, 47.
48. Not mine] Vain, vain *H.MS.*

430 Parnassus

Published *1889*, written 26 May (*Mat.* iv 214). *H.Nbk 55* has an epigram-matic version, a draft of ll. 9–12, 15–16; likewise, as *Fame*, in the *Trinity* trial edition or proofs. As *Fame*, it is in a *Lincoln* trial edition of *1889*, where it consisted of   ll. 1–4, 7–8. But other *Harvard* drafts suggest an earlier date. *Lpr 165* (*A* below) is on the back of part of *Becket* (printed 1879) and *The Northern Cobbler* (*1880*); and *Lpr 45* (*B*) is on the back of *De Profundis* (*1880*). Both these versions consist of section II only; T. extended and revised this in 1889, as is clear from another *Lincoln* trial edition of *1889*, where ll. 5–8 had the title *Fame* and where furthermore section III is shown to be a late addition. The poem's theme is common in T.; cp. the *Epilogue to The Charge of the Heavy Brigade* (III 96): 'Old Horace ... Earth passes, all is lost ... The man remains'. Also *Little Aubrey* (III 637). Jowett wrote to T., Dec. 1858, suggesting topics for poems: 'Have not many sciences such as Astronomy or Geology a side of feeling which is poetry?' (*Mem.* i 433). Herbert Warren (*Tennyson and His Friends*, pp. 136–8) compares a letter by FitzGerald to E. B. Cowell in 1847, and remarks on the 'extraordinarily close' parallel. Since this letter was published in July 1889 in FitzGerald's *Letters and Literary Remains* (ed. W. A. Wright, i 181–2), it may have influenced T. in his final drafting of the poem:
'Yet, as I often think, it is not the poetical imagination, but bare Science that every day more and more unrolls a greater Epic than the Iliad; the history of the World, the infinitudes of Space and Time! I never take up a book of Geology or Astronomy but this strikes me. And when we think that Man must go on to discover in the same plodding way, one fancies that the Poet of to-day may as well fold his hands, or turn them to dig and delve, considering how soon the march of discovery will distance all his imagina-tions, [and] dissolve the language in which they are uttered .... It is not only that this vision of Time must wither the Poet's hope of immortality; but it is in itself more wonderful than all the conceptions of Dante and Milton.'
On Astronomy and the Muses, M. Millhauser comments: 'It seems an ungracious quibble that Astronomy – Urania – was one of the original Muses; T. is presumably thinking of the difference in tone and human implications between the modern science ... and the Greek identification of constellations' (*Fire and Ice*, 1971, p. 25).
Epigraph: Horace prophesies his work's immortality, epilogue to *Odes* iii ('I have finished a monument ... that the countless chain of years and the ages' flight cannot destroy').

> *Exegi monumentum ...*
> *Quod non ...*
> *Possit diruere ...*
>   *... innumerabilis*
> *Annorum series et fuga temporum.*
>   **HORACE**

I

What be those crowned forms high over the sacred fountain?
Bards, that the mighty Muses have raised to the heights of the mountain,
And over the flight of the Ages! O Goddesses, help me up thither!
Lightning may shrivel the laurel of Cæsar, but mine would not wither.
5 Steep is the mountain, but you, you will help me to overcome it,
And stand with my head in the zenith, and roll my voice from the
summit,
Sounding for ever and ever through Earth and her listening nations,
And mixt with the great Sphere-music of stars and of constellations.

II

What be those two shapes high over the sacred fountain,
10 Taller than all the Muses, and huger than all the mountain?
On those two known peaks they stand ever spreading and heightening;
Poet, that evergreen laurel is blasted by more than lightning!
Look, in their deep double shadow the crowned ones all disappearing!
Sing like a bird and be happy, nor hope for a deathless hearing!
15 'Sounding for ever and ever?' pass on! the sight confuses –
These are Astronomy and Geology, terrible Muses!

III

If the lips were touched with fire from off a pure Pierian altar,
Though their music here be mortal need the singer greatly care?
Other songs for other worlds! the fire within him would not falter;
20 Let the golden Iliad vanish, Homer here is Homer there.

[1889. *Crossing the Bar*–see p. *665*]

¶430. *1.* The Castalian fountain on Mount Parnassus, sacred to the Muses.
4. The superstition that laurels are proof against lightning; cp. Marvell,
Horatian Ode 23-4: 'And *Caesars* head at last / Did through his Laurels
blast.'

Section II] A begins:
O little poet who fain would be fussy, and bristle, and rave
Of the glory implied in the slander that even follows the grave –
O little poet, of all little poets the least and the latest,
One little solace is thine, that thou wilt die with the greatest.

9. those two] the two vast *A*; the two great *B*.
11. On those] There on the *A-B*.
12. Poet . . . is] Look, little poet, thy laurels are *A-B*.
13-14] Not *A*, Notebook *45; B has here the third and fourth of the introductory
lines in A (see Section IIn).*
15. 'Sounding . . . ever?'] Look no more, little poet! *A-B*.
17. Pieria: a haunt of the Muses. Cp. Milton, *Nativity Ode* 28: 'From out
his secret Altar toucht with hallow'd fire'. Hence Pope, *Messiah* 6:
'Who touch'd *Isaiah's* hallow'd Lips with Fire!' Based on the seraph,
Isaiah vi 6-7. The link with the mountain may be a reminiscence of *The
Lover's Tale* i 315-17: 'and touched far-off / His mountain-altars, his high
hills, with flame / Milder and purer.'

434 The Roses on the Terrace

Published *1889*. It is not in the *Virginia* trial edition of *1889*. As a late addition to a *Lincoln* trial edition, it had the title *The Rose*. Written into an earlier *Lincoln* trial edition, it consisted only of four lines which told how the memory 'warms my heart today'. It is to Rosa Baring (see *Thy rosy lips*, II 59). Rader (p. 33) remarks that it may have been written in the spring–or summer–of 1889 after Tennyson heard the news of Rosa's husband's death in March, or perhaps at some time during the previous few years. T. combines the terrace at Aldworth with the terraced garden of Rosa's Harrington Hall. Cp. the blush in *Locksley Hall* 25–6.

Rose, on this terrace fifty years ago,
    When I was in my June, you in your May,
Two words, '*My* Rose' set all your face aglow,
    And now that I am white, and you are gray,
5 That blush of fifty years ago, my dear,
    Blooms in the Past, but close to me today
As this red rose, which on our terrace here
    Glows in the blue of fifty miles away.

450 June Bracken and Heather

TO –

Published *1892*. A dedication to T.'s wife Emily (as was *A Dedication*, II 683), it was written June 1891. The date is deduced from l. 6 (Emily was born 9 July 1813), and confirmed by *T.Nbk 37*. Martin (p. 576) notes that it is a wedding-anniversary tribute (June 1850).

There on the top of the down,
    The wild heather round me and over me June's high
        blue,
When I looked at the bracken so bright and the
        heather so brown,
I thought to myself I would offer this book to you,
5 This, and my love together,
    To you that are seventy-seven,
With a faith as clear as the heights of the June-blue
        heaven,
And a fancy as summer-new
    As the green of the bracken amid the gloom of the
        heather.

462 Crossing the Bar

Published *1889*. It is not in the *Virginia* trial edition of *1889*. Written Oct.
1889 while crossing the Solent: 'When he repeated it to me in the evening,
I said, "That is the crown of your life's work." He answered, "It came in a
moment"' (H.T.). P. L. Elliott notes that in *MS Mat. (Lincoln)* H.T.'s words
had been: 'That is one of the most beautiful poems ever written' (*The Making
of the Memoir*, 1978, p. 14). T. said to W. F. Rawnsley that he 'began and
finished it in twenty minutes' (*Nineteenth Century* xcvii (1925) 195). It had
been in T.'s mind since April or May 1889, when his nurse suggested he write
a hymn after his recovery from a serious illness (J. Tennyson, *The Times*, 5
Nov. 1936). For the image, cp. *De Profundis* (III 67), and *The Passing of
Arthur* 445: 'From the great deep to the great deep he goes.' The 'bar' is the
sandbank across the harbour-mouth. All variants from *H.Nbk 54* are below.
D. Sonstroem argues that the poem is a reconciliation of a great many of T.'s
earlier poems (*VP* viii, 1970, 55–60). The poem is here printed out of
sequence because of T.'s wish: 'Mind you put my *Crossing the Bar* at the end
of all editions of my poems.'

> Sunset and evening star,
>   And one clear call for me!
> And may there be no moaning of the bar,
>   When I put out to sea,
>
> 5 But such a tide as moving seems asleep,
>   Too full for sound and foam,
> When that which drew from out the boundless deep
>   Turns again home.

¶462. *2. And*] But *H.MS*. The 'call' is a marine term, a summons to duty,
here suggesting that of God; but it is ominous too. Cp. the death of Enoch
Arden, when 'There came so loud a calling of the sea' (*p. 615* and *n*).
3. Cp. Charles Kingsley's *The Three Fishers*, a poem on death: 'And the
harbour bar be moaning'. T. had a copy (*Lincoln*) of *Andromeda and Other
Poems* (1858), in which this poem appeared. He read some of Kingsley's
poems to E.T. in 1858 (her Journal). P. Hope-Wallace suggests that Kingsley
referred to the common estuary in Barnstaple Bay, where the joining of two
rivers' waters and the incoming sea can produce a loud moaning sound above
the sand-bar at the mouth of the inlet (*Tennyson*, ed. K. Amis, 1973, p. 218).
7. drew] came *MS*. 'The boundless deep' recurs often in T., with something
of the same mood and theme in *The Ancient Sage* 189–94; and cp. *Sea
Dreams* 85–6: 'such a tide', 'from out the boundless outer deep'. Cp.
In Memoriam: Epilogue 123–4: 'A soul shall draw from out the vast / And
strike his being into bounds.'

Twilight and evening bell,
10   And after that the dark!
And may there be no sadness of farewell,
    When I embark;

For though from out our bourne of Time and Place
    The flood may bear me far,
15 I hope to see my Pilot face to face
    When I have crost the bar.

10. after that] then *MS 1st reading.*

11. And] But *MS.*

13. For . . . our] Alone from out the *MS.*   *bourne*: suggested by Hamlet on death, 'from whose bourn / No traveller returns', III i 79–80.

13–16. J. H. Buckley (p. 287) compares H. F. Lyte's famous hymn: 'Praise, my soul, the King of Heaven . . . / Ye behold him face to face . . . / Dwellers all in time and space.' Also *1 Corinthians* xiii 12: 'For now we see through a glass, darkly; but then face to face.' As so often, T.'s mind may have gone back to Arthur Hallam, to *In Memoriam* cxxxi: 'And come to look on those we loved / And that which made us, face to face' *H.MS.* Hallam's poem *To Two Sisters* (Mary and at this point Emily T.) had said: 'Till our souls see each other face to face' (Motter, p. 90).

14] Alone I sail, and far, *MS.*

15. I] But *MS.* 'The pilot has been on board all the while, but in the dark I have not seen him' (T.). 'He explained the Pilot as "that Divine and Unseen Who is always guiding us"' (H.T.). T. J. Assad discusses the objections to the image, *Tulane Studies in English* viii (1958) 153–63. P. L. Elliott notes that H.T., at an earlier stage of *Mem.*, deleted: 'They [T. and Herbert Warren in 1892] spoke together of *Crossing the Bar* and of the absurdity of the "Pilot" being Arthur Hallam or my brother Lionel' (*The Making of the Memoir*, p. 27).

463–476 Idylls of the King

H.T. introduces the *Idylls* as follows:

'With the publication of *Gareth and Lynette* in 1872 my father thought that he had completed the cycle of the *Idylls*; but later he felt that some further introduction to *Merlin and Vivien* was necessary, and so wrote *Balin and Balan*.

'From his earliest years he had written out in prose various histories of Arthur. His prefatory MS note about the historical Arthur is: "He lived about 500 A.D. and defeated his enemies in a pitched battle in the Welsh kingdom of Strathclyde: and the earliest allusions to him are to be found in the Welsh bards of the seventh century. In the twelfth century Geoffrey of Monmouth collected the legends about him as an European conqueror in his *History of the Britons*: and translated them from Celtic into Latin. [*note*: Wace translated them into French and added the story of the Round Table.] The *Morte d'Arthur* by Sir Thomas Malory was printed by Caxton in 1485." On Malory, on Layamon's *Brut*, on Lady Charlotte Guest's translation of the *Mabinogion*, on the old Chronicles, on old French Romance, on Celtic folklore, and largely on his own imagination, my father founded his epic; he has made the old legends his own, restored the idealism, and infused into them a spirit of modern thought and an ethical significance, setting his characters in a rich and varied landscape; as indeed otherwise these archaic stories, "loosely strung together without art," would not have appealed to the modern world.

'In 1832 appeared the first of the Arthurian poems in the form of a lyric, *The Lady of Shalott* (another version of the story of Lancelot and Elaine), and this was followed in 1842 by the other lyrics, *Sir Launcelot and Queen Guinevere* (partly if not wholly written in 1830) and *Sir Galahad*.

'The 1842 volume also contained the *Morte d' Arthur*, which now forms part of the *Passing of Arthur*.

'The earliest fragment of an epic [*note*: My father told me he was prevented from doing his Arthur Epic, in twelve books, by John Sterling's review in the *Quarterly* [Sept. 1842]. "I had it all in my mind, could have done it without any trouble. But then I thought that a small vessel, built on fine lines, is likely to float further down the stream of Time than a big raft."] that I can find among my father's MSS in my possession was probably written about 1833, and is a sketch in prose. I give it as it stands.'

King Arthur

On the latest limit of the West in the land of Lyonnesse, where, save the rocky Isles of Scilly, all is now wild sea, rose the sacred Mount of Camelot. It rose from the deeps with gardens and bowers and palaces, and at the top of the Mount was King Arthur's hall, and the holy Minster with the Cross of gold. Here dwelt the King in glory apart, while the Saxons whom he had overthrown in twelve battles ravaged the land, and ever came nearer and nearer.

The Mount was the most beautiful in the world, sometimes green and fresh in the beam of morning, sometimes all one splendour, folded in the golden mists of the West. But all underneath it was hollow, and the mountain trembled, when the seas rushed bellowing through the porphyry caves; and there ran a prophecy that the mountain and the city on some wild morning would topple into the abyss and be no more.

It was night. The King sat in his Hall. Beside him sat the sumptuous Guinevere and about him were all his lords and knights of the Table Round. There they feasted, and when the feast was over the Bards sang to the King's glory.

'The following memorandum was presented by my father to Sir James Knowles at Aldworth on October 1, 1869, who told him that it was between thirty and forty years old. It was probably written at the same time as the fragment which I have just quoted. However, the allegorical drift here marked out was fundamentally changed in the later scheme of the *Idylls*.

From an original MS, about 1833:

K.A. Religious Faith

King Arthur's three Guineveres.

The Lady of the Lake?

Two Guineveres. The first prim. Christianity. 2ᵈ Roman Catholicism. The first is put away and dwells apart. 2ᵈ Guinevere flies. Arthur takes to the first again but finds her changed by lapse of Time.

Modred, the sceptical understanding. He pulls Guinevere, Arthur's latest wife, from the throne.

Merlin Emrys, the enchanter. Science. Marries his daughter to Modred. Excalibur, war.

The sea, the people.   ⎱ The S. are a sea-people and it is theirs and a
The Saxons, the people. ⎰ type of them.

The Round Table: liberal institutions.

Battle of Camlan.

2ᵈ Guinevere with the enchanted book and cup.

'Before 1840 it is evident that my father wavered between casting the Arthurian legends into the form of an epic or into that of a musical masque; for in one of his 1833–1840 MS books there is the following first rough draft of a scenario, into which the Lancelot and Elaine scenes were afterwards introduced.'

First Act

Sir Mordred and his party. Mordred inveighs against the King and the Round Table. The knights, and the quest. Mordred scoffs at the Ladies of the Lake, doubts whether they are supernatural beings, etc. Mordred's cringing interview with Guinevere. Mordred and the Lady of the Lake. Arthur lands in Albyn.

Second Act

Lancelot's embassy and Guinevere. The Lady of the Lake meets Arthur and endeavours to persuade him not to fight with Sir Mordred. Arthur will not be moved from his purpose. Lamentation of the Lady of the Lake. Elaine. Marriage of Arthur.

Third Act

Oak tomb of Merlin. The song of Nimuë. Sir Mordred comes to consult Merlin. Coming away meets Arthur. Their fierce dialogue. Arthur consults Sir L. and Sir Bedivere. Arthur weeps over Merlin and is reproved by Nimuë, who inveighs against Merlin. Arthur asks Merlin the issue of the battle. Merlin will not enlighten him. Nimuë requests Arthur to question Merlin again. Merlin tells him he shall bear rule again, but that the Ladies of the Lake can return no more. Guinevere throws away the diamonds into the river. The Court and the dead Elaine.

Fourth Act

Discovery by Mordred and Nimue of Lancelot and Guinevere. Arthur and Guinevere's meeting and parting.

Fifth Act

The battle. Chorus of the Ladies of the Lake. The throwing away of Excalibur and departure of Arthur.

———

'After this my father began to study the epical King Arthur in earnest. He had travelled in Wales, and meditated a tour in Cornwall. He thought, read, talked about King Arthur. He made a poem on Lancelot's quest of the San Graal; "in as good verse," he said, "as I ever wrote–no, I did not write, I made it in my head, and it has altogether slipt out of memory." [*note*: Letter from my father to the Duke of Argyll, 1859.] What he called "the greatest of all poetical subjects" perpetually haunted him. But it was not till 1855 that he determined upon the final shape of the poem, and not until 1859 that he published the first instalment, *Enid, Vivien, Elaine, Guinevere*. In spite of the public applause he did not rush headlong into the other *Idylls of the King*, although he had carried a more or less perfected scheme of them in his head over thirty years. For one thing, he did not consider that the time was ripe. In addition to this, he did not find himself in the proper mood to write them, and he never could work except at what his heart impelled him to do.–Then, however, he devoted himself with all his energies and with infinite enthusiasm to that work alone.

'He also gave some other reasons for pausing in the production of the *Idylls*. "One," he wrote, "is because I could hardly light upon a finer close than that ghostlike passing away of the king" (in *Guinevere*), although the *Morte d'Arthur* was the natural close. The second was that he was not sure he could keep up to the same high level throughout the remaining *Idylls*. "I have thought about it for two years," he writes in 1862, "and arranged all the intervening Idylls, but I dare not set to work for fear of a failure, and time lost." [see *Letters* ii 297, to the Duke of Argyll, [25] Feb. 1862.] The third was, to give it in his own words, '"I doubt whether such a subject as the San Graal could be handled in these days without incurring a charge of irreverence. It would be too much like playing with sacred things." *The Holy Grail*, however, later on seemed to come suddenly, as if by a breath of inspiration; and that volume was given to the world in 1869, containing *The Coming of Arthur, The Holy Grail, Pelleas and Ettarre*, and *The Passing of Arthur*.

'In 1871 *The Last Tournament* was privately printed, and then published in the *Contemporary Review*: re-published with *Gareth and Lynette* in 1872. These with *Balin and Balan* (published in 1885) make up the "twelve books,"–the number mentioned in the Introduction to the *Morte d'Arthur*.

'In 1870 an article on the *Idylls* by Dean Alford, the old college friend of Arthur Hallam and of my father, came out in the *Contemporary*: an able letter also by J. T. Knowles appeared in the *Spectator*. [*note*: See *Contemporary Review*, May 1873.] These reviews my father considered the best. But in later years he often said, "They have taken my hobby, and ridden it too hard, and have explained some things too allegorically, although there is an allegorical or perhaps rather a parabolic drift in the poem." "Of course Camelot for instance, a city of shadowy palaces, is everywhere symbolic of the gradual growth of human beliefs and institutions, and of the spiritual development of man. Yet there is no single fact or incident in the *Idylls*, however seemingly mystical, which cannot be explained as without any mystery or allegory whatever." The Bishop of Ripon (Boyd Carpenter) once asked him whether they were right who interpreted the three Queens, who accompanied King Arthur on his last voyage, as Faith, Hope and Charity. He answered: "They are right, and they are not right. They mean that and they do not. They are three of the noblest of women. They are also those three Graces, but they are much more. I hate to be tied down to say, ' *This* means *that*,' because the thought within the image is much more than any one interpretation."

'As for the many meanings of the poem my father would affirm, "Poetry is like shot-silk with many glancing colours. Every reader must find his own interpretation according to his ability, and according to his sympathy with the poet." The general drift of the *Idylls* is clear enough. "The whole," he said, "is the dream of man coming into practical life and ruined by one sin. Birth is a mystery and death is a mystery, and in the midst lies the tableland of life, and its struggles and performances. It is not the history of one man or of one generation but of a whole cycle of generations." . . . My father said on his eightieth birthday: "My meaning in the *Idylls of the King* was spiritual. I took the legendary stories of the Round Table as illustrations. I intended Arthur to represent the Ideal Soul of Man coming into contact with the warring elements of the flesh." . . . '"The vision of an ideal Arthur as I have drawn him," my father said, "had come upon me when, little more than a boy, I first lighted upon Malory" [*note*: My father's MS]; and it dwelt with him to the end; and we may perhaps say that now the completed poem, regarded as a whole, gives his innermost being more fully, though not more truly, than *In Memoriam*. He felt himself justified in having always pictured Arthur as the Ideal man by such passages as this from Joseph of Exeter: "The old world knows not his peer, nor will the future show us his equal: he alone towers over other kings, better than the past ones and greater than those that are to be." So this from Alberic:

> "Hic jacet Arturus, flos regum, gloria regni,
> Quem probitas morum commendat laude perenni."

'. . . On the other hand, having this vision of Arthur, my father thought that perhaps he had not made the real humanity of the King sufficiently clear in his epilogue; so he inserted in 1891, as his last correction, "Ideal manhood closed in real man," before the lines:

> Rather than that gray king, whose name, a ghost,
> Streams like a cloud, man-shaped, from mountain peak,
> And cleaves to cairn and cromlech still.

'. . . To sum up: if Epic unity is looked for in the *Idylls*, we find it not in the wrath of an Achilles, nor in the wanderings of an Ulysses, but in the unending war of humanity in all ages, – the world-wide war of Sense and Soul, typified in individuals, with the subtle interaction of character upon character, the central dominant figure being the pure, generous, tender, brave, human-hearted Arthur – so that the links (with here and there symbolic accessories) which bind the *Idylls* into an artistic whole, are perhaps somewhat intricate. . . .'
T.Nbk 26 has a page of notes, headed by H.T. 'ıst draft of Play Scenario', on Arthur, Guinevere, Merlin and others.

In her important detailed study of 'Tennyson's Serial Poem' (*Mid-Victorian Studies*, 1965, pp. 80–109), Kathleen Tillotson points out that one of T.'s difficulties was 'that his matter was new. In 1842, Arthurian story was still strange to the ordinary reader, and even felt to be unacceptable as a subject for poetry; and this was undoubtedly one reason for the first long interval of seventeen years between the serial appearances.' John Sterling's criticisms in *QR* (Sept. 1842) bring this home, and T. explicitly referred to Sterling when talking to Allingham in 1867: 'I had it all in my mind, could have done it without any trouble. The King is the complete man, the Knights are the passions' (W. Allingham, *Diary*, 1907, p. 150). T. said to Knowles: 'When I was twenty-four I meant to write a whole great poem on it, and began it in the *Morte d'Arthur*. I said I should do it in twenty years; but the Reviews stopped me . . . By King Arthur I always meant the soul, and by the Round Table the passions and capacities of a man. There is no grander subject in the world than King Arthur' (*Nineteenth Century* xxxiii (1893) 181–2). FitzGerald (his *Letters* i 623) reported in Nov. 1848: 'Not but he meditates new poems; and now the Princess is done, he turns to King Arthur–a worthy subject indeed–and has consulted some histories of him, and spent some time in visiting his traditionary haunts in Cornwall.' T. wrote to W. B. Donne, ? Feb. 1854: 'My wife has a great fancy for books about King Arthur, so oblige her as far as you can. She thinks I can write about the old king. I don't think books can help me to it, nevertheless oblige her' (*Mat.* ii 181; *Letters* ii 78). 'By 1855 Tennyson had planned the final shape of his long poem; but the two items that he chose to write first were as distant as possible from the *Morte d'Arthur*: in order of writing they were *Nimuë* (afterwards *Vivien*), and *Enid*, from the *Mabinogion*, partly written during two months in Wales, exploring Welsh manuscripts and studying the language' (K. Tillotson). E.T. wrote to G. S. Venables, 19 April 1856: '*Merlin* is all written down, quite finished I think, but not much else done. He troubles himself that the *Idylls* do not form themselves into a whole in his mind and moreover that the subject has not reality enough' (*Letters* ii 148).

In May 1857, there was set up *Enid and Nimuë: the True and the False* (*Mat.* ii 180). The British Library copy, which includes corrections by T., has a note by F. T. Palgrave: 'These two Idylls it was A.T.'s original intention to publish by themselves. Six copies were struck off, but owing to a remark upon *Nimuë* which reached him, he at once recalled the copies out: giving me leave, however, to retain the present.' (An edition was printed from this copy in 1902.) In June 1857, T. wrote to the Duchess of Argyll that he had 'heard of a "blustering mouth" . . . a man, a friend it was said, to whom I read or showed the Nimuë; who in lieu of giving his opinion honestly at the moment, appears to have gone brawling about town, saying that such a poem would corrupt the young, that no ladies could buy it or read it etc. etc. Such chatter is as unhandsome, as the criticism is false. Nevertheless why should I expose myself to the folly of fools (in an age which Byron and Wordsworth made and left undramatic?) [*n*. This is put too strongly but is it not in a measure true?]. I should indeed have thought that the truth and purity of the wife in the first poem might well have served as antidote to the untruth of the woman in the second. Perhaps I shall wait till I get a larger volume together and then bring out these with others' (*Letters* ii 179). On 11 Dec. 1858, T. wrote to Ticknor & Fields: 'I wish that you would disabuse your own minds and those of others, as far as you can, of the fancy that I am about an Epic of King Arthur. I should be crazed to attempt such a thing in the heart of the 19th Century' (*Letters* ii 212).

In spring 1859, he prepared the four *Idylls* for publication (*Mem.* i 436); on 8 March 1859, he wrote to the Duchess of Argyll: 'I could be well content to be silent for ever: however the Poems–there are four of them (Your Grace heard two) are finished and, for want of a better name, to be called *the King's*

Idylls' (*Letters* ii 215–6). T. wrote to Knowles, 20 or 21 Aug. 1868: '*Idylls of the King* implies something more and other than mere legends of Arthur: else why did I not name the book Idylls of King *Arthur*? It should have been clearer to my readers that in the very title there is an allusion to the King within us' (*Letters* ii 501). For trial editions of *1859*, see Richard Jones, *The Growth of the Idylls of the King* (1895), and *Virginia*.

In a letter of 23 Feb. 1862, the Duke of Argyll said that the Princess Royal 'is very anxious that you should make the *Morte d'Arthur* the ending of the Idylls–adding only something to connect it with the ending of *Guinevere*' (*Lincoln*). T. replied: 'As to joining these with the *Morte d'Arthur*, there are two objections,–one that I could scarcely light upon a finer close than that ghostlike passing away of the king, and the other that the *Morte* is older in style. I have thought about it and arranged all the intervening Idylls, but I dare not set to work for fear of a failure, and time lost' (*Mem.* i 482–3). (A note to this letter quotes T.: '*The Coming* and *The Passing of Arthur* are simpler and more severe in style, as dealing with the awfulness of Birth and Death'.) But the Duke persisted: 'I wonder whether you are right about the Idylls–I don't see any incongruity between them and the *Morte*' (26 Feb., *Lincoln*). Sir Charles Tennyson (p. 403) points out that T.'s later changes of *1859* archaized the text, and brought it closer to the style of *Morte d'Arthur*. When *The Passing of Arthur*, expanding *1842*, was published in *1869* ('*1870*'), a note read: 'This last, the earliest written of the Poems, is here connected with the rest in accordance with an early project of the author's.' In Dec. 1868, T. had said of *The Holy Grail*: 'I shall write three or four more of the *Idylls*, and link them together as well as I may' (*Mem.* ii 62). It was in *1869* ('*1870*') that T. provided the collective title *The Round Table*, and gave a note on the ordering of the series. (On the 1869 / 1870 datings, see *Book Collector* xvii, 1968, 218–19, 490–91.) In April 1873, R. H. Hutton warned T. not to add or alter, and T. said, with a grim smile, "I must have two more Idylls at the least to make *Vivien* come later into the Poem, as it comes in far too soon as it stands"' (*Diary of Alfred Domett*, 1953, p. 79). In fact, the only major modification was T.'s addition of *Balin and Balan*, which he wrote in 1872–4, but did not publish till 1885, 'whether for the sake of purchasers or because he had not decided whether to make it into one or two' (K. Tillotson).

Sources. See John Churton Collins, *Illustrations of Tennyson* (1891). Some of the school and university editions of individual poems, by F. J. Rowe, W. T. Webb and G. C. Macaulay, were submitted to T. and H.T. for approval (*Lincoln*); T. suggested changes, and H.T. draws heavily on their notes for *Eversley*. See also A. Hamann, *An Essay on Tennyson's Idylls of the King* (1887); H. Littledale, *Essays on Tennyson's Idylls of the King* (1893); and Richard Jones, *The Growth of the Idylls of the King* (1895). T. owned both the 1816 reprints of Malory (the Wilks and the Walker editions, *Lincoln*); all quotations from Malory below are from the Walker edition, preceded by Caxton's numbering for convenience. This Walker edition was given to T. by Leigh Hunt in 1835, and was 'much used' by T. (*Mem.* i 156). It is clear that T. also knew Southey's edition (1817) and Thomas Wright's (1858). On his knowledge of Geoffrey of Monmouth, see J. M. Gray, *Notes and Queries* (Feb. 1967). See also Tom Peete Cross, 'Tennyson as a Celticist', *MP* xviii (1921) 149–56; and W. D. Paden.

J. Pfordresher edited *A Variorum Edition of Tennyson's Idylls of the King* (1973). J. B. McCullough and C. C. Brew provide a very informative 'Study of the Publication of Tennyson's *Idylls of the King*', *Papers of the Bibliographical Society of America* lxv (1971) 156–69.

On the MSS, see Sir Charles Tennyson, *Cornhill* cliii (1936) 534–57, reprinted in *Six Tennyson Essays* (1954). Also Wise, *Bibliography*, passim. On T.'s textual changes, Richard Jones, *The Growth of the Idylls of the King* (1895), is instructive. For T.'s prose drafts, see *Mem.* ii 134–41, *Eversley* v 425–32 and D. Staines's exact transcript of all these prose drafts (*Harvard Library Bulletin* xxii, 1974, 280–308). Staines (see also his *Tennyson's Camelot*, 1983) shows that 'the completed poem is the union of two different modes of composition. The *Morte d'Arthur* and the first quartet of *Idylls* were first written out in poetic drafts. The ten-year delay in the progress of his Arthurian poem led to a new form of composition. For many of the remaining idylls, T. wrote out his first drafts in prose. The prose drafts offer an important perspective on the poet's method of composition. They reveal the central ideas that form the nucleus of the idyll; they exhibit a closer dependence upon source material than the final poetic form suggests; they present the poet experimenting with different approaches to the stories he selects.'

Of modern criticism of the *Idylls*, the most important items are F. E. L. Priestley (*University of Toronto Quarterly*, xix, 1949); J. H. Buckley (*Tennyson: the Growth of a Poet*, 1960); J. D. Rosenberg (*The Fall of Camelot*, 1973); J. M. Gray (*Thro' the Vision of the Night*, 1980). On the influence of Theocritus, see Turner (pp. 164–5); and on the idyll as a kind, R. Pattison, *Tennyson and Tradition* (1979). Theodore Watts recorded: 'Tennyson does not approve of my calling the Idylls an epic. Thinks the Idylls more original. Used Idylls for Idyls to denote a new kind of idyl' (15 Jan. 1886; W. Baker, *TRB* iii, 1979, 122). On the relations between *Morte d'Arthur, In Memoriam, Ode on the Death of the Duke of Wellington*, and *Idylls of the King* (each honouring an Arthur), see C. Y. Lang, *Tennyson's Psycho-drama* (1983); of *Idylls*, Lang says (p. 11): 'The real subject of this great poem is the British Empire.' Also Mark Girouard, *The Return to Camelot: Chivalry and the English Gentleman* (1981).

Idylls of the King

IN TWELVE BOOKS

Flos Regum Arthurus (JOSEPH OF EXETER)

463 Dedication

Published 1862. 'To the Prince Consort' (T.), who had died on 14 Dec. 1861. It was written by about Christmas 1861 (*Tennyson and His Friends*, p. 208), and sent 7 Jan. 1862 (*Letters* ii 291). On 23 Jan., T. wrote to the Duchess of Argyll: 'I am altogether, I assure you, out of love with my Dedication – but I suppose as the Queen has approved of it it must stand as it is' (*Letters* ii 294).

> These to His Memory – since he held them dear,
> Perchance as finding there unconsciously
> Some image of himself – I dedicate,
> I dedicate, I consecrate with tears –
> These Idylls.

¶463. *1.* Prince Albert had asked T. to inscribe a copy of the *Idylls*, 17 May 1860 (*Mem.* i 455).

4. Cp. Catullus, *Fragmenta* 2: *tibi dedico consecroque.* J. Ferguson says this 'may have an echo of Landor's *Rose Aylmer*': 'A night of memories and of sighs / I consecrate to thee' (*English Studies in Africa* xii, 1969, 48).

5. Idylls: 'Regarding the Greek derivation, I spelt my Idylls with two *l*'s mainly to divide them from the ordinary pastoral idyls usually spelt with one *l*. These idylls group themselves round one central figure' (T.). T. pronounced the word with an I as in 'idle'.

> 5   And indeed He seems to me
>   Scarce other than my king's ideal knight,
>   'Who reverenced his conscience as his king;
>   Whose glory was, redressing human wrong;
>   Who spake no slander, no, nor listened to it;
> 10   Who loved one only and who clave to her—'
>   Her—over all whose realms to their last isle,
>   Commingled with the gloom of imminent war,
>   The shadow of His loss drew like eclipse,
>   Darkening the world. We have lost him: he is gone:
> 15   We know him now: all narrow jealousies
>   Are silent; and we see him as he moved,
>   How modest, kindly, all-accomplished, wise,
>   With what sublime repression of himself,
>   And in what limits, and how tenderly;
> 20   Not swaying to this faction or to that;
>   Not making his high place the lawless perch
>   Of winged ambitions, nor a vantage-ground
>   For pleasure; but through all this tract of years
>   Wearing the white flower of a blameless life,
> 25   Before a thousand peering littlenesses,
>   In that fierce light which beats upon a throne,

6. *king's*] *1882*; own *1862–81*. 'The first reading ... was altered because Leslie Stephen and others called King Arthur a portrait of the Prince Consort' (H.T.).

12. 'Owing to the *Trent* affair [1861], when two Southern Commissioners accredited to Great Britain and France by the Confederate States were taken off a British steamship, the *Trent*, by the captain of the Federal man-of-war *San Jacinto*. The Queen and the Prince Consort were said to have averted war by their modification of a dispatch' (T.).

13. *drew*] *1863*; moved *1862*.

14. *We . . . gone*] That maiden-manly soul *H.Lpr 95 2nd reading*.

15 ∧ 16. The MS had included a reference to 'The fume and babble of a petulant hour'. The Duke and Duchess of Argyll (to whom T. sent the *Dedication* in Jan. 1862; *Letters* ii 291) criticised this, and other lines: 'Worthy the sacred name of gentleman', and l. 25. The Duke thought it 'expedient to omit all very direct allusion to *Jealousies* of the Prince'; 'I would not advise the insertion of the line "The sudden fume and petulance of an hour" ... Let it be forgotten, if possible' (14, 18 Jan. 1862; *Lincoln*).

17. In his letter of 23 Jan. 1862, T. wrote: 'I missed out the word "bounteous" in the lines I sent to the Queen and inserted "kindly" simply because I thought the line sounded better—some unhappy critic, possibly, would say that I struck out the word because the Prince had been called *near*' (*Letters* ii 294–5).

And blackens every blot: for where is he,
Who dares foreshadow for an only son
A lovelier life, a more unstained, than his?
30 Or how should England dreaming of *his* sons
Hope more for these than some inheritance
Of such a life, a heart, a mind as thine,
Thou noble Father of her Kings to be,
Laborious for her people and her poor –
35 Voice in the rich dawn of an ampler day –
Far-sighted summoner of War and Waste
To fruitful strifes and rivalries of peace –
Sweet nature gilded by the gracious gleam
Of letters, dear to Science, dear to Art,
40 Dear to thy land and ours, a Prince indeed,
Beyond all titles, and a household name,
Hereafter, through all times, Albert the Good.

Break not, O woman's-heart, but still endure;
Break not, for thou art Royal, but endure,
45 Remembering all the beauty of that star
Which shone so close beside Thee that ye made
One light together, but has past and leaves
The Crown a lonely splendour.

                    May all love,
His love, unseen but felt, o'ershadow Thee,
50 The love of all Thy sons encompass Thee,
The love of all Thy daughters cherish Thee,
The love of all Thy people comfort Thee,
Till God's love set Thee at his side again!

464 The Coming of Arthur

Published *1869* ('*1870*'). T.'s wife records that on 13 Feb. 1869 T. 'read what he had done of the birth and marriage of Arthur'; the poem was

36–7. 'The Prince Consort's work in the planning of the International Exhibitions of 1851 and 1862' (H.T.).
40. *thy land*: 'Saxe-Coburg Gotha' (T.).
41] Worthy the great old name of gentleman. *H.Lpr 96 1st reading*; Loving the sacred name of gentleman. *Yale MS*. Cp. *In Memoriam* cxi 22: 'The grand old name of gentleman'.
47. *leaves*] *1863*; left *1862*.
49. *o'ershadow*: OED 2, to protect. T. wrote to the Duchess of Argyll, 23 Jan. 1862: 'I added a line in the copy which I sent to Her [The Queen] – this – at the conclusion' (*Letters* ii 294).

finished 'before the end of Feb.' (*Mem.* ii 63–4). The title in the trial edition was *The Birth of Arthur* (Wise, *Bibliography* i 197–201). Based on Malory i. 'In this Idyll the poet lays bare the main lines of his story and of his parable' (H.T.). T. comments:

'How much of history we have in the story of Arthur is doubtful. Let not my readers press too hardly on details whether for history or for allegory. Some think that King Arthur may be taken to typify conscience. He is anyhow meant to be a man who spent himself in the cause of honour, duty and self-sacrifice, who felt and aspired with his nobler knights, though with a stronger and a clearer conscience than any of them, "reverencing his conscience as his king." "In short, God has not made since Adam was, the man more perfect than Arthur," as an old writer says. "Major praeteritis majorque futuris Regibus." The vision of Arthur as I have drawn him came upon me when, little more than a boy, I first lighted upon Malory.

> þe time cõ þe wes icoren:
> þa wes Arður iboren.
> Sone swa he com an eorðe:
> aluen hine iuengen.
> heo bigolen þat child:
> mid galdere swiðe stronge.
> heo ȝeuē him mihte:
> to beon bezst alre cnihten.
> heo ȝeuen him an oðer þing:
> þat he scolde beon riche king.
> heo ȝiuen hī þat þridde:
> þat he scolde longe libben.
> heo ȝifen him þat kine-bern:
> custen swiðe gode.
> þat he wes mete-custi:
> of alle quikemonnen.
> þis þe alue him ȝef:
> And al swa þat child iþæh.

Layamon's *Brut*, Madden, vol. ii 384.

'(The time came that was chosen, then was Arthur born. So soon as he came on earth, elves took him; they enchanted the child with magic most strong, they gave him might to be the best of all knights; they gave him another thing, that he should be a rich king; they gave him the third, that he should live long; they gave to him, the child, virtues most good, so that he was *most* generous of all men alive: This the elves gave him, and thus the child thrived.)

'The Coming of Arthur is on the night of the New Year; when he is wedded "the world is white with May"; on a summer night the vision of the Holy Grail appears; and the "Last Tournament" is in the "yellowing autumn-tide." Guinevere flees through the mists of autumn, and Arthur's death takes place at midnight in mid-winter. The form of the

Coming of Arthur and of the *Passing* is purposely more archaic than that of the other Idylls. The blank verse throughout each of the twelve Idylls varies according to the subject.'

See J. M. Gray, 'A Study in Idyl: Tennyson's *The Coming of Arthur*', *Renaissance and Modern Studies* xiv (1970) 111–59. D. Staines notes that this is the only one of the *Idylls* written after 1859 that does not survive in any form of a prose draft (*Harvard Library Bulletin* xxii, 1974, 308).

> Leodogran, the King of Cameliard,
> Had one fair daughter, and none other child;
> And she was fairest of all flesh on earth,
> Guinevere, and in her his one delight.
>
> 5   For many a petty king ere Arthur came
> Ruled in this isle, and ever waging war
> Each upon other, wasted all the land;
> And still from time to time the heathen host
> Swarmed overseas, and harried what was left.
> 10 And so there grew great tracts of wilderness,
> Wherein the beast was ever more and more,
> But man was less and less, till Arthur came.
> For first Aurelius lived and fought and died,
> And after him King Uther fought and died,
> 15 But either failed to make the kingdom one.
> And after these King Arthur for a space,
> And through the puissance of his Table Round,
> Drew all their petty princedoms under him.
> Their king and head, and made a realm, and reigned.
>
> 20 And thus the land of Cameliard was waste,
> Thick with wet woods, and many a beast therein,
> And none or few to scare or chase the beast;
> So that wild dog, and wolf and boar and bear

¶464. 5. 'This explains the existence of Leodogran, one of the petty princes. "Cameliard is apparently", according to Wright, "the district called Carmelide in the English metrical romance of *Merlin*, on the border of which was a town called 'Breckenho' (Brecknock)" – T. Wright's edition of the *Mort d'Arthure*' (T.).

13. 'Aurelius (Emrys) Ambrosius was brother of King Uther' (T.). H.T. adds: 'For the histories of Aurelius and Uther see Geoffrey of Monmouth's *Chronicle*, Bks v and vi.'

17. 'A table called King Arthur's is kept at Winchester. It was supposed to symbolise the world, being flat and round' (T.).

18. 'The several petty princedoms were under one head, the "pendragon"' (T.).

Came night and day, and rooted in the fields,
25 And wallowed in the gardens of the King.
And ever and anon the wolf would steal
The children and devour, but now and then,
Her own brood lost or dead, lent her fierce teat
To human sucklings; and the children, housed
30 In her foul den, there at their meat would growl,
And mock their foster-mother on four feet,
Till, straightened, they grew up to wolf-like men,
Worse than the wolves. And King Leodogran
Groaned for the Roman legions here again,
35 And Cæsar's eagle: then his brother king,
Urien, assailed him: last a heathen horde,
Reddening the sun with smoke and earth with blood,
And on the spike that split the mother's heart
Spitting the child, brake on him, till, amazed,
40 He knew not whither he should turn for aid.

But–for he heard óf Arthur newly crowned,
Though not without an uproar made by those
Who cried, 'He is not Uther's son'–the King
Sent to him, saying, 'Arise, and help us thou!
45 For here between the man and beast we die.'

And Arthur yet had done no deed of arms,
But heard the call, and came: and Guinevere
Stood by the castle walls to watch him pass;
But since he neither wore on helm or shield
50 The golden symbol of his kinglihood,
But rode a simple knight among his knights,
And many of these in richer arms than he,
She saw him not, or marked not, if she saw,
One among many, though his face was bare.
55 But Arthur, looking downward as he past,
Felt the light of her eyes into his life
Smite on the sudden, yet rode on, and pitched
His tents beside the forest. Then he drave

31. 'Imitate the wolf by going on four feet' (T.).
32. 'Compare what is told of in some parts of India (*Journal of Anthropological Society of Bombay*, vol. i) and of the loup-garous and were-wolves of France and Germany' (T.).
34. 'Cf. *Groans of the Britons*, by Gildas' (T.).
36. Urien] 1873; Rience *1869–70.* 'King of North Wales' (T.).
50. 'The golden dragon' (T.).
58. Then] 1873; And *1869–70.*

The heathen; after, slew the beast, and felled
60 The forest, letting in the sun, and made
Broad pathways for the hunter and the knight
And so returned.

For while he lingered there,
A doubt that ever smouldered in the hearts
Of those great Lords and Barons of his realm
65 Flashed forth and into war: for most of these,
Colleaguing with a score of petty kings,
Made head against him, crying, 'Who is he
That he should rule us? who hath proven him
King Uther's son? for lo! we look at him,
70 And find nor face nor bearing, limbs nor voice,
Are like to those of Uther whom we knew.
This is the son of Gorlois, not the King;
This is the son of Anton, not the King.'

And Arthur, passing thence to battle, felt
75 Travail, and throes and agonies of the life,
Desiring to be joined with Guinevere;
And thinking as he rode, 'Her father said
That there between the man and beast they die.
Shall I not lift her from this land of beasts
80 Up to my throne, and side by side with me?
What happiness to reign a lonely king,
Vext–O ye stars that shudder over me,
O earth that soundest hollow under me,
Vext with waste dreams? for saving I be joined
85 To her that is the fairest under heaven,
I seem as nothing in the mighty world,
And cannot will my will, nor work my work
Wholly, nor make myself in mine own realm
Victor and lord. But were I joined with her,
90 Then might we live together as one life,
And reigning with one will in everything
Have power on this dark land to lighten it,
And power on this dead world to make it live.'

Thereafter–as he speaks who tells the tale–
95 When Arthur reached a field-of-battle bright

59. ;after] 1873; ,and he 1869–70.   heathen: 'Angles, Jutes, and Saxons'
(T.).
60. letting] 1873; and let 1869–70.
66] 1873; not 1869–70.
94–133] 1873; not 1869–70. On the Lincoln MS of these lines, see C. Ricks, TRB
ii (1973) 68–72.

With pitched pavilions of his foe, the world
Was all so clear about him, that he saw
The smallest rock far on the faintest hill,
And even in high day the morning star.
100 So when the King had set his banner broad,
At once from either side, with trumpet-blast,
And shouts, and clarions shrilling unto blood,
The long-lanced battle let their horses run.
And now the Barons and the kings prevailed,
105 And now the King, as here and there that war
Went swaying; but the Powers who walk the world
Made lightnings and great thunders over him,
And dazed all eyes, till Arthur by main might,
And mightier of his hands with every blow,
110 And leading all his knighthood threw the kings
Carádos, Urien, Cradlemont of Wales,
Claudias, and Clariance of Northumberland,
The King Brandagoras of Latangor,
With Anguisant of Erin, Morganore,
115 And Lot of Orkney. Then, before a voice
As dreadful as the shout of one who sees
To one who sins, and deems himself alone
And all the world asleep, they swerved and brake
Flying, and Arthur called to stay the brands
120 That hacked among the flyers, 'Ho! they yield!'
So like a painted battle the war stood
Silenced, the living quiet as the dead,
And in the heart of Arthur joy was lord.
He laughed upon his warrior whom he loved
125 And honoured most. 'Thou dost not doubt me King,
So well thine arm hath wrought for me today.'
'Sir and my liege,' he cried, 'the fire of God
Descends upon thee in the battle-field:
I know thee for my King!' Whereat the two,
130 For each had warded either in the fight,
Sware on the field of death a deathless love.
And Arthur said, 'Man's word is God in man:
Let chance what will, I trust thee to the death.'

Then quickly from the foughten field he sent

---

100. Gray (p. 47): 'fuses the Biblical "and in the name of our God we will set up our banners" [*Psalm* xx 5] and Spenser's "with scutchins gilt and banners broad displayd" [*Faerie Queene* IV iii V]'.

111–15. On these names and modification of Malory, see J. M. Gray, *VP* viii (1970) 339–41; and Gray (pp. 47–8).

135 Ulfius, and Brastias, and Bedivere,
His new-made knights, to King Leodogran,
Saying, 'If I in aught have served thee well,
Give me thy daughter Guinevere to wife.'

Whom when he heard, Leodogran in heart
140 Debating—'How should I that am a king,
However much he holp me at my need,
Give my one daughter saving to a king,
And a king's son?'—lifted his voice, and called
A hoary man, his chamberlain, to whom
145 He trusted all things, and of him required
His counsel: 'Knowest thou aught of Arthur's birth?'

Then spake the hoary chamberlain and said,
'Sir King, there be but two old men that know:
And each is twice as old as I; and one
150 Is Merlin, the wise man that ever served
King Uther through his magic art; and one
Is Merlin's master (so they call him) Bleys,
Who taught him magic; but the scholar ran
Before the master, and so far, that Bleys
155 Laid magic by, and sat him down, and wrote
All things and whatsoever Merlin did
In one great annal-book, where after-years
Will learn the secret of our Arthur's birth.'

To whom the King Leodogran replied,
160 'O friend, had I been holpen half as well
By this King Arthur as by thee today,
Then beast and man had had their share of me:
But summon here before us yet once more
Ulfius, and Brastias, and Bedivere.'

165   Then, when they came before him, the King said,
'I have seen the cuckoo chased by lesser fowl,
And reason in the chase: but wherefore now
Do these your lords stir up the heat of war,
Some calling Arthur born of Gorloïs,
170 Others of Anton? Tell me, ye yourselves,
Hold ye this Arthur for King Uther's son?'

And Ulfius and Brastias answered, 'Ay.'
Then Bedivere, the first of all his knights
Knighted by Arthur at his crowning, spake—
175 For bold in heart and act and word was he,
Whenever slander breathed against the King—

134] 1873; And Arthur from the field of battle sent 1869–70.

'Sir, there be many rumours on this head:
For there be those who hate him in their hearts,
Call him baseborn, and since his ways are sweet,
180 And theirs are bestial, hold him less than man:
And there be those who deem him more than man,
And dream he dropt from heaven: but my belief
In all this matter—so ye care to learn—
Sir, for ye know that in King Uther's time
185 The prince and warrior Gorloïs, he that held
Tintagil castle by the Cornish sea,
Was wedded with a winsome wife, Ygerne:
And daughters had she borne him,—one whereof,
Lot's wife, the Queen of Orkney, Bellicent,
190 Hath ever like a loyal sister cleaved
To Arthur,—but a son she had not borne.
And Uther cast upon her eyes of love:
But she, a stainless wife to Gorloïs,
So loathed the bright dishonour of his love,
195 That Gorloïs and King Uther went to war:
And overthrown was Gorloïs and slain.
Then Uther in his wrath and heat besieged
Ygerne within Tintagil, where her men,
Seeing the mighty swarm about their walls,
200 Left her and fled, and Uther entered in,
And there was none to call to but himself.
So, compassed by the power of the King,
Enforced she was to wed him in her tears,
And with a shameful swiftness: afterward,
205 Not many moons, King Uther died himself,
Moaning and wailing for an heir to rule
After him, lest the realm should go to wrack.
And that same night, the night of the new year,
By reason of the bitterness and grief
210 That vext his mother, all before his time
Was Arthur born, and all as soon as born
Delivered at a secret postern-gate
To Merlin, to be holden far apart
Until his hour should come; because the lords
215 Of that fierce day were as the lords of this,
Wild beasts, and surely would have torn the child
Piecemeal among them, had they known; for each
But sought to rule for his own self and hand,

185–222. See Malory i 1–5, which T. modifies considerably.
189. 'The kingdom of Orkney and Lothian composed the North and East of Scotland' (T.).

And many hated Uther for the sake
220 Of Gorloïs. Wherefore Merlin took the child,
And gave him to Sir Anton, an old knight
And ancient friend of Uther; and his wife
Nursed the young prince, and reared him with her own;
And no man knew. And ever since the lords
225 Have foughten like wild beasts among themselves,
So that the realm has gone to wrack: but now,
This year, when Merlin (for his hour had come)
Brought Arthur forth, and set him in the hall,
Proclaiming, "Here is Uther's heir, your king,"
230 A hundred voices cried, "Away with him!
No king of ours! a son of Gorloïs he,
Or else the child of Anton, and no king,
Or else baseborn." Yet Merlin through his craft,
And while the people clamoured for a king,
235 Had Arthur crowned; but after, the great lords
Banded, and so brake out in open war.'

Then while the King debated with himself
If Arthur were the child of shamefulness,
Or born the son of Gorloïs, after death,
240 Or Uther's son, and born before his time,
Or whether there were truth in anything
Said by these three, there came to Cameliard,
With Gawain and young Modred, her two sons,
Lot's wife, the Queen of Orkney, Bellicent;
245 Whom as he could, not as he would, the King
Made feast for, saying, as they sat at meat,

'A doubtful throne is ice on summer seas.
Ye come from Arthur's court. Victor his men
Report him! Yea, but ye–think ye this king–
250 So many those that hate him, and so strong,
So few his knights, however brave they be–
Hath body enow to hold his foemen down?'

'O King,' she cried, 'and I will tell thee: few,
Few, but all brave, all of one mind with him;
255 For I was near him when the savage yells
Of Uther's peerage died, and Arthur sat

234. T. quotes Malory i 7: 'Wherefore all the commons cried at once,
"We will have Arthur unto our king".'
248–9] 1873; Ye come from Arthur's court: think ye this king–1869–70.
250] 1873; not 1869–70.
252. hold] 1873; beat 1869–70.   body enow: 'strength' (T.).

Crowned on the daïs, and his warriors cried,
"Be thou the king, and we will work thy will
Who love thee." Then the King in low deep tones,
260   And simple words of great authority,
Bound them by so strait vows to his own self,
That when they rose, knighted from kneeling, some
Were pale as at the passing of a ghost,
Some flushed, and others dazed, as one who wakes
265   Half-blinded at the coming of a light.

'But when he spake and cheered his Table Round
With large, divine, and comfortable words,
Beyond my tongue to tell thee—I beheld
From eye to eye through all their Order flash
270   A momentary likeness of the King:
And ere it left their faces, through the cross
And those around it and the Crucified,
Down from the casement over Arthur, smote
Flame-colour, vert and azure, in three rays,
275   One falling upon each of three fair queens,
Who stood in silence near his throne, the friends
Of Arthur, gazing on him, tall, with bright
Sweet faces, who will help him at his need.

'And there I saw mage Merlin, whose vast wit
280   And hundred winters are but as the hands
Of loyal vassals toiling for their liege.

'And near him stood the Lady of the Lake,
Who knows a subtler magic than his own—
Clothed in white samite, mystic, wonderful.
285   She gave the King his huge cross-hilted sword,
Whereby to drive the heathen out: a mist
Of incense curled about her, and her face
Wellnigh was hidden in the minster gloom;
But there was heard among the holy hymns
290   A voice as of the waters, for she dwells
Down in a deep; calm, whatsoever storms
May shake the world, and when the surface rolls,
Hath power to walk the waters like our Lord.

282. 'The Lady of the Lake in the old legends is the Church' (T.).
290. T. compares *Revelation* xiv 2: 'I heard a voice from heaven, as the
voice of many waters.'

'There likewise I beheld Excalibur
295 Before him at his crowning borne, the sword
    That rose from out the bosom of the lake,
    And Arthur rowed across and took it—rich
    With jewels, elfin Urim, on the hilt,
    Bewildering heart and eye—the blade so bright
300 That men are blinded by it—on one side,
    Graven in the oldest tongue of all this world,
    "Take me," but turn the blade and ye shall see,
    And written in the speech ye speak yourself,
    "Cast me away!" And sad was Arthur's face
305 Taking it, but old Merlin counselled him,
    "Take thou and strike! the time to cast away
    Is yet far-off." So this great brand the king
    Took, and by this will beat his foemen down.'

    Thereat Leodogran rejoiced, but thought
310 To sift his doubtings to the last, and asked,
    Fixing full eyes of question on her face,
    'The swallow and the swift are near akin,
    But thou art closer to this noble prince,
    Being his own dear sister;' and she said,
315 'Daughter of Gorloïs and Ygerne am I;'
    'And therefore Arthur's sister?' asked the King.
    She answered, 'These be secret things,' and signed
    To those two sons to pass, and let them be.
    And Gawain went, and breaking into song
320 Sprang out, and followed by his flying hair
    Ran like a colt, and leapt at all he saw:
    But Modred laid his ear beside the doors,
    And there half-heard; the same that afterward
    Struck for the throne, and striking found his doom.

325 And then the Queen made answer, 'What know I?
    For dark my mother was in eyes and hair,

294. *Excalibur*: 'Said to mean "cut-steel". In the Romance of *Merlin* the sword bore the following inscription: "Ich am y-hote Escalabore / Unto a king a fair tresore", and it is added: "On Inglis is this writing / Kerve steel and yren and al thing"' (T.).
298. *Urim*: *Exodus* xxviii 30: 'And thou shalt put in the breastplate of judgment the Urim and the Thummim' (oraculous gems). *Paradise Lost* vi 761 (Gray, p. 44).
302, 303. ye] 1873; you 1869-70.
306-7. *Ecclesiastes* iii 6: 'A time to get, and a time to lose; a time to keep, and a time to cast away.'

And dark in hair and eyes am I; and dark
Was Gorloïs, yea and dark was Uther too,
Wellnigh to blackness; but this King is fair
330 Beyond the race of Britons and of men.
Moreover, always in my mind I hear
A cry from out the dawning of my life,
A mother weeping, and I hear her say,
"O that ye had some brother, pretty one,
335 To guard thee on the rough ways of the world."'

'Ay,' said the King, 'and hear ye such a cry?
But when did Arthur chance upon thee first?'

'O King!' she cried, 'and I will tell thee true:
He found me first when yet a little maid:
340 Beaten I had been for a little fault
Whereof I was not guilty; and out I ran
And flung myself down on a bank of heath,
And hated this fair world and all therein,
And wept, and wished that I were dead; and he—
345 I know not whether of himself he came,
Or brought by Merlin, who, they say, can walk
Unseen at pleasure—he was at my side,
And spake sweet words, and comforted my heart,
And dried my tears, being a child with me.
350 And many a time he came, and evermore
As I grew greater grew with me; and sad
At times he seemed, and sad with him was I,
Stern too at times, and then I loved him not,
But sweet again, and then I loved him well.
355 And now of late I see him less and less,
But those first days had golden hours for me,
For then I surely thought he would be king.

'But let me tell thee now another tale:
For Bleys, our Merlin's master, as they say,
360 Died but of late, and sent his cry to me,
To hear him speak before he left his life.
Shrunk like a fairy changeling lay the mage;
And when I entered told me that himself
And Merlin ever served about the King,
365 Uther, before he died; and on the night
When Uther in Tintagil past away
Moaning and wailing for an heir, the two
Left the still King, and passing forth to breathe,
Then from the castle gateway by the chasm

370 Descending through the dismal night—a night
     In which the bounds of heaven and earth were lost—
     Beheld, so high upon the dreary deeps
     It seemed in heaven, a ship, the shape thereof
     A dragon winged, and all from stem to stern
375 Bright with a shining people on the decks,
     And gone as soon as seen. And then the two
     Dropt to the cove, and watched the great sea fall,
     Wave after wave, each mightier than the last,
     Till last, a ninth one, gathering half the deep
380 And full of voices, slowly rose and plunged
     Roaring, and all the wave was in a flame:
     And down the wave and in the flame was borne
     A naked babe, and rode to Merlin's feet,
     Who stoopt and caught the babe, and cried "The King!
385 Here is an heir for Uther!" And the fringe
     Of that great breaker, sweeping up the strand,
     Lashed at the wizard as he spake the word,
     And all at once all round him rose in fire,
     So that the child and he were clothed in fire.
390 And presently thereafter followed calm,
     Free sky and stars: "And this same child," he said,
     "Is he who reigns; nor could I part in peace
     Till this were told." And saying this the seer
     Went through the strait and dreadful pass of death,
395 Not ever to be questioned any more
     Save on the further side; but when I met
     Merlin, and asked him if these things were truth—
     The shining dragon and the naked child
     Descending in the glory of the seas—
400 He laughed as is his wont, and answered me
     In riddling triplets of old time, and said:

     "'Rain, rain, and sun! a rainbow in the sky!
     A young man will be wiser by and by;

377] Dropt from the castle to the cove, and saw
     Far off a light at sea such as the moon
     Crost by a cloud may cast upon the wave
                                    British Library MS
379. 'Every ninth wave is supposed by the Welsh bards to be larger than
those that go before' (H.T.).
402. 'The truth appears in different guise to divers persons. The one fact is
that man comes from the great deep and returns to it. This is an echo of the
triads of the Welsh bards' (T.). O. L. Jiriczek (*Anglia, Beiblatt,* 1926, p. 120)

An old man's wit may wander ere he die.
405 Rain, rain, and sun! a rainbow on the lea!
And truth is this to me, and that to thee;
And truth or clothed or naked let it be.
Rain, sun, and rain! and the free blossom blows:
Sun, rain, and sun! and where is he who knows?
410 From the great deep to the great deep he goes."

'So Merlin riddling angered me; but thou
Fear not to give this King thine only child,
Guinevere: so great bards of him will sing
Hereafter; and dark sayings from of old
415 Ranging and ringing through the minds of men,
And echoed by old folk beside their fires
For comfort after their wage-work is done,
Speak of the King; and Merlin in our time
Hath spoken also, not in jest, and sworn
420 Though men may wound him that he will not die,
But pass, again to come; and then or now
Utterly smite the heathen underfoot,
Till these and all men hail him for their king.'

She spake and King Leodogran rejoiced,
425 But musing 'Shall I answer yea or nay?'
Doubted, and drowsed, nodded and slept, and saw,
Dreaming, a slope of land that ever grew,
Field after field, up to a height, the peak
Haze-hidden, and thereon a phantom king,
430 Now looming, and now lost; and on the slope
The sword rose, the hind fell, the herd was driven,
Fire glimpsed; and all the land from roof and rick,
In drifts of smoke before a rolling wind,
Streamed to the peak, and mingled with the haze
435 And made it thicker; while the phantom king
Sent out at times a voice; and here or there
Stood one who pointed toward the voice, the rest
Slew on and burnt, crying, 'No king of ours,
No son of Uther, and no king of ours;'

quotes a triad's reference to 'the Great Deep or Lowest Point of Existence',
and suggests that T. was indebted to the notes to Southey's *Madoc*. H.T.
compares *Gareth and Lynette* 280–2.

420. Malory xxi 7: 'Some men yet say, in many parts of England, that
king Arthur is not dead; but, by the will of our Lord Jesu Christ, into
another place: and men say, that he will come again, and he shall win the
holy cross.'

440 Till with a wink his dream was changed, the haze
Descended, and the solid earth became
As nothing, but the King stood out in heaven,
Crowned. And Leodogran awoke, and sent
Ulfius, and Brastias and Bedivere,
445 Back to the court of Arthur answering yea.

Then Arthur charged his warrior whom he loved
And honoured most, Sir Lancelot, to ride forth
And bring the Queen;–and watched him from the
gates:
And Lancelot past away among the flowers,
450 (For then was latter April) and returned
Among the flowers, in May, with Guinevere.
To whom arrived, by Dubric the high saint,
Chief of the church in Britain, and before
The stateliest of her altar-shrines, the King
455 That morn was married, while in stainless white,
The fair beginners of a nobler time,
And glorying in their vows and him, his knights
Stood round him, and rejoicing in his joy.
Far shone the fields of May through open door,
460 The sacred altar blossomed white with May,
The Sun of May descended on their King,
They gazed on all earth's beauty in their Queen,
Rolled incense, and there past along the hymns
A voice as of the waters, while the two
465 Sware at the shrine of Christ a deathless love:
And Arthur said, 'Behold, thy doom is mine.
Let chance what will, I love thee to the death!'
To whom the Queen replied with drooping eyes,
'King and my lord, I love thee to the death!'
470 And holy Dubric spread his hands and spake,
'Reign ye, and live and love, and make the world
Other, and may thy Queen be one with thee,
And all this Order of thy Table Round
Fulfil the boundless purpose of their King!'

440. Rosenberg (p. 91) notes *1 Corinthians* xv 51–2: 'Behold, I show you a
mystery; We shall not all sleep, but we shall be changed, In a moment, in the
twinkling of an eye, at the last trump.'
442. but] 1873; and 1869-70.
451. Cp. the May scene in Malory xx 1.
452. Dubric: 'Archbishop of Caerleon. His crozier is said to be at St David's'
(T.).
454. 'According to Malory, the Church of St Stephen at Camelot' (T.).
459-69] 1873; not 1869-70.

475   So Dubric said; but when they left the shrine
Great Lords from Rome before the portal stood,
In scornful stillness gazing as they past;
Then while they paced a city all on fire
With sun and cloth of gold, the trumpets blew,
480   And Arthur's knighthood sang before the King:–

'Blow trumpet, for the world is white with May;
Blow trumpet, the long night hath rolled away!
Blow through the living world–"Let the King reign."

'Shall Rome or Heathen rule in Arthur's realm?
485   Flash brand and lance, fall battleaxe upon helm,
Fall battleaxe, and flash brand! Let the King reign.

'Strike for the King and live! his knights have heard
That God hath told the King a secret word.
Fall battleaxe, and flash brand! Let the King reign.

490   'Blow trumpet! he will lift us from the dust.
Blow trumpet! live the strength and die the lust!
Clang battleaxe, and clash brand! Let the King reign.

'Strike for the King and die! and if thou diest,
The King is King, and ever wills the highest.
495   Clang battleaxe, and clash brand! Let the King reign.

'Blow, for our Sun is mighty in his May!
Blow, for our Sun is mightier day by day!
Clang battleaxe, and clash brand! Let the King reign.

'The King will follow Christ, and we the King
500   In whom high God hath breathed a secret thing.
Fall battleaxe, and flash brand! Let the King reign.'

So sang the knighthood, moving to their hall.
There at the banquet those great Lords from Rome,
The slowly-fading mistress of the world,

475–502] *1873*; *not 1869–70*. 'My father wrote to my mother that this
Viking song, a pendant to Merlin's song, "rings like a grand music".
This and Leodogran's dream give the drift and grip of the poem, which
describes the aspirations and ambitions of Arthur and his knights, doomed
to downfall–the hints of coming doom being heard throughout' (H.T.).
T. wrote the song in Nov. 1872 (*Mem.* ii 117; *Letters* iii, 6 Nov., 8 Nov.,
10 Nov.)
476–7. 'Because Rome had been the Lord of Britain' (T.).
499. *1 Corinthians* xi 1: 'Be ye followers of me, even as I also am of Christ.'
503] *1873*; Then at the marriage feast came in from Rome, *1869–70*.

505 Strode in, and claimed their tribute as of yore.
But Arthur spake, 'Behold, for these have sworn
To wage my wars, and worship me their King;
The old order changeth, yielding place to new;
And we that fight for our fair father Christ,
510 Seeing that ye be grown too weak and old
To drive the heathen from your Roman wall,
No tribute will we pay:' so those great lords
Drew back in wrath, and Arthur strove with Rome.

And Arthur and his knighthood for a space
515 Were all one will, and through that strength the King
Drew in the petty princedoms under him,
Fought, and in twelve great battles overcame
The heathen hordes, and made a realm and reigned.

465 Gareth and Lynette

Published *1872*. In Feb. 1861, T. 'read of Sir Gareth in the *Morte d'Arthur*' (*Mem.* i 471). T.'s wife records, 7 Oct. 1869: 'He gave me his beginning of Beaumains . . . (the golden time of Arthur's Court) to read (written, as was said jokingly, "to describe a pattern youth for his boys").' T. set it aside for a while. On 5 April 1872, he wrote to Knowles (*Letters* iii; *Mem.* ii 113*n*): '*Gareth* is not finished yet. I left him off once altogether, finding him more difficult to deal with than anything I had ever tried, excepting perhaps *Aylmer's Field*. If I were at liberty, which I think I am not, to print the names of the speakers 'Gareth', 'Linette', over the short snip-snap of their talk, and so avoid the perpetual 'said' and its varieties, the work would be much easier. I have made out the plan, however, and perhaps some day it will be completed; and it will be then to consider whether or no it should go into the *Contemporary* or elsewhere.' T. sent it to press, 9 July 1872 (*Letters* iii; *Mat.* iii 186). Based on Malory vii; T.'s lines 1–430 have no counterpart in Malory. For the MSS and trial edition, see Wise, *Bibliography* i 216–21; E. F. Shannon, *Bibliographical Society of America* xli (1947) 321–40; and J. E. Hartman, *Harvard Library Bulletin* xiii (1959) 239–64. There is also a MS in the Bodleian Library. For T.'s prose drafts (*H.Nbk 40* and *32*, and fragments at the University of Texas at Austin), see D. Staines, *Harvard Library Bulletin*

505. *Strode in, and*] *1873*; Great lords, who *1869–70*.
506. Based on Malory v 2.
507. *wage*] *1873*; fight *1869–70*.
511. 'A line of forts built by Agricola betwixt the Firth of Forth and the Clyde, forty miles long' (T.).

xxii (1974) 294–306. Staines shows that T.'s original plan would have deprived the completed series of any idyll which features the full glory of the Order.

> The last tall son of Lot and Bellicent,
> And tallest, Gareth, in a showerful spring
> Stared at the spate. A slender-shafted Pine
> Lost footing, fell, and so was whirled away.
> 'How he went down,' said Gareth, 'as a false
> 5   knight
> Or evil king before my lance if lance
> Were mine to use – O senseless cataract,
> Bearing all down in thy precipitancy –
> And yet thou art but swollen with cold snows
> 10 And mine is living blood: thou dost His will,
> The Maker's, and not knowest, and I that know,
> Have strength and wit, in my good mother's hall
> Linger with vacillating obedience,
> Prisoned, and kept and coaxed and whistled to –
> 15 Since the good mother holds me still a child!
> Good mother is bad mother unto me!
> A worse were better; yet no worse would I.
> Heaven yield her for it, but in me put force
> To weary her ears with one continuous prayer,
> 20 Until she let me fly discaged to sweep
> In ever-highering eagle-circles up
> To the great Sun of Glory, and thence swoop
> Down upon all things base, and dash them dead,
> A knight of Arthur, working out his will,
> To cleanse the world. Why, Gawain, when he
> 25   came
> With Modred hither in the summertime,
> Asked me to tilt with him, the proven knight.
> Modred for want of worthier was the judge.
> Then I so shook him in the saddle, he said,
> "Thou hast half prevailed against me," said so –
> 30   he –
> Though Modred biting his thin lips was mute,
> For he is alway sullen: what care I?'

¶465. *3. the spate*: 'the river in flood' (T.).

18. H.T. compares *Antony and Cleopatra* IV ii 33: 'And the gods yield you for't.'

21. -highering]-widening *H.Nbk 40*. 'He invents a verb in his youthful exuberance' (T.).

25. 'Gawain and Modred, brothers of Gareth' (T.).

And Gareth went, and hovering round her chair
Asked, 'Mother, though ye count me still the child,
35 Sweet mother, do ye love the child?' She laughed,
'Thou art but a wild-goose to question it.'
'Then, mother, an ye love the child,' he said,
'Being a goose and rather tame than wild,
Hear the child's story.' 'Yea, my well-beloved,
40 An 'twere but of the goose and golden eggs.'

And Gareth answered her with kindling eyes,
'Nay, nay, good mother, but this egg of mine
Was finer gold than any goose can lay;
For this an Eagle, a royal Eagle, laid
45 Almost beyond eye-reach, on such a palm
As glitters gilded in thy Book of Hours.
And there was ever haunting round the palm
A lusty youth, but poor, who often saw
The splendour sparkling from aloft, and thought
50 "An I could climb and lay my hand upon it,
Then were I wealthier than a leash of kings."
But ever when he reached a hand to climb,
One, that had loved him from his childhood,
         caught
And stayed him, "Climb not lest thou break thy
         neck,
55 I charge thee by my love," and so the boy,
Sweet mother, neither clomb, nor brake his neck,
But brake his very heart in pining for it,
And past away.'

                    To whom the mother said,
'True love, sweet son, had risked himself and
         climbed,
60 And handed down the golden treasure to him.'

And Gareth answered her with kindling eyes,
'Gold? said I gold?—ay then, why he, or she,
Or whosoe'er it was, or half the world
Had ventured—*had* the thing I spake of been
65 Mere gold—but this was all of that true steel,
Whereof they forged the brand Excalibur,
And lightnings played about it in the storm,
And all the little fowl were flurried at it,
And there were cries and clashings in the nest,
70 That sent him from his senses: let me go.'

51. 'Three kings. Cf. a leash of dogs'. (T.).

Then Bellicent bemoaned herself and said,
'Hast thou no pity upon my loneliness?
Lo, where thy father Lot beside the hearth
Lies like a log, and all but smouldered out!
75 For ever since when traitor to the King
He fought against him in the Barons' war,
And Arthur gave him back his territory,
His age hath slowly droopt, and now lies there
A yet-warm corpse, and yet unburiable,
No more; nor sees, nor hears, nor speaks, nor
80   knows.
And both thy brethren are in Arthur's hall,
Albeit neither loved with that full love
I feel for thee, nor worthy such a love:
Stay therefore thou; red berries charm the bird,
85 And thee, mine innocent, the jousts, the wars,
Who never knewest finger-ache, nor pang
Of wrenched or broken limb—an often chance
In those brain-stunning shocks, and tourney-falls,
Frights to my heart; but stay: follow the deer
90 By these tall firs and our fast-falling burns;
So make thy manhood mightier day by day;
Sweet is the chase: and I will seek thee out
Some comfortable bride and fair, to grace
Thy climbing life, and cherish my prone year,
95 Till falling into Lot's forgetfulness
I know not thee, myself, nor anything.
Stay, my best son! ye are yet more boy than man.'

Then Gareth, 'An ye hold me yet for child,
Hear yet once more the story of the child.
100 For, mother, there was once a King, like ours.
The prince his heir, when tall and marriageable,
Asked for a bride; and thereupon the King
Set two before him. One was fair, strong, armed—
But to be won by force—and many men
105 Desired her; one, good lack, no man desired.
And these were the conditions of the King:
That save he won the first by force, he needs
Must wed that other, whom no man desired,
A red-faced bride who knew herself so vile,
110 That evermore she longed to hide herself,
Nor fronted man or woman, eye to eye—
Yea—some she cleaved to, but they died of her.
And one—they called her Fame; and one,—
    O Mother,

How can ye keep me tethered to you – Shame.
_115_ Man am I grown, a man's work must I do.
Follow the deer? follow the Christ, the King,
Live pure, speak true, right wrong, follow the King –
Else, wherefore born?'

            To whom the mother said,
'Sweet son, for there be many who deem him not,
_120_ Or will not deem him, wholly proven King –
Albeit in mine own heart I knew him King,
When I was frequent with him in my youth,
And heard him Kingly speak, and doubted him
No more than he, himself; but felt him mine,
_125_ Of closest kin to me: yet – wilt thou leave
Thine easeful biding here, and risk thine all,
Life, limbs, for one that is not proven King?
Stay, till the cloud that settles round his birth
Hath lifted but a little. Stay, sweet son.'

_130_   And Gareth answered quickly, 'Not an hour,
So that ye yield me – I will walk through fire,
Mother, to gain it – your full leave to go.
Not proven, who swept the dust of ruined Rome
From off the threshold of the realm, and crushed
_135_ The Idolaters, and made the people free?
Who should be King save him who makes us free?'

    So when the Queen, who long had sought in vain
To break him from the intent to which he grew,
Found her son's will unwaveringly one,
_140_ She answered craftily, 'Will ye walk through fire?
Who walks through fire will hardly heed the smoke.
Ay, go then, an ye must: only one proof,
Before thou ask the King to make thee knight,
Of thine obedience and thy love to me,
Thy mother, – I demand.'

_145_   And Gareth cried,
'A hard one, or a hundred, so I go.
Nay – quick! the proof to prove me to the quick!'

117. Rosenberg (p. 158) notes _1 Corinthians_ xi 1: 'Be ye followers of me, even
as I also am of Christ'.
124] _H.Nbk 40 has, of the King's birth:_
      dropt out of heaven
  So say the people – are the people wise?
  From the great deep, another said to me.
136. Rosenberg notes _John_ viii 32: 'the truth shall make you free'.

But slowly spake the mother looking at him,
'Prince, thou shalt go disguised to Arthur's hall,
150 And hire thyself to serve for meats and drinks
Among the scullions and the kitchen-knaves,
And those that hand the dish across the bar.
Nor shalt thou tell thy name to anyone.
And thou shalt serve a twelvemonth and a day.'

155 For so the Queen believed that when her son
Beheld his only way to glory lead
Low down through villain kitchen-vassalage,
Her own true Gareth was too princely-proud
To pass thereby; so should he rest with her,
160 Closed in her castle from the sound of arms.

Silent awhile was Gareth, then replied,
'The thrall in person may be free in soul,
And I shall see the jousts. Thy son am I,
And since thou art my mother, must obey.
165 I therefore yield me freely to thy will;
For hence will I, disguised, and hire myself
To serve with scullions and with kitchen-knaves;
Nor tell my name to any—no, not the King.'

Gareth awhile lingered. The mother's eye
170 Full of the wistful fear that he would go,
And turning toward him wheresoe'er he turned,
Perplext his outward purpose, till an hour,
When wakened by the wind which with full voice
Swept bellowing through the darkness on to dawn,
175 He rose, and out of slumber calling two
That still had tended on him from his birth,
Before the wakeful mother heard him, went.

The three were clad like tillers of the soil.
Southward they set their faces. The birds made
180 Melody on branch, and melody in mid air.
The damp hill-slopes were quickened into green,
And the live green had kindled into flowers,
For it was past the time of Easterday.

So, when their feet were planted on the plain
185 That broadened toward the base of Camelot,
Far off they saw the silver-misty morn
Rolling her smoke about the Royal mount,

172. outward purpose: 'purpose to go' (T.).
182. Cp. *In Memoriam* xxxix 11 and *n* (p. *382*).

That rose between the forest and the field.
At times the summit of the high city flashed;
190 At times the spires and turrets half-way down
Pricked through the mist; at times the great gate
    shone
Only, that opened on the field below:
Anon, the whole fair city had disappeared.

Then those who went with Gareth were amazed,
195 One crying, 'Let us go no further, lord.
Here is a city of Enchanters, built
By fairy Kings.' The second echoed him,
'Lord, we have heard from our wise man at home
To Northward, that this King is not the King,
200 But only changeling out of Fairyland,
Who drave the heathen hence by sorcery
And Merlin's glamour.' Then the first again,
'Lord, there is no such city anywhere,
But all a vision.'

               Gareth answered them
205 With laughter, swearing he had glamour enow
In his own blood, his princedom, youth and hopes,
To plunge old Merlin in the Arabian sea;
So pushed them all unwilling toward the gate.
And there was no gate like it under heaven.
210 For barefoot on the keystone, which was lined
And rippled like an ever-fleeting wave,
The Lady of the Lake stood: all her dress
Wept from her sides as water flowing away;
But like the cross her great and goodly arms
215 Stretched under all the cornice and upheld:
And drops of water fell from either hand;
And down from one a sword was hung, from one
A censer, either worn with wind and storm;
And o'er her breast floated the sacred fish;
220 And in the space to left of her, and right,
Were Arthur's wars in weird devices done,
New things and old co-twisted, as if Time
Were nothing, so inveterately, that men
Were giddy gazing there; and over all

198. man] 1875; men 1872-4.
212. 'The Lady of the Lake in the old romances of Lancelot instructs him
in the mysteries of the Christian faith' (T.).
219. fish: ancient symbol of Christianity.

High on the top were those three Queens, the
225   friends
Of Arthur, who should help him at his need.

Then those with Gareth for so long a space
Stared at the figures, that at last it seemed
The dragon-boughts and elvish emblemings
230 Began to move, seethe, twine and curl: they called
To Gareth, 'Lord, the gateway is alive.'

And Gareth likewise on them fixt his eyes
So long, that even to him they seemed to move.
Out of the city a blast of music pealed.
235 Back from the gate started the three, to whom
From out thereunder came an ancient man,
Long-bearded, saying, 'Who be ye, my sons?'

Then Gareth, 'We be tillers of the soil,
Who leaving share in furrow come to see
240 The glories of our King: but these, my men,
(Your city moved so weirdly in the mist)
Doubt if the King be King at all, or come
From Fairyland; and whether this be built
By magic, and by fairy Kings and Queens;
245 Or whether there be any city at all,
Or all a vision: and this music now
Hath scared them both, but tell thou these the
     truth.'

Then that old Seer made answer playing on him
And saying, 'Son, I have seen the good ship sail
250 Keel upward, and mast downward, in the heavens,
And solid turrets topsy-turvy in air:
And here is truth; but an it please thee not,
Take thou the truth as thou hast told it me.
For truly as thou sayest, a Fairy King
255 And Fairy Queens have built the city, son;
They came from out a sacred mountain-cleft

---

229. *dragon-boughts*: 'folds of the dragons' tails' (T.). H.T. compares
Faerie Queene I xi stanza 11: 'His huge long tayle wound up in hundred
foldes, / Does overspred his long bras-scaly backe, / Whose wreathed
boughts when ever he unfoldes, / Bespotted as with shields of red and
blacke . . .'.
236. 'Merlin' (T.).
249. 'Refraction by mirage' (T.).
253. 'Ironical' (T.).

Toward the sunrise, each with harp in hand,
And built it to the music of their harps.
And, as thou sayest, it is enchanted, son,
260 For there is nothing in it as it seems
Saving the King; though some there be that hold
The King a shadow, and the city real:
Yet take thou heed of him, for, so thou pass
Beneath this archway, then wilt thou become
265 A thrall to his enchantments, for the King
Will bind thee by such vows, as is a shame
A man should not be bound by, yet the which
No man can keep; but, so thou dread to swear,
Pass not beneath this gateway, but abide
270 Without, among the cattle of the field.
For an ye heard a music, like enow
They are building still, seeing the city is built
To music, therefore never built at all,
And therefore built for ever.'

Gareth spake
275 Angered, 'Old Master, reverence thine own beard
That looks as white as utter truth, and seems
Wellnigh as long as thou art statured tall!
Why mockest thou the stranger that hath been
To thee fair-spoken?'

But the Seer replied,
280 'Know ye not then the Riddling of the Bards?
"Confusion, and illusion, and relation,
Elusion, and occasion, and evasion"?
I mock thee not but as thou mockest me,
And all that see thee, for thou art not who
285 Thou seemest, but I know thee who thou art.
And now thou goest up to mock the King,
Who cannot brook the shadow of any lie.'

Unmockingly the mocker ending here
Turned to the right, and past along the plain;
290 Whom Gareth looking after said, 'My men,
Our one white lie sits like a little ghost
Here on the threshold of our enterprise.

257. 'The religions and the arts that came from the East' (T.).
269-70. 'Be a mere beast' (T.).
272-3. 'By the Muses' (T.).
285. *Luke* iv 34: 'I know thee who thou art; the Holy One of God.'

Let love be blamed for it, not she, nor I:
Well, we will make amends.'

                     With all good cheer
295 He spake and laughed, then entered with his twain
Camelot, a city of shadowy palaces
And stately, rich in emblem and the work
Of ancient kings who did their days in stone;
Which Merlin's hand, the Mage at Arthur's court,
300 Knowing all arts, had touched, and everywhere
At Arthur's ordinance, tipt with lessening peak
And pinnacle, and had made it spire to heaven.
And ever and anon a knight would pass
Outward, or inward to the hall: his arms
305 Clashed; and the sound was good to Gareth's ear.
And out of bower and casement shyly glanced
Eyes of pure women, wholesome stars of love;
And all about a healthful people stept
As in the presence of a gracious king.

310   Then into hall Gareth ascending heard
A voice, the voice of Arthur, and beheld
Far over heads in that long-vaulted hall
The splendour of the presence of the King
Throned, and delivering doom—and looked no
      more—
315 But felt his young heart hammering in his ears,
And thought, 'For this half-shadow of a lie
The truthful King will doom me when I speak.'
Yet pressing on, though all in fear to find
Sir Gawain or Sir Modred, saw nor one
320 Nor other, but in all the listening eyes
Of those tall knights, that ranged about the throne,
Clear honour shining like the dewy star
Of dawn, and faith in their great King, with pure
Affection, and the light of victory,
325 And glory gained, and evermore to gain.
   Then came a widow crying to the King,
'A boon, Sir King! Thy father, Uther, reft
From my dead lord a field with violence:
For howsoe'er at first he proffered gold,
330 Yet, for the field was pleasant in our eyes,
We yielded not; and then he reft us of it
Perforce, and left us neither gold nor field.'

302. 'Symbolizing the divine' (T.).

Said Arthur, 'Whether would ye? gold or field?'
To whom the woman weeping, 'Nay, my lord,
335 The field was pleasant in my husband's eye.'

And Arthur, 'Have thy pleasant field again,
And thrice the gold for Uther's use thereof,
According to the years. No boon is here,
But justice, so thy say be proven true.
340 Accursed, who from the wrongs his father did
Would shape himself a right!'

                     And while she past,
Came yet another widow crying to him,
'A boon, Sir King! Thine enemy, King, am I.
With thine own hand thou slewest my dear lord,
345 A knight of Uther in the Barons' war,
When Lot and many another rose and fought
Against thee, saying thou wert basely born.
I held with these, and loathe to ask thee aught.
Yet lo! my husband's brother had my son
350 Thralled in his castle, and hath starved him dead;
And standeth seized of that inheritance
Which thou that slewest the sire hast left the son.
So though I scarce can ask it thee for hate,
Grant me some knight to do the battle for me,
355 Kill the foul thief, and wreak me for my son.'

Then strode a good knight forward, crying to
     him,
'A boon, Sir King! I am her kinsman, I.
Give me to right her wrong, and slay the man.'

Then came Sir Kay, the seneschal, and cried,
360 'A boon, Sir King! even that thou grant her none,
This railer, that hath mocked thee in full hall—
None; or the wholesome boon of gyve and gag.'

But Arthur, 'We sit King, to help the wronged
Through all our realm. The woman loves her lord.
365 Peace to thee, woman, with thy loves and hates!
The kings of old had doomed thee to the flames,
Aurelius Emrys would have scourged thee dead,

347. *basely*] bastard- *H.Nbk 40.*
359. 'In the *Roman de la Rose* Sir Kay is given as a pattern of rough
discourtesy' (T.).
367. Uther's brother, who preceded him as king.

And Uther slit thy tongue: but get thee hence—
Lest that rough humour of the kings of old
370   Return upon me! Thou that art her kin,
Go likewise; lay him low and slay him not,
But bring him here, that I may judge the right,
According to the justice of the King:
Then, be he guilty, by that deathless King
375   Who lived and died for men, the man shall die.'

Then came in hall the messenger of Mark,
A name of evil savour in the land,
The Cornish king. In either hand he bore
What dazzled all, and shone far-off as shines
380   A field of charlock in the sudden sun
Between two showers, a cloth of palest gold,
Which down he laid before the throne, and knelt,
Delivering, that his lord, the vassal king,
Was even upon his way to Camelot;
385   For having heard that Arthur of his grace
Had made his goodly cousin, Tristram, knight,
And, for himself was of the greater state,
Being a king, he trusted his liege-lord
Would yield him this large honour all the more;
390   So prayed him well to accept this cloth of gold,
In token of true heart and feälty.

Then Arthur cried to rend the cloth, to rend
In pieces, and so cast it on the hearth.
An oak-tree smouldered there. 'The goodly knight!
395   What! shall the shield of Mark stand among these?'
For, midway down the side of that long hall
A stately pile,—whereof along the front,
Some blazoned, some but carven, and some blank,
There ran a treble range of stony shields,—
400   Rose, and high-arching overbrowed the hearth.
And under every shield a knight was named:
For this was Arthur's custom in his hall;
When some good knight had done one noble deed,
His arms were carven only; but if twain
405   His arms were blazoned also; but if none,
The shield was blank and bare without a sign
Saving the name beneath; and Gareth saw
The shield of Gawain blazoned rich and bright,

And Modred's blank as death; and Arthur cried
410   To rend the cloth and cast it on the hearth.

'More like are we to reave him of his crown
Than make him knight because men call him king.
The kings we found, ye know we stayed their hands
From war among themselves, but left them kings;
415   Of whom were any bounteous, merciful,
Truth-speaking, brave, good livers, them we enrolled
Among us, and they sit within our hall.
But Mark hath tarnished the great name of king,
As Mark would sully the low state of churl:
420   And, seeing he hath sent us cloth of gold,
Return, and meet, and hold him from our eyes,
Lest we should lap him up in cloth of lead,
Silenced for ever – craven – a man of plots,
Craft, poisonous counsels, wayside ambushings –
425   No fault of thine: let Kay the seneschal
Look to thy wants, and send thee satisfied –
Accursed, who strikes nor lets the hand be seen!'

And many another suppliant crying came
With noise of ravage wrought by beast and man,
430   And evermore a knight would ride away.

Last, Gareth leaning both hands heavily
Down on the shoulders of the twain, his men,
Approached between them toward the King,
      and asked,
'A boon, Sir King (his voice was all ashamed),
435   For see ye not how weak and hungerworn
I seem – leaning on these? grant me to serve

422. Cp. *The Passionate Pilgrim, As it fell upon a day* 23-4: 'King Pandion
he is dead; / All thy friends are lapped in lead.'

431-6. Malory vii 1: 'Right so came into the hall two men, well beseen
and richly, and upon their shoulders there leaned the goodliest young man,
and the fairest that ever they saw, and he was large, long and broad in the
shoulders, and well visaged, and the fairest and the largest hands that ever
man saw; but he fared as though he might not go, nor bear himself, but if
he leaned upon their shoulders.'

436-40. Malory vii 1: '"Now, sir," said he, "this is my petition for this
feast, that ye will give me meat and drink sufficiently for these twelve-
months; and at that day I will ask mine other two gifts." – "My fair son,"
said king Arthur, "ask better, I counsel thee, for this is but a simple asking;
for my heart giveth me to thee greatly that thou art come of men of
worship . . . Ye shall have meat and drink enough; I never offended none,

For meat and drink among thy kitchen-knaves
A twelvemonth and a day, nor seek my name.
Hereafter I will fight.'

                        To him the King,
440 'A goodly youth and worth a goodlier boon!
But so thou wilt no goodlier, then must Kay,
The master of the meats and drinks, be thine.'

    He rose and past; then Kay, a man of mien
Wan-sallow as the plant that feels itself
Root-bitten by white lichen,

445   'Lo ye now!
This fellow hath broken from some Abbey, where,
God wot, he had not beef and brewis enow,
However that might chance! but an he work,
Like any pigeon will I cram his crop,
450 And sleeker shall he shine than any hog.'

    Then Lancelot standing near, 'Sir Seneschal,
Sleuth-hound thou knowest, and gray, and all the
          hounds;
A horse thou knowest, a man thou dost not know:
Broad brows and fair, a fluent hair and fine,
455 High nose, a nostril large and fine, and hands
Large, fair and fine!—Some young lad's mystery—
But, or from sheepcot or king's hall, the boy
Is noble-natured. Treat him with all grace,
Lest he should come to shame thy judging of him.'

neither my friend nor foe. But what is thy name? I would fain know."–
"I cannot tell you," said he. "That have I marvel of thee," said the king,
"that thou knowest not thine own name, and thou art one of the goodliest
young men that ever I saw."'

441. *so*] *1873*; an *1872*.

441–2. Malory vii 1: 'Then the noble king Arthur betook him unto the
steward, sir Kaye, and charged him that he should give him of all manner
of meats and drinks of the best; and, also, that he have all manner of finding,
as though he were a lord's son.'

446–50. Malory vii 1–2: '"Pain of my life he was brought up and fostered
in some abbey; and howsomever it was they failed of meat and drink, and
so hither he is come for sustenance ... And into the kitchen I shall bring
him, and there he shall have fat brewis every day, that he shall be as fat by
twelvemonth's end as a pork hog."'   *brewis*: 'broth' (T.).

451–9. Malory vii 2 includes: 'And especially sir Launcelot, for he bid sir
Kaye leave his mocking, "for I dare lay my head he shall prove a man of
great worship".'

460   Then Kay, 'What murmurest thou of mystery?
Think ye this fellow will poison the King's dish?
Nay, for he spake too fool-like: mystery!
Tut, an the lad were noble, he had asked
For horse and armour: fair and fine, forsooth!
465   Sir Fine-face, Sir Fair-hands? but see thou to it
That thine own fineness, Lancelot, some fine day
Undo thee not—and leave my man to me.'

So Gareth all for glory underwent
The sooty yoke of kitchen-vassalage;
470   Ate with young lads his portion by the door,
And couched at night with grimy kitchen-knaves.
And Lancelot ever spake him pleasantly,
But Kay the seneschal, who loved him not,
Would hustle and harry him, and labour him
475   Beyond his comrade of the hearth, and set
To turn the broach, draw water, or hew wood,
Or grosser tasks; and Gareth bowed himself
With all obedience to the King, and wrought
All kind of service with a noble ease
480   That graced the lowliest act in doing it.
And when the thralls had talk among themselves,
And one would praise the love that linkt the King
And Lancelot—how the King had saved his life
In battle twice, and Lancelot once the King's—
485   For Lancelot was the first in Tournament,
But Arthur mightiest on the battle-field—
Gareth was glad. Or if some other told,
How once the wandering forester at dawn,
Far over the blue tarns and hazy seas,

463–5. Malory vii 1: '"That shall little need," said sir Kaye, "to do such cost upon him, for I dare well undertake that he is a villain born, and never will make man; for and he had been come of a gentleman, he would have asked of you horse and harness, but such as he is he hath asked. And sithence he hath no name, I shall give him a name, that shall be Beaumains; that is to say fair hands."'

470–2. Malory vii 2: 'And so sir Kaye had got him a place, and sat down to eat. So Beaumains went to the hall door, and sat him down among boys and lads, and there he eat sadly.'

473] H.Nbk 40, of Kay:
        but Kay the sour, a man
    Of visage sallow as the shrub that feels
    The touch of some white lichen at the root—

476. broach: 'spit' (T.).

490   On Caer-Eryri's highest found the King,
        A naked babe, of whom the Prophet spake,
        'He passes to the Isle Avilion,
        He passes and is healed and cannot die'–
        Gareth was glad. But if their talk were foul,
495   Then would he whistle rapid as any lark,
        Or carol some old roundelay, and so loud
        That first they mocked, but, after, reverenced him.
        Or Gareth telling some prodigious tale
        Of knights, who sliced a red life-bubbling way
500   Through twenty folds of twisted dragon, held
        All in a gap-mouthed circle his good mates
        Lying or sitting round him, idle hands,
        Charmed; till Sir Kay, the seneschal, would come
        Blustering upon them, like a sudden wind
505   Among dead leaves, and drive them all apart.
        Or when the thralls had sport among themselves,
        So there were any trial of mastery,
        He, by two yards in casting bar or stone
        Was counted best; and if there chanced a joust,
510   So that Sir Kay nodded him leave to go,
        Would hurry thither, and when he saw the knights
        Clash like the coming and retiring wave,
        And the spear spring, and good horse reel, the boy
        Was half beyond himself for ecstasy.

515   So for a month he wrought among the thralls;
        But in the weeks that followed, the good Queen,
        Repentant of the word she made him swear,
        And saddening in her childless castle, sent,
        Between the in-crescent and de-crescent moon,
520   Arms for her son, and loosed him from his vow.

           This, Gareth hearing from a squire of Lot
        With whom he used to play at tourney once,
        When both were children, and in lonely haunts
        Would scratch a ragged oval on the sand,
525   And each at either dash from either end–
        Shame never made girl redder than Gareth joy.

---

490. 'Snowdon' (T.).
506–14. Malory vii 2: 'But ever when he knew of any jousting of knights,
that would he see and he might . . . And whereas were any masteries done,
there would he be, and there might none cast the bar or stone to him by two
yards.'
515–72. Added to Malory.

He laughed; he sprang. 'Out of the smoke, at once
I leap from Satan's foot to Peter's knee –
These news be mine, none other's – nay, the King's –
530 Descend into the city:' whereon he sought
The King alone, and found, and told him all.

    'I have staggered thy strong Gawain in a tilt
For pastime; yea, he said it: joust can I.
Make me thy knight – in secret! let my name
535 Be hidden, and give me the first quest, I spring
Like flame from ashes.'

                        Here the King's calm eye
Fell on, and checked, and made him flush, and bow
Lowly, to kiss his hand, who answered him,
'Son, the good mother let me know thee here,
540 And sent her wish that I would yield thee thine.
Make thee my knight? my knights are sworn to
        vows
Of utter hardihood, utter gentleness,
And, loving, utter faithfulness in love,
And uttermost obedience to the King.'

545   Then Gareth, lightly springing from his knees,
'My King, for hardihood I can promise thee.
For uttermost obedience make demand
Of whom ye gave me to, the Seneschal,
No mellow master of the meats and drinks!
550 And as for love, God wot, I love not yet,
But love I shall, God willing.'

                        And the King
'Make thee my knight in secret? yea, but he,
Our noblest brother, and our truest man,
And one with me in all, he needs must know.'

555   'Let Lancelot know, my King, let Lancelot know,
Thy noblest and thy truest!'

                        And the King –
'But wherefore would ye men should wonder at you?
Nay, rather for the sake of me, their King,
And the deed's sake my knighthood do the deed,
Than to be noised of.'

560   Merrily Gareth asked,
'Have I not earned my cake in baking of it?
Let be my name until I make my name!'

My deeds will speak: it is but for a day.'
So with a kindly hand on Gareth's arm
565 Smiled the great King, and half-unwillingly
Loving his lusty youthhood yielded to him.
Then, after summoning Lancelot privily,
'I have given him the first quest: he is not proven.
Look therefore when he calls for this in hall,
570 Thou get to horse and follow him far away.
Cover the lions on thy shield, and see
Far as thou mayest, he be nor ta'en nor slain.'

Then that same day there past into the hall
A damsel of high lineage, and a brow
575 May-blossom, and a cheek of apple-blossom,
Hawk-eyes; and lightly was her slender nose
Tip-tilted like the petal of a flower;
She into hall past with her page and cried,

'O King, for thou hast driven the foe without,
580 See to the foe within! bridge, ford, beset
By bandits, everyone that owns a tower
The Lord for half a league. Why sit ye there?
Rest would I not, Sir King, an I were king,
Till even the lonest hold were all as free
585 From cursèd bloodshed, as thine altar-cloth
From that best blood it is a sin to spill.'

'Comfort thyself,' said Arthur, 'I nor mine
Rest: so my knighthood keep the vows they swore,
The wastest moorland of our realm shall be

573–96. Malory vii 2: 'Right so there came in a damsel and saluted the
king, and prayed him for succour. "For whom?" said the king: "what is
the adventure?"–"Sir," said she, "I have a lady of great worship and
renown, and she is besieged with a tyrant, so that she may not go out of her
castle; and, because that here in your court are called the noblest knights
of the world, I come unto you and pray you for succour."–"What call
ye your lady? where dwelleth she? and what is his name that hath besieged
her?"–"Sir king," said she, "as for my lady's name, that shall not be
known for me as at this time; but I let you wit she is a lady of great wor-
ship, and of great lands: and, as for the tyrant that besiegeth her, and
destroyeth her land, he is called the red knight of the red lands."–"I
know him not," said the king ... "there be knights here that would do
their power to rescue your lady, but because ye will not tell her name, nor
where she dwelleth; therefore, none of my knights that be here now shall
go with you by my will."–"Then must I speak [seek] further," said the
damsel.'

590 Safe, damsel, as the centre of this hall.
What is thy name? thy need?'

'My name?' she said—
'Lynette my name; noble; my need, a knight
To combat for my sister, Lyonors,
A lady of high lineage, of great lands,
595 And comely, yea, and comelier than myself.
She lives in Castle Perilous: a river
Runs in three loops about her living-place;
And o'er it are three passings, and three knights
Defend the passings, brethren, and a fourth
600 And of that four the mightiest, holds her stayed
In her own castle, and so besieges her
To break her will, and make her wed with him:
And but delays his purport till thou send
To do the battle with him, thy chief man
605 Sir Lancelot whom he trusts to overthrow,
Then wed, with glory: but she will not wed
Save whom she loveth, or a holy life.
Now therefore have I come for Lancelot.'

Then Arthur mindful of Sir Gareth asked,
610 'Damsel, ye know this Order lives to crush
All wrongers of the Realm. But say, these four,
Who be they? What the fashion of the men?'

'They be of foolish fashion, O Sir King,
The fashion of that old knight-errantry
615 Who ride abroad, and do but what they will;
Courteous or bestial from the moment, such
As have nor law nor king; and three of these
Proud in their fantasy call themselves the Day,
Morning-Star, and Noon-Sun, and Evening-Star,
620 Being strong fools; and never a whit more wise
The fourth, who alway rideth armed in black,
A huge man-beast of boundless savagery.
He names himself the Night and oftener Death,
And wears a helmet mounted with a skull,
625 And bears a skeleton figured on his arms,
To show that who may slay or scape the three,
Slain by himself, shall enter endless night.
And all these four be fools, but mighty men,
And therefore am I come for Lancelot.'

624. Cp. Maleger, *Faerie Queene* II xi st. 22.

630   Hereat Sir Gareth called from where he rose,
          A head with kindling eyes above the throng,
          'A boon, Sir King–this quest!' then–for he marked
          Kay near him groaning like a wounded bull–
          'Yea, King, thou knowest thy kitchen-knave am I,
635   And mighty through thy meats and drinks am I,
          And I can topple over a hundred such.
          Thy promise, King,' and Arthur glancing at him,
          Brought down a momentary brow. 'Rough, sudden,
          And pardonable, worthy to be knight–
640   Go therefore,' and all hearers were amazed.

          But on the damsel's forehead shame, pride, wrath
          Slew the May-white: she lifted either arm,
          'Fie on thee, King! I asked for thy chief knight,
          And thou hast given me but a kitchen-knave.'
645   Then ere a man in hall could stay her, turned,
          Fled down the lane of access to the King,
          Took horse, descended the slope street, and past
          The weird white gate, and paused without, beside
          The field of tourney, murmuring 'kitchen-knave.'

650   Now two great entries opened from the hall,
          At one end one, that gave upon a range
          Of level pavement where the King would pace
          At sunrise, gazing over plain and wood;
          And down from this a lordly stairway sloped
655   Till lost in blowing trees and tops of towers;
          And out by this main doorway past the King.
          But one was counter to the hearth, and rose
          High that the highest-crested helm could ride
          Therethrough nor graze: and by this entry fled
660   The damsel in her wrath, and on to this

630–49. Malory vii 3: 'Then with these words came before the king
Beaumains, while the damsel was there, and thus he said: "Sir king, God
thank you, I have been these twelvemonths in your kitchen, and have had
my full sustenance; and now I will ask my two gifts that be behind."–
"Ask upon my peril," said the king. "Sir, these shall be my two gifts:
first, that ye will grant me to have this adventure of the damsel, for it
belongeth to me."–"Thou shalt have it," said the king; "I grant it thee."–
"Then, sir, this is now the other gift: that ye shall bid sir Launcelot du
Lake to make me a knight, for of him I will be made knight, or else of
none. And when I am past, I pray you let him ride after me, and make me
knight when I require him."–"All this shall be done," said the king.–
"Fie on thee," said the damsel; "shall I have none but one that is your
kitchen page." Then was she wrath, and took her horse and departed.'

Sir Gareth strode, and saw without the door
King Arthur's gift, the worth of half a town,
A warhorse of the best, and near it stood
The two that out of north had followed him:
665 This bare a maiden shield, a casque; that held
The horse, the spear; whereat Sir Gareth loosed
A cloak that dropt from collar-bone to heel,
A cloth of roughest web, and cast it down,
And from it like a fuel-smothered fire,
That lookt half-dead, brake bright, and flashed as
670 those
Dull-coated things, that making slide apart
Their dusk wing-cases, all beneath there burns
A jewelled harness, ere they pass and fly.
So Gareth ere he parted flashed in arms.
675 Then as he donned the helm, and took the shield
And mounted horse and graspt a spear, of grain
Storm-strengthened on a windy site, and tipt
With trenchant steel, around him slowly prest
The people, while from out of kitchen came
680 The thralls in throng, and seeing who had worked
Lustier than any, and whom they could but love,
Mounted in arms, threw up their caps and cried,
'God bless the King, and all his fellowship!'
And on through lanes of shouting Gareth rode
685 Down the slope street, and past without the gate.

So Gareth past with joy; but as the cur
Pluckt from the cur he fights with, ere his cause
Be cooled by fighting, follows, being named,
His owner, but remembers all, and growls

665–85. Malory vii 3–4: 'And with that there came one to Beaumains, and told him that his horse and armour was come for him, and there was a dwarf come with all things that him needeth, in the richest manner; thereat, all the court had much marvel from whence came all that jeer [gear]. So when he was armed, there was none but few so goodly a man as he was. And right so he came into the hall and took his leave of king Arthur, and of sir Gawaine, and of sir Launcelot, and prayed him that he would hie after him; and so departed and rode after the damsel. But there went many after to behold how well he was horsed and trapped in cloth of gold, but he had neither shield nor spear.'
671–2. 'Certain insects which have brilliant bodies underneath dull wing-cases' (T.). H.T. compares *The Two Voices* 8–15. *H.Nbk 32* specified 'the beetle'.
675. *as*] *1873*; while *1872*.
679. *while*] *1873*; and *1872*.

690   Remembering, so Sir Kay beside the door
       Muttered in scorn of Gareth whom he used
       To harry and hustle.

                         'Bound upon a quest
       With horse and arms—the King hath past his time—
       My scullion knave! Thralls to your work again,
695   For an your fire be low ye kindle mine!
       Will there be dawn in West and eve in East?
       Begone!—my knave!—belike and like enow
       Some old head-blow not heeded in his youth
       So shook his wits they wander in his prime—
700   Crazed! How the villain lifted up his voice,
       Nor shamed to bawl himself a kitchen-knave.
       Tut: he was tame and meek enow with me,
       Till peacocked up with Lancelot's noticing.
       Well—I will after my loud knave, and learn
705   Whether he know me for his master yet.
       Out of the smoke he came, and so my lance
       Hold, by God's grace, he shall into the mire—
       Thence, if the King awaken from his craze,
       Into the smoke again.'

                         But Lancelot said,
710   'Kay, wherefore wilt thou go against the King,
       For that did never he whereon ye rail,
       But ever meekly served the King in thee?
       Abide: take counsel; for this lad is great
       And lusty, and knowing both of lance and sword.'
715   'Tut, tell not me,' said Kay, 'ye are overfine
       To mar stout knaves with foolish courtesies:'
       Then mounted, on through silent faces rode
       Down the slope city, and out beyond the gate.

       But by the field of tourney lingering yet
720   Muttered the damsel, 'Wherefore did the King
       Scorn me? for, were Sir Lancelot lackt, at least
       He might have yielded to me one of those
       Who tilt for lady's love and glory here,
       Rather than—O sweet heaven! O fie upon him—
       His kitchen-knave.'

690–718. Malory vii 4: 'Then sir Kaye said openly in the hall, "I will ride after my boy of the kitchen, for to wit whether he will know me for his better." Sir Launcelot and sir Gawaine said, "Yet abide at home." So sir Kaye made him ready, and took his horse and his spear, and rode after him.'

710. wilt thou] 1873; will ye 1872. Likewise l. 813.

725 　　　　　To whom Sir Gareth drew
　　　(And there were none but few goodlier than he)
　　　Shining in arms, 'Damsel, the quest is mine.
　　　Lead, and I follow.' She thereat, as one
　　　That smells a foul-fleshed agaric in the holt,
730 And deems it carrion of some woodland thing,
　　　Or shrew, or weasel, nipt her slender nose
　　　With petulant thumb and finger, shrilling, 'Hence!
　　　Avoid, thou smellest all of kitchen-grease.
　　　And look who comes behind,' for there was Kay.
735 'Knowest thou not me? thy master? I am Kay.
　　　We lack thee by the hearth.'

　　　　　　　　　　　　And Gareth to him,
　　　'Master no more! too well I know thee, ay—
　　　The most ungentle knight in Arthur's hall.'
　　　'Have at thee then,' said Kay: they shocked, and
　　　　　Kay
740 Fell shoulder-slipt, and Gareth cried again,
　　　'Lead, and I follow,' and fast away she fled.

　　　But after sod and shingle ceased to fly
　　　Behind her, and the heart of her good horse
　　　Was nigh to burst with violence of the beat,
745 Perforce she stayed, and overtaken spoke.

　　　'What doest thou, scullion, in my fellowship?
　　　Deem'st thou that I accept thee aught the more

729. 'An evil-smelling fungus of the wood common at Aldworth' (T.).
733. Malory vii 5: 'What doest thou here? thou stinkest all of the kitchen,
thy clothes be all bawdy of the grease and tallow.'
735–40. Malory vii 4: 'And right as Beaumains overtook the damsel,
right so came sir Kaye and said, "What, sir Beaumains, know ye not
me?" Then he turned his horse, and knew that it was sir Kaye, which had
done him all the despite that ye have heard afore. "Ye?" said sir Beau-
mains, "I know you for an ungentle knight of the court, and therefore
beware of me." Therewith sir Kaye put his spear in the rest, and ran upon
him with his sword in his hand; and so he put away the spear with his
sword, and with a foin thrust him through the side, that sir Kaye fell down
as though he had been dead; and he alighted down and took sir Kaye's
shield and his spear, and started upon his own horse, and rode his way.'
746–52. Malory vii 5: '"Weenest thou," said she, "that I allow thee for
yonder knight that thou hast slain? nay, truly, for thou slewest him
unhappily and cowardly; therefore, return again bawdy kitchen page. I
know thee well; for sir Kaye named thee Beaumains: what art thou but a
lusk and turner of broaches, and a washer of dishes?"'

Or love thee better, that by some device
Full cowardly, or by mere unhappiness,
750   Thou hast overthrown and slain thy master—thou!—
Dish-washer and broach-turner, loon!—to me
Thou smellest all of kitchen as before.'

'Damsel,' Sir Gareth answered gently, 'say
Whate'er ye will, but whatsoe'er ye say,
755   I leave not till I finish this fair quest,
Or die therefore.'

'Ay, wilt thou finish it?
Sweet lord, how like a noble knight he talks!
The listening rogue hath caught the manner of it.
But, knave, anon thou shalt be met with, knave,
760   And then by such a one that thou for all
The kitchen brewis that was ever supt
Shalt not once dare to look him in the face.'

'I shall assay,' said Gareth with a smile
That maddened her, and away she flashed again
765   Down the long avenues of a boundless wood,
And Gareth following was again beknaved.

'Sir Kitchen-knave, I have missed the only way
Where Arthur's men are set along the wood;
The wood is nigh as full of thieves as leaves:
770   If both be slain, I am rid of thee; but yet,
Sir Scullion, canst thou use that spit of thine?
Fight, an thou canst: I have missed the only way.'

So till the dusk that followed evensong
Rode on the two, reviler and reviled;
775   Then after one long slope was mounted, saw,
Bowl-shaped, through tops of many thousand pines
A gloomy-gladed hollow slowly sink
To westward—in the deeps whereof a mere,
Round as the red eye of an Eagle-owl,
780   Under the half-dead sunset glared; and shouts

753–6. Malory vii 5: '"Damsel," said sir Beaumains, "say to me what ye
list, I will not go from you whatsoever ye say; for I have undertaken of
king Arthur for to achieve your adventure, and I shall finish it to the end,
or I shall die therefore."'
756–62. Malory vii 5: 'Fie on thee, kitchen knave, wilt thou finish mine
adventure? thou shalt anon be met withal, that thou wouldest not, for all
the broth that ever thou suppest, once look him in the face.'
763. Malory vii 5: '"I shall assay," said Beaumains.'

Ascended, and there brake a servingman
Flying from out of the black wood, and crying,
'They have bound my lord to cast him in the mere.'
Then Gareth, 'Bound am I to right the wronged,
785 But straitlier bound am I to bide with thee.'
And when the damsel spake contemptuously,
'Lead, and I follow,' Gareth cried again,
'Follow, I lead!' so down among the pines
He plunged; and there, blackshadowed nigh the
      mere,
790 And mid-thigh-deep in bulrushes and reed,
Saw six tall men haling a seventh along,
A stone about his neck to drown him in it.
Three with good blows he quieted, but three
Fled through the pines; and Gareth loosed the stone
795 From off his neck, then in the mere beside
Tumbled it; oilily bubbled up the mere.
Last, Gareth loosed his bonds and on free feet
Set him, a stalwart Baron, Arthur's friend.

'Well that ye came, or else these caitiff rogues
800 Had wreaked themselves on me; good cause is theirs
To hate me, for my wont hath ever been
To catch my thief, and then like vermin here
Drown him, and with a stone about his neck;
And under this wan water many of them
805 Lie rotting, but at night let go the stone,
And rise, and flickering in a grimly light
Dance on the mere. Good now, ye have saved a life
Worth somewhat as the cleanser of this wood.
And fain would I reward thee worshipfully.

781–3. Malory vii 5: 'So, as they thus rode in the wood, there came a
knight flying all that he might. "Whether [Whither] wilt thou", said
Beaumains. "O Lord!" said he, "help me; for hereby in a sludge [slade]
are six thieves, which have taken my lord and bound him, and I am afraid
lest they will slay him."' T.'s ll. 789–96 were presumably suggested by
'sludge'.
791–6. Malory vii 5: 'And so they rode together, till they came there as
the knight was bound, and then he rode unto the thieves, and struck one
at the first stroke to death, and then another; and, at the third stroke, he
slew the third thief: and then the other three fled, and he rode after and
overtook them; and then those three thieves turned again, and hard
assailed sir Beaumains; but, at the last, he slew them, and then returned
and unbound the knight.'
796. Tumbled] He cast *H.Nbk 32 1st reading.*
809–23. Malory vii 5: '"Sir," said sir Beaumains, "I will no reward have:

What guerdon will ye?'
810   Gareth sharply spake,
'None! for the deed's sake have I done the deed,
In uttermost obedience to the King.
But wilt thou yield this damsel harbourage?'

Whereat the Baron saying, 'I well believe
815 You be of Arthur's Table,' a light laugh
Broke from Lynette, 'Ay, truly of a truth,
And in a sort, being Arthur's kitchen-knave!—
But deem not I accept thee aught the more,
Scullion, for running sharply with thy spit
820 Down on a rout of craven foresters.
A thresher with his flail had scattered them.
Nay—for thou smellest of the kitchen still.
But an this lord will yield us harbourage,
Well.'

So she spake. A league beyond the wood,
825 All in a full-fair manor and a rich,
His towers where that day a feast had been
Held in high hall, and many a viand left,
And many a costly cate, received the three.
And there they placed a peacock in his pride
830 Before the damsel, and the Baron set
Gareth beside her, but at once she rose.

'Meseems, that here is much discourtesy,
Setting this knave, Lord Baron, at my side.
Hear me—this morn I stood in Arthur's hall,
835 And prayed the King would grant me Lancelot
To fight the brotherhood of Day and Night—

I was this day made knight of the noble sir Launcelot; and, therefore, I
will have no reward, but God reward me: and, also, I must follow this
damsel." And when he came nigher, she bid him ride from her, "for thou
smellest all of the kitchen. Weenest thou that I have joy of thee? for all
this deed that thou hast done is but mishappened thee: but thou shalt see a
sight that shall make thee to turn again, and that lightly."'

815. *You*] *1873*; Ye *1872*. Likewise ll. 996, 1142, 1143, 1145, 1227, 1266,
1296.

824–46. Malory vii 5: 'Then the same knight, which was rescued of the
thieves, rode after the damsel, and prayed her to lodge with him all that
night; and, because it was near night, the damsel rode with him to his
castle, and there they had great cheer. And, at supper, the knight set sir
Beaumains before the damsel. "Fie, fie," said she, "sir knight, ye are
uncourteous for to set a kitchen page before me: him beseemeth better to
stick a swine, than to sit before a damsel of high parentage."'

The last a monster unsubduable
Of any save of him for whom I called –
Suddenly bawls this frontless kitchen-knave,
840 "The quest is mine; thy kitchen-knave am I,
And mighty through thy meats and drinks am I."
Then Arthur all at once gone mad replies,
"Go therefore," and so gives the quest to him –
Him – here – a villain fitter to stick swine
845 Than ride abroad redressing women's wrong,
Or sit beside a noble gentlewoman.'

Then half-ashamed and part-amazed, the lord
Now looked at one and now at other, left
The damsel by the peacock in his pride,
850 And, seating Gareth at another board,
Sat down beside him, ate and then began.

'Friend, whether thou be kitchen-knave, or not,
Or whether it be the maiden's fantasy,
And whether she be mad, or else the King,
855 Or both or neither, or thyself be mad,
I ask not: but thou strikest a strong stroke,
For strong thou art and goodly therewithal,
And saver of my life; and therefore now,
For here be mighty men to joust with, weigh
860 Whether thou wilt not with thy damsel back
To crave again Sir Lancelot of the King.
Thy pardon; I but speak for thine avail,
The saver of my life.'

And Gareth said,
'Full pardon, but I follow up the quest,
865 Despite of Day and Night and Death and Hell.'

So when, next morn, the lord whose life he saved
Had, some brief space, conveyed them on their way

839. frontless: 'shameless' (T.).
847–51. Malory vii 5: 'Then the knight was ashamed of her words, and took him up and sat before him at a sideboard, and set himself before him: and so all that night they had good and merry rest.'
849. 'Brought in on the trencher with his tail-feathers left' (T.). H.T. quotes Edward Stanley's *History of Birds*: when it was served, 'all the guests, male and female, took a solemn vow; the knights vowing bravery, and the ladies engaging to be loving and faithful.'
852. thou] *1873*; ye *1872*.
862. Malory vii 6: 'I say it for thine avail.'

And left them with God-speed, Sir Gareth spake,
'Lead, and I follow.' Haughtily she replied.
870   'I fly no more: I allow thee for an hour.
Lion and stoat have isled together, knave,
In time of flood. Nay, furthermore, methinks
Some ruth is mine for thee. Back wilt thou, fool?
For hard by here is one will overthrow
875   And slay thee: then will I to court again,
And shame the King for only yielding me
My champion from the ashes of his hearth.'

To whom Sir Gareth answered courteously,
'Say thou thy say, and I will do my deed.
880   Allow me for mine hour, and thou wilt find
My fortunes all as fair as hers who lay
Among the ashes and wedded the King's son.'

Then to the shore of one of those long loops
Wherethrough the serpent river coiled, they came.
Rough-thicketed were the banks and steep; the
885   stream
Full, narrow; this a bridge of single arc
Took at a leap; and on the further side
Arose a silk pavilion, gay with gold
In streaks and rays, and all Lent-lily in hue,
890   Save that the dome was purple, and above,
Crimson, a slender banneret fluttering.
And therebefore the lawless warrior paced
Unarmed, and calling, 'Damsel, is this he,
The champion thou hast brought from Arthur's
        hall?
895   For whom we let thee pass.' 'Nay, nay,' she said,
'Sir Morning-Star. The King in utter scorn

881–2. 'Cinderella's' (T.).
883. 'The three loops of the river typify the three ages of life; and the
guardians at the crossing the temptations of these ages' (T., *1913*).
886–7. Cp. *The Coach of Death* 147–8: 'It takes the ocean at a leap / And
in its leap is fixed.'
889. *Lent-lily*: 'daffodil' (T.).
893–900. Malory vii 7: 'With that the black knight came to the damsel and
said, "Fair damsel, have ye brought this knight from king Arthur's court
to be your champion?"–"Nay, fair knight," said she, "this is but a kitchen
knave, that hath been fed in king Arthur's kitchen for alms."'
894. *thou hast*] *1873*; ye have *1872*.
896. In Malory, there is a succession of knights, among them the Black
Knight, the Green Knight, and the Red Knight.

Of thee and thy much folly hath sent thee here
His kitchen-knave: and look thou to thyself:
See that he fall not on thee suddenly,
900 And slay thee unarmed: he is not knight but knave.'

Then at his call, 'O daughters of the Dawn,
And servants of the Morning-Star, approach,
Arm me,' from out the silken curtain-folds
Bare-footed and bare-headed three fair girls
905 In gilt and rosy raiment came: their feet
In dewy grasses glistened; and the hair
All over glanced with dewdrop or with gem
Like sparkles in the stone Avanturine.
These armed him in blue arms, and gave a shield
910 Blue also, and thereon the morning star.
And Gareth silent gazed upon the knight,
Who stood a moment, ere his horse was brought,
Glorying; and in the stream beneath him, shone
Immingled with Heaven's azure waveringly,
915 The gay pavilion and the naked feet,
His arms, the rosy raiment, and the star.

Then she that watched him, 'Wherefore stare
    ye so?
Thou shakest in thy fear: there yet is time:
Flee down the valley before he get to horse.
920 Who will cry shame? Thou art not knight but knave.'

Said Gareth, 'Damsel, whether knave or knight,
Far liefer had I fight a score of times
Than hear thee so missay me and revile.
Fair words were best for him who fights for thee;
925 But truly foul are better, for they send
That strength of anger through mine arms, I know
That I shall overthrow him.'

904. Malory vii 8: 'And there he blew three deadly notes, and there came three damsels that lightly armed him.'
908. *Avanturine*: 'sometimes called the Panther-stone–a kind of gray-green or brown quartz with sparkles in it' (T.). H.T. quotes the first reading: 'Like stars within the stone Avanturine'.
918–20. Malory vii 7: 'When the damsel saw the black knight she bade sir Beaumains flee down the valley; for his horse was not saddled. "I thank you," said sir Beaumains; "for always ye will have me a coward."'
921–4. Malory vii 11: '"Damsel," said sir Beaumains, "ye are to blame so to rebuke me; for I had rather to do five battles than be so rebuked: let him come, and then let him do his worst ... All the missaying that ye missayed furthered me in my battles."'

                       And he that bore
     The star, when mounted, cried from o'er the bridge,
     'A kitchen-knave, and sent in scorn of me!
930   Such fight not I, but answer scorn with scorn.
     For this were shame to do him further wrong
     Than set him on his feet, and take his horse
     And arms, and so return him to the King.
     Come, therefore, leave thy lady lightly, knave.
935   Avoid: for it beseemeth not a knave
     To ride with such a lady.'

                       'Dog, thou liest.
     I spring from loftier lineage than thine own.'
     He spake; and all at fiery speed the two
     Shocked on the central bridge, and either spear
940   Bent but not brake, and either knight at once,
     Hurled as a stone from out of a catapult
     Beyond his horse's crupper and the bridge,
     Fell, as if dead; but quickly rose and drew,
     And Gareth lashed so fiercely with his brand
945   He drave his enemy backward down the bridge,
     The damsel crying, 'Well-stricken, kitchen-knave!'
     Till Gareth's shield was cloven; but one stroke
     Laid him that clove it grovelling on the ground.

       Then cried the fallen, 'Take not my life: I yield.'
950   And Gareth, 'So this damsel ask it of me

928. *when*] *1886*; *being 1872–84.*
929–36. Malory vii 7: '"Wherefore cometh he in such array?" said the
knight: "it is a great shame that he beareth your company . . . I shall put
him down upon his feet, and his horse and his armour he shall leave with
me; for it were shame for me to do him any more harm . . . For it be-
seemeth not a kitchen knave to ride with such a lady."'
930. Gray (p. 45) compares *Paradise Lost* iv 834: 'To whom thus *Zephon*,
answering scorn with scorn'.
936–48. Malory vii 7: '"Thou liest," said sir Beaumains: "I am a gentleman
born, and of more high lineage than thou art, and that I will prove upon
thy body." Then in great wrath they departed with their horses, and came
together as it had been thunder: and the black knight's spear broke; and
sir Beaumains thrust him through both his sides, and therewith his spear
brake, and the truncheon stuck still in his side; but, nevertheless, the black
knight drew his sword, and smote many eager strokes and of great might,
and hurt sir Beaumains full sore. But at the last the black knight, within an
hour and a half, fell down from his horse in a swoon, and there died
forthwith.'
949–59. Based on Malory vii 8.

Good–I accord it easily as a grace.'
She reddening, 'Insolent scullion: I of thee?
I bound to thee for any favour asked!'
'Then shall he die.' And Gareth there unlaced
955   His helmet as to slay him, but she shrieked,
'Be not so hardy, scullion, as to slay
One nobler than thyself.' 'Damsel, thy charge
Is an abounding pleasure to me. Knight,
Thy life is thine at her command. Arise
960   And quickly pass to Arthur's hall, and say
His kitchen-knave hath sent thee. See thou crave
His pardon for thy breaking of his laws.
Myself, when I return, will plead for thee.
Thy shield is mine–farewell; and, damsel, thou,
Lead, and I follow.'

965   And fast away she fled.
Then when he came upon her, spake, 'Methought,
Knave, when I watched thee striking on the bridge
The savour of thy kitchen came upon me
A little faintlier: but the wind hath changed:
970   I scent it twenty-fold.' And then she sang,
'"O morning star" (not that tall felon there
Whom thou by sorcery or unhappiness
Or some device, hast foully overthrown),
"O morning star that smilest in the blue,
975   O star, my morning dream hath proven true,
Smile sweetly, thou! my love hath smiled on me."

'But thou begone, take counsel, and away,
For hard by here is one that guards a ford–
The second brother in their fool's parable–
980   Will pay thee all thy wages, and to boot.
Care not for shame: thou art not knight but
knave.'

To whom Sir Gareth answered, laughingly,
'Parables? Hear a parable of the knave.
When I was kitchen-knave among the rest
985   Fierce was the hearth, and one of my co-mates

967–9. Malory vii 7: '"Away, kitchen knave! go out of the wind; for the smell of thy bawdy clothes grieveth me."'
972. Malory vii 7: '"Alas! that ever such a knight as thou art should, by mishap, slay so good a knight as thou hast slain."'
980. Malory vii 7: '"But hereby is a knight that shall pay thee all thy payment."'

Owned a rough dog, to whom he cast his coat,
"Guard it," and there was none to meddle with it.
And such a coat art thou, and thee the King
Gave me to guard, and such a dog am I,
990   To worry, and not to flee–and–knight or knave–
The knave that doth thee service as full knight
Is all as good, meseems, as any knight
Toward thy sister's freeing.'

                     'Ay, Sir Knave!
Ay, knave, because thou strikest as a knight,
995   Being but knave, I hate thee all the more.'

     'Fair damsel, you should worship me the more,
That, being but knave, I throw thine enemies.'

     'Ay, ay,' she said, 'but thou shalt meet thy match.'

     So when they touched the second river-loop,
1000   Huge on a huge red horse, and all in mail
Burnished to blinding, shone the Noonday Sun
Beyond a raging shallow. As if the flower,
That blows a globe of after arrowlets,
Ten thousand-fold had grown, flashed the fierce
        shield,
1005   All sun; and Gareth's eyes had flying blots
Before them when he turned from watching him.
He from beyond the roaring shallow roared,
'What doest thou, brother, in my marches here?'
And she athwart the shallow shrilled again,
1010   'Here is a kitchen-knave from Arthur's hall
Hath overthrown thy brother, and hath his arms.'
'Ugh!' cried the Sun, and vizoring up a red
And cipher face of rounded foolishness,
Pushed horse across the foamings of the ford,
1015   Whom Gareth met midstream: no room was there

1000. *Revelation* vi 4: 'And there went out another horse that was red'. On the
Horsemen of the Apocalypse, see W. D. Shaw, *VN* No. 34 (1968) 34–5,
and Rosenberg (pp. 106, 161).
1002. 'The dandelion' (T.).
1008–11. Malory vii 8: '"Is that my brother, the black knight, that ye
have brought with you?"–"Nay, nay," said she, "this unhappy kitchen
knave hath slain your brother through unhappiness."'
1015–31. Malory vii 6: 'And therewith he rushed into the water, and in the
midst of the water either broke their spears to their hands, and then they
drew their swords, and smote at each other eagerly: and, at the last, sir
Beaumains smote the other upon the helm, that his head was stunned, and

For lance or tourney-skill: four strokes they struck
With sword, and these were mighty; the new knight
Had fear he might be shamed; but as the Sun
Heaved up a ponderous arm to strike the fifth,
1020 The hoof of his horse slipt in the stream, the stream
Descended, and the Sun was washed away.

Then Gareth laid his lance athwart the ford;
So drew him home; but he that fought no more,
As being all bone-battered on the rock,
1025 Yielded; and Gareth sent him to the King.
'Myself when I return will plead for thee.'
'Lead, and I follow.' Quietly she led.
'Hath not the good wind, damsel, changed again?'
'Nay, not a point: nor art thou victor here.
1030 There lies a ridge of slate across the ford;
His horse thereon stumbled–ay, for I saw it.

'"O Sun" (not this strong fool whom thou, Sir
      Knave,
Hast overthrown through mere unhappiness),
"O Sun, that wakenest all to bliss or pain,
1035 O moon, that layest all to sleep again,
Shine sweetly: twice my love hath smiled on me."

What knowest thou of lovesong or of love?
Nay, nay, God wot, so thou wert nobly born,
Thou hast a pleasant presence. Yea, perchance, –

therewith he fell down into the water, and there was drowned ... "Alas,"
said she, "that ever kitchen page should have the fortune to destroy two
such doughty knights: thou weenest thou hast done doughtily, and that is
not so; for the first knight's horse stumbled, and there he was drowned in
the water, and never it was by thy force and might: and the last knight,
by mishap thou camest behind him, and shamefully thou slewest him."'
1032–51. Cp. *Be merry*, an unpublished song by T. in the *Hn MSS* (HM
194 87):

> Be merry, be merry: the woods begin to blow;
> Be merry the lark aloft, the thrush below;
> Be merry my heart, as merry as heart can be.
>
> Be merry, be merry: the world begins to love;
> Be merry the jay, the tit, the pink, the dove;
> Be merry my heart, for love has smiled on me.
>
> Be merry my little heart as lambs at play,
> And merry as birds are merry among the may;
> Be merry my heart, as ever a heart can be.

1033. unhappiness: 'mischance' (T.).

1040 '"O dewy flowers that open to the sun,
  O dewy flowers that close when day is done,
  Blow sweetly: twice my love hath smiled on me."

  'What knowest thou of flowers, except, belike,
  To garnish meats with? hath not our good King
1045 Who lent me thee, the flower of kitchendom,
  A foolish love for flowers? what stick ye round
  The pasty? wherewithal deck the boar's head?
  Flowers? nay, the boar hath rosemaries and bay.

  '"O birds, that warble to the morning sky,
1050 O birds that warble as the day goes by,
  Sing sweetly: twice my love hath smiled on me."

  'What knowest thou of birds, lark, mavis, merle,
  Linnet? what dream ye when they utter forth
  May-music growing with the growing light,
1055 Their sweet sun-worship? these be for the snare
  (So runs thy fancy) these be for the spit,
  Larding and basting. See thou have not now
  Larded thy last, except thou turn and fly.
  There stands the third fool of their allegory.'

1060 For there beyond a bridge of treble bow,
  All in a rose-red from the west, and all
  Naked it seemed, and glowing in the broad
  Deep-dimpled current underneath, the knight,
  That named himself the Star of Evening, stood.

1065 And Gareth, 'Wherefore waits the madman there
  Naked in open dayshine?' 'Nay,' she cried,
  'Not naked, only wrapt in hardened skins
  That fit him like his own; and so ye cleave
  His armour off him, these will turn the blade.'

1070 Then the third brother shouted o'er the bridge,
  'O brother-star, why shine ye here so low?
  Thy ward is higher up: but have ye slain
  The damsel's champion?' and the damsel cried,

  'No star of thine, but shot from Arthur's heaven
1075 With all disaster unto thine and thee!

1051. 'Because of his having overthrown two knights. A light has broken
on her. Her morning dream has twice proved true, that she should find a
worthy champion' (H.T.).
1067. 'Allegory of habit' (T.).
1071. 'Gareth has taken the shield of the Morning-Star' (H.T.).

For both thy younger brethren have gone down
Before this youth; and so wilt thou, Sir Star;
Art thou not old?'
                    'Old, damsel, old and hard,
Old, with the might and breath of twenty boys.'
1080 Said Gareth, 'Old, and over-bold in brag!
But that same strength which threw the Morning
      Star
Can throw the Evening.'
                        Then that other blew
A hard and deadly note upon the horn.
'Approach and arm me!' With slow steps from out
1085 An old storm-beaten, russet, many-stained
Pavilion, forth a grizzled damsel came,
And armed him in old arms, and brought a helm
With but a drying evergreen for crest,
And gave a shield whereon the Star of Even
1090 Half-tarnished and half-bright, his emblem, shone.
But when it glittered o'er the saddle-bow,
They madly hurled together on the bridge;
And Gareth overthrew him, lighted, drew,
There met him drawn, and overthrew him again,
1095 But up like fire he started: and as oft
As Gareth brought him grovelling on his knees,
So many a time he vaulted up again;
Till Gareth panted hard, and his great heart,
Foredooming all his trouble was in vain,
1100 Laboured within him, for he seemed as one
That all in later, sadder age begins
To war against ill uses of a life,
But these from all his life arise, and cry,
'Thou hast made us lords, and canst not put us
       down!'
1105 He half despairs; so Gareth seemed to strike
Vainly, the damsel clamouring all the while,
'Well done, knave-knight, well stricken, O good
       knight-knave—
O knave, as noble as any of all the knights—
Shame me not, shame me not. I have prophesied—
1110 Strike, thou art worthy of the Table Round—
His arms are old, he trusts the hardened skin—
Strike—strike—the wind will never change again.'
And Gareth hearing ever stronglier smote,
And hewed great pieces of his armour off him,

1092ff. Cp. the fight with Maleger, *Faerie Queene* II xi sts 20–46.

1115 But lashed in vain against the hardened skin,
And could not wholly bring him under, more
Than loud Southwesterns, rolling ridge on ridge,
The buoy that rides at sea, and dips and springs
For ever; till at length Sir Gareth's brand
1120 Clashed his, and brake it utterly to the hilt.
'I have thee now;' but forth that other sprang,
And, all unknightlike, writhed his wiry arms
Around him, till he felt, despite his mail,
Strangled, but straining even his uttermost
1125 Cast, and so hurled him headlong o'er the bridge
Down to the river, sink or swim, and cried,
'Lead, and I follow.'

                But the damsel said,
'I lead no longer; ride thou at my side;
Thou art the kingliest of all kitchen-knaves.

1130   ' "O trefoil, sparkling on the rainy plain,
O rainbow with three colours after rain,
Shine sweetly: thrice my love hath smiled on me."

     'Sir,–and, good faith, I fain had added–Knight,
But that I heard thee call thyself a knave,–
1135 Shamed am I that I so rebuked, reviled,
Missaid thee; noble I am; and thought the King
Scorned me and mine; and now thy pardon, friend,
For thou hast ever answered courteously,
And wholly bold thou art, and meek withal
1140 As any of Arthur's best, but, being knave,
Hast mazed my wit: I marvel what thou art.'

     'Damsel,' he said, 'you be not all to blame,
Saving that you mistrusted our good King
Would handle scorn, or yield you, asking, one
1145 Not fit to cope your quest. You said your say;
Mine answer was my deed. Good sooth! I hold
He scarce is knight, yea but half-man, nor meet
To fight for gentle damsel, he, who lets
His heart be stirred with any foolish heat
1150 At any gentle damsel's waywardness.
Shamed? care not! thy foul sayings fought for me:

1135–6. Malory vii 11: '"Alas!" said she, "fair sir Beaumains forgive me
all that I have missayed and misdone against you."'
1144. you] *1873*; thee *1872*.
1145. your quest] *1873*; thy quest *1872*.

And seeing now thy words are fair, methinks
There rides no knight, not Lancelot, his great self,
Hath force to quell me.'
                              Nigh upon that hour
1155 When the lone hern forgets his melancholy,
Lets down his other leg, and stretching, dreams
Of goodly supper in the distant pool,
Then turned the noble damsel smiling at him,
And told him of a cavern hard at hand,
1160 Where bread and baken meats and good red wine
Of Southland, which the Lady Lyonors
Had sent her coming champion, waited him.

Anon they past a narrow comb wherein
Were slabs of rock with figures, knights on horse
1165 Sculptured, and deckt in slowly-waning hues.
'Sir Knave, my knight, a hermit once was here,
Whose holy hand hath fashioned on the rock
The war of Time against the soul of man.
And yon four fools have sucked their allegory
1170 From these damp walls, and taken but the form.
Know ye not these?' and Gareth lookt and read –
In letters like to those the vexillary
Hath left crag-carven o'er the streaming Gelt –
'PHOSPHORUS,' then 'MERIDIES'–'HESPERUS'–
1175 'NOX'–'MORS,' beneath five figures, armèd men,
Slab after slab, their faces forward all,
And running down the Soul, a Shape that fled
With broken wings, torn raiment and loose hair,
For help and shelter to the hermit's cave.
1180 'Follow the faces, and we find it. Look,
Who comes behind?'
                              For one–delayed at first
Through helping back the dislocated Kay

1172–3] In Roman lettering such as that which lasts
    Though worn beside the southward Roman walls

                                                H.Nbk 32

1172–5. T. comments: 'Years ago when I was visiting the Howards at
Naworth Castle, I drove over to the little river Gelt to see the inscription
carved upon the crags. It seemed to me very pathetic, this sole record of
the vexillary or standard-bearer of the sacred Legion (Augusta). This is the
inscription: VEX.LLEG.II AVG. ON. AP. APRO E MAXIMO CONSULIBUS SUB
AGRICOLA OP. OFICINA MERCATI.' Of the 'figures', H.T. says: 'Symbolical of
the temptations of youth, of middle-age, of later life, and of death overcome
by the youthful and joyous Gareth.'

To Camelot, then by what thereafter chanced,
The damsel's headlong error through the wood—
1185 Sir Lancelot, having swum the river-loops—
His blue shield-lions covered—softly drew
Behind the twain, and when he saw the star
Gleam, on Sir Gareth's turning to him, cried,
'Stay, felon knight, I avenge me for my friend.'
1190 And Gareth crying pricked against the cry;
But when they closed—in a moment—at one touch
Of that skilled spear, the wonder of the world—
Went sliding down so easily, and fell,
That when he found the grass within his hands
1195 He laughed; the laughter jarred upon Lynette:
Harshly she asked him, 'Shamed and overthrown,
And tumbled back into the kitchen-knave,
Why laugh ye? that ye blew your boast in vain?'
'Nay, noble damsel, but that I, the son
1200 Of old King Lot and good Queen Bellicent,
And victor of the bridges and the ford,
And knight of Arthur, here lie thrown by whom
I know not, all through mere unhappiness—
Device and sorcery and unhappiness—
Out, sword; we are thrown!' And Lancelot answered,
1205   'Prince,
O Gareth—through the mere unhappiness
Of one who came to help thee, not to harm,
Lancelot, and all as glad to find thee whole,
As on the day when Arthur knighted him.'

1210   Then Gareth, 'Thou—Lancelot!—thine the hand
That threw me? An some chance to mar the boast
Thy brethren of thee make—which could not chance—
Had sent thee down before a lesser spear,
Shamed had I been, and sad—O Lancelot—thou!'

1215   Whereat the maiden, petulant, 'Lancelot,
Why came ye not, when called? and wherefore now
Come ye, not called? I gloried in my knave,
Who being still rebuked, would answer still
Courteous as any knight—but now, if knight,
1220 The marvel dies, and leaves me fooled and tricked,

1185–93. Suggested by Gareth's jousting with Lancelot, Malory vii 4.
1198. Malory vii 11: "'Fie, fie!' said the damsel, "that ever such a stinking
knave should blow such a boast."'

And only wondering wherefore played upon:
And doubtful whether I and mine be scorned.
Where should be truth if not in Arthur's hall,
In Arthur's presence? Knight, knave, prince
    and fool,
I hate thee and for ever.'

1225   And Lancelot said,
'Blessèd be thou, Sir Gareth! knight art thou
To the King's best wish. O damsel, be you wise
To call him shamed, who is but overthrown?
Thrown have I been, nor once, but many a time.
1230 Victor from vanquished issues at the last,
And overthrower from being overthrown.
With sword we have not striven; and thy good horse
And thou are weary; yet not less I felt
Thy manhood through that wearied lance of thine.
1235 Well hast thou done; for all the stream is freed,
And thou hast wreaked his justice on his foes,
And when reviled, hast answered graciously,
And makest merry when overthrown. Prince,
    Knight,
Hail, Knight and Prince, and of our Table Round!'

1240   And then when turning to Lynette he told
The tale of Gareth, petulantly she said,
'Ay well–ay well–for worse than being fooled
Of others, is to fool one's self. A cave,
Sir Lancelot, is hard by, with meats and drinks
1245 And forage for the horse, and flint for fire.
But all about it flies a honeysuckle.
Seek, till we find.' And when they sought and found,
Sir Gareth drank and ate, and all his life
Past into sleep; on whom the maiden gazed.
'Sound sleep be thine! sound cause to sleep hast
1250   thou.
Wake lusty! Seem I not as tender to him
As any mother? Ay, but such a one
As all day long hath rated at her child,
And vext his day, but blesses him asleep–
1255 Good lord, how sweetly smells the honeysuckle
In the hushed night, as if the world were one
Of utter peace, and love, and gentleness!
O Lancelot, Lancelot'–and she clapt her hands–
'Full merry am I to find my goodly knave
1260 Is knight and noble. See now, sworn have I,
Else yon black felon had not let me pass,

To bring thee back to do the battle with him.
Thus an thou goest, he will fight thee first;
Who doubts thee victor? so will my knight-knave
1265 Miss the full flower of this accomplishment.'

Said Lancelot, 'Peradventure he, you name,
May know my shield. Let Gareth, an he will,
Change his for mine, and take my charger, fresh,
Not to be spurred, loving the battle as well
1270 As he that rides him.' 'Lancelot-like,' she said,
'Courteous in this, Lord Lancelot, as in all.'

And Gareth, wakening, fiercely clutched the shield;
'Ramp ye lance-splintering lions, on whom all spears
Are rotten sticks! ye seem agape to roar!
1275 Yea, ramp and roar at leaving of your lord!—
Care not, good beasts, so well I care for you.
O noble Lancelot, from my hold on these
Streams virtue—fire—through one that will not
        shame
Even the shadow of Lancelot under shield.
Hence: let us go.'

1280   Silent the silent field
They traversed. Arthur's harp though summer-wan,
In counter motion to the clouds, allured
The glance of Gareth dreaming on his liege.
A star shot: 'Lo,' said Gareth, 'the foe falls!'
1285 An owl whoopt: 'Hark the victor pealing there!'
Suddenly she that rode upon his left
Clung to the shield that Lancelot lent him, crying,
'Yield, yield him this again: 'tis he must fight:
I curse the tongue that all through yesterday
1290 Reviled thee, and hath wrought on Lancelot now
To lend thee horse and shield: wonders ye have
        done;
Miracles ye cannot: here is glory enow
In having flung the three: I see thee maimed,
Mangled: I swear thou canst not fling the fourth.'

1295   'And wherefore, damsel? tell me all ye know.
You cannot scare me; nor rough face, or voice,
Brute bulk of limb, or boundless savagery
Appal me from the quest.'

                            'Nay, Prince,' she cried,

1281. 'Lyra' (T.).

'God wot, I never looked upon the face,
1300 Seeing he never rides abroad by day;
But watched him have I like a phantom pass
Chilling the night: nor have I heard the voice.
Always he made his mouthpiece of a page
Who came and went, and still reported him
1305 As closing in himself the strength of ten,
And when his anger tare him, massacring
Man, woman, lad and girl–yea, the soft babe!
Some hold that he hath swallowed infant flesh,
Monster! O Prince, I went for Lancelot first,
1310 The quest is Lancelot's: give him back the shield.'

Said Gareth laughing, 'An he fight for this,
Belike he wins it as the better man:
Thus–and not else!'

           But Lancelot on him urged
All the devisings of their chivalry
1315 When one might meet a mightier than himself;
How best to manage horse, lance, sword and shield,
And so fill up the gap where force might fail
With skill and fineness. Instant were his words.

Then Gareth, 'Here be rules. I know but one–
1320 To dash against mine enemy and to win.
Yet have I watched thee victor in the joust,
And seen thy way.' 'Heaven help thee,' sighed
    Lynette.

Then for a space, and under cloud that grew
To thunder-gloom palling all stars, they rode
1325 In converse till she made her palfrey halt,
Lifted an arm, and softly whispered, 'There.'
And all the three were silent seeing, pitched
Beside the Castle Perilous on flat field,
A huge pavilion like a mountain peak
1330 Sunder the glooming crimson on the marge,
Black, with black banner, and a long black horn
Beside it hanging; which Sir Gareth graspt,

1315. When] *1873*; Where *1872*.
1330. crimson: 'sunrise' (T.).
1331. Malory vii 6–7 (where this encounter takes place earlier): 'And then
they came to a black land, and there was a black hawthorn, and thereon
hung a black banner; and on the other side there hung a black shield, and
by it stood a black spear and a long, and a great black horse covered with

And so, before the two could hinder him,
Sent all his heart and breath through all the horn.
1335 Echoed the walls; a light twinkled; anon
Came lights and lights, and once again he blew;
Whereon were hollow tramplings up and down
And muffled voices heard, and shadows past;
Till high above him, circled with her maids,
1340 The Lady Lyonors at a window stood,
Beautiful among lights, and waving to him
White hands, and courtesy; but when the Prince
Three times had blown – after long hush – at last –
The huge pavilion slowly yielded up,
Through those black foldings, that which housed
1345   therein.
High on a nightblack horse, in nightblack arms,
With white breast-bone, and barren ribs of Death,
And crowned with fleshless laughter – some ten
        steps –
In the half-light – through the dim dawn – advanced
1350 The monster, and then paused, and spake no word.

But Gareth spake and all indignantly,
'Fool, for thou hast, men say, the strength of ten,
Canst thou not trust the limbs thy God hath given,
But must, to make the terror of thee more,
1355 Trick thyself out in ghastly imageries
Of that which Life hath done with, and the clod,
Less dull than thou, will hide with mantling
        flowers
As if for pity?' But he spake no word;
Which set the horror higher: a maiden swooned;
1360 The Lady Lyonors wrung her hands and wept,
As doomed to be the bride of Night and Death;
Sir Gareth's head prickled beneath his helm;

silk, and black stone fast by it. There sat a knight all armed in black harness,
and his name was the knight of the black lands.'
1340. Malory vii 16: '"Sir," said the damsel, Linet, unto sir Beaumains,
"look that ye be merry and light, for yonder is your deadly enemy, and
at yonder window is my lady, my sister, dame Lyons." – "Where?" said
sir Beaumains. "Yonder," said the damsel, and pointed with her finger.
"That is sooth," said sir Beaumains, "she seemeth a far the fairest lady that
ever I looked upon; and truly," said he, "I ask no better quarrel, than now
to do battle: for truly she shall be my lady, and for her will I fight."'
1348. 'With a grinning skull' (T.).

And even Sir Lancelot through his warm blood
    felt
Ice strike, and all that marked him were aghast.

1365   At once Sir Lancelot's charger fiercely neighed,
And Death's dark war-horse bounded forward
    with him.
Then those that did not blink the terror, saw
That Death was cast to ground, and slowly rose.
But with one stroke Sir Gareth split the skull.
1370   Half fell to right and half to left and lay.
Then with a stronger buffet he clove the helm
As throughly as the skull; and out from this
Issued the bright face of a blooming boy
Fresh as a flower new-born, and crying, 'Knight,
1375   Slay me not: my three brethren bad me do it,
To make a horror all about the house,
And stay the world from Lady Lyonors.
They never dreamed the passes would be past.'
Answered Sir Gareth graciously to one
1380   Not many a moon his younger, 'My fair child,
What madness made thee challenge the chief knight
Of Arthur's hall?' 'Fair Sir, they bad me do it.
They hate the King, and Lancelot, the King's
    friend,
They hoped to slay him somewhere on the stream,
1385   They never dreamed the passes could be past.'

Then sprang the happier day from underground;
And Lady Lyonors and her house, with dance
And revel and song, made merry over Death,
As being after all their foolish fears
1390   And horrors only proven a blooming boy.
So large mirth lived and Gareth won the quest.

And he that told the tale in older times
Says that Sir Gareth wedded Lyonors,
But he, that told it later, says Lynette.

466 The Marriage of Geraint

Printed privately in 1857. Published *1859*, the first half of *Enid*. The title *Enid* was expanded to *Geraint and Enid* in *1870* ('*1869*'); the poem was divided into

1366. *And . . . war-*] *1873*; At once the black *1872*.
1392-4. H.T. glosses this: 'Malory' and 'my father'.

two parts in *1873*; and the final titles given in *1886*. H.T. notes: 'In 1857 six copies of *Enid and Nimuë: the True and the False* were printed. This Idyll is founded on *Geraint, son of Erbin*, in the *Mabinogion*, translated by Lady Charlotte Guest [1840, collected 1849, vol. ii], and has "brought the story within compass". It was begun on 16 April 1856, and first published in 1859 in the *Idylls of the King*. My father had also read *Erec and Enid*, by Chrestien de Troyes. The greater part of the Idylls contained in the volume of 1859 was written at Farringford. But the end of *Geraint and Enid* was written in July and August of 1856 in Wales, where he read, in the original, *Hanes Cymru* (Welsh history), the *Mabinogion*, and Llywarch Hen.' T. is very close in incidents and often in wording to the Guest translation; for a detailed comparison, see H. G. Wright, *Essays and Studies* xiv (1929) 80–103. G. C. Macaulay's edition (1892), pp. xxviii–xxx, lists T.'s possible debts to the French versions. For a detailed account of T.'s textual changes, see Richard Jones, *The Growth of the Idylls of the King* (1895), chapter ii. There is a copy of *Enid and Nimuë* (1857) in the British Library; an edition was printed from this in 1902.

> The brave Geraint, a knight of Arthur's court,
> A tributary prince of Devon, one
> Of that great Order of the Table Round,
> Had married Enid, Yniol's only child,
> 5 And loved her, as he loved the light of Heaven.
> And as the light of Heaven varies, now
> At sunrise, now at sunset, now by night
> With moon and trembling stars, so loved Geraint
> To make her beauty vary day by day,
> 10 In crimsons and in purples and in gems.
> And Enid, but to please her husband's eye,
> Who first had found and loved her in a state
> Of broken fortunes, daily fronted him
> In some fresh splendour; and the Queen herself,
> 15 Grateful to Prince Geraint for service done,
> Loved her, and often with her own white hands
> Arrayed and decked her, as the loveliest,
> Next after her own self, in all the court.
> And Enid loved the Queen, and with true heart
> 20 Adored her, as the stateliest and the best
> And loveliest of all women upon earth.
> And seeing them so tender and so close,
> Long in their common love rejoiced Geraint.

¶466. *4. married*] *1862*; wedded *1859–61*. 'He found out that the "E" in "Enid" was pronounced short (as if it were spelt "Ennid"), and so altered the phrase in the proofs "wedded Enid" to "married Enid"' (H.T.). J. M. Gray points out that the first U.S. edition has the correction.

But when a rumour rose about the Queen,
25 Touching her guilty love for Lancelot,
Though yet there lived no proof, nor yet was heard
The world's loud whisper breaking into storm,
Not less Geraint believed it; and there fell
A horror on him, lest his gentle wife,
30 Through that great tenderness for Guinevere,
Had suffered, or should suffer any taint
In nature: wherefore going to the King,
He made this pretext, that his princedom lay
Close on the borders of a territory,
35 Wherein were bandit earls, and caitiff knights,
Assassins, and all flyers from the hand
Of Justice, and whatever loathes a law:
And therefore, till the King himself should please
To cleanse this common sewer of all his realm,
40 He craved a fair permission to depart,
And there defend his marches; and the King
Mused for a little on his plea, but, last,
Allowing it, the Prince and Enid rode,
And fifty knights rode with them, to the shores
45 Of Severn, and they past to their own land;
Where, thinking, that if ever yet was wife

24–9. Added to *Mabinogion,* so that T. could link these two idylls with his main theme.

33–41. In *Mabinogion,* this is no pretext; Geraint needs 'to protect his dominions and his boundaries, seeing that his father was unable to do so'.

45. 'Geraint was at Caerleon, and would have to cross the Bristol Channel to go to Devon' (T.). 'I like the *t*–the strong perfect in verbs ending in *s, p,* and *x*–past, slipt, vext' (T.).

46–68. Mabinogion: 'He began to love ease and pleasure, for there was no one who was worth his opposing. And he loved his wife, and liked to continue in the palace, with minstrelsy and diversions. And for a long time he abode at home. And after that he began to shut himself up in the chamber of his wife, and he took no delight in anything besides, insomuch that he gave up the friendship of his nobles, together with his hunting and his amusements, and lost the hearts of all the host in his Court; and there was murmuring and scoffing concerning him among the inhabitants of the palace, on account of his relinquishing so completely their companionship for the love of his wife ... "There is nothing more hateful to me than this." And she knew not what she should do, for, although it was hard for her to own this to Geraint, yet was it not more easy for her to listen to what she heard, without warning Geraint concerning it. And she was very sorrowful.'

True to her lord, mine shall be so to me,
He compassed her with sweet observances
And worship, never leaving her, and grew
50 Forgetful of his promise to the King,
Forgetful of the falcon and the hunt,
Forgetful of the tilt and tournament,
Forgetful of his glory and his name,
Forgetful of his princedom and its cares.
55 And this forgetfulness was hateful to her.
And by and by the people, when they met
In twos and threes, or fuller companies,
Began to scoff and jeer and babble of him
As of a prince whose manhood was all gone,
60 And molten down in mere uxoriousness.
And this she gathered from the people's eyes:
This too the women who attired her head,
To please her, dwelling on his boundless love,
Told Enid, and they saddened her the more:
65 And day by day she thought to tell Geraint,
But could not out of bashful delicacy;
While he that watched her sadden, was the more
Suspicious that her nature had a taint.

At last, it chanced that on a summer morn
70 (They sleeping each by either) the new sun
Beat through the blindless casement of the room,
And heated the strong warrior in his dreams;
Who, moving, cast the coverlet aside,
And bared the knotted column of his throat,
75 The massive square of his heroic breast,
And arms on which the standing muscle sloped,
As slopes a wild brook o'er a little stone,

69–108. *Mabinogion*: 'And one morning in the summer time, they were
upon their couch, and Geraint lay upon the edge of it. And Enid was
without sleep in the apartment which had windows of glass. And the sun
shone upon the couch. And the clothes had slipped from off his arms and
his breast, and he was asleep. Then she gazed upon the marvellous beauty
of his appearance, and she said, "Alas, and am I the cause that these arms
and this breast have lost their glory and the warlike fame which they once
so richly enjoyed!"' T. adds words capable of misconstruction.

70. *either*] *1870* ('*1869*'); other *1859–69*.

77. T. remarks: 'I made this simile from a stream, and it is different, though
like Theocritus, *Idyll* xxii 48ff: ἐν δὲ μύες στερεοῖσι βραχίοσιν ἄκρον
ὑπ' ὦμον ἔστασαν, ἠΰτε πέτροι ὀλοίτροχοι, οὔστε κυλίνδων
χειμάρρους ποταμὸς μεγάλαις περιέξεσε δίναις.' ('Moreover, the sinews

Running too vehemently to break upon it.
And Enid woke and sat beside the couch,
80   Admiring him, and thought within herself,
Was ever man so grandly made as he?
Then, like a shadow, past the people's talk
And accusation of uxoriousness
Across her mind, and bowing over him,
85   Low to her own heart piteously she said:

    'O noble breast and all-puissant arms,
Am I the cause, I the poor cause that men
Reproach you, saying all your force is gone?
I *am* the cause, because I dare not speak
90   And tell him what I think and what they say.
And yet I hate that he should linger here;
I cannot love my lord and not his name.
Far liefer had I gird his harness on him,
And ride with him to battle and stand by,
95   And watch his mightful hand striking great blows
At caitiffs and at wrongers of the world.
Far better were I laid in the dark earth,
Not hearing any more his noble voice,
Not to be folded more in these dear arms,
100   And darkened from the high light in his eyes,
Than that my lord through me should suffer shame.
Am I so bold, and could I so stand by,
And see my dear lord wounded in the strife,
Or maybe pierced to death before mine eyes,
105   And yet not dare to tell him what I think,
And how men slur him, saying all his force
Is melted into mere effeminacy?
O me, I fear that I am no true wife.'

    Half inwardly, half audibly she spoke,
110   And the strong passion in her made her weep

upon his brawny arms upstood beside the shoulder like the boulder-stones some torrent hath rolled and rounded in his swirling eddies.') H.T. adds: 'When some one objected that he had taken this simile from Theocritus, he answered: "It is quite different. Geraint's muscles are not compared to the rounded stones, but to the stream pouring vehemently over them."'
107. effeminacy] uxoriousness *H.Nbk 35*. The old sense of 'effeminacy' (which this MS has in its next line).
109–18. Mabinogion: 'And as she said this, the tears dropped from her eyes, and they fell upon his breast. And the tears she shed, and the words she had spoken, awoke him; and another thing contributed to awaken him, and

True tears upon his broad and naked breast,
And these awoke him, and by great mischance
He heard but fragments of her later words,
And that she feared she was not a true wife.
115 And then he thought, 'In spite of all my care,
For all my pains, poor man, for all my pains,
She is not faithful to me, and I see her
Weeping for some gay knight in Arthur's hall.'
Then though he loved and reverenced her too much
120 To dream she could be guilty of foul act,
Right through his manful breast darted the pang
That makes a man, in the sweet face of her
Whom he loves most, lonely and miserable.
At this he hurled his huge limbs out of bed,
125 And shook his drowsy squire awake and cried,
'My charger and her palfrey;' then to her,
'I will ride forth into the wilderness;
For though it seems my spurs are yet to win,
I have not fallen so low as some would wish.
130 And thou, put on thy worst and meanest dress
And ride with me.' And Enid asked, amazed,
'If Enid errs, let Enid learn her fault.'
But he, 'I charge thee, ask not, but obey.'
Then she bethought her of a faded silk,
135 A faded mantle and a faded veil,
And moving toward a cedarn cabinet,
Wherein she kept them folded reverently
With sprigs of summer laid between the folds,
She took them, and arrayed herself therein,
140 Remembering when first he came on her

that was the idea that it was not in thinking of him that she spoke thus, but
that it was because she loved some other man more than him.'
124-33. Mabinogion: 'And thereupon Geraint was troubled in his mind,
and he called his squire; and when he came to him, "Go quickly," said he,
"and prepare my horse and my arms, and make them ready. And do thou
arise," said he to Enid, "and apparel thyself; and cause thy horse to be
accoutred, and clothe thee in the worst riding-dress that thou hast in
thy possession." . . . So she arose, and clothed herself in her meanest gar-
ments. "I know nothing, Lord", said she, "of thy meaning". "Neither
wilt thou know at this time", said he.'
129 ∧ 30] And we will both begin our lives afresh *T.Nbk 30, deleted.*
130. thou . . . thy] 1873; you . . . your *1859-70.*
133. thee] 1873; you *1859-70.*
138. 'Lavender' (T.).

Drest in that dress, and how he loved her in it,
And all her foolish fears about the dress,
And all his journey to her, as himself
Had told her, and their coming to the court.

145 For Arthur on the Whitsuntide before
Held court at old Caerleon upon Usk.
There on a day, he sitting high in hall,
Before him came a forester of Dean,
Wet from the woods, with notice of a hart
150 Taller than all his fellows, milky-white,
First seen that day: these things he told the King.
Then the good King gave order to let blow
His horns for hunting on the morrow morn.
And when the Queen petitioned for his leave
155 To see the hunt, allowed it easily.
So with the morning all the court were gone.
But Guinevere lay late into the morn,
Lost in sweet dreams, and dreaming of her love
For Lancelot, and forgetful of the hunt;
160 But rose at last, a single maiden with her,
Took horse, and forded Usk, and gained the wood;
There, on a little knoll beside it, stayed
Waiting to hear the hounds; but heard instead
A sudden sound of hoofs, for Prince Geraint,
165 Late also, wearing neither hunting-dress
Nor weapon, save a golden-hilted brand,
Came quickly flashing through the shallow ford
Behind them, and so galloped up the knoll.
A purple scarf, at either end whereof
170 There swung an apple of the purest gold,
Swayed round about him, as he galloped up
To join them, glancing like a dragon-fly
In summer suit and silks of holiday.
Low bowed the tributary Prince, and she,
175 Sweetly and statelily, and with all grace
Of womanhood and queenhood, answered him:
'Late, late, Sir Prince,' she said, 'later than we!'
'Yea, noble Queen,' he answered, 'and so late

146. 'Arthur's capital, *castra Legionis*, is in Monmouthshire on the Usk,
which flows into the Bristol Channel' (T.).
157–9. Mabinogion: 'And Arthur wondered that Gwenhwyvar did not
awake, and did not move in her bed; and the attendants wished to awaken
her. "Disturb her not", said Arthur, "for she had rather sleep than go to
see the hunting."' T.'s addition stresses a theme of the *Idylls*.

That I but come like you to see the hunt,
180   Not join it.' 'Therefore wait with me,' she said;
'For on this little knoll, if anywhere,
There is good chance that we shall hear the hounds:
Here often they break covert at our feet.'

And while they listened for the distant hunt,
185   And chiefly for the baying of Cavall,
King Arthur's hound of deepest mouth, there rode
Full slowly by a knight, lady, and dwarf;
Whereof the dwarf lagged latest, and the knight
Had vizor up, and showed a youthful face,
190   Imperious, and of haughtiest lineaments.
And Guinevere, not mindful of his face
In the King's hall, desired his name, and sent
Her maiden to demand it of the dwarf;
Who being vicious, old and irritable,
195   And doubling all his master's vice of pride,
Made answer sharply that she should not know.
'Then will I ask it of himself,' she said.
'Nay, by my faith, thou shalt not,' cried the dwarf;
'Thou art not worthy even to speak of him;'
200   And when she put her horse toward the knight,
Struck at her with his whip, and she returned
Indignant to the Queen; whereat Geraint
Exclaiming, 'Surely I will learn the name,'
Made sharply to the dwarf, and asked it of him,
205   Who answered as before; and when the Prince
Had put his horse in motion toward the knight,
Struck at him with his whip, and cut his cheek.
The Prince's blood spirted upon the scarf,
Dyeing it; and his quick, instinctive hand
210   Caught at the hilt, as to abolish him:
But he, from his exceeding manfulness
And pure nobility of temperament,

186. T. compares *Midsummer Night's Dream* IV i 122: 'matched in mouth like bells'.
190. haughtiest lineaments: *The Princess* ii 425.
201. Mabinogion: 'Then the maiden turned her horse's head towards the knight, upon which the dwarf struck her with the whip that was in his hand across the face and the eyes, until the blood flowed forth.'
202. whereat] *1870* ('*1869*'); at which *1859–69*.
211–4. Mabinogion: 'But he took counsel with himself, and considered that it would be no vengeance for him to slay the dwarf, and to be attacked

Wroth to be wroth at such a worm, refrained
From even a word, and so returning said:

215   'I will avenge this insult, noble Queen,
Done in your maiden's person to yourself:
And I will track this vermin to their earths:
For though I ride unarmed, I do not doubt
To find, at some place I shall come at, arms
220   On loan, or else for pledge; and, being found,
Then will I fight him, and will break his pride,
And on the third day will again be here,
So that I be not fallen in fight. Farewell.'

    'Farewell, fair Prince,' answered the stately Queen.
225   'Be prosperous in this journey, as in all;
And may you light on all things that you love,
And live to wed with her whom first you love:
But ere you wed with any, bring your bride,
And I, were she the daughter of a king,
230   Yea, though she were a beggar from the hedge,
Will clothe her for her bridals like the sun.'

    And Prince Geraint, now thinking that he heard
The noble hart at bay, now the far horn,
A little vext at losing of the hunt,
235   A little at the vile occasion, rode,
By ups and downs, through many a grassy glade
And valley, with fixt eye following the three.
At last they issued from the world of wood,
And climbed upon a fair and even ridge,
240   And showed themselves against the sky, and sank.
And thither came Geraint, and underneath
Beheld the long street of a little town
In a long valley, on one side whereof,
White from the mason's hand, a fortress rose;
245   And on one side a castle in decay,
Beyond a bridge that spanned a dry ravine:
And out of town and valley came a noise
As of a broad brook o'er a shingly bed

unarmed by the armed knight, so he returned to where Gwenhwyvar
was.'
226–31. No equivalent in *Mabinogion.*
239. Mabinogion: 'And they went along a fair, and even, and lofty ridge of
ground.'
242–55. Expanding *Mabinogion.*
243. whereof] *1870* ('*1869*'); of which *1859–69.*

Brawling, or like a clamour of the rooks
250   At distance, ere they settle for the night.

And onward to the fortress rode the three,
And entered, and were lost behind the walls.
'So,' thought Geraint, 'I have tracked him to his
    earth.'
And down the long street riding wearily,
255   Found every hostel full, and everywhere
Was hammer laid to hoof, and the hot hiss
And bustling whistle of the youth who scoured
His master's armour; and of such a one
He asked, 'What means the tumult in the town?'
260   Who told him, scouring still, 'The sparrow-hawk!'
Then riding close behind an ancient churl,
Who, smitten by the dusty sloping beam,
Went sweating underneath a sack of corn,
Asked yet once more what meant the hubbub here?
265   Who answered gruffly, 'Ugh! the sparrow-hawk.'
Then riding further past an armourer's,
Who, with back turned, and bowed above his work,
Sat riveting a helmet on his knee,
He put the self-same query, but the man
270   Not turning round, nor looking at him, said:
'Friend, he that labours for the sparrow-hawk
Has little time for idle questioners.'
Whereat Geraint flashed into sudden spleen:
'A thousand pips eat up your sparrow-hawk!
275   Tits, wrens, and all winged nothings peck him dead!
Ye think the rustic cackle of your bourg
The murmur of the world! What is it to me?
O wretched set of sparrows, one and all,
Who pipe of nothing but of sparrow-hawks!
280   Speak, if ye be not like the rest, hawk-mad,
Where can I get me harbourage for the night?
And arms, arms, arms to fight my enemy? Speak!'
Whereat the armourer turning all amazed

255–92. *Mabinogion*: 'And every house he saw was full of men, and arms, and horses. And they were polishing shields, and burnishing swords, and washing armour, and shoeing horses.' In *Mabinogion*, Geraint's enemies (the knight, the lady and the dwarf) are warmly welcomed in the city.
274. *pips*: 'a bird-disease' (T.).
280. *ye*] *1870* ('*1869*'); *you 1859–69*. Likewise ll. 304, 421, 684, 719, 726.
283. *Whereat*] *1873*; At this *1859–70*.

And seeing one so gay in purple silks,
285 Came forward with the helmet yet in hand
And answered, 'Pardon me, O stranger knight;
We hold a tourney here tomorrow morn,
And there is scantly time for half the work.
Arms? truth! I know not: all are wanted here.
290 Harbourage? truth, good truth, I know not, save,
It may be, at Earl Yniol's, o'er the bridge
Yonder.' He spoke and fell to work again.

Then rode Geraint, a little spleenful yet,
Across the bridge that spanned the dry ravine.
295 There musing sat the hoary-headed Earl,
(His dress a suit of frayed magnificence,
Once fit for feasts of ceremony) and said:
'Whither, fair son?' to whom Geraint replied,
'O friend, I seek a harbourage for the night.'
300 Then Yniol, 'Enter therefore and partake
The slender entertainment of a house
Once rich, now poor, but ever open-doored.'
'Thanks, venerable friend,' replied Geraint;
'So that ye do not serve me sparrow-hawks
305 For supper, I will enter, I will eat
With all the passion of a twelve hours' fast.'
Then sighed and smiled the hoary-headed Earl,
And answered, 'Graver cause than yours is mine
To curse this hedgerow thief, the sparrow-hawk:
310 But in, go in; for save yourself desire it,
We will not touch upon him even in jest.'

Then rode Geraint into the castle court,
His charger trampling many a prickly star
Of sprouted thistle on the broken stones.
315 He looked and saw that all was ruinous.
Here stood a shattered archway plumed with fern;
And here had fallen a great part of a tower,
Whole, like a crag that tumbles from the cliff,

290-7. *Mabinogion*: 'At a little distance from the town he saw an old palace in ruins, wherein was a hall that was falling to decay. And as he knew not anyone in the town, he went towards the old palace; and when he came near to the palace, he saw but one chamber, and a bridge of marble-stone leading to it. And upon the bridge he saw sitting a hoary-headed man, upon whom were tattered garments.'
298-311. Expanding *Mabinogion*.

And like a crag was gay with wilding flowers:
320 And high above a piece of turret stair,
Worn by the feet that now were silent, wound
Bare to the sun, and monstrous ivy-stems
Claspt the gray walls with hairy-fibred arms,
And sucked the joining of the stones, and looked
325 A knot, beneath, of snakes, aloft, a grove.

And while he waited in the castle court,
The voice of Enid, Yniol's daughter, rang
Clear through the open casement of the hall,
Singing; and as the sweet voice of a bird,
330 Heard by the lander in a lonely isle,
Moves him to think what kind of bird it is
That sings so delicately clear, and make
Conjecture of the plumage and the form;
So the sweet voice of Enid moved Geraint;
335 And made him like a man abroad at morn
When first the liquid note beloved of men
Comes flying over many a windy wave
To Britain, and in April suddenly
Breaks from a coppice gemmed with green and red,
340 And he suspends his converse with a friend,
Or it may be the labour of his hands,
To think or say, 'There is the nightingale;'
So fared it with Geraint, who thought and said,
'Here, by God's grace, is the one voice for me.'

345   It chanced the song that Enid sang was one
Of Fortune and her wheel, and Enid sang:

'Turn, Fortune, turn thy wheel and lower the
        proud;

319. 'These lines were made at Middleham Castle' (T.) (*Mem.* i 487). For the influence of Francis Grose's plates and commentary on the castle, and for the general influence of Grose on T., see W. D. Shaw, *ELN* v (1968) 269–77.
322–3. 'Tintern Abbey' (T.). These lines had originally been part of *The Princess: Prologue*, in MS.
326–60. Not in *Mabinogion*.
347–58. H.T. notes: 'This song of noble and enduring womanhood has its refrain in "Però giri Fortuna la sua ruota, / Come le piace"' (Dante, *Inferno* xv 95–6). But when John Churton Collins originally suggested this, T. wrote alongside '!!!' (*Cornhill*, Jan. 1880, Lincoln). Sir Charles Tennyson (*Cornhill* cliii (1936) 535) quotes from *H.MS* another version of the song:
Come in, the ford is roaring on the plain,
The distant hills are pale across the rain;
Come in, come in, for open is the gate.

Turn thy wild wheel through sunshine, storm, and
    cloud;
Thy wheel and thee we neither love nor hate.

350   'Turn, Fortune, turn thy wheel with smile or frown;
With that wild wheel we go not up or down;
Our hoard is little, but our hearts are great.

'Smile and we smile, the lords of many lands;
Frown and we smile, the lords of our own hands;
355   For man is man and master of his fate.

'Turn, turn thy wheel above the staring crowd;
Thy wheel and thou are shadows in the cloud;
Thy wheel and thee we neither love nor hate.'

'Hark, by the bird's song ye may learn the nest,'
360   Said Yniol; 'enter quickly.' Entering then,
Right o'er a mount of newly-fallen stones,
The dusky-raftered many-cobwebbed hall,
He found an ancient dame in dim brocade;

    Come in, poor man, and let the tempest blow.
    Let Fortune frown and old possession go,
      But health is wealth in high or low estate;
      Though Fortune frown thou shalt not hear us rail,
    The frown of Fortune never turned us pale,
    For man is man and master of his fate.
    Turn, Fortune, turn thy wheel with smile or frown,
    With thy false wheel we go not up or down,
    Our hoard is little but our hearts are great.
    Smile and we smile, the lords of many lands,
    Frown and we smile, the lords of our own hands,
    For man is man and master of his fate.
    The river ford will fall on yonder plain,
    The flying rainbow chase the flying rain,
    The sun at last will smile however late;
    Come in, come in, whoever lingers there,
    Nor scorn the ruined house and homely fare,
    The house is poor but open is the gate.

359. ye] *1873*; you *1859–70.* Likewise ll. 430, 698.
360–8. Mabinogion: 'And in the chamber he beheld an old decrepit woman,
sitting on a cushion, with old, tattered garments of satin upon her; and it
seemed to him that he had never seen a woman fairer than she must have
been, when in the fulness of youth. And beside her was a maiden, upon
whom were a vest and a veil, that were old, and beginning to be worn out.
And truly, he never saw a maiden more full of comeliness, and grace, and
beauty, than she.'

And near her, like a blossom vermeil-white,
365   That lightly breaks a faded flower-sheath,
Moved the fair Enid, all in faded silk,
Her daughter. In a moment thought Geraint,
'Here by God's rood is the one maid for me.'
But none spake word except the hoary Earl:
370   'Enid, the good knight's horse stands in the court;
Take him to stall, and give him corn, and then
Go to the town and buy us flesh and wine;
And we will make us merry as we may.
Our hoard is little, but our hearts are great.'

375   He spake: the Prince, as Enid past him, fain
To follow, strode a stride, but Yniol caught
His purple scarf, and held, and said, 'Forbear!
Rest! the good house, though ruined, O my son,
Endures not that her guest should serve himself.'
380   And reverencing the custom of the house
Geraint, from utter courtesy, forbore.

So Enid took his charger to the stall;
And after went her way across the bridge,
And reached the town, and while the Prince and Earl
385   Yet spoke together, came again with one,
A youth, that following with a costrel bore
The means of goodly welcome, flesh and wine.
And Enid brought sweet cakes to make them cheer,
And in her veil enfolded, manchet bread.
390   And then, because their hall must also serve
For kitchen, boiled the flesh, and spread the board,
And stood behind, and waited on the three.
And seeing her so sweet and serviceable,
Geraint had longing in him evermore
395   To stoop and kiss the tender little thumb,
That crost the trencher as she laid it down:
But after all had eaten, then Geraint,

---

368. 'Rood (originally the same as "rod") is the old word for cross' (T.).
375–81. Not in *Mabinogion*.
386–9. *Mabinogion*: 'And a youth with her, bearing on his back a costrel
full of good purchased mead, and a quarter of a young bullock. And in the
hands of the maiden was a quantity of white bread, and she had some
manchet bread in her veil, and she came into the chamber.'   *costrel:*
'a bottle with ear or ears, by which it could be hung from the waist
(*costrer*, by the side), hence sometimes called "pilgrim's bottle"' (T.).
manchet bread: 'little loaves or rolls made of fine wheat flour' (T.).

For now the wine made summer in his veins,
Let his eye rove in following, or rest
400 On Enid at her lowly handmaid-work,
Now here, now there, about the dusky hall;
Then suddenly addrest the hoary Earl:

'Fair Host and Earl, I pray your courtesy;
This sparrow-hawk, what is he? tell me of him.
405 His name? but no, good faith, I will not have it:
For if he be the knight whom late I saw
Ride into that new fortress by your town,
White from the mason's hand, then have I sworn
From his own lips to have it–I am Geraint
410 Of Devon–for this morning when the Queen
Sent her own maiden to demand the name,
His dwarf, a vicious under-shapen thing,
Struck at her with his whip, and she returned
Indignant to the Queen; and then I swore
415 That I would track this caitiff to his hold,
And fight and break his pride, and have it of him.
And all unarmed I rode, and thought to find
Arms in your town, where all the men are mad;
They take the rustic murmur of their bourg
420 For the great wave that echoes round the world;
They would not hear me speak: but if ye know
Where I can light on arms, or if yourself
Should have them, tell me, seeing I have sworn
That I will break his pride and learn his name,
425 Avenging this great insult done the Queen.'

Then cried Earl Yniol, 'Art thou he indeed,
Geraint, a name far-sounded among men
For noble deeds? and truly I, when first
I saw you moving by me on the bridge,
430 Felt ye were somewhat, yea, and by your state
And presence might have guessed you one of those
That eat in Arthur's hall at Camelot.
Nor speak I now from foolish flattery;
For this dear child hath often heard me praise
435 Your feats of arms, and often when I paused
Hath asked again, and ever loved to hear;
So grateful is the noise of noble deeds
To noble hearts who see but acts of wrong:
O never yet had woman such a pair
440 Of suitors as this maiden; first Limours,
A creature wholly given to brawls and wine,

Drunk even when he wooed; and be he dead
I know not, but he past to the wild land.
The second was your foe, the sparrow-hawk,
445 My curse, my nephew—I will not let his name
Slip from my lips if I can help it—he,
When I that knew him fierce and turbulent
Refused her to him, then his pride awoke;
And since the proud man often is the mean,
450 He sowed a slander in the common ear,
Affirming that his father left him gold,
And in my charge, which was not rendered to him;
Bribed with large promises the men who served
About my person, the more easily
455 Because my means were somewhat broken into
Through open doors and hospitality;
Raised my own town against me in the night
Before my Enid's birthday, sacked my house;
From mine own earldom foully ousted me;
460 Built that new fort to overawe my friends,
For truly there are those who love me yet;
And keeps me in this ruinous castle here,
Where doubtless he would put me soon to death,
But that his pride too much despises me:
465 And I myself sometimes despise myself;
For I have let men be, and have their way;
Am much too gentle, have not used my power:
Nor know I whether I be very base

447ff. H.T. comments: 'In the *Mabinogion* Earl Yniol is the wrong-doer,
and has earned his reward; but the poet has made the story more interesting
and more poetic by making the tale of wrong-doing a calumny on the
part of the Earl's nephew.

'And when they had finished eating, Geraint talked with the hoary-headed
man, and he asked him in the first place, to whom belonged the palace
that he was in. "Truly", said he, "it was I that built it, and to me also
belonged the city and the castle which thou sawest". "Alas!" said Geraint,
"how is it that thou hast lost them now?" "I lost a great Earldom as well
as these", said he, "and this is how I lost them. I had a nephew, the son of
my brother, and I took his possessions to myself; and when he came to his
strength, he demanded of me his property, but I withheld it from him.
So he made war upon me, and wrested from me all that I possessed."'

In the Idyll, for the greater unity of the tale, the nephew and the knight of
the Sparrow-hawk are one.'

Or very manful, whether very wise
470 Or very foolish; only this I know,
That whatsoever evil happen to me,
I seem to suffer nothing heart or limb,
But can endure it all most patiently.'

'Well said, true heart,' replied Geraint, 'but arms,
475 That if the sparrow-hawk, this nephew, fight
In next day's tourney I may break his pride.'

And Yniol answered, 'Arms, indeed, but old
And rusty, old and rusty, Prince Geraint,
Are mine, and therefore at thine asking, thine.
480 But in this tournament can no man tilt,
Except the lady he loves best be there.
Two forks are fixt into the meadow ground,
And over these is placed a silver wand,
And over that a golden sparrow-hawk,
485 The prize of beauty for the fairest there.
And this, what knight soever be in field
Lays claim to for the lady at his side,
And tilts with my good nephew thereupon,
Who being apt at arms and big of bone
490 Has ever won it for the lady with him,
And toppling over all antagonism
Has earned himself the name of sparrow-hawk.
But thou, that hast no lady, canst not fight.'

To whom Geraint with eyes all bright replied,
495 Leaning a little toward him, 'Thy leave!
Let *me* lay lance in rest, O noble host,

475] *1870* ('*1869*'); That if, as I suppose, your nephew fights *1859–69.*
479. *thine . . . thine*] *1873*; your . . . yours *1859–70.*
480–5. *Mabinogion*: 'In the midst of a meadow which is here, two forks will be set up, and upon the two forks a silver rod, and upon the silver rod a Sparrow-Hawk . . . and no man can joust for the Sparrow-Hawk, except the lady he loves best be with him.'
483. *placed*] *1873*; laid *1859–70.*
484. *a golden*] *1873*; is placed the *1859–70.*
493. *thou . . . hast . . . canst*] *1873*; you . . . have . . . cannot *1859–70.*
495. *Thy*] *1873*; Your *1859–70.* Likewise l. 780.
495–503. *Mabinogion*: 'And if . . . thou wilt permit me, Sir, to challenge for yonder maiden that is thy daughter, I will engage, if I escape from the tournament to love the maiden as long as I live; and if I do not escape, she will remain unsullied as before.'

For this dear child, because I never saw,
Though having seen all beauties of our time,
Nor can see elsewhere, anything so fair.
500   And if I fall her name will yet remain
Untarnished as before; but if I live,
So aid me Heaven when at mine uttermost,
As I will make her truly my true wife.'

Then, howsoever patient, Yniol's heart
505   Danced in his bosom, seeing better days.
And looking round he saw not Enid there,
(Who hearing her own name had stolen away)
But that old dame, to whom full tenderly
And folding all her hand in his he said,
510   'Mother, a maiden is a tender thing,
And best by her that bore her understood.
Go thou to rest, but ere thou go to rest
Tell her, and prove her heart toward the Prince.'

So spake the kindly-hearted Earl, and she
515   With frequent smile and nod departing found,
Half disarrayed as to her rest, the girl;
Whom first she kissed on either cheek, and then
On either shining shoulder laid a hand,
And kept her off and gazed upon her face,
520   And told her all their converse in the hall,
Proving her heart: but never light and shade
Coursed one another more on open ground
Beneath a troubled heaven, than red and pale
Across the face of Enid hearing her;
525   While slowly falling as a scale that falls,
When weight is added only grain by grain,
Sank her sweet head upon her gentle breast;
Nor did she lift an eye nor speak a word,
Rapt in the fear and in the wonder of it;
530   So moving without answer to her rest
She found no rest, and ever failed to draw
The quiet night into her blood, but lay
Contemplating her own unworthiness;
And when the pale and bloodless east began

504–32. Not in *Mabinogion*.
507. *stolen*] *1873*; *slipt 1859–70*.
531–2. H.T. compares *Aeneid* iv 529–31: *neque umquam | solvitur in somnos, oculisve aut pectore noctem | accipit.* ('She never sinks to sleep, nor draws the night into eyes or heart.')

535 To quicken to the sun, arose, and raised
    Her mother too, and hand in hand they moved
    Down to the meadow where the jousts were held,
    And waited there for Yniol and Geraint.

        And thither came the twain, and when Geraint
540 Beheld her first in field, awaiting him,
    He felt, were she the prize of bodily force,
    Himself beyond the rest pushing could move
    The chair of Idris. Yniol's rusted arms
    Were on his princely person, but through these
545 Princelike his bearing shone; and errant knights
    And ladies came, and by and by the town
    Flowed in, and settling circled all the lists.
    And there they fixt the forks into the ground,
    And over these they placed the silver wand,
550 And over that the golden sparrow-hawk.
    Then Yniol's nephew, after trumpet blown,
    Spake to the lady with him and proclaimed,
    'Advance and take, as fairest of the fair,
    What I these two years past have won for thee,
555 The prize of beauty.' Loudly spake the Prince,
    'Forbear: there is a worthier,' and the knight
    With some surprise and thrice as much disdain
    Turned, and beheld the four, and all his face
    Glowed like the heart of a great fire at Yule,
560 So burnt he was with passion, crying out,
    'Do battle for it then,' no more; and thrice
    They clashed together, and thrice they brake their
        spears.
    Then each, dishorsed and drawing, lashed at each
    So often and with such blows, that all the crowd
565 Wondered, and now and then from distant walls
    There came a clapping as of phantom hands.
    So twice they fought, and twice they breathed, and
        still
    The dew of their great labour, and the blood
    Of their strong bodies, flowing, drained their force.

543. 'Idris was one of the three primitive Bards. Cader Idris, the noblest
mountain next to Snowdon in N. Wales' (T.).
549, 550. the] 1873; a 1859–70.
554. What] 1886; For 1859–84.   won] 1886; won it 1859–84.
562–74. The combat is based closely on Mabinogion.
565–6. 'This is the echo of the sword-clash' (T.).

570   But either's force was matched till Yniol's cry,
      'Remember that great insult done the Queen,'
      Increased Geraint's, who heaved his blade aloft,
      And cracked the helmet through, and bit the bone,
      And felled him, and set foot upon his breast,
575   And said, 'Thy name?' To whom the fallen man
      Made answer, groaning, 'Edyrn, son of Nudd!
      Ashamed am I that I should tell it thee.
      My pride is broken: men have seen my fall.'
      'Then, Edyrn, son of Nudd,' replied Geraint,
580   'These two things shalt thou do, or else thou diest.
      First, thou thyself, with damsel and with dwarf,
      Shalt ride to Arthur's court, and coming there,
      Crave pardon for that insult done the Queen,
      And shalt abide her judgment on it; next,
585   Thou shalt give back their earldom to thy kin.
      These two things shalt thou do, or thou shalt die.'
      And Edyrn answered, 'These things will I do,
      For I have never yet been overthrown,
      And thou hast overthrown me, and my pride
590   Is broken down, for Enid sees my fall!'
      And rising up, he rode to Arthur's court,
      And there the Queen forgave him easily.
      And being young, he changed and came to loathe
      His crime of traitor, slowly drew himself
595   Bright from his old dark life, and fell at last
      In the great battle fighting for the King.

      But when the third day from the hunting-morn
      Made a low splendour in the world, and wings
      Moved in her ivy, Enid, for she lay
600   With her fair head in the dim-yellow light,

---

581. *with . . . with*] *1873*; thy lady, and thy *1859–70*.
582. *coming*] *1873*; being *1859–70*.
584–5. This addition to *Mabinogion* was necessitated by T.'s changes.
592–6. *Mabinogion* later gives a detailed account of Edyrn's return to the
court, which suggested T.'s handling of the close of *Geraint and Enid*.
593. *and . . . loathe*] *1870* ('*1869*'); himself, and grew *1859–69*.
594–5] *1870* ('*1869*');
          To hate the sin that seemed so like his own
          Of Modred, Arthur's nephew, and fell at last *1859–69*.
598] Beneath the swelling bosom of the cloud
     Had cast her golden zone along the dark
                                    H.Nbk 35 draft of these lines

Among the dancing shadows of the birds,
Woke and bethought her of her promise given
No later than last eve to Prince Geraint—
So bent he seemed on going the third day,
605 He would not leave her, till her promise given—
To ride with him this morning to the court,
And there be made known to the stately Queen,
And there be wedded with all ceremony.
At this she cast her eyes upon her dress,
610 And thought it never yet had looked so mean.
For as a leaf in mid-November is
To what it was in mid-October, seemed
The dress that now she looked on to the dress
She looked on ere the coming of Geraint.
615 And still she looked, and still the terror grew
Of that strange bright and dreadful thing, a court,
All staring at her in her faded silk:
And softly to her own sweet heart she said:

'This noble prince who won our earldom back,
620 So splendid in his acts and his attire,
Sweet heaven, how much I shall discredit him!
Would he could tarry with us here awhile,
But being so beholden to the Prince,
It were but little grace in any of us,
625 Bent as he seemed on going this third day,
To seek a second favour at his hands.
Yet if he could but tarry a day or two,
Myself would work eye dim, and finger lame,
Far liefer than so much discredit him.'

630 And Enid fell in longing for a dress
All branched and flowered with gold, a costly gift
Of her good mother, given her on the night

609ff. H.T. quotes *Mabinogion*: '"Where is the Earl Ynywl", said Geraint, "and his wife, and his daughter?". "They are in the chamber yonder", said the Earl's chamberlain, "arraying themselves in garments which the Earl has caused to be brought for them". "Let not the damsel array herself", said he, "except in her vest and her veil, until she come to the Court of Arthur, to be clad by Gwenhwyvar, in such garments as she may choose". So the maiden did not array herself.' From this point T. considerably expands, through to l. 826.
615. Cp. Goldsmith, *The Deserted Village* 215: 'And still they gazed, and still the wonder grew'.

Before her birthday, three sad years ago,
That night of fire, when Edyrn sacked their house,
635   And scattered all they had to all the winds:
For while the mother showed it, and the two
Were turning and admiring it, the work
To both appeared so costly, rose a cry
That Edyrn's men were on them, and they fled
640   With little save the jewels they had on,
Which being sold and sold had bought them bread:
And Edyrn's men had caught them in their flight,
And placed them in this ruin; and she wished
The Prince had found her in her ancient home;
645   Then let her fancy flit across the past,
And roam the goodly places that she knew;
And last bethought her how she used to watch,
Near that old home, a pool of golden carp;
And one was patched and blurred and lustreless
650   Among his burnished brethren of the pool;
And half asleep she made comparison
Of that and these to her own faded self
And the gay court, and fell asleep again;
And dreamt herself was such a faded form
655   Among her burnished sisters of the pool;
But this was in the garden of a king;
And though she lay dark in the pool, she knew
That all was bright; that all about were birds
Of sunny plume in gilded trellis-work;
660   That all the turf was rich in plots that looked
Each like a garnet or a turkis in it;
And lords and ladies of the high court went
In silver tissue talking things of state;
And children of the King in cloth of gold
665   Glanced at the doors or gamboled down the walks;
And while she thought 'They will not see me,' came
A stately queen whose name was Guinevere,
And all the children in their cloth of gold
Ran to her, crying, 'If we have fish at all
670   Let them be gold; and charge the gardeners now
To pick the faded creature from the pool,
And cast it on the mixen that it die.'
And therewithal one came and seized on her,
And Enid started waking, with her heart
675   All overshadowed by the foolish dream,

672. *mixen*: dung-hill.

And lo! it was her mother grasping her
To get her well awake; and in her hand
A suit of bright apparel, which she laid
Flat on the couch, and spoke exultingly:

680 'See here, my child, how fresh the colours look,
How fast they hold like colours of a shell
That keeps the wear and polish of the wave.
Why not? It never yet was worn, I trow:
Look on it, child, and tell me if ye know it.'

685 And Enid looked, but all confused at first,
Could scarce divide it from her foolish dream:
Then suddenly she knew it and rejoiced,
And answered, 'Yea, I know it; your good gift,
So sadly lost on that unhappy night;

690 Your own good gift!' 'Yea, surely,' said the dame,
'And gladly given again this happy morn.
For when the jousts were ended yesterday,
Went Yniol through the town, and everywhere
He found the sack and plunder of our house

695 All scattered through the houses of the town;
And gave command that all which once was ours
Should now be ours again: and yester-eve,
While ye were talking sweetly with your Prince,
Came one with this and laid it in my hand,

700 For love or fear, or seeking favour of us,
Because we have our earldom back again.
And yester-eve I would not tell you of it,
But kept it for a sweet surprise at morn.
Yea, truly is it not a sweet surprise?

705 For I myself unwillingly have worn
My faded suit, as you, my child, have yours,
And howsoever patient, Yniol his.
Ah, dear, he took me from a goodly house,
With store of rich apparel, sumptuous fare,

710 And page, and maid, and squire, and seneschal,
And pastime both of hawk and hound, and all
That appertains to noble maintenance.
Yea, and he brought me to a goodly house;
But since our fortune swerved from sun to shade,

715 And all through that young traitor, cruel need
Constrained us, but a better time has come;
So clothe yourself in this, that better fits

714. *swerved*] *1882*; slipt *1859–81*.

Our mended fortunes and a Prince's bride:
For though ye won the prize of fairest fair,
720 And though I heard him call you fairest fair,
Let never maiden think, however fair,
She is not fairer in new clothes than old.
And should some great court-lady say, the Prince
Hath picked a ragged-robin from the hedge,
725 And like a madman brought her to the court,
Then were ye shamed, and, worse, might shame the
          Prince
To whom we are beholden; but I know,
When my dear child is set forth at her best,
That neither court nor country, though they sought
730 Through all the provinces like those of old
That lighted on Queen Esther, has her match.'

Here ceased the kindly mother out of breath;
And Enid listened brightening as she lay;
Then, as the white and glittering star of morn
735 Parts from a bank of snow, and by and by
Slips into golden cloud, the maiden rose,
And left her maiden couch, and robed herself,
Helped by the mother's careful hand and eye,
Without a mirror, in the gorgeous gown;
740 Who, after, turned her daughter round, and said,
She never yet had seen her half so fair;
And called her like that maiden in the tale,
Whom Gwydion made by glamour out of flowers
And sweeter than the bride of Cassivelaun,
745 Flur, for whose love the Roman Cæsar first
Invaded Britain, 'But we beat him back,
As this great Prince invaded us, and we,
Not beat him back, but welcomed him with joy
And I can scarcely ride with you to court,
750 For old am I, and rough the ways and wild;

---

731. *Esther* ii 3.

742. T. quotes from *Mabinogion*, 'The Tale of Math, son of Mathonwy':
'So they took the blossoms of the oak, and the blossoms of the broom,
and the blossoms of the meadow-sweet, and produced from them a
maiden, the fairest and most graceful that man ever saw. And they baptized
her and gave her the name of Blodeuwedd' (flower-vision).

744. H.T. comments: 'The love of a British maiden named Flur, who was
betrothed to Cassivelaunus, according to the Welsh legend, led Caesar to
invade Britain', from *Mabinogion*, 'Manawyddan the Son of Llyr'.

But Yniol goes, and I full oft shall dream
I see my princess as I see her now,
Clothed with my gift, and gay among the gay.'

But while the women thus rejoiced, Geraint
755 Woke where he slept in the high hall, and called
For Enid, and when Yniol made report
Of that good mother making Enid gay
In such apparel as might well beseem
His princess, or indeed the stately Queen,
760 He answered: 'Earl, entreat her by my love,
Albeit I give no reason but my wish,
That she ride with me in her faded silk.'
Yniol with that hard message went; it fell
Like flaws in summer laying lusty corn:
765 For Enid, all abashed she knew not why,
Dared not to glance at her good mother's face,
But silently, in all obedience,
Her mother silent too, nor helping her,
Laid from her limbs the costly-broidered gift,
770 And robed them in her ancient suit again,
And so descended. Never man rejoiced
More than Geraint to greet her thus attired;
And glancing all at once as keenly at her
As careful robins eye the delver's toil,
775 Made her cheek burn and either eyelid fall,
But rested with her sweet face satisfied;
Then seeing cloud upon the mother's brow,
Her by both hands he caught, and sweetly said,

'O my new mother, be not wroth or grieved
780 At thy new son, for my petition to her.
When late I left Caerleon, our great Queen,
In words whose echo lasts, they were so sweet,
Made promise, that whatever bride I brought,
Herself would clothe her like the sun in Heaven.
785 Thereafter, when I reached this ruined hall,
Beholding one so bright in dark estate,
I vowed that could I gain her, our fair Queen,

764. H.T. compares *Hamlet* V i 210: 'the winter's flaw'–gusts of wind.
774. Cp. *Early Spring* (1833) 11–12 (I 538), which must modify H.T.'s note:
'This line was made one day while my father was digging . . . at Farring-
ford.'
785. *hall*] *1873*; hold *1859–70*.
787. *fair*] *1873*; kind *1859–70*.

No hand but hers, should make your Enid burst
Sunlike from cloud—and likewise thought perhaps,
790   That service done so graciously would bind
The two together; fain I would the two
Should love each other: how can Enid find
A nobler friend? Another thought was mine;
I came among you here so suddenly,
795   That though her gentle presence at the lists
Might well have served for proof that I was loved,
I doubted whether daughter's tenderness,
Or easy nature, might not let itself
Be moulded by your wishes for her weal;
800   Or whether some false sense in her own self
Of my contrasting brightness, overbore
Her fancy dwelling in this dusky hall;
And such a sense might make her long for court
And all its perilous glories: and I thought,
805   That could I someway prove such force in her
Linked with such love for me, that at a word
(No reason given her) she could cast aside
A splendour dear to women, new to her,
And therefore dearer; or if not so new,
810   Yet therefore tenfold dearer by the power
Of intermitted usage; then I felt
That I could rest, a rock in ebbs and flows,
Fixt on her faith. Now, therefore, I do rest,
A prophet certain of my prophecy,
815   That never shadow of mistrust can cross
Between us. Grant me pardon for my thoughts:
And for my strange petition I will make
Amends hereafter by some gaudy-day,
When your fair child shall wear your costly gift
820   Beside your own warm hearth, with, on her knees,
Who knows? another gift of the high God,
Which, maybe, shall have learned to lisp you thanks.'

791. *fain I would*] *1873*; for I wish *1859–70*.
792. *Should*] *1873*; To *1859–70*.   *can*] *1873*; should *1859–70*.
793. *was mine*] *1873*; I had *1859–70*.
797. *daughter's*] *1873*; filial *1859–70*.
798. *might*] *1873*; did *1859–70*.
804. *perilous*] *1873*; dangerous *1859–70*.
811. *usage*] *1873*; custom *1859–70*.
818. *gaudy-day*: 'Holiday – now only used of special feast-days at the Universities' (H.T.).

He spoke: the mother smiled, but half in tears,
Then brought a mantle down and wrapt her in it,
825 And claspt and kissed her, and they rode away.

Now thrice that morning Guinevere had climbed
The giant tower, from whose high crest, they say,
Men saw the goodly hills of Somerset,
And white sails flying on the yellow sea;
830 But not to goodly hill or yellow sea
Looked the fair Queen, but up the vale of Usk,
By the flat meadow, till she saw them come;
And then descending met them at the gates,
Embraced her with all welcome as a friend,
835 And did her honour as the Prince's bride,
And clothed her for her bridals like the sun;
And all that week was old Caerleon gay,
For by the hands of Dubric, the high saint,
They twain were wedded with all ceremony.

840 And this was on the last year's Whitsuntide.
But Enid ever kept the faded silk,
Remembering how first he came on her,
Drest in that dress, and how he loved her in it,
And all her foolish fears about the dress,
845 And all his journey toward her, as himself
Had told her, and their coming to the court.

And now this morning when he said to her,
'Put on your worst and meanest dress,' she found
And took it, and arrayed herself therein.

467 Geraint and Enid

Enid was privately printed in 1857. Published *1859*, the second half of *Enid*.
The title *Enid* was expanded to *Geraint and Enid* in *1870* ('*1869*'); the poem
was divided into two parts in *1873*; and the final titles given in *1886*. See
headnote to *The Marriage of Geraint* (p. *735*). 'The sin of Lancelot and
Guinevere begins to breed, even among those who would "rather die than
doubt", despair and want of trust in God and man' (H.T.).

826. In *Mabinogion*, Guinevere places a watch on the ramparts.
836. Mabinogion: 'And the choicest of all Gwenhwyvar's apparel was given
to the maiden.'

O purblind race of miserable men,
How many among us at this very hour
Do forge a life-long trouble for ourselves,
By taking true for false, or false for true;
5   Here, through the feeble twilight of this world
Groping, how many, until we pass and reach
That other, where we see as we are seen!

So fared it with Geraint, who issuing forth
That morning, when they both had got to horse,
10 Perhaps because he loved her passionately,
And felt that tempest brooding round his heart,
Which, if he spoke at all, would break perforce
Upon a head so dear in thunder, said:
'Not at my side. I charge thee ride before,
15 Ever a good way on before; and this
I charge thee, on thy duty as a wife,
Whatever happens, not to speak to me,
No, not a word!' and Enid was aghast;
And forth they rode, but scarce three paces on,
20 When crying out, 'Effeminate as I am,
I will not fight my way with gilded arms,
All shall be iron;' he loosed a mighty purse,
Hung at his belt, and hurled it toward the squire.
So the last sight that Enid had of home
25 Was all the marble threshold flashing, strown
With gold and scattered coinage, and the squire
Chafing his shoulder: then he cried again,
'To the wilds!' and Enid leading down the tracks
Through which he bad her lead him on, they past

¶467. *1*. H.T. compares Lucretius ii 14: *O miseras hominum mentes, O
pectora caeca*. ('O pitiable minds of men, O blind intelligences!') R. W.
King, *RES* n.s. xiii (1962) 439, suggests that T.'s opening adapts that of
Paradiso xi.

7. *1 Corinthians* xiii 12: 'Now we see through a glass, darkly; but then face
to face: now I know in part; but then shall I know even as also I am known.'
14. thee] *1873*; you *1859–70*. Likewise ll. 16, 230, 231, 347.
14–18. Mabinogion: 'And he desired Enid to mount her horse, and to ride
forward, and to keep a long way before him. "And whatever thou mayest
see, and whatever thou mayest hear concerning me", said he, "do thou
not turn back. And unless I speak unto thee, say not thou one word
either".'
16. thy] *1873*; your *1859–70*.
20–6. Not in *Mabinogion*.

30 The marches, and by bandit-haunted holds,
      Gray swamps and pools, waste places of the hern,
      And wildernesses, perilous paths, they rode:
      Round was their pace at first, but slackened soon:
      A stranger meeting them had surely thought
35 They rode so slowly and they looked so pale,
      That each had suffered some exceeding wrong.
      For he was ever saying to himself,
      'O I that wasted time to tend upon her,
      To compass her with sweet observances,
40 To dress her beautifully and keep her true'—
      And there he broke the sentence in his heart
      Abruptly, as a man upon his tongue
      May break it, when his passion masters him.
      And she was ever praying the sweet heavens
45 To save her dear lord whole from any wound.
      And ever in her mind she cast about
      For that unnoticed failing in herself,
      Which made him look so cloudy and so cold;
      Till the great plover's human whistle amazed
50 Her heart, and glancing round the waste she feared
      In every wavering brake an ambuscade.
      Then thought again, 'If there be such in me,
      I might amend it by the grace of Heaven,
      If he would only speak and tell me of it.'

55 But when the fourth part of the day was gone,
      Then Enid was aware of three tall knights
      On horseback, wholly armed, behind a rock
      In shadow, waiting for them, caitiffs all;
      And heard one crying to his fellow, 'Look,
60 Here comes a laggard hanging down his head,
      Who seems no bolder than a beaten hound;
      Come, we will slay him and will have his horse
      And armour, and his damsel shall be ours.'

      Then Enid pondered in her heart, and said:
65 'I will go back a little to my lord,

30. Mabinogion: 'And he did not choose the pleasantest and most frequented road, but that which was the wildest and most beset by thieves.'
31. Adapted from an unpublished stanza of *Come not, when I am dead* (II 131). Verbatim as *Sir John Oldcastle* 9 ∧ 10.
35–54. Not in *Mabinogion*.
51. Suggesting Juvenal x 19–21.
55–100. Based closely on *Mabinogion*, where however there are four attackers.

And I will tell him all their caitiff talk;
For, be he wroth even to slaying me,
Far liefer by his dear hand had I die,
Than that my lord should suffer loss or shame.'

70   Then she went back some paces of return,
Met his full frown timidly firm, and said;
'My lord, I saw three bandits by the rock
Waiting to fall on you, and heard them boast
That they would slay you, and possess your horse
75   And armour, and your damsel should be theirs.'

He made a wrathful answer: 'Did I wish
Your warning or your silence? one command
I laid upon you, not to speak to me,
And thus ye keep it! Well then, look—for now,
80   Whether ye wish me victory or defeat,
Long for my life, or hunger for my death,
Yourself shall see my vigour is not lost.'

Then Enid waited pale and sorrowful,
And down upon him bare the bandit three.
85   And at the midmost charging, Prince Geraint
Drave the long spear a cubit through his breast
And out beyond; and then against his brace
Of comrades, each of whom had broken on him
A lance that splintered like an icicle,
90   Swung from his brand a windy buffet out
Once, twice, to right, to left, and stunned the twain
Or slew them, and dismounting like a man
That skins the wild beast after slaying him,
Stript from the three dead wolves of woman born
95   The three gay suits of armour which they wore,
And let the bodies lie, but bound the suits
Of armour on their horses, each on each,
And tied the bridle-reins of all the three
Together, and said to her, 'Drive them on
100   Before you;' and she drove them through the waste.

He followed nearer; ruth began to work
Against his anger in him, while he watched
The being he loved best in all the world,
With difficulty in mild obedience
105   Driving them on: he fain had spoken to her,

77. *warning . . . silence*] *1862; transposed 1859–61.*
79, 80. *ye*] *1873;* you *1859–70. Likewise ll. 310, 321, 339, 625.*
101–15. Not in *Mabinogion.*

And loosed in words of sudden fire the wrath
And smouldered wrong that burnt him all within;
But evermore it seemed an easier thing
At once without remorse to strike her dead,
110 Than to cry 'Halt,' and to her own bright face
Accuse her of the least immodesty:
And thus tongue-tied, it made him wroth the more
That she *could* speak whom his own ear had heard
Call herself false: and suffering thus he made
115 Minutes an age: but in scarce longer time
Than at Caerleon the full-tided Usk,
Before he turn to fall seaward again,
Pauses, did Enid, keeping watch, behold
In the first shallow shade of a deep wood,
120 Before a gloom of stubborn-shafted oaks,
Three other horsemen waiting, wholly armed,
Whereof one seemed far larger than her lord,
And shook her pulses, crying, 'Look, a prize!
Three horses and three goodly suits of arms,
125 And all in charge of whom? a girl: set on.'
'Nay,' said the second, 'yonder comes a knight.'
The third, 'A craven; how he hangs his head.'
The giant answered merrily, 'Yea, but one?
Wait here, and when he passes fall upon him.'

130 And Enid pondered in her heart and said,
'I will abide the coming of my lord,
And I will tell him all their villainy.
My lord is weary with the fight before,
And they will fall upon him unawares.
135 I needs must disobey him for his good;
How should I dare obey him to his harm?
Needs must I speak, and though he kill me for it,
I save a life dearer to me than mine.'

And she abode his coming, and said to him
140 With timid firmness, 'Have I leave to speak?'
He said, 'Ye take it, speaking,' and she spoke.

'There lurk three villains yonder in the wood,
And each of them is wholly armed, and one
Is larger-limbed than you are, and they say
145 That they will fall upon you while ye pass.'

118–45. Based closely on *Mabinogion*.
141. Ye] *1870* ('*1869*'); You *1859–69*. Likewise in ll. 145, 221, 262, 412,
415, 417, 425, 445, 488, 547, 550, 670, 676, 681, 813, 887, 895, 896.

To which he flung a wrathful answer back:
'And if there were an hundred in the wood,
And every man were larger-limbed than I,
And all at once should sally out upon me,
150   I swear it would not ruffle me so much
As you that not obey me. Stand aside,
And if I fall, cleave to the better man.'

And Enid stood aside to wait the event,
Not dare to watch the combat, only breathe
155   Short fits of prayer, at every stroke a breath.
And he, she dreaded most, bare down upon him.
Aimed at the helm, his lance erred; but Geraint's,
A little in the late encounter strained,
Struck through the bulky bandit's corselet home,
160   And then brake short, and down his enemy rolled,
And there lay still; as he that tells the tale
Saw once a great piece of a promontory,
That had a sapling growing on it, slide
From the long shore-cliff's windy walls to the beach,
165   And there lie still, and yet the sapling grew:
So lay the man transfixt. His craven pair
Of comrades making slowlier at the Prince,
When now they saw their bulwark fallen, stood;
On whom the victor, to confound them more,
170   Spurred with his terrible war-cry; for as one,
That listens near a torrent mountain-brook,
All through the crash of the near cataract hears
The drumming thunder of the huger fall
At distance, were the soldiers wont to hear
175   His voice in battle, and be kindled by it,
And foemen scared, like that false pair who turned
Flying, but, overtaken, died the death
Themselves had wrought on many an innocent.

Thereon Geraint, dismounting, picked the lance
That pleased him best, and drew from those dead
180   wolves
Their three gay suits of armour, each from each,
And bound them on their horses, each on each,
And tied the bridle-reins of all the three

146–52. Not in *Mabinogion.*
153–78. Expanding *Mabinogion.*
163. slide] *1873*; slip *1859–70.*
170–75. 'A memory of what I heard near Festiniog, but the scenery
imagined is vaster' (T.).

Together, and said to her, 'Drive them on
185 Before you,' and she drove them through the wood.

He followed nearer still: the pain she had
To keep them in the wild ways of the wood,
Two sets of three laden with jingling arms,
Together, served a little to disedge
190 The sharpness of that pain about her heart:
And they themselves, like creatures gently born
But into bad hands fallen, and now so long
By bandits groomed, pricked their light ears, and
felt
Her low firm voice and tender government.

195 So through the green gloom of the wood they past,
And issuing under open heavens beheld
A little town with towers, upon a rock,
And close beneath, a meadow gemlike chased
In the brown wild, and mowers mowing in it:
200 And down a rocky pathway from the place
There came a fair-haired youth, that in his hand
Bare victual for the mowers: and Geraint
Had ruth again on Enid looking pale:
Then, moving downward to the meadow ground,
205 He, when the fair-haired youth came by him, said,
'Friend, let her eat; the damsel is so faint.'
'Yea, willingly,' replied the youth; 'and thou,
My lord, eat also, though the fare is coarse,
And only meet for mowers;' then set down
210 His basket, and dismounting on the sward
They let the horses graze, and ate themselves.
And Enid took a little delicately,
Less having stomach for it than desire
To close with her lord's pleasure; but Geraint
215 Ate all the mowers' victual unawares,
And when he found all empty, was amazed;
And 'Boy,' said he, 'I have eaten all, but take

186–94. Not in *Mabinogion*, which has a further episode with five attackers,
thus making Enid drive twelve horses in all.
195–9. *Mabinogion*: 'And early in the day they left the wood, and they came
to an open country, with meadows on one hand, and mowers mowing the
meadows.'
198. *chased*: set like a jewel.
201–31. Based on *Mabinogion*.
207. *thou*] *1873*; you *1859–70*. Likewise ll. 228, 491.

A horse and arms for guerdon; choose the best.'
He, reddening in extremity of delight,
220 'My lord, you overpay me fifty-fold.'
'Ye will be all the wealthier,' cried the Prince.
'I take it as free gift, then,' said the boy,
'Not guerdon; for myself can easily,
While your good damsel rests, return, and fetch
225 Fresh victual for these mowers of our Earl;
For these are his, and all the field is his,
And I myself am his; and I will tell him
How great a man thou art: he loves to know
When men of mark are in his territory:
230 And he will have thee to his palace here,
And serve thee costlier than with mowers' fare.'

Then said Geraint, 'I wish no better fare:
I never ate with angrier appetite
Than when I left your mowers dinnerless.
235 And into no Earl's palace will I go.
I know, God knows, too much of palaces!
And if he want me, let him come to me.
But hire us some fair chamber for the night,
And stalling for the horses, and return
240 With victual for these men, and let us know.'

'Yea, my kind lord,' said the glad youth, and
        went,
Held his head high, and thought himself a knight,
And up the rocky pathway disappeared,
Leading the horse, and they were left alone.

245   But when the Prince had brought his errant eyes
Home from the rock, sideways he let them glance
At Enid, where she droopt: his own false doom,
That shadow of mistrust should never cross
Betwixt them, came upon him, and he sighed;
250 Then with another humorous ruth remarked
The lusty mowers labouring dinnerless,
And watched the sun blaze on the turning scythe,
And after nodded sleepily in the heat.
But she, remembering her old ruined hall,
255 And all the windy clamour of the daws

228. *art*] *1873*; are *1859-70*.
245-60. Not in *Mabinogion*.
247. *doom*: 'judgment' (T.).

About her hollow turret, plucked the grass
There growing longest by the meadow's edge,
And into many a listless annulet,
Now over, now beneath her marriage ring,
260 Wove and unwove it, till the boy returned
And told them of a chamber, and they went;
Where, after saying to her, 'If ye will,
Call for the woman of the house,' to which
She answered, 'Thanks, my lord;' the two remained
265 Apart by all the chamber's width, and mute
As creatures voiceless through the fault of birth,
Or two wild men supporters of a shield,
Painted, who stare at open space, nor glance
The one at other, parted by the shield.

270 On a sudden, many a voice along the street,
And heel against the pavement echoing, burst
Their drowse; and either started while the door,
Pushed from without, drave backward to the wall,
And midmost of a rout of roisterers,
275 Femininely fair and dissolutely pale,
Her suitor in old years before Geraint,
Entered, the wild lord of the place, Limours.
He moving up with pliant courtliness,
Greeted Geraint full face, but stealthily,
280 In the mid-warmth of welcome and graspt hand,
Found Enid with the corner of his eye,
And knew her sitting sad and solitary.
Then cried Geraint for wine and goodly cheer
To feed the sudden guest, and sumptuously
285 According to his fashion, bad the host
Call in what men soever were his friends,
And feast with these in honour of their Earl;
'And care not for the cost; the cost is mine.'

And wine and food were brought, and Earl
Limours
290 Drank till he jested with all ease, and told

6–7. In *Mabinogion*, the Earl is not her previous suitor, though 'he set
all his thoughts and his affections upon her'. G. C. Macaulay points out that
T. transposes the names of Earl Limours and Earl Doorm; on a possibly
intended Doorm / doom resonance, see J. M. Gray, *VP* iv (1966) 131–2.
R. J. Fertel adds that the name Limours 'echoes the pastoral service of his
vassals: Limours, the mowers. The echo is not only phonetic but semantic,
for in Old French "*li mours*" means "turf grounds"' (*VP* xix, 1981, 344).

Free tales, and took the word and played upon it,
And made it of two colours; for his talk,
When wine and free companions kindled him,
Was wont to glance and sparkle like a gem
295 Of fifty facets; thus he moved the Prince
To laughter and his comrades to applause.
Then, when the Prince was merry, asked Limours,
'Your leave, my lord, to cross the room, and speak
To your good damsel there who sits apart, .
300 And seems so lonely?' 'My free leave,' he said;
'Get her to speak: she doth not speak to me.'
Then rose Limours, and looking at his feet,
Like him who tries the bridge he fears may fail,
Crost and came near, lifted adoring eyes,
305 Bowed at her side and uttered whisperingly:

 'Enid, the pilot star of my lone life,
Enid, my early and my only love,
Enid, the loss of whom hath turned me wild –
What chance is this? how is it I see you here?
310 Ye are in my power at last, are in my power.
Yet fear me not: I call mine own self wild,
But keep a touch of sweet civility
Here in the heart of waste and wilderness.
I thought, but that your father came between,
315 In former days you saw me favourably.
And if it were so do not keep it back:
Make me a little happier: let me know it:
Owe you me nothing for a life half-lost?
Yea, yea, the whole dear debt of all you are.
320 And, Enid, you and he, I see with joy,
Ye sit apart, you do not speak to him,
You come with no attendance, page or maid,
To serve you – doth he love you as of old?
For, call it lovers' quarrels, yet I know
325 Though men may bicker with the things they love,
They would not make them laughable in all eyes,
Not while they loved them; and your wretched
  dress,

301. doth] 1873; does 1859–70.
303] Like one that tries new ice if it will bear T.Nbk 30.
306–47. Expanding and modifying Mabinogion.
308. hath] 1873; has 1859–70.
320. see] 1873; sec it 1859–70.
323. doth] 1873; docs 1859–70.

A wretched insult on you, dumbly speaks
Your story, that this man loves you no more.
330 Your beauty is no beauty to him now:
A common chance–right well I know it–palled–
For I know men: nor will ye win him back,
For the man's love once gone never returns.
But here is one who loves you as of old;
335 With more exceeding passion than of old:
Good, speak the word: my followers ring him round:
He sits unarmed; I hold a finger up;
They understand: nay; I do not mean blood:
Nor need ye look so scared at what I say:
340 My malice is no deeper than a moat,
No stronger than a wall: there is the keep;
He shall not cross us more; speak but the word:
Or speak it not; but then by Him that made me
The one true lover whom you ever owned,
345 I will make use of all the power I have.
O pardon me! the madness of that hour,
When first I parted from thee, moves me yet.'

At this the tender sound of his own voice
And sweet self-pity, or the fancy of it,
350 Made his eye moist; but Enid feared his eyes,
Moist as they were, wine-heated from the feast;
And answered with such craft as women use,
Guilty or guiltless, to stave off a chance
That breaks upon them perilously, and said:

355 'Earl, if you love me as in former years,
And do not practise on me, come with morn,
And snatch me from him as by violence;
Leave me tonight: I am weary to the death.'

Low at leave-taking, with his brandished plume
360 Brushing his instep, bowed the all-amorous Earl,
And the stout Prince bad him a loud good-night.
He moving homeward babbled to his men,
How Enid never loved a man but him,
Nor cared a broken egg-shell for her lord.

332. ye] *1870*; you *1859–69*.
338. nay] *1873*; no *1859–70*.
344. whom] *1873*; which *1859–70*.   *owned*] *1873*; had *1859–70*.
348–51. Not in *Mabinogion*.
352. Mabinogion: 'and she considered that it was advisable to encourage him in his request.'
359–64. Not in *Mabinogion*.

365   But Enid left alone with Prince Geraint,
Debating his command of silence given,
And that she now perforce must violate it,
Held commune with herself, and while she held
He fell asleep, and Enid had no heart
370   To wake him, but hung o'er him, wholly pleased
To find him yet unwounded after fight,
And hear him breathing low and equally.
Anon she rose, and stepping lightly, heaped
The pieces of his armour in one place,
375   All to be there against a sudden need;
Then dozed awhile herself, but overtoiled
By that day's grief and travel, evermore
Seemed catching at a rootless thorn, and then
Went slipping down horrible precipices,
380   And strongly striking out her limbs awoke;
Then thought she heard the wild Earl at the door,
With all his rout of random followers,
Sound on a dreadful trumpet, summoning her;
Which was the red cock shouting to the light,
385   As the gray dawn stole o'er the dewy world,
And glimmered on his armour in the room.
And once again she rose to look at it,
But touched it unawares: jangling, the casque
Fell, and he started up and stared at her.
390   Then breaking his command of silence given,
She told him all that Earl Limours had said,
Except the passage that he loved her not;
Nor left untold the craft herself had used;
But ended with apology so sweet,
395   Low-spoken, and of so few words, and seemed
So justified by that necessity,
That,though he thought 'was it for him she wept
In Devon?' he but gave a wrathful groan,
Saying, 'Your sweet faces make good fellows fools
400   And traitors. Call the host and bid him bring
Charger and palfrey.' So she glided out
Among the heavy breathings of the house,
And like a household Spirit at the walls
Beat, till she woke the sleepers, and returned:
405   Then tending her rough lord, though all unasked,
In silence, did him service as a squire;

373–5. Mabinogion: 'At midnight she arose, and placed all Geraint's armour together, so that it might be ready to put on.' T.'s ll. 387–9 are his addition.

Till issuing armed he found the host and cried,
'Thy reckoning, friend?' and ere he learnt it, 'Take
Five horses and their armours;' and the host
410 Suddenly honest, answered in amaze,
'My lord, I scarce have spent the worth of one!'
'Ye will be all the wealthier,' said the Prince,
And then to Enid, 'Forward! and today
I charge you, Enid, more especially,
415 What thing soever ye may hear, or see,
Or fancy (though I count it of small use
To charge you) that ye speak not but obey.'

And Enid answered, 'Yea, my lord, I know
Your wish, and would obey; but riding first,
420 I hear the violent threats you do not hear,
I see the danger which you cannot see:
Then not to give you warning, that seems hard;
Almost beyond me: yet I would obey.'

'Yea so,' said he, 'do it: be not too wise;
425 Seeing that ye are wedded to a man,
Not all mismated with a yawning clown,
But one with arms to guard his head and yours,
With eyes to find you out however far,
And ears to hear you even in his dreams.'

430 With that he turned and looked as keenly at her
As careful robins eye the delver's toil;
And that within her, which a wanton fool,
Or hasty judger would have called her guilt,
Made her cheek burn and either eyelid fall.
435 And Geraint looked and was not satisfied.

Then forward by a way which, beaten broad,
Led from the territory of false Limours
To the waste earldom of another earl,
Doorm, whom his shaking vassals called the Bull,
440 Went Enid with her sullen follower on.
Once she looked back, and when she saw him ride
More near by many a rood than yestermorn,
It wellnigh made her cheerful; till Geraint
Waving an angry hand as who should say
445 'Ye watch me,' saddened all her heart again.

---

409. In *Mabinogion*, the remaining eleven.
418–35. Not in *Mabinogion*.
426. all] *1873*; quite *1859–70*.

But while the sun yet beat a dewy blade,
The sound of many a heavily-galloping hoof
Smote on her ear, and turning round she saw
Dust, and the points of lances bicker in it.
450   Then not to disobey her lord's behest,
And yet to give him warning, for he rode
As if he heard not, moving back she held
Her finger up, and pointed to the dust.
At which the warrior in his obstinacy,
455   Because she kept the letter of his word,
Was in a manner pleased, and turning, stood.
And in the moment after, wild Limours,
Borne on a black horse, like a thunder-cloud
Whose skirts are loosened by the breaking storm,
460   Half ridden off with by the thing he rode,
And all in passion uttering a dry shriek,
Dashed on Geraint, who closed with him, and bore
Down by the length of lance and arm beyond
The crupper, and so left him stunned or dead,
465   And overthrew the next that followed him,
And blindly rushed on all the rout behind.
But at the flash and motion of the man
They vanished panic-stricken, like a shoal
Of darting fish, that on a summer morn
470   Adown the crystal dykes at Camelot
Come slipping o'er their shadows on the sand,
But if a man who stands upon the brink
But lift a shining hand against the sun,
There is not left the twinkle of a fin
475   Betwixt the cressy islets white in flower;
So, scared but at the motion of the man,
Fled all the boon companions of the Earl,
And left him lying in the public way;
So vanish friendships only made in wine.

480   Then like a stormy sunlight smiled Geraint,
Who saw the chargers of the two that fell
Start from their fallen lords, and wildly fly,
Mixt with the flyers. 'Horse and man,' he said,
'All of one mind and all right-honest friends!

450–6. In *Mabinogion*, Enid simply speaks.
458. 'The horse's mane is compared to the skirts of the rain-cloud' (T.).
467–79. Not in *Mabinogion*, where Geraint has hereafter various combats,
is wounded, meets Arthur, rests and is healed.
475. T. had 'cressy islet' in a revision of *The Miller's Daughter* 48 ∧ 9.

485 Not a hoof left: and I methinks till now
Was honest – paid with horses and with arms;
I cannot steal or plunder, no nor beg:
And so what say ye, shall we strip him there
Your lover? has your palfrey heart enough
490 To bear his armour? shall we fast, or dine?
No? – then do thou, being right honest, pray
That we may meet the horsemen of Earl Doorm,
I too would still be honest.' Thus he said:
And sadly gazing on her bridle-reins,
495 And answering not one word, she led the way.

But as a man to whom a dreadful loss
Falls in a far land and he knows it not,
But coming back he learns it, and the loss
So pains him that he sickens nigh to death;
500 So fared it with Geraint, who being pricked
In combat with the follower of Limours,
Bled underneath his armour secretly,
And so rode on, nor told his gentle wife
What ailed him, hardly knowing it himself,
505 Till his eye darkened and his helmet wagged;
And at a sudden swerving of the road,
Though happily down on a bank of grass,
The Prince, without a word, from his horse fell.

And Enid heard the clashing of his fall,
510 Suddenly came, and at his side all pale
Dismounting, loosed the fastenings of his arms,
Nor let her true hand falter, nor blue eye
Moisten, till she had lighted on his wound,
And tearing off her veil of faded silk
515 Had bared her forehead to the blistering sun,
And swathed the hurt that drained her dear lord's
        life.
Then after all was done that hand could do,
She rested, and her desolation came
Upon her, and she wept beside the way.

490. 'Shall we go hungry, or shall we take his spoils and pay for our dinner with them?' (T.).
491. 'Enid shrinks from taking anything from her old lover' (T.).
500. In *Mabinogion*, Geraint is wounded by giants, and faints. Doorm (there named Limours) comes upon Enid who is with a damsel whose husband has been killed by the giants.

520   And many past, but none regarded her,
For in that realm of lawless turbulence,
A woman weeping for her murdered mate
Was cared as much for as a summer shower:
One took him for a victim of Earl Doorm,
525 Nor dared to waste a perilous pity on him:
Another hurrying past, a man-at-arms,
Rode on a mission to the bandit Earl;
Half whistling and half singing a coarse song,
He drove the dust against her veilless eyes:
530 Another, flying from the wrath of Doorm
Before an ever-fancied arrow, made
The long way smoke beneath him in his fear;
At which her palfrey whinnying lifted heel,
And scoured into the coppices and was lost,
535 While the great charger stood, grieved like a man.

    But at the point of noon the huge Earl Doorm,
Broad-faced with under-fringe of russet beard,
Bound on a foray, rolling eyes of prey,
Came riding with a hundred lances up;
540 But ere he came, like one that hails a ship,
Cried out with a big voice, 'What, is he dead?'
'No, no, not dead!' she answered in all haste.
'Would some of your kind people take him up,
And bear him hence out of this cruel sun?
545 Most sure am I, quite sure, he is not dead.'

    Then said Earl Doorm: 'Well, if he be not dead,
Why wail ye for him thus? ye seem a child.
And be he dead, I count you for a fool;
Your wailing will not quicken him: dead or not,
550 Ye mar a comely face with idiot tears.
Yet, since the face *is* comely—some of you,
Here, take him up, and bear him to our hall:
An if he live, we will have him of our band;
And if he die, why earth has earth enough
555 To hide him. See ye take the charger too,
A noble one.'
               He spake, and past away,
But left two brawny spearmen, who advanced,
Each growling like a dog, when his good bone

542. In *Mabinogion*, Enid thought Geraint was dead, and it was the Earl
who 'thought that there still remained some life in Geraint'.
546–78. Expanding *Mabinogion*.

Seems to be plucked at by the village boys
560 Who love to vex him eating, and he fears
To lose his bone, and lays his foot upon it,
Gnawing and growling: so the ruffians growled,
Fearing to lose, and all for a dead man,
Their chance of booty from the morning's raid,
565 Yet raised and laid him on a litter-bier,
Such as they brought upon their forays out
For those that might be wounded; laid him on it
All in the hollow of his shield, and took
And bore him to the naked hall of Doorm,
570 (His gentle charger following him unled)
And cast him and the bier in which he lay
Down on an oaken settle in the hall,
And then departed, hot in haste to join
Their luckier mates, but growling as before,
575 And cursing their lost time, and the dead man,
And their own Earl, and their own souls, and her.
They might as well have blest her: she was deaf
To blessing or to cursing save from one.

So for long hours sat Enid by her lord,
580 There in the naked hall, propping his head,
And chafing his pale hands, and calling to him.
Till at the last he wakened from his swoon,
And found his own dear bride propping his head,
And chafing his faint hands, and calling to him;
585 And felt the warm tears falling on his face;
And said to his own heart, 'She weeps for me:'
And yet lay still, and feigned himself as dead,
That he might prove her to the uttermost,
And say to his own heart, 'She weeps for me.'

590 But in the falling afternoon returned
The huge Earl Doorm with plunder to the hall.
His lusty spearmen followed him with noise:
Each hurling down a heap of things that rang
Against the pavement, cast his lance aside,
595 And doffed his helm: and then there fluttered in,
Half-bold, half-frighted, with dilated eyes,
A tribe of women, dressed in many hues,

568. Mabinogion: 'He had him carried with him in the hollow of his shield.'
579–607. Not in *Mabinogion.*
582. Till] *1873;* And *1859–70.*

And mingled with the spearmen: and Earl Doorm
Struck with a knife's haft hard against the board,
600   And called for flesh and wine to feed his spears.
And men brought in whole hogs and quarter beeves,
And all the hall was dim with steam of flesh:
And none spake word, but all sat down at once,
And ate with tumult in the naked hall,
605   Feeding like horses when you hear them feed;
Till Enid shrank far back into herself,
To shun the wild ways of the lawless tribe.
But when Earl Doorm had eaten all he would,
He rolled his eyes about the hall, and found
610   A damsel drooping in a corner of it.
Then he remembered her, and how she wept;
And out of her there came a power upon him;
And rising on the sudden he said, 'Eat!
I never yet beheld a thing so pale.
615   God's curse, it makes me mad to see you weep.
Eat! Look yourself. Good luck had your good man,
For were I dead who is it would weep for me?
Sweet lady, never since I first drew breath
Have I beheld a lily like yourself.
620   And so there lived some colour in your cheek,
There is not one among my gentlewomen
Were fit to wear your slipper for a glove.
But listen to me, and by me be ruled,
And I will do the thing I have not done,
625   For ye shall share my earldom with me, girl,
And we will live like two birds in one nest,
And I will fetch you forage from all fields,
For I compel all creatures to my will.'

He spoke: the brawny spearman let his cheek
Bulge with the unswallowed piece, and turning
630   stared;
While some, whose souls the old serpent long had
          drawn
Down, as the worm draws in the withered leaf
And makes it earth, hissed each at other's ear
What shall not be recorded – women they,
635   Women, or what had been those gracious things,

617–717. T. greatly expands this, though the main events are in *Mabinogion*
(the brief commands to eat, drink, and change apparel, and the blow).
631. *old serpent*: *Revelation* xii 9.
632. 'My father would quote this simile as good' (H.T.).

But now desired the humbling of their best,
Yea, would have helped him to it: and all at once
They hated her, who took no thought of them,
But answered in low voice, her meek head yet
640 Drooping, 'I pray you of your courtesy,
He being as he is, to let me be.'

She spake so low he hardly heard her speak,
But like a mighty patron, satisfied
With what himself had done so graciously,
645 Assumed that she had thanked him, adding, 'Yea,
Eat and be glad, for I account you mine.'

She answered meekly, 'How should I be glad
Henceforth in all the world at anything,
Until my lord arise and look upon me?'

650 Here the huge Earl cried out upon her talk,
As all but empty heart and weariness
And sickly nothing; suddenly seized on her,
And bare her by main violence to the board,
And thrust the dish before her, crying, 'Eat.'

655 'No, no,' said Enid, vext, 'I will not eat
Till yonder man upon the bier arise,
And eat with me.' 'Drink, then,' he answered.
     'Here!'
(And filled a horn with wine and held it to her,)
'Lo! I, myself, when flushed with fight, or hot,
660 God's curse, with anger—often I myself,
Before I well have drunken, scarce can eat:
Drink therefore and the wine will change your will.'

'Not so,' she cried, 'by Heaven, I will not drink
Till my dear lord arise and bid me do it,
665 And drink with me; and if he rise no more,
I will not look at wine until I die.'

At this he turned all red and paced his hall,
Now gnawed his under, now his upper lip,
And coming up close to her, said at last:
670 'Girl, for I see ye scorn my courtesies,
Take warning: yonder man is surely dead;
And I compel all creatures to my will.
Not eat nor drink? And wherefore wail for one,
Who put your beauty to this flout and scorn
675 By dressing it in rags? Amazed am I,
Beholding how ye butt against my wish,

That I forbear you thus: cross me no more.
At least put off to please me this poor gown,
This silken rag, this beggar-woman's weed:
680   I love that beauty should go beautifully:
For see ye not my gentlewomen here,
How gay, how suited to the house of one
Who loves that beauty should go beautifully?
Rise therefore; robe yourself in this: obey.'

685   He spoke, and one among his gentlewomen
Displayed a splendid silk of foreign loom,
Where like a shoaling sea the lovely blue
Played into green, and thicker down the front
With jewels than the sward with drops of dew,
690   When all night long a cloud clings to the hill,
And with the dawn ascending lets the day
Strike where it clung: so thickly shone the gems.

But Enid answered, harder to be moved
Than hardest tyrants in their day of power,
695   With life-long injuries burning unavenged,
And now their hour has come; and Enid said:

'In this poor gown my dear lord found me first,
And loved me serving in my father's hall:
In this poor gown I rode with him to court,
700   And there the Queen arrayed me like the sun:
In this poor gown he bad me clothe myself,
When now we rode upon this fatal quest
Of honour, where no honour can be gained:
And this poor gown I will not cast aside
705   Until himself arise a living man,
And bid me cast it. I have griefs enough:
Pray you be gentle, pray you let me be:
I never loved, can never love but him:
Yea, God, I pray you of your gentleness,
710   He being as he is, to let me be.'

Then strode the brute Earl up and down his hall,
And took his russet beard between his teeth;
Last, coming up quite close, and in his mood
Crying, 'I count it of no more avail,

679. *weed*: 'garment' (T.).
688-9. 'I made these lines on the High Down one morning at Freshwater'
(T.).
694. 'The worst tyrants are those who have long been tyrannised over, if
they have tyrannous natures' (T.).

715 Dame, to be gentle than ungentle with you;
Take my salute,' unknightly with flat hand,
However lightly, smote her on the cheek.

Then Enid, in her utter helplessness,
And since she thought, 'He had not dared to do it,
720 Except he surely knew my lord was dead,'
Sent forth a sudden sharp and bitter cry,
As of a wild thing taken in the trap,
Which sees the trapper coming through the wood.

This heard Geraint, and grasping at his sword,
725 (It lay beside him in the hollow shield),
Made but a single bound, and with a sweep of it
Shore through the swarthy neck, and like a ball
The russet-bearded head rolled on the floor.
So died Earl Doorm by him he counted dead.
730 And all the men and women in the hall
Rose when they saw the dead man rise, and fled
Yelling as from a spectre, and the two
Were left alone together, and he said:

'Enid, I have used you worse than that dead man;
735 Done you more wrong: we both have undergone
That trouble which has left me thrice your own:
Henceforward I will rather die than doubt.
And here I lay this penance on myself,
Not, though mine own ears heard you yestermorn—
740 You thought me sleeping, but I heard you say,
I heard you say, that you were no true wife:
I swear I will not ask your meaning in it:
I do believe yourself against yourself,
And will henceforward rather die than doubt.'

745 And Enid could not say one tender word,
She felt so blunt and stupid at the heart:
She only prayed him, 'Fly, they will return
And slay you; fly, your charger is without,
My palfrey lost.' 'Then, Enid, shall you ride
750 Behind me.' 'Yea,' said Enid, 'let us go.'
And moving out they found the stately horse,
Who now no more a vassal to the thief,

718–21. As in *Mabinogion*.
727–8. In *Mabinogion*, merely 'he clove him in twain'.
734–44. *Mabinogion*: 'He was grieved for two causes; one was, to see that
Enid had lost her colour and her wonted aspect; and the other, to know
that she was in the right.'

But free to stretch his limbs in lawful fight,
Neighed with all gladness as they came, and stooped
755 With a low whinny toward the pair: and she
Kissed the white star upon his noble front,
Glad also; then Geraint upon the horse
Mounted, and reached a hand, and on his foot
She set her own and climbed; he turned his face
760 And kissed her climbing, and she cast her arms
About him, and at once they rode away.

And never yet, since high in Paradise
O'er the four rivers the first roses blew,
Came purer pleasure unto mortal kind
765 Than lived through her, who in that perilous hour
Put hand to hand beneath her husband's heart,
And felt him hers again: she did not weep,
But o'er her meek eyes came a happy mist
Like that which kept the heart of Eden green
770 Before the useful trouble of the rain:
Yet not so misty were her meek blue eyes
As not to see before them on the path,
Right in the gateway of the bandit hold,
A knight of Arthur's court, who laid his lance
775 In rest, and made as if to fall upon him.
Then, fearing for his hurt and loss of blood,
She, with her mind all full of what had chanced,
Shrieked to the stranger 'Slay not a dead man!'
'The voice of Enid,' said the knight; but she,
780 Beholding it was Edyrn son of Nudd,
Was moved so much the more, and shrieked again,
'O cousin, slay not him who gave you life.'
And Edyrn moving frankly forward spake:
'My lord Geraint, I greet you with all love;
785 I took you for a bandit knight of Doorm;
And fear not, Enid, I should fall upon him,
Who love you, Prince, with something of the love
Wherewith we love the Heaven that chastens us.
For once, when I was up so high in pride
790 That I was halfway down the slope to Hell,
By overthrowing me you threw me higher.
Now, made a knight of Arthur's Table Round,
And since I knew this Earl, when I myself
Was half a bandit in my lawless hour,

762ff. In *Mabinogion* there are other adventures, but the rest of T.'s poem is
his own.

795 I come the mouthpiece of our King to Doorm
     (The King is close behind me) bidding him
     Disband himself, and scatter all his powers,
     Submit, and hear the judgment of the King.'

     'He hears the judgment of the King of kings,'
800 Cried the wan Prince; 'and lo, the powers of Doorm
     Are scattered,' and he pointed to the field,
     Where, huddled here and there on mound and
        knoll,
     Were men and women staring and aghast,
     While some yet fled; and then he plainlier told
805 How the huge Earl lay slain within his hall.
     But when the knight besought him, 'Follow me,
     Prince, to the camp, and in the King's own ear
     Speak what has chanced; ye surely have endured
     Strange chances here alone;' that other flushed,
810 And hung his head, and halted in reply,
     Fearing the mild face of the blameless King,
     And after madness acted question asked:
     Till Edyrn crying, 'If ye will not go
     To Arthur, then will Arthur come to you,'
815 'Enough,' he said, 'I follow,' and they went.
     But Enid in their going had two fears,
     One from the bandit scattered in the field,
     And one from Edyrn. Every now and then,
     When Edyrn reined his charger at her side,
820 She shrank a little. In a hollow land,
     From which old fires have broken, men may fear
     Fresh fire and ruin. He, perceiving, said:

     'Fair and dear cousin, you that most had cause
     To fear me, fear no longer, I am changed.
825 Yourself were first the blameless cause to make
     My nature's prideful sparkle in the blood
     Break into furious flame; being repulsed
     By Yniol and yourself, I schemed and wrought
     Until I overturned him; then set up
830 (With one main purpose ever at my heart)
     My haughty jousts, and took a paramour;
     Did her mock-honour as the fairest fair,
     And, toppling over all antagonism,
     So waxed in pride, that I believed myself
835 Unconquerable, for I was wellnigh mad:
     And, but for my main purpose in these jousts,
     I should have slain your father, seized yourself.

I lived in hope that sometime you would come
To these my lists with him whom best you loved;
840 And there, poor cousin, with your meek blue eyes,
The truest eyes that ever answered Heaven,
Behold me overturn and trample on him.
Then, had you cried, or knelt, or prayed to me,
I should not less have killed him. And you came, —
845 But once you came, — and with your own true eyes
Beheld the man you loved (I speak as one
Speaks of a service done him) overthrow
My proud self, and my purpose three years old,
And set his foot upon me, and give me life.
850 There was I broken down; there was I saved:
Though thence I rode all-shamed, hating the life
He gave me, meaning to be rid of it.
And all the penance the Queen laid upon me
Was but to rest awhile within her court;
855 Where first as sullen as a beast new-caged,
And waiting to be treated like a wolf,
Because I knew my deeds were known, I found,
Instead of scornful pity or pure scorn,
Such fine reserve and noble reticence,
860 Manners so kind, yet stately, such a grace
Of tenderest courtesy, that I began
To glance behind me at my former life,
And find that it had been the wolf's indeed:
And oft I talked with Dubric, the high saint,
865 Who, with mild heat of holy oratory,
Subdued me somewhat to that gentleness,
Which, when it weds with manhood, makes a man.
And you were often there about the Queen,
But saw me not, or marked not if you saw;
870 Nor did I care or dare to speak with you,
But kept myself aloof till I was changed;
And fear not, cousin; I am changed indeed.'

He spoke, and Enid easily believed,
Like simple noble natures, credulous
875 Of what they long for, good in friend or foe,
There most in those who most have done them ill.
And when they reached the camp the King himself
Advanced to greet them, and beholding her
Though pale, yet happy, asked her not a word,
880 But went apart with Edyrn, whom he held
In converse for a little, and returned,
And, gravely smiling, lifted her from horse,

And kissed her with all pureness, brother-like,
And showed an empty tent allotted her,
885 And glancing for a minute, till he saw her
Pass into it, turned to the Prince, and said:

'Prince, when of late ye prayed me for my leave
To move to your own land, and there defend
Your marches, I was pricked with some reproof,
890 As one that let foul wrong stagnate and be,
By having looked too much through alien eyes,
And wrought too long with delegated hands,
Not used mine own: but now behold me come
To cleanse this common sewer of all my realm,
895 With Edyrn and with others: have ye looked
At Edyrn? have ye seen how nobly changed?
This work of his is great and wonderful.
His very face with change of heart is changed.
The world will not believe a man repents:
900 And this wise world of ours is mainly right.
Full seldom doth a man repent, or use
Both grace and will to pick the vicious quitch
Of blood and custom wholly out of him,
And make all clean, and plant himself afresh.
905 Edyrn has done it, weeding all his heart
As I will weed this land before I go.
I, therefore, made him of our Table Round,
Not rashly, but have proved him everyway
One of our noblest, our most valorous,
910 Sanest and most obedient: and indeed
This work of Edyrn wrought upon himself
After a life of violence, seems to me
A thousand-fold more great and wonderful
Than if some knight of mine, risking his life,
915 My subject with my subjects under him,
Should make an onslaught single on a realm
Of robbers, though he slew them one by one,
And were himself nigh wounded to the death.'

So spake the King; low bowed the Prince, and
felt
920 His work was neither great nor wonderful,
And past to Enid's tent; and thither came
The King's own leech to look into his hurt;
And Enid tended on him there; and there
Her constant motion round him, and the breath

901. doth] 1873; does 1859–70.

925 Of her sweet tendance hovering over him,
  Filled all the genial courses of his blood
  With deeper and with ever deeper love,
  As the south-west that blowing Bala lake
  Fills all the sacred Dee. So past the days.

930 But while Geraint lay healing of his hurt,
  The blameless King went forth and cast his eyes
  On each of all whom Uther left in charge
  Long since, to guard the justice of the King:
  He looked and found them wanting; and as now
935 Men weed the white horse on the Berkshire hills
  To keep him bright and clean as heretofore,
  He rooted out the slothful officer
  Or guilty, which for bribe had winked at wrong,
  And in their chairs set up a stronger race
940 With hearts and hands, and sent a thousand men
  To till the wastes, and moving everywhere
  Cleared the dark places and let in the law,
  And broke the bandit holds and cleansed the land.

  Then, when Geraint was whole again, they past
945 With Arthur to Caerleon upon Usk.
  There the great Queen once more embraced her
    friend,
  And clothed her in apparel like the day.
  And though Geraint could never take again
  That comfort from their converse which he took
950 Before the Queen's fair name was breathed upon,
  He rested well content that all was well.
  Thence after tarrying for a space they rode,
  And fifty knights rode with them to the shores
  Of Severn, and they past to their own land.
955 And there he kept the justice of the King
  So vigorously yet mildly, that all hearts
  Applauded, and the spiteful whisper died:

929. T. compares *Lycidas* 55: 'Where Deva spreads her wisard stream'.
930–43. C. Y. Lang (*Tennyson's Arthurian Psycho-drama*, 1983, p. 7) notes that
these lines derive from *Ode on the Death of the Duke of Wellington* 107–10 (with
MS reading including 'wasted . . . back . . . bandit').
932. each . . . whom] *1870* ('*1869*'); whom his father *1859–69*.
935. 'The white horse near Wantage on the Berkshire hills which com-
memorates the victory at Ashdown of the English under Alfred over the
Danes (871). The white horse was the emblem of the English or Saxons,
as the raven was of the Danes, and as the dragon was of the Britons' (T.).

And being ever foremost in the chase,
And victor at the tilt and tournament,
960 They called him the great Prince and man of men.
But Enid, whom her ladies loved to call
Enid the Fair, a grateful people named
Enid the Good; and in their halls arose
The cry of children, Enids and Geraints
965 Of times to be; nor did he doubt her more,
But rested in her fëalty, till he crowned
A happy life with a fair death, and fell
Against the heathen of the Northern Sea
In battle, fighting for the blameless King.

468 Balin and Balan

Published *1885*. H.T. comments: 'Partly founded on Book II of Malory,
written mostly at Aldworth, soon after *Gareth and Lynette* [completed
1872] . . . The story of the poem is largely original. "Loyal natures are
wrought to anger and madness against the world".' Written 1872–4
(according to *CT*, pp. 402, 484). Apart from the final fight between Balin
and Balan, T. takes very little from Malory; the theme of Guinevere's
guilt and the appearance by Vivien are additions. The poem was to lead
into *Merlin and Vivien*; in *H.MS*, T. incorporated an account by Vivien at
court (*Cornhill* cliii (1936) 552–3):
    'I bring thee here a message from the dead'.
    And therewithal shewing Sir Balan's hair,
    'Know ye not this? not so, belike; but this
    A most strange red, is easier known'. The Queen
    Took the dead hair and slightly shuddering asked
    'Sir Balin's? is he slain?' 'Yea, noble Queen,
    Likewise his brother, Balan: for they fought,
    Not knowing–some misprision of their shields –
    I know not what. I found them side by side
    And wounded to the death, unlaced their helms,
    And gave them air and water, held their heads,
    Wept with them; and thy Balin joyed my heart
    Calling thee stainless wife and perfect Queen,
    Heaven's white earth-angel; then they bade me clip
    One tress from either head and bring it thee,

967. H.T. quotes, from the notes to *Mabinogion*, Llywarch Hen's elegy on
Geraint's death in the battle of Llongborth. Mrs Patmore, by request, sent
a copy of the elegy to T. in Nov. 1857 (Patmore, *Memoir* (1900) ii 308).

Proof that my message is not feigned; and prayed
King Arthur would despatch some holy man,
As these had lain together in one womb,
To give them burial in a single grave—
Sent their last blessings to their King and thee,
And therewithal their dying word, that thou,
For that good service I had done thy knights,
Wouldst yield me shelter for mine innocency'.
To whom the Queen made answer, 'We must hear
Thy story further; thou shalt bide the while.
I know no more of thee than that thy tale
Hath chilled me to the heart. Ghastly mischance,
Enough to make all childless mc herhood
Fain so to bide for ever. Where do they lie?'
And Vivien's voice was broken answering her.
'Dead in a nameless corner of the woods,
Each locked in either's arms. I know the place,
But scarce can word it plain for thee to know'.
'And therefore damsel shalt thou ride at once
With Arthur's knights and guide them through the woods.
Thy wish, and these dead men's, if such were theirs,
Must bide mine answer till we meet again.'
After, when Vivien on returning came
To Guinevere and spake 'I saw the twain
Buried, and wept above their woodland grave.
But grant me now my wish and theirs', . . .

For T.'s prose draft of the story of Pellam (H.Nbk 37), see D. Staines, *Harvard
Library Bulletin* xxii (1974) 306–7. Staines is persuasive that T.'s prose
account of the poem, 'The "Dolorous Stroke"' (*Eversley* v 425–32; *Mem.* ii
134–41), is not a prose draft but a recollection of the synopsis of the plot. See
J. M. Gray, 'Tennyson's Doppelgänger: *Balin and Balan*' (1971); also Gray
(pp. 37–42). D. F. Goslee has traced 'The Stages in Tennyson's Composition
of *Balin and Balan*', thirteen stages through the MSS (*Huntington Library
Quarterly* xxxviii, 1975, 247–68).

Pellam the King, who held and lost with Lot
In that first war, and had his realm restored
But rendered tributary, failed of late
To send his tribute; wherefore Arthur called
5   His treasurer, one of many years, and spake,
'Go thou with him and him and brĭng it to us,
Lest we should set one truer on his throne.
Man's word is God in man.'
                                        His Baron said
'We go but harken: there be two strange knights
10 Who sit near Camelot at a fountain-side,

A mile beneath the forest, challenging
And overthrowing every knight who comes.
Wilt thou I undertake them as we pass,
And send them to thee?'
                       Arthur laughed upon him.
15 'Old friend, too old to be so young, depart,
Delay not thou for aught, but let them sit,
Until they find a lustier than themselves.'

    So these departed. Early, one fair dawn,
The light-winged spirit of his youth returned
20 On Arthur's heart; he armed himself and went,
So coming to the fountain-side beheld
Balin and Balan sitting statuelike,
Brethren, to right and left the spring, that down,
From underneath a plume of lady-fern,
25 Sang, and the sand danced at the bottom of it.
And on the right of Balin Balin's horse
Was fast beside an alder, on the left
Of Balan Balan's near a poplartree.
'Fair Sirs,' said Arthur, 'wherefore sit ye here?'
30 Balin and Balan answered 'For the sake
Of glory; we be mightier men than all
In Arthur's court; that also have we proved;
For whatsoever knight against us came
Or I or he have easily overthrown.'
35 'I too,' said Arthur, 'am of Arthur's hall,
But rather proven in his Paynim wars
Than famous jousts; but see, or proven or not,
Whether me likewise ye can overthrow.'
And Arthur lightly smote the brethren down,
40 And lightly so returned, and no man knew.

    Then Balin rose, and Balan, and beside
The carolling water set themselves again,
And spake no word until the shadow turned;
When from the fringe of coppice round them burst

¶468. *16. aught*] ought *Eversley, 1885.* Emended here for consistency with
T.'s 'aught' in *Merlin and Vivien* 387.
23–5. Cp. Robert Bloomfield's *Rosy Hannah* (*Rural Tales,* 1801,
Lincoln), which begins: 'A spring, o'erhung with many a flower, / The grey
sand dancing in its bed.' Also Coleridge, *Inscription for a Fountain*: 'Nor
ever cease / Yon tiny cone of sand its soundless dance, / Which at the
bottom . . . dances still.' 'Suggested by a spring which rises near the house
at Aldworth' (H.T.).

45 A spangled pursuivant, and crying 'Sirs,
Rise, follow! ye be sent for by the King,'
They followed; whom when Arthur seeing asked
'Tell me your names; why sat ye by the well?'
Balin the stillness of a minute broke
50 Saying 'An unmelodious name to thee,
Balin, "the Savage"–that addition thine–
My brother and my better, this man here,
Balan. I smote upon the naked skull
A thrall of thine in open hall, my hand
55 Was gauntleted, half slew him; for I heard
He had spoken evil of me; thy just wrath
Sent me a three-years' exile from thine eyes.
I have not lived my life delightsomely:
For I that did that violence to thy thrall,
60 Had often wrought some fury on myself,
Saving for Balan: those three kingless years
Have past–were wormwood-bitter to me. King,
Methought that if we sat beside the well,
And hurled to ground what knight soever spurred
65 Against us, thou would'st take me gladlier back,
And make, as ten-times worthier to be thine
Than twenty Balins, Balan knight. I have said.
Not so–not all. A man of thine today
Abashed us both, and brake my boast. Thy will?'
70 Said Arthur 'Thou hast ever spoken truth;
Thy too fierce manhood would not let thee lie.
Rise, my true knight. As children learn, be thou
Wiser for falling! walk with me, and move
To music with thine Order and the King.
75 Thy chair, a grief to all the brethren, stands
Vacant, but thou retake it, mine again!'

    Thereafter, when Sir Balin entered hall,
The Lost one Found was greeted as in Heaven
With joy that blazed itself in woodland wealth
80 Of leaf, and gayest garlandage of flowers,
Along the walls and down the board; they sat,
And cup clashed cup; they drank and some one sang,
Sweet-voiced, a song of welcome, whereupon
Their common shout in chorus, mounting, made
85 Those banners of twelve battles overhead
Stir, as they stirred of old, when Arthur's host
Proclaimed him Victor, and the day was won.

    Then Balan added to their Order lived

A wealthier life than heretofore with these
90 And Balin, till their embassage returned.

'Sir King' they brought report 'we hardly found,
So bushed about it is with gloom, the hall
Of him to whom ye sent us, Pellam, once
A Christless foe of thine as ever dashed
95 Horse against horse; but seeing that thy realm
Hath prospered in the name of Christ, the King
Took, as in rival heat, to holy things;
And finds himself descended from the Saint
Arimathæan Joseph; him who first
100 Brought the great faith to Britain over seas;
He boasts his life as purer than thine own;
Eats scarce enow to keep his pulse abeat;
Hath pushed aside his faithful wife, nor lets
Or dame or damsel enter at his gates
105 Lest he should be polluted. This gray King
Showed us a shrine wherein were wonders – yea –
Rich arks with priceless bones of martyrdom,
Thorns of the crown and shivers of the cross,
And therewithal (for thus he told us) brought
110 By holy Joseph hither, that same spear
Wherewith the Roman pierced the side of Christ.
He much amazed us; after, when we sought
The tribute, answered "I have quite foregone
All matters of this world: Garlon, mine heir,
115 Of him demand it," which this Garlon gave
With much ado, railing at thine and thee.

'But when we left, in those deep woods we found
A knight of thine spear-stricken from behind,
Dead, whom we buried; more than one of us
120 Cried out on Garlon, but a woodman there
Reported of some demon in the woods
Was once a man, who driven by evil tongues
From all his fellows, lived alone, and came
To learn black magic, and to hate his kind
125 With such a hate, that when he died, his soul
Became a Fiend, which, as the man in life
Was wounded by blind tongues he saw not whence,
Strikes from behind. This woodman showed the cave
From which he sallies, and wherein he dwelt.
130 We saw the hoof-print of a horse, no more.'

126–8. 'Symbolic of slander' (H.T.).

Then Arthur, 'Let who goes before me, see
He do not fall behind me: foully slain
And villainously! who will hunt for me
This demon of the woods?' Said Balan, 'I'!
135 So claimed the quest and rode away, but first,
Embracing Balin, 'Good my brother, hear!
Let not thy moods prevail, when I am gone
Who used to lay them! hold them outer fiends,
Who leap at thee to tear thee; shake them aside,
140 Dreams ruling when wit sleeps! yea, but to dream
That any of these would wrong thee, wrongs thyself.
Witness their flowery welcome. Bound are they
To speak no evil. Truly save for fears,
My fears for thee, so rich a fellowship
145 Would make me wholly blest: thou one of them,
Be one indeed: consider them, and all
Their bearing in their common bond of love,
No more of hatred than in Heaven itself,
No more of jealousy than in Paradise.'

150 So Balan warned, and went; Balin remained:
Who–for but three brief moons had glanced away
From being knighted till he smote the thrall,
And faded from the presence into years
Of exile–now would strictlier set himself
155 To learn what Arthur meant by courtesy,
Manhood, and knighthood; wherefore hovered round
Lancelot, but when he marked his high sweet smile
In passing, and a transitory word
Make knight or churl or child or damsel seem
160 From being smiled at happier in themselves–
Sighed, as a boy lame-born beneath a height,
That glooms his valley, sighs to see the peak
Sun-flushed, or touch at night the northern star;
For one from out his village lately climbed
165 And brought report of azure lands and fair,
Far seen to left and right; and he himself
Hath hardly scaled with help a hundred feet
Up from the base: so Balin marvelling oft
How far beyond him Lancelot seemed to move,
170 Groaned, and at times would mutter, 'These be gifts,
Born with the blood, not learnable, divine,
Beyond *my* reach. Well had I foughten–well–
In those fierce wars, struck hard–and had I crowned
With my slain self the heaps of whom I slew–
175 So–better!–But this worship of the Queen,

That honour too wherein she holds him–this,
This was the sunshine that hath given the man
A growth, a name that branches o'er the rest,
And strength against all odds, and what the King
180 So prizes–overprizes–gentleness.
Her likewise would I worship an I might.
I never can be close with her, as he
That brought her hither. Shall I pray the King
To let me bear some token of his Queen
185 Whereon to gaze, remembering her–forget
My heats and violences? live afresh?
What, if the Queen disdained to grant it! nay
Being so stately-gentle, would she make
My darkness blackness? and with how sweet grace
190 She greeted my return! Bold will I be–
Some goodly cognizance of Guinevere,
In lieu of this rough beast upon my shield,
Langued gules, and toothed with grinning savagery.'

And Arthur, when Sir Balin sought him, said
195 'What wilt thou bear?' Balin was bold, and asked
To bear her own crown-royal upon shield,
Whereat she smiled and turned her to the King,
Who answered 'Thou shalt put the crown to use.
The crown is but the shadow of the King,
200 And this a shadow's shadow, let him have it,
So this will help him of his violences!'
'No shadow' said Sir Balin 'O my Queen,
But light to me! no shadow, O my King,
But golden earnest of a gentler life!'

205 So Balin bare the crown, and all the knights
Approved him, and the Queen, and all the world
Made music, and he felt his being move
In music with his Order, and the King.

The nightingale, full-toned in middle May,
210 Hath ever and anon a note so thin
It seems another voice in other groves;
Thus, after some quick burst of sudden wrath,
The music in him seemed to change, and grow
Faint and far-off.
                        And once he saw the thrall
215 His passion half had gauntleted to death,
That causer of his banishment and shame,

193. *Langued gules*: 'red-tongued – language of heraldry' (H.T.).

Smile at him, as he deemed, presumptuously:
His arm half rose to strike again, but fell:
The memory of that cognizance on shield
220 Weighted it down, but in himself he moaned:

'Too high this mount of Camelot for me:
These high-set courtesies are not for me.
Shall I not rather prove the worse for these?
Fierier and stormier from restraining, break
225 Into some madness even before the Queen?'

Thus, as a hearth lit in a mountain home,
And glancing on the window, when the gloom
Of twilight deepens round it, seems a flame
That rages in the woodland far below,
230 So when his moods were darkened, court and King
And all the kindly warmth of Arthur's hall
Shadowed an angry distance: yet he strove
To learn the graces of their Table, fought
Hard with himself, and seemed at length in peace.

235 Then chanced, one morning, that Sir Balin sat
Close-bowered in that garden nigh the hall.
A walk of roses ran from door to door;
A walk of lilies crost it to the bower:
And down that range of roses the great Queen
240 Came with slow steps, the morning on her face;
And all in shadow from the counter door
Sir Lancelot as to meet her, then at once,
As if he saw not, glanced aside, and paced
The long white walk of lilies toward the bower.
245 Followed the Queen; Sir Balin heard her 'Prince,
Art thou so little loyal to thy Queen,
As pass without good morrow to thy Queen?'
To whom Sir Lancelot with his eyes on earth,
'Fain would I still be loyal to the Queen.'
250 'Yea so' she said 'but so to pass me by—
So loyal scarce is loyal to thyself,
Whom all men rate the king of courtesy.
Let be: ye stand, fair lord, as in a dream.'

Then Lancelot with his hand among the flowers
255 'Yea—for a dream. Last night methought I saw
That maiden Saint who stands with lily in hand

226-9. 'Suggested by what he often saw from his own study at Aldworth'
(H.T.).

In yonder shrine. All round her prest the dark,
And all the light upon her silver face
Flowed from the spiritual lily that she held.
260   Lo! these her emblems drew mine eyes – away:
For see, how perfect-pure! As light a flush
As hardly tints the blossom of the quince
Would mar their charm of stainless maidenhood.'

'Sweeter to me' she said 'this garden rose
265   Deep-hued and many-folded! sweeter still
The wild-wood hyacinth and the bloom of May.
Prince, we have ridden before among the flowers
In those fair days – not all as cool as these,
Though season-earlier. Art thou sad? or sick?
270   Our noble King will send thee his own leech –
Sick? or for any matter angered at me?'

Then Lancelot lifted his large eyes; they dwelt
Deep-tranced on hers, and could not fall: her hue
Changed at his gaze: so turning side by side
275   They past, and Balin started from his bower.

'Queen? subject? but I see not what I see.
Damsel and lover? hear not what I hear.
My father hath begotten me in his wrath.
I suffer from the things before me, know,
280   Learn nothing; am not worthy to be knight;
A churl, a clown!' and in him gloom on gloom
Deepened: he sharply caught his lance and shield,
Nor stayed to crave permission of the King,
But, mad for strange adventure, dashed away.

285   He took the selfsame track as Balan, saw
The fountain where they sat together, sighed

266–7]   . . . See thy hand
Is kindled with the glowing dust of these!
Thy maiden emblems have a heart as warm
As other maids who look as white as they.
All white is rare in aught that lives: in snow
We find it, but the firstlings of the snow –
Fair-maids of February, as we say –
Have in them, looked to close, a spark of fire:
And this a damsel, seven small summers old,
Showed me at Cameliarde – where first we met.
                                        H.Nbk 33, deleted
Cp. *The Snowdrop* 2, 4: 'February fair-maid', 'Solitary firstling'.

'Was I not better there with him?' and rode
The skyless woods, but under open blue
Came on the hoarhead woodman at a bough
290 Wearily hewing. 'Churl, thine axe!' he cried,
Descended, and disjointed it at a blow:
To whom the woodman uttered wonderingly
'Lord, thou couldst lay the Devil of these woods
If arm of flesh could lay him.' Balin cried
295 'Him, or the viler devil who plays his part,
To lay that devil would lay the Devil in me.'
'Nay' said the churl, 'our devil is a truth,
I saw the flash of him but yestereven.
And some *do* say that our Sir Garlon too
300 Hath learned black magic, and to ride unseen.
Look to the cave.' But Balin answered him
'Old fabler, these be fancies of the churl,
Look to thy woodcraft,' and so leaving him,
Now with slack rein and careless of himself,
305 Now with dug spur and raving at himself,
Now with droopt brow down the long glades he rode;
So marked not on his right a cavern-chasm
Yawn over darkness, where, nor far within,
The whole day died, but, dying, gleamed on rocks
310 Roof-pendent, sharp; and others from the floor,
Tusklike, arising, made that mouth of night
Whereout the Demon issued up from Hell.
He marked not this, but blind and deaf to all
Save that chained rage, which ever yelpt within,
315 Past eastward from the falling sun. At once
He felt the hollow-beaten mosses thud
And tremble, and then the shadow of a spear,
Shot from behind him, ran along the ground.
Sideways he started from the path, and saw,
320 With pointed lance as if to pierce, a shape,
A light of armour by him flash, and pass
And vanish in the woods; and followed this,
But all so blind in rage that unawares
He burst his lance against a forest bough,
325 Dishorsed himself, and rose again, and fled
Far, till the castle of a King, the hall
Of Pellam, lichen-bearded, grayly draped
With streaming grass, appeared, low-built but strong;
The ruinous donjon as a knoll of moss,
330 The battlement overtopt with ivytods,
A home of bats, in every tower an owl.
    Then spake the men of Pellam crying 'Lord,

Why wear ye this crown-royal upon shield?'
Said Balin 'For the fairest and the best
335 Of ladies living gave me this to bear.'
So stalled his horse, and strode across the court,
But found the greetings both of knight and King
Faint in the low dark hall of banquet: leaves
Laid their green faces flat against the panes,
340 Sprays grated, and the cankered boughs without
Whined in the wood; for all was hushed within,
Till when at feast Sir Garlon likewise asked
'Why wear ye that crown-royal?' Balin said
'The Queen we worship, Lancelot, I, and all,
345 As fairest, best and purest, granted me
To bear it!' Such a sound (for Arthur's knights
Were hated strangers in the hall) as makes
The white swan-mother, sitting, when she hears
A strange knee rustle through her secret reeds,
350 Made Garlon, hissing; then he sourly smiled.
'Fairest I grant her: I have seen; but best,
Best, purest? *thou* from Arthur's hall, and yet
So simple! hast thou eyes, or if, are these
So far besotted that they fail to see
355 This fair wife-worship cloaks a secret shame?
Truly, ye men of Arthur be but babes.'

A goblet on the board by Balin, bossed
With holy Joseph's legend, on his right
Stood, all of massiest bronze: one side had sea
360 And ship and sail and angels blowing on it:
And one was rough with wattling, and the walls
Of that low church he built at Glastonbury.
This Balin graspt, but while in act to hurl,
Through memory of that token on the shield
365 Relaxed his hold: 'I will be gentle' he thought
'And passing gentle' caught his hand away,
Then fiercely to Sir Garlon 'Eyes have I
That saw today the shadow of a spear,
Shot from behind me, run along the ground;
370 Eyes too that long have watched how Lancelot draws

357–62. 'The goblet is embossed with scenes from the story of Joseph of
Arimathea, his voyage, and the wattle-built church he raised at Glaston-
bury. King Pellam represents the type of asceticism and superstition'
(H.T.).
361. *wattling, and the walls*] 1886; pole and scaffoldage 1885.

From homage to the best and purest, might,
Name, manhood, and a grace, but scantly thine,
Who, sitting in thine own hall, canst endure
To mouth so huge a foulness – to thy guest,
375   Me, me of Arthur's Table. Felon talk!
Let be! no more!'
              But not the less by night
The scorn of Garlon, poisoning all his rest,
Stung him in dreams. At length, and dim through
     leaves
Blinkt the white morn, sprays grated, and old
     boughs
380   Whined in the wood. He rose, descended, met
The scorner in the castle court, and fain,
For hate and loathing, would have past him by;
But when Sir Garlon uttered mocking-wise;
'What, wear ye still that same crown-scandalous?'
385   His countenance blackened, and his forehead veins
Bloated, and branched; and tearing out of sheath
The brand, Sir Balin with a fiery 'Ha!
So thou be shadow, here I make thee ghost,'
Hard upon helm smote him, and the blade flew
390   Splintering in six, and clinkt upon the stones.
Then Garlon, reeling slowly backward, fell,
And Balin by the banneret of his helm
Dragged him, and struck, but from the castle a cry
Sounded across the court, and – men-at-arms,
395   A score with pointed lances, making at him –
He dashed the pummel at the foremost face,
Beneath a low door dipt, and made his feet
Wings through a glimmering gallery, till he marked
The portal of King Pellam's chapel wide
400   And inward to the wall; he stept behind;
Thence in a moment heard them pass like wolves
Howling; but while he stared about the shrine,
In which he scarce could spy the Christ for Saints,
Beheld before a golden altar lie
405   The longest lance his eyes had ever seen,
Point-painted red; and seizing thereupon
Pushed through an open casement down, leaned on it,
Leapt in a semicircle, and lit on earth;

380–420. Picked out by T. as 'a passage of rapid blank verse (where the pauses are light, and the accentuated syllables under the average – some being short in quantity, and the narrative brief and animated)'.

Then hand at ear, and harkening from what side
410 The blindfold rummage buried in the walls
Might echo, ran the counter path, and found
His charger, mounted on him and away.
An arrow whizzed to the right, one to the left,
One overhead; and Pellam's feeble cry
415 'Stay, stay him! he defileth heavenly things
With earthly uses'–made him quickly dive
Beneath the boughs, and race through many a mile
Of dense and open, till his goodly horse,
Arising wearily at a fallen oak,
420 Stumbled headlong, and cast him face to ground.

Half-wroth he had not ended, but all glad,
Knightlike, to find his charger yet unlamed,
Sir Balin drew the shield from off his neck,
Stared at the priceless cognizance, and thought
425 'I have shamed thee so that now thou shamest me,
Thee will I bear no more,' high on a branch
Hung it, and turned aside into the woods,
And there in gloom cast himself all along,
Moaning 'My violences, my violences!'

430 But now the wholesome music of the wood
Was dumbed by one from out the hall of Mark,
A damsel-errant, warbling, as she rode
The woodland alleys, Vivien, with her Squire.

'The fire of Heaven has killed the barren cold,
435 And kindled all the plain and all the wold.

402ff. Altogether modifying Malory ii 15–16: 'And when Balin was weaponless, he came into a chamber for to seek some weapon, and so from chamber to chamber, and no weapon could he find; and always king Pellam followed him, and at the last he entered into a chamber that was marvellously well dight and richly, and a bed arrayed with cloth of gold, the richest that might be thought, and one lying therein, and thereby stood a table of clean gold, with four pillars of silver that bear up the table, and upon the table stood a marvellous spear, strangely wrought. And when Balin saw the spear, he gat it in his hand, and turned him to king Pellam, and smote him passingly sore with that spear, that king Pellam fell down in a swoon; and therewith the castle rove and walls break, and fell to the earth, and Balin fell down, so that he might not stir hand nor foot: and so the most part of the castle that was fallen down, through that dolorous stroke, lay upon king Pellam and Balin three days ... And that was the same spear that Longius smote our Lord to the heart; and king Pellam was nigh of Joseph's kin.'

The new leaf ever pushes off the old.
The fire of Heaven is not the flame of Hell.

'Old priest, who mumble worship in your quire –
Old monk and nun, ye scorn the world's desire,
440   Yet in your frosty cells ye feel the fire!
The fire of Heaven is not the flame of Hell.

'The fire of Heaven is on the dusty ways.
The wayside blossoms open to the blaze.
The whole wood-world is one full peal of praise.
445   The fire of Heaven is not the flame of Hell.

'The fire of Heaven is lord of all things good,
And starve not thou this fire within thy blood,
But follow Vivien through the fiery flood!
The fire of Heaven is not the flame of Hell!'

450   Then turning to her Squire 'This fire of Heaven,
This old sun-worship, boy, will rise again,
And beat the cross to earth, and break the King
And all his Table.'
                              Then they reached a glade,
Where under one long lane of cloudless air
455   Before another wood, the royal crown
Sparkled, and swaying upon a restless elm
Drew the vague glance of Vivien, and her Squire;
Amazed were these; 'Lo there' she cried – 'a crown –
Borne by some high lord-prince of Arthur's hall,
460   And there a horse! the rider? where is he?
See, yonder lies one dead within the wood.
Not dead; he stirs! – but sleeping. I will speak.
Hail, royal knight, we break on thy sweet rest,
Not, doubtless, all unearned by noble deeds.
465   But bounden art thou, if from Arthur's hall,
To help the weak. Behold, I fly from shame,
A lustful King, who sought to win my love
Through evil ways: the knight, with whom I rode,
Hath suffered misadventure, and my squire
470   Hath in him small defence; but thou, Sir Prince,
Wilt surely guide me to the warrior King,
Arthur the blameless, pure as any maid,
To get me shelter for my maidenhood.
I charge thee by that crown upon thy shield,
475   And by the great Queen's name, arise and hence.'

And Balin rose, 'Thither no more! nor Prince

Nor knight am I, but one that hath defamed
The cognizance she gave me: here I dwell
Savage among the savage woods, here die—
480 Die: let the wolves' black maws ensepulchre
Their brother beast, whose anger was his lord.
O me, that such a name as Guinevere's,
Which our high Lancelot hath so lifted up,
And been thereby uplifted, should through me,
485 My violence, and my villainy, come to shame.'

Thereat she suddenly laughed and shrill, anon
Sighed all as suddenly. Said Balin to her
'Is this thy courtesy—to mock me, ha?
Hence, for I will not with thee.' Again she sighed
490 'Pardon, sweet lord! we maidens often laugh
When sick at heart, when rather we should weep.
I knew thee wronged. I brake upon thy rest,
And now full loth am I to break thy dream,
But thou art man, and canst abide a truth,
495 Though bitter. Hither, boy—and mark me well.
Dost thou remember at Caerleon once—
A year ago—nay, then I love thee not—
Ay, thou rememberest well—one summer dawn—
By the great tower—Caerleon upon Usk—
500 Nay, truly we were hidden: this fair lord,
The flower of all their vestal knighthood, knelt
In amorous homage—knelt—what else?—O ay
Knelt, and drew down from out his night-black hair
And mumbled that white hand whose ringed caress
505 Had wandered from her own King's golden head,
And lost itself in darkness, till she cried—
I thought the great tower would crash down on both—
"Rise, my sweet King, and kiss me on the lips,
Thou art my King." This lad, whose lightest word
510 Is mere white truth in simple nakedness,
Saw them embrace: he reddens, cannot speak,
So bashful, he! but all the maiden Saints,
The deathless mother-maidenhood of Heaven,
Cry out upon her. Up then, ride with me!
515 Talk not of shame! thou canst not, an thou would'st,
Do these more shame than these have done
          themselves.'

She lied with ease; but horror-stricken he,
Remembering that dark bower at Camelot,
Breathed in a dismal whisper 'It is truth.'

520   Sunnily she smiled 'And even in this lone wood, .
       Sweet lord, ye do right well to whisper this.
       Fools prate, and perish traitors. Woods have tongues,
       As walls have ears: but thou shalt go with me,
       And we will speak at first exceeding low.
525   Meet is it the good King be not deceived.
       See now, I set thee high on vantage ground,
       From whence to watch the time, and eagle-like
       Stoop at thy will on Lancelot and the Queen.'

       She ceased; his evil spirit upon him leapt,
530   He ground his teeth together, sprang with a yell,
       Tore from the branch, and cast on earth, the shield,
       Drove his mailed heel athwart the royal crown,
       Stampt all into defacement, hurled it from him
       Among the forest weeds, and cursed the tale,
       The told-of, and the teller.
535   That weird yell,
       Unearthlier than all shriek of bird or beast,
       Thrilled through the woods; and Balan lurking there
       (His quest was unaccomplished) heard and thought
       'The scream of that Wood-devil I came to quell!'
540   Then nearing 'Lo! he hath slain some brother-knight,
       And tramples on the goodly shield to show
       His loathing of our Order and the Queen.
       My quest, meseems, is here. Or devil or man
       Guard thou thine head.' Sir Balin spake not word,
545   But snatched a sudden buckler from the Squire,
       And vaulted on his horse, and so they crashed
       In onset, and King Pellam's holy spear,
       Reputed to be red with sinless blood,
       Reddened at once with sinful, for the point
550   Across the maiden shield of Balan pricked
       The hauberk to the flesh; and Balin's horse
       Was wearied to the death, and, when they clashed,
       Rolling back upon Balin, crushed the man
       Inward, and either fell, and swooned away.

555   Then to her Squire muttered the damsel 'Fools!
       This fellow hath wrought some foulness with his
               Queen:
       Else never had he borne her crown, nor raved
       And thus foamed over at a rival name:
       But thou, Sir Chick, that scarce hast broken shell,
560   Art yet half-yolk, not even come to down—

547. Not so in Malory.

Who never sawest Caerleon upon Usk –
And yet hast often pleaded for my love –
See what I see, be thou where I have been,
Or else Sir Chick – dismount and loose their casques
565   I fain would know what manner of men they be.'
And when the Squire had loosed them, 'Goodly!
    – look!
They might have cropt the myriad flower of May,
And butt each other here, like brainless bulls,
Dead for one heifer!'
                                  Then the gentle Squire
570   'I hold them happy, so they died for love:
And, Vivien, though ye beat me like your dog,
I too could die, as now I live, for thee.'

'Live on, Sir Boy,' she cried. 'I better prize
The living dog than the dead lion: away!
575   I cannot brook to gaze upon the dead.'
Then leapt her palfrey o'er the fallen oak,
And bounding forward 'Leave them to the wolves.'

But when their foreheads felt the cooling air,
Balin first woke, and seeing that true face,
580   Familiar up from cradle-time, so wan,
Crawled slowly with low moans to where he lay,
And on his dying brother cast himself

573–4. Rosenberg (p. 162) notes *Eccles.* ix 4.
578–620. Malory ii 18: 'Then said Balin le Savage, "What knight art
thou? for ere now I found never no knight that matched me".–"My name
is", said he, "Balan, brother to the good knight Balin".–"Alas!" said
Balin, "that ever I should see this day". And therewith he fell backward in
a swoon. Then Balan went on all four, feet and hands, and put off the helm
of his brother, and might not know him by the visage, it was so full hewn
and bebled [be-bled]; but when he awoke, he said, "O Balan, my brother,
thou hast slain me, and I thee, wherefore all the wide world shall speak of
us both".–"Alas!" said Balin, "that ever I saw this day, that through
mishap I might not know you; for I espied well your two swords, but
because ye had another shield, I deemed you had been another knight".–
"Alas!" said Balin, "all that made an unhappy knight in the castle, for he
caused me to leave mine own shield to the destruction of us both; and if I
might live I would destroy that castle for the ill customs". . . "We came
both out of one womb, that is to say, mother's belly, and so shall we lie
both in one pit". . . "Now", said Balin, "when we are buried in one
tomb, and the mention made over us how two brethren slew each other,
there will never good knight, nor good man, see our tomb, but they will
pray for our souls".'

Dying; and *he* lifted faint eyes; he felt
One near him; all at once they found the world,
585 Staring wild-wide; then with a childlike wail,
And drawing down the dim disastrous brow
That o'er him hung, he kissed it, moaned and spake;

'O Balin, Balin, I that fain had died
To save thy life, have brought thee to thy death.
590 Why had ye not the shield I knew? and why
Trampled ye thus on that which bare the Crown?'

Then Balin told him brokenly, and in gasps,
All that had chanced, and Balan moaned again.

'Brother, I dwelt a day in Pellam's hall:
595 This Garlon mocked me, but I heeded not.
And one said "Eat in peace! a liar is he,
And hates thee for the tribute!" this good knight
Told me, that twice a wanton damsel came,
And sought for Garlon at the castle-gates,
600 Whom Pellam drove away with holy heat.
I well believe this damsel, and the one
Who stood beside thee even now, the same.
"She dwells among the woods" he said "and meets
And dallies with him in the Mouth of Hell."
605 Foul are their lives; foul are their lips; they lied.
Pure as our own true Mother is our Queen.'

'O brother' answered Balin 'woe is me!
My madness all thy life has been thy doom,
Thy curse, and darkened all thy day; and now
610 The night has come. I scarce can see thee now.

Goodnight! for we shall never bid again
Goodmorrow–Dark my doom was here, and dark
It will be there. I see thee now no more.
I would not mine again should darken thine,
Goodnight, true brother.'
615 　　　　　　　　Balan answered low
'Goodnight, true brother here! goodmorrow there!
We two were born together, and we die
Together by one doom:' and while he spoke
Closed his death-drowsing eyes, and slept the sleep
620 With Balin, either locked in either's arm.

469 Merlin and Vivien

Published *1859* as *Vivien* (the final title in *1870* ['*1869*']). 'Begun in Feb. and finished on March 31st, 1856' (H.T.). On 15 July 1856, James Spedding wrote to T. objecting to Merlin's seduction by Vivien (*Lincoln*). Sir Charles Tennyson says that in 1854 T. 'had already begun work on a poem about the enchantment of Merlin, but he laid this aside for *Maud*' (*CT*, p. 282); T. wrote to Simeon, *c.* 20 March 1856: 'I have done some of my Merlin Idyl which promises well I think' (*Letters* ii 147). T.'s trial edition of *Enid and Nimuë: the True and the False* was set up in the summer of 1857; there is a copy in the British Library (from which an edition was printed in 1902). For details of T.'s revisions, see Richard Jones, *The Growth of the Idylls of the King* (1895), Chapter ii; and Sir Charles Tennyson, *Cornhill* cliii (1936) 534–57. H.T. comments: 'My father created the character of Vivien with much care – as the evil genius of the Round Table [*note:* Even to the last. See *Guinevere* 97–8.] – who in her lustfulness of the flesh could not believe in anything either good or great. The story of the poem ... is essentially original, and was founded on the following passage from Malory' [iv 1, slightly bowdlerized by H.T., here restored]:

'She was one of the damsels of the lake, which hight Nimue. But Merlin would let her have no rest, but always he would be with her in every place; and ever she made Merlin good cheer, till she had learned of him all manner of things that she desired, and he was so sore assotted upon her, that he might not be from her . . . And then he departed from king Arthur. And within a while the damsel of the lake departed, and Merlin went evermore with her wheresoever she went. And oftentimes Merlin would have had her privily away by his subtle crafts . . . And by the way as they went Merlin shewed her many wonders, and came into Cornwall. And always Merlin lay about the lady, for to have her maidenhead; and she was ever passing weary of him, and fain would have been delivered of him; for she was afraid of him, because he was a devil's son, and she could not put him away by any means. And so, upon a time, it happened that Merlin shewed to her in a rock where was a great wonder, and wrought by enchantment, which went under a stone. So, by her subtle craft and working, she made Merlin to go under that stone to let her wit of the marvels there; but she wrought so there for him, that he came never out, for all the craft that he could do: and so she departed, and left Merlin.'

'For the name of Vivien my father is indebted to the old *Romance of Merlin*' (H.T.). G. S. Haight (*SP* xliv (1947) 550–7) discusses the Vulgate *Merlin*, much of which is translated in Southey's edition of Malory (1817, pp. xliv–xlvi), where the relevant passage runs:

'When Merlin related all this to his master Blaise, who seems to have been his confessor as well as historiographer, Blaise was much troubled, and censured him greatly, and gave him good advice; but good advice was lost upon Merlin, who saw his own fate, and with all his wisdom was unable to avoid it. Accordingly one day the enchanter took leave of his old master, telling him "it was the last time he would ever see him, for from thenceforth he must abide with his mistress, and should never more have the power of leaving her, nor of going and coming at his pleasure. When Blaise heard this, he said to him full sorrowfully, Since then it is so that you will not be able to depart when once you shall have gone there, fair friend go not there at all, for you well know the thing that must happen to you. Certes, answered Merlin, I needs must go, for so I have covenanted and promised; and even if I had not covenanted, I am so taken with her love that I could not forbear going. All this have I done myself, for I have taught her great part of what I know, and she will still learn more from me, for I have no power to withhold myself. With that Merlin departed from Blaise his master, and travelled so long in few hours, that he came to Viviane his mistress." This was good travelling, for Blaise lived in Northumberland, and Viviane in France. They dwelt a long while together, and "she showed him greater semblance of love than she had ever done before, as one who knew so many enchantments that never other woman knew so much. So she devised within herself how she might detain him for ever more; but never could she compass nor achieve this: then was she full sorrowful and vexed, and cast about how she might discover it. Then began she to fawn and to flatter Merlin more than before; and she said to him, My sweet friend, I do not yet know one thing which I would fain know, I pray you teach me it. And Merlin, who well knew what it was, and to what she tended, said to her, Mistress, what is it? Sir, said Viviane, I would have you teach and show me how to inclose and imprison a man without a tower, without walls, without chains, but by enchantments alone, in such manner that he may never be able to go out, except by me. When Merlin heard her he shook his head, and began to sigh deeply; and Viviane, when she perceived it, asked of him wherefore he sighed thus. Dame, said Merlin, I will tell you. Well I know that you are devising how you may detain me; but I am so taken, that perforce will I or not, it behoves me to do your will. When Viviane heard this, for her great treason, and the better to delude and deceive him, she put her arms round his neck, and began to kiss him, saying, that he might well be hers, seeing that she was his: You well know, said she, that the great love which I have in you, has made me leave father and mother that I may have you in my arms day and night. All my desire and thought is in you; without you I have neither joy nor good. I have placed all my hope upon you, and I never look to have joy or good except from you. Seeing then that I love you, and you love me, is it not right that you should do my will and I yours? Certes, lady, yes, said Merlin, and I will do it; tell me what you would have. Sir, said she, I would that we should make a fair place and a suitable, so contrived by art and by cunning, that it might never be undone, and that you and I should be there in joy and in solace. My lady, said Merlin, I will perform all this. Sir, said she, I would not have you do it, but you shall teach me, and I will do it, and then it will be more to my will. I grant you this, said Merlin. Then he began to devise, and the damsel put it all in writing. And when he had devised the whole, then had the damsel full great joy, and showed him greater semblance of loving him than she had ever before made; and they sojourned together a long while. At length it fell out that as they were going one day hand in hand through the forest of Broceliande, they found a bush of white thorn which was laden with flowers; and they seated themselves under the shade of this white thorn upon the green grass, and they disported together and took their solace, and Merlin laid his head upon the damsel's lap, and then she began to feel if he were asleep. Then the damsel rose and made a ring with her wimple round the bush and round Merlin, and began her enchantments such as he himself had taught her; and nine times she made the ring, and nine times she made the enchantment; and then she went and sate down by him, and placed his head again upon her lap; and when he awoke and looked round him, it seemed to him that he was inclosed in the strongest tower in the world, and laid upon a fair bed; then said he to the dame, My lady, you have deceived me unless you abide with me, for no one hath power to unmake this tower, save you alone. Fair friend, she replied, I shall often be here, and you shall hold me in your arms, and I will hold you in mine. And in this she held her covenant to him, for afterwards there was never night nor day in which she was not there. And Merlin never went out of that tower where his mistress Viviane had inclosed him. But she entered and went out again when she listed; and often time she regretted what she had done, for she had thought that the thing which he taught her could not be true, and willingly would she have let him out if she could."

'The writer very properly remarks upon Merlin, for having taught his mistress so much, *quil en fut depuis, et est encore tenu pour fol.*'

Richard Jones had suggested that this version came to T. from the notes to Lady Charlotte Guest's *Mabinogion*. T. commented on the poem: ·'Some even among the highest intellects become the slaves of the evil which is at first half disdained.' On the lifelong diverse importance of Merlin to T., see C. B. Stevenson, *VN* No. 57 (1980) 14–23.

> A storm was coming, but the winds were still,
> And in the wild woods of Broceliande,
> Before an oak, so hollow, huge and old
> It looked a tower of ivied masonwork,
> 5   At Merlin's feet the wily Vivien lay.

¶469. 2. *Broceliande*: 'The forest of Broceliand in Brittany near St Malo' (T.).
4. *ivied*] *1885*; ruined *1859–84*.

　　　For he that always bare in bitter grudge
　　The slights of Arthur and his Table, Mark
　　The Cornish King, had heard a wandering voice,
　　A minstrel of Caerleon by strong storm
10　Blown into shelter at Tintagil, say
　　That out of naked knightlike purity
　　Sir Lancelot worshipt no unmarried girl
　　But the great Queen herself, fought in her name,
　.　Sware by her—vows like theirs, that high in heaven
15　Love most, but neither marry, nor are given
　　In marriage, angels of our Lord's report.

　　　He ceased, and then—for Vivien sweetly said
　　(She sat beside the banquet nearest Mark),
　　'And is the fair example followed, Sir,
20　In Arthur's household?'—answered innocently:

　　　'Ay, by some few—ay, truly—youths that hold
　　It more beseems the perfect virgin knight
　　To worship woman as true wife beyond
　　All hopes of gaining, than as maiden girl.
25　They place their pride in Lancelot and the Queen.
　　So passionate for an utter purity
　　Beyond the limit of their bond, are these,
　　For Arthur bound them not to singleness.
　　Brave hearts and clean! and yet—God guide them—
　　　　young.'

30　　Then Mark was half in heart to hurl his cup
　　Straight at the speaker, but forbore: he rose
　　To leave the hall, and, Vivien following him,
　　Turned to her: 'Here are snakes within the grass;
　　And you methinks, O Vivien, save ye fear
35　The monkish manhood, and the mask of pure
　　Worn by this court, can stir them till they sting.'

　　　And Vivien answered, smiling scornfully,
　　'Why fear? because that fostered at *thy* court
　　I savour of thy—virtues? fear them? no.
40　As Love, if Love be perfect, casts out fear,
　　So Hate, if Hate be perfect, casts out fear.

6–146] 1874, *Cabinet Works; not 1859–73.* Until the final reading in *1885,* these added lines began: 'Whence came she? One that bare in bitter grudge / The scorn of Arthur....'

14–16. Matthew xxii 30.

40. 1 John iv 18: 'perfect love casteth out fear.' Gray (p. 53) adds *Psalm* cxxxix

My father died in battle against the King,
My mother on his corpse in open field;
She bore me there, for born from death was I
45 Among the dead and sown upon the wind –
And then on thee! and shown the truth betimes,
That old true filth, and bottom of the well,
Where Truth is hidden. Gracious lessons thine
And maxims of the mud! "This Arthur pure!
50 Great Nature through the flesh herself hath made
Gives him the lie! There is no being pure,
My cherub; saith not Holy Writ the same?" –
If I were Arthur, I would have thy blood.
Thy blessing, stainless King! I bring thee back,
55 When I have ferreted out their burrowings,
The hearts of all this Order in mine hand –
Ay–so that fate and craft and folly close,
Perchance, one curl of Arthur's golden beard.
To me this narrow grizzled fork of thine
60 Is cleaner-fashioned – Well, I loved thee first,
That warps the wit.'

      Loud laughed the graceless Mark.
But Vivien, into Camelot stealing, lodged
Low in the city, and on a festal day
When Guinevere was crossing the great hall
65 Cast herself down, knelt to the Queen, and wailed.

'Why kneel ye there? What evil have ye wrought?
Rise!' and the damsel bidden rise arose
And stood with folded hands and downward eyes
Of glancing corner, and all meekly said,
70 'None wrought, but suffered much, an orphan maid!

21–2: 'Do not I hate them, O Lord, that hate thee? Yea, I hate them with
perfect hatred'.
45. Gray (p. 53) notes *Hosea* viii 7: 'for they have sown the wind, and they
shall reap the whirlwind'.
47–8. Sir Thomas Browne: 'Truth, which wise men say doth lye in a well'
(Tilley's *Proverbs*, T582).
51–2. *Proverbs* xx 9: 'Who can say, I have made my heart clean, I am pure
from my sin?'
51] I hate the man that wears the mask of pure,
 I front him with a countermask of pure; *H.Nbk 34*
61]   Loud laughed the graceless king,
  And like some long stilt-walker of the fens,
  More wood than man, shambled away to sleep. *H.Nbk 34*
70–83. Sir Charles Tennyson quotes from *H.Nbk 34* the first draft of Vivien's

My father died in battle for thy King,
My mother on his corpse–in open field,
The sad sea-sounding wastes of Lyonnesse–
Poor wretch–no friend!–and now by Mark the King
75 For that small charm of feature mine, pursued–
If any such be mine–I fly to thee.
Save, save me thou–Woman of women–thine
The wreath of beauty, thine the crown of power,
Be thine the balm of pity, O Heaven's own white
80 Earth-angel, stainless bride of stainless King–
Help, for he follows! take me to thyself!
O yield me shelter for mine innocency
Among thy maidens!'

                  Here her slow sweet eyes
Fear-tremulous, but humbly hopeful, rose
85 Fixt on her hearer's, while the Queen who stood
All glittering like May sunshine on May leaves
In green and gold, and plumed with green replied,
'Peace, child! of overpraise and overblame
We choose the last. Our noble Arthur, him
90 Ye scarce can overpraise, will hear and know.
Nay–we believe all evil of thy Mark–
Well, we shall test thee farther; but this hour
We ride a-hawking with Sir Lancelot.
He hath given us a fair falcon which he trained;
95 We go to prove it. Bide ye here the while.'

    She past; and Vivien murmured after 'Go!
I bide the while.' Then through the portal-arch
Peering askance, and muttering broken-wise,
As one that labours with an evil dream,
100 Beheld the Queen and Lancelot get to horse.

    'Is that the Lancelot? goodly–ay, but gaunt:
Courteous–amends for gauntness–takes her hand–
That glance of theirs, but for the street, had been
A clinging kiss–how hand lingers in hand!
105 Let go at last!–they ride away–to hawk
For waterfowl. Royaller game is mine.
For such a supersensual sensual bond

speech, in which she tells of the death of Balin and Balan (*Cornhill* cliii (1936)
552–3); see *p. 787.*
104 ∧ 5] Bruise not the little fingers, courtesy–*H.Nbk 34.*
107. supersensual sensual] supersexual sexless *H.Nbk 34.*

As that gray cricket chirpt of at our hearth –
Touch flax with flame – a glance will serve – the
        liars!
110 Ah little rat that borest in the dyke
Thy hole by night to let the boundless deep
Down upon far-off cities while they dance –
Or dream – of thee they dreamed not – nor of me
These – ay, but each of either: ride, and dream
115 The mortal dream that never yet was mine –
Ride, ride and dream until ye wake – to me!
Then, narrow court and lubber King, farewell!
For Lancelot will be gracious to the rat,
And our wise Queen, if knowing that I know,
120 Will hate, loathe, fear – but honour me the more.'

Yet while they rode together down the plain,
Their talk was all of training, terms of art,
Diet and seeling, jesses, leash and lure.
'She is too noble' he said 'to check at pies,
125 Nor will she rake: there is no baseness in her.'
Here when the Queen demanded as by chance
'Know ye the stranger woman?' 'Let her be,'
Said Lancelot and unhooded casting off
The goodly falcon free; she towered; her bells,
130 Tone under tone, shrilled; and they lifted up
Their eager faces, wondering at the strength,
Boldness and royal knighthood of the bird
Who pounced her quarry and slew it. Many a time
As once – of old – among the flowers – they rode.

135 But Vivien half-forgotten of the Queen
Among her damsels broidering sat, heard, watched
And whispered: through the peaceful court she crept

---

108 ∧ 9] When all the heat and force were out of him H.Nbk 34 1st reading;
The heat and force of life were out of him, H.Nbk 34.
109]   Touch flax with fire – a glance will do – no more.
        Lies, lies! for which I hate the world – and him
        That made me hate it, though he spake the truth –
        Him least perchance – fool! for he wronged me most. H.Nbk 34
114–116. 'The only real bit of feeling, and the only pathetic line which
Vivien speaks' (T.).
123. seeling: 'sewing up eyes of hawk' (H.T.).   jesses: 'straps of leather
fastened to legs' (H.T.).
124. check at pies: 'fly at magpies' (H.T.).
125. Nor will she rake: 'nor will she fly at other game' (H.T.).

And whispered: then as Arthur in the highest
Leavened the world, so Vivien in the lowest,
140 Arriving at a time of golden rest,
And sowing one ill hint from ear to ear,
While all the heathen lay at Arthur's feet,
And no quest came, but all was joust and play,
Leavened his hall. They heard and let her be.

145 Thereafter as an enemy that has left
Death in the living waters, and withdrawn,
The wily Vivien stole from Arthur's court.

She hated all the knights, and heard in thought
Their lavish comment when her name was named.
150 For once, when Arthur walking all alone,
Vext at a rumour issued from herself
Of some corruption crept among his knights,
Had met her, Vivien, being greeted fair,
Would fain have wrought upon his cloudy mood
155 With reverent eyes mock-loyal, shaken voice,
And fluttered adoration, and at last
With dark sweet hints of some who prized him more
Than who should prize him most; at which the King
Had gazed upon her blankly and gone by:
160 But one had watched, and had not held his peace:
It made the laughter of an afternoon
That Vivien should attempt the blameless King.
And after that, she set herself to gain
Him, the most famous man of all those times,
165 Merlin, who knew the range of all their arts,
Had built the King his havens, ships, and halls,
Was also Bard, and knew the starry heavens;
The people called him Wizard; whom at first
She played about with slight and sprightly talk,
170 And vivid smiles, and faintly-venomed points
Of slander, glancing here and grazing there;
And yielding to his kindlier moods, the Seer
Would watch her at her petulance, and play,

145-6. 'Poisoned the wells' (T.).

150-62. Gray (p. 13): 'Vivien's attempt to seduce Arthur is not T.'s addition
to the legend, but is drawn from an episode in Malory when a similar
enchantress, Annowre, tries hard to seduce the king' (ix 15).

151. *issued from herself*] 1873, *Imperial Library Edition*; rife about the Queen,
1859-73.

152] 1873, *Imperial Library Edition*; not 1859-73.

Even when they seemed unloveable, and laugh
175 As those that watch a kitten; thus he grew
Tolerant of what he half disdained, and she,
Perceiving that she was but half disdained,
Began to break her sports with graver fits,
Turn red or pale, would often when they met
180 Sigh fully, or all-silent gaze upon him
With such a fixt devotion, that the old man,
Though doubtful, felt the flattery, and at times
Would flatter his own wish in age for love,
And half believe her true: for thus at times
185 He wavered; but that other clung to him,
Fixt in her will, and so the seasons went.

Then fell on Merlin a great melancholy;
He walked with dreams and darkness, and he found
A doom that ever poised itself to fall,
190 An ever-moaning battle in the mist,
World-war of dying flesh against the life,
Death in all life and lying in all love,
The meanest having power upon the highest,
And the high purpose broken by the worm.

195 So leaving Arthur's court he gained the beach,
There found a little boat, and stept into it;
And Vivien followed, but he marked her not.
She took the helm and he the sail; the boat
Drave with a sudden wind across the deeps,
200 And touching Breton sands, they disembarked.
And then she followed Merlin all the way,
Even to the wild woods of Broceliande.
For Merlin once had told her of a charm,
The which if any wrought on anyone
205 With woven paces and with waving arms,
The man so wrought on ever seemed to lie
Closed in the four walls of a hollow tower,

187. on Merlin] 1873; upon him 1859–70.
188–94] 1873, Imperial Library Edition; not 1859–73. H.Nbk 39 had two lines not
adopted in this passage:
     Faint cries for him who fainted in his faith,
     And dimly felt the King who cannot die.
188. Gray (p. 53) notes Proverbs ii 13: 'who leave the paths of uprightness, to
walk in the ways of darkness'.
190. 'The vision of the battle at the end' (T.).
195. So] 1873; And 1859–70.

From which was no escape for evermore;
And none could find that man for evermore,
210 Nor could he see but him who wrought the charm
Coming and going, and he lay as dead
And lost to life and use and name and fame.
And Vivien ever sought to work the charm
Upon the great Enchanter of the Time,
215 As fancying that her glory would be great
According to his greatness whom she quenched.

There lay she all her length and kissed his feet,
As if in deepest reverence and in love.
A twist of gold was round her hair; a robe
220 Of samite without price, that more exprest
Than hid her, clung about her lissome limbs,
In colour like the satin-shining palm
On sallows in the windy gleams of March:
And while she kissed them, crying, 'Trample me,
225 Dear feet, that I have followed through the world,
And I will pay you worship; tread me down
And I will kiss you for it;' he was mute:
So dark a forethought rolled about his brain,
As on a dull day in an Ocean cave
230 The blind wave feeling round his long sea-hall
In silence: wherefore, when she lifted up
A face of sad appeal, and spake and said,
'O Merlin, do ye love me?' and again,
'O Merlin, do ye love me?' and once more,
235 'Great Master, do ye love me?' he was mute.
And lissome Vivien, holding by his heel,
Writhed toward him, slided up his knee and sat,
Behind his ankle twined her hollow feet
Together, curved an arm about his neck,
240 Clung like a snake; and letting her left hand
Droop from his mighty shoulder, as a leaf,
Made with her right a comb of pearl to part
The lists of such a beard as youth gone out

228. Cp. *Hail Briton* 96 ∧ 7, MS: 'The forethought of a working brain'.
229–31. 'This simile is taken from what I saw in the Caves of Ballybunion'
(T.). This was in 1842 (*Mem.* i 218). In his copy of John Churton Collins's
article (*Cornhill*, Jan. 1880, *Lincoln*), T. said that he had 'no thought of
[Homer's] κῦμα κωφόν'.
233. *ye*] *1870* ('*1869*'); *you 1859–69*. Likewise in ll. 234–5, 267, 313–14,
353, 358, 397, 442, 540, 551, 700–1.
235. *Master*] master *Eversley, presumably in error*.

Had left in ashes: then he spoke and said,
245 Not looking at her, 'Who are wise in love
Love most, say least,' and Vivien answered quick,
'I saw the little elf-god eyeless once
In Arthur's arras hall at Camelot:
But neither eyes nor tongue–O stupid child!
250 Yet you are wise who say it; let me think
Silence is wisdom: I am silent then,
And ask no kiss;' then adding all at once,
'And lo, I clothe myself with wisdom,' drew
The vast and shaggy mantle of his beard
255 Across her neck and bosom to her knee,
And called herself a gilded summer fly
Caught in a great old tyrant spider's web,
Who meant to eat her up in that wild wood
Without one word. So Vivien called herself,
260 But rather seemed a lovely baleful star
Veiled in gray vapour; till he sadly smiled:
'To what request for what strange boon,' he said,
'Are these your pretty tricks and fooleries,
O Vivien, the preamble? yet my thanks,
265 For these have broken up my melancholy.'

And Vivien answered smiling saucily,
'What, O my Master, have ye found your voice?
I bid the stranger welcome. Thanks at last!
But yesterday you never opened lip,
270 Except indeed to drink: no cup had we:
In mine own lady palms I culled the spring
That gathered trickling dropwise from the cleft,
And made a pretty cup of both my hands
And offered you it kneeling: then you drank
275 And knew no more, nor gave me one poor word;
O no more thanks than might a goat have given
With no more sign of reverence than a beard.
And when we halted at that other well,
And I was faint to swooning, and you lay
280 Foot-gilt with all the blossom-dust of those
Deep meadows we had traversed, did you know

280–81. Adapted from *The Brook*, MS related to 166–7: 'through the fields /
Came all foot-gilt with yellow meadow-dust'.
282. Rosenberg (pp. 164–5) notes *John* xiii 5–16, Jesus washing the feet of the
disciples; and *Luke* vii 37–8, a sinner bathing Jesus' feet 'with tears, and did
wipe them with the hairs of her head, and kissed his feet'.

That Vivien bathed your feet before her own?
And yet no thanks: and all through this wild wood
And all this morning when I fondled you:
285 Boon, ay, there was a boon, one not so strange –
How had I wronged you? surely ye are wise,
But such a silence is more wise than kind.'

And Merlin locked his hand in hers and said:
'O did ye never lie upon the shore,
290 And watch the curled white of the coming wave
Glassed in the slippery sand before it breaks?
Even such a wave, but not so pleasurable,
Dark in the glass of some presageful mood,
Had I for three days seen, ready to fall.
295 And then I rose and fled from Arthur's court
To break the mood. You followed me unasked;
And when I looked, and saw you following still,
My mind involved yourself the nearest thing
In that mind-mist: for shall I tell you truth?
300 You seemed that wave about to break upon me
And sweep me from my hold upon the world,
My use and name and fame. Your pardon, child.
Your pretty sports have brightened all again.
And ask your boon, for boon I owe you thrice,
305 Once for wrong done you by confusion, next
For thanks it seems till now neglected, last
For these your dainty gambols: wherefore ask;
And take this boon so strange and not so strange.'

And Vivien answered smiling mournfully:
310 'O not so strange as my long asking it,
Not yet so strange as you yourself are strange,
Nor half so strange as that dark mood of yours.
I ever feared ye were not wholly mine;
And see, yourself have owned ye did me wrong.
315 The people call you prophet: let it be:
But not of those that can expound themselves.
Take Vivien for expounder; she will call
That three-days-long presageful gloom of yours
No presage, but the same mistrustful mood

285. ay] 1873; yes 1859–70.
286. ye] 1873; you 1859–70. Likewise in ll. 289, 324, 334, 373, 381, 464,
466, 486, 514, 523, 547, 650, 686, 688, 770, 776.
311. Not] 1880; Nor 1859–78.

320 That makes you seem less noble than yourself,
Whenever I have asked this very boon,
Now asked again: for see you not, dear love,
That such a mood as that, which lately gloomed
Your fancy when ye saw me following you,
325 Must make me fear still more you are not mine,
Must make me yearn still more to prove you mine,
And make me wish still more to learn this charm
Of woven paces and of waving hands,
As proof of trust. O Merlin, teach it me.
330 The charm so taught will charm us both to rest.
For, grant me some slight power upon your fate,
I, feeling that you felt me worthy trust,
Should rest and let you rest, knowing you mine.
And therefore be as great as ye are named,
335 Not muffled round with selfish reticence.
How hard you look and how denyingly!
O, if you think this wickedness in me,
That I should prove it on you unawares,
That makes me passing wrathful; then our bond
340 Had best be loosed for ever: but think or not,
By Heaven that hears I tell you the clean truth,
As clean as blood of babes, as white as milk:
O Merlin, may this earth, if ever I,
If these unwitty wandering wits of mine,
345 Even in the jumbled rubbish of a dream,
Have tript on such conjectural treachery—
May this hard earth cleave to the Nadir hell
Down, down, and close again, and nip me flat,
If I be such a traitress. Yield my boon,
350 Till which I scarce can yield you all I am;
And grant my re-reiterated wish,
The great proof of your love: because I think,
However wise, ye hardly know me yet.'

    And Merlin loosed his hand from hers and said,
355 'I never was less wise, however wise,
Too curious Vivien, though you talk of trust,
Than when I told you first of such a charm.
Yea, if ye talk of trust I tell you this,
Too much I trusted when I told you that,
360 And stirred this vice in you which ruined man
Through woman the first hour; for howsoe'er

338 ∧ 9] To make you lose your use and name and fame, *1859–70*.
339. *passing wrathful*] *1873*; most indignant *1859–70*.

In children a great curiousness be well,
Who have to learn themselves and all the world,
In you, that are no child, for still I find
365 Your face is practised when I spell the lines,
I call it,—well, I will not call it vice:
But since you name yourself the summer fly,
I well could wish a cobweb for the gnat,
That settles, beaten back, and beaten back
370 Settles, till one could yield for weariness:
But since I will not yield to give you power
Upon my life and use and name and fame,
Why will ye never ask some other boon?
Yea, by God's rood, I trusted you too much.'

375 And Vivien, like the tenderest-hearted maid
That ever bided tryst at village stile,
Made answer, either eyelid wet with tears:
'Nay, Master, be not wrathful with your maid;
Caress her: let her feel herself forgiven
380 Who feels no heart to ask another boon.
I think ye hardly know the tender rhyme
Of "trust me not at all or all in all."
I heard the great Sir Lancelot sing it once,
And it shall answer for me. Listen to it.

385 "In Love, if Love be Love, if Love be ours,
Faith and unfaith can ne'er be equal powers:
Unfaith in aught is want of faith in all.

"It is the little rift within the lute,
That by and by will make the music mute,
390 And ever widening slowly silence all.

"The little rift within the lover's lute
Or little pitted speck in garnered fruit,
That rotting inward slowly moulders all.

"It is not worth the keeping: let it go:
395 But shall it? answer, darling, answer, no.
And trust me not at all or all in all."

O Master, do ye love my tender rhyme?'

369] Settles and breaks the just beginning dream
  With twang twang twang in [on?] one bloodsucking note *H.Lpr 153*
Cp. *Lancelot and Elaine* 137–8.
396. Gray (p. 160) notes *Taming of the Shrew* II i 130: 'That is, her love; for
that is all in all'.

And Merlin looked and half believed her true,
So tender was her voice, so fair her face,
400 So sweetly gleamed her eyes behind her tears
Like sunlight on the plain behind a shower:
And yet he answered half indignantly:

'Far other was the song that once I heard
By this huge oak, sung nearly where we sit:
405 For here we met, some ten or twelve of us,
To chase a creature that was current then
In these wild woods, the hart with golden horns.
It was the time when first the question rose
About the founding of a Table Round,
410 That was to be, for love of God and men
And noble deeds, the flower of all the world.
And each incited each to noble deeds.
And while we waited, one, the youngest of us,
We could not keep him silent, out he flashed,
415 And into such a song, such fire for fame,
Such trumpet-blowings in it, coming down
To such a stern and iron-clashing close,
That when he stopt we longed to hurl together,
And should have done it; but the beauteous beast
420 Scared by the noise upstarted at our feet,
And like a silver shadow slipt away
Through the dim land; and all day long we rode
Through the dim land against a rushing wind,
That glorious roundel echoing in our ears,
425 And chased the flashes of his golden horns
Until they vanished by the fairy well
That laughs at iron – as our warriors did –
Where children cast their pins and nails, and cry,
"Laugh, little well!" but touch it with a sword,
430 It buzzes fiercely round the point; and there
We lost him: such a noble song was that.
But, Vivien, when you sang me that sweet rhyme,

403. 'The song about the clang of battle-axes, etc., in the *Coming of Arthur*' (T.).
426–31. Gray (pp. 14–15): 'The hart that Arthur's knights chase at the time of the Round Table's foundation stems from Malory, but where it vanishes comes from the *Mabinogion*': 'The fountain of Baranton is supplied by a mineral spring, and it bubbles up on a piece of iron or copper being thrown into it. "Les enfans s'amusent à y jeter des épingles, et disent par commun proverbe: 'Ris donc, fontaine de Berendon, et je te donnerai une épingle'"'.
430. *fiercely*] 1873; wildly 1859–70.

I felt as though you knew this cursèd charm,
Were proving it on me, and that I lay
435 And felt them slowly ebbing, name and fame.'

And Vivien answered smiling mournfully:
'O mine have ebbed away for evermore,
And all through following you to this wild wood,
Because I saw you sad, to comfort you.
440 Lo now, what hearts have men! they never mount
As high as woman in her selfless mood.
And touching fame, howe'er ye scorn my song,
Take one verse more—the lady speaks it—this:

'"My name, once mine, now thine, is closelier
mine,
445 For fame, could fame be mine, that fame were thine,
And shame, could shame be thine, that shame were
mine.
So trust me not at all or all in all."

'Says she not well? and there is more—this rhyme
Is like the fair pearl-necklace of the Queen,
450 That burst in dancing, and the pearls were spilt;
Some lost, some stolen, some as relics kept.
But nevermore the same two sister pearls
Ran down the silken thread to kiss each other
On her white neck—so is it with this rhyme:
455 It lives dispersedly in many hands,
And every minstrel sings it differently;
Yet is there one true line, the pearl of pearls:
"Man dreams of Fame while woman wakes to love."
Yea! Love, though Love were of the grossest, carves
460 A portion from the solid present, eats
And uses, careless of the rest; but Fame,
The Fame that follows death is nothing to us;
And what is Fame in life but half-disfame,
And counterchanged with darkness? ye yourself
465 Know well that Envy calls you Devil's son,
And since ye seem the Master of all Art,
They fain would make you Master of all vice.'

And Merlin locked his hand in hers and said,
'I once was looking for a magic weed,

459. Yea!] 1873; True: 1859–70.

470 And found a fair young squire who sat alone,
Had carved himself a knightly shield of wood,
And then was painting òn it fancied arms,
Azure, an Eagle rising or, the Sun
In dexter chief; the scroll "I follow fame."
475 And speaking not, but leaning over him,
I took his brush and blotted out the bird,
And made a Gardener putting in a graff,
With this for motto, "Rather use than fame."
You should have seen him blush; but afterwards
480 He made a stalwart knight. O Vivien,
For you, methinks you think you love me well;
For me, I love you somewhat; rest: and Love
Should have some rest and pleasure in himself,
Not ever be too curious for a boon,
485 Too prurient for a proof against the grain
Of him ye say ye love: but Fame with men,
Being but ampler means to serve mankind,
Should have small rest or pleasure in herself,
But work as vassal to the larger love,
490 That dwarfs the petty love of one to one.
Use gave me Fame at first, and Fame again
Increasing gave me use. Lo, there my boon!
What other? for men sought to prove me vile,
Because I fain had given them greater wits:
495 And then did Envy call me Devil's son:
The sick weak beast seeking to help herself
By striking at her better, missed, and brought
Her own claw back, and wounded her own heart.
Sweet were the days when I was all unknown,
500 But when my name was lifted up, the storm
Brake on the mountain and I cared not for it.
Right well know I that Fame is half-disfame,
Yet needs must work my work. That other fame,
To one at least, who hath not children, vague,
505 The cackle of the unborn about the grave,
I cared not for it: a single misty star,

494. fain ... wits] 1873; wished to give them greater minds 1859-70.
501. Brake] 1873; Broke 1859-70.
506-8. 'θ Orionis—the nebula in which is imbedded the great multiple
star. When this was written some astronomers fancied that this nebula in
Orion was the vastest object in the Universe—a firmament of suns too far
away to be resolved into stars by the telescope, and yet so huge as to be seen
by the naked eye' (T.).

Which is the second in a line of stars
That seem a sword beneath a belt of three,
I never gazed upon it but I dreamt
510 Of some vast charm concluded in that star
To make fame nothing. Wherefore, if I fear,
Giving you power upon me through this charm,
That you might play me falsely, having power,
However well ye think ye love me now
515 (As sons of kings loving in pupilage
Have turned to tyrants when they came to power)
I rather dread the loss of use than fame;
If you—and not so much from wickedness,
As some wild turn of anger, or a mood
520 Of overstrained affection, it may be,
To keep me all to your own self,—or else
A sudden spurt of woman's jealousy,—
Should try this charm on whom ye say ye love.'

And Vivien answered smiling as in wrath:
525 'Have I not sworn? I am not trusted. Good!
Well, hide it, hide it; I shall find it out;
And being found take heed of Vivien.
A woman and not trusted, doubtless I
Might feel some sudden turn of anger born
530 Of your misfaith; and your fine epithet
Is accurate too, for this full love of mine
Without the full heart back may merit well
Your term of overstrained. So used as I,
My daily wonder is, I love at all.
535 And as to woman's jealousy, O why not?
O to what end, except a jealous one,
And one to make me jealous if I love,
Was this fair charm invented by yourself?
I well believe that all about this world
540 Ye cage a buxom captive here and there,
Closed in the four walls of a hollow tower
From which is no escape for evermore.'

Then the great Master merrily answered her:
'Full many a love in loving youth was mine;
545 I needed then no charm to keep them mine
But youth and love; and that full heart of yours
Whereof ye prattle, may now assure you mine;
So live uncharmed. For those who wrought it first,
The wrist is parted from the hand that waved,
550 The feet unmortised from their ankle-bones

Who paced it, ages back: but will ye hear
The legend as in guerdon for your rhyme?

'There lived a king in the most Eastern East,
Less old than I, yet older, for my blood
555 Hath earnest in it of far springs to be.
A tawny pirate anchored in his port,
Whose bark had plundered twenty nameless isles;
And passing one, at the high peep of dawn,
He saw two cities in a thousand boats
560 All fighting for a woman on the sea.
And pushing his black craft among them all,
He lightly scattered theirs and brought her off,
With loss of half his people arrow-slain;
A maid so smooth, so white, so wonderful,
565 They said a light came from her when she moved:
And since the pirate would not yield her up,
The King impaled him for his piracy;
Then made her Queen: but those isle-nurtured eyes
Waged such unwilling though successful war
570 On all the youth, they sickened; councils thinned,
And armies waned, for magnet-like she drew
The rustiest iron of old fighters' hearts;
And beasts themselves would worship; camels knelt
Unbidden, and the brutes of mountain back
575 That carry kings in castles, bowed black knees
Of homage, ringing with their serpent hands,
To make her smile, her golden ankle-bells.
What wonder, being jealous, that he sent
His horns of proclamation out through all
580 The hundred under-kingdoms that he swayed
To find a wizard who might teach the King
Some charm, which being wrought upon the Queen
Might keep her all his own: to such a one
He promised more than ever king has given,
585 A league of mountain full of golden mines,
A province with a hundred miles of coast,
A palace and a princess, all for him:
But on all those who tried and failed, the King

553–97. 'People have tried to discover this legend, but there is no legend
of the kind that I know of' (T.).
558. Gray (p. 149) notes Gray's *Elegy* 98: 'Oft have we seen him at the peep of
dawn'.
576. *serpent hands: anguimanus*, as in Lucretius v 1303.

Pronounced a dismal sentence, meaning by it
590   To keep the list low and pretenders back,
Or like a king, not to be trifled with –
Their heads should moulder on the city gates.
And many tried and failed, because the charm
Of nature in her overbore their own:
595   And many a wizard brow bleached on the walls:
And many weeks a troop of carrion crows
Hung like a cloud above the gateway towers.'

And Vivien breaking in upon him, said:
'I sit and gather honey; yet, methinks,
600   Thy tongue has tript a little: ask thyself.
The lady never made *unwilling* war
With those fine eyes: she had her pleasure in it,
And made her good man jealous with good cause.
And lived there neither dame nor damsel then
605   Wroth at a lover's loss? were all as tame,
I mean, as noble, as the Queen was fair?
Not one to flirt a venom at her eyes,
Or pinch a murderous dust into her drink,
Or make her paler with a poisoned rose?
610   Well, those were not our days: but did they find
A wizard? Tell me, was he like to thee?'

She ceased, and made her lithe arm round his
      neck
Tighten, and then drew back, and let her eyes
Speak for her, glowing on him, like a bride's
615   On her new lord, her own, the first of men.

He answered laughing, 'Nay, not like to me.
At last they found – his foragers for charms –
A little glassy-headed hairless man,
Who lived alone in a great wild on grass;
620   Read but one book, and ever reading grew
So grated down and filed away with thought,
So lean his eyes were monstrous; while the skin
Clung but to crate and basket, ribs and spine.
And since he kept his mind on one sole aim,
625   Nor ever touched fierce wine, nor tasted flesh,
Nor owned a sensual wish, to him the wall
That sunders ghosts and shadow-casting men
Became a crystal, and he saw them through it,

600. *Thy ... thyself*] *1873*; Your ... yourself *1859–70*.
616–48. 'Nor is this a legend to be found' (T.).

And heard their voices talk behind the wall,
630 And learnt their elemental secrets, powers
And forces; often o'er the sun's bright eye
Drew the vast eyelid of an inky cloud,
And lashed it at the base with slanting storm;
Or in the noon of mist and driving rain,
635 When the lake whitened and the pinewood roared,
And the cairned mountain was a shadow, sunned
The world to peace again: here was the man.
And so by force they dragged him to the King.
And then he taught the King to charm the Queen
640 In such-wise, that no man could see her more,
Nor saw she save the King, who wrought the charm,
Coming and going, and she lay as dead,
And lost all use of life: but when the King
Made proffer of the league of golden mines,
645 The province with a hundred miles of coast,
The palace and the princess, that old man
Went back to his old wild, and lived on grass,
And vanished, and his book came down to me.'

And Vivien answered smiling saucily:
650 'Ye have the book: the charm is written in it:
Good: take my counsel: let me know it at once:
For keep it like a puzzle chest in chest,
With each chest locked and padlocked thirty-fold,
And whelm all this beneath as vast a mound
655 As after furious battle turfs the slain
On some wild down above the windy deep,
I yet should strike upon a sudden means
To dig, pick, open, find and read the charm:
Then, if I tried it, who should blame me then?'

660 And smiling as a master smiles at one
That is not of his school, nor any school
But that where blind and naked Ignorance
Delivers brawling judgments, unashamed,
On all things all day long, he answered her:

665 'Thou read the book, my pretty Vivien!
O ay, it is but twenty pages long,

633. *lashed*: 'like an eyelash' (T.).
634-6. A draft of these lines appears as a fragment in *H.Nbk 26*.
647. Gray (p. 53) notes Nebuchadnezzar: 'and he was driven from men, and did eat grass as oxen' (*Daniel* iv 33).
665-81. C. Y. Lang argues 'that the text is the English Constitution. "None

But every page having an ample marge,
And every marge enclosing in the midst
A square of text that looks a little blot,
670   The text no larger than the limbs of fleas;
And every square of text an awful charm,
Writ in a language that has long gone by.
So long, that mountains have arisen since
With cities on their flanks – thou read the book!
675   And every margin scribbled, crost, and crammed
With comment, densest condensation, hard
To mind and eye; but the long sleepless nights
Of my long life have made it easy to me.
And none can read the text, not even I;
680   And none can read the comment but myself;
And in the comment did I find the charm.
O, the results are simple; a mere child
Might use it to the harm of anyone,
And never could undo it: ask no more:
685   For though you should not prove it upon me,
But keep that oath ye sware, ye might, perchance,
Assay it on some one of the Table Round,
And all because ye dream they babble of you.'

And Vivien, frowning in true anger, said:
690   'What dare the full-fed liars say of me?
They ride abroad redressing human wrongs!
They sit with knife in meat and wine in horn!
They bound to holy vows of chastity!
Were I not woman, I could tell a tale.
695   But you are man, you well can understand
The shame that cannot be explained for shame.
Not one of all the drove should touch me: swine!'

can read the text, not even I" – and this is the literal truth, for the English
Constitution (unlike the American, for example) is "the whole body of
common and statutory law of the realm" plus "the knowledge of the
working of the government"'; the commentaries are then Coke, Bacon,
Blackstone, and others, and the 'hairless man' of ll. 618–31 suggests both T.'s
friend James Spedding (who edited Bacon) and Bacon himself (*Tennyson's
Arthurian Psycho-drama*, 1983, pp. 11–12).
665. Thou] *1873*; *You 1859–70.*
674. thou] *1873*; *you 1859–70.*
686. sware] *1873*; *swore 1859–70.*
690] 'The filthy swine! what do they say of me? *MS*. Cp. the published
text with the end of *The Lady of Shalott*, *1832* text: 'The wellfed wits at
Camelot'.

Then answered Merlin careless of her words:
'You breathe but accusation vast and vague,
700 Spleen-born, I think, and proofless. If ye know,
Set up the charge ye know, to stand or fall!'

And Vivien answered frowning wrathfully:
'O ay, what say ye to Sir Valence, him
Whose kinsman left him watcher o'er his wife
705 And two fair babes, and went to distant lands;
Was one year gone, and on returning found
Not two but three? there lay the reckling, one
But one hour old! What said the happy sire?
A seven-months' babe had been a truer gift.
710 Those twelve sweet moons confused his fatherhood.'

Then answered Merlin, 'Nay, I know the tale.
Sir Valence wedded with an outland dame:
Some cause had kept him sundered from his wife: ·
One child they had: it lived with her: she died:
715 His kinsman travelling on his own affair
Was charged by Valence to bring home the child.
He brought, not found it therefore: take the truth.'

'O ay,' said Vivien, 'overtrue a tale.
What say ye then to sweet Sir Sagramore,
720 That ardent man? "to pluck the flower in season,"
So says the song, "I trow it is no treason."
O Master, shall we call him overquick
To crop his own sweet rose before the hour?'

And Merlin answered, 'Overquick art thou
725 To catch a loathly plume fallen from the wing
Of that foul bird of rapine whose whole prey
Is man's good name: he never wronged his bride.
I know the tale. An angry gust of wind
Puffed out his torch among the myriad-roomed
730 And many-corridored complexities
Of Arthur's palace: then he found a door,
And darkling felt the sculptured ornament
That wreathen round it made it seem his own;
And wearied out made for the couch and slept,
735 A stainless man beside a stainless maid;

700. *Letters* i 148 (8 or 9 Jan. 1837) has 'spleen-born', and notes that *OED* cites
Merlin and Vivien.
707. *reckling*: 'the puny infant' (H.T.).
724. *art thou*] *1873*; are you *1859–70*.

And either slept, nor knew of other there;
Till the high dawn piercing the royal rose
In Arthur's casement glimmered chastely down,
Blushing upon them blushing, and at once
740   He rose without a word and parted from her:
But when the thing was blazed about the court,
The brute world howling forced them into bonds,
And as it chanced they are happy, being pure.'

'O ay,' said Vivien, 'that were likely too.
745   What say ye then to fair Sir Percivale
And of the horrid foulness that he wrought,
The saintly youth, the spotless lamb of Christ,
Or some black wether of St Satan's fold.
What, in the precincts of the chapel-yard,
750   Among the knightly brasses of the graves,
.   And by the cold Hic Jacets of the dead!'

And Merlin answered careless of her charge,
'A sober man is Percivale and pure;
But once in life was flustered with new wine,
755   Then paced for coolness in the chapel-yard;
Where one of Satan's shepherdesses caught
And meant to stamp him with her master's mark;
And that he sinned is not believable;
For, look upon his face!—but if he sinned,
760   The sin that practice burns into the blood,
And not the one dark hour which brings remorse,
Will brand us, after, of whose fold we be:
Or else were he, the holy king, whose hymns
Are chanted in the minster, worse than all.
765   But is your spleen frothed out, or have ye more?'

And Vivien answered frowning yet in wrath:
'O ay; what say ye to Sir Lancelot, friend
Traitor or true? that commerce with the Queen,
I ask you, is it clamoured by the child,
770   Or whispered in the corner? do ye know it?'

To which he answered sadly, 'Yea, I know it.
Sir Lancelot went ambassador, at first,
To fetch her, and she watched him from her walls.

763. 'David' (T.).
773–4] 1873, *Imperial Library Edition*; To fetch her, and she took him for the
King; 1859–73.

A rumour runs, she took him for the King,
775 So fixt her fancy on him: let them be.
But have ye no one word of loyal praise
For Arthur, blameless King and stainless man?'

She answered with a low and chuckling laugh:
'Man! is he man at all, who knows and winks?
780 Sees what his fair bride is and does, and winks?
By which the good King means to blind himself,
And blinds himself and all the Table Round
To all the foulness that they work. Myself
Could call him (were it not for womanhood)
785 The pretty, popular name such manhood earns,
Could call him the main cause of all their crime;
Yea, were he not crowned King, coward, and fool.'

Then Merlin to his own heart, loathing, said:
'O true and tender! O my liege and King!
790 O selfless man and stainless gentleman,
Who wouldst against thine own eye-witness fain
Have all men true and leal, all women pure;
How, in the mouths of base interpreters,
From over-fineness not intelligible
795 To things with every sense as false and foul
As the poached filth that floods the middle street,
Is thy white blamelessness accounted blame!'

But Vivien, deeming Merlin overborne
By instance, recommenced, and let her tongue
800 Rage like a fire among the noblest names,
Polluting, and imputing her whole self,
Defaming and defacing, till she left
Not even Lancelot brave, nor Galahad clean.

Her words had issue other than she willed.
805 He dragged his eyebrow bushes down, and made
A snowy penthouse for his hollow eyes,
And muttered in himself, 'Tell *her* the charm!
So, if she had it, would she rail on me
To snare the next, and if she have it not

775. them] *1873*; him *1859–70.*
775 ∧ 6] There yet is nothing proved against the Queen. *HnMS.*
779. Man!] *1873*; Him? *1859–70.*
796. *poached*: trampled into mire.
806. Cp. Coleridge, *The Raven* 25: 'His brow, like a pent-house, hung over his eyes.'

810 So will she rail. What did the wanton say?
"Not mount as high;" we scarce can sink as low:
For men at most differ as Heaven and earth,
But women, worst and best, as Heaven and Hell.
I know the Table Round, my friends of old;
815 All brave, and many generous, and some chaste.
She cloaks the scar of some repulse with lies;
I well believe she tempted them and failed,
Being so bitter: for fine plots may fail,
Though harlots paint their talk as well as face
820 With colours of the heart that are not theirs.
I will not let her know: nine tithes of times
Face-flatterer and backbiter are the same.
And they, sweet soul, that most impute a crime
Are pronest to it, and impute themselves,
825 Wanting the mental range; or low desire
Not to feel lowest makes them level all;
Yea, they would pare the mountain to the plain,
To leave an equal baseness; and in this
Are harlots like the crowd, that if they find
830 Some stain or blemish in a name of note,
Not grieving that their greatest are so small,
Inflate themselves with some insane delight,
And judge all nature from her feet of clay,
Without the will to lift their eyes, and see
835 Her godlike head crowned with spiritual fire,
And touching other worlds. I am weary of her.'

He spoke in words part heard, in whispers part,
Half-suffocated in the hoary fell
And many-wintered fleece of throat and chin.
840 But Vivien, gathering somewhat of his mood,
And hearing 'harlot' muttered twice or thrice,
Leapt from her session on his lap, and stood
Stiff as a viper frozen; loathsome sight,
How from the rosy lips of life and love,
845 Flashed the bare-grinning skeleton of death!
White was her cheek; sharp breaths of anger puffed

---

811 ∧ 2] Tact, craft and malice working to one end – *H.Nbk 31.*
816] *1873*; I think she cloaks the wounds of loss with lies; *1859–70.*
817. well] *1873*; do *1859–70.*
818. Being] *1873*; She is *1859–70.*
822. Face-flatterer and backbiter] *1873*; Face-flatterers and back-biters
1859–70.

Her fairy nostril out; her hand half-clenched
Went faltering sideways downward to her belt,
And feeling; had she found a dagger there
850 (For in a wink the false love turns to hate)
She would have stabbed him; but she found it not:
His eye was calm, and suddenly she took
To bitter weeping like a beaten child,
A long, long weeping, not consolable.
855 Then her false voice made way, broken with sobs:

'O crueller than was ever told in tale,
Or sung in song! O vainly lavished love!
O cruel, there was nothing wild or strange,
Or seeming shameful—for what shame in love,
860 So love be true, and not as yours is—nothing
Poor Vivien had not done to win his trust
Who called her what he called her—all her crime,
All—all—the wish to prove him wholly hers.'

She mused a little, and then clapt her hands
865 Together with a wailing shriek, and said:
'Stabbed through the heart's affections to the heart!
Seethed like the kid in its own mother's milk!
Killed with a word worse than a life of blows!
I thought that he was gentle, being great:
870 O God, that I had loved a smaller man!
I should have found in him a greater heart.
O, I, that flattering my true passion, saw
The knights, the court, the King, dark in your
      light,
Who loved to make men darker than they are,
875 Because of that high pleasure which I had
To seat you sole upon my pedestal
Of worship—I am answered, and henceforth
The course of life that seemed so flowery to me
With you for guide and master, only you,
880 Becomes the sea-cliff pathway broken short,
And ending in a ruin—nothing left,
But into some low cave to crawl, and there,
If the wolf spare me, weep my life away,
Killed with inutterable unkindliness.'

885 She paused, she turned away, she hung her head,
The snake of gold slid from her hair, the braid

867. *Exodus* xxiii 19: 'Thou shalt not seethe a kid in his mother's milk.'

Slipt and uncoiled itself, she wept afresh,
And the dark wood grew darker toward the storm
In silence, while his anger slowly died
890 Within him, till he let his wisdom go
For ease of heart, and half believed her true:
Called her to shelter in the hollow oak,
'Come from the storm,' and having no reply,
Gazed at the heaving shoulder, and the face
895 Hand-hidden, as for utmost grief or shame;
Then thrice essayed, by tenderest-touching terms,
To sleek her ruffled peace of mind, in vain.
At last she let herself be conquered by him,
And as the cageling newly flown returns,
900 The seeming-injured simple-hearted thing
Came to her old perch back, and settled there.
There while she sat, half-falling from his knees,
Half-nestled at his heart, and since he saw
The slow tear creep from her closed eyelid yet,
905 About her, more in kindness than in love,
The gentle wizard cast a shielding arm.
But she dislinked herself at once and rose,
Her arms upon her breast across, and stood,
A virtuous gentlewoman deeply wronged,
910 Upright and flushed before him: then she said:

'There must be now no passages of love
Betwixt us twain henceforward evermore;
Since, if I be what I am grossly called,
What should be granted which your own gross heart
915 Would reckon worth the taking? I will go.
In truth, but one thing now – better have died
Thrice than have asked it once – could make me stay –
That proof of trust – so often asked in vain!
How justly, after that vile term of yours,
920 I find with grief! I might believe you then,
Who knows? once more. Lo! what was once to me
Mere matter of the fancy, now hath grown
The vast necessity of heart and life.

891] He, where the current ran so low that even
     Dim eyes could see the bottom, let his will
     Drift and looked on and half believed her true
                                        H.MS (Amy Lowell 1827.12)

921. Lo!] 1873; O, 1859–70.
922. hath] 1873; has 1859–70.

Farewell; think gently of me, for I fear
925 My fate or folly, passing gayer youth
For one so old, must be to love thee still.
But ere I leave thee let me swear once more
That if I schemed against thy peace in this,
May yon just heaven, that darkens o'er me, send
930 One flash, that, missing all things else, may make
My scheming brain a cinder, if I lie.'

Scarce had she ceased, when out of heaven a bolt
(For now the storm was close above them) struck,
Furrowing a giant oak, and javelining
935 With darted spikes and splinters of the wood
The dark earth round. He raised his eyes and saw
The tree that shone white-listed through the gloom.
But Vivien, fearing heaven had heard her oath,
And dazzled by the livid-flickering fork,
940 And deafened with the stammering cracks and claps
That followed, flying back and crying out,
'O Merlin, though you do not love me, save,
Yet save me!' clung to him and hugged him close;
And called him dear protector in her fright,
945 Nor yet forgot her practice in her fright,
But wrought upon his mood and hugged him close.
The pale blood of the wizard at her touch
Took gayer colours, like an opal warmed.
She blamed herself for telling hearsay tales:
950 She shook from fear, and for her fault she wept
Of petulancy; she called him lord and liege,
Her seer, her bard, her silver star of eve,
Her God, her Merlin, the one passionate love
Of her whole life; and ever overhead
955 Bellowed the tempest, and the rotten branch
Snapt in the rushing of the river-rain
Above them; and in change of glare and gloom
Her eyes and neck glittering.went and came;
Till now the storm, its burst of passion spent,
960 Moaning and calling out of other lands,
Had left the ravaged woodland yet once more
To peace; and what should not have been had been,

924. *gently*] *1873*; kindly *1859–70*.
925. *folly, passing*] *1873*; fault, omitting *1859–70*.
926, 927. *thee*] *1873*; you *1859–70*.
928. *thy*] *1873*; your *1859–70*.
937. *white-listed*: 'striped with white' (T.).

For Merlin, overtalked and overworn,
Had yielded, told her all the charm, and slept.

965   Then, in one moment, she put forth the charm
Of woven paces and of waving hands,
And in the hollow oak he lay as dead,
And lost to life and use and name and fame.

Then crying 'I have made his glory mine,'
970   And shrieking out 'O fool!' the harlot leapt
Adown the forest, and the thicket closed
Behind her, and the forest echoed 'fool.'

470 Lancelot and Elaine

Published *1859* as *Elaine* (the final title in *1870* ['*1869*']). 'Begun ... in July 1858' (H.T.). Thomas Woolner wrote to T.'s wife Emily, 7 June 1858: 'I most earnestly wish you could persuade him to do the *Maid of Astolat*' (A. Woolner, *Thomas Woolner*, 1917, p. 149). She wrote, 15 Feb. 1859 (p. 163): '*The Maid of Astolat* is quite finished now, all but last touches.' Cp. *The Lady of Shalott (p. 18)*. 'The tenderest of all natures sinks under the blight, that which is of the highest in her working her doom' (T.). The source is Malory xviii 9–20, beginning: 'This old baron had a daughter at that time, that was called the fair maid of Astolat, and ever she beheld sir Launcelot wonderfully; and she cast such a love unto sir Launcelot, that she could not withdraw her love, wherefore she died; and her name was Elaine la Blaunch.' M. G. Wiebe discusses a trial printing of *Elaine* and *Guinevere* (*The Maid of Astolat; British Library*), which 'must be regarded as forming the second half of the 1857 trial printing' (and not, as Pfordresher describes it, as proofs); Wiebe shows that changes from the trial edition often are 'concerned to capture the full range of nuances of personalities and the interplay between them' (*Book Collector* xxiii, 1974, 355–60).

Elaine the fair, Elaine the loveable,
Elaine, the lily maid of Astolat,
High in her chamber up a tower to the east
Guarded the sacred shield of Lancelot;
5   Which first she placed where morning's earliest ray
Might strike it, and awake her with the gleam;
Then fearing rust or soilure fashioned for it
A case of silk, and braided thereupon
All the devices blazoned on the shield
10   In their own tint, and added, of her wit,
A border fantasy of branch and flower,

And yellow-throated nestling in the nest.
Nor rested thus content, but day by day,
Leaving her household and good father, climbed
15 That eastern tower, and entering barred her door,
Stript off the case, and read the naked shield,
Now guessed a hidden meaning in his arms,
Now made a pretty history to herself
Of every dint a sword had beaten in it,
20 And every scratch a lance had made upon it,
Conjecturing when and where: this cut is fresh;
That ten years back; this dealt him at Caerlyle;
That at Caerleon; this at Camelot:
And ah God's mercy, what a stroke was there!
25 And here a thrust that might have killed, but God
Broke the strong lance, and rolled his enemy down,
And saved him: so she lived in fantasy.

How came the lily maid by that good shield
Of Lancelot, she that knew not even his name?
30 He left it with her, when he rode to tilt
For the great diamond in the diamond jousts,
Which Arthur had ordained, and by that name
Had named them, since a diamond was the prize.

For Arthur, long before they crowned him King,
35 Roving the trackless realms of Lyonnesse,
Had found a glen, gray boulder and black tarn.
A horror lived about the tarn, and clave
Like its own mists to all the mountain side:
For here two brothers, one a king, had met
40 And fought together; but their names were lost;
And each had slain his brother at a blow;
And down they fell and made the glen abhorred:
And there they lay till all their bones were bleached,
And lichened into colour with the crags:
45 And he, that once was king, had on a crown
Of diamonds, one in front, and four aside.
And Arthur came, and labouring up the pass,

¶470. 34] *1870* ('*1869*');
        For Arthur when none knew from whence he came,
        Long ere the people chose him for their king, *1859–69*
35. *Lyonnesse*: 'A land that is said to have stretched between Land's End
and Scilly, and to have contained some of Cornwall as well' (T.).
39–55. This episode is not in Malory.
45. *he . . . was*] *1862*; one of these, the *1859–61*.

All in a misty moonshine, unawares
Had trodden that crowned skeleton, and the skull
50   Brake from the nape, and from the skull the crown
Rolled into light, and turning on its rims
Fled like a glittering rivulet to the tarn:
And down the shingly scaur he plunged, and caught,
And set it on his head, and in his heart
55   Heard murmurs, 'Lo, thou likewise shalt be King.'

Thereafter, when a King, he had the gems
Plucked from the crown, and showed them to his
     knights,
Saying, 'These jewels, whereupon I chanced
Divinely, are the kingdom's, not the King's—
60   For public use: henceforward let there be,
Once every year, a joust for one of these:
For so by nine years' proof we needs must learn
Which is our mightiest, and ourselves shall grow
In use of arms and manhood, till we drive
65   The heathen, who, some say, shall rule the land
Hereafter, which God hinder.' Thus he spoke:
And eight years past, eight jousts had been, and still
Had Lancelot won the diamond of the year,
With purpose to present them to the Queen,
70   When all were won; but meaning all at once
To snare her royal fancy with a boon
Worth half her realm, had never spoken word.

Now for the central diamond and the last
And largest, Arthur, holding then his court
75   Hard on the river nigh the place which now
Is this world's hugest, let proclaim a joust
At Camelot, and when the time drew nigh
Spake (for she had been sick) to Guinevere,
'Are you so sick, my Queen, you cannot move

53. *scaur*: 'precipitous bank', variant of scar (*OED*, from 1805, Scott).
79–83. Malory xviii 8: 'So king Arthur made him ready to depart to these jousts and would have had the queen with him, but at that time she would not go she said, for she was sick, and might not ride at that time. "Then me repenteth," said the king, "for these seven years ye saw not such a fellowship together, except at Whitsuntide, when sir Galahad departed from the court." – "Truly," said the queen unto the king, "ye must hold me excused, I may not be there, and that me repenteth." And many deemed that the queen would [not] be there, because of sir Launcelot du Lake, for sir Launcelot would not ride with the king, for he said that he was not whole

80   To these fair jousts?' 'Yea, lord,' she said, 'ye know it.'
'Then will ye miss,' he answered, 'the great deeds
Of Lancelot, and his prowess in the lists,
A sight ye love to look on.' And the Queen
Lifted her eyes, and they dwelt languidly
85   On Lancelot, where he stood beside the King.
He thinking that he read her meaning there,
'Stay with me, I am sick; my love is more
Than many diamonds,' yielded; and a heart
Love-loyal to the least wish of the Queen
90   (However much he yearned to make complete
The tale of diamonds for his destined boon)
Urged him to speak against the truth, and say,
'Sir King, mine ancient wound is hardly whole,
And lets me from the saddle;' and the King
95   Glanced first at him, then her, and went his way.
No sooner gone than suddenly she began:

    'To blame, my lord Sir Lancelot, much to blame!
Why go ye not to these fair jousts? the knights
Are half of them our enemies, and the crowd
100   Will murmur, "Lo the shameless ones, who take
Their pastime now the trustful King is gone!"'
Then Lancelot vext at having lied in vain:
'Are ye so wise? ye were not once so wise,
My Queen, that summer, when ye loved me first.
105   Then of the crowd ye took no more account
Than of the myriad cricket of the mead,
When its own voice clings to each blade of grass,
And every voice is nothing. As to knights,
Them surely can I silence with all ease.

of the wound, the which sir Mador had given him.'
80. ye] *1870* ('*1869*'); you *1859–69*. Likewise in ll. 81, 83, 98, 103–5, 135, 154,
197–8, 222, 227–8, 574, 657, 675–6, 711–12, 750, 763, 792, 910, 955, 1030,
1032–3, 1035, 1038, 1055, 1057, 1104, 1300, 1383.
91. tale: tally.
94. lets: hinders.
97–101. Malory xviii 8: '"Sir Launcelot, ye are greatly to blame, thus to
hold you behind my lord; what trow ye what your enemies and mine will
say and deem? nought else but see how sir Launcelot holdeth him ever
behind the king, and so doth the queen, for that they would have their
pleasure together, and thus they will say," said the queen unto sir
Launcelot.'
103–4. Malory xviii 9: '"Madam," said sir Launcelot to the queen, "I
allow your wit, it is of late come sith ye were wise."'

110   But now my loyal worship is allowed
      Of all men: many a bard, without offence,
      Has linked our names together in his lay,
      Lancelot, the flower of bravery, Guinevere,
      The pearl of beauty: and our knights at feast
115   Have pledged us in this union, while the King
      Would listen smiling. How then? is there more?
      Has Arthur spoken aught? or would yourself,
      Now weary of my service and devoir,
      Henceforth be truer to your faultless lord?'

120   She broke into a little scornful laugh:
      'Arthur, my lord, Arthur, the faultless King,
      That passionate perfection, my good lord—
      But who can gaze upon the Sun in heaven?
      He never spake word of reproach to me,
125   He never had a glimpse of mine untruth,
      He cares not for me: only here today
      There gleamed a vague suspicion in his eyes:
      Some meddling rogue has tampered with him—else
      Rapt in this fancy of his Table Round,
130   And swearing men to vows impossible,
      To make them like himself: but, friend, to me
      He is all fault who hath no fault at all:
      For who loves me must have a touch of earth;
      The low sun makes the colour: I am yours,
135   Not Arthur's, as ye know, save by the bond.
      And therefore hear my words: go to the jousts:
      The tiny-trumpeting gnat can break our dream
      When sweetest; and the vermin voices here
      May buzz so loud—we scorn them, but they sting.'

140   Then answered Lancelot, the chief of knights:
      'And with what face, after my pretext made,
      Shall I appear, O Queen, at Camelot, I
      Before a King who honours his own word,
      As if it were his God's?'

123 ∧ 4] He hath all faults who hath no fault at all. *Virginia MS, deleted.*
134. The colours of sunrise and sunset.
140–57. Malory xviii 9: '"But, wit ye well," said sir Launcelot unto queen Guenever, "that at those jousts I will be against the king and all his fellowship."—"Ye may there do as ye list," said queen Guenever, "but by my counsel ye shall not be against your king and your fellowship, for therein are many hardy knights of your blood."'

                              'Yea,' said the Queen,
145   'A moral child without the craft to rule,
        Else had he not lost me: but listen to me,
        If I must find you wit: we hear it said
        That men go down before your spear at a touch,
        But knowing you are Lancelot; your great name,
150   This conquers: hide it therefore; go unknown:
        Win! by this kiss you will: and our true King
        Will then allow your pretext, O my knight,
        As all for glory; for to speak him true,
        Ye know right well, how meek soe'er he seem,
155   No keener hunter after glory breathes.
        He loves it in his knights more than himself:
        They prove to him his work: win and return.'

            Then got Sir Lancelot suddenly to horse,
        Wroth at himself. Not willing to be known,
160   He left the barren-beaten thoroughfare,
        Chose the green path that showed the rarer foot,
        And there among the solitary downs,
        Full often lost in fancy, lost his way;
        Till as he traced a faintly-shadowed track,
165   That all in loops and links among the dales
        Ran to the Castle of Astolat, he saw
        Fired from the west, far on a hill, the towers.
        Thither he made, and blew the gateway horn.
        Then came an old, dumb, myriad-wrinkled man,
170   Who let him into lodging and disarmed.
        And Lancelot marvelled at the wordless man;
        And issuing found the Lord of Astolat
        With two strong sons, Sir Torre and Sir Lavaine,
        Moving to meet him in the castle court;
175   And close behind them stept the lily maid
        Elaine, his daughter: mother of the house
        There was not: some light jest among them rose
        With laughter dying down as the great knight
        Approached them: then the Lord of Astolat:
180   'Whence comest thou, my guest, and by what name
        Livest between the lips? for by thy state
        And presence I might guess thee chief of those,
        After the King, who eat in Arthur's halls.

168. blew] *1873*; wound *1859–70*.
180–1. An epic formula, as in *Aeneid* xii 235. Cp. *The Gardener's Daughter*
49–50: 'Among us lived / Her fame from lip to lip.'

Him have I seen: the rest, his Table Round,
185 Known as they are, to me they are unknown.'

Then answered Lancelot, the chief of knights:
'Known am I, and of Arthur's hall, and known,
What I by mere mischance have brought, my shield.
But since I go to joust as one unknown
190 At Camelot for the diamond, ask me not,
Hereafter ye shall know me – and the shield –
I pray you lend me one, if such you have,
Blank, or at least with some device not mine.'

Then said the Lord of Astolat, 'Here is Torre's:
195 Hurt in his first tilt was my son, Sir Torre.
And so, God wot, his shield is blank enough.
His ye can have.' Then added plain Sir Torre,
'Yea, since I cannot use it, ye may have it.'
Here laughed the father saying, 'Fie, Sir Churl,
200 Is that an answer for a noble knight?
Allow him! but Lavaine, my younger here,
He is so full of lustihood, he will ride,
Joust for it, and win, and bring it in an hour,
And set it in this damsel's golden hair,
205 To make her thrice as wilful as before.'

'Nay, father, nay good father, shame me not
Before this noble knight,' said young Lavaine,
'For nothing. Surely I but played on Torre:
He seemed so sullen, vext he could not go:
210 A jest, no more! for, knight, the maiden dreamt
That some one put this diamond in her hand,
And that it was too slippery to be held,
And slipt and fell into some pool or stream,
The castle-well, belike; and then I said
215 That *if* I went and *if* I fought and won it
(But all was jest and joke among ourselves)
Then must she keep it safelier. All was jest.
But, father, give me leave, an if he will,
To ride to Camelot with this noble knight:
220 Win shall I not, but do my best to win:
Young as I am, yet would I do my best.'

188. The borrowing of the shield is in Malory.
191. ye] *1873;* you *1859–70.* Likewise in ll. 546, 665, 695, 766, 966.
210–13. 'A vision prophetic of Guinevere hurling the diamonds into the
Thames' (T.).

'So ye will grace me,' answered Lancelot,
Smiling a moment, 'with your fellowship
O'er these waste downs whereon I lost myself,
225 Then were I glad of you as guide and friend:
And you shall win this diamond, – as I hear
It is a fair large diamond, – if ye may,
And yield it to this maiden, if ye will.'
'A fair large diamond,' added plain Sir Torre,
230 'Such be for queens, and not for simple maids.'
Then she, who held her eyes upon the ground,
Elaine, and heard her name so tost about,
Flushed slightly at the slight disparagement
Before the stranger knight, who, looking at her,
235 Full courtly, yet not falsely, thus returned:
'If what is fair be but for what is fair,
And only queens are to be counted so,
Rash were my judgment then, who deem this maid
Might wear as fair a jewel as is on earth,
240 Not violating the bond of like to like.'

He spoke and ceased: the lily maid Elaine,
Won by the mellow voice before she looked,
Lifted her eyes, and read his lineaments.
The great and guilty love he bare the Queen,
245 In battle with the love he bare his lord,
Had marred his face, and marked it ere his time.
Another sinning on such heights with one,
The flower of all the west and all the world,
Had been the sleeker for it: but in him
250 His mood was often like a fiend, and rose
And drove him into wastes and solitudes
For agony, who was yet a living soul.
Marred as he was, he seemed the goodliest man
That ever among ladies ate in hall,
255 And noblest, when she lifted up her eyes.
However marred, of more than twice her years,

243. Gray (p. 52, noting also ll. 255, 258): 'echoes a powerfully expectant Biblical expression, for example "Lot lifted up his eyes and beheld all the plain of Jordan"'.
249–52. Cp. *Luke* viii 29: 'For he had commanded the unclean spirit to come out of the man. For oftentimes it had caught him: and he was kept bound with chains and in fetters; and he brake the bands, and was driven of the devil into the wilderness.'
255. Gray (p. 22) notes T.'s 'use of a Biblical expression to convey expectation', e.g. *Genesis* xiii 10.

Seamed with an ancient swordcut on the cheek,
And bruised and bronzed, she lifted up her eyes
And loved him, with that love which was her doom.

260   Then the great knight, the darling of the court,
Loved of the loveliest, into that rude hall
Stept with all grace, and not with half disdain
Hid under grace, as in a smaller time,
But kindly man moving among his kind:
265   Whom they with meats and vintage of their best
And talk and minstrel melody entertained.
And much they asked of court and Table Round,
And ever well and readily answered he:
But Lancelot, when they glanced at Guinevere,
270   Suddenly speaking of the wordless man,
Heard from the Baron that, ten years before,
The heathen caught and reft him of his tongue.
'He learnt and warned me of their fierce design
Against my house, and him they caught and maimed;
275   But I, my sons, and little daughter fled
From bonds or death, and dwelt among the woods
By the great river in a boatman's hut.
Dull days were those, till our good Arthur broke
The Pagan yet once more on Badon hill.'

280   'O there, great lord, doubtless,' Lavaine said, rapt
By all the sweet and sudden passion of youth
Toward greatness in its elder, 'you have fought.
O tell us—for we live apart—you know
Of Arthur's glorious wars.' And Lancelot spoke
285   And answered him at full, as having been
With Arthur in the fight which all day long
Rang by the white mouth of the violent Glem;
And in the four loud battles by the shore
Of Duglas; that on Bassa; then the war
290   That thundered in and out the gloomy skirts
Of Celidon the forest; and again
By castle Gurnion, where the glorious King
Had on his cuirass worn our Lady's Head,

286–302. H.T. quotes from Nennius the account of these battles. On T.'s
modifications, see J. M. Gray, *Notes and Queries* ccxi (1966) 341–2. (H.T., it
should be added, was indebted to F. J. Rowe's edn of the poem in 1895,
p. 57.) Also Gray (pp. 48–50).
288. loud] 1873; wild 1859–70.
293. In Nennius, the tradition was that Arthur bore the image of the Virgin
Mary upon his shoulders (usually it was upon his shield). For the 'cuirass'

Carved of one emerald centered in a sun
295   Of silver rays, that lightened as he breathed;
And at Caerleon had he helped his lord,
When the strong neighings of the wild white Horse
Set every gilded parapet shuddering;
And up in Agned-Cathregonion too,
300   And down the waste sand-shores of Trath Treroit,
Where many a heathen fell; 'and on the mount
Of Badon I myself beheld the King
Charge at the head of all his Table Round,
And all his legions crying Christ and him,
305   And break them; and I saw him, after, stand
High on a heap of slain, from spur to plume
Red as the rising sun with heathen blood,
And seeing me, with a great voice he cried,
"They are broken, they are broken!" for the King,
310   However mild he seems at home, nor cares
For triumph in our mimic wars, the jousts—
For if his own knight cast him down, he laughs
Saying, his knights are better men than he—
Yet in this heathen war the fire of God
315   Fills him: I never saw his like: there lives
No greater leader.'

                While he uttered this,
Low to her own heart said the lily maid,
'Save your great self, fair lord;' and when he fell
From talk of war to traits of pleasantry—
320   Being mirthful he, but in a stately kind—
She still took note that when the living smile
Died from his lips, across him came a cloud
Of melancholy severe, from which again,
Whenever in her hovering to and fro
325   The lily maid had striven to make him cheer,
There brake a sudden-beaming tenderness
Of manners and of nature: and she thought
That all was nature, all, perchance, for her.
And all night long his face before her lived,

(breastplate), cp. *Faerie Queene* I vii st.29–30: 'Athwart his brest a bauldrick
brave he ware, / That shynd, like twinkling stars, with stons most pretious
rare. // And in the midst thereof one pretious stone / Of wondrous worth,
and eke of wondrous mights, / Shapt like a Ladies head, exceeding shone.'
297. The emblem of the Saxons was a white horse.

320 ∧ 1] Not double-sided in a decent phrase
             Nor dipping into mud for graceless tales *Virginia MS*

330   As when a painter, poring on a face,
Divinely through all hindrance finds the man
Behind it, and so paints him that his face,
The shape and colour of a mind and life,
Lives for his children, ever at its best

335   And fullest; so the face before her lived,
Dark-splendid, speaking in the silence, full
Of noble things, and held her from her sleep.
Till rathe she rose, half-cheated in the thought
She needs must bid farewell to sweet Lavaine.

340   First as in fear, step after step, she stole
Down the long tower-stairs, hesitating:
Anon, she heard Sir Lancelot cry in the court,
'This shield, my friend, where is it?' and Lavaine
Past inward, as she came from out the tower.

345   There to his proud horse Lancelot turned, and smoothed
The glossy shoulder, humming to himself.
Half-envious of the flattering hand, she drew
Nearer and stood. He looked, and more amazed
Than if seven men had set upon him, saw

350   The maiden standing in the dewy light.
He had not dreamed she was so beautiful.
Then came on him a sort of sacred fear,
For silent, though he greeted her, she stood
Rapt on his face as if it were a God's.

355   Suddenly flashed on her a wild desire,
That he should wear her favour at the tilt.
She braved a riotous heart in asking for it.

338. rathe: 'early' (T.).

341. '"Stairs" is to be read as a monosyllable, with a pause after it' (T.).
H.T. quotes James Spedding: 'The art with which A.T. has represented
Elaine's action by the slow and lingering movement, the sudden arrest,
and the hesitating advance of the metre, has been altogether lost on some
critics.'

355–82. Malory xviii 9: 'So thus as she came to and fro, she was so hot in
her love, that she thought sir Launcelot should wear upon him at the jousts
a token of her's. "Fair damsel," said sir Launcelot, "and if I grant you that,
ye may say I do more for your love than ever I did for lady or damsel."
Then he remembered him that he would ride unto the jousts disguised,
and for because he had never before that time borne no manner of token
of no damsel; then he bethought him that he would bear one of her's,
that none of his blood thereby might know him. And then he said, "fair
damsel, I will grant you to wear a token of yours upon my helmet; and,
therefore, what it is, shew me."–"Sir," said she, "it is a red sleeve of mine
of scarlet, well embroidered with great pearls"; and so she brought it him.

'Fair lord, whose name I know not–noble it is,
I well believe, the noblest–will you wear
360 My favour at this tourney?' 'Nay,' said he,
'Fair lady, since I never yet have worn
Favour of any lady in the lists.
Such is my wont, as those, who know me, know.'
'Yea, so,' she answered; 'then in wearing mine
365 Needs must be lesser likelihood, noble lord,
That those who know should know you.' And he turned
Her counsel up and down within his mind,
And found it true, and answered, 'True, my child.
Well, I will wear it: fetch it out to me:
370 What is it?' and she told him 'A red sleeve
Broidered with pearls,' and brought it: then he bound
Her token on his helmet, with a smile
Saying, 'I never yet have done so much
For any maiden living,' and the blood
375 Sprang to her face and filled her with delight;
But left her all the paler, when Lavaine
Returning brought the yet-unblazoned shield,
His brother's; which he gave to Lancelot,
Who parted with his own to fair Elaine:
380 'Do me this grace, my child, to have my shield
In keeping till I come.' 'A grace to me,'
She answered, 'twice today. I am your squire!'
Whereat Lavaine said, laughing, 'Lily maid,
For fear our people call you lily maid
385 In earnest, let me bring your colour back;
Once, twice, and thrice: now get you hence to bed:'
So kissed her, and Sir Lancelot his own hand,
And thus they moved away: she stayed a minute,
Then made a sudden step to the gate, and there–
390 Her bright hair blown about the serious face
Yet rosy-kindled with her brother's kiss–
Paused by the gateway, standing near the shield
In silence, while she watched their arms far-off
Sparkle, until they dipt below the downs.

So sir Launcelot received it and said, "Never or this time did I so much for
no damsel." And then sir Launcelot betook the fair damsel his shield in
keeping, and prayed her to keep it until he came again. And so that night
he had merry rest and great cheer, for ever the fair damsel Elaine was about
sir Launcelot all the while that she might be suffered.'

392. by . . . near] 1873; in . . . by 1859-70.

395   Then to her tower she climbed, and took the shield,
There kept it, and so lived in fantasy.

Meanwhile the new companions past away
Far o'er the long backs of the bushless downs,
To where Sir Lancelot knew there lived a knight
400   Not far from Camelot, now for forty years
A hermit, who had prayed, laboured and prayed,
And ever labouring had scooped himself
In the white rock a chapel and a hall
On massive columns, like a shorecliff cave,
405   And cells and chambers: all were fair and dry;
The green light from the meadows underneath
Struck up and lived along the milky roofs;
And in the meadows tremulous aspen-trees
And poplars made a noise of falling showers.
410   And thither wending there that night they bode.

But when the next day broke from underground,
And shot red fire and shadows through the cave,
They rose, heard mass, broke fast, and rode away:
Then Lancelot saying, 'Hear, but hold my name
415   Hidden, you ride with Lancelot of the Lake,'
Abashed Lavaine, whose instant reverence,
Dearer to true young hearts than their own praise,
But left him leave to stammer, 'Is it indeed?'
And after muttering 'The great Lancelot,'
420   At last he got his breath and answered, 'One,
One have I seen – that other, our liege lord,
The dread Pendragon, Britain's King of kings,
Of whom the people talk mysteriously,
He will be there – then were I stricken blind
425   That minute, I might say that I had seen.'

So spake Lavaine, and when they reached the
     lists
By Camelot in the meadow, let his eyes
Run through the peopled gallery which half round
Lay like a rainbow fallen upon the grass,
430   Until they found the clear-faced King, who sat
Robed in red samite, easily to be known,
Since to his crown the golden dragon clung,
And down his robe the dragon writhed in gold,
And from the carven-work behind him crept
435   Two dragons gilded, sloping down to make
Arms for his chair, while all the rest of them
Through knots and loops and folds innumerable

Fled ever through the woodwork, till they found
The new design wherein they lost themselves,
440 Yet with all ease, so tender was the work:
And, in the costly canopy o'er him set,
Blazed the last diamond of the nameless king.

Then Lancelot answered young Lavaine and said,
'Me you call great: mine is the firmer seat,
445 The truer lance: but there is many a youth
Now crescent, who will come to all I am
And overcome it; and in me there dwells
No greatness, save it be some far-off touch
Of greatness to know well I am not great:
450 There is the man.' And Lavaine gaped upon him
As on a thing miraculous, and anon
The trumpets blew; and then did either side,
They that assailed, and they that held the lists,
Set lance in rest, strike spur, suddenly move,
455 Meet in the midst, and there so furiously
Shock, that a man far-off might well perceive,
If any man that day were left afield,
The hard earth shake, and a low thunder of arms.
And Lancelot bode a little, till he saw
460 Which were the weaker; then he hurled into it
Against the stronger: little need to speak
Of Lancelot in his glory! King, duke, earl,
Count, baron—whom he smote, he overthrew.

But in the field were Lancelot's kith and kin,
465 Ranged with the Table Round that held the lists,
Strong men, and wrathful that a stranger knight
Should do and almost overdo the deeds
Of Lancelot; and one said to the other, 'Lo!

447–50. T. said, 'When I wrote that, I was thinking of Wordsworth and myself' (*Tennyson and His Friends*, p. 210).

462–3. Gray (p. 46): 'this stems from an incidental list in Malory: "and there was a great press of kings, dukes, earls, and barons, and many noble knights". T. has omitted the last item, and inserted one of his own: "count", which is the European equivalent of "earl" ... These jousts may be international, but Lancelot is supreme champion'.

468–74. Malory xviii 11: '"O mercy, Jesu," said sir Gawaine, "what knight is that I see yonder, that doth so marvellous deeds of arms in the fields?"—"I wot well who is that," said king Arthur, "but all this time I will not name him."—"Sir," said sir Gawaine, "I would say it were sir Launcelot, by the riding, and by his buffets that I see him deal. But always

What is he? I do not mean the force alone –
470 The grace and versatility of the man!
Is it not Lancelot?' 'When has Lancelot worn
Favour of any lady in the lists?
Not such his wont, as we, that know him, know.'
'How then? who then?' a fury seized them all,
475 A fiery family passion for the name
Of Lancelot, and a glory one with theirs.
They couched their spears and pricked their steeds,
        and thus,
Their plumes driven backward by the wind they
        made
In moving, all together down upon him
480 Bare, as a wild wave in the wide North-sea,
Green-glimmering toward the summit, bears, with all
Its stormy crests that smoke against the skies,
Down on a bark, and overbears the bark,
And him that helms it, so they overbore
485 Sir Lancelot and his charger, and a spear
Down-glancing lamed the charger, and a spear
Pricked sharply his own cuirass, and the head
Pierced through his side, and there snapt, and
        remained.

Then Sir Lavaine did well and worshipfully;
490 He bore a knight of old repute to the earth,
And brought his horse to Lancelot where he lay.
He up the side, sweating with agony, got,
But thought to do while he might yet endure,
And being lustily holpen by the rest,
495 His party, – though it seemed half-miracle
To those he fought with, – drave his kith and kin,
And all the Table Round that held the lists,
Back to the barrier; then the trumpets blew

me seemeth it should not be he, because he beareth the red sleeve upon the
helm, for I wist him never yet bear token at no jousts of lady or gentle-
woman."–"Let him be," said king Arthur, "for he will be better known,
and do more, or he depart."'
474. *them all*] *1873*; on them *1859–70*.
480–3. 'Seen on a voyage of mine to Norway' (T.). H.T. quotes a letter
by T., 24 July 1858: 'the green sea looking like a mountainous country,
far-off waves with foam at the top looking like snowy mountains bounding
the scene; one great wave, green-shining, past with all its crests smoking
high up beside the vessel.'
498. *trumpets*] *1873*; heralds *1859–70*.

Proclaiming his the prize, who wore the sleeve
500 Of scarlet, and the pearls; and all the knights,
His party, cried 'Advance and take thy prize
The diamond;' but he answered, 'Diamond me
No diamonds! for God's love, a little air!
Prize me no prizes, for my prize is death!
505 Hence will I, and I charge you, follow me not.'

He spoke, and vanished suddenly from the field
With young Lavaine into the poplar grove.
There from his charger down he slid, and sat,
Gasping to Sir Lavaine, 'Draw the lance-head:'
510 'Ah my sweet lord Sir Lancelot,' said Lavaine,
'I dread me, if I draw it, you will die.'
But he, 'I die already with it: draw–
Draw,'–and Lavaine drew, and Sir Lancelot gave
A marvellous great shriek and ghastly groan,
515 And half his blood burst forth, and down he sank
For the pure pain, and wholly swooned away.
Then came the hermit out and bare him in,
There stanched his wound; and there, in daily doubt
Whether to live or die, for many a week
520 Hid from the wide world's rumour by the grove
Of poplars with their noise of falling showers,
And ever-tremulous aspen-trees, he lay.

But on that day when Lancelot fled the lists,
His party, knights of utmost North and West,

501. *thy*] *1873*; *your 1859–70*. Likewise in l. 603.
502–5. Malory xviii 12, after Launcelot has been offered the prize: '"If I
have deserved thanks, I have sore bought it, and that me repenteth, for I
am like never to escape with my life; therefore, fair lords, I pray you that
ye will suffer me to depart where me liketh, for I am sore hurt, I take no
force of none honour; for I had lever to rest me, than to be lord of all the
world."'
509–16. Malory xviii 12: '"O gentle knight, sir Lavaine, help me, that this
truncheon were out of my side, for it sticketh so sore, that it almost slayeth
me."–"O, mine own lord," said sir Lavaine, "I would fain help you, but
it dreads me sore; and I draw out the truncheon, that ye shall be in peril of
death."–"I charge you," said sir Launcelot, "as ye love me, draw it out."
And therewith he descended from his horse, and so did sir Lavaine; and
forthwith sir Lavaine drew the truncheon out of his side: and sir Launcelot
gave a great shriek, and a marvellous ghastly groan, and his blood burst out
nigh a pint at once, that at the last he sunk down upon his buttocks and
swooned, pale and deadly.'
513. *Sir Lancelot*] *1873*; *that other 1859–70*.

525 Lords of waste marches, kings of desolate isles,
Came round their great Pendragon, saying to him,
'Lo, Sire, our knight, through whom we won the day,
Hath gone sore wounded, and hath left his prize
Untaken, crying that his prize is death.'
530 'Heaven hinder,' said the King, 'that such an one,
So great a knight as we have seen today—
He seemed to me another Lancelot—
Yea, twenty times I thought him Lancelot—
He must not pass uncared for. Wherefore, rise,
535 O Gawain, and ride forth and find the knight.
Wounded and wearied needs must he be near.
I charge you that you get at once to horse.
And, knights and kings, there breathes not one of you
Will deem this prize of ours is rashly given:
540 His prowess was too wondrous. We will do him
No customary honour: since the knight
Came not to us, of us to claim the prize,
Ourselves will send it after. Rise and take
This diamond, and deliver it, and return,
545 And bring us where he is, and how he fares,
And cease not from your quest until ye find.'

So saying, from the carven flower above,
To which it made a restless heart, he took,
And gave, the diamond: then from where he sat
550 At Arthur's right, with smiling face arose,
With smiling face and frowning heart, a Prince
In the mid might and flourish of his May,
Gawain, surnamed The Courteous, fair and strong,
And after Lancelot, Tristram, and Geraint
555 And Gareth, a good knight, but therewithal
Sir Modred's brother, and the child of Lot,
Nor often loyal to his word, and now
Wroth that the King's command to sally forth
In quest of whom he knew not, made him leave
560 The banquet, and concourse of knights and kings.

So all in wrath he got to horse and went;
While Arthur to the banquet, dark in mood,

534. *Wherefore*] *1870* ('*1869*'); Gawain *1859–69*.
535. *O Gawain*] *1870* ('*1869*'); My nephew *1859–69*.
543. *Rise and*] *1870* ('*1869*'); Wherefore *1859–69*.
545. *where*] *1870* ('*1869*'); what *1859–69*.
555. *Gareth*] *1873*; Lamorack *1859–70*.
556. *and . . . Lot*] *1873*; of a crafty house *1859–70*.

Past, thinking 'Is it Lancelot who hath come
Despite the wound he spake of, all for gain
565   Of glory, and hath added wound to wound,
And ridden away to die?' So feared the King,
And, after two days' tarriance there, returned.
Then when he saw the Queen, embracing asked,
'Love, are you yet so sick?' 'Nay, lord,' she said.
570   'And where is Lancelot?' Then the Queen amazed,
'Was he not with you? won he not your prize?'
'Nay, but one like him.' 'Why that like was he.'
And when the King demanded how she knew,
Said, 'Lord, no sooner had ye parted from us,
575   Than Lancelot told me of a common talk
That men went down before his spear at a touch,
But knowing he was Lancelot; his great name
Conquered; and therefore would he hide his name
From all men, even the King, and to this end
580   Had made the pretext of a hindering wound,
That he might joust unknown of all, and learn
If his old prowess were in aught decayed;
And added, "Our true Arthur, when he learns,
Will well allow my pretext, as for gain
Of purer glory."'

585   Then replied the King:
'Far lovelier in our Lancelot had it been,
In lieu of idly dallying with the truth,
To have trusted me as he hath trusted thee.
Surely his King and most familiar friend
590   Might well have kept his secret. True, indeed,
Albeit I know my knights fantastical,
So fine a fear in our large Lancelot
Must needs have moved my laughter: now remains
But little cause for laughter: his own kin—
595   Ill news, my Queen, for all who love him, this!—
His kith and kin, not knowing, set upon him;
So that he went sore wounded from the field:
Yet good news too: for goodly hopes are mine
That Lancelot is no more a lonely heart.
600   He wore, against his wont, upon his helm
A sleeve of scarlet, broidered with great pearls,
Some gentle maiden's gift.'

563. hath] *1873*; has *1859–70*. Likewise in ll. 565, 588, 826.
588. thee] *1873*; you *1859–70*.
595. this] *1873*; these *1859–70*.

                                        'Yea, lord,' she said,
        'Thy hopes are mine,' and saying that, she choked,
        And sharply turned about to hide her face,
605   Past to her chamber, and there flung herself
        Down on the great King's couch, and writhed upon
              it,
        And clenched her fingers till they bit the palm,
        And shrieked out 'Traitor' to the unhearing wall,
        Then flashed into wild tears, and rose again,
610   And moved about her palace, proud and pale.

        Gawain the while through all the region round
        Rode with his diamond, wearied of the quest,
        Touched at all points, except the poplar grove,
        And came at last, though late, to Astolat:
615   Whom glittering in enamelled arms the maid
        Glanced at, and cried,'What news from Camelot, lord?
        What of the knight with the red sleeve?' 'He won.'
        'I knew it,' she said. 'But parted from the jousts
        Hurt in the side,' whereat she caught her breath;
620   Through her own side she felt the sharp lance go;
        Thereon she smote her hand: wellnigh she swooned:
        And, while he gazed wonderingly at her, came
        The Lord of Astolat out, to whom the Prince
        Reported who he was, and on what quest
625   Sent, that he bore the prize and could not find
        The victor, but had ridden a random round
        To seek him, and had wearied of the search.
        To whom the Lord of Astolat, 'Bide with us,
        And ride no more at random, noble Prince!
630   Here was the knight, and here he left a shield;
        This will he send or come for: furthermore
        Our son is with him; we shall hear anon,
        Needs must we hear.' To this the courteous Prince
        Accorded with his wonted courtesy,
635   Courtesy with a touch of traitor in it,
        And stayed; and cast his eyes on fair Elaine:
        Where could be found face daintier? then her shape

605. *Past*] *1870* ('*1869*'); Moved *1859–69*.
608. Malory xviii 15: "'Ah! sir Bors, have ye heard say how falsely sir
Launcelot hath betrayed me? . . . he is but a false, traitorous knight.'"
626. *a random*] *1873*; wildly *1859–70*.
627. *had*] *1873*; was *1859–70*.
629. *more at random*] *1873*; longer wildly *1859–70*.
636. As F. J. Rowe notes, in Malory Gawain appears as a loyal friend of

From forehead down to foot, perfect—again
From foot to forehead exquisitely turned:
640 'Well—if I bide, lo! this wild flower for me!'
And oft they met among the garden yews,
And there he set himself to play upon her
With sallying wit, free flashes from a height
Above her, graces of the court, and songs,
645 Sighs, and slow smiles, and golden eloquence
And amorous adulation, till the maid
Rebelled against it, saying to him, 'Prince,
O loyal nephew of our noble King,
Why ask you not to see the shield he left,
Whence you might learn his name? Why slight
650 your King,
And lose the quest he sent you on, and prove
No surer than our falcon yesterday,
Who lost the hern we slipt her at, and went
To all the winds?' 'Nay, by mine head,' said he,
655 'I lose it, as we lose the lark in heaven,
O damsel, in the light of your blue eyes;
But an ye will it let me see the shield.'
And when the shield was brought, and Gawain saw
Sir Lancelot's azure lions, crowned with gold,
660 Ramp in the field, he smote his thigh, and mocked:
'Right was the King! our Lancelot! that true man!'
'And right was I,' she answered merrily, 'I,
Who dreamed my knight the greatest knight of all.'
'And if I dreamed,' said Gawain, 'that you love
665 This greatest knight, your pardon! lo, ye know it!
Speak therefore: shall I waste myself in vain?'
Full simple was her answer, 'What know I?
My brethren have been all my fellowship;
And I, when often they have talked of love,
670 Wished it had been my mother, for they talked,
Meseemed, of what they knew not; so myself—
I know not if I know what true love is,
But if I know, then, if I love not him,
I know there is none other I can love.'
675 'Yea, by God's death,' said he, 'ye love him well,

Lancelot; these lines 'illustrate the increasing corruption of the Round Table'. T. departs from Malory throughout this episode.
653. her] 1882; him 1859–81.
660. field: surface of the shield.
674. I know] 1873; Methinks 1859–70.

But would not, knew ye what all others know,
And whom he loves.' 'So be it,' cried Elaine,
And lifted her fair face and moved away:
But he pursued her, calling, 'Stay a little!
680 One golden minute's grace! he wore your sleeve:
Would he break faith with one I may not name?
Must our true man change like a leaf at last?
Nay–like enow: why then, far be it from me
To cross our mighty Lancelot in his loves!
685 And, damsel, for I deem you know full well
Where your great knight is hidden, let me leave
My quest with you; the diamond also: here!
For if you love, it will be sweet to give it;
And if he love, it will be sweet to have it
690 From your own hand; and whether he love or not,
A diamond is a diamond. Fare you well
A thousand times!–a thousand times farewell!
Yet, if he love, and his love hold, we two
May meet at court hereafter: there, I think,
695 So ye will learn the courtesies of the court,
We two shall know each other.'

                              Then he gave,
And slightly kissed the hand to which he gave,
The diamond, and all wearied of the quest
Leapt on his horse, and carolling as he went
700 A true-love ballad, lightly rode away.

    Thence to the court he past; there told the King
What the King knew, 'Sir Lancelot is the knight.'
And added, 'Sire, my liege, so much I learnt;
But failed to find him, though I rode all round
705 The region: but I lighted on the maid
Whose sleeve he wore; she loves him; and to her,
Deeming our courtesy is the truest law,
I gave the diamond: she will render it;
For by mine head she knows his hiding-place.'

710   The seldom-frowning King frowned, and replied,
'Too courteous truly! ye shall go no more
On quest of mine, seeing that ye forget
Obedience is the courtesy due to kings.'

683. *Nay–like enow*] *1873*; May it be so? *1859–62*; Nay–like enough *1863–70*.
686. The leaving of the diamond and the king's anger with Gawain
(ll. 710–13) are additions to Malory.

He spake and parted. Wroth, but all in awe,
715   For twenty strokes of the blood, without a word,
Lingered that other, staring after him;
Then shook his hair, strode off, and buzzed abroad
About the maid of Astolat, and her love.
All ears were pricked at once, all tongues were
      loosed:
720   'The maid of Astolat loves Sir Lancelot,
Sir Lancelot loves the maid of Astolat.'
Some read the King's face, some the Queen's, and all
Had marvel what the maid might be, but most
Predoomed her as unworthy. One old dame
725   Came suddenly on the Queen with the sharp news.
She, that had heard the noise of it before,
But sorrowing Lancelot should have stooped so low,
Marred her friend's aim with pale tranquillity.
So ran the tale like fire about the court,
730   Fire in dry stubble a nine-days' wonder flared:
Till even the knights at banquet twice or thrice
Forgot to drink to Lancelot and the Queen,
And pledging Lancelot and the lily maid
Smiled at each other, while the Queen, who sat
735   With lips severely placid, felt the knot
Climb in her throat, and with her feet unseen
Crushed the wild passion out against the floor
Beneath the banquet, where the meats became
As wormwood, and she hated all who pledged.

740   But far away the maid in Astolat,
Her guiltless rival, she that ever kept
The one-day-seen Sir Lancelot in her heart,
Crept to her father, while he mused alone,
Sat on his knee, stroked his gray face and said,
745   'Father, you call me wilful, and the fault
Is yours who let me have my will, and now,
Sweet father, will you let me lose my wits?'
'Nay,' said he, 'surely.' 'Wherefore, let me hence,'
She answered, 'and find out our dear Lavaine.'
750   'Ye will not lose your wits for dear Lavaine:
Bide,' answered he: 'we needs must hear anon
Of him, and of that other.' 'Ay,' she said,
'And of that other, for I needs must hence
And find that other, wheresoe'er he be,
755   And with mine own hand give his diamond to him,

728. aim] 1873; point 1859-70.

Lest I be found as faithless in the quest
As yon proud Prince who left the quest to me.
Sweet father, I behold him in my dreams
Gaunt as it were the skeleton of himself,
760 Death-pale, for lack of gentle maiden's aid.
The gentler-born the maiden, the more bound,
My father, to be sweet and serviceable
To noble knights in sickness, as ye know
When these have worn their tokens: let me hence
765 I pray you.' Then her father nodding said,
'Ay, ay, the diamond: wit ye well, my child,
Right fain were I to learn this knight were whole,
Being our greatest: yea, and you must give it—
And sure I think this fruit is hung too high
770 For any mouth to gape for save a queen's—
Nay, I mean nothing: so then, get you gone,
Being so very wilful you must go.'

Lightly, her suit allowed, she slipt away,
And while she made her ready for her ride,
775 Her father's latest word hummed in her ear,
'Being so very wilful you must go,'
And changed itself and echoed in her heart,
'Being so very wilful you must die.'
But she was happy enough and shook it off,
780 As we shake off the bee that buzzes at us;
And in her heart she answered it and said,
'What matter, so I help him back to life?'
Then far away with good Sir Torre for guide
Rode o'er the long backs of the bushless downs
785 To Camelot, and before the city-gates
Came on her brother with a happy face
Making a roan horse caper and curvet
For pleasure all about a field of flowers:
Whom when she saw, 'Lavaine,' she cried,
        'Lavaine,
790 How fares my lord Sir Lancelot?' He amazed,
'Torre and Elaine! why here? Sir Lancelot!
How know ye my lord's name is Lancelot?'

786–92. Malory xviii 15: 'By fortune sir Lavaine was ridden to play him
and to enchase his horse. And anon as fair Elaine saw him, she knew him,
and then she cried aloud unto him: and when he heard her, anon he came
unto her, and then she asked her brother, "How fareth my lord, sir
Launcelot?"—"Who told you, sister, that my lord's name was sir
Launcelot!"'

But when the maid had told him all her tale,
Then turned Sir Torre, and being in his moods
795 Left them, and under the strange-statued gate,
Where Arthur's wars were rendered mystically,
Past up the still rich city to his kin,
His own far blood, which dwelt at Camelot;
And her, Lavaine across the poplar grove
800 Led to the caves: there first she saw the casque
Of Lancelot on the wall: her scarlet sleeve,
Though carved and cut, and half the pearls away,
Streamed from it still; and in her heart she laughed,
Because he had not loosed it from his helm,
805 But meant once more perchance to tourney in it.
And when they gained the cell wherein he slept,
His battle-writhen arms and mighty hands
Lay naked on the wolfskin, and a dream
Of dragging down his enemy made them move.
810 Then she that saw him lying unsleek, unshorn,
Gaunt as it were the skeleton of himself,
Uttered a little tender dolorous cry.
The sound not wonted in a place so still
Woke the sick knight, and while he rolled his eyes
815 Yet blank from sleep, she started to him, saying,
'Your prize the diamond sent you by the King:'
His eyes glistened: she fancied 'Is it for me?'
And when the maid had told him all the tale
Of King and Prince, the diamond sent, the quest
820 Assigned to her not worthy of it, she knelt
Full lowly by the corners of his bed,
And laid the diamond in his open hand.
Her face was near, and as we kiss the child
That does the task assigned, he kissed her face.
825 At once she slipt like water to the floor.
'Alas,' he said, 'your ride hath wearied you.
Rest must you have.' 'No rest for me,' she said;
'Nay, for near you, fair lord, I am at rest.'
What might she mean by that? his large black
   eyes,
830 Yet larger through his leanness, dwelt upon her,
Till all her heart's sad secret blazed itself
In the heart's colours on her simple face;
And Lancelot looked and was perplext in mind,

806. *wherein*] *1873*; in which *1859–70*.
807. Cp. *Sense and Conscience* 57: 'battle-writhen sinews'.

And being weak in body said no more;
835 But did not love the colour; woman's love,
Save one, he not regarded, and so turned
Sighing, and feigned a sleep until he slept.

Then rose Elaine and glided through the fields,
And past beneath the weirdly-sculptured gates
840 Far up the dim rich city to her kin;
There bode the night: but woke with dawn, and
        past
Down through the dim rich city to the fields,
Thence to the cave: so day by day she past
In either twilight ghost-like to and fro
845 Gliding, and every day she tended him,
And likewise many a night: and Lancelot
Would, though he called his wound a little hurt
Whereof he should be quickly whole, at times
Brain-feverous in his heat and agony, seem
850 Uncourteous, even he: but the meek maid
Sweetly forbore him ever, being to him
Meeker than any child to a rough nurse,
Milder than any mother to a sick child,
And never woman yet, since man's first fall,
855 Did kindlier unto man, but her deep love
Upbore her; till the hermit, skilled in all
The simples and the science of that time,
Told him that her fine care had saved his life.
And the sick man forgot her simple blush,
860 Would call her friend and sister, sweet Elaine,
Would listen for her coming and regret
Her parting step, and held her tenderly,
And loved her with all love except the love   .
Of man and woman when they love their best,
865 Closest and sweetest, and had died the death
In any knightly fashion for her sake.
And peradventure had he seen her first
She might have made this and that other world
Another world for the sick man; but now
870 The shackles of an old love straitened him,

833 ∧ 4] Brake the sad cloud of maiden truthfulness *Virginia MS.*
839. *weirdly-*] *1873*; wildly- *1859–70*.
843–56. Malory xviii 15: 'So this maid Elaine never went from sir Launce-
lot, but watched him day and night, and gave such attendance upon him,
there was never woman did more kindlier for man than she did.'

His honour rooted in dishonour stood,
And faith unfaithful kept him falsely true.

Yet the great knight in his mid-sickness made
Full many a holy vow and pure resolve.
875 These, as but born of sickness, could not live:
For when the blood ran lustier in him again,
Full often the bright image of one face,
Making a treacherous quiet in his heart,
Dispersed his resolution like a cloud.
880 Then if the maiden, while that ghostly grace
Beamed on his fancy, spoke, he answered not,
Or short and coldly, and she knew right well
What the rough sickness meant, but what this
meant
She knew not, and the sorrow dimmed her sight,
885 And drave her ere her time across the fields
Far into the rich city, where alone
She murmured, 'Vain, in vain: it cannot be.
He will not love me: how then? must I die?'
Then as a little helpless innocent bird,
890 That has but one plain passage of few notes,
Will sing the simple passage o'er and o'er
For all an April morning, till the ear
Wearies to hear it, so the simple maid
Went half the night repeating, 'Must I die?'
895 And now to right she turned, and now to left,
And found no ease in turning or in rest;
And 'Him or death,' she muttered, 'death or
him,'
Again and like a burthen, 'Him or death.'

But when Sir Lancelot's deadly hurt was whole,
900 To Astolat returning rode the three.
There morn by morn, arraying her sweet self
In that wherein she deemed she looked her best,
She came before Sir Lancelot, for she thought
'If I be loved, these are my festal robes,
905 If not, the victim's flowers before he fall.'
And Lancelot ever prest upon the maid
That she should ask some goodly gift of him
For her own self or hers; 'and do not shun
To speak the wish most near to your true heart;

877. bright] 1873; sweet 1859–70.
880. 'Vision of Guinevere' (T.).

910   Such service have ye done me, that I make
       My will of yours, and Prince and Lord am I
       In mine own land, and what I will I can.'
       Then like a ghost she lifted up her face,
       But like a ghost without the power to speak.
915   And Lancelot saw that she withheld her wish,
       And bode among them yet a little space
       Till he should learn it; and one morn it chanced
       He found her in among the garden yews,
       And said, 'Delay no longer, speak your wish,
920   Seeing I go today:' then out she brake:
       'Going? and we shall never see you more.
       And I must die for want of one bold word.'
       'Speak: that I live to hear,' he said, 'is yours.'
       Then suddenly and passionately she spoke:
925   'I have gone mad. I love you: let me die.'
       'Ah, sister,' answered Lancelot, 'what is this?'
       And innocently extending her white arms,
       'Your love,' she said, 'your love–to be your wife.'
       And Lancelot answered, 'Had I chosen to wed,
930   I had been wedded earlier, sweet Elaine:
       But now there never will be wife of mine.'
       'No, no,' she cried, 'I care not to be wife,
       But to be with you still, to see your face,
       To serve you, and to follow you through the
            world.'
       And Lancelot answered, 'Nay, the world, the
935   world,
       All ear and eye, with such a stupid heart
       To interpret ear and eye, and such a tongue
       To blare its own interpretation–nay,
       Full ill then should I quit your brother's love,
940   And your good father's kindness.' And she said,

920. go] 1873; must go 1859–70.
922–42. Malory xviii 19: '"Have mercy upon me, and suffer me not to
die for your love."–"What would you that I did?" said sir Launcelot.
"I would have you unto my husband," said the maid Elaine. "Fair damsel,
I thank you," said sir Launcelot; "but certainly," said he, "I cast me never
to be married."–"Then, fair knight," said she, "will ye be my para-
mour?"–"Jesu defend me!" said sir Launcelot; "for then should I reward
your father and your brother full evil for their great goodness."–"Alas!"
said she, "then must I needs die for your love. . . . For but if ye will wed
me, or else be my paramour at the least, wit ye well, sir Launcelot, my
good days are done."'

'Not to be with you, not to see your face—
Alas for me then, my good days are done.'
'Nay, noble maid,' he answered, 'ten times nay!
This is not love: but love's first flash in youth,
945 Most common: yea, I know it of mine own self:
And you yourself will smile at your own self
Hereafter, when you yield your flower of life
To one more fitly yours, not thrice your age:
And then will I, for true you are and sweet
950 Beyond mine old belief in womanhood,
More specially should your good knight be poor,
Endow you with broad land and territory
Even to the half my realm beyond the seas,
So that would make you happy: furthermore,
955 Even to the death, as though ye were my blood,
In all your quarrels will I be your knight.
This will I do, dear damsel, for your sake,
And more than this I cannot.'

                While he spoke
She neither blushed nor shook, but deathly-pale
960 Stood grasping what was nearest, then replied:
'Of all this will I nothing;' and so fell,
And thus they bore her swooning to her tower.

    Then spake, to whom through those black walls
        of yew
Their talk had pierced, her father: 'Ay, a flash,
965 I fear me, that will strike my blossom dead.
Too courteous are ye, fair Lord Lancelot.
I pray you, use some rough discourtesy
To blunt or break her passion.'

                Lancelot said,
'That were against me: what I can I will;'
970 And there that day remained, and toward even
Sent for his shield: full meekly rose the maid,
Stript off the case, and gave the naked shield;
Then, when she heard his horse upon the stones,
Unclasping flung the casement back, and looked
975 Down on his helm, from which her sleeve had gone.

951-2. Malory xviii 19: '"that wheresoever ye will set your heart upon
some good knight that will wed you, I shall give you together a thousand
pounds yearly to you and to your heirs."'
966-9. Added to Malory.

And Lancelot knew the little clinking sound;
And she by tact of love was well aware
That Lancelot knew that she was looking at him.
And yet he glanced not up, nor waved his hand,
980 Nor bad farewell, but sadly rode away.
This was the one discourtesy that he used.

So in her tower alone the maiden sat:
His very shield was gone; only the case,
Her own poor work, her empty labour, left.
985 But still she heard him, still his picture formed
And grew between her and the pictured wall.
Then came her father, saying in low tones,
'Have comfort,' whom she greeted quietly.
Then came her brethren saying, 'Peace to thee,
990 Sweet sister,' whom she answered with all calm.
But when they left her to herself again,
Death, like a friend's voice from a distant field
Approaching through the darkness, called; the owls
Wailing had power upon her, and she mixt
995 Her fancies with the sallow-rifted glooms
Of evening, and the moanings of the wind.

And in those days she made a little song,
And called her song 'The Song of Love and Death,'
And sang it: sweetly could she make and sing.

1000 'Sweet is true love though given in vain, in vain;
And sweet is death who puts an end to pain:
I know not which is sweeter, no, not I.

'Love, art thou sweet? then bitter death must be:
Love, thou art bitter; sweet is death to me.
1005 O Love, if death be sweeter, let me die.

'Sweet love, that seems not made to fade away,
Sweet death, that seems to make us loveless clay,
I know not which is sweeter, no, not I.

'I fain would follow love, if that could be;
1010 I needs must follow death, who calls for me;
Call and I follow, I follow! let me die.'

998. The song takes the place of Elaine's religious meditation, Malory
xviii 19.

High with the last line scaled her voice, and this,
All in a fiery dawning wild with wind
That shook her tower, the brothers heard, and
    thought
1015   With shuddering, 'Hark the Phantom of the house
That ever shrieks before a death,' and called
The father, and all three in hurry and fear
Ran to her, and lo! the blood-red light of dawn
Flared on her face, she shrilling, 'Let me die!'

1020   As when we dwell upon a word we know,
Repeating, till the word we know so well
Becomes a wonder, and we know not why,
So dwelt the father on her face, and thought
'Is this Elaine?' till back the maiden fell,
1025   Then gave a languid hand to each, and lay,
Speaking a still good-morrow with her eyes.
At last she said, 'Sweet brothers, yesternight
I seemed a curious little maid again,
As happy as when we dwelt among the woods,
1030   And when ye used to take me with the flood
Up the great river in the boatman's boat.
Only ye would not pass beyond the cape
That has the poplar on it: there ye fixt
Your limit, oft returning with the tide.
1035   And yet I cried because ye would not pass
Beyond it, and far up the shining flood
Until we found the palace of the King.
And yet ye would not; but this night I dreamed
That I was all alone upon the flood,
1040   And then I said, "Now shall I have my will:"
And there I woke, but still the wish remained.
So let me hence that I may pass at last
Beyond the poplar and far up the flood,
Until I find the palace of the King.
1045   There will I enter in among them all,
And no man there will dare to mock at me;
But there the fine Gawain will wonder at me,
And there the great Sir Lancelot muse at me;
Gawain, who bad a thousand farewells to me,
1050   Lancelot, who coldly went, nor bad me one:
And there the King will know me and my love,
And there the Queen herself will pity me,

1015. The Banshee, as described in J. Brand's *Popular Antiquities* (of which
the 1810 edn is at *Lincoln*).

And all the gentle court will welcome me,
And after my long voyage I shall rest!'

1055   'Peace,' said her father, 'O my child, ye seem
Light-headed, for what force is yours to go
So far, being sick? and wherefore would ye look
On this proud fellow again, who scorns us all?'

Then the rough Torre began to heave and move,
1060   And bluster into stormy sobs and say,
'I never loved him: an I meet with him,
I care not howsoever great he be,
Then will I strike at him and strike him down,
Give me good fortune, I will strike him dead,
1065   For this discomfort he hath done the house.'

To whom the gentle sister made reply,
'Fret not yourself, dear brother, nor be wroth,
Seeing it is no more Sir Lancelot's fault
Not to love me, than it is mine to love
1070   Him of all men who seems to me the highest.'

'Highest?' the father answered, echoing 'highest?'
(He meant to break the passion in her) 'nay,
Daughter, I know not what you call the highest;
But this I know, for all the people know it,
1075   He loves the Queen, and in an open shame:
And she returns his love in open shame;
If this be high, what is it to be low?'

Then spake the lily maid of Astolat:
'Sweet father, all too faint and sick am I
1080   For anger: these are slanders: never yet
Was noble man but made ignoble talk.
He makes no friend who never made a foe.
But now it is my glory to have loved
One peerless, without stain: so let me pass,
1085   My father, howsoe'er I seem to you,
Not all unhappy, having loved God's best
And greatest, though my love had no return:
Yet, seeing you desire your child to live,
Thanks, but you work against your own desire;
1090   For if I could believe the things you say
I should but die the sooner; wherefore cease,
Sweet father, and bid call the ghostly man
Hither, and let me shrive me clean, and die.'

1092. *ghostly man*: priest.

So when the ghostly man had come and gone,
1095 She with a face, bright as for sin forgiven,
Besought Lavaine to write as she devised
A letter, word for word; and when he asked
'Is it for Lancelot, is it for my dear lord?
Then will I bear it gladly;' she replied,
1100 'For Lancelot and the Queen and all the world,
But I myself must bear it.' Then he wrote
The letter she devised; which being writ
And folded, 'O sweet father, tender and true,
Deny me not,' she said—'ye never yet
1105 Denied my fancies—this, however strange,
My latest: lay the letter in my hand
A little ere I die, and close the hand
Upon it; I shall guard it even in death.
And when the heat is gone from out my heart,
1110 Then take the little bed on which I died
For Lancelot's love, and deck it like the Queen's
For richness, and me also like the Queen
In all I have of rich, and lay me on it.
And let there be prepared a chariot-bier
1115 To take me to the river, and a barge
Be ready on the river, clothed in black.
I go in state to court, to meet the Queen.
There surely I shall speak for mine own self,
And none of you can speak for me so well.
1120 And therefore let our dumb old man alone
Go with me, he can steer and row, and he
Will guide me to that palace, to the doors.'

1096–1129. Malory xviii 19: 'And then she called her father, sir Bernard, and her brother, sir Tirre; and heartily she prayed her father, that her brother might write a letter like as she would indite it. And so her father granted it her. And, when the letter was written, word by word, as she had devised, then she prayed her father that she might be watched until she were dead. "And while my body is whole let this letter be put into my right hand, and my hand bound fast with the letter until that I be cold; and let me be put in a fair bed, with all the richest clothes that I have about me. And so let my bed, with all my rich clothes, be laid with me in a chariot to the next place whereas the Thames is; and there let me be put in a barge, and but one man with me, such as ye trust to steer me thither, and that my barge be covered with black samite over and over. Thus, father, I beseech you let be done." So her father granted her faithfully that all this thing should be done like as she had devised. Then her father and her brother made great dole; for, when this was done, anon she died.' See ll. 1239–47n.

She ceased: her father promised; whereupon
She grew so cheerful that they deemed her death
1125   Was rather in the fantasy than the blood.
But ten slow mornings past, and on the eleventh
Her father laid the letter in her hand,
And closed the hand upon it, and she died.
So that day there was dole in Astolat.

1130   But when the next sun brake from underground,
Then, those two brethren slowly with bent brows
Accompanying, the sad chariot-bier
Past like a shadow through the field, that shone
Full-summer, to that stream whereon the barge,
1135   Palled all its length in blackest samite, lay.
There sat the lifelong creature of the house,
Loyal, the dumb old servitor, on deck,
Winking his eyes, and twisted all his face.
So those two brethren from the chariot took
1140   And on the black decks laid her in her bed,
Set in her hand a lily, o'er her hung
The silken case with braided blazonings,
And kissed her quiet brows, and saying to her
'Sister, farewell for ever,' and again
1145   'Farewell, sweet sister,' parted all in tears.
Then rose the dumb old servitor, and the dead,
Oared by the dumb, went upward with the flood—
In her right hand the lily, in her left
The letter—all her bright hair streaming down—
1150   And all the coverlid was cloth of gold
Drawn to her waist, and she herself in white
All but her face, and that clear-featured face
Was lovely, for she did not seem as dead,
But fast asleep, and lay as though she smiled.

1155   That day Sir Lancelot at the palace craved
Audience of Guinevere, to give at last
The price of half a realm, his costly gift,
Hard-won and hardly won with bruise and blow,
With deaths of others, and almost his own,
1160   The nine-years-fought-for diamonds: for he saw

1130–54. Malory xviii 19: 'And so, when she was dead, the corpse and the
bed, and all, were led the next way unto the Thames; and there a man,
and the corpse and all, were put in a barge on the Thames: and so the man
steered the barge to Westminster, and there he rode a great while to and
fro, or any man discovered it.'
1147. Oared] 1870 ('1869'); Steered 1859–69.

One of her house, and sent him to the Queen
Bearing his wish, whereto the Queen agreed
With such and so unmoved a majesty
She might have seemed her statue, but that he,
1165 Low-drooping till he wellnigh kissed her feet
For loyal awe, saw with a sidelong eye
The shadow of some piece of pointed lace,
In the Queen's shadow, vibrate on the walls,
And parted, laughing in his courtly heart.

1170 All in an oriel on the summer side,
Vine-clad, of Arthur's palace toward the stream,
They met, and Lancelot kneeling uttered, 'Queen,
Lady, my liege, in whom I have my joy,
Take, what I had not won except for you,
1175 These jewels, and make me happy, making them
An armlet for the roundest arm on earth,
Or necklace for a neck to which the swan's
Is tawnier than her cygnet's: these are words:
Your beauty is your beauty, and I sin
1180 In speaking, yet O grant my worship of it
Words, as we grant grief tears. Such sin in words
Perchance, we both can pardon: but, my Queen,
I hear of rumours flying through your court.
Our bond, as not the bond of man and wife,
1185 Should have in it an absoluter trust
To make up that defect: let rumours be:
When did not rumours fly? these, as I trust
That you trust me in your own nobleness,
I may not well believe that you believe.'

1190 While thus he spoke, half turned away, the Queen
Brake from the vast oriel-embowering vine
Leaf after leaf, and tore, and cast them off,
Till all the place whereon she stood was green;
Then, when he ceased, in one cold passive hand
1195 Received at once and laid aside the gems
There on a table near her, and replied:

'It may be, I am quicker of belief
Than you believe me, Lancelot of the Lake.

1167. *some*] *1873*; a *1859–70*.
1170–1235. Malory xviii 20: 'So, by fortune, king Arthur and queen Guenever were speaking together at a window; and so as they looked into the Thames, they espied the black barge, and had marvel what it might mean. . . . And she lay as though she had smiled.'

Our bond is not the bond of man and wife.
1200   This good is in it, whatsoe'er of ill,
It can be broken easier. I for you
This many a year have done despite and wrong
To one whom ever in my heart of hearts
I did acknowledge nobler. What are these?
Diamonds for me! they had been thrice their
1205   worth
Being your gift, had you not lost your own.
To loyal hearts the value of all gifts
Must vary as the giver's. Not for me!
For her! for your new fancy. Only this
1210   Grant me, I pray you: have your joys apart.
I doubt not that however changed, you keep
So much of what is graceful: and myself
Would shun to break those bounds of courtesy
In which as Arthur's Queen I move and rule:
1215   So cannot speak my mind. An end to this!
A strange one! yet I take it with Amen.
So pray you, add my diamonds to her pearls;
Deck her with these; tell her, she shines me
     down:
An armlet for an arm to which the Queen's
1220   Is haggard, or a necklace for a neck
O as much fairer—as a faith once fair
Was richer than these diamonds—hers not mine—
Nay, by the mother of our Lord himself,
Or hers or mine, mine now to work my will—
She shall not have them.'

1225   Saying which she seized,
And, through the casement standing wide for heat,
Flung them, and down they flashed, and smote the
     stream.
Then from the smitten surface flashed, as it were,
Diamonds to meet them, and they past away.
1230   Then while Sir Lancelot leant, in half disdain
At love, life, all things, on the window ledge,
Close underneath his eyes, and right across
Where these had fallen, slowly past the barge.
Whereon the lily maid of Astolat
1235   Lay smiling, like a star in blackest night.

1230. *disdain*] *1873*; disgust *1859–70*.
1234–5. G. H. Ford compares *Endymion* i 990–1: 'faint-smiling like a star /
Through autumn mists' (*Keats and the Victorians*, 1944, p. 25*n*).

But the wild Queen, who saw not, burst away
To weep and wail in secret; and the barge,
On to the palace-doorway sliding, paused.
There two stood armed, and kept the door; to
      whom,
1240 All up the marble stair, tier over tier,
Were added mouths that gaped, and eyes that asked
'What is it?' but that oarsman's haggard face,
As hard and still as is the face that men
Shape to their fancy's eye from broken rocks
1245 On some cliff-side, appalled them, and they said,
'He is enchanted, cannot speak—and she,
Look how she sleeps—the Fairy Queen, so fair!
Yea, but how pale! what are they? flesh and blood?
Or come to take the King to Fairyland?
1250 For some do hold our Arthur cannot die,
But that he passes into Fairyland.'

While thus they babbled of the King, the King
Came girt with knights: then turned the tongueless
      man
From the half-face to the full eye, and rose
1255 And pointed to the damsel, and the doors.
So Arthur bad the meek Sir Percivale
And pure Sir Galahad to uplift the maid;
And reverently they bore her into hall.
Then came the fine Gawain and wondered at her,
1260 And Lancelot later came and mused at her,
And last the Queen herself, and pitied her:
But Arthur spied the letter in her hand,
Stoopt, took, brake seal, and read it; this was all:

'Most noble lord, Sir Lancelot of the Lake,
1265 I, sometime called the maid of Astolat,

1239–47. Malory xviii 20: 'And there they found the fairest corpse, lying
in a rich bed, that ever they saw, and a poor man sitting in the end of the
barge, and no word would speak.'
1247–51] *For an unadopted passage, T.Nbk 28, see Appendix A,* III 602.
1262. Malory xviii 20: 'Then the queen espied the letter in the right hand,
and told the king thereof. Then the king took it in his hand.'
1264–74. Malory xviii 20: '"Most noble knight, my lord, sir Launcelot du
Lake, now hath death made us two at debate for your love. I was your
lover, that men called the Fair Maiden of Astolat; therefore unto all
ladies I make my moan. Yet for my soul that ye pray, and bury me at the
least, and offer me my mass penny. This is my last request: and a clean

Come, for you left me taking no farewell,
Hither, to take my last farewell of you.
I loved you, and my love had no return,
And therefore my true love has been my death.
1270   And therefore to our Lady Guinevere,
And to all other ladies, I make moan:
Pray for my soul, and yield me burial.
Pray for my soul thou too, Sir Lancelot,
As thou art a knight peerless.'

                  Thus he read;
1275   And ever in the reading, lords and dames
Wept, looking often from his face who read
To hers which lay so silent, and at times,
So touched were they, half-thinking that her lips,
Who had devised the letter, moved again.

1280   Then freely spoke Sir Lancelot to them all:
'My lord liege Arthur, and all ye that hear,
Know that for this most gentle maiden's death
Right heavy am I; for good she was and true,
But loved me with a love beyond all love
1285   In women, whomsoever I have known.
Yet to be loved makes not to love again;
Not at my years, however it hold in youth.
I swear by truth and knighthood that I gave
No cause, not willingly, for such a love:
1290   To this I call my friends in testimony,
Her brethren, and her father, who himself
Besought me to be plain and blunt, and use,
To break her passion, some discourtesy
Against my nature: what I could, I did.

maid I died, I take God to my witness. Pray for my soul, sir Launcelot, as thou art a knight peerless."'

1275–9. Malory xviii 20: 'And when it was read, the queen and all the knights wept for pity of the doleful complaints.'

1281–98. Malory xviii 20: '"My lord, king Arthur, wit you well that I am right heavy of the death of this fair damsel. God knoweth I was never causer of her death by my will; and that I will report me unto her own brother here, he is sir Lavaine. I will not say nay", said sir Launcelot, "but that she was both fair and good; and much was I beholden unto her: but she loved me out of measure."'

1284–5. Gray (p. 52) compares *2 Samuel* i 26: 'love was wonderful, passing the love of women'.

1295 I left her and I bad her no farewell;
Though, had I dreamt the damsel would have died,
I might have put my wits to some rough use,
And helped her from herself.'
                                    Then said the Queen
(Sea was her wrath, yet working after storm)
1300 'Ye might at least have done her so much grace,
Fair lord, as would have helped her from her death.'
He raised his head, their eyes met and hers fell,
He adding,
                    'Queen, she would not be content
Save that I wedded her, which could not be.
Then might she follow me through the world, she
1305   asked;
It could not be. I told her that her love
Was but the flash of youth, would darken down
To rise hereafter in a stiller flame
Toward one more worthy of her – then would I,
1310 More specially were he, she wedded, poor,
Estate them with large land and territory
In mine own realm beyond the narrow seas,
To keep them in all joyance: more than this
I could not; this she would not, and she died.'

1315   He pausing, Arthur answered, 'O my knight,
It will be to thy worship, as my knight,
And mine, as head of all our Table Round,
To see that she be buried worshipfully.'

        So toward that shrine which then in all the realm
1320 Was richest, Arthur leading, slowly went

1298–301. Malory xviii 20: '"Ye might have shewed her," said the queen, "some bounty and gentleness, that ye might have preserved her life."'
1303–14. Malory xviii 20: '"Madam," said sir Launcelot, "she would none other way be answered, but that she would be my wife, or else my paramour; and of these two I would not grant her; but I proffered her for her good love, which she shewed me, a thousand pounds yearly to her and her heirs, and to wed any manner of knight that she could find best to love in her heart. For, madam," said sir Launcelot, "I love not to be constrained to love; for love must arise of the heart, and not by constraint."'
1315–8. Malory xviii 20: 'Said the king unto sir Launcelot, "it will be your worship that ye oversee that she be buried worshipfully."'
1316. thy] 1870 ('1869'); your 1859–69.
1319–35. Malory xviii 20: 'And so many knights went thither to behold the fair dead maid. And on the morrow she was richly buried, and sir

The marshalled Order of their Table Round,
And Lancelot sad beyond his wont, to see
The maiden buried, not as one unknown,
Nor meanly, but with gorgeous obsequies,
1325 And mass, and rolling music, like a queen.
And when the knights had laid her comely head
Low in the dust of half-forgotten kings,
Then Arthur spake among them, 'Let her tomb
Be costly, and her image thereupon,
1330 And let the shield of Lancelot at her feet
Be carven, and her lily in her hand.
And let the story of her dolorous voyage
For all true hearts be blazoned on her tomb
In letters gold and azure!' which was wrought
1335 Thereafter; but when now the lords and dames
And people, from the high door streaming, brake
Disorderly, as homeward each, the Queen,
Who marked Sir Lancelot where he moved apart,
Drew near, and sighed in passing, 'Lancelot,
1340 Forgive me; mine was jealousy in love.'
He answered with his eyes upon the ground,
'That is love's curse; pass on, my Queen, forgiven.'
But Arthur, who beheld his cloudy brows,
Approached him, and with full affection said,

1345   'Lancelot, my Lancelot, thou in whom I have
Most joy and most affiance, for I know
What thou hast been in battle by my side,
And many a time have watched thee at the tilt
Strike down the lusty and long practised knight,
1350 And let the younger and unskilled go by
To win his honour and to make his name,
And loved thy courtesies and thee, a man
Made to be loved; but now I would to God,

Launcelot offered her mass penny; and all the knights of the round table
that were there, at that time, offered with sir Launcelot.' T. says of ll. 1319–
27: 'This passage and the "tower-stair" passage [l. 341] are among the
best blank verse in *Lancelot and Elaine*, I think' (T.).
1337–42. Malory xviii 20: 'Then the queen sent for sir Launcelot, and
prayed him of mercy, for because she had been wrath with him causeless.–
"This is not the first time", said sir Launcelot, "that ye have been dis-
pleased with my counsels [me causeless]; but, madam, ever I must suffer
you, but what sorrow that I endure, ye take no force."'
1344. *said*,] *1873*; flung *1859–70*.
1344 ∧ 5] One arm about his neck, and spake and said. *1859–70*

Seeing the homeless trouble in thine eyes,
1355 Thou couldst have loved this maiden, shaped, it
        seems,
By God for thee alone, and from her face,
If one may judge the living by the dead,
Delicately pure and marvellously fair,
Who might have brought thee, now a lonely man
1360 Wifeless and heirless, noble issue, sons
Born to the glory of thy name and fame,
My knight, the great Sir Lancelot of the Lake.'

Then answered Lancelot, 'Fair she was, my King,
Pure, as you ever wish your knights to be.
1365 To doubt her fairness were to want an eye,
To doubt her pureness were to want a heart—
Yea, to be loved, if what is worthy love
Could bind him, but free love will not be bound.'

'Free love, so bound, were freëst,' said the King.
1370 'Let love be free; free love is for the best:
And, after heaven, on our dull side of death,
What should be best, if not so pure a love
Clothed in so pure a loveliness? yet thee
She failed to bind, though being, as I think,
1375 Unbound as yet, and gentle, as I know.'

And Lancelot answered nothing, but he went,
And at the inrunning of a little brook
Sat by the river in a cove, and watched
The high reed wave, and lifted up his eyes
1380 And saw the barge that brought her moving down,
Far-off, a blot upon the stream, and said
Low in himself, 'Ah simple heart and sweet,
Ye loved me, damsel, surely with a love
Far tenderer than my Queen's. Pray for thy soul?
1385 Ay, that will I. Farewell too—now at last—
Farewell, fair lily. "Jealousy in love?"
Not rather dead love's harsh heir, jealous pride?
Queen, if I grant the jealousy as of love,
May not your crescent fear for name and fame
1390 Speak, as it waxes, of a love that wanes?

1354] *1873*; For the wild people say wild things of thee, *1859–70.*
1363] And Lancelot answered, 'She was beautiful,
      Most tender, and I knew it; though methinks
      How beautiful I never knew till now: *Virginia MS*

Why did the King dwell on my name to me?
Mine own name shames me, seeming a reproach,
Lancelot, whom the Lady of the Lake
Caught from his mother's arms–the wondrous one
1395   Who passes through the vision of the night–
She chanted snatches of mysterious hymns
Heard on the winding waters, eve and morn
She kissed me saying, "Thou art fair, my child,
As a king's son," and often in her arms
1400   She bare me, pacing on the dusky mere.
Would she had drowned me in it, where'er it be!
For what am I? what profits me my name
Of greatest knight? I fought for it, and have it:
Pleasure to have it, none; to lose it, pain;
1405   Now grown a part of me: but what use in it?
To make men worse by making my sin known?
Or sin seem less, the sinner seeming great?
Alas for Arthur's greatest knight, a man
Not after Arthur's heart! I needs must break
1410   These bonds that so defame me: not without
She wills it: would I, if she willed it? nay,
Who knows? but if I would not, then may God,
I pray him, send a sudden Angel down
To seize me by the hair and bear me far,
1415   And fling me deep in that forgotten mere,
Among the tumbled fragments of the hills.'

So groaned Sir Lancelot in remorseful pain,
Not knowing he should die a holy man.

1394–5] *1873*; Stole from his mother–as the story runs–*1859–70*.
1396. hymns] *1873*; song *1859–70*.
1401]   But these are dreams.
    Yet somewhere I remember the waste gleam
    On some deep water, whence I came, but now
    I have dreamed a dream which seemed as deep as truth
    And that will drown my soul. *T.Nbk 39, del.*
1418. 'I asked my father why he did not write an Idyll "How Sir Lancelot
came unto the hermitage, and how he took the habit unto him; how he
went to Almesbury and found Queen Guinevere dead, whom they brought
to Glastonbury; and how Sir Lancelot died a holy man"; and he answered,
"Because it could not be done better than by Malory". My father loved
his own great imaginative knight, the Lancelot of the *Idylls*' (H.T.). Gray
(pp. 23–4) notes that T.'s ending 'echoes the words of a hermit of Lancelot's
during his Grail quest: "But God knoweth his thought and his unstableness,
and yet shall he die right an holy man'" (Malory xvi 5).

471 The Holy Grail

Published *1869* ('*1870*'). H.T. quotes his mother's journal: '1868, *Sept. 9th.* A. read a bit of his *San Graal*, which he has just begun. *Sept. 14th.* He has almost finished the *San Graal*. It came like a breath of inspiration. *Sept. 23rd* ... A. read the *San Graal* MS complete in the garden ... I doubt whether the *San Graal* would have been written but for my endeavour, and the Queen's wish, and that of the Crown Princess. Thank God for it. He has had the subject in his mind for years, ever since he began to write about Arthur and his knights.' As long ago as 3 Oct. 1859, T. had written to the Duke of Argyll: 'As to Macaulay's suggestion of the Sangreal, I doubt whether such a subject could be handled in these days, without incurring a charge of irreverence' (*Mem.* i 456; *Mat.* ii 236). Emily wrote to Woolner, 24 Oct. 1863: 'I long for him to be at the *San Graal*, feeling sure that is his work'; and again, 11 July 1864: 'I hope you think he has given your stories well. I wish he would give mine now and do the *San Graal* for me' (*Letters of E.T.*, pp. 176, 185). In April 1868 he wrote Ambrosius's speech (*Mem.* ii 53). Sir Charles Tennyson has pointed out the odd discrepancy between T.'s reluctance to tackle *The Holy Grail* and the statement in 1859 (*Eversley* v 440): 'He made a poem on Lancelot's quest of the San Graal; "in as good verse", he said, "as I ever wrote – no, I did not write, I made it in my head, and it has altogether slipt out of memory"'. See the MS stanzas of *Sir Launcelot and Queen Guinevere* (pp. 99–100). The source of *Eversley* is T.'s letter to the Duke of Argyll, 3 Oct. 1859. 'As to Macaulay's suggestion of the Sangraal I doubt whether such a subject could be handled in these days, without incurring a charge of irreverence. It would too much like playing with sacred things. The old writers *believed* in the Sangraal. Many years ago I did write Lancelot's Quest of the Grail in as good verses as I ever wrote – no, I did not write – I made it in my head, and it has now altogether slipt out of memory' (*Letters* ii 244). Walter White specifies that this amounted to 'three hundred lines' (14 Aug. 1860; *Journals*, 1898, pp. 151–2). Cp. *Sir Galahad* (p. 165).

The MS in *H.Nbk 38* includes a long prose draft, which 'carries the narrative to the close, but does not include Percival's meeting with Bors and his account of his meeting with Lancelot; and Percival's confession is evidently a later addition' (K. Tillotson, *Mid-Victorian Studies*, 1965, p. 98*n*). The beginning of the prose draft is quoted in *Mat.* iii 141–5. For a transcript of the prose draft with a few short poetic passages interspersed (*H.Nbk 38*), see D. Staines, *Harvard Library Bulletin* xxii (1974) 281–92. There is also a MS in *T.Nbk 29*. T.'s source was Malory xiii–xvii, which he modified very considerably. T. says of the poem: 'Faith declines, religion in many turns from practical goodness to the quest after the supernatural and marvellous and selfish religious excitement. Few are those for whom the quest is a source of spiritual strength... *The Holy Grail* is one of the most imaginative of my poems. I have expressed there my strong feeling as to the

Reality of the Unseen. The end, where the King speaks of his work and of his visions, is intended to be the summing up of all in the highest note by the highest of men.' 'My father looked on this description of Sir Galahad's quest, and on that of Sir Lancelot's, as among the best blank verse he had written. He pointed out the difference between the five visions of the Grail, as seen by the Holy Nun, Sir Galahad, Sir Percivale, Sir Lancelot, Sir Bors, according to their different, their own peculiar natures and circumstances, their selflessness, and the perfection or imperfection of their Christianity. He dwelt on the mystical treatment of every part of his subject, and said the key is to be found in a careful reading of Sir Percivale's visions. He would also call attention to the babbling homely utterances of the village priest Ambrosius as a contrast to the sweeping passages of blank verse that set forth the visions of spiritual enthusiasm' (H.T.). Gray (p. 28) suggests that T.'s major modification of his source, the singling out of Percivale to narrate the whole, was suggested to T. by Milton's Raphael; 'in Malory the narrators are the self-abnegating Bors and Lancelot'.

> From noiseful arms, and acts of prowess done
> In tournament or tilt, Sir Percivale,
> Whom Arthur and his knighthood called The Pure,
> Had passed into the silent life of prayer,
> 5   Praise, fast, and alms; and leaving for the cowl
> The helmet in an abbey far away
> From Camelot, there, and not long after, died.
>
> And one, a fellow-monk among the rest,
> Ambrosius, loved him much beyond the rest,
> 10   And honoured him, and wrought into his heart
> A way by love that wakened love within,
> To answer that which came: and as they sat
> Beneath a world-old yew-tree, darkening half
> The cloisters, on a gustful April morn
> 15   That puffed the swaying branches into smoke
> Above them, ere the summer when he died,
> The monk Ambrosius questioned Percivale:
>
> 'O brother, I have seen this yew-tree smoke,
> Spring after spring, for half a hundred years:

¶471. 2. G. C. Macaulay points out that 'Sir Percivale was the original hero of the Grail legend, and always a most important person in it, though his place was in the later form of the story partly taken by Galahad. Tennyson generally follows the later legend, but by making Percivale the narrator he has in fact given to him and to his adventures the chief degree of prominence.' For an amplification of this, see D. Staines on 'the tragedy of Percivale', *MLR* lxix (1974) 745–56.

18. 'The pollen in Spring, which, blown abroad by the wind, looks like smoke' (T. compares *Mem.* ii 53, and *In Memoriam* xxxix).

20 For never have I known the world without,
Nor ever strayed beyond the pale: but thee,
When first thou camest–such a courtesy
Spake through the limbs and in the voice–I knew
For one of those who eat in Arthur's hall;
25 For good ye are and bad, and like to coins,
Some true, some light, but every one of you
Stamped with the image of the King; and now
Tell me, what drove thee from the Table Round,
My brother? was it earthly passion crost?'

30 'Nay,' said the knight; 'for no such passion mine.
But the sweet vision of the Holy Grail
Drove me from all vainglories, rivalries,
And earthly heats that spring and sparkle out
Among us in the jousts, while women watch
Who wins, who falls; and waste the spiritual
35 strength
Within us, better offered up to Heaven.'

To whom the monk: 'The Holy Grail!–I trust
We are green in Heaven's eyes; but here too much
We moulder–as to things without I mean–
40 Yet one of your own knights, a guest of ours,
Told us of this in our refectory,
But spake with such a sadness and so low
We heard not half of what he said. What is it?
The phantom of a cup that comes and goes?'

45 'Nay, monk! what phantom?' answered Percivale.
'The cup, the cup itself, from which our Lord
Drank at the last sad supper with his own.
This, from the blessèd land of Aromat–
After the day of darkness, when the dead
50 Went wandering o'er Moriah–the good saint
Arimathæan Joseph, journeying brought
To Glastonbury, where the winter thorn

48. Aromat: 'Used for Arimathea, the home of Joseph of Arimathea, who, according to the legend, received in the Grail the blood that flowed from our Lord's side' (T.).
49–50. Matthew xxvii 45 and 52–3: 'Now from the sixth hour there was darkness over all the land unto the ninth hour ... And the graves were opened; and many bodies of the saints which slept arose, And came out of the graves after his resurrection, and went into the holy city, and appeared unto many.'
52–3. 'It was believed to have been grown from the staff of Joseph of Arimathea' (H.T.).

Blossoms at Christmas, mindful of our Lord.
And there awhile it bode; and if a man
55　Could touch or see it, he was healed at once,
By faith, of all his ills. But then the times
Grew to such evil that the holy cup
Was caught away to Heaven, and disappeared.'

To whom the monk: 'From our old books I
　　　know
60　That Joseph came of old to Glastonbury,
And there the heathen Prince, Arviragus,
Gave him an isle of marsh whereon to build;
And there he built with wattles from the marsh
A little lonely church in days of yore,
65　For so they say, these books of ours, but seem
Mute of this miracle, far as I have read.
But who first saw the holy thing today?'

'A woman,' answered Percivale, 'a nun,
And one no further off in blood from me
70　Than sister; and if ever holy maid
With knees of adoration wore the stone,
A holy maid; though never maiden glowed,
But that was in her earlier maidenhood,
With such a fervent flame of human love,
75　Which being rudely blunted, glanced and shot
Only to holy things; to prayer and praise
She gave herself, to fast and alms. And yet,
Nun as she was, the scandal of the Court,
Sin against Arthur and the Table Round,
80　And the strange sound of an adulterous race,
Across the iron grating of her cell
Beat, and she prayed and fasted all the more.

'And he to whom she told her sins, or what
Her all but utter whiteness held for sin,
85　A man wellnigh a hundred winters old,
Spake often with her of the Holy Grail,
A legend handed down through five or six,
And each of these a hundred winters old,
From our Lord's time. And when King Arthur made
90　His Table Round, and all men's hearts became
Clean for a season, surely he had thought

61. *Arviragus*: king of the Britons.

That now the Holy Grail would come again;
But sin broke out. Ah, Christ, that it would come,
And heal the world of all their wickedness!
95 "O Father!" asked the maiden, "might it come
To me by prayer and fasting?" "Nay," said he,
"I know not, for thy heart is pure as snow."
And so she prayed and fasted, till the sun
Shone, and the wind blew, through her, and I
    thought
100 She might have risen and floated when I saw her.

    'For on a day she sent to speak with me.
And when she came to speak, behold her eyes
Beyond my knowing of them, beautiful,
Beyond all knowing of them, wonderful,
105 Beautiful in the light of holiness.
And "O my brother Percivale," she said,
"Sweet brother, I have seen the Holy Grail:
For, waked at dead of night, I heard a sound
As of a silver horn from o'er the hills
110 Blown, and I thought, 'It is not Arthur's use
To hunt by moonlight;' and the slender sound
As from a distance beyond distance grew
Coming upon me—O never harp nor horn,
Nor aught we blow with breath, or touch with
    hand,
115 Was like that music as it came; and then
Streamed through my cell a cold and silver beam,
And down the long beam stole the Holy Grail,
Rose-red with beatings in it, as if alive,
Till all the white walls of my cell were dyed
120 With rosy colours leaping on the wall;
And then the music faded, and the Grail
Past, and the beam decayed, and from the walls
The rosy quiverings died into the night.
So now the Holy Thing is here again
125 Among us, brother, fast thou too and pray,
And tell thy brother knights to fast and pray,
That so perchance the vision may be seen
By thee and those, and all the world be healed."

    'Then leaving the pale nun, I spake of this
130 To all men; and myself fasted and prayed
Always, and many among us many a week
Fasted and prayed even to the uttermost,
Expectant of the wonder that would be.

'And one there was among us, ever moved
135 Among us in white armour, Galahad.
"God make thee good as thou art beautiful,"
Said Arthur, when he dubbed him knight; and none,
In so young youth, was ever made a knight
Till Galahad; and this Galahad, when he heard
140 My sister's vision, filled me with amaze;
His eyes became so like her own, they seemed
Hers, and himself her brother more than I.

'Sister or brother none had he; but some
Called him a son of Lancelot, and some said
145 Begotten by enchantment–chatterers they,
Like birds of passage piping up and down,
That gape for flies–we know not whence they come;
For when was Lancelot wanderingly lewd?

'But she, the wan sweet maiden, shore away
150 Clean from her forehead all that wealth of hair
Which made a silken mat-work for her feet;
And out of this she plaited broad and long
A strong sword-belt, and wove with silver thread
And crimson in the belt a strange device,
155 A crimson grail within a silver beam;
And saw the bright boy-knight, and bound it on him,
Saying, "My knight, my love, my knight of heaven,
O thou, my love, whose love is one with mine,

137. Malory xiii 1: 'And on the morrow, at the hour of prime, at Galahad's desire, he [Lancelot] made him a knight, and said, "God make him a good man, for beauty faileth him not as any that liveth."'
144–5. Malory xi 2 tells of the enchantment by which Lancelot was made to sleep with Elaine (daughter of King Pelles), believing her to be Guinevere: 'and for this intent; the king knew well that sir Launcelot should get a child upon his daughter, the which should be named sir Galahad, the good knight, by whom all the foreign country should be brought out of danger, and by him the holy grail would be achieved.'
149–60. Malory xvii 7, in which Percival's sister speaks to Galahad: '"Lo! lords", said the gentlewoman, "here is a girdle that ought to be set about the sword; and wit ye well that the greatest part of this girdle was made of my hair, the which I loved full well while I was a woman of the world; but as soon as I wist that this adventure was ordained me, I clipped off my hair, and made this girdle ... Now reck I not, though I die; for now I hold me [one of] the blessed maidens of the world, which hath made thee now the worthiest knights of the world."'
151. Cp. Keats, *Hyperion* i 82: 'A soft and silken mat for Saturn's feet.'

I, maiden, round thee, maiden, bind my belt.
160 Go forth, for thou shalt see what I have seen,
And break through all, till one will crown thee king
Far in the spiritual city:" and as she spake
She sent the deathless passion in her eyes
Through him, and made him hers, and laid her
      mind
165 On him, and he believed in her belief.

'Then came a year of miracle: O brother,
In our great hall there stood a vacant chair,
Fashioned by Merlin ere he past away,
And carven with strange figures; and in and out
170 The figures, like a serpent, ran a scroll
Of letters in a tongue no man could read.
And Merlin called it "The Siege perilous,"
Perilous for good and ill; "for there," he said,
"No man could sit but he should lose himself:"
175 And once by misadvertence Merlin sat
In his own chair, and so was lost; but he,
Galahad, when he heard of Merlin's doom,
Cried, "If I lose myself, I save myself!"

'Then on a summer night it came to pass,
180 While the great banquet lay along the hall,
That Galahad would sit down in Merlin's chair.

'And all at once, as there we sat, we heard
A cracking and a riving of the roofs,
And rending, and a blast, and overhead
185 Thunder, and in the thunder was a cry.
And in the blast there smote along the hall
A beam of light seven times more clear than day:
And down the long beam stole the Holy Grail

162. 'In the Grail legends "the spiritual city" is the city of Sarras, where
Joseph of Arimathaea converted King Evelac' (G. C. Macaulay).
172. 'The perilous seat which stands for the spiritual imagination' (T.).
See Malory xiii 4 for the empty seat at the Round Table, the letters on
which came to read: 'This is the siege of sir Galahad the good knight.'
178. *Matthew* x 39: 'He that findeth his life shall lose it: and he that loseth
his life for my sake shall find it.'
182–202. Malory xiii 7: 'Then anon they heard cracking and crying of
thunder, that they thought the place should all to rive. In the midst of the
blast entered a sun beam more clear by seven times than ever they saw
day, and all they were alighted of the grace of the Holy Ghost. Then
began every knight to behold other, and either saw other by their seeming

All over covered with a luminous cloud.
190 And none might see who bare it, and it past.
But every knight beheld his fellow's face
As in a glory, and all the knights arose,
And staring each at other like dumb men
Stood, till I found a voice and sware a vow.

195   'I sware a vow before them all, that I,
Because I had not seen the Grail, would ride
A twelvemonth and a day in quest of it,
Until I found and saw it, as the nun
My sister saw it; and Galahad sware the vow,
200 And good Sir Bors, our Lancelot's cousin, sware,
And Lancelot sware, and many among the knights,
And Gawain sware, and louder than the rest.'

Then spake the monk Ambrosius, asking him,
'What said the King? Did Arthur take the vow?'

205   'Nay, for my lord,' said Percivale, 'the King,

fairer than ever they saw other, not for then there was no knight that might
speak any word a great while; and so they looked every man on other as
they had been dumb. Then they [there] entered into the hall, the holy
grail covered with white samite, but there was none that might see it, nor
who bear it, and there was all the hall fulfilled with great odours, and
every knight had such meat and drink as he best loved in this world, and
when the holy grail had been borne through the hall, then the holy vessel
departed suddenly, that they wist not where it became. Then had they
breath to speak, and then the king yielded thanks unto God of his grace
that he had sent them. "Certainly," said king Arthur, "we ought greatly
to thank our Lord, Jesus Christ, for that he hath shewed us this day at the
reverence of this high feast of Pentecost".–"Now", said sir Gawaine,
"we have been served this day of what meats and drinks we thought on,
but one thing beguiled us, we might not see the holy grail, it was so
preciously covered, wherefore I will make here a vow, that to-morrow,
without any longer abiding, I shall labour in quest of the Sancgreal, that I
shall hold me out a twelvemonth and a day, or more if need be, and never
shall I return again unto the court till I have seen it more openly than it
hath been seen here. And if I may not speed I shall return again, as he that
may not be against the will of our Lord Jesus Christ". When they of the
round table heard sir Gawaine say so, they arose the most part of them and
avowed the same. And anon as king Arthur heard this, he was greatly
displeased, for he wist well that they [he] might not again say [gainsay]
their vows.'

205–6. Gray (p. 29): 'In Malory, Arthur is present with his knights when the
Grail comes'; Gray discusses the implications of T.'s change.

Was not in hall: for early that same day,
Scaped through a cavern from a bandit hold,
An outraged maiden sprang into the hall
Crying on help: for all her shining hair
210 Was smeared with earth, and either milky arm
Red-rent with hooks of bramble, and all she wore
Torn as a sail that leaves the rope is torn
In tempest: so the King arose and went
To smoke the scandalous hive of those wild bees
215 That made such honey in his realm. Howbeit
Some little of this marvel he too saw,
Returning o'er the plain that then began
To darken under Camelot; whence the King
Looked up, calling aloud, "Lo, there! the roofs
220 Of our great hall are rolled in thunder-smoke!
Pray Heaven, they be not smitten by the bolt."
For dear to Arthur was that hall of ours,
As having there so oft with all his knights
Feasted, and as the stateliest under heaven.

225   'O brother, had you known our mighty hall,
Which Merlin built for Arthur long ago!
For all the sacred mount of Camelot,
And all the dim rich city, roof by roof,
Tower after tower, spire beyond spire,
230 By grove, and garden-lawn, and rushing brook,
Climbs to the mighty hall that Merlin built.
And four great zones of sculpture, set betwixt
With many a mystic symbol, gird the hall:
And in the lowest beasts are slaying men,
235 And in the second men are slaying beasts,
And on the third are warriors, perfect men,
And on the fourth are men with growing wings,
And over all one statue in the mould
Of Arthur, made by Merlin, with a crown,
240 And peaked wings pointed to the Northern Star.
And eastward fronts the statue, and the crown
And both the wings are made of gold, and flame
At sunrise till the people in far fields,
Wasted so often by the heathen hordes,
245 Behold it, crying, "We have still a King."

232–7. 'The four zones represent human progress: the savage state of
society; the state where man lords it over the beast; the full development
of man; the progress toward spiritual ideals' (H.T.).

'And, brother, had you known our hall within,
Broader and higher than any in all the lands!
Where twelve great windows blazon Arthur's wars,
And all the light that falls upon the board
250   Streams through the twelve great battles of our
        King.
Nay, one there is, and at the eastern end,
Wealthy with wandering lines of mount and mere,
Where Arthur finds the brand Excalibur.
And also one to the west, and counter to it,
And blank: and who shall blazon it? when and
255   how?—
O there, perchance, when all our wars are done,
The brand Excalibur will be cast away.

'So to this hall full quickly rode the King,
In horror lest the work by Merlin wrought,
260   Dreamlike, should on the sudden vanish, wrapt
In unremorseful folds of rolling fire.
And in he rode, and up I glanced, and saw
The golden dragon sparkling over all:
And many of those who burnt the hold, their arms
Hacked, and their foreheads grimed with smoke,
265   and seared,
Followed, and in among bright faces, ours,
Full of the vision, prest: and then the King
Spake to me, being nearest, "Percivale,"
(Because the hall was all in tumult—some
270   Vowing, and some protesting), "what is this?"

'O brother, when I told him what had chanced,
My sister's vision, and the rest, his face
Darkened, as I have seen it more than once,
When some brave deed seemed to be done in vain,
275   Darken; and "Woe is me, my knights," he cried,
"Had I been here, ye had not sworn the vow."
Bold was mine answer, "Had thyself been here,
My King, thou wouldst have sworn." "Yea, yea,"
        said he,
"Art thou so bold and hast not seen the Grail?"

'"Nay, lord, I heard the sound, I saw the
280   light,
But since I did not see the Holy Thing,
I sware a vow to follow it till I saw."

261. 'This line gives onomatopoeically the "unremorseful flames"' (T.).

'Then when he asked us, knight by knight, if any
Had seen it, all their answers were as one:
285 "Nay, lord, and therefore have we sworn our vows."

'"Lo now," said Arthur, "have ye seen a cloud?
What go ye into the wilderness to see?"

'Then Galahad on the sudden, and in a voice
Shrilling along the hall to Arthur, called,
290 "But I, Sir Arthur, saw the Holy Grail,
I saw the Holy Grail and heard a cry –
'O Galahad, and O Galahad, follow me.'"

'"Ah, Galahad, Galahad," said the King, "for such
As thou art is the vision, not for these.
295 Thy holy nun and thou have seen a sign –
Holier is none, my Percivale, than she –
A sign to maim this Order which I made.
But ye. that follow but the leader's bell"
(Brother, the King was hard upon his knights)
300 "Taliessin is our fullest throat of song,
And one hath sung and all the dumb will sing.
Lancelot is Lancelot, and hath overborne
Five knights at once, and every younger knight,
Unproven, holds himself as Lancelot,
305 Till overborne by one, he learns – and ye,
What are ye? Galahads? – no, nor Percivales"
(For thus it pleased the King to range me close
After Sir Galahad); "nay," said he, "but men
With strength and will to right the wronged, of power
310 To lay the sudden heads of violence flat,
Knights that in twelve great battles splashed and
    dyed
The strong White Horse in his own heathen blood –

---

287. Christ says of John the Baptist: 'What went ye out into the wilderness to see? A reed shaken with the wind?' (*Matthew* xi 7).

290. Sir Charles Tennyson suggests that Galahad is here Arthur's equal, since this is the only time he calls him 'Sir Arthur'.

293–4. 'The king thought that most men ought to do the duty that lies closest to them, and that to few only is given the true spiritual enthusiasm. Those who have it not ought not to affect it' (T.).

298. ye] *1873;* you *1869–70.* Likewise in ll. 319, 325.

300. Taliessin: greatest of the ancient Welsh bards.

301. Gray (p. 55) notes *Isaiah* xxxv 6: 'Then shall the tongue of the dumb sing'.

But one hath seen, and all the blind will see.
Go, since your vows are sacred, being made:
315 Yet – for ye know the cries of all my realm
Pass through this hall – how often, O my knights,
Your places being vacant at my side,
This chance of noble deeds will come and go
Unchallenged, while ye follow wandering fires
320 Lost in the quagmire! Many of you, yea most,
Return no more: ye think I show myself
Too dark a prophet: come now, let us meet
The morrow morn once more in one full field
Of gracious pastime, that once more the King,
325 Before ye leave him for this Quest, may count
The yet-unbroken strength of all his knights,
Rejoicing in that Order which he made."

    'So when the sun broke next from under ground,
All the great table of our Arthur closed
330 And clashed in such a tourney and so full,
So many lances broken – never yet
Had Camelot seen the like, since Arthur came;
And I myself and Galahad, for a strength
Was in us from the vision, overthrew
335 So many knights that all the people cried,
And almost burst the barriers in their heat,
Shouting, "Sir Galahad and Sir Percivale!"

    'But when the next day brake from under ground –
O brother, had you known our Camelot,
340 Built by old kings, age after age, so old
The King himself had fears that it would fall,
So strange, and rich, and dim; for where the roofs
Tottered toward each other in the sky,
Met foreheads all along the street of those
345 Who watched us pass; and lower, and where the long
Rich galleries, lady-laden, weighed the necks

315–27. Malory xiii 7: "'Alas', said king Arthur unto sir Gawaine, "ye have nigh slain me with the vow and promise that ye have made, for through you ye have bereft me of the fairest fellowship, and the truest of knighthood, that ever were seen together in any realm of the world, for when they shall depart from hence I am sure that all shall never meet more in this world, for there shall many die in the quest, and so it forethinketh me a little, for I have loved them as well as my life; wherefore it shall grieve me right sore the separation of this fellowship, for I have had an old custom to have them in my fellowship.''

Of dragons clinging to the crazy walls,
Thicker than drops from thunder, showers of flowers
Fell as we past; and men and boys astride
350 On wyvern, lion, dragon, griffin, swan,
At all the corners, named us each by name,
Calling "God speed!" but in the ways below
The knights and ladies wept, and rich and poor
Wept, and the King himself could hardly speak
355 For grief, and all in middle street the Queen,
Who rode by Lancelot, wailed and shrieked aloud,
"This madness has come on us for our sins."
So to the Gate of the three Queens we came,
Where Arthur's wars are rendered mystically,
360 And thence departed every one his way.

   'And I was lifted up in heart, and thought
Of all my late-shown prowess in the lists,
How my strong lance had beaten down the knights,
So many and famous names; and never yet
365 Had heaven appeared so blue, nor earth so green,
For all my blood danced in me, and I knew
That I should light upon the Holy Grail.

   'Thereafter, the dark warning of our King,
That most of us would follow wandering fires,
370 Came like a driving gloom across my mind.
Then every evil word I had spoken once,
And every evil thought I had thought of old,
And every evil deed I ever did,
Awoke and cried, "This Quest is not for thee."
375 And lifting up mine eyes, I found myself
Alone, and in a land of sand and thorns,
And I was thirsty even unto death;
And I, too, cried, "This Quest is not for thee."

   'And on I rode, and when I thought my thirst

350. *wyvern*: 'two-legged dragon. Old French *wivre*, viper' (T.).
352. *ways*] *1873*; street *1869–70*.
353. Malory xiii 7: 'Then the queen departed into her chamber, so that
no man should perceive her great sorrows . . . And there was weeping of
the rich and poor, and the king returned [turned] away, and might not
speak for weeping.'
355. *all in*] *1873*; in the *1869–70*.
358] *1873*; And then we reached the weirdly-sculptured gate, *1869–70*.
359. *are*] *1873*; were *1869–70*.
379–90. Gray (p. 26) notes that this is from Ector's dream about Lancelot
(Malory xvi 2).

380   Would slay me, saw deep lawns, and then a brook,
       With one sharp rapid, where the crisping white
       Played ever back upon the sloping wave,
       And took both ear and eye; and o'er the brook
       Were apple-trees, and apples by the brook
385   Fallen, and on the lawns. "I will rest here,"
       I said, "I am not worthy of the Quest;"
       But even while I drank the brook, and ate
       The goodly apples, all these things at once
       Fell into dust, and I was left alone,
390   And thirsting, in a land of sand and thorns.

           'And then behold a woman at a door
       Spinning; and fair the house whereby she sat,
       And kind the woman's eyes and innocent,
       And all her bearing gracious; and she rose
395   Opening her arms to meet me, as who should say,
       "Rest here;" but when I touched her, lo! she, too,
       Fell into dust and nothing, and the house
       Became no better than a broken shed,
       And in it a dead babe; and also this
400   Fell into dust, and I was left alone.

           'And on I rode, and greater was my thirst.
       Then flashed a yellow gleam across the world,
       And where it smote the plowshare in the field,
       The plowman left his plowing, and fell down
405   Before it; where it glittered on her pail,
       The milkmaid left her milking, and fell down
       Before it, and I knew not why, but thought
       "The sun is rising," though the sun had risen.
       Then was I ware of one that on me moved
410   In golden armour with a crown of gold
       About a casque all jewels; and his horse
       In golden armour jewelled everywhere:
       And on the splendour came, flashing me blind;
       And seemed to me the Lord of all the world,
415   Being so huge. But when I thought he meant

387-90. 'The gratification of sensual appetite brings Percivale no content'
(T., who comments on the ensuing episodes: 'Nor does wifely love and
the love of the family; nor does wealth, which is worshipt by labour; nor
does glory; nor does Fame').

409-20. Gray (p. 26) notes that this is from Percivale's 'dreaming that he had
to fight "with the strongest champion of the world"' (Malory xiv 6).

To crush me, moving on me, lo! he, too,
Opened his arms to embrace me as he came,
And up I went and touched him, and he, too,
Fell into dust, and I was left alone
420 And wearying in a land of sand and thorns.

'And I rode on and found a mighty hill,
And on the top, a city walled: the spires
Pricked with incredible pinnacles into heaven.
And by the gateway stirred a crowd; and these
425 Cried to me climbing, "Welcome, Percivale!
Thou mightiest and thou purest among men!"
And glad was I and clomb, but found at top
No man, nor any voice. And thence I past
Far through a ruinous city, and I saw
430 That man had once dwelt there; but there I found
Only one man of an exceeding age.
"Where is that goodly company," said I,
"That so cried out upon me?" and he had
Scarce any voice to answer, and yet gasped,
435 "Whence and what art thou?" and even as he spoke
Fell into dust, and disappeared, and I
Was left alone once more, and cried in grief,
"Lo, if I find the Holy Grail itself
And touch it, it will crumble into dust."

440 'And thence I dropt into a lowly vale,
Low as the hill was high, and where the vale
Was lowest, found a chapel, and thereby
A holy hermit in a hermitage,
To whom I told my phantoms, and he said:

445 '"O son, thou hast not true humility,
The highest virtue, mother of them all;
For when the Lord of all things made Himself
Naked of glory for His mortal change,
'Take thou my robe,' she said, 'for all is thine,'
450 And all her form shone forth with sudden light
So that the angels were amazed, and she
Followed Him down, and like a flying star
Led on the gray-haired wisdom of the east;
But her thou hast not known: for what is this
455 Thou thoughtest of thy prowess and thy sins?
Thou hast not lost thyself to save thyself
As Galahad." When the hermit made an end,
In silver armour suddenly Galahad shone

453. 'The Magi' (T.).

Before us, and against the chapel door
460   Laid lance, and entered, and we knelt in prayer.
And there the hermit slaked my burning thirst,
And at the sacring of the mass I saw
The holy elements alone; but he,
"Saw ye no more? I, Galahad, saw the Grail,
465   The Holy Grail, descend upon the shrine:
I saw the fiery face as of a child
That smote itself into the bread, and went;
And hither am I come; and never yet
Hath what thy sister taught me first to see,
470   This Holy Thing, failed from my side, nor come
Covered, but moving with me night and day,
Fainter by day, but always in the night
Blood-red, and sliding down the blackened marsh
Blood-red, and on the naked mountain top
475   Blood-red, and in the sleeping mere below
Blood-red. And in the strength of this I rode,
Shattering all evil customs everywhere,
And past through Pagan realms, and made them mine,
And clashed with Pagan hordes, and bore them down,
480   And broke through all, and in the strength of this
Come victor. But my time is hard at hand,
And hence I go; and one will crown me king
Far in the spiritual city; and come thou, too,
For thou shalt see the vision when I go."

485   'While thus he spake, his eye, dwelling on mine,
Drew me, with power upon me, till I grew
One with him, to believe as he believed.
Then, when the day began to wane, we went.

       'There rose a hill that none but man could climb,
490   Scarred with a hundred wintry water-courses—
Storm at the top, and when we gained it, storm
Round us and death; for every moment glanced
His silver arms and gloomed: so quick and thick

462. sacring: 'consecration' (T.).
462-7. Malory xvii 20: 'And then the bishop made semblance as though he would have gone to the sakering of the mass; and then he took a wafer, which was made in the likeness of bread, and at the lifting up there came a figure in the likeness of a child, and the visage was as red and as bright as any fire, and smote himself into that bread, so that they all saw that the bread was formed of a fleshly man.'
491. 'It was a time of storm when men could imagine miracles, and so storm is emphasized' (T.).

The lightnings here and there to left and right
495 Struck, till the dry old trunks about us, dead,
Yea, rotten with a hundred years of death,
Sprang into fire: and at the base we found
On either hand, as far as eye could see,
A great black swamp and of an evil smell,
500 Part black, part whitened with the bones of men,
Not to be crost, save that some ancient king
Had built a way, where, linked with many a bridge,
A thousand piers ran into the great Sea.
And Galahad fled along them bridge by bridge,
505 And every bridge as quickly as he crost
Sprang into fire and vanished, though I yearned
To follow; and thrice above him all the heavens
Opened and blazed with thunder such as seemed
Shoutings of all the sons of God: and first
510 At once I saw him far on the great Sea,
In silver-shining armour starry-clear;
And o'er his head the Holy Vessel hung
Clothed in white samite or a luminous cloud.
And with exceeding swiftness ran the boat,
515 If boat it were—I saw not whence it came.
And when the heavens opened and blazed again
Roaring, I saw him like a silver star—
And had he set the sail, or had the boat
Become a living creature clad with wings?
520 And o'er his head the Holy Vessel hung
Redder than any rose, a joy to me,
For now I knew the veil had been withdrawn.
Then in a moment when they blazed again
Opening, I saw the least of little stars
525 Down on the waste, and straight beyond the star
I saw the spiritual city and all her spires
And gateways in a glory like one pearl—
No larger, though the goal of all the saints—
Strike from the sea; and from the star there shot
530 A rose-red sparkle to the city, and there
Dwelt, and I knew it was the Holy Grail,
Which never eyes on earth again shall see.
Then fell the floods of heaven drowning the deep.
And how my feet recrost the deathful ridge

509. *Job* xxxviii 7: 'When the morning stars sang together, and all the sons
of God shouted for joy.'
526-7. Cp. *Revelation* xxi.

535   No memory in me lives; but that I touched
The chapel-doors at dawn I know; and thence
Taking my war-horse from the holy man,
Glad that no phantom vext me more, returned
To whence I came, the gate of Arthur's wars.'

540   'O brother,' asked Ambrosius, – 'for in sooth
These ancient books – and they would win thee – teem,
Only I find not there this Holy Grail,
With miracles and marvels like to these,
Not all unlike; which oftentime I read,

545   Who read but on my breviary with ease,
Till my head swims; and then go forth and pass
Down to the little thorpe that lies so close,
And almost plastered like a martin's nest
To these old walls – and mingle with our folk;

550   And knowing every honest face of theirs
As well as ever shepherd knew his sheep,
And every homely secret in their hearts,
Delight myself with gossip and old wives,
And ills and aches, and teethings, lyings-in,

555   And mirthful sayings, children of the place,
That have no meaning half a league away:
Or lulling random squabbles when they rise,
Chafferings and chatterings at the market-cross,
Rejoice, small man, in this small world of mine,

560   Yea, even in their hens and in their eggs –
O brother, saving this Sir Galahad,
Came ye on none but phantoms in your quest,
No man, no woman?'

                Then Sir Percivale:
   'All men, to one so bound by such a vow,

565   And women were as phantoms. O, my brother,
Why wilt thou shame me to confess to thee
How far I faltered from my quest and vow?
For after I had lain so many nights,
A bedmate of the snail and eft and snake,

570   In grass and burdock, I was changed to wan
And meagre, and the vision had not come;
And then I chanced upon a goodly town
With one great dwelling in the middle of it;
Thither I made, and there was I disarmed

575   By maidens each as fair as any flower:

575–605. See the temptation of Percivale in Malory xiv 9.

But when they led me into hall, behold,
The Princess of that castle was the one,
Brother, and that one only, who had ever
Made my heart leap; for when I moved of old
580 A slender page about her father's hall,
And she a slender maiden, all my heart
Went after her with longing: yet we twain
Had never kissed a kiss, or vowed a vow.
And now I came upon her once again,
585 And one had wedded her, and he was dead,
And all his land and wealth and state were hers.
And while I tarried, every day she set
A banquet richer than the day before
By me; for all her longing and her will
590 Was toward me as of old; till one fair morn,
I walking to and fro beside a stream
That flashed across her orchard underneath
Her castle-walls, she stole upon my walk,
And calling me the greatest of all knights,
595 Embraced me, and so kissed me the first time,
And gave herself and all her wealth to me.
Then I remembered Arthur's warning word,
That most of us would follow wandering fires,
And the Quest faded in my heart. Anon,
600 The heads of all her people drew to me,
With supplication both of knees and tongue:
"We have heard of thee: thou art our greatest knight,
Our Lady says it, and we well believe:
Wed thou our Lady, and rule over us,
605 And thou shalt be as Arthur in our land."
O me, my brother! but one night my vow
Burnt me within, so that I rose and fled,
But wailed and wept, and hated mine own self,
And even the Holy Quest, and all but her;
610 Then after I was joined with Galahad
Cared not for her, nor anything upon earth.'

Then said the monk, 'Poor men, when yule is cold,
Must be content to sit by little fires.
And this am I, so that ye care for me
615 Ever so little; yea, and blest be Heaven
That brought thee here to this poor house of ours
Where all the brethren are so hard, to warm
My cold heart with a friend: but O the pity
To find thine own first love once more–to hold,
620 Hold her a wealthy bride within thine arms,

Or all but hold, and then – cast her aside,
Foregoing all her sweetness, like a weed.
For we that want the warmth of double life,
We that are plagued with dreams of something sweet
625　Beyond all sweetness in a life so rich, –
Ah, blessèd Lord, I speak too earthlywise,
Seeing I never strayed beyond the cell,
But live like an old badger in his earth,
With earth about him everywhere, despite
630　All fast and penance. Saw ye none beside,
None of your knights?'

　　　　　　　'Yea so,' said Percivale:
'One night my pathway swerving east, I saw
The pelican on the casque of our Sir Bors
All in the middle of the rising moon:
635　And toward him spurred, and hailed him, and he me,
And each made joy of either; then he asked,
"Where is he? hast thou seen him – Lancelot? – Once,"
Said good Sir Bors, "he dashed across me – mad,
And maddening what he rode: and when I cried,
640　'Ridest thou then so hotly on a quest
So holy,' Lancelot shouted, 'Stay me not!
I have been the sluggard, and I ride apace,
For now there is a lion in the way.'
So vanished."

　　　　　　　'Then Sir Bors had ridden on
645　Softly, and sorrowing for our Lancelot,
Because his former madness, once the talk
And scandal of our table, had returned;
For Lancelot's kith and kin so worship him
That ill to him is ill to them; to Bors
650　Beyond the rest: he well had been content
Not to have seen, so Lancelot might have seen,
The Holy Cup of healing; and, indeed,
Being so clouded with his grief and love,
Small heart was his after the Holy Quest:

642–3. *Proverb* xxvi 13: 'The slothful man saith, There is a lion in the way;
a lion is in the streets.'
646. Malory xii 3–4, on Lancelot's madness and his cure by the Grail.
649–52. Gray (p. 26) notes that this 'derives from an admission Malory's Bors
makes to a hermit: "... there is nothing in the world but I had lever do it
than to see my lord, Sir Launcelot du Lake, to die in my default"' (Malory
xvi 11).

655   If God would send the vision, well: if not,
     The Quest and he were in the hands of Heaven.

     'And then, with small adventure met, Sir Bors
     Rode to the lonest tract of all the realm,
     And found a people there among their crags,
660   Our race and blood, a remnant that were left
     Paynim amid their circles, and the stones
     They pitch up straight to heaven: and their wise men
     Were strong in that old magic which can trace
     The wandering of the stars, and scoffed at him
665   And this high Quest as at a simple thing:
     Told him he followed—almost Arthur's words—
     A mocking fire: "what other fire than he,
     Whereby the blood beats, and the blossom blows,
     And the sea rolls, and all the world is warmed?"
670   And when his answer chafed them, the rough crowd,
     Hearing he had a difference with their priests,
     Seized him, and bound and plunged him into a cell
     Of great piled stones; and lying bounden there
     In darkness through innumerable hours
675   He heard the hollow-ringing heavens sweep
     Over him till by miracle—what else?—
     Heavy as it was, a great stone slipt and fell,
     Such as no wind could move: and through the gap
     Glimmered the streaming scud: then came a night
680   Still as the day was loud; and through the gap
     The seven clear stars of Arthur's Table Round—
     For, brother, so one night, because they roll
     Through such a round in heaven, we named the stars,
     Rejoicing in ourselves and in our King—
685   And these, like bright eyes of familiar friends,
     In on him shone: "And then to me, to me,"
     Said good Sir Bors, "beyond all hopes of mine,
     Who scarce had prayed or asked it for myself—
     Across the seven clear stars—O grace to me—
690   In colour like the fingers of a hand

658] Down to the last tongue-tip of Lyoness rode, *T.Nbk 29*.
661–2. 'The temples and upright stones of the Druidic religion' (T.).
666–9] Till our fair father Christ should pass away
       And their diviner worship be restored. *HnMS*
667. 'The sun-worshippers that were said to dwell on Lyonnesse scoffed at Percivale' (T.).
675. *heavens*] 1869–94; heaven *Eversley*.
681. 'The Great Bear' (T.).

Before a burning taper, the sweet Grail
Glided and past, and close upon it pealed
A sharp quick thunder." Afterwards, a maid,
Who kept our holy faith among her kin
695   In secret, entering, loosed and let him go.'

To whom the monk: 'And I remember now
That pelican on the casque: Sir Bors it was
Who spake so low and sadly at our board;
And mighty reverent at our grace was he:
700   A square-set man and honest; and his eyes,
An out-door sign of all the warmth within,
Smiled with his lips—a smile beneath a cloud,
But heaven had meant it for a sunny one:
Ay, ay, Sir Bors, who else? But when ye reached
705   The city, found ye all your knights returned,
Or was there sooth in Arthur's prophecy,
Tell me, and what said each, and what the King?'

Then answered Percivale: 'And that can I,
Brother, and truly; since the living words
710   Of so great men as Lancelot and our King
Pass not from door to door and out again,
But sit within the house. O, when we reached
The city, our horses stumbling as they trode
On heaps of ruin, hornless unicorns,
715   Cracked basilisks, and splintered cockatrices,
And shattered talbots, which had left the stones
Raw, that they fell from, brought us to the hall.

'And there sat Arthur on the dais-throne,
And those that had gone out upon the Quest,
720   Wasted and worn, and but a tithe of them,
And those that had not, stood before the King,
Who, when he saw me, rose, and bad me hail,
Saying, "A welfare in thine eye reproves
Our fear of some disastrous chance for thee
725   On hill, or plain, at sea, or flooding ford.
So fierce a gale made havoc here of late
Among the strange devices of our kings;
Yea, shook this newer, stronger hall of ours,
And from the statue Merlin moulded for us
730   Half-wrenched a golden wing; but now—the Quest,

691–2. 'It might have been a meteor' (T.).
715. *basilisks*: 'the fabulous crowned serpent whose look killed' (T.).
cockatrices: 'in heraldry, winged snakes' (T.).
716. *talbots*: 'heraldic dogs' (T.).

This vision—hast thou seen the Holy Cup,
That Joseph brought of old to Glastonbury?"

'So when I told him all thyself hast heard,
Ambrosius, and my fresh but fixt resolve
735 To pass away into the quiet life,
He answered not, but, sharply turning, asked
Of Gawain, "Gawain, was this Quest for thee?"

'"Nay, lord," said Gawain, "not for such as I.
Therefore I communed with a saintly man,
740 Who made me sure the Quest was not for me;
For I was much awearied of the Quest:
But found a silk pavilion in a field,
And merry maidens in it; and then this gale
Tore my pavilion from the tenting-pin,
745 And blew my merry maidens all about
With all discomfort; yea, and but for this,
My twelvemonth and a day were pleasant to me."

'He ceased; and Arthur turned to whom at first
He saw not, for Sir Bors, on entering, pushed
750 Athwart the throng to Lancelot, caught his hand,
Held it, and there, half-hidden by him, stood,
Until the King espied him, saying to him,
"Hail, Bors! if ever loyal man and true
Could see it, thou hast seen the Grail;" and Bors,
755 "Ask me not, for I may not speak of it:
I saw it;" and the tears were in his eyes.

'Then there remained but Lancelot, for the rest
Spake but of sundry perils in the storm;
Perhaps, like him of Cana in Holy Writ,
760 Our Arthur kept his best until the last;
"Thou, too, my Lancelot," asked the King, "my friend,
Our mightiest, hath this Quest availed for thee?"

'"Our mightiest!" answered Lancelot, with a groan;
"O King!"—and when he paused, methought I spied

738. Based on Malory xvi 5, though here and elsewhere T. worsened the
character of Gawain. Gray (p. 27): 'The adventure with maidens in a
pavilion, not in Malory, was perhaps suggested by a like incident in a
famous collection concerning the knight' ('The Jeaste of Sir Gawain', in *Sir
Gawayne*, ed. Madden, 1839).
759. *John* ii 1–10.
763. H.T. compares Malory xiii 19: 'And there he said, "My sin and my
wretchedness hath brought me unto great dishonour: for when I sought
worldly adventures, and worldly desires, I ever achieved them, and had the
better in every place, and never was I discomfited in any quarrel, were it right

765   A dying fire of madness in his eyes—
         "O King, my friend, if friend of thine I be,
         Happier are those that welter in their sin,
         Swine in the mud, that cannot see for slime,
         Slime of the ditch: but in me lived a sin
770   So strange, of such a kind, that all of pure,
         Noble, and knightly in me twined and clung
         Round that one sin, until the wholesome flower
         And poisonous grew together, each as each,
         Not to be plucked asunder; and when thy knights
775   Sware, I sware with them only in the hope
         That could I touch or see the Holy Grail
         They might be plucked asunder. Then I spake
         To one most holy saint, who wept and said,
         That save they could be plucked asunder, all
780   My quest were but in vain; to whom I vowed
         That I would work according as he willed.
         And forth I went, and while I yearned and strove
         To tear the twain asunder in my heart,
         My madness came upon me as of old,
785   And whipt me into waste fields far away;
         There was I beaten down by little men,
         Mean knights, to whom the moving of my sword
         And shadow of my spear had been enow
         To scare them from me once; and then I came
790   All in my folly to the naked shore,
         Wide flats, where nothing but coarse grasses grew;
         But such a blast, my King, began to blow,
         So loud a blast along the shore and sea,
         Ye could not hear the waters for the blast,
795   Though heapt in mounds and ridges all the sea
         Drove like a cataract, and all the sand
         Swept like a river, and the clouded heavens
         Were shaken with the motion and the sound.
         And blackening in the sea-foam swayed a boat,
800   Half-swallowed in it, anchored with a chain;
         And in my madness to myself I said,
         'I will embark and I will lose myself,

or wrong; and now I take upon me the adventures of holy things: and now I see and understand that mine old sin hindereth me; and also shamed me, so that I had no power to stir, nor to speak, when the holy blood appeared before me." So thus he sorrowed till it was day, and heard the fowls of the air sing; then was he somewhat comforted.'

777–9. Based on Malory xiii 20, where the hermit refers specifically to Lancelot's love of Guinevere (which in T.'s context cannot be mentioned).

And in the great sea wash away my sin.'
I burst the chain, I sprang into the boat.
805 Seven days I drove along the dreary deep,
And with me drove the moon and all the stars;
And the wind fell, and on the seventh night
I heard the shingle grinding in the surge,
And felt the boat shock earth, and looking up,
810 Behold, the enchanted towers of Carbonek,
A castle like a rock upon a rock,
With chasm-like portals open to the sea,
And steps that met the breaker! there was none
Stood near it but a lion on each side
815 That kept the entry, and the moon was full.
Then from the boat I leapt, and up the stairs.
There drew my sword. With sudden-flaring manes
Those two great beasts rose upright like a man,
Each gript a shoulder, and I stood between;
820 And, when I would have smitten them, heard a voice,
'Doubt not, go forward; if thou doubt, the beasts
Will tear thee piecemeal.' Then with violence
The sword was dashed from out my hand, and fell.
And up into the sounding hall I past;
825 But nothing in the sounding hall I saw,
No bench nor table, painting on the wall

808. Cp. 'I seemed to hear the shingle grind / For ever in the boundless froth'
(*A foolish book*, III 626).
810. The legendary home of the Grail.
810–14. Malory xvii 14: 'So it befel, upon a night, at midnight, he arrived
afore a castle, on the back side, which was rich and fair; and there was a
postern that opened toward the sea, and was open without any keeping,
save two lions kept the entry; and the moon shined clear.'
815–22. Malory xvii 14: 'Then he ran to his arms, and armed him, and so he
went unto the gate, and saw the two lions; then he set hands to his sword,
and drew it. Then came there suddenly a dwarf, that smote him upon the
arm so sore, that the sword fell out of his hand. Then he heard a voice,
that said, "Oh, man of evil faith and poor belief, wherefore believest
thou more in thy harness than in thy Maker; for he might more avail
thee than thine armour, in whose service thou art set". Then said sir
Launcelot, "Fair father, Jesu Christ, I thank thee, of thy great mercy, that
thou reprovest me of my misdeed. Now see I well that thou holdest me
for thy servant". Then took he again his sword, and put it upon his
shield, and made a cross on his forehead, and came to the lions; and they
made attempt to do him harm; notwithstanding, he passed by them
without hurt, and entered into the castle, to the chief fortress.'

Or shield of knight; only the rounded moon
Through the tall oriel on the rolling sea.
But always in the quiet house I heard,
830   Clear as a lark, high o'er me as a lark,
A sweet voice singing in the topmost tower
To the eastward: up I climbed a thousand steps
With pain: as in a dream I seemed to climb
For ever: at the last I reached a door,
835   A light was in the crannies, and I heard,
'Glory and joy and honour to our Lord
And to the Holy Vessel of the Grail.'
Then in my madness I essayed the door;
It gave; and through a stormy glare, a heat
840   As from a seventimes-heated furnace, I,
Blasted and burnt, and blinded as I was,
With such a fierceness that I swooned away –
O, yet methought I saw the Holy Grail,
All palled in crimson samite, and around
845   Great angels, awful shapes, and wings and eyes.

827–8. 'My father was fond of quoting these lines for the beauty of the
sound. "The lark" in the tower toward the rising sun symbolizes Hope'
(H.T.). C. Y. Lang notes rather, *pace* H.T., that the lark is Lancelot's vision
of Elaine and Elaine's song of love and death.
833–6. Malory xvii 15: 'Then he listened, and heard a voice, which sung so
sweetly, that it seemed none earthly thing; and thought that the voice
said, "Joy and honour be to the Father of heaven."'
838–48. Malory xvii 15: 'And with that he saw the chamber-door open,
and with that there came out a great clearness, that the house was as bright
as though all the torches of the world had been there. So came he to the
chamber-door, and would have entered, and anon a voice said unto him,
"Flee, sir Launcelot, and enter not, for thou oughtest not to do it; and, if
thou enter, thou shalt forethink it". And he withdrew him back, and was
right heavy in his mind. Then he looked up in the midst of the chamber,
and saw a table of silver, and the holy vessel covered with red samite, and
many angels about it, whereof one of them held a candle of wax burning,
and the other held a cross, and the ornaments of the altar . . . Right so he
entered into the chamber, and came toward the table of silver. And when
he came nigh he felt a breath, that him thought was intermeddled with fire,
which smote him so sore in the visage, that him thought it all to break his
visage; and therewith he fell to the ground, and had no power to arise.'
840. Daniel iii 19, 'heat the furnace one seven times more than it was wont
to be heated' (the story of Shadrach, Meshach, and Abednego).
845. Ezekiel x 12, 'And their whole body, and their backs, and their hands,
and their wings, and the wheels, were full of eyes round about.'

And but for all my madness and my sin,
And then my swooning, I had sworn I saw
That which I saw; but what I saw was veiled
And covered; and this Quest was not for me."

850 'So speaking, and here ceasing, Lancelot left
The hall long silent, till Sir Gawain–nay,
Brother, I need not tell thee foolish words,–
A reckless and irreverent knight was he,
Now boldened by the silence of his King,–
855 Well, I will tell thee: "O King, my liege," he said,
"Hath Gawain failed in any quest of thine?
When have I stinted stroke in foughten field?
But as for thine, my good friend Percivale,
Thy holy nun and thou have driven men mad,
860 Yea, made our mightiest madder than our least.
But by mine eyes and by mine ears I swear,
I will be deafer than the blue-eyed cat,
And thrice as blind as any noonday owl,
To holy virgins in their ecstasies,
Henceforward."

865   '"Deafer," said the blameless King,
"Gawain, and blinder unto holy things
Hope not to make thyself by idle vows,
Being too blind to have desire to see.
But if indeed there came a sign from heaven,
870 Blessèd are Bors, Lancelot and Percivale,
For these have seen according to their sight.
For every fiery prophet in old times,
And all the sacred madness of the bard,
When God made music through them, could but speak
875 His music by the framework and the chord;
And as ye saw it ye have spoken truth.

'"Nay–but thou errest, Lancelot: never yet
Could all of true and noble in knight and man
Twine round one sin, whatever it might be,
880 With such a closeness, but apart there grew,
Save that he were the swine thou spakest of,
Some root of knighthood and pure nobleness;
Whereto see thou, that it may bear its flower.

862. H.T. quotes the first chapter of Darwin's *Origin of Species*: 'Thus cats which are entirely white and have blue eyes are generally deaf; but it has lately been pointed out by Mr Tait that this is confined to the males.'

'"And spake I not too truly, O my knights?
885 Was I too dark a prophet when I said
To those who went upon the Holy Quest,
That most of them would follow wandering fires,
Lost in the quagmire?—lost to me and gone,
And left me gazing at a barren board,
890 And a lean Order—scarce returned a tithe—
And out of those to whom the vision came
My greatest hardly will believe he saw;
Another hath beheld it afar off,
And leaving human wrongs to right themselves,
895 Cares but to pass into the silent life.
And one hath had the vision face to face,
And now his chair desires him here in vain,
However they may crown him otherwhere.

'"And some among you held, that if the King
900 Had seen the sight he would have sworn the vow:
Not easily, seeing that the King must guard
That which he rules, and is but as the hind
To whom a space of land is given to plow.
Who may not wander from the allotted field
905 Before his work be done; but, being done,
Let visions of the night or of the day
Come, as they will; and many a time they come,
Until this earth he walks on seems not earth,
This light that strikes his eyeball is not light,
910 This air that smites his forehead is not air
But vision—yea, his very hand and foot—
In moments when he feels he cannot die,
And knows himself no vision to himself,
Nor the high God a vision, nor that One
915 Who rose again: ye have seen what ye have seen."

'So spake the King: I knew not all he meant.'

908. 'Arthur suggests that all the material universe may be but vision' (T.).
911–3. H.T. compares *The Ancient Sage*.
913–14. 'My father said (I think) about this passage: "There is something miraculous in man, and there is more in Christianity than some people think. It is enough to look on Christ as Divine and Ideal without defining more. They will not easily beat the character of Christ, that union of man and woman, strength and sweetness"' (H.T.).

472 Pelleas and Ettarre

Published *1869* ('*1870*'). On 28 June 1859, T. 'read *Sir Pelleas and Ettarre* [Malory iv 21-4] . . . with a view to a new poem' (*Mat.* ii 220). Written 1869 (*CT*, pp. 381-2). R. W. Rader (*Tennyson's 'Maud'*, 1963, pp. 54-5) argues that T. associated this poem 'consciously or unconsciously with memories of Rosa [Baring]', especially the rose-song (ll. 391-400). 'Almost the saddest of the Idylls. The breaking of the storm' (T.). For evidence from the stubs in *H.Nbk 39* that T. wrote a prose draft of at least a major section, see D. Staines, *Harvard Library Bulletin* xxii (1974) 292.

King Arthur made new knights to fill the gap
Left by the Holy Quest; and as he sat
In hall at old Caerleon, the high doors
Were softly sundered, and through these a youth,
5   Pelleas, and the sweet smell of the fields
Past, and the sunshine came along with him.

'Make me thy knight, because I know, Sir King,
All that belongs to knighthood, and I love.'
Such was his cry: for having heard the King
10   Had let proclaim a tournament – the prize
A golden circlet and a knightly sword,
Full fain had Pelleas for his lady won
The golden circlet, for himself the sword:
And there were those who knew him near the King,
15   And promised for him: and Arthur made him knight.

And this new knight, Sir Pelleas of the isles –
But lately come to his inheritance,
And lord of many a barren isle was he –
Riding at noon, a day or twain before,
20   Across the forest called of Dean, to find
Caerleon and the King, had felt the sun
Beat like a strong knight on his helm, and reeled
Almost to falling from his horse; but saw
Near him a mound of even-sloping side,
25   Whereon a hundred stately beeches grew,
And here and there great hollies under them;
But for a mile all round was open space,
And fern and heath: and slowly Pelleas drew
To that dim day, then binding his good horse

¶472. *10-11*. Malory iv 21: 'And who that proved him the best knight should have a passing good sword and a circlet of gold; and the circlet the knight should give it to the fairest lady that was at those jousts.'

30 To a tree, cast himself down; and as he lay
　　At random looking over the brown earth
　　Through that green-glooming twilight of the grove,
　　It seemed to Pelleas that the fern without
　　Burnt as a living fire of emeralds,
35 So that his eyes were dazzled looking at it.
　　Then o'er it crost the dimness of a cloud
　　Floating, and once the shadow of a bird
　　Flying, and then a fawn; and his eyes closed.
　　And since he loved all maidens, but no maid
40 In special, half-awake he whispered, 'Where?
　　O where? I love thee, though I know thee not.
　　For fair thou art and pure as Guinevere,
　　And I will make thee with my spear and sword
　　As famous–O my Queen, my Guinevere,
45 For I will be thine Arthur when we meet.'

　　Suddenly wakened with a sound of talk
　　And laughter at the limit of the wood,
　　And glancing through the hoary boles, he saw,
　　Strange as to some old prophet might have seemed
50 A vision hovering on a sea of fire,
　　Damsels in divers colours like the cloud
　　Of sunset and sunrise, and all of them
　　On horses, and the horses richly trapt
　　Breast-high in that bright line of bracken stood:
55 And all the damsels talked confusedly,
　　And one was pointing this way, and one that,
　　Because the way was lost.

　　　　　　　　And Pelleas rose,
　　And loosed his horse, and led him to the light.
　　There she that seemed the chief among them said,
60 'In happy time behold our pilot-star!
　　Youth, we are damsels-errant, and we ride,
　　Armed as ye see, to tilt against the knights
　　There at Caerleon, but have lost our way:
　　To right? to left? straight forward? back again?
　　Which? tell us quickly.'

33–4. 'Seen as I lay in the New Forest' (T.). *Mat.* iii 89, 13 Sept. 1868.
46–54. Not in Malory. Cp. *Sir Orfeo*, long extracts from which are given
in Thomas Keightley's *Fairy Mythology* (1833, i 82–6). Part of this from
Keightley was copied out in *H.Nbk* 7. Heurodis sleeps under the trees, and
then meets knights and ladies on fine horses.
61–2. damsels-errant: from *Faerie Queene* II i XIX, iii i XXI (Gray, p. 31).

65   Pelleas gazing thought,
   'Is Guinevere herself so beautiful?'
   For large her violet eyes looked, and her bloom
   A rosy dawn kindled in stainless heavens,
   And round her limbs, mature in womanhood;
70 And slender was her hand and small her shape;
   And but for those large eyes, the haunts of scorn,
   She might have seemed a toy to trifle with,
   And pass and care no more. But while he gazed
   The beauty of her flesh abashed the boy,
75 As though it were the beauty of her soul:
   For as the base man, judging of the good,
   Puts his own baseness in him by default
   Of will and nature, so did Pelleas lend
   All the young beauty of his own soul to hers,
80 Believing her; and when she spake to him,
   Stammered, and could not make her a reply.
   For out of the waste islands had he come,
   Where saving his own sisters he had known
   Scarce any but the women of his isles,
   Rough wives, that laughed and screamed against the
85   gulls,
   Makers of nets, and living from the sea.

   Then with a slow smile turned the lady round
   And looked upon her people; and as when
   A stone is flung into some sleeping tarn,
90 The circle widens till it lip the marge,
   Spread the slow smile through all her company.
   Three knights were thereamong; and they too smiled,
   Scorning him; for the lady was Ettarre,
   And she was a great lady in her land.

95   Again she said, 'O wild and of the woods,
   Knowest thou not the fashion of our speech?
   Or have the Heavens but given thee a fair face,
   Lacking a tongue?'

65. *Pelleas*] *1886*; And Pelleas *1869–85*.
70] And slenderer miracles of hand and foot
      Never had woman: and herself was small, *Texas MS*
82–6. Suggested by Malory iv 22: 'My name is sir Pelles, born in the isles, and of many isles I am lord, and never have I loved lady nor damsel till now.'
94. Malory iv 21: 'He loveth a great lady in this country, and her name is Ettarde.'

                    'O damsel,' answered he,
'I woke from dreams; and coming out of gloom
100   Was dazzled by the sudden light, and crave
Pardon: but will ye to Caerleon? I
Go likewise: shall I lead you to the King?'

     'Lead then,' she said; and through the woods they
        went.
And while they rode, the meaning in his eyes,
105   His tenderness of manner, and chaste awe,
His broken utterances and bashfulness,
Were all a burthen to her, and in her heart
She muttered, 'I have lighted on a fool,
Raw, yet so stale!' But since her mind was bent
110   On hearing, after trumpet blown, her name
And title, 'Queen of Beauty,' in the lists
Cried – and beholding him so strong, she thought
That peradventure he will fight for me,
And win the circlet: therefore flattered him,
115   Being so gracious, that he wellnigh deemed
His wish by hers was echoed; and her knights
And all her damsels too were gracious to him,
For she was a great lady.

                   And when they reached
Caerleon, ere they past to lodging, she,
120   Taking his hand, 'O the strong hand,' she said,
'See! look at mine! but wilt thou fight for me,
And win me this fine circlet, Pelleas,
That I may love thee?'

               Then his helpless heart
Leapt, and he cried, 'Ay! wilt thou if I win?'
125   'Ay, that will I,' she answered, and she laughed,
And straitly nipt the hand, and flung it from her;
Then glanced askew at those three knights of hers,
Till all her ladies laughed along with her.

     'O happy world,' thought Pelleas, 'all, meseems,
130   Are happy; I the happiest of them all.'
Nor slept that night for pleasure in his blood,
And green wood-ways, and eyes among the leaves;
Then being on the morrow knighted, sware
To love one only. And as he came away,
135   The men who met him rounded on their heels
And wondered after him, because his face
Shone like the countenance of a priest of old
Against the flame about a sacrifice
Kindled by fire from heaven: so glad was he.

Then Arthur made vast banquets, and strange
140   knights
From the four winds came in: and each one sat,
Though served with choice from air, land, stream, and
    sea,
Oft in mid-banquet measuring with his eyes
His neighbour's make and might: and Pelleas looked
145 Noble among the noble, for he dreamed
His lady loved him, and he knew himself
Loved of the King: and him his new-made knight
Worshipt, whose lightest whisper moved him more
Than all the rangèd reasons of the world.

150 Then blushed and brake the morning of the jousts,
And this was called 'The Tournament of Youth:'
For Arthur, loving his young knight, withheld
His older and his mightier from the lists,
That Pelleas might obtain his lady's love,
155 According to her promise, and remain
Lord of the tourney. And Arthur had the jousts
Down in the flat field by the shore of Usk
Holden: the gilded parapets were crowned
With faces, and the great tower filled with eyes
160 Up to the summit, and the trumpets blew.
There all day long Sir Pelleas kept the field
With honour: so by that strong hand of his
The sword and golden circlet were achieved.

Then rang the shout his lady loved: the heat
165 Of pride and glory fired her face; her eye
Sparkled; she caught the circlet from his lance,
And there before the people crowned herself:
So for the last time she was gracious to him.

Then at Caerleon for a space – her look
170 Bright for all others, cloudier on her knight –
Lingered Ettarre: and seeing Pelleas droop,
Said Guinevere, 'We marvel at thee much,
O damsel, wearing this unsunny face
To him who won thee glory!' And she said,

150–63. Malory iv 21: 'And this knight, sir Pelles, was the best knight that was there, and there five hundred knights; but there was never man that ever sir Pelles met withal, but that he struck him down, or else from his horse. And every day of the three days he struck down twenty knights; therefore, they gave him the prize.'

175 'Had ye not held your Lancelot in your bower,
My Queen, he had not won.' Whereat the Queen,
As one whose foot is bitten by an ant,
Glanced down upon her, turned and went her way.

But after, when her damsels, and herself,
180 And those three knights all set their faces home,
Sir Pelleas followed. She that saw him cried,
'Damsels—and yet I should be shamed to say it—
I cannot bide Sir Baby. Keep him back
Among yourselves. Would rather that we had
185 Some rough old knight who knew the worldly way,
Albeit grizzlier than a bear, to ride
And jest with: take him to you, keep him off,
And pamper him with papmeat, if ye will,
Old milky fables of the wolf and sheep,
190 Such as the wholesome mothers tell their boys.
Nay, should ye try him with a merry one
To find his mettle, good: and if he fly us,
Small matter! let him.' This her damsels heard,
And mindful of her small and cruel hand,
195 They, closing round him through the journey home,
Acted her hest, and always from her side
Restrained him with all manner of device,
So that he could not come to speech with her.
And when she gained her castle, upsprang the bridge,
200 Down rang the grate of iron through the groove,
And he was left alone in open field.

'These be the ways of ladies,' Pelleas thought,
'To those who love them, trials of our faith.
Yea, let her prove me to the uttermost,
205 For loyal to the uttermost am I.'
So made his moan; and, darkness falling, sought
A priory not far off, there lodged, but rose
With morning every day, and, moist or dry,
Full-armed upon his charger all day long
210 Sat by the walls, and no one opened to him.

182–3. Malory iv 22: 'But she was so proud that she had scorn of him, and said, "That she would never love him, though he would die for her."'
188. Cp. *What Thor Said* 4: 'But pap-meat-pamper not the time.'
189 ∧ *90*] And tales that have a moral twang and tang *Texas MS, deleted.*
202–10. Malory iv 22: 'And so this knight promised the lady Ettarde to follow her into this country, and never to leave her till she loved him; and thus he is here the most part nigh her, and lodged by a priory.'

And this persistence turned her scorn to wrath.
Then calling her three knights, she charged them,
  'Out!
And drive him from the walls.' And out they came,
But Pelleas overthrew them as they dashed
215 Against him one by one; and these returned,
But still he kept his watch beneath the wall.

Thereon her wrath became a hate; and once,
A week beyond, while walking on the walls
With her three knights, she pointed downward, 'Look,
220 He haunts me—I cannot breathe—besieges me;
Down! strike him! put my hate into your strokes,
And drive him from my walls.' And down they went,
And Pelleas overthrew them one by one;
And from the tower above him cried Ettarre,
'Bind him, and bring him in.'

225   He heard her voice;
Then let the strong hand, which had overthrown
Her minion-knights, by those he overthrew
Be bounden straight, and so they brought him in.

Then when he came before Ettarre, the sight
230 Of her rich beauty made him at one glance
More bondsman in his heart than in his bonds.
Yet with good cheer he spake, 'Behold me, Lady,
A prisoner, and the vassal of thy will;
And if thou keep me in thy donjon here,
235 Content am I so that I see thy face
But once a day: for I have sworn my vows,
And thou hast given thy promise, and I know
That all these pains are trials of my faith,
And that thyself, when thou hast seen me strained
240 And sifted to the utmost, wilt at length
Yield me thy love and know me for thy knight.'

Then she began to rail so bitterly,
With all her damsels, he was stricken mute;
But when she mocked his vows and the great King,
245 Lighted on words: 'For pity of thine own self,
Peace, Lady, peace: is he not thine and mine?'
'Thou fool,' she said, 'I never heard his voice

211–28. Malory iv 22: 'And every week she sendeth knights to fight with
him; and when he hath put them to the worst, then will he suffer them
wilfully to take him prisoner, because he would have a sight of this lady.'

But longed to break away. Unbind him now,
And thrust him out of doors; for save he be
250 Fool to the midmost marrow of his bones,
He will return no more.' And those, her three,
Laughed, and unbound, and thrust him from the gate.

And after this, a week beyond, again
She called them, saying, 'There he watches yet,
255 There like a dog before his master's door!
Kicked, he returns: do ye not hate him, ye?
Ye know yourselves: how can ye bide at peace,
Affronted with his fulsome innocence?
Are ye but creatures of the board and bed,
260 No men to strike? Fall on him all at once,
And if ye slay him I reck not: if ye fail,
Give ye the slave mine order to be bound,
Bind him as heretofore, and bring him in:
It may be ye shall slay him in his bonds.'

265 She spake; and at her will they couched their spears,
Three against one: and Gawain passing by,
Bound upon solitary adventure, saw
Low down beneath the shadow of those towers
A villainy, three to one: and through his heart
270 The fire of honour and all noble deeds
Flashed, and he called, 'I strike upon thy side—
The caitiffs!' 'Nay,' said Pelleas, 'but forbear;
He needs no aid who doth his lady's will.'

So Gawain, looking at the villainy done,
275 Forbore, but in his heat and eagerness
Trembled and quivered, as the dog, withheld
A moment from the vermin that he sees
Before him, shivers, ere he springs and kills.

And Pelleas overthrew them, one to three;
280 And they rose up, and bound, and brought him in.
Then first her anger, leaving Pelleas, burned
Full on her knights in many an evil name
Of craven, weakling, and thrice-beaten hound:
'Yet, take him, ye that scarce are fit to touch,

266. In Malory, Gawain is told of Pelleas and seeks him out; Pelleas is not
being attacked, and simply tells Gawain of Ettarde's treatment. The details
are T.'s; in Malory, Pelleas says: 'When I am brought before her she
rebuketh me in the foulest manner'.

285 Far less to bind, your victor, and thrust him out,
And let who will release him from his bonds.
And if he comes again' – there she brake short;
And Pelleas answered, 'Lady, for indeed
I loved you and I deemed you beautiful,
290 I cannot brook to see your beauty marred
Through evil spite: and if ye love me not,
I cannot bear to dream you so forsworn:
I had liefer ye were worthy of my love,
Than to be loved again of you – farewell;
295 And though ye kill my hope, not yet my love,
Vex not yourself: ye will not see me more.'

While thus he spake, she gazed upon the man
Of princely bearing, though in bonds, and thought,
'Why have I pushed him from me? this man loves,
300 If love there be: yet him I loved not. Why?
I deemed him fool? yea, so? or that in him
A something—was it nobler than myself?
Seemed my reproach? He is not of my kind.
He could not love me, did he know me well.
305 Nay, let him go – and quickly.' And her knights
Laughed not, but thrust him bounden out of door.

Forth sprang Gawain, and loosed him from his
bonds,
And flung them o'er the walls; and afterward,
Shaking his hands, as from a lazar's rag,
310 'Faith of my body,' he said, 'and art thou not –
Yea thou art he, whom late our Arthur made
Knight of his table; yea and he that won
The circlet? wherefore hast thou so defamed
Thy brotherhood in me and all the rest,
315 As let these caitiffs on thee work their will?'

And Pelleas answered, 'O, their wills are hers
For whom I won the circlet; and mine, hers,
Thus to be bounden, so to see her face,
Marred though it be with spite and mockery now,
320 Other than when I found her in the woods;
And though she hath me bounden but in spite,
And all to flout me, when they bring me in,
Let me be bounden, I shall see her face;
Else must I die through mine unhappiness.'

325 And Gawain answered kindly though in scorn,
'Why, let my lady bind me if she will,

And let my lady beat me if she will:
But an she send her delegate to thrall
These fighting hands of mine – Christ kill me then
330   But I will slice him handless by the wrist,
And let my lady sear the stump for him,
Howl as he may. But hold me for your friend:
Come, ye know nothing: here I pledge my troth,
Yea, by the honour of the Table Round,
335   I will be leal to thee and work thy work,
And tame thy jailing princess to thine hand.
Lend me thine horse and arms, and I will say
That I have slain thee. She will let me in
To hear the manner of thy fight and fall;
340   Then, when I come within her counsels, then
From prime to vespers will I chant thy praise
As prowest knight and truest lover, more
Than any have sung thee living, till she long
To have thee back in lusty life again,
345   Not to be bound, save by white bonds and warm,
Dearer than freedom. Wherefore now thy horse
And armour: let me go: be comforted:
Give me three days to melt her fancy, and hope
The third night hence will bring thee news of gold.'

350   Then Pelleas lent his horse and all his arms,
Saving the goodly sword, his prize, and took
Gawain's, and said, 'Betray me not, but help –
Art thou not he whom men call light-of-love?'

      'Ay,' said Gawain, 'for women be so light.'
355   Then bounded forward to the castle walls,

332–53. Malory iv 22–3: '"Well", said sir Gawaine, "all this shall I amend, and ye will do as I shall devise: I will have your horse and your armour, and so will I ride to her castle, and tell her that I have slain you; and so shall I come within to her, to cause her to cherish me, and then shall I do my true part, that ye shall not fail to have her love". And therewithal sir Gawaine plight his troth unto sir Pelles to be true and faithful unto him. When they had plight their troth, the one to the other, they changed their horses and harness.'
342. prowest: 'noblest' (T.).
355–81. Malory iv 23: 'And sir Gawaine departed and came to the castle, whereas stood the pavilions of this lady without the gate: and, as soon as Ettarde had espied sir Gawaine, she fled towards the castle. Then sir Gawaine spake on high and bid her abide, for he was not sir Pelles; "I am another knight, that hath slain sir Pelles". "Do off your helm", said the lady

And raised a bugle hanging from his neck,
And winded it, and that so musically
That all the old echoes hidden in the wall
Rang out like hollow woods at hunting-tide.

360   Up ran a score of damsels to the tower;
'Avaunt,' they cried, 'our lady loves thee not.'
But Gawain lifting up his vizor said,
'Gawain am I, Gawain of Arthur's court,
And I have slain this Pelleas whom ye hate:
365   Behold his horse and armour. Open gates,
And I will make you merry.'

                    And down they ran,
Her damsels, crying to their lady, 'Lo!
Pelleas is dead—he told us—he that hath
His horse and armour: will ye let him in?
370   He slew him! Gawain, Gawain of the court,
Sir Gawain—there he waits below the wall,
Blowing his bugle as who should say him nay.'

        And so, leave given, straight on through open door
Rode Gawain, whom she greeted courteously.
375   'Dead, is it so?' she asked. 'Ay, ay,' said he,
'And oft in dying cried upon your name.'
'Pity on him,' she answered, 'a good knight,
But never let me bide one hour at peace.'
'Ay,' thought Gawain, 'and you be fair enow:
380   But I to your dead man have given my troth,
That whom ye loathe, him will I make you love.'

        So those three days, aimless about the land,
Lost in a doubt, Pelleas wandering
Waited, until the third night brought a moon
385   With promise of large light on woods and ways.

Ettarde, "that I may behold your visage". And when she saw it was not
sir Pelles, she made him to alight, and led him unto her castle, and asked
him faithfully whether he had slain sir Pelles? and he said yea. And then
sir Gawaine told her that his name was sir Gawaine, and of the court of
king Arthur, and his sister's son. "Truly", said she, "that is great pity, for
he was a passing good knight of his body, but of all men on live I hated
him most, for I never could be quiet for [quit of] him; and for that ye have
slain him I shall be your woman, and do any thing that may please you".
So she made sir Gawaine good cheer.'
365. gates] 1873; gate 1869–70.

Hot was the night and silent; but a sound
Of Gawain ever coming, and this lay –
Which Pelleas had heard sung before the Queen,
And seen her sadden listening – vext his heart,
390 And marred his rest – 'A worm within the rose.'

'A rose, but one, none other rose had I,
A rose, one rose, and this was wondrous fair,
One rose, a rose that gladdened earth and sky,
One rose, my rose, that sweetened all mine air –
395 I cared not for the thorns; the thorns were there.

'One rose, a rose to gather by and by,
One rose, a rose, to gather and to wear,
No rose but one – what other rose had I?
One rose, my rose; a rose that will not die, –
400 He dies who loves it, – if the worm be there.'

This tender rhyme, and evermore the doubt,
'Why lingers Gawain with his golden news?'
So shook him that he could not rest, but rode
Ere midnight to her walls, and bound his horse
405 Hard by the gates. Wide open were the gates,
And no watch kept; and in through these he past,
And heard but his own steps, and his own heart
Beating, for nothing moved but his own self,
And his own shadow. Then he crost the court,
410 And spied not any light in hall or bower,
But saw the postern portal also wide
Yawning; and up a slope of garden, all
Of roses white and red, and brambles mixt
And overgrowing them, went on, and found,
415 Here too, all hushed below the mellow moon,
Save that one rivulet from a tiny cave
Came lightening downward, and so spilt itself
Among the roses, and was lost again.

386–403] *1873* (see l. *397n*); The night was hot: he could not rest, but rode *1869–70*. T. wrote to F. Locker, Nov. 1872: 'I am thinking of writing a Song for Pelleas' (*Mat.* iii 198; *Letters* iii).

395] He laughs who loves it – though the thorns be there *Hn MS, replacing the published line*; T. wrote: 'This makes the song more perfect as a Song – but the old reading has more pathos and will, I think, be retained'.

397. a] *1882*; one *1873–81*.

410] *1873*; *not 1869–70*.

411. But] *1873*; And *1869–70*.

413. brambles] *1873*; wild ones *1869–70*.

Then was he ware of three pavilions reared
420　Above the bushes, gilden-peakt: in one,
　　　Red after revel, droned her lurdane knights
　　　Slumbering, and their three squires across their feet:
　　　In one, their malice on the placid lip
　　　Frozen by sweet sleep, four of her damsels lay:
425　And in the third, the circlet of the jousts
　　　Bound on her brow, were Gawain and Ettarre.

　　　Back, as a hand that pushes through the leaf
　　　To find a nest and feels a snake, he drew:

419. of . . . reared] *1873*; that white pavilions rose, *1869–70*.

419–26. Malory iv 23: 'And then it was in the month of May, that she and
sir Gawaine went out of the castle and supped in a pavilion, and there was a
bed made, and there sir Gawaine and the lady Ettarde went to bed together;
and in another pavilion she laid her damsels; and in the third pavilion she
laid part of her knights: for then she had no dread nor fear of sir Pelles.
And there sir Gawaine lay with her, doing his pleasure in that pavilion,
two days and two nights, against the faithful promise that he made to sir
Pelles. And, on the third day, in the morning early, sir Pelles armed him,
for he had not slept sith that sir Gawaine departed from him; for sir Gawaine
had promised, by the faith of his body, to come unto him to his pavilion
by the priory within the space of a day and a night. Then sir Pelles mounted
on horseback, and came to the pavilions that stood without the castle,
and found, in the first pavilion, three knights in their beds, and three
squires lying at their feet; then went he to the second pavilion and found
four gentlewomen lying in four beds: and then he went to the third pavilion,
and found sir Gawaine lying in a bed with his lady Ettarde, and either
clasping other in their arms.'

420. Above] *1873*; Three from *1869–70*.

421. lurdane: 'from Old French *lourdin*, heavy' (T.). H.T. compares Scott's
Abbot iv: 'I found the careless lurdane feeding him with unwashed flesh'.

427–46. Malory iv 23: 'And when he saw that his heart almost burst for
sorrow, and said, "Alas! that ever a knight should be found so false".
And then he took his horse, and might no longer abide for sorrow. And
when he had ridden nigh half a mile, he turned again, and thought to
slay them both; and when he saw them both lie so fast sleeping, unneth
he might hold him on horseback for sorrow, and said thus to himself:
"Though he be never so false I will not slay him sleeping; for I will never
destroy the high order of knighthood". And therewith he departed again,
and left them sleeping. And or he had ridden half a mile he returned again,
and thought then to slay them, making the greatest sorrow that any man
might make; and when he came to the pavilions he tied his horse to a tree,
and pulled out his sword, naked in his hand, and went straight to them
whereas they lay together, and yet he thought that it were great shame

Back, as a coward slinks from what he fears
430   To cope with, or a traitor proven, or hound
Beaten, did Pelleas in an utter shame
Creep with his shadow through the court again,
Fingering at his sword-handle until he stood
There on the castle-bridge once more, and thought,
435   'I will go back, and slay them where they lie.'

And so went back, and seeing them yet in sleep
Said, 'Ye, that so dishallow the holy sleep,
Your sleep is death,' and drew the sword, and thought,
'What! slay a sleeping knight? the King hath bound
440   And sworn me to this brotherhood;' again,
'Alas that ever a knight should be so false.'
Then turned, and so returned, and groaning laid
The naked sword athwart their naked throats,
There left it, and them sleeping; and she lay,
445   The circlet of the tourney round her brows,
And the sword of the tourney across her throat.

And forth he past, and mounting on his horse
Stared at her towers that, larger than themselves
In their own darkness, thronged into the moon.
450   Then crushed the saddle with his thighs, and clenched
His hands, and maddened with himself and moaned:

'Would they have risen against me in their blood
At the last day? I might have answered them
Even before high God. O towers so strong,
455   Huge, solid, would that even while I gaze
The crack of earthquake shivering to your base
Split you, and Hell burst up your harlot roofs
Bellowing, and charred you through and through
          within,
Black as the harlot's heart—hollow as a skull!
460   Let the fierce east scream through your eyelet-holes,
And whirl the dust of harlots round and round
In dung and nettles! hiss, snake—I saw him there—

for him to slay them sleeping, and laid the naked sword overthwart their
throats, and then he took his horse and rode forth his way.'
446. 'The line gives the quiver of the sword across their throats' (T.).
462] Various MS drafts hereabouts:
                    and let the churl
     Tending his goats, stung with old Nature's sting
     Chalk his true filth upon your rotting stones
                                   British Library MS (Ashley)

Let the fox bark, let the wolf yell. Who yells
Here in the still sweet summer night, but I—
465 I, the poor Pelleas whom she called her fool?
Fool, beast—he, she, or I? myself most fool;
Beast too, as lacking human wit—disgraced,
Dishonoured all for trial of true love—
Love?—we be all alike: only the King
470 Hath made us fools and liars. O noble vows!
O great and sane and simple race of brutes
That own no lust because they have no law!
For why should I have loved her to my shame?
I loathe her, as I loved her to my shame.
475 I never loved her, I but lusted for her—
Away—'
    He dashed the rowel into his horse,
And bounded forth and vanished through the night.

Then she, that felt the cold touch on her throat,
Awaking knew the sword, and turned herself
480 To Gawain: 'Liar, for thou hast not slain
This Pelleas! here he stood, and might have slain
Me and thyself.' And he that tells the tale
Says that her ever-veering fancy turned
To Pelleas, as the one true knight on earth,
485 And only lover; and through her love her life
Wasted and pined, desiring him in vain.

---

          and helpless churl
Stung with the sting of his own rams and goats [deleted]
Chalk nature's filth upon your rotting stones—
                      Texas MS
469] True love, true lust. We are all of us alike. *British Library MS.*
472. Rosenberg (p. 108) notes *Romans* vii 7: 'I had not known sin, but by the
law: for I had not known lust, except the law had said, Thou shalt not covet'.
478–82. Malory iv 23: 'Then sir Gawaine and the lady Ettarde awakened
out of their sleep, and found the naked sword overthwart both their throats;
then she knew well that it was sir Pelles' sword. "Alas!" said she to sir
Gawaine, "ye have betrayed me and sir Pelles also; for ye told me that ye
had slain him, and now I know well it is not so, he is alive: and if sir Pelles
had been as courteous to you as you have been to him ye had been a dead
knight, but ye have deceived me and betrayed me falsely, that all ladies and
damsels may beware by you and me."'
482–6. Malory iv 23: 'The damsel of the Lake . . . cast such an enchant-
ment upon her [Ettarde], that she loved him out of measure, that well
nigh she was out of her mind. "Oh! Lord Jesus", said the lady Ettarde,
"how is it befallen me that I now love him which I before most hated of

But he by wild and way, for half the night,
And over hard and soft, striking the sod
From out the soft, the spark from off the hard,
490   Rode till the star above the wakening sun,
Beside that tower where Percivale was cowled,
Glanced from the rosy forehead of the dawn.
For so the words were flashed into his heart
He knew not whence or wherefore: 'O sweet star,
495   Pure on the virgin forehead of the dawn!'
And there he would have wept, but felt his eyes
Harder and drier than a fountain bed
In summer: thither came the village girls
And lingered talking, and they come no more
500   Till the sweet heavens have filled it from the heights
Again with living waters in the change
Of seasons: hard his eyes; harder his heart
Seemed; but so weary were his limbs, that he,
Gasping, 'Of Arthur's hall am I, but here,
505   Here let me rest and die,' cast himself down,
And gulfed his griefs in inmost sleep; so lay,
Till shaken by a dream, that Gawain fired
The hall of Merlin, and the morning star
Reeled in the smoke, brake into flame, and fell.

510   He woke, and being ware of some one nigh,
Sent hands upon him, as to tear him, crying,
'False! and I held thee pure as Guinevere.'

But Percivale stood near him and replied,
'Am I but false as Guinevere is pure?
515   Or art thou mazed with dreams? or being one
Of our free-spoken Table hast not heard
That Lancelot'–there he checked himself and paused.

Then fared it with Sir Pelleas as with one
Who gets a wound in battle, and the sword
520   That made it plunges through the wound again,
And pricks it deeper: and he shrank and wailed,
'Is the Queen false?' and Percivale was mute.
'Have any of our Round Table held their vows?'

all men living?"–"This is the right wise [righteous] judgment of God",
said the lady of the lake'. Pelleas then spurns her. 'So the lady Ettarde died
for sorrow, and the damsel of the lake rejoiced sir Pelles, and loved
together during their lives.' T. completely changes this ending, and
continues the tale of the bitter and violent sir Pelleas in *The Last Tourna-
ment*.

And Percivale made answer not a word.
525 'Is the King true?' 'The King!' said Percivale.
'Why then let men couple at once with wolves.
What! art thou mad?'
                    But Pelleas, leaping up,
Ran through the doors and vaulted on his horse
And fled: small pity upon his horse had he,
530 Or on himself, or any, and when he met
A cripple, one that held a hand for alms—
Hunched as he was, and like an old dwarf-elm
That turns its back on the salt blast, the boy
Paused not, but overrode him, shouting, 'False,
535 And false with Gawain!' and so left him bruised
And battered, and fled on, and hill and wood
Went ever streaming by him till the gloom,
That follows on the turning of the world,
Darkened the common path: he twitched the reins,
540 And made his beast that better knew it, swerve
Now off it and now on; but when he saw
High up in heaven the hall that Merlin built,
Blackening against the dead-green stripes of even,
'Black nest of rats,' he groaned, 'ye build too high.'

545 Not long thereafter from the city gates
Issued Sir Lancelot riding airily,
Warm with a gracious parting from the Queen,
Peace at his heart, and gazing at a star
And marvelling what it was: on whom the boy,
550 Across the silent seeded meadow-grass
Borne, clashed: and Lancelot, saying, 'What name
        hast thou
That ridest here so blindly and so hard?'
'No name, no name,' he shouted, 'a scourge am I
To lash the treasons of the Table Round.'
555 'Yea, but thy name?' 'I have many names,' he cried:
'I am wrath and shame and hate and evil fame,
And like a poisonous wind I pass to blast
And blaze the crime of Lancelot and the Queen.'
'First over me,' said Lancelot, 'shalt thou pass.'
560 'Fight therefore,' yelled the youth, and either knight
Drew back a space, and when they closed, at once

550. *meadow-*] *1869–94*; mellow- *Eversley.*
553. *No name,*] *1890*; I have *1869–89.*
560. *youth*] *1886*; other *1869–84.*

The weary steed of Pelleas floundering flung
His rider, who called out from the dark field,
'Thou art false as Hell: slay me: I have no sword.'
565 Then Lancelot, 'Yea, between thy lips – and sharp;
But here will I disedge it by thy death.'
'Slay then,' he shrieked, 'my will is to be slain,'
And Lancelot, with his heel upon the fallen,
Rolling his eyes, a moment stood, then spake:
570 'Rise, weakling; I am Lancelot; say thy say.'

And Lancelot slowly rode his warhorse back
To Camelot, and Sir Pelleas in brief while
Caught his unbroken limbs from the dark field,
And followed to the city. It chanced that both
575 Brake into hall together, worn and pale.
There with her knights and dames was Guinevere.
Full wonderingly she gazed on Lancelot
So soon returned, and then on Pelleas, him
Who had not greeted her, but cast himself
580 Down on a bench, hard-breathing. 'Have ye fought?'
She asked of Lancelot. 'Ay, my Queen,' he said.
'And thou hast overthrown him?' 'Ay, my Queen.'
Then she, turning to Pelleas, 'O young knight,
Hath the great heart of knighthood in thee failed
585 So far thou canst not bide, unfrowardly,
A fall from *him?*' Then, for he answered not,
'Or hast thou other griefs? If I, the Queen,
May help them, loose thy tongue, and let me know.'
But Pelleas lifted up an eye so fierce
590 She quailed; and he, hissing 'I have no sword,'
Sprang from the door into the dark. The Queen
Looked hard upon her lover, he on her;
And each foresaw the dolorous day to be:
And all talk died, as in a grove all song
595 Beneath the shadow of some bird of prey;
Then a long silence came upon the hall,
And Modred thought, 'The time is hard at hand.'

473 The Last Tournament

Published *Contemporary Review*, Dec. 1871; then *1872*. T. thought of
writing 'a poem on Tristram and Isolt' in 1859 (*Mat.* ii 218). Sir Charles

565. H.T. compares *Cymbeline* III iv 33–4: 'No, 'tis slander, / Whose edge
is sharper than the sword.'

597. Rosenberg (p. 86) notes *Matthew* xxvi 18: 'My time is at hand'.

Tennyson points out that the germ of it is in prose in the *H.MS* of *Gareth and Lynette*, written 1869–72. On this, see D. Staines, who gives a transcript of this prose draft (*H.Nbk 40*) in *Harvard Library Bulletin* xxii (1974) 300–301. On 8 Nov. 1870, 'he repeated some of *The Last Tournament* which he had just written' (*Mem.* ii 100); the poem was read aloud 2 May 1871 (E.T. to H.T., Lincoln), and completed by 21 May 1871 (*Mem.* ii 104). 'The bare outline of the story and of the vengeance of Mark is taken from Malory [viii–x]; my father often referred with pleasure to his creation of the half-humorous, half-pathetic fool Dagonet' (H.T.). J. M. Gray shows that the Red Knight 'is carefully modelled on selected details in Malory' (*Notes and Queries* ccxxii, 1977, 405–7).

> Dagonet, the fool, whom Gawain in his mood
> Had made mock-knight of Arthur's Table Round,
> At Camelot, high above the yellowing woods,
> Danced like a withered leaf before the hall.
> 5   And toward him from the hall, with harp in hand,
> And from the crown thereof a carcanet
> Of ruby swaying to and fro, the prize
> Of Tristram in the jousts of yesterday,
> Came Tristram, saying, 'Why skip ye so, Sir Fool?'
>
> 10   For Arthur and Sir Lancelot riding once
> Far down beneath a winding wall of rock
> Heard a child wail. A stump of oak half-dead,
> From roots like some black coil of carven snakes,
> Clutched at the crag, and started through mid air
> 15   Bearing an eagle's nest: and through the tree
> Rushed ever a rainy wind, and through the wind
> Pierced ever a child's cry: and crag and tree
> Scaling, Sir Lancelot from the perilous nest,
> This ruby necklace thrice around her neck,
> 20   And all unscarred from beak or talon, brought
> A maiden babe; which Arthur pitying took,
> Then gave it to his Queen to rear: the Queen
> But coldly acquiescing, in her white arms
> Received, and after loved it tenderly,
> 25   And named it Nestling; so forgot herself
> A moment, and her cares; till that young life

¶473. *1. mood*] *1872*; moods *1871*.
10. Kathleen Tillotson discusses as a source for the story of Nestling a legend of King Alfred told in Sharon Turner's *History* (*Mid-Victorian Studies*, 1965, p. 84*n*). *Mat.* provides evidence that T. read Turner. The source was noted by H. Littledale (1893).
12–15. These lines of description were written July 1866 (*Mem.* ii 39).

Being smitten in mid heaven with mortal cold
Past from her; and in time the carcanet
Vext her with plaintive memories of the child:
30   So she, delivering it to Arthur, said,
'Take thou the jewels of this dead innocence,
And make them, an thou wilt, a tourney-prize.'

To whom the King, 'Peace to thine eagle-borne
Dead nestling, and this honour after death,
35   Following thy will! but, O my Queen, I muse
Why ye not wear on arm, or neck, or zone
Those diamonds that I rescued from the tarn,
And Lancelot won, methought, for thee to wear.'

'Would rather you had let them fall,' she cried,
40   'Plunge and be lost–ill-fated as they were,
A bitterness to me!–ye look amazed,
Not knowing they were lost as soon as given–
Slid from my hands, when I was leaning out
Above the river–that unhappy child
45   Past in her barge: but rosier luck will go
With these rich jewels, seeing that they came
Not from the skeleton of a brother-slayer,
But the sweet body of a maiden babe.
Perchance–who knows?–the purest of thy knights
50   May win them for the purest of my maids.'

She ended, and the cry of a great jousts
With trumpet-blowings ran on all the ways
From Camelot in among the faded fields
To furthest towers; and everywhere the knights
55   Armed for a day of glory before the King.

But on the hither side of that loud morn
Into the hall staggered, his visage ribbed
From ear to ear with dogwhip-weals, his nose
Bridge-broken, one eye out, and one hand off,
60   And one with shattered fingers dangling lame,
A churl, to whom indignantly the King,

'My churl, for whom Christ died, what evil beast
Hath drawn his claws athwart thy face? or fiend?
Man was it who marred heaven's image in thee thus?'

Then, sputtering through the hedge of splintered
65   teeth,

39. *you*] *1873;* ye *1871–2.*

Yet strangers to the tongue, and with blunt stump
Pitch-blackened sawing the air, said the maimed churl,

'He took them and he drave them to his tower—
Some hold he was a table-knight of thine—
70   A hundred goodly ones—the Red Knight, he—
Lord, I was tending swine, and the Red Knight
Brake in upon me and drave them to his tower;
And when I called upon thy name as one
That doest right by gentle and by churl,
75   Maimed me and mauled, and would outright have slain,
Save that he sware me to a message, saying,
"Tell thou the King and all his liars, that I
Have founded my Round Table in the North,
And whatsoever his own knights have sworn
80   My knights have sworn the counter to it—and say
My tower is full of harlots, like his court,
But mine are worthier, seeing they profess
To be none other than themselves—and say
My knights are all adulterers like his own,
85   But mine are truer, seeing they profess
To be none other; and say his hour is come,
The heathen are upon him, his long lance
Broken, and his Excalibur a straw."'

Then Arthur turned to Kay the seneschal,
90   'Take thou my churl, and tend him curiously
Like a king's heir, till all his hurts be whole.
The heathen—but that ever-climbing wave,
Hurled back again so often in empty foam,
Hath lain for years at rest—and renegades,
95   Thieves, bandits, leavings of confusion, whom
The wholesome realm is purged of otherwhere,
Friends, through your manhood and your fealty,—now
Make their last head like Satan in the North.
My younger knights, new-made, in whom your flower
100   Waits to be solid fruit of golden deeds,
Move with me toward their quelling, which achieved,
The loneliest ways are safe from shore to shore.
But thou, Sir Lancelot, sitting in my place
Enchaired tomorrow, arbitrate the field;

66. *strangers to the tongue*: 'rough' (T.).   *blunt stump*: 'where the hand
had been cut off and the stump had been pitched' (T.).
70. *the Red Knight*: 'Pelleas' (T.).
86. Rosenberg (p. 86) notes *John* xii 23.
98. *Isaiah* xiv 13.

105 For wherefore shouldst thou care to mingle with it,
Only to yield my Queen her own again?
Speak, Lancelot, thou art silent: is it well?'

Thereto Sir Lancelot answered, 'It is well:
Yet better if the King abide, and leave
110 The leading of his younger knights to me.
Else, for the King has willed it, it is well.'

Then Arthur rose and Lancelot followed him,
And while they stood without the doors, the King
Turned to him saying, 'Is it then so well?
115 Or mine the blame that oft I seem as he
Of whom was written, "A sound is in his ears"?
The foot that loiters, bidden go, – the glance
That only seems half-loyal to command, –
A manner somewhat fallen from reverence –
120 Or have I dreamed the bearing of our knights
Tells of a manhood ever less and lower?
Or whence the fear lest this my realm, upreared,
By noble deeds at one with noble vows,
From flat confusion and brute violences,
125 Reel back into the beast, and be no more?'

He spoke, and taking all his younger knights,
Down the slope city rode, and sharply turned
North by the gate. In her high bower the Queen,
Working a tapestry, lifted up her head,
130 Watched her lord pass, and knew not that she sighed.
Then ran across her memory the strange rhyme
Of bygone Merlin, 'Where is he who knows?
From the great deep to the great deep he goes.'

But when the morning of a tournament,
135 By these in earnest those in mockery called
The Tournament of the Dead Innocence,
Brake with a wet wind blowing, Lancelot,
Round whose sick head all night, like birds of prey,
The words of Arthur flying shrieked, arose,
140 And down a streetway hung with folds of pure
White samite, and by fountains running wine,
Where children sat in white with cups of gold,

---

116. Job xv 20–1: 'The wicked man travaileth with pain all his days, and the number of years is hidden to the oppressor. A dreadful sound is in his ears: in prosperity the destroyer shall come upon him.'

Moved to the lists, and there, with slow sad steps
Ascending, filled his double-dragoned chair.

145   He glanced and saw the stately galleries,
Dame, damsel, each through worship of their Queen
White-robed in honour of the stainless child,
And some with scattered jewels, like a bank
Of maiden snow mingled with sparks of fire.
150   He looked but once, and vailed his eyes again.

The sudden trumpet sounded as in a dream
To ears but half-awaked, then one low roll
Of Autumn thunder, and the jousts began:
And ever the wind blew, and yellowing leaf
155   And gloom and gleam, and shower and shorn plume
Went down it. Sighing weariedly, as one
Who sits and gazes on a faded fire,
When all the goodlier guests are past away,
Sat their great umpire, looking o'er the lists.
160   He saw the laws that ruled the tournament
Broken, but spake not; once, a knight cast down
Before his throne of arbitration cursed
The dead babe and the follies of the King;
And once the laces of a helmet cracked,
165   And showed him, like a vermin in its hole,
Modred, a narrow face: anon he heard
The voice that billowed round the barriers roar
An ocean-sounding welcome to one knight,
But newly-entered, taller than the rest,
170   And armoured all in forest green, whereon
There tript a hundred tiny silver deer,
And wearing but a holly-spray for crest,
With ever-scattering berries, and on shield
A spear, a harp, a bugle – Tristram – late
175   From overseas in Brittany returned,
And marriage with a princess of that realm,
Isolt the White – Sir Tristram of the Woods –
Whom Lancelot knew, had held sometime with pain
His own against him, and now yearned to shake

150. *vailed*: 'drooped' (T.). H.T. compares *Hamlet* I ii 70–1: 'Do not
ever with thy vailed lids / Seek for thy noble father in the dust.'
153. 'The·autumn of the Round Table' (T.).
174–5. 'He was a harper and a hunter' (T.). H.T. quotes Malory viii 3. Gray
(pp. 36–7) notes that 'the knight appears on one occasion in green armour,
with green trappings' (Malory x 67–8).

180   The burthen off his heart in one full shock
        With Tristram even to death: his strong hands gript
        And dinted the gilt dragons right and left,
        Until he groaned for wrath—so many of those,
        That ware their ladies' colours on the casque,
185   Drew from before Sir Tristram to the bounds,
        And there with gibes and flickering mockeries
        Stood, while he muttered, 'Craven crests! O shame!
        What faith have these in whom they sware to love?
        The glory of our Round Table is no more.'

190   So Tristram won, and Lancelot gave, the gems,
        Not speaking other word than 'Hast thou won?
        Art thou the purest, brother? See, the hand
        Wherewith thou takest this, is red!' to whom
        Tristram, half plagued by Lancelot's languorous mood,
195   Made answer, 'Ay, but wherefore toss me this
        Like a dry bone cast to some hungry hound?
        Let be thy fair Queen's fantasy. Strength of heart
        And might of limb, but mainly use and skill,
        Are winners in this pastime of our King.
200   My hand—belike the lance hath dript upon it—
        No blood of mine, I trow; but O chief knight,
        Right arm of Arthur in the battlefield,
        Great brother, thou nor I have made the world;
        Be happy in thy fair Queen as I in mine.'

205   And Tristram round the gallery made his horse
        Caracole; then bowed his homage, bluntly saying,
        'Fair damsels, each to him who worships each
        Sole Queen of Beauty and of love, behold
        This day my Queen of Beauty is not here.'
210   And most of these were mute, some angered, one
        Murmuring, 'All courtesy is dead,' and one,
        'The glory of our Round Table is no more.'

        Then fell thick rain, plume droopt and mantle clung,
        And pettish cries awoke, and the wan day
215   Went glooming down in wet and weariness:
        But under her black brows a swarthy one

---

192. T. refers to ll. 49-50.
205-12. 'It was the law to give the prize to some lady on the field, but the
laws are broken, and Tristram the courteous has lost his courtesy, for the
great sin of Lancelot was sapping the Round Table' (T.).
216. one] 1872; dame 1871.

Laughed shrilly, crying, 'Praise the patient saints,
Our one white day of Innocence hath past,
Though somewhat draggled at the skirt. So be it.
220 The snowdrop only, flowering through the year,
Would make the world as blank as Winter-tide.
Come—let us gladden their sad eyes, our Queen's
And Lancelot's, at this night's solemnity
With all the kindlier colours of the field.'

225 So dame and damsel glittered at the feast
Variously gay: for he that tells the tale
Likened them, saying, as when an hour of cold
Falls on the mountain in midsummer snows,
And all the purple slopes of mountain flowers
230 Pass under white, till the warm hour returns
With veer of wind, and all are flowers again;
So dame and damsel cast the simple white,
And glowing in all colours, the live grass,
Rose-campion, bluebell, kingcup, poppy, glanced
235 About the revels, and with mirth so loud
Beyond all use, that, half-amazed, the Queen,
And wroth at Tristram and the lawless jousts,
Brake up their sports, then slowly to her bower
Parted, and in her bosom pain was lord.

240 And little Dagonet on the morrow morn,
High over all the yellowing Autumn-tide,
Danced like a withered leaf before the hall.
Then Tristram saying, 'Why skip ye so, Sir Fool?'
Wheeled round on either heel, Dagonet replied,
245 'Belike for lack of wiser company;
Or being fool, and seeing too much wit
Makes the world rotten, why, belike I skip
To know myself the wisest knight of all.'
'Ay, fool,' said Tristram, 'but 'tis eating dry
250 To dance without a catch, a roundelay
To dance to.' Then he twangled on his harp,
And while he twangled little Dagonet stood
Quiet as any water-sodden log
Stayed in the wandering warble of a brook;

217. Gray (p. 55) notes *Revelation* xiii 10: 'Here is the patience and faith of the
saints'.

220. 'Because they were dressed in white' (T.).

222. *gladden*] *1872*; comfort *1871*.

227-8. 'Seen by me at Mürren in Switzerland' (T.).

255   But when the twangling ended, skipt again;
      And being asked, 'Why skipt ye not, Sir Fool?'
      Made answer, 'I had liefer twenty years
      Skip to the broken music of my brains
      Than any broken music thou canst make.'
260   Then Tristram, waiting for the quip to come,
      'Good now, what music have I broken, fool?'
      And little Dagonet, skipping, 'Arthur, the King's;
      For when thou playest that air with Queen Isolt,
      Thou makest broken music with thy bride,
265   Her daintier namesake down in Brittany—
      And so thou breakest Arthur's music too.'
      'Save for that broken music in thy brains,
      Sir Fool,' said Tristram, 'I would break thy head.
      Fool, I came late, the heathen wars were o'er,
270   The life had flown, we sware but by the shell—
      I am but a fool to reason with a fool—
      Come, thou art crabbed and sour: but lean me down,
      Sir Dagonet, one of thy long asses' ears,
      And harken if my music be not true.

275   '"Free love—free field—we love but while we may:
      The woods are hushed, their music is no more:
      The leaf is dead, the yearning past away:
      New leaf, new life—the days of frost are o'er:
      New life, new love, to suit the newer day:
280   New loves are sweet as those that went before:
      Free love—free field—we love but while we may."

      'Ye might have moved slow-measure to my tune,
      Not stood stockstill. I made it in the woods,
      And heard it ring as true as tested gold.'

285   But Dagonet with one foot poised in his hand,
      'Friend, did ye mark that fountain yesterday
      Made to run wine?—but this had run itself
      All out like a long life to a sour end—
      And them that round it sat with golden cups
290   To hand the wine to whosoever came—

259. *thou canst*] *1873*; ye can *1871–2*.
265. 'Isolt of the white hands' (T.).
270. *shell*: 'husk' (T.).
271. Gray (p. 56) notes *Proverbs* xxvi 4: 'Answer not a fool according to his folly, lest thou also be like him'.
290. *whosoever*] *1872*; whomsoever *1871*.

The twelve small damosels white as Innocence,
In honour of poor Innocence the babe,
Who left the gems which Innocence the Queen
Lent to the King, and Innocence the King
295 Gave for a prize—and one of those white slips
Handed her cup and piped, the pretty one,
"Drink, drink, Sir Fool," and thereupon I drank,
Spat—pish—the cup was gold, the draught was mud.'

And Tristram, 'Was it muddier than thy gibes?
300 Is all the laughter gone dead out of thee?—
Not marking how the knighthood mock thee, fool—
"Fear God: honour the King—his one true knight—
Sole follower of the vows"—for here be they
Who knew thee swine enow before I came,
305 Smuttier than blasted grain: but when the King
Had made thee fool, thy vanity so shot up
It frighted all free fool from out thy heart;
Which left thee less than fool, and less than swine,
A naked aught—yet swine I hold thee still,
310 For I have flung thee pearls and find thee swine.'

And little Dagonet mincing with his feet,
'Knight, an ye fling those rubies round my neck
In lieu of hers, I'll hold thou hast some touch
Of music, since I care not for thy pearls.
315 Swine? I have wallowed, I have washed—the world
Is flesh and shadow—I have had my day.
The dirty nurse, Experience, in her kind
Hath fouled me—an I wallowed, then I washed—
I have had my day and my philosophies—
320 And thank the Lord I am King Arthur's fool.
Swine, say ye? swine, goats, asses, rams and geese
Trooped round a Paynim harper once, who thrummed
On such a wire as musically as thou
Some such fine song—but never a king's fool.'

325 And Tristram, 'Then were swine, goats, asses, geese
The wiser fools, seeing thy Paynim bard
Had such a mastery of his mystery
That he could harp his wife up out of hell.'

Then Dagonet, turning on the ball of his foot,
330 'And whither harp'st thou thine? down! and thyself
Down! and two more: a helpful harper thou,

322. 'Orpheus' (T.).   *Paynim*: pagan.

That harpest downward! Dost thou know the star
We call the harp of Arthur up in heaven?'

　　And Tristram, 'Ay, Sir Fool, for when our King
335　Was victor wellnigh day by day, the knights,
Glorying in each new glory, set his name
High on all hills, and in the signs of heaven.'

　　And Dagonet answered, 'Ay, and when the land
Was freed, and the Queen false, ye set yourself
340　To babble about him, all to show your wit—
And whether he were King by courtesy,
Or King by right—and so went harping down
The black king's highway, got so far, and grew
So witty that ye played at ducks and drakes
345　With Arthur's vows on the great lake of fire.
Tuwhoo! do ye see it? do ye see the star?'

　　'Nay, fool,' said Tristram, 'not in open day.'
And Dagonet, 'Nay, nor will: I see it and hear.
It makes a silent music up in heaven,
350　And I, and Arthur and the angels hear,
And then we skip.' 'Lo, fool,' he said, 'ye talk
Fool's treason: is the King thy brother fool?'
Then little Dagonet clapt his hands and shrilled,
'Ay, ay, my brother fool, the king of fools!
355　Conceits himself as God that he can make
Figs out of thistles, silk from bristles, milk
From burning spurge, honey from hornet-combs,
And men from beasts—Long live the king of fools!'

　　And down the city Dagonet danced away;
360　But through the slowly-mellowing avenues
And solitary passes of the wood
Rode Tristram toward Lyonnesse and the west.
Before him fled the face of Queen Isolt
With ruby-circled neck, but evermore
365　Past, as a rustle or twitter in the wood
Made dull his inner, keen his outer eye
For all that walked, or crept, or perched, or flew.
Anon the face, as, when a gust hath blown,
Unruffling waters re-collect the shape
370　Of one that in them sees himself, returned;

---

333. 'Lyra' (T.).
357. *burning spurge*: 'the juice of the common spurge' (T.).
366. *outer eye*: 'the hunter's eye' (T.).

But at the slot or fewmets of a deer,
Or even a fallen feather, vanished again.

So on for all that day from lawn to lawn
Through many a league-long bower he rode. At length
375 A lodge of intertwisted beechen-boughs
Furze-crammed, and bracken-rooft, the which himself
Built for a summer day with Queen Isolt
Against a shower, dark in the golden grove
Appearing, sent his fancy back to where
380 She lived a moon in that low lodge with him:
Till Mark her lord had past, the Cornish King,
With six or seven, when Tristram was away,
And snatched her thence; yet dreading worse than shame
Her warrior Tristram, spake not any word,
385 But bode his hour, devising wretchedness.

And now that desert lodge to Tristram lookt
So sweet, that halting, in he past, and sank
Down on a drift of foliage random-blown;
But could not rest for musing how to smoothe
390 And sleek his marriage over to the Queen.
Perchance in lone Tintagil far from all
The tonguesters of the court she had not heard.
But then what folly had sent him overseas
After she left him lonely here? a name?
395 Was it the name of one in Brittany,
Isolt, the daughter of the King? 'Isolt
Of the white hands' they called her: the sweet name
Allured him first, and then the maid herself,
Who served him well with those white hands of hers,
400 And loved him well, until himself had thought
He loved her also, wedded easily,
But left her all as easily, and returned.
The black-blue Irish hair and Irish eyes
Had drawn him home—what marvel? then he laid
405 His brows upon the drifted leaf and dreamed.

He seemed to pace the strand of Brittany
Between Isolt of Britain and his bride,
And showed them both the ruby-chain, and both
Began to struggle for it, till his Queen
410 Graspt it so hard, that all her hand was red.
Then cried the Breton, 'Look, her hand is red!

371. *slot*: 'trail' (T.).   *fewmets*: 'droppings' (T.).

These be no rubies, this is frozen blood,
And melts within her hand – her hand is hot
With ill desires, but this I gave thee, look,
415 Is all as cool and white as any flower.'
Followed a rush of eagle's wings, and then
A whimpering of the spirit of the child,
Because the twain had spoiled her carcanet.

He dreamed; but Arthur with a hundred spears
420 Rode far, till o'er the illimitable reed,
And many a glancing plash and sallowy isle,
The wide-winged sunset of the misty marsh
Glared on a huge machicolated tower
That stood with open doors, whereout was rolled
425 A roar of riot, as from men secure
Amid their marshes, ruffians at their ease
Among their harlot-brides, an evil song.
'Lo there,' said one of Arthur's youth, for there,
High on a grim dead tree before the tower,
430 A goodly brother of the Table Round
Swung by the neck: and on the boughs a shield
Showing a shower of blood in a field noir,
And therebeside a horn, inflamed the knights
At that dishonour done the gilded spur,
435 Till each would clash the shield, and blow the horn.
But Arthur waved them back. Alone he rode.
Then at the dry harsh roar of the great horn,
That sent the face of all the marsh aloft
An ever upward-rushing storm and cloud
440 Of shriek and plume, the Red Knight heard, and all,
Even to tipmost lance and topmost helm,
In blood-red armour sallying, howled to the King,

'The teeth of Hell flay bare and gnash thee flat! –
Lo! art thou not that eunuch-hearted King
445 Who fain had clipt free manhood from the world –

421. sallowy: having willows.
423. machicolated: machicolation, 'an opening between the corbels which
support a projecting parapet, or in the vault of a portal, through which
combustibles, molten lead, stones, etc., were dropped on the heads of the
assailants' (OED).
439. Arthur Hallam had written of 'the upward rushing tempest' in a
poem to T.'s sister Emily, *Oh save me* (VP iii (1965) Suppt.).
445 ∧ 6] And overslimes all with hypocrisy *Berg MS 1st reading*;
            Who got himself made wittol, while he strove
            To slime the world with his hypocrisy? *Berg MS*

The woman-worshipper? Yea, God's curse, and I!
Slain was the brother of my paramour
By a knight of thine, and I that heard her whine
And snivel, being eunuch-hearted too,
450 Sware by the scorpion-worm that twists in hell,
And stings itself to everlasting death,
To hang whatever knight of thine I fought
And tumbled. Art thou King?—Look to thy life!'

He ended: Arthur knew the voice; the face
455 Wellnigh was helmet-hidden, and the name
Went wandering somewhere darkling in his mind.
And Arthur deigned not use of word or sword,
But let the drunkard, as he stretched from horse
To strike him, overbalancing his bulk,
460 Down from the causeway heavily to the swamp
Fall, as the crest of some slow-arching wave,
Heard in dead night along that table-shore,
Drops flat, and after the great waters break
Whitening for half a league, and thin themselves,
465 Far over sands marbled with moon and cloud,
From less and less to nothing; thus he fell
Head-heavy; then the knights, who watched him, roared
And shouted and leapt down upon the fallen;
There trampled out his face from being known,
470 And sank his head in mire, and slimed themselves:
Nor heard the King for their own cries, but sprang
Through open doors, and swording right and left
Men, women, on their sodden faces, hurled
The tables over and the wines, and slew
475 Till all the rafters rang with woman-yells,
And all the pavement streamed with massacre:
Then, echoing yell with yell, they fired the tower,
Which half that autumn night, like the live North,
Red-pulsing up through Alioth and Alcor,

447–52. Gray (p. 36) notes that this is 'carefully modelled on selected details in Malory'.
450. Gray (p. 55) notes *Revelation* ix 3: 'As the scorpions of the earth have power', and *Mark* ix 44: 'where their worm dieth not'.
455. *the name*: 'Pelleas' (T.).
461–6. 'As I have heard and seen the sea on the shore of Mablethorpe' (T.).
467. ; *then*] 1873; , while 1871–2.
477. *echoing . . . yell*] 1886; yell with yell echoing 1871–84.
479. *Alioth and Alcor*: 'two stars in the Great Bear' (T.).

480 Made all above it, and a hundred meres
       About it, as the water Moab saw
       Come round by the East, and out beyond them flushed
       The long low dune, and lazy-plunging sea.

       So all the ways were safe from shore to shore,
485 But in the heart of Arthur pain was lord.

       Then, out of Tristram waking, the red dream
       Fled with a shout, and that low lodge returned,
       Mid-forest, and the wind among the boughs.
       He whistled his good warhorse left to graze
490 Among the forest greens, vaulted upon him,
       And rode beneath an ever-showering leaf,
       Till one lone woman, weeping near a cross,
       Stayed him. 'Why weep ye?' 'Lord,' she said, 'my man
       Hath left me or is dead;' whereon he thought—
495 'What, if she hate me now? I would not this.
       What, if she love me still? I would not that.
       I know not what I would'—but said to her,
       'Yet weep not thou, lest, if thy mate return,
       He find thy favour changed and love thee not'—
500 Then pressing day by day through Lyonnesse
       Last in a roky hollow, belling, heard
       The hounds of Mark, and felt the goodly hounds
       Yelp at his heart, but turning, past and gained
       Tintagil, half in sea, and high on land,
       A crown of towers.

505   Down in a casement sat,
       A low sea-sunset glorying round her hair
       And glossy-throated grace, Isolt the Queen.
       And when she heard the feet of Tristram grind
       The spiring stone that scaled about her tower,
510 Flushed, started, met him at the doors, and there
       Belted his body with her white embrace,
       Crying aloud, 'Not Mark—not Mark, my soul!
       The footstep fluttered me at first: not he:

---

481. 2 Kings iii 22: 'And the sun shone upon the water, and the Moaʟ.
saw the water on the other side as red as blood.'
495, 496. if] *1875*; an *1871–4.   she*: 'his wife' (T.).
501. roky: 'misty'; H.T. compares *Macbeth* III ii 51: 'th' rooky wood'.
T. used the word in a fragment (III 631).   *belling*: bellowing, with OED
2 specifically of deer.
509. 'Winding stone staircase' (T.).

Catlike through his own castle steals my Mark,
515 But warrior-wise thou stridest through his halls
Who hates thee, as I him – even to the death.
My soul, I felt my hatred for my Mark
Quicken within me, and knew that thou wert nigh.'
To whom Sir Tristram smiling, 'I am here.
520 Let be thy Mark, seeing he is not thine.'

And drawing somewhat backward she replied,
'Can he be wronged who is not even his own,
But save for dread of thee had beaten me,
Scratched, bitten, blinded, marred me somehow –
Mark?
525 What rights are his that dare not strike for them?
Not lift a hand – not, though he found me thus!
But harken! have ye met him? hence he went
Today for three days' hunting – as he said –
And so returns belike within an hour.
530 Mark's way, my soul! – but eat not thou with Mark,
Because he hates thee even more than fears;
Nor drink: and when thou passest any wood
Close vizor, lest an arrow from the bush
Should leave me all alone with Mark and hell.
535 My God, the measure of my hate for Mark
Is as the measure of my love for thee.'

So, plucked one way by hate and one by love,
Drained of her force, again she sat, and spake
To Tristram, as he knelt before her, saying,
540 'O hunter, and O blower of the horn,
Harper, and thou hast been a rover too,
For, ere I mated with my shambling king,
Ye twain had fallen out about the bride
Of one – his name is out of me – the prize,
545 If prize she were – (what marvel – she could see) –
Thine, friend; and ever since my craven seeks
To wreck thee villainously: but, O Sir Knight,
What dame or damsel have ye kneeled to last?'

And Tristram, 'Last to my Queen Paramount,
550 Here now to my Queen Paramount of love
And loveliness – ay, lovelier than when first

530. Mark] 1872; him 1871.
542. shambling: Sir Charles Tennyson notices this detail in the MS of
Merlin and Vivien (p. 809).

Her light feet fell on our rough Lyonnesse,
Sailing from Ireland.'

Softly laughed Isolt;
'Flatter me not, for hath not our great Queen
555   My dole of beauty trebled?' and he said,
'Her beauty is her beauty, and thine thine,
And thine is more to me—soft, gracious, kind—
Save when thy Mark is kindled on thy lips
Most gracious; but she, haughty, even to him,
560   Lancelot; for I have seen him wan enow
To make one doubt if ever the great Queen
Have yielded him her love.'

To whom Isolt,
'Ah then, false hunter and false harper, thou
Who brakest through the scruple of my bond,
565   Calling me thy white hind, and saying to me
That Guinevere had sinned against the highest,
And I—misyoked with such a want of man—
That I could hardly sin against the lowest.'

He answered, 'O my soul, be comforted!
570   If this be sweet, to sin in leading-strings,
. If here be comfort, and if ours be sin,
Crowned warrant had we for the crowning sin
That made us happy: but how ye greet me—fear
And fault and doubt—no word of that fond tale—
575   Thy deep heart-yearnings, thy sweet memories
Of Tristram in that year he was away.'

And, saddening on the sudden, spake Isolt,
'I had forgotten all in my strong joy
To see thee—yearnings?—ay! for, hour by hour,
580   Here in the never-ended afternoon,
O sweeter than all memories of thee,
Deeper than any yearnings after thee
Seemed those far-rolling, westward-smiling seas,
Watched from this tower. Isolt of Britain dashed
585   Before Isolt of Brittany on the strand,
Would that have chilled her bride-kiss? Wedded her?

553. 'Tristram had told his uncle Mark of the beauty of Isolt, when he saw
her in Ireland, so Mark demanded her hand in marriage, which he obtained.
Then Mark sent Tristram to fetch her as in my *Idylls* Arthur sent Lancelot
for Guinevere' (T.).
569. Gray (p. 56) notes *Psalm* xvi 2.

Fought in her father's battles? wounded there?
The King was all fulfilled with gratefulness,
And she, my namesake of the hands, that healed
590   Thy hurt and heart with unguent and caress –
Well – can I wish her any huger wrong
Than having known thee? her too hast thou left
To pine and waste in those sweet memories.
O were I not my Mark's, by whom all men
595   Are noble, I should hate thee more than love.'

And Tristram, fondling her light hands, replied,
'Grace, Queen, for being loved: she loved me well.
Did I love her? the name at least I loved.
Isolt? – I fought his battles, for Isolt!
600   The night was dark; the true star set. Isolt!
The name was ruler of the dark – Isolt?
Care not for her! patient, and prayerful, meek,
Pale-blooded, she will yield herself to God.'

And Isolt answered, 'Yea, and why not I?
605   Mine is the larger need, who am not meek,
Pale-blooded, prayerful. Let me tell thee now.
Here one black, mute midsummer night I sat,
Lonely, but musing on thee, wondering where,
Murmuring a light song I had heard thee sing,
610   And once or twice I spake thy name aloud.
Then flashed a levin-brand; and near me stood,
In fuming sulphur blue and green, a fiend –
Mark's way to steal behind one in the dark –
For there was Mark: "He has wedded her," he said,
615   Not said, but hissed it: then this crown of towers
So shook to such a roar of all the sky,
That here in utter dark I swooned away,
And woke again in utter dark, and cried,
"I will flee hence and give myself to God" –
620   And thou wert lying in thy new leman's arms.'

Then Tristram, ever dallying with her hand,
'May God be with thee, sweet, when old and gray,

599–600]   And sweet, ye know, there be so many rungs
            Between the lowest in the scale of love,
            And this whereon we stand and breathe the heaven.
            Seemed there a treachery of the body too?
            Not all a treachery of the heart. Isolt–

                                              Berg MS

And past desire!' a saying that angered her.
'"May God be with thee, sweet, when thou art old,
625 And sweet no more to me!" I need Him now.
For when had Lancelot uttered aught so gross
Even to the swineherd's malkin in the mast?
The greater man, the greater courtesy.
Far other was the Tristram, Arthur's knight!
630 But thou, through ever harrying thy wild beasts –
Save that to touch a harp, tilt with a lance
Becomes thee well – art grown wild beast thyself.
How darest thou, if lover, push me even
In fancy from thy side, and set me far
635 In the gray distance, half a life away,
Her to be loved no more? Unsay it, unswear!
Flatter me rather, seeing me so weak,
Broken with Mark and hate and solitude,
Thy marriage and mine own, that I should suck
640 Lies like sweet wines: lie to me: I believe.
Will ye not lie? not swear, as there ye kneel,
And solemnly as when ye sware to him,
The man of men, our King – My God, the power
Was once in vows when men believed the King!
645 They lied not then, who sware, and through their vows
The King prevailing made his realm: – I say,
Swear to me thou wilt love me even when old,
Gray-haired, and past desire, and in despair.'

       Then Tristram, pacing moodily up and down,
650 'Vows! did you keep the vow you made to Mark
More than I mine? Lied, say ye? Nay, but learnt,
The vow that binds too strictly snaps itself –
My knighthood taught me this – ay, being snapt –
We run more counter to the soul thereof
655 Than had we never sworn. I swear no more.
I swore to the great King, and am forsworn.
For once – even to the height – I honoured him.
"Man, is he man at all?" methought, when first
I rode from our rough Lyonnesse, and beheld
660 That victor of the Pagan throned in hall –
His hair, a sun that rayed from off a brow
Like hillsnow high in heaven, the steel-blue eyes,
The golden beard that clothed his lips with light –

627. 'Slut among the beech nuts' (T.).
629] 1873; not 1871–2.
650. you . . . you] 1873; ye . . . ye 1871–2.

Moreover, that weird legend of his birth,
665 With Merlin's mystic babble about his end
Amazed me; then, his foot was on a stool
Shaped as a dragon; he seemed to me no man,
But Michaël trampling Satan; so I sware,
Being amazed: but this went by – The vows!
670 O ay – the wholesome madness of an hour –
They served their use, their time; for every knight
Believed himself a greater than himself,
And every follower eyed him as a God;
Till he, being lifted up beyond himself,
675 Did mightier deeds than elsewise he had done,
And so the realm was made; but then their vows –
First mainly through that sullying of our Queen –
Began to gall the knighthood, asking whence
Had Arthur right to bind them to himself?
680 Dropt down from heaven? washed up from out the deep?
They failed to trace him through the flesh and blood
Of our old kings: whence then? a doubtful lord
To bind them by inviolable vows,
Which flesh and blood perforce would violate:
685 For feel this arm of mine – the tide within
Red with free chase and heather-scented air,
Pulsing full man; can Arthur make me pure
As any maiden child? lock up my tongue
From uttering freely what I freely hear?
690 Bind me to one? The wide world laughs at it.
And worldling of the world am I, and know
The ptarmigan that whitens ere his hour
Woos his own end; we are not angels here
Nor shall be: vows – I am woodman of the woods,
695 And hear the garnet-headed yaffingale

666–8. Gray (p. 56) notes *Psalm* cx 1: 'I make thine enemies my footstool';
Matthew v 35: 'Behold, I give unto you power to tread on serpents'; *Psalm* xci
13: 'the dragon shalt thou trample under feet'; and *Revelation* xii 7: 'Michael
and his angels fought against the dragon'.
672. 'When the man had an ideal before him' (T.).
690. *wide*] *1872*; great *1871*.
692. 'Seen by me in the Museum at Christiania in Norway' (T.).
692, 695. C. Y. Lang considers the relation of these lines to Darwin and to the
Duke of Argyll's *The Reign of Law*, 1866 (*Tennyson's Arthurian Psycho-drama*,
p. 16).
695. *yaffingale*: 'old word, and still provincial for the green wood-pecker
(so called from its laughter). In Sussex "yaffel"' (T.).

Mock them: my soul, we love but while we may;
And therefore is my love so large for thee,
Seeing it is not bounded save by love.'

Here ending, he moved toward her, and she said,
700 'Good: an I turned away my love for thee
To some one thrice as courteous as thyself—
For courtesy wins woman all as well
As valour may, but he that closes both
Is perfect, he is Lancelot—taller indeed,
705 Rosier and comelier, thou—but say I loved
This knightliest of all knights, and cast thee back
Thine own small saw, "We love but while we may,"
Well then, what answer?'

He that while she spake,
Mindful of what he brought to adorn her with,
710 The jewels, had let one finger lightly touch
The warm white apple of her throat, replied,
'Press this a little closer, sweet, until—
Come, I am hungered and half-angered—meat,
Wine, wine—and I will love thee to the death,
715 And out beyond into the dream to come.'

So then, when both were brought to full accord,
She rose, and set before him all he willed;
And after these had comforted the blood
With meats and wines, and satiated their hearts—
720 Now talking of their woodland paradise,
The deer, the dews, the fern, the founts, the lawns;
Now mocking at the much ungainliness,
And craven shifts, and long crane legs of Mark—
Then Tristram laughing caught the harp, and sang:

725 'Ay, ay, O ay—the winds that bend the brier!
A star in heaven, a star within the mere!
Ay, ay, O ay—a star was my desire,
And one was far apart, and one was near:
Ay, ay, O ay—the winds that bow the grass!
730 And one was water and one star was fire,
And one will ever shine and one will pass.
Ay, ay, O ay—the winds that move the mere.'

Then in the light's last glimmer Tristram showed
And swung the ruby carcanet. She cried,

725–32. 'Like an old Gaelic song – the two stars symbolic of the two Isolts'
(T.).

735   'The collar of some Order, which our King
       Hath newly founded, all for thee, my soul,
       For thee, to yield thee grace beyond thy peers.'

       'Not so, my Queen,' he said, 'but the red fruit
       Grown on a magic oak-tree in mid-heaven,
740   And won by Tristram as a tourney-prize,
       And hither brought by Tristram for his last
       Love-offering and peace-offering unto thee.'

       He spoke, he turned, then, flinging round her neck,
       Claspt it, and cried 'Thine Order, O my Queen!'
745   But, while he bowed to kiss the jewelled throat,
       Out of the dark, just as the lips had touched,
       Behind him rose a shadow and a shriek–
       'Mark's way,' said Mark, and clove him through the
       brain.

       That night came Arthur home, and while he climbed,
750   All in a death-dumb autumn-dripping gloom,
       The stairway to the hall, and looked and saw
       The great Queen's bower was dark,– about his feet
       A voice clung sobbing till he questioned it,
       'What art thou?' and the voice about his feet
755   Sent up an answer, sobbing, 'I am thy fool,
       And I shall never make thee smile again.'

474 Guinevere

Published *1859*. H.T. records: '"Some one", writes my father, "asks how
long it took to *write Guinevere?* About a fortnight" . . . My mother notes
in her Journal: "*July 9th*, 1857. A. has brought me as a birthday present the
first two lines that he has made of *Guinevere*, which might be the nucleus
of a great poem. Arthur is parting from Guinevere, and says:

> But hither shall I never come again,
> Never lie by thy side; see thee no more–
> Farewell! [575–7]".'

743. *spoke*] *1882*; rose *1871–81.*   *then,*] *1872*; and *1871.*
744–5] *1872*; Claspt it; but while he bowed himself to lay
       Warm kisses in the hollow of her throat, *1871*
Compare Malory xx 6: '"That is hard to do", said sir Launcelot; "for
by sir Tristram I may have a warning: for when by means of the treaty
sir Tristram brought again la beale Isoude unto king Marke, from Joyous
Gard, look what fell on the end, how shamefully that false traitor (king
Marke) slew that noble knight as he sat harping before his lady, la beale
Isoude, with a sharp grounded glaive thrust him behind to the heart."'

T. does not seem to have proceeded till 1858; in Jan. '*The Parting of Arthur and Guinevere* was finished'; the song [166–77] was written on 8 March; and on 15 March *Guinevere* was 'finally completed' (*Mem.* i 424). The dates rule out G. S. Haight's suggestion that T. was concerned to counteract William Morris's *Defence of Guenevere* (pub. early March 1858). H.T. comments: 'This Idyll is largely original, being founded on the following passage from Malory [xxi 7, the beginning of the sentence being here added]':

'And when queen Guenever understood that her lord, king Arthur, was slain, and all the noble knights, sir Mordred and all the remnant, then she stole away, and five ladies with her: and so she went to Almesbury, and there she let make herself a nun, and wore white clothes and black: and great penance she took, as ever did sinful lady in this land, and never creature could make her merry, but lived in fastings, prayers, and alms-deeds, that all manner of people marvelled how virtuously she was changed. Now leave we queen Guenever in Almesbury, that was a nun in white clothes and in black, and there she was abbess and ruler as reason would.'

'Guinevere was called Gwenhwyvar (the white ghost) by the bards, and is said by Taliessin to have been "of a haughty disposition even in her youth". Malory calls her the daughter of Leodogran of the land of Camelyard' (H.T.). In Malory, the only interview at Almesbury is between Lancelot and Guinevere, since Guinevere does not go there till after hearing of the death of Arthur. Gray (p. 19): T. 'follows Geoffrey of Monmouth in having Guinevere enter a nunnery before the last battle'.

> Queen Guinevere had fled the court, and sat
> There in the holy house at Almesbury
> Weeping, none with her save a little maid,
> A novice: one low light betwixt them burned
> 5 Blurred by the creeping mist, for all abroad,
> Beneath a moon unseen albeit at full,
> The white mist, like a face-cloth to the face,
> Clung to the dead earth, and the land was still.
>
> For hither had she fled, her cause of flight
> 10 Sir Modred; he that like a subtle beast
> Lay couchant with his eyes upon the throne,
> Ready to spring, waiting a chance: for this
> He chilled the popular praises of the King
> With silent smiles of slow disparagement;
> 15 And tampered with the Lords of the White Horse,
> Heathen, the brood by Hengist left; and sought

¶474. 10] *1870* ('*1869*');   Sir Modred; he the nearest to the King,
                              His nephew, ever like a subtle beast *1859–69*

To make disruption in the Table Round
Of Arthur, and to splinter it into feuds
Serving his traitorous end; and all his aims
20 Were sharpened by strong hate for Lancelot.

For thus it chanced one morn when all the court,
Green-suited, but with plumes that mocked the may,
Had been, their wont, a-maying and returned,
That Modred still in green, all ear and eye,
25 Climbed to the high top of the garden-wall
To spy some secret scandal if he might,
And saw the Queen who sat betwixt her best
Enid, and lissome Vivien, of her court
The wiliest and the worst; and more than this
30 He saw not, for Sir Lancelot passing by
Spied where he couched, and as the gardener's hand
Picks from the colewort a green caterpillar,
So from the high wall and the flowering grove
Of grasses Lancelot plucked him by the heel,
35 And cast him as a worm upon the way;
But when he knew the Prince though marred with dust,
He, reverencing king's blood in a bad man,
Made such excuses as he might, and these
Full knightly without scorn; for in those days
40 No knight of Arthur's noblest dealt in scorn;
But, if a man were halt or hunched, in him
By those whom God had made full-limbed and tall,
Scorn was allowed as part of his defect,
And he was answered softly by the King
45 And all his Table. So Sir Lancelot holp
To raise the Prince, who rising twice or thrice
Full sharply smote his knees, and smiled, and went:
But, ever after, the small violence done
Rankled in him and ruffled all his heart,
50 As the sharp wind that ruffles all day long
·   A little bitter pool about a stone
On the bare coast.

But when Sir Lancelot told
This matter to the Queen, at first she laughed
Lightly, to think of Modred's dusty fall,
55 Then shuddered, as the village wife who cries

21–35. J. M. Gray discusses the literary echoes of Spenser, Milton, Malory,
Chaucer and Shakespeare (*TRB* iii, 1978, 75–6; and Gray, pp. 59–60).
55–6. J. M. Gray compares Francis Grose, *A Provincial Glossary* (Somersby,
Lincoln): 'A person being suddenly taken with a shivering, is a sign that

'I shudder, some one steps across my grave;'
Then laughed again, but faintlier, for indeed
She half-foresaw that he, the subtle beast,
Would track her guilt until he found, and hers
60   Would be for evermore a name of scorn.
Henceforward rarely could she front in hall,
Or elsewhere, Modred's narrow foxy face,
Heart-hiding smile, and gray persistent eye:
Henceforward too, the Powers that tend the soul,
65   To help it from the death that cannot die,
And save it even in extremes, began
To vex and plague her. Many a time for hours,
Beside the placid breathings of the King,
In the dead night, grim faces came and went
70   Before her, or a vague spiritual fear—
Like to some doubtful noise of creaking doors,
Heard by the watcher in a haunted house,
That keeps the rust of murder on the walls—
Held her awake: or if she slept, she dreamed
75   An awful dream; for then she seemed to stand
On some vast plain before a setting sun,
And from the sun there swiftly made at her
A ghastly something, and its shadow flew
Before it, till it touched her, and she turned—
80   When lo! her own, that broadening from her feet,
And blackening, swallowed all the land, and in it
Far cities burnt, and with a cry she woke.
And all this trouble did not pass but grew;
Till even the clear face of the guileless King,
85   And trustful courtesies of household life,
Became her bane; and at the last she said,
'O Lancelot, get thee hence to thine own land,
For if thou tarry we shall meet again,
And if we meet again, some evil chance
90   Will make the smouldering scandal break and blaze
Before the people, and our lord the King.'
And Lancelot ever promised, but remained,
And still they met and met. Again she said,
'O Lancelot, if thou love me get thee hence.'
95   And then they were agreed upon a night
(When the good King should not be there) to meet
And part for ever. Vivien, lurking, heard.

someone has just then walked over the spot of their future grave' (*TRB* ii,
1975, 172).
97–8] *1890*; And part for ever. Passion-pale they met *1859–89.*

She told Sir Modred. Passion-pale they met
And greeted. Hands in hands, and eye to eye,
100 Low on the border of her couch they sat
Stammering and staring. It was their last hour,
A madness of farewells. And Modred brought
His creatures to the basement of the tower
For testimony; and crying with full voice
105 'Traitor, come out, ye are trapt at last,' aroused
Lancelot, who rushing outward lionlike
Leapt on him, and hurled him headlong, and he fell
Stunned, and his creatures took and bare him off,
And all was still: then she, 'The end is come,
110 And I am shamed for ever;' and he said,
'Mine be the shame; mine was the sin: but rise,
And fly to my strong castle overseas:
There will I hide thee, till my life shall end,
There hold thee with my life against the world.'
115 She answered, 'Lancelot, wilt thou hold me so?
Nay, friend, for we have taken our farewells.
Would God that thou couldst hide me from myself!
Mine is the shame, for I was wife, and thou
Unwedded: yet rise now, and let us fly,
120 For I will draw me into sanctuary,
And bide my doom.' So Lancelot got her horse,
Set her thereon, and mounted on his own,
And then they rode to the divided way,
There kissed, and parted weeping: for he past,
125 Love-loyal to the least wish of the Queen,
Back to his land; but she to Almesbury
Fled all night long by glimmering waste and weald,
And heard the Spirits of the waste and weald
Moan as she fled, or thought she heard them moan:
130 And in herself she moaned 'Too late, too late!'
Till in the cold wind that foreruns the morn,
A blot in heaven, the Raven, flying high,
Croaked, and she thought, 'He spies a field of death;
For now the Heathen of the Northern Sea,
135 Lured by the crimes and frailties of the court,
Begin to slay the folk, and spoil the land.'

102–24. Based on Malory xx 1–4. Gray (p. 20) notes that T. 'has changed the place of discovery from the queen's chamber to a tower'.
127] So fled the sad Queen through the moony night
In which no moon appeared, but one vast fleece
Of all the Heavens, moon white from verge to verge.
H.Nbk 36

And when she came to Almesbury she spake
There to the nuns, and said, 'Mine enemies
Pursue me, but, O peaceful Sisterhood,
140   Receive, and yield me sanctuary, nor ask
Her name to whom ye yield it, till her time
To tell you:' and her beauty, grace and power,
Wrought as a charm upon them, and they spared
To ask it.

So the stately Queen abode
145   For many a week, unknown, among the nuns;
Nor with them mixed, nor told her name, nor sought,
Wrapt in her grief, for housel or for shrift,
But communed only with the little maid,
Who pleased her with a babbling heedlessness
150   Which often lured her from herself; but now,
This night, a rumour wildly blown about
Came, that Sir Modred had usurped the realm,
And leagued him with the heathen, while the King
Was waging war on Lancelot: then she thought,
155   'With what a hate the people and the King
Must hate me,' and bowed down upon her hands
Silent, until the little maid, who brooked
No silence, brake it, uttering 'Late! so late!
What hour, I wonder, now?' and when she drew
160   No answer, by and by began to hum
An air the nuns had taught her; 'Late, so late!'
Which when she heard, the Queen looked up, and said,
'O maiden, if indeed ye list to sing,
Sing, and unbind my heart that I may weep.'
165   Whereat full willingly sang the little maid.

'Late, late, so late! and dark the night and chill!
Late, late, so late! but we can enter still.
Too late, too late! ye cannot enter now.

'No light had we: for that we do repent;
170   And learning this, the bridegroom will relent.
Too late, too late! ye cannot enter now.

'No light: so late! and dark and chill the night!
O let us in, that we may find the light!
Too late, too late: ye cannot enter now.

147. *housel*: 'Anglo-Saxon *husel*, the Eucharist' (T.).
163. *ye*] *1870* ('*1869*'); *you 1859–69.*
166–77. Based on *Matthew* xxv 1–13, the parable of the virgins.

175   'Have we not heard the bridegroom is so sweet?
         O let us in, though late, to kiss his feet!
         No, no, too late! ye cannot enter now.'

         So sang the novice, while full passionately,
         Her head upon her hands, remembering
180   Her thought when first she came, wept the sad Queen.
         Then said the little novice prattling to her,
         'O pray you, noble lady, weep no more;
         But let my words, the words of one so small,
         Who knowing nothing knows but to obey,
185   And if I do not there is penance given—
         Comfort your sorrows; for they do not flow
         From evil done; right sure am I of that,
         Who see your tender grace and stateliness.
         But weigh your sorrows with our lord the King's,
190   And weighing find them less; for gone is he
         To wage grim war against Sir Lancelot there,
         Round that strong castle where he holds the Queen;
         And Modred whom he left in charge of all,
         The traitor—Ah sweet lady, the King's grief
195   For his own self, and his own Queen, and realm,
         Must needs be thrice as great as any of ours.
         For me, I thank the saints, I am not great.
         For if there ever come a grief to me
         I cry my cry in silence, and have done.
200   None knows it, and my tears have brought me good:
         But even were the griefs of little ones
         As great as those of great ones, yet this grief
         Is added to the griefs the great must bear,
         That howsoever much they may desire
205   Silence, they cannot weep behind a cloud:
         As even here they talk at Almesbury
         About the good King and his wicked Queen,
         And were I such a King with such a Queen,
         Well might I wish to veil her wickedness,
210   But were I such a King, it could not be.'

         Then to her own sad heart muttered the Queen,
         'Will the child kill me with her innocent talk?'
         But openly she answered, 'Must not I,
         If this false traitor have displaced his lord,
215   Grieve with the common grief of all the realm?'

         'Yea,' said the maid, 'this is all woman's grief,
         That *she* is woman, whose disloyal life

Hath wrought confusion in the Table Round
Which good King Arthur founded, years ago,
220 With signs and miracles and wonders, there
At Camelot, ere the coming of the Queen.'

Then thought the Queen within herself again,
'Will the child kill me with her foolish prate?'
But openly she spake and said to her,
225 'O little maid, shut in by nunnery walls,
What canst thou know of Kings and Tables Round,
Or what of signs and wonders, but the signs
And simple miracles of thy nunnery?'

To whom the little novice garrulously,
230 'Yea, but I know: the land was full of signs
And wonders ere the coming of the Queen.
So said my father, and himself was knight
Of the great Table—at the founding of it;
And rode thereto from Lyonnesse, and he said
235 That as he rode, an hour or maybe twain
After the sunset, down the coast, he heard
Strange music, and he paused, and turning—there,
All down the lonely coast of Lyonnesse,
Each with a beacon-star upon his head,
240 And with a wild sea-light about his feet,
He saw them—headland after headland flame
Far on into the rich heart of the west:
And in the light the white mermaiden swam,
And strong man-breasted things stood from the sea,
245 And sent a deep sea-voice through all the land,
To which the little elves of chasm and cleft
Made answer, sounding like a distant horn.
So said my father—yea, and furthermore,
Next morning, while he past the dim-lit woods,
250 Himself beheld three spirits mad with joy
Come dashing down on a tall wayside flower,
That shook beneath them, as the thistle shakes
When three gray linnets wrangle for the seed:
And still at evenings on before his horse
255 The flickering fairy-circle wheeled and broke
Flying, and linked again, and wheeled and broke
Flying, for all the land was full of life.
And when at last he came to Camelot,

235–47. On possible sources, see W. D. Paden (p. 158), and J. Ferguson on
Catullus lxiv 16–18 (*English Studies in Africa* xii, 1969, 52).

A wreath of airy dancers hand-in-hand
260 Swung round the lighted lantern of the hall;
And in the hall itself was such a feast
As never man had dreamed; for every knight
Had whatsoever meat he longed for served
By hands unseen; and even as he said
265 Down in the cellars merry bloated things
Shouldered the spigot, straddling on the butts
While the wine ran: so glad were spirits and men
Before the coming of the sinful Queen.'

Then spake the Queen and somewhat bitterly,
270 'Were they so glad? ill prophets were they all,
Spirits and men: could none of them foresee,
Not even thy wise father with his signs
And wonders, what has fallen upon the realm?'

To whom the novice garrulously again,
275 'Yea, one, a bard; of whom my father said,
Full many a noble war-song had he sung,
Even in the presence of an enemy's fleet,
Between the steep cliff and the coming wave;
And many a mystic lay of life and death
280 Had chanted on the smoky mountain-tops,
When round him bent the spirits of the hills
With all their dewy hair blown back like flame:
So said my father—and that night the bard
Sang Arthur's glorious wars, and sang the King
285 As wellnigh more than man, and railed at those
Who called him the false son of Gorloïs:
For there was no man knew from whence he came;
But after tempest, when the long wave broke
All down the thundering shores of Bude and Bos,
290 There came a day as still as heaven, and then
They found a naked child upon the sands
Of dark Tintagil by the Cornish sea;

262-3. As happens when the Grail appears (*The Holy Grail* 182–202n, pp. 881–2).
266. *spigot*: 'bung' (T.). Suggested by T. Crofton Croker's *Fairy Legends* (1834 edn, *Lincoln*, p. 82), 'The Haunted Cellar': 'and on advancing perceived a little figure, about six inches in height, seated astride upon the pipe of the oldest port in the place, and bearing a spigot upon his shoulder'.
289. *Bude and Bos*: 'north of Tintagil' (T.).
292. *dark Tintagil*] *1865 Selection*; wild Dundagil *1859–61*; dark Dundagil *1862–5*.

And that was Arthur; and they fostered him
Till he by miracle was approven King:
295   And that his grave should be a mystery
From all men, like his birth; and could he find
A woman in her womanhood as great
As he was in his manhood, then, he sang,
The twain together well might change the world.
300   But even in the middle of his song
He faltered, and his hand fell from the harp,
And pale he turned, and reeled, and would have fallen,
But that they stayed him up; nor would he tell
His vision; but what doubt that he foresaw
305   This evil work of Lancelot and the Queen?'

Then thought the Queen, 'Lo! they have set her on,
Our simple-seeming Abbess and her nuns,
To play upon me,' and bowed her head nor spake.
Whereat the novice crying, with clasped hands,
310   Shame on her own garrulity garrulously,
Said the good nuns would check her gadding tongue
Full often, 'and, sweet lady, if I seem
To vex an ear too sad to listen to me,
Unmannerly, with prattling and the tales
315   Which my good father told me, check me too
Nor let me shame my father's memory, one
Of noblest manners, though himself would say
Sir Lancelot had the noblest; and he died,
Killed in a tilt, come next, five summers back,
320   And left me; but of others who remain,
And of the two first-famed for courtesy—
And pray you check me if I ask amiss—
But pray you, which had noblest, while you moved
Among them, Lancelot or our lord the King?'

325   Then the pale Queen looked up and answered her,
'Sir Lancelot, as became a noble knight,
Was gracious to all ladies, and the same
In open battle or the tilting-field
Forbore his own advantage, and the King
330   In open battle or the tilting-field
Forbore his own advantage, and these two
Were the most nobly-mannered men of all;
For manners are not idle, but the fruit
Of loyal nature, and of noble mind.'

335   'Yea,' said the maid, 'be manners such fair fruit?
Then Lancelot's needs must be a thousand-fold

Less noble, being, as all rumour runs,
The most disloyal friend in all the world.'

To which a mournful answer made the Queen:
340 'O closed about by narrowing nunnery-walls,
What knowest thou of the world, and all its lights
And shadows, all the wealth and all the woe?
If ever Lancelot, that most noble knight,
Were for one hour less noble than himself,
345 Pray for him that he scape the doom of fire,
And weep for her who drew him to his doom.'

'Yea,' said the little novice, 'I pray for both;
But I should all as soon believe that his,
Sir Lancelot's, were as noble as the King's,
350 As I could think, sweet lady, yours would be
Such as they are, were you the sinful Queen.'

So she, like many another babbler, hurt
Whom she would soothe, and harmed where she would
    heal;
For here a sudden flush of wrathful heat
355 Fired all the pale face of the Queen, who cried,
'Such as thou art be never maiden more
For ever! thou their tool, set on to plague
And play upon, and harry me, petty spy
And traitress.' When that storm of anger brake
360 From Guinevere, aghast the maiden rose,
White as her veil, and stood before the Queen
As tremulously as foam upon the beach
Stands in a wind, ready to break and fly,
And when the Queen had added 'Get thee hence,'
365 Fled frighted. Then that other left alone
Sighed, and began to gather heart again,
Saying in herself, 'The simple, fearful child
Meant nothing, but my own too-fearful guilt,
Simpler than any child, betrays itself.
370 But help me, heaven, for surely I repent.
For what is true repentance but in thought—
Not even in inmost thought to think again
The sins that made the past so pleasant to us:
And I have sworn never to see him more,
To see him more.'

375   And even in saying this,
Her memory from old habit of the mind
Went slipping back upon the golden days

In which she saw him first, when Lancelot came,
Reputed the best knight and goodliest man,
380 Ambassador, to lead her to his lord
Arthur, and led her forth, and far ahead
Of his and her retinue moving, they,
Rapt in sweet talk or lively, all on love
And sport and tilts and pleasure, (for the time
385 Was maytime, and as yet no sin was dreamed,)
Rode under groves that looked a paradise
Of blossom, over sheets of hyacinth
That seemed the heavens upbreaking through the earth,
And on from hill to hill, and every day
390 Beheld at noon in some delicious dale
The silk pavilions of King Arthur raised
For brief repast or afternoon repose
By couriers gone before; and on again,
Till yet once more ere set of sun they saw
395 The Dragon of the great Pendragonship,
That crowned the state pavilion of the King,
Blaze by the rushing brook or silent well.

But when the Queen immersed in such a trance,
And moving through the past unconsciously,
400 Came to that point where first she saw the King
Ride toward her from the city, sighed to find
Her journey done, glanced at him, thought him cold,
High, self-contained, and passionless, not like him,
'Not like my Lancelot' – while she brooded thus
405 And grew half-guilty in her thoughts again,
There rode an armèd warrior to the doors.
A murmuring whisper through the nunnery ran,
Then on a sudden a cry, 'The King.' She sat
Stiff-stricken, listening; but when armèd feet
410 Through the long gallery from the outer doors
Rang coming, prone from off her seat she fell,
And grovelled with her face against the floor:
There with her milkwhite arms and shadowy hair
She made her face a darkness from the King:
415 And in the darkness heard his armèd feet
Pause by her; then came silence, then a voice,

395. 'The headship of the tribes who had confederated against the Lords of the White Horse. "Pendragon" not a dactyl as some make it, but Pén-drágon' (T.).
400. *where*] *1870* ('*1869*'); when *1859–69.*

Monotonous and hollow like a Ghost's
Denouncing judgment, but though changed, the King's:

'Liest thou here so low, the child of one
420 I honoured, happy, dead before thy shame?
Well is it that no child is born of thee.
The children born of thee are sword and fire,
Red ruin, and the breaking up of laws,
The craft of kindred and the Godless hosts
425 Of heathen swarming o'er the Northern Sea;
Whom I, while yet Sir Lancelot, my right arm,
The mightiest of my knights, abode with me,
Have everywhere about this land of Christ
In twelve great battles ruining overthrown.
430 And knowest thou now from whence I come—from him
From waging bitter war with him: and he,
That did not shun to smite me in worse way,
Had yet that grace of courtesy in him left,
He spared to lift his hand against the King
435 Who made him knight: but many a knight was slain;
And many more, and all his kith and kin
Clave to him, and abode in his own land.
And many more when Modred raised revolt,
Forgetful of their troth and fealty, clave
440 To Modred, and a remnant stays with me.
And of this remnant will I leave a part,
True men who love me still, for whom I live,
To guard thee in the wild hour coming on,
Lest but a hair of this low head be harmed.
445 Fear not: thou shalt be guarded till my death.
Howbeit I know, if ancient prophecies
Have erred not, that I march to meet my doom.
Thou hast not made my life so sweet to me,
That I the King should greatly care to live;
450 For thou hast spoilt the purpose of my life.
Bear with me for the last time while I show,
Even for thy sake, the sin which thou hast sinned.
For when the Roman left us, and their law
Relaxed its hold upon us, and the ways
455 Were filled with rapine, here and there a deed
Of prowess done redressed a random wrong.
But I was first of all the kings who drew
The knighthood-errant of this realm and all
The realms together under me, their Head,
460 In that fair Order of my Table Round,
A glorious company, the flower of men,

To serve as model for the mighty world,
And be the fair beginning of a time.
I made them lay their hands in mine and swear
465 To reverence the King, as if he were
Their conscience, and their conscience as their King,
To break the heathen and uphold the Christ,
To ride abroad redressing human wrongs,
To speak no slander, no, nor listen to it,
470 To honour his own word as if his God's,
To lead sweet lives in purest chastity,
To love one maiden only, cleave to her,
And worship her by years of noble deeds,
Until they won her; for indeed I knew
475 Of no more subtle master under heaven
Than is the maiden passion for a maid,
Not only to keep down the base in man,
But teach high thought, and amiable words
And courtliness, and the desire of fame,
480 And love of truth, and all that makes a man.
And all this throve before I wedded thee,
Believing, "lo mine helpmate, one to feel
My purpose and rejoicing in my joy."
Then came thy shameful sin with Lancelot;
485 Then came the sin of Tristram and Isolt;
Then others, following these my mightiest knights,
And drawing foul ensample from fair names,
Sinned also, till the loathsome opposite
Of all my heart had destined did obtain,
490 And all through thee! so that this life of mine
I guard as God's high gift from scathe and wrong,
Not greatly care to lose; but rather think
How sad it were for Arthur, should he live,
To sit once more within his lonely hall,
495 And miss the wonted number of my knights,
And miss to hear high talk of noble deeds
As in the golden days before thy sin.
For which of us, who might be left,·could speak
Of the pure heart, nor seem to glance at thee?
500 And in thy bowers of Camelot or of Usk
Thy shadow still would glide from room to room,
And I should evermore be vext with thee
In hanging robe or vacant ornament,

470] *1873; not 1859–70.*
481. before] *1873;* until *1859–70.*

Or ghostly footfall echoing on the stair.
505 For think not, though thou wouldst not love thy lord,
Thy lord has wholly lost his love for thee.
I am not made of so slight elements.
Yet must I leave thee, woman, to thy shame.
I hold that man the worst of public foes
510 Who either for his own or children's sake,
To save his blood from scandal, lets the wife
Whom he knows false, abide and rule the house:
For being through his cowardice allowed
Her station, taken everywhere for pure,
515 She like a new disease, unknown to men,
Creeps, no precaution used, among the crowd,
Makes wicked lightnings of her eyes, and saps
The fealty of our friends, and stirs the pulse
With devil's leaps, and poisons half the young.
520 Worst of the worst were that man he that reigns!
Better the King's waste hearth and aching heart
Than thou reseated in thy place of light,
The mockery of my people, and their bane.'

He paused, and in the pause she crept an inch
525 Nearer, and laid her hands about his feet.
Far off a solitary trumpet blew.
Then waiting by the doors the warhorse neighed
As at a friend's voice, and he spake again:

'Yet think not that I come to urge thy crimes,
530 I did not come to curse thee, Guinevere,
I, whose vast pity almost makes me die
To see thee, laying there thy golden head,
My pride in happier summers, at my feet.
The wrath which forced my thoughts on that fierce law,
535 The doom of treason and the flaming death,
(When first I learnt thee hidden here) is past.
The pang—which while I weighed thy heart with one
Too wholly true to dream untruth in thee,
Made my tears burn—is also past—in part.
540 And all is past, the sin is sinned, and I,
Lo! I forgive thee, as Eternal God
Forgives: do thou for thine own soul the rest.
But how to take last leave of all I loved?
O golden hair, with which I used to play

534-6. In Malory, Arthur condemned Guinevere to be burnt to death, and
she was rescued by Lancelot.

545 Not knowing! O imperial-moulded form,
      And beauty such as never woman wore,
      Until it came a kingdom's curse with thee—
      I cannot touch thy lips, they are not mine,
      But Lancelot's: nay, they never were the King's.
550 I cannot take thy hand; that too is flesh,
      And in the flesh thou hast sinned; and mine own flesh,
      Here looking down on thine polluted, cries
      "I loathe thee:" yet not less, O Guinevere,
      For I was ever virgin save for thee,
555 My love through flesh hath wrought into my life
      So far, that my doom is, I love thee still.
      Let no man dream but that I love thee still.
      Perchance, and so thou purify thy soul,
      And so thou lean on our fair father Christ,
560 Hereafter in that world where all are pure
      We two may meet before high God, and thou
      Wilt spring to me, and claim me thine, and know
      I am thine husband—not a smaller soul,
      Nor Lancelot, nor another. Leave me that,
565 I charge thee, my last hope. Now must I hence.
      Through the thick night I hear the trumpet blow:
      They summon me their King to lead mine hosts
      Far down to that great battle in the west,
      Where I must strike against the man they call
570 My sister's son—no kin of mine, who leagues
      With Lords of the White Horse, heathen, and knights,
      Traitors—and strike him dead, and meet myself
      Death, or I know not what mysterious doom.
      And thou remaining here wilt learn the event;
575 But hither shall I never come again,
      Never lie by thy side; see thee no more—
      Farewell!'

              And while she grovelled at his feet,
      She felt the King's breath wander o'er her neck,
      And in the darkness o'er her fallen head,
580 Perceived the waving of his hands that blest.

         Then, listening till those armèd steps were gone,
      Rose the pale Queen, and in her anguish found

569–72] *1870* ('*1869*');
         Where I must strike against my sister's son,
         Leagued with the lords of the White Horse and knights
         Once mine, and strike him dead, and meet myself *1859–69.*

The casement: 'peradventure,' so she thought,
'If I might see his face, and not be seen.'
585 And lo, he sat on horseback at the door!
And near him the sad nuns with each a light
Stood, and he gave them charge about the Queen,
To guard and foster her for evermore.
And while he spake to these his helm was lowered,
590 To which for crest the golden dragon clung
Of Britain; so she did not see the face,
Which then was as an angel's, but she saw,
Wet with the mists and smitten by the lights,
The Dragon of the great Pendragonship
595 Blaze, making all the night a steam of fire.
And even then he turned; and more and more
The moony vapour rolling round the King,
Who seemed the phantom of a Giant in it,
Enwound him fold by fold, and made him gray
600 And grayer, till himself became as mist
Before her, moving ghostlike to his doom.

Then she stretched out her arms and cried aloud
'Oh Arthur!' there her voice brake suddenly,
Then – as a stream that spouting from a cliff
605 Fails in mid air, but gathering at the base
Re-makes itself, and flashes down the vale –
Went on in passionate utterance:

'Gone – my lord!
Gone through my sin to slay and to be slain!
And he forgave me, and I could not speak.
610 Farewell? I should have answered his farewell.
His mercy choked me. Gone, my lord the King,
My own true lord! how dare I call him mine?
The shadow of another cleaves to me,
And makes me one pollution: he, the King,
615 Called me polluted: shall I kill myself?
What help in that? I cannot kill my sin,
If soul be soul; nor can I kill my shame;
No, nor by living can I live it down.
The days will grow to weeks, the weeks to months,
620 The months will add themselves and make the years,
The years will roll into the centuries,
And mine will ever be a name of scorn.
I must not dwell on that defeat of fame.

591–2. *Acts* vi 15, of Stephen: 'And all that sat in the council, looking stedfastly on him, saw his face as it had been the face of an angel.'

Let the world be; that is but of the world.
625 What else? what hope? I think there was a hope,
Except he mocked me when he spake of hope;
His hope he called it; but he never mocks,
For mockery is the fume of little hearts.
And blessèd be the King, who hath forgiven
630 My wickedness to him, and left me hope
That in mine own heart I can live down sin
And be his mate hereafter in the heavens
Before high God. Ah great and gentle lord,
Who wast, as is the conscience of a saint
635 Among his warring senses, to thy knights—
To whom my false voluptuous pride, that took
Full easily all impressions from below,
Would not look up, or half-despised the height
To which I would not or I could not climb—
640 I thought I could not breathe in that fine air
That pure severity of perfect light—
I yearned for warmth and colour which I found
In Lancelot—now I see thee what thou art,
Thou art the highest and most human too,
645 Not Lancelot, nor another. Is there none
Will tell the King I love him though so late?
Now—ere he goes to the great Battle? none:
Myself must tell him in that purer life,
But now it were too daring. Ah my God,
650 What might I not have made of thy fair world,
Had I but loved thy highest creature here?
It was my duty to have loved the highest:
It surely was my profit had I known:
It would have been my pleasure had I seen.
655 We needs must love the highest when we see it,
Not Lancelot, nor another.'

Here her hand
Grasped, made her vail her eyes: she looked and saw
The novice, weeping, suppliant, and said to her,
'Yea, little maid, for am *I* not forgiven?'
660 Then glancing up beheld the holy nuns
All round her, weeping; and her heart was loosed
Within her, and she wept with these and said,

'Ye know me then, that wicked one, who broke
The vast design and purpose of the King.

---

642. *yearned for*] *1886*; wanted *1859–84*. *Eversley* accidentally omits 'for'.

665 O shut me round with narrowing nunnery-walls,
Meek maidens, from the voices crying "shame."
I must not scorn myself: he loves me still.
Let no one dream but that he loves me still.
So let me, if you do not shudder at me,
670 Nor shun to call me sister, dwell with you;
Wear black and white, and be a nun like you,
Fast with your fasts, not feasting with your feasts;
Grieve with your griefs, not grieving at your joys,
But not rejoicing; mingle with your rites;
675 Pray and be prayed for; lie before your shrines;
Do each low office of your holy house;
Walk your dim cloister, and distribute dole
To poor sick people, richer in His eyes
Who ransomed us, and haler too than I;
680 And treat their loathsome hurts and heal mine own;
And so wear out in almsdeed and in prayer
The sombre close of that voluptuous day,
Which wrought the ruin of my lord the King.'

She said: they took her to themselves; and she
685 Still hoping, fearing 'is it yet too late?'
Dwelt with them, till in time their Abbess died.
Then she, for her good deeds and her pure life,
And for the power of ministration in her,
And likewise for the high rank she had borne,
690 Was chosen Abbess, there, an Abbess, lived
For three brief years, and there, an Abbess, past
To where beyond these voices there is peace.

475 The Passing of Arthur

Published *1869* ('*1870*'). Written 1869 (*CT*, p. 382). T. created it from his
Morte d'Arthur (*1842*), which forms ll. 170–440 of *The Passing of Arthur*.
(For the only changes in wording, see ll. 175 ∧ 6*n*, and l. 373*n*.) For detailed
notes to these lines, including the relevant passages from Malory, see
Morte d'Arthur (p. *148*). T. comments:"The temporary triumph of evil,
the confusion of moral order, closing in the Great Battle of the West.'
The title had been *The Death of Arthur* in the trial edition (1869), for details
of which see Wise, *Bibliography* i 197–209. Anne Ritchie, *Harper's Magazine*
vii (1883) 31, reports: 'The first *Idyll* and the last, I have heard Mr Tenny-
son say, are intentionally more archaic than the others.' J. Pfordresher describes
a MS draft of ll. 1–5, 80–97 (*Georgetown University*) not listed in his edition,
'an early stage in the composition of the poem' (*TRB* ii, 1976, 203–4). For

T.'s prose draft of the opening (*H.Nbk 37*), see D. Staines, *Harvard Library Bulletin* xxii (1974) 292–3.

> That story which the bold Sir Bedivere,
> First made and latest left of all the knights,
> Told, when the man was no more than a voice
> In the white winter of his age, to those
> 5 With whom he dwelt, new faces, other minds.
>
> For on their march to westward, Bedivere,
> Who slowly paced among the slumbering host,
> Heard in his tent the moanings of the King:
>
> 'I found Him in the shining of the stars,
> 10 I marked Him in the flowering of His fields,
> But in His ways with men I find Him not.
> I waged His wars, and now I pass and die.
> O me! for why is all around us here
> As if some lesser god had made the world,
> 15 But had not force to shape it as he would,
> Till the High God behold it from beyond,
> And enter it, and make it beautiful?
> Or else as if the world were wholly fair,
> But that these eyes of men are dense and dim,
> 20 And have not power to see it as it is:
> Perchance, because we see not to the close; –
> For I, being simple, thought to work His will,
> And have but stricken with the sword in vain;
> And all whereon I leaned in wife and friend
> 25 Is traitor to my peace, and all my realm
> Reels back into the beast, and is no more.
> My God, thou hast forgotten me in my death;
> Nay – God my Christ – I pass but shall not die.'

¶475. *6–28*] 1873; not 1869–70.

9–28. For a MS of these lines (*Lincoln*), see A. Day, *The Library* Sixth Ser. iii (1981) 343–6.

14. 'Cf. the demiurge of Plato, and the gnostic belief that lesser Powers created the world' (T.).

21 ∧ *2*] Or else as if there were no God at all – *Lincoln MS*.

23. P. Metcalf compares *Romans* xiii 4: 'For he beareth not the sword in vain'.

25–6. Cp. *Locksley Hall Sixty Years After* 148: 'Then back into the beast again'.

27] My God my God thou hast forsaken me. *Lincoln MS*. *Psalm* xxii 1, and *Matthew* xxvii 46: 'My God, my God, why hast thou forsaken me?'

        Then, ere that last weird battle in the west,
30   There came on Arthur sleeping, Gawain killed
        In Lancelot's war, the ghost of Gawain blown
        Along a wandering wind, and past his ear
        Went shrilling, 'Hollow, hollow all delight!
        Hail, King! tomorrow thou shalt pass away.
35   Farewell! there is an isle of rest for thee.
        And I am blown along a wandering wind,
        And hollow, hollow, hollow all delight.'
        And fainter onward, like wild birds that change
        Their season in the night and wail their way
40   From cloud to cloud, down the long wind the dream
        Shrilled; but in going mingled with dim cries
        Far in the moonlit haze among the hills,
        As of some lonely city sacked by night,
        When all is lost, and wife and child with wail
45   Pass to new lords; and Arthur woke and called,
        'Who spake? A dream. O light upon the wind,
        Thine, Gawain, was the voice—are these dim cries
        Thine? or doth all that haunts the waste and wild
        Mourn, knowing it will go along with me?'

50   This heard the bold Sir Bedivere and spake:
        'O me, my King, let pass whatever will,

29. Then, ere] *1873*; Before *1869–70*.
30–49. For T.'s earlier version of the ghost of Gawain (a version closer to
Malory xxi 3), see *Morte d'Arthur* 13 ∧ 14 (*p. 150*). In Malory xxi 4, the
ghost of Gawain warned Arthur not to fight that day: 'How by mis-
adventure of an adder the battle began'.
36. T. compares *Aeneid* vi 740–1, on the fate of the dead: *aliae panduntur
inanes / suspensae ad ventos* ('Some are hung stretched out to the empty
winds').
37. Cp. *Locksley Hall* 75, MS (*p. 186*): 'Hollow, hollow, hollow comfort'.
50–78] Not trial edition (*1869*). See Wise, *Bibliography* i 207.
        This heard the bold Sir Bedivere and past
    Within the tent and spake 'My Lord, the King,
    I find a feeble whiteness as of dawn.
    In the far East
    Wilt thou not rise and follow to the West
    And
    That all the sooner we may turn again
    And see the sunrise light the golden wings
    That Merlin gave thine image on the hill'.
        Then spake King Arthur
    'O thinkst thou we shall ever turn again

Elves, and the harmless glamour of the field;
But in their stead thy name and glory cling
To all high places like a golden cloud
55 For ever: but as yet thou shalt not pass.
Light was Gawain in life, and light in death
Is Gawain, for the ghost is as the man;
And care not thou for dreams from him, but rise—
I hear the steps of Modred in the west,
60 And with him many of thy people, and knights
Once thine, whom thou hast loved, but grosser grown
Than heathen, spitting at their vows and thee.
Right well in heart they know thee for the King.
Arise, go forth and conquer as of old.'

65   Then spake King Arthur to Sir Bedivere:
'Far other is this battle in the west
Whereto we move, than when we strove in youth,
And brake the petty kings, and fought with Rome,
Or thrust the heathen from the Roman wall,
70 And shook him through the north. Ill doom is mine
To war against my people and my knights.
The king who fights his people fights himself.
And they my knights, who loved me once, the stroke
That strikes them dead is as my death to me.
75 Yet let us hence, and find or feel a way
Through this blind haze, which ever since I saw
One lying in the dust at Almesbury,
Hath folded in the passes of the world.'

Then rose the King and moved his host by night,
80 And ever pushed Sir Modred, league by league,

To light and sunrise in the golden East.
We follow night and sunset in the West
And those who love the King will die with me'.
    And therewithal returned on Bedivere
The burthen of a hymn himself had sung.
He clashed his arms together and he said·
        'King art thou in East and West,
Strike for the King and die: let the King reign'.
                                        H.Nbk 39 draft

Cp. *The Coming of Arthur* 481–501.
52. 'The legends which cluster round the King's name' (T.).
57. 'The spirit' (T.).
68] *1873; not 1869–70.*
69. Or] *1873;* And *1869–70.*

Back to the sunset bound of Lyonnesse –
A land of old upheaven from the abyss
By fire, to sink into the abyss again;
Where fragments of forgotten peoples dwelt,
85 And the long mountains ended in a coast
Of ever-shifting sand, and far away
The phantom circle of a moaning sea.
There the pursuer could pursue no more,
And he that fled no further fly the King;
90 And there, that day when the great light of heaven
Burned at his lowest in the rolling year,
On the waste sand by the waste sea they closed.
Nor ever yet had Arthur fought a fight
Like this last, dim, weird battle of the west.
95 A deathwhite mist slept over sand and sea:
Whereof the chill, to him who breathed it, drew
Down with his blood, till all his heart was cold
With formless fear; and even on Arthur fell
Confusion, since he saw not whom he fought.
100 For friend and foe were shadows in the mist,
And friend slew friend not knowing whom he slew;
And some had visions out of golden youth,
And some beheld the faces of old ghosts
Look in upon the battle; and in the mist
105 Was many a noble deed, many a base,
And chance and craft and strength in single fights,
And ever and anon with host to host
Shocks, and the splintering spear, the hard mail hewn,
Shield-breakings, and the clash of brands, the crash
110 Of battleaxes on shattered helms, and shrieks
After the Christ, of those who falling down
Looked up for heaven, and only saw the mist;
And shouts of heathen and the traitor knights,
Oaths, insult, filth, and monstrous blasphemies,

84. 'Perhaps old Celts' (T.).
87. T. had thought of using this line in 1868 for *The Lover's Tale* iv 141: 'A world of reed and rush, and far away / The phantom circle of a moaning sea.' He had originally created the line as part of *Lines [Here often]*: 'The phantom-circle of the moaning main' (I 541).
91. 'The winter solstice' (T.).
93–4. 'A Vision of Death (T.).
99 ∧ 100] Nor whence he was nor whether he were king
And still the heathen shouted in the haze
Proclaiming Modred lord of all the realm. *Texas MS*
114. T. compares *Revelation* xvi 21: 'and men blasphemed God', after

115 Sweat, writhings, anguish, labouring of the lungs
In that close mist, and cryings for the light,
Moans of the dying, and voices of the dead.

Last, as by some one deathbed after wail
Of suffering, silence follows, or through death
120 Or deathlike swoon, thus over all that shore,
Save for some whisper of the seething seas,
A dead hush fell; but when the dolorous day
Grew drearier toward twilight falling, came
A bitter wind, clear from the North, and blew
125 The mist aside, and with that wind the tide
Rose, and the pale King glanced across the field
Of battle: but no man was moving there;
Nor any cry of Christian heard thereon,
Nor yet of heathen; only the wan wave
130 Brake in among dead faces, to and fro
Swaying the helpless hands, and up and down
Tumbling the hollow helmets of the fallen,
And shivered brands that once had fought with Rome,
And rolling far along the gloomy shores
135 The voice of days of old and days to be.

Then spake King Arthur to Sir Bedivere,
And whiter than the mist that all day long
Had held the field of battle was the King:

'Hearest thou this great voice that shakes the world,
140 And wastes the narrow realm whereon we move,
And beats upon the faces of the dead,
My dead, as though they had not died for me?—
O Bedivere, for on my heart hath fallen
Confusion, till I know not what I am,
145 Nor whence I am, nor whether I be King.
Behold, I seem but King among the dead.'

Then spake the bold Sir Bedivere: 'My King,

the battle of Armageddon. 'This grim battle in the mist contrasts with
Arthur's glorious battle in the *Coming of Arthur*, fought on a bright day
when "he saw the smallest rock far on the faintest hill"' (T.). The landscape
and the mist are additions to Malory. On the Homeric echo in this battle
(*Iliad* xvii 645–7), see Turner (p. 164); and on Layamon's *Brut*, see Gray
(p. 145).

134] And sending far along the dreary shores *Texas MS 1st reading.*

King everywhere! and so the dead have kings,
There also will I worship thee as King.
150 Yet still thy life is whole, and still I live
Who love thee; but who hates thee, he that brought
The heathen back among us, yonder stands,
Modred, unharmed, the traitor of thine house.'

Then spake the King: 'My house hath been my doom.
155 But call not thou this traitor of my house
Who hath but dwelt beneath one roof with me.
My house are rather they who sware my vows,
Yea, even while they brake them, owned me King.
And well for thee, saying in my dark hour,
160 When all the purport of my throne hath failed,
That quick or dead thou holdest me for King.
King am I, whatsoever be their cry;
And one last act of kinghood shalt thou see
Yet, ere I pass.' And uttering this the King
165 Made at the man: then Modred smote his liege
Hard on that helm which many a heathen sword
Had beaten thin; while Arthur at one blow,
Striking the last stroke with Excalibur,
Slew him, and all but slain himself, he fell.

170   So all day long the noise of battle rolled
Among the mountains by the winter sea;
Until King Arthur's Table, man by man,
Had fallen in Lyonnesse about their lord,
King Arthur. Then, because his wound was deep,
175 The bold Sir Bedivere uplifted him,
And bore him to a chapel nigh the field,
A broken chancel with a broken cross,
That stood on a dark strait of barren land:
On one side lay the Ocean, and on one
180 Lay a great water, and the moon was full.

Then spake King Arthur to Sir Bedivere:
'The sequel of today unsolders all
The goodliest fellowship of famous knights
Whereof this world holds record. Such a sleep
185 They sleep—the men I loved. I think that we
Shall never more, at any future time,
Delight our souls with talk of knightly deeds,
Walking about the gardens and the halls

175 ∧ 6] Sir Bedivere, the last of all his knights, *Morte d'Arthur*.

Of Camelot, as in the days that were.
190 I perish by this people which I made, –
Though Merlin sware that I should come again
To rule once more; but, let what will be, be,
I am so deeply smitten through the helm
That without help I cannot last till morn.
195 Thou therefore take my brand Excalibur,
Which was my pride: for thou rememberest how
In those old days, one summer noon, an arm
Rose up from out the bosom of the lake,
Clothed in white samite, mystic, wonderful,
200 Holding the sword – and how I rowed across
And took it, and have worn it, like a king;
And, wheresoever I am sung or told
In aftertime, this also shall be known:
But now delay not: take Excalibur,
205 And fling him far into the middle mere:
Watch what thou seëst, and lightly bring me word.'

To him replied the bold Sir Bedivere:
'It is not meet, Sir King, to leave thee thus,
Aidless, alone, and smitten through the helm –
210 A little thing may harm a wounded man;
Yet I thy hest will all perform at full,
Watch what I see, and lightly bring thee word.'

So saying, from the ruined shrine he stept,
And in the moon athwart the place of tombs,
215 Where lay the mighty bones of ancient men,
Old knights, and over them the sea-wind sang
Shrill, chill, with flakes of foam. He, stepping down
By zigzag paths, and juts of pointed rock,
Came on the shining levels of the lake.

220 There drew he forth the brand Excalibur,
And o'er him, drawing it, the winter moon,
Brightening the skirts of a long cloud, ran forth
And sparkled keen with frost against the hilt:
For all the haft twinkled with diamond sparks,
225 Myriads of topaz-lights, and jacinth-work
Of subtlest jewellery. He gazed so long
That both his eyes were dazzled as he stood,
This way and that dividing the swift mind,
In act to throw: but at the last it seemed
230 Better to leave Excalibur concealed
There in the many-knotted waterflags,

That whistled stiff and dry about the marge.
So strode he back slow to the wounded King.

Then spake King Arthur to Sir Bedivere:
235 'Hast thou performed my mission which I gave?
What is it thou hast seen? or what hast heard?'

And answer made the bold Sir Bedivere:
'I heard the ripple washing in the reeds,
And the wild water lapping on the crag.'

240 To whom replied King Arthur, faint and pale:
'Thou hast betrayed thy nature and thy name,
Not rendering true answer, as beseemed
Thy fëalty, nor like a noble knight:
For surer sign had followed, either hand,
245 Or voice, or else a motion of the mere.
This is a shameful thing for men to lie.
Yet now, I charge thee, quickly go again,
As thou art lief and dear, and do the thing
I bade thee, watch, and lightly bring me word.'

250 Then went Sir Bedivere the second time
Across the ridge, and paced beside the mere,
Counting the dewy pebbles, fixed in thought;
But when he saw the wonder of the hilt,
How curiously and strangely chased, he smote
255 His palms together, and he cried aloud:

'And if indeed I cast the brand away,
Surely a precious thing, one worthy note,
Should thus be lost for ever from the earth,
Which might have pleased the eyes of many men.
260 What good should follow this, if this were done?
What harm, undone? Deep harm to disobey,
Seeing obedience is the bond of rule.
Were it well to obey then, if a king demand
An act unprofitable, against himself?
265 The King is sick, and knows not what he does.
What record, or what relic of my lord
Should be to aftertime, but empty breath
And rumours of a doubt? But were this kept,
Stored in some treasure-house of mighty kings,
270 Some one might show it at a joust of arms,
Saying, "King Arthur's sword, Excalibur,
Wrought by the lonely maiden of the Lake.

Nine years she wrought it, sitting in the deeps
Upon the hidden bases of the hills."
275 So might some old man speak in the aftertime
To all the people, winning reverence.
But now much honour and much fame were lost.'

So spake he, clouded with his own conceit,
And hid Excalibur the second time,
280 And so strode back slow to the wounded King.

Then spoke King Arthur, breathing heavily:
'What is it thou hast seen? or what hast heard?'

And answer made the bold Sir Bedivere:
'I heard the water lapping on the crag,
285 And the long ripple washing in the reeds.'

To whom replied King Arthur, much in wrath:
'Ah, miserable and unkind, untrue,
Unknightly, traitor-hearted! Woe is me!
Authority forgets a dying king,
290 Laid widowed of the power in his eye
That bowed the will. I see thee what thou art,
For thou, the latest-left of all my knights,
In whom should meet the offices of all,
Thou wouldst betray me for the precious hilt;
295 Either from lust of gold, or like a girl
Valuing the giddy pleasure of the eyes.
Yet, for a man may fail in duty twice,
And the third time may prosper, get thee hence:
But, if thou spare to fling Excalibur,
300 I will arise and slay thee with my hands.'

Then quickly rose Sir Bedivere, and ran,
And, leaping down the ridges lightly, plunged
Among the bulrush beds, and clutched the sword,
And strongly wheeled and threw it. The great brand
305 Made lightnings in the splendour of the moon,
And flashing round and round, and whirled in an arch,
Shot like a streamer of the northern morn,
Seen where the moving isles of winter shock
By night, with noises of the Northern Sea.
310 So flashed and fell the brand Excalibur:
But ere he dipt the surface, rose an arm

306. 'The extra syllable gives the rush of the sword as it is whirled in
parabolic curve' (T.).

Clothed in white samite, mystic, wonderful,
And caught him by the hilt, and brandished him
Three times, and drew him under in the mere.
315 And lightly went the other to the King.

Then spoke King Arthur, drawing thicker breath:
'Now see I by thine eyes that this is done.
Speak out: what is it thou hast heard, or seen?'

And answer made the bold Sir Bedivere:
320 'Sir King, I closed mine eyelids, lest the gems
Should blind my purpose, for I never saw,
Nor shall see, here or elsewhere, till I die,
Not though I live three lives of mortal men,
So great a miracle as yonder hilt.
325 Then with both hands I flung him, wheeling him;
But when I looked again, behold an arm,
Clothed in white samite, mystic, wonderful,
That caught him by the hilt, and brandished him
Three times, and drew him under in the mere.'

330 And answer made King Arthur, breathing hard:
'My end draws nigh; 'tis time that I were gone.
Make broad thy shoulders to receive my weight,
And bear me to the margin; yet I fear
My wound hath taken cold, and I shall die.'

335 So saying, from the pavement he half rose,
Slowly, with pain, reclining on his arm,
And looking wistfully with wide blue eyes
As in a picture. Him Sir Bedivere
Remorsefully regarded through his tears,
340 And would have spoken, but he found not words;
Then took with care, and kneeling on one knee,
O'er both his shoulders drew the languid hands,
And rising bore him through the place of tombs.

But, as he walked, King Arthur panted hard,
345 Like one that feels a nightmare on his bed
When all the house is mute. So sighed the King,
Muttering and murmuring at his ear, 'Quick, quick!
I fear it is too late, and I shall die.'
But the other swiftly strode from ridge to ridge,
350 Clothed with his breath, and looking, as he walked,
Larger than human on the frozen hills.
He heard the deep behind him, and a cry
Before. His own thought drove him like a goad.

Dry clashed his harness in the icy caves
355   And barren chasms, and all to left and right
The bare black cliff clanged round him, as he based
His feet on juts of slippery crag that rang
Sharp-smitten with the dint of armèd heels –
And on a sudden, lo! the level lake,
360   And the long glories of the winter moon.

Then saw they how there hove a dusky barge,
Dark as a funeral scarf from stem to stern,
Beneath them; and descending they were ware
That all the decks were dense with stately forms,
365   Black-stoled, black-hooded, like a dream – by these
Three Queens with crowns of gold: and from them rose
A cry that shivered to the tingling stars,
And, as it were one voice, an agony
Of lamentation, like a wind that shrills
370   All night in a waste land, where no one comes,
Or hath come, since the making of the world.

Then murmured Arthur, 'Place me in the barge.'
So to the barge they came. There those three Queens
Put forth their hands, and took the King, and wept.
375   But she, that rose the tallest of them all
And fairest, laid his head upon her lap,
And loosed the shattered casque, and chafed his hands,
And called him by his name, complaining loud,
And dropping bitter tears against a brow
380   Striped with dark blood: for all his face was white
And colourless, and like the withered moon
Smote by the fresh beam of the springing east;
And all his greaves and cuisses dashed with drops
Of onset; and the light and lustrous curls –
385   That made his forehead like a rising sun
High from the daïs-throne – were parched with dust;
Or, clotted into points and hanging loose,
Mixed with the knightly growth that fringed his lips.
So like a shattered column lay the King;
390   Not like that Arthur who, with lance in rest,
From spur to plume a star of tournament,
Shot through the lists at Camelot, and charged
Before the eyes of ladies and of kings.

373. So] And *Morte d'Arthur*.
379. a] *1873*; his *1869–70*.

Then loudly cried the bold Sir Bedivere:
395 'Ah! my Lord Arthur, whither shall I go?
Where shall I hide my forehead and my eyes?
For now I see the true old times are dead,
When every morning brought a noble chance,
And every chance brought out a noble knight.
400 Such times have been not since the light that led
The holy Elders with the gift of myrrh.
But now the whole Round Table is dissolved
Which was an image of the mighty world,
And I, the last, go forth companionless,
405 And the days darken round me, and the years,
Among new men, strange faces, other minds.'

And slowly answered Arthur from the barge:
'The old order changeth, yielding place to new,
And God fulfils himself in many ways,
410 Lest one good custom should corrupt the world.
Comfort thyself: what comfort is in me?
I have lived my life, and that which I have done
May He within himself make pure! but thou,
If thou shouldst never see my face again,
415 Pray for my soul. More things are wrought by prayer
Than this world dreams of. Wherefore, let thy voice
Rise like a fountain for me night and day.
For what are men better than sheep or goats
That nourish a blind life within the brain,
420 If, knowing God, they lift not hands of prayer
Both for themselves and those who call them friend?
For so the whole round earth is every way
Bound by gold chains about the feet of God.
But now farewell. I am going a long way
425 With these thou seëst—if indeed I go
(For all my mind is clouded with a doubt)—
To the island-valley of Avilion;
Where falls not hail, or rain, or any snow,
Nor ever wind blows loudly; but it lies
430 Deep-meadowed, happy, fair with orchard lawns
And bowery hollows crowned with summer sea,
Where I will heal me of my grievous wound.'

408–32. T. wrote to Knowles, late Dec. 1872: 'I hope they are not printed off:
for I have come to the conclusion that the *whole* of Arthur's last speech
"The old order" etc. ought to remain' (*Letters* iii).

So said he, and the barge with oar and sail
Moved from the brink, like some full-breasted swan
435   That, fluting a wild carol ere her death,
Ruffles her pure cold plume, and takes the flood
With swarthy webs. Long stood Sir Bedivere
Revolving many memories, till the hull
Looked one black dot against the verge of dawn,
440   And on the mere the wailing died away.

But when that moan had past for evermore,
The stillness of the dead world's winter dawn
Amazed him, and he groaned, 'The King is gone.'
And therewithal came on him the weird rhyme,
445   'From the great deep to the great deep he goes.'

Whereat he slowly turned and slowly clomb
The last hard footstep of that iron crag;
Thence marked the black hull moving yet, and cried,
'He passes to be King among the dead,
450   And after healing of his grievous wound
He comes again; but–if he come no more–
O me, be yon dark Queens in yon black boat,
Who shrieked and wailed, the three whereat we gazed
On that high day, when, clothed with living light,
455   They stood before his throne in silence, friends
Of Arthur, who should help him at his need?'

Then from the dawn it seemed there came, but faint
As from beyond the limit of the world,
Like the last echo born of a great cry,
460   Sounds, as if some fair city were one voice
Around a king returning from his wars.

Thereat once more he moved about, and clomb
Even to the highest he could climb, and saw,
Straining his eyes beneath an arch of hand,
465   Or thought he saw, the speck that bare the King,

441–5] 1873; not 1869–70.
445. 'Merlin's song when he was born' (T.). Cp. De Profundis (III 67).
446] 1873; At length he groaned, and turning slowly clomb 1869–70.
457. 'From (the dawn) the East, whence have sprung all the great religions
of the world. A triumph of welcome is given to him who has proved
himself "more than conqueror"' (T.).
463. Even] Ev'n 1873; E'en 1869–70.

Down that long water opening on the deep
Somewhere far off, pass on and on, and go
From less to less and vanish into light.
And the new sun rose bringing the new year.

476 To the Queen

Published *1873*, Imperial Library Edition. T. had sent it to Knowles prior to 18 Dec. 1872 (*Letters* iii); T. is described as having 'just written' it, 25 Dec. 1872 (*Mem.* ii 119). Cp. *To the Queen* (*p. 485*). Knowles hoped to be allowed to publish it in the *Contemporary Review*, New Year 1873. 'After considering the idea of letting it appear first in the *Contemporary*, T. wrote to Knowles from Farringford just before Christmas that there would then be no time for the Queen to see it first, and that he preferred to let it find its own way "silently among the people"' (P. Metcalf, *James Knowles*, 1980, p. 259; *Letters* iii).

O loyal to the royal in thyself,
And loyal to thy land, as this to thee—
Bear witness, that rememberable day,
When, pale as yet, and fever-worn, the Prince
5   Who scarce had plucked his flickering life again

463–5. J. Hollander compares *Aeneid* vi 454: *aut videt aut vidisse putat*, and *Paradise Lost* i 783–4: 'sees, / Or dreams he sees' (*The Figure of Echo*, 1981, pp. 110–11).
468. 'The purpose of the individual man may fail for a time, but his work cannot die' (T.). T. compares Malory xxi 7: 'Some men yet say, in many parts of England, that king Arthur is not dead; but, by the will of our Lord Jesu Christ, into another place: and men say, that he will come again, and he shall win the holy cross.' T. adds: 'And cf. what Arthur says in Layamon's *Brut*, 28619, Madden's Edition iii 144: "And seothe ich cumen wulle / to mine kineriche, / and wunien mid Brutten, / mid muchelere wunne." (And afterwards I will come (again) to my kingdom, and dwell with the Britons with much joy).'
469. Wise, *Bibliography* i 207–8, quotes the trial edition (1869), which followed l. 467 with:

> Then rose the new sun bringing the new year,
> And on the heart of Bedivere returned
> A rhyme of Merlin, 'Where is he who knows?
> From the great deep to the great deep he goes'.

¶476. 3. 'When the Queen and the Prince of Wales went to the thanksgiving at St Paul's (after the Prince's dangerous illness) in Feb. 1872' (T.).

     From halfway down the shadow of the grave,
     Past with thee through thy people and their love,
     And London rolled one tide of joy through all
     Her trebled millions, and loud leagues of man
10   And welcome! witness, too, the silent cry,
     The prayer of many a race and creed, and clime–
     Thunderless lightnings striking under sea
     From sunset and sunrise of all thy realm,
     And that true North, whereof we lately heard
15   A strain to shame us 'keep you to yourselves;
     So loyal is too costly! friends–your love
     Is but a burthen: loose the bond, and go.'
     Is this the tone of empire? here the faith
     That made us rulers? this, indeed, her voice
20   And meaning, whom the roar of Hougoumont
     Left mightiest of all peoples under heaven?
     What shock has fooled her since, that she should speak
     So feebly? wealthier–wealthier–hour by hour!
     The voice of Britain, or a sinking land,
25   Some third-rate isle half-lost among her seas?
     There rang her voice, when the full city pealed
     Thee and thy Prince! The loyal to their crown
     Are loyal to their own far sons, who love
     Our ocean-empire with her boundless homes
30   For ever-broadening England, and her throne
     In our vast Orient, and one isle, one isle,
     That knows not her own greatness: if she knows
     And dreads it we are fallen.—But thou, my Queen,
     Not for itself, but through thy living love
35   For one to whom I made it o'er his grave
     Sacred, accept this old imperfect tale,
     New-old, and shadowing Sense at war with Soul,
     Ideal manhood closed in real man,
     Rather than that gray king, whose name, a ghost,

14–17. 'Canada. A leading London journal had written advocating that
Canada should sever her connection with Great Britain, as she was
"too costly": hence these lines' (T.). Referring to *The Times.* T. wrote to
E.T., 8 Nov. 1872: 'Lady F[ranklin] has sent me that Canadian bit of the
Times. Villa[i]nous!' (*Letters* iii); see also T.'s letter to William Kirby, 18
March 1873 (*Letters* iii).
20. Hougoumont: 'Waterloo' (T.).
35. See the *Dedication* to the Prince Consort (*p. 675*).
38] *1899*; not *1873–98*. See *p. 671*.

Streams like a cloud, man-shaped, from mountain
40   peak,
And cleaves to cairn and cromlech still; or him
Of Geoffrey's book, or him of Malleor's, one
Touched by the adulterous finger of a time
That hovered between war and wantonness,
45 And crownings and dethronements: take withal
Thy poet's blessing, and his trust that Heaven
Will blow the tempest in the distance back
From thine and ours: for some are scared, who mark,
Or wisely or unwisely, signs of storm,
50 Waverings of every vane with every wind,
And wordy trucklings to the transient hour,
And fierce or careless looseners of the faith,
And Softness breeding scorn of simple life,
Or Cowardice, the child of lust for gold,
55 Or Labour, with a groan and not a voice,
Or Art with poisonous honey stolen from France,
And that which knows, but careful for itself,
And that which knows not, ruling that which knows.
To its own harm: the goal of this great world
60 Lies beyond sight: yet–if our slowly-grown
And crowned Republic's crowning common-sense,
That saved her many times, not fail–their fears
Are morning shadows huger than the shapes
That cast them, not those gloomier which forego
65 The darkness of that battle in the West,
Where all of high and holy dies away.

---

39. 'The legendary Arthur from whom many mountains, hills, and cairns throughout Great Britain are named' (H.T.).

42. 'Geoffrey of Monmouth's', and 'Malory's name is given as Maleorye, Maleore, and Malleor' (T.).

43. Kathleen Tillotson points out that F. J. Furnivall in 1864 had drawn attention to Arthur's incest: 'It was perhaps because of such reference to the incest episode that Tennyson made the disclaimer' (*Mid-Victorian Studies*, 1965, p. 98).

Appendix I

ALTERNATIVE DRAFTS

*THE PRINCESS (p. 219)

Sir Charles Tennyson has described the MSS in *Nineteenth Century* cix
(1931) 632–6, and *Cornhill* cliii (1936) 672–80. He notes the Cambridge
flavour of these fragments (*H.Nbk 23*) which sketch the layout. Arundel
is 'in some degree a portrait of Tennyson himself'. See J. H. Buckley
(p. 94).

[introducing ii]

  I said my say; when Walter with a glance
  At Lilia, meditating malice, took
  The person of the Prince; but months have gone,
  I can but give the substance not the words.

[iii]

  The third that spoke, though steersman of our boat
  At college, feared to steer the tale and cried
  Against it – nothing could be done – but urged
  By common voice, continued as he might.

[iv]

  The next that spoke, a wild November fool,
  Twice had he been convened and once had fought
  A bargeman – he was Irish out of Clare.
  For every prize he wrote and failed in all,
  And many a song he made which no man knew –
  The cleverest man in all our set was he,
  And something like the Cyril in the tale.

[vi]

  The next that spoke was Arthur Arundel
  The Poet: rough his hair but fine to feel,
  And dark his skin but softer than a babe's,
  And large his hand as of the plastic kind,
  And early furrows in his face he had:
  Small were his themes – low builds the nightingale –
  But promised more: and mellow was his voice,
  He pitched it like a pipe to all he would;
  And thus he brought our story back to life.

[vii]

The last that spoke was one we used to call
The lady: lady-like he read the parts
Of Viola, Beatrice, Hermione:
We thought he fancied Lilia: who could tell?
He coloured at the name of any girl.
He plucked a flower that like a moral grew
From *miserere* on the broken tomb
Beside us and he held it as he spoke.

[Conclusion]

Here closed our tale: I give it, not as told
But drest in words by Arthur Arundel
In aftertimes, a medley, which at first
Perhaps but meant &c.

H.Lpr 196 has an unadopted passage which relates to [vi] above and to i 176ff:

We called our set The Shakespeare: we were wont
To meet and read him far into the night,
Half-read, half-act together. Arthur Clive
Was as our central star: we loved him well
5   For candid even to folly were his moods:
His locks were rough to see but fine to feel:
And swarthy his skin but soft as is a child's,
And early furrows in his face he had:
And large his hand and mellow was his voice,
10   He toucht it like a pipe to all he would.
The rest were young men full of health and scorn.
And there we seven had met at Vivian Place.

ii ∧ iii (*p. 253*)

Two alternative versions of *Sweet and low. H.Lpr 192* was printed by W. F.
Rawnsley, *Nineteenth Century* xcvii (1925) 191:

Who claps the gate
So late, so late,
Who claps the gate on the windy wold?
O were it he
5   Come back from sea!
Sleep, sleep, my blossom; the night is cold –

Sleep, dearest dear!
The moon is clear
To light him back to my babe and me

10   And he'll come soon
            All under the moon,
     A thousand miles on the silver sea.

Mem. i 255 : 'Two versions of *Sweet and low* were made, and were sent to my mother to choose which should be published. She chose the published one in preference to that which follows, because it seemed to her more song-like'. This is dated 24 Nov. 1849 (formerly *Lincoln*); for an earlier draft of it, with minor variants, written on a proof of *The Princess* (1847, *Lincoln*), see C. B. Stevenson, *TRB* ii (1974) 130–31. There are other drafts and versions in *ULC MS*.

           Bright is the moon on the deep,
           Bright are the cliffs in her beam,
              Sleep, my little one, sleep!
           Look he smiles, and opens his hands,
     5   He sees his father in distant lands,
           And kisses him there in a dream,
              Sleep, sleep.

           Father is over the deep,
           Father will come to thee soon,
     10   Sleep, my pretty one, sleep!
           Father will come to his babe in the nest,
           Silver sails all out of the West,
           Under the silver moon,
              Sleep, sleep!

iv ∧ v (*p. 283*)

Three alternative versions of *Thy voice is heard through rolling drums.* 'My first version of this song was published in *Selections, 1865*' (T.); he reprinted it in the Miniature Edition, 1870, only.

           Lady, let the rolling drums
           Beat to battle where thy warrior stands:
           Now thy face across his fancy comes,
              And gives the battle to his hands.

     5   Lady, let the trumpets blow,
           Clasp thy little babes about thy knee:
           Now their warrior father meets the foe,
              And strikes him dead for thine and thee.

Sir Charles Tennyson has printed two further versions, *Nineteenth Century* cix (1931) 635–6, describing them as probably the second and third versions. *H.Lpr 197*. (There is another draft in *ULC MS*.)

When all among the fifes and the thundering drums
Thy soldier in the battlefield, my Ada, stands,
Thy woman's face, believe it, across his fancy comes
And gives the battle, the battle to his hands.

5 Then though many a fatal bullet may whistle near,
And round him half his comrades may reel, may roll,
Thy whispers, O my life, will tremble at his ear,
Thy kisses, ah my darling, burn within his soul.

When the cannons roar and the trumpets, trumpets blow;
10 He will hear his young ones call him o'er the sea;
When the word is given, like a fire he meets the foe
And strikes a thousand dead for them and for thee.

When roars the fight to left and right
And on the field thy soldier stands,
When far and wide the cannon booms,
And shrill the fifes and beat the drums,
5 Thy face across his fancy comes
And gives the battle to his hands.

When roars the fight to left and right
And round him half his comrades roll,
Though many a bullet whistles near,
10 He fears not death, he knows not fear—
Thy whispers tremble at his ear,
Thy kisses burn within his soul.

When roars the fight to left and right,
He sees his young ones at thy knee.
15 The word is given; the trumpets blow;
The word is given, and on they go;
He heads the charge, he meets the foe
And strikes a thousand dead for thee.

v ∧ vi (*p. 301*)

An alternative version of *Home they brought her warrior dead* was published
in *A Selection* (1865); it was reprinted in the Miniature Edition, 1870, and
then only in *Songs* (1872). (There are other drafts in *ULC MS.*)

> Home they brought him slain with spears.
> They brought him home at even-fall:
> All alone she sits and hears
> Echoes in his empty hall,
> 5   Sounding on the morrow.
>
> The Sun peeped in from open field,
> The boy began to leap and prance,
> Rode upon his father's lance,
> Beat upon his father's shield –
> 10   'O hush, my joy, my sorrow.'

*IN MEMORIAM A. H. H. (*p. 331*)

The eight following sections which T. did not publish are printed (in the
order of the published poem) in this Appendix, since they might distract
from the final sequence of the poem. Two unpublished fragments follow.

(i) 'SPEAK TO ME FROM THE STORMY SKY!'

Printed *Mem.* ii 517. In *H.Lpr 104* it is on the sheet facing vii (*p. 351*).

> Speak to me from the stormy sky!
> The wind is loud in holt and hill.
> It is not kind to be so still.
> Speak to me, dearest, lest I die.
>
> 5 Speak to me: let me hear or see!
> Alas my life is frail and weak.
> Seest thou my faults and wilt not speak?
> They are not want of love for thee.

(ii) 'THE PATH BY WHICH I WALKT ALONE'

Unpublished, *H.Lpr 103*. (S & S note that this is a detached leaf from *T.MS.*)
It is written above xxii (*p. 367*), with which it has obvious affinities. Cp.
Youth (I 633).

i 2. T. wrote to W. H. Brookfield, mid-March 1832: 'You came to see us
when there was an utter dearth of all beauty in holt and hill' (*Letters* i 71).

The path by which I walkt alone
Ere yet thy motion caught mine eye
Was rich with many a prophecy
In every gale about me blown.

5 The blackbird warbled, 'Make thee whole
In spirit. Hear how glad I am.'
The lark on golden vapour swam
And chanted, 'Find a kindred soul.'

And yearning woke and was not stilled.
10 I could not find thee here or there.
I cried to all the breezes, 'Where?',
For all my want was unfulfilled.

But freshly did my feet advance
For twenty summers all but two
15 Till when the time was full I drew
To where I met thee as by chance.

(iii) 'O SORROWER FOR THE FADED LEAF'

Unpublished, *Lincoln MS*, deleted. It follows lvi (p. *398*), and acts as an
introduction to lvii which is on the same page.

'O Sorrower for the faded leaf',
A dark and slothful spirit said,
'Why lingerest thou beside the dead?
Thy songs are fuel to thy grief.

5 They help not thee, and who will thank
Thy labour? What are these indeed
But sighings of the withered reed?
A little cry from off a plank

Of shipwreck, lost in shoreless seas,
10 A print in ever-shifting sands,
A spreading out of feeble hands
To that which hears not?' Ill at ease

I faltered in my toil and broke
The moulds that Fancy made; and turned
15 To that fair soul that with me mourned
About his tomb, and sighing spoke.

ii 7. *golden vapour*: *Youth* 106.
iii 8-9. Cp. *Queen Mary* V ii: 'A voice of shipwreck on a shoreless sea'.

(iiiA) 'THE LIGHT THAT SHONE WHEN HOPE WAS BORN'

Printed *TLS*, 22 Aug. 1969; *T.MS* of *In Memoriam*, where it follows xxx
(*p. 373*). This fragmentary section opens by repeating the last line of xxx.

> 'The light that shone when Hope was born':
>   So whispers my Melpomene,
>   'It was the light that lighted thee,
> And it shall make me less forlorn.
>
> 5   And where is hope like this', she cries
>   'That changes human spites and scorns
>   And all a poor man's crown of thorns
>   To glory when the beggar dies;
>
>   Who looks upon his girl and boy:
> 10   How will they live when he is dead?
>
>   Where turn to gain a little bread?
>   Yet – O the wonder – parts in joy;
>
>   A hope that, spite of tribe and clan

(iv) THE PHILOSOPHER

Printed *Mat.* ii 274–5. *Mem.* i 457 omitted ll. 5–8, 13–16, and placed it as a
poem of 1859. But it is in a MS of *The Princess* (mainly the songs–*Univer-
sity Library, Cambridge*), which shows that it belongs to *c.* 1849. It is pre-
sumably about Arthur Hallam and connected with *In Memoriam*; cp. in
particular xcvi (*p. 440*). In Nov. 1882, T. sent four unidentified semi-legible
lines in H.T.'s hand (together with *England and America in 1782* 1–5 and *Enoch
Arden* 906–9) to A. T. Claflin to help raise money to buy Longfellow's house
(*Letters* iii). The lines have affinities with *The Philosopher*:

> Brave truth [?], somewhat hard to know,
>   For though not mailed in jealous pride
>   He shunned to wear his heart outside
> Like brides [?] at a new [?] show.

> He was too good and kind and sweet,
>   Even when I knew him in his hour
>   Of darkest doubt, and in his power,
> To fling his doubts into the street.

iiiA. *2. Melpomene*: the Muse of Tragedy, and of Elegy, who speaks too in
xxxvii.
12] *MS has no punctuation.*

5 Our modern authors young and vain
    Must print or preach their doubts aloud
    And blurt to every passing crowd
    Those indigestions of the brain.

    Truth-seeking he and not afraid,
10   But questions that perplex us now –
    What time (he thought) have loom or plough
    To weigh them as they should be weighed?

    But we that are not kind or just
    We scatter seeds that spring in flame,
15   Or bear their fruit in London's shame –
    The Sabbath journal mixt with lust.

    We help the blatant voice abroad
    To preach the freedom of despair,
    And from the heart of all things fair
20   To pluck the sanction of a God.

(v) 'YOUNG IS THE GRIEF I ENTERTAIN'

Printed *Mem.* i 306–7, from *T.MS* of *In Memoriam*, with the title *To A.H.H.*
('originally No. cviii'). In the MS it comes between cxi (*p. 458*) and *Are
these the far-famed Victor Hours* (*p. 985*). H.T. wrote in *T.MS*: '(Omitted
because the thought did not seem coherent enough)'.

    Young is the grief I entertain,
        And ever new the tale she tells,
        And ever young the face that dwells
    With reason cloistered in the brain.

5   Yet grief deserves a nobler name.
        She spurs an imitative will.
        'Tis shame to fail so far and still
    My failing shall be less my shame,

    Considering what mine eyes have seen,
10   And all the sweetness which thou wast
        And thy beginnings in the past
    And all the strength thou wouldst have been –

iv 6. *print or*] *MS*; point and *Mat.*
iv 14. *in*] *MS*; or *Mat.*
v 6 Adapted as 'That spurs an imitative will', cx 20.
11. *And*] *T.MS, Eversley*; In *Mem. Mem.* inaccurately transcribed *T.MS.* The
correct reading was supplied by T. (*Eversley* proofs, *Lincoln*).

> A master mind with master minds,
> An orb repulsive of all hate,
> *15* A will concentric with all fate,
> A life four-square to all the winds.

(vi) 'LET DEATH AND MEMORY KEEP THE FACE'

Printed, from *Lincoln MS* of *In Memoriam,* by Valerie Pitt, *Tennyson Laureate* (1962), p. 97. It comes between cxvii (*p. 463*) and cxxii. The MS does not include cxvi (which incorporated a line from *Let Death*) or cxix (for which *Let Death* furnished the concluding stanza).

> Let Death and Memory keep the face
> Of three and twenty summers, fair.
> I see it and no grief is there,
> Nor Time can wrong the youthful grace.
>
> *5* I see it and I scarce repine.
> I hear the voice that held me fast.
> The voice is pleasant in the past,
> It speaks to me of me and mine.
>
> The face is bright, the lips are bland,
> *10* He smiles upon me eye to eye,
> And in my thoughts with scarce a sigh
> I take the pressure of his hand.

(vii) 'I KEEP NO MORE A LONE DISTRESS'

Printed *Mem.* i 306, from *T.MS* of *In Memoriam,* with the title *The Grave* ('originally No. lvii'). In the MS it comes between cxxvi and cxxv (*p. 471*).

15. Cp. *On a Mourner* 19–20, MS (also on the death of Hallam, written Oct. 1833): 'Till all my soul concentric shine / With that wide will that closes mine.'

16. Adapted as 'Which stood four-square to all the winds that blew!', *Ode on Wellington* 39. For the epithet, T. compares Simonides, 'though I did not think of this parallel when I wrote it.'

vi 2. Arthur Hallam was in his twenty-third year when he died.

7–8. Adapted as cxvi 11–12: 'And that dear voice, I once have known, / Still speak to me of me and mine.'

9–12. Adapted as cxix 9–12: 'And bless thee, for thy lips are bland, / And bright the friendship of thine eye; / And in my thoughts with scarce a sigh / I take the pressure of thine hand.'

I keep no more a lone distress.
The crowd have come to see thy grave.
Small thanks or credit shall I have
But these shall see it not the less.

5   The happy maiden's tears are free
And she will weep and give them way:
Yet one unschooled in want will say,
'The dead are dead and let them be.'

Another whispers, sick with loss,
10   'O let the simple slab remain,
The MERCY JESU in the rain,
The MISERERE in the moss!

I love the daisy weeping dew,
I hate the trim-set plots of Art!'
15   My friend, thou speakest from the heart,
But look, for these are Nature too.

(viii) 'ARE THESE THE FAR-FAMED VICTOR HOURS'

Printed *Mem.* i 307, from *T.MS* of *In Memoriam*, with the title *The Victor Hours* ('originally No. cxxvii'). In the MS it comes between *Young is the grief I entertain* (p. 983) and cxxviii (p. 474).

Are these the far-famed Victor Hours
That ride to death the griefs of men?
I fear not, if I feared them then.
Is this blind flight the wingèd Powers?

5   Behold, ye cannot bring but good,
And see, ye dare not touch the truth,
Nor Sorrow beauteous in her youth,
Nor Love that holds a constant mood.

Ye must be wiser than your looks,
10   Or wise yourselves, or wisdom-led,
Else this wide whisper round my head
Were idler than a flight of rooks.

vii 4. *not*] *T.MS*; none *Mem.*
11–12. 'As seen by me in Tintern Abbey' (T.); xix was 'written at Tintern Abbey', and is on the same theme of the relationship of the poems to T.'s sense of loss. Cp. *The Princess: Prologue*, MS (Appendix I, p. 977): 'He plucked a flower that like a moral grew / From *miserere* on the broken tomb.'
viii 1. *these*] *T.MS*; those *Mem.*, *Eversley.*
11. *wide*] *T.MS*, *Eversley*; wild *Mem.*

> Go forward: crumble down a throne,
> Dissolve a world, condense a star,
> *15*   Unsocket all the joints of war,
> And fuse the peoples into one.

Fragments

Unpublished, *H.Nbk 17*, where it follows ix (*p. 353*), after a stub. Presumably from the earliest fragments, when *In Memoriam* was still in the *abab* stanza (cp. iii *n*, II 320). Cp. the third line with *The Lover's Tale*, MS (Appendix A, III *580*), draft iii 8–9: 'and night and day / The hearts of men and angels ache for men'.

> Time is not merely lapse of hours.
> This yearning is not idly given.
> The hearts of angels ache for ours.
> Earth's laws are recognized in Heaven.

Unpublished; *H.Nbk 19*, facing xcvii; little more than a syntax and an asseveration, but cp. *Some pleasure and exceeding pain* (III 13).

> If love of   power [?]
> But mean to [I?] fertilize the sod [?]
> God knows if then
> I would not brook

*TO THE QUEEN (*p. 485*)

In the Appendix to *The Growth of the Idylls of the King* (1895), Richard Jones printed 'a hitherto unpublished version' of *To the Queen* (1851), from the MS at the *Drexel Institute, Philadelphia*. (This MS was sold at the Parke-Bernet Galleries, Oct. 1944.) Lines that subsequently became part of the published poem are merely listed below, without their variants being given.

> The noblest men are born and bred
> Among the Saxo-Norman race,
> And in this world the noblest place
> Madam, is yours, our Queen and Head.
>
> *5*   Your name is blown on every wind,
> Your flag through Austral ice is borne
> And glimmers to the Northern morn
> And floats in either golden Ind.

The poets, they that often seem
10   So wretched, touching mournful strings,
      They likewise are a kind of kings,
      Nor is their empire all a dream.

      Their words fly over land and main,
      Their warblings make the distance glad,
15   Their voices heard hereafter add
      A glory to a glorious reign.

      A work not done by flattering state,
      Nor such a lay should kings receive,
      And kingly poets should believe
20   The king's heart true as he is great.

      The taskwork ode has ever failed:
      Not less the king in time to come
      Will seem the greater under whom
      The sacred poets have prevailed.

[ll. 5–8 of *1851*]

      I would I were as those of old,
30   A mellow mouth of song to fill
      Your reign with music which might still
      Be music when my lips were cold.

      That after-men might turn the page
      And light on fancies true and sweet,
35   And kindle with a loyal heat
      To fair Victoria's golden age.

      But he your Laureate who succeeds
      A master such as all men quote
      Must feel as one of slender note
40   And piping low among the reeds.

[ll. 9–12, 17–20, 21–4, of *1851*]

As the dedication of *Mem.*, H.T. printed a draft of ll. 1–8 (*Drexel* text) plus a draft of ll. 17–20 (*1851*), as 'An Unpublished Version'. As the dedication of *Mat.*, he had printed a different draft, where the second stanza (ll. 5–8, *Drexel*) had run: 'Your power about the world is blown / From under icy Boreal moons, / Through our mid-planet's sweet lagoons / And downward to the central zone.' The MS in the *Charterhouse School Library* (*The Greyfriar*, Dec. 1921) consists of a draft of five stanzas, one of which praises the International Exhibition: 'A sight more noble on the tides / Of changing time, that forward flow, / Than all your ships of war that blow / The battle from their oaken sides!' These lines were adapted from *Hail Briton* 5–8, and the year after *To the Queen* they became *Britons, Guard Your Own* 37–8 (II 472). The above account makes no attempt to give all the variants in these drafts, but it quotes all such stanzas as did not appear in *1851*. A torn leaf in a MS at *University Library, Cambridge* (6346) has a scrap of a draft with links ('Saxo-Norman', 'freedom', 'good or sweet').

MAUD: 227 *'OH! THAT 'TWERE POSSIBLE' (*p. 571*)

Published, as *Stanzas*, in *The Tribute* (ed. Lord Northampton), Sept. 1837. T. created it by adding to a poem he had written after the death of Arthur Hallam, 1833–4; this exists in two drafts in *Heath MS* (*A, B*). *H.Nbk 13* has a draft of ll. 1–16, 23–35, 42–8, 58–64. Later T. took it as the 'germ' of *Maud* (1855), where *Oh! that 'twere possible* falls into place (*p. 511*). A decision where to place it chronologically is difficult; there are few disadvantages if the poem is given under 1833–4, but in the text which T. published, that of *1837*. All the variants between the later version in *Heath* (*B*) and *1837* are given below, and the concluding stanzas added in *1837* are placed within square brackets. A full collation of *H.MS, Heath A* and *B, 1837*, and *1855* is given under *Maud*, together with other notes. G. O. Marshall discusses the changes in *PMLA* lxxviii (1963) 225–9.

In its original form of 1833–4, the poem is plainly precipitated by the death of Hallam, and it has many links with *In Memoriam*. *Heath A* is 'an incomplete fragment', dated 1833, consisting of 41 lines (6 stanzas). *Heath B* has 68 lines (10 stanzas). On 19 Sept. 1834 Spedding acknowledged to T., 'I have also the alterations of *Oh that it were possible*, improvements I must admit though I own I did not think that could have been' (*Letters* i 118; *Mem.* i 139). Then in Dec. 1836, T. angered Richard Monckton Milnes by refusing to contribute to *The Tribute* (*Letters* i 146, *c.*21 Dec.; *Mem.* i 157–60). T. relented: 'I will either bring or send you something for your Annual' (8 or 9 Jan. 1837); and then wrote (? March 1837): 'I have *not* been forgetful: these two poems have been causing me confounded bother to get them into shape. One I cannot send: it is too raw, but as I made the other double its former size, I hope it will do' (*Letters* i 148–9). R. W. Rader (p. 6) comments: 'Tennyson finished and published his poem in 1837 against his will, cobbling up an ending for it under pressure because he wished to pacify Milnes and had no other poem to do it with. But that he continued to think of his poem as incomplete (the 1834 version ended unsatisfactorily with "And weep / My whole soul out to thee") is suggested by the existence of a fair copy, dated April, 1838, in which it has been returned to its pre-1837 form; and by the fact that he did not reprint this lovely lyric in the *1842* volumes or in any other collection before *Maud*'. Shatto argues that this transcript (by Spedding) need not imply T.'s thinking the poem incomplete. Reviewing *The Tribute*, the *Edinburgh*

Review said: 'We do not profess perfectly to understand the somewhat mysterious contribution of Mr Alfred Tennyson, entitled *Stanzas*' (E. F. Shannon, *Tennyson and the Reviewers*, 1952, p. 29). T. later assented to Jowett's opinion that these were his most touching lines (*Mem.* ii 466). A. Day notes that the poem has something in common with *Fair face! fair form* (III 610), not least the word 'archetype' (not to be found elsewhere in T.).

> Oh! that 'twere possible,
>   After long grief and pain,
> To find the arms of my true-love
>   Round me once again!
>
> 5 When I was wont to meet her
>   In the silent woody places
>   Of the land that gave me birth,
> We stood tranced in long embraces,
> Mixt with kisses sweeter, sweeter,
> 10   Than any thing on earth.
>
> A shadow flits before me –
>   Not thou, but like to thee.
> Ah God! that it were possible
>   For one short hour to see
> 15 The souls we loved, that they might tell us
>   What and where they be.
>
> It leads me forth at Evening,
>   It lightly winds and steals
>   In a cold white robe before me,
> 20   When all my spirit reels
> At the shouts, the leagues of lights,
>   And the roaring of the wheels.
>
> Half the night I waste in sighs,
>   In a wakeful doze I sorrow
> 25 For the hand, the lips, the eyes –
>   For the meeting of tomorrow,
>   The delight of happy laughter,
> The delight of low replies.

¶ *227.13. God*] Christ *Heath B, 1855.*
17–22] Not *Heath A.*
18. It] And *Heath B.*
24] Half, in dreams I sorrow after *Heath B, 1855.*
25. For] Not *Heath B.*
26] Not *Heath B.*
27] The winsome laughter. *Heath B.*
28] Not *Heath B.*

Do I hear the pleasant ditty,
30   That I heard her chant of old?
But I wake—my dream is fled.
Without knowledge, without pity—
In the shuddering dawn behold,
By the curtains of my bed,
35   That abiding phantom cold.

Then I rise: the eave-drops fall
And the yellow-vapours choke
The great city sounding wide;
The day comes—a dull red ball,
40   Wrapt in drifts of lurid smoke,
On the misty river-tide.

Through the hubbub of the market
I steal, a wasted frame;
It crosseth here, it crosseth there—
45   Through all that crowd, confused and loud,
The shadow still the same;
And on my heavy eyelids
My anguish hangs like shame.

Alas for her that met me,
50   That heard me softly call—
Came glimmering through the laurels
At the quiet even-fall,
In the garden by the turrets
Of the old Manorial Hall.

55   Then the broad light glares and beats,
And the sunk eye flits and fleets,
And will not let me be.
I loathe the squares and streets,
And the faces that one meets,
60   Hearts with no love for me;

29. *Do*] And *Heath B.*
30. *old?*] old; *Heath B.*
33. *dawn*] grey *Heath B.*
35. *abiding*] dreadful *Heath B.*
35 ∧ 6] *Heath B, like 1855, had ll. 65–70 here (they are not in Heath A).*
36–41] *Not Heath A.*
39. *The*] And *Heath B.*
40. *Wrapt in drifts*] In a drift *Heath B.*
49–57] *Not Heath A.*
55. *Then*] *Not Heath B.*

Always I long to creep
To some still cavern deep,
And to weep, and weep and weep
My whole soul out to thee.
65　Get thee hence, nor come again,
Pass and cease to move about –
Pass, thou death-like type of pain,
Mix not memory with doubt.
'Tis the blot upon the brain
70　That *will* show itself without.

[Would the happy Spirit descend
In the chamber or the street
As she looks among the blest;
Should I fear to greet my friend,
75　Or to ask her, 'Take me, sweet,
To the region of thy rest.'

But she tarries in her place,
And I paint the beauteous face
Of the maiden, that I lost,
80　In my inner eyes again,
Lest my heart be overborne
By the thing I hold in scorn,
By a dull mechanic ghost
And a juggle of the brain.

85　I can shadow forth my bride
As I knew her fair and kind,
As I wooed her for my wife;
She is lovely by my side
In the silence of my life –
90　'Tis a phantom of the mind.
'Tis a phantom fair and good;
I can call it to my side,
So to guard my life from ill,
Though its ghastly sister glide
95　And be moved around me still

63. And to] And *Heath B.*
65–70] *See ll. 35 ∧ 6n.*
66, 68] *Transposed in Heath B* (Mixing . . .).
71–6] *Not Heath B. In 1855 these lines were incorporated* (ll. 54 ∧ 5).
77–110] *Not Heath B. These lines of 1837 found no place in 1855, except
that ll. 83–4 became Maud ii 82, 90.*
78–9. A. Day compares *In Memoriam* lxx 2–3: 'When on the gloom I strive
to paint / The face I know'.

       With the moving of the blood,
         That is moved not of the will.

       Let it pass, the dreary brow,
         Let the dismal face go by.
100   Will it lead me to the grave?
         Then I lose it: it will fly:
       Can it overlast the nerves?
       Can it overlive the eye?
       But the other, like a star,
105   Through the channel windeth far
         Till it fade and fail and die,
       To its Archetype that waits,
       Clad in light by golden gates–
       Clad in light the Spirit waits
110   To embrace me in the sky.]

TITHONUS: 218 *TITHON (*p. 583*)

Printed from *Heath MS* by M. J. Donahue, *PMLA* lxiv (1949) 401–2.
Written 1833, it is an early, shorter version of *Tithonus* (1860, *p. 583*). The
major revisions are noted below, and the details under *Tithonus*. There
are earlier drafts in *T.Nbks 20–21* (1833). T.'s revisions are extensively
discussed by Miss Donahue and by L. Hughes, *PQ* lviii, 1979, 82–9. T.
remarks that Tithonus was 'beloved by Aurora, who gave him eternal life
but not eternal youth. He grew old and infirm, and as he could not die,
according to the legend, was turned into a grasshopper.' Cp. *The
Grasshopper* 5, 28 (*1830*): 'No Tithon thou as poets feign . . . / No withered
immortality.' Written after the shock of Arthur Hallam's death, the poem
is a companion to *Ulysses*, which was begun at the same time (*Mem.* ii 9).
The theme may have been influenced by the grief of T.'s sister Emily
(Hallam's betrothed); she wrote to T., 12 July 1834, 'What is life to me! If I
die (which the Tennysons never do)' (*Mem.* i 135, cited by Miss Donahue).

       Ay me! ay me! the woods decay and fall,
       The vapours weep their substance to the ground,
       Man comes and tills the earth and lies beneath,
       And after many summers dies the rose.
5   Me only fatal immortality
       Consumes: I wither slowly in thine arms,
       Here at the quiet limit of the world,
       A white-haired shadow roaming like a dream
       The ever-silent spaces of the East,
10   Far-folded mists, and gleaming halls of morn.
       Ay me! ay me! what everlasting pain,

Being immortal with a mortal heart,
To live confronted with eternal youth:
To look on what is beautiful nor know
15 Enjoyment save through memory. Can thy love,
Thy beauty, make amends, though even now,
Close over us, the silver star, thy guide,
Shines in those tremulous eyes that fill with tears?
Release me: let me go: take back thy gift:
20 Why should a man desire in any shape
To vary from his kind, or beat the roads
Of life, beyond the goal of ordinance
Where all should pause, as is most meet for all?
Or let me call thy ministers, the hours,
25 To take me up, to wind me in their arms,
To shoot the sunny interval of day,
And lap me deep within the lonely west.
A soft air fans the cloud apart; there comes
A glimpse of that dark world where I was born.
30 Once more the old mysterious glimmer steals
From thy pure brows, and from thy shoulders pure,
And bosom throbbing with a fresher heart.
Thy cheek begins to bloom a fuller red,
Thy sweet eyes brighten slowly close to mine,
35 Ere yet they blind the stars, and thy wild team,
Spreading a rapid glow with loosened manes,
Fly, trampling twilight into flakes of fire.
'Tis ever thus: thou growest more beautiful,
Thou partest: when a little warmth returns
40 Thou partest, and thy tears are on my cheek.
Ay me! ay me! with what another heart,
By thy divine embraces circumfused,
Thy black curls burning into sunny rings,

¶218. 11–15] *Expanded in 1860.*
24–7] Not 1860.
29–32] Not T.Nbk 20 1st draft.
36–7] Not T.Nbk 20 1st draft.
35 ∧ 6] 1860 added a line.
40 ∧ 41] 1860 added four lines. T.Nbk 20 1st draft, from here to the end, differs considerably from *Heath MS.* It has eight lines, threatening Aurora that he will call up Death; then a shorter version of the closing lines, ending with l. 63 but incorporating a description of Aurora's horses (different from *Heath MS*). T.MS 2nd draft has the eight lines on Death following l. 53, and then breaks off.
42] Expanded in 1860.

With thy change changed, I felt this wondrous glow
45 That, gradually blooming, flushes all
Thy pale fair limbs: what time my mortal frame
Molten in thine immortal, I lay wooed,
Lips, forehead, eyelids, growing dewy-warm
With kisses balmier than opening buds;
50 Anon the lips that dealt them moved themselves
In wild and airy whisperings more sweet
Than that strange song I heard Apollo sing,
While Ilion like a mist rose into towers.
  Ah! keep me not for ever in the East:
55 How can my nature longer mix with thine?
Coldly thy rosy shadows bathe me, cold
Are all thy lights, and cold my wrinkled feet
Upon these glimmering thresholds, when the steam
Floats up from those still fields that dream below.
60 Release me! so restore me to the ground;
Thou seest all things, thou wilt see my grave:
Thou wilt renew thy beauty with the morn;
I earth in earth forget these empty courts,
And thee returning on thy silver wheels.

*IDYLLS OF THE KING:
LANCELOT AND ELAINE (*p. 869*)

Some lines on 'Avalon' (the 'Avilion' of *The Passing of Arthur* 427) are in
T.Nbk 28 (1859); they relate to *Lancelot and Elaine* 1247–51.

And she, how fast she sleeps! What is it? truth
Or glamour? fairies come from fairyland
To fetch the king to Avalon

And what is Avalon? Avalon is an isle
5 All made of apple-blossom in the West,
And all the waves are fragrant and the winds
About it and the fairies live upon it
And there are those have seen it far away
Shine like a rose upon the summer sea
10 And thither goes the king and thence returns
And reigns: some hold he cannot die

59 ∧ 60] 1860 added two lines.
Lancelot and Elaine
11. some] hereafter written above in MS.

*IDYLLS OF THE KING

Printed by J. Pfordresher, *A Variorum Edition of Tennyson's Idylls of the King* (1973), with a few errors of transcription. Pfordresher says 'written in another hand', but the hand is unquestionably T.'s, *H.Lpr 97*. Presumably Modred speaks.

Not without reason have we raised the land
And drawn a force together, worthy men,
That think with us. If ancient prophecies
(As human providence forecalculates
5 The possible) and dim presentiments
That racing with a people's blood foretell
And fashion sequent change – if these hold firm –
The time is come wherein this state of things
Should fail or alter. Better it should fail
10 Than not to alter. Who that sees the court
At full spring-tide of profligacy, who
That looks upon the land, the husbandman
Withdrawn from wholesome tillage of the soil
To gaze on pomps and shows – the whole long year
15 Almost one holiday – so week by week
Much treasure lavisht and the people drained –
Who last, that contemplates our greatest grief
The table round, two hundred knights, maintained
At public charge – who by their vows are bound
20 To deeds of honour, yet at license ride
And pillage, wringing half the little left
From worthier men – who sees all this can doubt
But that the time is here? Up then and do.
For since the older sort with Arthur keep
25 We younger bloods, that make and suit the time
Must turn it where the choice of judgement leads.

Appendix II

CONTENTS PAGES OF THE
COMPLETE EDITION

This Appendix gives the Contents pages of the Complete Edition, retaining the original numbering sequence and pagination used in each volume. A dagger (†) indicates a poem included in this Selected Edition.

VOLUME ONE

VOLUME TWO

VOLUME THREE

APPENDICES

Index of Titles and First Lines

This includes the sections of *In Memoriam*, and the songs from *The Princess, Idylls of the King* and elsewhere. A dagger indicates a poem included in this Selected Edition.